lonely planet

 W9-DEW-727

# Mediterranean Europe

Duncan Garwood, Fiona Adams, Carolyn Bain, Joe Bindloss,
Terry Carter, Vesna Maric, Amy Marr, Jeanne Oliver, Tom Parkinson,
Josephine Quintero, Andrew Stone

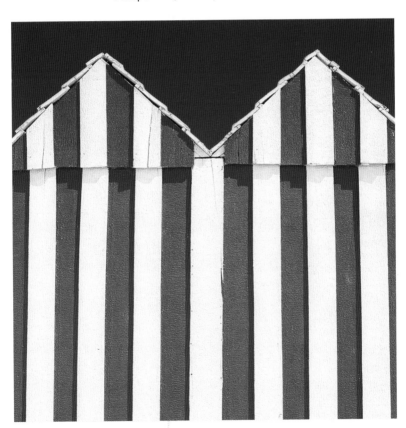

# Contents

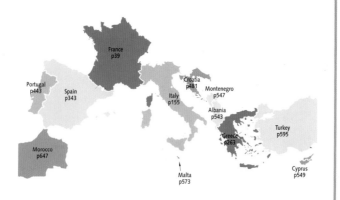

Portugal p443
Spain p343
France p39
Croatia p481
Montenegro p547
Italy p155
Albania p543
Turkey p595
Greece p263
Morocco p647
Malta p573
Cyprus p549

Lonely Planet books provide independent advice. Lonely Planet does not accept advertising in guidebooks, nor do we accept payment in exchange for listing or endorsing any place or business. Lonely Planet writers do not accept discounts or payments in exchange for positive coverage of any sort.

# Destination Mediterranean Europe

Mediterranean Europe is a region of bold colours and fiery passions. The brilliant blues of sea and sky, the burning yellows and bleached whites sear themselves onto the memory in an indelible image of shimmering beauty. But just as the ancient landscapes lull you into a state of delightful inertia so the region's exuberant vitality takes you by storm.

You need only dive into a teeming marketplace or join the crowds at a traditional festival to witness the frenzy of noise, colour and chaos that's as much a part of Mediterranean life as its glorious seascapes.

Stretching 3000km, from the Strait of Gibraltar to Turkey's west coast, the Mediterranean offers a multitude of pleasures. To many, the winning combination of sun-drenched beaches, beautiful bodies and party nights is lure enough. Others are drawn by the region's unparalleled cultural heritage. You can visit the Parthenon in Athens and the Colosseum in Rome, the Alhambra in Granada and the Aya Sofya in Istanbul before you've even started on the thousands of galleries and museums that house a considerable chunk of the Western world's artistic legacy.

When the weight of the culture and the coastal crowds starts to overwhelm you, head for the mountains. Skiing is widely available in winter and the many trekking opportunities provide a rare chance to get away from the summer hordes.

Exercising your taste buds is rightly considered one of the Mediterranean's great pleasures. To eat pizza in Italy, paella in Spain or couscous in Morocco is to know that you can't beat the real thing. Fine French wines, port in Portugal – there really is no better place to drink.

DALLAS STRIBLEY

NICE (p124)
Party with the beautiful
people in the capital of
the French Riviera

THE ALGARVE (p460)
Vast sandy beaches,
surfing and golf attract
sunseekers and sports fans

BARCELONA (p374)
High culture, thumping nightlife
and wacky modern architecture
in the Catalan capital

RABAT (p667)
Muslim architecture,
a 17th-century medina and
ancient fortifications tell
of an imperial heritage

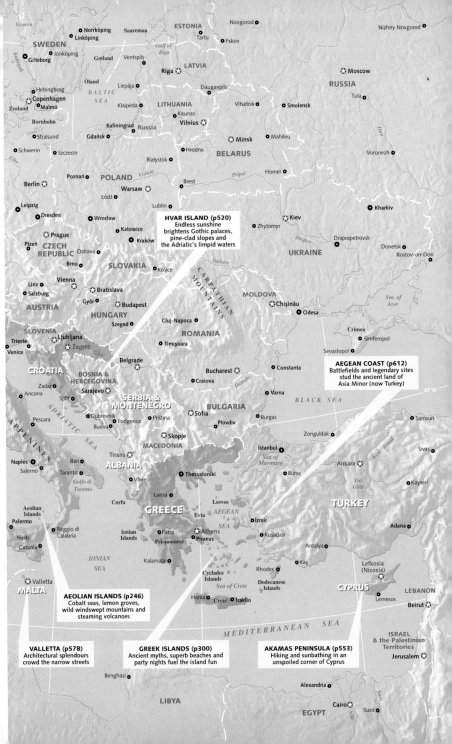

**HVAR ISLAND (p520)**
Endless sunshine brightens Gothic palaces, pine-clad slopes and the Adriatic's limpid waters

**AEGEAN COAST (p612)**
Battlefields and legendary sites stud the ancient land of Asia Minor (now Turkey)

**AEOLIAN ISLANDS (p246)**
Cobalt seas, lemon groves, wild windswept mountains and steaming volcanoes

**VALLETTA (p578)**
Architectural splendours crowd the narrow streets

**GREEK ISLANDS (p300)**
Ancient myths, superb beaches and party nights fuel the island fun

**AKAMAS PENINSULA (p553)**
Hiking and sunbathing in an unspoiled corner of Cyprus

Blessed with a beautiful climate and stunning scenery, Mediterranean Europe is a modern hedonist's dream. The islands of Mykonos, Greece and Ibiza, Spain rock to a bacchanalian beat, while the swish resorts of France's Côte d'Azur promise elegant evenings. Sunseekers can brown themselves on the fabulous beaches of Turkey's Mediterranean coast and cool off with a dip in the alluring waters off Croatia's Dalmatian coast. For one of Europe's most stunning coastlines head to the Amalfi Coast, Italy. For more cerebral pursuits take your pick from the monumental Acropolis, Gaudí's wacky architecture in Barcelona or the timeless wonders of Rome. The Mediterranean is a laid-back place and strolling the lovely streets of Valletta, Malta or walking in the unspoiled wilds of the Akamas Peninsula, Cyprus is not a bad way to build up an appetite. Lovers of seafood can tuck into *bouillabaisse* in Marseilles, France while for a quick bite on the hoof you can't beat the tasty tapas of Andalucìa, Spain.

Hire boats at a beach pier, Turkey (p622)

JON DAVISON

PAUL DAVID HELLANDER

Spend languorous days on the beach at Pafos (p561), Cyprus

Get ready for the evening party in Mykonos town (p301) in the Cyclades, Greece

CHRIS CHRISTO

DALLAS STRIBLEY

Cool off in the shallows at Cagliari's Poetto Beach (p251) on Sardinia, Italy

STEPHEN SAKS

Hit the road along the Amalfi Coast (p231), Italy

Feast at crowded outdoor eateries in old town (p409) in Ibiza City, Spain

BILL WASSMAN

See the Acropolis now (p276), Athens, Greece

ANDERS BLOMQVIST

JON DAVISON

Bask in gentle rays at Cavtat (p530),
Dubrovnik, Croatia

GREG ELMS

Dine outdoors on *bouillabaisse*,
Marseille (p118), Provence, France

Ask why – Gaudí's La Pedrera (rooftop
chimney pots; p378), Barcelona, Spain

MARTIN HUGHES

Relish the Basque Country tapas in
San Sebastián (p394), Spain

OLIVER STREWE

# Getting Started

To travel in Mediterranean Europe is to give your senses a thorough going over. You'll be dazzled by the magnificent landscapes, the colours and rich smells, by the simple delights of the cuisine, while the high concentration of art and architecture, the result of human activity that dates back thousands of years, is unparalleled anywhere.

Fortunately, though, the region is not stuck in the past. Transport is efficient, accommodation easy to find and although language difficulties can arise they are rarely insurmountable. In the major tourist areas English is widely spoken even if locals will greatly appreciate any efforts to speak their language. It's not, however, the cheapest of areas but with a bit of prior knowledge and careful planning you can make your budget stretch further.

See Climate Charts (p703) for more information.

## WHEN TO GO

Any time is a good time to visit Mediterranean Europe, although the best times are the months either side of summer. The weather is sunny without being deadly hot, it's far less crowded and prices are lower than in the high summer season. If you really want to visit in summer, which lasts roughly from early June to mid-September, try to avoid August. Temperatures are at their highest (in some parts they can hit 45°C) and the crowds are stifling. Everyone in France, Spain and Italy takes their holidays in August, which means that prices are sky-high, accommodation fully booked and the major attractions are packed. However, visiting in August does have its compensations: there are any number of festivals to catch, cities tend to empty making them less chaotic and the holiday atmosphere is undeniably contagious.

If you're keen on winter sports, ski resorts begin operating in November and move into full swing after the New Year, closing down again when the snow begins to melt in March or April. Expect to pay high season rates in the period between Christmas and the first week in January and then from late January through to late March. Away from the mountain resorts and major cities, winter in the Mediterranean can be rather melancholy. The weather, if not cold by northern standards, is often grim and frequently wet, and many resorts simply shut up shop until the next season.

---

### WHAT TO TAKE

Travelling as light as possible is the key. There's not a lot you can't find in Mediterranean Europe if you run out and it's better to buy what you need when you need it than to lug around a backpack full of crumpled clothes that you're not going to wear.

Clearly what you take depends on when you're going – heavy coats aren't top of the list in high summer – and what you're planning to do – summer trekking still requires walking shoes even if daytime temperatures are sweltering. Some things, though, are always a good idea:

- Your ID card or passport and visa if required (p714)
- Valid travel insurance (p707)
- Your driving licence (p726) if you're planning to hire a car
- Photocopies of all important documents
- Stuff to read. They might be heavy but English-language books are not always readily available.
- A set of smart casual clothes for evenings out – looks count on the Mediterranean

The Climate and When to Go sections in the individual country chapters explain what weather to expect and when to expect it, and the climate charts in the Regional Directory (p703) will help you compare the weather in different destinations. As a general rule though, the Mediterranean coast is hotter and drier than the Atlantic seaboard with most rain falling in the winter. For the purposes of this book, summer and winter correspond to high and low tourist seasons, respectively; for summer read roughly May to September and for winter read October to April.

## COSTS & MONEY

Mediterranean Europe is not particularly cheap, although compared to the north of Europe the situation doesn't seem so bad. As a general rule, Morocco and the eastern Mediterranean countries are cheaper than France, Italy and Spain.

Of your expenses, accommodation is by far the greatest. However, the massive variety of available options means that you don't necessarily need to pay through the nose. At the budget end of the scale, you should reckon on spending between €6 and €15 for a bed in a youth hostel dormitory; camping costs less, from about €5 per adult per night but to this you have to add the cost of getting to and from the campsite if you're without your own wheels. A double room in a budget hotel will cost anywhere between €15 and €40. Further up the scale and the sky's the limit, but for a double room in an average three-star hotel you could easily be looking at a high season rate of €100. Clearly these prices depend on the season (August costs more than December) and the place (Barcelona is more expensive than Istanbul).

Eating out, one of the true pleasures of the Mediterranean, need not cost a bomb. Grab a bite from a roadside snack bar and you could pay as little as €1. Alternatively, sit down to a full meal in a city-centre restaurant and you should reckon on about €25. Many places do set lunchtime menus, which are often considerably cheaper than ordering off the regular menu. Drinking the local wine rather than beer will also keep costs down.

As a rough guide, a backpacker cutting all the corners – sticking to youth hostels, snacking at noon and travelling slowly should reckon on about €40 a day. Travelling on a moderate budget, you should be able to manage on between €70 and €80 a day. This would allow you to stay in a cheap hotel or pension, eat in a modest restaurant and down the occasional beer.

Public transport throughout the region is largely efficient and not desperately expensive. Buses and long-distance coaches are generally cheaper than trains, especially for cross-border travel, while travelling by ferry is reasonably priced. If you're planning on using the ferries in summer make sure you book ahead – they get extremely busy. Car hire, however, is expensive and the cost of petrol anything but cheap. To save on car hire, it's always best to organise it before you leave home (p725).

Shoppers looking to pick up bargain buys in the region might find themselves a little disappointed. Consumer products are not especially cheap and although Rome and Madrid cost less than London, you're unlikely to be won over by the price tags.

The best way to manage your money is to use a cash card. ATMs are widely available throughout the region and with a cash card you can withdraw what you need without having to cart huge wads of cash around. However, you shouldn't depend entirely on plastic (cash and/or credit card) as in some more out-of-the-way places you might not be able to use it. It's always wise to have a little spare cash for emergencies both in the local currency and in an easily exchanged currency such as US dollars. About €150 should be sufficient. For further details on money matters see p709 and the individual country chapters.

## READING UP

Writers have been waxing lyrical about the Mediterranean for thousands of years. Setting the ball rolling, the ancient Greeks were great travellers and writers: Homer's epic *The Odyssey* is a masterpiece of Mediterranean adventure, Herodotus reported on his experiences in Egypt and Asia Minor, while historian and geographer Pausanius wrote the world's first travel guide some 2000 years ago.

Two of the greatest Mediterranean travel writers, however, sought their fame elsewhere. The great Moroccan explorer Abu Abdullah Muhammed Ibn Battuta (1304–69) is said to have covered some 75,000 miles in 30 years of travel in Asia and the eastern Mediterranean, while Venetian adventurer Marco Polo (1254–1324) thrilled with his tales of Asian exotica.

Just as homegrown voyagers have set out for unknown pastures, so the Mediterranean has lured a succession of northern authors to its summer shores. In more recent times, Goethe and Stendhal, Byron, Dickens and DH Lawrence have all travelled to the Mediterranean seeking inspiration.

### Books

To get a feel for the region there are any number of books to choose from. Here we've highlighted some of the best.

- *Mediterranean Winter* (Robert Kaplan) Better known for his Yugoslav history *Balkan Ghosts*, Kaplan evokes a wonderful sense of time and place as he recalls a trip he took as a youth through the off-season Mediterranean.
- *On the Shores of the Mediterranean* (Eric Newby) Newby turns his sparkling eye to the Italian mafia, Arabian harems and communist Albania in this wonderfully compelling exploration of Mediterranean life. It's guaranteed to entertain.
- *Pillars of Hercules* (Paul Theroux) With his usual dry wit and languid style, veteran traveller Theroux leads the reader along the shores of Spain to the French Riviera, Sardinia and Sicily.
- *Travel Reader* (Lawrence Durrell) A collection of Durrell's travel writing, this book reflects the author's lifelong love of the Mediterranean. He paints a hugely appealing picture of life in the area without ever lapsing into cliché.
- *Labels: A Mediterranean Journal* (Evelyn Waugh) The Mediterranean provides the foreign backdrop for Waugh's quintessentially English take on life. From Malta to Morocco, the locations change but Waugh's wit remains as pointed as ever.
- *The Ancient Mediterranean* (Michael Grant) Classical scholar Grant provides a highly readable analysis of the Mediterranean's ancient civilisations. From the earliest beginnings until the Roman Empire, Grant covers the region's greatest era.
- *The Odyssey* (Homer) Homer's ripping yarn of derring-do traces Odysseus's desperate attempts to return home after 10 years on the road. On the way he encounters a cast of deadly monsters and malevolent magicians.

## Websites
**Ferry To** (www.aferry.to) Details ferry routes, rates and ports throughout Europe.
**Lonely Planet** (www.lonelyplanet.com) Read up on where you want to go and hear from folk who've already been there.
**Rail Europe** (www.raileurope.com) European rail passes, prices and routes.
**Tourist Offices** (www.towd.com) Lists tourist offices for most countries.
**Travel City** (www.travelocity.com) What airlines fly where, when and for how much.
**World Heritage Sites** (www.worldheritagesite.org) Unesco's list of the world's cultural and natural treasures.

## MUST-SEE MOVIES
The crystal clear light and photogenic landscape has made Mediterranean Europe a firm favourite with film directors. Here's a selection of teasing celluloid tempters to take you on a tour of the region from the comfort of your own home.

- *Jean de Florette* (1986; Claude Berri) French stars Gérard Depardieu and Daniel Auteuil feature in this tragic tale of crushed dreams in rural France. The acting is wonderful and the landscape a picture.
- *Mediterraneo* (1991; Gabriele Salvatores) Italian director Salvatores snatched an Oscar for his beautifully shot film of a group of sailors stranded on a Greek island during WWII.
- *Land and Freedom* (1995; Ken Loach) The Spanish Civil war as told by left-wing Brit director Ken Loach. Inspired by George Orwell's *Homage to Catalonia*, it's a tragic portrait of a brutal period.
- *Il Postino* (1994; Michael Radford) Filmed on the Aeolian Islands this is a visual feast of a film. Starring a wonderfully laconic Massimo Troisi, it's the tale of Chilean poet Pablo Neruda's Italian exile.
- *Casablanca* (1942; Michael Curtiz) Quite simply, the greatest love story of them all. When Bogart and Bergman meet in wartime Casablanca the on-screen passion burns as fiercely as any Moroccan sun.

## RESPONSIBLE TRAVEL
Without going out of your way, you can, and should, behave in a way that's not likely to offend the local people or damage the environment. Some 220 million tourists pour into the region each year and while it is well-prepared to receive them, the environment is suffering. Desertification, deforestation and bushfires are becoming ever more serious, while increasingly dry summers are adversely affecting the region's water resources.

The key rule for the environment is to preserve natural resources and to leave the countryside as you find it. Some simple guidelines to follow include:

---

**CONDUCT IN MEDITERRANEAN EUROPE**

Most Mediterranean countries are fundamentally conservative and attach a great deal of importance to appearance, so your clothes may well have some bearing on how you're treated, especially in Spain, Portugal, Italy and Greece. By all means dress casually, but keep your clothes clean and ensure sufficient body cover (trousers or a knee-length dress) if your sightseeing includes churches, monasteries, mosques or synagogues. Also keep in mind that in most Muslim countries, such as Morocco, Western women or men in shorts or sleeveless shirts are virtually in their underwear in the eyes of more traditional locals.

On the beach, nude bathing is generally limited to particular areas, but topless bathing is common in many parts of Mediterranean Europe. Nevertheless, if nobody else seems to be doing it, you shouldn't do it either.

## FAVOURITE FESTIVALS & EVENTS

No-one knows how to put on a show better than the party folk of the Mediterranean. And there's really no better way of witnessing the ancient passions of the region than by partaking in one of the many annual festivals.

What follows is not meant to be a comprehensive festival guide; it's simply a list of our top annual events.

- **Carnevale** (p204) Venice; February. Revellers take to Venice's atmospheric streets every February to celebrate Carnevale. During the 10 days leading up to Ash Wednesday, the cold winter squares fill with party-goers sporting spectacular period costumes and elaborate masks.
- **Il Palio** (p258) Italy; July and August. Costumed jockeys career round Siena's Piazza del Campo in Italy's most famous horse race. Festivities begin with a huge parade of medieval pomp and finish off with streetside banquets.
- **San Fermines** (p436) Spain; early June. Running bulls and macho posturing attract TV crews from all over the world to Spain's most high-profile fiesta. Folk music, religious services and bullfighting add to Pamplona's high-octane fun.
- **Hellenic Festival** (p336) Greece; June to September. The highlight of the cultural calendar in Athens, this summer festival features international music, dance and theatre in one of the city's most atmospheric venues.
- **Cannes Film Festival** (p149) France; May. Stars parade up and down the Croisette at the film world's most glitzy get-together. Paparazzi and stargazers feast on the celebrity spectacle.
- **International Istanbul Music Festival** (p642) Turkey; June and July. Catch a concert in a sultan's palace or a 4th-century church. International artists descend on Istanbul to perform everything from classical music to jazz, rock to opera.

- Don't leave litter. If you're trekking in the mountains, stick to prepared paths whenever possible and always carry your rubbish away with you.
- Light fires only in fireplaces provided at picnic areas and camping grounds.
- Leave wildflowers where they are. Many are protected species and they all look much better in the countryside than squashed inside your pocket.
- Save water where possible – for example, turn the tap off while brushing your teeth.
- Don't use detergents or toothpaste (even if they are biodegradable) in or near watercourses. If you just gotta go when you're out in the wilderness, bury it in a hole at least 15cm deep and at least 100m from any watercourse.
- Use recycling bins if they are available.
- Do yourself and residents a favour and use public transport. Urban traffic congestion is a major problem.

# Itineraries
## CLASSIC ROUTES

### THE GRAND TOUR
One Month / Italy & Greece

A month is not a long time to take in all the treasures of Italy and Greece, but follow this Mediterranean itinerary for just a glimpse of what makes these countries so enduringly fascinating.

Starting with a couple of days in **Rome** (p163) you can admire some of the world's most photographed sights including St Peter's Basilica (where St Peter was buried), the Sistine Chapel and the Colosseum. From Rome head north to **Florence** (p215), the Renaissance capital of the world, where the Galleria Degli Uffizi (Uffuzi Gallery) on its own displays more masterpieces than most countries have in their posession. After a quick day trip to the leaning tower of **Pisa** (p223) it's off to **Venice** (p198) for a couple of days' exploring the picturesque waterways and marvelling at the majesty of Basilica di San Marco (St Mark's Basilica).

In the second week, head south for some dazzling ruins and startling coastline. **Naples** (p231) offers a high-voltage shot of art, culture and

food on the way to the ancient sites of **Herculaneum** (p236) and **Pompeii** (p236). With Mt Vesuvius looming menacingly in the background, the ruins provide an intriguing glimpse into ancient Roman life. Continuing southwards, the **Amalfi Coast** (p238) is one of Europe's most dramatic stretches of coastline. It incorporates beautiful towns such as **Positano** (p239) and **Amalfi** (p239), while further south, **Paestum** (p240) boasts three magnificent Greek temples.

From Paestum you'll need to double back 35km up the coast to Salerno before heading cross-country to **Brindisi** (p241) on the Adriatic coast. From here, take a ferry trip to **Patra** (p287) in Greece. On your arrival, don't hang around but head straight for the sacred site of **Olympia** (p293), where the first Olympic Games were staged in 776 BC. Continuing southeast you'll reach **Mystras** (p291), famed for the beauty of its Byzantine palaces and monasteries. Before leaving the mountainous islands of the Peloponnese, you shouldn't miss the mythical **Mycenae** (p291) and the ruins of **Ancient Corinth** (p290).

Across the water, the Greek capital **Athens** (p272) provides a chaotic mix of the ancient and the modern. Not to be missed, the Parthenon dominates the cityscape from its position over the Acropolis while the National Archaeological Museum houses the country's most important collection of ancient artefacts. After a couple of full days here make for stunning, ancient **Delphi** (p294) in the northwest. Home to the legendary oracle, this place has been attracting visitors in search of a prophesy since the 6th century BC. Continue further north for the spectacular monasteries of **Meteora** (p294).

For the last stretch of your Grand Tour, don your sea legs for some island hopping through the **Cyclades islands** (p300). For all-day sunbathing and all-night drinking head for Mykonos (a popular spot for gay revellers), Ios and the blue and white loveliness of Santorini. There's a quieter time to be had in Paros (p303) and Naxos (p305).

For transport information see the Italy (p260) and Greece (p339) chapters and the Transport in Mediterranean Europe chapter (p717).

This journey of ancient wonders and natural beauty covers 2295km and more than 3000 years of history. It requires considerable stamina but can easily be broken down into week-long segments.

## A MOORISH ADVENTURE    One Month / Spain, Morocco & Portugal

Combining Christian and Islamic traditions, Spain and Portugal's artistic heritage owes much to the Islamic influence of the Moroccan Moors.

A vibrant blend of nightlife and culture, **Madrid** (p351) is the place to start. From here head south, via **Toledo** (p372) and its remarkable cathedral, to Andalucía. Moorish marvels not to miss include the Mezquita in **Córdoba** (p418), **Seville's** 10th-century Alcázar (p414) and the Alhambra in **Granada** (p421).

Continuing southwards to Málaga you can pick up a ferry for **Melilla** (p665), a Spanish territorial port on the north coast of Morocco. From here, make for **Fès** (p682) where chances are you'll get completely lost in the massive ancient quarter (the medina). Once you've emerged, push on towards **Marrakesh** (p676), Morocco's red centre. Watch the sun set on the blood-red walls before hitting the road for the country's most cosmopolitan city, **Casablanca** (p671).

Returning to the Spanish mainland via **Tangier** (p653) and the great limestone lump of British **Gibraltar** (p430), it's time to turn west for Portugal. First stop is the resort of **Lagos** (p462), where the sandy beaches and watersports provide a welcome break for travel-weary bones. Further north, the unpretentious fortngese capital **Lisbon** (p448) marks the end of the road.

For transport information see the Spain (p439) and Portugal (p478) chapters and the Transport in Mediterranean Europe chapter (p717).

Taking anything from three weeks to one month, this route stretches 1590km over two continents, from Spain's religious architecture to Morocco's *souqs* and Portugal's beaches.

# ROADS LESS TRAVELLED

## TURKISH DELIGHTS
Two Weeks / Istanbul to Göreme

Bridging the gap between Europe and Asia, Turkey is an intriguing mix of East and West with a long history of Christian and Muslim rule. It boasts a spectacular landscape and some superb sandy beaches.

The obvious starting point is **Istanbul** (p603). Straddling the Bosphorus, it's a bubbling cauldron of a city, featuring the Aya Sofya and the Blue Mosque. Further round the Aegean **Çanakkale** (p613) is a popular base for visiting nearby **Gallipoli** (p613), scene of vicious WWI fighting, and the legendary town of **Troy** (p613).

Following the coast round to the southeast, you arrive at **Selçuk** (p617), 3km from the monumental Roman ruins at **Ephesus** (p617). About three hours' drive away **Bodrum** (p620) is home to the Mausoleum, the tomb of King Mausolus and one of the Seven Wonders of the Ancient World.

Sunseekers should push on for the magnificent beaches of Patara (p626) and take a moment here to visit the ruins, Kaş (p627) and Antayla (p629), some of the best beaches in the Mediterranean. Inland from the coast Konya (p637) is the historical home of the whirling dervishes, while further northeast the rocky landscape around Göreme (p638) is eerily breathtaking.

For transport information see the Turkey chapter (p644) and the Transport in Mediterranean Europe chapter (p717).

Two weeks is long enough to cover the 1100km of this Turkish tour but it could be extended for as long as you have available. The beautiful beaches are an ideal rest-cure after days of heavyweight sightseeing.

## CROATIAN COASTLINE

One Week / Dubrovnik to Zadar

Characterised by thousands of rocky inlets and islets, wonderfully clear waters and a number of historic towns, Croatia's 6000km coastline offers classic Mediterranean charm. Follow this northbound itinerary and you'll get at least some of the picture.

Described by Byron as the 'pearl of the Adriatic', **Dubrovnik** (p525) is a magical medieval town of ornamental fountains, palaces, churches and monasteries. Almost back to its best after shelling in 1992, it's a charming introduction to Croatia's coastal splendours.

From Dubrovnik, jump on a ferry for the short hop to the island of **Mljet** (p523), where you can hike, bike and boat in and around the lakes of the pine-clad national park.

Back on the mainland, continue northwards for **Split** (p513), Croatia's largest coastal city. Despite the less-than-beautiful suburbs, Split merits a visit for its historic centre and the imposing Roman palace of Diocletian. A ferry crossing away, the island of **Hvar** (p520) virtually guarantees sunshine in which to enjoy the many water sports on offer. From Split push on up the coast. Five kilometres northeast of town the ruins of **Solin** (p518) constitute Croatia's top archaeological site.

The last stop is Zadar (p510), whose strategic position has made it a target for hostile raiders throughout its long history. The high walls running along the harbour and massive 16th-century fortifications attest to the town's resilient spirit.

For transport information see the Croatia chapter (p535) and the Transport in Mediterranean Europe chapter (p717).

Stretching 300km, this exploration of Croatia's southern Dalmatian coast could take anything from one to two weeks, depending on how long you spend soaking up the sun.

## EXPLORE MONTENEGRO & ALBANIA   Two Weeks / Kotor to Saranda

Montenegro is one half of Europe's youngest nation (Serbia & Montenegro). A country of mountains, fjords and rivers, it's not exactly unexplored but it's still off the traditional tourist track.

One of the Balkans' great secrets, **Kotor** (p548) makes for a dramatic starting point. Situated at the head of southern Europe's deepest fjord, it boasts a Unesco-listed medieval city and some stunning mountain scenery. Heading southwards towards Albania the road leads to Montenegro's best beach resort **Budva** (p547) where you can sunbathe on the fine beaches and walk through the picturesque old town.

From Budvar head inland to Podgorica and the border crossing at Han i Hotit. A closed communist country until 1990, Albania provides relatively untrodden paths and a genuine travelling experience. From Shkodra, 30km south of the border, it's 116km to **Tirana** (p545). One of Europe's less-glamorous capitals, it's a bustling city of street markets and bulky 1930s Italian-style architecture. For a more laid-back feel head for **Durrës** (p545) on the Ionian coast. Here you can join the citizens on their early evening stroll and check out the impressive Roman amphitheatre. The road continues south, by way of the immaculate sandy beaches of **Dhërmi** and **Drymades** (p546) to the port of **Saranda** (p546), a favourite Albanian holiday resort.

For transport information see the Albania chapter (p546).

A couple of weeks is enough to cover the 380km trail that leads from southern Europe's deepest fjord in Montenegro down Albania's Ionian coast to the southern port of Saranda.

# TAILORED TRIPS

## A GASTRONOMIC WORKOUT
One Month / France, Italy & Spain

As good a place as any to start eating your way around the Mediterranean is **Montpellier** (p136) in France. Here you can tuck into cassoulet, a casserole of beans, pork sausage and goose conserve. For a seafood speciality make for **Marseille** (p116) whose *bouillabaisse* has been a staple of Provence fishing folk for centuries.

First stop on the Italian leg is **Bologna** (p209). Home of bolognese sauce,

known in Italy as *ragú*, this gourmet town also first cooked tortellini and lasagne. Overdosed on pasta, it's time for pizza and that means **Naples** (p231). Cooked in a traditional wood-fired oven, nothing beats this masterfully simple dish.

Jumping across the water to Spain, the first port of call is **Valencia** (p399), where paella was originally cooked. Then go southwards to **Seville** (p414) where you'll discover why tapas is such an irresistible Spanish snack.

Sate your thirst as you eat with the robust red wines of France and Italy and Spain's free-flowing sherry.

For transport information see the France (p151), Italy (p260) and Spain (p439) chapters and Transport in Mediterranean Europe (p717).

## ISLAND HERITAGE SITES
One Week / Cyprus, Rhodes, Patmos & Delos

Mediterranean Europe boasts a wealth of Unesco World Heritage Sites and you need only hop on a ferry to discover that there's more to the Aegean Islands than package resorts and heaving beaches.

In **Cyprus** (p549), head up to the beautiful Troodos mountains and their 10 Byzantine churches. Two striking examples are the Church of Archangelos in Pedoulas and Agios Nikolaos tis Stegis (St Nikolaos of the Roof) near Kakopetria. Down on the coast, the 3rd-century mosaics of **Pafos** (p561) are a major attraction.

Next stop is **Rhodes** (p317). A magnificent ensemble of Gothic and

Ottoman architecture, the old town in Rhodes City provides the island's historical highlight.

From Rhodes, it's a ferry journey to the holy island of **Patmos** (p323), where, in the Cave of the Apocalypse, St John is said to have written the *Book of Revelations*. The Monastery of St John the Theologian should not be missed.

Further east, the uninhabited **Delos** (p303) is the mythological birthplace of Apollo. Of the archaeological treasures that litter this ancient island, it's the 7th-century BC Sanctuary of Apollo that stands out.

For transport information see the Greece (p339) and Cyprus (p570) chapters and Transport in Mediterranean Europe (p717).

# The Authors

## DUNCAN GARWOOD
**Coordinating Author**

It was island-hopping around the Greek islands as a student that first opened Duncan's eyes to the charms of Mediterranean life. So when an opportunity arose for a move to Italy in 1997 he grabbed his chance. A two-year stint in Bari provided a full-immersion crash course in the ways of southern Italian life, before Rome claimed him in 1999. Currently living in the hills to the south of the capital, Duncan has explored Italy extensively, from the lakes and Alps of the north to the art cities of the centre and the coastal stretches of the deep south.

**My Favourite Trip**

Rome (p163) in early June is a lovely place to be. The sun's out, temperatures are bearable and the crowds are yet to hit their stifling worst. After my fill of ruins and baroque piazzas I head north towards Venice (p178), stopping on the way in Bologna (p209) to wolf down some of Italy's best pasta. Leaving the canals of Venice for a day I quickly nip off to the romantic city of Verona (p196) before the call of the sea proves too strong. Of the Mediterranean's coastal delights, I go for Croatia – sunshine is virtually guaranteed on the island of Hvar (p520), the picturesque port of Dubrovnik (p525) always charms and the Adriatic waters are just too tempting to resist.

Verona

Venice

Bologna

Rome

Hvar
Dubrovnik

## FIONA ADAMS
**Spain**

In love with all things Latin, Fiona worked as a journalist in South America for three years. More memorable adventures involve piranha fishing in the Amazon, lunch in a Bolivian jail and joining an expedition in search of Atlantis.

She has a degree in archaeology and anthropology, a masters in Latin American Studies and has worked on editions of Lonely Planet's *Spain*, *Italy* and *South America on a shoestring*.

Fiona and her husband Jamie live in the Scottish Highlands but are considering swapping cock-a-leekie broth for gazpacho and upping sticks to Andalucía.

## CAROLYN BAIN
**Malta**

Carolyn updated the Malta chapter. She grew up in a small country town outside Melbourne, Australia. Many of her classmates were the children of Maltese postwar immigrants – part of a mass migration that resulted in almost as many Maltese people living in Australia as in Malta! Carolyn eagerly signed up for the chance to visit this wee speck on the world map – what could be more perfect than a small, sunny island in the Med where everyone speaks English? Once there she fell in love with ricotta *pastizzi*, big old yellow buses and Gozitan farmhouses.

## JOE BINDLOSS                                    Cyprus

Joe was born in Famagusta and took refuge in Lefkosia during the conflict in 1974. He now lives in the UK, but he still makes regular trips to Cyprus to see friends and family and enjoy food that actually tastes of something. His favourite spot on the island is the Akamas Peninsula – he volunteered here on a sea turtle conservation project as one of his first solo travelling experiences as a teenager. Over the years, Joe has spear-fished off Cape Greko, gone rock-climbing in the Troodos and learned to cook *kleftiko* (baked lamb) from refugee chefs on the Green Line.

## TERRY CARTER                                    Greece

Terry's first visit to Greece was with a Greek-Australian friend returning to his local village in Rhodes for their annual festival. He quickly learnt that even the coolest Greek guys only need a couple of ouzos for the inner *zeïmbekiko* dancer to surface. While still preferring to play the Turkish *saz* than the bouzouki, he now has a clear understanding of how making Greek coffee differs from brewing Turkish coffee. When not dreaming of hiding away in Monemvasia with a few good books, Terry is a freelance writer and designer based in Dubai.

## VESNA MARIC                          Albania & Montenegro

Vesna Maric was born in Mostar, Bosnia–Hercegovina in 1976 and moved to Britain at the age of 16. She studied Czech Literature in London and lived in Prague for a year, before working for the BBC World Service for 3½ years. She has written magazine articles, produced radio features and worked on short films, and likes to photograph insignificant things. Her latest and, as she claims, most exciting project was travelling to Albania.

## AMY MARR                                        Italy

Boston-bred Amy's love affair with Italy began with an early addiction to Sicilian-style pizza. She studied Art History and Italian at Williams College and in Florence. After working as a business writer and PR director, she led and researched biking/hiking trips throughout Italy. In 1998 she moved to Santa Fe, where she managed Outside Online. Now a writer for magazines and a publisher of food and entertaining books, she is firmly rooted in Marin County, CA, but still shows signs of restlessness, tempered by cooking Italian feasts for friends, and regular trips to her favourite country.

### JEANNE OLIVER
Croatia

Jeanne is a freelance journalist, born in New Jersey and living in the south of France. She has been visiting and writing about Croatia since 1996, shortly after the new country was 'born'. Travelling the country by bus, boat, train and car, she's swum in its waters, hiked its trails and stuffed her backpack full of local cheese, homemade brandy and a handful of recipes to keep her going until the next trip. She's looking forward to eventually visiting every one of Croatia's islands, especially now that she's finally figured out how to read the Jadrolinija schedule.

### TOM PARKINSON
Turkey

Having lived on a street full of kebab shops in the second-biggest Turkish community in the world (Berlin, Germany), it was only a matter of time before Tom graduated to the real thing. For this book he took in the full scope of the Turkish Mediterranean experience, from haggling in Istanbul to hitching round the coast, with the occasional bomb alert thrown in. Thanks to diligent research, he remains an unrivalled authority on the relative merits of doner kebabs worldwide.

### JOSEPHINE QUINTERO
Portugal

Josephine updated the Portugal chapter. Born in England, she started travelling with a backpack and guitar in the late '60s (didn't everyone?), stopping off in Israel on a kibbutz for a year. Further travels took her to Kuwait where she edited the *Kuwaiti Digest* and was held hostage during the Iraq invasion of Kuwait.

Josephine then moved to the relaxed shores of Andalucía, Spain, from where she has enjoyed exploring neighbouring Portugal.

Josephine has contributed to more than 20 travel guidebooks and writes regularly for in-flight magazines and travel websites.

### ANDREW STONE
France

Andrew Stone updated the France chapter. Andrew's first experience of Southern France was as a schoolboy barely out of short trousers. A large extended French family (10 cousins) scattered around the country and an addiction to the country's wine and food ensures he remains a regular visitor.

### MARA VORHEES
**Morocco**

On her first day of her first trip to Morocco, Mara called home in tears. She had been propositioned, harassed and followed – all on a short stroll down Ave Mohammed V. Despite the harsh initiation, she successfully completed her field research on foreign aid programs, producing a fascinating thesis on cereals market deregulation. The experience led to nine years working in international development and extensive travel in Spain and Morocco. The pen-wielding traveller has since been lost and found in many medinas, drunk gallons of mint tea, and strolled down Ave Mohammed V in every town on the map.

# Snapshots

## CURRENT EVENTS

It's been a busy period for European leaders. On 1 May 2004 they cheerfully welcomed 10 new member states to the European Union, of which Cyprus, Malta and Slovenia bore the standard for Mediterranean Europe. Then, little more than a month later, it was once again smiles all round as they announced agreement on a new European Constitution.

Further afield, continuing hostilities in Iraq continued to dominate European headlines.

On a lighter note, armchair athletes enjoyed a summer of sporting excess as the European Football Championships kicked off in Portugal and the 24th Olympic Games returned to Athens, their historical hometown.

In Spain a royal wedding provided monarchists with an opportunity to wave their flags and the paparazzi with a chance to snap Europe's assembled royalty.

### France

Talk in France is centred on a new law that bans the wearing of Islamic veils in state schools. The controversial law, which also forbids students to wear Jewish skullcaps or large Christian crosses, has provoked outcry in the Muslim community which claims that it amounts to religious persecution. The government argues that France is a secular state and religious wear has no place in state schools. The controversy is set to continue as critics fear it will lead to an increase in religious extremism.

Elsewhere in France, a mayor of a small provincial town set tongues wagging when he married a homosexual couple and forced the left wing into coming out in favour of gay weddings and adoption by gay couples.

'The 24th Olympic Games returned to Athens, their historical hometown.'

### Italy

The release of three Italian hostages in Iraq after a blitz by US forces provoked a huge sigh of relief throughout the country. Shocked to the core when a fourth captive was shot dead within days of their capture, the government immediately requested a media blackout and Italy waited with uncharacteristic quiet. News of the release when it came was, however, curiously sketchy and led to much gossip and political speculation.

On the domestic front, the charismatic leader of the Lega Nord (Northern League) and major political player Umberto Bossi has been noticeable by his absence. Hit by a massive heart attack he has been in hospital for several months and although his supporters talk of a return to the scene, it seems unlikely in the near future. However, even from his bed, he managed to scare the living daylights out of Prime Minister Silvio Berlusconi when he resigned as Minister for Institutional Reform to take up a seat in the European Parliament. This left the government in a decidedly precarious position, with a full-blown crisis only avoided after several days of fevered negotiation between coalition members.

### Greece

When conservative Costas Karamanlis became the youngest ever Greek prime minister, he inherited something of a hot potato. Preparations for the 24th Olympic Games in Athens were not going well and sniping in the international press had become a daily sport. Defiant organisers continued to assure critics that yes, despite appearances, everything would be ready on time (it was). Three small bomb explosions 100 days before the opening ceremony did little to allay security fears.

Athenians had mixed feelings over the whole business. Glad of the benefits of an improved transport system, they couldn't help but feel an opportunity had been lost to brighten the city as only one-seventh of the planned greening of Athens was actually completed. All grumbles were put to one side though as Greeks took to the streets to celebrate the improbable victory of their national football team in the 2004 European Championships.

## Spain

Heavy rain did little to dampen Spanish enthusiasm as Crown Prince Felipe married former TV anchorwoman Letizia Ortiz Rocasolano at a sumptuous ceremony in Madrid. Coming little more than two months after the Spanish capital had been ripped apart by a series of bomb attacks, it provided some much needed light relief.

On 11 March 2004, 10 bombs exploded on four Madrid commuter trains killing 191 people. The al-Qaeda attacks were seen as a direct consequence of Spain's participation in the Iraq war and proved a major factor in the victory of socialist Luis Rodríguez Zapatero in the general elections of 14 March. Within a month Zapatero had ordered the withdrawal of Spain's troops from Iraq, thus reversing his predecessor's pro-war policy.

## Portugal

It's a good time to be a football fan in Portugal. Club side Porto are European champions and the national side reached the final of the 2004 European Championship, finishing runners-up to unlikely champions Greece. The tournament, involving 16 teams in 31 matches, provided Portuguese security forces with their biggest headache in living memory. Faced with an influx of an estimated one million spectators for the 3½-week football frenzy, organisers spent some €450 million on ensuring the tournament is remembered for the quality of the sport rather than any terrorist or hooligan-inspired violence.

## Croatia

Out of the flurry of headlines emerging from a two-day summit of European leaders in Brussels, the announcement that Croatia had become an official candidate for entry to the EU didn't make much of a splash. However, if the entry talks that are due to start in 2005 are successful Croatia will become only the second former Yugoslav republic to join the Union. (Slovenia became a member on 1 May 2004.)

European leaders said they'd been impressed by Croatia's willingness to cooperate with the UN War Crimes Tribunal in The Hague but that it was still necessary to improve minority rights and to speed up the return of Serb refugees who escaped the country in the 1990s.

## Cyprus

There's to be no end to the schism that has divided Cyprus for more than 30 years. Following the failure of a UN-sponsored unification plan and much to the chagrin of the Turkish north, the Greek-controlled half of the island became one of 10 new members of the EU on 1 May 2004.

Islanders were invited to vote on the UN proposals in a referendum in April 2004. Turkish Cypriots, eager to rejoin the international fold, voted overwhelmingly in favour of the plan but, at the urging of their president Tassos Papadopoulos, Greek Cypriots gave it the thumbs down. The effect that membership of the EU will have on the island remains to be seen.

Letizia Ortiz Rocasolano, now known as Princess Letizia of Asturias, is the first commoner ever to be in line to the Spanish throne.

## Malta

A spectacular fireworks display lit up the Grand Harbour in Valletta as Malta celebrated its newly acquired membership of the EU. The question of the island's EU application had been the central issue in the April 2003 general election, which was won by the veteran leader Eddie Fenech Adami. On retiring in March 2004, Adami was replaced by Lawrence Gonzi.

On a more glamorous note, islanders were thrilled when Brad Pitt and crew sauntered into town to film the blockbuster *Troy*. The Hollywood producers were drawn to the island's dramatic cliffs and rock formations, which they felt were a suitably spectacular setting for Brad's chiselled looks.

Malta's branch of the Manchester United Supporters Club is the oldest in the world.

## Turkey

As the 10 new EU nations celebrated their membership status on 1 May 2004, Turkey took a rueful look at its own European position. The country has long held aspirations to join the Union but human rights issues and the complex Kurdish question have proved obstacles. EU leaders are set to decide in December 2004 if entry talks can begin in March 2005.

The cream of Europe's singing talent rocked into Istanbul in May 2004 for the 49th edition of Europe's much-maligned musical bonanza, the Eurovision Song Contest.

## Morocco

A collective wave of disappointment swept through the country when it was announced that the 2010 World Cup would be held in South Africa. Morocco's bid to host the massive money-spinner that is the world's largest football tournament was generally regarded to have been in with a serious chance but the commercial aspirations of FIFA (football's governing body) played into South Africa's hands.

The event would have proved a welcome diversion in a country that has been hit hard by the upsurge in international terrorism. Casablanca was hit by suicide bombers in May 2003 and Moroccan citizens have been linked with the Madrid bombings of March 2004.

On a lighter note, Moroccan rastas flocked to the town of Essaouira to let their dreads down at the annual Gnawa festival. The star attraction was Bob Marley's reggae band, the Wailers, now fronted by Aston Family Man Barret.

# HISTORY

Any exploration of the Mediterranean's tempestuous past starts in the realm of myth. The Sirens were said to have seduced sailors in the waters off southern Italy, Homer wrote of Odysseus island-hopping from one adventure to another, while in Crete legend has the half-man, half-bull Minotaur feasting on human flesh.

It is with the emergence of the Greek Empire, the first of the Mediterranean's great superpowers, that myth begins to merge into history. Successive centuries bore witness to the rise and fall of various power blocs of which the Roman Empire was the most spectacular example. Emerging some time later the Muslim Ottoman Empire dominated Turkey and much of the Balkans until the early 20th century.

The history of the region is also one of exploration and colonialisation. The 15th and 16th centuries were full of tales of derring-do on the high seas and it was largely thanks to the discoveries of Columbus and Magellan, da Gama and Diaz that Spain and Portugal were able to build their massive overseas empires.

Revolution and civil war have plagued Mediterranean countries. Most famously, revolution undid the 18th-century French monarchy and paved the way for Napolean and his imperial ambitions. Similarly, in Spain, civil war led to the lengthy Franco dictatorship. Military-backed regimes also affected Portugal and Greece.

What follows is not intended to be a chronological history of the region but rather a brief look at some of the major historical themes.

## Ancient Civilisations

The ancient history of the Mediterranean is dominated by the two great empires of Greece and Rome.

Based on the city-state, or polis, the Greek Empire more closely resembled a confederation of often competing rivals than a unified political entity. Athens and, to a lesser extent, Sparta became the dominant powers, maintaining a hold over colonies as far afield as southern Italy and Sicily.

Despite the fragmented nature of the Empire, intercity rivalries were put on hold in times of danger as the Persians discovered to their cost when they were defeated by the Greeks at the battles of Marathon (490 BC) and Salamis (480 BC). A period of unprecedented enlightenment and prosperity, known as the Classical Age, followed. The Athenians in particular had never had it so good. Pericles revealed a common touch by championing democracy, and a visionary nature by commissioning the Parthenon; Sophocles, Aeschylus and Euripides established their literary reputations and Socrates turned his mind to the nature of knowledge.

Alas, the good times were not to last and in 431 BC the Spartans, driven by a consuming jealousy of their rich Athenian neighbours, sparked off the Peloponnesian War. Ending in defeat for Athens in 404 BC, the war was of limited value to the Spartans who themselves were defeated shortly after by the Thebans. Theban rule was also shortlived as King Philip II of Macedonia stormed in from the north taking control of the exhausted city-states.

Philip's ambitions were obvious but they were nothing compared to those of his son, Alexander the Great. Succeeding his father in 336 BC at the age of 20, Alexander took only 13 years to conquer Asia Minor, Egypt, Persia and parts of India and Afghanistan. His death at the age of 33, however, ensured the break-up of the largest empire the world had ever seen as his generals divided the imperial spoils between themselves.

Greek power was on the wane and by 146 BC both Greece and Macedonia had become Roman provinces.

Tradition has Romulus founding Rome in 753 BC although it wasn't until the end of the 3rd century BC that the young Roman Republic managed to overpower the Etruscans. By 218 BC, all of Italy south of the Alps, except the northwest, was under Roman control.

It was the Alps that provided the unexpected gateway for the Carthaginian general Hannibal and his elephants to march into Italy during the second Punic War (218–202 BC). Ending in defeat for Carthage, the war whet the Romans' appetite for expansion, and Spain, much of North Africa, and Greece rapidly fell to the rampant legionnaires.

Less than a hundred years later, Julius Caesar was at the helm, orchestrating victories in Gaul and Egypt. An imposing fellow, Julius Caesar eventually became too powerful for his own good and on the Ides of March (15 March) 44 BC was stabbed to death. A power struggle ensued between Mark Antony and Octavian, Caesar's great-nephew. Inheriting something of the family nous, Octavian proved too strong for Antony who, together with his Egyptian lover Cleopatra, died in 31 BC.

David Childress leads readers on a fascinating exploration of the ancient past in his book *Lost Cities of Atlantis, Ancient Europe and the Mediterranean.*

Octavian became the first Roman to bear the title of Augustus (Your Eminence) and was, in effect, the first Roman emperor. Unlike many of his successors, he ruled well and oversaw great advances in engineering and architecture as well as a flourishing literary scene, of which Virgil, Horace and Ovid were the leading lights.

By the end of the 3rd century the Empire had become so vast that Emperor Diocletion divided it into two parts – the Eastern Empire and the Western Empire. His successor Constantine went further by founding Constantinople (modern-day Istanbul) in Byzantium as his Eastern capital.

But the Empire was by now in full decline. German tribes entered Rome in AD 476 and the barbarian leader Odoacer proclaimed himself ruler of Italy. The Eastern Empire lasted a little longer hanging on until it was effectively incorporated into the Byzantine Empire.

## Exploration

The late 15th century marked the great era of European exploration. Admittedly, Marco Polo (1254–1324) had already travelled from his native Venice to China and the Far East but it wasn't until the Portuguese master mariners started stretching the navigational limits of the day that exploration became big business.

The Portuguese benefitted hugely from the trade routes that their explorers opened up. The spice route was already a well-established overland trail when Vasco da Gama (1469–1524) became the first European to reach India by sea. Setting off from Portugal in 1497 he followed the route Bartolomeu Diaz (died 1500) had pioneered around the Cape of Good Hope in 1488 before crossing the Indian Ocean to Calicut. Successive ships of Portuguese traders wasted little time in grabbing control of the lucrative spice trade.

Ferdinand Magellan (1480–1521) may have been Portuguese but it was the Spanish who financed his westward voyage to the Pacific, via the Strait that bears his name. Setting out from Spain in 1519 Magellan himself died in the Philippines but one of his five ships eventually made it back to Spain via the Indian Ocean and Cape of Good Hope and so completed the first circumnavigation of the world.

Spanish money also sponsored the most famous of all explorers, Christopher Columbus (1451–1506). Genoan by birth, Columbus had long dreamed of sailing westwards to discover a new route to the Indies. Unfortunately, the financiers of the day were less idealistic and it took years of begging until he finally got the green light. His plan, however, failed and on 12 October 1492 he landed on a small island in what is now the Bahamas. He had discovered America.

America was named after Florentine explorer Amerigo Vespucci (1454–1512). Vespucci explored much of the South American coastline and earned a reputation as an exceptional navigator.

## Revolution & Religion

At the same time as the sea breezes were propelling Europeans across the seven seas, the winds of religious discontent were sweeping over Europe.

The Catholic popes may have been delighted at the missionary zeal of the European colonialists, but they were less happy at the religious doctrines seeping down from northern Europe. Top of their hit list was the German monk Martin Luther (1483–1546) whose ideas inspired the Protestant Reformation and fuelled the violent backlash of the Catholic Counter-Reformation. History, however, shows that although the Catholic masters of the day failed to eradicate Protestantism completely, it never seriously threatened their hold in the Mediterranean.

Not so Islam, which had been introduced into Spain as early as the eighth century. By AD 714 Muslim armies from Morocco had occupied virtually all of the Spanish Peninsula establishing a hold that they would not fully relinquish for almost 800 years. But just as their control over Spain was on the wane, so, further east, the seeds of Ottoman power were being sown in Turkey. Reaching the peak of its power in the 16th century, the Muslim Ottoman Empire was long a thorn in the side of Catholic dominion.

The guillotine was not created by Joseph Guillotin (1738–1814) but by Tobias Schmidt, a German harpsichord player, and Leon Berger, a French carpenter.

Despite the threats from outside, much of the Mediterranean remained in the hands of Catholic royalty. An extravagant lot, the European monarchs were given a severe wake-up call when Louis XVI of France and his wife Marie-Antoinette quite literally lost their heads to the guillotine. The French Revolution broke out in 1789 setting off a series of bloody events that culminated in Napoleon declaring himself Emperor of France in 1804.

In Spain it was the Fascist General Franco who emerged victorious from his country's three-year Civil War (1936–39). A bitter affair that pitted the Nationalist coalition of army, Church and Fascist party against the factious left-wing Republicans, it left up to 350,000 Spaniards dead and the country isolated. It wasn't until 1977, two year's after Franco's death, that the first post-dictatorship elections were held.

Across the border in Portugal, the military were busy arming their guns with flowers. In 1974, the so-called Revolution of the Carnations put paid to 48 years of military rule, as the army effectively led a peaceful mutiny against its dictatorial leaders. In the same year the Greek colonels were forced out of power after a brutal seven-year incumbency.

## PEOPLE
### Minority Cultures

The ethnic map of Mediterranean Europe presents a complex picture. Migration, both within the area and from outside, has led to the creation of hundreds of small communities – there are, for example, pockets of Albanians in Italy, Turks in Greece, and North Africans in Spain and France. Add to this the strong regional affiliations felt in many parts – a Catalan is first a Catalan and then a Spaniard – and the profusion of traditional dialects, and clear-cut national boundaries begin to seem increasingly blurred.

Film stars Yul Brynner, Charlie Chaplin, Michael Caine, Bob Hoskins and Rita Hayworth have all claimed Roma ancestry.

Throughout the Balkan Peninsula, but also elsewhere, there are numerous Roma communities. No official figures exist for their population, but estimates put it at around 12 million worldwide. Originally from India – the original Romany language is based on Hindi – the Roma arrived in Europe in the 14th century.

Over the centuries the various groups that constitute the Roma have adopted their own customs and dialects, even if most adhere to a system of social standards known as the Romaniya. It is this system that lies at the heart of the Roma's reluctance to integrate in other societies, stressing as it does the need for social and cultural independence.

## SPORT

Competitive sport in Mediterranean Europe dates back to 776 BC when the original Olympic Games were first celebrated in Olympia. More than 2½ millennia later and they returned to Greece as Athens hosted the 2004 Olympic Games. As in all modern sporting events, even if lip service is paid to sporting ideals, they play a poor second fiddle to the ruthless demands of the real masters of world sport – the TV bosses.

The commercialisation of sport, and football in particular, has reached ludicrous heights. Far and away the most popular sport, football is followed by millions of fans throughout the region. It follows that,

Mediterranean Europe produces some of the best teams in the world – the French national team regularly wins top tournaments, while club sides from Spain and Italy dominate the European tournaments. Basking in the international spotlight, Portugal is enjoying its moment of glory – not only did it host the 2004 European championships but its club side Porto are reigning European champions.

There are other sports followed in the region. Cycling is big in Spain, France and Italy and the world famous Tour de France is recognised as *the* premier cycling race. Past champions include Spain's cycling legend Miguel Indurain, five-times winner between 1991 and 1995, and Marco Pantani, an Italian cyclist who died just before the 2004 Tour de France.

Basketball is also widely followed. Big in the Balkans, leagues in Croatia, Serbia & Montenegro, and Greece enjoy considerable popular support. Elsewhere, top games in Spain and Italy regularly pull in the punters.

Considered by many to be barbaric and cruel, by others a noble act of courage and tradition, bullfighting continues to arouse passions. The bullfighting centre of Mediterranean Europe is the southern Spanish region of Andalucía where some 70 bullrings play host to regular events. Over the border in France up to 40 towns in the south of the country have bullrings.

## RELIGION

The arm of the Church is long in southern Europe. Although Roman Catholicism is not the state religion in any of the major Mediterranean countries, its influence is considerable. At the heart of many local customs and beliefs lies the Church's ideology and even if church attendance is not exactly high (roughly 20% in Spain, 35% in Italy), most people in these parts consider themselves Roman Catholic. A question of form, perhaps, but one that plays an important role in the fundamentally conservative societies of the Mediterranean – first communions, church weddings and religious feast days are an integral part of life. The sheer number of churches in the region is also a noticeable feature – from the seat of papal power, St Peter's Basilica in Rome, to the humblest of village chapels, the physical presence of the Church is never far away.

'The arm of the Church is long in southern Europe.'

The Eastern Orthodox Church is the major denomination in Greece and Serbia & Montenegro. Divided into self-governing national churches, of which the most important are headed by a patriarch, it is, theologically speaking, fairly close to Catholicism. Services are based on the Byzantine Rite, which includes communion and confession and differs only in detail from its Roman Catholic counterpart. The Orthodox Church does not, however, accept the authority of the pope.

Morocco, Turkey and Albania are the major standard bearers for Islam in the region. As in the worldwide Muslim community, the overwhelming majority are Sunni Muslim. Sunnis differ from the Shiite minority in their interpretation of the Sunna, Islam's second most important holy text, which, put crudely, acts as a reader's guide to the Qur'an.

Throughout the region there are also a number of Jewish and Protestant communities.

## ARTS
### Art & Architecture

Repository for much of the Western world's artistic and architectural heritage, Mediterranean Europe is a dream destination for art lovers. Not only is it home to some of the world's most recognisable paintings – Leonardo da Vinci's *Mona Lisa*, for example, and Picasso's *Guernica* –

but it also boasts an architectural appeal unparalleled anywhere in the world. The Acropolis and the Colosseum tell of past glories, Gothic churches tower into the sky while baroque palaces dazzle with their ornate beauty and Moorish mosques offer a mesmerising glimpse of the East.

It was the Renaissance of the 15th and 16th centuries which more than any other period marked the high point in European art. Spurred on by the Medici family in Florence and the popes in Rome, Leonardo da Vinci, Michelangelo and Raphael were the star players, creating a body of work that still inspires awe today. The world's single greatest collection of Renaissance art is housed in Florence's Uffizi Gallery.

Europe's artistic and architectural traditions date back thousands of years. The wealth of Greek and Roman ruins across the region attest to the importance that people attached to public buildings and private displays. Roman innovations on Greek architectural styles tended to be more a case of technique than art although in the dying days of the Empire, eastern influences began to creep into Roman art as the Byzantine hold tightened.

In Spain the influence of Islamic styles is all too evident. The famous Mezquita (Great Mosque) in Córdoba is one of many stunning examples of Moorish architecture that survive to this day. Over the water in Morocco, the *medersas* (religious schools) of Fès are a visual feast.

For something completely different head north. Gaudí's Sagrada Família church in Barcelona is an icon to the modernist spirit that swept through Spain and France in the late 19th and early 20th centuries. In France, Monet, Renoir and co. gifted the world with impressionism, which Cézanne and Gauguin later developed into post-impressionism. Picasso and Braque heralded in cubism, while in Spain Dalí and Miró went down their own decidedly original paths.

France's contribution to European architecture dates back to the 11th century when the Normans' Christian zeal led to the construction of many Romanesque churches. Characterised by thick walls and round arches they can be found throughout France and as far afield as Sicily, a one-time Norman province. Towards the end of the 12th century, churches began to get increasingly bigger and more dramatic. The Gothic architects believed that the higher you went the nearer you got to God, so they built big, with huge pointed arches signalling the way to heaven and ornate stained glass windows providing a touch of colour. For confirmation, try Notre Dame in Paris or Seville's gigantic cathedral for size.

Equally as exuberant but considerably lighter on the eye, the baroque offerings of the 17th century continue to dazzle. Many of the ornate sculptures that grace Rome's city centre were sculpted by baroque master Gianlorenzo Bernini.

*The Penguin Book of the Renaissance* by JH Plumb examines the artistic energy and bloody machinations of this remarkable period.

# ENVIRONMENT
## The Land

The Mediterranean nations covered in this guide encompass more than three million sq km of land. In the west, Portugal marks the last stop on the European mainland, while just a short hop over the water from neighbouring Spain lies the North African kingdom of Morocco. Three thousand kilometres to the east and by way of France, Italy, the Balkan Peninsula and Greece, Turkey bridges the passage from Europe to Asia.

Characterised by low-lying sandy beaches, the coastline of the Mediterranean does, in fact, offer plenty of variety. Head to the Amalfi Coast in Italy, for example, and you'll find spectacular cliffs plummeting into blue waters; further east and the 6000km of craggy Croatian coast offers a seemingly infinite number of rocky inlets.

Travel inland from the coast and much of the region's interior is mountainous. The best known of Europe's mountain ranges is the Alps, which run from southern France across the north of Italy and east into Austria. In Slovenia, the Dinaric Alps branch southeast off the main range and continue down through the Balkans into Greece where they become the Pindos Mountains. Other major ranges include the four chains of the Atlas Mountains in Morocco, the Pyrenees in Spain, and the Italian Apennines. The most famous and most expensive Alpine resorts are to be found in Italy and France, but skiing and summer trekking are available throughout the region.

Although under threat from acid rain and summer fires, great forests still cover large swathes of the Balkan Peninsula. Up to 50% of Slovenia is covered by forest, while neighbouring Croatia boasts some wonderfully preserved oak forests. Further south, 40% of Albania's land surface is forest. In order to conserve these massive natural habitats, environmentalists are continuously pushing for increased protection.

One of the region's most spectacular natural phenomena is provided by Mt Etna in Sicily. One of four active volcanoes in Italy (the others are Stromboli and Vulcano in the Aeolian Islands and Vesuvius near Naples), Etna is a regular, if unpredictable, blower. Eruptions are frequent and although spectacular, are often highly disruptive to local life.

A much more serious risk is posed by the threat of earthquakes. Particularly vulnerable are Greece and Turkey, which lie at the heart of one of the world's most seismically active areas. In 1999 three massive earthquakes, two in Turkey and one in Greece, left thousands of people dead. The most powerful, measuring 7.4 on the Richter scale, hit Izmit in northwest Turkey on 17 August, killing some 17,000 people. The activity is caused by the convergence of the Eurasian, African and Arabian continental plates deep below the eastern Mediterranean. As the plates wear away at each other, they rise and fall, creating tremors that, depending on their force, result in quakes on the earth's surface.

## Wildlife

Much of the region's wildlife quietly goes about its business in inland areas away from the spotlight. Wolves and brown bears, chamois, deer and lynx are all present, although numbers are limited and recent research has warned that the Iberian lynx (indigenous to Spain and Portugal) is on the verge of extinction. Wild boars roam the wooded parklands of southern Europe and the Atlas Mountains of Morocco, while various species of

Spain boasts the region's cleanest beaches. Some 370 have won the prestigious Blue Flag beach rating awarded by the Foundation for Environmental Action in Europe.

---

**MEDITERRANEAN FACT FILE**

The third largest sea in the world after the South China Sea and the Caribbean, the Mediterranean covers an area of 2,510,000 sq km, measuring 3900km at its longest point and 1600km at the widest. Almost entirely landlocked, it's connected to the Atlantic Ocean by the Strait of Gibraltar; to the Black Sea in the east by the Dardanelles and the Bosphorus; and to the Red Sea by the Suez Canal. Because of these limited oceanic connections tidal activity in the Mediterranean is minimal.

Within the Mediterranean there are a number of smaller seas, of which the most important are: the Tyrrhenian (running down the west coast of Italy); the Adriatic (between the east coast of Italy and the Dalmatian coast); the Ionian (between Italy and Greece); and the Aegean (between Greece and Turkey).

A characteristic feature is the huge number of islands that litter the seascape. Greece alone has about 2000, many of which are little more than rocks and sea gulls. The biggest islands are, from east to west: Cyprus, Rhodes, Crete, Malta, Sicily, Sardinia, Corsica, Menorca, Mallorca and Ibiza.

For an introduction to the region's flora and fauna read Paul Sterry's *Complete Mediterranean Wildlife*. It covers everything from seashells to reptiles and wildflowers.

vipers lie coiled in the region's rocky nooks and crannies. On some beaches in Turkey and Cyprus you might even spot a nesting turtle.

The Mediterranean skies are home to a rich assortment of bird life and are particularly impressive in spring and autumn as flocks of migrating birds pass through. Ornithologists can marvel at the huge numbers of storks that stop for a breather in Morocco or at the eagles and hawks that haughtily swoop the skies. Menacing vultures can be spotted in Croatia, France and Greece.

Dive into the deep blue sea and you discover a thriving marine ecosystem. In the Ligurian Sea above Corsica whale watchers have counted up to 2000 whales and up to 45,000 dolphins in summer. In fact, it is here that a 32,000-sq-m safe haven was established in 1999 for whales and dolphins. A permanent home to seven species, it welcomes an additional five species in summer. White sharks have also been spotted in the Mediterranean but attacks are almost unheard of.

## National Parks

The best of the flora and fauna is found in the region's national parks and nature reserves. Conservationists are continually lobbying to increase the amount of land protected but despite an increased awareness of environmental issues it remains an uphill struggle.

The following areas are classified as Unesco World Heritage sites.

**Croatia** Plitvice Lakes National Park
**France** Scandola Nature Reserve in Corsica
**Italy** Aeolian Islands
**Slovenia** Škocjan Caves
**Spain** Garajonay National Park; Doñana National Park

## Environmental Issues

Since ancient times, human activity has been taking its toll on the Mediterranean. Today, one of the biggest environmental issues, both on land and sea, is traffic. Many of the major cities in the region suffer from the choking effects of uncontrolled traffic and while attempts are made to curb the flow of cars into city centres, they tend to be half-hearted at best.

On the high seas the situation is little better. The seaways are heavily used and although the Mediterranean constitutes just 1% of the earth's marine surface, about 20% of the world's oil tanker traffic passes through, spilling, on average, 635,000 tonnes of crude oil a year. This naturally does little for the health of the maritime fauna, which is already suffering from overfishing. Approximately 1.5 million tonnes of fish are caught each year, which, while good news for the restaurant business, is less so for ever-depleting fish stocks.

It is a bitter irony that one of the biggest threats to the region's environment is posed by one of its biggest money-spinners – mass tourism. To cater to the annual influx of 220 million holiday-makers, increasingly large areas are being taken over by developers keen to cash in. One of the side effects is an increase in soil erosion and desertification. Already a problem thanks to road-building, climate change and industrial-scale farming, its effects are estimated at US$200 million a year in Spain alone.

Such a large seasonal increase in population levels also adds to the pressure on the region's water resources and increases the risk of bushfires. Each year more than 50,000 fires consume up to 8000 hectares of land, destroying natural habitats and indigenous forests. Of these fires, 95% are said to be caused by human activity.

# FOOD & DRINK

To enjoy your food in these parts is to partake in a tradition that goes back thousands of years. Ever since the ancient Greek hedonists raised the pursuit of pleasure to a philosophy and the Romans discovered the fun to be had at a good dinner orgy, food and its enjoyment have had a special place in Mediterranean hearts.

Few regions in the world offer such a variety of cuisines in such a small area. Dishes range from the spicy couscous concoctions of Morocco to the meaty kebabs so favoured by Turkish diners, from the best pizza you'll ever taste to seafood plucked straight off the fishing boat.

You'll also be spoiled for choice when selecting your tipple. France and Italy produce the top wines in the world – Champagne and Chianti, Burgundy and Barolo – and while buffs will have a field day, you need not pay a fortune for good wine. In many places the house wine will be a decent, local drop that costs little more than mineral water. In Spain, try the sherry or sangría; Portugal is famous for its port, while both Turkey (*rakı*) and Greece (*ouzo*) specialise in super-strong aniseed spirits.

To fully enjoy your meal in the Mediterranean you should follow a few simple guidelines: first, ensure you're in congenial company; second, select a suitable spot, whether it's a seafront trattoria or kerbside café; and thirdly, sit back, slow down and relax. Rush your meal and you're missing the point.

Elizabeth David's *Mediterranean Cooking* is a classic of kitchen literature. To bring the taste of the Mediterranean into your own home follow her recipes.

## Staples & Specialities

### BREAD

Bread is fundamental to the Mediterranean diet. Coming in all shapes and sizes – from the flat pitta bread used in Turkish kebabs to the long baguettes baked by the French *boulangers* – it's served as a matter of course at all meals except breakfast. When eating out, don't take it personally when a basket is plonked on your table and you're later charged for it even though you neither asked for it nor ate it. It's standard practice.

### PASTA

To an Italian, a meal without pasta is as meaningless as a game of football without the ball. But although pasta is largely produced, and eaten, in Italy, it's served throughout the Mediterranean. A reliable choice for diners on a budget, it's served with a mouthwatering array of sauces, many of which are disarmingly simple. There's nothing complicated, for example, about adding cherry tomatoes, fresh basil, garlic and olive oil to spaghetti.

### GRAINS & PULSES

Much of the health of the Mediterranean diet is thanks to the profusion of lentils, chickpeas and beans. Decidedly unglamorous, they crop up in a number of regional dishes, including pastas, soups, and salads, and are a mainstay of Moroccan cooking.

Of the grains, couscous forms the bedrock of many North African dishes while across the water, rice is used in many traditional dishes – paella in Spain or risotto in Italy.

### FRUIT & VEGETABLES

The key to much regional cooking is the quality of the fruit and vegetables. Blessed with a favourable climate, the Mediterranean producers put on an enviable display of home-grown goodies. These include onions, aubergines, tomatoes, garlic, capsicums, mushrooms, artichokes and cucumbers, oranges, lemons, melons, apricots, dates and figs.

To gauge the importance of these products, try to imagine Italian cuisine without the tomato or Greek cooking without the aubergine. Life simply wouldn't be the same without *ragú* (the meat-flavoured tomato sauce known outside Italy as bolognese) or moussaka (the ubiquitous Greek dish of aubergine, mince and béchamel sauce).

### OLIVES & OLIVE OIL

Thousands of hectares across the Mediterranean are given over to growing olives, which are used for eating, cooking and making oil. Olive oil is no luxury in these parts, but rather a staple without which cooking would simply be unthinkable. The colour and consistency vary, ranging from a gloopy petrol green to a less viscous golden yellow, depending on the type of olives used, the ripeness at which they're picked and how they're crushed. Likewise, quality varies enormously.

'Mediterranean Europe is a dream for seafood aficionados.'

### MEAT

In the Muslim areas, lamb is the meat of choice. Turkish cooks like to shred it into pitta bread to make their famous kebabs, while in Morocco it is stewed in earthenware pots for the national dish, *tagine*. You'll also find it roasted, often over an open fire.

In the southern European countries, ham is a favourite. Cured using traditional techniques, it appears in various guises – in Spain ask for *jamón serrano*, in France for *jambon* and in Italy for *prosciutto*.

### SEAFOOD

Mediterranean Europe is a dream for aficionados of seafood. Despite overfishing and pollution, the Mediterranean still supplies a dazzling array of edible treasures: fresh prawns, mussels, clams, octopus and squid are all menu mainstays popping up in various sauces and salads or simply fried or grilled. Cod is another favourite, particularly in Portugal where *bacalhau* (dried salt cod) has been a staple since the 16th century.

---

## TOP TEN MEDITERRANEAN DELIGHTS

- **France** Provence fisher folk have been cooking the fish stew *bouillabaisse* for centuries.
- **Spain** Paella is the national dish but foodies go mad for tapas, the small savoury dishes served with drinks at many bars.
- **Portugal** For a fish dish, *bacalhau* (dried salt cod) appears in dozens of dishes.
- **Italy** Pizza aficionados claim you can't beat pizza margherita. The topping of tomato (red), mozzarella (white) and basil (green) reflects the national flag.
- **Greece** Vegetarians will enjoy the *horiatiki salata* (read Greek salad), a mix of cucumbers, olives, red onions, tomatoes and feta cheese.
- **Croatia** On the coast, the Dalmatian speciality *brodet* (a broth of mixed fish and rice) is a perennial favourite.
- **Albania & Montenegro** Meat served with sour cream or yogurt is common. A local speciality is *rosto me salcë kosi* (roast beef with sour cream).
- **Turkey** Kebabs are king. For a simple bite go for the *durum döner kebab*, sliced lamb packed into pitta bread.
- **Cyprus** To sample a bit of everything go for meze, a multicourse spread of cheese, hummus (a chickpea purée), *koupepia* (stuffed vine leaves), *seftalia* (local sausage) and much more.
- **Malta** The national speciality is *fenech* (rabbit), which is fried or baked in a casserole.

## HERBS & SPICES

Freshly cut herbs are used in many Mediterranean dishes. Basil, bay laurel, parsley, sage, rosemary and thyme grow freely in the warm southern European climate and are found in all well-stocked kitchens.

Over the water, Moroccan cuisine uses a rich variety of spices. These include coriander and cumin, saffron, cinnamon and paprika. Chillis are liberally used to add a kick to many dishes.

## DESSERTS

Fruit is often served as a dessert or is incorporated into the cakes and pastries that are so beloved by sweet-toothed locals. Small family-run pastry shops do a flourishing trade in cakes, tarts and biscuits, especially on Sundays and special occasions.

Honey, nuts and raisins are often used to sweeten North African desserts.

## Drinks

### WINES & SPIRITS

Wine buffs will have their work cut out in Mediterranean Europe. France and Italy are the two largest wine producers in the world and many other Mediterranean nations make their own wines. But don't worry if you're not an expert; wine drinking is not the preserve of the well-heeled or well-informed, it's a fundamental part of many people's everyday routines. Most restaurants, bars and cafés serve decent local wines that are often a much better bet than beer or soft drinks (even on a budget).

Other tipples worth tasting include sherry and sangría in Spain, port in Portugal, ouzo in Greece, and *rakı* in Turkey.

Although Islam forbids the drinking of alcoholic beverages, they are nevertheless widely available in Morocco and Turkey.

### BEER

Even though there is no great tradition of beer drinking in most Mediterranean countries, beer is never hard to find. Local brews abound and are usually cheaper than the imported lagers which can be very expensive. Similarly, drinking draught beer is cheaper than quaffing the bottled stuff.

### TEA & COFFEE

Drunk in massive quantities, coffee is the favoured breakfast drink in most Mediterranean countries. But ask for a coffee in these parts and you

> 'Other tipples worth tasting include sherry and sangría in Spain, port in Portugal, ouzo in Greece, and *rakı* in Turkey.'

---

### WINES BY THE COUNTRY

- **France** Burgundy, Bordeaux, Champagne or Chablis – red, white or fizzy, France has got it all.
- **Spain** Try the *jerez* (sherry), *cava* (sparkling wine) or sangría (wine punch).
- **Portugal** The Lagoa area in the Algarve is the centre of Portugal's wine country.
- **Italy** In Tuscany the Chianti's a winner; in Piedmont Barolo rules.
- **Greece** Retsina is produced in Attica and central Greece.
- **Croatia** Producing more than 700 wines, Croatia is more famous for its selection of brandies.
- **Turkey** Turkish drinkers prefer their local firewater *rakı*.
- **Cyprus** The sweet *komandaria* hails from the Troödos mountains.
- **Malta** A bargain tipple is the local Pinot Grigio.

won't be sipping from a large mug of instant coffee, you'll be downing a small dose of almost pure caffeine. Not to everybody's taste, it's guaranteed to wake you up and can become alarmingly addictive.

Likewise, tea is rarely served with milk unless you specifically ask for it. Fruit teas are popular and in Morocco the ubiquitous mint tea is considered the national drink.

The Italians are the biggest consumers of bottled water in the world. On average they drink 107 litres each a year.

### WATER

In many countries, tap water is safe to drink but, if in doubt, bottled water is readily available throughout the region.

## Where to Eat & Drink

If deciding what to eat is a tough call, choosing where to eat can be equally demanding. The variety of choices range from superexpensive designer bistros to family-run restaurants, from seafront cafés to roadside kiosks.

Prices also vary enormously. The cheapest places for a decent meal are often the self-service restaurants in department stores. University restaurants are also dirt cheap, but the food tends to be bland and you may not be allowed in if you're not a local student. Kiosks are often a good bet, selling cheap snacks that, if you're lucky, are every bit as tasty as anything served up in the smarter restaurants.

Self-catering can be a cheap and wholesome as well as fun way of eating. Dive into a local market and you'll often find fresh produce that tastes as good as it invariably looks. Even without cooking you can eat well. Pick up a loaf of bread, some ripe cheese and a slice or two of salami; add a juicy tomato and a bottle of local wine and you've got the recipe for the perfect picnic.

## Vegetarians & Vegans

If you have dietary restrictions, you're a vegetarian or you keep kosher, for example, tourist organisations may be able to advise you or provide lists of suitable restaurants.

In general, vegetarians need not worry in Mediterranean Europe; many restaurants have one or two vegetarian dishes, and southern European menus in particular tend to contain many vegetable dishes and salads.

## Habits & Customs

Lunch is traditionally the main meal of the day in most Mediterranean countries. Although modern working hours are eroding the old ways, at weekends and on holidays lunch often remains the focal point of the day. Old habits die hard and it is still common in many places for shops and businesses to close for three to four hours in the early afternoon. Depending on your mood, this is either a distinctly civilised habit or a complete pain in the neck.

It's also worth noting that meals are taken considerably later in southern Europe than in more northerly areas. Sit down to dinner at 6pm and you'll find yourself the only one in the restaurant; that's assuming you can find one that's open.

# France

CONTENTS

Paris may be France's political and cultural centre but the south is where everyone wants to live. Official projections predict the population in the southern regions around the Mediterranean are set to grow by a third in the coming decades, at the expense of the north and it's hardly surprising.

Where else in France can you enjoy warm sea, mountains to ski in, vineyards to sample wine in and ancient Roman market towns to explore, all within an afternoon's drive of each other? France's southern coasts are also the destinations for the chic and the moneyed (the two don't always go together) in celebrated celebrity haunts such as Cannes, Monaco and St Tropez.

The southern regions are also some of the richest culturally. You'll find it peppered with fine Roman buildings and with art (prodigious quantities of it left behind by some of the most celebrated modern painters) in the area's museums and galleries.

The coastal area also benefits from all of France's culinary bounty, best sampled in its many excellent markets. As well as being an important and increasingly respected wine-growing region, it's also the best place to enjoy treats from inland, such as the sharp, herb-infused flavours from Provence, which are often married perfectly with fresh catches from the Mediterranean.

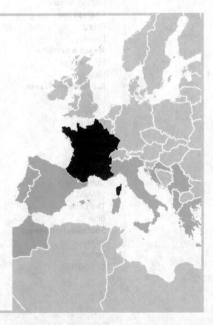

## FAST FACTS

- **Area** 551,000 sq km
- **Capital** Paris
- **Currency** euro (€); A$1 = €0.58; ¥100 = €0.76; NZ$ = €0.54; UK£1 = €1.50; US$1 = €0.83
- **Famous for** Napoleon Bonaparte, fabulous food, world-class wine, cheese, bad plumbing
- **Key Phrases** *merci* (thank you); *parlez-vous Anglais?* (do you speak English?); *excusez-moi* (excuse me); *s'il vous plaît* (please); *pardon* (sorry)
- **Official Language** French
- **Population** 60.2 million
- **Telephone Codes** country code ☎ 33; international access code ☎ 00
- **Visas** none needed for EU citizens, prospective EU member states, Switzerland, Iceland, Norway, Australia, the USA, Canada, New Zealand, Japan and Israel

FRANCE

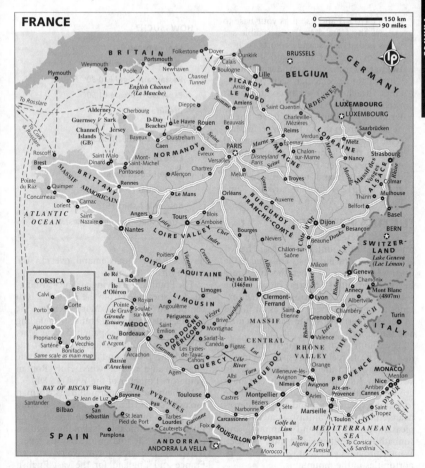

## HIGHLIGHTS

- Drop in to **Nice** (p124) down south for mild climes, heavenly sea, inexpensive accommodation, great art, good food and happening nightlife, which more than make up for its pebbly beach.
- Discover the wilder, more savage beauty and solitude (at times other than summer's silly season) of **Corsica** (p139), with its jagged coasts, magnificent harbours, spectacular mountainous trails and dazzling seas.
- Get a sniff of how the other 0.01% live by visiting stylish, manicured **Monaco** (p134), home to gambling high-rollers, Formula One drivers, tax-dodging entrepreneurs and bejewelled royalty.

- Spoil yourself in chic, romantic, demure **Paris** (p48); you'll need several days just to scratch its lovely cultural surfaces.
- Lavish treats on your tastebuds in **Burgundy** (p97) – in the Côte d'Or's world-class wine country or the gastronomic powerhouse of Dijon.

## ITINERARIES

- **One week** You'll find it hard to leave Paris' beauty, charm and cultural riches. Two days isn't time enough for even an introduction to the museums and sights but make time for the Musée d'Orsay (p52), the Louvre (p53) and for strolling the capital's lovely boulevards and along the banks of the river Seine. Then head south to Nice (p124) and use it as your base to explore the Côte d'Azur's incredible sea vistas and stylish seaside resorts such as Monaco, Antibes, Cannes and St Tropez.

■ **Two weeks** From Nice consider sailing to Corsica for spectacular scenery, often-empty beaches and pretty coastal towns where it will be easy to fill a week. Alternatively cut this short to leave time to head west from the Côte d'Azur, to Marseille's buzzing streets and handsome old port, to the elegant café-filled squares of nearby Aix-en-Provence (p119) and then further inland, to the roman ruins at Arles (p123) and the striking Papal fortress city of Avignon (p120).

## CLIMATE & WHEN TO GO

France's climate is generally temperate and mild except in mountainous areas. The Atlantic brings rain and persistent wind to the northwest. Except for when the sometimes fierce, often biting, Mistral blows in the south, a pleasant Mediterranean climate extends from the southern coast as far inland as the southern Alps, the Massif Central and the eastern Pyrenees.

The country is at its best in spring. Summer can be fiercely hot, especially in the south away from the coast. Even Paris can swelter in July and August. It can be a crowded, traffic-choked and expensive time to travel, especially around the Mediterranean. Autumn, by contrast, is mellow and pleasant everywhere, and swimming and sunbathing are often viable until October. Winter provides excellent winter sport opportunities in the mountains.

## HISTORY
### Prehistoric People

Animal-hunting, cave-dwelling Neanderthals were the first to live in France (about 90,000 to 40,000 BC). Cro-Magnons, a taller *Homo sapiens* variety, followed 35,000 years ago and left behind cave paintings and engravings. Neolithic people (about 7500 to 4000 years ago) created France's incredible menhirs (single standing stones) and dolmens (monolithic tombs).

The Celtic Gauls moved into the region between 1500 and 500 BC. They were superceded by the Romans for five centuries after Julius Caesar took control around 52 BC, until the Franks (hence the name

---

**HOW MUCH?**

■ **Loaf of bread** €1

■ **Bottle of table wine** €3

■ **Restaurant meal** €20-30

■ **Espresso in a café** €1.50

■ **Breakfast** €4-5

**LONELY PLANET INDEX**

■ **Litre of petrol** €1.15

■ **Litre of bottled water** €0.80

■ **Beer at bar (25cl)** €3

■ **Souvenir T-shirt** €9

■ **Street snack (pommes frites)** €1

---

'France') and the Alemanii overran the country from the east.

The Frankish Merovingian and Carolingian dynasties ruled from the 5th to the 10th century. In 732 Charles Martel defeated the Moors, thus preventing France from falling under Muslim rule as Spain had done. Martel's grandson, Charlemagne (742–814), extended the power and boundaries of the kingdom and was crowned Holy Roman Emperor (Emperor of the West) in 800.

William the Conqueror and his Norman forces occupied England in 1066, making Normandy (and, later, Plantagenet-ruled England) a formidable rival of the kingdom of France, a tale told on the Bayeux tapestry (p79). The subsequent rivalry between France and England for the vast English territories in France lasted three centuries, degenerating into the Hundred Years' War (1337–1453).

Five years later, the dukes of Burgundy (allied with the English) occupied Paris and in 1422 John Plantagenet, duke of Bedford, was made regent of France for England's King Henry VI. Less than a decade later he was crowned king of France at Paris' Notre Dame (p53).

In 1429, a 17-year-old virginal warrior in the shape of Jeanne d'Arc (Joan of Arc) persuaded French legitimist Charles VII that she had a divine mission from God to expel the English from France and bring about Charles' coronation in Reims. Convicted of witchcraft and heresy following her capture and sale to the English, Joan was burned at the stake in Rouen in 1431.

The Reformation swept through Europe in the 1530s, the ideology of Jean (John) Calvin (1509–64) – a Frenchman born in Noyon (Picardie) but exiled to Geneva. The Wars of Religion (1562–98) broke out between the Huguenots (French Protestants who received help from the English), the Catholic League (led by the House of Guise) and the Catholic monarchy.

## The Sun King

*Le Roi Soleil* (the Sun King) ascended the throne as Louis XIV (ruled 1643–1715), involving France in wars that gained it territory, terrified its neighbours and nearly bankrupted the treasury.

Sun-king grandson Louis XV (ruled 1715–74) was an oafish buffoon whose regent, the duke of Orléans, shifted the royal court back to Paris. As the 18th century progressed, the *ancien régime* (old order) became increasingly out of step with the needs of the country. Enlightened anti-establishment and anticlerical ideas expressed by Voltaire, Rousseau and Montesquieu further threatened the royal regime.

## Revolution to Republic

Popular discontent and the lack of political progress under Louis XVI culminated in a Parisian mob storming the prison at Bastille (now a busy roundabout; p56). France was declared a constitutional monarchy but before long, the moderate republican Girondins lost power to the radical Jacobins. Louis XVI was publicly guillotined in January 1793 on Paris' place de la Concorde (p56).

The terrifying Reign of Terror between September 1793 and July 1794 saw religious freedoms revoked, churches closed, cathedrals turned into 'Temples of Reason' and thousands beheaded. In the chaos a dashing young Corsican general named Napoleon Bonaparte (1769–1821) emerged.

## Napoleon Bonaparte

In 1799 Napoleon assumed power as consul and in 1804 Pope Pius VII crowned him emperor of the French at Notre Dame. To consolidate and legitimise his authority, Napoleon waged several wars in which France gained control over most of Europe. Two years later, Allied armies entered Paris,

exiled Napoleon to Elba and restored the House of Bourbon to the French throne at the Congress of Vienna (1814–15).

In 1815 Napoleon escaped, entering Paris on 20 May. His glorious 'Hundred Days' back in power ended with the Battle of Waterloo and his return to exile where he died in 1821.

## Second Republic to Second Empire

A struggle between extreme monarchists who sought a return to the *ancien régime,* people who saw the changes post-Revolution as irreversible, and the radicals of the poor working-class neighbourhoods of Paris dominated the reign of Louis XVIII (ruled 1814–24). Charles X's rule (1824–30) was inept and he was overthrown.

Louis-Philippe (ruled 1830–48), a constitutional monarch of bourgeois sympathies and tastes, was chosen by parliament, only to be ousted by the 1848 Revolution. The Second Republic was established and elections instated Napoleon's useless nephew, Louis Napoleon Bonaparte, as president. But in 1851 Louis Napoleon led a coup d'etat and proclaimed himself Emperor Napoleon III of the Second Empire (1852–70).

France enjoyed significant economic growth at this time. Paris was transformed under urban planner Baron Haussmann (1809–91) who, among other things, created the 12 huge boulevards radiating from the Arc de Triomphe (p56).

But Napoleon III embroiled France in various catastrophic conflicts, including the Crimean War (1853–56) and the humiliating Franco-Prussian War (1870–71) which ended with Prussia taking the emperor prisoner. Upon hearing the news, defiant Parisian masses took to the streets demanding a republic be declared – the Third Republic.

## The Great War

A trip to the Somme (p74) battlefields goes some way to revealing the unimaginable human cost of WWI. Of the eight million French men called to arms, 1.3 million were killed and almost one million crippled. Much of the war took place in northeastern France – trench warfare using thousands of soldiers as cannon fodder to gain a few metres of territory.

The Great War officially ended in November 1918 but the details were not meted out until 1919 when the Treaty of Versailles was signed. Its harsh terms included the return of Alsace-Lorraine to France and a reparations bill of US$33 billion for Germany.

## WWII

In 1939, France joined Britain in declaring war on Germany. By June 1940, France had capitulated. Germany divided France into a zone under direct German occupation (in the north and along the western coast) and a puppet state centred on the spa town of Vichy.

## The Fourth Republic

Elections in 1945 created a national assembly composed largely of pro-resistant Communists. The wartime leader of the Free French, General Charles de Gaulle, was appointed head of the government, but quickly sensed that the tide was turning against his idea of a strong presidency and in 1946 he resigned.

Progress rebuilding France's shattered economy and infrastructure was slow. By 1947 France was forced to turn to the USA for loans as part of the Marshall Plan to rebuild Europe. The economy gathered steam in the 1950s but the decade marked the end of French colonialism in Vietnam and in Algeria, where the struggle for independence was nastier. The resulting Algerian War (1954–62) was brutal, characterised by torture and massacre meted out to nationalist Algerians.

## The Fifth Republic

De Gaulle assumed the presidency in 1958 and drafted a new constitution – the Fifth Republic – which gave considerable powers to the president at the expense of the National Assembly.

Georges Pompidou (1911–74), prime minister under de Gaulle, stepped onto the podium as president and was followed by Valéry Giscard d'Estaing (born 1926). In 1981 he was ousted by long-time head of the Parti Socialiste (Socialist Party), François Mitterrand (1916–96).

By 1986 the economy was weakening and in parliamentary elections that year the right-wing opposition led by Jacques Chirac (Paris mayor since 1977) won a majority in the National Assembly.

Presidential elections in 1995 ushered in Jacques Chirac who was re-elected with an overwhelming majority in 2002 after French voters boxed themselves into a corner by setting up National Front right winger Jean Marie Le Pen as the only alternative.

## PEOPLE

France is not really densely populated – 107 people inhabit every square kilometre – although 20% of the national population is packed into the Paris area.

The last 10 years have seen rural and suburban areas steadily gaining population; and Paris and the northeast (except Alsace) losing inhabitants to southern France, where populations are predicted to rise by 30% over the next 30 years.

For much of the last two centuries, France has had a considerably lower rate of population growth than its neighbours. In the last decade, that trend has changed and the birth rate is now 2.1%. By 2050 the population of mainland France is expected to reach 64 million – five million more than in 2000.

Multicultural France has always drawn immigrants from other parts of Europe and more recently from Africa. Immigrants today form 7.4% (4.3 million) of the population yet only 36% have French citizenship, which is not conferred automatically at birth.

The French republican code, while inclusive and non-discriminatory on one hand, does little to accommodate a multicultural society. Racial tensions are fuelled by the extreme-right Front National (National Front).

This dichotomy exploded in a riot of demonstrations in 2004 when the Islamic headscarf (along with Jewish skullcaps, crucifixes and other religious symbols) was banned in French schools. The law, avowedly intended to protect the secular nature of state education, was also seen as proof that the French state is not prepared to integrate Muslims into French society.

Some 90% of France's Muslim community are non-citizens; many are illegal immigrants, and most live in depressing poverty-stricken *bidonvilles* (tinpot towns) surrounding major metropolitan centres.

## RELIGION

Secular France maintains a rigid distinction between the church and state. Some 55% of

French identify themselves as Catholic, although no more than 10% attend church regularly. Another one million are Protestant.

Coexisting uneasily with this nominally Christian majority is France's five million-strong Muslim community. Over half of France's 600,000-strong Jewish population (Europe's largest) lives in and around Paris. Marseille has the next-largest Jewish community.

# ARTS
## Literature
The philosophical work of Voltaire (1694–1778), and of Swiss-born philosopher Jean-Jacques Rousseau, dominated the 18th century. A century on the poems and novels of Victor Hugo – *Les Misérables* and *Notre Dame de Paris* (The Hunchback of Notre Dame) among them – became landmarks of French Romanticism.

In 1857 two literary landmarks were published: *Madame Bovary* by Gustave Flaubert (1821–80) and Charles Baudelaire's collection of poems, *Les Fleurs du Mal* (The Flowers of Evil). Émile Zola (1840–1902) meanwhile strove to convert novel-writing from an art to a science in his powerful series, *Les Rougon-Macquart*.

The expression of mental states was the aim of symbolists Paul Verlaine (1844–96) and Stéphane Mallarmé (1842–98). Verlaine's poems – alongside those of Arthur Rimbaud (1854–91) – are seen as French literature's first modern poems.

After WWII, existentialism developed around the lively debates of Jean-Paul Sartre (1905–80), Simone de Beauvoir (1908–86) and Albert Camus (1913–60) in Paris' left-bank cafés of St-Germain des Prés.

Contemporary authors include Françoise Sagan, Pascal Quignard, Jean Auel, Emmanuel Carrère and Stéphane Bourguignon. Also popular are Frédéric Dard (alias San Antonio), Léo Malet and Daniel Pennac.

## Cinema
Cinematographic pioneers, the Lumière brothers, shot the world's first-ever motion picture in March 1895 and French film flourished in the following decades. The post-WWII *nouvelle vague* (new wave) filmmakers, such as Claude Chabrol and François Truffaut, produced uniquely personal films using real-life subject matter.

Big-name stars, slick production values and nostalgia were the dominant motifs in the 1980s as filmmakers switched to costume dramas, comedies and 'heritage movies'. Claude Berri's depiction of pre-war Provence in *Jean de Florette* (1986), Jean-Paul Rappeneau's *Cyrano de Bergerac* (1990) and *Bon Voyage* (2003) set in 1940s Paris – all starring France's best known (and biggest-nosed) actor Gérard Depardieu – found huge audiences in France and abroad.

*Le Fabuleux Destin de Amélie Poulain* (*Amélie*; 2001), a feel-good story of a winsome Parisian do-gooder, directed by Jean-Pierre Jeunet, proved an instant hit everywhere. French film has enjoyed a massive renaissance abroad ever since.

## Music
There's more to French music than accordions and Edith Piaf.

French musical luminaries – Charles Gounod (1818–93), César Franck (1822–90) and *Carmen*-creator Georges Bizet (1838–75) among them – were a dime a dozen in the 19th century.

Claude Debussy (1862–1918) revolutionised classical music with his *Prélude à l'Après-Midi d'un Faune* (Prelude to the Afternoon of a Faun), creating a light, almost Asian musical impressionism; while impressionist comrade Maurice Ravel (1875–1937) peppered his work, including *Boléro*, with sensuousness and tonal colour.

Jazz hit 1920s Paris, which post–WWI hoisted the likes of Sidney Bechet, Kenny Clarke, Bud Powell and Dexter Gordon.

The *chanson française* was revived in the 1930s by Piaf and Charles Trenet. In the 1950s the Left Bank cabarets nurtured *chansonniers* (cabaret singers) such as Léo Ferré, Georges Brassens, Claude Nougaro, Jacques Brel and Serge Gainsbourg.

French pop music has evolved massively since the 1960s *yéyé* (imitative rock) days of Johnny Halliday. Particularly strong is world music, from Algerian *rai* and other North African music (artists include Natacha Atlas) to Senegalese *mbalax* (Youssou N'Dour) and West Indian *zouk* (Kassav, Zouk Machine). One musician who combines many of these elements is Paris-born Manu Chao.

Another hot musical export is Parisian electronic music from bands such as Daft

FRANCE

Punk and Air. French rap was spearheaded in the 1990s by Senegal-born Paris-reared rapper MC Solaar, and today is a popular genre in its own right.

## Architecture

Southern France is the place to find France's Gallo-Roman legacy: at the Pont du Gard (p139), amphitheatres in Nimes and Arles and the theatre at Orange.

Several centuries later, architects adopted Gallo-Roman architectural elements to create *roman* (Romanesque) masterpieces such as Poitier's Église Notre Dame la Grande (p88).

Impressive 12th-century Gothic structures include Avignon's massive pontifical palace (p121).

Under Napoleon, many of Paris' best-known sights – the Arc de Triomphe, the Arc du Carrousel at the Louvre and the Assemblée Nationale building – were designed.

Art Nouveau (1850–1910) combined iron, brick, glass and ceramics in new ways. See for yourself in Paris's noodle-like metro entrances and inside the Musée d'Orsay (p52).

French political leaders have long sought to immortalise themselves by building public edifices. Georges Pompidou commissioned the once-reviled – now much-revered – Centre Beaubourg (p53) in Paris while François Mitterrand commissioned several contemporary architectural landmarks, including IM Pei's glass pyramid (p53) at the Louvre.

## Painting

An extraordinary flowering of artistic talent occurred in 19th- and 20th-century France. The Impressionists, who endeavoured to capture the ever-changing aspects of reflected light, included Edouard Manet, Claude Monet, Edgar Degas, Camille Pisarro, and Pieree-Auguste Renoir.

They were followed by the likes of Paul Cézanne, Paul Gauguin and Georges Seurat. A little later the Fauves, the most famous of whom was Henri Matisse, became known for their radical use of vibrant colour.

France was also where Cubism, a form of art based on abstract and geometric representation, was pioneered by Pablo Picasso and Georges Braque.

# ENVIRONMENT
## The Land

Hexagon-shaped France, the largest country in Western Europe, is hugged by water or mountains along every side except its northeastern boundary – a relatively flat frontier abutting Germany, Luxembourg and Belgium. Inland, five major river systems crisscross the country.

Mountains run riot. Europe's highest peak, Mt Blanc (4807m), spectacularly tops the French Alps which stagger along France's eastern border from Lake Geneva to the Côte d'Azur. North of Lake Geneva the gentle limestone Jura Range runs along the Swiss frontier to reach heights of around 1700m, while the rugged Pyrenees lace France's entire 450km-long border with Spain.

The ancient Massif Central covers one-sixth (91,000 sq km) of the country and is renowned for its chain of extinct volcanoes.

## Wildlife

The Alps and Pyrenees are blessed with a rich variety of flora and fauna; France has more mammalian species to see (around 110) than other country in Europe. Couple this with its 363 bird species, 30 amphibian types, 36 varieties of reptiles and 72 kinds of fish, and wildlife watchers are in paradise.

The mountains shelter marmots, nimble *chamois* (mountain antelopes) with dark-striped heads and the *bouquetin* (Alpine ibexes). Roe deer and wild boar are common in lower-altitude forested areas.

The wolf, which disappeared from France in the 1930s, was spotted in the Parc National du Mercantour in 1992. The brown bear also disappeared from the Alps in the mid-1930s and no more than five remain in France today.

## National Parks

The proportion of land protected in France is low relative to the country's size: six small national parks *(parcs nationaux)* fully protect just 0.8% of the country. Another 7% is protected to a substantially lesser degree by 42 *parcs naturals régionaux* (regional parks) and a further 0.4% by 136 smaller *réserves naturelles* (nature reserves).

## Environmental Issues

Summer forest fires are an annual hazard; great tracts of forest burn each year. Wetlands, essential for the survival of a great number of species, are shrinking. More than two million hectares – 3% of French territory – are considered important wetlands, but only 4% of this land is protected. Hunters with dogs and guns pose an equal threat to French animal life. Many traditional animal habitats have been destroyed by the damming of rivers to produce electricity.

# FOOD & DRINK
## Staples & Specialties
French cuisine has long stood apart for its great use of a variety of foods – beef, lamb, pork, poultry, fish and shellfish, cereals, vegetables and legumes – but its staple 'trinity' is bread, cheese and *charcuterie* (cured, smoked or processed meat products).

Nothing is more French than *pain* (bread). More than 80% of all French people eat it at every meal. All bakeries have long thin *baguettes* (and the similar but fatter *flûtes*) and wider loaves which are simply called *pains*. There are countless other heavenly varieties.

France has nearly 500 varieties of *fromage* (cheese). The choice on offer at a *fromagerie* (cheese shop) can be overwhelming, but *fromagers* (cheese merchants) always allow you to sample and are usually happy to advise.

Traditionally charcuterie is made only from pork, though a number of other meats – from beef and veal to chicken and goose – are used in making sausages, blood puddings, hams and other cured and salted meats. *Pâtés, terrines* and *rillettes* are essentially charcuterie and are prepared in many different ways.

### REGIONAL SPECIALTIES
There are all sorts of reasons for the amazing variety of France's regional cuisine. Climatic and geographical factors have been particularly important: the hot south tends to favour olive oil, garlic and tomatoes, while the cooler, pastoral northern regions favour cream and butter. Coastal areas specialise in mussels, oysters and saltwater fish.

### DRINKS
There are dozens of wine-producing regions throughout France, and seven principal regions. These are Alsace, Bordeaux, Burgundy, Champagne, Languedoc-Roussillon, the Loire and the Rhône. Areas such as Burgundy comprise many well-known districts, including Chablis, Beaujolais and Mâcon, while Bordeaux encompasses Médoc, Saint Émilion and Sauternes – to name just a few of its many subregions.

The *bière à la pression* (draft beer) is served by the *demi* (about 33cl). Northern France and Alsace produce some excellent local beers.

The most popular nonalcoholic beverages consumed in France are coffee and mineral water. If you prefer tap water (perfectly safe) rather than pricey bottled water, make sure you ask for *de l'eau* (some water), or *une carafe d'eau* (a jug of water).

## Where to Eat & Drink
### BISTROS & BRASSERIES
A *bistro* (often spelled *bistrot*) is not clearly defined in France. It can be simply a pub or bar with snacks and light meals, or a fully fledged restaurant. *Brasseries* – which can look very much like cafés – serve full meals, drinks and coffee from morning till late at night.

### RESTAURANTS
The *restaurant* comes in many guises and price ranges in France. Generally they specialise in a particular variety of food (eg regional, traditional, Vietnamese). You can generally get an excellent French meal for under €30.

Restaurants almost always have a *carte* (menu) posted outside so you can decide before going in whether the selection and prices are to your liking. Most offer at least one fixed-price, multicourse and usually good-value meal known in French as a *menu, menu à prix fixe* or *menu du jour* (daily menu), usually offering an entrée, such as salad, paté or soup; a main dish (several meat, poultry or fish dishes, including the *plat du jour* (daily special); and a final course (cheese or dessert).

*Boissons* (drinks), including wine, cost extra unless the menu says *boisson comprise* (drink included), in which case you may get a beer or a glass of mineral water. If the *menu* has *vin compris* (wine included), you'll probably be served a 25cl *pichet* (jug) of wine.

Restaurant meals are almost always served with bread.

**FRANCE**

## Vegetarians & Vegans

Vegetarians and vegans are not particularly well catered for; specialist vegetarian restaurants are few and far between. On the bright side, more and more restaurants are offering vegetarian choices on their set menus, and *produits biologiques* (organic products) are springing up.

# PARIS

**pop 2.147 million (urban area)**

Everyone has an opinion on Paris, whether they have travelled there or not. Other towns are quick to adopt its moniker: Maastricht styles itself the 'Paris of the Netherlands'; Melbourne is affectionately referred to as 'Paris on the Yarra'; while Bucharest, St Petersburg, Shanghai and Hanoi all lay claim to being the 'Paris of the East'.

Oft imitated, but never duplicated, Paris remains the benchmark for beauty, culture and class the world over. Even the most cynical traveller, sceptical that any city could live up to Paris' reputation, can't help but be charmed by its magnificent avenues and cosy café life, its unparalleled arts scene and energetic but composed pace. Paris is the Paris of the Parisians, the Paris of France, the one and only Paris. Nothing comes close.

## HISTORY

The Parisii, a tribe of Celtic Gauls, settled the Île de la Cité in the 3rd century BC. In 508 AD, Frankish king Clovis I made Paris his seat in the newly united Gaul. Paris prospered during the Middle Ages and flourished during the Renaissance when many of city's most famous buildings were erected.

The excesses of Louis XVI and his capricious queen, Marie-Antoinette, led to an uprising of Parisians on 14 July 1789 and the storming of the Bastille prison. This kickstarted the French Revolution.

In 1851 emperor Napoleon III oversaw the construction of a more modern Paris, with wide boulevards, sculptured parks and a sewer system. The disastrous 1870 war with Prussia led to the emperor's capture. When the news reached Paris, the masses took to the streets, demanding that the republic be restored.

This, the Third Republic, ushered in the glittering *belle époque* (beautiful era), famed for its Art Nouveau architecture and its artistic and scientific advances. By the 1930s, Paris had become a centre for the artistic avant-garde, an era cut short by the Nazi occupation of 1940 to 1944.

## ORIENTATION

Central Paris is relatively small: approximately 9.5km (north to south) by 11km (east to west). Not including the Bois de Boulogne and the Bois de Vincennes, its total area is 105 sq km. Within the 'oval' of central Paris, which Parisians call *intramuros* (Latin for 'within the walls'), the Rive Droite (Right Bank) is north of the Seine, while the Rive Gauche (Left Bank) is south of it since the river flows from east to west.

Paris is divided into 20 *arrondissements* (districts), which spiral clockwise from the centre. City addresses always include the number of the arrondissement, as streets with the same name exist in different districts.

The city has 372 metro stations and there is almost always one station within a maximum of 500m of where you need to go.

### Maps

The most useful map of Paris is the 1:10,000-scale *Paris Plan* published by Michelin.

## INFORMATION
### Emergency

**SOS Helpline** ( ☎ 01 47 23 80 80, in English)
**SOS Médecins** ( ☎ 01 47 07 77 77, 0 820 332 424) Provide 24-hour house calls.
**Urgences Médicales de Paris** (Paris Medical Emergencies; ☎ 01 53 94 94 94, 01 48 28 40 40) Provides 24-hour house calls.

### Internet Access

Some metro and RER stations offer free Internet access. Fifty post offices have Internet centres called Cyberposte Internet, which generally open from 8am or 9am to 7pm weekdays and till noon Saturday.

Among the best and/or most central commercial Internet cafés in Paris are:
**Access Academy** (Map pp54-5; ☎ 01 43 25 23 80; www .accessacademy.com; 60-61 rue St-André des Arts, 6e; metro Odéon; per hr €3.50, per day/week/month €6.80/14.90/35.70; ☽ 8-2am) This is France's largest Internet café, with 400 screens in the heart of St-Germain.

**XS Arena Les Halles** (Map pp54–5; ☎ 01 40 13 02 60; 43 rue Sébastopol, 1er; metro Les Halles) Just down from the Forum des Halles.

**XS Arena Luxembourg** (Map pp54–5; ☎ 01 43 44 55 55; 17 rue Soufflot, 5e; metro Luxembourg; per 1/2/3/4/5 hr €3/6/8/10/12; ☼ 24hr) This mini-chain of Internet cafés is bright, buzzy and open round the clock.

### Internet Resources

**Metropole Paris** (www.metropoleparis.com) Excellent online magazine in English.

**Paris Pages** (www.paris.org) Good links to museums and cultural events.

**Paris tourist office** (www.paris-touristoffice.com) Super site with more links than you'll ever need.

### Laundry

There's a *laverie libre-service* (self-service laundrette) around every corner in Paris; your hotel or hostel can point you to one in the neighbourhood.

### Left Luggage

All the train stations have left-luggage offices or lockers. Most are closed from about 11.15pm to about 6.30am.

### Medical Services

There are some 50 *assistance publique* (public health service) hospitals in Paris. Major hospitals include:

**American Hospital** (Map pp50–1; ☎ 01 46 41 25 25; www.american-hospital.org; 63 blvd Victor Hugo, 92200 Neuilly-sur-Seine; metro Pont de Levallois Bécon) Offers emergency 24-hour medical and dental care.

**Hertford British Hospital** (Map pp50–1; ☎ 01 46 39 22 22; hbh.free.fr; 3 rue Barbès, 92300 Levallois-Perret; metro Anatole France) Less expensive English-speaking option than the American Hospital.

### Money

In general you'll find that post offices in Paris can offer the best exchange rates, and will accept banknotes in various currencies as well as travellers cheques issued by American Express or Visa. The commission for travellers cheques is 1.5% (minimum about €4).

Commercial banks usually charge a stiff €3 to €4.50 per foreign-currency transaction. The rates offered vary, so it pays to compare. In Paris, bureaux de change are faster and easier, open longer hours and give better rates than most banks. Some good central choices include:

**Best Change** (Map pp54–5; ☎ 01 42 21 46 05; 21 rue du Roule, 1er; metro Louvre Rivoli; ☼ 10am–1pm & 2–7pm Mon-Sat) This bureau de change is three blocks southwest of Forum des Halles.

**Bureau de Change** (Map pp50–1; ☎ 01 42 25 38 14; 25 av des Champs-Élysées, 8e; metro Franklin D Roosevelt; ☼ 9am-8pm)

**Thomas Cook** (Map pp50–1; ☎ 01 47 20 25 14; 125 av des Champs-Élysées, 8e; metro Charles de Gaulle-Étoile; ☼ 9.15am-8.30pm)

### Post

Most post offices (*bureaux de poste*) in Paris are open 8am to 7pm weekdays and 8am or 9am till noon on Saturday. *Tabacs* (tobacconists) usually sell postage stamps.

The **main post office** (Map pp54–5; ☎ 01 40 28 76 00; 52 rue du Louvre, 1er; metro Sentier or Les Halles; ☼ 24hr) opens round the clock for basic services such as sending letters and picking up poste restante mail (window Nos 5 to 7; €0.46 per letter). Other services, including currency exchange, are available during regular opening hours.

### Tourist Information

**Office de Tourisme et de Congrès de Paris** (Paris Convention & Visitors Bureau; Map pp50–1; ☎ 0 892 683 3000; www.paris-touristoffice.com; 25-27 rue de Pyramides, 1er; metro Pyramides; ☼ 9am-8pm Apr-Oct, 9am-8pm Mon-Sat & 11am-7pm Sun Nov-Mar) This main branch is about 500m northwest of the Louvre. Closed 1 May only.

## DANGERS & ANNOYANCES

In general, Paris is a safe city. As you'll notice, women *do* travel alone on the metro late at night in most areas. Metro stations that are probably best avoided late at night include: Châtelet-Les Halles; Château Rouge in Montmartre; Gare du Nord; Strasbourg St-Denis; Réaumur Sébastopol; and Montparnasse Bienvenüe.

---

#### AH, LA CARTE!

The **Carte Musées-Monuments** (Museums-Monuments Card; %01 44 61 96 60; €18/36/54 for one/three/five days) is valid for entry to three dozen sights in Paris – including the Louvre, the Centre Pompidou and the Musée d'Orsay. It's available from tourist offices, Fnac outlets, RATP information desks and major metro stations.

# PARIS

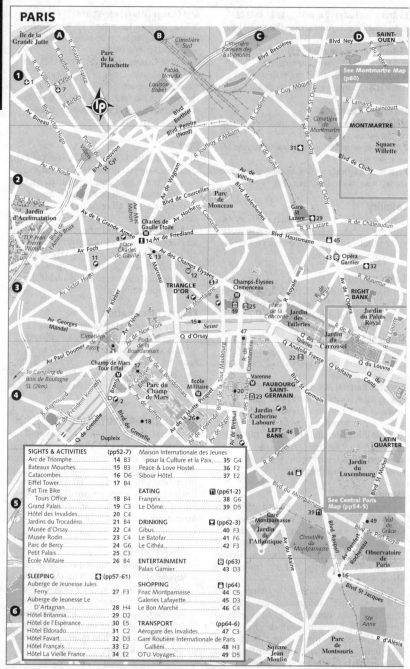

FRANCE

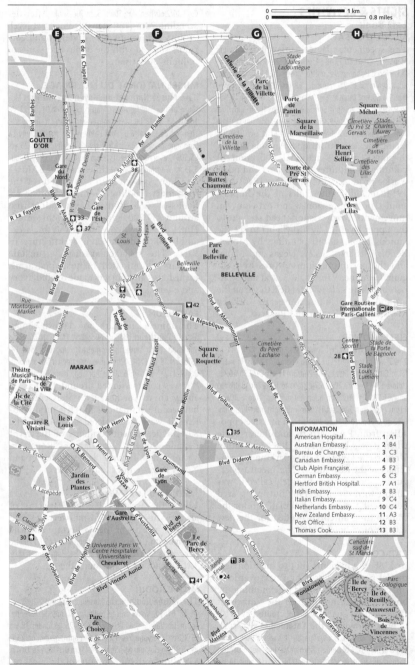

0 — 1 km
0 — 0.8 miles

**INFORMATION**

| | |
|---|---|
| American Hospital | **1** A1 |
| Australian Embassy | **2** B4 |
| Bureau de Change | **3** C3 |
| Canadian Embassy | **4** B3 |
| Club Alpin Française | **5** F2 |
| German Embassy | **6** C3 |
| Hertford British Hospital | **7** A1 |
| Irish Embassy | **8** B3 |
| Italian Embassy | **9** C4 |
| Netherlands Embassy | **10** C4 |
| New Zealand Embassy | **11** A3 |
| Post Office | **12** B3 |
| Thomas Cook | **13** B3 |

## SIGHTS & ACTIVITIES
### Left Bank
#### MUSÉE D'ORSAY

The spectacular **Musée d'Orsay** (Orsay Museum; Map50-1; ☎ 01 40 49 48 84; www.musee-orsay.fr; 1 rue de la Légion d'Honneur, 7e; metro Musée d'Orsay or Solférino; adult/senior & 18-25 yrs/under 18 yrs €7/5/free, everyone free 1st Sun of month; 9am-6pm Tue, Wed, Fri & Sat, to 9.45pm Thu, to 6pm Sun late Jun-Sep; 10am-6pm Tue, Wed, Fri & Sat, 10am-9.45pm Thu, 9am-6pm Sun Oct-late Jun), housed in a former train station (1900) facing the Seine from quai Anatole France, displays France's national collection of paintings, sculptures, *objets d'art* and other works produced between the 1840s and 1914, including the fruits of the Impressionist, postimpressionist and Art Nouveau movements. Many visitors head straight to the upper level (lit by a skylight) to see the famous Impressionist paintings by Monet, Renoir, Pissarro, Sisley, Degas and Manet and the postimpressionist works by Gauguin, Cézanne, Van Gogh, Seurat and Matisse, but there's also a great deal to see on the ground floor, including some early works by Manet, Monet, Renoir and Pissarro.

#### EIFFEL TOWER

The **Tour Eiffel** (Eiffel Tower; Map pp50-1; ☎ 01 44 11 23 23; www.tour-eiffel.fr; metro Champ de Mars-Tour Eiffel or Bir Hakeim; lifts to 1st/2nd/3rd levels €4/7.30/10.40, children 3-11 yrs €2.20/4/5.70, stairs to 1st & 2nd platforms only €3.50; lifts 9am-midnight mid-Jun–Aug, 9.30am-11pm Sep–mid-Jun, stairs 9am-midnight mid-Jun–Aug, 9.30am-6.30pm Sep–mid-Jun) faced massive opposition from Paris' artistic and literary elite when it was built for the 1889 Exposition Universelle (World Fair), marking the centenary of the Revolution. The 'metal asparagus', as some Parisiens snidely called it, was almost torn down in 1909 but was spared because it proved an ideal platform for the transmitting antennas needed for the new science of radiotelegraphy.

#### CATACOMBES

In 1785, the hygienic (not to mention aesthetic) problems posed by Paris' overflowing cemeteries was solved by exhuming the bones and storing them in the tunnels of three disused quarries. One, created in 1810, is now known as the **Catacombes** (Map pp50-1; ☎ 01 43 22 47 63; www.paris.fr/musees/musee_carnavalet, in French; 1 pl Denfert Rochereau, 14e; metro Denfert Rochereau; adult/senior & student/14-25 yrs/under 14 yrs €5/3.30/2.60/free; 10am-5pm Tue-Sun). After descending 20m (130 steps) from street level, visitors follow 1.6km of underground corridors stacked with the bones and skulls of millions of Parisians.

#### MUSÉE NATIONAL DU MOYEN AGE

The **Musée National du Moyen Age** (National Museum of the Middle Ages; Map pp54-5; ☎ 01 53 73 78 16, 01 53 73 78 00; www.musee-moyenage.fr, in French; Thermes de Cluny, 6 pl Paul Painlevé, 5e; metro Cluny-La Sorbonne or St-Michel; adult/senior, student & 18-25 yrs €5.50/4, everyone free 1st Sun of month; 9.15am-5.45pm Wed-Mon), sometimes called the Musée de Cluny, is housed in two structures: the **frigidarium** (cooling room) and other remains of Gallo-Roman baths dating from around AD 200, and the late-15th-century Hôtel de Cluny, considered the finest example of medieval civil architecture in Paris. The spectacular displays include statuary, illuminated manuscripts, arms, furnishings and objects made of gold, ivory and enamel.

#### PANTHÉON

The domed landmark now known simply as the **Pantheon** (Map pp54-5; ☎ 01 44 32 18 00; www.monum.fr; pl du Panthéon, 5e; metro Luxembourg; adult/18-25/under 18 yrs €7/4.50/free, everyone free 1st Sun of month Oct-Mar; 9.30am-6.30pm Apr-Sep, 10am-6.15pm Oct-Mar) was commissioned around 1750 as an abbey church dedicated to Ste-Geneviève, but because of financial and structural problems it wasn't completed until 1789. The 80-odd permanent residents of the crypt include Voltaire, Jean-Jacques Rousseau, Victor Hugo, Émile Zola, Jean Moulin and Nobel Prize-winner Marie Curie.

#### JARDIN DU LUXEMBOURG

When the weather is fine Parisians of all ages flock to the formal terraces and chestnut groves of the 23-hectare **Jardin du Luxembourg** (Luxembourg Garden; Map pp50-1; metro Luxembourg; 7am-9.30pm Apr-Oct, 8am-sunset Mar-Nov) to read, relax and sunbathe.

#### MUSÉE RODIN

The **Musée Rodin** (Rodin Museum; Map pp50-1; ☎ 01 44 18 61 10; www.musee-rodin.fr; 77 rue de Varenne, 7e; metro Varenne; adult/senior & 18-25 yrs/under 18 yrs €5/3/free, everyone free 1st Sun of month, garden only €1; 9.30am-5.45pm Apr-Sep, to 4.45pm Oct-Mar) is both a sublime museum and one of the most relaxing spots in the city, with a lovely **garden** full of sculptures and shade trees.

### HÔTEL DES INVALIDES

The **Hôtel des Invalides** (Map pp50-1; metro Varenne or La Tour Maubourg) was built in the 1670s by Louis XIV to provide housing for 4000 *invalides* (disabled war veterans). On 14 July 1789, a mob forced its way into the building and, after fierce fighting, seized 28,000 rifles before heading on to the prison at Bastille, and revolution.

### CHAMP DE MARS

Running southeast from the Eiffel Tower, the grassy **Champ de Mars** (Field of Mars; Map pp50-1; metro Champ de Mars-Tour Eiffel or École Militaire), named after the Roman god of war, was originally a parade ground for the cadets of the 18th-century **École Militaire** (Military Academy). This is a vast, French-classical building (1772) at the southeast end of the park, which counted Napoleon among its graduates.

## The Islands

### ÎLE DE LA CITÉ

The site of the first settlement in Paris around the 3rd century BC and later the Roman town of Lutèce (Lutetia), the **Île de la Cité** (Map pp54-5) remained the centre of royal and ecclesiastical power even after the city spread to both banks of the Seine during the Middle Ages.

### CATHÉDRALE DE NOTRE DAME DE PARIS

The **Cathédrale de Notre Dame de Paris** (Cathedral of Our Lady of Paris; Map pp54-5; ☎ 01 42 34 56 10; pl du Parvis Notre Dame, 4e; metro Cité; ☒ 8am-6.45pm Mon-Fri, to 7.45pm Sat & Sun) is the true heart of Paris; in fact, distances from Paris to every part of metropolitan France are measured from **place du Parvis Notre Dame**, the square in front of Notre Dame, and a bronze star, set in the pavement across the street from the cathedral's main entrance, marks the exact location of **point zéro des routes de France** (point zero of French roads).

Notre Dame is not only a masterpiece of French Gothic architecture but has also been the focus of Catholic Paris for seven centuries. Built on a site occupied by earlier churches – and, a millennium before that, a Gallo-Roman temple – it was begun in 1163 and largely completed by the middle of the 14th century.

### STE-CHAPELLE

The most exquisite of Paris' Gothic monuments, **Ste-Chapelle** (Holy Chapel; Map pp54-5; ☎ 01 53 40 60 97; www.monum.fr; 4 blvd du Palais, 1er; metro Cité; adult/18-25/under 18 yrs €6.10/4.10/free, everyone free 1st Sun of month Oct-Mar, joint ticket with Conciergerie €10.40/7.40; ☒ 9.30am-6pm Mar-Oct, 9am-5pm Nov-Feb) is tucked away within the walls of the **Palais de Justice** (Law Courts). Built in just under three years, Ste-Chapelle was consecrated in 1248. The chapel was conceived by Louis IX to house his personal collection of sacred relics.

## Right Bank

### MUSÉE DU LOUVRE

The vast Palais du Louvre was constructed as a fortress by Philippe-Auguste in the early 13th century and rebuilt in the mid-16th century. In 1793, the Convention turned it into the **Musée du Louvre** (Louvre Museum; Map pp54-5; ☎ 01 40 20 53 17 or ☎ 01 40 20 51 51; www.louvre.fr; metro Palais Royal-Musée du Louvre; permanent collections/permanent collections & temporary exhibits €7.50/11.50, after 3pm & all day Sun €5/9.50, everyone free on 1st Sun of month; ☒ 9am-6pm Thu-Sun, 9.45pm Mon & Wed).

The paintings, sculptures and artefacts on display include works of art and artisanship from all over Europe and important collections of Assyrian, Etruscan, Greek, Coptic and Islamic art and antiquities. Traditionally the Louvre's raison d'être is to present Western art from the Middle Ages to about the year 1848 (at which point the Musée d'Orsay takes over).

### CENTRE GEORGES POMPIDOU

The **Centre National d'Art et de Culture Georges Pompidou** (Georges Pompidou National Centre of Art & Culture; Map pp54-5; ☎ 01 44 78 12 33; www.centre pompidou.fr; pl Georges Pompidou, 4e; metro Rambuteau) also known as the Centre Beaubourg, has amazed and delighted visitors since it was inaugurated in 1977, not just for its outstanding collection of modern art, but for its radical architectural statement; it was among the first buildings to have its 'insides' turned outside. The **Forum du Centre Pompidou** (admission free; ☒ 11am-10pm Wed-Mon), the open space at ground level, has temporary exhibits.

The 4th and 5th floors are taken up by the **Musée National d'Art Moderne** (MNAM, National Museum of Modern Art; adult/senior & 18-25/under 18 yrs €7/5/free, everyone free 1st Sun of month, day pass

FRANCE

# CENTRAL PARIS

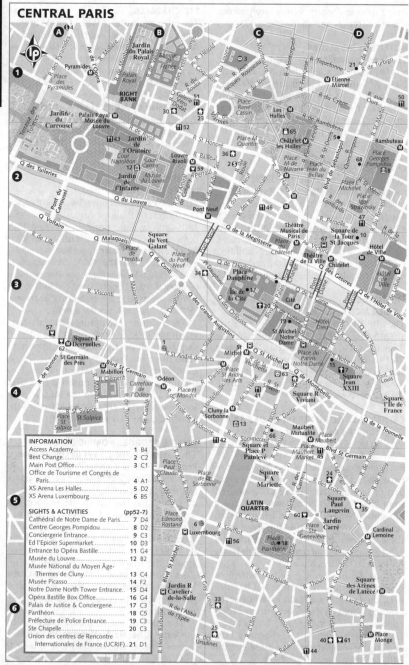

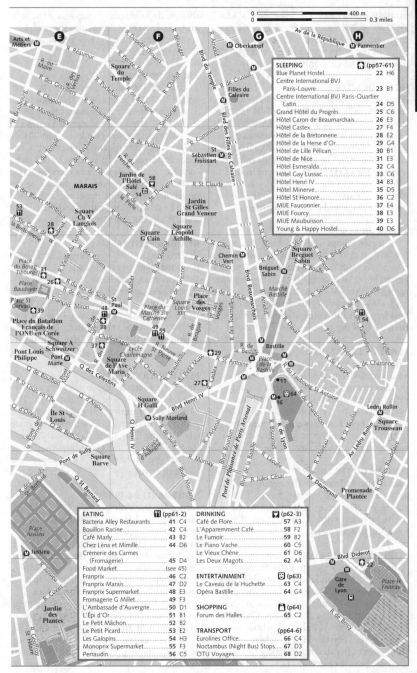

incl MNAM & temp exhibits €10/8, permanent collection (☽ 11am-9pm Wed-Mon), which exhibits art dating from 1905 onward and including the work of the Surrealists and Cubists as well as pop art and contemporary works.

### HÔTEL DE VILLE

After it was gutted during the Paris Commune of 1871, Paris' **Hôtel de Ville** (city hall; Map pp54-5; ☎ 0 820 007 575; www.paris.fr; pl de l'Hôtel de Ville, 4e; metro Hôtel de Ville; ☽ 9.30am-6pm to 7pm Mon-Sat) was rebuilt in the neo-Renaissance style (1874–82). The Hôtel de Ville faces the majestic **place de l'Hôtel de Ville**, used from the Middle Ages to the 19th century to stage many of Paris' celebrations, rebellions, book burnings and public executions.

### MUSÉE PICASSO

The **Musée Picasso** (Picasso Museum; Map pp54-5; ☎ 01 42 71 25 21; 5 rue de Thorigny, 3e; metro St-Paul or Chemin Vert; adult/18-25 yrs & everyone Sun €6.70/5.20, everyone free 1st Sun of month; ☽ 9.30am-6pm Wed-Mon Apr-Sep, to 5.30pm Wed-Mon Oct-Mar), housed in the mid-17th-century Hôtel Salé, is one of Paris' best loved art museums and includes more than 3500 of the *grand maître's* works.

### PLACE DE LA BASTILLE

The Bastille, built during the 14th century as a fortified royal residence, is the most famous monument in Paris that no longer exists; the notorious prison was demolished by a Revolutionary mob on 14 July 1789. The **place de la Bastille** (Map pp54-5; metro Bastille) in the 12e, where the prison once stood, is now a very busy traffic roundabout.

### JARDINS DU TROCADÉRO

The **Jardins du Trocadéro** (Trocadero Gardens; Map pp50-1; metro Trocadéro), whose fountains and statue garden are grandly illuminated at night, are accessible across Pont d'Iéna from the Eiffel Tower.

### ÉTOILE & CHAMPS-ÉLYSÉES

A dozen avenues radiate from the world's largest traffic roundabout, **place de l'Étoile** (Map pp50-1; metro Charles de Gaulle Étoile) – officially place Charles de Gaulle and – and first among them is the av des Champs-Élysées. This broad boulevard, whose name refers to the 'Elysian Fields', where happy souls dwelt after death according to Greek mythology, links place de la Concorde with the Arc de Triomphe. Symbolising the style and *joie de vivre* of Paris since the mid-19th century, the avenue remains a popular tourist destination.

### ARC DE TRIOMPHE

The **Arc de Triomphe** (Triumphal Arch; Map pp50-1; ☎ 01 55 37 73 77 or ☎ 01 44 95 02 10; www.monum .fr; metro Charles de Gaulle-Étoile; viewing platform adult/18-25 yrs €7/4.50, admission free for under-18 & everyone on 1st Sun of month; ☽ 9.30am-11pm Apr-Sep, 10am-10.30pm Oct-Mar) is 2.2km northwest of place de la Concorde in the middle of place Charles de Gaulle (or place de l'Étoile). It was commissioned in 1806 by Napoleon to commemorate his imperial victories but remained unfinished when he started losing battles and then entire wars. It was not completed until 1836.

### GRAND & PETIT PALAIS

Erected for the 1900 Exposition Universelle, the **Grand Palais** (Great Palace; Map pp50-1; ☎ 01 44 13 17 17; www.rmn.fr; 3 av du Général Eisenhower, 8e; metro Champs-Élysées Clemenceau; adult without/with booking €9/10, student & senior €7/8, everyone Mon €7/8, free 1st Sun of month; ☽ without booking 1-8pm Thu-Mon, to 10pm Wed, with booking from 10am) houses the **Galeries Nationales du Grand Palais** beneath its huge, Art Nouveau glass roof.

### PLACE DE LA CONCORDE

**Place de la Concorde** (Map pp50-1; metro Concorde) was laid out between 1755 and 1775. The 3300-year-old pink granite **obelisk** with the gilded top in the middle of the square once stood in the Temple of Ramses at Thebes (today's Luxor) and was given to France in 1831 by Muhammad Ali, viceroy and pasha of Egypt.

### MONTMARTRE & PIGALLE

During the late 19th and early 20th centuries the bohemian lifestyle of **Montmartre** (Map p60) in the 18e attracted a number of important writers and artists, including Picasso, who lived at the studio called **Bateau Lavoir** (Map p60; 11bis Émile Goudeau) from 1908 to 1912. Montmartre retains an upbeat ambience that all the tourists in the world couldn't spoil.

Only a few blocks southwest of the tranquil, residential streets of Montmartre is lively, neon-lit **Pigalle** (Map p60), 9e and 18e, a red-light district that also boasts plenty of trendy nightspots, including clubs and cabarets.

### BASILIQUE DU SACRÉ CŒUR

The **Basilique du Sacré Cœur** (Basilica of the Sacred Heart; Map p60; ☎ 01 53 41 89 00; www.sacre-coeur -montmartre.com; pl du Parvis du Sacré Cœur, 18e; metro Anvers; ☼ 6am-11pm), perched at the very top of the Butte de Montmartre (Montmartre Hill), was built from contributions pledged by Parisian Catholics as an act of contrition after the humiliating Franco-Prussian War of 1870 to 1871. Construction began in 1873, but the basilica was not consecrated until 1919. Some 234 spiralling steps lead you to the basilica's **dome** (admission €5; ☼ 9am-7pm Apr-Sep, to 6pm Oct-Mar), which affords one of Paris' most spectacular panoramas.

### CIMETIÈRE DU PÈRE LACHAISE

The world's most visited graveyard, the **Cimetière Père Lachaise** (Père Lachaise Cemetery; Map pp50-51; ☎ 01 55 25 82 10; metro Philippe Auguste, Gambetta or Père Lachaise; ☼ 8am-6pm Mon-Fri, 8.30am-6pm Sat, 9am-6pm Sun mid-Mar—early Nov; 8am-5.30pm Mon-Fri, 8.30am-5.30pm Sat, 9am-5.30pm Sun early Nov—mid-Mar) opened its oneway doors in 1804. Its 70,000 ornate – even ostentatious – tombs form a verdant, open-air sculpture garden. Among the mortal remains of the one million people buried here are Chopin, Molière, Oscar Wilde, Balzac, Proust, Gertrude Stein, Colette, Pissarro, Seurat, Modigliani, Sarah Bernhardt, Yves Montand, Delacroix, Edith Piaf and even the immortal 12th-century lovers, Abélard and Héloïse. One particularly frequented grave is that of 1960s rock star **Jim Morrison** (1943–71), who is buried in division No 6.

## TOURS

An English-speaking company that consistently gets rave reviews from readers is **Fat Tire Bike Tours** (Map pp50-51; ☎ 01 56 58 10 54; www .fattirebiketoursparis.com; 24 rue Edgar Faure, 15e; metro La Motte-Piquet Grenelle; ☼ 9am-7pm), offering day tours of the city (adult/student €24/22) lasting about four hours from March to September.

Based on the Right Bank just east of Pont de l'Alma, **Bateaux Mouches** (Map pp50-51; ☎ 01 42 25 96 10; www.bateauxmouches.com; Port de la Conférence, 8e; metro Alma Marceau; adult/senior & child 4-12 yrs €7/4, child under 4 yrs free; ☼ every half-hour 10am-8pm, every 20 min 8-11pm mid-Mar—mid-Nov, at 11am, 2.30pm, 4pm, 6pm & 9pm mid-Nov—mid-Mar), the most famous river boat company in Paris, runs 1000-seat tour boats.

## SLEEPING

The student travel agency **OTU Voyages** (Map pp54-55; ☎ 01 40 29 12 22 or ☎ 0 825 004 024; www .otu.fr, in French; 119 rue St-Martin, 4e; metro Rambuteau; ☼ 9.30am-6.30pm Mon-Fri, 10am-5pm Sat; Luxembourg Map pp50-51; ☎ 0 825 004 027; 39 av Georges Bernanos, 5e; metro Port Royal; ☼ 9am-6.30pm Mon-Fri, 10am-noon & 1.15-5pm Sat), directly across the *parvis* (square) from the Centre Pompidou, can *always* find you accommodation.

An agency that arranges bed and breakfast accommodation in Paris and gets good reviews from readers is **Alcôve & Agapes** ( ☎ 01 44 85 06 05; fax 01 44 85 06 14; info@paris-bedandbreakfast .com). Expect to pay between €45 and €100 for a double. Prices for budget accommodation include shared bathroom unless stated. All mid-range and top end accommodation has en-suite bathroom unless stated.

### Louvre & Les Halle

**BUDGET**

**Centre International BVJ Paris-Louvre** (Map pp54-5; ☎ 01 53 00 90 90; bvj@wanadoo.fr; 20 rue Jean-Jacques Rousseau, 1er; metro Louvre-Rivoli; dm €25, d per person €28; ✗ ) This modern, 200-bed hostel run by the Bureau des Voyages de la Jeunesse, has bunks in a single-sex room for two to eight people; rates include breakfast. Guests should be aged under 35.

**Hôtel de Lille Pélican** (Map pp54-5; ☎ 01 42 33 33 42; 8 rue du Pélican, 1er; metro Palais Royal-Musée du Louvre; s/d/tr with washbasin €35/43/65, d with shower €50; ✗ ) This old-fashioned but clean 13-room hotel down a quiet side street has recently been given a face-lift. The helpful manager speaks good English.

**MID-RANGE**

Between the Palais Royal and the Seine and at the eastern end of a very upmarket shopping street, **Hôtel St-Honoré** (Map pp54-5; ☎ 01 42 36 20 38; paris@hotelsthonore.com; 85 rue St-Honoré, 1er; metro Châtelet; s/d/tw/q €59/74/83/92) offers some fairly cramped rooms and a few more spacious ones for three and four people.

### Marais & Bastille

**BUDGET**

**Maison Internationale de la Jeunesse et des Étudiants** (MIJE; ☎ 01 42 74 23 45; www.mije.com) runs three hostels in attractively renovated 17th- and 18th-century *hôtels particuliers* (private mansions) in the heart of the Marais, and it's difficult to think of a better budget deal

**FRANCE**

in Paris. Costs are the same for all three (see following listings); rooms are closed from noon to 3pm, and curfew is from 1am to 7am.

**MIJE Le Fourcy** (6 rue de Fourcy, 4e; metro St-Paul; dm with shower €27, s/d/tr €42/32/28; ✖ 🖳 ) This 207-bed branch is the largest of the three. There's a cheap eatery here called Le Restaurant with a three-course *menu* including a drink for €10.50 and a two-course *formule* plus drink for €8.50.

**MIJE Le Fauconnier** (11 rue du Fauconnier, 4e; metro St-Paul or Pont Marie; dm with shower €27, s/d/tr €42/32/28; ✖ 🖳 ) This 125-bed hostel is two blocks south of MIJE Le Fourcy.

**MIJE Maubuisson** (12 rue des Barres, 4e; metro Hôtel de Ville or Pont Marie; dm with shower €27, s/d/tr €42/32/28; ✖ 🖳 ) This 103-bed place – and the pick of the three in our opinion – is half a block south of the *mairie* (town hall) of the 4e.

**Maison Internationale des Jeunes pour la Culture et la Paix** (Map pp50-1; ☎ 01 43 71 99 21; mij .cp@wanadoo.fr; 4 rue Titon, 11e; metro Faidherbe Chaligny; dm €20; ✖ 🖳 ) This hostel with 166 beds is 1.3km east of place de la Bastille. It offers accommodation in comfortable but institutional-like dormitory rooms for up to eight people.

**Hôtel de la Herse d'Or** (Map pp54-5; ☎ 01 48 87 84 09; hotel.herse.dor@wanadoo.fr; 20 rue St-Antoine, 4e; metro Bastille; d €58/60, s/d with washbasin €38/45) This friendly, 35-room place on busy rue St-Antoine has serviceable rooms.

**MID-RANGE**

**Hôtel de la Bretonnerie** (Map pp54-5; ☎ 01 48 87 77 63; www.bretonnerie.com; 22 rue Ste-Croix de la Bretonnerie, 4e; metro Hôtel de Ville; s & d €110-145, tr & q €170, ste €180-205) A charming three-star hotel in the heart of the Marais nightlife area dating from the 17th century. Decorations in each of the 22 rooms and seven-suites are unique and some rooms have four poster and canopy beds.

**Hôtel Caron de Beaumarchais** (Map pp54-5; ☎ 01 42 72 34 12; www.carondebeaumarchais.com; 12 rue Vieille du Temple, 4e; metro St-Paul; d €120-152; ✖ ) You have to see this award-winning themed hotel to believe it. The hotel has a prized 18th-century pianoforte, gilded mirrors and candelabras in its front room and 44 stylish (though somewhat small) guestrooms.

**Hôtel Castex** (Map pp54-5; ☎ 01 42 72 31 52; www.castexhotel.com; 5 rue Castex, 4e; metro Bastille;

s €95-115, d €120-140, ste €190-220; ✖ ) This former budget hotel, equidistant from Bastille and the Marais, had a major face-lift in 2003 and has retained some of its 17th-century elements

**Hôtel de Nice** (Map pp54-5; ☎ 01 42 78 55 29; fax 01 42 78 36 07; 42bis rue de Rivoli, 4e; metro Hôtel de Ville; s/d/tr €65/100/120) This is an especially warm, family-run place with 23 comfortable rooms. Some rooms have balconies high above busy rue de Rivoli. Reception is on the 1st floor.

## The Islands
### BUDGET

Popular for its terrific location on the tip of the Île de la Cité, **Hôtel Henri IV** (Map pp54-5; ☎ 01 43 54 44 53; 25 pl Dauphine, 1er; metro Pont Neuf or Cité; s €24-31, d €31-36, tr with washbasin €42, d with shower €44, d with shower & toilet €55/68) is a decrepit place with 20 tattered and worn rooms. But it would be impossible to find something this romantic at such a price elsewhere. Hall showers cost €2.50. Breakfast included. Book well in advance.

## Latin Quarter & Jardin des Plantes
### BUDGET
**Centre International BVJ Paris-Quartier Latin** (Map pp54-5; ☎ 01 43 29 34 80; bvj@wanadoo.fr; 44 rue des Bernardins, 5e; metro Maubert Mutualité; 1-/2-/6-bed per person €35/28/26; ✖ ) This 38-bed Left Bank hostel is a branch of the Centre International BVJ Paris-Louvre (see p57) and has the same rules. All the rooms here have en-suite showers and telephones.

**Grand Hôtel du Progrès** (Map pp54-5; ☎ 01 43 54 53 18; fax 01 56 24 87 80; 50 rue Gay Lussac, 5e; metro Luxembourg; s/d/tr €35/42/55, s/d with shower & toilet €46/54) This budget, 26-room hotel has been a favourite of students for generations. There are washbasin-equipped singles and large, old-fashioned doubles with a view and morning sun. Rates include breakfast. Hall showers are free.

**Young & Happy Hostel** (Map pp54-5; ☎ 01 47 07 47 07; www.youngandhappy.fr; 80 rue Mouffetard, 5e; metro Pl Monge; dm €20-22, d per person €23-25; ✖ 🖳 ) A friendly though slightly tatty place in the centre of the most happening area of the Latin Quarter. The 2am curfew is strictly enforced. Beds are in smallish rooms for two to four people. In summer, the easiest way to get a bed is to stop by at about 9am.

## MID-RANGE

**Hôtel Esmeralda** (Map pp54-5; ☎ 01 43 54 19 20; fax 01 40 51 00 68; 4 rue St-Julien le Pauvre, 5e; metro St-Michel; s with washbasin/shower/bath €35/65/80, d with shower & toilet €80, & with bath & toilet €85-95, tr/q from €110/180) This renovated 19-room inn, tucked away in a quiet street with full views of Notre Dame, has been well and truly discovered, so book ahead.

**Hôtel de l'Espérance** (Map pp50-1; ☎ 01 47 07 10 99; hotel.esperance@wanadoo.fr; 15 rue Pascal, 5e; metro Censier Daubenton; s with shower/bath & toilet €68/76, d with shower/bath & toilet €73/84, tw €84, tr €99) The 'Hotel of Hope', just a couple of minutes' walk south of lively rue Mouffetard, is a quiet and immaculately kept 38-room place with faux antique furnishings and a warm welcome.

**Hôtel Gay Lussac** (Map pp54-5; ☎ 01 43 54 23 96; fax 01 40 51 79 49; 29 rue Gay Lussac, 5e; metro Luxembourg; s/d €33/49, s/d with shower €55/64, s/d with shower & toilet €59/68.50, tr/q with shower & toilet €90/95) A 35-room, family-run hotel with a lot of character in the southern part of the Latin Quarter.

**Hôtel Minerve** (Map pp54-5; ☎ 01 43 26 26 04; www .hotel-paris-minerve.com; 13 rue des Écoles, 5e; metro Cardinal Lemoine; s with shower & toilet €79-101, d with shower €93, d with bath €109-125, tr €145; 🖳 ) Reception is kitted out with Oriental carpets and antique books, attractive frescoes and reproduction 18th-century wallpaper. There are 10 rooms with small balconies, eight with views of Notre Dame and two have tiny courtyards that are swooningly romantic.

## Clichy & Gare St-Lazare
### BUDGET

A great find: the **Hôtel Eldorado** (Map pp50-1; ☎ 01 45 22 35 21; eldoradohotel@wanadoo.fr; 18 rue des Dames, 17e; metro Pl de Clichy; s/d/tr with shower €45/60/80) is a welcoming, well-run hotel with 40 colourfully decorated rooms on a quiet street with a private garden at the back. Is this really Paris?

### MID-RANGE

**Hôtel Britannia** (Map pp50-1; ☎ 01 42 85 36 36; fax 01 42 85 16 93; 24 rue d'Amsterdam, 9e; metro St-Lazare; s & d with shower/bath €78/85, tr €94) A 46-room place with narrow hallways but pleasant, clean rooms just opposite the Gare St-Lazare and an easy walk to the *grands magasins* on blvd Haussmann.

**Hôtel Favart** (Map pp50-1; ☎ 01 42 97 59 83; www .hotel-paris-favart.com; 5 rue Marivaux, 2e; metro Richelieu Drouot; s/d/tr €85/108/130) With 37 rooms facing the Opéra Comique, the Favart is a stylish Art Nouveau hotel that feels like it never let go of the *belle époque*.

## Gare du Nord, Gare de l'Est & République
### BUDGET

**Auberge de Jeunesse Jules Ferry** (Map pp50-1; ☎ 01 43 57 55 60; www.fuaj.fr; 8 blvd Jules Ferry, 11e; metro République or Goncourt; dm €19.50, d per person €20 ✖ 🖳 ) It's somewhat institutional and the rooms could be cleaner, but the atmosphere is relaxed. Beds are in rooms for two to six people. There is no curfew. Those without a Hostelling International card or equivalent pay an extra €3 per night.

**Auberge de Jeunesse Le D'Artagnan** (Map pp50-1; ☎ 01 40 32 34 56; www.fuaj.fr; 80 rue Vitruve, 20e; metro Porte de Bagnolet; dm €20.60; ✖ 🖳 ) Far from the centre of the action but just one metro stop from the Gare Routière Internationale de Paris-Gallieni (international bus terminal), this is the largest hostel in France, with 439 beds. The D'Artagnan has rooms with two to eight beds, big lockers, laundry facilities, a bar and cinema.

**Peace & Love Hostel** (Map pp50-1; ☎ 01 46 07 65 11; www.paris-hostels.com; 245 rue La Fayette, 10e; metro Jaurès or Louis Blanc; dm €17-21, d per person €21-26; 🖳 ) This modern-day hippy hangout is rather chaotically run with beds in small-ish, shower-equipped rooms for two to four people. There's a great kitchen and eating area and a lively ground floor bar (open till 2am).

**Sibour Hôtel** (Map pp50-1; ☎ 01 46 07 20 74; sibour .hotel@wanadoo.fr; 4 rue Sibour, 10e; metro Gare de l'Est; s & d with washbasin €35, s & d with toilet €40, s/d/tr/q with shower & toilet €50/58/63/80; 🅿 ) This homely and friendly place has 45 well-kept rooms, including some old-fashioned ones. Hall showers cost €3.

**Hôtel La Vieille France** (Map pp50-1; ☎ 01 45 26 42 37; la.vieille.france@wanadoo.fr; 151 rue La Fayette, 10e; metro Gare du Nord; d with washbasin €42, d with shower/bath & toilet €58/64, tr €78-90) 'The Old France' is a 34-room place with relatively spacious and pleasant rooms. At least one reader has written to complain about the noise, however. Hall showers are free.

### MID-RANGE

Facing the Gare de l'Est, the two-star **Hôtel Français** (Map pp50-1; ☎ 01 40 35 94 14; www.hotel francais.com; 13 rue du 8 Mai 1945, 10e; metro Gare de l'Est;

s €77-81, d €84-91, tr €109-116; 😭 🖳 (P)) has 71 attractive, almost luxurious, rooms (some with balconies).

## Gare de Lyon, Nation & Bercy
### BUDGET
The 43-room **Blue Planet Hostel** (Map pp54-5; 📞 01 43 42 06 18; www.hostelblueplanet.com; 5 rue Hector Malot, 12e; metro Gare de Lyon; dm €18.30-21; 🖳 ) is very close to Gare de Lyon – convenient if you're heading south or east. Dorm beds are in rooms for three or four people. There's no curfew.

## Montmartre & Pigalle
### BUDGET
**Hôtel Bonséjour** (Map p60; 📞 01 42 54 22 53; fax 01 42 54 25 92; 11 rue Burq, 18e; metro Abbesses; s/d with washbasin €22-25/30-32, d with shower €38-40, tr €53) The 'Good Stay' is at the end of a quiet street in Montmartre. Some rooms (eg No 14, 23, 33, 43 & 53) have little balconies and at least one room (No 55) offers a fleeting glimpse of Sacré Cœur. It's a simple place to stay – no lift, linoleum floors – but comfortable and very friendly. The Hall showers cost €2.

**Le Village Hostel** (Map p60; 📞 01 42 64 22 02; www.villagehostel.fr; 20 rue d'Orsel, 18e; metro Anvers; dm/d/tr per person €20/23/21.50 Nov–mid-Mar, €21.50/25/23 mid-Mar–Oct; 🖳 ) 'The Village' is a fine 25-room hostel with beamed ceilings and views of Sacré Coeur. Dorm beds are in rooms for four to six people and all rooms have showers and toilet. Kitchen facilities are available, and there is a lovely outside terrace. Curfew is 2am.

**Woodstock Hostel** (Map p60; 📞 01 48 78 87 76; www.woodstock.fr; 48 rue Rodier, 9e; metro Anvers; dm/d per person €15/17 Oct-Mar, €20/23 Apr-Sep; 🖳 ) Woodstock is just down the hill from raucous Pigalle in a quiet, residential quarter. Dorm beds are in rooms for four to six people and there's a kitchen. Curfew is at 2am.

### MID-RANGE
**Hôtel des Arts** (Map p60; 📞 01 46 06 30 52; www.arts-hotel-paris.com; 5 rue Tholozé, 18e; metro Abbesses or Blanche; s/d/tr €64/78/94; (P)) Part of the Logis de France group, the 'Arts Hotel' is a friendly and attractive 50-room place convenient for both Pigalle and Montmartre. Towering over it is the old-style Moulin de la Galette windmill.

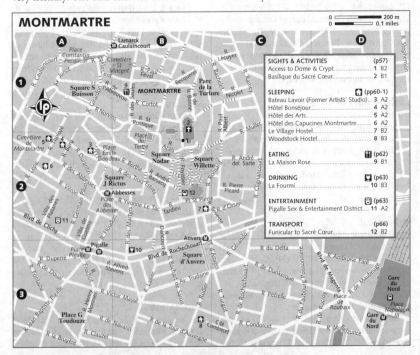

MONTMARTRE

| | |
|---|---|
| **SIGHTS & ACTIVITIES** | **(p57)** |
| Access to Dome & Crypt......................... 1 B2 |
| Basilique du Sacré Cœur........................ 2 B1 |
| **SLEEPING** | **(pp60-1)** |
| Bateau Lavoir (Former Artists' Studio)... 3 A2 |
| Hôtel Bonséjour...................................... 4 A2 |
| Hôtel des Arts........................................ 5 A2 |
| Hôtel des Capucines Montmartre........... 6 A2 |
| Le Village Hostel.................................... 7 B2 |
| Woodstock Hostel................................. 8 B3 |
| **EATING** | **(p62)** |
| La Maison Rose...................................... 9 B1 |
| **DRINKING** | **(p63)** |
| La Fourmi............................................ 10 B3 |
| **ENTERTAINMENT** | **(p63)** |
| Pigalle Sex & Entertainment District..... 11 A2 |
| **TRANSPORT** | **(p66)** |
| Funicular to Sacré Cœur...................... 12 B2 |

**FRANCE**

---

**CAMPING IN PARIS**

**Camping du Bois de Boulogne** ( ☎ 01 45 24 30 81; www.abccamping.com/boulogne.htm; 2 allée du Bord de l'Eau, 16e; camp sites Oct-Mar/ Apr-Jun & Nov/Jul & Aug €11/14.20/15.40, with vehicle per d €18.50/22.50/24.50, with electricity €22.50/26.50/31.70, 1st-time booking fee €12; ⌚ 6-2am) The only campsite within the Paris city limits lies along the Seine at the far western edge of the Bois de Boulogne. It gets crowded in the summer, but there's always space for a small tent. Fully equipped caravans sleeping four to five cost around €49 to €85. Porte Maillot metro station, 4.5km to the northeast through the wood, is linked to the site by RATP bus No 244, which runs from 6am to 8.30pm daily, and from April to October by a privately operated shuttle bus charging about €2.

---

**Hôtel des Capucines Montmartre** (Map p60; ☎ 01 42 52 89 80; fax 01 42 52 29 57; 5 rue Aristide Bruant, 18e; metro Abbesses or Blanche; s €45-50, d €54-60, tr €60-70) A decent, family-run hotel with 30 rooms on a small street awash with places to stay.

# EATING

Parisian restaurants generally specialise in a particular variety of food (eg traditional or regional French, north African, Vietnamese), whereas a brasserie always serves more standard French and/or Alsatian fare. One of the delights of visiting Paris is stocking up on fresh bread, pastries, cheese, fruit, and prepared dishes and sitting down for a gourmet *pique-nique*.

## Louvre & Les Halles

**Café Marly** (Map pp54-5; ☎ 01 46 26 06 60; cour Napoléon du Louvre, 93 rue de Rivoli, 1er; metro Palais Royal-Musée du Louvre; starters €8-21, sandwiches & snacks €10-14, mains €16-30; ⌚ noon-1am) This classic venue serves contemporary French fare under the colonnades of the Louvre, and overlooks the glass pyramid.

**L'Épi d'Or** (Map pp54-5; ☎ 01 42 36 38 12; 25 rue Jean-Jacques Rousseau, 1er; metro Louvre-Rivoli; starters €5-15, mains €14-20, set menu €18; ⌚ lunch & dinner Mon-Fri, Sat dinner only) This oh-so-Parisian bistro serves well-prepared, classic dishes – such as *gigot d'agneau* (leg of lamb), which is cooked for seven hours.

**Le Petit Mâchon** (Map pp54-5; ☎ 01 42 60 08 06; 158 rue St-Honoré, 1er; metro Palais Royal-Musée du Louvre; starters €6.50-12.50, mains €14-21, lunch menu €16.50; ⌚ lunch & dinner to 11pm Tue-Sun) This is an upbeat bistro convenient to the Louvre, with Lyon-inspired specialities.

Self-catering options include **Ed l'Épicier** (Map pp54-5; 80 rue de Rivoli, 4e; ⌚ 9am-8pm Mon-Sat) and **Franprix** (Map pp54-5; 35 rue Berger, 1er; ⌚ 8.30am-7.50pm Mon-Sat).

## Marais & Bastille

**L'Ambassade d'Auvergne** (Map pp54-5; ☎ 01 42 72 31 22; 22 rue du Grenier St-Lazare, 3e; metro Rambuteau; starters €9-18, mains €14-19, menu €27; ⌚ lunch & dinner to 10.30pm) The place to go if you're really hungry; the sausages and hams of this region, the lentils from Puy and the *clafoutis*, a custard and cherry tart, are sublime.

**Les Galopins** (Map pp54-5; ☎ 01 47 00 45 35; 24 des Taillandiers, 11e; metro Bastille or Voltaire; starters €6-10.50, mains €11.50-18, lunch menu €11.50 & €15; ⌚ lunch Mon-Fri, dinner to 11pm Mon-Thu, to 11.30pm Fri & Sat) This neighbourhood bistro serves dishes in the best tradition of French cuisine: *poêlée de pétoncles* (pan-fried scallops), *magret de canard* (duck breast fillet), *cœur de rumsteck* (tenderloin rump steak).

**Le Petit Picard** (Map pp54-5; ☎ 01 42 78 54 03; 42 rue Ste-Croix de la Bretonnerie, 4e; metro Hôtel de Ville; lunch menu €12, dinner menu €14.50 & €21.50; ⌚ lunch Tue-Fri, dinner to 11pm Tue-Sun) This popular little restaurant in the centre of Marais serves traditional French cuisine. If you're very hungry, try the generous *menu traditionel* (€21.50).

In the Marais, there are several food shops and Asian delicatessens on rue St-Antoine, 4e, as well as a number of supermarkets. For cheese, try the excellent **Fromagerie G Millet** (Map pp54-5; ☎ 01 42 78 48 78; 77 rue St-Antoine, 4e; ⌚ 7.30am-1pm & 3.30-8pm Mon-Fri, 7.30am-1pm Sat). Supermarkets include:
**Franprix** (Map pp54-5; 135 rue St-Antoine, 4e; ⌚ 9am-8.30pm Mon-Sat)
**Franprix Marais** (Map pp54-5; 87 rue de la Verrerie, 4e)
**Monoprix** (Map pp54-5; 71 rue St-Antoine, 4)

## Latin Quarter & Jardin Des Plantes

The restaurants between rue St-Jacques, blvd St-Germain and blvd St-Michel attract mainly foreign tourists, who appear to be unaware that some people refer to the area as 'Bacteria Alley'.

**Bouillon Racine** (Map pp54-5; ☎ 01 44 32 15 60; 3 rue Racine, 6e; metro Cluny La Sorbonne; starters €7-11.50, mains €12-17, lunch menu €15 & dinner menu €25; ⊙ lunch & dinner to 11pm) This 'soup kitchen' built in 1906 to feed city workers is an Art Nouveau palace, though the classic French dishes like *caille confite* (preserved quail) and *cochon de lait* (milk-fed pork) can't hold a candle to the surrounds.

**Chez Léna et Mimille** (Map pp54-5; ☎ 01 47 07 72 47; 32 rue Tournefort, 5e; metro Censier Daubenton; lunch starters/mains/desserts €7/14/7, dinner menu with wine €3; ⊙ lunch Tue-Fri, dinner to 11pm Mon-Sat) This cosy but elegant French restaurant has excellent food and one of the most fabulous terraces in Paris, overlooking a little park with a fountain.

**Perraudin** (Map pp54-5; ☎ 01 46 33 15 75; 157 rue St-Jacques, 5e; metro Luxembourg; starters €6-15, mains €14-23, lunch/dinner menu €18/26; ⊙ lunch & dinner to 10.30pm Mon-Fri) Perraudin is a traditional French restaurant that hasn't changed much since the late 19th century and is great for classics such as *bœuf bourguignon* (€14), *gigot d'agneau* (€15) or *confit de canard* (€15).

Place Maubert, 5e, becomes a lively **food market** four mornings a week. There are also some great provisions shops here, including a cheese shop called **Crémerie des Carmes** (Map pp54-5; ☎ 01 43 54 50 93; 47 ter blvd St-Germain, 5e; metro Maubert Mutualité; ⊙ 7.30am-1pm & 3.30pm-8pm Mon-Fri, to 1pm Sat).

## Montparnasse

**La Coupole** (Map pp54-5; ☎ 01 43 20 14 20; 102 blvd du Montparnasse, 14e; metro Vavin; starters €7.50-12.50, mains €13.50-18.50, lunch menu €17.50, dinner menu €22.90 & €32.90; ⊙ 8-1am Sun-Thu, to 1.30am Fri & Sat) This 450-seat brasserie, which opened in 1927, has mural-covered columns painted by such artists as Brancusi and Chagall.

**Le Dôme** (Map pp50-1; ☎ 01 43 35 25 81; 108 blvd du Montparnasse, 14e; metro Vavin; starters €12.50-23, mains €30.50-56; ⊙ lunch & dinner to 12.30am) An Art Deco extravaganza dating from the 1930s, The Dome is a monumental place for a meal, with the emphasis on the freshest of oysters, shellfish and fish dishes such as *sole meunière*.

## Montmartre & Pigalle

If you are looking for the quintessential intimate Montmartre bistro, head for the tiny **La Maison Rose** (Map p60; ☎ 01 42 57 66 75; 2 rue de l'Abreuvoir, 18e; metro Lamarck Caulaincourt; starters €7.80-13, mains €14.50-16.50, menu €14.50; ⊙ lunch & dinner to 10.30pm Mar-Oct, lunch Thu-Mon, dinner to 9pm Mon, Thu-Sat Nov-Feb), the 'Pink House', just north of the place du Tertre.

# DRINKING
## Louvre & Les Halles

Just opposite the Louvre, **Le Fumoir** (The Smoking Room Map pp54-5; ☎ 01 42 92 00 24; 6 rue de l'Amiral Coligny, 1er; metro Louvre-Rivoli; ⊙ 11pm-2am), is a huge bar/café with a gentleman's club/library theme. It's a friendly, lively place and quite good fun. Happy hour is 6pm to 8pm daily.

## Marais & Bastille

An absolute oasis of peace, **L'Apparemment Café** (Map p60; ☎ 01 48 87 12 22; 18 rue des Coutures St-Gervais, 3e; metro St-Sébastien Froissart; ⊙ noon-2am Mon-Fri, 4pm-2am Sat, 12.30pm-midnight Sun), tucked not so 'apparently' behind the Musée Picasso, looks and feels like a private living room.

## Latin Quarter & Jardin des Plantes

**Le Piano Vache** (Map pp54-5; ☎ 01 46 33 75 03; 8 rue Laplace, 5e; metro Maubert Mutualité; ⊙ noon-2am Mon-Fri, 9pm-2am Sat & Sun) Just down the hill from the Panthéon, 'The Mean Piano' plays great music (guest DJs) and attracts a good crowd of mixed ages. Happy hour is from opening to 9pm Monday to Friday.

**Le Vieux Chêne** (Map pp54-5; ☎ 01 43 37 71 51; 69 rue Mouffetard, 5e; metro Pl Monge; ⊙ 4pm-2am Sun-Thu, to 5am Fri & Sat) 'The Old Oak' is popular with students and has jazz at the weekend. Happy hour is from opening to 9pm daily.

## St-Germain, Odéon & Luxembourg

**Café de Flore** (Map pp54-5; ☎ 01 45 48 55 26; 172 blvd St-Germain, 6e; metro St-Germain des Prés; ⊙ 7.30-1.30am) The Flore is an Art Deco café where the red upholstered benches, mirrors and marble walls haven't changed since the days when Sartre, de Beauvoir, Camus and Picasso bent their elbows here. The terrace is a much sought-after place to sip beer (€7.50 for 400ml), the house Pouilly Fumé (€7.50 a glass or €29 a bottle) or coffee (€4).

**Les Deux Magots** (Map pp54-5; ☎ 01 45 48 55 25; 170 blvd St-Germain, 6e; metro St-Germain des Prés; ⊙ 7-1am) This erstwhile literary haunt is best known as the favoured hangout of Sartre, Hemingway, Picasso and André Breton. Everyone has to sit on the terrace here at least once and have a coffee (€4), beer (€5.50) or the famous hot chocolate served in porcelain jugs (€6).

## Montmartre & Pigalle

A trendy Pigalle hang-out, **La Fourmi** (Map pp54-5; ☎ 01 42 64 70 35; 74 rue des Martyrs, 18e; metro Pigalle; ☼ 8-2am Mon-Thu, 10-4am Fri-Sun), the 'Ant', buzzes (marches?) all day and night and is a convenient place to meet before heading off to the clubs.

## ENTERTAINMENT

It's virtually impossible to sample the richness of Paris' entertainment scene without first studying *Pariscope* (€0.40) or *Officiel des Spectacles* (€0.35), both of which come out on Wednesday. *Pariscope* includes a six-page insert in English at the back, courtesy of London's *Time Out* magazine. The weekly magazine *Zurban* (www.zurban .com – in French; €0.80), which also appears on Wednesday, offers a fresher look at entertainment in the capital. For up-to-date information on clubs and the music scene, pick up a copy of *LYLO*

You can buy tickets for cultural events at many ticket outlets, including **Fnac** ( ☎ 08 92 68 36 22; www.fnac.com, in French) and **Virgin Megastore branches** (www.virginmega.fr, in French), for a small commission.

## Cinemas

Expect to pay between €6 and €8 for a first-run film. Students and those aged under 18 or over 60 usually get discounts of about 25% except on Friday, Saturday and Sunday nights.

## Live Music

### OPERA & CLASSICAL

**Opéra National de Paris** (ONP; ☎ 08 92 89 90 90; www .opera-de-paris.fr, in French) splits its performance schedule between the Palais Garnier and the modern Opéra Bastille, which opened in 1989. Both opera houses also stage ballets and classical-music concerts (September to July) performed by the ONP's affiliated orchestra and ballet companies.

**Opéra Bastille** (Map pp54-5; 2-6 pl de la Bastille, 12e; metro Bastille) Tickets are available from the **box office** (Map pp54-5; 130 rue de Lyon, 12e; ☼ 11am-6.30pm Mon-Sat) some 14 days before the date of the performance, but the only way to ensure a seat is by **post** (120 rue de Lyon, 75576 Paris CEDEX 12) some two months in advance. Operas cost €6 to €114. Ballets cost €13 to €70; seats, with limited or no visibility, available at the box office only are €6 to €9. Unsold

tickets are offered to people aged under 26 or over 65 and students for €20 only 15 minutes before the curtain goes up.

**Palais Garnier** (Map pp50-1; pl de l'Opéra, 9e; metro Opéra) Ticket prices and conditions (including last-minute discounts) at the **box office** (pl de l'Opéra, 9e; ☼ 11am-6.30pm Mon-Sat) of the city's original opera house are almost exactly the same as those at the Opéra Bastille.

### JAZZ & BLUES

After WWII, Paris was Europe's most important jazz centre and it is again very much à la mode; the city's better clubs attract top international stars.

**Le Caveau de la Huchette** (Map pp54-5; ☎ 01 43 26 65 05; 5 rue de la Huchette, 5e; metro St-Michel; adult Sun-Thu €10.50, Fri & Sat €13, student €9; ☼ 9pm-2.30am Sun-Thu, to 3.30am Fri, 9pm-4am Sat) Housed in a medieval *caveau* (cellar) that was used as a courtroom and torture chamber during the Revolution, this club is where virtually all the jazz greats since the end of WWII have played.

### Nightclubs

Paris is great for music (techno remains very popular) and there are some mighty fine DJs based here. Latino and Cuban salsa music is also huge.

**Le Batofar** (Map pp50-1; ☎ 01 56 29 10 33; www .batofar.net, in French; opposite 11 quai François Mauriac, 13e; metro Quai de la Gare or Bibliothèque; admission free-€12; ☼ 9pm-midnight Mon & Tue, 9pm or 10pm-4am, 5am or 6am Wed-Sun) What looks like an unassuming tugboat moored near the imposing Bibliothèque Nationale de France is a rollicking dancing spot that attracts some top international techno and funk DJ talent.

**Le Cithéa** (Map pp50-1; ☎ 01 40 21 70 95; www .cithea.com, in French; 114 rue Oberkampf, 11e; metro Parmentier or Ménilmontant; admission free-€4; ☼ 5pm-5.30am Tue-Thu, 10pm-6.30am Fri & Sat) This popular concert venue has bands playing soul, Latin and funk but especially world music and jazz, usually from 10.30pm, with DJs from 1am.

**Gibus** (Map pp50-1; ☎ 01 47 00 78 88; www.gibus .fr, in French; 18 rue du Faubourg du Temple, 11e; metro République; admission free-€18; ☼ 11pm-dawn Tue-Sat) Gibus, an enormously popular cave-like venue halfway between the Canal St-Martin and place de la République, has hard techno on Tuesday, acid and trance on Wednesday, techno on Thursday.

## SHOPPING

**Le Bon Marché** (Map pp50-1; ☎ 01 44 39 80 00; www .bonmarche.fr, in French; 24 rue de Sèvres, 7e; metro Sèvres Babylone; ⊙ 9.30am-7pm Mon-Wed & Fri, 10am-9pm Thu, 9.30am-8pm Sat) Grandly opened by Gustave Eiffel as Paris' first department store in 1852.

**Galeries Lafayette** (Map pp50-1; ☎ 01 42 82 34 56; www.galerieslafayette.com; 40 blvd Haussmann, 9e; metro Auber or Chaussée d'Antin; ⊙ 9.30am-7.30pm Mon-Wed, Fri & Sat, to 9pm Thu) A vast grand magasin in two adjacent buildings, Galeries Lafayette features a wide selection of fashion and accessories.

## GETTING THERE & AWAY
### Air
#### AÉROPORT D'ORLY

The airport **Orly** (code ORY; ☎ 01 49 75 15 15, flight info 0 892 681 515; www.adp.fr) is about 18km south of the city.

#### AÉROPORT ROISSY CHARLES DE GAULLE

Located 30km northeast of Paris in the suburb of Roissy is **Roissy Charles de Gaulle** (code CDG; ☎ 01 48 62 22 80, 0 892 681 515; www.adp.fr). Terminals (Aérogares) 1 and 25 are used by international and domestic carriers.

#### AÉROPORT PARIS-BEAUVAIS

The international airport at **Beauvais** (code BVA; ☎ 03 44 11 46 86; www.aeroportbeauvais.com), 80km north of Paris, is used by the discount airline Ryanair for its European flights, including those between Paris and Dublin, Shannon and Glasgow.

### Bus

Eurolines links Paris with points all over Western and Central Europe, Scandinavia and Morocco. The main **Eurolines office** (Map pp54-5; ☎ 01 43 54 11 99 or 0 892 899 091; www.euro lines.fr; 55 rue St-Jacques, 5e; metro Cluny-La Sorbonne; ⊙ 9.30am-6.30pm Mon-Fri, 10am-1pm & 2-6pm Sat). The **Gare Routière Internationale** (Map pp50-1; ☎ 0 892 899 091; 28 av du Général de Gaulle; metro Gallieni), the city's international bus terminal, is in the inner suburb of Bagnolet.

### Train

Mainline train information is available round the clock at **SNCF** (www.sncf.fr; ☎ 0 892 353 535). Paris has six major train stations, each of which handles passenger traffic to different parts of France and Europe.

**Gare d'Austerlitz** (Map pp50-1; blvd de l'Hôpital, 13e; metro Gare d'Austerlitz) Spain and Portugal; Loire Valley and non-TGV trains to southwestern France (eg Bordeaux and Basque Country)

**Gare de l'Est** (Map pp50-1; blvd de Strasbourg, 10e; metro Gare de l'Est) Luxembourg, parts of Switzerland (Basel, Lucerne, Zurich), southern Germany (Frankfurt, Munich) and points further east; areas of France east of Paris (Champagne, Alsace and Lorraine)

**Gare de Lyon** (Map pp50-1; blvd Diderot, 12e; metro Gare de Lyon) Parts of Switzerland (eg Bern, Geneva, Lausanne), Italy and points beyond; regular and TGV Sud-Est trains to areas southeast of Paris, including Dijon, Lyon, Provence, the Côte d'Azur and the Alps.

**Gare du Nord** (Map p60; rue de Dunkerque, 10e; metro Gare du Nord) UK, Belgium, northern Germany, Scandinavia, Moscow etc (terminus of the high-speed Thalys trains to/from Amsterdam, Brussels, Cologne and Geneva and Eurostar to London); trains to the northern suburbs of Paris and northern France, including TGV Nord trains to Lille and Calais.

**Gare Montparnasse** (Map pp50-1; av du Maine & blvd de Vaugirard, 15e; metro Montparnasse Bienvenüe) Brittany and places en route from Paris, TGV Atlantique trains to Nantes, Bordeaux and other destinations in southwestern France.

**Gare St-Lazare** (Map pp50-1; rue St-Lazare & rue d'Amsterdam, 8e; metro St-Lazare) Normandy (eg Dieppe, Le Havre, Cherbourg).

## GETTING AROUND
### To/from the Airports
#### AÉROPORT D'ORLY

There are half a dozen public transport options to get to/from Orly airport. Apart from RATP bus No 183, all services call at both terminals. Tickets for the bus services are sold on board.

---

### GETTING TO THE COAST FROM PARIS

**By Train** The fast TGV trains link Paris' Gare de Lyon with Nice (€81, 5½ hours, three daily) and Marseille (€83.90, three hours, 17 daily)

**By Bus** French transport policy is biased in favour of the trains so there are no intercity bus services for the south coast.

**By Car** By autoroute, the drive from Paris to Nice (about 950km) takes eight or nine hours and costs at least €130 in fuel and tolls. Useful websites include www.viami chelin.com and www.autoroutes.fr which both itemise routes, distances and tolls.

**Air France Bus No 1** ( ☎ 0 892 350 820; www.cars -airfrance.com, in French; one way/return €7.50/12.75; 🕑 every 15min 6am-11.30pm to Paris, 5.45am-11pm to Orly; journey time 30-45min) This *navette* (shuttle bus) runs to/from the eastern side of Gare Montparnasse as well as **Aérogare des Invalides** (Map pp50-1; metro Invalides) in the 7e. On your way into the city, you can ask to get off at metro Porte d'Orléans or metro Duroc.

**Jetbus** ( ☎ 01 69 01 00 09; €5.15; 🕑 every 15-20min 6.43am-10.49pm to Paris, 6.15am-10.15pm to Orly; journey time 55min) With the exception of RATP bus No 183, Jetbus is the cheapest way to get to/from Orly. It runs to/from metro Villejuif Louis Aragon, south of the 13e on the city's southern fringe.

**Orlybus** ( ☎ 0 892 687 714; €5.70; 🕑 every 15-20min 6am-11.30pm to Paris, 5.35am-11pm to Orly; journey time 30min) This RATP bus runs to/from metro Denfert Ro-chereau in the 14e and makes several stops in the eastern 14e in each direction.

**Orlyval** ( ☎ 0 892 687 714; €8.80 to/from Paris, €10.65 to/from La Défense; 🕑 every 4-12min 6am-11pm each direction; journey time 33min to Paris, 50min to La Défense) This RATP service links Orly with the city centre via a shuttle train and the RER. A driverless shuttle train runs between the airport and Antony RER station (eight minutes) on RER line B, from where it's an easy journey into the city; to get to Antony from the city (26 minutes), take line B4 towards St-Rémy-lès-Chevreuse. Orlyval tickets are valid for travel on the RER and for metro travel within the city.

**RATP Bus No 183** ( ☎ 0 892 687 714; €1.30 or one metro/bus ticket; 🕑 every 35min 5.35am-8.35pm each direction; journey time 1hr) This is a slow public bus that links Orly-Sud (only) with metro Porte de Choisy, at the southern edge of the 13e.

**RER C** ( ☎ 0 890 361 010; €5.35; 🕑 every 12-20 min 5.45am-11pm each direction; journey time 50min) An Aéroports de Paris (ADP) shuttle bus links the airport with RER line C at Pont de Rungis-Aéroport d'Orly RER station. From the city, take a C2 train towards Pont de Rungis or Massy-Palaiseau. Tickets are valid for onward travel on the metro.

Along with public transport the follow-ing private options provide door-to-door service for about €25 for a single person (from about €15 to €18 per person for two or more). Book in advance and allow for numerous pick-ups and drop-offs:

**Allô Shuttle** ( ☎ 01 34 29 00 80; www.alloshuttle.com)

**Paris Airports Service** ( ☎ 01 46 80 14 67; www.paris airportservice.com)

**Shuttle Van PariShuttle** ( ☎ 0 800 699 699; www .parishuttle.com)

**Taxi** A taxi between central Paris and Orly costs about €40 and takes 20 to 30 minutes.

**World Shuttle** ( ☎ 01 46 80 14 67; www.world -shuttles.com)

## AÉROPORT ROISSY CHARLES DE GAULLE

Roissy Charles de Gaulle has two train stations: Aéroport Charles de Gaulle 1 (CDG1) and the sleek Aéroport Charles de Gaulle 2 (CDG2). Both are served by commuter trains on RER line B3. A free shuttle bus links the terminals with the train stations; otherwise there are various public-transport options for travel be-tween Aéroport Roissy Charles de Gaulle and Paris. Tickets for the bus services are sold on board.

**Air France bus No 2** ( ☎ 0 892 350 820; www.cars-air france.com, in French; one way/return €10/17; 🕑 every 15 min 5.45am-11pm each direction; journey time 35-50mins) Air France bus No 2 links the airport with two locations on the Right Bank: near the Arc de Triomphe just outside 2 av Carnot, 17e (metro Charles de Gaulle-Étoile) and the Palais des Congrès de Paris (blvd Gouvion St-Cyr, 17e; metro Porte Maillot).

**Air France bus No 4** ( ☎ 0 892 350 820; www.cars -airfrance.com, in French; one way/return €11.50/19.55; 🕑 every 30min to Paris 7am-9pm, to Roissy Charles de Gaulle 7am-9.30pm; journey time 45-55min) Air France bus No 4 links the airport with Gare de Lyon and with the Gare Montparnasse

**RATP Bus Nos 350** ( ☎ 0 892 687 714; €3.90 or three metro/bus tickets; 🕑 every 30min 5.45am-7pm each direction; journey time 1¼hrs) This public bus links Aérog-ares 1 & 2 with Gare de l'Est and with Gare du Nord

**RATP Bus No 351** ( ☎ 0 892 687 714; €3.90 or three metro/bus tickets; 🕑 every 30min 6am-9.30pm to Paris, 6am-8.20pm to Roissy Charles de Gaulle; journey time 55min) Links the eastern side of place de la Nation with the Roissy Charles de Gaulle.

**RER B** ( ☎ 0 890 361 010; €7.75; 🕑 every 4-15min 4.56am-11.40pm in each direction; journey time 30mins) RER line B3 links CDG1 and CDG2 with the city. To get to the airport take any RER line B train whose four-letter destination code begins with E (eg EIRE) and a shuttle bus (every 5-8min) will ferry you to the appropriate terminal. Regular metro ticket windows can't always sell RER tickets as far as the airport so you may have to buy one at the RER station where you board.

**Roissybus** ( ☎ 0 892 687 714; €8.20; 🕑 every 15-20 min 5.45am-11pm in each direction; journey time 60min) This public bus links both terminals with rue Scribe (metro Opéra) behind the Palais Garnier in the 9e.

**Shuttle Van** The four companies in the Orly section will take you from Roissy Charles de Gaulle to your hotel for similar prices. Book in advance.

**Taxi** Taxis to/from the city centre cost from €40 to €55.

FRANCE

## Car & Motorcycle

While driving in Paris is nerve-racking, it's not impossible. The fastest way to get across the city by car is via the blvd Périphérique, the ring road that encircles the city.

In many parts of Paris you pay €1.50 to €2 an hour to park your car on the street. Large municipal parking garages usually charge €2.60 an hour and between €20 and €23 for 24hrs.

Car rental companies include:

**Avis** ( ☎ 0 802 050 505; www.avis.fr)

**Budget** ( ☎ 0 825 003 564; www.budget.fr, in French)

**Europcar** ( ☎ 0 825 358 358; www.europcar.fr, in French)

**Hertz** ( ☎ 0 825 861 861; www.hertz.fr)

Smaller agencies can offer much more attractive deals. Check the *Yellow Pages* under 'Location d'Automobiles: Tourisme et Utilitaires'.

## Public Transport

### BUS

Paris' bus system, also operated by the RATP, runs from 5.45am to 12.30am Monday to Saturday. Services are drastically reduced on Sunday. After the metro lines have finished their last runs at about 1am, the Noctambus network of night buses links the place du Châtelet (1er) and av Victoria just west of the Hôtel de Ville in the 4e with most parts of the city. Short bus rides cost one metro/bus ticket; longer rides require two. Whatever kind of single-journey ticket you have, you must cancel *(oblitérer)* it in the *composteur* (cancelling machine) next to the driver.

### METRO & RER

Paris' underground network consists of two separate but interlinked systems: the **Métropolitain**, known as the metro, with 14 lines and 372 stations; and the **RER** (Réseau Express Régional), a network of suburban lines designated A to E and then numbered, that pass through the city centre.

### Metro Network

Each metro train is known by the name of its terminus. On lines that split into several branches (eg line Nos 3, 7 and 13), the terminus served by each train is indicated with back-lit panels on the cars. The last metro trains run between 12.35am and 1.04am and start again around 5.30am.

### RER Network

The RER is faster than the metro, but the stops are much further apart. RER lines are known by an alphanumeric combination – the letter (A to E) refers to the line, the number to the spur it will follow somewhere out in the suburbs. The same RATP tickets are valid on the metro, the RER (for travel within the city limits), buses, the Montmartre funicular and Paris' two tram lines. They cost €1.30 if bought individually and €10 (€5 for children aged four to 11) for a carnet of 10.

Always keep your ticket until you exit from your station; you may be stopped by a *contrôleur* (ticket inspector).

### TOURIST PASSES

The Mobilis card and its coupon allows unlimited travel for one day in two to eight zones (€5.20 to €18.30), but you would have to make at least six metro trips in a day (based on the carnet price) in zones 1 and 2 to break even on this pass.

Paris Visite passes, which allow the holder discounted entry to certain museums and activities as well as discounts on transport fares, are valid for one, two, three or five consecutive days of travel in either three, five or eight zones. The version covering one to three zones costs €8.35/13.70/18.25/26.65 for one/two/three/five days.

### TRAVEL PASSES

The cheapest and easiest way to use public transport in Paris is to get a Carte Orange, a weekly or monthly combined metro, RER and bus pass. The basic ticket valid for zones 1 and 2 should be sufficient. To buy your first Carte Orange, take a passport-size photograph to any metro or RER ticket window.

## Taxi

The *prise en charge* (flag-fall) in a Parisian taxi is €2. Within the city limits, it costs €0.62 per kilometre for travel between 7am and 7pm Monday to Saturday and €1.06 per kilometre from 7pm to 7am at night, all day Sunday and on public holidays. Pick-ups from SNCF mainline stations cost another €0.70.

Radio-dispatched taxi companies, on call 24 hours, include:

**Alpha Taxis** ( ☎ 01 45 85 85 85)

**Taxis Bleus** ( ☎ 01 49 36 10 10)

**Taxis Radio 7000** ( ☎ 01 42 70 00 42)

# CHAMPAGNE

Only bubbly from the Champagne region – grown in designated areas, then aged and bottled according to the strictest standards – can be labelled as champagne. The town of Épernay, south of Reims, is the de facto capital of champagne (the drink) and is the best place to head for *dégustation* (tasting).

## REIMS

**pop 206, 000**

Meticulously reconstructed after the two world wars, Reims is a neat and orderly city with wide avenues and well-tended parks.

### Orientation & Information

The train station is about 1km northwest of the cathedral, across square Colbert from place Drouet d'Erlon, the city's major nightlife centre. Virtually every street in the city centre is oneway.

The **tourist office** ( ☎ 03 26 77 45 00; www.reims -tourisme.com; 2 rue Guillaume de Machault; ⏱ 9am-7pm Mon-Sat, 10am-6pm Sun & hols early Apr–mid-Oct, 10am-5pm Mon-Sat, 11am-4pm Sun & hols mid-Oct–early Apr) has an Internet post that runs on a France Télécom *télécarte*.

The **post office** (2 rue Cérès; ⏱ 8.30am-6pm Mon-Fri, 8am-noon Sat) has currency exchange and a Cyberposte.

**Clique et Croque Cybercafé** ( ☎ 03 26 86 93 92; 27 rue de Vesle; per hr €4.20; ⏱ 10am-12.30am Mon-Sat, 2pm-9pm Sun) has Internet access.

### Sights & Activities

The heavily restored Reims' **Cathédrale Notre Dame** ( ⏱ approx 7.30am-7.30pm closed during Sun morning Mass) is a 138m-long Gothic edifice where the coronation of Charles VII took place – with Joan of Arc at his side – on 17 July 1429. The **Palais du Tau** ( ☎ 03 26 47 81 79; adult/18-25 yrs/under 18 yrs €6.10/4.10/free; ⏱ 9.30am-6.30pm Tue-Sun early May-early Sep, to 12.30pm & 2-5.30pm Tue-Sun early Sep-early May), displays truly exceptional statues, ritual objects and tapestries from the cathedral. Also see the **Basilique St-Rémi** (pl St-Rémi) – its Romanesque nave and transept date mainly from the mid-11th century.

#### CHAMPAGNE CELLARS

You can visit the *caves* (cellars) of about a dozen Reims-area champagne houses, on guided tours (with tastings) in English.

**Taittinger** ( ☎ 03 26 85 84 33; www.taittinger.com; 9 place St-Niçaise; adult/child under 12 yrs €7/free; tours ⏱ 9.30am-11.45am and 2pm-4.20pm, closed weekends Dec–mid-Mar) An excellent place for a straightforward presentation on how champagne is made.

**Mumm** ( ☎ 03 26 49 59 70; www.mumm.com; 34 rue du Champ de Mars; adult/child under 16y rs €7/free; tours ⏱ 9-11am & 2-5pm Mar-Oct) Pronounced 'moom', this is

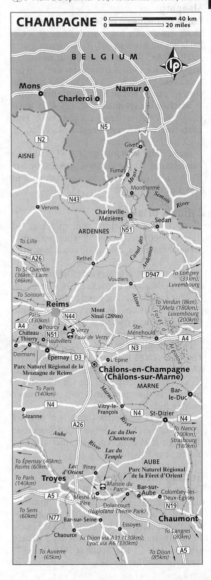

CHAMPAGNE

now the worlds 3rd-largest producer of champagne (eight million bottles a year).

**Pommery** ( ☎ 03 26 61 62 55; www.pommery.com; 5 pl du Général Gouraud; adult/student/child under 12 €7.50/6/free; tours ⊗ 10am-5pm, to 4 or 4.30pm mid-Nov–Mar) Cellar tours take you 30m underground to Gallo-Roman quarries and 25 million bottles of bubbly.

## Sleeping

**Centre International de Séjour** (CIS; ☎ 03 26 40 52 60; www.cis-reims.com; chaussée Bocquaine; s €28, bed in a 2/3-5 person dm, €12/11, with shower & toilet 16/13; ⊗ 24hr; 🖳 ) A friendly atmosphere makes up for the institutional rooms. To get there take bus B, K, M or N to the Comédie stop or bus H to the Pont De Gaulle stop.

**Hôtel de la Cathédrale** ( ☎ 03 26 47 28 46; fax 03 26 88 65 81; 20 rue Libergier; d/q from €56/77) This charming family-run two-star place, has 17 high-ceilinged rooms.

**Grand Hôtel du Nord** ( ☎ 03 26 47 39 03; www .hotelreims.com; 75 pl Drouet d'Erlon; d from €55) Boasts 50 cheerful, upbeat rooms, some with grand views of the square.

## Eating & Drinking

Place Drouet d'Erlon, the epicentre of Reims' nightlife, is overflowing with pizzerias, brasseries, cafés, pubs and sandwich places.

**L'Apostrophe** ( ☎ 03 26 79 19 89; 59 pl Drouet d'Erlon; 2-course weekday menu €13, salads €11-14, mains €12.50-23) This bustling, book-lined brasserie serves generous portions of international cuisine and some mean cocktails. There's a chic atmosphere and a summertime terrace.

**Le Continental** ( ☎ 03 26 47 01 47; 95 pl Drouet d'Erlon; menu €18.50-36, some incl wine; ⊗ noon-2.30pm & 7-11pm or later) Panoramic views complement classic French dishes at Le Continental – seafood is the speciality from September to May here.

**Brasserie Le Boulingrin** ( ☎ 03 26 40 96 22; 48 rue de Mars; menu €16-23; ⊗ Mon-Sat). Check out the original 1920s décor here, including an old-time zinc bar.

## Getting There & Away

Direct train destinations from Reims include Épernay (€5.20, 21 to 45 minutes, 23 daily weekdays, 14 daily weekends) and Paris' Gare de l'Est (€20.30, 1¾ hours, 12 to 16 daily). Information and tickets are available at the **Boutique SNCF** (1 cours JB Langlet; ⊗ 10am-7pm Mon-Sat).

# ÉPERNAY

pop 26,000

Home to some of the world's most famous champagne houses, Épernay, is 25km south of Reims. Beneath the streets, 200 million of bottles of champagne are being aged in 100km of subterranean cellars.

## Orientation & Information

Mansion-lined ave de Champagne, where many of Épernay's champagne houses are based, stretches eastwards from the town's commercial heart (around place des Arcades), whose liveliest streets are rue Général Leclerc and rue St-Thibault.

The **tourist office** ( ☎ 03 26 53 33 00; www.ot -epernay.fr; 7 ave de Champagne; ⊗ 9.30am-12.30pm & 1.30-7pm Mon-Sat, 11am-4pm Sun & hols mid-Apr–mid-Oct; 9.30am-12.30pm & 1.30-5.30pm Mon-Sat mid-Oct–mid-Apr) supplies details on activities in the region, including cellar visits.

## Champagne Houses

Must-see champagne houses of Épernay include **Moët & Chandon** ( ☎ 03 26 51 20 20; www.moet .com; adult/12-16 yrs €7.50/4.50; 18 ave de Champagne; tours ⊗ 9.30-11.30am & 2-4.30pm, closed weekends mid-Nov–mid-Mar), the number one champagne producer; **De Castellane** ( ☎ 03 26 51 19 19; www .castellane.com; 64 ave de Champagne; adult/10-18 yrs €6/4.50; tours ⊗ 10.30-11.15am & 2.30-5.15pm Apr-Nov) is recommended for the panoramic view from the top of the 60m tower. **Mercier** ( ☎ 03 26 51 22 22; www.champagnemercier.com; 68-70 ave de Champagne; adult/12-15 yrs €6.50/3; ⊗ mid-Jan–about 20 Dec, closed Tue & Wed except mid-Mar–mid-Nov, tours 9.30-11.30am & 2-4.30pm) has the most glitzy and impressive tour.

## Sleeping

Épernay's hotels are especially full-on weekends from Easter to September and on weekdays in May, June and September.

**Hôtel St-Pierre** ( ☎ 03 26 54 40 80; fax 03 26 57 88 68; 1 rue Jeanne d'Arc; s/d from €21/24, d with shower & toilet from €34; 🅿 ) In an early-20th-century mansion that has hardly changed in half a century, this place has 15 simple rooms that retain the charm and atmosphere of yesteryear.

**Hôtel Les Berceaux** ( ☎ 03 26 55 28 84; les .berceaux@wanadoo.fr; 13 rue des Berceaux; d €66-75) The 27 rooms of this three-star institution, founded in 1889, are endowed with a certain Champenoise ambience.

## Eating

**La Cave à Champagne** ( ☎ 03 26 55 50 70; 16 rue Gambetta; menu €14.50-28; 🕙 Thu-Tue) Designed to look like a wine cellar, this place specialises in Champenoise cuisine.

**Chez Ali** ( ☎ 03 26 51 80 82; 27 rue de la Fauvette; mains €12-18.50; 🕙 closed Sun night & Mon) Chez Ali serves up steaming Algerian couscous (€12-18.50).

Self-catering options include the **covered market** (Halle St-Thibault; rue Gallice; 🕙 8am-noon Wed & Sat), and **Traiteur** (9 pl Hugues Plomb; 🕙 8am-12.45pm & 3pm-7.30pm except Sun & Wed), which sells scrumptious prepared dishes.

## Getting There & Around

The **train station** (pl Mendès-France) has direct services to Reims (€5.20, 21 to 45 minutes, 23 daily weekdays, 14 daily weekends) and Paris' Gare de l'Est (€17.50, 1¼ hours, 10 to 16 daily). Cars can be hired from **Europcar** ( ☎ 03 26 54 90 61; 20 rempart Perrier).

# ALSACE & LORRAINE

Though they are often spoken of as if they were one, Alsace and Lorraine, neighbouring regions in France's northeastern corner, are linked by little more than a common border through the Vosges Mountains and the imperial ambitions of late-19th-century Germany. In 1871, after the Franco-Prussian War, the newly created German Reich annexed Alsace and part of Lorraine, making their return to rule from Paris a rallying cry of French nationalism.

## STRASBOURG

pop 427,000

Situated just a few kilometres west of the Rhine, prosperous, cosmopolitan Strasbourg (City of the Roads) is France's great northeastern metropolis and the intellectual and cultural capital of Alsace. Strasbourg serves as an important European crossroads thanks to the presence of the European Parliament, the Council of Europe, the European Court of Human Rights and 48,000 students.

## Orientation

Strasbourg's train station is approximately 400m west of the Grande Île (Big Island), the core of ancient and modern Strasbourg. The quaint Petite France area in the Grande Île's southwestern corner is subdivided by canals. Much of the city centre is for pedestrians only. The European Parliament building and Palais de l'Europe are about 2km northeast of the cathedral. The city centre is about 3.5km west of pont de l'Europe, the bridge that links the French bank of the Rhine with the German city of Kehl.

### INTERNET ACCESS

**NeT SuR CouR** ( ☎ 03 88 35 66 76; 18 quai des Pêcheurs; tram stop Gallia; per hr €2; 🕙 9.30am-9.30pm Mon-Fri, 2-8pm Sat & Sun) Situated at the end of a narrow courtyard.

### TOURIST INFORMATION

**Tourist office** ( ☎ 03 88 52 28 28; www.ot-strasbourg .fr; 17 pl de la Cathédrale; 🕙 9am-7pm) The Strasbourg Pass (€10.60), a coupon book valid for three consecutive days, may save you a fair bit of cash.

## Information

**Tourist office annexe** ( ☎ 03 88 32 51 49; tram stop Gare Centrale; 🕙 9am-7pm Jun-Sep & Dec, to 12.30pm & 1.45-6pm Apr, May, Oct & Nov, closed Sun Jan-Mar & Nov) In the subterranean Galerie de l'En-Verre (underneath place de la Gare); there are plans to move it into the train station building.

## Sights & Activities

The enchanting **Grande Île** is a paradise for an aimless amble through bustling public squares, busy pedestrianised areas and upmarket shopping. The narrow streets of the **old city**, crisscrossed by narrow lanes, canals and locks, have a fairytale feel. The romantic Terrasse Panoramique atop **Barrage Vauban** (admission free; 🕙 9am-7.30pm), a dam built to prevent river-borne attacks on the city, affords panoramas of the Ill River.

Strasbourg's lacy, fragile-looking Gothic **Cathédrale Notre Dame** ( 🕙 7am-7pm) is one of the marvels of European architecture. The west façade was completed in 1284, but the 142m spire, the tallest of its time, was not in place until 1439; its southern companion was never built. The 30m-high Gothic and Renaissance contraption just inside the southern entrance is the *horloge astronomique* (astronomical clock), a late-16th-century clock that strikes solar noon every day at 12.30pm. The 66m-high **platform** ( ☎ 03 88 43 60 40; adult/student & under-18 yrs €3/1.50; 🕙 9am-5pm Mon-Fri, 10am-5pm Sat & Sun Apr-Oct, to 4.30pm Nov-Mar) above the façade affords a spectacular stork's-eye view of Strasbourg.

# STRASBOURG

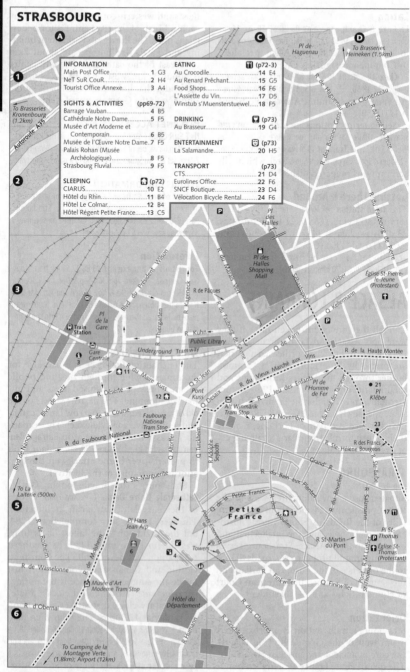

**INFORMATION**
Main Post Office.....................1 G3
NeT SuR CouR........................2 H4
Tourist Office Annexe...............3 A4

**SIGHTS & ACTIVITIES** (pp69-72)
Barrage Vauban......................4 B5
Cathédrale Notre Dame............5 F5
Musée d'Art Moderne et
    Contemporain......................6 B5
Musée de l'Œuvre Notre Dame..7 F5
Palais Rohan (Musée
    Archéologique)....................8 F5
Strasbourg Fluvial..................9 F5

**SLEEPING** (p72)
CIARUS................................10 E2
Hôtel du Rhin.......................11 B4
Hôtel Le Colmar....................12 B4
Hôtel Régent Petite France.....13 C5

**EATING** (p72-3)
Au Crocodile........................14 E4
Au Renard Prêchant...............15 G5
Food Shops..........................16 F6
L'Assiette du Vin...................17 D5
Winstub s'Muensterstuewel.....18 F5

**DRINKING** (p73)
Au Brasseur.........................19 G4

**ENTERTAINMENT** (p73)
La Salamandre......................20 H5

**TRANSPORT** (p73)
CTS....................................21 D4
Eurolines Office....................22 F6
SNCF Boutique......................23 D4
Vélocation Bicycle Rental........24 F6

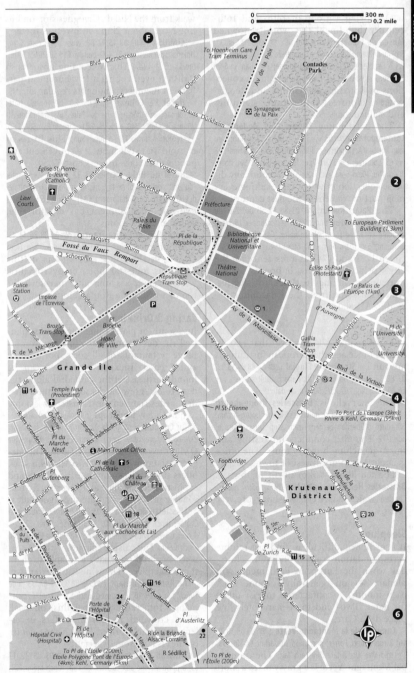

Occupying a group of 14th- and 16th-century buildings, the world-renowned **Musée de l'Œuvre Notre Dame** ( ☎ 03 88 32 88 17; 3 pl du Château; adult/student-under-26 & senior/under 18 yrs & disabled €4/2/free incl audioguide; ✆ 10am to 6pm Tue-Sun) has one of Europe's premier collections of Romanesque, Gothic and Renaissance sculptures, 15th-century paintings and stained glass.

The outstanding **Musée d'Art Moderne et Contemporain** ( ☎ 03 88 23 31 31; pl Hans Jean Arp; tram stop Musée d'Art Moderne; adult/student/over 60 & under 18 yrs €5/2.50/free; ✆ 11am-7pm Tue, Wed, Fri & Sat, noon-10pm Thu, 10am-6pm Sun) has an exceptionally diverse collection of works representing every major art movement of the past century.

The **Palais Rohan** ( ☎ 03 88 52 50 00; 2 pl du Château; adult/student under 26 & senior/under 18 yrs & disabled €6/3/free for whole complex, €4/2/free for each museum; ✆ 10am-6pm Wed-Mon) was built between 1732 and 1742 as a residence for the city's princely bishops. It houses several museums including the **Musée Archéologique**, which takes you from the Palaeolithic period to AD 800.

## Tours

Boat excursions (70 minutes) that take in Petite France and the European institutions are run by **Strasbourg Fluvial** ( ☎ 03 88 84 13 13, 03 88 32 75 25; behind Palais Rohan; adult/student day €6.80/3.40, night €7.20/3.60; 4 tours daily).

The marvellous **Brasseries Kronenbourg** ( ☎ 03 88 27 41 59; siege.visites@kronenbourg-fr.com; 68 route d'Oberhausbergen; tram stop Ducs d'Alsace; adult/12-18 yrs €3/2) conducts interesting and thirst-quenching brewery tours. The office is about 1.2km northwest of town.

Located about 1.5km north of town is **Brasseries Heineken** ( ☎ 03 88 19 57 55; 4 rue St-Charles) which has free, two-hour brewery tours.

## Sleeping

It is *extremely* difficult to find last-minute accommodation from Monday to Thursday when the European Parliament is in plenary session (generally for one week each month) – contact the tourist office for dates. Two- and three-star hotels line place de la Gare.

**Camping de la Montagne Verte** ( ☎ 03 88 30 25 46; 2 rue Robert Forrer; per camp site/adult €4.50/3.35; ✆ mid-Mar–Oct & late Nov-early Jan) The municipal Montagne Verte is a grassy place a short walk from the Nid de Cigognes stop on bus line No 2, about 2km southwest of town.

**CIARUS** ( ☎ 03 88 15 27 88; www.ciarus.com; 7 rue Finkmatt; per person in 8-/4-/2-bed dm €16.50/20/22.50 incl breakfast; P ▢ ) This welcoming hostel is so stylish it even counts a few European parliament members among its regular clients.

**Hôtel Le Colmar** ( ☎ 03 88 32 16 89; hotel .le.colmar@wanadoo.fr; 1 rue du Maire Kuss; tram stop Alt Winmärik; s/d €37/40, with shared bathroom €24.50/27.50; ✆ reception closed 1.30-5.30pm Sun) This 15-room cheapie isn't stylish but it's convenient and good value. Hall showers cost €2.50.

**Hôtel du Rhin** ( ☎ 03 88 32 35 00; www.hotel -du -rhin.com; 7-8 pl de la Gare; tram stop Gare Centrale; d €60, with shared bathroom €34) This 61-room two-star establishment has comfortable, sound-proofed rooms.

**Hôtel Régent Petite France** ( ☎ 03 88 76 43 43; www.regent-hotels.com; 5 rue des Moulins; s/d from €223/243, ste €366-455; P ✿ ) Guests of this luxurious four-star hotel enjoy romantic watery views, a sauna and marble bathrooms worthy of a Roman emperor.

## Eating & Drinking

Just south of place Gutenberg, pedestrianised rue des Tonneliers is lined with mid-range restaurants of all sorts, both ethnic and French. Inexpensive places can be found northeast of the cathedral along rue des Frères. A few blocks south of the cathedral, pedestrianised rue d'Austerlitz is home to quite a few **food shops** (rue d'Austerlitz) also.

**Au Crocodile** ( ☎ 03 88 32 13 02; 10 rue de l'Outre; 3-/4-course weekday lunch menu €53/74, with wine €77/104, dinner menu €80 & €122; ✆ Tue-Sat) This elegant restaurant, holder of two Michelin stars, offers all-out gastronomique indulgence and sophisticated elegance at a surprisingly reasonable price. Reservations are a good idea.

**L'Assiette du Vin** ( ☎ 03 88 32 00 92; 5 rue de la Chaîne; lunch menu €19.90, 2-/3-course menu €21/26, 4-course menu with 4 wines €45; ✆ closed Sat lunch, Mon lunch & Sun) The cuisine changes with the seasons, inspired by what's available fresh in the marketplace. The wine list is extensive.

**Au Renard Prêchant** ( ☎ 03 88 35 62 87; 33 pl de Zurich; mains €9-16; ✆ closed lunch Sat & Sun) Occupying a 16th-century chapel, this convivial, often crowded restaurant, offers excellent, reasonably priced French fare. *Gibier* (game) is a seasonal speciality.

**Winstub s'Muensterstuewel** ( ☎ 03 88 32 17 63; 8 pl du Marché aux Cochons de Lait; lunch menu €23;

Tue-Sat) This winstub has an excellent reputation – for mains and desserts – thanks to its English-speaking Paul Bocuse-trained owner, who's happy to whip up vegetarian options on demand.

**Au Brasseur** ( ☎ 03 88 36 12 13; 22 rue des Veaux; 11am-1am) Four beers – *brune, ambrée, blonde* and *blanche* – are brewed on the premises of this warm, dimly lit microbrewery, which also has some of the best deals in town on Alsatian treats.

## Entertainment

Strasbourg's entertainment options are legion. Details on cultural events appear in the free monthly **Spectacles** (www.spectacles-publications.com), available at the tourist office.

**La Salamandre** ( ☎ 03 88 25 79 42; www.lasalamandre-strasbourg.fr, in French; 3 rue Paul Janet; adult/student, incl drink €10/6; 10pm-4am Wed-Sun) Billed as a *bar-club-spectacles*, this discotheque has theme nights each Friday (salsa, disco, 1980s etc).

## Getting There & Away

Eurolines buses stop 2.5km south of the **Eurolines office** ( ☎ 03 90 22 14 60; 6D pl d'Austerlitz; 10am-6.30pm Mon-Fri, to noon & 2pm-5pm Sat) near Stade de la Meinau (the city's main football stadium), on rue du Maréchal Lefèbvre, about 200m west of avenue de Colmar and the Lycée Couffignal tram stop.

Strasbourg city bus No 21 (€1.20) links place Gutenberg with the Stadthalle in Kehl, the German town just across the Rhine.

Train information and tickets are available on the Grande Île at the **SNCF Boutique** (5 rue des France-Bourgeois; 10am-7pm Mon-Fri, to 5pm Sat). The train station is linked to Lyon (€42.30, five hours) and Paris' Gare de l'Est (€40.90, four hours); and, internationally, to Basel (Bâle; €17.40, 1¼ hours) and Frankfurt (€35.60, 2½ hours).

## Getting Around

Four tram lines form the centrepiece of Strasbourg's public transport network, run by **CTS** ( ☎ 03 88 77 70 70; 31 pl Kléber). The main hub is at place de l'Homme de Fer. Strasbourg is a bicycle-friendly place and **Vélocation Bicycle Rental** ( ☎ 03 88 23 56 75; 4 rue du Maire Kuss; 6am-7.30pm Mon-Fri, 9am-noon & 2-7.30pm Sat) rents well-maintained single-speed bikes for €4/7 per half/full day (€100 deposit).

# NANCY

pop 331,000

Delightful Nancy has an air of refinement unique in Lorraine. With a magnificent central square, several fine museums and sparkling shop windows, the former capital of the dukes of Lorraine seems as opulent today as it did in the 16th to 18th centuries, when much of the centre was built.

## Orientation & Information

Place Stanislas connects the narrow, twisting streets of the medieval Vieille Ville (Old Town), centred on the Grande Rue, with the rigid right angles of the 16th-century Ville Neuve (New Town) to the south. The train station is 800m southwest of place Stanislas.

There's a **tourist office** ( ☎ 03 83 35 22 41; www.ot-nancy.fr; pl Stanislas; 9am-7pm Mon-Sat, 10am-5pm Sun & hols Apr-Oct, 9am-6pm Mon-Sat, 10am-1pm Sun & hols Nov-Mar)

## Sights

Beautifully proportioned, the neoclassical **place Stanislas** is impressively illuminated at night. The opulent buildings that surround the square, dazzling gilded wrought-iron gateways, rococo fountains and **d'Amphitrite** form one of the finest ensembles of 18th-century architecture and decorative arts anywhere in France.

The highlight of a visit to Nancy is the brilliant **Musée de l'École de Nancy** (School of Nancy Museum: ☎ 03 83 40 14 86; 36-38 rue du Sergent Blandan; adult/student & senior €4.75/2.29; 10.30am-6pm Tue-Sat), which brings together a collection of furnished rooms and glass produced by the Art Nouveau movement.

The 16th-century Palais Ducal, splendid former residence of the dukes of Lorraine, now houses the **Musée Historique Lorrain** ( ☎ 03 83 32 18 74; 64 & 66 Grande Rue; adult/student €4.60/3.10 for both sections, €3.10/2.30 for one section; 10am-12.30pm & 2p,-6pm Wed-Mon), dedicated to fine arts and history and to regional art and folklore.

## Sleeping

**Auberge de Jeunesse Château de Remicourt** ( ☎ 03 83 27 73 67; aubergeremicourt@mairie-nancy.fr; 149 rue de Vandoeuvre in Villers-lès-Nancy; dm €13.50, d per person incl sheets & breakfast €15.50) This fantastic old chateau, with 60 beds, is 4km south of the centre.

**Hôtel des Portes d'Or** ( ☎ 03 83 35 42 34; www .hotel-lesportesdor.com; 21 rue Stanislas; d from €51) This welcoming and very cosy two-star hostelry, superbly situated just metres from place Stanislas, has 20 charming rooms.

### Eating & Drinking

Rue des Maréchaux is lined in its entirety with restaurants.

**La Basse Cour** ( ☎ 03 83 36 67 29; 23 Grande Rue; menu €16; ☽ 6.30-11pm or later Mon-Sat) A former 16th- and 17th-century townhouse this homely place specialises in mouth-watering Lorraine-style *cuisine de campagne* (farm-fresh country cuisine).

**Le Ch'timi** ( ☎ 03 83 32 82 76; 17 pl St-Epvre; ☽ 9am-2am Mon-Sat, to 8pm Sun) This unpretentious, mellow bar offers 200 different beers.

### Getting There & Away

The **train station** (pl Thiers; tram stop Nancy Gare) is on the main line linking Paris' Gare de l'Est (€35.30, three hours, 12 to 14 daily) with Strasbourg (€18.40, 1¼ hours, nine to 12 daily).

# FAR NORTHERN FRANCE

Le Nord de France, densely populated and laden with declining rust-belt industries, is made up of three historical regions, Flanders (Flandre or Flandres), Artois and Picardy (Picardie), and has lots to offer visitors willing to explore.

## LILLE

**pop 1 million**
Long an industrial centre, Lille's recent history shows how a grimy metropolis, its economy based on declining technologies, can transform itself with the help of generous government investment into a glittering and self-confident cultural hub. Highlights include an attractive old town with a strong Flemish flavour, two renowned art museums, some fine dining and a happening student-driven nightlife scene.

### Orientation

Lille is centred around three public squares: place du Général de Gaulle (also called the Grand' Place), place du Théâtre and place Rihour. The area of narrow streets north of place du Général de Gaulle is known as

Vieux Lille (Old Lille). Gare Lille-Flandres is about 400m southeast of place du Général de Gaulle; ultra-modern Gare Lille-Europe is 500m further east.

### Information
#### INTERNET ACCESS
**Cybercafé Le Smiley** ( ☎ 03 20 21 12 19; 2 rue Royale; per hr €6.10; ☽ noon-3am Mon-Sat, 4pm-midnight Sun)

#### TOURIST INFORMATION
**Tourist office** ( ☎ 03 59 57 95 00; www.lilletourism .com; pl Rihour; ☽ 9.30am-6.30pm Mon-Sat, 10am-noon & 2pm-5pm Sun & hols).

### Sights

North of place du Général de Gaulle, **Vieux Lille** gleams with restored 17th- and 18th-century houses. Other equally atmospheric streets include **rue de la Grande Chaussée** and **rue Esquermoise**.

The ornate, Flemish-Renaissance **Vieille Bourse** (Old Stock Exchange; pl du Général de Gaulle), built in 1652, actually consists of 24 separate buildings. The courtyard in the middle hosts a **book market** ( ☽ 2-7pm Tue-Sun).

The world-renowned **Palais des Beaux-Arts** ( ☎ 03 20 06 78 00; pl de la République; metro République; adult/12-25 yrs/child under 12 €4.60/3/free; ☽ 2-6pm Mon, 10am-6pm Wed, Thu, Sat & Sun, to 7pm Fri) possesses a superb collection of 15th- to 20th-century paintings.

### Sleeping

**Auberge de Jeunesse** ( ☎ 03 20 57 08 94; lille@fuaj.org; 12 rue Malpart; metro Mairie de Lille; dm 1st/subsequent nights incl breakfast €16.25/13.45; ☽ closed late-Dec–late Jan) The spartan rooms house 165 beds (up to six beds per room).

**Hôtel de France** ( ☎ 03 20 57 14 78; fax 03 20 57 06 01; 10 rue de Béthune; s/d €39/46, with shared bathroom from €30/35) You can't get more central than this two-star place, whose 32 airy, functional rooms are one of the best deals in town.

**Hôtel Le Globe** ( ☎ 03 20 57 29 58; 1 blvd Vauban; d/q €35/50.50) The 20 large rooms have French windows that look out on the Citadelle and (in most cases) chimneys, adding a dollop of old-fashioned charm.

### Eating & Drinking

Rue Royale is *the* place for ethnic cuisine. The rue d'Amiens area is full of restaurants and pizzerias.

**À l'Huîtrière** ( ☎ 03 20 55 43 41; www.huitriere.fr; 3 rue des Chats Bossus; lunch menu €43, mains €30-48; ☯ noon-2pm & 7-9.30pm except Sun dinner & 21 Jul-22 Aug). The original sea-themed Art-Deco mosaics, stained glass and ceramics haven't changed since this family-owned fish shop, situated in the heart of Vieux Lille, opened in 1928. Nor has the family's commitment to culinary excellence: the restaurant has held one or two Michelin stars continuously since 1930 for super-fresh seafood, accompanied by a wine or two from the 40,000-bottle cellar. Book ahead at weekends.

**Le Hochepot** ( ☎ 03 20 54 17 59; 6 rue du Nouveau Siècle; menu €18-25; ☯ closed Sat lunch & Sun) This rustic but elegant restaurant specialises in Flemish dishes such as *coq à la bière* (chicken cooked in beer) and carbonnade.

**Brasserie La Chicorée** ( ☎ 03 20 54 81 52; 15 pl Rihour; menu €9.50-25.50; ☯ 10-4.30am Sun-Thu, 10-6.30am Fri & Sat) Dine on regional treats such as carbonnade and *waterzoë* (three kinds of fish prepared with beer) at practically any time of the day or night.

Self-catering options include **Carrefour hypermarket** ( ☯ 9am-10pm Mon-Sat), on the upper level of the Euralille shopping mall, and **Wazemmes food market** (pl Nouvelle Aventure; metro Gambetta; ☯ 7am-6pm Tue-Thu, to 8pm Fri & Sat, to 2pm Sun), a lively covered market 1.2km southwest of the centre.

**L'Illustration Café** ( ☎ 03 20 12 00 90; 18 rue Royale; ☯ 12.30pm-3am) This mellow but smoky bar is decorated with Art Nouveau woodwork and paintings by local artists.

## Getting There & Away

Buses with **Eurolines** ( ☎ 03 20 78 18 88; 23 parvis St-Maurice; ☯ 9am-7pm Mon-Fri, to 6pm Sat Jun–mid-Sep) go to destinations that include Brussels (€10, two hours), Amsterdam (€34, six hours) and London (€39, six hours). Buses depart from the unsignposted bus parking lane on rue de Turin, on the northeast side of Gare Lille-Europe.

Lille's two train stations are one stop apart on metro line No 2. **Gare Lille-Flandres** is used by almost all regional services and most TGVs to Paris' Gare du Nord (€33.70 or €45.80, 62 minutes) while **Gare Lille-Europe** handles pretty much everything else, including Eurostar trains to London, TGVs/Eurostars to Brussels (weekdays/weekends €22.40/14.40, 38 minutes) and TGVs to Nice (€104.90 or €123.70, 7¼ hours).

## Getting Around

Lille's two speedy metro lines, two tramways and bus lines (several cross into Belgium) are run by **Transpole** ( ☎ 08 20 42 40 40), which has an **information window** ( ☯ closed Sunday) in the Gare Lille-Flandres metro station.

# CALAIS
### pop 75,000

But for two small museums and Rodin's *The Burghers of Calais*, there's little to encourage the 22 million people who go through grim, industrial Calais each year to stay.

## Orientation & Information

Gare Calais-Ville (the train station) is 650m south of the main square, place d'Armes, and 700m north of Calais' commercial district (around blvd Léon Gambetta and the Place du Théâtre bus hub). The Car Ferry Terminal is 1.5km northeast of place d'Armes; the Hoverport (for SeaCats) is another 1.5km further out. The Channel Tunnel's vehicle loading area is about 6km southwest of the town centre.

The **tourist office** ( ☎ 03 21 96 62 40; www.calais -cotedopale.com; 12 blvd Georges Clemenceau; ☯ 9am-7pm Mon-Sat, 10am-1pm Sun & hols Easter-August, 10am-1pm & 2-6.30pm Mon-Sat Sep-Easter) can provide information.

## Sights

Calais' Flemish Renaissance-style **town hall** (1911–25) contains Rodin's *Les Bourgeois de Calais* (1895), honouring six local citizens who, in 1347, after eight months of holding off the besieging English forces, surrendered themselves and the keys of the starving city to Edward III of England. Their hope: that by sacrificing themselves they might save the town and its people. Moved by his wife Philippa's entreaties, Edward eventually spared both the Calaisiens and their six brave leaders.

The exhibits at **Musée des Beaux-Arts et de la Dentelle** (Museum of Fine Arts & Lace; ☎ 03 21 46 48 40; 25 rue Richelieu; adult/student €3/1.50, free Wed; ☯ 10am-noon & 2-5.30pm Mon & Wed-Fri, to noon & 2-6.30pm Sat, 2-6.30pm Sun) focus on mechanised lacemaking.

## Sleeping

**Auberge de Jeunesse** (Centre Européen de Séjour; ☎ 03 21 34 70 20; www.auberge-jeunesse-calais.com; ave Maréchal de Lattre de Tassigny; dm €15.20 incl breakfast; ☯ 24hr;

**P** ) The modern, well-equipped 162-bed hostel just 200m from the beach is a good source of information on local events.

**Hôtel Richelieu** ( ☎ 03 21 34 61 60; www.hotel richelieu-calais.com; 17 rue Richelieu; d/q from €46/92) At this quiet two-star place the 15 cheery rooms, each one unique, are outfitted with antique furniture redeemed by the owner from local markets.

## Eating
Rue Royal and place d'Armes are lined with touristy places.

**La Pléiade** ( ☎ 03 21 34 03 70; 32 rue Jean Quéhen; 3-/4-/6-course menu €22/35/50; ☽ closed Sun & Mon) The *filet de bar rôti* (sea bass with almond sauce and a dollop of pistou) is very popular.

**Aux Mouettes** ( ☎ 03 21 34 67 59; 10 rue Jean Pierre Avron; menu €15-32; ☽ closed Sun dinner & Mon) Fishers sell their daily catch across the street at the quay – easy to see why this unassuming place is known for serving only the freshest fish.

There's a **food market** (pl d'Armes; ☽ Wed & Sat morning) and a **Match supermarket** (pl d'Armes; ☽ 9am-7.30pm Mon-Sat).

## Getting There & Around
For details on getting across the Channel, see p152.

### BOAT
Every day, 45 to 54 car ferries from Dover dock at the busy **Car Ferry Terminal**, about 1.5km northeast of place d'Armes. Companies at the ferry terminal are:

**P&O Ferries** ( ☎ 03 21 46 10 10; ☽ 24hr)
**SeaFrance** ( ☎ 03 21 46 80 05; ☽ 6am-10.45pm)
Their offices in town are:
**P&O Ferries** ( ☎ 01 55 69 82 28; 41 pl d'Armes)
**SeaFrance** ( ☎ 03 21 19 42 42; 2 pl d'Armes)

Shuttle buses (€1.50 for P&O), coordinated with departure times, link Gare Calais-Ville and each company's office at place d'Armes with the Car Ferry Terminal.

Hoverspeed's car-carrying SeaCats to Dover (operational from mid-March to 22 December) use the **Hoverport** (High Speed Ferry Terminal; ☎ 03 21 46 14 00 or ☎ 00800 1211 1211), which is 3km northeast of the town centre.

### BUS
**Inglard** ( ☎ 03 21 96 49 54), at the Car Ferry Terminal, links Calais' train station with the beautiful Côte d'Opale and Boulogne.

**Cariane Littoral** ( ☎ 03 21 34 74 40; 10 rue d'Amsterdam) operates express BCD services from Calais' train station to Boulogne and Dunkirk.

### CAR & MOTORCYCLE
To reach the Channel Tunnel's vehicle loading area at Coquelles, follow the road signs on the A16 to the 'Tunnel Sous La Manche' (Tunnel under the Channel) at exit No 13.

### TRAIN
Calais has two train stations: Gare Calais-Ville in the city centre; and Gare Calais-Fréthun, a TGV station 10km southwest of town near the Channel Tunnel entrance. They are linked by the free Navette TER, a bus service operated by Cariane Littoral.

Gare Calais-Ville has services to Boulogne (€6.60, 27 to 48 minutes, 15 to 19 daily Monday to Saturday, nine daily Sunday), Dunkirk (€7, 50 minutes, four daily Monday to Friday, two on Saturday) and Lille-Flandres (€14, 1¼ hours, 18 daily Monday to Friday, 11 on Saturday, seven on Sunday).

Calais-Fréthun is served by TGVs to Paris' Gare du Nord (€35.50 or €47.90, 1½ hours, five daily Monday to Saturday, two on Sunday) as well as the Eurostar to London.

## DUNKIRK
pop 209,000

Dunkirk (Dunkerque), flattened during WWII, was rebuilt during one of the most uninspired periods in Western architecture (the 1950s), so unless you want to hang out on the Malo-les-Bains beach or plan to join in a colourful pre-Lent carnival, there's little reason to linger.

## Orientation & Information
The train station is 600m southwest of Dunkirk's main square, place Jean Bart. The beach and esplanade are 2km northeast of the centre in the rather faded resort of Malo-les-Bains.

There's a **tourist office** ( ☎ 03 28 66 79 21; www .ot-dunkerque.fr; rue de l'Amiral Ronarc'h; ☽ 9am-12.30pm & 1.3pm0-6.30pm Mon-Fri, to 6.30pm Sat, 10am-noon & 2pm-4pm Sun & hols, no midday closure Jul & Aug).

The **Musée Portuaire** (Harbour Museum; ☎ 03 28 63 33 39; 9 quai de la Citadelle; adult/child €4/3;

🕓 10am-12.45pm & 1.30-6pm), housed in a one-time tobacco warehouse, will delight ship-model lovers.

### Getting There & Away

For details on links to Calais, see p76. Almost all trains to Lille use Lille-Flandres (€11.60, 1¼ hours, nine to 21 daily).

Ferries run by **Norfolk Line** (☎ 03 28 59 01 01; www.norfolkline.com) link Loon Plage, about 25km west of the town centre, with Dover.

# NORMANDY

Often compared with the countryside of southern England, Normandy (Normandie) is the land of the *bocage*, farmland subdivided by hedges and trees. Winding through these hedgerows are sunken lanes, whose grassy sides are covered with yellow primroses and gorse. In 911 the Rouen region became home to the invading Viking Norsemen (or Normans), who gave their name to the region.

## ROUEN

The city of Rouen, for centuries the furthest point downriver where you could cross the Seine by bridge, is known for its many spires, church towers and half-timbered houses. Rouen also has a renowned Gothic cathedral and a number of excellent museums. The city was occupied by the English during the Hundred Years' War when the young Joan of Arc (Jeanne d'Arc) was tried for heresy and burned at the stake here.

### Orientation & Information

The main train station (Gare Rouen-Rive Droite) is at the northern end of rue Jeanne d'Arc, the main thoroughfare running south to the Seine. The old city is centred around rue du Gros Horloge between the place du Vieux Marché and the cathedral.

The **tourist office** (☎ 02 32 08 32 40; www.mairie -rouen.fr; 25 pl de la Cathédrale; 🕓 9am-7pm Mon-Sat, 9.30am-12.30pm & 2pm-6pm Sun May-Sep; 9am-6pm Mon-Sat, 10am-1pm Sun Oct-Apr) is opposite the western façade of the Cathédrale Notre Dame.

### Sights & Activities

The main street of the old city is rue du Gros Horloge, running from the cathedral to **place du Vieux Marché**, where 19-year-old Joan of

Arc was executed in 1431. The striking **Église Jeanne d'Arc** (🕓 10am-12.15pm & 2pm-6pm, closed Fri & Sun am) marks the site and has marvellous 16th-century stained-glass windows.

Rouen's **Cathédrale Notre Dame** (🕓 8am-6pm Tue-Sun, 2-6pm Mon) is considered a masterpiece of French Gothic architecture. There are several guided visits each day to the crypt and ambulatory.

The fascinating **Musée Le Secq des Tournelles** (☎ 02 35 71 28 40; 2 rue Jacques Villon; adult/student €2.30/1.55; 🕓 10am-1pm & 2-6pm Wed-Mon), devoted to the blacksmith's craft, displays some 12,000 locks, keys, scissors, tongs and other wrought-iron utensils made between the 3rd and 19th centuries.

The **Musée des Beaux-Arts** (Fine Arts Museum; ☎ 02 35 71 28 40; 26 bis rue Jean Lecanuet; adult/student €3/2; 🕓 10am-6pm Wed-Mon) features paintings from the 15th to the 20th centuries.

The **Tour Jeanne d'Arc** (☎ 02 35 98 16 21; rue du Donjon; adult/student €1.50/free; 🕓 10am-12.30pm & 2-6pm Mon & Wed-Sat, 2-6.30pm Sun Apr-Sep; 10am-12.30pm & 2-5pm Mon & Wed-Sat, 2-5.30pm Sun Oct-Mar) is where Joan of Arc was imprisoned before her execution.

### Sleeping

If you're staying over a weekend, ask the tourist office about its 'Bon Weekend' offer of two nights for the price of one in some hotels, but you'll have to reserve eight days in advance.

**Camping Municipal** (☎ 02 35 74 07 59; rue Jules Ferry; camp sites per tent/car/child €4/1.50/1; 🕓 year-round). You'll find the camping ground 5km northwest of Gare Rouen-Rive Droite in Déville-lès-Rouen.

**Hôtel des Flandres** (☎ /fax 02 35 71 56 88; 5 rue des Bons Enfants; d with shower/shower & toilet €26/29) This is the pick of the budget options with comfy, newly renovated doubles.

**Hôtel Le Palais** (☎ 02 35 71 41 40; 12 rue du Tambour; s/d €32/34, with washbasin only €25) Well-situated hotel near the Palais de Justice and the Gros Horloge.

### Eating

**Les Maraîchers** (☎ 02 35 71 57 73; 37 pl du Vieux Marché; menu €14.95-21) Always busy and the very best of the Vieux Marché's many restaurants, this place has a lively pavement terrace and varied *menus*.

**Le P'tit Bec** (☎ 02 35 07 63 33; 182 rue Eau de Robec; lunch menu €11 & €13.50, mains €7-9; 🕓 closed dinner

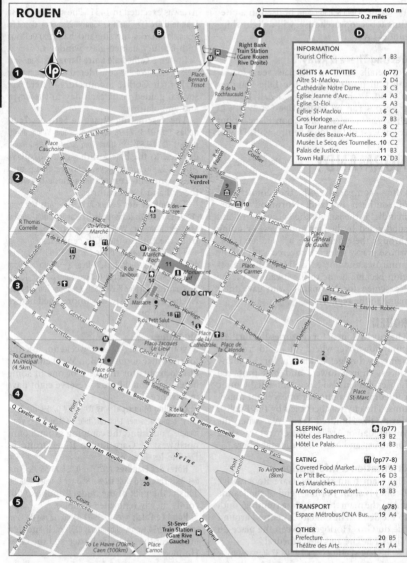

**ROUEN**

0 _____ 400 m
0 _____ 0.2 miles

| INFORMATION | |
|---|---|
| Tourist Office | 1 B3 |

| SIGHTS & ACTIVITIES | (p77) |
|---|---|
| Aître St-Maclou | 2 D4 |
| Cathédrale Notre Dame | 3 C3 |
| Église Jeanne d'Arc | 4 A3 |
| Église St-Éloi | 5 A3 |
| Église St-Maclou | 6 C4 |
| Gros Horloge | 7 B3 |
| La Tour Jeanne d'Arc | 8 C2 |
| Musée des Beaux-Arts | 9 C2 |
| Musée Le Secq des Tournelles | 10 C2 |
| Palais de Justice | 11 B3 |
| Town Hall | 12 D3 |

| SLEEPING | (p77) |
|---|---|
| Hôtel des Flandres | 13 B2 |
| Hôtel Le Palais | 14 B3 |

| EATING | (pp77-8) |
|---|---|
| Covered Food Market | 15 A3 |
| Le P'tit Bec | 16 D3 |
| Les Maraîchers | 17 A3 |
| Monoprix Supermarket | 18 B3 |

| TRANSPORT | (p78) |
|---|---|
| Espace Métrobus/CNA Bus | 19 A4 |

| OTHER | |
|---|---|
| Prefecture | 20 B5 |
| Théâtre des Arts | 21 A4 |

Mon-Thu & all day Sun) On a peaceful square, this restaurant offers a delicious array of dishes including some vegetarian specialities.

Dairy products, fish and fresh produce are on sale at the **covered food market** (pl du Vieux Marché; 6am-1.30pm Tue-Sun), and there's a **Monoprix supermarket** (65 rue du Gros Horloge; 8.30am-9pm Mon-Sat)

## Getting There & Away

Find regional bus info at **Espace Métrobus** ( 02 35 52 92 00; 9 rue Jeanne d'Arc). Buses leave from quai du Havre and quai de la Bourse.

Trains to Paris and far-flung destinations depart from Gare Rouen-Rive Droite. The Gare Rouen-Rive Gauche south of the river has mainly regional services.

# BAYEUX

**pop 15,000**

Bayeux is celebrated for two trans-Channel invasions: the conquest of England by the Normans under William the Conqueror in 1066 (an event chronicled in the celebrated Bayeux Tapestry) and the Allied D-day landings of 6 June 1944, which launched the liberation of Nazi-occupied France. It was the first town in France to be freed and, remarkably, survived virtually unscathed.

## Orientation & Information

The Cathédrale Notre Dame, the major landmark in the centre of Bayeux and visible throughout the town, is 1km northwest of the train station.

Just off the northern end of rue Larcher is the **tourist office** ( ☎ 02 31 51 28 28; fax 02 31 51 28 29; www.bayeux-tourism.com; Pont St-Jean; ⏰ 9.30am-12.30pm & 2pm-6pm Mon-Sat, 10am-12.30pm & 2pm-5.30pm Sun Apr-Jun, 9am-7pm Mon-Sat, 9am-12.30pm & 2pm-6.30pm Sun Jul-Sep, 9.30am-12.30pm & 2pm-5.30pm Mon-Sat Jan-Mar & Oct-Dec).

## Sights & Activities

The world-famous Bayeux Tapestry was commissioned by Bishop Odo of Bayeux, half-brother to William the Conqueror, sometime between the successful Norman invasion of England in 1066 and 1082. The tapestry recounts the dramatic story of the Norman invasion and the events that led up to it (from the Norman perspective).

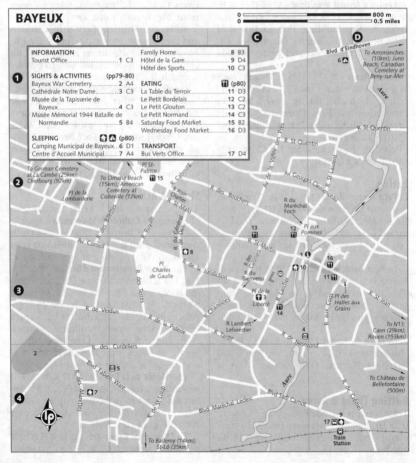

| BAYEUX | | 0 —— 800 m |
| --- | --- | --- |
| | | 0 —— 0.5 miles |

| INFORMATION | |
| --- | --- |
| Tourist Office.................................1 C3 | |

| SIGHTS & ACTIVITIES (pp79-80) | |
| --- | --- |
| Bayeux War Cemetery...............2 A4 | |
| Cathédrale Notre Dame............3 C3 | |
| Musée de la Tapisserie de | |
| Bayeux.....................................4 C3 | |
| Musée Mémorial 1944 Bataille de | |
| Normandie..............................5 B4 | |

| SLEEPING 🏠 🛏 (p80) | |
| --- | --- |
| Camping Municipal de Bayeux..6 D1 | |
| Centre d'Accueil Municipal.......7 A4 | |

| Family Home..............................8 B3 |
| --- |
| Hôtel de la Gare.........................9 D4 |
| Hôtel des Sports.........................10 C3 |

| EATING 🍴 (p80) |
| --- |
| La Table du Terroir.....................11 D3 |
| Le Petit Bordelais.......................12 C2 |
| Le Petit Glouton.........................13 C2 |
| Le Petit Normand.......................14 C3 |
| Saturday Food Market................15 B2 |
| Wednesday Food Market............16 D3 |

| TRANSPORT |
| --- |
| Bus Verts Office.........................17 D4 |

The tapestry is housed in the **Musée de la Tapisserie de Bayeux** ( ☎ 02 31 51 25 50; rue de Nesmond; adult/student €6.40/2.60; ⊗ 9am-7pm May-Aug; 9am-6.30pm mid-Mar–Apr, Sep & Oct; 9.30am-12.30pm & 2pm-6pm Nov–mid-Mar).

The totally spectacular **Cathédrale Notre Dame** ( ⊗ 8am-7pm July & Aug, 8.30am-6pm Sep-Jun) is a fine example of Norman Gothic architecture, dating from the 13th century.

## Sleeping

**Camping Municipal de Bayeux** ( ☎ 02 31 92 08 43; camp sites per adult/tent & car €2.85/3.50; ⊗ mid-Mar–mid-Nov; check-in 7am-9pm Jul & Aug, 8am-9am & 5pm-7pm Sep-Jun) is about 2km to the north of the town centre, and just south of blvd d'Eindhoven.

**Centre d'Accueil Municipal** ( ☎ 02 31 92 08 19; fax 02 31 92 12 40; 21 rue des Marettes; s €11.90) In a large, modern building, 1km southwest of the cathedral, the singles (all that's available) are a great deal and prices include breakfast.

**Family Home** ( ☎ 02 31 92 15 22; 39 rue du Général de Dais; dm with/without HI card €16/18, s €25) An excellent old hostel, this is a great place to meet other travellers. Dorm rates include breakfast. Multicourse French dinners cost €10 including wine. A few tents can be pitched in the back garden for €5 per person. There's a laundry.

## Eating

**Le Petit Normand** ( ☎ 02 31 22 88 66; 35 rue Larcher; lunch menu €8.85, dinner menu €12.95 & €22.10; ⊗ closed Thu Nov-Apr) Traditional Norman food is served here, including dishes such as mussels with apple cider, or ham with camembert sauce.

**Le Petit Bordelais** ( ☎ 02 31 92 06 44; 15 rue du Maréchal Foch; plat du jour €7.20; ⊗ noon-2pm Tue-Sat) This tiny extension of an old wine shop serves good home-cooked meals, local cheeses and homemade pâté for lunch only.

**La Table du Terroir** ( ☎ 02 31 92 05 53; Alleé de l'Orangerie; menu €11-20; ⊗ closed Sun dinner & Mon) Excellent Norman-style *menus*. Meat is king here.

## Getting There & Away

Train services include Paris' Gare St-Lazare (€28.50, 2½ hours) via Caen (€4.98, 20 minutes, 15 daily) as well as Cherbourg (€14.30, one hour, 10 daily).

# BRITTANY

Brittany stands slightly aloof from the rest of France, set apart by its Celtic roots and a stubborn independent streak. Brittany's shoreline possesses some of France's finest coastal scenery, while its festivals of traditional music and culture are among the liveliest and most colourful in Europe. Brittany boasts dozens of classic seaside resorts and offers some of the best yachting, windsurfing, sea-kayaking and coastal hiking in France.

## QUIMPER
### pop 59,400

Quimper (kam-*pair*), lying where the small rivers Odet and Steïr meet, takes its name from the Breton word *kemper*, meaning 'confluence'. Strongly Breton in character and the administrative capital of the *département* of Finistère, Quimper is very much the cultural and artistic capital, with its cobbled streets, half-timbered houses, waterways and magnolias imparting a pleasing village feel.

The **tourist office** ( ☎ 02 98 53 04 05; www .quimper-tourisme.com, in French; pl de la Résistance; ⊗ 9am-7pm Mon-Sat, 10am-1pm & 3-5.45pm Sun Jul-Aug; 9.30am-12.30pm & 1.30-6 or 6.30pm Mon-Sat Sep-Jun, 10am-12.45pm Sun Jun & 1-15 Sep) can reserve accommodation and arrange weekly guided city tours in English in July and August.

## Sights & Activities

The twin spires and soaring vertical lines of Quimper's **Cathédrale St-Corentin** dominate the city centre. Begun in 1239, it wasn't fully completed until the 1850s. The inside gives an extraordinary feeling of light and space.

The **Musée Départemental Breton** ( ☎ 02 98 95 21 60; 1 rue du Roi Gradlon; adult/child €3.80/2.50; ⊗ 9am-6pm Jun-Sep; to noon & 2pm-5pm Tue-Sat & 2pm-5pm Sun Oct-May) is in what used to be the bishop's palace, beside the cathedral. It has superb exhibits on the history, furniture, costumes, crafts and archaeology of the area. Adjoining the museum is the **Jardin de l'Évêché** (Bishop's Palace Garden; admission free; ⊗ 9am-5pm or 6pm).

The **Musée de la Faïence** ( ☎ 02 98 90 12 72; 14 rue Jean-Baptiste Bousquet; adult/child €4/2.30; ⊗ 10am-6pm Mon-Sat mid-Apr–mid-Oct) occupies a one-time ceramics factory and displays over 2000 pieces of choice china.

The **Musée des Beaux-Arts** ( ☎ 02 98 95 45 20; 40 pl St-Corentin; adult/child €4/2.50; ⊗ 10am-7pm Jul-Aug;

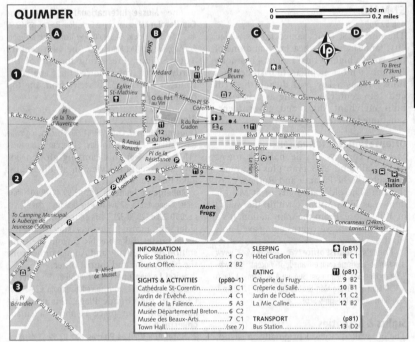

**QUIMPER**

| INFORMATION | | |
| --- | --- | --- |
| Police Station | 1 | C2 |
| Tourist Office | 2 | B2 |

| SIGHTS & ACTIVITIES | (pp80–1) | |
| --- | --- | --- |
| Cathédrale St-Corentin | 3 | C1 |
| Jardin de l'Évêché | 4 | C1 |
| Musée de la Faïence | 5 | A3 |
| Musée Départemental Breton | 6 | C2 |
| Musée des Beaux-Arts | 7 | C1 |
| Town Hall | (see 7) | |

| SLEEPING | (p81) |
| --- | --- |
| Hôtel Gradlon | 8 C1 |

| EATING | (p81) |
| --- | --- |
| Crêperie du Frugy | 9 B2 |
| Crêperie du Sallé | 10 B1 |
| Jardin de l'Odet | 11 C2 |
| La Mie Câline | 12 B2 |

| TRANSPORT | (p81) |
| --- | --- |
| Bus Station | 13 D2 |

to noon & 2-6pm Wed-Mon Apr-Jun & Sep-Oct; to noon & 2-6pm Wed-Sat & Mon, 2-6pm Sun Nov-Mar), in the town hall, displays European paintings from the 16th to early 20th centuries.

## Sleeping

**Camping Municipal** ( ☎ /fax 02 98 55 61 09; ave des Oiseaux; person/tent/car €3.26/0.75/1.55; ☺ year-round) is 1km west of the old city. Take bus No 1 from the train station to the Chaptal stop.

**Auberge de Jeunesse** ( ☎ 02 98 64 97 97; quimper@fuaj.org; 6 ave des Oiseaux; dm €8.90) The hostel is beside the camping ground, on the edge of a wooded park.

**Hôtel Gradlon** ( ☎ 02 98 95 04 39; www.hotel-gradlon.com, in French; 30 rue de Brest; d €82-99; ☺ closed 20 Dec-20 Jan) Rooms are set around a pretty courtyard with a rose garden at its heart, and there's a convivial bar with an open fire for winter evenings.

## Eating

**Crêperie du Frugy** ( ☎ 02 98 90 32 49; 9 rue Ste-Thérèse; galettes €3.70-6.55; ☺ closed Sun & Mon lunch) This tiny place, in the shadow of Mont Frugy, dishes up excellent inexpensive crepes and galettes.

**Crêperie du Sallé** ( ☎ 02 98 95 95 80; 6 rue du Sallé; galettes €3-9; ☺ Tue-Sat) Locals crowd into this bright and breezy crêperie at lunchtime, so arrive early to guarantee a table. Sample some real Breton specialities such as *saucisse fumée* (smoked sausage; €6.60) and *coquilles St-Jacques* (scallops; €8.60).

**Jardin de l'Odet** ( ☎ 02 98 95 76 76; 39 blvd Amiral de Kerguélen; menu €19-35; ☺ Mon-Sat) This stylish Art Deco restaurant overlooks part of the Jardin de l'Évêché. Specialising in Breton and French cuisine, it takes familiar dishes and modifies them creatively.

**La Mie Câline** (14 quai du Steir) A hugely popular bakery where you can get a whopping filled baguette, pastry and soft drink for only €5.20.

## Getting There & Away

Bus destinations with **CAT** ( ☎ 02 98 90 68 40) are Brest (€13.30, 1¼ hours) and Douarnenez (€6, 35 minutes, six to 10 daily).

There are frequent trains to Brest (€13.80, 1¼ hours, up to 10 daily) and Paris (Gare Montparnasse; €63.30, 4¾ hours, eight daily).

FRANCE

## ST-MALO
pop 52,700

The port of St-Malo, famed for its walled city, fantastic nearby beaches – and one of the world's highest tidal ranges – is among Brittany's most popular tourist destinations. It was a key port during the 17th and 18th centuries, serving as a base for both merchant ships and government-sanctioned pirates.

### Orientation & Information

St-Malo consists of the harbour towns of St-Malo and St-Servan plus the modern suburbs of Paramé and Rothéneuf to the east. The old walled city of St-Malo is known as Intra-Muros ('within the walls') or Ville Close. From the train station, it's a 15-minute walk westwards along ave Louis Martin.

There's a **tourist office** ( ☎ 02 99 56 64 48; www .saint-malo-tourisme.com; esplanade St-Vincent;  9am-7.30pm Mon-Sat, 10am-6pm Sun Jul-Aug; 9am-12.30pm & 1.30-6pm or 6.30pm Mon-Sat Sep-Jun, 10am-12.30pm & 2.30-6pm Sun Easter-Jun & Sep).

### Sights & Activities

The old walled city was originally an island, which became linked to the mainland by the sandy isthmus of Le Sillon in the 13th century. During 1944, the battle to drive German forces out of St-Malo destroyed around 80% of it. The main historical monuments were faithfully reconstructed, while the rest of the area was rebuilt in the style of the 17th and 18th centuries.

The town's centrepiece (which was constructed between the 12th and 18th centuries) is **Cathédrale St-Vincent** (pl J de Châtillon;  9.30am-6pm), severely damaged by the 1944 bombing. If the narrow streets become claustrophobic, escape to the **ramparts,** constructed at the end of the 17th century. You can make a complete circuit (around 2km); there's free access at several places, including all the main city gates. From their northern stretch, you can look across to the remains of **Fort National** (admission free;  Jun-Sep).

Walk to the rocky islet of Île du Grand Bé, where the great 18th-century writer Chateaubriand is buried, via the Porte des Bés. Once the tide rushes in, the causeway remains impassable for about six hours, so check tide times with the tourist office.

The **Musée International du Long Cours Cap-Hornier** (Museum of the Cape Horn Route; ☎ 02 99 40 71 58; adult/child €4.8/2.40;  10am-noon & 2-6pm Apr-Sep, Tue-Sun Oct-Mar) is in the 14th-century Tour Solidor. Presenting the life of the hardy sailors who followed the Cape Horn route, it offers superb views from the top of the tower.

### Sleeping

**Camping Aleth** ( ☎ 02 99 81 60 91; camping@ville -saint-malo.fr; Allée Gaston Buy, St-Servan; camp sites €11.10;  Apr-Sep) This camping ground enjoys an exceptional view in all directions. Take bus No 6.

**Auberge de Jeunesse** ( ☎ 02 99 40 29 80; info@ centrevarangot.com; 37 ave du Père Umbricht; dm €13.20, s €20.70-22, d €29.40-32) This place offers a considerably more luxurious stay than the usual hostel. Take bus No 5 from the train station or No 1 (July and August only) from the bus station and tourist office.

**Hôtel Le Neptune** ( ☎ 02 99 56 82 15; 21 rue de l'Industrie; d €27-42, with shared bathroom €20-27.50) Close to the Grande Plage, this comfortable, family-run place is above a small, cheerful bar.

**Hôtel Aux Vieilles Pierres** ( ☎ 02 99 56 46 80; 4 rue des Lauriers; d €45, with shared bathroom €29) This friendly, intimate, family-run hotel, the cheapest in the old city, has a cosy downstairs restaurant but only six rooms, so book ahead.

**Hôtel San Pedro** ( ☎ 02 99 40 88 57; www.san -pedro.hotel.com; 1 rue Sainte-Anne; s/d €50/55;  Feb-Nov) Tucked at the back of the old city, the San Pedro offers impeccable rooms, the warmest of welcomes and sea views.

### Eating

**Le Petit Crêpier** ( ☎ 02 99 40 93 19; 6 rue Ste-Barbe; dishes €5.50-8;  closed Tue-Wed except Jul-Aug) This famous creperie is known for its gourmet specialities such as a galette with plaice in a seaweed and Muscadet sauce, or a crepe with a mousse of dates and spices.

**La Coquille d'Oeuf** ( ☎ 02 99 40 92 62; 20 rue de la Corne de Cerf; menu €12-23.50) Neat, trim and with a nautical theme, this small restaurant with its tables for two makes for intimate, good-value dining.

Among the food shops along rue de l'Orme is a truly excellent **cheese shop** (  Tue-Sat) at No 9. Just down the street is **Hall au Blé**, a covered market.

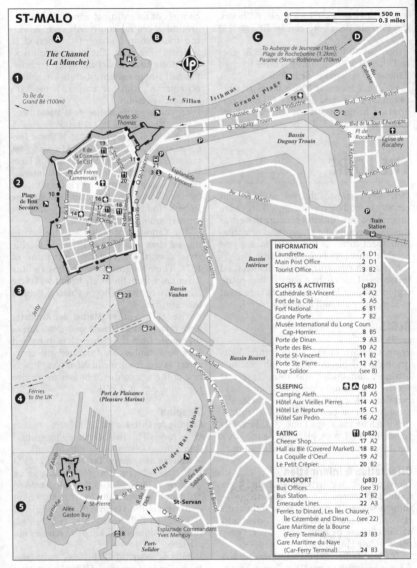

**ST-MALO**

0 — 500 m
0 — 0.3 miles

| INFORMATION | |
|---|---|
| Laundrette | 1 D1 |
| Main Post Office | 2 D1 |
| Tourist Office | 3 B2 |

| SIGHTS & ACTIVITIES | (p82) |
|---|---|
| Cathédrale St-Vincent | 4 A2 |
| Fort de la Cité | 5 A5 |
| Fort National | 6 B1 |
| Grande Porte | 7 B2 |
| Musée International du Long Cours Cap-Hornier | 8 B5 |
| Porte de Dinan | 9 A3 |
| Porte des Bés | 10 A2 |
| Porte St-Vincent | 11 B2 |
| Porte Ste Pierre | 12 A2 |
| Tour Solidor | (see 8) |

| SLEEPING | (p82) |
|---|---|
| Camping Aleth | 13 A5 |
| Hôtel Aux Vieilles Pierres | 14 A2 |
| Hôtel Le Neptune | 15 C1 |
| Hôtel San Pedro | 16 A2 |

| EATING | (p82) |
|---|---|
| Cheese Shop | 17 A2 |
| Hall au Blé (Covered Market) | 18 B2 |
| La Coquille d'Oeuf | 19 A2 |
| Le Petit Crêpier | 20 B2 |

| TRANSPORT | (p83) |
|---|---|
| Bus Offices | (see 3) |
| Bus Station | 21 B2 |
| Émeraude Lines | 22 A3 |
| Ferries to Dinard, Les Îles Chausey, Île Cézembre and Dinan | (see 22) |
| Gare Maritime de la Bourse (Ferry Terminal) | 23 B3 |
| Gare Maritime du Naye (Car-Ferry Terminal) | 24 B3 |

## Getting There & Away

The company **Brittany Ferries** (reservations ☎ France 08 25 82 88 28, ☎ UK 0870 556 1600; www .brittany-ferries.com) runs ferries between St-Malo and Portsmouth, and **Condor Ferries** (☎ France 08 25 16 03 00, ☎ UK 0845 345 2000; www .condorferries.co.uk) to/from both Poole and Weymouth via Jersey or Guernsey.

Hydrofoils and catamarans depart from the Gare Maritime de la Bourse; car ferries leave from the Gare Maritime du Naye.

There are services with **Courriers Bretons** (☎ 02 99 19 70 80) to Cancale (€3.80, 30 minutes), Fougères (€13.90, 1¾ hours, one to three daily) and Pontorson (€8.30, one hour).

Buses to Rennes (€9.90, one to 1½ hours, three to six daily) are run by **TIV** (☎ 02 99 82 26 26).

Bus No 10 for **CAT** (☎ 02 99 82 26 26) goes to Dinan (€5.70, 50 minutes, three to eight daily) via the Barrage de la Rance.

Frequent trains or SNCF buses run between St-Malo and Rennes (€11.40, one hour). Change at Rennes for Paris' Gare Montparnasse (€53, 4¼ hours, eight to 10 daily).

# THE LOIRE

Defensive fortresses thrown up in the 9th century to fend off marauding Vikings were superseded by whimsical pleasure palaces as this area became the playground of nobles who spent fortunes turning it into a vast neighbourhood of lavish chateaux. The result is a rich concentration of architectural treasures (Unesco has named the entire region a World Heritage site) that are great to explore by car and especially bicycle.

## BLOIS

**pop 49,300**

From the 15th to the 17th century, Blois (pronounced blwah) was a hub of court intrigue, and during the 16th century it served as a second capital of France. Several dramatic events involving some of the most important personages in French history such as the kings Louis XII, François I and Henri III, took place inside the city's outstanding attraction, Château de Blois.

### Orientation & Information

Blois, on the northern bank of the River Loire, is a compact town – almost everything is within 10 minutes' walk of the train station. The old city is the area south and east of Château de Blois, which towers over place Victor Hugo.

The **tourist office** (☎ 02 54 90 41 41; www.ville-blois .fr & www.loiredeschateaux.com; 23 pl du Château; 9am-7pm Mon-Sat, 10am-7pm Sun Apr-Sep; 9am-12.30pm & 2pm-6pm Mon-Sat, 9.30am-12.30pm Sun Oct-Mar) charges €2.30 to make hotel or B&B reservations.

### Sights & Activities

The **Château de Blois** (☎ 02 54 90 33 32; adult/ student/child €6.50/4.50/2; 9am-7pm Jul & Aug; to 6pm Apr-Jun, Sep & Oct; to 12.30pm & 2-5.30pm Nov-Mar)

consists of four distinct wings constructed around a central courtyard, each reflecting the favoured style of the period in which it was built. The distinctive brick-and-stone **Louis XII section**, which includes the hall where entrance tickets are sold, is ornamented with porcupines, Louis XII's heraldic symbol.

Opposite is the **Maison de la Magie** (House of Magic; ☎ 02 54 55 26 26; 1 pl du Château; adult/12-17 yrs/6-11 yrs €7.50/6.50/5; 10am-12.30pm & 2pm-6.30pm Jul & Aug, to 12.30pm & 2pm-6pm Tue-Sun Apr-Jun, to noon & 2pm-6pm Wed, Thu, Sat & Sun Sep-Mar) faces the chateau and has magic shows, interactive exhibits and displays of clocks invented by the Blois-born magician Jean-Eugène Robert-Houdin (1805-71), after whom the great Houdini named himself.

The **Cathédrale St-Louis** ( 7.30am-6pm) in the **old town** was rebuilt in a late Gothic style after the devastating hurricane of 1678. There's a great view of Blois and the River Loire from the lovely **Jardins de l'Évêché** (Gardens of the Bishop's Palace), behind the cathedral.

The 15th-century **Maison des Acrobates** (House of the Acrobats; 3 bis rue Pierre de Blois), across the square from the cathedral, is so-named because its timbers are decorated with characters taken from medieval farces. It was one of the few medieval houses to survive the bombings of WWII.

### Sleeping

**Camping des Châteaux** (☎ 02 54 78 82 05; camp sites €9; Jul-Sep) This two-star camping ground is in Vineuil, about 4km south of Blois.

**Auberge de Jeunesse Les Grouëts** (☎ 02 54 78 27 21; blois@fuaj.org; 18 rue de l'Hôtel Pasquier; dm €7, sheets €2.70, breakfast €3.20; Mar–mid-Nov) This youth hostel is in Les Grouëts, 4.5km southwest of Blois train station – call ahead as it's often full. Beds are in two 24-bed, single-sex dorms and kitchen facilities are available.

**Hôtel du Bellay** (☎ 02 54 78 23 62; hoteldubellay .free.fr; 12 rue des Minimes; d/tr/q €35/45/55, d with shared bathroom €23-25) Some of the rooms are tiny, but all have charm, lovingly adorned with older-style, mumsy wallpaper.

**Hôtel St-Jacques** (☎ 02 54 78 04 15; www.hotel saintjacquesblois.com; 7 rue Ducoux; s/d €35/37, with shared bathroom with washbasin €25/27) A functional but friendly one-star hotel next to the station with ample-sized but uninspiring rooms.

# BLOIS

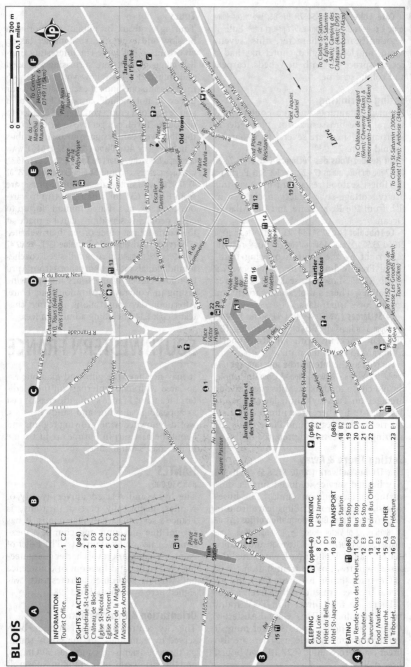

| | | |
|---|---|---|
| **INFORMATION** | | |
| Tourist Office.................... | 1 | C2 |
| | | |
| **SIGHTS & ACTIVITIES** | | (p84) |
| Cathédrale St-Louis............. | 2 | F2 |
| Château de Blois................ | 3 | D3 |
| Église St-Nicolas............... | 4 | D4 |
| Église St-Vincent.............. | 5 | C2 |
| Maison de la Magie............. | 6 | D3 |
| Maison des Acrobates.......... | 7 | E2 |

| | | |
|---|---|---|
| **SLEEPING** | | (pp84–6) |
| Côté Loire....................... | 8 | C4 |
| Hôtel du Bellay................. | 9 | D1 |
| Hôtel St-Jaques................ | 10 | B3 |
| | | |
| **EATING** | | (p86) |
| Au Rendez-Vous des Pêcheurs.. | 11 | C4 |
| Charcuterie...................... | 12 | E3 |
| Charcuterie...................... | 13 | D1 |
| Food Market..................... | 14 | D2 |
| Intermarché..................... | 15 | A3 |
| Le Triboulet.................... | 16 | D3 |

| | | |
|---|---|---|
| **DRINKING** | | (p86) |
| Le St James..................... | 17 | F2 |
| | | |
| **TRANSPORT** | | (p86) |
| Bus Station..................... | 18 | B2 |
| Bus Stop........................ | 19 | E3 |
| Bus Stop........................ | 20 | D3 |
| Bus Stop........................ | 21 | E1 |
| Point Bus Office................ | 22 | D2 |
| | | |
| **OTHER** | | |
| Préfecture....................... | 23 | E1 |

**Côté Loire** ( ☎ 02 54 78 07 86; www.coteloire .com; 2 pl de la Grève; r from €39, Apr-Oct €46) Full of wooden-beamed character, this seven-room, higgledy-piggledy hotel has had a recent spruce-up with new beds, carpets and colour scheme.

### Eating & Drinking
Popular restaurants line rue Foulerie and several café-brasseries dot place de la Résistance. There are several good bars in the old town.

**Au Rendez-Vous des Pêcheurs** ( ☎ 02 54 74 67 48; 27 rue du Foix; mains €21-28; ☺ Tue-Sat) Perhaps the finest seafood restaurant in town, this pretty cottage-style place specialises in fish from the River Loire and the Atlantic Ocean.

**Le Triboulet** ( ☎ 02 54 74 11 23; Pl du Château; menu €16.50-23.50; ☺ closed Sun & Mon) A busy restaurant right by the château offering traditional French dining. The tasty *menu du terroir* (€23.50) showcases seasonal Loire area specialities. There's a pleasant garden and terrace for warmer days.

**Le St James** ( ☎ 02 54 74 44 99; 50 rue Foulerie; ☺ 10pm-5am Thu-Sun) A lively bar serving 162 different cocktails with an atmospheric courtyard to enjoy them in.

As well as the **Intermarché supermarket** (ave Gambetta; ☺ 9am-12.30pm & 3pm-7.15pm Mon-Sat), in the old city, a food market fills rue Anne de Bretagne on Tuesday, Thursday and Saturday until 1pm. There are a number of charcuteries in the area around Place Louis XII offering cold meats and prepared dishes.

### Getting There & Away
The **TLC bus network** ( ☎ 02 54 58 55 44) has a very limited service, reduced further during the holidays and on Sunday. TLC buses to destinations around Blois leave from in front of the **Point Bus information office** ( ☎ 02 54 78 15 66; 2 pl Victor Hugo; ☺ 1.30-6pm Mon, 8am-noon & 1.30-6pm Tue-Fri, 1.30-4.30pm Sat) and the bus station – a patch of car park with schedules posted – in front of the train station.

The train station is on ave Dr Jean Laigret at the western end of the street.

There are four direct non-TGV trains daily from Blois to Paris' Gare d'Austerlitz (€20.80, two hours), plus several more if you change trains in Orléans. There are also direct trains to Nantes (€27.10, two hours, three daily).

### Tours
Touring chateaux by public transport can be slow and expensive, so consider taking an organised bus tour. The interesting English-language tours are surprisingly relaxed and informal. Most allow you between 45 minutes and one hour at each chateau. Tour prices do not include entrance fees, but if you're part of a group you may be entitled to discounts. If you can get five to seven people together, you can design your own minibus itinerary. Try **Acco-Dispo** ( ☎ 06 82 00 64 51; www .accodispo-tours.com), **Quart de Tours** ( ☎ 06 85 72 16 22; www.quartdetours.com) and **St-Eloi Excursions** ( ☎ 02 47 37 08 04; www.saint-eloi.com). Typical prices are from €18 to €31 for a half-day trip to various chateaux, in a shared minibus for up to eight people. Reservations can be made at the Tours tourist office or via their website.

**Services Touristiques de Touraine** (STT; ☎ 02 47 05 46 09; www.stt-millet.fr) runs full-sized coaches for individuals rather than groups from April to mid-October. Many tours include wine tasting in Vouvray or Montlouis-sur-Loire. Afternoon/day tours taking in three chateaux cost €34, including admission fees.

# SOUTHWESTERN FRANCE

It may not have the glitz and glamour associated with its counterpart on the Mediterranean, but France's Atlantic coast is just as appealing: sunshine and sandy beaches, world-renowned wine-growing regions and about the best surf in Europe are just some of the coast's attractions.

## NANTES
**pop 550,000**
The lively and relaxed university city of Nantes, historically part of Brittany, is France's seventh-largest metropolis. It has several fine museums and countless inexpensive cafés and restaurants. The Edict of Nantes, a landmark royal charter guaranteeing civil rights and freedom of conscience and worship to France's Protestants, was signed here by Henri IV in 1598.

### Orientation & Information
The city centre's two main arteries, both served by tram lines, are the north–south, partly pedestrianised, cours des 50 Otages, and the east–west Cours Franklin Roosevelt

that connects the train station (to the east) with quai de la Fosse (to the west).

The commercial centre runs from the Gare Centrale bus/tram hub northeast to rue de la Marne and northwest to rue du Calvaire. The old city is to the east, between cours des 50 Otages and the chateau. There is Internet access at **Cyber Planet** ( ☎ 02 51 82 47 97; 18 rue de l'Arche Sèche; Internet per hr €3; 🕙 10am-midnight Mon-Sat, 2-8pm Sun). The **tourist office** ( ☎ 02 40 20 60 00; www.nantes-tourisme.com; pl du Commerce; 🕙 10am-7pm Mon-Sat) is in the Palais de la Bourse. In July and August there is also an **annexe** (2 pl St-Pierre) next to the cathedral.

## Sights

This renowned **Musée des Beaux-Arts** ( ☎ 02 51 17 45 00; adult €3.30; 10 rue Georges Clemenceau; 🕙 10am-6pm Wed-Mon, to 8pm Fri) showcases one of the finest French collections of paintings outside Paris, with works by Georges de La Tour, Ingres and Monet, Picasso and Kandinsky.

From the outside, the **Château des Ducs de Bretagne** (Chateau of the Dukes of Brittany; ☎ 02 51 17 49 00; adult/child €10/free, admission to grounds free; 🕙 10am-6pm) looks like your standard medieval castle. Inside, the parts facing the courtyard are in the style of a Renaissance pleasure palace. Walking along part of the ramparts is free.

Inside the flamboyant Gothic **Cathédrale St-Pierre et St-Paul** (pl St-Pierre), the **tomb of François II** (reigned 1458–88), duke of Brittany, and his second wife, Marguerite de Foix, is considered a masterpiece of Renaissance art.

## Sleeping

**Hôtel St-Daniel** ( ☎ 02 40 47 41 25; hotel.st.daniel@ wanadoo.fr; 4 rue du Bouffay; d from €29) In the heart of the old town, this great-value budget place offers rooms with un-budget extras like spaciousness, TV, hairdryer and double-glazing. Some rooms have been renovated and boast flashy wooden floors. There are a few family rooms for €39.

**Hôtel Fourcroy** ( ☎ 02 40 44 68 00; 11 rue Fourcroy; s/d with shower & toilet €30/32; **P** ) In a nondescript building tucked away down a side-street, this great-value hotel has 19 exceptionally well-kept rooms, with modern bathrooms and upholstered doors.

**Hôtel Pommeraye** ( ☎ 02 40 48 78 79; www.hotel -pommeraye.com; 2 rue Boileau; s/d from €49/59 Mon-Fri, €35/43 Sat & Sun; **P** 🖵 ) A stylish boutique hotel within an older building, mixing the classic and the contemporary with great success in the heart of Nantes' shopping district. Comfortable, well-equipped rooms are presented in warm, modern colours. Cheaper rooms are a bit small but there's free lobby Internet.

## Eating & Drinking

There are dozens of cafés, bars and small restaurants, many of them French-regional or ethnic, a couple of blocks west of the chateau in the lively area around rue de la Juiverie, rue des Petites Écuries and rue de la Bâclerie.

**Brasserie La Cigale** ( ☎ 02 51 84 94 94; 4 pl Graslin; menu €15.20-24.80; 🕙 7.30-12.30am) A trip to Nantes wouldn't be complete without a stop at the exquisite Cigale, grandly decorated with 1890s tilework and painted ceilings that mix baroque with Art Nouveau. If you can't get there for a meal (traditional French), drop in for afternoon tea.

The small **covered market** (pl du Bouffay) and the huge **Marché de Talensac** (rue Talensac) are open until about 1pm (closed Monday).

**La Maison** ( ☎ 02 40 37 04 12; 4 rue Lebrun; 🕙 3pm-2am) An entertaining send-up of a home furnished in very bad taste c 1970, this convivial bar plays mainly house music and is a lively place popular with students.

## Entertainment

Listings of cultural events appear in *Nantes Poche* and *Pil'* (both €0.50). *Le Mois Nantais*, available at the tourist office and at tobacconists, has day-by-day details of cultural events. What's-on websites include www.vivanantes.com. The six-screen **Cinéma Katorza** ( ☎ 02 51 84 90 60; 3 rue Corneille) offers nondubbed films.

## Getting There & Away

The southbound **bus station** ( ☎ 0825 08 71 56), across from 13 allée de la Maison Rouge, is used by CTA buses serving areas of the Loire-Atlantique *département* south of the Loire River. The northbound **bus office** ( ☎ 0825 08 71 56; 1 allée Duquesne, on cours des 50 Otages), run by Cariane Atlantique, handles buses to destinations north of the Loire. There's also a **Eurolines office** ( ☎ 02 51 72 02 03; allée de la Maison Rouge; 🕙 8am-6pm Mon-Fri, to 12.30pm Sat).

The **train station** ( ☎ 36 35; 27 blvd de Stalingrad) is well connected to most of France.

FRANCE

Destinations include Paris' Gare Montparnasse (€49.10 to €61.40, 2¼ hours by TGV, 15 to 20 daily), Bordeaux (€37, four hours, three or four daily) and La Rochelle (€21, 1¾ hours, three or four daily). Tickets and information are available at the **SNCF ticket office** (12 pl de la Bourse; ☒ 10am-7pm Mon, 9am-7pm Tue-Sat; allée Brancas; ☒ 8.30am-6.45pm Mon-Fri).

## Getting Around

The **TAN network** ( ☎ 0801 44 44 44; www.tan.fr), which has an **information office** (2 allée Brancas, pl du Commerce; ☒ Mon-Sat), includes three modern tram lines that intersect at the Gare Centrale (Commerce), the main bus/tram transfer point. Buses run from 7.15am to 9pm. Night services continue until 12.30am.

Bus/tram tickets, sold individually (€1.20) by bus (but not tram) drivers and at tram stop ticket machines, are valid for one hour after being time-stamped. A *ticket journalier*, good for 24hrs, costs €3.30; time-stamp it only the first time you use it.

# POITIERS

**pop 120,000**

Poitiers, the former capital of Poitou, is home to some of France's most remarkable Romanesque churches. It's not a particularly fetching city although the pedestrian-only shopping precinct has its charms. In AD 732, somewhere near Poitiers (the exact site is not known), the cavalry of Charles Martel defeated the Muslim forces of Abd ar-Rahman, governor of Córdoba, thereby ending Muslim attempts to conquer France.

## Orientation & Information

The train station is about 600m west and down the slope from the old city and commercial centre, which begins just north of Poitiers' main square, place du Maréchal Leclerc, and stretches northeast to Église Notre Dame la Grande. Rue Carnot heads south from place du Maréchal Leclerc.

The **tourist office** ( ☎ 05 49 41 21 24; accueil@ ot-poitiers.fr; 45 pl Charles de Gaulle; ☒ 9.30am-7pm Mon-Sat, 10am-6pm Sun Jun-Sep; 10am-6pm Mon-Sat Oct-May) is near the Église Notre Dame.

## Sights

The renowned Romanesque **Église Notre Dame la Grande** (pl Charles de Gaulle; ☒ 8.30am-7pm Mon-Sat, 2pm-5pm Sun) is in the pedestrianised

old city. It dates mostly from the 11th and 12th centuries. The atrocious, painted decoration in the nave is from the mid-19th century; the only original **frescoes** are the faint 12th- or 13th-century works that adorn the U-shaped dome above the choir.

The worthwhile **Musée Ste-Croix** ( ☎ 05 49 41 07 53; www.musees-poitiers.org; 3 rue Jean Jaurès; adult/ child €3.50/free; ☒ 1.15pm-6pm Mon, 10am-noon & 1.15pm-6pm Tue-Fri, 10am-noon & 2pm-6pm Sat & Sun Jun-Sep; only to 5pm Mon-Fri & afternoons Sat & Sun Oct-May) is across the lawn from Baptistère St-Jean, and was built atop Gallo-Roman walls that were excavated and left *in situ*. It has exhibits on the history of Poitou from prehistoric times to the 19th century.

## Sleeping

Other than a couple of nasty places near the station, Poitiers is short on budget accommodation.

**Hôtel de l'Europe** ( ☎ 05 49 88 12 00; www.hotel deleuropepoitiers.com; 39 rue Carnot; s/d from €47.50/53; **P** ) This charming hotel is worth more than its official two stars. The main building, dating from 1710, has a sweeping staircase, oversized rooms and pleasing older-style décor. Breakfast is served in the lovely garden room.

**Le Grand Hôtel** ( ☎ 05 49 60 90 60; www.grand hotelpoitiers.fr; 28 rue Carnot; s/d €65.50/80.50; **P** ⚇ ) Faux Art Deco furnishings and fittings give this three-star hotel some character. The rooms, popular with business travellers, are spacious and well-equipped.

## Eating & Drinking

The most promising area for dining is south of place du Maréchal Leclerc, especially rue Carnot. The Grand'Rue also has some good eateries. Bars and pubs can be found along rue Carnot and one block north of place du Maréchal Leclerc along rue du Chaudron d'Or.

**La Serrurerie** ( ☎ 05 49 41 05 14; 28 rue des Grandes Ecoles; mains €10-14) This atmospheric, lively and hugely popular café bistro does great meals and huge weekend brunches (€14). Temporary exhibitions showcase local art and sculpture.

**La Joyeuse Marmite** ( ☎ 05 49 88 14 59; 66 Grand'Rue; menu €10; ☒ lunch only Mon-Fri) A merry local bistro serving hearty lunch meals including wine. It's just north of Place de la Cathédrale.

## Getting There & Away

The modern **train station** (☎ 0836 35 35 35; blvd du Grand Cerf) has direct links to Bordeaux (€28.70, 1¾ hours), La Rochelle (€19.80, one hour 20 minutes) and many other cities. TGV tickets from Paris' Gare Montparnasse (1½ hours, 12 daily) cost from €43. SNCF buses go to Nantes (€23, 3¼ hours).

# LA ROCHELLE

pop 120,000

The focal point of La Rochelle, a lively and increasingly chic port city midway down France's Atlantic coast, is the old port lined with picturesque cafés and restaurants, which basks in the bright Atlantic sunlight by day and is grandly illuminated at night.

## Orientation & Information

The train station is linked to the Vieux Port by the 500m-long ave du Général de Gaulle. Place du Marché and place de Verdun are at the northern edge of the old city. The **tourist office** (☎ 05 46 41 14 68; www.larochelle-tourisme.com or www.ville-larochelle.fr; ◷ 9am-8pm Mon-Sat, 11am-5.30pm Sun Jul & Aug; 9am-7pm Mon-Sat, 11am-5pm Sun Jun & Sep; 9am-6pm Mon-Sat, 10am-1pm Sun Oct-May) is on the southern side of the Vieux Port in an area of brightly painted wooden buildings known as Le Gabut.

## Sights & Activities

To protect the harbour at night and defend it in times of war, an enormous chain used to be stretched between the two 14th-century stone towers at the harbour entrance. **Tour de la Chaîne** affords fine views from the top and has displays on the history of the local Protestant community in the basement. Across the harbour you can also climb to the top of the 36m-high pentagonal **Tour St-Nicolas**, if you don't get lost in the maze of stairs and corridors.

West of Tour de la Chaîne, the medieval wall leads to the steeple-topped, 15th-century **Tour de la Lanterne**, also known as Tour des Quatre Sergents in memory of four sergeants from the local garrison who were executed in 1822 for plotting to overthrow the newly reinstated monarchy.

The **three towers** (☎ 05 46 34 11 81; admission per tower adult/18-25 yrs/child €4.60/3.10/free; ◷ 10am-7pm Apr-Sep, to 12.30pm & 2pm-5.30pm Tue-Sun Oct-May, closed hols) can be visited on a combined ticket which costs €10/6.50.

## Sleeping

**Centre International de Séjour-Auberge de Jeunesse** (☎ 05 46 44 43 11; fax 05 46 45 41 48; ave des Minimes; bus No 10; dm/d €13/32; ◷ check-in 8am-midnight) This hostel is 2km southwest of the train station in Les Minimes.

**Hôtel François 1er** (☎ 05 46 41 28 46; www.hotelfrancois1er.fr; 15 rue Bazoges; d €50-85; **P** ) A charming, quiet hotel with a cobbled courtyard entrance and traditionally furnished rooms. In the 15th and 16th centuries, a number of French kings stayed in this building.

**Hôtel La Marine** (☎ 05 46 50 51 63; www.hotel-marine.com; 30 quai Duperré; r May-Sep €70-95, Oct-May €59-75) This two-star hotel is in a fantastic location overlooking the port. Most rooms have recently been refurbished with neutral tones and designer furniture – rooms 1, 6, 9 and 13 stand out, with first class views.

## Eating

**André** (☎ 05 46 41 28 24; 5 rue St-Jean du Perot; mains €12-22) Something of an institution, this restaurant has been serving up fresh seafood for more than 50 years, and is usually packed with fish-hungry punters enjoying innovative creations like Monkfish infused with mango and Indian spices, or the knockout *Cassate Charentaise* (regional fruit flan) both on the €35 menu.

**Café de la Paix** (☎ 05 46 41 39 79; 54 rue Chaudrier; breakfast €6.50, menu €14/19, children €8, mains €15-20; ◷ 7am-9.30pm) This century-old place is an atmospheric brasserie-bar with high, painted ceilings, gold-edged mirrors and all the traditional choices: beef, duck, foie gras and salads. Also a good spot for breakfast or afternoon tea.

The best place to pick up your own edibles is at the lively, 19th-century **covered market** (pl du Marché; ◷ 7am-1pm). Food shops in the vicinity include two cheap East Asian **takeaways** (4 & 10 rue Gambetta). In the old city, there's **Monoprix supermarket** (30-36 rue du Palais; ◷ 8.30am-8pm Mon-Sat).

## Getting There & Away

From **La Rochelle Airport** (☎ 05 46 42 30 26; www.larochelle.aeroport.fr; north of the city centre off the N237) there are flights throughout France and to London (with Ryanair) and Southampton (with Flybe) in the UK.

The **bus station** and bus information offices are at place de Verdun. Eurolines ticketing is handled by **Citram Littoral** ( ☎ 05 46 50 53 57; 30 cours des Dames; ✆ closed Sat afternoon, Mon morning & all day Sun).

The **train station** ( ☎ 0836 35 35 35) is linked by TGV to Paris' Gare Montparnasse (€53.60, three hours, five or six direct daily). Other destinations served by direct trains include Nantes (€22, two hours, five or six daily), and Bordeaux (€22.60, two hours, five to seven daily).

### Getting Around
The innovative local transport system, **Autoplus** ( ☎ 05 46 34 02 22), has a bus hub and **information office** (pl de Verdun; ✆ 7am-7.30pm Mon-Sat). Tickets are €1.20. Bus No 21 runs from place Verdun to the train station, returning via the Vieux Port. No 10 links place de Verdun with the youth hostel and Les Minimes.

## BORDEAUX
**pop 735,000**
Bordeaux is buzzing, thank in part to a massive renovation programme: streets have been pedestrianised, squares re-paved, trees planted and a state-of-the-art tram system installed. Against a backdrop of neoclassical architecture, wide avenues and pretty parks, the city boasts excellent museums, a vibrant nightlife, an ethnic diversity population and a lively university community.

### Orientation
The city centre lies between place Gambetta and the tidal, 350m- to 500m-wide Garonne. From place Gambetta, place de Tourny is 500m northeast, and the tourist office is 400m to the east.

The train station, Gare St-Jean, is in a seedy area about 3km southeast of the city centre. Cours de la Marne stretches from the train station to place de la Victoire, which is linked to place de la Comédie by the long and straight pedestrianised shopping street, rue Ste-Catherine. Banks offering currency exchange can be found near the tourist office on cours de l'Intendance, rue de l'Esprit des Lois and cours du Chapeau Rouge.

### Information
**Laundrette** (31 rue du Palais Gallien; ✆ 8am-9pm)
**Self-service** ( ✆ 7am-9pm; 32 rue des Augustins; 5 rue de Fondaudège; 8 rue Lafaurie de Monbadon)
**Main post office** (37 rue du Château d'Eau)

**NetZone** ( ☎ 05 57 59 01 25; 209 rue Ste-Catherine; Internet access per hr €3; ✆ 9.30am-midnight daily)
**Tourist office** ( ☎ 05 56 00 66 00; www.bordeaux-tour isme.com; 12 cours du 30 Juillet; ✆ 9am-7.30pm Mon-Sat Jul-Aug, to 7pm May-Jun & Sep-Oct, 9.30am-6.30pm Sun May-Oct; 9am-6.30pm Mon-Sat, 9.45am-4.30pm Sun Nov-Apr) Next to the tram stop Comédie.

### Sights & Activities
The sights mentioned below appear pretty much from north to south.

Entrepôts Lainé was built in 1824 as a warehouse for the rare and exotic products of France's colonies (such as coffee, cocoa, peanuts and vanilla). Its capacious spaces now house the **CAPC Musée d'Art Contemporain** (Museum of Contemporary Art; ☎ 05 56 00 81 50; Entrepôt 7, rue Ferrère; ✆ 11am-6pm Tue, Thu-Sun, to 8pm Wed, closed Mon). Most of the exhibits and installations are temporary, presenting major artistic movements over the last 30 years.

The beautifully landscaped **Jardin Public** (cours de Verdun), established in 1755 and laid out in the English style a century later, includes the meticulously catalogued **Jardin Botanique** ( ☎ 05 56 52 18 77; admission free; ✆ 8.30am-6pm), founded in 1629 and at its present site since 1855; and the nearby **Musée d'Histoire Naturelle** (Natural History Museum; ☎ 05 56 48 29 86; ✆ 11am-6pm Mon & Wed-Fri, 2-6pm Sat & Sun). There's a **children's playground** on the island.

Nearby, off rue de Fondaudège, is the city's most impressive Roman site, the **Palais Gallien** (rue du Dr Albert Barraud; adult/under-12 yrs €1.50/free; ✆ 3-7pm Jun-Sep), the ruins of a 3rd-century amphitheatre.

The **esplanade des Quinconces**, a vast square laid out in 1820, features the fountain monument to the Girondins, a group of moderate, bourgeois National Assembly deputies during the French Revolution, 22 of whom were executed in 1793 when convicted of counter-revolutionary activities.

Nowadays, **place Gambetta** is an island of greenery in the midst of the city centre's hustle and bustle, but during the Reign of Terror that followed the Revolution, a guillotine placed here severed the heads of 300 alleged counter-revolutionaries.

A few blocks south of place Gambetta, the **Musée des Arts Décoratifs** (Museum of Decorative Arts; ☎ 05 56 00 72 50; 39 rue Bouffard; museum ✆ 2-6pm Wed-Mon, temporary exhibits from 11am Mon-Fri) specialises in faïence, porcelain, silverwork, glasswork, furniture and the like.

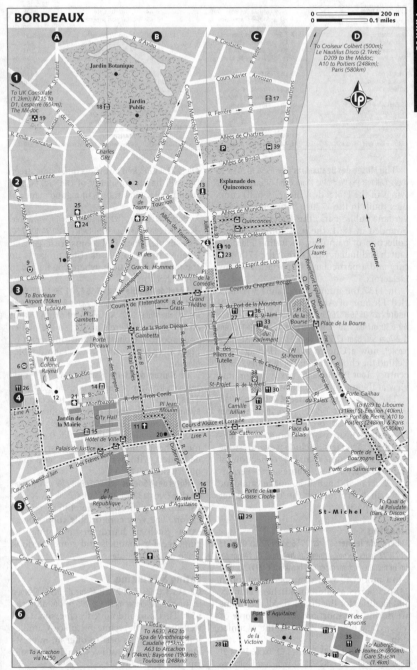

# BORDEAUX

0 — 200 m
0 — 0.1 miles

**A** **B** **C** **D**

R. d'Aviau

Jardin Botanique

R. Constantin

To Croiseur Colbert (500m);
Le Nautilus Disco (2.1km);
D209 to the Médoc;
A10 to Poitiers (248km);
Paris (580km)

**1**
Jardin
Public

Cours Xavier Arnozan

17 🏛

To UK Consulate
(1.2km); N215 to
D1, Lesparre (65km);
The Médoc

18 🏛

19 🏨

R. Ferrère

R. Foy

Allées de Chartres

R. Emile Fourcand

Pl
Charles
GRt

Allées de Bristol

39 🏨

R. de Fondaudège

Cours de Verdun

R. Bouffard

Cours du Maréchal Foch

**2**
R. Turenne

2 •

13 🏨

Esplanade des
Quinconces

Cours de Tournon

Allées de Munich

R. de l'Abbé de l'Épée

Pl
de
Tourny

Cours de Tourny

Quinconces 🚇

Pl
Jean
Jaurès

Garonne

25 🏨
R. Huguerie
24 🏨

22 🏨

Allées de Tourny

Allées d'Orléans

5 •

7 🏨

Cours Georges Clémenceau

9 ⓘ

14 •

R. Castéja

Pl des
Grands Hommes

10 🏨
23 🏨

R. du Palais Gallien

R. Montméjan

R. Mautrec

Pl
de la
Comédie

R. de l'Esprit des Lois

**3**
To Bordeaux
Airport (10km)

37 🏨

Cours de l'Intendance

Grand
Théâtre

Cours du Chapeau Rouge

R. Judaïque

Pl
Gambetta

R. de
Grassi

R. du Port de la Mousque

36 🏨
27 🏨 R. St-Rémi

Pl
de la
Bourse

Place de la Bourse

Porte
Dijeaux

R. de la Porte Dijeaux
Gambetta

33 🏨
Pl
du
Parlement

Q. de la Douane

Ligne C

R. de Cheverus

R. des
Piliers de
Tutelle

Pl
St-Pierre

6 ⓘ
Pl du
Colonel
Raynal

R. la Boétie

R. Vital Carles

R. du Cancera

R. de Chartres

Porte Cailhau

**4**
26 🏨
12 •
21 🏨
R. Boulan

14 🏨

R. Montbazon

R. des Trois Conils

38 🏨
Pl
St-Projet

R. de la Merci

30 🏨

Pl
du Palais

Ligne A

Jardin de
la Mairie

15 🏨
City Hall

11 🏛
20 🏨

Pl Jean
Moulin

Pl
Camille
Jullian

32 🏨

To N89 to Libourne
(31km) St-Émilion (40km);
Pont de Pierre; A10 to
Poitiers (248km) & Paris
(580km)

Hôtel de Ville 🏛

Cours d'Alsace et Lorraine

Ste-Catherine

Place du
Palais

Palais de Justice 🏛

Ligne A

Porte de
Bourgogne

R. des Frères Bonie

R. du Hâ

Porte des Salinières •

**5**
Cours du Maréchal Juin

Pl
de la
République

16 🏨

Musée
d'Aquitaine

R. de Cursol

Porte de la
Grosse Cloche •

St-Michel

To Quai de
la Paludate
(Bars & Discos;
1.3km)

R. Lucande

R. de Belfort

R. Mouneyra

Cours d'Albret

R. Jean Burguet

Cours Pasteur

29 🏨

Cours Victor Hugo

R. des Faures

Cours de la Libération

8 @

R. St-François

R. des Menuts

**6**
R. du Tondu

R. de Pessac

Cours Aristide Briand

R. Henri IV

R. des Augustins

3 •

Victoire 🚇

Porte d'Aquitaine

Pl des
Capucins

31 🏨

To Arcachon
via N250

R. Villedieu
To A630, A62 to
Spa de Vinothérapie
Caudalie (15km);
A63 to Arcachon
(74km); Bayonne (190km);
Toulouse (248km)

28 🏨

Pl
de la
Victoire

4 •
R. Élie Gintrec

Cours de la Marne

34 🏨

35 🏨

To Auberge
de Jeunesse (800m);
Gare St-Jean
(1.4km)

The **Musée des Beaux-Arts** ( ☎ 05 56 10 20 56; 20 cours d'Albret; 🕑 Wed-Mon 11am-6pm) occupies two wings of the Hôtel de Ville (city hall) complex (built in the 1770s); between them is a verdant public park, the **Jardin de la Mairie**. Founded in 1801, the museum has a large collection of paintings, including Flemish, Dutch and Italian works from the 17th century and a particularly important work by Delacroix.

In 1137 the future King Louis VII married Eleanor of Aquitaine in **Cathédrale St-André** ( ☎ 05 56 81 26 25; admission free; 🕑 10-11.30am & 2-6.30pm Mon, 7.30-11.30am & 2-6pm Tue-Fri, 9-11.30am & 2-7pm Sat, 8am-12.30pm Sun; 2.30-5.30pm 1st Sun of month), now a Unesco World Heritage Site. Behind the choir, the 50m-high belfry, 15th-century **Tour Pey-Berland**, has a panoramic view at the top of 232 narrow steps.

The outstanding **Musée d'Aquitaine** (Museum of Aquitaine; ☎ 05 56 01 51 00; 20 cours Pasteur; 🕑 11am-6pm Tue-Sun) presents 25,000 years of Bordeaux's history and ethnography. Exceptional artefacts include several stone carvings of women and a collection of Gallo-Roman steles, statues and ceramics. A detailed, English-language catalogue is worth borrowing at the ticket counter (€1.50 deposit).

## Sleeping

**Auberge de Jeunesse** ( ☎ 05 56 33 00 70; fax 05 56 33 00 71; 22 cours Barbey, annexe at 208 cours de l'Argonne; dm HI member/nonmember incl breakfast €16/17.50; 🖳 ) Ultra-modern, well-equipped and open 24hrs, there's a café-bar, kitchen, laundry and facilities for the disabled. All the rooms are dorms, but most are for four people or fewer. Take bus Nos 7 or 8 to the Meunier stop.

**Hôtel Boulan** ( ☎ 05 56 52 23 62; fax 05 56 44 91 65; 28 rue Boulan; s/d €28.25/28.50, with shared bathroom €20.25/23.50) Tucked away in a quiet side-street, but still handy for many of the sights, this friendly place has rooms of a good standard for this price.

**Hôtel Excelsior** ( ☎ 05 56 48 00 14; www.hotel-bordeaux.com; 26 rue Huguerie; d/tw/tr €22.80/24.40/27.50) The simple, functional rooms are larger and brighter than those at its sister property up the road, Hôtel Studio, where you'll need to go to check in.

**Hôtel de Famille** ( ☎ 05 56 52 11 28; fax 05 56 51 94 43; 76 cours Georges Clemenceau; s & d €29-36, with shared bathroom €18-22) A variety of ordinary but comfy rooms. There's no lift, so the higher your room, the cheaper (and smaller) it is. Light sleepers beware – there's no double-glazing.

**La Maison du Lierre** ( ☎ 05 56 51 92 71; www.maisondulierre.com; 57 rue Huguerie; s/d €63/73; 🅿 ) This is truly a delightful hotel. It occupies a sympathetically restored townhouse which has a beautiful Bordeaux stone staircase and pretty courtyard for breakfast in summer. The 12 mid-sized rooms are nicely decorated with warm colours and parquetry floors.

**Hôtel des 4 Soeurs** ( ☎ 05 57 81 19 20; www.4soeurs.free.fr; 6 cours du 30 Juillet; s/d from €60/70; 🍽 🐾 🖳 ) An appealing three-star hotel in a great location. The very comfortable rooms boast extras such as hairdryers and English-language TV channels and some overlook place de la Comédie.

## Eating & Drinking

**Claret's** ( ☎ 05 56 01 21 21; 46 rue du Pas St Georges; lunch menu €10, dinner menu €16-20; 🕑 closed Sat lunch & Sun) This is an undoubtedly chic, smart and well-priced little venue on place Camille-Jullian. It does its best to offer an interesting selection of southwestern French and Japanese specialities.

**Cassolette Café** ( ☎ 05 56 92 94 96; www.cassolette café.com; 20 pl de la Victoire; cassolette €10.50, lunch/ dinner menu €8.50/10.50; ☒ noon-midnight) Extremely popular and great value, you order your menu or the (five) ingredients of your *cassolette* (casserole cooked on a terracotta plate) using a check-off form – and your choices appear promptly.

**Le Bistrot d'Édouard** ( ☎ 05 56 81 48 87; 16 pl du Parlement; menu €11-20) The great-value three-course menu at €11 (available lunch and dinner) keeps this bistrot packed. Outside tables are in a calming spot by the fountain in place du Parlement.

**La Petite Brasserie** ( ☎ 05 56 52 19 79; 43 rue du Pas St Georges; menu €25/35; ☒ Wed-Sun) An unpretentious place offering fine brasserie-style dining in a relaxed and cosy atmosphere. The traditional bordelaise cuisine, extensive wine list and attentive service all get top marks.

**Le Fournil des Capucins** (62-64 cours de la Marne) Near place de la Victoire, this bakery never closes.

**Bodega Bodega** ( ☎ 05 56 01 24 24; 4 rue des Piliers de Tutelle; ☒ noon-3.15pm & 7pm-2am Mon-Sat, 7pm-2am Sun) With two floors of tapas, tunes and trendy types, this is the biggest and best Spanish bar in town.

**Café Brun** ( ☎ 05 56 52 20 49; 45 rue St-Rémi; ☒ 10-2am) This bar-bistro with a warm atmosphere and cool jazz is great for an evening aperitif.

**Marché des Capucins** ( ☒ 6am-1pm Tue-Sun) is a few blocks east of place de la Victoire, and is a one-time wholesale market. Nearby rue Élie Gintrec has super-cheap **fruit & vegie stalls** ( ☒ to 1pm or 1.30pm Mon-Sat).

Also recommended:

**Champion supermarket** (pl des Grands Hommes; ☒ 8.30am-7.30pm Mon-Sat) In the basement of the Marché des Grands Hommes.

**Auchan supermarket** ( ☒ 8.30am-10pm Mon-Sat; opposite 58 rue du Château d'Eau)In the Centre Commercial Mériadeck.

## Entertainment

Bordeaux has a vibrant nightlife scene; details of events appear in *Bordeaux Plus* and *Clubs & Concerts* (French website at www .clubsetconcerts.com), both free and available at the tourist office.

Nondubbed films are screened at two art cinemas, **Centre Jean Vigo** ( ☎ 05 56 44 35 17; 6 rue Franklin), and the popular, five-screen **Cinéma Utopia** ( ☎ 05 56 52 00 03; 3 pl Camille Jullian).

## Getting There & Away

The **Bordeaux airport** ( ☎ 05 56 34 50 50; www .bordeaux.aeroport.fr) is in Mérignac, 10km west of the city centre. Air France and **Ryanair** (www.ryanair.com) operate regular flights from the UK and low-cost Dutch airline **Basiq Air** (www.basiqair.com) flies from Amsterdam.

Buses to places all over the Gironde (and parts of nearby *départements*) leave from the **Halte Routière** (bus terminal; allées de Chartres), in the northeast corner of esplanade des Quinconces; schedules are posted. **Citram Aquitaine** runs buses to destinations in the Gironde and has an **information kiosk** ( ☎ 05 56 43 68 43; ☒ 1-8pm Mon-Fri, 9am-1.30pm & 5-8pm Sat) at the Halte Routière.

Facing the train station is **Eurolines** ( ☎ 05 56 92 50 42; 32 rue Charles Domercq; ☒ Mon-Sat).

The train station, **Gare St-Jean**, is about 3km from the city centre at the southern terminus of cours de la Marne. Destinations include Paris' Gare Montparnasse (€58.90, three hours, at least 16 daily), Bayonne (€24.40, 13/4hrs, eight daily), La Rochelle (€22.50, two hours, five to seven daily) and Toulouse (€27.70, two to three hours, nine to 14 daily).

# BORDEAUX WINE-GROWING REGION

The 1000-sq-km wine-growing area around the city of Bordeaux is, along with Burgundy, France's most important producer of top-quality wines. Bordeaux has over 5000 chateaux (also known as *domaines*, *crus* or *clos*); the properties where grapes are raised, picked, fermented and then matured as wine. The smaller chateaux often accept walk-in visitors, but at many places, especially the better-known ones, you have to make advance reservations by phone. Many chateaux are closed during the *vendange* (grape harvest) in October.

## Information & Tours

In Bordeaux, the **Maison du Vin de Bordeaux** ( ☎ 05 56 00 22 88; 3 cours du 30 Juillet; ☒ 8.30am-4.30pm Mon-Fri), across the street from the tourist office, can supply you with a free, colour-coded map of production areas, details on chateau visits, and the addresses of local *maisons du vin* (tourist offices that deal mainly with winery visits).

Every Wednesday and Saturday (daily from May to October) at about 1.30pm, the Bordeaux tourist office runs five-hour bus tours in French and English to wine chateaux in the area (adult/student/child under 12 €26/23/11.50). From May to October, all-day trips (adult/student/child €47/40/23.50) to wine chateaux, starting with a tour and lunch in Bordeaux, begin at 9.15am on Wednesday and Saturday.

# BAYONNE

pop 42,000

The cultural and economic capital of the French Basque Country Bayonne, unlike the upmarket seaside resort of Biarritz, retains much of its Basqueness: you'll hear almost as much Euskara (the Basque language) as French in certain quarters. The town's premier fiesta is the five-day **Fêtes de Bayonne** in early August – like Pamplona's running of the bulls, only with cows.

## Orientation & Information

The Rivers Adour and Nive split Bayonne into three: St-Esprit, the area north of the Adour; Grand Bayonne, the oldest part of the city, on the western bank of the Nive; and the very Basque Petit Bayonne quarter to its east. Check your email at the **tourist office** ( ☎ 05 59 46 01 46; www.bayonne-tourisme.com; pl des Basques; ⊙ 9am-7pm Mon-Sat, 10am-1pm Sun Jul & Aug; 9am-6.30pm Mon-Fri, 10am-6pm Sat Sep-Jun) for free brochures including *Fêtes*, listing French Basque Country cultural and sporting events and *Tout à Loisir*, and information on hiking, biking and other activities.

## Sights

Construction of Bayonne's Gothic **Cathédrale Ste-Marie** ( ⊙ 7.30am-11.45am & 3pm-5.45pm Mon-Sat, 3.30-5.45pm Sun) began in the 13th century, when Bayonne was ruled by the Anglo-Normans, and was completed well after France assumed control in 1451.

The **Musée Basque et de l'Histoire de Bayonne** ( ☎ 05 59 46 61 90; 37 quai des Corsaires; adult/student/ under 18 yrs €5.50/3/free; ⊙ 10am-6.30pm Tue-Sun May-Oct, to 12.30pm & 2pm-6pm Tue-Sun Nov-Apr) presents the history and culture of this unique people.

There is a **combined ticket** (adult/student €9/4.50) to both the Musée Basque and **Musée Bonnat** ( ☎ 05 59 59 08 52; 5 rue Jacques Lafitte; adult/student/child €5.50/3/free; ⊙ 10am-6.30pm Wed-Mon May-Oct, to 12.30pm & 2-6pm Wed-Mon Nov-Apr), an art gallery featuring canvases by El Greco, Goya and Degas, and Rubens.

## Sleeping

**Auberge de Jeunesse** ( ☎ 05 59 58 70 00; anglet@fuaj .org; 19 route des Vignes, Anglet; dm €17 first night, €14.20 subsequent nights; ⊙ mid-Feb–mid-Nov) This hostel, in Anglet, complete with a Scottish pub, is lively and popular. Reservations are essential in summer. The hostel has **camping** (sites per adult incl breakfast €10). From Bayonne station, take STAB bus No 2 towards Anglet. At the Cinq Cantons stop, change to No 72, direction Les Plages, which stops outside the hostel. Alternatively – and in high season when bus No 72 doesn't run – take No 2 to the Moulin Barbot stop, from where the hostel is a 10-minute signposted walk. On Sunday take line C from the town hall.

**Hôtel Paris-Madrid** ( ☎ 05 59 55 13 98; sorbois@ wanadoo.fr; pl de la Gare; d from €25, s/d with shared bathroom from €16/22; **P** ) This friendly place is highly recommended, especially for those arriving at the station opposite. The owners speak English and the rooms, decorated with flair, are good value.

**Adour Hôtel** ( ☎ 05 59 55 11 31; www.adourhotel .fr; 13 pl Ste-Ursule; d/tr/q from €47/50/64) Just north of the River Adour and convenient for the station, this welcoming establishment has bright, airy rooms decorated with bullfighting, rugby and gastronomy memorabilia.

## Eating & Drinking

A good selection of medium-priced restaurants surround the covered market and all along quai Amiral Jauréguiberry.

**Bodega Ibaia** ( ☎ 05 59 59 86 66; 45 quai Jauréguiberry; mains €8-12; ⊙ closed Sun & Mon lunch) Atmospheric Basque restaurant/tapas bar with wooden benches, sawdust on the floor and traditional Spanish tiling.

**Bistrot Ste-Cluque** ( ☎ 05 59 55 82 43; 9 rue Hugues; menu €16) There's only one *menu* here on a large chalkboard. Noisy, smoky and bustling, it's atmospheric and unpretentious.

The **covered market** (quai Commandant Roquebert; ⊙ 7am-1pm & 3.30pm-7pm Fri, 8am-1pm Mon-Thu & Sat) occupies an imposing riverside building. There are several tempting food shops and delicatessens along rue Port Neuf and rue d'Espagne. The greatest concentration of pubs and bars is in Petit Bayonne, especially along rue Pannecau, rue des Cordeliers and quai Galuperie. Every Thursday in July and August, there's traditional **Basque music** (admission free; 9.30pm) in place Charles de Gaulle.

## Getting There & Away

The **Biarritz-Anglet-Bayonne airport** ( ☎ 05 59 43 83 83; www.biarritz.aeroport.fr) is 5km southwest of central Bayonne and 3km southeast of Biarritz. Air France flies to/from Paris Orly about eight times daily and less frequently to Lyon and Geneva. Ryanair flies daily to/from London Stansted.

From place des Basques, **ATCRB buses** ( ☎ 05 59 26 06 99) follow the coast to the Spanish border. Transportes Pesa buses leave twice a day for Irún and San Sebastián in Spain (€6.20, 1¾ hours). **Eurolines** ( ☎ 05 59 59 19 33; 3 pl Charles de Gaulle) buses stop opposite the company office.

TGVs run between Bayonne and Paris' Gare Montparnasse (€71.60, five hours, five daily). There are frequent trains to Biarritz (€2.10, 10 minutes), Bordeaux (€24.40, 2¼ hours, at least 10 daily), and Toulouse (€33.10, 3 hours, at least four daily).

## BIARRITZ

**pop 30,000**

The stylish coastal town of Biarritz, 8km west of Bayonne, is known for its fine beaches and some of Europe's best surfing. If travelling on a budget, consider staying in Bayonne and visiting Biarritz from there. Many surfers camp or stay at one of the two excellent youth hostels in Biarritz and in Anglet.

## Orientation & Information

Place Clemenceau, at the heart of Biarritz, is just south of the main beach (Grande Plage). Pointe St-Martin, topped with a lighthouse, rounds off Plage Miramar, the northern continuation of the Grande Plage. Both train station and airport are about 3km southeast of the centre.

The **tourist office** ( ☎ 05 59 22 37 10; www.biarritz .fr; 1 square d'Ixelles; ⏱ 8am-8pm Jul & Aug; 9am-6pm Mon-Sat, 10am-5pm Sun Sep-Jun) publishes *Biarritzcope*, a free monthly what's-on guide.

For surfing of the electronic kind, visit **Génius Informatique** ( ☎ 05 59 24 39 07; 60 ave Édouard VII; per hr €5).

## Sights

**Musée de la Mer** ( ☎ 05 59 22 75 40; www.museedelamer.com; Esplanade de la Vierge; adult/child €7.20/4.60; ⏱ 9.30am-12.30pm & 2-6pm Tue-Sat) has an aquarium seething with life from the Bay of Biscay (Golfe de Gascogne) and exhibits on commercial fishing and Biarritz' whaling past.

Biarritz' fashionable beaches – the **Grande Plage** and **Plage Miramar** to its north – are lined with striped bathing tents and are often packed in summer. Beyond Pointe St-Martin, the superb surfing beaches of **Anglet** stretch northwards for over 4km. Take eastbound bus No 9 from place Clemenceau. The best board rental and instruction bargains are to be had at the **Auberge de Jeunesse** in Anglet. The French-language **Swell Line** ( ☎ 08 36 68 40 64; www.swell-line.com) details surf conditions.

## Sleeping

**Camping de Parme** ( ☎ 05 59 23 03 00; www.camping deparme.com; route de l'Aviation; camp sites €15.50-23) The area's only year-round camp site is in a quiet, leafy spot 1.25km northeast of the train station. It's normally fully booked months in advance for July and August.

**Biarritz Camping** ( ☎ 05 59 23 00 12; www.biarritz-camping.fr; 28 rue d'Harcet; camp sites €13.50-19.50; ⏱ mid-May–mid-Sep; 🖳 ) This summer campsite has spacious and shady sites, 3km southwest of the centre. Take westbound bus No 9 to the Biarritz Camping stop.

**Auberge de Jeunesse** ( ☎ 05 59 41 76 00; biarritz@fuaj.org; 8 rue Chiquito de Cambo; dm €14.90; ⏱ mid-Jan–mid-Dec) This highly popular place offers a host of outdoor activities including surfing and sailing. To get here, follow the railway westwards from the train station for 800m.

**Hôtel Plaza** ( ☎ 05 59 24 74 00; hotel.plaza.biarritz@wanadoo.fr; 20 ave Edouard VII; s/d from €81/103; 🖳 ) A three-star Art Deco delight overlooking Grande Plage with the feel of a glamorous heyday hotel. The spacious rooms (many with beach views) are decked out in grand style.

## Eating

**Le Corsaire** ( ☎ 05 59 24 63 72; Port des Pêcheurs; mains €9-22) It's all about seafood down here by the waters edge on a delightful harbourside terrace, with dishes including *dorade à l'Espagnole* (€14.50) and *grilled cod with chorizo* (€12.20).

**Le Lodge** ( ☎ 05 59 24 73 78; 1 rue de Port-Vieux; mains €13-17) A buzzing new restaurant and gallery featuring traditional cuisine and contemporary art.

Just downhill from Bistrot des Halles, **La Table de Don Quichotte** (12 ave Victor Hugo) sells Spanish hams and sausages.

FRANCE

## Drinking & Entertainment

There are several good bars along rue du Port Vieux and the streets radiating from it. **Le Surfing** ( ☎ 05 59 24 78 72; 9 blvd Prince des Galles) is the place to come to discuss waves and wipe-outs. There's an outside terrace with decent views.

Two discos near the town centre are **Le Caveau** ( ☎ 05 59 24 16 17; 4 rue Gambetta; ♥ 11pm-5am) and **Biarritz Latino** ( ☎ 05 59 22 77 59; ♥ 11pm-5am Tue-Sat), in the Casino Municipal.

## Getting There & Away

Stopping outside the tourist office, nine **ATCRB buses** ( ☎ 05 59 26 06 99) daily follow the coast southwestwards. For other destinations, it's better to go from Bayonne – znot least to ensure a seat in high season. Biarritz-La Négresse train station is about 3km from the town centre. Bus Nos 2 and 9 connect the two. **SNCF** has a town-centre office (13 ave du Maréchal Foch; ♥ Mon-Fri).

# THE DORDOGNE

Known to the French as Périgord, this region was one of the prehistoric cradles of human civilisation. The remains of Neanderthal and Cro-Magnon people have been discovered throughout the area and quite a number of local caves, including the world-famous Lascaux, are decorated with extraordinary works of prehistoric art. During the warmer months the Dordogne, famed for its rich cuisine (such as truffles and *foie gras*), attracts vast numbers of tourists.

## PÉRIGUEUX
pop 33,294

Founded over 2000 years ago on a hill bounded by a curve in the gentle River Isle, Périgueux has one of France's best museums of prehistory. The city is at its liveliest during the Wednesday and Saturday truffle and *foie gras* markets. The medieval and Renaissance old city, Puy St-Front, is on the hillside between the Isle (to the east) and blvd Michel Montaigne and place Bugeaud (to the west). The train station is about 1km northwest of the old city. The **tourist office** ( ☎ 05 53 53 10 63; tourisme. perigueux@perigord.tm.fr; 26 pl Francheville; ♥ 9am-1pm & 2-6pm Mon-Sat year-round, 10am-1pm & 2-6pm

Sun mid-Jun–mid-Sep) is next to the medieval Tour Mataguerre.

**Hôtel des Voyageurs** ( ☎ 05 53 53 17 44; 26 rue Denis Papin; s/d from €14/16) is one of six inexpensive hotels near the train station, along rue Denis Papin and rue des Mobiles de Coulmiers. The rock-bottom prices here equate to tiny rooms, flimsy furniture and noise from the rowdy bar next door.

**Hôtel de l'Univers** ( ☎ 05 53 53 34 79; fax 05 53 06 70 76; 18 cours Michel Montaigne; s €42.70, d €45-53.35; ♥ Feb-Dec) is a welcoming, two-star hotel has a varied selection of generously sized rooms. Most have high ceilings and bathrooms; the two attic rooms are a touch cheaper. There's a decent **restaurant** downstairs.

The **bus station** (pl Francheville) is on the southern side of the square; hours are posted at the bus stops. One of the carriers, **CFTA** ( ☎ 05 53 08 43 13; ♥ Mon-Fri), has an office on the storey overlooking the waiting room. The tourist office and the train station information office can supply you with schedules.

The **train station** (rue Denis Papin) is served by local bus Nos 1, 4 and 5. Destinations with direct services include Bordeaux (€16.30, 1¼ hours, nine to 13 daily). Services to Paris' Gare d'Austerlitz (€45.90, three to five hours, 12 to 16 daily) are via Limoges. To get to Sarlat-la-Canéda (€12) you have to change at Brive.

## SARLAT-LA-CANÉDA
pop 10,000

The beautiful, well-restored town of Sarlat, administratively twinned with nearby La Canéda, is the capital of Périgord Noir.

## Orientation & Information

The heart-shaped Medieval Town (Cité Médiévale) is bisected by the ruler-straight rue de la République (La Traverse), which (along with its continuations) stretches for 2km north from the viaduct and nearby train station to the Auberge de Jeunesse. The Medieval Town is centred on place de la Liberté, rue de la Liberté and place du Peyrou.

Sarlat's **main tourist office** ( ☎ 05 53 31 45 45; www.ot-sarlat-perigord.fr; rue Tourny; ♥ 9am-7pm Mon-Sat, 10am-noon Sun Apr-Oct, 9am-noon & 2-7pm Mon-Sat Nov-Mar) is in a building attached to the cathedral. In summer, it charges €2 for hotel and B&B bookings.

## Sleeping & Eating

**Auberge de Jeunesse** ( ☎ 05 53 59 47 59, 05 53 30 21 27; 77 ave de Selves; dm €10) At this modest but friendly 15-bed hostel kitchen facilities are available; call ahead for a reservation.

**Hôtel Les Récollets** ( ☎ 05 53 31 36 00; www.hotel -recollets-sarlat.com; 4 rue Jean-Jacques Rousseau; d from €39) Lost in the narrow alleys of the Medieval Town, this delightful old building has been freshly renovated inside with 18 fully-equipped two-star rooms.

## Getting There & Away

Bus services are very limited; schedules are available at the tourist office. Departures are from the train station, place Pasteur or place de la Petite Rigaudie. There are one or two buses daily (fewer in July and August) to Périgueux (€6.80, 1½ hours) via Montignac.

The **train station** ( ☎ 05 53 59 00 21), 1.3km south of the old city at the southern end of ave de la Gare, is poorly linked with the rest of the region.

Destinations served include Bordeaux (€19.90, 2½ hours, two to four direct daily) which is on the same line as Bergerac, Périgueux (change at Le Buisson; €12.00, 1½ hours, two daily). The SNCF bus to Souillac (€4.90, 40 minutes, two to four daily) links up with trains on the Paris (Gare d'Austerlitz)-Limoges-Toulouse line.

# BURGUNDY & THE RHÔNE

Best-known for its cooking and world class wine, you'll find Burgundy is also one of France's most varied *départements* – an enticing blend of hilltop villages and bustling market towns, grand châteaux and tiny churches, rolling fields and abandoned abbeys.

## DIJON

**pop 230,000**

Dijon is one of France's most appealing provincial cities, with an inviting centre graced by elegant medieval and Renaissance buildings. It served as the capital for the dukes of Burgundy from the 11th to 15th centuries during which time Dijon was turned into one of the great centres of European art. Modern Dijon is a lively, dynamic city with 24,000 university students and a thriving cultural scene.

## Orientation

Dijon's commercial centre stretches from the tourist office eastwards to Église St Michel; the main shopping streets here are rue de la Liberté and rue du Bourg. Place Grangier, with its many bus stops, is north of rue de la Liberté, while the train station is at the western end of ave Maréchal Foch. The old city is around place François Rude and the surrounding streets.

## Information

**Laundrette** (41 rue Auguste Comte; 28 rue Berbisey; 55 rue Berbisey; 8 pl de la Banque; ⏲ 7.30am-9pm)

**Main post office** (pl Grangier; ⏲ 8am-7pm Mon-Fri, to noon Sat)

**Multi-Rezo** ( ☎ 03 80 66 33 21; 74 rue Vannerie; ⏲ 9am-midnight Mon-Sat, 2-10pm Sun; Internet per 12 min/hr €1/5)

**Tourist office** ( ☎ 03 80 44 11 44; dijon-tourism. com; pl Darcy; ⏲ 9am-7pm May–mid-Oct; 10am-6pm mid-Oct–Apr)

## Sights & Activities

Once home to rulers, the elaborate **Palais des Ducs et des États de Bourgogne** palace complex lies at the heart of old Dijon. The eastern wing houses the Musée des Beaux-Arts (see p99). The 46m-high, 15th-century **Tour Philippe-le-Bon** (Tower of Philip the Good; adult/concession €2.30/1.20; ⏲ 9am-noon, 1.45pm-5.30pm Easter-end Nov, to 11pm, 1.30-3.30pm Wed afternoon, Sat & Sun Nov-Easter) affords fantastic views over the city.

A little way north of the Palais des Ducs, **Église Notre Dame** was built between 1220 and 1240. The façade's three tiers are decorated with leering gargoyles. Outside, **rue de la Chouette** is named after the small stone *chouette* (owl) carved into the north wall of the church. It is said to grant happiness and wisdom to those who stroke it.

Situated above the tomb of St Benignus (who brought Christianity to Burgundy in the 2nd century), Dijon's 13th-century **Cathédrale St Bénigne** was originally built as an abbey church.

Dijon has several outstanding museums. The Dijon Card (€8/11/14 for 24/48/72hrs) gets you into the main ones, and includes a guided city tour and use of public transport. Several museums are free to students and to everyone on Sunday.

FRANCE

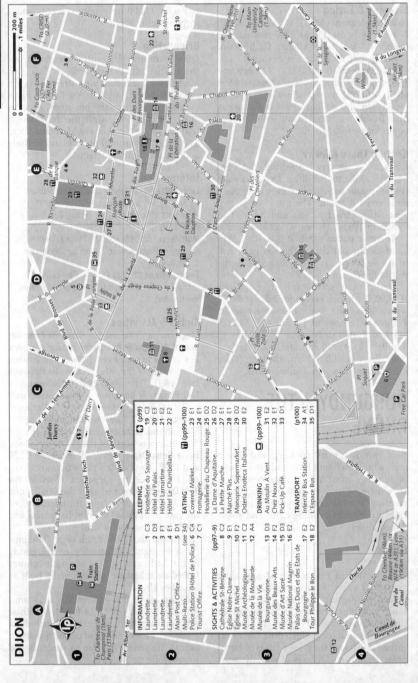

# DIJON

| INFORMATION | | |
| --- | --- | --- |
| Laundrette | 1 | C3 |
| Laundrette | 2 | D3 |
| Laundrette | 3 | F1 |
| Laundrette | 4 | E1 |
| Laundrette | 5 | D1 |
| Main Post Office | (see 34) |
| Multi-Rezo | 6 | C4 |
| Police Station (Hôtel de Police) | 6 | C4 |
| Tourist Office | 7 | C1 |

| SIGHTS & ACTIVITIES | (pp97–9) | |
| --- | --- | --- |
| Cathédrale St-Bénigne | 8 | C2 |
| Église Notre-Dame | 9 | E1 |
| Église St Michel | 10 | F2 |
| Musée Archéologique | 11 | C2 |
| Musée de la Vie | 12 | A4 |
| Bourguignonne | 13 | D3 |
| Musée des Beaux-Arts | 14 | F2 |
| Musée d'Art Sacré | 15 | D3 |
| Musée National Magnin | 16 | E2 |
| Palais des Ducs et des états de | | |
| Bourgogne | 17 | E2 |
| Tour Philippe le Bon | 18 | E2 |

| SLEEPING | ☐ (p99) | |
| --- | --- | --- |
| Hostellerie du Sauvage | 19 | C3 |
| Hôtel du Palais | 20 | E3 |
| Hôtel Lamartine | 21 | E2 |
| Hôtel Le Chambellan | 22 | F2 |

| EATING | 🍴 (pp99–100) | |
| --- | --- | --- |
| Covered Market | 23 | E1 |
| Fromagerie | 24 | E1 |
| Hostellerie du Chapeau Rouge | 25 | D2 |
| La Dame d'Aquitaine | 26 | D2 |
| La Petite Marche | 27 | E1 |
| Marché Plus | 28 | E1 |
| Monoprix Supermarket | 29 | D2 |
| Osteria Enoteca Italiana | 30 | E2 |

| DRINKING | ☐ (pp99–100) | |
| --- | --- | --- |
| Au Moulin A Vent | 31 | E2 |
| Chez Nous | 32 | E1 |
| Pick-Up Café | 33 | D1 |

| TRANSPORT | (p100) | |
| --- | --- | --- |
| Intercity Bus Station | 34 | A1 |
| L'Espace Bus | 35 | D1 |

Housed in the eastern wing of the Palais des Ducs, **Musée des Beaux-Arts** ( ☎ 03 80 74 52 70; adult/senior/student €3.40/1.60/free, admission free Sun; ⏰ 9.30am-6pm Wed-Mon May-Oct, 10am-5pm Wed-Mon Nov-Apr) is one of the most renowned museums in France – considered by many to be second only to the Louvre. The museum has important collections of French, Flemish and Italian art.

The city's archaeological museum, **Musée Archéologique** ( ☎ 03 80 30 88 54; 5 rue du Docteur Maret; adult/senior/student €2.20/1.10/free, free Sun; ⏰ 9.30am-12.30pm & 1.30-6pm Wed-Sun Oct-May, to 6pm Jun-Sep) displays Celtic artefacts and a particularly fine 1st-century bronze of the goddess Sequana standing on a boat. The 11th-century chamber on the lowest level was once part of a Benedictine abbey.

Housed in a 17th-century *hotel particulier*, **Musée National Magnin** ( ☎ 03 80 67 11 10; 4 rue des Bons Enfants; adult/student €3/2.30, Sun €2.30, first Sun of the month free; ⏰ 10am-noon & 2-6pm Tue-Sun) displays works of art donated to the city in 1938 by the brother and sister team of Jeanne and Maurice Magnin.

In the copper-domed chapels of a neo-classical church (1709), the **Musée d'Art Sacré** ( ☎ 03 80 44 12 69; 15 rue Ste Anne; adult/senior/student €2.80/1.60/free, admission free Sun; ⏰ 9am-noon & 2pm-6pm Wed-Mon) displays ecclesiastical objects from the 12th to 19th centuries. Almost next door and included in the ticket price, the **Musée de la Vie Bourguignonne** ( ☎ 03 80 44 12 69; 17 rue Ste Anne; ⏰ 9am-noon & 2-6pm Wed-Mon) occupies a 17th-century Cistercian convent and explores rural life in Burgundy in past centuries.

You couldn't really leave Dijon without paying homage to the city's most famous export. Visits to the **Musée de la Moutarde** (48 quai Nicolas Rolin; adult/child €3/free) at the factory of Amora, Dijon's main mustard company, can be arranged at the tourist office.

## Sleeping

**Centre de Rencontres Internationales et de Séjour de Dijon** (CRISD; ☎ 03 80 72 95 20; reservation@auberge -cri-dijon.com; 1 blvd Champollion; s/d/q per person €26/16/13.50) An institutional, 260-bed place 2.8km northeast of the centre. Take bus No 5 (towards Épirey) from place Grangier; at night take line A to Épirey.

**Hôtel Lamartine** ( ☎ 03 80 30 37 47; ot-dijon.fr; 12 rue Jules Mercier; s/d €31/47; ⏰ reception closed noon-3pm) On a shabby backstreet just off rue du Bourg, the 14 rooms are plain and the street views are uninspiring, but the location is unbeatable – the Palace des Ducs is a few steps from the front door.

**Hôtel du Palais** ( ☎ 03 80 67 16 26; fax 03 80 65 12 16; 23 rue du Palais; s/d with shower €30-37/34-43, s/d/tr with bath €40-45/48-65/52-70) One of Dijon's best-kept secrets oozes old-fashioned charm in a former *hotel particulier* near the Quartier d'Antiquaires. The rooms are spacious and welcoming (the best are on the first floor).

**Hôtel le Chambellan** ( ☎ 03 80 67 12 67; hotelchambellan@aol.com; 92 rue Vannerie; s €34-48, d €42-52) A great deal on one of the city's oldest streets. The pretty building is typical, with flower-boxes and shuttered windows, and there is a small 17th-century courtyard where breakfast is served in summer.

**Hostellerie du Sauvage** ( ☎ 03 80 41 31 21; hoteldusauvage@free.fr; 64 rue Monge; d from €41; Ⓟ ) On an idyllic cobbled courtyard in a 15th-century *relais de poste* (relay posthouse), this great-value hotel is off buzzy rue Monge. Parking is available in the old carriage-houses for €4.

## Eating & Drinking

**Au Moulin à Vent** ( ☎ 03 80 30 81 43; 8 pl François Rude; ⏰ closed Sun dinner & Mon) A quintessentially French street-side café opposite the fountain on place François Rude. There's a large terrace outside and a snug restaurant upstairs, serving local specialities.

**Chez Nous** ( ☎ 03 80 50 12 98; 8 impasse Quentin; plat du jour €7; ⏰ Tue-Sat) A tiny neighbourhood bistro down an alleyway off place du Marché. Locals come for the coffee and lunch-time menu; the décor and atmosphere could have been lifted from a café on Paris' Left Bank.

**Hostellerie du Chapeau Rouge** ( ☎ 03 80 50 88 88; bourgogne.net/chapeaurouge; 5 rue Michelet; menu without/with wine €35/42) Bold, creative French cuisine based on traditional ingredients and top-quality local produce. For gastrophiles, the restaurant offers two gourmet menus; €75 buys seven sumptuous courses, while €100 gets a belt-busting 11.

**La Dame d'Aquitaine** ( ☎ 03 80 30 45 65; 23 pl Bossuet; menu €18-35.90; ⏰ closed lunch Sun & Mon) Excellent Burgundian and southwestern French cuisine and the atmospheric location in a vaulted 13th-century cellar make this one of Dijon's most renowned restaurants.

**FRANCE**

**La Petite Marche** ( ☎ 03 80 30 15 10; 27-29 rue Musette; menu €10-15; 7am-9pm Mon-Sat, 9am-noon Sun) Vegetarians tired of Burgundy's meat-heavy menus should head for this popular organic restaurant.

**Osteria Enoteca Italiana** ( ☎ 03 80 50 07 36; 32 rue Amiral Roussin; lunch menu €14; Tue-Sun) A small Italian diner with delicious pasta and fish dishes.

**Pick-Up Café** ( ☎ 03 80 30 61 44; 9 rue Mably; 8am-2am) A typically French idea of an American bar-diner, complete with juke-boxes and pinball machines.

**Coco-Loco** ( ☎ 03 80 73 29 44; 18 ave Garibaldi; 6pm-2am Tue-Sat) This friendly, noisy bar attracts legions of students.

For picnic supplies, head for the 19th-century **covered market** (Halles du Marché; until 1pm Tue, Thu-Sat) and the nearby **fromagerie** (28 rue Musette; closed Sun & Mon morning). Supermarkets include **Monoprix** (11-13 rue Piron; 9am-9pm Mon-Sat) and **Marché Plus** (Rue Bannelier; 7am-9pm Mon-Sat, 9am-noon Sun).

## Entertainment

For the latest on Dijon's cultural scene, pick up *Spectacles,* available free from the tourist office. Dijon's club scene is centred on place de la République.

**L'An-Fer** ( ☎ 03 80 70 03 69; 8 rue Marceau; Wed-Thu €5-7, Fri €9.50, Sat & Sun €8; 11pm-5am Wed-Sun, closed Wed mid-Jul–mid-Sep) achieved fame for pioneering techno music (Laurent Garnier worked here for four years); house music takes centre stage on Saturday.

## Getting There & Away

Five km southeast of the city centre, **Dijon-Bourgogne airport** ( ☎ 03 80 67 67 67) has regular flights to many French cities, as well as Strasbourg and Amsterdam.

The bus station is in the train station complex. Details on services are available at the **Transco information counter** ( ☎ 03 80 42 11 00; 5.30am-8.30pm Mon-Fri, 6.45am-12.30pm & 4-8.30pm Sat, 10am-1pm & 4-8.30pm Sun). Timetables are posted on the platforms; tickets are sold on board.

Paris' Gare de Lyon is just 1¾ hours away by TGV (€46.20, nine to 16 daily). Most trains to Lyon (€22.50, two hours, at least 12 daily) go to Gare de la Part-Dieu. Other long-haul destinations include Nice (€76.20, six hours, two daily) and Strasbourg (€34.60, four hours, three or four non-direct daily).

## Getting Around

To get to the airport, take bus No 1 (towards Longvic) and get off at the Longvic Mairie stop, from where it's a 500m walk Details on Dijon's bus network, operated by **STRD**, are available from **L'Espace Bus** ( ☎ 03 80 30 60 90; pl Grangier; 7.15am-7.15pm Mon-Fri, to 12.15pm & 2.15pm-7.15pm Sat). Single tickets, sold by drivers, cost €0.80 and last for an hour; a Forfait Journée ticket is valid all day and costs €2.70 (available from the tourist office or Espace Bus).

## CÔTE D'OR VINEYARDS

Burgundy's finest vintages come from the vine-covered Côte d'Or (Golden Hillside), the narrow, eastern slopes of a limestone, flint and clay ridge that runs south from Dijon for about 60km. The northern section, the **Côte de Nuits**, stretches from the village of Fixin south to Corgoloin and produces full-bodied, robust reds. The southern section, the **Côte de Beaune** between Aloxe-Corton and Santenay produces great reds and whites.

**Wine & Voyages** ( ☎ 03 80 61 15 15; www.wineand voyages.com) runs minibus tours from Dijon in French and English, including two-hour/three-hour/full-day circuits to the Côte de Nuits vineyards (€45/50/95) from early March to mid-December. It's essential to reserve ahead.

## LYON

**pop 415,000**

Grand old Lyon (Lyons in English) is the focus of a prosperous urban area of almost two million people; France's second-largest conurbation. Lyon boasts museums, dynamic cultural life, hot clubbing and bars, a large university, fantastic shopping and an historical centre precious enough to be protected as a Unesco world heritage site. Gourmets can indulge their wildest gastronomic fantasies here. The city centre is on the Presqu'île, a 500m- to 800m-wide peninsula bounded by the Rivers Rhône and Saône. On the western bank of the Saône, Vieux Lyon (Old Lyon) is sandwiched between the river and the hilltop area of Fourvière.

## Information
### INTERNET ACCESS

**The Albion** ( ☎ 04 78 28 33 00; 12 rue Ste-Catherine, 1er; metro Hôtel de Ville; 7pm-2am Sun-Thu, to 3am Fri & Sat) English pub with free WiFi zone and free Internet access on two terminals.

**LAUNDRY**
**Laundrette** (10 rue Ste-Catherine, 1er; metro Hôtel de Ville; ☉ 6.30am-8.30pm)

**MONEY**
Commercial banks abound on rue Victor Hugo, 2e; rue du Bât d'Argent, 1er; and rue de la République, 1er.
**AOC Exchange** (20 rue Gasparin, 2e; metro Bellecour; ☉ 9.30am-6.30pm Mon-Sat)

**POST**
**Central post office** (10 pl Antonin Poncet, 2e; metro Bellecour)

**TOURIST INFORMATION**
**Tourist office** ( ☎ 04 72 77 69 69; www.lyon-france.com; pl Bellecour, 2e; metro Bellecour; ☉ 9am-7pm Mon-Sat, 10am-6pm Sun mid-Apr–mid-Oct; 10am-6pm Mon-Sat, to 5.30pm Sun mid-Oct–mid-Apr) Buy the **Lyon City Card** (€15/25/30 for 1/2/3 days) here. It allows entry to every museum in Lyon, onto the roof of Basilique Notre Dame de Fourvière, and up Fourvière's Tour de l'Observatoire, also unlimited travel on buses, trams, the funicular and the metro, guided or audioguided city tours, and – between April and October – a free river excursion.

## Sights & Activities
### VIEUX LYON
Old Lyon, with its cobbled streets and **medieval** and **Renaissance houses** below Fourvière hill, is split into three quarters: St-Paul at the northern end, St-Jean in the middle and St-Georges in the south. Facing the river is the **Palais de Justice** (Law Courts; quai Romain Rolland).

The partly Romanesque **Cathédrale St-Jean** (pl St-Jean, 5e; metro Vieux Lyon; ☉ 8am-noon & 2pm-7.30pm Mon-Fri, to noon & 2pm-5pm Sat & Sun), seat of Lyon's 133rd bishop, was built from the late 11th to the early 16th centuries. The portals of its Flamboyant Gothic façade (completed in 1480) are decorated with 280 square stone medallions (early 14th century).

### FOURVIÈRE
Over two millennia ago, the Romans built the city of Lugdunum on the slopes of Fourvière. Today, Lyon's 'hill of prayer' – topped by a basilica and the **Tour Métallique**, a grey, Eiffel Tower-like structure erected in 1893 and used as a TV transmitter – affords spectacular views of Lyon and its two rivers. The funicular departing from place Édouard Commette in Vieux Lyon is the easiest way

up; use a metro ticket or buy a funicular return ticket (€2.20).

Crowning the hill is the ornate **Basilique Notre Dame de Fourvière** (www.lyon-fourviere.com; ☉ 8am-7pm), a superb example of the enthusiasm for embellishment that dominated French ecclesiastical architecture during the late 19th century. **Guided tours** ( ☎ 04 78 25 86 19; adult/child €4/2.50; ☉ 2.30pm & 4pm Mon-Sun Jun-Sep, 2.30pm Oct & Nov, 2.30pm & 4pm Apr-May) last 1¼ hours and take in the roof and various bits inside, and end up at the top of the **Tour de l'Observatoire** (Observatory Tower).

Several sumptuous mosaics and lots of Latin inscriptions are displayed in the **Musée de la Civilisation Gallo-Romaine** (Museum of Gallo-Roman Civilisation; ☎ 04 72 38 81 90; 17 rue Cléberg, 5e; Fourvière funicular station; adult/under 18 yrs €3.80/free, admission free Thu; ☉ 10am-6pm Tue-Sun Mar-Oct, to 5pm Tue-Sun Nov-Feb). Next door to the museum is the **Théâtre Romain,** built around 15 BC and enlarged in AD 120 to seat an audience of 10,000, and the smaller **odéon** where Romans held poetry readings and musical recitals.

### PRESQU'ÎLE
The centrepiece of beautiful **place des Terreaux** (metro Hôtel de Ville) is a 19th-century fountain made of 21 tonnes of lead and sculpted by Frédéric-Auguste Bartholdi, creator of New York's Statue of Liberty.

Next door, the **Musée des Beaux-Arts** (Museum of Fine Arts; ☎ 04 72 10 17 40; 20 pl des Terreaux, 1er; metro Hôtel de Ville; adult/under 18 yrs €6/free; ☉ 10am-6pm Wed-Mon, from 10.30am Fri) showcases France's finest collection of sculptures and paintings – from every period of European art – outside Paris. The free **cloister garden** is a great picnic venue.

Extraordinary Lyonnais silks, French and Asian textiles, and carpets are included in the collection of the **Musée des Tissus** (Textile Museum; ☎ 04 78 38 42 00; www.musee-des-tissus.com; 34 rue de la Charité, 2e; metro Ampère; adult/under 18 yrs €4.60/free; ☉ 10am-5.30pm Tue-Sun). Next door, the **Musée des Arts Décoratifs** (Decorative Arts Museum; free with Textile Museum ticket; ☉ 10am-noon & 2-5.30pm Tue-Sun) showcases 18th-century furniture, tapestries, wallpaper, ceramics and silver.

### OTHER ATTRACTIONS
The brick-and-glass **Cité Internationale** was designed by Italian architect Renzo Piano to host the G7 summit in 1996. Inside, the **Musée d'Art Contemporain** (Museum of Contemporary

FRANCE

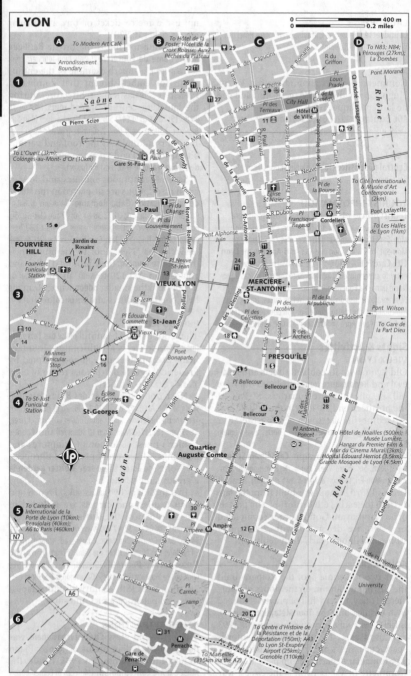

# LYON

0 ————— 400 m
0 ————— 0.2 miles

**A** To Modern Art Café

**B** To Hôtel de la
Poste; Hôtel de la
Croix Rousse; Aux7
Pêchés du Plateau

**C**

**D** To N83; N84;
Pérouges (27km);
La Dombes

Arrondissement
Boundary

**1**

R du
Griffon

R du Capucins

R Romain

Pl
Louis
Pradel

Pont Morand

29

22

26

R de la Martinière

R Terme

R Ste-Catherine

R des Capucins

R d'Algérie

Pl des
Terreaux

3 6

City Hall

Pl de la
Comédie

Rhône

27

Hôtel
de Ville

R André Lassagne

Saône

Q Pierre Scize

11

19

R Constantine

R Lanterne

21

R du Garet

R Paul
Chenavard

R du Président Édouard Herriot

R Neuve

Pl St-
Paul

Pl du
Change

Q de la Pêcherie

Q de Bondy

R d'Octavio Mey

R François Vernay

R Juiverie

R Romain Rolland

Église
St Nizier

R Gentil

Pl de
la Bourse

To Cité Internationale
& Musée d'Art
Contemporain
(2km)

**2**

To L'Ouest (3km);
Colonges-au-Mont-d'Or (10km)

Gare St-Paul

St-Paul

R St-Barthélemy

Pont Lafayette

Pl du
Gouvernement

R de Brest

R Dubois

Pl
Francisque
Regaud

Cordeliers

To Les Halles
de Lyon (1km)

15

Pont Alphonse
Juin

Q St-Antoine

**FOURVIÈRE
HILL**

Jardin du
Rosaire

Montée du Chemin Neuf

R du Bœuf

Pl Neuve
St-Jean

24

17

23 25

R Mercière

R Ferrandière

Pont Wilson

Fourvière
Funicular
Station

B

13

**VIEUX LYON**

**MERCIÈRE-
ST-ANTOINE**

**3**

R Roger Radisson

R Cléberg

10

14

Minimes
Funicular
Stop

Pl
St-Jean

Pl Édouard
Commette

9

**St-Jean**

R des Célestins

Pl des
Jacobins

Pl des
Célestins

Pl de la
République

R Childebert

To Gare de
la Part Dieu

16

Vieux Lyon

R Romain Rolland

18

R des
Archers

**PRESQU'ÎLE**

To St-Just
Funicular
Station

Pont
Bonaparte

R Émile Zola

R Gasparin

1

**4**

Église
St Georges

R du Doyenné

R Tupin

R du Plat

5

Pl Bellecour

Bellecour

28

R de la Barre

**St-Georges**

R St-Georges

Saône

Bellecour

7

Pl Antonin
Poncet

R des Marronniers

To Hôtel de Noailles (500m);
Musée Lumière;
Hangar du Premier Film &
Mur du Cinéma Mural (3km);
Hôpital Édouard Herriot (3.5km);
Grande Mosquée de Lyon (4.5km)

**Quartier
Auguste Comte**

2

R Ste-Hélène

R Sala

Victor Hugo

R de la Charité

Rhône

**5**

To Camping
International de la
Porte de Lyon (10km);
Beaujolais (40km);
A6 to Paris (460km)

N7

R Jarente

30

Ampère

Ampère

12

R Auguste Comte

Q du Docteur Gailleton

Pont de l'Université

R de l'Université

R Aubépin

R d'Enghien

R Henri IV

Ampère

R des Remparts d'Ainay

R Franklin

Claude Bernard

University

A6

R Général Plessier

Pl
Carnot

ramp

R de Condé

R Duhamel

R Pasteur

R Chevreul

**6**

Q Rambaud

31

Perrache

To Centre d'Histoire de
la Résistance et de la
Déportation (150m); A43
to Lyon St-Exupéry
Airport (25km);
Grenoble (110km)

Claude Bernard

Gare de
Perrache

To Marseilles
(315km via the A7)

Av Berthelot

| INFORMATION | | | |
|---|---|---|---|
| AOC Exchange | 1 C4 | Palais de Justice | 13 B3 |
| Central Post Office | 2 C4 | Théâtre Romain | 14 A3 |
| Laundrette | 3 C1 | Tour Métallique | 15 A2 |
| Police Station | 4 C6 | | |
| SNCF Boutique | 5 C4 | SLEEPING ⚅ (p103) | |
| The Albion | 6 C1 | Auberge de Jeunesse du Vieux Lyon | 16 A4 |
| Tourist Office | 7 C4 | Comfort Hôtel St-Antoine | 17 C3 |
| | | Hôtel des Artistes | 18 C3 |
| SIGHTS & ACTIVITIES (pp101–3) | | Hôtel Iris | 19 D1 |
| Basilique Notre Dame de Fourvière | 8 A3 | Sofitel Royal Lyon | 20 C6 |
| Cathédrale St-Jean | 9 B3 | | |
| Musée de la Civilisation Gallo-Romaine | 10 A3 | EATING 🍴 (p104) | |
| Musée des Arts Décoratifs | (see 12) | Café des Fédérations | 21 C2 |
| Musée des Beaux-Arts | 11 C1 | Café-Restaurant des Deux Places | 22 B1 |
| Musée des Tissus | 12 C5 | Commanderie des Antonins | 23 C3 |
| | | Food Market | 24 C3 |

| | |
|---|---|
| Gaston Restaurant Agricole | 25 C3 |
| La Halle de la Martinière | 26 B1 |
| La Table d'Hippolyte | 27 C1 |
| Maison Perroudon | 28 D4 |
| DRINKING 🍸 (p104) | |
| Palais de la Bière | 29 C1 |
| Thé Cha Yuan | 30 B5 |
| TRANSPORT (p105) | |
| Bus Station | 31 B6 |
| Eurolines | (see 31) |
| Intercars | (see 31) |
| Linebús | (see 31) |
| OTHER | |
| Centre d'Échange | (see 31) |

Art; ☎ 04 72 69 17 17; www.moca-lyon.org; 81 quai Charles de Gaulle, 6e; adult/under 18 yrs €3.80/free; ☷ noon-7pm Wed-Sun) displays works created after 1960.

The WWII headquarters of Gestapo chief Klaus Barbie house the evocative **Centre d'Histoire de la Résistance et de la Déportation** ( ☎ 04 78 72 23 11; 14 ave Berthelot, 7e; metro Perrache or Jean Macé; adult/under 18 yrs €3.80/free; ☷ 9am-5.30pm Wed-Sun). Multimedia exhibits present the history of Nazi atrocities and the heroism of French Resistance fighters.

Cinema's glorious beginnings are featured at the **Musée Lumière** ( ☎ 04 78 78 18 95; www.institut-lumiere.org; 25 rue du Premier Film, 8e; metro Monplaisir-Lumière; adult/student €6/5; ☷ 11am-6.30pm Tue-Sun), 3km southeast of place Bellecour along cours Gambetta. It occupies the home of Antoine Lumière who, together with his sons Auguste and Louis, shot the first reels of the world's first motion picture, *La Sortie des Usines Lumières* (Exit of the Lumières Factories) on 19 March 1895. Classic films are screened at the **Hangar du Premier Film**.

## Sleeping

**Camping International de la Porte de Lyon** ( ☎ 04 78 35 64 55; camping-lyon@marie-lyon.fr; allée du Camping, Portes de Lyon; camp sites €13.70; reception ☷ 8am-8pm Mon-Fri, 12.30-8pm Sat & Sun; ☕ ) About 10km northwest of central Lyon in Dardilly, this 215-place camping ground can be reached by bus No 3 from metro Hôtel de Ville or bus No 89 from metro Gare de Vaise.

**Auberge de Jeunesse du Vieux Lyon** ( ☎ 04 78 15 05 50; lyon@fuaj.org; 41-45 montée du Chemin Neuf, 5e; metro Vieux Lyon; dm €12.70; reception ☷ 7am-1pm & 9pm or 10pm-1am) Rates include breakfast at this superbly located hostel above Vieux Lyon. Its 180 beds are split between rooms for two to seven people.

**Hôtel de la Poste** ( ☎ /fax 04 78 28 62 67; 1 rue Victor Fort, 4e; metro Croix Rousse; d/tr €33/46, s/d/q

with shared bath from €17/17/33; reception ☷ 6.30am-8.30pm) Rooms share toilets on the corridor (some showers too) at this back-to-basics hotel where price – not prettiness – pulls in the punters.

**Hôtel Iris** ( ☎ 04 78 39 93 80; hoteliris@freesurf.fr; 36 rue de l'Arbre Sec, 1er; metro Hôtel de Ville; s/d from €36/39, with shared bathroom €29/32) The location of this two-star hotel, inside a wonderful, four-century-old convent, could not be better – so get in quick to snag one of its 11 simple rooms overlooking a quiet courtyard.

**Hôtel de la Croix Rousse** ( ☎ 04 78 28 29 85; 157 blvd de la Croix Rousse, 4e; metro Croix Rousse; d €46; Ⓟ ) Croix Rousse's simple, village-style hotel touts 18 rooms – furnished several decades ago but spick, span and spotlessly clean

**Hôtel de Noailles** ( ☎ 04 78 72 40 72; hotel-de-noailles-lyon@wanadoo.fr; 30 cours Gambetta, 7e; metro Saxe-Gambetta; s/d from €54/62; ☒ Ⓟ ) This charming 24-room hotel is a comfortable choice for those seeking a bed on the *rive gauche* (left bank).

**Comfort Hôtel St-Antoine** ( ☎ 04 78 92 91 91; www.hotel-saintantoine.fr; 1 rue du Port du Temple, 2e; metro Cordeliers; s/d from €63/66; ☒ Ⓟ 💻 ) A stylish mix of old and new – a WiFi zone and period furnishings – greet guests at this thoroughly modern hotel which languishes inside an 18th-century townhouse.

**Hotel des Artistes** ( ☎ 04 78 42 04 88; www.hotel desartistes.fr; 8 rue Gaspard André, 2e; metro Bellecour or Hôtel de Ville; s €70-102, d €79-108) Theatrically furnished rooms are the trademark of this very red, very charming, three-star pad in the heart of Presqu'île shopping land.

**Sofitel Royal Lyon** ( ☎ 04 78 37 57 31; fax 04 78 37 01 36; H2952@accor-hotels.com; 20 pl Bellecour, 2e; metro Bellecour; s/d from €136/150, lux s/d from €215/241, ste €492; Ⓟ ☒ ☒ 💻 ) The most prestigious address on place Bellecour has lavished tender loving luxurious care upon its guests since 1895.

## Eating

**Café des Fédérations** ( ☎ 04 78 28 26 00; www.lesfederationsdelyon.com; 8 rue Major Martin, 1er; metro Hôtel de Ville; dinner menu €23; ☺ Mon-Fri) For proof of the pudding that some things never change, plop yourself down at this splendid little place and feast on *caviar de la Croix Rousse* (lentils dressed in a creamy sauce) and other age-old dishes.

**Café-Restaurant des Deux Places** ( ☎ 04 78 28 95 10; 5 pl Fernand Rey, 1er; metro Hôtel de Ville; menu €22; ☺ Mon-Fri) Checked curtains and an interior crammed with antiques and old photographs contribute to the overwhelmingly traditional feel of this well-placed *bouchon*. Its pavement-terrace beneath trees on a quiet village-like square is a major drawcard.

**L'Ouest** ( ☎ 04 37 64 64 64; www.bocuse.com; 1 quai du Commerce, 9e; metro Gare de Vaise; starters/mains €14/20; ☺ lunch & dinner) Run by the legendary chef Paul Bocuse, one of the oldest and most respected names in the business, the focus is on everything from crab 'n saffron soup to Indonesian-inspired cod and straightforward lamb chops prepared in front of diners in a state-of-the-art open kitchen. Décor is minimalist and avant garde (think glass and wood), and a vast decking space outside overlooks the Saône.

**Aux 7 Péchés du Plateau** ( ☎ 04 78 28 48 82; pl Tapis 3, 4e; metro Croix Rousse; menu €18 & €30; ☺ Mon-Sat) Make no bones about it – diners come here for the meat, not the décor which is strictly bare-bones. This butcher's restaurant serves *salade de rognons blancs et ris d'agneau* (white kidney salad with sweet breads), *tête de veau* (calf's head) and several beef cuts.

**Commanderie des Antonins** ( ☎ 04 78 37 19 21; www.commanderie-antonons.fr; 30 quai St-Antoine, 2e; metro Cordeliers; lunch/dinner menu €15/19.90) Another meaty choice, albeit it a highly refined one, this ode to the carnivorous sees meat cooked the old-fashioned way – slowly over a low heat in a wood-burning oven – and serves it with a flourish in a medieval banquet hall.

**La Table d'Hippolyte** ( ☎ 04 78 27 75 59; 22 rue Hippolyte Flandrin, 1er; metro Hôtel de Ville; lunch menu €17, full dinner around €45; closed Sat lunch, Sun & Mon) Traditional French cuisine is concocted with the freshest seasonal ingredients at this pocket-sized place with a pocket-sized pavement terrace in summer. What's at the market dictates what is chalked up on the board.

**Gaston Restaurant Agricole** ( ☎ 04 72 41 87 86; 41 rue Mercière, 2e; metro Cordeliers; lunch buffet €12; ☺ Mon-Sat) Pack a hearty thirst and giant-sized appetite before venturing into this feisty agricultural restaurant complete with rusty old tractor parked at the front and a liberal scattering of veg-filled wheelbarrows. Dining is around shared wooden tables and the feast-until-your-full lunchtime buffet of cold meat and veg is a steal.

**Maison Perroudon** ( ☎ 04 78 37 37 56; 6 rue de la Barre, 2e; metro Bellecour; ☺ 7am-7.30pm Tue-Sun ✗ ) A predominantly female crowd lunches on light salads. Its cakes are to die for.

Central Lyon has two fantastic **outdoor food markets** (quai St-Antoine, 2e; metro Bellecour or Cordeliers; ☺ Tue-Sun morning; blvd de la Croix Rousse, 4e; metro Croix Rousse; ☺ Tue-Sun morning). The main indoor food markets are **Les Halles de Lyon** (102 cours Lafayette, 3e; metro Part-Dieu; ☺ 7am-noon & 3-7pm Tue-Thu, to 7pm Fri & Sat, to noon Sun) and **La Halle de la Martinière** (24 rue de la Martinière, 1er; metro Hôtel de Ville; ☺ 8am-12.30pm & 4-7.30pm Tue-Sun).

## Drinking

The bounty of café-terraces on place des Terreaux, 1er, buzz with drinkers day and night. English-style pubs are clustered on rue Ste-Catherine, 1er (metro Hôtel de Ville) and in Vieux Lyon.

**Modern Art Café** ( ☎ 04 72 87 06 82; www.modernartcafé.net; 65 blvd de la Croix Rousse, 4e; metro Croix Rousse; ☺ 5-1am Mon-Fri, 11-1am Sat & Sun) Retro furnishings, changing art on the walls, a *plage* (beach) with deckchairs, weekend brunch and a clutch of music- and video-driven happenings make this art bar one cool place to lounge.

**Palais de la Bière** ( ☎ 04 78 27 94 00; 1 rue Terme, 1er; metro Hôtel de Ville; ☺ 6pm-2am Tue-Thu, 6pm-3am Fri & Sat) With 15 beers on tap (€3.40/4.20 for a 25cl glass before/after 9pm) and 300 different types of bottled beers, pint lovers won't go thirsty. An Ardèche-brewed *bière aux marrons* (chestnut beer) is about the only beer produced in the wine-loving Rhône Valley. The truly thirsty can embark on a 15-beer *tour du monde* (world tour).

**Thé Cha Yuan** ( ☎ 04 72 41 04 60; 7-9 rue des Remparts d'Ainay, 2e; metro Ampère; ☺ 9am-7pm Tue-Sat) Some 300 kinds of tea are brewed at this tea room which also serves dim sum – a sublime combination of French elegance and traditional Chinese serenity.

## Entertainment

The tourist office has loads of information on Lyon's rich and varied entertainment scene. Locally published listings guides include the weekly *Lyon Poche* (www.lyon poche.com; €1 at newsagents); the quarterly *Progrescope* (www.progrescope.com) distributed every three months with the local daily newspaper *Le Progrès* (www.leprogres. fr; €0.80 at newsagents); and the free weekly *Le Petit Bulletin* (www.petit-bulletin.fr) available at the tourist office.

## Getting There & Away

Flights from cities around Europe land at **Lyon-St Exupéry airport** (formerly Lyon-Satolas; ☎ 0800 826 826; www.lyon.aeroport.fr), 25km east of the city.

In the Perrache complex **Eurolines** ( ☎ 04 72 56 95 30), **Intercars** ( ☎ 04 78 37 20 80) and Spain-oriented **Linebús** ( ☎ 04 72 41 72 27) have on the bus-station level of the Centre d'Échange (follow the 'Lignes Internationales' signs).

Lyon has two mainline train stations: **Gare de la Part-Dieu** (metro Part-Dieu), 1.5km east of the Rhône, which handles all long-haul trains; and **Gare de Perrache** (metro Perrache), on the Presqu'île, which is increasingly just a regional station. Many long-distance trains stop at both. Just a few local trains stop at **Gare St-Paul** (metro Vieux Lyon) in Vieux Lyon. Tickets are sold at all three stations and in town at the **SNCF Boutique** (2 pl Bellecour, 2e; metro Bellecour; 🕑 9am-6.45pm Mon-Fri, 10am-6.30pm Sat).

Destinations accessible by direct TGV include Paris' Gare de Lyon (€55.60, two hours, every 30 to 60 minutes), Nantes (€102.20, 4¾ hours, six daily), Dijon (€24.20, 1¾ to two hours, at least 12 daily) and Strasbourg (€42.30, five hours, four or five direct daily).

## Getting Around

Public transport – buses, trams, a four-line metro and two funiculars linking Vieux Lyon to Fourvière and St-Just – is run by **TCL** ( ☎ 08 20 42 70 00, www.tcl.fr; 7 bis blvd Vivier Merle, 3e; metro Part-Dieu; 🕑 8.30am-5pm Mon-Fri). It operates from around 5am to midnight. Tickets cost €1.40/11.50 for one/10 and are available from bus and tram drivers and from machines at metro entrances. Tickets allowing unlimited travel for two hours/one day €2/4.20 are also available, as are *tickets jumelés* combining a return a public transport ticket with admission to the Musée Lumière (adult/child €7/6) or aquarium (€11/7).

# THE FRENCH ALPS

The French Alps, where green valleys meet soaring peaks topped with craggy, snowbound summits, form one of the most awesome mountain ranges in the world. Skiing and snowboarding are the region's most obvious attractions, but in summer, visitors can explore hundreds of kilometres of hiking trails and engage in warm-weather sports ranging from paragliding to white-water rafting.

## CHAMONIX

**pop 10,000 / elevation 1037m**

Chamonix is surrounded by the most spectacular scenery in the French Alps. It's almost Himalayan: deeply crevassed glaciers point towards the valley from the icy crown of Mont Blanc, which soars 3.8km above the valley floor.

## Information

### INTERNET ACCESS

**Le CyBar** ( ☎ 04 50 53 69 70; www.cybarchamonix.com; 80 rue des Moulins; 🕑 10am-1.30am; per min €0.10) Computers spread over two floors.

### LAUNDRY

**Laundromats** (40 impasse Primavère; also at 174 ave de l'Aiguille du Midi; 🕑 9am-8pm)

### MONEY

**Le Change** (21 pl Balmat; 🕑 9am-1pm & 3-7pm May, Jun, early Sep-Nov, 8am-8pm Jul-early Sep & Dec-Apr) Generally offers the best rate in town. A 24-hour automated exchange machine accepts banknotes in15 currencies.

### POST

**Post office** (pl Balmat; 🕑 8am-noon & 2pm-6pm Mon-Fri, to noon Sat Sep-Jun, to 7pm Mon-Fri, to noon Sat Jul-Aug)

### TOURIST INFORMATION

**Centrale de Réservation** ( ☎ 04 50 53 23 33; reservation @chamonix.com; 🕑 24hr) Usually takes accommodation bookings for stays of three nights minimum.

**Maison de la Montagne** (190 pl de l'Église) Across the square from the tourist office, and should be your first port of call for finding out about the Mont Blanc area and about winter sports, ski lessons and guided tours and activities.

**Office de Haute Montagne** ( ☎ 04 50 53 22 08; www
.ohm-chamonix.com; 2nd fl, 190 pl de l'Église; ☑ 9am-
12.30pm & 2.30-6.30pm Mon-Sat) Serves walkers, hikers
and mountain climbers, providing information on trails,
hiking conditions and *refuges* (huts).

**Tourist office** ( ☎ 04 50 53 00 24; www.chamonix.com;
85 pl du Triangle de l'Amitié; ☑ 8.30am-12.30pm & 2pm-
7pm Jun-Sep & Dec-Apr, 9am-12.30pm & 2pm-6.30pm
off-season) Offers hundreds of brochures on accommodation and activities, and also sells ski passes. Weather
bulletins are posted here.

## Sights

### AIGUILLE DU MIDI

A jagged pinnacle of rock rising above
glaciers, snowfields and rocky crags, 8km
from the domed summit of Mont Blanc, the

Aiguille du Midi is one of Chamonix's most
famous landmarks. The panoramic views
you'll enjoy from the summit are absolutely
breathtaking.

Return cable-car tickets from Chamonix to the Aiguille du Midi cost adult/child
€34/24. A ride to the téléphérique's halfway point, Plan de l'Aiguille (2317m) – a
top place to start hikes in summer – costs
€12.30/14.40 one way/return.

The *téléphérique*, which leaves from the
end of ave de l'Aiguille du Midi, runs year-
round from 8am (7am in summer). The last
ride up is at 3.30pm (5.30pm in summer).
Be prepared for long queues. You can make
advance reservations 24 hours a day ( ☎ 08
92 68 00 67 premium rate number; booking fee €2).

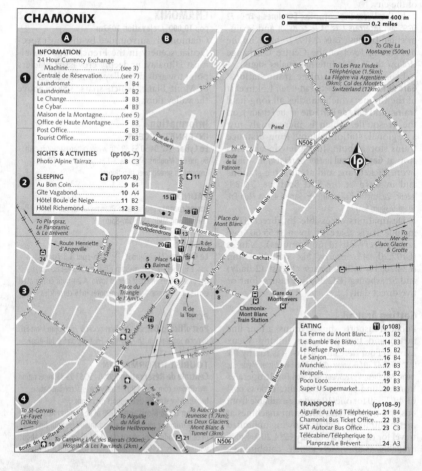

### CHAMONIX

| INFORMATION | |
|---|---|
| 24 Hour Currency Exchange | |
| Machine.....................(see 3) | |
| Centrale de Réservation...........(see 7) | |
| Laundromat.............................1 B4 | |
| Laundromat.............................2 B2 | |
| Le Change.............................3 B3 | |
| Le Cybar.................................4 B3 | |
| Maison de la Montagne............(see 5) | |
| Office de Haute Montagne......5 B3 | |
| Post Office.............................6 B3 | |
| Tourist Office........................7 B3 | |

| SIGHTS & ACTIVITIES (pp106-7) | |
|---|---|
| Photo Alpine Tairraz..................8 C3 | |

| SLEEPING (pp107-8) | |
|---|---|
| Au Bon Coin............................9 B4 | |
| Gîte Vagabond.......................10 A4 | |
| Hôtel Boule de Neige.............11 B2 | |
| Hôtel Richemond....................12 B3 | |

| EATING (p108) | |
|---|---|
| La Ferme du Mont Blanc.........13 B2 | |
| Le Bumble Bee Bistro.............14 B3 | |
| Le Refuge Payot.....................15 B2 | |
| Le Sanjon.............................16 B4 | |
| Munchie...............................17 B3 | |
| Neapolis...............................18 B2 | |
| Poco Loco.............................19 B3 | |
| Super U Supermarket.............20 B3 | |

| TRANSPORT (pp108-9) | |
|---|---|
| Aiguille du Midi Téléphérique....21 B4 | |
| Chamonix Bus Ticket Office.....22 B3 | |
| SAT Autocar Bus Office.........23 C3 | |
| Télécabine/Téléphérique to | |
| Planpraz/Le Brévent.............24 A3 | |

From the Aiguille du Midi, between May and September, you can make the 5km ride in the Panoramic Mont Blanc cable car to **Pointe Helbronner** (3466m) on the Italian border, crossing a vista of glaciers, snow plains and shimmering icefields en route.

### LE BRÉVENT
The highest peak on the western side of the valley (2525m) has fabulous views of the Mont-Blanc massif. It can be reached by **télécabine** and **téléphérique** ( ☎ 04 50 53 13 18; adult/child return €15.50/11) from the end of Chemin de la Mollard. The lifts are open 8am to 5.45pm in summer, 9am to 5pm in winter.

Several hiking trails can be picked up at Le Brévent or at the *télecabine*'s midway station, **Planpraz** (1999m; €8.50/10.50 one way/return).

### MER DE GLACE
The Mer de Glace (Sea of Ice), the second largest glacier in the Alps, is 14km long, 1800m wide and up to 400m deep. The glacier moves 45m a year at the edges, and up to 90m a year in the centre, and has become a popular tourist attraction thanks to the rack-and-pinion railway line built between 1897 and 1908.

Since 1946, the **Grotte de la Mer de Glace** (ice cave; ☼ late May-late Sep) has been carved every spring – work begins in February and takes three months. The interior temperature is between -2 and -5°C. Look down the slope for last year's cave to see how far the glacier has moved.

With avalanche proofing over parts of the tracks, the train – which leaves from **Gare du Montenvers** ( ☎ 04 50 53 12 54) in Chamonix and creeps up to Montenvers (1913m) – runs year-round. Trains run from 10am to 4pm in winter (longer in summer). The 20-minute trip costs €14 return. From Montenvers, a *téléphérique* takes tourists to the cave. A combined ticket valid for the train, *téléphérique,* and admission to the cave costs adult/child €21/15.

The Mer de Glace can be reached on foot via the Grand Balcon Nord trail from Plan de l'Aiguille. The uphill trail from Chamonix (two hours) begins near the summer luge track. Traversing the glacier and its crevasses requires proper equipment and an experienced guide.

## Activities
In late spring and summer (about mid-June to October), 310km of spectacular walking trails open up around Chamonix. The most rewarding are the high-altitude trails reached by cable car. The *téléphériques* shut down in the late afternoon, but in June and July there is enough light to walk until 9pm or later.

The combined map and guide *Carte des Sentiers du Mont Blanc* (Mountain Trail Map; €4) is ideal for straightforward day walks. The most useful map is the 1:25,000 IGN map entitled *Chamonix-Massif du Mont Blanc* (No 3630OT; €9). Both are sold at Photo Alpine Tairraz. *The Most Beautiful Hikes for Everyone* (Editions Aio; €4.50) details easy day hikes in the Mont Blanc region.

The **Grand Balcon Sud** trail along the western side of the valley stays at around 2000m and affords great views of Mont Blanc. On foot, it can be reached from behind Le Brévent's *télécabine* station. For less uphill walking, take either the Planpraz or La Flégère lifts.

### CANYONING
Summer canyoning expeditions are offered by **Yannick Seigneur** (mobile ☎ 06 09 48 51 77; info@yannickseigneur.com), in the Mont Blanc mountains. A half-/full day canyoning course costs €54.90/83.85.

## Sleeping
### BUDGET
Because of the altitude, it's nearly always chilly at night if you're camping. Most mountain *refuges* (huts; €14-20 a night) are accessible to hikers, though some can be reached only by mountain climbers. Breakfast and dinner, prepared by the warden, are often available for an extra fee. It's essential to reserve a place – you don't want to hike halfway across Mont Blanc to find the *refuge* full. For information, contact the CAF (see Maison de la Montagne; p105). *Gîte* accommodation can also be a good way to cut costs.

**L'Île des Barrats** ( ☎ 04 50 53 51 44; 185 chemin d'Ile des Barrats; ☼ May-Oct) This three-star site is in a quiet clearing, near the base of the Aiguille du Midi *téléphérique*.

**Les Deux Glaciers** ( ☎ 04 50 53 15 84; glaciers@clubinter net.fr; 80 route des Tissières; ☼ closed mid-Nov–mid-Dec)

Another three-star place in Les Bossons, 3km south of Chamonix. To get there, take the train to Les Bossons or the Chamonix Bus to the Tremplin-le-Mont stop.

**Auberge de Jeunesse** ( ☎ 04 50 53 14 52; chamonix@fuaj.org; 127 montée Jacques Balmat; dm with breakfast €17; ☺ check in 8am-noon & 5-10pm, closed early May & Oct–mid-Dec) In Les Pélerins, 2km south-west of Chamonix, this hostel can be reached by bus. Take the Chamonix-Les Houches line and get off at the Pélerins École stop. In winter, only weekly packages are available, including bed, food, ski pass and ski hire for six days. There's no kitchen.

**Gîte La Montagne** ( ☎ 04 50 53 11 60; www.leva gabond.co.uk; 789 promenade des Crémeries; dm €12; ☺ closed 11 Nov-20 Dec) An attractive *gîte* in a traditional alpine-style building on a for-ested site, 1.5km north of the train station (near La Frasse bus-stop).

**Gîte Vagabond** ( ☎ 04 50 53 15 43; fax 04 50 53 68 21; 365 ave Ravanel-le-Rouge; dm €12.50, half-board €28; 🖳 ) A neat hostelry with a kitchen, bar/restaurant with Internet access, BBQ area, climbing wall and parking. Beds are in four- or six-person dorms.

### MID-RANGE
During July, August and the ski season, ho-tels are heavily booked, so reserve ahead.

**Hôtel Boule de Neige** ( ☎ 04 50 53 04 48; 362 rue Joseph Vallot; s/d from €36/56) A chalet-style hotel halfway up the lively rue Joseph Vallot. The rooms are as basic as they come, but there's an attractive mountain-town feel helped by the little local bar downstairs.

**Au Bon Coin** ( ☎ 04 50 53 15 67; hotelauboncoin@ wanadoo.fr; 80 ave de l'Aiguille du Midi; d €54.50-62; 🅿 ) One of the best year-round deals in Cha-monix. Perched above busy shops, it looks drab from the front; but the rear rooms are south-facing, and most have small balco-nies offering views of Mont Blanc.

**Hôtel Richemond** ( ☎ 04 50 53 08 85; fax 04 50 55 91 69; 228 rue du Docteur Paccard; d low/high €66/80; 🅿 ) A vast, austere hotel where the prices stay low even in high season, which means it's nearly always full. The best rooms have mountain views; the worst have a view of the car park.

## Eating
**Neapolis** ( ☎ 04 50 53 98 41; 79 Gallerie Alpina; pizza & pasta €6.40-9.90; ☺ Mon-Sat) Simply Italian this restaurant overlooks the river and has

cheap, wholesome cooking – which makes it very popular.

**Le Sanjon** ( ☎ 04 50 53 56 44; 5 ave Ravanel-le-Rouge; menu €15-25) A picturesque wooden chalet res-taurant serving *raclette* – a block of melted cheese, usually eaten with potatoes and cold meats (€12) and fondue (€11 to €21).

**Munchie** ( ☎ 04 50 53 45 41; 87 rue des Moulins; mains €10-25; ☺ closed lunchtimes) A trendy place with excellent pan-Asian food, exciting mains include blackened salmon *sashimi*, Thai Chicken with pimento and ginger and sushi.

**Le Bumble Bee Bistro** ( ☎ 04 50 53 50 03; 65 rue des Moulins) A tiny, welcoming café which serves hot, hearty meals throughout the day. Cod fritters, chargrilled chicken, steak and ale pie and potato wedges are ideal after a hard day on the slopes, but veggies should try the Red Dragon Pie, stuffed full of vegetables, lentils and spicy beans.

**Poco Loco** ( ☎ 04 50 53 43 03; 47 rue du Docteur Paccard; pizza €5-7, menu from €7) One of several sandwich shops near place Balmat, with hot paninis (from €3.80), sweet crepes (from €1.50) and huge burgers.

There's a **Super U Supermarket** (117 rue Joseph Vallot; ☺ 8.15am-7.30pm Mon-Sat, to 12.45pm Sun in winter). **Le Refuge Payot** (166 rue Joseph Vallot) and **La Ferme du Mont Blanc** (202 rue Joseph Vallot) stock an excellent range of cheeses, meats and other local products.

## Getting There & Away
The bus station is in the train-station build-ing. The office of **SAT Autocar** ( ☎ 04 50 53 01 15; www.satobus-alps.com; ☺ 6.45-10.30pm & 1.25pm-4.45pm Mon-Fri, to 11pm & 1.25pm-4.45pm Sat & Sun in winter, hrs vary summer) is near the train station en-trance. Buses operate to Geneva bus station (€33, 1½ to two hours) and Geneva airport (€33, 2¼ hours). Services to Italy, through the Mont Blanc tunnel, include Courmayeur (€18 return) and Aoste (€22 return).

The Chamonix-Mont Blanc **train station** ( ☎ 04 50 53 12 98) is at the end of ave Michel Croz. Here you'll find a **left-luggage counter** (☺ 6am-8pm).

Major destinations include Paris' Gare de Lyon (€86.50, six to seven hours, five daily), Lyon (€31.70, 4½ hours via Annecy), Geneva (€16.60, four hours via Annecy or Chambéry), and Grenoble (27.90, five hours via Annecy). There's an overnight train to Paris (€98.90, 10hrs) year-round.

## Getting Around

Bus transport is handled by **Chamonix Bus** (☎ 04 50 53 05 55; pl du Triangle de l'Amitié; ⏰ 7am-7pm in winter, 8am-noon & 2pm-7pm Jun-Aug).

## ANNECY

**pop 50,000 / elevation 448m**

Annecy, the chic capital of Haute-Savoie, is an unquestionably pretty lakeside town, criss-crossed with ancient canals and lined with arched alleyways and medieval houses. Visitors in a languid mood can stroll along the lakefront or mosey around the old city, admiring the Alpine peaks or the geranium-covered bridges, while more active types can take to the waters of Lac d'Annecy in pedalos, canoes and cruise-boats.

## Orientation

The train and bus stations are 500m northwest of the Vieille Ville (Old City), which is huddled around the River Thiou (split into Canal du Thiou to the south and Canal du Vassé to the north). The town centre is between the post office and the purpose-built Centre Bonlieu, which houses the city's theatre and the tourist office, near the shores of Lac d'Annecy.

## Information

**Main post office** (4 bis rue des Glières; ⏰ 8am-7pm Mon-Fri, 9am-noon Sat)

**Syndrome Cybercafé** (☎ 04 50 45 39 75; infos@syndrome.com; 3 bis ave de Chevêne; ⏰ noon-midnight daily; Internet per 15min/hr €2/6)

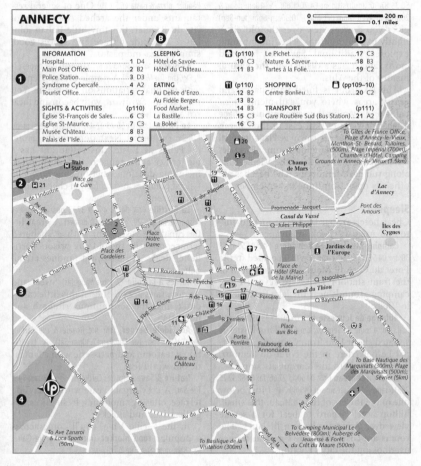

ANNECY

| | | 0 | 200 m |
| | | 0 | 0.1 miles |

**INFORMATION**
Hospital........................................1 D4
Main Post Office.........................2 B2
Police Station.............................3 D3
Syndrome Cybercafé..................4 A2
Tourist Office.............................5 C2

**SIGHTS & ACTIVITIES** (p110)
Église St-François de Sales.........6 C3
Église St-Maurice.......................7 C3
Musée Château..........................8 B3
Palais de l'Isle............................9 C3

**SLEEPING** (p110)
Hôtel de Savoie........................10 C3
Hôtel du Château.....................11 B3

**EATING** (p110)
Au Delice d'Enzo......................12 B2
Au Fidéle Berger.......................13 B2
Food Market.............................14 B3
La Bastille.................................15 C3
La Bolée...................................16 C3

Le Pichet..................................17 C3
Nature & Saveur.......................18 B3
Tartes à la Folie........................19 C2

**SHOPPING** (pp109–10)
Centre Bonlieu.........................20 C2

**TRANSPORT** (p111)
Gare Routière Sud (Bus Station)...21 A2

To Gîtes de France Office,
Plage d'Annecy-le-Vieux,
Menthon-St-Benard, Talloires,
(500m); Plage Impérial (700m);
Chambre d'Hôtel, Camping
Grounds in Annecy-le-Vieux (1.5km)

To Base Nautique des
Marquisats (300m); Plage
des Marquisats (500m);
Sévrier (5km)

To Ave Zanaroi
& Loca Sports
(50m)

To Basilique de la
Visitation (300m)

To Camping Municipal Le
Belvédère (800m); Auberge de
Jeunesse & Forêt
du Crêt du Maure (500m)

**FRANCE**

**Tourist office** ( ☎ 04 50 45 00 33; www.lac-annecy.com; 1 rue Jean Jaurès;  9am-12.30pm & 1.45-6pm Mon-Sat mid-Sep–mid-May, to 6.30pm Mon-Sat mid-May–mid-Sep, to 12.30pm & 1.45-6pm Sun Jul-Sep, 10am-1pm Sun Oct) In the Centre Bonlieu.

## Sights & Activities

The **Vieille Ville**, a warren of narrow streets and colonnaded passageways, retains much of its 17th-century appearance. On the central island, the imposing **Palais de l'Isle** ( ☎ 04 50 33 87 31; adult/student €3.05/0.75;  10am-6pm Jun-Sep, to noon & 2-6pm Wed-Mon Oct-May) was once a prison, but now houses local history displays.

Located in the 13th-16th century castle above the town, **Musée Château** ( ☎ 04 50 33 87 30; adult/student €4.70/1.60;  10am-noon & 2pm-6pm Wed-Mon Oct-May, 10.30am-6pm Jun-Sep) gives you a great view over the old city's tightly packed rooftops. The fine museum explores traditional Savoyard art and crafts, and it has a display on the natural history of the Alps.

The lakefront is lined with parks and grassy areas where you can picnic, sunbathe and swim in the warm months. **Plage d'Annecy-le-Vieux** is 1km east of the Champ de Mars. Closer to town is **Plage Impérial** (€3), which has changing rooms. **Plage des Marquisats** is 1km south of the Vieille Ville along rue des Marquisats. The beaches are officially open from June to September.

## Sleeping

Cheap hotels are hard to find from mid-July to mid-August – book in advance.

**Camping Municipal Le Belvédère** ( ☎ 04 50 45 48 30; fax 04 50 45 55 56; camp sites €13) Located in the Forêt du Crêt du Maure, is 2.5km south of the train station. There are several other camping grounds near the lake in Annecy-le-Vieux.

**Auberge de Jeunesse** ( ☎ 04 50 45 33 19; annecy@ fuaj.com; 4 route du Semnoz; dm €12) This hostel is situated about 1km from Camping Municipal Le Belvédère in the Forêt du Semnoz. Take bus No 1 to the Marquisats stop.

**Hôtel du Château** ( ☎ 04 50 45 27 66; fax 04 50 52 75 26; 16 rampe du Château; s/d €45-60;  ) Just below one of the towers of the château, this small, hilltop hotel is hard to beat for a serene view over Annecy's lantern-lit lanes. The rooms are cosy and there's a great terrace overlooking the city's rooftops.

**Chambre d'hôte** ( ☎ 04 50 45 72 28; rampe du Château; d €60-80) A good choice in a big period house next to Hôtel du Château.

**Hôtel de Savoie** ( ☎ 04 50 45 15 45; fax 04 50 45 11 99; 1 pl de St-François; s/d €45-70) Once a convent, this little hotel (full of character) has its entrance on the left side of Église St-François de Sales. It is a small, friendly place with relatively simple rooms and a great location.

## Eating

In the Vieille Ville, the quays along both sides of Canal du Thiou are lined with cafés and restaurants. There are lots of cheap places along rue du Pâquier.

**Au Delice d'Enzo** ( ☎ 04 50 45 35 36; 17 rue du Pâquier; pizza & pasta €6.50-10) One of several restaurants under the arched colonnades of rue du Paquier, this tiny little Italian joint has a streetside terrace and serves good, simple pizza and pasta.

**La Bolée** ( ☎ 04 50 45 26 62; 14 rue de l'Isle; crepes €7-9;  Thu-Tue May-Sep) A simple Breton creperie with regional variations on the theme. You must try the *Savoyard*, with bacon and local *reblochon* cheese.

**Le Pichet** ( ☎ 04 50 45 32 41; 13 rue Perrière; menu €18-29;  Thu-Mon) Next door to the Hôtel du Palais de L'Isle, this restaurant has a big terrace and a range of Savoyard dishes, including delicious, diet-busting *tartiflette* (sliced potatoes and *reblochon* cheese baked in the oven).

**La Bastille** ( ☎ 04 50 45 09 37; 3 quai des Vieilles Prison; menu €11-20;  lunch & dinner) A great little canalside restaurant with a sheltered terrace, opposite the old city prison. Tartiflette, steaks and Savoyard fondues are all delicious.

**Tartes à la Folie** (7-9 rue Vaugelas) Sweet and savoury tarts are on offer at this little café – don't miss the scrumptious rhubarb and nut tarts.

**Au Fidèle Berger** (cnr rue Royale & rue Carnot;  9.15am-7pm Tue-Fri, 9am-7.30pm Sat) A traditional tearoom and patisserie with a fantastic old-world feel.

**Nature & Saveur** (pl des Cordeliers;  8.30am-7pm Tue-Sat) A cosy organic café with a quayside terrace, offering smoothies, fresh juices, organic salads and snacks.

In the Vieille Ville, you'll come across a popular **food market** (rue Faubourg Ste-Claire;  8am-noon Sun, Tue & Fri).

## Getting There & Away

Annecy's small **airport** ( ☎ 04 50 27 30 06; 8 route Côte Merle) is north of the city in Meythet, just west of the autoroute to Geneva. The airport has daily flights to Paris' Orly Sud, Lilles, Nantes, Bordeaux and Toulouse.

The bus station, **Gare Routière Sud** (rue de l'Industrie) is next to the train station. Exits from the train-station platforms lead directly to the bus station.

The **Voyages Crolard** ( ☎ 04 50 45 08 12; ⌚ 7.15am-12.15pm & 1.30-7.30pm Mon-Sat, 7.45am-noon Sun) serves various points around Lake Annecy, including Menthon, Talloires and Roc de Chère on the eastern shore; Sévrier on the western shore; and Bout du Lac on the southern tip. Other destinations include La Clusaz (€9.20, 50 minutes), Albertville (€7.70, 1¼ hours) and Chamonix (€15.80, two hours).

**Autocars Frossard** ( ☎ 04 50 45 73 90; ⌚ 7.45am-11am & 2-7.15pm Mon-Fri, to 1pm Sat) sells tickets to Annemasse, Chambéry, Évian, Geneva, Grenoble, Nice and Thonon.

The information counters at the **train station** ( ☎ 08 36 35 35 35; pl de la Gare) are open 9am to noon and 2pm to 7pm daily, and the ticket windows are open 5am to 10.30pm Monday to Friday, 9am to 7.30pm Saturday and Sunday.

There are frequent trains to Paris' Gare de Lyon (€76.40 by TGV, 3¾ hours), Nice (€65.50, 7½ hours), Lyon (€19, three hours). The night train to Paris (€70.30, eight hours), often full at weekends, leaves between 9pm and 10pm.

## GRENOBLE

pop 156,000

The elegant, modern city of Grenoble is the intellectual and economic capital of the Alps, spectacularly sited in a broad valley surrounded by snow-capped mountains. The city's modern shops, broad boulevards and varied architecture make it a great place to spend a few days soaking up the big-city atmosphere. The large university serves a student body of 50,000.

## Orientation

The old city is centred around place Grenette and place Notre-Dame, both about 1km east of the train and bus stations. The main university campus is a couple of kilometres east of the old centre on the southern side of the River Isère.

## Information

### INTERNET ACCESS

**Neptune Internet Services** ( ☎ 04 76 63 94 18; 2 de la Paix; ⌚ 9am-9pm Mon-Fri, to 8pm Sat, 1-8pm Sun; salle-Internet@neptune.fr; per 15min/hr €2/3.50) Wireless networking and laptop connection points. Discounts from noon to 2pm and 7pm to 9pm.

### LAUNDRY

**Lavomatique** (14 rue Thiers; ⌚ 7am-10pm) Opposite Hôtel Victoria.

### POST

**Main post office** (7 blvd Maréchal Lyautey; ⌚ 8am-6.45pm Mon-Fri, to noon Sat)

### TOURIST INFORMATION

**Cargo Kiosk** ( ⌚ 1pm-6.30pm Tue-Sat) Events tickets.
**SNCF Counter** ( ⌚ 8.30am-6.30pm Mon-Fri, 9am-6pm Sat) For train information.
**TAG office** ( ⌚ 8.30am-6.30pm Mon-Fri, 9am-6pm Sat) Local bus information.
**Tourist office** ( ☎ 04 76 42 41 41; www.grenoble-isere .info; 14 rue de la République; ⌚ 9.30am-6pm year-round, 10am-1pm Sun Oct-Apr, 10am-1pm & 2pm-4pm May-Sep) Located inside the large purpose-built Maison du Tourisme on rue de la Republique.

## Sights

Looming above the old city on the northern side of the Isère river, the 16th century **Fort de la Bastille** is Grenoble's best-known landmark. The views are spectacular, with vast mountains on every side and the bridges and grey waters of the Isère river below. To get to the fort, a **téléphérique** ( ☎ 04 76 44 33 65; oneway/return €3.80/5.50, students €3/4.40) leaves from Quai Stéphane Jay between the Marius Gontard and St-Laurent bridges. It gets crowded in summer – leave early to avoid the worst queues.

The sleek glass and steel exterior of Grenoble's boldest museum, the **Musée des Beaux-Arts** ( ☎ 04 76 63 44 44; 5 pl de Lavalette; www.museedegrenoble.fr; adult/student €5/2; ⌚ 10am-6.30pm, closed Tue), stands at the southern end of place Notre-Dame. It's renowned for its distinguished modern collection, which includes work by Chagall, Matisse, Modigliani, Monet, Picasso, Pissaro, Gauguin and others.

**Musée Dauphinois** ( ☎ 04 76 85 19 01; www .musee-dauphinois.fr; 30 rue Maurice Gignoux; ⌚ 10am-7pm Wed-Mon May-Oct, to 6pm Nov-Apr) documents the cultures, crafts and traditions of Alpine

# GRENOBLE

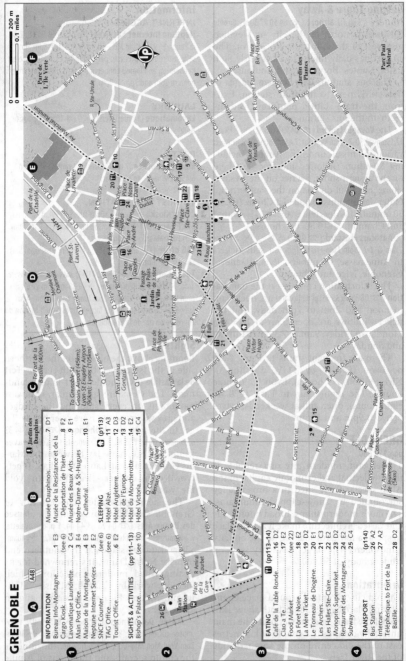

**INFORMATION**
| | |
|---|---|
| Bureau Info-Montagne.........................1 | E3 |
| Cargo Kiosk.................................(see 6) | |
| Lavomatic Laundrette.......................2 | C4 |
| Main Post Office.............................3 | E4 |
| Maison de la Montagne......................4 | E3 |
| Neptune Internet Services...................5 | E2 |
| SNCF Counter...............................(see 6) | |
| TAG Office..................................6 | E2 |
| Tourist Office...............................6 | E2 |

**SIGHTS & ACTIVITIES (pp111-13)**
| | |
|---|---|
| Bishop's Palace.............................(see 10) | |
| Jardin des Dauphins.........................7 | D1 |
| Musée Dauphinois...........................7 | D1 |
| Musée de la Resistance et de la | |
|   Déportation de l'Isère......................8 | F2 |
| Musée des Beaux Arts........................9 | E1 |
| Notre-Dame & St-Hugues | |
|   Cathedral.................................10 | E1 |

**SLEEPING (p113)**
| | |
|---|---|
| Hôtel Alize................................11 | A3 |
| Hôtel Angleterre...........................12 | D3 |
| Hôtel de l'Europe...........................13 | D2 |
| Hôtel du Moucherotte......................14 | E2 |
| Hôtel Victoria.............................15 | C4 |

**EATING (pp113-14)**
| | |
|---|---|
| Café de la Table Ronde......................16 | D2 |
| Ciao a Te..................................17 | E2 |
| Food Market.............................(see 22) | |
| La Forêt Noire.............................18 | E2 |
| La Mère Ticket............................19 | D2 |
| Le Tonneau de Diogène......................20 | E1 |
| Les Archers...............................21 | C3 |
| Les Halles Ste-Claire.......................22 | E2 |
| Monoprix Supermarket.....................23 | D2 |
| Restaurant des Montagnes..................24 | E2 |
| Subway..................................25 | C4 |

**TRANSPORT (p114)**
| | |
|---|---|
| Bus Station................................26 | A2 |
| Intercars.................................27 | A2 |
| Téléphérique to Fort de la | |
|   Bastille................................28 | D2 |

life. The museum occupies a beautiful 17th-century convent, nestled at the foot of the hill below Fort de la Bastille. From the city centre, it is most easily reached by the Pont St-Laurent footbridge.

The **Notre Dame and St-Hugues Cathedral** (pl Notre Dame) and the adjoining 14th-century **Bishop's Palace** ( ☎ 04 76 03 15 25; 2 rue Très Cloîtres; ancien-eveche-isere.com; admission free; ❧ 9am-6pm Mon-Sat except Tue, 10am-7pm Sun) have had complete facelifts and now contain three museums: the **crypte archéologique**, with Roman walls and a baptistery dating from the 4th to 10th century; the **Musée d'Art Sacré**, which contains liturgical and religious objects; and the **Centre Jean Achard**, with exhibits of art from the Dauphiné region.

This moving **Musée de la Résistance et de la Déportation de l'Isère** ( ☎ 04 76 42 38 53; 14 rue Hébert; admission free; ❧ 9am-7pm Wed-Mon Jun-Aug; to noon & 2-6pm Wed-Mon, from 10am Sun Sep-May) examines the deportation of Jews and other 'undesirables' from Grenoble to Nazi camps during WWII, and explores the role of the Vercors region in the French Resistance. Captions are in French, English and German.

## Activities

For information on outdoor activities, head for the **Maison de Montagne** ( ☎ 08 25 82 55 88; 3 rue Raoul Blanchard). All the main organisations are housed under one roof. The **Bureau Info-Montagne** ( ☎ 04 76 42 45 90; fax 04 76 42 87 08; ❧ 9am-noon & 2pm-6pm Mon-Fri, 10am-1pm & 2-6pm Sat) can give advice on just about every imaginable mountain activity except skiing. It sells hiking maps and has information on *gîtes d'étape* and *refuges* (huts).

The tourist office has comprehensive information, including accommodation lists, for all of Grenoble's surrounding ski resorts.

## Sleeping

**Auberge de Jeunesse** ( ☎ 04 76 09 33 52; grenoble@ fuaj.org; 10 ave du Grésivaudan; dm €12; reception ❧ 7.30am-11pm) This hostel is 5km south of the train station in the Echirolles district. From Cours Jean Jaurès, take bus No 1 to the Quinzaine stop (look for the Casino supermarket). Breakfast is included.

**Hôtel du Moucherotte** ( ☎ 04 76 54 61 40; fax 04 76 44 62 52; 1 rue Auguste Gaché; s/d from €28.20/30.25) If you're budgeting, the murky Moucherotte is one of the cheapest options near the city centre. Despite its dingy exterior, the rooms are clean but basic.

**Hôtel de l'Europe** ( ☎ 04 76 46 16 94; www.hoteleurope .fr; 22 pl Grenette; s €26-53, d €28-59) One of the city's oldest establishments, housed in a classic Grenoblois building above pl Grenette. It's a great value hotel with big rooms and a fabulous spiral staircase to the top floor. The front rooms have balconies with great views.

**Hôtel Alizé** ( ☎ 04 76 43 12 91; fax 04 76 47 62 79; 1 rue Amiral Courbet; s/d €31/36, tr €44-48) Small, simple and very cheap hotel which makes it popular – book in advance.

**Hôtel Victoria** ( ☎ 04 76 46 06 36; 17 rue Thiers; s/d from €32/36.30; ❧ Sep-Jul; ⓟ ) Tucked away in a quiet courtyard in the Place Condorcet Area, this place has old-fashioned floral décor and friendly owners. The lively place Condorcet area has lots of low-rent restaurants and scruffy bars.

**Hôtel Angleterre** ( ☎ 04 76 87 37 21; www.hotel -angleterre.fr; 5 pl Victor-Hugo; s/d €88-150) The pick of several three-star hotels in the area, thanks to its luxurious rooms and a great location opposite the fountain-adorned pl Victor-Hugo. Accepts 'Bon-Weekend' reservations.

## Eating

**Le Tonneau de Diogène** ( ☎ 04 76 42 38 40; 6 pl Notre Dame; menu from €6, plat du jour €10; ❧ 8.30-1am) A cramped, wonderfully atmospheric place, decked out with polished wood, leather booths, and lots of tightly packed tables.

**Café de la Table Ronde** ( ☎ 04 76 44 51 41; 7 pl St-André; lunch menu €10; ❧ 7am-midnight Mon-Sat) Another of Grenoble's most famous cafés, it was a favoured haunt of Stendhal and Rousseau, and the old-world atmosphere and period furnishings don't seem to have changed much since they were around.

**La Forêt Noire** (pl Ste-Claire) A Grenoble institution for afternoon tea. The café serves a lavish range of cakes, tarts and *viennoiseries*, as well as light meals. Look no further for something sweet and sticky.

**La Mère Ticket** ( ☎ 04 76 44 45 40; 13 rue Jean-Jacques Rousseau; ❧ lunch & 8-11pm Mon-Sat) A tiny, traditional French restaurant tucked away on a busy shopping street. The homely country cooking is fantastic value, especially at lunchtime (€10, 11 with dessert). The delicious *poulet aux écrevisses* (chicken with crayfish) and *gratin dauphinois* come highly recommended.

**Restaurant des Montagnes** ( ☎ 04 76 15 20 72; 5 rue Brocherie; ☻ 7pm-midnight Sep-Jun) Grenoble's premier place for fondue and *tartiflette*. Loosen your belt and order one of the 13 kinds of sumptuous fondue (€12.50 to €21 per person – minimum two people).

**Les Archers** ( ☎ 04 76 46 27 76; 2 rue Docteur Bailly; ☻ 11-1am) A brasserie with great outside seating in summer. Fish and seafood are especially good, with delicacies including pan-fried trout and grilled sea bass.

**Ciao a Te** ( ☎ 04 76 42 54 41; 2 rue de la Paix; ☻ Tue-Sat) A vibrant Italian restaurant which serves great pasta from around €10. If you're feeling hungry, try the filling, delicious cannelloni.

**Les Halles Ste-Claire** ( ☻ 6am-1pm Tue-Sun) is Grenoble's lovely old covered market. Even if you're not going there to shop, the market atmosphere is worth investigating. There's also a busy **food market place Ste-Claire** ( ☻ Wed-Mon). There's a **Monoprix supermarket** (cnr rue de la République & rue Lafayette; ☻ 8.30am-7.30pm Mon-Sat).

## Getting There & Away
### AIR
Domestic flights are handled by **Grenoble-St-Geoirs airport** ( ☎ 04 76 65 48 48), 41km northwest of Grenoble. International flights operate to/from **Lyon-St Exupéry airport** ( ☎ 08 26 80 08 26), 90km from the city off the A43 to Lyon.

### BUS
The **bus station** ( ☎ 04 76 87 90 31; rue Émile Gueymard; ☻ 6.30am-7pm Mon-Sat, 7.15am-7pm Sun) is next to the train station, and is the main terminus for several bus companies. **VFD** ( ☎ 08 20 83 38 33; www.vfd.fr; ☻ 8am-6pm Tue-Fri, to noon & 1.30pm-4.30pm Sat & Mon) serves most Alpine destinations; tariffs are worked out on a zone system according to how far you travel. Destinations include the Vercors ski stations.

**Intercars** ( ☎ 04 76 46 19 77; www.intercars.fr; station office ☻ 9am-noon & 2-6pm Mon-Fri, to noon & 2pm-5pm Sat) handles long-haul destinations including Budapest (€88, 22hrs), Munich (€72, 10½ hours), Rome (€48, 13½ hours), Milan (€23, 5½ hours), Zurich (€31, five) and Geneva (€12, 2½ hours).

### TRAIN
The huge, modern **train station** ( ☎ 08 36 35 35 35; rue Émile Gueymard; ☻ 4.30am-2am) is next to the Gare Europole tram stop, which is served by both tramlines (see Getting Around).

Destinations served include Paris' Gare de Lyon (from €63.30, 3½ hours by TGV), Chambéry (€9, one hour, 14 daily) and Lyon (€16.30, 1½ hours, five daily), from where you can catch trains to Nice and Monaco. There are also daily trains to Turin (€44), Milan (€54, change at Chambéry), and Geneva (€19.70, two hours).

## Getting Around
### TO/FROM THE AIRPORT
The bus ( ☎ 04 76 87 90 31) to Lyon-St Exupéry airport stops at the bus station (€20/30 one way/return, 65 minutes). Buses to the Grenoble-St-Geoirs domestic airport depart from the bus station (€13/20 one way/return, 45 minutes).

### BUS & TRAM
Grenoble's two tram lines – sensibly called A and B – both stop at the tourist office and the train station, and run through the heart of town. Bus and tram tickets cost €1.20 and are available from ticket machines at tram stops or from drivers. They must be time-stamped in the blue machines located at each stop before boarding. Tickets are valid for transfers – but not return trips – within one hour.

A *carnet* of 10 tickets costs €9.50. Daily/five-day passes (Visitag) are available for €3.20/11 at the **TAG information desk** ( ☎ 04 76 20 66 66) at the tourist office, or from the TAG office outside the train station.

Most of the buses on the 20 different lines stop running quite early, usually between 6pm and 9pm. Trams run daily from 5am (6.15am on Sunday) to just after midnight.

# THE JURA

The dark wooded hills and granite plateaus of the Jura Mountains stretch for 360km along the Franco-Swiss border from the Rhine to the Rhône. Part of the historic Franche-Comté region, the Jura is one of the least explored regions in France, which makes it a fine place to escape the Alpine crowds. If you're looking for a taste of traditional mountain life, the Jura makes a far better destination than the ruthlessly modernised and tourist-orientated resorts elsewhere in the Alps.

# BESANÇON

**pop 125,000**

Noted for its vast parks, clean streets and few tourists, Besançon is considered one of the most liveable cities in France. It has one of the country's largest foreign student populations and the old town's cobbled streets hum with bars and bistros. Victor Hugo, author of *Les Misérables*, and the film-pioneering Lumière brothers, were all born on the square now known as place Victor Hugo in Besançon's old town.

## Orientation

Besançon's old city is neatly encased by the curve of the River Doubs called the Boucle du Doubs. The tourist office and train station are both just outside this loop to the north-west and north. The Battant quarter straddles the northwest bank of the river around rue Battant. Grande Rue, the pedestrianised main street, slices through the old city from the river to the gates of the citadel.

## Information

### INTERNET ACCESS

**Optimum** ( ☎ 03 81 82 13 07; www.optimum.fr; 31 rue d'Arènes; ☺ 10am-10.30pm Mon-Sat, 2-10pm Sun; per 10 min/hr €1/3.50).

### LAUNDRY

**Blanc-Matic** (14 rue de la Madeleine; ☺ 7am-8pm)

### POST

**Post office** (23 rue Proudhon; ☺ 9am-noon & 2pm-6pm) In the old city. There is another branch on rue Battant.

### TOURIST INFORMATION

**Tourist office** ( ☎ 03 81 80 92 55; www.besancon -tourisme.com; 2 place de la 1ère Armée Française; ☺ 10am-7pm Mon, 9am-7pm Tue-Sat, 10am-noon & 3-5pm Sun Apr-Sep; 10am-6pm Mon, 9am-6pm Tue-Sat Oct-Mar; 10am-noon Sun mid-Sep–mid-Jun).

## Sights

Thought to be France's oldest museum, the **Musée des Beaux-Arts** ( ☎ 03 81 87 80 49; 1 pl de la Révolution; adult/student €3/free; ☺ 9.30am-noon & 2pm-6pm Wed-Mon) houses an impressive collection of paintings, including primitive and Renaissance works. Franche-Comté's long history of clock-making is also displayed here.

Built by Vauban for Louis XIV between 1688 and 1711, Besançon's **citadel** ( ☎ 03 81 87 83 33; adult/concession/child €7/6/4; ☺ 9am-7pm

Jul-Aug; to 6pm Apr-Jun, Sep & Oct; 10am-5pm Nov-Mar) sits at the top of rue des Fusillés de la Résistance. It's a steep 15-minute walk from the **Porte Noire** (Black Gate), a triumphal arch left over from Besançon's Roman days, dating from the 2nd century AD.

## Sleeping

**Auberge de Jeunesse Les Oiseaux** ( ☎ 03 81 40 32 00; 48 rue des Cras; dm €20) The hostel is 2km east of the train station. Rates include breakfast and bedding; subsequent nights cost €2 less. Take bus No 7 from the tourist office in the direction of Orchamps and get off at Les Oiseaux.

**Hôtel Regina** ( ☎ 03 81 81 18 30; 91 Grande Rue; d €35-50) Down a quiet alley in the heart of the old city, this two-star hotel offers cosy, floral rooms with shower, toilet and TV.

**Hôtel de Paris** ( ☎ 03 81 81 36 56; hoteldeparis@hotmail .com; 33 rue des Granges; d €45-60; P ) One of the best deals in Besancon, this efficient, comfortable hotel has 60 rooms which vary in quality – ask to see one before you choose.

## Eating & Drinking

**Carpe Diem** ( ☎ 03 81 83 11 18; 2 pl Jean Gigoux; salads from €2.60, plats du jour €8) A small, rough-and-ready café-bar with a smoky atmosphere, wooden bar, and tattered posters.

**La Femme du Boulanger** ( ☎ 03 81 82 86 93; 6 rue Morand) Scrumptious bakery and coffee bar offering homemade breads, sweet and savoury tarts, healthy breakfasts and not-so-healthy cakes.

**Al Sirocco** ( ☎ 03 81 82 24 05; 1 rue Chifflet; ☺ closed Sun & Mon lunch) Great, traditional Italian diner with little tables and fishing nets hanging from the ceiling. Locals come here for the best pizza and pasta in Besançon.

**Le Vin et l'Assiette** ( ☎ 03 81 81 48 18; 97 rue Battant; menu €18; ☺ Tue-Sat) An intimate bistro and wine bar, located above the Caves Marcellin (Marcellin wine cellars). Sample local Jura wine accompanied by meats and cheeses.

**Pierre qui Mousse** ( ☎ 03 81 81 15 25; 1 pl Jouffrey; ☺ daily until late) A popular bar-brasserie right on the riverfront, where you can sup Belgian beer (€3.50) under low wooden beams. Happy hour is usually from 6pm to 7pm.

Fresh fish, meat, vegetables and cheeses are sold at the large **indoor market** (cnr rue Paris & rue Claude Goudimel). The nearby **outdoor market** (pl de la Révolution) sells mainly fresh fruit and vegetables.

## Getting There & Away

Buses operated by **Monts Jura** ( ☎ 08 25 00 22 44) depart from the **bus station** (9 rue Proudhon; ⌚ 8-10am & 4pm-6.30pm Mon-Fri, 8am-1pm & 2.30pm-5.30pm Sat). There are daily services to Ornans and Pontarlier.

Up the hill, 800m from the city centre, is **Besançon Gare Viotte** ( ☎ 08 36 35 35 35; ticket office ⌚ 5am-10.30pm). Train tickets can be bought in advance at the **SNCF office** (44 Grande Rue). Major connections include Paris' Gare de Lyon (from €45.10 non-TGV, three hours, three daily), Dijon (€13.80, 50 minutes, 20 daily), Lyon (€31.40, three hours, eight daily).

## Getting Around

Local buses are run by **CTB** ( ☎ 03 81 48 12 12), which has a **ticket/information kiosk** (pl du 8 Septembre; ⌚ 9am-12.30pm & 1-7pm Mon-Sat). A single ticket/day ticket/*carnet* of 10 costs €0.95/3.20/8. Bus Nos 8 and 24 link the train station with the centre.

# PROVENCE

First-time visitors may be as captivated by this ruggedly lovely chunk of France as the painter Van Gogh was. 'What intensity of colours, what pure air, what vibrant serenity,' he wrote on arrival from a gloomy Paris. 'Nature here is extraordinarily beautiful, everything and everywhere.'

It's a culturally and historically rich region too. The Romans were among the earliest to spot its charms, invading it then sending their favourite legions to retire here. They left many unmissable monuments behind, including theatres and thermal baths (some still in use) in places like Arles and Aix.

## MARSEILLE
pop 807,071

In parts African, in others Middle-eastern but in its entirety unmistakeably French, the cosmopolitan port of Marseille is a brusque, bustling place with character. There's the attractive old port, the gritty (and often stinking) back streets, lively markets with the atmosphere of a Moroccan *souq* and heavenly harbourside restaurants.

France's second city and its third-largest metropolitan area, Marseille has not been prettified for the benefit of tourists and its old (and mostly outdated) reputation as a place of crime and racial tension dies hard. Yet visitors who enjoy exploring on foot will be rewarded with more sights, sounds, smells and big-city commotion than almost anywhere else in the country.

## Orientation & Information

The city's main thoroughfare, the wide boulevard called La Canebière, stretches eastwards from the Vieux Port (Old Port). The train station is north of La Canebière at the northern end of blvd d'Athènes. Just a few blocks south of La Canebière is the bohemian cours Julien, a large pedestrianised square. The ferry terminal is west of place de la Joliette, a few minutes walk north of the Nouvelle Cathédrale. Addresses given below include arondissements (1er being the most central).

Surf the Web at **Info Cafe** ( ☎ 04 91 33 74 98; 1 quai du Rive Neuve, 1e; Internet per hr €3.60; ⌚ 9am-10pm Mon-Sat, 2.30pm-7.30pm Sun). The overwhelmed and understaffed **tourist office** ( ☎ 04 91 13 89 00; www.marseille-tourisme.com; 4 La Canebière, 1er; ⌚ 9am-7pm Mon-Sat, 10am-5pm Sun, 9am-7.30pm daily mid-Jun–mid-Sep) can make hotel reservations. There's an **annexe** ( ☎ 04 91 50 59 18; ⌚ 10am-1pm & 2-6pm Mon-Sat) at the main train station.

### DANGERS & ANNOYANCES

Despite its reputation for crime, Marseille is not significantly more dangerous than other French cities. Avoid walking alone at night in the Belsunce area, a poor neighbourhood southwest of the train station bounded by La Canebière, cours Belsunce and rue d'Aix, rue Bernard du Bois and blvd d'Athènes.

## Sights & Activities

Unless noted otherwise, the museums open from 10am to 5pm Tuesday to Sunday October to May and 11am to 6pm June to September. Admission to each museum's permanent exhibitions cost adult/child €2/1.

The **Centre de la Vieille Charité** (Old Charity Cultural Centre; ☎ 04 91 14 58 80; 2 rue de la Charité, 2e) in the mostly North African Panier Quarter is home to **Musée d'Archéologie** ( ☎ 04 91 14 58 80) with some worthwhile exhibits on ancient Egypt and Greece.

Just north of La Canebière, **Musée d'Histoire de Marseille** ( ☎ 04 91 90 42 22; Centre Bourse shopping centre, 1er; ⌚ noon-7pm Mon-Sat) a smallish place

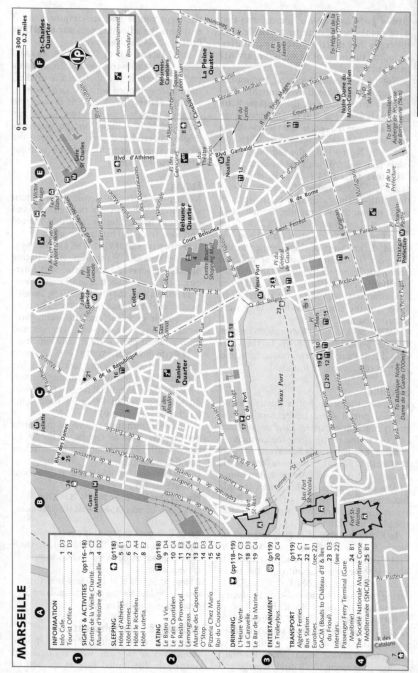

# MARSEILLE

| INFORMATION | |
| --- | --- |
| Info Cafe | 1 D3 |
| Tourist Office | 2 D3 |

| SIGHTS & ACTIVITIES | (pp116–18) |
| --- | --- |
| Centre de la Vieille Charité | 3 C2 |
| Musée d'Histoire de Marseille | 4 D2 |

| SLEEPING | (p118) |
| --- | --- |
| Hôtel d'Athènes | 5 E1 |
| Hôtel Hermes | 6 C3 |
| Hôtel le Richelieu | 7 A4 |
| Hôtel Lutetia | 8 E2 |

| EATING | (p118) |
| --- | --- |
| Le Bistro à Vin | 9 D4 |
| Le Pain Quotidien | 10 C4 |
| Le Resto Provençal | 11 E3 |
| Lemongrass | 12 C4 |
| Marché des Capucins | 13 E3 |
| O'Stop | 14 D3 |
| Pizzeria Chez Mario | 15 D4 |
| Roi du Couscous | 16 C1 |

| DRINKING | (pp118–19) |
| --- | --- |
| L'Heure Verte | 17 C3 |
| La Caravelle | 18 D3 |
| Le Bar de la Marine | 19 C4 |

| ENTERTAINMENT | (p119) |
| --- | --- |
| Le Trolleybus | 20 C4 |

| TRANSPORT | (p119) |
| --- | --- |
| Algérie Ferries | 21 C1 |
| Bus Station | 22 E1 |
| Eurolines | (see 22) |
| GACM (Boats to Château d'If & Îles du Frioul) | 23 D3 |
| Intercars | (see 22) |
| Passenger Ferry Terminal (Gare Maritime) | 24 B1 |
| The Société Nationale Maritime Corse Méditerranée (SNCM) | 25 B1 |

FRANCE

gives a good overview of the cultures that have made their home in Marseille, and the crafts they practised over the centuries, including the remains of a 3rd century AD merchant vessel.

Not to be missed for great panoramas and some handsome, if overwrought, 19th-century architecture is the **Basilique Notre Dame de la Garde** ( ☎ 04 91 13 40 80; admission free; basilica & crypt 🕑 7am-8pm, to 10pm mid-Jun–mid-Aug, to 7pm winter). Dress conservatively when you visit. Bus No 60 links the old port (from cours Jean Ballard) with the basilica.

**Château d'If** ( ☎ 04 91 59 02 30; adult/student €4.60/3.10; 🕑 9.30am-6pm Sep-Mar, to 6.30pm Jun-Aug), the 16th-century fortress-turned-prison made infamous by Alexandre Dumas' classic novel, *Le Comte de Monte Cristo* (The Count of Monte Cristo), is on a 30-sq-km island, 3.5km west of the entrance to the old port. In reality all sorts of political prisoners, hundreds of Protestants (many of whom perished in the dungeons), the Revolutionary hero Mirabeau, the rebels of 1848 and the Communards of 1871 were imprisoned here.

**GACM** ( ☎ 04 91 55 50 09, www.answeb.net/gacm; 1 quai des Belges, 1er) runs boats to the Château d'If at 9am, 10.30am, noon, 2pm, and 3.30pm (€9 return, 20 minutes).

## Sleeping

Generally, the better hotels cluster around the old port (where budget options are pretty much non-existent) and as you head east out of the centre along the corniche.

**Auberge de Jeunesse de Bonneveine** ( ☎ 04 91 17 63 30; fax 04 91 73 97 23; impasse du Docteur Bonfils, 8e; dm €14.55; 🕑 Feb-Dec) About 4.5km south of the centre, rates at this hostel include breakfast. Take bus No 44 from the Rond Point du Prado metro stop and get off at the place Bonnefons stop.

**Le Richelieu** ( ☎ 04 91 31 01 92; hotelmer@club -Internet.fr; 52 Corniche Président John F Kennedy, 7e; r €34-41, sea-facing €41-53) An idyllic, two-star place with ace views, built onto the rocks right next to plage des Catalans. Road-facing rooms can be noisy. Some sea-facing rooms have balconies. Book ahead.

**Hôtel d'Athènes** ( ☎ 04 91 90 12 93; fax 04 91 90 72 03; 37-39 blvd d'Athènes, 1er; s/d with shower €24/34, s/d/tr with shower & toilet 39/46/56) At the foot of the grand staircase leading from the train station into town you'll find average but

well-kept rooms and an elevator here. It also runs the adjoining one-star **Hôtel Little Palace** (r €25-34 with shower only).

**Hôtel Lutetia** ( ☎ 04 91 50 81 78; www.hotel lutetia13.com; 38 allées Léon Gambetta, 1er; s/d/tr from €46/51/70) Homely and spotless, the smallish rooms are equipped with TV and phone.

**Hôtel Hermes** ( ☎ 04 96 11 63 63; www.hotel .hermes@wanadoo.fr; 2 rue Bonneterie, 1er; s/d from €45/67; 🔀 ✕ 🅿 ) Right on the quayside, bright, cheerful and good value given the location overlooking the harbour and Basilique Notre Dame.

## Eating

No trip to Marseille is complete without sampling *bouillabaisse*, a rich red soup full of chunks of Mediterranean fish – the old port area is a good hunting ground.

**Lemongrass** ( ☎ 04 91 33 97 65; 8 rue Fort-Notre-Dame, 1e; menu €20; 🕑 closed Sun) An exciting newcomer serving inexpensive and interesting menus of fusion Asian/French food.

**Le Bistro à Vin** ( ☎ 04 91 54 02 20; 17 rue Sainte, 6e; mains around €12; 🕑 closed Sun & Sat lunch) The wine selection is excellent and the accompaniments – *tapenade*, artisanal cheeses and unusual meat parts – are equally enticing.

**Le Resto Provençal** ( ☎ 04 91 48 85 12; 64 cours Julien, 1er; 🕑 closed Sat lunch & Sun) A winning combination of an outside dining terrace, a *menu* offering regional fare for €21, a plat du jour for around €9 and a good-value lunchtime *menu* for €12.

Get your fresh fruit and veg at the **Marche des Capucins** (place des Capucins; 🕑 Mon-Sat), a block south of La Canabiére. For snackier fare take your pick:

**Le Pain Quotidien** ( ☎ 04 91 33 55 00; 18 Pl Aux Huiles; breakfast €5-8) For a decent breakfast.

**Pizzeria Chez Mario** ( ☎ 04 91 54 48 54; 8 rue Euthymènes,1er; mains €8.50-15) Good fish, grilled meats, pizza and pasta.

**Roi du Couscous** ( ☎ 04 91 91 45 46; 63 rue de la République, 2e; couscous €8-12; 🕑 Tue-Sun) Serves large and delicious portions of steamed semolina with meats and vegetables.

**O'Stop** ( ☎ 04 91 33 85 34, 15 rue Saint-Saëns, 1er; menu €9; 🕑 24hr) Non-stop sandwiches, pasta and simple, authentic regional specialities.

## Drinking & Entertainment

Cultural event listings appear in the monthly *Vox Mag* and weekly *Taktik* and *Sortir*, all distributed free at the tourist office. It's also worth consulting the website www.marseillebynight.com.

There are plenty of venues (and variety). Two hotspots are the bars and clubs around quayside, especially along the Quai de Rive Neuve, and, a fair hike away, the bars and cafés around Place Jean Jaurés

**Le Trolleybus** ( ☎ 04 91 54 30 45; 24 Quai Rive Neuve; ☺ 11pm-dawn Wed-Sat) Inside the various sections of this tunnel-like club by the harbour there could be techno, funk and indie playing at the same time.

**Le Bar de la Marine** ( ☎ 04 91 54 95 42; 15 Quai de Rive Neuve) Chic metropolitan espresso sippers mix it with grizzled pastis-gulping sailor types at this gregarious bar right on the water.

**La Caravelle** ( ☎ 04 91 90 36 64, 34 quai du Port, 2e) Upstairs at the Hôtel Bellevue, this is in a marvellous location overlooking the port with a small balcony.

**L'Heure Verte** ( ☎ 04 91 90 12 73; 108 quai du Port; ☺ 11am-11pm high season) The place to go to sample many different types of pastis and some fierce absinthe.

## Getting There & Away
### AIR
The **Marseille-Provence airport** ( ☎ 04 42 14 14 14), also known as the Marseille-Marignane airport, is 28km northwest of the city in Marignane.

### BOAT
Marseille's **passenger ferry terminal** (gare maritime; ☎ 04 91 56 38 63; fax 04 91 56 38 70) is 250m south of place de la Joliette (2e).

The **Société Nationale Maritime Corse Méditerranée** (SNCM; ☎ 08 36 67 95 00; fax 04 91 56 35 86; 61 blvd des Dames, 2e; ☺ 8am-6pm Mon-Fri, 8.30am-noon & 2-5.30pm Sat) links Marseille with Corsica, Sardinia and Tunisia.

There is an office for **Algérie Ferries** ( ☎ 04 91 90 64 70; 29 blvd des Dames, 2e; ☺ 9am-11.45 & 1pm-4.45pm Mon-Fri). Ticketing and reservations for the Tunisian and Moroccan ferry companies, **Compagnie Tunisienne de Navigation** (CTN) and **Compagnie Marocaine de Navigation** (COMANAV; ☎ 04 67 46 68 00; departures from 4 quai d'Alger in Sète) are handled by SNCM.

### BUS
The **bus station** (gare des autocars; ☎ 04 91 08 16 40; 3 pl Victor Hugo, 3e) is 150m to the right as you exit the train station. Services include

Aix-en-Provence (€4.20, 35 minutes via the autoroute/one hour via the N8, every five to 10 minutes); Avignon (€17, 35 minutes, one daily); and Nice (€22, 2¾ hours).

**Eurolines** ( ☎ 08 92 28 99 091 or 04 91 50 57 55) has buses to Spain, Belgium, the Netherlands, Italy, Morocco, the UK and other countries. **Intercars** ( ☎ 04 91 50 08 66), whose office is next to Eurolines in the bus station, has buses to the UK, Spain, Portugal, Morocco, Poland and Slovakia. Both firms share offices at the bus station and at 3 alles Leon Gambetta ( ☎ 04 91 50 57 55).

### TRAIN
Marseille's passenger train station, served by both metro lines, is called **Gare St-Charles.** There's a large information and ticket **reservation office** ( ☺ 9am-8pm Mon-Sat; ticket sales 4-1am). Destinations include Paris' Gare de Lyon (€83.90, three hours, 17 daily); Avignon (€19.40, 30mins, 27 daily); Lyon (€39.40, 3¼ hours, 16 daily) and Nice (€25, 2½ hours, 21 daily).

Luggage may be left at the **left-luggage office** ( ☺ 7.15am-10pm; €3.40 for 72hrs), next to platform A.

## Getting Around
### TO/FROM THE AIRPORT
**Navette Shuttle Buses** (Marseille ☎ 04 91 50 59 34; airport ☎ 04 42 14 31 27) link Marseille-Provence airport (€8.50, one hour) with Marseille's train station. Airport-bound buses leave from the train station's main entrance every 20 minutes.

### BUS & METRO
Marseille is served by two fast, well-maintained metro lines (Métro 1 and Métro 2) and an extensive bus network. The metro and most buses run from about 5am to 9pm. From 9.25pm to 12.30am, metro and tram routes are covered every 15 minutes by buses M1 and M2.

Bus/metro tickets cost €1.50. A pass for one/three days costs €4/9.50.

## AIX-EN-PROVENCE
pop 137,067

Aix-en-Provence, or just Aix (pronounced like the letter 'x'), is one of France's most graceful, popular cities, boasting the art heritage of Cezanne who lived and painted here (although sadly the Musée Granet which exhibits some of his work is closed for a massive rebuild until at least 2006), a lively nightlife (sustained by the presence of 30,000 students) and plenty of charm.

The Cours Mireabeau, a graceful plane tree-lined boulevard is the perfect place to watch the world pass as you nurse a slow espresso on one of the many large cafés lining it. The warren of streets running off it into the old town are full of ethnic restaurants and specialist shops, mingled with handsome old 17th- and 18th-century mansions.

Aix's **Cathédrale St-Sauveur** (rue J de Laroque; ☻8am-noon & 2pm-6pm) is an interesting ragtag of styles through the ages, incorporating architectural features of every major period from the 5th to 18th centuries stuck onto one another.

## Sleeping

Despite being a student town, Aix is not cheap. Even so, the centre can fill up fast so book ahead.

**Camping Arc-en-Ciel** ( ☎ 04 42 26 14 28; route de Nice; camp sites €17.10; ☻ Apr-Sep) There are peaceful wooded hills out back but a busy motorway out front. It's 2km southeast of town, at Pont des Trois Sautets. Take bus No 3 to Les Trois Sautets stop

**Auberge de Jeunesse du Jas de Bouffan** ( ☎ 04 42 20 15 99; fax 04 42 59 36 12; 3 ave Marcel Pagnol; dm incl breakfast & sheets €15) A smart, modern place with great views of a distant Mont Ventoux. It's 2km west of the centre. Rooms are locked between 9am and 5pm. Take bus line No 4 from La Rotonde to the Vasarely stop.

**Hôtel Paul** ( ☎ 04 42 23 23 89; hotel.paul@wanadoo .fr; 10 ave Pasteur; s/d/tr €35/45/55) Welcoming rooms and a pleasant courtyard garden make this an appealing budget option just north of blvd Jean Jaurès and a 10-minute walk from the tourist office, or take minibus No 2 from La Rotonde or the bus station.

**Hôtel Cardinal** ( ☎ 04 42 38 32 30; fax 04 42 26 39 05; 24 rue Cardinale; s/d €47/60, self-catering ste €76) A charming place with large (mostly) en-suite rooms and a mix of modern and period furniture. The upper rooms offer pretty views across town.

## Eating

Aix is known for its superb markets. A mass of fruit and vegetable stands are set up each morning on place Richelme, just as they have been for centuries.

Aix's cheapest dining street is rue Van Loo, lined with tiny restaurants offering Italian, Chinese, Thai and other Asian cuisines.

**Le Dernier Bistrot** ( ☎ 04 42 21 13 02; 15-19 rue Constantin; lunch menu €10, dinner menu €16/19/23; ☻ Mon-Sat) Mixes traditional bistro recipes with Provençal culinary fodder such as beef *daubes* (stew) and carpaccios, *soupe au pistou* (pesto soup) and courgette flan.

**Yôji** ( ☎ 04 42 38 84 48; 7 ave Victor Hugo; lunch menu from €9.50, dinner menu €16-20) Often packed and you'll taste why if you can get in (book ahead). The sushi is first rate but for real theatre choose the sizzling Korean barbecues brought to your table. There are some great fusion twists too, including the toothsome green tea brulée.

# AVIGNON

**pop 88,312**

Avignon is synonymous in France with the annual performing arts festival held here each summer, but there's plenty to see in this bustling walled city year-round, including a number of interesting museums and the massive fortress of the medieval popes, the Palais des Papes.

The city first acquired wealth and power, its mighty ramparts and its reputation as a city of art and culture during the 14th century, when Pope Clement V and his court fled political turmoil in Rome and established themselves near Avignon. From 1309 to 1377 seven French-born popes based themselves here. Even after the pontifical court returned to Rome, Avignon remained under papal rule until 1791.

## Orientation & Information

The main avenue within the walled city *(intra-muros)* runs northwards from the train station to place de l'Horloge; it's called cours Jean Jaurès south of the tourist office and rue de la République north of it.

Place de l'Horloge is 300m south of place du Palais, which abuts the Palais des Papes. The city gate nearest the train station is Porte de la République, while the city gate next to pont Édouard Daladier, which leads to Villeneuve-lès-Avignon, is Porte de l'Oulle. Check out the Internet at **Webzone** ( ☎ 04 32 76 29 47; 3 rue St Jean le Vieux; Internet per hr €4.57; ☻ 11am-10pm Mon-Sat, noon-5pm Sun). For local information visit the **tourist office**

( ☎ 04 32 74 32 74; fax 04 90 82 95 03; www.ot-avignon
.fr; 41 cours Jean Jaurès; ☯ 9am-6pm Mon-Sat, 9am-5pm
Sun Apr-Jun & Aug-Oct; to 6pm Mon-Fri, to 5pm Sat, 10am-
noon Sun Nov-Mar; to 7pm Mon-Sat, 10am-5pm Sun Jul),
300m north of the train station; during the
Avignon Festival it opens 9am to 7pm daily
(till 5pm on Sunday).

## Sights & Activities

Ask at the tourist office about the Avignon
Passion museum pass, which entitles you to
special discounts.

The **Pont St Bénézet** (Le Pont d'Avignon; ☎ 04 90
27 51 16; full price/pass €3.50/3; ☯ 9am-7pm Apr-May,
Oct-Nov, to 8pm Jul-Sep, 9.30am-5.45pm Nov-Mar) was
built between 1177 and 1185 to link Avignon
with the settlement across the Rhône that
later became Villeneuve-lès-Avignon. Yes,
this is also the **Pont d'Avignon** in the French
nursery rhyme. Many people find a distant
view of the bridge from the Rocher des Doms
(also known as the Pont Édouard Daladier)
much more interesting (and it's free).

The huge **Palais des Papes** ( ☎ 04 90 27 50 00;
pl du Palais; full price/pass €9.50/7.50; ☯ 9am-7pm Apr-
May, Oct-Nov, to 8pm Jul-Sep, 9.30am-5.45pm Nov-Mar)
was built during the 14th century as a fortified palace for the pontifical court. The
cavernous stone halls testify to the enormous wealth amassed by the papacy while
it resided here.

The **Musée du Petit Palais** ( ☎ 04 90 86 44 58;
pl du Palais; full price/pass €6/3; ☯ 10am-1pm & 2-6pm
Wed-Mon Jun-Sep, 9.30am-1pm & 2-5.30pm Wed-Mon Oct-
May), a former archbishop's palace, houses
an outstanding collection of lavishly coloured 13th- to 16th-century Italian religious paintings.

Just up the hill from the cathedral is
**Rocher des Doms**, a delightful bluff-top park
that affords great views of the Rhône, Pont
St-Bénézet, Villeneuve-lès-Avignon and the
Alpilles. There's shade, breeze and benches
aplenty up here – a good spot for a picnic.

The **Musée Lapidaire** ( ☎ 04 90 86 33 84; 27 rue de
la Republic; full price/pass €2/1; ☯ 10am-1pm & 2pm-6pm
Wed-Mon), close to the tourist office, is well
worth a quick look for its somewhat random collection of Egyptian, Roman, Etruscan and early Christian marble statuary,
delicate vases and bronze figurines.

Founded towards the late 13th century,
**Villeneuve-lès-Avignon**, across the Rhône and
in a different *département* from Avignon,
is where you'll find the **Musée Pierre de**

Luxembourg ( ☎ 04 90 27 49 66; rue de la République; full
price/pass €3/1.90; ☯ 10am-12.30 & 2-6.30pm, closed Mon
mid-Sep–mid-Jun). If you're remotely interested
in religious art it's well worth the visit for
Enguerrand Quarton's lavish and dramatic
1453 painting *The Crowning of the Virgin*.

**Tour Philippe-le-Bel** ( ☎ 04 32 70 08 57; full price/
pass €1.60/0.90; ☯ 10am-12.30pm & 2-6.30pm, closed
Mon mid-Sep–mid-Jun), a 14th century defensive
tower offering great views of Avignon's
walled city, the river and the surrounding
countryside, is a five-minute walk away. The
spiral stairs up are narrow and numerous.

## Festivals & Events

Avignon's streets buzz with life, street theatre, buskers and leafleters enticing you into
the hundreds of shows held during the
city's now world-famous **Festival d'Avignon**,
held every year from early July to early August. Information on the official festival can
be obtained from the **Bureau du Festival** ( ☎ 04
90 27 66 50; www.festival-avignon.com; Espace St-Louis, 20
rue du Portail Boquier) and for the fringe events
contact **Avignon Public Off** ( ☎ 01 48 05 01 19; www
.avignon-off.org).

## Sleeping

During the festival it's practically impossible
to find a hotel room at short notice. Rooms
are readily available in August, however.

**Camping Bagatelle** ( ☎ 04 90 86 30 39; camping
.bagatelle@wanadoo.fr; Île de la Barthelasse; s/d camp sites
€11/13; ☯ year-round, reception 8am-9pm) An attractive, shaded camping ground just north
of pont Édouard Daladier, 850m from the
walled city. Take bus No 10 to the La Barthelasse stop. Follow the river to the camp site.

**Auberge Bagatelle** ( ☎ 04 90 85 78 45; auberge
.bagatelle@wanadoo.fr; Île de la Barthelasse; dm €11-11.50,
d €34, d with shared bathroom €26.50) This hostel has
210 beds and is part of a large, park-like
area that includes Camping Bagatelle.

**YMCA-UCJG** ( ☎ 04 90 25 46 20; www.ymca-avignon
.com; 7 bis Chemin de la Justice; s/d/tr €33/42/51, s/d/tr/q
with shared bathroom €22/28/33/44) A good hostel in
Villeneuve-lès-Avignon with well-maintained
rooms in a variety of sizes. Take bus No 10 to
the Pont d'Avignon stop Monteau.

**Hôtel Monclar** ( ☎ 04 90 86 20 14; www.hotel
-monclar.com; 13 Ave Monclar; s/d €26/45, with shared
bathroom €20/30; **P** ) Occupies a handsome,
peppermint-shuttered 18th-century building by the train station (next to the tracks
in fact, so noise can be a problem).

FRANCE

# AVIGNON

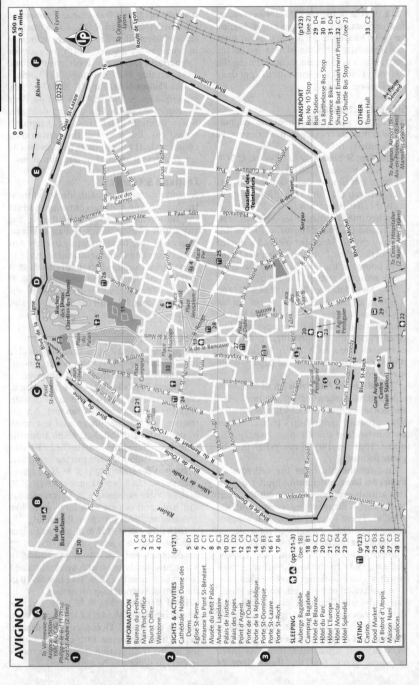

**Hôtel du Parc** ( ☎ 04 90 82 71 55; www.hotelduparc .fr.fm; 18 rue Agricol Perdiguier; s/d with shower €35/43, with shower & toilet €47/47) Comfortable one-star rooms and its location close to the tourist office are the main attractions for this hotel.

**Hôtel Splendid** ( ☎ 04 90 86 14 46; www.avignon -splendid-hotel.com; 17 rue Agricol Perdiguier; s/d with shower €37/49, with shower & toilet 43/54). Near the Hôtel du Parc, this is a friendly hotel with recently renovated rooms.

**Hôtel de Blauvac** ( ☎ 04 90 86 34 11; www.hotel -blauvac.com; 13 rue Joseph Vernet; s/d/tr €48/51/65) Just off the main square you'll find the lovely 17th century former townhouse of the Marqui de Blauvac, now a friendly, comfortable and central hotel with convivial and stylish rooms.

**Hôtel L'Europe** ( ☎ 04 90 14 76 76; www.heurope .com; 12 pl Crillon; r €129-410; ✖ P ✖ ) A great four-star place with bags of charm. Napoleon Bonaparte is just one of the famous folk to have stayed here.

## Eating

From Easter until mid-November, half of place de l'Horloge is taken over by tourist restaurants and cafés. *Menus* around these parts start at about €14.

**Tapalocas** ( ☎ 04 90 82 56 84; 15 rue Galante; dishes from €2; ✖ 11.45-1am) A down-to-earth Spanish tapas bar selling cheap, beer-session ballast.

**Maison Nani** ( ☎ 04 90 82 60 90; 29 rue Théodore Aubanel; plat du jour €9; ✖ lunch Mon-Sat, dinner Fri-Sun) A cheerful, popular bistro serving Provençal salads, grilled meat and fresh fish.

**Le Bistrot d'Utopia** ( ☎ 04 90 27 04 96; 4 rue des Escaliers Ste-Anne; mains from €13) Great for atmosphere and simple, tasty food like mushroom tarts with buttery pastry and ace desserts such as a slender lemon curd tart topped with a sliver of crystallised orange.

Les Halles has a great **food market** (pl Pie; ✖ 7am-1pm Tue-Sun). For groceries there's **Casino** (22 rue St-Agricol; ✖ 8am-12.45pm & 3pm-7.30pm Mon-Sat).

## Getting There & Away
### BUS

The **bus station** (halte routière; ☎ 04 90 82 07 35; information window ✖ 10.15am-1pm Mon-Fri, 2-6pm Mon-Fri) is in the basement of the building down the ramp to the right as you exit the train station on blvd St-Roch. Destinations include Aix-en-Provence (via the highway €13.90, one hour; on secondary

roads €11.70, 1½ hours, four to six daily); Arles (€8.50, 1½ hours, six daily); Marseille (€16.40, 35 minutes direct, one daily) and Nice (€27, three hours, one daily).

Long-haul bus companies **Linebus** ( ☎ 04 90 85 30 48) and **Eurolines** ( ☎ 04 90 85 27 60; www .eurolines.fr) have offices at the far end of the bus platforms.

### TRAIN

The **main train station** (information counters ✖ 9am-6.15pm Mon-Sat) is located across blvd St-Roch from Porte de la République. The **left-luggage** (from €3; ✖ 6am-10pm) is to the left as you exit the station.

The brand new **TGV station** is a few kilometres from town. A **shuttle bus** (€2; ✖ half-hourly from 5.30am-10.50pm) takes you from the TGV station to the bus stop just outside the main post office.

There are trains to Arles (€5.70, 20 minutes, 14 to 18 daily); Marseille (€15.50, 40 minutes); Nice (€38.80, three hours); Nîmes (€7.40, 30 min, 15 daily); and by TGV, Paris' Gare de Lyon (€67, 2½ hours) and Lyon (€29.60, one hour).

## Getting Around

Local TCRA bus tickets cost €1.05 each if bought from the driver. The two most important bus transfer points are the Poste stop at the main post office and place Pie. Bus No 10, which stops in front of the main post office and on the western side of the walled city near Porte de l'Oulle, heads to Villeneuve-lès-Avignon.

Rent a bike, scooter and larger motorbike from **Provence Bike** ( ☎ 04 90 27 92 61; 52 bd St Roch).

## AROUND AVIGNON
### Arles
pop 51,614

Arles began its ascent to prosperity and political importance in 49 BC, when the victorious Julius Caesar – to whom the city had given its support – captured and plundered Marseille, which had backed Caesar's rival, the general and statesman Pompey the Great.

Arles soon replaced Marseille as the region's major port and became the sort of Roman provincial centre that, within a century and a half, needed a 12,000-seat theatre and a 20,000-seat amphitheatre to entertain its citizens. Known as the **Arénes** and the **Théâtre Antique** they are still used to stage cultural events and bullfights. The town's most famous resident was Vincent van Gogh (1853-90) who painted many of his most celebrated works here.

The **tourist office** ( ☎ 04 90 18 41 20; www.tour isme.ville-arles.fr; Esplanade Charles de Gaulle; 9am-6.45pm Apr-Sep; to 4.45pm Mon-Sat, 10.30am-2.30pm Sun Oct-Mar) is a short trip along blvd des Lices. There is a **tourist office annexe** ( ☎ 04 90 49 36 90; 9am-1pm Jun-Sep) at the train station.

Arles' **train station** (information office 9am-12.30pm & 2-6.30pm Mon-Sat) is opposite the bus station. Major rail destinations include Nîmes (€6.60, 30min), Montpellier (€12.20, one hour), Marseille (€11.60, 40min) and Avignon (€5.70, 20min).

The **bus station** (information office ☎ 08 00 19 94 13, 08 10 00 08 16; 7.30am-4pm Mon-Sat), at the end of ave Paulin Talabot, is about 1km north of les Arènes. **Telleschi** ( ☎ 04 42 28 40 22; 16 bd de la Durance) runs services to Aix-en-Provence (€11.30, 1¾ hours).

# CÔTE D'AZUR

The beautiful Côte d'Azur (Azure Coast), also known as the French Riviera, stretches along the Mediterranean coast from Toulon to the Italian border. Many towns along the coast – Nice, Monaco, Cannes, St-Tropez – are well known as the playgrounds of the rich, famous and tanned. The reality is usually less glamorous but the Côte d'Azur still has a great deal to attract visitors: sun, 40km of beach, sea water as warm as 25°C, and numerous cultural activities.

East of Nice, the foothills of the Alps plummet into the Mediterranean. Three heart stopping roads, known as *corniches,* take you eastwards from Nice to Menton and the Italian border. The tiny Principality of Monaco is roughly midway between Nice and Menton.

## NICE
pop 345,892

The capital of the Riviera, Nice makes a great base from which to explore the rest of the Côte d'Azur. The city has lots of relatively cheap places to stay and is only a short train or bus ride from Monaco, Cannes and other Riviera hot spots. It's also blessed

with fine museums, a lively night life in the old city's narrow warren of streets, an old harbour and great markets.

### Orientation

Ave Jean Médecin runs south from near the train station to place Masséna. The modern city centre, the area north and west of place Masséna, includes the upmarket pedestrianised streets of rue de France and rue Masséna. The Station Centrale and intercity bus station are three blocks east of place Masséna. The famous promenade des Anglais follows the gently curved beachfront from the city centre to the airport, 6km west.

### Information

**Le Change** ( ☎ 04 93 88 56 80; 17 ave Thiers; 7.30am-8pm) Opposite the Gare Nice Ville, to the right as you leave the terminal building; offers decent rates.

**Main post office** (23 ave Thiers; 8am-7pm Mon-Fri, to noon Sat) Exchanges foreign currency.

**Tourist office** ( ☎ 04 92 70 74 07; www.nicetourism.com; ave Thiers; 8am-8pm Mon-Sat, 9am-7pm Sun Jun-Sep; 8am-7pm Mon-Sat, 9am-6pm Sun Oct-May) Next to the Gare Nice Ville (the main train station). There's another, less crowded **office** ( ☎ 08 92 70 74 07; fax 04 92 14 48 03; 5 promenade des Anglais; 8am-8pm Mon-Sat, 9am-7pm Sun Jun-Sep; 9am-6pm Mon-Sat Oct-May).

**Worldwide Web Service** ( ☎ 04 93 80 51 12; 32 rue Assalit; 10am-7pm Mon-Sat)

### Sights

The Carte Musées Côte d'Azur is an excellent-value pass that gives free admission to some 60 Côte d'Azur museums. It costs €8/15/25 for one/five/seven days and is available at tourist offices and participating museums. Alternatively the Carte Musées Ville de Nice, which allows entry into all of Nice's museums except the Chagall, costs €6/18.30 for seven/15 days.

The **Musée d'Art Moderne et d'Art Contemporain** ( ☎ 04 93 62 61 62; ave St-Jean Baptiste; adult/student €4/2.50; 10am-6pm Wed-Mon) specialises in French and American avant-garde works from the 1960s to the present, which explode with colour in the light, large display spaces. Featured artists include Nice-born Yves Klein (1928-62), Andy Warhol, Christo, Marseille-born sculptor César and sculptor Nikki St-Phalle.

The **Musée National Message Biblique Marc Chagall** ( ☎ 04 93 53 87 20; adult/student €5.50/4, in Jul & Aug €5.80/4.25; 10am-6pm Wed-Mon Jul-Sep, to 5pm Wed-Mon Oct-Jun) contains a series of large, impressive and colourful series of paintings of Old Testament scenes. Take bus No 15 from place Masséna to the front of the museum or walk.

The **Musée Matisse** ( ☎ 04 93 81 08 08; 164 ave des Arènes de Cimiez; adult/student €4/2.50; ☺ 10am-6pm Wed-Mon) has a fine collection of works by Henri Matisse in the bourgeois district Cimiez. Well-known permanent pieces include Matisse's blue paper cutouts of *Blue Nude IV* and *Woman with Amphora*. Take bus No 15, 17, 20, 22 or 25 from the Station Centrale to the Arènes stop.

The multicoloured **Russian Orthodox Cathedral of St-Nicolas** ( ☎ 04 93 96 88 02; ave Nicolas II; ☺ 9am-noon & 2.30-6pm, closed Sun morning), crowned by six onion domes, is opposite 17 blvd du Tzaréwich. Step inside and you're transported to Imperial Russia. Shorts, miniskirts and sleeveless shirts are forbidden.

## Activities

A good way to see Nice is aboard the open-topped buses of **Le Grand Tour** ( ☎ 04 92 29 17 00; adult/student/child €17/13/9). Tours, with headphone commentary, last 1½ hours.

Free sections of **public beach** alternate with 15 **plages concédées** (private beaches), for which you have to pay by renting a chair (around €11 a day) or mattress (around €9).

On the beach you can hire a catamaran, paddleboats, sailboards and jet skis, go parascending and water-skiing, or give paragliding a go. There are outdoor showers on every beach, and indoor showers and toilets opposite 50 promenade des Anglais.

## Festivals & Events

The colourful **Carnaval de Nice**, held every spring around Mardi Gras (Shrove Tuesday), fills the streets with floats and musicians. The week-long **Nice Jazz Festival** (www.nicejazzfest.com) takes up the entire Arènes de Cimiez, Roman ruins and all.

## Sleeping

Nice has a surfeit of reasonably priced places to stay, particularly in the city centre, around the main railway station, and along rue d'Angleterre, rue d'Alsace-Lorraine and ave Durante. Accommodation is plentiful (and pricier) close to and on the seafront. In summer budget places can be hard to find after 10am or 11am.

### BUDGET

**Auberge de Jeunesse** ( ☎ 04 93 89 23 64; fax 04 92 04 03 10; route Forestière de Mont Alban; dm €14; ☺ curfew midnight) This is 4km east of the Gare Nice Ville. Rooms are locked from noon to 5pm. Take bus No 14 (last one at 8.20pm) from the Station Centrale bus terminal on place Général Leclerc, which is linked to the Gare Nice Ville by bus Nos 15 and 17, and get off at L'Auberge stop.

**Villa St Exupery** ( ☎ 04 93 84 42 83; www.villasaintexupery.com; 22 ave Gravier; dm/s/d from €18/28/44; P ☐) Out of town, this hostel in a lovely old former monastery has been recommended by a number of readers. There's no curfew, a friendly vibe and free Internet access, breakfast and station shuttle.

**Backpackers Chez Patrick** ( ☎ 04 93 80 30 72; chezpatrick@voila.fr; 32 rue Pertinax; dm €18-21, r with 2-3 beds per person €20-25) A popular 24-bed spot. There's no curfew and Patrick, who runs the place, can direct party-mad backpackers to the hot spot of the moment.

The following budget hotels are near the train station – walk straight down the steps opposite the Gare Nice Ville onto ave Durante.

**Hôtel Belle Meunière** ( ☎ 04 93 88 66 15; fax 04 93 82 51 76; 21 ave Durante; dm with shower & toilet for under-26 yrs €15, d with shower/shower & toilet €47/51) A great and central option. The large four-bed dorm rooms are posh, panelled affairs and the place touts a tree-studded garden to lounge in. Rates include breakfast.

**Hôtel Les Orangers** ( ☎ 04 93 87 51 41; fax 04 93 82 57 82; 10 bis ave Durante; dm €16, s/d with shower €25/40) Les Orangers is recommended for its large-windowed, sunlit rooms, although this scruffy old place could do with a refit. Rooms come with a fridge (and hotplate on request).

### MID-RANGE & TOP END

**Hôtel du Centre** ( ☎ 04 93 88 83 85; hotel-centre@webstore.fr; 2 rue de Suisse; s/d €50/59, d with hall shower €28.50) This is an attractively renovated place with very neat rooms.

**Hôtel Notre Dame** ( ☎ 04 93 88 70 44; fax 04 93 82 20 38; 22 rue de Russie; s/d/q €39/42/60) A basic but popular place (so book ahead) offering spacious rooms.

**Hôtel Claire Meublé** ( ☎ 04 93 87 87 61; hotel_clair_meuble@hotmail.com; 6 rue d'Italie; 2-/3-/4-/5-person studios €42/50/64/70) A spotless place near the train station with compact, fully equipped studios well suited for self-catering families and couples.

# NICE

**INFORMATION**
Le Change................................ 1 D3
Main Post Office....................... 2 C3
Main Tourist Office................... 3 D2
Police Headquarters.................. 4 F3
Tourist Office Annexe................ 5 D5
Worldwide Web Service............ 6 D2

**SIGHTS & ACTIVITIES** (pp124-5)
Flower Market......................... 7 F5
Musée d'Art Moderne et d'Art
   Contemporain...................... 8 G3
Musée National Message Biblique Marc
   Chagall............................... 9 E1
Russian Orthodox Cathedral of
   St-Nicolas.......................... 10 B2
WW1 Memorial...................... 11 G5

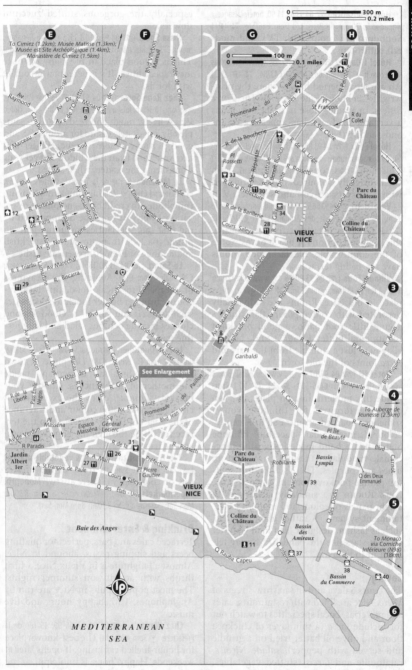

0       300 m
0       0.2 miles

E
To Cimiez (1.2km); Musée Matisse (1.3km);
Musée est Site Archéologique (1.4km);
Monastère de Cimiez (1.5km)

F

G

H

0       100 m
0       0.1 miles

Promenade du
Blvd Jean Jaurès
Paillon
41
Pl
St François
R du
Collet
R Ste Claire
R de la Boucherie
32
R de la Loge
Pl
Rossetti
33
R Benoît Bunico
R Rossetti
R Ste Réparate
R Centrale
R Droite
30
R de la Préfecture
34
R de la Barillerie
Gilly
28
Cours Saleya
VIEUX
NICE

24
23
R Prefolière

Parc du
Château

Colline du
Château

Av George-V
R George-V
Av Dr de l'Olivetto
Av de Menard
Montée de Cimiez
Blvd Vittorio Manuel
Av Raymond
Cimbroul
9
R Marceau
Autoroute Urbaine Sud
Raimbaldi
Blvd
R Assalit
R Pertinax
R de Paris
R de Cimiez
Blvd de Cimiez
Av Emile Chemin du Bois
Av de Normandie
R Moriez
Av Moriez
12
21
Av Notre Dame
Miron
Av Malaussena
Foch
R E Trianlu
R Lamartine
Av Maréchal
R Biscarra
29
4
Blvd Carabacel
R Dubouchage
R Pierre Devoluy
R Brancheatti
R Gallieni
Av Georges Clemenceau
Blvd
R Delille
R Tondut de l'Escarène
R A Mortier
Av St Jean Baptiste
8
Esplanade des
Av de la République
Pl
Garibaldi
R Barla
Pl Anson
R Arson
R Aubanne Gal
3
R Clair Av Delory
R de l'Hôtel des Postes
R Gioffredo
R Alberti
R Chauvain
R Cabernails
R Pastorelli
See Enlargement
Av Félix Faure
Promenade du Paillon
Blvd Jean Jaurès
R Cassini
R Bonaparte
Blvd P Riquier
4
To Auberge de
Jeunesse (2.5km)
R Foderi
Pl Île
de Beauté
Blvd
R de la Liberté
Pass Emile Negrin
R Masséna
Espace
Général
Leclerc
Sq
Général
Leclerc
R de la
31
R Rossetti
Parc du
Château
Pl
Robilante
Bassin
Lympia
Q des Deux
Emmanuel
Av de Verdun
R Paradis
Jardin
Albert
1er
R St François de Paule
R A Mari
26
27
Cours Saleya
7
Préfecture
Pl Pierre
Gautier
VIEUX
NICE
Colline du
Château
Q Lunel
Q Papacino
Q des Docks
39
Bassin
des
Amiraux
Carnot
5
Baie des Anges
11
Q Rauba Capeu
Q Infernet
Internet
37
Q du Commerce
To Monaco
via Corniche
Inférieure (N98)
(18km)
38
40
Bassin
du Commerce
6
MEDITERRANEAN
SEA
LP

**Hôtel Plaisance** ( ☎ 04 93 85 11 90; hotelplaisance@ wanadoo.fr; 20 rue de Paris; s/d from €46/56; ✂ P ) Soundproofed rooms with TVs, and modern bathrooms.

**Hôtel L'Oasis** ( ☎ 04 93 88 12 29; www.hotel-oasis -nice.com.fr; 23 rue Gounod; s/d from €43/84; ✂ P ✗ ) An attractive period house where the playwright Chekhov wrote his play *The Three Sisters*. In a quiet close near the sea, it has a verdant, shady garden, appealing rooms and parking (€8).

**Hôtel Félix** ( ☎ 04 93 88 67 73; www.hotel-felix.com; 41 rue Masséna; rooms low/high season €50/70; ✂ ▯ ) This hotel has considerable appeal, with small brightly coloured rooms equipped with hairdryers, air-con and satellite TV.

**Villa Eden** ( ☎ 04 93 86 53 70; hotelvilllaeden@caramail .com; 99 bis promenade des Anglais; s/d/tr €50/75/90; ✂ P ) Across the street from the beach, this is a good option for beach bums. Some of the comfortable, old-fashioned rooms have sea-facing terraces.

**Villa la Tour** ( ☎ 04 93 80 08 15; www.villa-la-tour .com; 4 rue de la Tour; r from €56; ✂ ) A great new place in old Nice. Rooms are individually decorated with contemporary flair, there's a cute little roof patio, a good breakfast (continental/buffet €3.50/7) and, best of all, you're just a stumble from the bars and *socca* joints of the old town.

**Hotel Hi** ( ☎ 04 97 07 26 26; www.hi-hotel.com; 3 ave des Fleurs; rooms €175-500; ▯ ✂ ▯ ✗ ) Step inside this modern, hi-tech place and you could be forgiven for thinking you've somehow boarded an ultra-stylish, candy-coloured, inter-stellar spaceship. Philippe Starck had a hand in designing the functional, modular panelling in ice-cream limes and purples. There's a modish rooftop plunge pool overlooking town and the Alps. Rooms are similarly striking with bright panels of colour and modern entertainment systems. A rather glam clientele, such as fashion designer Jean Paul Gaultier or rock stars like the band REM, may teleport in to join you.

## Eating

The cours Saleya and the narrow streets of Vieux Nice are lined with restaurants, cafés and pizzerias. Local specialties to watch out for include *socca* (a thin layer of chickpea flour and olive oil batter fried on a griddle and served with pepper), *salade Niçoise*, ratatouille and *farcis* (stuffed vegetables,

especially the gorgeous stuffed zucchini flowers).

**Nissa Socca** ( ☎ 04 93 80 18 35; 5 rue Ste-Réparate; menu €13, dishes from €6; ✆ closed Mon lunch & Sun) This is a good place to try many of those local specialities. It's a perennial favourite with locals.

**Chez Rene Socca** ( ☎ 04 93 92 05 73; rue Pairolière; ✆ 9am-10.30pm Jul-Aug, to 9pm rest of the year, closed Mon) A lively, rough and ready place to sample oily, tapas-style dishes for around €2, and good portions of *socca* (crepe). Order and take your food from the window but get your drinks from the waiters when seated.

**Le Merenda** (4 rue de la Terrasse; starters from €9, mains around €16; ✆ Mon-Fri) Tiny and annoying (no phone, no credit cards, no phone reservations) but you won't be disappointed by the first-rate specialities including *pâte au pistou* (pasta with pesto sauce), stockfish and a range of French/Provençale dishes.

**Le Safari** ( ☎ 04 93 80 18 44; 1 cours Saleya; menu €28, mains from €14) Avoiding the heaviness of cheaper Provençale food, this local favourite brings a lighter touch to specialities such as *farcis* and stockfish. Good seafood choices include octopus salad and langoustine pasta.

**Le Pain Quotidien** (cnr rue Louis Gassin & Cours Saleya; breakfast from €6, brunch €18) *The* place in town to have some breakfast, or perhap – tackle the mother of all brunches. Choose your breakfast *formule*, enjoy the excellent hot chocolate, take in the colour and fragrance of the adjacent flower market from the terrace (or inside through the large windows) and be happy.

There's a fantastic **fruit & vegetable market** ( ✆ 7am-1pm Tue-Sun) in front of the prefecture on cours Saleya. There are two **Monoprix supermarkets** (33 ave Jean Médecin; ✆ 8.30am-8.30pm Mon-Sat; pl Garibaldi; ✆ 8.30am-8pm Mon-Sat).

## Drinking & Entertainment

Terraced cafés and bars, perfect for quaffing beers and sipping pastis, abound in Nice. Almost all nightlife is in Vieux Nice, which throbs with activity on summer nights. The most popular pubs in Nice are run by Anglophones, with happy hours and live music.

**Chez Wayne's** ( ☎ 04 93 13 46 99; 15 rue de la Préfecture; ✆ 3pm-midnight) The best-known place for liquor-fuelled carousing. It opens later at weekends. Happy 'hour' is until 9pm.

**Nocy-Bé** (rue de la Prefecture) Cool, dark Moroccan-style tea house where you can sit low on cushions and sip sweet, refreshing mint teas.

**Le Bar des Oiseaux** ( ☎ 04 93 80 27 33; 5 rue St-Vincent; ☾ Mon-Sat) Offers a changing programme of music, theatre and philosophical discussion sessions. Jazz is the strong point. Expect to pay around €5 for admission when there's live music.

**Jonathan's** ( ☎ 04 93 62 57 62; 1 rue de la Loge) Another live music hot spot every night in summer.

## Getting There & Away
### AIR
Nice's international airport, **Aéroport International Nice-Côte d'Azur** ( ☎ 08 20 42 33 33), is located about 6km west of the city centre. The free shuttle bus connects both terminals.

### BUS
Lines operated by some two dozen bus companies stop at the **intercity bus station** ( ☎ 04 93 85 61 81; 5 blvd Jean Jaurès). There's a busy information counter.

There are slow but frequent services until about 7.30pm daily to Cannes (€5.90, 1½ hours), Menton (€5.10, 1¼ hours) and Monaco (€3.90 return, 45 min). For long-haul travel, **Intercars** ( ☎ 04 93 80 08 70), at the bus station, takes you to various European destinations; it sells Eurolines tickets for buses to London, Brussels and Amsterdam.

### TRAIN
Nice's main train station, **Gare Nice Ville** (or Gare Thiers; ave Thiers), is 1.2km north of the beach. There are fast and frequent services (up to 40 trains a day in each direction) to towns along the coast including Cannes (€5.20, 40 minutes), Menton (€3.90, 35 minutes) and Monaco (€3, 20 minutes).

Two or three TGVs link Nice with Paris' Gare de Lyon (€81, 5½ hours), via Lyon (€55.50, 4½ hours).

## Getting Around
Sunbus route No 23 (€1.30), which runs to the airport every 20 or 30 minutes from about 6am to 8pm, can be picked up at the Gare Nice Ville or on blvd Gambetta, rue de France or rue de la Californie.

Local buses, operated by Sunbus, cost €1.30/16 for a single/14 rides. After you

---

**WHERE TO TAKE A BOAT RIDE**

The eucalyptus- and pine-covered **Île Ste-Marguerite** 1km from Cannes is where the enigmatic Man in the Iron Mask – immortalised by Alexandre Dumas in his novel *Le Vicomte de Bragelonne* (The Viscount of Bragelonne) – was held during the late 17th century. The museum in the Fort Royal tells the story (p129).

---

time-stamp your ticket, it's valid for one hour and can be used for one transfer or return. The Nice by Bus pass, valid for one/five/seven days costs €4/12.95/16.75 and includes a return trip to the airport. You can buy single trips, 14-trip cards and a day card on the bus.

## CANNES
pop 68,214
The harbour, the bay, the hill west of the port called Le Suquet, the beachside promenade, the beaches and the people sunning themselves provide more than enough natural beauty to make at least a day trip here worth the effort.

Cannes is famous for its cultural activities and many festivals, the most renowned being the 10-day **Cannes Film Festival** in mid-May, which sees the city's population treble overnight.

The **tourist office** ( ☎ 04 92 99 84 22; www.cannes .com; ☾ 9am-8pm daily Jul- Aug, to 7pm Mon-Sat Sep-Jun) is on the ground floor of the Palais des Festivals. There's an **annexe** ( ☎ 04 93 99 19 77; ☾ 9am-7pm Mon-Sat) next to the train station.

Check email at **Cybercafé Webstation** ( ☎ 04 93 68 72 37; 26 rue Hoche; ☾ 10am-11pm Mon-Sat; 30min/1 hr €3/6).

## Sights & Activities
One of the best ways to spend time here is to meander aimlessly east from the **Vieux Port** and its massive yachts, along the **Croisette** where you can sit and watch Cannes' human circus pass by in all its expensively-but-strangely-dressed, perma-tanned, facelifted, small-yappy-dog-carrying glory.

Housed in the chateau atop Le Suquet, the **Musée de la Castre** ( ☎ 04 93 38 55 26; adult/concession €3/2; ☾ 10am-1pm & 3-7pm Tue-Sun Jun-Aug; to 1pm & 2-6pm Tue-Sun Apr, May & Sep; to 1pm & 2-5pm

FRANCE

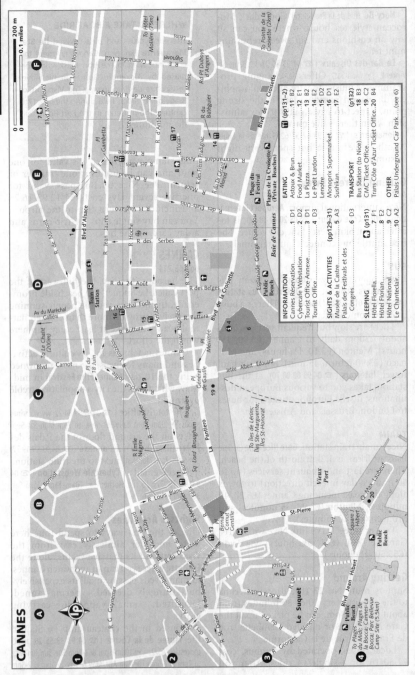

# CANNES

Wed-Mon Oct-Mar) has a diverse collection of Mediterranean and Middle Eastern antiquities, as well as objects of ethnographic interest from all over the world.

Unlike Nice, Cannes is endowed with sandy **beaches**; most are sectioned off for guests of the fancy hotels lining blvd de la Croisette. Sun worshippers pay around €19 a day for the privilege of stretching out on a lounge chair. There's only a small strip of public sand near the Palais des Festivals. However, free public beaches, **Plages du Midi** and **Plages de la Bocca**, stretch westward from the Vieux Port along blvd Jean Hibert and blvd du Midi.

Cannes makes a good base for boat trips up and down the coast. **Trans Côte d'Azur** ( ☎ 04 92 98 71 30; www.trans-cote-azur.com; quai St-Pierre) runs boats to St-Tropez or Monaco (adult/child €31/16 return), Île de Porquerolles (€46/21) and San Remo (€41/19.50) in Italy.

A good trip from Cannes is to the nearby **Îles de Lérins**. The eucalyptus- and pine-covered **Île Ste-Marguerite**, 1km from the mainland is where the enigmatic Man in the Iron Mask – immortalised by Alexandre Dumas in his novel *Le Vicomte de Bragelonne* (The Viscount of Bragelonne) – was held during the late 17th century. The **Musée de la Mer** ( ☎ 04 93 38 55 26; adult/child €3/2; museum & cells ⊙ 10.30am-1.15pm & 2.15pm-5.45pm Wed-Mon Apr-Sep, closes 4.45pm Wed-Mon Oct-Mar), in the Fort Royal, has interesting exhibits dealing with the fort's history.

The smaller, forested 1.5km long and 400m wide **Île St-Honorat** is home to Cistercian monks who own the island but welcome people to visit their monastery and seven small chapels dotted around the island.

All boats for the isles leave from the same point on the quai des îles at the far end of the western arm of the harbour. **Compagnie Maritime Cannoise** (CMC; ☎ 04 93 38 66 33) runs ferries to Île Ste-Marguerite (€9 return, 20 minutes) and **Compagnie Esterel Chanteclair** ( ☎ 04 93 39 11 82) boat has sevices to Île St-Honorat (€10 return, 20 minutes).

## Sleeping

Tariffs rise by up to 50% in July and August. During the film festival hotel rooms, many booked months in advance, are virtually impossible to find.

**Parc Bellevue** ( ☎ 04 93 47 28 97; fax 04 93 48 66 25; 67 ave Maurice Chevalier; camp sites per €20; ⊙ Apr-Sep) In Cannes-La Bocca, this is the nearest place to camp, 5.5km west of the centre. Take No 9 from the bus station on place Bernard Cornut Gentille stops 400m away.

**Le Chalit** ( ☎ 04 93 99 22 11; www.lechalit.com; 27 ave du Maréchal Galliéni; dm in 4-/6-bed rooms €16/20; ⊙ Jan-Oct, ⊙ reception 8.30am-7.30pm) Around 300m northwest of the station, this is a friendly, pleasant private hostel. Sheets cost €3. There is no curfew.

**Le Chanteclair** ( ☎ /fax 04 93 39 68 88; 12 rue Forville; s/d €40/42, with shared bathroom €33/36) A well-run hotel with functional whitewashed rooms in the colourful Le Suquet area, so it's well located for many of the restaurants and the harbour.

**Hôtel Florella** ( ☎ 04 93 38 48 11; fax 04 93 99 22 15; 55 blvd de la République; s/d €60/64, with shared bathroom €40/45) A slightly tatty hotel but friendly, homely and good value.

**Hôtel National** ( ☎ 04 93 39 91 92; fax 04 92 98 44 06; 8 rue Maréchal Joffre; s/d 45/60; ✖ ) The well-equipped and newly refurbished rooms at this friendly hotel are soundproofed and have TVs and hairdryers. Book ahead and try to get a room overlooking the courtyard.

**Hôtel Florian** ( ☎ 04 93 39 24 82; fax 04 92 99 18 30; 31 rue Commandant André; s/d €62/72; ✖ ) A central, neat and modern hotel. All rooms have private bath, TV, telephone and hairdryers.

**Hôtel Moliére** ( ☎ 04 93 38 16 16; www.hotel-moliere .com; 5 rue Moliére; s/d from €79/97; ✖ ) This immaculate, comfortable period place has a picture-postcard garden and a pastel-pink wedding cake exterior. Some rooms have balconies.

## Eating

**Le petit Lardon** ( ☎ 04 93 39 06 28; 3 rue du Batéguier; menu €21) A small, intimate, friendly and reliable place. Here you'll discover reasonably priced local fare, such as *soupe de poisson* and *anchoiade*.

**Astoux & Brun** ( ☎ 04 93 39 21 87; 21 rue Félix Faure; menu €28; ⊙ 10am-1am) This is the place for seafood. Every type and size of oyster is available by the dozen here, as well as elaborate fish platters, scallops, and mussels stuffed with garlic and parsley. In summer, chefs draw the crowds by preparing the shellfish out front.

**La Piazza** ( ☎ 04 92 98 60 80; 9 pl Bernard Cornut Gentille; menu €19, mains €12) This sprawling, friendly establishment offers the best homemade pasta, risotto and pizza in town.

**Sushikan** ( ☎ 04 93 39 86 13; 5 rue Florian; dishes €2.50-4.50) A smart sushi-on-a-conveyor-belt place, which also does takeaways.

**Lenotre** ( ☎ 04 92 92 56 00; 63 rue d'Antibes; breakfast €7, lunch €12; ☽ 8am-4.30pm) With a serene, classy dining room above the patisserie counter, this is a great place to sip espresso, take breakfast or enjoy a light lunch of tarts and pastries among well-to-do ladies who lunch.

**Food markets** (pl Gambetta & rue du Marché Forville) are held every morning except Monday. Large supermarkets include **Monoprix** (9 rue Maréchal Foch).

### Getting There & Away

Buses to Nice (€5.90, 1½ hours, every 20 minutes) leave from place Bernard Cornut Gentille. There is an **information office** ( ☎ 04 93 39 11 39).

From the **train station** ( ☎ 36 35; rue Jean Jaurès) there are regular services to Nice (€5.20,

---

## TOP FIVE SEASIDE SPOTS

■ **Nice** It may be pebbly but Nice's beach extends for miles and the clear water is lovely (p124)

■ **St Tropez** The quintessential Côte d'Azur beach experience is the Plage de Tahiti and Plage de Pampelonne, a magnificent stretch of sand about 4km out of town (p132)

■ **Cannes** Less of a good sun bathing spot (the public beach is tiny and unlovely) but the stylish Croissette is a peerless people-watching location (p129)

■ **Bonifacio** An unforgettable Corsican fortress town perched on steep cliffs 70m above the Mediterranean on a rock promontory sometimes called 'Corsica's Gibraltar' whose tall ancient houses lean precariously over the water (p144)

■ **The Corniches** East of Nice, three heart stopping roads, known as *corniches*, thread through the foothills of the Alps which plummet into the Mediterranean between Nice and the Italian border. The views are spectacular (p124)

---

40 minutes, two an hour) and Marseille (€22.30, two hours).

## ST TROPEZ
pop 5542

A destination for the jet-set (and in summer too many visitors for comfort) St Tropez has long since ceased to be the quiet, charming, isolated fishing village that attracted artists, writers and the gliteratti here in the 20th century. The year things really changed for good was 1956, when *Et Dieu Créa la Femme* (And God Created Woman) starring Brigitte Bardot was shot here. Its stunning success brought about St-Tropez's rise to stardom – or destruction, depending on your point of view.

Away from the conspicuous consumption going on aboard the harbourside yachts, it can still be a place of charm. Sitting in a café on place des Lices in late May, watching the locals play *pétanque* (bowls) in the shade of the age-old plane trees, you could be in any little Provençal village (if you squint to ignore those exclusive boutiques). There is a helpful **tourist office** ( ☎ 04 94 97 45 21; www.saint-tropez.st; quai Jean Jaurès; ☽ 9.30am-8.30pm Jul-Aug, to 12.30pm & 2-7pm Apr-Jun, Sep & Oct, to 12.30pm & 2-6pm Nov-Mar) overlooking the boats.

### Sights & Activities

The **Musée de l'Annonciade** ( ☎ 04 94 97 04 01; pl Grammont, Vieux Port; adult/student €4.50/2.50; ☽ 10am-noon & 3-7pm Wed-Mon Jun-Sep, to noon & 2-6pm Wed-Mon Oct-May, closed Nov) contains a large collection of modern art – be impressed by its works including those by Matisse, Bonnard, Dufy, Derain and Rouault and Signac.

If you're bored with watching the antics of the rich and (maybe not so) famous, the **Citadelle de Saint Tropez** ( ☎ 04 94 97 59 43; adult/concession €4/2.50; ☽ 10am-12.30pm & 1.30-6.30pm Apr-Sep, to 12.30pm & 1.30-5.30pm Oct-Mar) is worth strolling to for the views across the bay, a view you may share with the resident peacocks. Inside the citadelle there are displays on the town's maritime history and the Allied landings that took place here in 1944.

About 4km southeast of the town is the start of a magnificent sandy beach, **Plage de Tahiti**, and its continuation, Plage de Pampelonne. It runs for about 9km between Cap du Pinet and the rocky Cap Camarat.

## Sleeping & Eating

There's not a cheap hotel to be found in St-Tropez. However, to the southeast along Plage de Pampelonne there are plenty of multi-star camping grounds.

**Le Baron** ( ☎ 04 94 97 06 57; fax 04 94 97 58 72; 23 rue de l'Aïoli; r €54-100; 🐾 ) Well worth the cash, Le Baron is calm and quiet. Rooms – all with TV and private bath – overlook the citadel. Some have balconies. Book ahead.

**Lou Cagnard** ( ☎ 04 94 97 04 24; www.hotel-lou-cagnard.com; 18 ave Paul Roussel; rooms €44-100; 🐾 P ) A very pleasant option with attractive rooms containing TV and telephone in a traditional Provençal *mas* (farmhouse), surrounded by shrubs and plants.

**Hôtel La Méditerranée** ( ☎ 04 94 97 00 44; www.hotelmediterranee.org; 21 blvd Louis Blanc; rooms low/high season €50/150; 🐾 ) This solid, period house has recently refurbished rooms, a cosy restaurant and courtyard garden, and a proprietor who can tell you where all the St Trop hotspots are.

**La Table du Marché** ( ☎ 04 94 97 85 20; 38 rue Georges Clemenceau; lunch/dinner formule of main, dessert & glass of wine €18, menu €25; 🕙 lunch & dinner) A stylish place for great pastries in the café at the front (daytime only), for sushi upstairs (summer only) or excellent, reasonably priced brasserie-style food (like scallop raviolis in thyme butter or tomato and basil tart) at the back.

**Le Fregate** ( ☎ 04 94 97 07 08; 52-54 rue Allard; menu €19-27; 🕙 Thu-Tue) The blue and white décor heralds excellent fish dishes. Try the *aïoli* at €15 if it's on the daily menu.

**Le Café** ( ☎ 04 94 97 44 69; pl des Lices) St-Tropez' most historic café was one of the former haunts of BB and her glam friends.

## Getting There & Away

St-Tropez **bus station** (ave Général de Gaulle) is on the southwest edge of town on the main road out. There's an **information office** ( ☎ 04 94 54 62 36; 🕙 8am-noon & 2-6pm Mon-Fri, to noon Sat). A day trip by boat from Nice or Cannes can be a good way to avoid St-Tropez' notorious traffic jams and high hotel prices.

## MENTON
pop 29,266

Menton, a confection of elegant historic buildings in sugared-almond pastels, is only a few kilometres from the Italian border and reputed to be the warmest spot on the Côte d'Azur (especially during winter). It's popular with older holiday-makers, the town's after-dark entertainment is a tad tranquil compared to other spots along the coast. Artist Jean Cocteau lived here from 1956 to 1958. Today, Menton retains a sedate charm free of the airs and pretensions found in other areas of the Côte d'Azur.

The **tourist office** ( ☎ 04 92 41 76 76; www.menton.fr; 8 ave Boyer; 🕙 9am-7pm Mon-Sat, 10am-noon Sun Jul-Aug; 8.30am-12.30pm & 2-6pm Mon-Fri, 9am-noon & 2-6pm Sat low season) is inside the Palais de l'Europe.

The early-17th-century **Église St-Michel** (Church of St Michael; 🕙 10am-noon & 3-5.15pm, closed Sat morning), the grandest and possibly prettiest Baroque church in this part of France, is perched in the centre of the Vieille Ville.

## Sleeping

**Camping Saint Michel** ( ☎ 04 93 35 81 23; route des Ciappes de Castellar; 🕙 1 Apr-15 Oct) This two-star camping ground is 1km northeast of the train station up Plateau St-Michel, close to the youth hostel.

**Auberge de Jeunesse** ( ☎ 04 93 35 93 14; fax 04 93 35 93 07; Plateau St-Michel; dm with breakfast €14.40; 🕙 closed noon-5pm, 10am to 5pm in winter; P ) This hostel occupies a lovely spot high on a hill overlooking town and bay. The walk from the train station is quite a hike uphill. Otherwise take a Line 6 bus and get off at the camping ground. Curfew is midnight (or 10pm in winter).

**Hôtel Le Terminus** ( ☎ 04 92 10 49 80; fax 04 92 10 49 81; pl de la Gare; s/d €30/40, with shared bathroom €28/31; P ) A welcoming, clean place with a few rooms right next to the station. Hall showers are free.

**Hôtel de Londres** ( ☎ 04 93 35 74 62; www.hotel-de-londres.com; 15 ave Carnot; s/d from €53/58, with shared bathroom from €35/38; P 🐾 ) This appealing place has a dining terrace and a garden near the seafront.

## Getting There & Away

The **bus station** ( ☎ 04 93 28 43 27) is next to 12 promenade Maréchal Leclerc, the northern continuation of ave Boyer. There's an **information office** ( ☎ 04 93 35 93 60). There are buses to Monaco (€2.10 return, 30 min), Nice (€5.10 return, 1¼ hours). Trains to Ventimiglia cost €2.10 and take 10 minutes.

# MONACO (PRINCIPAUTÉ DE MONACO)

**pop 30,000**

Tiny, glamorous Monaco, covering a mere 1.95 sq km, is a fantasy land of perfectly groomed streets, lush gardens, chic boutiques and extravagantly opulent 19th-century pleasure palaces. With a photogenic royal family whose heritage stretches back to the 13th century and a stream of high-rollers filling its famous casino or gathering for the annual Formula One Grand Prix race, Monaco never seems to go out of style.

The Principality of Monaco has been under the rule of the Grimaldi family for most of the period since 1297 and is a sovereign state with close ties to France. It has been ruled since 1949 by Prince Rainier III (born 1923), whose sweeping constitutional powers make him much more than a mere figurehead. Rainier's rule modernised Monaco and weaned it from its dependence on gambling revenue, and his marriage to the much beloved Grace Kelly (remembered from her Hollywood days as an actress) restored Monaco's glamour. **Direction du Tourisme et des Congrès de la Principauté de Monaco** ( ☎ 92 16 61 16; www.monaco-tourisme.com; 2a blvd des Moulins; ☺ 9am-7pm Mon-Sat, 10am-noon Sun) is across the public gardens from the casino. From mid-June to late-September several tourist information kiosks open around the harbour.

## Sights & Activities

The changing of the guard takes place daily outside the **Palais du Prince** ( ☎ 93 25 18 31), at the southern end of rue des Remparts in Monaco Ville, at precisely 11.55am. You can also visit the **state apartments** (adult/child €6/3; ☺ 9.30am-6.30pm Jun-Sep, 10am-5pm Oct, closed Nov-May) with commentary through audioguides.

If you're planning to see just one aquarium on your whole trip, the world-renowned **Musée Océanographique de Monaco** ( ☎ 93 15 36 00; ave St-Martin, Monaco Ville; adult/student €11/6; ☺ 9.30am-7pm Jul-Aug, to 6.30pm Apr-Jun, to 7pm Sep) should be it. It has 90 tanks, and upstairs there are all sorts of exhibits on ocean exploration. Bus Nos 1 and 2 are

the alternatives to a relatively long walk up the hill.

Although not all that spectacular, the 1875 Romanesque-Byzantine **cathedral** (4 rue Colonel) has one draw: the grave of former Hollywood film star Grace Kelly (1929–82), which lies on the western side of the cathedral choir. Her modest tombstone, inscribed with the Latin words *Gratia Patricia Principis Rainerii III*, is heavily adorned with flowers.

## Sleeping

Monaco has no hostels or cheap hotels so neighbouring Beausoleil is where to head. When calling these hotels from Monaco (eg from the train station), dial ☎ 00 33, then the listed phone number (dropping the first 0).

**Azur Hotel** ( ☎ 04 93 78 01 25; www.azurhotel.biz; 12 blvd de la Republique; s/d/tr from €42/52/62; 🖳 ) This is probably the pick of places in the area for value, appealing décor and location.

**Hôtel Cosmopolite** ( ☎ 04 93 78 36 00; fax 04 93 41 84 22; 19 blvd du Général Leclerc; s/d €51/54) Cosmopolite has comfortable rooms with TV, telephone, minibars and hairdryers.

## Eating

There are a few sandwich and snack places inside the Centre Commercial Le Métropole. One closely kept local secret, until now, is the very reasonable food available in the quiet little bar above the **rowing club** (quai des Etats Unis; mains €9-12), where locals smoke and play cards.

**Planet Pasta** ( ☎ 93 50 97 02; 6 rue Imberty; pizza/pasta €9-13, mains €17-22) This is a reliable choice, serving filling portions of what its name advertises in a busy, often hot and stuffy dining room.

**U Cavagnetu** ( ☎ 93 30 35 80; 14 rue Comte Félix-Gastaldi; lunch menu €14.50, dinner menu €20-25) One of the few affordable restaurants specialising in Monégasque dishes.

## Getting There & Away

Intercity buses leave from various stops around the city. There's an **information desk** (ave Prince Pierre) at Monaco train station. Taking the train along the coast is highly recommended – the sea and the mountains provide a truly magnificent sight. There are frequent trains eastwards to Menton (€1.70, 10 min), Nice (€2.90, 20 min) and Ventimiglia in Italy (€3, 25 min).

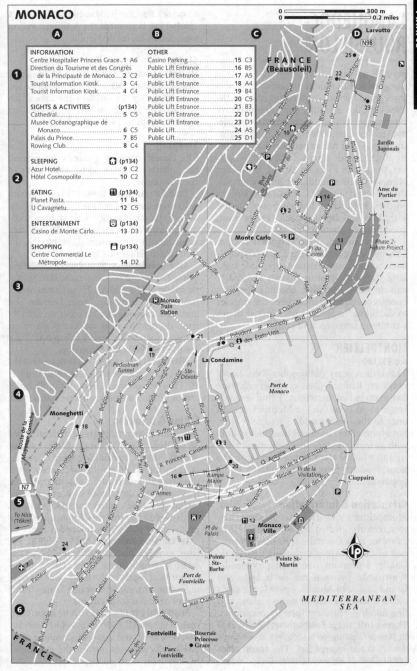

**MONACO**

0 — 300 m
0 — 0.2 miles

**A**    **B**    **C**    **D** Larvotto
N98

**INFORMATION**
Centre Hospitalier Princess Grace..1 A6
Direction du Tourisme et des Congrès
  de la Principauté de Monaco....2 C2
Tourist Information Kiosk............3 C4
Tourist Information Kiosk............4 C4

**SIGHTS & ACTIVITIES** (p134)
Cathedral.................................5 C5
Musée Océanographique de
  Monaco.................................6 C5
Palais du Prince........................7 B5
Rowing Club............................8 C4

**SLEEPING** (p134)
Azur Hotel...............................9 C2
Hôtel Cosmopolite...................10 C2

**EATING** (p134)
Planet Pasta............................11 B4
U Cavagnetu...........................12 C5

**ENTERTAINMENT** (p134)
Casino de Monte Carlo.............13 D3

**SHOPPING** (p134)
Centre Commercial Le
  Métropole...........................14 D2

**OTHER**
Casino Parking.........................15 C3
Public Lift Entrance...................16 B5
Public Lift Entrance...................17 A5
Public Lift Entrance...................18 A4
Public Lift Entrance...................19 B4
Public Lift Entrance...................20 C5
Public Lift Entrance...................21 B3
Public Lift Entrance...................22 D1
Public Lift Entrance...................23 D1
Public Lift.................................24 A5
Public Lift.................................25 D1

FRANCE
(Beausoleil)

Jardin
Japonais

Anse du
Portier

Phase 2-
Future Project

Monte Carlo

Pl du
Casino

Monaco Train
Station

La Condamine

Port de
Monaco

Moneghetti

Ciappaira

To Nice
(16km)

Rampe
Major

Pl
d'Armes

Monaco
Ville

Pl du
Palais

Pointe
Ste-Barbe

Pointe St-
Martin

Port de
Fontvieille

MEDITERRANEAN
SEA

Fontvieille

Roseraie
Princesse
Grace

Parc
Fontvieille

FRANCE

FRANCE

# LANGUEDOC-ROUSSILLON

**pop 2.295 million**

Languedoc-Roussillon is something of a three-eyed hybrid, cobbled together in the 1960s by the merging, for administrative purposes, of two historic regions. **Bas Languedoc** (Lower Languedoc), land of bullfighting, rugby and robust red wines and home to all the major towns, such as Montpellier, the region's vibrant capital, sun-baked Nîmes with its magnificent Roman amphitheatre – and fairytale Carcassonne, with its witches' hat turrets, hovering over the hot plain like a medieval mirage. On the coast, good beaches abound.

Deeper inland, **Haut Languedoc** (Upper Languedoc) occupies rugged, sparsely populated mountainous terrain, great for trekking, mountain pasture, forests and hearty cuisine while **Roussillon**, abutting the Pyrenees, constantly glances over the frontier to Catalonia, in Spain, with which it shares a common language and culture.

## MONTPELLIER

**pop 230,000**

The 17th-century philosopher John Locke may have had one glass of Minervois wine too many when he wrote: 'I find it much better to go twise (sic) to Montpellier than once to the other world'. Paradise it ain't, but Montpellier continues to attract visitors with its reputation for innovation and vitality and a public transport system second to none. Students form nearly a quarter of the population.

### Orientation & Information

Montpellier's mostly pedestrianised historic centre, girdled by wide boulevards, has place de la Comédie at its heart. Northeast of this square is esplanade Charles de Gaulle, a pleasant tree-lined promenade. Westwards, between rue de la Loge and Grand Rue Jean Moulin, sprawls the city's oldest quarter, a web of narrow alleys and fine *hôtels particuliers* (private mansions). There's Internet at **Point Internet** ( ☎ 04 67 54 57 60; 54 rue de l'Aiguillerie; per hr €1.60 ☼ 9.30am-midnight Mon-Sat, 10.30am-midnight Sun). The **tourist office** ( ☎ 04 67 60 60 60; www.ot-montpellier.fr; ☼ 9am-

6.30pm or 7.30pm Mon-Fri, 10am-6pm Sat, 10am-1pm & 2pm-5pm Sun) is towards the southern end of esplanade Charles de Gaulle.

### Sights

**Musée Languedocien** ( ☎ 04 67 52 93 03; 7 rue Jacques Cœur; adult/student €5/3; ☼ 3-6pm Mon-Sat Jul-Aug, 2-5pm Mon-Sat Sep-Jun) displays the area's rich archaeological finds as well as *objets d'art* from the 16th to 19th centuries.

### Sleeping

The closest camping grounds are around the suburb of Lattes, some 4km south of the city centre.

**Oasis Palavasienne** ( ☎ 04 67 15 11 61; www.oasis-palavasienne.com; route de Palavas; camp sites €16.70-24.50; ☼ mid-May–Aug; ☙ ) This shady camping ground has a large pool. Prices vary according to the season. Take bus No 17 from Montpellier bus station.

**Auberge de Jeunesse** ( ☎ 04 67 60 32 22; montpellier@fuaj.org; 2 impasse de la Petite Corraterie; dm €8.90; ☼ mid-Jan–mid-Dec) Montpellier's HI-affiliated youth hostel is just off rue des Écoles Laïques. The grandiose mosaic entrance contrasts with its basic dorms but who can complain when there's a friendly bar and a cheap bed? Take the tram to the Louis Blanc stop.

**Hôtel des Étuves** ( ☎ 04 67 60 78 19; www.hoteldesetuves.fr, in French; 24 rue des Étuves; s €20.50-31, d €32-38) This welcoming, 13-room family hotel creeps around a spiral staircase like a vine.

### Eating & Drinking

You'll find plenty of cheap and cheerful places on rue de l'Université, rue des Écoles Laïques and the streets interlinking them. Place de la Comédie is alive with cafés where you can drink and watch street entertainers strut their stuff. Smaller, more intimate, squares include place Jean Jaurès and place St-Ravy. With over 60,000 students, Montpellier has a profusion of places to drink and dance.

**Le Ban des Gourmands** ( ☎ 04 67 65 00 85; 5 pl Carnot; menu €25, mains €16-18; ☼ Tue-Fri & Sat dinner Sep-Jul) South of the train station and a favourite of locals in the know, this appealing restaurant, run by a young family team, serves delicious local cuisine.

**Tripti Kulai** ( ☎ 04 67 66 30 51; 20 rue Jacques Coeur; salads €8.50, menu €11 & €15; ☼ noon-9.30pm Mon-Sat) Barrel-vaulted and cosy, this popular vegetarian place stands out for the inventiveness of many of its dishes.

**Mannekin-Pis** (110 rue des Balances) This little neighbourhood bar serves eight brands on draught and around 100 in bottles.

The city's **food markets** include **Halles Castellane** (rue de la Loge), the biggest, and **Halles Laissac** (rue Anatole France).

## Getting There & Away

Montpellier's **airport** ( ☎ 04 67 20 85 00) is 8km southeast of town. British Airways flies three times per week (daily in summer) to/from London (Gatwick) and Ryanair operates daily to/from London (Stansted). Air France has up to 10 daily flights to Paris.

The **bus station** ( ☎ 04 67 92 01 43; rue du Grand St-Jean) is an easy walk from the train station. **Hérault Transport** ( ☎ 08 25 34 01 34) runs hourly buses to La Grande Motte (No 106; €1.25, 35 minutes) from Odysseum at the end of the tram line.

**Eurolines** ( ☎ 04 67 58 57 59; ticketing & information office 8 rue de Verdun) has buses to most European destinations including Barcelona (€27, five hours), London (€93, 17hrs) and Amsterdam (€87, 21hrs). **Linebus** ( ☎ 04 67 58 95 00) mainly operates services to destinations in Spain.

Major destinations from Montpellier's two-storey **train station** include Paris' Gare de Lyon by TGV (€70 to €83, 3½ hours, 12 daily), Carcassonne (€19.50, 1½ hours, six to eight daily), Millau (€21.80, 1½ hours, two daily). Over 20 trains daily go northwards to Nîmes (€7.50, 30 minutes).

## CARCASSONNE

pop 46,250

From afar, Carcassonne looks like some fairytale medieval city. Bathed in late-afternoon sunshine and highlighted by dark clouds, La Cité, as the old walled city is known, is truly breathtaking. Once you're inside the fortified walls, La Cité is far less magical. Luring over two million visitors each year, it can be a tourist hell in high summer.

## Orientation & Information

The River Aude separates the Ville Basse from the Cité, up on a hill 500m southeast. Pedestrianised rue Georges Clemenceau leads from the train station and Canal du Midi southwards through the heart of the lower town.

The **tourist office** ( ☎ 04 68 10 24 30; www.carcassonne-tourisme.com; 28 rue Verdun; ☉ 9am-7pm Jul-Aug, to 6pm Sep-Jun) has local information.

## Sights

Dramatically illuminated at night, **La Cité** is one of Europe's largest city fortifications. Only the lower sections of the walls are original; the rest, including the anachronistic witch's-hat roofs (the originals were altogether flatter and weren't covered with slate), were stuck on by Viollet-le-Duc in the 19th century.

The entrance fee to the 12th-century **Château Comtal** (adult/student/child €6.10/4.10/free; ☉ 9.30am-6.30pm Apr-Sep; to 5pm Oct-Mar) lets you visit the castle itself and also join a 30 to 40-minute **guided tour** of both castle and ramparts.

## Sleeping

**Camping de la Cité** ( ☎ 04 68 25 11 77; www.campeoles .com; route de St-Hilaire; camp sites €13.50-19 according to season; ☉ mid-Mar–mid-Oct) A walking and cycling trail leads from the camping ground to both La Cité and the Ville Basse. From mid-June to mid-September, bus No 8 connects it with La Cité and the train station.

**Auberge de Jeunesse** ( ☎ 04 68 25 23 16; carcassonne@ fuaj.org; rue Vicomte Trencavel; dm €15.50; ☉ Feb–mid-Dec; ▣ ) Carcassonne's cheery, welcoming, HI-affiliated youth hostel is in the heart of La Cité. It has a members kitchen, snack bar offering light meals and a great outside terrace. Breakfast is included. Although it has 120 beds, it's smart to reserve year-round.

**Hôtel au Royal** ( ☎ 04 68 25 19 12; godartcl@wanadoo .fr; 22 blvd Jean Jaurès; d €36-65; ☉ Jan-Nov; Ⓟ ) At this attractive mid-range option you're guaranteed a copious, varied breakfast. Rooms are comfortable, well appointed and equipped with ceiling fans and those facing the busy street all have double glazing.

## Eating

**Au Bon Pasteur** ( ☎ 04 68 25 49 63; 29 rue Armagnac; menu €13-22; ☉ closed Sun-Mon Jul-Aug, Sun & Wed Sep-Jun) At this welcoming, intimate family restaurant, you can warm yourself in winter with their yummy cassoulet or *choucroute* (sauerkraut). Year-round, their *menu classique* (€13) and *formules de midi* (lunch specials; €9.50 to €11) both represent excellent value.

**Restaurant Gil** ( ☎ 04 68 47 85 23; 32 route Minervoise; menu €15-33, mains €9-19) At this place you're sure to enjoy quality, Catalan-influenced cuisine. Its particular strength is the sheer quality of its fresh seafood and fish dishes (€10-15), mostly served grilled and unsmothered by superfluous sauces or adornment.

There's a **covered market** (rue Verdun; Mon-Sat) and an **open-air market** (pl Carnot; Tue, Thu & Sat).

## Getting There & Away

**Carcassonne-Salvaza airport** ( ☎ 04 68 71 96 46), 5km from town, has precisely two flights daily – **Ryanair** ( ☎ 04 68 71 96 65) to/from London (Stansted) and to/from Brussels (Charleroi). Carcassonne is on the main line linking Toulouse (€12.10, 50 min) and Montpellier (€18.90, 1½ hours).

## NÎMES

**pop 134,000**

Nîmes is graced by some of France's best-preserved Roman buildings. Founded by Emperor Augustus, the Roman Colonia Nemausensis reached its zenith during the 2nd century AD, receiving its water from a Roman aqueduct system that included the Pont du Gard, a magnificent arched bridge 23km northeast of town. Ransacked by the Vandals in the early 5th century, the city began a downward spiral from which it has never quite recovered. For information drop in to the **tourist office** ( ☎ 04 66 58 38 00; www.ot-nimes.fr; 6 rue Auguste; 8.30am-7pm Mon-Fri, 8am-8pm Jul-Aug, 9am-7pm Sat & 10am-5pm Sun year-round).

## Sights

A **combination ticket** (adult/child €5.70/4.65) admits you to both Les Arènes and Tour Magne. Alternatively, pick up a **three-day pass** (adult/child €10/5), giving access to all of Nîmes' museums and sites, from the tourist office or the first place you visit.

### LES ARÈNES

This superb Roman amphitheatre (adult/child €4.65/3.40; 9am-7pm mid-Mar–mid-Oct, 10am-5pm mid-Oct–mid-Mar), built around AD 100 to seat 24,000 spectators, is wonderfully preserved, even retaining its upper storey, unlike its counterpart in Arles.

### MAISON CARRÉE

This remarkably preserved rectangular Roman temple, today called the Maison Carrée (Square House; as for Les Arènes), was constructed around AD 5 to honour Emperor Augustus' two adopted sons. It has

survived the centuries as a medieval meeting hall, private residence, stable, church and, after the Revolution, archive.

The striking glass and steel building across the square, completed in 1993, is the **Carré d'Art** (Square of Art), which houses the municipal library and Musée d'Art Contemporain. The work of British architect Sir Norman Foster, it's a wonderful, airy building good just to float around.

## Sleeping

**Auberge de Jeunesse** ( ☎ 04 66 68 03 20; nimes@fuaj .org; 257 chemin de l'Auberge de Jeunesse, la Cigale; dm €13.25) Freshly and comprehensively renovated, this hostel is in a lovely park 3.5km northwest of the train station. Take bus No 2, direction Alès or Villeverte, and get off at the Stade stop.

**Hôtel Amphithéâtre** ( ☎ 04 66 67 28 51; hotel -amphitheatre@wanadoo.fr; 4 rue des Arènes; s €37-40, d €47-59; Feb-Dec; ) The welcoming Amphithéatre, once a pair of 18th-century mansions, has recently been taken over by a young family. Rooms are decorated in warm, woody colours and named after writers or painters; we suggest Montesquieu or Arrabal (€59), both large and with balconies overlooking pedestrian place du Marché.

## Eating

**La Truye qui Filhe** ( ☎ 04 66 21 76 33; 9 rue Fresque; menu €8.70; noon-2pm Mon-Sat, closed Aug) Within the vaults of a restored 14th-century inn, this, the bargain of Nîmes, blends a self-service format with a homely atmosphere and does a superb-value menu.

There are colourful Thursday markets in the old city in July and August. The large covered food market is in rue Général Perrier.

## Getting There & Away

Nîmes' **airport** ( ☎ 04 66 70 49 49), 10km southeast of the city on the A54, handles precisely one plane daily – the Ryanair flight to/from London Stansted.

The **bus station** (rue Ste-Félicité) is immediately south of the train station. Regional destinations include Pont du Gard (€5.40, 45 minutes, up to seven daily). There are also buses to/from Avignon (€7.30, 1½ hours, seven daily).

Long-haul operator **Eurolines** ( ☎ 04 66 29 49 02) covers most European destinations including London (€95) and Amsterdam (€87) and, together with **Line Bus** ( ☎ 04 66 29 50 62), services to/from Spain.

There's an **SNCF sales office** (11 rue de l'Aspic). Ten TGVs daily run to/from Paris' Gare de Lyon (€68.90-82.80, three hours). There are frequent services to/from Arles (€6.60, 30 min), Avignon (€7.40, 30 min), Marseille (€16.20, 1¼ hours) and Montpellier (€7.50, 30 min).

## AROUND NÎMES
### Pont du Gard

The Pont du Gard, a Unesco World Heritage site, is an exceptionally well-preserved, three-tiered Roman aqueduct that was once part of a 50km-long system of canals built about 19 BC by the Romans to bring water from near Uzès to Nîmes. The scale is huge: the 35 arches of the 275m-long upper tier, running 50m above the River Gard, contain a watercourse designed to carry 20,000 cubic metres of water per day and the largest construction blocks weigh over five tonnes.

From car parks (€5) either side of the River Gard, you can walk along the road bridge, built in 1743 and running parallel with the aqueduct's lower tier. The best view of the Pont du Gard is from upstream, beside the river, where you can swim on hot days.

# CORSICA (CORSE)

Though Corsica has been governed by mainland France for over 200 years, the island remains a nation apart, with its own distinctive language, customs and character and an entirely unique landscape: 1000km of seaswept coastline, snowcapped mountain-ranges, a world-renowned marine reservation, uninhabited desert and a 'continental divide' running down the island's centre.

A single day's travel can carry you through secret coves, booming waterfalls, plunging canyons, sweeping bays, megalithic menhirs and dense forests of chestnut and pine. Away from the main holiday resorts, you'll discover the quiet fishing villages, remote mountain towns and deserted beaches that died out in the rest of the Mediterranean long ago.

## Dangers & Annoyances

When Corsica makes the headlines, it's often because nationalist militants have turned nasty (previous acts include bombings, bank robberies and the murder of the prefect). But the violence is not targeted at tourists, and visitors have no need to worry about their safety.

## BASTIA
**pop 37,800**

Bustling Bastia, once the seat of Corsica's Genoese governors and retaining a distinctly Italian atmosphere, is Corsica's main centre of business and commerce. Little effort has been made to smarten up the city for tourists, making it an authentic and atmospheric introduction to modern-day Corsica. You can easily spend a day exploring – the old port being Bastia's highlight – but most visitors move on pretty quickly. The focal point of the city is place St-Nicolas. Bastia's main thoroughfares are the busy shopping street of boulevard Paoli and ave Maréchal Sébastiani, which links the ferryport with the train station.

### Information

**Cyber Space** ( ☎ 04 95 30 70 83; 3 blvd Paoli; Internet per 15min/hr €1/3.80; ✆ 9am-midnight Mon-Sat, 4pm-midnight Sun)

**Oxy Cybercafé** ( ☎ 04 95 58 27 96; rue Salvatore Viale; Internet per hr €3.10; ✆ 9am-midnight Mon-Sat)

**Post office** (ave Maréchal Sébastiani; ✆ 8am-7pm Mon-Fri, to noon Sat)

**Tourist office** ( ☎ 04 95 55 96 85; www.bastia-tourisme .com; pl St-Nicolas; ✆ 8am-6pm Mon-Sat, to 1pm Sun)

### Sights & Activities

Bastia can be covered in a half-day stroll starting with **place St-Nicolas**, a vast seafront esplanade laid out in the 19th century. The square is lined with trees and cafés, and at the southern end, a bizarre statue of **Napoleon Bonaparte** depicted as a muscle-bound Roman emperor stands guard.

Between place St-Nicolas and the old port lies **Terra Vecchia**, a historic neighbourhood of old houses and tumbledown tenement blocks.

The **old port** is an atmospheric jumble of boats, restaurants and crumbling buildings, dominated by the twin towers of the **Eglise St-Jean-Baptiste**, which loom over the north side of the harbour.

Bastia's most historic quarter juts out above the old port. The **citadel** (Terra Nova), built by the Genoese between the 15th and 17th centuries to protect Bastia's harbour, can be reached by climbing the stairs through **Jardin Romieu**, the hillside park on the southern side of the harbour.

## Sleeping

**Camping San Damiano** ( ☎ 04 95 33 68 02; www .campingsandamiano.com; camp sites low/high season €5.50/6.50; ☼ Apr-Oct) A shady seaside camping graound 5km south of Bastia, with furnished bungalows available. Served by the airport bus.

**Hôtel Central** ( ☎ 04 95 31 71 12; www.centralhotel .fr; 3 rue Miot; s/d €40-55/50-78 low/high season; ☒ ) As its name suggests, it's right in the city centre and the rooms have all been refurbished: the best have balconies and kitchenettes. You can also rent apartments (€50-65/ 305-420 per day/week).

**Hôtel d'Univers** ( ☎ 04 95 31 03 38; fax 04 95 31 19 91; 3 ave Maréchal Sébastiani; low season s/d/tr €45/55/65, high season €60/70/80; ☒ ) The pick of Bastia's mid-range hotels, tucked between old and new towns. Tasteful rooms have white walls, colourful bedspreads and wood floors.

## Eating

Cafés and restaurants line place St-Nicolas, the old port, quai des Martyrs and place de l'Hôtel de Ville.

**La Marine** ( ☎ 06 12 21 38 09; 8 rue St-Jean; menu €12-21; ☼ Mon-Sat) An informal seafood restaurant which also offers pizzas and Corsican fare on its portside terrace: most of the fish comes literally straight off the boats.

**Chez Mémé** ( ☎ 04 95 31 44 12; quai des Martyrs; menu €14-17) One of many seafront restaurants near the old port, this is a simple, unpretentious place that specialises in fish and shellfish: the €14 *Menu Corse* includes Corsican meats and cheeses.

There's a lively **food market** (Tue-Sun) on place de l'Hôtel de Ville. The large **Spar supermarket** (rue César Campinchi) is the most convenient place for supplies. Out of town, there is a **Casino supermarket** (Géant Port Toga Centre Commercial).

## Getting There & Away

### AIR
**Bastia-Poretta airport** ( ☎ 04 95 54 54 54; bastia. aeroport.fr) is 24km south of the city. Buses (€8, seven to nine daily, fewer on Sunday)

depart from outside the prefecture building. The tourist office has schedules, and timetables are posted at the bus-stop. A taxi to the airport costs €20-30.

### BOAT
The southern ferry terminal is at the eastern end of ave François Pietri. There's an **SNCM office** ( ☎ 04 95 54 66 81; www.sncm.fr; ☼ 8am-11.45am & 2-5.45pm Mon-Fri, to noon Sat) in the southern terminal. **Moby Lines** ( ☎ 04 95 34 84 94; www.mobylines .it; 4 rue du Commandant Luce de Casabianca; ☼ 8am-noon & 2-6pm Mon-Fri, to noon Sat) has a bureau in the ferry terminal, open two hours before each sailing. **Corsica Ferries** ( ☎ 04 95 32 95 95; www .corsicaferries.com; 15 bis rue Chanoine Leschi; ☼ 8.30am-noon & 2-6pm Mon-Fri, 9am-noon Sat) is across the road from the ferry terminal.

### BUS
Buses leave from several locations around town – consult the tourist office. **Eurocorse** ( ☎ 04 95 31 73 76) travels to Ajaccio (€18, three hours) via Corte (€10, two hours) twice daily except Sunday. **Rapides Bleus** ( ☎ 04 95 31 03 79; 1 ave Maréchal Sébastiani) runs buses to Porto-Vecchio (€18.50) with connections to Bonifacio and Sarténe. It sells tickets for the Eurocorse service to Corte and Ajaccio. **Les Beaux Voyages** ( ☎ 04 95 65 11 35) travels to Calvi (€12.50, two hours) daily except Sunday.

### TRAIN
The **train station** ( ☎ 04 95 32 80 61; ave Maréchal Sébastiani; ☼ 6am-8.40pm Mon-Sat, 8.40am-12.40pm & 4.15-8.40pm Sun) is beside the large roundabout on Square Mal-Leclerc. Main destinations include Ajaccio (€20.70, four hours) via Corte, and Calvi (€15.70, four hours).

## CALVI
pop 4800

On a sparkling crescent-shaped bay and backed by snowy peaks, Calvi is a thriving pleasure port that attracts sun-seekers and weekend sailors from all over the Mediterranean, though the towers, bastions and clustered houses of its 15th-century citadel remain as relics of its martial past.

In 1794, a British expeditionary fleet assisting Pasquale Paoli's Corsican nationalist forces besieged and bombarded Calvi during which the legendary British sailor Horatio Nelson was wounded and lost the use of his right eye.

## Orientation & Information

The citadel – also known as the Haute Ville (upper city) – is on a rocky promontory northeast of the Basse Ville (lower city). Blvd Wilson, the major thoroughfare through town, is uphill from the marina.

The **main tourist office** ( ☎ 04 95 65 16 67; omt .calvi@wanadoo.fr; ❨ 8.30am-1pm & 2.30-7pm Jun–mid-Sep, 9am-noon & 2-6pm Mon-Sat Oct-May) is near the marina.

## Sights & Activities

Calvi's massively fortified 15th-century **citadel** dominates the harbour skyline and affords great views. The **Palais des Gouverneurs** (Governors' Palace; pl d'Armes), once the seat of power for the Genoese administration, now serves as a base for the French Foreign Legion.

Uphill from Caserne Sampiero is the 13th-century **Église St-Jean Baptiste**, rebuilt in 1570.

Calvi's 4km of beach begins at the marina and stretches east around the Golfe de Calvi. Other good beaches are west of town, including **Algajola**.

## Sleeping

Calvi's hotels aren't cheap at any time of year, and most are closed in winter.

**Camping La Clé des Champs** ( ☎ 04 95 65 00 86; camagni2@wanadoo.fr; route de Pietra Maggiore; adult/ car/tent €6/2/2.50; ❨ Apr-Oct, reception 9am-10.30pm) South of Les Castors, but still only a short walk to the beach.

**Auberge de Jeunesse BVJ Corsotel** ( ☎ 04 95 65 14 15; bvjhotel.com; ave de la République; dm €22; ❨ Mar-Nov) The hostel offers 120 budget beds, including breakfast.

**Hôtel Le Magnolia** ( ☎ 04 95 65 19 16; fax 04 95 65 08 02; cnr pl du Marché & rue Alsace-Lorraine; s/d low season €65/77-97, high season €85/100-120; ❨ Apr-Jan; ❇ ) An elegant hotel ideally placed just behind the harbour, near Église Ste-Marie. The impeccable rooms have garden or sea views, and you can have breakfast or supper in the tree-covered courtyard.

**Hôtel Le Rocher** ( ☎ 04 95 65 20 04, hotel.le rocher@wanadoo.fr; blvd Wilson; d €90-190; 2-person apt per week €389-793, 4-person apt per week €645-1080; ❨ Apr-Sep; ❇ ) Rooms and mini-apartments with kitchenettes, fridges, TV and telephone.

## Eating

**Île de Beauté** ( ☎ 04 95 65 00 46; quai Landry; menu €20) The best of the romantic waterfront cafés and restaurants. It specialises in fish

and Corsican cuisine: delicacies include red mullet salad, sea bream in pesto sauce, and crab soup.

**U Minellu** ( ☎ 04 95 65 05 52; Traverse á l'Église; menu €14-16; ❨ closed Sun in winter) A delightful family-run restaurant opposite Église Ste-Marie, serving Corsican dishes under a wooden awning lit by lanterns. The menu Corse (€16) includes regional specialties such as *brocciu* cannelloni, Corsican cooked pork, and chestnut and apple cake.

**Best Of** (1 rue Clemenceau; snacks €4-6; ❨ 11.30am-10pm) Head here for something light, such as sandwiches and paninis.

The **Marché Couvert** (covered market; ❨ 8am-noon Mon-Sat) is near Église Ste-Marie Majeure. There's a large **Casino Supermarket** (ave Christophe Colomb) south of the train station. Alternatively, try the well-stocked **Alimentation du Golfe** (rue Clemenceau).

## Getting There & Away

The tourist office has bus information and can supply timetables. Buses to Bastia (€12.50, 2¼ hours) are run by **Les Beaux Voyages** ( ☎ 04 95 65 15 02; pl de la Porteuse d'Eau). From mid-May to mid-October, **Autocars SAIB** ( ☎ 04 95 22 41 99) runs buses from Calvi's Monument aux Morts (war memorial) to Galéria (1¼ hours) and Porto (three hours). There are no buses on Sunday.

Calvi's **train station** ( ☎ 04 95 65 00 61; ❨ until 7.30pm) is off ave de la République. There are two departures daily to Ajaccio (€24.10), Bastia (€15.70) and the stations between. From April to October, the single-car trains of CFC's **Tramway de la Balagne** make 19 stops along the coast between Calvi and Île Rousse (45 minutes).

The ferry terminal is below the southern side of the citadel. From Calvi there are express NGV ferries to Nice (2½ hours, five weekly). Ferry tickets can be bought at the port two hours before departure. At other times, SNCM tickets are handled by **Tramar** ( ☎ 04 95 65 01 38; quai Landry; ❨ 9am-noon & 2pm-6pm Mon-Fri, to noon Sat). Tickets for Corsica Ferries are handled by Les Beaux Voyages.

## PORTO

pop 460

The seaside village of Porto (Portu), which nestles among huge outcrops of red granite and fragrant groves of eucalyptus, is renowned for its fiery sunsets and proximity to the Scandola nature reserve. Hotel prices are reasonable, making it a good base for exploring Les Calanques, a spectacular mountain landscape of orange and red granite, and the mountain villages of Ota and Évisa.

## Orientation & Information

Porto is split into three sections: the marina area, the Vaita quarter further uphill, and the main road from Calvi. Shops, hotels and restaurants are located in all three districts. From the Calvi road to the marina is a walk of about 1km.

The **main tourist office** ( ☎ 04 95 26 10 55; www .porto-tourisme.com; ☺ 9am-noon & 2-6pm Mon-Sat Apr-Jun, Sep & Oct; to 6pm Jul-Aug) is built into the wall below the marina's upper car park. It publishes a good English brochure, *Hikes & Walks in the Area of Porto* (€2.50).

## Sights & Activities

A short trail leads up the rocks to a **Genoese tower** (€2.50; ☺ 10am-noon & 2-7pm Apr-Jun, Sep & Oct; 9am-9pm Jul-Aug). Nearby, the marina overlooks the estuary of the Porto river. On the far side, across a footbridge, there's a modest pebbly **beach** and one of Corsica's best-known **eucalyptus groves**.

From April to October, **Nave Va Promenades en Mer** ( ☎ 04 95 26 15 16; www.naveva.com) and **Porto Linéa** ( ☎ 04 95 26 11 50, ☎ 06 08 16 89 71) offer excursions (€35 to €40 depending on season) to the **Réserve Naturelle de Scandola** (Scandola Nature Reserve), listed by Unesco for its unique marine environment.

## Sleeping

**Le Funtana al' Ora** ( ☎ 04 95 26 11 65; fax 04 95 26 15 48; per person/tent/car €5.50/2.20/2.20; ☺ Apr-Oct) This camping ground, 2km east of Porto on the road to Évisa, has four-person bungalows from €300/540 in low/high season

**Le Golfe** ( ☎ 04 95 26 13 33; Marina; r low/high season €35-50/55-70) This cheap hotel above a café offers basic rooms, some with little balconies overlooking the bay.

**Le Colombo** ( ☎ 04 95 26 10 14; www.hotelcolombo .com; route de Calvi; d with breakfast low/high season €59/120; ☺ Apr-Oct; 🅿 🕸 ) Charming little hotel on the Calvi road, with quirky décor and valley views. Get a balcony if you can.

## Getting There & Away

The **Autocars SAIB** ( ☎ 04 95 22 41 99) has two buses daily, linking Porto and Ota with Ajaccio (€11, two hours, none on Sunday). From May to October a bus runs from Porto to Calvi (€16, three hours). **Transports Mordiconi** ( ☎ 04 95 48 00 44) connects Porto with Corte (€19, 2½ hours, one daily) via Evisa and Ota.

# PIANA

**pop 500 / elevation 438m**

The quiet hillside village of Piana affords breathtaking views of the Golfe de Porto and the soaring central mountains, and makes an excellent base for exploring Les Calanques.

**Hôtel Continental** ( ☎ 04 95 27 83 12; www.cont inentalpiana.com; d low/high season €29-35/32-38, ☺ Apr-Sep) An old, converted townhouse 100m uphill from the church, with 17 old-fashioned rooms and antique décor to match.

**Hôtel des Roches Rouges** (Red Rocks; ☎ 04 95 27 81 81; fax 04 95 27 81 76; d from €69; ☺ Apr–mid-Nov) A grand old 30-room hotel dating from 1912, and without doubt one of Corsica's most romantic places to stay. The elegant double rooms have panoramic views of sea and hills while the antique dining room and period furnishings conjure the air of a bygone age.

Buses between Porto and Ajaccio stop near the church and the post office.

# LES CALANQUES

One of Corsica's most stunning natural sights is just outside Piana: Les Calanques de Piana (E Calanche in Corsican), a spectacular landscape of red granite cliffs and spiky outcrops, carved into bizarre shapes by the forces of wind, water and weather. Less rocky areas support pine and chestnut forests, whose green foliage contrasts dramatically with the technicoloured granite.

# AJACCIO

**pop 60,000**

The pastel-shaded port of Ajaccio or Ajaciv pronounced Ajaxio is the most cosmopolitan city in Corsica. with designer shops, fashionable restaurants and hectic traffic. Inland from the harbour, the modern shopping streets lead into the alleyways and narrow lanes of the old city crowded with 18th-century townhouses. For educational value there are several museums dedicated to Ajaccio's most famous native son, Napoleon Bonaparte.

FRANCE

## Orientation

Ajaccio's main street is cours Napoléon, which stretches from place de Gaulle northwards to the train station and beyond. The old city is south of place Foch. The port is on the east side of town – a tree-lined promenade leads west along plage St-Francois.

## Information

**Game Net** ( ☎ 04 95 50 72 79; 2 ave de Paris; Internet per 15min/1hr €2/5; 🕙 9am-noon & 2pm-9pm Mon-Fri, 2pm-9pm Sat & Sun)

**Main post office** (13 cours Napoléon; 🕙 8am-6.45pm Mon-Fri, to noon Sat)

**Tourist office** ( ☎ 04 95 51 53 03; www.tourisme.fr/ajaccio; 3 blvd du Roi Jérôme; 🕙 8am-7pm Mon-Sat, 9am-1pm Sun)

## Sights & Activities

You can't walk far in Ajaccio without stumbling across some reference to the Ajaccio-born boy who became Emperor of France. In fact, Napoleon spent little of his adult life in Corsica. After crowning himself Emperor of France in 1804, he never returned to the island.

The saga begins at the **Maison Bonaparte** ( ☎ 04 95 21 43 89; rue St-Charles; adult/concession €4/2.60; 🕙 9am-noon & 2-6pm Tue-Sun, 2-6pm Mon Apr-Sep, 10am-noon & 2-5pm Tue-Sat, 2-5pm Mon Oct-Mar), the grand building in the old city where Napoleon was born and spent the first nine years of his childhood.

The impressive **Musée Fesch** ( ☎ 04 95 21 48 17; 50-52 rue du Cardinal Fesch; adult/student €5.35/3.80;

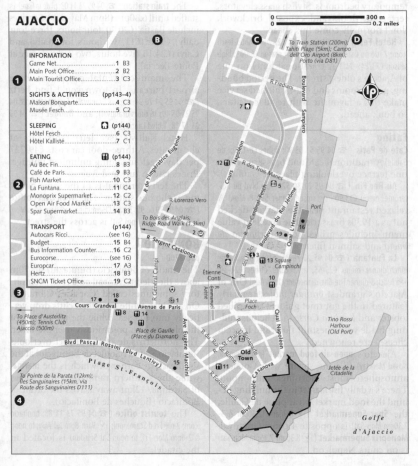

**AJACCIO**

0 — 300 m
0 — 0.2 miles

| INFORMATION | |
| --- | --- |
| Game Net | 1 B3 |
| Main Post Office | 2 B2 |
| Main Tourist Office | 3 C3 |

| SIGHTS & ACTIVITIES | (pp143–4) |
| --- | --- |
| Maison Bonaparte | 4 C3 |
| Musée Fesch | 5 C2 |

| SLEEPING | (p144) |
| --- | --- |
| Hôtel Fesch | 6 C3 |
| Hôtel Kallisté | 7 C1 |

| EATING | (p144) |
| --- | --- |
| Au Bec Fin | 8 B3 |
| Café de Paris | 9 B3 |
| Fish Market | 10 C3 |
| La Funtana | 11 C4 |
| Monoprix Supermarket | 12 C2 |
| Open Air Food Market | 13 C3 |
| Spar Supermarket | 14 B3 |

| TRANSPORT | (p144) |
| --- | --- |
| Autocars Ricci | (see 16) |
| Budget | 15 B4 |
| Bus Information Counter | 16 C2 |
| Eurocorse | (see 16) |
| Europcar | 17 A3 |
| Hertz | 18 B3 |
| SNCM Ticket Office | 19 C2 |

To Train Station (200m);
Tahiti Plage (5km); Campo
dell'Oro Airport (8km);
Porto (via D81)

R Frediani

Boulevard Sampiero

R de l'Impératrice Eugénie

Cours Napoléon

R des Trois Maries

R Lorenzo Vero

To Bois des Anglais;
Ridge Road Walk (1.3km)

R du Cardinal Fesch

Boulevard du Roi Jérôme

Quai l'Herminier

Port

R Sergent Casalonga

R Général Campi

Étienne
Conti

R des

Square
Campinchi

R Emmanuel Arène

Place
Foch

Quai Napoléon

To Place d'Austerlitz
(450m); Tennis Club
Ajaccio (500m)

Cours Grandval

Avenue de Paris

Place de Gaulle
(Place du Diamant)

Blvd Pascal Rossini (Blvd Lantivy)

Ave Eugène Macchini

R du Roi de Rome

R St-Charles

R de Rome

Bonaparte

Old
Town

R Forcioli Conti

R Danièle Casanova

Tino Rossi
Harbour
(Old Port)

Jetée de la
Citadelle

To Pointe de la Parata (12km);
îles Sanguinaires (15km, via
Route des Sanguinaires D111)

Plage St-François

Golfe
d'Ajaccio

FRANCE

☑ 1.15pm-5.15pm Mon, 9.15am-12.15pm & 2.15pm-5.15pm Tue-Sun Apr-Jun & Sep; 1.30pm-6pm Mon, 9am-6pm Tue-Fri, 10.30am-6pm Sat & Sun Jul-Aug; 9.15am-12.15pm & 2.15pm-5.15pm Tue-Sat Oct-Mar), established by Napoleon's uncle, has the finest collection in France of 14th- to 19th-century Italian art outside the Louvre (mostly looted during Napoléon's foreign campaigns), including works by Titian, Botticelli, Raphael, Poussin and Bellini.

## Sleeping

There are no budget options in Ajaccio. Reserve ahead in summer.

**Hôtel Kallisté** ( ☎ 04 95 51 34 45; 51 cours Napoléon; s/d low season €51/56, high season €58/68; ☒ ☒ ☒ ) Excellent city hotel with clean lines and contemporary bedrooms. Stylish glass elevators, terracotta floors and exposed brickwork don't normally come this cheap.

**Hôtel Fesch** ( ☎ 04 95 51 62 62; www.hotel-fesch .com; 7 rue du Cardinal Fesch; s/d low season €54/63, high season €73/84; ☒ ) A traditional hotel on one of Ajaccio's oldest streets. The period building, grand rooms and old-fashioned service make this a favourite with regular visitors, so book ahead.

## Eating

**Café de Paris** ( ☎ 04 95 51 03 90; dishes €8-15; pl de Gaulle) A traditional café and brasserie with a fine terrace overlooking place de Gaulle.

**Au Bec Fin** ( ☎ 04 95 21 30 52; 3 bis blvd du Roi-Jérôme; menu €13.90; ☑ closed dinner Sun & Mon) A relaxed restaurant near the market, decked out as a 1930s brasserie. The excellent value menu includes grilled tuna, *carpaccio de boeuf* and salmon fillet.

**La Funtana** ( ☎ 04 95 21 78 04; 7 rue Notre Dame; lunch/dinner menu €25/55, à la carte dishes €24-30; ☑ lunch & dinner Tue-Sat, dinner only Jul & Aug) One of Ajaccio's grandest *grandes tables*, regularly featured in the gourmet guides. The grilled lobster and *l'anima Corse* (a delicious pudding made with chestnut flour and brocciu cheese) are renowned.

Ajaccio's **open-air food market** (pl Campinchi; closed Monday) fills the square with Corsican atmosphere most mornings until noon. There's a daily **fish market** in the building behind the food market. Near place de Gaulle, the **Spar Supermarket** ( ☑ 8.30am-12.30pm & 3-7.30pm Mon-Sat) is opposite 4 cours Grandval. **Monoprix Supermarket** ( ☑ 8.30am-7.15pm Mon-Sat) is on cours Napoléon.

## Getting There & Away

The **Aéroport d'Ajaccio-Campo dell'Oro** ( ☎ 04 95 23 56 56; ajaccio.aeroport.fr) is 8km east of the city centre.

Bus companies operate from Terminal Maritime et Routier on quai l'Herminier. Most have ticket kiosks on the right as you enter the station. The **information counter** ( ☎ 04 95 51 55 45; ☑ 7am-7pm) provides schedules.

Companies **Eurocorse** ( ☎ 04 95 21 06 30) and **Autocars Ricci** ( ☎ 04 95 51 08 19) serve the main destinations, including Bastia (€18, three hours, two daily); Bonifacio (€19.50, four hours, two or three daily); Calvi (€19.85, change at Ponte Leccia); Corte (€10.50, 2¾ hours, two daily); Porto (€11.45, 2½ hours, two daily). Services run Monday to Saturday.

The **train station** ( ☎ 04 95 23 11 03; pl de la Gare) is staffed until 6.30pm (8pm May-Sep). Services include Bastia (€20.70, four hours, three-four daily), Corte (€11, two hours, four daily), and Calvi (€24.10, five hours, two daily; change at Ponte-Leccia).

The main car-rental companies have airport bureaus. In town you'll find **Hertz** ( ☎ 04 95 21 70 94; 8 cours Grandval); **Europcar** ( ☎ 04 95 21 05 49; 16 cours Grandval); and **Budget** ( ☎ 04 95 21 17 18; 1 blvd Lantivy).

Hôtel Kallisté (see left) rents cars at cheap rates. A three-door car costs €49/227 per day/week including unlimited mileage. Prices rise in July and August.

The ferry terminal is in the same building as the bus station. The **SNCM ticket office** ( ☎ 04 95 29 66 99; 3 quai l'Herminier; ☑ 8am-6pm Mon, to 8pm Tue-Fri, to 1pm Sat) is across the street.

## BONIFACIO
pop 2700

The citadel of Bonifacio (Bunifaziu) sits 70m above the Mediterranean on a rock promontory sometimes called 'Corsica's Gibraltar'. On all sides, white limestone cliffs drop vertically into the sea, while the tall houses of the old city lean precariously over the water. The northern side of the citadel overlooks Bonifacio Sound (Goulet de Bonifacio) at the southeastern corner of which is the **marina**, while the southern ramparts afford views of Sardinia, 12km away across the Strait of Bonifacio (Bouches de Bonifacio).

The **tourist office** ( ☎ 04 95 73 11 88; bonifacio .com; 2 rue Fred Scamaroni; ☑ 9am-8pm Jul-Aug; to noon & 2-6pm Mon-Fri, to noon Sat Sep-Jun) is located in the citadel.

## Sights

### CITADEL

The steps linking rue St-Érasme with Porte de Gênes are known as Montée Rastello and Montée St-Roch further up. At the top of Montée St-Roch stands the **Porte de Gênes**. Just inside the gateway, you can visit the **Grand Bastion** (admission €2; ☺ 9am-6pm Mon-Sat Apr & May, Sep-Oct; daily Jul-Aug) above Porte de Gênes.

Nearby, along the citadel's ramparts, there are great views from **place du Marché** and **place Manichella**.

Criss-crossed by meandering alleyways lined with tall stone houses, the old city has a distinctly medieval feel. **Rue des Deux Empereurs** is so named because Charles V and Napoleon once slept in the houses at Nos 4 and 7. **Église Ste-Marie Majeure**, a 14th-century Romanesque church, is known for its loggia (roofed porch).

From the citadel, the **Escalier du Roi d'Aragon** (Staircase of the King of Aragon; admission €2; ☺ 9am-6pm Mon-Sat Apr & May, Sep-Oct; daily Jul-Aug) leads down the cliff.

Outside the citadel, west along the limestone headland, stands **Église Ste-Dominique** – one of the only Gothic buildings in Corsica. Further west, near three ruined **mills**, the elaborate tombs of the **Cimetière Marin** stand out against a backdrop of crashing waves and wheeling gulls.

## Sleeping

**Camping L'Araguina** ( ☎ 04 95 73 02 96; ave Sylvére Bohn; per person/tent/car €5.50/1.70/1.85; ☺ Mar-Oct) Near the Hôtel des Étrangers, shaded by olive trees and only a short walk into town.

**Hôtel des Étrangers** ( ☎ 04 95 73 01 09; fax 04 95 73 16 97; ave Sylvére Bohn; d €43-71; ☺ Apr-Oct; P ⌘ ) The best deal in Bonifacio is just outside town. This large hotel offers 30 plain rooms and there's plenty of onsite parking – a rare treat in Bonifacio.

**Hotel du Roy d'Aragon** ( ☎ 04 95 73 03 99; royaragon.com; 13 quai Camporetti; d low season €45-79, high season €90-145; ⌘ ⌘ ) A refined hotel that stands out on the crowded quay. The lovely rooms with portside balconies are the best value in Bonifacio – book well ahead.

## Eating

**Le Voilier** ( ☎ 04 95 73 07 06; quai Jérôme Comparetti; menu €24.50, two courses €19) A reliable restaurant offering top-quality fish dishes, from *langoustines* roasted in butter to sea bream cooked with basil sauce.

**L'Archivolto** ( ☎ 04 95 73 17 58; rue de l'Archivolto; plats du jour €7-14; ☺ Mon-Sat) A wonderfully quirky restaurant-cum-antique shop in the citadel, serving imaginative food. Try the chicken in pietra beer and the fresh herb tart with brocciu.

**Super Marché Simoni** (93 quai Jérôme Comparetti; ☺ 8am-12.30pm & 3.30-7.30pm Mon-Sat, to 12.30pm Sun) is on the marina. Next door, **Coccinelle supermarket** (quai Jérôme Comparetti) has a fresh bakery counter.

## Getting There & Away

There are two buses to Ajaccio (€19.50, three to four hours) via Sarténe from Monday to Saturday, run by **Eurocorse** ( ☎ 04 95 70 13 83 in Porto-Vecchio). For Bastia, change at Porto-Vecchio (€6.50, 45 minutes, two to four daily). Buses leave from near the Eurocorse kiosk on the marina in summer only

Daily ferries to Santa Teresa in Sardinia are offered by **Saremar** ( ☎ 04 95 73 00 96) and **Moby Lines** ( ☎ 04 95 73 00 29) from Bonifacio's ferry-port (50 min, two to seven daily). Saremar charges €6.70/8.50 oneway in low/high season, while Moby Lines charges €22/30 return. Cars cost between €21 and €43. Port taxes are €3.

## CORTE

**pop 5700 / elevation 400m**

When Pasquale Paoli led Corsica to independence in 1755, one of his first acts was to make this fortified town at the centre of the island the country's capital. To this day, Corte (Corti) remains a potent symbol of Corsican independence. Paoli founded a national university here in 1765, with 3000 students today.

Ringed with mountains and bordered eastwards by the forest region of Castagniccia, it's also an excellent base for hiking. Some of the island's highest peaks are just west of town. There is Internet access at the **Grand Café** ( ☎ 04 95 46 00 33; 22 cours Paoli; ☺ 7pm-2am; per 15 min/hr €1/3.50). The **tourist office** ( ☎ 04 95 46 26 70; corte.tourisme@wanadoo.fr; La Citadelle; ☺ 9am-noon & 2pm-6pm Mon-Sat Apr & May; to 1pm & 2pm-7pm Mon-Sat Jun & Sep; to 8pm daily Jul & Aug; to noon & 2pm-6pm Mon-Fri Oct-Mar) can provide good local information.

## Sights

### CITADEL

Corte's citadel juts from a rocky outcrop above the Tavignanu and Restonica Rivers and the cobbled alleyways of the Ville Haute. The highest point is the **chateau** (known as the Nid d'Aigle, or Eagle's Nest), built in 1419 by a Corsican nobleman allied with the Aragonese. It was expanded during the 18th and 19th centuries and served as a Foreign Legion base from 1962 until 1983.

The **Museu di a Corsica** (Musée de la Corse; ☎ 04 95 45 25 45; museu@sitec.fr; adult/student €3/2.30; ☼ 10am-6pm Tue-Sun, to 5pm Nov-Apr, daily late Jun–late Sep) houses an outstanding exhibition (in French and Corsican) on Corsican traditions, crafts, agriculture, and anthropology. Outside the ramparts, a path leads to the **belvédère** (viewing platform), which has views of the city and the Eagle's Nest. Nearby, a precarious staircase leads down to the river.

## Sleeping

**Camping Alivetu** ( ☎ 04 95 46 11 09; fax 04 95 46 12 34; faubourg de St-Antoine; per person/car/tent €5/2/2; ☼ Apr-Oct) Attractive and shaded by olive trees.

**Hôtel de la Paix** ( ☎ 04 95 46 06 72; fax 04 95 46 23 84; ave du Général de Gaulle; s/d/tr from €35/42/55; **P** ) A big, comfortable hotel with 60 spic-and-span rooms on a quiet square off cours Paoli. The inhouse Corsican restaurant (menu €13) is decent too.

**Hôtel de la Poste** ( ☎ 04 95 46 01 37; 2 pl du Duc de Padoue; rooms €33.50) On the same square as Hôtel de la Paix, but looking rather worse for wear, this is a typically Corsican no-frills hotel with mismatched décor and run-down charm.

## Eating

**A Merenda** ( ☎ 04 95 46 30 99; 3 cours Paoli; ☼ 9am-midnight Mon-Sat) A popular café-bar and *salon du thé* with delicious coffee and light meals, including salads and *croques-monsieurs*.

**Grand Café** ( ☎ 04 95 46 00 33; 22 cours Paoli; ☼ 7-2am) A cosy student hangout underneath the Hotel du Nord where you can leave your backpacks for free.

**U Museu** ( ☎ 04 95 61 08 36; rampe Ribanelle; menu €13-15; ☼ closed Sun Oct-Jun) Corte's outstanding Corsican restaurant serves traditional cuisine on a gazebo-covered terrace. Its menus include *civet de sanglier aux myrtes sauvages* (wild boar with myrtle), *soissons*

*Corses* (Corsican lima beans), and *truite au peveronata* (trout in red pepper sauce).

**La Trattoria** ( ☎ 04 95 46 00 76; 6 cours Paoli; menu €9-14; ☼ closed Sun) A family-run restaurant loved by locals, which serves up classic Corsican meat dishes and enormous salads. The next-door patisserie is the best in town.

Corte's top boulangerie is **Casanova** (cours Paoli), next door to La Trattoria – practically the whole town comes here to buy their cakes. There's also a **Eurospar** (7 ave Xavier Luciani) and a **Casino Supermarket** (allée du 9 Septembre).

## Getting There & Away

Eurocorse travels through town twice daily from Ajaccio (€9.90, 2¾ hours) towards Bastia (€8.40, 1¼ hours) except Sunday.

The **train station** ( ☎ 04 95 46 00 97; ☼ 6.30am-8.30pm Mon-Sat, 9.45am-noon & 4.45-8.35pm Sun) is 1km east of the city centre. Destinations include Bastia (€9.70, two hours, three to four daily) and Ajaccio (€11, two hours, three-four daily).

# FRANCE DIRECTORY

## ACCOMMODATION

Accommodation is listed in this chapter in ascending order of price (ie from budget to top end). Hotels listed under 'budget' have doubles up to €40 (€50 in Paris). Most are equipped with a washbasin but lack private bath/shower or toilet. Hall showers usually cost €2. Prices quoted in this chapter for budget are for shared bathroom facilities unless otherwise stated.

Hotels listed under 'mid-range' are usually in the range of €40 to €100 for a double (up to €150 in Paris) and always have en-suite bathroom facilities. These places are comfortable and good value. 'Top end' accommodation will cost more than €100 (€150 in the capital). Prices quoted in this chapter for mid-range and top-end accommodation include en-suite bathroom unless stated.

During periods of heavy domestic or foreign tourism, popular destinations are packed out. Tourist offices will often reserve rooms (generally for a fee).

## Camping & Caravan Parks

Camping is immensely popular in France, and many of the thousands of camping grounds are near rivers, lakes or oceans.

Most close from October or November to March or April. Hostels sometimes let travellers pitch tents. Gîtes de France coordinates farm camping and publishes an annual guide *Camping à la Ferme*.

Camping in non-designated spots, or *camping sauvage*, is usually illegal. Camping on the beach is not a good idea in areas with high tidal variations.

### Gîtes Ruraux & B&Bs

A *gîte rural* is a self-contained holiday cottage (or part of a house) in a village or on a farm. A *chambre d'hôte*, basically a B&B (bed and breakfast), is a room in a private house, rented by the night. The website www.bbfrance.com is useful for arranging B&Bs and vacation rentals.

Ask about Gîtes de France offices and brochures and guides at local tourist offices, or contact the **Fédération Nationale des Gîtes de France** ( ☎ 01 49 70 75 75; www.gites-de-france.fr).

### Hostels

Official hostels are known as *auberges de jeunesse*. A hostel bed generally costs around €20 (including breakfast) in Paris, and €8 to €13 in the provinces.

The major hostel associations, **Fédération Unie des Auberges de Jeunesse** (FUAJ; ☎ 01 48 04 70 30; www.fuaj.org) and **Ligue Française pour les Auberges de la Jeunesse** (LFAJ; ☎ 01 44 16 78 78; www .auberges-de-jeunesse.com) need you to have or purchase a Hostelling International (HI) card or a nightly Welcome Stamp. Bring your own sleeping sheet or rent one for a small fee.

The non-profit organisation **Union des Centres de Rencontres Internationales de France** (UCRIF; ☎ 01 40 26 57 64; www.ucrif.asso.fr) has 'international holiday centres' with private rooms, dorms and restaurant facilities.

In university towns, student dormitories (*foyers d'étudiant*) are sometimes converted for travellers during summer. Relatively unknown, these places frequently have space when other hostels are full.

### Hotels

A double has one double bed, so specify if you prefer twin beds (*deux lits séparés*). Look out for great weekend deals to 33 cities and towns at www.bon-week-end-en-villes.com. **Logis de France** ( ☎ 01 45 84 83 84; www.logis-de-france.fr) publishes an annual guide with maps.

## ACTIVITIES

France's varied geography and climate make it a superb place for a wide range of outdoor pursuits. France's stunning scenery lends itself to adventure sports and exhilarating outdoor activities of all kinds.

### Cycling

The best areas for cycling (with varying grades of difficulty) are in the French Alps, the Jura, and the Pyrenees, the Dordogne, Quercy, Brittany, Normandy and the Atlantic coast. Lonely Planet's *Cycling France* includes maps, directions and technical tips.

### Walking

France is crisscrossed everywhere by a staggering 120,000km of *sentiers balisés* (marked walking paths), which pass through every imaginable kind of terrain. Make note that there are restrictions on where you can camp, especially in national parks.

Probably the best-known trails are the *sentiers de grande randonnée*, long-distance footpaths marked by red-and-white striped track indicators.

The **Club Alpin Français** (Map pp50-1; ☎ 01 53 72 87 00; www.clubalpin.com; 24 ave de Laumiére, 19e Paris; metro Laumiére) has a centre with useful information in Paris – joining is probably worthwhile if you're planning to do a great deal of hiking.

Lonely Planet's *Walking in France* is packed with essential practical information.

### Skiing

France has more than 400 ski resorts in the Alps, the Jura, the Pyrenees, the Vosges, the Massif Central and even Corsica. The ski season generally lasts from December to March or April. January and February tend to have the best overall conditions.

The Alps have some of Europe's finest – and priciest – ski facilities. Much cheaper and less glitzy, smaller, low-altitude stations are in the Pyrenees and the Massif Central.

One of the cheapest ways to ski in France is to buy a package deal before leaving home. Websites for online bookings include www .ski-europe.com and www.alpsweek.com.

### Watersports

France has lovely beaches. The fine, sandy beaches along the family-oriented Atlantic coast (eg near La Rochelle) are less crowded than their often pebbly counterparts on the Côte d'Azur. Corsica has some magnificent spots. Brittany and the north coast are also popular (though cooler) beach destinations.

The best surfing in France is on the Atlantic coast around Biarritz, where waves can reach heights of 4m. Windsurfing is popular wherever there's water and a breeze, and renting equipment is often possible on lakes.

White-water rafting and kayaking are practised on many French rivers, especially in Massif Central and the Alps. The **Fédération Française de Canoë-Kayak** (FFCK; ☎ 01 45 11 08 50; www.ffck.org) can supply information on canoeing and kayaking clubs around the country.

## BUSINESS HOURS

Shop hours are usually 9am or 10am to 6pm or 7pm, often (except in Paris) with a break from noon or 1pm to 2pm or 3pm. Most businesses close on Sunday; exceptions include grocery stores, *boulangeries* and patisseries. Many will also close on Monday.

Restaurants are usually open for lunch between noon and 2pm and for dinner from 7.30pm. Cafés open from early morning until around midnight. Bars usually open early evening and close at 1am or 2am.

Banks usually open from 9am to 1pm and 2pm to 5pm, Monday to Friday or Tuesday to Saturday. Post offices open 8.30am or 9am to 5pm or 6pm on weekdays (perhaps with a midday break) and Saturday morning.

Supermarkets open Monday to Saturday from about 9.30am to 7pm (plus a midday break in smaller towns); some open on Sunday morning.

## EMBASSIES & CONSULATES
### French Embassies & Consulates

France's diplomatic and consular representatives abroad are listed on the website www.france.diplomatie.fr.

**Australia** Canberra ( ☎ 02-6216 0100; www.ambafrance -au.org; 6 Perth Ave, Yarralumla, ACT 2600); Sydney ( ☎ 02-9261 5779; www.consulfrance-sydney.org; 20th floor, St Martin's Tower, 31 Market St, Sydney, NSW 2000)
**Canada** Ottawa ( ☎ 613-789 1795; www.ambafrance -ca.org; 42 Sussex Drive, Ottawa, Ont K1M 2C9); Toronto ( ☎ 416-925 8041; www.consulfrance-toronto.org; 130 Bloor West, Suite 400, Ont M5S 1N5)
**Germany** Berlin ( ☎ 030-590 039 000; www.botschaft -frankreich.de; Parizer Platz 5, 10117); Munich ( ☎ 089-419 4110; Möhlstrasse 5, 81675)

**Italy** ( ☎ 06-686 011; www.ambafrance-it.org; Piazza Farnese 67, Rome 00186)
**Netherlands** The Hague ( ☎ 070-312 5800; www .ambafrance-nl.org; Smidsplein 1, 2514 BT); Amsterdam ( ☎ 020-530 6969; www.consulfrance-amsterdam.org; Vijzelgracht 2, 1017 HR)
**New Zealand** ( ☎ 04-384 2555; www.ambafrance -nz.org; Rural Bank Building, 34-42 Manners St, Wellington)
**UK** London ( ☎ 020-7073 1000; www.ambafrance-uk.org; 58 Knightsbridge, London SW1X 7JT); Consulate ( ☎ 020-7073 1200; 21 Cromwell Rd, London SW7 2EN); Visa section ( ☎ 020-7838 2051; 6A Cromwell Place SW7 2EW)
**USA** Washington ( ☎ 202-944 6000; 4101 Reservoir Rd NW, DC 20007); New York ( ☎ 212-606 3600/89; www .consulfrance-newyork.org; 934 Fifth Ave, NY 10021) San Francisco ( ☎ 415-397 4330; www.consulfrance-san francisco.org; 540 Bush St, CA 94108)

### Embassies & Consulates in France

All foreign embassies can be found in Paris. Many countries – including the USA, Canada and most European countries – also have consulates in other major cities. To find an embassy or consulate not listed here, look up 'Ambassades et Consulats' in the *Yellow Pages* (*Pages Jaunes*; www.pages jaunes.fr) for Paris.

Countries represented in Paris include:
**Australia** (Map pp50-1; ☎ 01 40 59 33 00; www .austgov.fr; 4 rue Jean Rey, 15e; metro Bir Hakeim)
**Canada** (Map pp50-1; ☎ 01 44 43 29 00; www .amb-canada.fr; 35 ave Montaigne, 8e; metro Franklin D Roosevelt); Nice ( ☎ 04 93 92 93 22; 10 rue Lamartine)
**Germany** (Map pp50-1; ☎ 01 53 83 45 00; www.amb -allemagne.fr; 13-15 ave Franklin D Roosevelt, 8e; metro Franklin D Roosevelt)
**Ireland** (Map pp50-1; ☎ 01 70 20 00 20; 33 rue Miromesnil, 8e; metro Miromesnil)
**Italy** (Map pp50-1; ☎ 01 49 54 03 00; www.amb -italie.fr; 51 rue de Varenne, 7e; metro Rue du Bac)
**Netherlands** (Map pp50-1; ☎ 01 40 62 33 00; www .amb-pays-bas.fr; 7 rue Eblé, 7e; metro St-François Xavier)
**New Zealand** (Map pp50-1; ☎ 01 45 01 43 43; www .nzembassy.com; 7 ter rue Léonard de Vinci, 16e; metro Victor Hugo)
**UK** Paris ( ☎ 01 44 51 31 00; www.amb-grandebretagne .fr; 35 rue du Faubourg St-Honoré, 8e; metro Concorde); Paris ( ☎ 01 44 51 31 02; 16 bis rue d'Anjou, 8e metro Madeleine); Nice ( ☎ 04 93 62 13 56; 26 ave Notre Dame); Marseille ( ☎ 04 91 15 72 10; 24 ave du Prado)
**USA** Paris (Map pp50-1; ☎ 01 43 12 22 22; www.amb -usa.fr; 2 ave Gabriel, 8e metro Concorde); Paris ( ☎ 01 43 12 47 08; 2 rue St-Florentin, 1er metro Concorde); Nice ( ☎ 04 93 88 89 55; 7 ave Gustav V, 06000); Marseille ( ☎ 04 91 54 92 00; place Varian Fry)

## FESTIVALS & EVENTS

Most French cities, towns and villages have at least one major music, dance, theatre, cinema or art festival each year.

### May/June

**May Day** (France; 1 May) Workers day is celebrated with trade union parades, and diverse protests. People give each other *muguet* (lilies of the valley) for good luck. No one works (except waiters and muguet sellers).

**Cannes Film Festival** (Cannes; mid-May; www.festival -cannes.com) The stars walk the red carpet at Cannes, the epitome of see-and-be-seen cinema events in Europe.

**Fête de la Musique** (France; 21 June; www.fetedela musique.culture.fr) Bands, orchestras, crooners, buskers and spectators take to the streets for this national celebration of music.

### July

**National Day** (France; 14 July) Fireworks, parades and all-round hoo-ha to commemorate the storming of the Bastille in 1789, symbol of the French Revolution.

**Gay Pride** (Paris and other cities; www.gaypride.fr) Effervescent street parades, performances and parties through Paris and other major cities.

### August/September

**Festival Interceltique** (Lorient; www.festival-inter celtique.com) This massive August event pulls hundreds of thousands of Celts from all over Brittany and the UK for a massive celebration of their shared celtic culture.

### December

**Christmas Markets** (Alsace) Alsace is the place to be for a traditional-style festive season, with world-famous Christmas markets, decorations and celebrations.

## GAY & LESBIAN TRAVELLERS

France is one of Europe's most liberal countries when it comes to homosexuality. Paris has been a thriving gay and lesbian centre since the late 1970s. Montpellier, Lyon, Toulouse, Bordeaux and many others also have significant communities. Attitudes towards homosexuality tend to become more conservative in the countryside and villages. France's lesbian scene is much less public than its gay counterpart and is centred mainly around women's cafés and bars (the best places to find information).

Online, www.gayscape.com has hundreds of links, while www.france.qrd.org is a 'queer resources directory' for gay and lesbian travellers. Another good sight for finding out about gay events is http://citegay.fr.

## HOLIDAYS

The following *jours fériés* (public holidays) are observed in France.

**New Year's Day** (Jour de l'An) 1 January – parties in larger cities; fireworks are subdued by international standards

**Easter Sunday and Monday** (Pâques & lundi de Pâques) Late March/April

**May Day** (Fête du Travail) 1 May – traditional parades

**Victoire 1945** 8 May – the Allied WWII victory in Europe

**Ascension Thursday** (L'Ascension) May – celebrated on the 40th day after Easter

**Pentecost/Whit Sunday and Whit Monday** (Pentecôte & lundi de Pentecôte) Mid-May to mid-June – celebrated on the seventh Sunday after Easter

**Bastille Day/National Day** (Fête Nationale) 14 July – *the* national holiday

**Assumption Day** (L'Assomption) 15 August

**All Saints' Day** (La Toussaint) 1 November

**Remembrance Day** (L'onze novembre) 11 November – celebrates the WWI armistice

**Christmas** (Noël) 25 December

## LEGAL MATTERS

French police have wide powers of search and seizure, and can ask you to prove your identity at any time. Foreigners must be able to prove their legal status in France (eg passport, visa, residency permit) without delay. If the police stop you for any reason, be polite and remain calm. You may refuse to sign a police statement, and have the right to ask for a copy. French law does not officially distinguish between 'hard' and 'soft' drugs.

## MONEY

The official currency of France is the euro. You always get a better exchange rate in-country, though it's a good idea to arrive with enough local currency to take a taxi to a hotel. Automated Teller Machines (ATMs), or *distributeurs automatiques de billets* (DAB) are plentiful in all major cities and towns. Visa and MasterCard (Access or Eurocard) are widely accepted. In general cards can be used in shops, supermarkets, for train travel, car rentals, autoroute tolls and cash advances. Don't assume that you can pay for a meal or a budget hotel with a credit card – inquire first. For lost travellers cheques call **AmEx** ( ☎ 0 800 90 86 00) or **Thomas Cook** ( ☎ 0 800 90 83 30). For lost cards, these numbers operate 24 hours:

**FRANCE**

**AmEx** ( ☎ 01 47 77 72 00; AmEx offices arrange on-the-spot replacements)
**Diners Club** ( ☎ 0810 314 159)
**MasterCard, Eurocard & Access** (Eurocard France; ☎ 0 800 90 13 87)
**Visa** (Carte Bleue; ☎ 0 800 90 20 33)

## POST

Each of France's 17,000 post offices is marked with a yellow or brown sign reading 'La Poste'. Since La Post also has banking functions, queues can be very long, but there are automatic machines for postage.

### Postal Rates

Domestic letters of up to 20g cost €0.50. Internationally, there are three different zones: a letter/package under 20g/2kg costs €0.50/12.50 to Zone A (EU, Switzerland, Iceland, Norway); €0.75/14 to Zone B (the rest of Europe and Africa); and €0.90/20.50 to Zone C (North and South America, Asia & Middle East, Australasia). Worldwide express mail delivery **Chronopost** ( ☎ 0 825 80 18 01) costs a lot and is not as rapid as advertised.

### Receiving Mail

Picking up poste-restante mail costs €0.50; you must show your passport or national ID card. Mail will be kept for 15 days. Poste-restante mail not addressed to a particular branch goes to the city's main post office.

## TELEPHONE
### International Dialling

Phone cards offer better international rates than Country Direct services (which allow you to be billed by the long-distance carrier you use at home). To make a reverse-charges (collect) call *(en PCV)* or a person-to-person call *(avec préavis)*, dial ☎ 3123 or ☎ 0 800 990 011 (for the USA and Canada) and ☎ 0 800 990 061 for Australia. Expect about €12 for a three-minute call.

---

**EMERGENCY NUMBERS**

- Ambulance (SAMU) ☎ 15
- Fire ☎ 18
- Police ☎ 17
- EU-wide emergency hotline ☎ 112
- Rape crisis hotline ☎ 0 800 059 595

---

### National Dialling Areas

France has five telephone dialling areas. You dial the same 10-digit number no matter where you are, but it is cheaper to call locally. The five regional area codes are:

| | |
|---|---|
| ☎ 01 | Paris region |
| ☎ 02 | the northwest |
| ☎ 03 | the northeast |
| ☎ 04 | the southeast (including Corsica) |
| ☎ 05 | the southwest |

For France Telecom's directory inquiries *(services des renseignements)*, dial ☎ 12 (around €0.45 per minute). Not all operators speak English. Emergency numbers and 0800 numbers can be dialled free from public and private telephones.

### Public Phones & Telephone Cards

Almost all public telephones in France are card-operated. Cards can be purchased for €7.50 or €15 at post offices, *tabacs* (tobacconists) and anywhere that you see a blue sticker reading *'télécarte en vente ici'*. A whole bevy of other cards are available for cheap international calls.

### Mobile Phones

France uses GSM 900/1800, which is compatible with the rest of Europe and Australia but not with the North American GSM 1900 (though some North Americans have GSM 1900/900 phones that do work here).

The three major mobile networks are **Bouygues** ( ☎ 0 810 63 01 00; www.bouygtel.com), France Telecom's **Orange** ( ☎ 0 800 83 08 00; www.orange.fr) and **SFR** (0800 10 60 00; www.sfr.com). If you already have a compatible phone, you can buy a pre-paid phone SIM-card with a mobile phone number. When these run out you purchase a recharge card at most *tabacs*.

## VISAS

EU nationals and citizens of Switzerland, Iceland and Norway need only a passport or national identity card to enter France. Citizens of Australia, the USA, Canada, New Zealand, Japan and Israel do not need visas to visit France as tourists for up to three months; the same goes for citizens of EU candidate countries (except Turkey).

Those not exempt will need a visa allowing unlimited travel throughout the entire zone for 90 days. Apply to the consulate of the country you are entering first, or that of your main destination. Among other things, you will need medical insurance and proof of sufficient funds to support yourself. See www.eurovisa.com for information.

# TRANSPORT IN FRANCE

## GETTING THERE & AWAY
## Air
### AIRPORTS
**Air France** (www.airfrance.com), France's national carrier, and scores of other airlines link Paris with every part of the globe. France's two major international airports are Roissy-Charles de Gaulle (CDG, ☎ 01 48 62 12 12) and Orly (ORY; ☎ 01 49 75 15 15), both run by **Aeroports de Paris** ( ☎ 01 43 35 70 00; www.adp.fr). For details on these airports see the Paris chapter.

Other airports with significant international services (mostly within Europe) are:
**Bordeaux** (code BOD; ☎ 05 56 34 50 50; www .bordeaux.aeroport.fr)
**Lyon** (code LYS; ☎ 0826 800 826; www.lyon.aeroport.fr)
**Marseille** (code MRS; ☎ 04 42 14 14 14; www .marseille-provence.aeroport.fr)
**Nice** (code NCE; ☎ 0820 423 333; www.nice.aeroport.fr)
**Strasbourg** (code SXB; ☎ 03 88 64 67 67 www.strasbourg .aeroport.fr)
**Toulouse** (code TLS; ☎ 0825 380 000; www.toulouse .aeroport.fr)

Some airlines or budget carriers use provincial airports for UK, continental Europe and sometimes North African flights. Small airports taking international flights include Biarritz, Caen, Carcassone, Metz-Nancy-Lorraine, Montpellier, Rennes and Quimper.

### AIRLINES
Most of the world's major carriers serve Paris at the very least. Airlines flying to and from France include:
**Aer Lingus** (code EI; ☎ 01 70 20 00 72; www.aerlingus .com; hub Dublin)
**Air Canada** (code AC; ☎ 0 825 880 881; www.air canada.ca; hub Toronto)
**Air France** (code AF; ☎ 0 820 820 820; www.airfrance .com; hub Paris)
**Alitalia** (code AZ; ☎ 0 820 315 31; www.alitalia.com; hub Rome)
**American Airlines** (code AA; ☎ 0 810 872 872; www .americanairlines.com; hub Dallas)

**Basiqair** (code HV; www.basiqair.com; hub Amsterdam)
**BMI BritishMidland** (code BD; ☎ www.flybmi.com; hub London)
**British Airways** (code BA; ☎ 0 825 825 400; www .britishairways.com; hub London)
**Easyjet** (code EZY; ☎ 023-568 4880; www.easyjet.com; hub London Luton)
**Iberia** (code IB; ☎ 0 820 075 075; www.iberia.com; hub Madrid)
**Lufthansa** (code LH; ☎ 0 820 020 030; www.lufthansa .com; hub Frankfurt)
**Ryanair** (code FR; www.ryanair.com; hub London Stansted & Dublin)

## Land
If you are doing a lot of travel around Europe, look for discount bus and train passes, which can be conveniently combined with discount air fares.

### BUS
Buses are slower and less comfortable than trains, but they are cheaper, especially if you qualify for discount rates (youths under 26, seniors over 60, teachers and students).

The company **Eurolines** ( ☎ 08 92 69 52 52, ☎ 01 43 54 11 99; www.eurolines.com) groups together 31 European coach operators and links points all across Europe as well as Morocco and Russia. Eurolines' all-Europe website has links to each national company's site and gives detailed information on fares, routes, bookings and special deals. You can usually book online. Return tickets cost about 20% less than two oneways. In summer, make reservations at least two working days in advance. The main hub is Paris.

French coach company **Intercars** (www .intercars.fr, in French) links France with cities throughout Europe, including Eastern Europe and Russia. The office in **Paris** ( ☎ 01 42 19 99 35; 139 bis rue de Vaugirard, 15e; metro Falguière) links with Berlin (€77, 13hrs), Moscow (€234, 50hrs), and many places in between. From **Lyon** ( ☎ 04 78 37 20 80; Perrache bus station) you can reach Venice, Naples, Porto, Minsk or Zagreb. From **Nice** ( ☎ 04 93 80 08 70; Nice bus station) you can reach San Sebastian, Casablanca and Warsaw. Reserve by emailing the agency closest to your place of departure.

### CAR & MOTORCYCLE
Arriving in France by car is easy. At some border points you may be asked for your passport or identity card (a drivers' licence

will not be sufficient ID). Police searches are not uncommon for vehicles entering France, particularly from Spain and Belgium.

### Eurotunnel

The Channel Tunnel, inaugurated in 1994, is the first dry-land link between England and France since the Ice Age.

High-speed **Eurotunnel shuttle trains** (UK ☎ 0870 535 3535, France ☎ 03 21 00 61 00; www.eurotunnel.com) whisk cars, motorbikes and coaches from Folkestone through the Channel Tunnel to Coquelles, 5km southwest of Calais. Shuttles run 24 hours a day, with up to five departures an hour during peak periods.

Prices vary with market demand, but the regular oneway fare for a car and passengers costs from UK£150 (in February or March) to UK£250 (in July or August); return passage costs twice as much. Return fares valid for less than five days are much cheaper.

### TRAIN

Rail services link France with every country in Europe; schedules are available from major train stations in France and abroad. You can book tickets and get information from **Rail Europe** (www.raileurope.com) up to two months ahead. In France, ticketing is handled by the **SNCF** ( ☎ 08 92 35 35 35; www.sncf.fr).

### Eurostar

On the highly civilised **Eurostar** (France ☎ 08 92 35 35 39, UK ☎ 08705 186 186; www.eurostar.com), the trip from London to Paris will take just two hours and 35 minutes. There are direct services from London and Ashford to Paris and the three other stations in France: Calais-Fréthun and Lille. A full-fare, 2nd-class ticket from London to Paris can be as low as UK£50 (and as high as UK£300). Student travel agencies often have youth fares not available directly from Eurostar.

## Sea

Tickets for ferry travel to/from the UK, Channel Islands and Ireland are available from most travel agencies. Return fares sometimes cost less than two oneway tickets.

### IRELAND

Eurail pass holders pay 50% of the adult pedestrian fare for crossings between Ireland and France on Irish Ferries (make sure you book ahead).

**Irish Ferries** ( ☎ 01-638 3333; France 01 43 94 46 94; www.irishferries.ie) has overnight runs from Rosslare to either Cherbourg (18hrs) or Roscoff (16hrs) every other day. A pedestrian/car with two adults costs around €90/389.

From April to September, **Brittany Ferries** ( ☎ 0870 366 5333, France 0825 828 828; www.brittany-ferries.com) runs a car ferry every Saturday from Cork (Ringaskiddy) to Roscoff (14hrs) and every Friday in the other direction.

Freight ferries run by **P&O Irish Sea** ( ☎ 0870 242 4777; www.poirishsea.com) link Rosslare with Cherbourg (18hrs, three per week); cars with two passengers cost from €154. From April to September there is also a weekly Dublin–Cherbourg route (18hrs); cars with two adults cost €174. No foot passengers.

### ITALY

From late April to mid-October, the **Société Nationale Maritime Corse Méditerranée** (SNCM; ☎ 0891 70 18 01; www.sncm.fr) has five or six car ferries per week from Marseille or Toulon to Porto Torres on the island of Sardinia (Sardaigne in French). The oneway adult pedestrian fare is around €100 and takes about 11hrs.

### NORTH AFRICA

The SNCM and the **Compagnie Tunisienne de Navigation** (CTN; www.ctn.com.tn) link Marseille with the Tunisian capital, Tunis (about 24 hours, three or four a week). The standard adult fare is €300 one way with discounts for seniors and those under 25. In France, ticketing is handled by the SNCM. The SNCM also links Marseille with Alger (Algeria).

The **Compagnie Marocaine de Navigation** (CoMaNav; www.comanav.co.ma) links Sète, 29km (20 minutes by train) southwest of Montpellier, with the Moroccan port of Tangier (Tanger; 36hrs, five to seven a month). The cheapest berth costs €168 (€228 in August and for some other summer sailings) one way; return tickets cost 15%–20% less than two oneways. In France, ticketing is handled by SNCM.

### UK

Fares vary. Three- or five-day excursion (return) fares generally cost about the same as regular oneway tickets; special promotional return fares, often requiring advance booking, are sometimes cheaper than a standard oneway fare. Check out **Ferry Savers** ( ☎ 0870 990 8492; www.ferrysavers.com), which guarantees the lowest prices on Channel crossings.

### Normandy

The Newhaven–Dieppe route with **Hoverspeed** ( ☎ 0870 240 8070, France 00 800 1211 1211; www.hover speed.co.uk) and **Transmanche Ferries** ( ☎ 0800 917 1201; www.transmancheferries.com). The hovercraft trip (one to three daily) takes 2¼ hours; the ferry trip (two daily) takes four hours. Pedestrians pay from UK£30 one way (deals available).

Brittany Ferries also has car ferries from Portsmouth to Caen (Ouistreham; six hours, three per day). Tickets cost the same as for Poole–Cherbourg.

The crossing (three, 4¼ hours) from Poole to Cherbourg is via **Brittany Ferries** (UK ☎ 0870 366 5333, France 0825 82 88 28; www.brittany-ferries .com). Passengers pay from UK£33 one way.

Portsmouth–Cherbourg route is with Brittany Ferries, Condor Ferries and **P&O Portsmouth** (UK ☎ 0870 598 0555, France 08 25 01 30 13; www .poferries.com) – two car ferries a day (five hours by day, or eight hours overnight). April to September, there are two faster catamarans a day. Foot passengers pay UK£29 one way.

The Portsmouth–Le Havre crossing is handled by P&O Portsmouth (5½ hours by day, 7¾ hours overnight, three car ferries a day, fewer in winter). Passage costs somewhat more than Portsmouth–Cherbourg.

### Far Northern France

The fastest way to cross the English Channel is between Dover and Calais, served by Hoverspeed's SeaCats (catamarans), which take 50 minutes. For foot passengers, a one-way trip (or a return completed within five days) costs UK£39. From Calais, there are five daily trains to Le Tréport, the northernmost town in Normandy (€19, five hours).

The Dover–Calais crossing is also handled by car ferries, run by **SeaFrance** (UK ☎ 0870 571 1711, France 08 04 04 40 45; www.seafrance.com; 1½hrs, 15 daily) and **P&O Ferries** (UK ☎ 0870 520 20 20; www.posl .com; 1-1¼hrs, 29 daily) for about the same price.

A new 50-minute catamaran service between Dover and Boulogne is operated by **Speed One** (UK ☎ 01304 203000; www.speedferries .com) which makes five crossings daily and costs from £60 return for five passenger and car. It's cheaper the earlier you book.

### Brittany

Mid-March to mid-November, Plymouth is linked to Roscoff (six hours for day crossings, one to three per day) by Brittany Ferries. A oneway fare for foot passengers is UK£35.

Brittany Ferries also links Portsmouth and Plymouth with St-Malo (8¾ hours for day crossing, one per day). Pedestrians pay from UK£27 one way.

From April to September, **Condor Ferries** (uk ☎ 0845 345 2000, France ☎ 02 99 20 03 00; www .condorferries.com) has at least one daily ferry linking Weymouth with St-Malo (UK£35) that can take anywhere from seven to 10 hours, including a stopover in Guernsey.

## GETTING AROUND

### Air

The long-established **Air France** ( ☎ 0820 820 820; www.airfrance.com) continues to control the lion's share of France's long-protected domestic airline industry, although British budget carrier Easyjet has begun flights linking Paris with Marseille, Nice and Toulouse.

Any French travel agency or Air France office can make bookings for domestic flights and supply details on the complex fare options. Outside France, Air France representatives sell tickets for many domestic flights.

Up to 84% reduction is available if you fly during the week and purchase your ticket three weeks in advance. Significant discounts are available to children, young people, families and seniors. Special last-minute offers are posted on the Air France website every Wednesday.

### Bus

Within France, bus services are provided by numerous different companies, usually based within one *département*. For travel between regions, a train is your best bet since inter-regional bus services are limited. Buses are used quite extensively for short-distance travel within *départements*, especially in rural areas with relatively few train lines (eg Brittany and Normandy) – but services are often slow, and few and far between.

### Car & Motorcycle

Having your own wheels gives you exceptional freedom and allows you to visit more remote parts of France. Unfortunately, it can be expensive, and in cities parking and traffic are frequently a major headache. Motorcyclists will find France great for touring. The websites www.viamichelin .com and www.autoroutes.fr both calculate how much you will pay in petrol and tolls for specified journeys.

## DRIVING LICENCE & DOCUMENTS

All drivers must carry at all times: a national ID card or passport; a valid driver's licence; car ownership papers, known as a *carte grise* (grey card); and proof of third-party (liability) insurance.

## FUEL

*Essence* (petrol or gasoline), also known as *carburant* (fuel) costs around €1.10 a litre for 95 unleaded.

## HIRE

To hire a car in France you'll need to be over 21 years old and hold a valid drivers' licence and an international credit card. Arranging your car rental or fly/drive package before you leave home is often cheaper. Major rental companies include:

**ADA** ( ☎ 08 25 16 91 69; www.ada.fr)

**Avis** ( ☎ 08 02 05 05 05; www.avis.com)

**Budget** ( ☎ 08 00 10 00 01; www.budget.com)

**Easycar** ( ☎ 09 06 33 33 33 3; www.easycar.com) Cheap rates and offices in Paris and Nice.

**Europcar** ( ☎ 08 03 35 23 52; www.europcar.com)

**Hertz** ( ☎ 08 25 34 23 43; www.hertz.com)

**OTU Voyages** ( ☎ 01 40 29 12 12; www.otu.fr) Students.

Deals can be found on the Internet, with travel agencies and through companies like **Auto Europe** ( ☎ 1-888 223 5555; www.autoeurope .com) in the US, or **Holiday Autos** ( ☎ 08 70 5300 400; www.holidayautos.co.uk) in the UK.

## INSURANCE

Unlimited third-party liability insurance is mandatory for all vehicles entering France, whether the owner accompanies the vehicle or not. Third-party liability insurance is provided by car-rental companies, but collision-damage waivers (CDW) vary greatly. When comparing rates check the *franchise* (excess/deductible), which is usually €350 for a small car. Your credit card may cover CDW if you use it to pay for the car rental.

## ROAD RULES

Cars drive on the right in France. All passengers must wear seat belts, and children weighing less than 18kg must travel in backward-facing child seats. You will be fined for going 10km over the speed limit.

Any car entering an intersection (including a T-junction) from a road on your right has right-of-way, unless the intersection is marked *vous n'avez pas la priorité* (you do not have right of way) or *cédez le passage* (give way). *Priorité à droite* (give way to the right) is also suspended on priority roads, which are marked by an up-ended yellow square with a black square in the middle.

It's illegal to drive with a blood-alcohol concentration (BAC) over 0.05% (0.5g per litre of blood) – equal to two glasses of wine for a 75kg adult. Mobile phones may only be used with a hands-free or speakerphone.

Riders of any type of two-wheeled vehicle with a motor (except motor-assisted bicycles) must wear a helmet.

## Train

A superb rail network reaches almost every part of the country. Many towns and villages not on the SNCF train and bus network are linked by intra-departmental bus lines.

France's most important train lines radiate from Paris like the spokes of a wheel, making train travel between provincial towns situated on different spokes infrequent and rather slow. In some cases you have to transit through Paris.

### TGV Atlantique Sud-Ouest & TGV Atlantique Ouest

These link Paris' Gare Montparnasse with western and southwestern France, including Brittany (Rennes, Quimper, Brest), Nantes, Poitiers, La Rochelle, Bordeaux, Biarritz and Toulouse.

### TGV Nord, Thalys & Eurostar

These link Paris' Gare du Nord with Arras, Lille, Calais, Brussels, Amsterdam, Cologne and, via the Channel Tunnel, Ashford and London Waterloo.

### TGV Sud-Est & TGV Midi-Méditerranée

These link Paris' Gare de Lyon with the southeast, including Dijon, Lyon, Geneva, the Alps, Avignon, Marseille, Nice and Montpellier.

A train that is not a TGV is often referred to as a *corail*, a *classique* or a TER *(train express régional)*.

Fantastic deals are available exclusively on the website www.sncf.com: last minute offers up to 50% off, published every Tuesday; and *Prem's* early bird deals (eg Paris–Nice €25), available only through online bookings made at least three weeks in advance

Before boarding the train you must validate your ticket by time-stamping it in a *composteur*, one of those orange posts situated at the start of the platform. If you forget, find a conductor on the train so they can punch it for you (otherwise you're likely to be fined). Tickets *can* be purchased on board the train (straight away from the conductor) with cash but there is a surcharge.

# Italy

ITALY

Rare is the traveller who isn't smitten by Italy. Everyone loves the Italians – their quirky, outspoken zest for life, and their gorgeous country. Fringed with a glistening coastline, Italy teems with ancient history, artistic splendour, and divine food and wine. It's an intoxicating place, with a raw beauty and simple passions, but also rough around the edges, frustrating at times, and certainly entertaining. Where else would a wine maker conduct a contest for the ideal breast, the winning form to serve as the shape for a new line of wine glasses?

Italy's siesta-ready Mediterranean climate imbues an enticing romanticism, like a soft cashmere sweater tossed loosely over your shoulders. There's a fetching vibrancy to the coastal cities of Naples and Palermo. Sun-struck Sicily and Sardinia shelter gorgeous sandy beaches and pockets of wild splendour, while Capri and the Aeolian Islands are idyllic havens for isole-hoppers. The Ligurian and Amalfi coasts, pocked with tiny colourful villages, offer some of Europe's most beautiful coastline, with terraced, lemon-covered hillsides falling dramatically to the sea.

If you come looking for efficient systems, fast-paced living, and a low-carb menu, best leave your expectations and diets at the border. Italy is one big moveable feast – come prepared to indulge yourself.

## FAST FACTS

- **Area** 301, 230 sq km
- **Capital** Rome
- **Currency** euro (€); A$1 = €0.58; ¥100 = €0.76; NZ$ = €0.54; UK£1 = €1.50; US$1 = €0.83
- **Famous for** emperors, gladiators, Renaissance art, food and wine, romantic countryside, resplendent seaside
- **Key Phrases** buongiorno (hello); grazie (thanks); mi scusi (excuse me); come si chiama? (what's your name?); prego (no problem); andiamo (let's get going)
- **Official Language** Italian
- **Population** 57.8 million
- **Telephone Codes** country code ☎ 39; international access code ☎ 00; non-Europe reverse-charge code ☎ 170; Europe reverse-charge code ☎ 15
- **Visa** citizens of many countries, including the USA, Australia, Canada and New Zealand, don't need visas to enter Italy as tourists; a permesso di soggiorno is necessary if you plan to study, work or live in Italy. EU citizens with a passport or national identity card can stay in Italy for as long as they like.

# HIGHLIGHTS

- Love it or leave it, edgy **Naples** (p231) and its sparkling bay (not to mention the most perfect pizza) is sure to elicit strong emotions.
- Island-hop around the the sun-splashed **Aeolian Islands** (p246), with their lush lemon groves, aquamarine coves and steaming volcano.
- Discover the **Cinque Terre** (p189), a cluster of five tiny fishing villages strewn along the rocky Ligurian coast.
- Try these classics in **La Cucina**: *mozzarella di bufala*, *bruschetta*, pizza margherita, and *insalata caprese* (all washed down with *Vermentino*).
- Delve the **grottoes** (p254) on Sardinia's west coast, with its magnificent inner lakes and columns of organ pipes.

**HOW MUCH?**

- **Cappuccino at bar** €1
- **Glass of house vino** €2
- **Insalata Caprese** €5-8
- **Gelato** €1.50
- **A Baci chocolate** €0.50

**LONELY PLANET INDEX**

- **Litre of petrol** €1.40
- **Litre of bottled water** €1
- **Bottle of beer (Peroni)** €2
- **Souvenir T-shirt** €8-12
- **Slice of pizza** €1-3

## SOUTHERN SIESTA

- **One week** Sizzling and sultry, the Mezzogiorno is a rapturous place for the adventurous, sun-seeking traveller. The combination of vibrant cities, rich history and resplendent coastline is unbeatable. Begin your *giro* (trip) in edgy Naples, sitting pretty in the shadow of Mt Vesuvius and gazing out over the sparkling Gulf. From here, take day trips to see the ruins of two ancient Roman resort towns, Herculaneum and Pompeii. Hop on a boat for a swift ride to Capri, with gorgeous grottoes, lush landscape and two pretty villages. The Amalfi Coast boasts one of Europe's most dazzling coastlines, terraced with lemon trees and dotted with resorts such as Positano, Amalfi and Ravello.
- **Two weeks** If you've got another week to spare, continue south to Sicily and catch a boat to Palermo, full of creative masterpieces. On this sun-struck island, delight in incredible ancient ruins, gorgeous beaches, delicious cuisine, enticing cities and a fiery volcano.

## CLIMATE & WHEN TO GO

Italy lies comfortably in a temperate zone, but the climates of the north and south can vary considerably. Summers are uniformly hot (and sticky), and winters can be chilly and fickle, though mild in the south. May and October are the best months to visit – gentle weather, few crowds and better rates. Virtually all of Italy goes on vacation during the month of August – if you're planning a summer trip, book well in advance. Though you'll likely need a strong umbrella, winter is a peaceful and cost-effective time to visit the cities, with elbowroom to spare at star sights.

See Climate Charts p703.

## HISTORY

According to legend, the she-wolf-reared Romulus founded Rome in 753 BC, but the country had already been inhabited for thousands of years. By the start of the Bronze Age, around 2000 BC, the peninsula had been settled by several Italic tribes. From 900 BC, the Etruscan civilisation developed, while the southern reaches were settled by Greek traders in the 8th century BC, their independent city-states forming Magna Graecia. Etruscan civilisation flourished until the end of the 3rd century BC, when the Romans took over the last of the Etruscan cities.

### The New Roman Republic

Despite an occasional blow – such as the invasion of the Gauls in 390 BC – Rome steadily garnered strength and expanded south, claiming Sicily in 241 BC and Spain and Greece in 202 BC. Romans left their mark everywhere, planting olive trees and grape vines, establishing trade networks, building roads and aqueducts, and settling prosperous towns on the plains. Under Julius

# ITALY

0 — 100 m
0 — 0.1 miles

Caesar's rule, Rome conquered Gaul and moved into Egypt in the 1st century BC. After Caesar's assassination, his adopted son Octavius defeated rivals Mark Antony and Cleopatra. He established the Roman Empire in 27 BC and adopted the title of Augustus Caesar, kicking off a time of significant advancement in engineering and the arts.

## The Emergence of City-States & the Renaissance

By the end of the 3rd century AD, the Roman empire was so big that Emperor Diocletian divided it between east and west. His successor, Constantine, ruled from Byzantium (Istanbul) and was the first Christian emperor. From the 5th to 9th centuries, Goths, Huns and Arabs beset the empire from the south.

The Middle Ages were characterised by the development of powerful city-states in the north. In the 15th century the Renaissance spread throughout the country, fostering artistic geniuses such as Brunelleschi, Donatello, Bramante, Botticelli, da Vinci, Masaccio, Lippi, Raphael and Michelangelo. By the early 16th century much of Italy was under Habsburg rule. After Napoleon's invasion in 1796, a degree of unity was introduced for the first time in centuries. In the 1860s the unification movement (the Risorgimento) gained momentum, and in 1861 the Kingdom of Italy was declared under the rule of King Vittorio Emanuele. Venice was wrested from Austria in 1866, and Rome yanked from the papacy four years later and named the country's capital.

## Fascism, WWII & the Italian Republic

In 1921 Benito Mussolini's Fascist Party took control, and became a German ally in WWII. After several military disasters, the king led a coup against Mussolini and had him arrested. Italian partisans killed Mussolini in April 1945, and the monarchy was abolished a year later.

In 1957, Italy was a founding member of the European Economic Community, the forerunner of the European Union (EU). The '70s were marked by a spate of terrorism, including the assassination of Prime Minister Aldo Moro in 1978, but the following decade saw increased stability and significant economic growth, with Italy for a short time one of the world's leading economies.

## Modern Times

The country enjoyed economic growth for a while, but the 1990s heralded a period of crisis, both economically and politically. A national bribery scandal known as Tangentopoli ('kickback city') rocked the nation. Investigations implicated thousands of politicians, public officials and businesspeople, and left the main parties in tatters after the 1992 elections. A programme of fiscal austerity was ushered in to guarantee Italy's entry into the EMU, and Italy also moved decisively against the Sicilian Mafia.

Since 2001, media magnate Silvio Berluschoni – dubbed Il Cavaliere ('the Knight') by the press – has been prime minister, with his right-wing Forza Italia party. His tenure thus far has disappointed many and been marred by continued allegations of corruption, a well-worn path.

## La Mafiosa

Once a powerful entity, the Sicilian Mafia has gradually lost its steam. During the 1990s, Italy took decisive steps against La Cosa Nostra ('Our Thing'), prompted by the 1992 assassinations of two prominent anti-Mafia judges. Numerous testimonies took place, leading to several important arrests, including the life sentencing of Salvatore 'Toto' Riina, the Sicilian godfather himself. Riina's suspected successor, Giovanni Brusca, was arrested in 1996, implicated for murder and imprisoned for 30 years in 1999. While the high-profile arrests continue, and some claim the Mafia's confidence and power have been seriously undermined, others believe the entrenched system and family *segreti* (secrets) are far from cracked. However, the April 2004 death of a former leader, serving a life sentence in America, led to a public declaration that the *mafiosa* had seen its last days of power.

## PEOPLE

Italians have a legendary reputation for being impassioned, fiery, love-struck individuals who drive with reckless abandon, ooze charm, wear their hearts on the sleeve, siesta away the workday and feast daily on sinfully good food and wine. Scratch the stylish veneer and get to know Italy's remarkably diverse, and vigorously proud, inhabitants. Amongst one another, Italians are fiercely protective of their home towns, of regional dialects and cuisine; either Sicilian or Roman, but not both. Yet when faced with a foreigner, Italians exude more of a national pride, making those strong regional distinctions harder to discern for the unaware visitor.

Italy's population hovers around 57.8 million, and the country has the lowest birth rate in Europe.

Italians are supremely family oriented, and 'mamma's boys' do exist, with a high percentage of men living at home until married. Grandmothers *(nonne)* are downright revered, and there's even a 'coolest granny' title doled out annually (the most recent winner beat the competition by dancing a barefoot tarantella).

## SPORT

Football (soccer) is a national love, and there are stadiums in all major towns. Italy's club teams have traditionally done well in European tournaments. Check newspapers for details of who's playing where.

In May, the *Gazzetta dello Sport* sponsors the *Giro d'Italia,* held annually since 1909. This long-distance, multi-staged cycle race covers a great swatch of the countryside and draws legions of cheering fans.

Italy hosts two major motor races each year: the Italian Formula One Grand Prix is held each September at Monza, just north of Milan; and the San Marino Grand Prix is held at Imola in May. Team Ferrari is the long-time favourite; securing tickets can be a challenge.

## RELIGION

To most foreigners, Italy is synonymous with Catholicism. Just shy of 85% of Italians profess to be Catholic. While millions still flock to Rome to catch a glimpse of the pope each year, the role of religion in Italy has lessened in recent years, with more attention put towards formalities than actual faith. Still, first Communions, church weddings and regular feast days are an integral part of daily life, and pilgrimages continue to be big business. Beyond Catholics, there are about 700,000 Muslims, making Islam Italy's second religion. Italy is also home to 400,000 evangelical Protestants, 350,000 Jehovah's Witnesses and smaller numbers of Jews and Buddhists.

## ARTS

### Literature

Before Dante wrote his *Divina Commedia* (Divine Comedy) in the early 1300s, Latin was the language of writers. Among ancient Rome's greatest writers were Cicero, Ovid, Petronius and Virgil, whose *Aeneid* – an epic of the founding of Rome – is the most famous work of that time. Petrarch (1304–74) was a contemporary of Dante's. Giovanni Boccaccio (1313–75), author of the *Decameron,* is considered the first Italian novelist. Machiavelli's *The Prince,* a purely political work, has proved a lasting Renaissance piece.

Italy's richest contribution to modern literature has been in the novel and short story. Leonardo Sciascia's taut writings on Sicilian themes are enigmatically beautiful. Umberto Eco's best-known work, *The Name of the Rose,* is a highbrow murder mystery.

### Cinema

Despite a number of popular contemporary Italian films, such as Robert Benigni's Oscar-winning *Life is Beautiful* (1998) and *Cinema Paradiso,* the real heyday for Italian films was during the postwar 1940s, when a trio of brilliant neorealists – Roberto Rossellini (1906–77), Vittorio de Sica (1901–74) and Luchino Visconti (1907–76) – turned the camera on the everyday struggles of war-worn Italians and churned out classic masterpieces such as *Bicycle Thieves* (1948) and *Rome Open City* (1945). Schooled with the neorealist stars, Federico Fellini carried the creative torch onward with gems such as *La Dolce Vita* (1959). Other notable directors and films include Michelangelo Antonioni, with the 1967 hit *Blow-up* (1966); Bernardo

---

**READING UP**

For historical background, scoop up the *Concise History of Italy* by Vincent Cronin. Charles Richards' *The New Italians* offers a fascinating look at modern Italian life. E.M. Forster's *A Room with a View* gorgeously portrays Florence's romantic appeal, while George Negus' *The World from Italy: Football, Food and Politics,* is a light-hearted look at the country's charm.

Bertolucci, with *Last Tango in Paris* (1972), *The Last Emperor* (1987), *Stealing Beauty* (1996) and *Besieged* (1999); and Franco Zeffirelli, whose film *Tea with Mussolini* (1998) was an international hit.

Contemporary directors worth a look include the Taviani brothers, Giuseppe Tornatore, and Nanni Moretti. *L'Ultimo Bacio,* produced in 2001 by Gabriele Muccino, and a smash hit in Italy and abroad, portrayed a group of 30-something men grappling with life's poignant questions and a lack of ideals.

## Music & Theatre

Italian artists have taken a dominant place in the realms of opera and instrumental music. Antonio Vivaldi (1675–1741) created the concerto in its present form. Verdi, Puccini, Bellini, Donizetti and Rossini, composers from the 19th and early 20th centuries, are all stars of the modern operatic era. Tenor Luciano Pavarotti (1935–) has recently had his crown as 'King of Mother's Day CD Sales' taken by Andrea Bocelli (1958–), who soared to international stardom in the 1990s. With his bluesy voice, Zucchero (Adelmo Fornaciari) has also had a few international hits.

Sicilian Luigi Pirandello (1867–1936), author of the influential *Six Characters in Search of an Author,* is Italy's most renowned playwright and won the Nobel Prize in Literature in 1934. On the contemporary scene, actor/director Dario Fo (who won the Nobel Prize in Literature in 1998) is the most noteworthy, with luminous works such as *Mistero Buffo,* laced with social and political commentary.

## Architecture, Painting & Sculpture

Take a walk through any Italian town – Palermo, Siena, Florence, Pienza, Venice, Lecce, Rome – and you'll see glistening examples of Italy's rich artistic past before even stepping into a museum. In the south, where the Greeks left an indelible mark prior to Roman domination, there are important archaeological sites, with well-preserved temples at Paestum, in Campania, and the Valley of the Temples in Agrigento, Sicily. Pompeii and Herculaneum glean insight on the day-to-day lives of ancient Romans. In Ravenna, Venice and Palermo, gilded Byzantine mosaics adorn churches.

Patronised mainly by the Medici family in Florence and the popes in Rome, painters, sculptors, architects and writers flourished during the Renaissance. Filippo Brunelleschi's greatest achievement – the distinct red dome on the Florence Duomo – represented the greatest artistic feat of the day. The High Renaissance (1490–1520) was dominated by three brilliant artists: Leonardo da Vinci (1452–1519), Michelangelo Buonarrotti (1475–1564) and Raphael (1483–1520).

The baroque period followed in the 17th century, spawning numerous buildings with elaborately sumptuous façades and richly decorative painting and sculpture. Florence and the small city of Lecce, in the southern region of Puglia, offer countless displays of this luxuriant architectural style, while Rome literally teems with masterpieces by the brilliant baroque sculptor and architect Gianlorenzo Bernini (1598–1680) and Michelangelo Merisi da Caravaggio (1573–1610). During the neoclassic period, Canova (1757–1822) emerged as a star sculptor, his smooth white marble works sensual masterpieces. Rome's Spanish Steps and Trevi Fountain both date from this period, a reaction to the frivolous excesses of the baroque works.

Of Italy's modern artists, Amedeo Modigliani (1884–1920) is most famous. The early 20th century also produced a movement known as the futurists, which rejected the sentimental art of the past and was infatuated by new technology, including modern warfare. Fascism produced its own style of architecture, characterised by the EUR satellite city and the work of Marcello Piacentini (1881–1960).

## ENVIRONMENT

Boot-shaped Italy incorporates Sicily and Sardinia and is bound by the Adriatic, Ligurian, Tyrrhenian and Ionian Seas. There is more than 8000km of coastline. Inland, about 75% of the peninsula is mountainous, with the Alps dividing the country from France, Switzerland and Austria, and the Apennines forming a backbone that extends from the Alps into Sicily.

Italy has 20 national parks, with several more on the way, and over 400 smaller nature reserves, natural parks and wetlands. The national parks cover about 5% of the country's land, and include: Parco Nazionale del Gran Paradiso and Parco Nazionale dello Stelvio, both in the Alps; Parco Nazionale d'Abruzzo; Parco Nazionale del Pollino, straddling Basilicata and Calabria; and Umbria's Parco Nazionale dei Monti Sibillini, home to over 50 species of mammals and over 150 types of bird.

Not known for environmental awareness, Italy's major cities, and much of the industrialised north, suffer from air pollution, attributed to high car usage. Aesthetically, the result of industrious humankind is not always displeasing – much of Tuscany's beauty lies in the mazing of olive groves with vineyards. But centuries of tree clearing, combined with illegal building, have also led to severe land degradation and some serious erosion woes. Coupled with some people's passion for hunting, this has had a dire effect on native animals and birds, many now endangered. Fortunately, new laws are far more progressive, partly in response to EU directives. Italy also has its share of natural hazards, including landslides, mudflows, floods, earthquakes and volcanic eruptions, thanks to six active volcanoes. A rumble of quakes in the autumn of 1997 left severe damage and 10 dead in Umbria, particularly in the town of Assisi, and another devastating quake in 2002 killed 29 in Molise. Sicily and the Aeolian Islands have seen much nonfatal volcanic action since then, including a Stromboli eruption that caused an eight-metre tidal wave.

---

**COASTAL WALKS**

■ **Cinque Terre** – The 12km Via dell'Amore (Lovers' Lane) path links the five glistening fishing villages that comprise the dazzling Cinque Terre (p189)

■ **San Fruttuoso** – this Medieval monastery (fronted by a swimming beach) is a gorgeous a 2 ½ hour hike from either Portofino or Camogli (p188)

■ **Sorrento Peninsula** – Follow the stairs, lemon-terraced hills and staggering views from Positano to Nocelle (p239)

■ **Cala Gonone** – Hike the cliff-side path, past crescent beaches, from Cala Fiuli to Cala Luna (p254)

---

## FOOD & DRINK

Food enthusiasts will have a gastronomic heyday in Italy, where *la cucina* (the kitchen) revolves around season and region with additional variances between north and south. While rustic Tuscan cooking is characterised by simplicity and distinct flavours, in the south dishes are usually spicier. During spring, you'll see lots of fava beans, courgette (zucchini) flowers and asparagus pepper dishes, while autumn brings *porcini* (funghi) and *cinghiale* (wild boar). Vegetarians won't have a problem foraging in Italy, which prides itself on using garden-fresh produce and has open-air produce markets countrywide.

A full meal consists of an antipasto such as bruschetta, followed by the *primo piatto*, a pasta dish, and the *secondo piatto*, meat or fish. Next comes an *insalata* (salad) or *contorni* (side vegetable) before finishing with with *dolci* (cake) and *caffè* (coffee).

Italian wine is delicious, abundant, justifiably world-famous and reasonably priced, with a very drinkable bottle costing as little as €7. In Tuscany, sample chianti, *sangiovese* and *brunello* for reds, and *vernaccia* for white; Piedmont produces excellent Barolo, Sicily terrific *nero di avola,* and crisp *vermentino* hails from Sardinia and Liguria. Peroni is the national beer; for a draft, order it *alla spinna.*

### Where & When to Eat & Drink

Dining options are divided into several categories. A pizzeria serves the obvious, but sometimes a full menu as well, and the best sport a *forno a legna* sign, indicating a wood-fire oven. An *osteria* is the Italian equivalent of a tavern, with an equal doling of wine and local dishes, while an *enoteca* (wine library) specialises in wines by the glass accompanied by savoury pairings, such as platters of cheese, olives and cured meats. Trattorias are traditional neighbourhood eateries, often family-run with simple home cooking. A *ristorante* tends towards a more formal ambience and higher price bracket. For fast, cheap eating, there's *pizza a taglio* (pizza by the slice) and the *tavola calda* (literally 'hot table'), offering inexpensive dishes served caféteria-style. A *rosticceria* specialises in grilled meats and take-away food, *alimentari* and *salumerie* are small, delicatessen-style grocers, and fresh bread is baked at a *forno* or *panetteria*. Cafés serve any number of beverages and snacks, and often stay open from morning until late at night.

Keep an eye out for recent stickers from Italian restaurant guides (such as *Gambero Rosso*) posted in eating-establishment windows – almost always a sign of excellent, well-valued food.

Restaurants are usually open for lunch from 12.30pm to 3pm. For dinner, opening hours vary from north to south but are generally from 7.30pm to 11.30pm. Restaurants are closed one night a week and for much of August; in seasonal tourist areas, many also close between Christmas and April.

Most eating establishments charge a *pane e coperto* (cover charge), ranging from €1 to €4; some tack on a *servizio* (service charge) of 10% to 15% but when it's not included, tourists are expected to round up the bill or leave 10% (locals, however, don't).

### Habits & Customs

Italians don't tend to eat a sit-down *colazione* (breakfast), preferring instead a quick cappuccino and *cornetto* (croissant) grabbed at the bar. *Pranzo* (lunch) is traditionally the main meal, although more Italians are taking speedy lunches these days, and *cena* (dinner) is becoming the bigger meal. Italians are late diners, often not eating dinner until after 9pm.

# ROME

**pop 2.8 million**

If you had time for just one city in life, Rome's your spot – gloriously artistic, romantically beautiful, and endearingly *pazzo* (crazy). No other city so stylishly meshes its significant, visible history with its hip, contemporary, fun-loving self. Rome's more than 2500 years of history have produced a veritable archive of Western culture. There is simply a dizzying amount to see, between the remnants of ancient Rome and the artistic splendours from the Renaissance and baroque periods.

Whether you've got a weekend or a month, this beguiling city will swallow you whole, charm you to pieces, then leave you craving more.

## HISTORY

Rome's origins date to a group of Etruscan, Latin and Sabine settlements, scattered across the city's hills, but it is the legend of the she-wolf-reared twins – Romulus and Remus – that's the pervading tale. Having killed his brother over governing rights, Romulus established the city on the Palatine, one of the famed Seven Hills of Rome, and seeded an empire that eventually controlled almost all of Europe.

Modern Rome still gleams with evidence of the Western world's two great former rulers: the Roman Empire and the Christian Church. The sprawling Forum and majestic Colosseum are balanced by St Peter's and the Vatican, which give off an incredibly powerful energy. Between these two are countless layers of history, displayed in every piazza and church: some visible, some not. For example, St Peter's Basilica stands on the site of an earlier basilica built by the Emperor Constantine, on top of the necropolis where St Peter himself was buried.

## ORIENTATION

Despite Rome's vast size, it's a very walking-friendly city, with most of the major sights within the relatively small *centro storico* (historic centre), just west of Stazione Termini, the central train station. The Tiber River cuts through the city, with Vatican City and Trastevere lying on its west bank. Rome's best-known geographical features are its seven hills: Palatine, Capitoline, Aventine, Celian, Esquiline, Viminal and Quirinal – all part of the ancient city.

Rome's main bus terminus is in Piazza del Cinquecento, directly in front of the train station. Many intercity buses arrive and depart from the Piazzale Tiburtina, in front of Stazione Tiburtina, accessible from Termini on the Metro Linea B.

If your time is limited, it helps to plan an itinerary. Most of the major museums and galleries are open all day until 7pm or 8pm; some museums are closed on Monday, so check ahead.

## INFORMATION
### Bookshops

**Feltrinelli International** (Map p167; Via VE Orlando 84; 9am-8pm) An extensive selection of maps, travel books and titles in many different languages.

# ROME

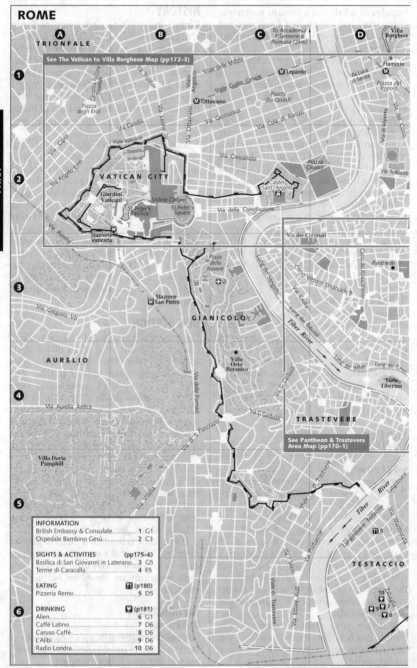

See The Vatican to Villa Borghese Map (pp172–3)

See Pantheon & Trastevere Area Map (pp170–1)

| INFORMATION | | |
| --- | --- | --- |
| British Embassy & Consulate | 1 | G1 |
| Ospedale Bambino Gesù | 2 | C3 |

| SIGHTS & ACTIVITIES | (pp175–6) | |
| --- | --- | --- |
| Basilica di San Giovanni in Laterano | 3 | G5 |
| Terme di Caracalla | 4 | F5 |

| EATING | (p180) | |
| --- | --- | --- |
| Pizzeria Remo | 5 | D5 |

| DRINKING | (p181) | |
| --- | --- | --- |
| Alien | 6 | G1 |
| Caffè Latino | 7 | D6 |
| Caruso Caffè | 8 | D6 |
| L'Alibi | 9 | D6 |
| Radio Londra | 10 | D6 |

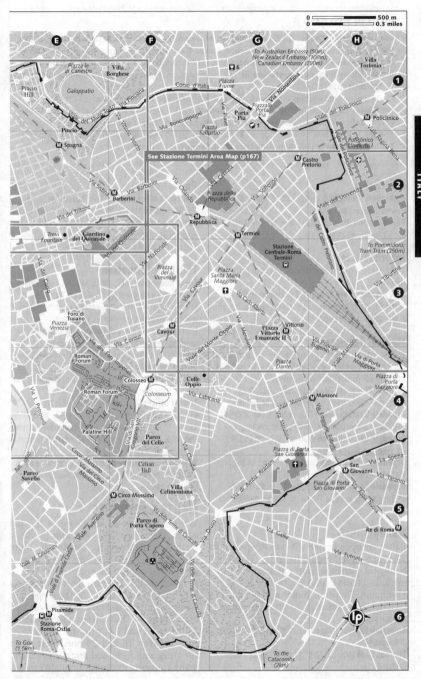

ITALY

---

**ROME IN TWO DAYS**

Visit the **Sistine Chapel** (p172), the **Vatican Museums** (p172) and **St Peter's Basilica** (p169), then recover over a leisurely lunch around **Piazza Navona** (p173). Traipse the afternoon away at the **Roman Forum** (p168) and **Colosseum** (p174), stopping for a *caffè* at **Café Café** (p180) before hitting vivacious **Trastevere** (p175) for dinner, an evening *passeggiata* and a nightcap at **Stardust** (p181).

On day two, take in the Roman morning vibe at the **Campo de'Fiori market** (p173), then tackle the **Musei Capitolini** (p170) and the **Pantheon** (p173) – with a *granita* break at **Tazza D'Oro** (p181). Refresh on a siesta walk to **Villa Borghese** (p174), via **Trevi Fountain** (p174) and **Piazza di Spagna** (p174), then window shop on **Via Condotti** (p182) and gallery hop on **Via Giulia** (p175). Eat hip at **'Gusto** (p179) then stroll back to **'Il Campo'** (p173) for the night vibe.

---

## Emergency

**Foreigners' Bureau** (Map p167; ☎ 06 468 62 977; Via Genova 2) Report thefts here.

**Police station** (Questura; Map p167; ☎ 06 468 61; Via San Vitale 11; ☼ 24hr)

## Internet Access

There are Internet cafés scattered all over town.

**Easy Internet Café** (Map pp172-3; Via Barberini 2; per 30min €1) Plenty of terminals, around-the-clock access, an actual café and good prices.

## Medical Services

A list of all-night pharmacies in the city centre is posted on www.romaturismo.it and in all pharmacy windows.

**24-Hour Pharmacy** (Map p167; ☎ 06 488 00 19; Piazza del Cinquecento 51) Opposite Stazione Termini.

**Ospedale Bambino Gesù** (Map pp164-5; ☎ 06 685 92 351; Piazza di Sant'Onofrio 4) Rome's paediatric hospital.

**Ospedale San Gallicano** (Map pp170-1; ☎ 06 588 23 90; Via di San Gallicano 25a, Trastevere)

**Ospedale San Giacomo** (Map pp172-3; ☎ 06 362 61; Via Canova 29) Near Piazza del Popolo.

**Ospedale Santo Spirito** (Map pp172-3; ☎ 06 65 09 01; Lungotevere in Sassia 1) Near the Vatican; multilingual staff.

## Money

Banks are open from 8.45am to 1.30pm and 2.45pm to 4pm Monday to Friday. There's a bank and exchange booths at Stazione Termini, and an exchange booth and ATMs at Fiumicino. There are numerous Bancomats (ATMs) and exchange booths throughout the city.

**American Express** (Map pp172-3; ☎ 06 676 41; Piazza di Spagna 38)

**Thomas Cook** (Map pp172-3; ☎ 06 482 81 82; Piazza Barberini 21)

## Post

**Main post office** (Map pp172-3; Piazza di San Silvestro 20; ☼ 9am-6.30pm Mon-Fri, 9am-1pm Sat) Off Via del Tritone.

**Vatican post office** (Map pp172-3; ☎ 06 69 88 34 06; Piazza di San Pietro; ☼ 8.30am-6pm Mon-Fri, to 1pm Sat) Said to offer faster and more reliable service.

## Tourist Information

**Enjoy Rome** (Map p167; ☎ 06 445 18 43; www.enjoy rome.com; Via Marghera 8a; ☼ 8.30am-7pm Mon-Sat, to 2pm Sun) Five minutes' walk northeast of the station; a well-run private tourist office with a free hotel-reservation service and travel agency. The English-speaking staff can help you find or book nearly anything and offer great biking and walking tours (in English) that cover all sorts of interests.

**Rome Online** (www.romatourismo.com) Everything you need to know about Rome.

**Tourist offices** Stazione Termini (Map p167; ☎ 06 48 90 63 00; ☼ 8am-9pm); Via Parigi 5 (Map p167; ☎ 06 36 00 43 99; ☼ 9am-7pm Mon-Sat) Good information on hotels and sights. Both offices provide maps and printed information about bus services.

**Vatican tourist office** (Map pp172-3; ☎ 06 69 88 16 62; Piazza San Pietro; ☼ 8.30am-7pm Mon-Sat) To the left of the basilica.

## SIGHTS & ACTIVITIES

When it comes to seeing the sights, that old adage, *Roma, non basta una vita* (Rome, a lifetime is not enough), couldn't be more true. It would take 900 days alone to visit all of Rome's churches, one per day. Whew, time for another espresso. Fortunately, you can briskly cover many of the important sights in three days. Entry to various attractions is free for EU citizens aged under 18 and over 65, and half-price for EU citizens aged between 18 and 25 plus those from countries with reciprocal arrangements and many university students. Cumulative tickets

# STAZIONE TERMINI AREA

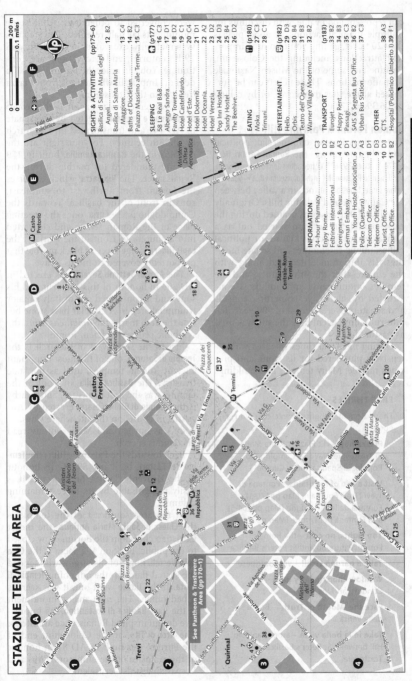

| | | |
|---|---|---|
| **INFORMATION** | | |
| 24-hour Pharmacy | 1 | C3 |
| Enjoy Rome | 2 | D2 |
| Feltrinelli International | 3 | B2 |
| Foreigners' Bureau | 4 | A3 |
| German Embassy | 5 | D1 |
| Italian Youth Hostel Association | 6 | C3 |
| Police (Questura) | 7 | A3 |
| Telecom Office | 8 | D1 |
| Telecom Office | 9 | D3 |
| Tourist Office | 10 | D3 |
| Tourist Office | 11 | B2 |

| | | |
|---|---|---|
| **SIGHTS & ACTIVITIES** | (pp175–6) | |
| Basilica di Santa Maria degli | | |
| Angeli | 12 | B2 |
| Basilica di Santa Maria | | |
| Maggiore | 13 | C4 |
| Baths of Diocletian | 14 | B2 |
| Palazzo Massimo alle Terme | 15 | C3 |

| | | |
|---|---|---|
| **SLEEPING** | (p177) | |
| 58 Le Real B&B | 16 | C3 |
| Albergo Sandra | 17 | D1 |
| Fawlty Towers | 18 | D2 |
| Hotel Castelfidardo | 19 | C1 |
| Hotel d'Este | 20 | D2 |
| Hotel Dolomiti | 21 | D1 |
| Hotel Oceania | 22 | A2 |
| Hotel Venezia | 23 | D2 |
| Pop Inn Hostel | 24 | D3 |
| Sandy Hostel | 25 | B4 |
| The Beehive | 26 | D2 |

| | | |
|---|---|---|
| **EATING** | (p180) | |
| Moka | 27 | C3 |
| Trimani | 28 | C1 |

| | | |
|---|---|---|
| **ENTERTAINMENT** | (p182) | |
| Hello | 29 | D3 |
| Orbis | 30 | B4 |
| Teatro dell'Opera | 31 | B3 |
| Warner Village Moderno | 32 | B2 |

| | | |
|---|---|---|
| **TRANSPORT** | (p183) | |
| Eurojet | 33 | B2 |
| Happy Rent | 34 | B3 |
| Passagi | 35 | C3 |
| SAIS & Segesta Bus Office | 36 | B2 |
| Urban Bus Station | 37 | C3 |

| | | |
|---|---|---|
| **OTHER** | | |
| CTS | 38 | A3 |
| Hospital (Policlinico Umberto I) | 39 | F1 |

can represent good value, with discounts for multiple main attractions. A good pick is the €20 ticket, getting you into nine important attractions, including the Colosseum, Palatine and some of the Museo Nazionale Romano locations. These tickets can be purchased at the sites they cover, or by calling ☎ 06 39 96 77 00.

## Roman Forum & Palatine Hill

The ancient Roman commercial, political and religious centre, the **Roman Forum** (Map pp170-1; ☎ 06 399 67 700; free admission to Roman Forum, admission to Palatine Hill with Colosseum €8; ☺ 9am-1hr before sunset Mon-Sat), stands in a valley between the Capitoline and Palatine hills. Originally marshland, the area was drained during the early republican era and started out as a typical piazza, a public centre for political rallies, public ceremonies and senate meetings. Its importance declined along with the empire after the 4th century, and the temples, monuments and buildings constructed by successive emperors, consuls and senators over a period of 900 years fell into ruin, until eventually the site was used as pasture land.

During medieval times the area was extensively plundered for its stone and precious marble. Many temples and buildings

---

**FREE THRILLS**

These Roman delights won't cost you a euro:

- **Piazza hop** – Hit Piazzas Santa Maria in Trastevere, Navona, Campidoglio, Popolo, di Spagna and 'Il Campo'
- **Visit a trio of fountains** – Fontana di Trevi (Trevi Fountain; Map pp170-1), Fontana delle Tartarughe (Map pp164-5) and Fontana del Tritone (Map pp172-3)
- **Top sights, no cost** – the Roman Forum, Pantheon and St Peter's Basilica
- **Take a garden stroll** – Villa Borghese
- **Window shop, gallery gaze** – Via Condotti and Via Giulia
- **Face the 'Mouth of Truth'** – Bocca della Verità
- **Take in la bella vista** – atop Gianicolo Hill between St Peter's Basilica and Trastevere

---

were converted to other uses, while some monuments lay half-revealed. The area was systematically excavated in the 18th and 19th centuries, and excavations are continuing. You can enter the Forum from Via dei Fori Imperiali, which leads from Piazza Venezia to the Colosseum.

As you enter, to your left is the **Tempio di Antonino e Faustina**, erected by the senate in AD 141 and transformed into a church in the 8th century. To your right are the remains of the **Basilica Aemilia**, built in 179 BC and plundered for marble during the Renaissance. The **Via Sacra**, which traverses the Forum from northwest to southeast, runs in front of the basilica. Towards the Campidoglio is the **Curia**, once the meeting place of the Roman senate and converted into a church. In front of the Curia is the **Lapis Niger**, a large piece of black marble that purportedly covered Romulus' grave.

The **Arco di Settimo Severo** was erected in AD 203 in honour of this emperor and his sons, and is considered one of Italy's major triumphal arches. A circular base stone beside the arch marks the *umbilicus urbis*, the symbolic centre of ancient Rome.

Just to the southwest of the arch is the **Tempio di Saturno**, one of the most important ancient Roman temples, used as the state treasury. The **Basilica Giulia**, in front of the temple, was the seat of justice, and nearby is the **Tempio di Giulio Cesare**, erected by Augustus in 29 BC on the site where Caesar's body was burned and Mark Antony read his famous speech.

Back towards the Palatine Hill is the **Tempio dei Castori**, built in 489 BC in honour of the Heavenly Twins, or Dioscuri. It is easily recognisable by its three remaining columns.

In the area southeast of the temple is the **Chiesa di Santa Maria Antiqua**, the oldest Christian church in the Forum, now closed to the public. Back on Via Sacra is the **Casa delle Vestali**, home of the virgins who tended the sacred flame in the adjoining **Tempio di Vesta**. If the flame went out, it was seen as a bad omen. The next major monument is the vast **Basilica di Costantino**. Its impressive design inspired Renaissance architects. The **Arco di Tito**, at the Colosseum end of the Forum, was built in AD 81 in honour of the victories of the emperors Titus and Vespasian against Jerusalem.

From here, climb the **Palatine** (admission costs apply from here; entrances are along Via di San Gregorio and Piazza dei Santa Maria Nova), where wealthy Romans built their homes and legend says that Romulus founded the city. Archaeological evidence demonstrates that the earliest settlements in the area were in fact on the Palatine. Like the Forum, the buildings of the Palatine fell into ruin and in the Middle Ages the hill became the site of convents and churches. During the Renaissance, wealthy families established gardens here. The Farnese gardens were built over the ruins of the Domus Tiberiana.

Worth a look is the impressive **Domus Augustana**, the private residence of the emperors; the **Domus Flavia**, the residence of Domitian; the **Tempio della Magna Mater**, built in 204 BC; and the fresco-adorned **Casa di Livia**, thought to belong to the wife of Emperor Augustus.

## Piazza del Campidoglio

Perched atop Capitoline Hill, this elegant **piazza** (Map pp170-1) was designed by Michelangelo in 1538. Formerly the seat of the ancient Roman government, it is now the seat of the city's municipal government. In addition Michelangelo designed the façades of the three palaces bordering the piazza. A modern copy of the bronze equestrian statue of Emperor Marcus Aurelius is at its centre; the original is on display in the ground-floor portico of the **Palazzo Nuovo** (Palazzo del Museo Capitolino; Map pp170-1). This forms part of the **Musei Capitolini** (Map pp170-1; ☎ 06 67 10 20 71; admission €6.20; ☯ 9am-8pm Tue-Sun), entirely worth visiting for the collections of ancient Roman sculpture.

Walk to the right of the Palazzo Senatorio for a lovely panorama of the Roman Forum. Walk to the left of the same building to reach the ancient Roman **Carcere Mamertino** (Mamertine Prison; Map pp170-1; ☯ 9am-noon & 2-5pm), where it's believed St Peter was imprisoned.

The **Chiesa di Santa Maria d'Aracoeli** (Map pp170-1) is between Piazza del Campidoglio and the Monumento Vittorio Emanuele II, at the highest point of the Capitoline Hill. It is built on the site where legend says the Tiburtine Sybil told the Emperor Augustus of the coming birth of Christ.

## Vatican City

After Italian unification in 1861, the Papal States of central Italy became part of the new Kingdom of Italy, causing a considerable rift between church and state. In 1929, Mussolini, under the Lateran Treaty, gave the pope full sovereignty over what is now called Vatican City. The smallest independent state in existence, the Vatican has considerable influence, along with its own postal service, currency, newspaper, radio station and even an army of Swiss Guards to watch over the pope's personal safety.

Guided tours of the Vatican City **gardens** (Map pp172-3; ☎ 06 69 88 44 66; €10) can be organised at the Vatican tourist office (p166) in advance.

### ST PETER'S BASILICA & SQUARE

Whatever your faith, the most famous, but no longer largest, church in Christendom will likely leave you awestruck. **St Peter's Basilica** (Map pp172-3; Piazza San Pietro; admission free; ☯ 7am-7pm Apr-Sep, to 6pm Oct-Mar) stands on the site where St Peter was buried. The first church on the site was built during Constantine's reign in the 4th century, and in 1506 work started on a new basilica, designed by Bramante.

Final kudos, however, went to Michelangelo, who took over the project in 1547, at the age of 72, and was responsible for the design of the grand dome, which soars 120m above the altar and was completed in 1590, long after the genius artist had died. The cavernous interior contains numerous treasures, including Michelangelo's superb *Pietà*, sculpted when he was only 24 years old and the only work to carry his signature.

Entrance to the dome is to the right as you climb the stairs to the basilica's atrium. Make the climb on foot for €4, or pay €5 for the lift. Dress rules and security are stringently enforced – no shorts, miniskirts or sleeveless tops, and be prepared to have your bags searched.

Equally impressive is Bernini's masterpiece **Piazza San Pietro**, laid out in the 17th century. The vast piazza is bound by two semicircular colonnades, each comprised of four rows of Doric columns, and in its centre stands an obelisk brought to Rome by Caligula from Heliopolis (in ancient Egypt). The pope usually gives a **public audience** at

# PANTHEON & TRASTEVERE AREA

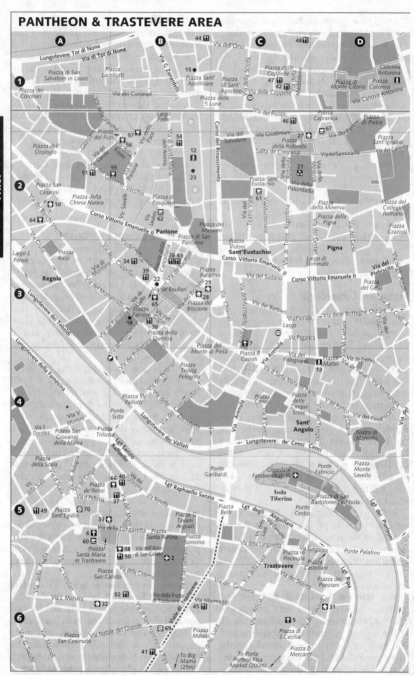

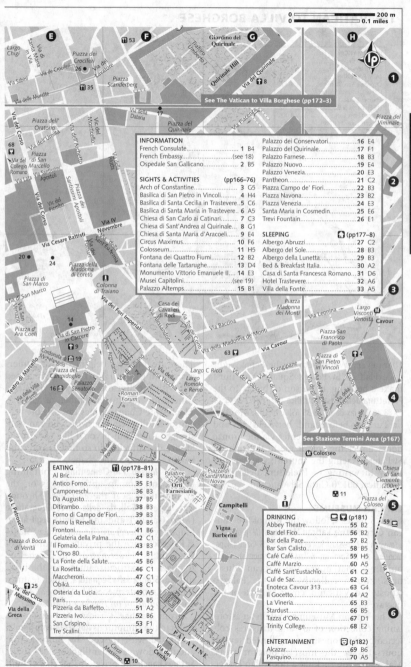

ITALY

**0 ——— 200 m**
**0 ——— 0.1 miles**

See The Vatican to Villa Borghese (pp172–3)

See Stazione Termini Area (p167)

| INFORMATION | |
|---|---|
| French Consulate | 1 B4 |
| French Embassy | (see 18) |
| Ospedale San Gallicano | 2 B5 |

| SIGHTS & ACTIVITIES | (pp166–76) |
|---|---|
| Arch of Constantine | 3 G5 |
| Basilica di San Pietro in Vincoli | 4 H4 |
| Basilica di Santa Cecilia in Trastevere | 5 C6 |
| Basilica di Santa Maria in Trastevere | 6 A5 |
| Chiesa di San Carlo ai Catinari | 7 C3 |
| Chiesa di Sant'Andrea al Quirinale | 8 G1 |
| Chiesa di Santa Maria d'Aracoeli | 9 E4 |
| Circus Maximus | 10 F6 |
| Colosseum | 11 H5 |
| Fontana dei Quattro Fiumi | 12 B2 |
| Fontana delle Tartarughe | 13 D4 |
| Monumento Vittorio Emanuele II | 14 E3 |
| Musei Capitolini | (see 19) |
| Palazzo Altemps | 15 B1 |
| Palazzo dei Conservatori | 16 E4 |
| Palazzo del Quirinale | 17 F1 |
| Palazzo Farnese | 18 B3 |
| Palazzo Nuovo | 19 E4 |
| Palazzo Venezia | 20 E3 |
| Pantheon | 21 C2 |
| Piazza Campo de' Fiori | 22 B3 |
| Piazza Navona | 23 B2 |
| Piazza Venezia | 24 E3 |
| Santa Maria in Cosmedin | 25 E6 |
| Trevi Fountain | 26 E1 |

| SLEEPING | (pp177–8) |
|---|---|
| Albergo Abruzzi | 27 C2 |
| Albergo del Sole | 28 B3 |
| Albergo della Lunetta | 29 B3 |
| Bed & Breakfast Italia | 30 A2 |
| Casa di Santa Francesca Romano | 31 D6 |
| Hotel Trastevere | 32 A6 |
| Villa della Fonte | 33 A5 |

| EATING | (pp178–81) |
|---|---|
| Al Bric | 34 B3 |
| Antico Forno | 35 E1 |
| Camponeschi | 36 B3 |
| Da Augusto | 37 B5 |
| Ditirambo | 38 B3 |
| Forno di Campo de' Fiori | 39 B3 |
| Forno la Renella | 40 B5 |
| Frontoni | 41 B6 |
| Gelateria della Palma | 42 C1 |
| Il Fornaio | 43 B3 |
| L'Orso 80 | 44 B1 |
| La Fonte della Salute | 45 B6 |
| La Rosetta | 46 C1 |
| Maccheroni | 47 C1 |
| Óbikà | 48 C1 |
| Osteria da Lucia | 49 A5 |
| Paris | 50 B5 |
| Pizzeria da Baffetto | 51 A2 |
| Pizzeria Ivo | 52 B6 |
| San Crispino | 53 F1 |
| Tre Scalini | 54 B2 |

| DRINKING | (p181) |
|---|---|
| Abbey Theatre | 55 B2 |
| Bar del Fico | 56 B2 |
| Bar della Pace | 57 B2 |
| Bar San Calisto | 58 B5 |
| Café Café | 59 H5 |
| Caffé Marzio | 60 A5 |
| Caffé Sant'Eustachio | 61 C2 |
| Cul de Sac | 62 B2 |
| Enoteca Cavour 313 | 63 G4 |
| Il Gocetto | 64 A2 |
| La Vineria | 65 B3 |
| Stardust | 66 B5 |
| Tazza d'Oro | 67 D1 |
| Trinity College | 68 E2 |

| ENTERTAINMENT | (p182) |
|---|---|
| Alcazar | 69 B6 |
| Pasquino | 70 A5 |

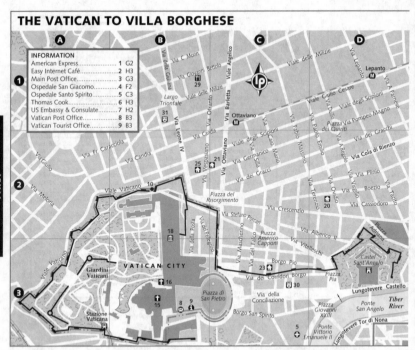

## THE VATICAN TO VILLA BORGHESE

**INFORMATION**
| | |
|---|---|
| American Express..................... 1 | G2 |
| Easy Internet Café.................. 2 | H3 |
| Main Post Office..................... 3 | G3 |
| Ospedale San Giacomo........... 4 | F2 |
| Ospedale Santo Spirito........... 5 | C3 |
| Thomas Cook......................... 6 | H3 |
| US Embassy & Consulate......... 7 | H2 |
| Vatican Post Office................. 8 | B3 |
| Vatican Tourist Office.............. 9 | B3 |

10am every Wednesday in the Papal Audience Hall or St Peter's Square. You must make a booking, in person or by fax to the **Prefettura della Casa Pontifica** (Map pp172-3; ☎ 06 69 88 46 31; fax 06 69 88 38 65) on the Monday or Tuesday beforehand, between 9am and 1pm. To go in person, enter via the bronze doors under the colonnade to the right of St Peter's (facing the church); you can also apply in writing to Prefettura della Casa Pontifica, 00120 Citta del Vaticano.

### VATICAN MUSEUMS

From St Peter's, follow the wall of the Vatican City to the **Vatican Museums** (Map pp172-3; admission €12, free last Sun of month; ☉ 8.45am-4.45pm Mon-Fri, to 1.45pm Sat & last Sun of month). The buildings that house the Vatican Museums, known collectively as the Palazzo Apostolico Vaticano, cover an area of 5½ hectares.

The Vatican Museums contain an astonishing collection of art and treasures collected by the popes, and you'll need several hours to see the most important areas. Make sure you pick up a floor-plan leaflet.

There are four very helpful 'oneway' itineraries, lasting from 1½ to five hours, mapped out with the aim of simplifying visits and containing the huge number of visitors. The Sistine Chapel comes towards the very end of a full visit; otherwise, you can walk straight there, but if you'd like to visit the Stanze di Raffaello, do so first as you can't backtrack once in the chapel.

The **Museo Pio-Clementino**, containing Greek and Roman antiquities, is on the ground floor near the entrance. Through the superb **Galleria delle Carte Geografiche** (Map Gallery) and the **Galleria degli Arazzi** (Tapestry Gallery) are the magnificent **Stanze di Rafaello**, once the private apartments of Pope Julius II, decorated with frescoes by Raphael. Of particular interest is the magnificent **Stanza della Segnatura**, which features Raphael's masterpieces *The School of Athens* and *Disputation on the Sacrament*.

From Raphael's rooms, go down the stairs to the sumptuous **Appartamento Borgia**, decorated with frescoes by Pinturicchio, and then down another flight of stairs to the **Sistine Chapel**, the private papal chapel built

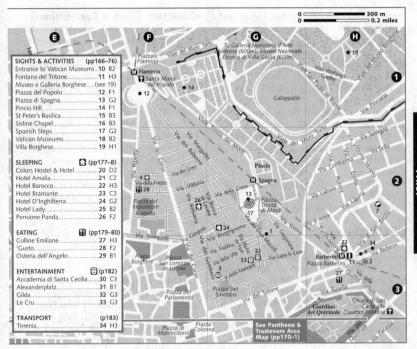

See Pantheon & Trastevere Area Map (pp170-1)

in 1473 for Pope Sixtus IV. Michelangelo's wonderful frescoes, *Creation* and *Last Judgment*, have been superbly restored to their original brilliance. It took Michelangelo four years, at the height of the Renaissance, to paint the *Creation*; 24 years later he painted the extraordinary *Last Judgment*. The other walls of the chapel were painted by artists including Botticelli, Ghirlandaio, Pinturicchio and Signorelli.

## Pantheon

The **Pantheon** (Map pp170-1; Piazza della Rotonda; admission free; 8.30am-7.30pm Mon-Sat, 9am-6pm Sun) is the best-preserved building of ancient Rome. The original temple was built in 27 BC by Marcus Agrippa, son-in-law of Emperor Augustus, and dedicated to the planetary gods. Agrippa's name remains inscribed over the entrance.

Over the centuries the temple was consistently plundered and damaged. The gilded-bronze roof tiles were removed by an emperor of the eastern empire, and Pope Urban VIII had the bronze ceiling of the portico melted down to make the canopy over the main altar of St Peter's and 80 cannons for Castel Sant' Angelo. The Pantheon's extraordinary dome is considered the most important achievement of ancient Roman architecture. The Italian kings Vittorio Emanuele II and Umberto I, and the painter Raphael, are buried here.

## Piazza Navona

A few blocks west of the Pantheon, this vast and beautiful **square** (Map pp170-1), lined with baroque palaces, was laid out on the ruins of Domitian's stadium and features three fountains. In its centre is Bernini's masterpiece, **Fontana dei Quattro Fiumi** (Fountain of the Four Rivers; Map pp170-1). Visit at different times of the day, and be sure to grab a *gelato*, relax on one of the stone benches in the sun, or enjoy a cappuccino at one of the many cafés – the expense is worth it to watch the various artists mingling in the piazza and to absorb the ever-vibrant hum.

## Campo de'Fiori

The colourful **Piazza Campo de'Fiori** (Map pp170-1), affectionately called 'Il Campo', was a

ITALY

place of execution during the Inquisition, and Caravaggio went on the run after killing a man who had the gall to beat him in tennis on this piazza. Nowadays a **flower and vegetable market** is held here Monday to Saturday, and revellers fill the many bars at night.

The **Palazzo Farnese** (Map pp170-1), in the piazza of the same name, is just off the Campo. A magnificent Renaissance building, it was started in 1514 by Antonio da Sangallo, carried on by Michelangelo and completed by Giacomo della Porta. Built for Cardinal Alessandro Farnese (later Pope Paul III), the palace is now the French embassy. The piazza has two fountains, which are enormous granite baths taken from the Baths of Caracalla (see opposite).

## Villa Borghese

This gorgeous **park** (Map pp172-3) was once the estate of Cardinal Scipione Borghese. His 17th-century villa houses the **Museo e Galleria Borghese** (Map pp172-3; ☎ 06 3 28 10; www .ticketeria.it; admission €8.50; ☉ 9am-7pm Tue-Sat), an impressive collection of paintings and sculptures. Take a walk through the lovely, leafy park, which has a zoo and a lake full of ducks, swans and turtles. You can hire boats at the lake and bicycles near the Porta Pinciana entrance. Just north of the park is the **Galleria Nazionale d'Arte Moderna** ( ☎ 06 32 34 000; Viale delle Belle Arti 131; admission €6.50; ☉ 8.30am-7.30pm Tue-Sun), a *belle époque* palace housing 19th- and 20th-century paintings. The Etruscan museum, **Museo Nazionale Etrusco di Villa Giulia** (admission €4; ☉ 8.30am-7.30pm Tue-Sun), is on the same street in Piazzale di Villa Giulia, in the former villa of Pope Julius III.

## Trevi Fountain

The high-baroque **Fontana di Trevi** (Map pp170-1; Piazza di Crociteri), about six blocks northeast of the Pantheon, was designed by Nicola Salvi in 1732 and immortalised in Fellini's *La Dolce Vita*. It sprawls over almost the entire piazza and depicts Neptune's chariot being led by Tritons, with sea horses representing the moods of the sea. Its water was supplied by one of Rome's earliest aqueducts, and the name refers to the three roads *(tre vie)* that converged here. The custom is to throw a coin into the fountain (over your shoulder while facing away) to ensure your return to Rome; a second coin grants a wish.

## Colosseum & Arch of Constantine

Originally known as the Flavian Amphitheatre, Rome's best-known monument, the **Colosseum** (Map pp170-1; ☎ 06 399 67 700; admission with Palatine Hill €8; ☉ 9am-1hr before sunset), was begun by Emperor Vespasian in AD 72. The massive structure could seat 80,000 and featured gory and deadly gladiatorial combat and wild beast shows.

During the Middle Ages, the Colosseum became a fortress, then later a quarry for travertine and marble to build Palazzo Venezia and other buildings. Restoration works have been under way since 1992. Skip paying the entrance fee for the barren interior.

On the west side of the Colosseum is the triumphal arch built to honour Constantine following his victory over his rival Maxentius at the battle of Milvian Bridge in AD 312. Its decorative reliefs were taken from earlier structures.

## Piazza di Spagna & Spanish Steps

The exquisite **Piazza di Spagna** (Map pp172-3), church and famous **Spanish Steps** (Scalinata della Trinità dei Monti; Map pp172-3) have long provided a major gathering place for foreigners and locals alike. Built with a legacy from the French in 1725, but named after the Spanish embassy to the Holy See, the steps lead to the church; the steps were constructed to link the piazza with the well-heeled folks living above it.

In the 18th century, beautiful Italians gathered here hoping to be chosen as artists' models. Beauties of both sexes still abound today. To the right as you face the steps is the house where Keats spent the last three months of his life, in 1821. In the piazza is the boat-shaped fountain of the **Barcaccia**, believed to be by Pietro Bernini, father of the famous Gian Lorenzo. One of Rome's most elegant, expensive shopping streets, **Via Condotti** (p182), runs off the piazza towards Via del Corso.

## Piazza del Popolo

The vast and impressive **Piazza del Popolo** (Map pp172-3) was laid out in the 16th century at the point of convergence of three roads – Via di Ripetta, Via del Corso and Via del Baubino – which form a trident at what was the city's main entrance from the north. Giuseppe Valadier redesigned it three centuries later, and today this neighbourhood is called 'the trident'. Rainaldi designed the seemingly twin baroque churches in the 17th century, and Bernini worked on the gate around the same time. **Santa Maria del Popolo** houses two magnificent Caravaggio paintings (of St Peter and of St Paul). The piazza is at the foot of the **Pincio Hill** (Map pp172-3), which affords a *bella vista* of the city, especially in the early hours; Keats, Strauss, Ghandi and Mussolini liked strolling here.

## Trastevere

Separated from *centro storico* by the Tiber, picturesque Trastevere exudes a sense of bonhomie. Wander through the narrow medieval streets, which retain the air of a typical Roman neighbourhood despite the influx of foreigners. Especially beautiful at night, this is a great area for eating and bar hopping.

Don't miss the **Basilica di Santa Maria in Trastevere** (Map pp170-1), in the lovely piazza of the same name, believed to be the oldest Roman church dedicated to the Virgin. Although the first church was built on the site in the 4th century, the present structure was built in the 12th century and features a Romanesque bell tower and façade, with a mosaic of the Virgin. Its interior was redecorated during the baroque period, but the vibrant mosaics in the apse and on the triumphal arch date from the 12th century. Also take a look at the **Basilica di Santa Cecilia in Trastevere** (Map pp170-1; admission free; ☉ 9am-12.30pm & 4.15-6.30pm Mon-Sat), with its magnificent 13th-century fresco.

## Via Giulia

Bramante designed this elegant street for Pope Julius II as a new approach to St Peter's. It runs parallel to the Tiber, south of Vittorio Emanuele II, and is lined with Renaissance palaces, antique shops and art galleries. Spanning the southern end is Michelangelo's ivy-draped **Arco Farnese.**

## Catacombs

There are several catacombs in Rome, consisting of miles of tunnels carved out of volcanic rock, which were the meeting and burial places of early Christians. The largest are along the Via Appia Antica (Appian Way), just southeast of the city and accessible on Metro Linea A to Colli Albani, then bus No 660. Via Appia Antica is traffic-free on Sundays if you want to walk or cycle it. The **Catacombs of San Callisto** (admission €5; ☉ 8.30am-noon & 2.30-5pm Thu-Tue Mar-Jan) and **Catacombs of San Sebastiano** (admission €5; ☉ 8.30am-noon & 2.30-5pm Mon-Sat mid-Dec–mid-Nov) are almost next to each other. Admission to each is with a guide only.

## Termi di Caracalla

The huge **Baths of Caracalla** (Map pp164-5; ☎ 06 399 67 70; Via delle Terme di Caracalla 52; admission €5; ☉ 9am-1hr before sunset Tue-Sun, to 2pm Mon) complex, covering 10 hectares, could hold 1600 people and included shops, gardens, libraries and entertainment. Begun by Antonius Caracalla and inaugurated in AD 217, the baths were used until the 6th century.

## Churches & Cathedrals

Down the road from Stazione Termini is the massive **Basilica di Santa Maria Maggiore** (Map p167; Via Cavour; ☉ 7am-6.30pm), originally named Santa Maria della Neve and built by Pope Liberius in 352 after the Virgin Mary

**STAY COOL UNDERGROUND**

While visitors queue on the streets for star attractions, head underground for some funky sights. Check out the underbellies of four cities while exploring Roman cisterns, former bomb shelters, haunted freezer chambers and rows of mummies. Added bonus: this makes a very cool activity on hot summer days.

**Naples** (www.napolisotterranea.com) An amazing 40m beneath the city streets are underground passages totalling more than 400km.

**Rome** (www.catacombe.roma.it, in Italian) The eternal city has over 50 catacombs, of which five are open for public visits – try a night-time foray.

**Palermo** ( ☎ 091 21 21 17) The Catacombe dei Cappucini, lined with adorned mummies sitting upright, are bizarrely ghoulish; there's even a separate section for virgins.

**Turin** (www.somewhere.it) Hidden passages tucked into 19th-century *palazzi* lead to a labyrinth of war-time shelters and tunnels, including the Porta Palazzo's natural ice caves, rumored to be haunted.

ITALY

instructed him to construct a church on the spot where the next snow fell. Its main baroque façade was added in the 18th century, preserving the 13th-century mosaics of the earlier façade. Its bell tower is Romanesque and the interior is baroque. There are 5th-century mosaics decorating the triumphal arch and nave.

Rome's cathedral, **Basilica di San Giovanni in Laterano** (Map pp164-5; Via Merulana; 7am-12.30pm & 3.30-7pm), was originally a church built in the 4th century, the first Christian basilica in Rome. Largely destroyed over a long period of time, it was rebuilt in the 17th century.

**Basilica di San Pietro in Vincoli** (Map pp170-1), just off Via Cavour, is worth a visit because it houses Michelangelo's *Moses* and his unfinished statues of Leah and Rachel, as well as the chains worn by St Peter during his imprisonment before being crucified; hence the church's name (St Peter in Chains).

**Chiesa di San Clemente** (Via San Giovanni in Laterano), east from the Colosseum, defines how history in Rome exists on many levels. The 12th-century church at street level was built over a 4th-century church that was, in turn, built over a 1st-century Roman house containing a temple dedicated to the pagan god Mithras.

**Santa Maria in Cosmedin** (Map pp170-1; Via del Circo Massimo; 10am-1pm & 2.30-6pm), northwest of **Circus Maximus** (Map pp170-1; Via del Circo Massimo), is regarded as one of the finest medieval churches in Rome. It has a seven-storey bell tower and its interior is heavily decorated with Cosmatesque inlaid marble, including the beautiful floor. The main attraction for masses of tourists is, however, the **Bocca della Verità** (Mouth of Truth). Legend has it that if you put your right hand into the mouth and tell a lie, it will snap shut.

## Piazza Venezia

A neoclassical monument dedicated to Vittorio Emanuele II overshadows the **Piazza Venezia** (Map pp170-1). Built to commemorate Italian unification, the piazza incorporates the **Altare della Patria** and the **tomb of the unknown soldier**, as well as the **Museo del Risorgimento** (admission free; 10am-6pm). Also in the piazza is the 15th-century **Palazzo Venezia** (9am-2pm Tue-Sat, to 1pm Sun), partially built with material quarried from the Colosseum, was once Mussolini's official residence and is now a museum housing medieval and Renaissance art.

## Baths of Diocletian & Basilica di Santa Maria degli Angeli

Just across the piazza from Termini, the **Baths of Diocletian** (Map p167; 06 488 05 30; Viale E De Nicola 79; admission €5; 9am-7.45pm Tue-Sun) were built at the turn of the 3rd century. Rome's largest baths could accommodate 3000 people; the complex also included libraries, concert halls and gardens and covered about 13 hectares. In AD 536, invaders destroyed the aqueduct that fed the baths and the complex fell into decay. Parts of the ruins are incorporated into the **Basilica di Santa Maria degli Angeli** (Map p167; Piazza della Repubblica; 7.30am-6.30pm).

Designed by Michelangelo, the basilica incorporates what was the great central hall and *tepidarium* (lukewarm room) of the original baths. Over the centuries his original work was drastically changed and little evidence of his design, apart from the great vaulted ceiling of the church, remains. An interesting feature of the church is a double meridian in the transept, one tracing the polar star and the other telling the precise time of the sun's zenith (visible at noon).

## Museo Nazionale Romano-Palazzo Altemps

This museum, in two separate buildings, houses an important collection of ancient art, including Greek and Roman sculpture. The restored 15th-century **Palazzo Altemps** (Map pp170-1; 06 683 37 59; Piazza Sant'Apollinare 44; admission €5; 9am-7.45pm Tue-Sun), near Piazza Navona, is home to most of the art, with numerous important pieces from the Ludovisi collection. **Palazzo Massimo alle Terme** (Map p167; 06 48 90 35 00; Largo di Villa Peretti 1; admission €6; 9am-7.45pm Tue-Sun), just off Piazza del Cinquecento, houses another part of the same museum and contains a collection of frescoes and mosaics from the Villa of Livia, excavated at Prima Porta, and a knockout numismatic (coin) collection.

## Villa Doria Pamphill

Rome's largest park, **Villa Doria Pamphill** (Via di San Pancrazio; sunrise-sunset), west of Trastevere, was laid out by Algardi in the 16th century, and offers a rejuvenating reprieve from the heady city pace. Relax by a baroque fountain, nap under a parasol pine or enjoy a stroll along the lovely walkways. To get there, you can take a bus to Via di San Pancrazio.

# SLEEPING

Rome has a wide range of accommodation, much of it charming, but the most popular and best-value options fill fast; book well ahead. The municipal government keeps a full list of accommodation options, including prices, on its excellent and very helpful website www.romaturismo.it.

The head office of the **Italian Youth Hostel Association** (Map p167; ☎ 06 487 11 52; www.ostel lionline.org; Via Cavour 44; ⊙ 9am-5pm Mon-Fri) has information about all the hostels in Italy and will assist with bookings to stay at universities during summer. You can also join HI here.

Still a new concept in Rome, B&Bs are growing in popularity. The tourist office has a list of private B&B operators.

## North of Stazione Termini

Most of the less-expensive options near the station are along Via Castro Pretorio, to the right as you leave the train platforms.

**Fawlty Towers** (Map p167; ☎ 06 445 03 74; www .fawltytowers.org; Via Magenta 39; dm/s/d €23/55/70, with shared bathroom €20/47/65; 🖳 ) This ever-popular spot offers hostel-style accommodation, lots of information about Rome, cheap Internet access and a lively common room with satellite TV – the flower-filled terrace and lack of curfew are icing on the cake.

**Beehive** (Map p167; ☎ 06 447 04 553; www.the-bee hive.com; Via Marghera 8; dm €20, d per person €40, with shared bathroom per person €35) This clean, cheery spot with a friendly American couple at the helm has a nice garden and communal kitchen. Walk-ins are not accepted, and party animals will be happier elsewhere.

**Albergo Sandra** (Map p167; ☎ 06 445 26 12; albergo sandra@libero.it; Via Villafranca 10; s/d €45/65) A mere 10-minute walk from Termini, this medium-sized *pensione* has clean and pleasant rooms and is lorded over by a house-proud Italian mamma and her English-speaking son.

**Pop Inn Hostel** (Map p167; ☎ 06 495 98 87; www .popinnhostel.com; Via Marsala 80; dm €17-25, s €35-95, d €20-49; 🖳 ) Comfortable and squeaky clean, this notch-above hostel has exceptionally helpful, friendly and multilingual staff; other simpatico features include no curfew, free breakfast, free luggage storage, and laundry.

**Hotel Castelfidardo** (Map p167; ☎ 06 446 46 38; castelfidardo@italmarke.it; Via Castelfidardo 31; s/d €55/74, with shared bathroom €46/65) Just off Piazza dell'Indipendenza, this well-run spot is one of Rome's better one-star hotels. The English-speaking staff are friendly and helpful.

**Hotel Dolomiti** (Map p167; ☎ 06 49 10 58; www .hotel-dolomiti.it; Via San Martino della Battaglia 11; s €58-90, d €78-125; 🔀 ) Two former run-down *pensioni* merged into one airy, good-value hotel with spotless, spacious and well-outfitted rooms. There's a snug bar, and the welcoming staff speak English, French and Spanish.

**Hotel Venezia** (Map p167; ☎ 06 445 71 01; www.hotel venezia.com; Via Varese 18; s €200-215, d €180-205; 🔀 ) The elegant Venezia is a delightful haven, beautifully furnished with antiques and pretty fabrics, and with a charming multilingual staff. It's excellent value, and the best spot in this hood; good for families too.

## South of Stazione Termini

This area can be a bit seedy but gets noticeably better closer to the Colosseum.

**Sandy Hostel** (Map p167; ☎ 06 488 45 85; www .sandyhostel.com; Via Cavour 136; dm €18, with bathroom €20) Rome's version of a backpackers' crash pad is on the 5th floor (no lift), has no curfew, not-great bathrooms, metal lockers without keys and a party atmosphere for the young and tolerant crowd; cash only.

**58 Le Real B&B** (Map p167; ☎ 06 48 23 566; www .58viacavour.it; Via Cavour 58; s €65-75, d €85-95; 🔀 ) Close to the Colosseum, this is a clean and pretty apartment, with airy rooms and a sun-drenched terrace. The friendly owners treat guests like friends, offering free access to a fridge loaded with juices, yogurt and water.

**Hotel Oceania** (Map p167; ☎ 06 48 24 696; www .hoteloceania.it; Via Firenze 38; s €52-104, d €62-135) You'll be greeted with a warm welcome at this small hotel with outstanding hospitality, smart rooms, wonderful owners and thoughtful extras such as English newspapers in the morning.

**Hotel d'Este** (Map p167; ☎ 06 446 56 07; d.este@taly hotel.com; Via Carlo Alberto 4b; s €72-145, d €83-196; 🔀 ) A short skip from Piazza Santa Maria Maggiore, this friendly spot with eager-to-please staff has nicely furnished rooms and a pleasant roof garden.

## City Centre

Truly budget rooms don't exist once you foray from the noisy Termini area. But what you lose in euros, you more than make up for in convenience and the unbeatable pleasure of staying in the heart of historic Rome.

ITALY

**Albergo della Lunetta** (Map pp170-1; ☎ 06 686 10 80; Piazza del Paradiso 68; d/tr €110/130, s/d/tr with shared bathroom €57/85/115) This central, old-school *pensione* is managed by *signori* who will either charm or irritate you, and the maze-like corridors and staircases lead to small, spotless rooms.

**Albergo Abruzzi** (Map pp170-1; ☎ 06 679 20 21; Piazza della Rotonda 69; s €125-150, with shared bathroom €55-75, d €175-195, with shared bathroom €90-115) There's nothing special about the rooms, but the position – overlooking the Pantheon – is hard to beat, even if the piazza can be noisy. Bookings are essential, and the chatty management makes this a perennial favourite.

**Pensione Panda** (Map pp172-3; ☎ 06 678 01 79; www.pensionepanda.com; Via della Croce 35; s/d €65/98, with shared bathroom €48/68) Close to the Spanish Steps, this 2nd-floor *pensione* has comfortable rooms with arched ceilings and helpful, English-speaking staff.

**Albergo del Sole** (Map pp170-1; ☎ 06 687 94 46; www.solealbiscione.it; Via del Biscione 76; s/d €83/125, with shared bathroom €65/95; **P** ) A short walk from Campo de'Fiori, this sunny spot dates from 1462. Cheery rooms, some with antiques, lots of communal space, a pretty patio and rooftop terrace make this hotel, one of Rome's oldest, a standout.

**Hotel Barocco** (Map pp172-3; ☎ 064872001; www.hotel barocco.com; Piazza Barberini 9; s/d €170/250; **P** ) Tucked into a quiet street off Piazza Barberini, this intimate and elegant pad has gentle staff and pretty rooms, some with a view of Bernini's baroque Triton fountain.

**Hotel D'Inghilterra** (Map pp172-3; ☎ 06 699 81 204; www.charminghotels.com; Via Bocca di Leone 14; d from €260; **P** ) This fashionable boutique hotel near the Spanish Steps is housed in a 16th-century *palazzo* and steeped in literary history – Hemingway, Twain and Henry James all bedded down here.

## Near the Vatican

Staying in this area is a good choice for those looking for quiet not too far from the main sights. Alas, bargains are rare, and bookings necessary because rooms are often filled with people attending Vatican conferences. The easiest way to reach the area is on Metro Linea A to Ottaviano; bus No 64 from Termini stops at St Peter's.

**Colors Hostel & Hotel** (Map pp172-3; ☎ 06 687 40 30; www.colorshotel.com; Via Boezio 31; dm €22, d/tr €85/90, d/tr with shared bathroom €75/85; ) Run by the people at Enjoy Rome (p166), Colors offers tidy rooms, a mini-gym and cooking facilities; the owners are opening a new mid-range hotel next door.

**Hotel Lady** (Map pp172-3; ☎ 06 324 21 12; 4th fl, Via Germanico 198; d €125, with shared bathroom €90) A quiet, old-world *pensione* with pleasant rooms and rustic antiques. The friendly and loquacious owners don't speak much English, but it's a good chance to practise *la lingua*.

**Hotel Amalia** (Map pp172-3; ☎ 06 397 23 356; www .hotelamalia.com; Via Germanico 66; s €95-130, d €150-210; ) Bright, clean rooms a coin's toss from the Vatican make this a popular, good-value option; look for last-minute specials online.

**Hotel Bramante** (Map pp172-3; ☎ 06 688 06 426; www.hotelbramante.com; Via delle Palline 24; s €105-150, d €150-210; ) With marble bathrooms and antique furnishings, this charming hotel is the nicest sleep spot in the area.

## Trastevere

One of Rome's most vibrant neighbourhoods makes an excellent base for the young (or young at heart).

**Casa di Santa Francesca Romano** (Map pp170-1; ☎ 06 581 21 21; istituto@sfromana.it; Via dei Vascellari 61; s/d/tr incl breakfast €70/100/123) This former noble home is now a gracious inn with pretty rooms and a cloistered garden.

**Hotel Trastevere** (Map pp170-1; ☎ 06 581 47 13; hoteltrastevere@tiscalinet.it; Via L Manara 24a-25; s €77-83, d €103-119, tr & q €129-154) This little gem offers great value and friendly service; many of the spotless rooms look out over Piazza San Cosimato.

**Villa della Fonte** (Map pp170-1; ☎ 06 580 37 97; www.villafonte.com; Via della Fonte d'olio 8; s/d €95/145; ) Five pretty and pristine rooms a hop from Piazza Santa Maria; the sunny garden terrace is lovely.

## EATING

Romans take visible pride in their *cucina* and traditional recipes. The roots of the local cuisine are the diet of the poor, hence a preponderance of *trippa* (tripe), and the Roman-Jewish tradition, with legacies such as stuffed *fiori di zucca* (zucchini/courgette flowers) and *carciofi alla romana* (artichokes with garlic, mint and parsley). Antipasto is a standout, particularly bruschetta, and classic Roman pastas include *cacio e pepe* (with pecorino, black pepper and olive oil) and the snappy *all'amatriciana* (with tomato, pancetta and chilli). The most beloved *secondo* is *saltimbocca alla romana* (escalopes of veal sautéed with white wine, sage and prosciutto).

Restaurant hours are generally noon to 3pm for lunch, and 7.30pm to 11.30pm for dinner; locals rarely eat dinner before 9pm.

## Snacks & Self-Catering

For quick and cheap eats, head to a bar, where you can wolf a *panini* (sandwich) for under €3, or a *pizza al taglio*, where a slab of oven-hot pizza, sold by weight, can cost as little as €1.50.

**Antico Forno** (Map pp170-1; Via del Muratte 8) Head here for delicious oven-hot slices and hearty sandwiches.

**Frontoni** (Map pp170-1; Viale di Trastevere) Good sandwiches made from local delicacies and sold by weight.

**Forno la Renella** (Map pp170-1; Via del Moro 15-16) This tiny spot churns out has some of Trastevere's top-notch slices.

**Forno di Campo de'Fiori** (Map pp170-1; Campo de'Fiori 22) Rome's best spot for metres of *pizza bianca* (white pizza, ie without tomato sauce).

Foragers will be orgasmic in the lively food markets, held off Viale delle Millizie, just north of the Vatican, and in Piazza Vittorio Emanuele, near Termini. There's also a well-stocked **24-hour supermarket** (Map p167; Stazione Termini) underneath the main concourse of the station, which is a handy stop for self-caterers.

## Restaurants, Trattorias & Pizzerias

With a few exceptions, the eating establishments near Stazione Termini are to be avoided, unless you're okay about paying high prices for mediocre food. In the historic centre, you'll pay dearly to eat in the A-list piazzas, sometimes a worthy splurge. For better value, hit the side streets off 'Il Campo' and Piazza Navona. San Lorenzo, to the east of Termini, and Testaccio are currently hot dining spots with locals. Trastevere simmers with eating options, but dodge the soulless tourist menus; expect to pay more near the Vatican.

### CITY CENTRE

**Pizzeria da Baffetto** (Map pp170-1; ☎ 06 686 16 17; Via del Governo Vecchio 114; pizza about €7) Any self-respecting pizza fan will make a stop at this Roman institution, always packed to the beams. Come very early or very late if you don't want to queue or share a table.

**Ditirambo** (Map pp170-1; ☎ 06 687 16 26; Piazza della Cancelleria 72; mains about €9) With wood-beamed ceilings, this cosy trattoria serves largely organic fare with funky twists, such as ravioli with *taleggio* (pungent soft cheese) and *radicchio* (chicory); the tall, dark and handsome waiters will charm you silly.

**Maccheroni** (Map pp170-1; ☎ 06 683 07 895; Piazza delle Coppelle 44; mains from €9) A hip trattoria that serves traditional Roman fare with new flair to the trendy set; on a hot night, the outdoor tables are coveted.

**Colline Emiliane** (Map pp172-3; ☎ 06 481 75 38; Via degli' Avignonesi 22; mains from €12) This small trattoria tucked into a cheerless street off Piazza Barberini serves superb Emilia-Romagnan food such as home-made pasta stuffed with pumpkin.

**'Gusto** (Map pp172-3; ☎ 06 322 62 73; Piazza Augusto Imperatore 9; pastas from €6) Slick and savvy, this place is a melange of pizzeria, *osteria*, wine

---

**MOZZARELLA DI BUFALA**

Springy on the outside, tantalisingly moist and buttery on the inside, *mozzarella di bufala* is a most singular (and surprisingly low-fat) cheese. And, to settle the debate, it really is made with milk from water buffalos, which have grazed the countryside south and west of Naples since the 2nd century AD. When the prized herds were destroyed during WWII, Italy brought in more of the animals from India. Today, thanks to healthy herds, there's a thriving water buffalo–milk industry ensuring a plentiful supply of the cheese. Although mozzarella is made from cow's milk as well, it lacks the nuttiness and depth of flavour.

You'll see fresh *mozzarella di bufala* on menus all over Italy, often tucked into *insalata caprese*, and in shops. Buy a mozzarella ball and eat it like an apple, doused with a little salt. Then head to the recently opened **Obikà** (Map pp170-1; Via dei Prefetti 26a; tasting plates from €12), a sushi-style 'mozzarella bar', to hone your taste.

bar and kitchen shop. It's a worthy stop any time, with an excellent wine list, an enormous cheese selection and good people-watching.

**L'Orso 80** (Map pp170-1; ☎ 06 686 4904; Via dell Orso 33; antipasti from €15) Delicious and plentiful antipasti are the stars at this popular spot, and the friendly waiters are happy to keep bringing small plates until you yell *basta* (enough); a good option for vegetarians.

**Al Bric** (Map pp170-1; ☎ 06 687 95 33; Via del Pellegrino 51-52; mains from €9) This snug dining space, with wood beams, wine box–lined walls and soft lighting, combined with excellent pastas served in big bowls, will make you feel like you're in a friend's home.

**Camponeschi** (Map pp170-1; ☎ 06 687 49 27; Piazza Farnese 50; mains from €15) Politicians, diplomats and glitterati swear by this spot, which has an ideal location – tucked onto Michelangelo's impossibly pretty piazza – and excellent Mediterranean fare served up with French flair.

**La Rosetta** (Map pp170-1; ☎ 06 686 10 02; Via della Rosetta 8-9; mains €25) Near the Pantheon, this oft-lauded star serves the best seafood in Rome. Trust your palate to owner-chef Massimo Riccioli, regarded as one of Italy's best, and his deliciously creative dishes such as fried *moscardini* (octopus) and mint. Expensive but oh so memorable.

### WEST OF THE TIBER: TRASTEVERE, TESTACCIO & THE VATICAN

**Café Café** (Map pp170-1; ☎ 06 700 87 43; Via dei Santi Quattro 44; salads & lights meals from €4) This low-key neighbourhood joint is not far from the Colosseum and offers excellent salads, light meals and sandwiches – as well as international newspapers, cups of brew

and wines by the glass. So likeable and comfortable, in fact, you may have trouble leaving.

**Pizzeria Remo** (Map pp164-5; ☎ 06 574 62 70; Piazza Santa Maria Liberatice 44; pizzas from €4.50) This place is loud and rowdy – filling with party types on weekend nights – but the cheap prices, pizza and *bruschette al pomodoro* (bruschettas with tomato) make the chaos and obligatory queues worth it.

**Osteria dell'Angelo** (Map pp172-3; ☎ 06 372 94 70; Via G Bettolo 24; mains from €12) Offering the best value near the Vatican, this popular spot serves delicious authentic Roman fare such as *salsicce al cinghiale* (wild boar sausage), and is run by a former rugby player.

**Pizzeria Ivo** (Map pp170-1; ☎ 06 581 70 82; Via di San Francesco a Ripa 158; pizza €4.75) Nice outdoor tables, excellent bruschetta and a spirited local crowd, who gather to watch soccer games, make up for the too-small-but-tasty pizzas and long queues.

**Da Augusto** (Map pp170-1; ☎ 06 580 37 98; Piazza de'Renzi 15; mains from €8) This bare-bones-but-beloved mamma's kitchen serves Roman classics with an occasionally surly attitude.

**Osteria da Lucia** (Map pp170-1; ☎ 06 580 36 01; Via del Mattinato 2; mains from €8) Dine under the stars, laundry flittering on the line, at this terrific neighbourhood trattoria serving a *trippa alla romano* (Roman tripe) that may well make you a convert.

**Paris** (Map pp170-1; ☎ 06 581 53 78; Piazza San Calisto 7; mains from €10) This elegant, old-world restaurant serves excellent Roman-Jewish cuisine such as *fritto misto con baccalà* (fried vegetables with salted cod).

### AROUND STAZIONE TERMINI & SAN LORENZO

**Trimani** (Map p167; ☎ 06 446 96 630; Via Cernaia 37; mains from €7) Rome's biggest *enoteca* (wine bar) has a vast selection of regional wines along with excellent soups, pasta and *torta rustica* (quiche).

**Pommidoro** (☎ 06 445 26 92; Piazza dei Sanniti 44; mains from €11) This San Lorenzo trattoria, 500m east of the Termini, is popular with artists and intellectuals; the grilled meats are particularly good.

**Moka** (Map p167; ☎ 06 474 22 11; Via Giovanni Giolitti 34; ☼ 24hr) If you've got some time at Termini, head to platform 24 for tasty, ready-made food.

---

### THE AUTHOR'S CHOICE

**Tram Tram** (☎ 064 470 25 85; Via dei Reti 44; mains from €10) In the heart of funky San Lorenzo, 500m east of the Stazione Termini, this small trattoria is worth the trek: friendly and *molta carina* (very sweet and charming), with high ceilings, big windows, cosy bar and loyal local clientele. The menu changes daily, but seafood dishes from southern Italy are the speciality; the swordfish is sublime and the excellent wine list lauds small producers.

## Gelati

**San Crispino** (Map pp170-1; Via della Panetteria 42)
The rumour that this *gelateria*, near Trevi
Fountain, has some of Rome's best *gelato*
is in fact true. The delicious fruit sorbets
change with the season – try *fichi* (fig) – but
it's the divine cream-based flavours – such
as ginger, honey, whisky and cinnamon –
that will make you an instant addict.

**Tre Scalini** (Map pp170-1; Piazza Navona 30) While
ogling in Piazza Navona, swing by Tre Scalini for good *gelato* and a memorable *tartufo
nero* (black truffle) concoction.

Also recommended (though not for the
indecisive), **Gelateria della Palma** (Map pp170-
1; Via della Maddalena 20) has 100 flavours –
the creamy mousses are a sure bet – and
Trastevere's **La Fonte della Salute** (Map pp170-
1; Via Cardinale Marmaggi 2-6) has excellent *gelati* (try the *marron glace*) and generous
scoops.

## DRINKING

Rome has an array of watering holes worthy of the gods. Much of the activity is in
the centre, where Campo de'Fiori fills with
young revellers, and there are nifty late-
night spots nestled in the alleyways fringing
Piazza Navona. Trastevere is packed with
friendly bars and co-mingling tourists and
locals; the Monti, Esquilino and Testaccio
districts also have lots of bars, including
some gay venues. Romans love their *enote-
cas,* and these cool places can offer a good-
value way to sample *vini* (wine) and meet
locals over a glass.

Just remember, the same cappucino
taken at the bar will cost less – but passing
an hour or so watching the world go by
over a wine in a beautiful location is hard to
beat and, despite what you may have heard,
Italians do it too. Often.

**Tazza d'Oro** (Map pp170-1; ☎ 06 679 27 68; Via degli
Orfani; ☽ Mon-Sat) Locals claim it's the water
from one of the city's original aqueducts
that makes the coffee here so outstanding;
in summer, try the *granita di caffè*.

**Caffè Sant'Eustachio** (Map pp170-1; ☎ 06 686 13
09; Piazza Sant'Eustachio 82) Also excellent, with
sublime, creamy coffee, served extra sweet.

**Bar del Fico** (Map pp170-1; ☎ 06 06 687 55 68; Piazza
del Fico 24; ☽ 8-2am Mon-Sat, from 6pm Sun) Popular
with local actors and artists, this pretty bar
has tables beneath its namesake fig tree –
providing shade on sunny days and a hit of

romance at night – and a snug interior with
tasteful music and local art.

**Cul de Sac** (Map pp170-1; Piazza Pasquino; ☽ noon-
4pm & 6-12.30am Tue-Sat) Tucked into a nook
off Piazza Navona, this *carina* wine bar has
communal wood benches out front, a chat-
tery interior, simple but good *enoteca* fare
and a robust wine list.

**Enoteca Cavour 313** (Map pp170-1; Via Cavour 313)
With wine-packed shelves, wood benches,
good antipasti and a very knowledgeable
owner, this simple and *buono* wine bar is
one of Rome's best.

**Caffè Marzio** (Map pp170-1; Piazza Santa Maria) In
Trastevere, this place has terrific coffee and
a gorgeous view onto one of Rome's presti-
est piazzas; perfection comes with a price,
though.

**Bar della Pace** (Map pp170-1; ☎ 06 686 12 16; Via
della Pace 3-7) With its gilded ambience and
dashing in-crowd, this is an atmospheric
drinking spot.

**La Vineria** (Map pp170-1; ☎ 06 68 80 32 68; Campo
de'Fiori 15; ☽ 9.30am-2pm & 6-1am Mon-Sat, to 2am
Sun) Hit the cosy Vineria on the Campo,
once the gathering place of the Roman lit-
erati.

**Bar San Calisto** (Map pp170-1; ☎ 06 583 58 69;
Piazza San Calisto) The slacker Trastevere set
hangs out at unglamorous Calisto. Besides
the cheap drinks and arty crowd, it has
memorable chocolate offerings.

**Il Gocetto** (Map pp170-1; ☎ 06 686 42 68; Via dei
Banchi Vecchi 14; ☽ 5.30-10pm Mon-Sat) This club-
like wine bar – one of the city's best – attracts locals dropping by after work. Slip
in and enjoy some of the 20 wines by the
glass.

**Trinity College** (Map pp170-1; ☎ 06 678 64 72; Via
del Collegio Romano 6; ☽ 11-3am) If you're hanker-
ing for pub night, try Trinity College; it has
a good selection of imported brews, great
food and an easy-going ambience; it also
gets packed at weekends.

---

**THE AUTHOR'S CHOICE**

**Stardust** (Map pp170-1; ☎ 06 583 20 875; Vic-
colo dei Renzi 4; ☽ 7.30pm-2am Mon-Sat, from
noon Sun) is a tiny Trastevere pub-meets-jazz
bar. This funky haunt purrs with sultry jazz
and impromptu jam sessions, and doesn't
close until the last customers tumble out
the door.

**ITALY**

ITALY

# ENTERTAINMENT

Gladiators are no longer fighting to their deaths, but Rome still has a lively entertainment scene. Though clubbing isn't as big in Rome as in other European capitals, sophisticates and hipsters are still well served.

The best entertainment guide is the Thursday-published *Roma C'è* (www.rom ace.it, in Italian), with an English-language section; *Wanted in Rome* (www.wanted inrome. com), published on alternate Wednesdays, is also good; *La Repubblica* and *Il Messagero*, daily newspapers, have cinema, theatre and concert listings. All are available at newsstands. Rome's entertainment schedule is particularly heady in summer, with numerous alfresco performances; be sure to catch one if possible.

For theatre, opera and sporting events, book ahead through **Hello** (Map p167; Stazione Termini) or **Orbis** (Map p167; Piazza dell'Esquilino 37).

## Nightclubs & Live Music

**Radio Londra** (Map pp164-5; ☎ 06 575 00 44; Via di Monte Testaccio 65b, Testaccio) Popular and decked out like an air-raid shelter, with live music four nights a week.

**Caruso Caffè** (Map pp164-5; Via di Monte Testaccio 36) Nearby and more sedate, with live music twice weekly and good DJs otherwise.

**Caffè Latino** (Map pp164-5; Via di Monte Testaccio 36) Live Latin music and a disco of Latin and funk.

For jazz and blues featuring top international musicians, head to **Alexanderplatz** (Map pp172-3; ☎ 06 397 42 171; Via Ostia 9; ☼ 8.30pm-2.30am Mon-Sat), near the Vatican, or **Big Mama** (☎ 06 581 24 51; Via San Francesco a Ripa 18; ☼ 9pm-1.30am), just south of Piazza Mastai in Trastevere.

At Roman nightclubs, expect to pay upwards of €20 to get in, which may or may not include one drink.

**Gilda** (Map pp172-3; ☎ 06 679 73 96; Via Mario de'Fiori 97) With plush décor and a vast dance floor, Gilda attracts a slightly older, jackets-required crowd.

**Le Cru** (Map pp172-3; ☎ 06 678 48 38; Via della Mercede 10/d) A newcomer, next door to Gilda, oozing smoke and bedecked with tapestries, mirrors, candle-lit tables and kissing couples; there's no cover, but the cocktails, served in voluptuous glasses, are steep.

**L'Alibi** (Map pp164-5; ☎ 06 574 34 48; Via di Monte Testaccio 44) Regarded as Rome's premier gay venue.

Popular stayers include **Alien** (Map pp164-5; ☎ 06 841 22 12; Via Velletri 13; ☼ 10.30pm-4am Tue & Thu-Sun), for sci-fi décor, dancers on raised platforms and hip-hop rhythms, and the far-flung **Goa** (☎ 06 574 82 77; Via Libetta 13; 11pm-3am Tue & Thu-Sun Oct-May), with its groovy ethnic décor and glam crowd but a distant location south of the city near metro stop Garbatella.

## Cinema

Several cinemas show films in English, including **Pasquino** (Map pp170-1; ☎ 06 580 36 22; Piazza Sant'Egidio), just off Piazza Santa Maria, and **Warner Village Moderno** (Map p167; ☎ 06 588 00 99; Via Merry del Val 14), a mega-plex showing Hollywood blockbusters and Italian films. Expect to pay €7, with discounts on Wednesday.

## Opera & Classical Music

**Teatro dell'Opera** (Map p167; ☎ 06 481 60 28 706; www.operaroma.it, in Italian; Piazza Beniamino Gigli) Rome's finest opera offerings from December to June; ticket prices are steep.

For a full season of concerts, there's the **Accademia di Santa Cecilia** (Map pp172-3; ☎ 06 361 10 64; Via della Conciliazione 4) and the **Accademia Filarmonica Romana** (☎ 06 323 48 90; www.tea troolimpico.it; Teatro Olimpico, Piazza Gentile da Fabriano 17), about 2km north of the city – take the bus from Piazza Manzini.

# SHOPPING

Shopping in Rome is undeniably fun and will no doubt lure your attention from ancient ruins. It's a very popular local pastime, with traffic banned on Saturdays to accommodate the thousands of window shoppers traipsing down the three ancient Roman roads radiating from Piazza del Popolo, the main shopping district.

Fashionistas will be happiest on Via Condotti and the narrow streets fanning from Piazza di Spagna to Via del Corso, lined with expensive boutiques full of clothing, footwear and accessories; most major designer labels are represented here. Via del Corso, with a nice mix of shops featuring designer knock-offs, is easier on the wallet, as is Via Nazionale. Via del Governo Vecchio is home to second-hand shops and up-and-coming designers.

If you're after art and antiques, wander the streets around Via Margutta, Via Ripetta, Via del Babuino, and Via dei Coronari, near Piazza Navona. For jewellery, the area between Ponte Sisto and Campo de'Fiori shines.

Across the Tiber, head to Via Cola di Rienzo, near the Vatican, for a good selection of clothing, shoes and food shops; the twisty streets of Trastevere harbour lots of little boutiques and design shops.

For funky finds and great bargains, head to Trastevere's **Porta Portese flea market** (Map pp170-1; 6.30am-2pm Sun), Rome's biggest and best known. It's just 300m south of Basilica di Santa Cecilia in Trastevere – even if you don't want to buy an antique vase or doll parts, go for the scene (but be aware of pickpockets). The excellent **market** (Via Sannio; Mon-Sat morning) near Porta San Giovanni sells new and second-hand clothes.

# GETTING THERE & AWAY
## Air
Rome's main airport is Leonardo da Vinci, at Fiumincino. Once in town, you'll find the main airline offices just north of Stazione Termini, in the area around Via Bissolati and Via Barberini.

## Boat
Tirrenia and the Ferrovie dello Stato (FS) ferries leave for various points in Sardinia (see p250) from Civitavecchia. A Tirrenia fast ferry leaves from Fiumicino and Civitavecchia in summer only. Bookings can be made at the Termini-based agency **Passagi** (Map p167; 7.15am-9pm), or any travel agency displaying the Tirrenia or FS sign. You can also book directly with **Tirrenia** (Map pp172-3; 06 42 00 98 03; Via San Nicola da Tolentino 5) or at the Stazione Marittima (ferry terminal) at the ports. Bookings can be made at Stazione Termini for FS ferries.

## Bus
The main terminal for intercity buses is in Piazzale Tiburtina, in front of the Stazione Tiburtina. Catch Metro Linea B from Termini to Tiburtina, or bus No 649 or 492 from the piazza in front of the station.

Numerous bus lines run to cities throughout Italy; all depart from the same area and the relevant ticket offices or agents are next to the bus terminus. For general information of which company services what area, go to the tourist office or Enjoy Rome (p166); for information and to make bookings, it's easiest to go through a travel agent.

**Cotral** ( 800 15 00 08; www.cotralspa.it, in Italian) services the Lazio region and departs from numerous points throughout the city, depending on the destinations.

**Lazzi** ( 06 884 08 40) runs services to other European cities and northern and central Italy.

**Eurojet** (Map p167; 06 474 28 01; Piazza della Repubblica 54) runs services to Bari, Brindisi, Sorrento, the Amalfi Coast and Pompeii, as well as to Matera. **SAIS & Segesta** (Map p167; 06 481 96 76; Piazza della Repubblica 42) has services to Sicily, and **SENA** ( 06 440 44 95) has services to Siena.

**Sulga Trioviaggi** ( 06 440 27 38) or **Sulga Perugia** ( 075 575 96 41) offer services to Perugia, Assisi and Romagna.

## Car & Motorcycle
It's no holiday trying to motor yourself into Rome's centre, which has many traffic restrictions and can be exceedingly nerve fraying to navigate. If you insist, the main road connecting Rome to the north and south is the Autostrada del Sole (A1), which extends from Milan to Reggio di Calabria. On the outskirts of the city it connects with the Grande Raccordo Anulare (GRA), the ring road encircling Rome. It's best to enter or leave Rome via the GRA and the major feeder roads that connect it to the city. If approaching from the north, take the Via Salaria, Via Nomentana or Via Flaminia exits. From the south, Via Appia Nuova, Via Cristoforo Colombo and Via del Mare (which connects Rome to the Lido di Ostia) all provide reasonably direct routes into the city. The A12 connects the city to both Civitavecchia and Fiumincino airport.

Car-rental offices at Stazione Termini include **Avis** ( 800 86 30 63; www.avis.com), **Europcar** ( 800 014410; www.europcar.com), **Hertz** ( 06 474 03 89; www.hertz.com) and **Maggiore National** ( 06 488 00 49; www.maggiore.it, in Italian). All rental offices at both airports as well. **Happy Rent** (Map p167; 06 481 81 85; www.happyrent.com; Via Farini 3) hires scooters (from €31 per day), motorcycles (around €104 and up) and bicycles (from €62 per week).

## Train
Almost all trains arrive at and depart from Stazione Termini, though some depart from the stations at Ostiense and Tiburtina. There are regular connections to all major cities in

Italy and throughout Europe. The tourist office in Stazione Termini (p166) can provide all timetables (English is spoken), however reservations must be made outside at Sportello 8. Italian speakers can book by phone on the **reservations line** ( ☎ 848 88 80 88; ☯ 7am-9pm). Most travel agents with a Trenitalia sign in the window can make reservations for you as well, and the **Trenitalia** (www.trenitalia.it) website is highly useful. You can also pick up an *orario* (timetable) at most newsstands in and around Termini for €4; this is particularly handy and a worthwhile investment if you are making multiple train journeys.

Services at Termini include telephones, money exchange, tourist information, post office, shops and **luggage storage** (per piece for 5hr €3.10, per piece per hr thereafter €0.52; ☯ 7am-midnight).

## GETTING AROUND
### To/From the Airport
There are several options for getting to and from Rome's main airport, Leonardo da Vinci (often simply called Fiumincino), about 30km southwest of the city centre. The least expensive transport is the convenient Leonardo Express train service (follow the signs to the station from the airport arrivals hall), which costs €8.80, arrives at and leaves from platform Nos 25 to 29 at Termini and takes 35 minutes. The first direct train leaves the airport at 6.37am, and then trains run half-hourly until the last one at 11.37pm. From Termini to the airport, trains start at 5:51am and run half-hourly until the last train at 10.51pm. Another train (€4.70) from Fiumincino (with destination Orte or Fara Sabina) stops at Trastevere, Ostiense and Tiburtina stations, but not at Termini, with a service from the airport every 20 minutes from 5.57am to 11.27pm, and from Tiburtina from 5.06am until 10.36pm. From midnight to 5am, an hourly bus runs from Stazione Tiburtina to the airport. Taxis from the airport to city centre run to about €47.

The **Airport Shuttle** ( ☎ 06 420 14 507; www .airportshuttle.it) offers transfers to/from Fiumincino for €28.50 for one or two passengers, €35 for three and €46.50 for four.

**Airport Connection Services** ( ☎ 06 338 32 21; www.airportconnection.it) offers a minivan shuttle to either airport for €30 per person, minimum two passengers. If driving yourself, the airport is connected to Rome by an autostrada, accessible from the GRA.

The other airport is Ciampino, 15km southeast of the city centre and used for most domestic and international charter flights. Blue Cotral buses (running from 6.50am to 11.40pm) connect with the Metro Linea A at Anagnina, where you can catch the subway to Termini or the Vatican. If you arrive very late at night, a taxi is your best bet. The FM4 metro line connects Termini with the Ciampino airport and Albano Laziale. The airport is connected to Rome by Via Appia Nuova.

### Car & Motorcycle
Negotiating Roman traffic by car is difficult enough, but you are in for enormous life-risking stress if you ride a motorcycle or Vespa. The rule in Rome is to look straight ahead to watch the vehicles in front and pray those behind are watching you. Pedestrians should always watch out for motorcycles, which often skip red lights.

Most of the historic centre is closed to normal traffic, and you are not permitted to drive into the centre from 6.30am to 6pm Monday to Friday and 2pm to 6pm Saturday without residency or special permission.

If your car goes missing after being parked illegally, check with the **traffic police** ( ☎ 06 6 76 91). It will cost about €95 to get it back, plus a hefty fine.

The major parking area closest to the centre is at the Villa Borghese; entrance is from Piazzale Brasile at the top of Via Vittorio Veneto. There's also a supervised car park at Stazione Termini. Other parks are at Piazza dei Partigiani, just outside Stazione Ostiense, and at Stazione Tiburtina, from where you can also catch the metro into the centre.

See p262 for information about car and scooter rental.

### Public Transport
Rome has an integrated public transport system, so the same **Metrebus** (www.metrebus.it) ticket is valid for all modes of transport. You can buy tickets at all *tabacchi*, newsstands and from vending machines at main bus stops. Single tickets cost €0.75 for 75 minutes, daily tickets cost €3.10 and weekly tickets cost €12.40. Tickets must be purchased before you go and validated in the orange machine as you board. Ticketless riders risk a hefty €53 fine – there's zero tolerance for tourists being or acting dumb.

ATAC ( ☎ 800 43 17 84; www.atac.roma.it) is the city's public transport company. Free transport maps and details on bus routes are available at the **ATAC information booth** (Piazza dei Cinquecento), where many of the main bus routes terminate. Largo di Torre Argentina, Piazza Venezia and Piazza San Silvestro are other hubs. Buses generally run from about 6am to midnight, with limited services throughout the night on some routes. A fast tram service, the No 8, connects Largo Argentina with Trastevere, Porta Portese and Monteverde Nuovo.

The Metropolitana has two lines, A and B. Both pass through Stazione Termini. Take Linea A for Piazza di Spagna, the Vatican (Ottaviano) and Villa Borghese (Flaminio), and Linea B for the Colosseum and Circus Maximus. Trains run approximately every five minutes between 5.30am and 11.30pm (12.30am on Saturday).

## Taxi

Roman taxi drivers can be at the top of the fleecing-foreigners game, so understand the rules before you and your bags get in the car. Make sure your taxi is licensed and metered, and always go with the metered fare, never an arranged price. Daytime trips within the centre can cost from €5 to €15.

**Cooperativa Radio Taxi Romana** ( ☎ 06 35 70) oversees many operators. Major taxi ranks are at the airports, Stazione Termini and Largo Argentina in the historical centre (look for the orange-and-black taxi signs). There are surcharges from €1 to €3 for luggage, night service, Sunday and public holidays; travel to/from Fiumicino airport has a surcharge of €7.45/6.10. The flagfall is around €2.75 (for the first 3km), then €0.75 for every kilometre. Taxis are on radio call 24 hours a day.

# AROUND ROME

## OSTIA ANTICA

The Romans founded this port city at the mouth of the Tiber in the 4th century BC and it became a strategically important centre of defence and trade. It was populated by merchants, sailors and slaves, and the ruins of the city provide a fascinating contrast to the ruins at Pompeii, which was a resort town for the wealthy. Barbarian invasions and the outbreak of malaria led to Ostia Antica's eventual abandonment, but Pope Gregory IV re-established the city in the 9th century AD.

Information about the town and ruins is available from the Rome tourist office or Enjoy Rome (p166).

Of particular note in the **excavated city** ( ☎ 06 56 35 80 99; admission €4.20; ⏰ 9am-5pm Tue-Sun winter, to 7pm summer) are the mosaics of the **Terme di Nettuno** (Baths of Neptune); a **Roman theatre** built by Agrippa; the **forum** and **Capitolium temple**, dedicated to Jupiter, Juno and Minerva; and the **Piazzale delle Corporazioni**, the offices of Ostia's 70 merchant guilds, distinguished by mosaics depicting their different trades.

To get to Ostia Antica from Rome, take the Metro Linea B to Piramide or Magliana, then the Ostia Lido train (getting off at Ostia Antica). By car, take the Via del Mare or the parallel-running Via Ostiense.

## TIVOLI

### pop 53,000

Set on a hill by the Aniene River, Tivoli was a resort town of the ancient Romans and became popular as a summer playground for the wealthy during the Renaissance. While the terraced gardens and fountains of the Villa d'Este are the main tourist draw, the ruins of Villa Adriana, built by the Roman emperor Hadrian, are far more interesting.

The **tourist office** ( ☎ 0774 31 12 49; Largo Garibaldi; ⏰ 8.30am-2.30pm Tue-Sat & 3-6pm Tue-Thu) is near the Cotral bus stop.

### Sights

Hadrian's spectacular summer villa, **Villa Adriana** ( ☎ 0774 53 02 03; admission €6.50; ⏰ 9am-1hr before sunset), built in the 2nd century AD, was one of the largest and most sumptuous in the Roman Empire. Although successively plundered by barbarians and Romans for building materials (many of its original decorations were used to embellish the Villa d'Este), enough resplendence remains to convey the villa's magnificence.

The Renaissance **Villa d'Este** (admission €6.50; ⏰ 9am-1hr before sunset Tue-Sun) was built in the 16th century for Cardinal Ippolito d'Este on the site of a Franciscan monastery. The villa's wonderful gardens are decorated with numerous fountains, its main attraction.

## Getting There & Away

Tivoli is 30km east of Rome and accessible by Cotral bus from outside the Ponte Mammolo station on Metro Linea B. Buses depart every 20 minutes, stopping at Villa Adriana, about 1km from Tivoli, along the way; the trip takes about one hour. Local bus No 4 goes to Villa Adriana from Tivoli's Piazza Garibaldi. The fastest route by car is on the Rome-L'Aquila autostrada (A24).

## TARQUINIA

pop 15,300

Believed to have been founded in the 12th century BC, and home of the Tarquin kings who ruled Rome before the creation of the republic, Tarquinia was an important economic and political centre of the Etruscan League. The major attractions here are the painted tombs of its *necropoli* (burial grounds), although the town itself is quite pretty and has a small medieval centre. There's a **tourist information office** ( ☎ 0766 85 63 84; Piazza Cavour 1; ⚐ 8am-2pm Mon-Sat) just past the medieval ramparts.

Tarquinia is about 90km northwest of Rome.

## Sights

The 15th-century Palazzo Vitelleschi houses the **Museo Nazionale Tarquiniense** ( ☎ 0766 85 60 36; admission incl necropolis €6.20; ⚐ 9am-7pm Tue-Sun), a significant collection of Etruscan treasures, including frescoes from the tombs. Keep an eye out for a few red-and-black plates featuring acrobatic sex acts. The **necropolis** ( ☎ 0766 85 63 08; ⚐ 8.30am-6.30pm Tue-Sun) is a 15- to 20-minute walk away (or catch one of four daily buses). Ask at the tourist office for directions. Some of the tombs are richly painted with frescoes, although many have deteriorated.

## Sleeping & Eating

Tarquinia has limited accommodation, so it's best to book ahead; it makes a very fine day trip from Rome.

**Hotel San Marco** ( ☎ 0766 84 22 34; Piazza Cavour 10; s/d €52/67) In the medieval centre, this pleasant hotel is the closest to the sights.

**Trattoria Arcadia** (Via Mazzini 6) Friendly and affordable for a good meal.

## Getting There & Away

Cotral buses leave approximately every hour for Tarquinia from outside the Lepanto stop on Metro Linea A, arriving at Barriera San Giusto, a short distance from the tourist office.

## CERVETERI

Ancient Caere, founded by the Etruscans, was one of the most important commercial centres in the Mediterranean from the 7th to 5th century BC. The present-day lures are the atmospheric tombs, known as *tumoli*, great mounds of earth with carved stone bases. Treasures taken from these tombs can be seen in the Vatican Museums, the Villa Giulia Museum and the Louvre. There is a **tourist office** ( ☎ 06 994 06 72; Piazza Risorgimento 19).

Once inside the main necropolis area, **Banditaccia** ( ☎ 06 994 00 01; Via del Necropoli; admission €4.20; ⚐ 9am-7pm Tue-Sun summer, 9am-4pm Tue-Sun winter), the *tumoli* are laid out in the form of a town. The best-preserved example is the 4th-century-BC **Tomba dei Rilievi**, adorned with painted reliefs depicting household items.

**Antica Locanda Le Ginestre** ( ☎ 06 994 06 72; Piazza Santa Maria 5) draws Romans just for a meal on the outdoor terrace; the pastas are especially good.

Cerveteri is accessible from Rome by Cotral bus (1¼ hours, every 30 minutes) from outside the Lepanto stop on Metro Linea A.

Get to Banditaccia by local bus (summer only) from the main square; otherwise it's a pleasant 2km walk west from town.

# NORTHERN ITALY

Italy's 'well-heeled' north isn't short of finery; from the imposing Alps to the jewelled beaches of Liguria and fairy-tale beauty of *La Serenissima* (Venice), its physical riches are matched by the cultural treasures concentrated here, due to Florence's role as the epicentre of the Renaissance. The only danger is lingering in bigger cities, when there are equal delights awaiting throughout Piedmont, Lombardy, Emilia-Romagna and the Veneto.

## GENOA

pop 628,800

Liguria's capital, the busy port of Genoa is simultaneously aristocratic, grandiose and dingy. Amid the contradictions, however, the mighty maritime republic once lauded as 'La Superba' retains a salty exuberance its most famous son, Christopher Columbus (1451–1506), would surely salute.

Vibrant Genoa was a EU–designated European City of Culture in 2004 and justly rewards a stop on any northern Italy itinerary.

## Orientation

Most trains stop at Genoa's main stations, Principe and Brignole. Brignole is closer to Genoa's centre and convenient to slightly better accommodation. Principe, nearer to the port, has many cheaper, if somewhat dingy, options nearby. It's no war zone, but it's somewhere best avoided at night by women travelling alone. From Brignole walk down Via Fiume towards Via XX Settembre and the historic centre. Local ATM buses service both stations.

## Information

**In-Centro IT** (Via XX Settembre 17-21; per hr €4; ☺ 10am-1pm & 2.30-7.30pm Mon-Fri, 10am-1pm & 3.30-7.30pm Sat) A tourism 'shop' with Internet access and good maps upstairs.

**Main post office** (☎ 5318708; Via Dante 4a; ☺ 8am-6.30pm Mon-Sat) Just off Piazza de Ferrari.

**Ospedale San Martino** (☎ 010 55 51; www.hsanmartino.liguria.it, in Italian; Largo Rosanna Benzi 10) East of the centre.

**Telecom office** (Piazza Verdi; ☺ 8am-9pm) To the left of Stazione Brignole.

**Tourist information office** Stazione Principe (☎ 010 2462633; www.apt.genova.it; ☺ 9.30am-1pm & 2.30-6pm Mon-Sat); Stazione Marittima (☎ 010 2463686; ☺ based on ship arrivals/departures); Airport (☎ 010 6015247; ☺ 9.30am-12.30pm & 1.30-5.30pm Mon-Sat)

## Sights

Any tour of Genoa should start in the backstreets around the old port. Newer parts of the harbour also appeal at night, when the hill-top lights form an appealing backdrop for the popular evening *passeggiata*.

Search out the gorgeous 12th-century, black-and-white marble **Cattedrale di San Lorenzo** (Piazza San Lorenzo; ☺ 8am-noon & 3.30-7pm) and the huge **Palazzo Ducale** (☎ 010 5574000; www.palazzoducale.genova.it; Piazza Matteotti 9; admission varies; ☺ 9am-9pm, ticket office to 8pm Tue-Sun), which doubles as the region's major exhibition space/arts hub.

Palaces line Via Garibaldi, many of which house galleries, including the 16th-century **Palazzo Bianco** (☎ 010 5572013; www.museopalaz-

zobianco.it; Via Garibaldi 11; 1-day/3-day card €8/12, bus surcharge €1/3; ☺ 9am-8pm Tue-Sun) and the 17th-century **Palazzo Rosso** (☎ 010 2476351; www.palazzorosso.it; Via Garibaldi 18; admission €3.10; ☺ 9am-7pm Tue-Fri, 10am-7pm Sat & Sun). **Galleria Nazionale di Palazzo Spinola** (☎ 010 2477061; Piazza Pellicceria 1; admission €4; ☺ 8.30am-7.30pm Tue-Sat, 1-8pm Sun) displays major Italian and Flemish Renaissance works, including Caravaggio's *Ecce Homo*.

**Acquario Di Genova** (☎ 010 234 52 67; www.acquario.ge.it; Ponte Spinola; adult/child €12.50/7.50; ☺ 9.30am-7.30pm Mon-Wed & Fri, to 10pm Thu, to 8.30pm Sat & Sun) is a highlight. The eye-catching Renzo Piano–designed aquarium jutting into the harbour is Europe's biggest, with typical beasties on display in an atypically interesting example of the genre.

## Sleeping

**Ostello Genova** (☎ 010 242 2457; hostelge@iol.it; Via Costanzi 120; dm with breakfast €13-18, dinner €8; ☺ closed Jan) In Righi, outside Genoa, is the nearest AIG (HI) hostel. Typically clean, but a little soulless (11.30pm curfew). There's a terrace with spectacular views of Genoa, though. Take bus No 40 from Brignole.

**Carola** (☎ 010 839 13 40; Via Gropallo 4; d/tr €55/70, s/d/tr with shared bathroom €30/45/60) On the 3rd floor of a gracious old *palazzo* near Brignole, Carola offers simple rooms and a warm welcome. Basic but functional, it's comfortable enough and a steal at the price. On a pleasant street north of Piazza Brignole, 1km from the old port.

**Hotel Bel Soggiorno** (☎ 010 542880; www.belsoggiornohotel.com; Via XX Settembre 19; s/d €73/93; ☒ ☐) The charming owner of this enchanting hotel works hard to ensure a pleasant stay, and rooms are bright and airy, if a little chintzy. Superbly located in the historic centre, a stone's throw from Brignole. The multilingual staff (Italian, German, French, English) are helpful, and there's a decent buffet breakfast. Ask about discounts for multinight stays.

## Eating

Genoa offers many Ligurian specialities, including the eponymous local 'dish', *pesto Genovese*. There's also delicious *pansoti* (ravioli in ground walnut sauce) and focaccia.

**Threegaio** (☎ 010 2465793; Piazza delle Erbe 17/19r; snacks €5-10; ☺ lunch & dinner Mon-Sat) Hip without being pretentious, accessible without being boring, and nicely placed on one of Genoa's coolest little piazzas, Threegaio is a bit of everything – bar, café, restaurant, meeting point. Best at *aperitivo* (cocktail hour) time.

**Il Panson** ( ☎ 010 2468903; Piazza delle Erbe 5; mains €9-11; ☽ dinner Mon-Sat) Il Panson has been serving up superb seafood to Genovese diners since 1790. Try the handmade basil ravioli in prawn sauce – insanely delicious and amazing value.

**Il Barbarossa** ( ☎ 010 2465097; Piano di Sant Andrea 21/23r; 2-course menu €12-18; ☽ 7.30-3.30am Mon, to 2.30am Tue-Fri, 12.30pm-2.30am Sat & Sun) In the shadows of the Porta Soprana, metres from Columbus' house, Barbarossa is small, popular and deliciously atmospheric. The fab wine and cocktail list offsets a menu of local specialities, though it's also great for a quick *panini* and a beer.

**Antica Cantina i Tre Merli** (The Three Crows; ☎ 010 2474095; www.itremerli.it; Vico dietro il Coro Maddalena 26r; 2-course menu €15-20; ☽ noon-3pm & 7pm-1am Mon-Fri, dinner Sat) For a protracted dining experience, this *antica cantina* (old-style eatery) offers moody, rustic ambience and serves up great, hearty Ligurian food with a sensational wine list; try the fantastic tomato pasta with *seppia* (cuttlefish ink) sauce.

**Oriental market** (Via XX Settembre) Fantastic fresh produce.

## Drinking & Entertainment

**Dueseiuno** ( ☎ 010 2511558; Mura della Marina, 21r; ☽ noon-2am) Genoa's nightlife is subdued; try the three floors here.

**Cosa Zapata** (Via Sampierdarena 36; ☽ 9pm-3am Fri & Sat) Live music fans should seek this place out, where a younger crowd mosh to modern music within medieval walls.

There are good bars clustered around Piazza Raibetta and Piazza delle Erbe – great places for an aperitif. There's also a cinema multiplex and abundant mainstream shops in the huge **Magazin del Cotone** (Cotton Shop; Porto Antico).

## Getting There & Around

### AIR

There are regular domestic and international flights from **Cristoforo Colombo Airport** ( ☎ 010 601 54 10; Sestri Ponente), 6km west of the city. The **Volabus** ( ☎ 558 24 14; ☽ 5.30am-11pm) airport bus service (line No 100) leaves from Piazza Verdi (€2.20, 25 minutes, every 30 minutes), just outside Stazione Brignole, also stopping at Stazione Principe.

### BUS

Buses for Rome, Florence, Milan and Perugia leave from Piazza della Vittoria, south of Stazione Brignole, where Eurolines coaches also depart for Barcelona, Madrid and Paris. Book tickets at **Geotravels** ( ☎ 010 58 71 81) in the piazza.

### TRAIN

Genoa is linked by train to Turin (€15.86, 1¾ hours, seven to 10 daily), Milan (€12.86, 1½ hours, eight daily), Pisa (€15.86, two hours, up to eight daily) and Rome (€34.51, 5¼ hours, six daily) and it makes little difference which of the two train stations (Principe or Brignole) you choose, except for trips along the two Rivieras. Fares quoted are Intercity fares.

### FERRIES

Genoa is a major embarkation point for ferries to Sicily, Sardinia and Corsica. Major companies are **Corsica Ferries** ( ☎ 019 21 55 11; www.corsicaférries.com) in Savona; **Moby Lines** ( ☎ 010 254 15 13; www.moby.it) at Ponte Asserato for Corsica; **Tirrenia** ( ☎ 199 12 31 99, 800 82 40 79; www.gruppotirrenia.it) at the Stazione Marittima, Ponte Colombo, for Sicily and Sardinia; and Grandi Navi Veloci and **Grandi Traghetti** ( ☎ 010 58 93 31; Via Fieschi 17) for Sardinia, Sicily, Malta and Tunisia.

# RIVIERA DI LEVANTE

The Ligurian coast from Genoa south to La Spezia is spectacular, rivalling the Amalfi Coast in its beauty. Summer here is congested; try going in spring and autumn when smaller crowds make sightseeing easier and the heat is less stifling. A good option is using either Santa Margherita Ligure in the north as a base or La Spezia in the south.

The **tourist office** ( ☎ 0185 28 74 85; www.aptcin queterre.sp.it; Via XXV Aprile 4) in Santa Margherita is central; the one in **La Spezia** ( ☎ 0187 77 09 00; Via Mazzini 45) is near the waterfront. Both have information on the Cinque Terre and surrounding coastal towns.

## Sights & Activities

From pretty Santa Margherita Ligure you can explore the nearby resorts of **Portofino**, a haunt of the glamour set, and **Camogli**, a gorgeous fishing village turned resort town. The medieval Benedictine monastery of **San Fruttuoso** is a hilly 2½-hour walk from Camogli or Portofino, with sensational views along the way; it's possible to catch the ferry back.

Don't miss the **Cinque Terre**, five tiny villages – Riomaggiore, Manorola, Corniglia, Vernazza and **Monterosso** – clustered along a section of eye-popping Unesco-protected coastline, easily among the most beautiful regions in Italy. Individually charming, collectively breathtaking, all are easily reached by train from La Spezia. Linked by a 12km path, the remarkable scenery of the **Via dell'Amore** (Lovers' Lane; toll €3) is a perfect, mildly challenging day walk.

Don't limit your sightseeing to land; in summer, swimming's permitted in some bays and coves (check before diving in), and bring snorkelling gear for an often-overlooked treat.

### Sleeping

**La Dolce Vita** ( ☎ 0187 760044; fax 0187 920935; Via Colombo 120; bed from €20) Giacomo Natale runs this bed-booking service in Riomaggiore, and he knows everyone and everywhere worth remembering in the area. Call him first or ask for him at Bar Centrale; if he can't find you a bed, no-one can. Rooms are generally excellent (most with views).

**Ostello 5 Terre** ( ☎ 0187 92 02 15; www.cinqueterre .net/ostello; Via B Riccobaldi 21; dm €17-22, breakfast €3.50, dinner €14) This is an orderly, well-run hostel in Manorola. Always crowded, so reserve. Manorola is a 15-minute, clearly-marked walk from Riomaggiore.

**Nuova Riviera** ( ☎ 0185 28 74 03; info@nuovariviera .com; Via Belvedere 10/2; s/d €75/90; P X R ) In Santa Margherita, this lovely old hotel is metres from the water and highly atmospheric for a seaside rendezvous. Splash out!

### Eating & Drinking

**A Pie De Ma** ( ☎ 338 2220088; Via dell' Amore; snacks €5-8; breakfast, lunch & dinner) Perched on a cliffside above the perfect teal of a tiny Riomaggiore bay, you'll seldom find a more beautiful backdrop for a snack, coffee or wine – or just whiling away hours – than the divine terrace vista here. Food and service are tops, too.

**Bar Centrale** ( ☎ 0187 920208; barcentr@tin.it; Via Colombo 144; Internet per hr €6) On the main drag, this hub of Riomaggiore hijinks is always open. Your only real carousing option in the off-season, certainly the most raucous one in summer; barman Ivo serves up drinks and sarcasm equally.

### Getting There & Away

All the coastal towns are easily accessible by train from Genoa. Buses leave from Santa Margherita's Piazza Martiri della Libertà for Portofino. **Servizio Marittimo del Tigullio** ( ☎ 0185 28 46 70; www.traghettiportofino.it) runs summer ferries from Santa Margherita to Portofino, San Fruttuoso and the Cinque Terre. From La Spezia many ferry routes service the coast. For the Cinque Terre, a *biglietto giornaliero Cinque Terre* (24-hour Cinque Terre rail pass; €5.80) allows unlimited travel between Monterosso and La Spezia.

## TURIN

pop 898,400

Set to host the 2006 Winter Olympics, Turin is a grand old city. The former capital of Italy (until 1945) and seat of the Savoys feels like a once-regal place whose glory won't *quite* fade; mostly thanks to the era of the Agnelli family's Fiat automobile empire, and to Italy's most notorious football team, Juventus. Memorable products occasionally originate in unexpected places, and Turin is the birthplace of Ferrero Rocher chocolates, Nutella and Tic Tacs.

Turin's other famous icon is Il Sindone, or the Shroud of Turin, believed to be Christ's burial cassock.

### Orientation

Porta Nuova train station is the usual point of arrival. For the centre, cross Corso Vittorio Emanuele II and walk through the grand Carlo Felice and San Carlo piazzas toward Piazza Castello.

### Information

**Tourist offices** Piazza Castello ( ☎ 011 53 51 81; www .turismotorino.org; Piazza Castello 161; 9.30am-7pm Mon-Sat, to 3pm Sun); Porta Nuova train station ( ☎ 011 53 13 27); Airport ( ☎ 011 567 81 24)

Museum enthusiasts should consider the **Torino Card** (48/72hr card €15/17), available at the Piazza Castello tourist office and valid for all public transport and discounts/entry to 120 museums, monuments and castles.

### Sights

Start at the central Piazza San Carlo, known as 'Turin's drawing room' and capped by the baroque churches of **San Carlo** and **Santa Cristina**. Nearby, the majestic **Piazza Castello**

ITALY

features the sumptuous **Palazzo Madama**, home to the **Museo Civico d'Arte Antica** ( ☎ 011 442 99 12; Piazza Castello; adult/child €6.20/3.10; ☺ 10am-8pm Tue-Fri & Sun, to 11pm Sat) and the 17th-century **Palazzo Reale** (Royal Palace; ☎ 011 436 14 55; Piazza Castello; adult/child €6.50/free; ☺ 9am-7pm Tue-Sun), where the gardens were designed in 1697 by Louis le Nôtre, noted for his work at Versailles.

Film buffs shouldn't miss the **Museo Nazionale del Cinema** ( ☎ 011 8125658; www.museo nazionaledelcinema.it; Via Montebello 20; adult/concession €5.20/4.20; ☺ 9am-8pm Tue-Fri & Sun, to 11pm Sat), Italy's most comprehensive archive of imaging history/materials. There are presound 'magic lantern' exhibits, original Charlie Chaplin storyboards, HR Giger–designed *Aliens* props and more, all in a cutting-edge gallery. It's 20 minutes from Porta Nuova on foot, or take bus No 61 (alight Via Po) or 68 (alight Via Rossini).

The nearby **Cattedrale di San Giovanni Battista** is home to a Catholic curiosity, the Shroud of Turin, the linen cloth purportedly used to wrap the crucified Christ. Carbon dating challenges this, showing the cloth to be from the 13th century, and, in 2004, Italian scientists discovered what appears to be a secondary image on the reverse of the iconograph. Rarely shown, check ahead if you're determined to see it. There's a copy displayed in the cathedral. The **Museo della Sindone** (Museum of the Shroud; ☎ 011 436 58 32; Via San Domenico 28; adult/child €5.50/2.50; ☺ 9am-noon & 3-7pm) answers most questions.

Turin's **Museo Egizio** (Egyptian Museum; ☎ 011 561 77 76; www.museoegizio.org; Via Accademia delle Scienze 6; admission €6.50; ☺ 8.30am-7.30pm Tue-Sun) is considered to be among the best museums of Egyptian artefacts after those in London and Cairo.

Outside town is the **Palazzina di Caccia di Stupinigi** (Savoy Hunting Lodge; ☎ 011 358 1220; www .stupinigi.it, in Italian; Piazza Principe Amedeo 7; ☺ 10am-5pm Tue-Sun, to 6pm summer), a stupefyingly rococo example of the French baroque architecture the Savoys applied to Turin more broadly during their reign.

## Sleeping

**Bologna** ( ☎ 011 562 02 90; www.hotelbolognasrl.it, in Italian; Corso Vittorio Emanuele II 60; s/d/tr €57/88/100) Near the station, and deservedly popular. Looking grim at first, rooms are actually clean and comfortable, if a little exposed to street noise.

**Hotel Roma e Rocco Cavour** ( ☎ 011 561 27 72; hotel@roma.tin.it; Piazza Carlo Felice 60; s/d/tr €70/88/99, s/d with shared bathroom €50/68) Something for everyone right on Turin's most engaging square. Basic décor and adequate service don't detract from a fundamentally pleasant night's accommodation.

**Dogana Vecchia** ( ☎ 011 436 67 52; Via Corte D'Appello 4; s/d €83/104; ✗ ✗ ▣ ) Dogana Vecchia has accommodated the likes of Verdi and Mozart. Rooms have all mod cons, yet still make you feel like you've stepped back in time. Splurge and see how it feels to live like minor royalty.

**Ostello Torino** ( ☎ 011 660 29 39; www.ostellion line.org; Via Alby 1; dm/d €12/17, dinner €8.50; ☺ closed 9.30am-2pm; ✗ ) To get to this quiet HI hostel, walk 1.5km up a steep hill or catch bus No 52 from Porta Nuova (No 64 on Sunday). Book ahead to snag a double room.

**Campeggio Villa Rey** ( ☎ 011 819 01 17; Strada Superiore Val San Martino 27; per person/tent €3.65/6; ☺ Mar-Oct) This camping ground in the hills east of the Po has access and bathrooms for disabled travellers. Bus No 52 from Porta Nuova (No 64 on Sunday).

## Eating

**Al Pigaron** ( ☎ 011 8125018; Via Accademia Albertina 27; set menus €8; ☺ lunch & dinner) The cheapest good three-course lunch in Turin. Décor is '70s shabby-tacky, but the service is excellent and the simple Piemontese dishes are delicious and served in decent portions.

**La Stua** ( ☎ 011 8178339; Via Giuseppe Mazzini 46; pizzas €7-9; ☺ noon-2pm & 6.45pm-midnight Tue-Sun) Wonderful pizzeria offering a fantastic range of the trademark dish, as well as excellent pasta and main meals. Warm atmosphere, great prices and friendly staff.

**Ristorante Perbacco** ( ☎ 011 882110; Via Giuseppe Mazzini 31; set menus €28; ☺ 7.45pm-1am Tue-Sun) Super stylish. Think low light, deep-red furnishings, first-rate cooking with the best local produce and a wine list longer than the Po. Try the rabbit with *dolcelatte* (sweet blue cheese), or the outstanding salmon in rocket sauce.

For *gelati* and chocolate you're spoiled for choice; get revolutionary at **Caffè Fiorio** (Via Po 8), which was good enough for Camillo Cavour, the father of Italian unification.

## Getting There & Around

Turin is serviced by the **Turin International Airport** ( ☎ 011 567 63 61; www.turin-airport.com) in

Caselle, with flights to European and national destinations. **Sadem** (☎ 011 300 01 66) runs buses to the airport (€5.40, 40 minutes, every 45 minutes) from the corner between Via Sacchi and Corso Vittorio Emanuele II, west of Porta Nuova. National and international buses use the terminal on Corso Castelfidardo. Regular daily trains connect with Milan (€14.57, 1¾ hours), Aosta (€6.80, two hours), Venice (€25, five hours), Genoa (€15.86, 1¾ hours) and Rome (€40.45, seven hours). The city is well serviced by buses and trams.

# MILAN
**pop 1.3 million**

Milan is a glitzy city, obsessed with money, looks and glamour. Sure enough, it offers the best in Italian theatre, nightlife and clothes, but little else. And you almost require the salary of one of its top models or football stars to fully indulge in its other great diversion: shopping.

Originally believed to be Celtic, it was conquered by the Romans in 222 BC and then became a major trading and transport centre. From the 13th century, the city flourished under the rule of two powerful families: the Visconti, followed by the Sforza.

Milan closes down almost completely in August, when most of the city's inhabitants take their buff bodies away for annual holidays.

## Orientation

From Milan's central train station (Stazione Centrale), approach the centre on its efficient underground railway, the Metropolitana Milanese (MM). Use the Duomo (cathedral) and the Castello Sforzesco as your landmarks; the main shopping areas and sights are around and between the two.

## Information

### BOOKSHOPS

**Feltrinelli International** (☎ 02 6595644; www.la feltrinelli.it, in Italian; Piazza Cavour 1) The foreign-language arm of Italy's best book chain.

### EMERGENCY

**Ambulance & Fire** (☎ 118)
**Milan City Council** (☎ 02 54 66 81 18; Via Friuli 30) For lost property.

**Police headquarters** (Questura; ☎ 02 622 61; Via Fatebenefratelli 11) English spoken.
**Ufficio Stranieri** (Foreigners' office; ☎ 02 622 61; Via Montebello 26)

### INTERNET ACCESS

**Grazia Internet** (☎ 02 6700543; Piazza Duca D'Aosta 40; per hr €4; ✆ 8-2am) Next to Stazione Centrale, this place is orange, like a mini Easy Internet.

### LAUNDRY

**Lavanderia Self Service** (Via Tadino 4; small/large load €3.10/6.10; ✆ 7.30am-9.30pm)

### MEDICAL SERVICES

**Farmacia Carlo Erba** (☎ 02 87 86 68; Piazza del Duomo 21; ✆ 24hr)
**Ospedale Maggiore Policlinico** (☎ 02 550 31; Via Francesco Sforza 35) A central public hospital.
**Pharmacy** (☎ 02 669 07 35; Stazione Centrale; ✆ 24hr)

### MONEY

**American Express** (Via Larga 4; ✆ 9am-5.30pm Mon-Fri)
**Banca Cesare Ponte** (19 Piazza del Duomo) Has an ATM.
**Exchange offices** (Stazione Centrale)

### POST

**Main post office** (Via Cordusio 4; ✆ 8am-7pm Mon-Fri, 8.30am-noon Sat) Off Via Dante, near Piazza del Duomo. There are other offices at the station and Linate airport.

### TELEPHONE

**Telecom office** Stazione Centrale (Upper level; ✆ 8am-9.30pm); Galleria Vittorio Emanuele II (✆ 8am-9.30pm) Both offices have international telephone directories. The Galleria Vittorio Emanuele II branch also has fax services and phonecards.

### TOURIST INFORMATION

**Tourist offices** Piazza del Duomo (☎ 02 72 52 43 01; www.milanoinfotourist.com; Via Marconi 1; ✆ 8.45am-1pm & 2-6pm Mon-Sat, 9am-1pm & 2-5pm Sun); Stazione Centrale (☎ 02 72 52 43 60; ✆ 9am-6.30pm Mon-Sat, 9am-12.30pm & 1.30-5pm Sun) Pick up free guides *Hello Milano* and *Milano Mese* here, and a *Milan is Milano* map. There are also tourist offices at both airports.

## Dangers & Annoyances

Milan's main shopping areas are haunts for thieves; some teams employ diversionary tactics. Be alert, particularly around Stazione Centrale, to people crowding you around the underground, especially when the platform seems oddly uncrowded.

# CENTRAL MILAN

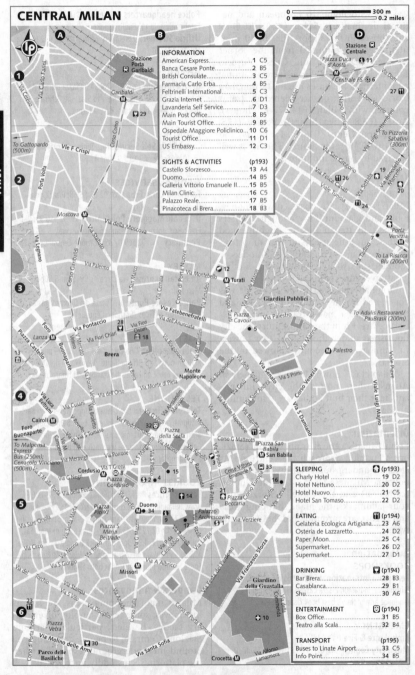

**INFORMATION**

| | |
|---|---|
| American Express | 1 C5 |
| Banca Cesare Ponte | 2 B5 |
| British Consulate | 3 C5 |
| Farmacia Carlo Erba | 4 B5 |
| Feltrinelli International | 5 C3 |
| Grazia Internet | 6 D1 |
| Lavanderia Self Service | 7 D3 |
| Main Post Office | 8 B5 |
| Main Tourist Office | 9 B5 |
| Ospedale Maggiore Policlinico | 10 C6 |
| Tourist Office | 11 D1 |
| US Embassy | 12 C3 |

| SIGHTS & ACTIVITIES | (p193) |
|---|---|
| Castello Sforzesco | 13 A4 |
| Duomo | 14 B5 |
| Galleria Vittorio Emanuele II | 15 B5 |
| Milan Clinic | 16 C5 |
| Palazzo Reale | 17 B5 |
| Pinacoteca di Brera | 18 B3 |

| SLEEPING | (p193) |
|---|---|
| Charly Hotel | 19 D2 |
| Hotel Nettuno | 20 D2 |
| Hotel Nuovo | 21 C5 |
| Hotel San Tomaso | 22 D2 |

| EATING | (p194) |
|---|---|
| Gelateria Ecologica Artigiana | 23 A6 |
| Osteria de Lazzaretto | 24 D2 |
| Paper Moon | 25 C4 |
| Supermarket | 26 D2 |
| Supermarket | 27 D1 |

| DRINKING | (p194) |
|---|---|
| Bar Brera | 28 B3 |
| Casablanca | 29 B1 |
| Shu | 30 A6 |

| ENTERTAINMENT | (p194) |
|---|---|
| Box Office | 31 B5 |
| Teatro alla Scala | 32 B4 |

| TRANSPORT | (p195) |
|---|---|
| Buses to Linate Airport | 33 C5 |
| Info Point | 34 B5 |

## Sights & Activities

The city's landmark **Duomo** (stairs/lift to roof €3.50/5; ☼ 9am-5.30pm) looks like the backdrop for an animated story (and seats 40,000!). Commissioned in 1386 to a florid French-Gothic design and finished nearly 600 years later, the resulting façade is an unforgettable marble mass of statues, spires and pillars. The view from the roof is wonderful.

Join the throngs for a *passeggiata* through the magnificent **Galleria Vittorio Emanuele II** towards **Teatro alla Scala** (see p194), the world's most famous opera house, recently reopened after – appropriately enough for Milan – a facelift.

The immense **Castello Sforzesco** (☎ 02 801410; www.milanocastello.it; Piazza Castello 3; admission free; ☼ 9.30am-5.30pm Tue-Sun), once a Visconti fortress, rebuilt by Francesco Sforza in 1450, now houses collections of furniture, artefacts and sculpture, notably Michelangelo's unfinished *Pietà Rondanini*. Nearby, on Via Brera, is the 17th-century Palazzo di Brera, home to the **Pinacoteca di Brera** (☎ 02 86 07 96; www.amicidibrera.milano.it, in Italian; Via Brera 28; admission €5; ☼ 8.30am-7.30pm Tue-Sun), whose collection includes Mantegna's masterpiece, the *Dead Christ*.

Leonardo's *Last Supper* is in the **Cenacolo Vinciano** (☎ 02 89 42 11 46; www.cenacolovinciano.org; Piazza Santa Maria delle Grazie 2; admission €6.50; ☼ 8am-7.30pm Tue-Sun), just west of the centre. Phone ahead to book; decide for yourself whether or not the apostle to Christ's left really is a woman, as Dan Brown implied in his controversial bestseller *The Da Vinci Code*.

## Festivals

**St Ambrose's Day** (7 December) is Milan's major festival, with celebrations at the Fiera di Milano (MM1 – red line: stop Amendola Fiera).

## Sleeping

Milan's hotels are among the most expensive and heavily booked in Italy, due to frequent trade fairs held here. Budget hotels of widely varying quality are concentrated around Stazione Centrale.

**Ostello Piero Rotta** (☎ 02 39 26 70 95; Viale Salmoiraghi 1; dm €16; ☼ lockout 9am-3.30pm, curfew 12.30am) An HI hostel northwest of the centre near San Siro; there are friendly multilingual staff and typically sterile ambience.

Take the MM1 (red line, direction Molino Dorino) to stop QT8.

**Hotel Due Giardini** (☎ 02 29 52 10 93; duegiardinihotel@libero.it; Via B Marcello 47; s/d/tr €68/115/155; ✵ ) One of Milan's nicest one-star hotels, this place has delightful rooms overlooking a tranquil back garden. Turn right off Via D Scarlatti, to the left as you leave the station. Note that these prices may be negotiable depending on season and trade fairs.

**Hotel Bagliori** (☎ 02 29 52 68 84; www.hotelme.it; Via Boscovich 43; s €80-140, d €130-200) For some three-star comfort, try the schmick Bagliori with its pretty little walled garden and attentive service. The tastefully decorated rooms have fridge, TV, direct-dial phone and the breakfast buffet is fab. The hotel is located about 15 minutes out of the city centre.

**Hotel Nettuno** (☎ 02 29 40 44 81; Via Tadino 27; s/d/tr/q €50/95/125/165, s/d/tr with shared bathroom €45/68/87; ✕ ✵ ) This modest outfit is much nicer than its spartan foyer might suggest. The gracious multilingual staff ensure a pleasant stay.

**Charly Hotel** (☎ /fax 02 20 47 190; www.hotelcharly.com; Via Settala 76; s €62-90, d €68-130, s with shared bathroom €45-60, d with shared bathroom €57-100; Ⓟ ✕ ✵ ) Small, friendly two-star on a quiet street, Charly Hotel is a bargain gem worth ferreting out. The terrace is dinky, but pleasant in fine weather.

**Hotel San Tomaso** (☎ 02 29 51 47 47; hotelsantomaso@tin.it; Viale Tunisia 6; d from €65, s/d with shared bathroom from €30/45; ✵ ▣ ) Just off Corso Buenos Aires, this super-friendly place is well located for shopping, and cosy as you like. Room prices vary because some have views, but all have TV and phone. It was renovated in 2004.

**Hotel Serena** (☎ 02 29404958; www.hotelserena.com; Via Boscovich 59; s €50-135, d €75-210, t €101-289; ✕ ✵ ▣ ) Rates vary hugely with trade-fair/seasonal demand at the neat, luxurious Serena. Rooms are excellent, the staff gruff yet likeable. Buffet breakfast included.

**Hotel Nuovo** (☎ 02 86 46 05 42; fax 02 72 00 17 52; Piazza Beccaria 6; d/tr €93/124, s/d with shared bathroom €31/51) Just off Corso Vittorio Emanuele II and the Duomo, you'll need to call ahead; the Nuovo is a perennial budget favourite in a city that doesn't care much for 'cheap'. A good deal at great rates for the simple yet comfortable rooms.

## Eating

If you're looking for a traditional trattoria, try streets south of the station and along Corso Buenos Aires.

**Osteria del Lazzaretto** ( ☎ /fax 02 669 6234; Via Lazzaretto 15; 3-course menu €9; ☽ lunch & dinner) Fantastic, understated restaurant whose daily special is a gobsmacking bargain. Heaping portions and gracious service, all in a rustic dining room on a quiet street off Viale Tunisia. Try the authentically eggy carbonara – it's a myth the dish contains cream.

**La Risacca Blu** ( ☎ 02 20480964; www.larisaccablu.it, in Italian; Viale Tunisia 13; mains €12-15; ☽ lunch Wed-Sun, dinner Tue-Sun) Splash out on a fish or shellfish feast at La Risacca, a fab seafood restaurant serving delights such as crayfish with *pilaf* rice (€16). The mouth-watering marine morsels are augmented by a great wine list and elegant, semi-formal dining rooms.

**Ristorante Pizzeria Sabatini** ( ☎ 02 29 40 28 14; www.ristorantesabatini.com; Via Boscovich 54; pizzas €15; ☽ lunch & dinner Mon-Sat) Around the corner from Corso Buenos Aires, this large, bland place does superior pizzas, more than compensating for the lack of ambience. Pasta and other mains are also available; seafood is a speciality.

**Adulis Restaurant/Pau Brasil** ( ☎ 02 29 51 58 16; Via Melzo 24; mains €12-16; ☽ lunch & dinner Tue-Sun) This Brazilian/Eritrean restaurant is great when you're all pizza and pastad out. A social and dining hub for afro-*sudamericano* expats, the atmosphere is as warm and inviting as the food. Great spicy rice and meat dishes at fair prices.

**Paper Moon** ( ☎ 02 796 083; Via Bagutta 1; mains €10-15; ☽ Mon-Sat) It may be 'only' a paper moon, but it's well worth seeking for its understated dishes, many vegetarian.

**Pastarito** ( ☎ 02 86 22 10; Via Verdi 6; mains €10) A chain restaurant (along with Pizzarito, usually adjacent) that compensates for a subdued atmosphere with huge portions and dependable quality. It's €1 to €2 extra for fresh (handmade) pasta; pay – it tastes better and cooks faster.

There are two supermarkets in Stazione Centrale, one on the upper level and one on the western side, as well as other **supermarkets** (Via D Vitruvio 32 & Via Casati 30) close by.

## Drinking

**Bar Brera** ( ☎ 02 877091; Via Brera 23; cocktail €6) Relaxed rendezvous nook before a night's dining and dancing, in the artsy precinct. Low-key and friendly.

**Casablanca** ( ☎ 02 62690186; Corso Como 14) 'Loop it, Sam' – a more appropriate paraphrase at this DJ-fuelled doof-den evoking the Bogey classic. Faux colonial décor; chic despite the potted palms.

**Gattopardo** ( ☎ 02 34537699; www.gattopardocafé .com; Via Piero della Francesca 47; ☽ 6pm-4am; happy-hour buffet €6) Elitist, looks-based entry is the only admission price to one of Milan's hottest nightspots; if you got 'it', bring it!

**Shu** ( ☎ 02 58315720; www.shucafé.it, in Italian; Via della Chiusa) This place is awesomely hipper than thou but bearably so, with cool art on the walls and foxy cocktails. If you're feeling fly – Shu.

## Entertainment

Music, theatre and cinema dominate Milan's entertainment calendar. The opera season at **Teatro alla Scala** ( ☎ 02 86 07 75; www.tea troallascala.org) runs from 7 December through to July. The **box office** ( ☎ 02 72 0 37 44; Galleria del Sagrato, Piazza del Duomo; ☽ noon-6pm Sep–mid-Jul) is in the metro underpass beneath Piazza del Duomo.

Nightlife is centred on Brera and, further south, Navigli. The club scene is exclusive, policed vigilantly by local fashionistas. Consult *Hello Milano* or *Milano Mese*, or ask in hip shops about what's going down. Note that most Italian bartenders don't use spirit measures, preferring the showy skilfulness of free-pouring – cocktails can be 'potent' value!

Football fans must visit the San Siro (official name Stadio Olympico Meazza), home-ground of both AC Milan (the *rossoneri*, 'red and blacks') and Inter (the *ner'azzuri*, 'black and blues'). Local rivalry is savage: confusing the two *will* offend. Tickets (from €15) are available at branches of Cariplo (AC Milan) and Banca Popolare di Milano (Inter) banks.

## Shopping

Looking good is religion; shopping is nearly a blood sport in Milan, and it's not cheap. Hit the streets behind the Duomo around Corso Vittorio Emanuele II for clothing, footwear and accessories, or dream on and window-shop along Via Monte Napoleone, Via della Spiga and Via Borgospesso. Street markets are held around the canals, notably on Viale Papiniano on Tuesday and Saturday morning. There's a **flea market** (Viale Gabriele d'Annunzio) each Saturday, and an **antique market** (Via Fiori Chiari) in Brera every third Saturday.

## Getting There & Away
### AIR
Most international flights use Malpensa Airport, about 50km northwest of Milan. Domestic and some European flights use Linate Airport, about 7km east of the city. Call **flight information** ( ☎ 02 74 85 22 00).

### CAR & MOTORCYCLE
Milan is the major junction of Italy's motorways, including the A1 (Rome), A4 (Milan–Turin), A7 (Milan–Genoa), the Serenissima (Verona and Venice) and the A8/A9 north to the lakes and Swiss border. All these join the Milan ring road – the Tangenziale Est and Tangenziale Ovest (the east and west bypasses). Directions to the centre are well marked. The A4 is particularly busy; accidents delay traffic interminably. In winter all roads can become hazardous.

### TRAIN
Regular trains depart Stazione Centrale for Venice, Florence, Bologna, Genoa, Turin, Rome and major European cities. For **timetable information** ( ☎ 848 88 80 88; 7am-9pm), call or visit the office in Stazione Centrale (English spoken). Regional trains stop at Stazione Porta Garibaldi and Stazione Nord in Piazzale Cadorna on the MM2 line.

## Getting Around
### TO/FROM THE AIRPORT
STAM buses leave for Linate Airport from Piazza Luigi di Savoia, on the east side of Stazione Centrale (€1.80, every 30 minutes 5.40am to 9.35pm) or use local bus No 73 from Piazza San Babila (€1, 20 minutes). For Malpensa Airport, the Malpensa Shuttle and Malpensa Bus Express both depart from Piazza Luigi di Savoia (€4 to €5, 50 minutes to one hour, every 20 minutes 4.30am to 12.15am). Buses also link the airports (hourly, 8am to 9.30pm). The Malpensa Express train connects Malpensa Airport with Cadorna underground station (€9.30, 40 minutes, 5.50am to 8.20pm from Cadorna, buses 8.20pm to 11.10pm).

### BUS & METRO
Milan's public transport is excellent, with underground (MM), tram and bus services (tickets €1 for one ride and/or 75 minutes on buses and trams). Buy tickets at MM stations and most tobacconists and newsstands.

### CAR & MOTORCYCLE
Entering Milan by car or motorcycle niggles, and the city car parks are expensive. An alternative is using one of the supervised car parks at the last stop on each MM line. In the centre there are private garages (€3 per hour). If your car is clamped or towed, call the **Polizia Municipale** ( ☎ 02 772 72 59). Hertz, Avis, Maggiore and Europcar all have offices at Stazione Centrale.

### TAXI
Don't hail passing taxis; they won't stop. Head for the taxi ranks, which have telephones, or call one of numerous radio **taxi companies** ( ☎ 02 40 40, 02 52 51, 02 53 53, 02 83 83 or 02 85 85).

## MANTUA
**pop 48,000**
Poised beside Lake Superior, Mantua is associated with the Gonzagas, who ruled from 1328 until 1707. These days, Mantua is considered a stronghold of Umberto Bossi's separatist *Lega Nord* party, though you'd barely notice in this sleepy township if it weren't for the odd spot of graffiti. The sumptuous Gonzaga family palaces justify a detour.

## Information
**Tourist office** ( ☎ 0376 32 82 53; www.aptmantova .it, in Italian; Piazza Andrea Mantegna 6; 8.30am-12.30pm & 3-6pm Mon-Sat, 9.30am-12.30pm Sun) A short walk from the station along Corso Vittorio Emanuele, which becomes Corso Umberto 1.

## Sights
Impressive buildings surround Piazza Sordello, including the eclectic **cattedrale**, but the focal point is the **Palazzo Ducale** (adult/concession €6.50/3.25; 8.45am-7.15pm Tue-Sun), the massive former seat of the Gonzaga family. Amongst its 500 rooms and 15 courtyards, its showpieces include the Gonzagas' private apartments and art collection, and the **Camera degli Sposi** (Bridal Chamber), with frescoes by Mantegna. The weekend **market** sprawls across four piazzas, and is more diverse than similar fare in cities twice Mantua's size.

## Sleeping & Eating

**Hotel ABC** ( ☎ 0376 32 23 29; www.hotelabcmantova
.it; Piazza Don Leoni 25; s €44-77, d €66-110) Conveniently located opposite the train station, Hotel ABC is basic but sufficient. Breakfast is included. All rooms feature TV, telephone and en-suite bathroom.

**Osteria Vecchia Mantova** (Piazza Sordello 26; 2-course menu €13-20; ☼ lunch & dinner Tue-Sun) This place is small and elegant, with rustic local specialities – such as the sensational pumpkin tortellini (€6.50) – at unbeatable prices.

**Ristorante Pavesi** ( ☎ 0376 32 36 27; Piazza delle Erbe 13; set menu €34) If all the Gonzaga luxury has stirred your sense of indulgence, Pavesi is the place; the classic Lombardy menu oozes as much class as the ambience, complemented by a fab wine list.

## Getting There & Away

Mantua is accessible by train and bus from Verona (40 minutes), and by train from Milan and Bologna (change at Modena).

## VERONA

**pop 256,100**

One of Italy's prettiest cities, Verona is perpetually associated with Romeo and Juliet. But the city was an important Roman centre long before the Della Scala (aka the Scaligeri) family took the reins around the mid-13th century, a period noted for the savage feuding between families, particularly the Guelphs and Ghibellines, on which Shakespeare based his tragedy. In centuries past, Verona was even referred to as *piccola Roma* ('little Rome').

Leave your preconceptions about *that* balcony aside, however, and you may just fall in love with Verona's real stars; its charming pedestrianised centre and amazing amphitheatre.

Buses to the centre leave from the train station; otherwise, it's a 2km walk. Turn right to leave the station, cross the river and follow Corso Porta Nuova to Piazza Brà.

## Information

Ask at the tourist office about the **Verona Card** (1/3 days €8/12) if you're cramming lots of sightseeing into a short time.

**Internet Fast** ( ☎ 045 803 32 12; Via Oberdan 16/b; per hr €4; ☼ 10am-10pm Mon-Fri, to 8pm Sat & 2-8pm Sun)

**Post office** (Piazza Viviani)

**Tourist offices** Via degli Alpini 9 ( ☎ 045 806 86 80; info@tourism.verona.it; ☼ 9am-6pm Mon-Sat, to 2pm Sun); Train station ( ☎ 045 800 08 61; ☼ 9am-6pm Mon-Sat); Airport ( ☎ 045 861 91 63; ☼ 11am-5pm Mon-Sat)

## Sights

Piazza Brà's Roman **amphitheatre**, known simply as the 'Arena', dates from the 1st century and is the world's third largest. Not as big as Rome's, but well preserved, it's now Verona's opera house, and regularly hosts contemporary artists from Pink Floyd to Bjork.

Walk along Via Mazzini to Via Cappello and the **Casa di Giulietta** (Juliet's House; ☎ 045 803 5645; Via Capello 23; courtyard free; Capulet museum €3; ☼ 9am-6.30pm Tue-Sun), where the balcony overlooks a graffiti-covered courtyard and statue of Juliet. Romantic superstition suggests that rubbing Juliet's 'heart' brings you a new lover. Further along the street is **Porta Leoni**, one of the gates to the old Roman Verona; the other, **Porta Borsari**, is north of the Arena.

The former site of the Roman forum, **Piazza delle Erbe** is lined with palaces and filled with questionable market stalls. Nearby is the elegant (and much quieter) **Piazza dei Signori**, flanked by the medieval town hall and the Della Scala (Scaligeri) residence, partly decorated by Giotto and nowadays known as the **Governor's Palace**.

## Sleeping

**Ostello Villa Francescatti** ( ☎ 045 59 03 60; fax 045 800 9127; Salita Fontana del Ferro 15; dm with breakfast €14, 2-course menu €8.50) Among the best HI hostels in Italy, this 500-year-old former church has vaulted roofs and remnants of original frescoes on some walls. Wonderfully evocative. A hostel/student card is required. Take bus No 73 from the station.

**Hotel Aurora** ( ☎ 045 597 834; www.hotelaurora .biz; Piazza Erbe; d €117, s/d with shared bathroom €56/108; ✗ ✗ ▯ ) Right on the city's prettiest piazza is this fantastic option. Most rooms have views and all are well-appointed. Great buffet breakfast included.

**Hotel All'Antica Porta Leona** ( ☎ 045 59 54 99; fax 045 59 52 14; htlanticaportaleona@tiscalinet.it; Corticella Leoni 3; s/d €91/129; ⓟ ✗ ✗ ) Bright, airy rooms are the signature of the once glorious, still good Porta Leona. Well located with superb amenities.

## Eating

Boiled meats are a Veronese speciality, as is the crisp Soave white wine.

**Hosteria All'Orso** ( ☎ 045 597214; Via Sottoriva 3/c; mains €14-20; ⊙ lunch Tue-Sat, dinner Mon-Sat) A warm, friendly restaurant nestled under the Sottoriva porticoes, serving hearty Veronese and northern Italian staples within a shout of the river. In the heart of Verona's night-life district, it's the perfect place to kick off with a substantial meal and drinks.

**Trattoria All'Isolo** ( ☎ 045 59 42 91; Piazza dell'Isolo 5a; menus €12) Dodge the tourist crowds and eat with a Veronese one, across the river at this pleasant place, which has challenging meat dishes: adventurers could try the horse-meat pie or the donkey stew.

**Il Desco** ( ☎ 045 801 00 15; Via Dietro San Sebastiano 7; mains €60-90; ⊙ Tue-Sat & lunch Sun) Among Italy's finest restaurants, this Michelin-starred stunner is the perfect place to dine. Il Desco's reputation is as grand as the décor. Try the amazing *petto di faraone con purea di topinambur, salsa all l'aceto balsamico e cioccolato* (breast of guinea fowl with Jerusalem artichoke purée and a chocolate and balsamic sauce).

## Drinking & Entertainment

Verona hosts events throughout the year, culminating in a season of opera and drama at the **Arena** (www.arena.it; tickets from €21.50; ⊙ Jul-Sep). There is a winter lyric-symphonic season at the 18th-century **Teatro Filarmonico** ( ☎ 800 28 80; Via dei Mutilati 4); box office ( ☎ 045 8005151; www.arena.it; Via Dietro Anfiteatro 6b).

For bar/late action, head for Via Sottoriva, with a variety of carousing options. Two goodies are the bizarrely cool 'lifestyle-bar' **square** ( ☎ 045 597 120; Via Sottoriva 15; ⊙ 6.30pm-2am Mon-Fri, 3.30pm-2am Sat & Sun), whose DJ-assisted options include shiatsu massage, perusing elegant homewares, sipping swanky cocktails, fusion snacks and free Internet, or the more traditional **Sottoriva 23** ( ☎ 045 800 99 04; Via Sottoriva 23; ⊙ 10-2am), a cosy, low-lit cavern for drinks and chatter, usually rammed with friendly locals.

## Getting There & Around

The **Verona-Villafranca airport** ( ☎ 045 809 56 66) is 16km away, accessible by bus and train. The APT airport bus (€4.20, every 20 minutes) departs from the train station. Bus Nos 11, 12, 13 and 14 (Nos 91, 92 and 98 on Sunday) connect the station (bus stop A) with Piazza Brà, and Nos 72 and 73 go to Piazza delle Erbe. The main bus station is in the piazza in front of Porta Nuova train station. Buses service surrounding towns, including Mantua, Ferrara and Brescia.

Verona is on the Brenner Pass train line to Austria/Germany, and directly linked by rail to Milan, Venice, Florence and Rome. There's a free car park in Via Città di Nimes.

## PADUA

**pop 211,500**

In millennia past, the most compelling reason to visit Padua was to see the tomb of Saint Anthony. These days, it's to marvel at Giotto's restored frescoes in the Cappella degli Scrovegni (Scrovegni Chapel), among the world's greatest works of figurative art. Masterpieces aside, Padua is a pleasant city, and – thanks to the students attending its university – always lively and engaging.

## Orientation & Information

It's a 15-minute walk from the train station to the centre, or take bus No 3 or 8 along Corso del Popolo (which becomes Corso Garibaldi). Padua's centre is easily covered on foot.

The **padovacard** (1 adult & 1 child €13) provides discounts on many sights and all public transport for 48 hours. Pick one up at the tourist office.

**Post office** (Corso Garibaldi 33)

**Tourist offices** Train station ( ☎ 049 875 20 77; ⊙ 9.15am-6.30pm Mon-Sat, 9am-12.30pm Sun); Galleria Pedrocchi ( ☎ 049 876 79 27; ⊙ 9am-12.30pm & 3-7pm Mon-Sat)

## Sights

The **Cappella degli Scrovegni** ( ☎ 049 201 00 20; www.cappelladegliscrovegni.it; Piazza Eremitani 8; admission €12, free Mar 25; ⊙ 9am-7pm, 30 min entry) is Padua's highlight, housing Giotto's transcendent frescoes. The 38 glorious panels movingly depict Christ's life. Booking ahead is mandatory, as is arriving at the chapel 10 minutes prior to your appointed time. The ticket accesses the neighbouring **Musei Civici agli Eremitani** ( ☎ 049 829 4550; www .padovanet.it/museicivici, in Italian; ⊙ 9am-6pm Tue-Sun winter, to 7pm spring-autumn).

Thousands of pilgrims annually seek out Padua's **Basilica di Sant'Antonio** (St Anthony's

Basilica) in the hope that St Anthony, patron saint of lost things (and Padua), will help them find whatever they're looking for. The saint's gaudy **tomb** is in the basilica, along with 14th-century frescoes, and sculptures by Donatello adorning the high altar. Just outside the basilica is an equestrian statue, the *Gattamelata* (Honeyed Cat), also by Donatello.

## Sleeping

**Ostello della Città di Padova** ( ☎ /fax 049 654 210; www.ctgveneto.it/ostello, in Italian; Via A Aleardi 30; dm with breakfast €15.50) The HI hostel is a five-minute bus ride from the station. Take bus No 3, 8 or 12 to Prato della Valle and then ask for directions.

**Hotel Sant'Antonio** ( ☎ 049 875 13 93; www.hotel santantonio.it; Via Santo Fermo 118; s/d €60/80, s with shared bathroom €40) In a fabulous central location near the river, all of the air-conditioned rooms in this neat-as-a-pin place are as comfy as they are charming; all have TV, telephone and en-suite facilities.

**Koko Nor Association** ( ☎ 049 864 33 94; www .bandb-veneto.it/kokonor; Via Selva 5; s/d from around €35/60) This is a good organisation to consult if you're after the privacy (and often friendlier touch) of lodging in *affittacamere* – rented rooms in private family homes. Also try the tourist office, which keeps similar lists of families offering such services.

## Eating

**Dalla Zita** (Via Gorizia 16; panini from €2.30) A great sandwich bar, popular with local workers and skint students alike. Value and quality are matched only by the variety; the details of over 100 types of *panini* cover the place more like wallpaper than a menu.

**Godenda** ( ☎ 049 877 41 92; www.godenda.it, in Italian; Via Squarcini 4/6; mains €10-15; ☺ lunch & dinner) A combination gourmet-everything locale, including a wine bar (more than 300 labels), a great sampling/tasting restaurant, and dozens of delicious pre-prepared takeaway dishes (sold by weight) to tempt the taste buds.

**Pe Pen** ( ☎ 049 875 94 83; www.pepen.it, in Italian; Piazza Cavour 15; pizzas & pastas €10-12; ☺ lunch & dinner) The last word in Padua posh nosh. Try Umbrian speciality *tagliolini* (hand-cut fresh pasta) with stunning variations such as *con ostriche e porri* (with oysters and leeks).

## Getting There & Away

Padua has direct rail links to Milan, Venice and Bologna, and is easily accessible from other major cities. Buses serve Venice, Milan, Trieste and surrounding towns. The **bus terminal** (Piazzale Boschetti) is off Via Trieste, near the train station. There is a car park in Prato della Valle, a massive piazza near the Basilica del Santo.

# VENICE

pop 272,100

It throws one of the best parties on earth (Carnevale), and you can drown crossing its roads. There's no doubt that Venice is extraordinary. In no other city is fantasy and reality so artfully combined. Ever since Casanova set the romance myth rolling, travellers, writers and even dictators have been beguiled by La Serenissima (the Most Serene Republic). Writers from Byron to Henry James to contemporary best-seller Jeanette Winterson have used Venice to bewitching effect. Even Napoleon pronounced Piazza San Marco (St Mark's Square) 'the finest drawing room in Europe'.

Obviously Venice wasn't always a living museum. The lagoon's islands were settled during barbarian invasions around 1500 years ago, when the Veneto's inhabitants sought refuge in the area, building the city on pole foundations pounded into the marshy subsoil. Following centuries of Byzantine rule, Venice evolved into a republic ruled by a succession of doges (chief magistrates) and enjoyed a period of independence that lasted 1000 years. It was the point where east met west, and the city grew in power to dominate half the Mediterranean, the Adriatic and the trade routes to the Levant. It was from Venice that Marco Polo set out on his voyage to China in 1271.

Today, delivery boats jostle chintzy gondolas, endless stalls tout bogus Carnevale masks, and the pigeons are only outnumbered by the swarms of tourists picking through all the wonderment. Regular flooding (*acqua alte*, 'high tides') and sky-high property prices make it a difficult place to actually live: most 'locals' commute from Mestre, linked by the bridge across the lagoon.

The secret to discovering Venice is walking. Dorsoduro and Castello rarely see many tourists; you can lose yourself for hours in the streets between the Accademia and the train station. Another groovy gambit is choosing your hours strategically; even San Marco, the glorious centrepiece heaving with thousands daily, is basically empty from midnight to dawn. At such moonlit moments, you'll be suddenly and irrevocably seduced by the Queen of the Seas.

## Orientation

Venice is built on 117 islands with 150-odd canals and 400 bridges. Only three bridges cross the Canal Grande (Grand Canal): the Rialto, the Accademia and, at the train station, the Scalzi. To cross the Grand Canal between the bridges, use a *traghetto* (basically a public gondola, but much cheaper).

The city is divided into six *sestieri* (quarters): Cannaregio, Castello, San Marco, Dorsoduro, San Polo and Santa Croce. A street can be a *calle, ruga* or *salizzada;* beside a canal it's a *fondamenta.* A canal is a *rio;* a filled canal-turned-street a *rio terra.* The only square in Venice called a *piazza* is San Marco – all the others are called *campo.* Venice's street numbering is unique, too. Instead of a system based on individual streets, each *sestiere* has a series of numbers; addresses are virtually meaningless unless you're a Venetian postie. Getting lost is inevitable – enjoy!

Public transport is via the canals, on *vaporetti* (water buses). The other mode of transportation is your feet. Walking from the *ferrovia* (train station) to San Marco along the main thoroughfare, Lista di Spagna (whose name changes frequently), takes about 30 minutes – follow the signs to San Marco. From San Marco the routes to the Rialto, the Accademia and the train station are well signposted but confusing, particularly in Dorsoduro and San Polo.

## Information

There are two types of discount cards available from tourist offices and various outlets. The **Rolling Venice Card** ( ☎ 041 241 39 08; €3) is for visitors aged 14 to 29; it offers discounts on food, accommodation, shopping, transport and museums. You'll need your passport and a colour photograph. The **Venice Card** ( ☎ 041 2424; www.venicecard.it; blue card under 29 yrs 1/3/7 days €9/22/49, over 29 yrs €14/29/51; orange card

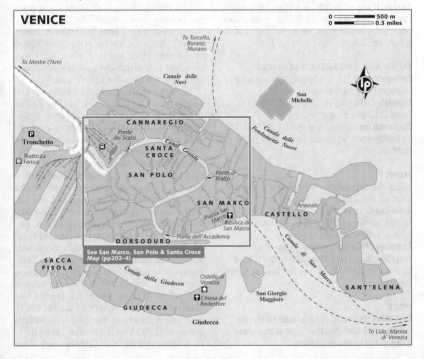

VENICE

0 — 500 m
0 — 0.3 miles

To Torcello;
Burano;
Murano

To Mestre (7km)

Canale delle
Navi

San
Michelle

CANNAREGIO

Ponte
dei Scalzi

Canal Grande

SANTA
CROCE

Canale delle
Fondamente Nuove

P
Tronchetto

Teatro La
Fenice

SAN POLO

Ponte di
Rialto

SAN MARCO

Arsenale

Piazza San
Marco

CASTELLO

Basilica di
San Marco

Ponte dell'Accademia

DORSODURO

Canale di San Marco

See San Marco, San Polo & Santa Croce
Map (pp202–4)

SACCA
FISOLA

Canale della Giudecca

Ostello di
Venezia

Chiesa del
Redentore

San Giorgio
Maggiore

SANT'ELENA

GIUDECCA

Giudecca

To Lido; Marina
di Venezia

ITALY

under 29 yrs €18/35/61, over 29 yrs €28/47/68) is a multi-purpose pass for museums, public transport, car parks and restrooms. The Venice Card *isn't* always a saving, so check its coverage against your itinerary before spending.

## INTERNET ACCESS

There are tons of Internet cafés in Venice, none of them cheap. The airport is a Wi-Fi hotspot.

**Casanova** (Map pp202-4; ☎ 041 524 06 64; Rio Tera Lista di Spagna, Cannaregio 158/a; per hr €7; ☿ 9am-11.30pm) A cheesy club and combined webcafé in one, close to the station.

**Netgate** (Map pp202-4; ☎ 041 244 02 13; Calle dei Preti Crosera 3812, Dorsoduro; per hr €6; ☿ 10.15am-8pm Mon-Fri, to 10pm Sat, 2.15-10pm Sun)

**Nethouse** (Map pp202-4; ☎ 041 277 11 90; Campo Santo Stefano 2967; per 20min/1hr €3/9; ☿ 24hr) Nethouse has tons of screens, plus printing and fax services.

**Planet Internet** (Map pp202-4; ☎ 041 524 41 88; Rio Tera San Leonardo, Cannaregio 1520; per hr €7; ☿ 8am-11pm) Good central location; the perfect place to surf while doing laundry.

## LAUNDRY

**Speedy Wash** (Map pp202-4; Rio Tera San Leonardo, Cannaregio 1520; 8kg wash/dry €4.50/3; ☿ 9am-10pm) Strangely, laundry is cheaper here than elsewhere in Italy.

## MEDICAL & EMERGENCY SERVICES

**Emergency** ( ☎ 112) An emergency service in foreign languages run by the *carabinieri*.

**Ospedale Civile** (Map pp202-4; ☎ 041 529 41 11; Campo SS Giovanni e Paolo)

**Police station** (Questura; Map pp202-4; ☎ 041 271 55 11; Fondamenta di San Lorenzo, Castello 5053) Handles thefts etc.

## MONEY

Most major banks have branches in the area around the Rialto and San Marco.

**American Express** (Map pp202-4; ☎ 041 520 08 44; Salizzada San Moisè 1471; ☿ 9am-5.30pm Mon-Fri, 9.30am-12.30pm Sat & Sun)

**Exchange office** (train station; ☿ 7am- 9pm)

**Travelex** (Thomas Cook; Map pp202-4; ☎ 041 522 47 51; Piazza San Marco 141; ☿ 9am-7pm Mon-Sat, 9.30am-5pm Sun)

## POST

**Post office** (Map pp202-4; Salizzada del Fontego dei Tedeschi; ☿ 8.10am-7pm Mon-Sat) In an atmospheric former trading house near the Rialto.

## TOURIST INFORMATION

**Tourist offices** Train station (Map pp202-4; ☎ 041 529 87 11; ☿ 8am-8pm); Piazzale Roma (Map pp202-4; ☿ 8am-8pm); Venice Pavilion (Map pp202-4; ☿ 10am-6pm); Piazza San Marco 71f (Map pp202-4; ☿ 9.45am-3.15pm Mon-Sat) There are also offices at the Lido and the airport. Get the useful guide *Un Ospite di Venezia* (A Guest of Venice).

# Sights & Activities

Before you visit Venice's monuments, churches and museums, take vaporetto No 1 along the **Grand Canal**, lined with rococo Gothic, Moorish and Renaissance palaces. Then stretch your legs with a decent walk: start at **San Marco** and either delve into the tiny lanes of tranquil **Castello** or head for the **Ponte dell'Accademia** (Accademia Bridge) to reach the narrow streets and squares of **Dorsoduro** and **San Polo**.

Most museums are closed Monday.

## PIAZZA & BASILICA DI SAN MARCO

The stunning Piazza San Marco is enclosed by the basilica and the elegant arcades of the **Procuratie Vecchie** and **Procuratie Nuove**. While you're taking it all in, you might see the bronze *mori* (Moors) strike the bell of the 15th-century **Torre dell'Orologio** (clock tower). Venice's lowest point, the Piazza is the first place to flood when tides rise. In *acque alte* of epochs past, the *gondolieri* could punt across the square itself!

From a distance, it looks like some sort of glorious ice-cream cake, but the **Basilica di San Marco** (St Mark's Basilica; Map pp202-4) was built to house St Mark's body. Stolen from his Egyptian burial place and smuggled to Venice in a barrel of pork, the saint has been reburied several times, his body now resting under the high altar. The present basilica, with its spangled spires, Byzantine domes and façade of mosaics and marble, is the result of centuries of redesigning and postdisaster renovations and was 'finished' in (approximately) its current form in 1071. The interior is richly decorated with mosaics, as well as looted embellishments from the ensuing five centuries. The bronze horses above the entrance are replicas of statues 'liberated' from Constantinople in the Fourth Crusade (1204). The originals are in the basilica's **Galleria** (admission €1.55). You'll never forget you're in a floating city; the 12th-century floor

SALLY DILLON

Picnic food (red wine and charcuterie), Ajaccio market (p142), Corsica, France

Poppies in early June, Provence (p116), France

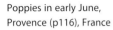

NICOLA WILLIAMS

OLIVIER CIRENDINI

Bonifacio (p144), Corsica, France

Casino, Monaco (p134), France

DAVID TOMLINSON

Vernazza (p189), Liguria, Italy

Golfo di Orosei (p253), Sardinia, Italy

Trevi Fountain (p174), Rome, Italy

Pizza margherita,
Naples (p234), Italy

undulates, wavelike, from centuries of tidal shifts affecting the foundation. Don't miss the **Pala d'Oro** (adult/child €1.50/1), a stunning gold altarpiece decorated with countless priceless jewels.

The 99m freestanding **campanile** (bell tower; Map pp202-4; adult/child €6/3; ☾ 9am-9pm late Jun-Aug, to 7pm Apr-Jun & Sep-Oct, to 4pm Nov-Mar) dates from the 10th century, although it suddenly collapsed on 14 July 1902 and had to be rebuilt. Photos of the actual collapse abound, as the piazza's barely been camera-free since the birth of photography.

### PALAZZO DUCALE

The official residence of the doges and the seat of the republic's government, the **Palazzo Ducale** (admission €9.50; ☾ 9am-7pm Apr-Oct, to 5pm Nov-Mar; ticket office closed 4.30pm) also housed municipal officials and Venice's prisons. The **Sala del Maggior Consiglio** features paintings by Tintoretto and Veronese. Tickets also cover entry to the Museo Correr (for Venetian art and history), Biblioteca Marciana and Museo Archeologico. A surcharge (€6) covers the Palazzo Mocenigo (San Stae area), and Burano and Murano museums.

The **Ponte dei Sospiri** (Bridge of Sighs) connects the palace to the old dungeons, and evokes romantic images, possibly through association with Casanova, a Venetian native who languished in the cells. Far bleaker is the real reason for the sighing; the sadness of condemned prisoners en route to their executions, seeing Venice for the last time.

### GALLERIA DELL'ACCADEMIA

Tracing the development of Venetian art, the **Galleria dell'Accademia** (Academy of Fine Arts; Map pp202-4; ☎ 041 522 2247; adult €6.50, EU citizens 18-25 yrs €3.25, child under 12 & EU citizens under 18 & over 65 free; ☾ 8.15am-2pm Mon, to 7.15pm Tue-Sun) includes masterpieces by Bellini, Titian, Carpaccio, Tintoretto, Giorgione and Veronese.

### COLLEZIONE PEGGY GUGGENHEIM

For a change of pace and style, visit the **Collezione Peggy Guggenheim** (Map pp202-4; ☎ 041 240 54 11; www.guggenheim-venice.it; Palazzo Venier dei Leoni, Dorsoduro 701; adult €8, student & child €5; ☾ 10am-6pm Wed-Fri & Sun-Mon, to 10pm Sat), displayed in the American heiress' former home. The brilliant collection runs the gamut of modern art (Bacon, Pollock, Picasso, Dali, Magritte and more) and the *palazzo* is in a sculpture garden where Peggy and her dogs are buried.

### CHURCHES

Venice has many gorgeous churches, most boasting an art treasure or two. The excellent **Chorus Pass** (adult €8, student & child €5) gets you into 15 of them; ask at a tourist office.

The **Chiesa del Redentore** (Church of the Redeemer; Map p199; Giudecca) was built by Palladio to commemorate the end of the great plague (1576) and is the scene of the annual Festa del Redentore (see p204). Longhena's **Chiesa di Santa Maria della Salute** (Map pp202-4) 'guards' the Grand Canal's entrance and contains works by Tintoretto and Titian. Definitely visit the great Gothic churches **SS Giovanni e Paolo** (Map pp202-4), with its glorious stained-glass windows, and the **Frari** (Map pp202-4), home to Titian's tomb and his uplifting *Assumption*.

### THE LIDO

This thin strip of land separating Venice from the Adriatic is easily accessible by vaporetto Nos 1, 6, 14, 61 and 82. Once *the* most fashionable resort and still very popular – it's almost impossible to find a space on the beach in summer.

### ISLANDS

The island of **Murano** is the home of Venetian glass. Tour a factory for a behind-the-scenes look at production, or visit the **Glassworks Museum** to see exquisite historical pieces. **Burano**, still a relatively sleepy fishing village, is renowned for its lace and colourful houses. **Torcello**, the republic's original island settlement, was abandoned due to malaria. Little remains on the hauntingly deserted island besides the Byzantine cathedral, its mosaics intact. Vaporetto No 12 services all three from Fondamente Nuove.

### GONDOLAS

Ask yourself what price for romance, and the rather alarming answer is €62 (€77.45 after 8pm) for a 50-minute ride. These are the official rates and are valid for the gondola (which can carry six people), not per person; it's entirely acceptable to split a gondola with friends.

ITALY

# SAN MARCO, SAN POLO & SANTA CROCE

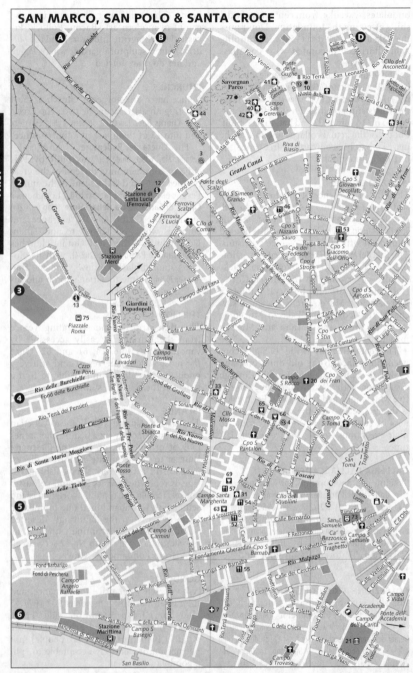

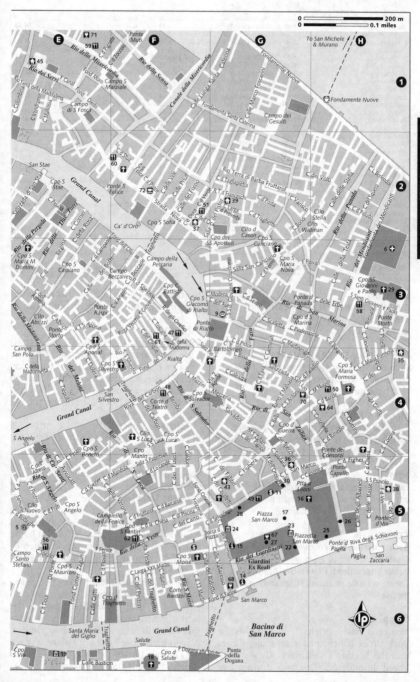

## Festivals

**EVERY EVEN-NUMBERED YEAR**
**Venice Biennale** A major, year-long exhibition of
international visual arts.

**LATE FEBRUARY–EARLY MARCH**
**Carnevale** Venice's famed last-knees-up-before-Lent.
Everyone dons spectacular masks and costumes for a
10-day street party.

**MARCH & NOVEMBER**
**Feste del' Laure** Students lampoon their graduating
comrades by putting up caricatured posters all over town,
and singing while parading drunkenly through the streets.

**JULY**
**Festa del Redentore** (Festival of the Redeemer) Held
on the third weekend in July to celebrate the plague's end;
features a spectacular fireworks display.

**SEPTEMBER**
**Regata Storica** A wildly colourful gondola race on the
Grand Canal. First Sunday in September.
**Venice International Film Festival** Italy's take on
Cannes; held at the atmospheric Palazzo del Cinema, on
the Lido.

## Sleeping

Venice is Italy's priciest city – highest in
peak times (Christmas, Carnevale, Easter
and the height of summer). Always book
ahead. Litorale del Cavallino, northeast of
the city on the Adriatic coast, has numerous
camping grounds, many with bungalows.

### BUDGET

**Ostello di Venezia** (Map p199; ☎ 041 523 82 11; fax 041
523 56 89; Fondamenta delle Zitelle 86; dm €16, dinner €8;
 curfew 11.30pm) On the island of Giudecca,
the HI hostel is for members only, although
you can buy membership there. Take vaporetto No 41, 42 or 82 from the station,
alighting at Zitelle.

**Foresteria Valdese** (Map pp202-4; ☎ 041 528
67 97; fax 041 241 6238; Castello 5170; dm €20, d €75,
d with shared bathroom €55) Behave yourself at
this popular option in the former Palazzo
Cavagnis. Follow Calle Lunga from Campo
Santa Maria Formosa.

**Ostello Santa Fosca** (Map pp202-4; ☎ 041 71 57
75; cpu@iuav.unive.it; Cannaregio 2372; dm €18, s/d with
shared bathroom €21;  check-in 5-8pm) Students
and travellers on the cheap will feel at home
in these basic university dorms less than 15
minutes from the station through Campo
Santa Fosca.

**Marina di Venezia** ( ☎ 041 530 09 55; camping@
marinadivenezia.it; Via Montello 6, Punta Sabbioni; per
person/tent €7.50/19;  mid-Apr–end Aug) A decent camping ground for the fine weather
months, with many facilities (shop, cinema,
playground) close by. It's out of the way, on
the Littorale Cavallino, but accessible by vaporetto No 12 (from Fondamenta Nuove).

**Hotel Marte & Biasin** ( ☎ 041 522 72 57; Fondamenta di Cannaregio 338; d €65, s/d with shared bathroom €35/45; ⊠ ⊠ ) A pair of very basic but clean and friendly one-star hotels in a great location near the Ponte delle Guglie in Cannaregio. Beds are slightly limp and the appointments spartan, but rooms are clean and quiet and the bilingual staff are just lovely. It's also cheap.

**Hotel Bernardo Semenzato** ( ☎ 041 522 72 57; www .hotelbernardi.com; SS Apostoli, 4363-4366 Cannaregio; s €45-50, d €78-88, s with shared bathroom €28-33, d with shared bathroom €58-68) Sweet place especially suited to families, with a popular couple-plus-kids annex. Hosts Leonardo and Maria Theresa are simply wonderful, and the rooms they preside over beautifully tended. A stunning bargain for this standard in Venice.

**Hotel Doni** (Map pp202-4; ☎ /fax 041 522 42 67; www.albergodoni.it; Calle del Vin, Castello 4656; d €120, s/d with shared bathroom €60/90) A lovely, family-run canal-side hotel with basic, spotless rooms. Book well ahead to secure room No 8, with an original 18th-century fresco. Highly recommended.

**Albergo Antico Capon** (Map pp202-4; ☎ 041 528 5292; www.casaperon.com; Campo Santa Margherita, Dorsoduro 3004b; s €25-90, d €45-90) In Venice's coolest square, 'the old (fat) cockerel' provides airy, colourful rooms – many with *campo* views – to roost in. Opposite some of Venice's most understatedly fun cafés and cheap eateries, it's central, yet off the obvious tourist trail.

**MID-RANGE**

**Hotel Santa Lucia** (Map pp202-4; ☎ 041 71 51 80; www.hotelslucia.com; Calle della Misericordia, Cannaregio 358; d/tr/q from €110/140/170, s/d with shared bathroom from €60/70) The friendly owners and multilingual staff (Italian, French and English) ensure a carefree stay at Santa Lucia. Ask for a room with a view of the charming garden. Breakfast is included.

**Hotel Minerva & Nettuno** (Map pp202-4; ☎ 041 71 59 68; www.minervaenettuno.it; Lista di Spagna, Cannaregio 230; s/d/tr/q €58/92/114/136, with shared bathroom €50/61/80/98; ⊠ ⊠ ) Modest, friendly hotel run by the same family for 66 years. The half-board rates are worthwhile; they also run a good restaurant in the Ghetto Nuovo.

**Hotel Guerrini** (Map pp202-4; ☎ 041 71 53 33; www.hotelguerrini.it; Lista di Spagna, Cannaregio 265; d €110-140, tr €130-160, q €140-170, s with shared bathroom €45-60, d with shared bathroom €65-85) With rooms ranging from simple singles without bath-room to lushly appointed suites, Guerrini has something for everyone.

**Casa Gerotto & Alloggi Calderan** (Map pp202-4; ☎ 041 71 55 62; www.casagerottocalderan.com; Campo San Geremia 283; dm/s/d/tr €21/46/90/108, s/d with shared bathroom €36/65) A popular choice, whether for the prices or location on a buzzing *campo* near a morning produce market. A pleasantly ramshackle atmosphere most suited to travellers used to the delightful chaos of hostelling. Single-sex dorms.

**Hotel Noemi** (Map pp202-4; ☎ 041 523 81 44; www.hotelnoemi.com; Calle dei Fabbri, San Marco 909; s/d/tr €100/150/200, s/d with shared bathroom from €40/50; ⊠ ⊠ ⊠ ) Superbly located just 50m from Piazza San Marco is this comfy hotel. All rooms with en-suite bathroom, TV, telephone and pleasant décor.

**Casa Peron** (Map pp202-4; ☎ 041 71 10 21; www .casaperon.com; Salizzada San Pantalon, San Polo 84; s/d/tr €48/75/105) You get some idea of the relaxed atmosphere at Casa Peron after being greeted by Pierino, the owner's enormous parrot, presiding calmly over the reception. The place is no menagerie, though. Neat as a pin and in a lovely area close to happenin' Campo Santa Margherita.

**Hotel ai Do Mori** (Map pp202-4; ☎ 041 520 48 17; www.hotelaidomori.com; Calle Larga San Marco 658; s €50-100, d €80-135, d with shared bathroom €60-90; ⊠ ⊠ ) Up some alarmingly steep stairs, the rooms here have views of St Mark's, plus there's a breakfast terrace practically in the shadow of the campanile. Simple rooms and friendly staff make this sensational for the price.

**TOP END**

**Hotel Giorgione** (Map pp202-4; ☎ 041 522 58 10; www .hotelgiorgione.com; Calle Larga dei Proverbi, Campo SS Apostoli 4587; s from €105-173, d from €120-200, ste from €250; ⊠ ⊠ ⊠ ) A sybaritic sensation, superb for splurging, this former 15th-century palace impresses. When you're not sightseeing, you can sip Bellinis in the billiard room, or a *sprizze* on the sun deck. Conservatively decorated rooms sport every luxury.

**Ca' San Marcuola** (Map pp202-4; ☎ 041 71 60 48; www.casanmarcuola.com; Cannaregio 1763; s €70-150, d €100-200, tr €130-250, q €160-300; ⊠ ⊠ ⊠ ) Newly expanded, the marble interior of Ca' San Marcuola leads to fabulous rooms – many with *campo* views – matching varied budgets, but all featuring rococo Venetian décor and mod cons. Free Internet and great breakfast included.

## Eating

Wherever you choose to eat in Venice it will be expensive, but quality can vary greatly, so sniff around and be selective. There are good-value restaurants tucked away from the big landmarks, and excellent self-catering options. Staples of Venetian cuisine are rice and beans, and, naturally, seafood. Try *risotto con piselli* (risotto with baby peas) followed by a glass of *fragolino*, a fragrant strawberry wine.

### RESTAURANTS

**Hosteria Ai Promessi Sposi** (Map pp202-4; ☎ 041 522 86 09; Calle De L'Oca 4367; mains €15-20; ☺ lunch & dinner Tue-Sun) Tucked away down a tiny alley is this lovely place where the mixed fish antipasti – among the many mouthwatering Venetian specialities displayed – is a thing of particular wonder. You're on Venetian time in this place where the old boys serving you glide around with graceful, practised ease.

**Sahara** (Map pp202-4; ☎ 041 72 10 77; Fondamenta della Misericordia, Cannaregio 2519; mains €10, set menus €20; ☺ lunch & dinner Tue-Sun) In what passes for a nightlife district in Cannaregio, Sahara is an excellent Arabic eatery offering an alternative to Italian food. The Syrian cooking is delicious, and there's belly dancing every Saturday night.

**Al Buso** (Map pp202-4; ☎ 041 528 90 78; Ponte Di Rialto, San Marco 5338; set menus €15; ☺ lunch & dinner) If you must eat by the Grand Canal, Venetians themselves recommend Al Buso, in the shadow of the Rialto (literally). The set menu is good; try the *spaghetti al scoglio* (spaghetti with seafood) for an ample, tasty meal.

**Vino Vino** (Map pp202-4; ☎ 041 523 70 27; www .vinovino.co.it; Calle della Veste, San Marco 2007; mains €10; ☺ 10.30am-midnight Wed-Mon) At Ponte Veste, near Teatro La Fenice, this fantastic wine bar also does excellent food. Typical Venetian specialities abound; a great, moodily evocative place to try some polenta or *pasta con nero di seppia* (pasta in shellfish ink). There's a choice of 350 wines available by the bottle/glass.

**Antica Carbonera** (Map pp202-4; ☎ 041 22 54 79; Calle Bembo, San Marco 4648; mains €30; ☺ lunch & dinner) This popular bar/*osteria* on the continuation of Calle dei Fabbri has old-school charm. Ambience in abundance lies within its little booths, but at a price. Seafood is a speciality – the *tagliolini ai granseola* (hand-cut pasta with spider crab) is outstanding.

**Cip Ciap** (Map pp202-4; ☎ 041 523 66 21; Calle del Mondo Novo, Castello, 5799; pizza slice €2.30) Cip Ciap is cheap and cheerful, just right for a quick takeaway pizza slice, and near buzzy Campo Santa Maria Formosa.

**Ae Oche** (Three Geese; Map pp202-4; ☎ 041 524 11 61; Calle del Tintor, Santa Croce 1552a/b; pizzas €7; ☺ lunch & dinner) Venice's best pizzeria; easily the most welcoming and always busy. Enjoy one of 90 (!) pizzas or its excellent pastas in the cosy saloon-style dining room. Then chase it all with a little dollop of Venetian wonder: *sgroppino*. This cool, creamy, alcoholic lemon sorbet is *heavenly* after a meal.

**La Zucca** (The Pumpkin; Map pp202-4; ☎ 041 524 15 70; San Giacomo dell'Orio, Santa Croce 1762; mains €10-16; ☺ lunch & dinner Mon-Sat) A smashing *hosteria*, purveying innovative dishes using seasonal vegetables. The vegetarian lasagne is stunning, the fennel in spicy olive sauce transcendent. Rabbit, wild fowl and even horse are also offered in traditional preparations. Lovely rustic ambience and magnificent service make this tiny restaurant worth seeking. Book ahead.

**Trattoria alla Madonna** (Map pp202-4; ☎ 041 522 38 24; Calle della Madonna 594; meal about €30; ☺ lunch & dinner Thu-Tue) In a city of seafood restaurants, this is among the best. You'll spend a bit, but there's no faulting the food or super-friendly service – it's great value at the price.

**Osteria ai 4 Ferri** (Map pp202-4; ☎ 041 520 69 78; Calle Lunga San Barnaba, Dorsoduro 2754/a; mains €12-17; ☺ lunch & dinner) A great *osteria* off Campo San Barnaba. 'The Four Irons' is well-respected for its regional seafood delights (fantastic scampi, prawns and shellfish). The mix of young owners and traditional outlook is successful; booking required.

**Pizza al Volo** (Map pp202-4; ☎ 041 522 54 30; Campo Santa Margherita, Dorsoduro 2944; pizza slice €1.50, whole pizzas €4-6; ☺ lunch & dinner) Venice's favourite cheapie pizza takeaway serves slices the size of sails for under €2. The 'normal' pizza is enormous; don't even contemplate the *familiare* (family-size) unless you have friends handy.

### GELATI & PASTRIES

There's no shortage of great pastries and *gelato* in Venice.

**Il Doge** (Map pp202-4; ☎ 041 523 46 07; Campo Santa Margherita, Dorsoduro 3058/a; sml/lge gelato €1.50/3; ☺ 10-2am Feb-Nov) The finest *gelato* on the sweetest piazza.

**Pasticceria Marchini** (Map pp202-4; ☎ 041 522 91 09; www.golosessi.com; Calle Spadaria, San Marco 2769; ☼ 9am-10pm Mon-Sat) Popular, pricey spot for pastries just off Campo Santo Stefano. Kitschy but cute are Le Baute Veneziane – chocolates shaped like Carnevale masks.

**Rosa Salva** (Map pp202-4; ☎ 041 522 79 49; rsalva@doge.it; Campo SS Giovanni e Paolo, Castello 6779; ☼ 7.30am-8.30pm Thu-Tue) More than 100 years after launching as a 'travelling kitchen', delivering hot meals by gondola, Rosa Salva's reputation is unmatched; some of the best coffee and pastries in Venice can be enjoyed while perusing local artists' exhibits.

### SELF-CATERING

For fruit and vegetables, as well as deli items, head for the markets in the streets on the San Polo side of the Rialto, or the Rio Terrà San Leonardo in Cannaregio. There are also supermarkets: Mega 1, off Campo Santa Margherita, and **Standa** (Strada Nova).

## Drinking

### BARS

Around 4pm you'll notice everyone drinking *sprizze* – an aperitif of *prosecco* (Venetian sparkling white), soda and a bitter mixer (usually the gaudy Aperol) giving the drink its trademark colour. The best ones come with a fat olive. Delicious!

**Harry's Bar** (Map pp202-4; ☎ 041 528 57 77; www .cipriani.com; Calle Vallaresso, San Marco 1323; cocktails €8-13; ☼ 10.30am-11.15pm) Venice's star-magnet seems stalled in time, a sepia-toned scene, gilt-edged but amber-mellow. The ambience in Harry's isn't really inviting, but it oozes style. Writers and celebrities from Hemingway and Capote to Woody Allen, Orson Welles and Marlene Dietrich have all dined here. Although Harry's is first and foremost a bar, the menu's star is the Bellini (€13) – a divine cocktail of white-peach pulp and *prosecco*, invented here.

**Il Caffè** (Map pp202-4; ☎ 041 528 79 98; Campo San Margherita, Dorsoduro 2963; ☼ late) Better known as Café Rosso for the big red sign, this fantastic hub on Venice's most delightful square is popular with young and old. The cool staff make great *sprizze* and might even let you assault the piano if you can convince them you can wail – jams aren't uncommon.

**Café Blue** (Map pp202-4; ☎ 041 711 02 27; cafébleu venezia@hotmail.co; Salizzada San Pantalon, Dorsoduro 3778; ☼ late Mon-Sat) A pub-like drinking den not far from Santa Margherita, Café Blue usually figures somewhere in a Dorsoduro *giro d'ombra* (Venetian-style low-key pub crawl). Dark and atmospheric, it's a slightly shabby option, but still warm and inviting. Free Internet access is a cool feature.

**Café Noir** (Map pp202-4; ☎ 041 71 09 25; Calle San Pantalon 3805; ☼ 7-2am Mon-Sat, 9-2am Sun) A laid-back, more studenty hang-out, usually occupied night and day with locals catching up on gossip, flirting, drinking, eating and generally enjoying the wonderfully casual atmosphere of this pub-like bar/café.

**Paradiso Perduto** (Paradise Lost; Map pp202-4; ☎ 041 72 05 81; Fondamenta della Misericordia, Cannaregio 2540; ☼ 7pm-late, happy hour 6.30-7.30pm Thu-Mon, lunch Sat & Sun) Popular dim, bohemian bar/eatery/club with live and DJ-fuelled music. It's queer-friendly, self-consciously outré and does an awesome quasi-buffet lunch on weekends.

**Inishark** (Map pp202-4; ☎ 041 523 53 00; Calle Mondo Novo, Castello 5787; ☼ 5.30pm-2am Tue-Sun, closed Aug) A fun Irish bar so low-lit you'll need the light from the TV screens showing football (soccer) games to even *see* your Guinness.

**Bar Du Champ** (Map pp202-4; ☎ 041 528 62 55; Campo Santa Margherita, Dorsoduro 3019; ☼ 10-2am) Hip bar considered studenty because of the location, but really pulling a mixed crowd. Cheap *panini* for €1 to €2 and Tetley's on tap. It's swisher than it sounds.

**Barbanera** (Map pp202-4; ☎ 041 541 07 17; Calle de le Bande, Castello 5356; ☼ 11am-midnight) A *bir-reria/enoteca* (specialist wine and beer bar) also doing good food. The fish soup is cheap (€5) and authentic, the deep-fried olives (€3) pure salty deliciousness. Try them with warm crusty bread and a cold ale.

### CAFÉS

**Caffè Florian** (Map pp202-4; ☎ 041 520 56 41; www .caffeflorian.com; Piazza San Marco 56/59; coffee €7-10; ☼ late daily) If you can cope with paying at least €7 for a cappuccino, spend an hour or so sitting at an outdoor table in Piazza San Marco, listening to the orchestra and taking in the sights at leisure.

**Caffè Quadri** (Map pp202-4; ☎ 041 528 92 99; www .quadrivenice.com; Piazza San Marco 120; coffee €7-10; ☼ late) Another piazza café with a pedigree stretching back centuries.

**Torrefazione Costarica** (Map pp202-4; ☎ 041 716 371; Strada Nuovo, Cannaregio 1337; ☼ 8am-6.30pm) Perhaps surprisingly, Venice's best coffee is also the cheapest, prepared by the sweetest, most unassuming purveyors. Camillo Marchi and family do espresso for €0.65, cappuccino for €1.05.

## Entertainment

**Teatro La Fenice** (Map p199; ☎ 041 78 6511; www .teatrolafenice.it; Campo San Fantin, San Marco 1970) Like the phoenix it's named after, Venice's opera house recently re-emerged – literally – from the ashes of its previous incarnation: fire damage in 1996 saw the theatre closed for repairs for seven years. Back to its sumptuous best, it's once again the nexus of grand musical and theatrical performances in Venice.

**Palazzo Grassi** (Map pp202-4; www.palazzograssi .it; San Samuele, San Marco 3231; tickets adult/concession €9/6.50; ⏱ 10am-7pm) Palazzo Grassi is *the* schmick venue for major art exhibitions, from ancient to modern, in the city throughout the year.

## Shopping

Venice is synonymous with elaborate crafts, primarily glassware from the island of Murano and Venetian lace. Marbled paper and luscious velvet fabrics are other Venetian specialities, as are hand-bound books. There are several workshops and showrooms in Venice, but quality's inconsistent – there are a lot of knock offs. A good rule of thumb is to go to the source. If you're after Murano glass, visit Murano. And for lace, just remember that the authentic stuff is expensive – if it ain't pricey, it ain't genuine.

For designer-label clothing, shoes, accessories and jewellery, head for the narrow streets between San Marco and the Rialto. Luxury items can be found in the area near La Fenice.

**Studio Livio De Marchi** (Map pp202-4; ☎ 041 528 56 94; www.liviodemarchi.com; Salizzada San Samuele, San Marco 3157/a) Step into the fairy-tale world of surrealist sculptor Livio De Marchi, a dazzling showcase of his playfulness with wood and glass. When not turning trees into treasures, he's sometimes found 'driving' on the canals in his 'car': a vaporetto that's an exact, life-size, hand-carved wooden replica of a Ferrari F50!

## Getting There & Away

Some 12km from Venice is **Marco Polo Airport** ( ☎ 041 260 61 11, flight info ☎ 041 260 92 60), servic-

ing domestic and European flights. From Piazzale Roma use **ATVO** ( ☎ 041 520 55 30; €2.70) buses or **ACTV** ( ☎ 899 90 90 90; Intercity Bus Station) bus No 5 (€0.80).

The ACTV buses also service surrounding areas, including Mestre and Chioggia, a fishing port at the southernmost point of the lagoon, and also Padua and Treviso. Tickets and information are available at the office in Piazzale Roma.

The train station, **Stazione Santa Lucia** ( ☎ 848 88 80 88) is directly linked to Padua, Verona, Trieste, Milan and Bologna, and easily accessible for Florence and Rome. You can also reach points in France, Germany, Austria, Switzerland, Slovenia and Croatia. The Venice Simplon *Orient Express* (London ☎ 020 7805 5100; www.orient-express .com) runs twice weekly between Venice and London, via Innsbruck, Zurich and Paris.

**Minoan Lines** ( ☎ 041 240 71 01; Porto Venezia, Zona Santa Marta) run ferries to Greece (one way summer €72, daily in summer and four times a week in winter).

## Getting Around

Cars must be parked on Tronchetto or at Piazzale Roma (cars are allowed on the Lido – take car ferry No 17 from Tronchetto). The car parks are not cheap – €18 per day – so leave the car at Fusina, near Mestre, and catch vaporetto No 16 to Zattere, then No 82 either to Piazza San Marco or the train station. Ask for information at the tourist office just before the bridge to Venice.

The city's mode of public transport is the vaporetti (single/return ticket €3.10/5.20, 24-/72-hour unlimited-use ticket €19/31). Full timetables (€0.50) are available at vaporetto ticket offices. The most useful vaporetti are:

No 1: From Piazzale Roma, the No 1 zigzags along the Grand Canal to San Marco, then the Lido.

No 12: Departs from Fondamenta Nuove for the islands of Murano, Burano and Torcello.

No 82: Faster than the No 1 if you are in a hurry to get to St Mark's. Also services Giudecca.

*Traghetti* (€0.50 per crossing) are the public gondolas used by Venetians for crossing the Grand Canal – they get you a less romanticised gondola experience. Use them; they're quick, cheap, fun and you'll be getting around Venetian-style.

# FERRARA

pop 131,600

Lovely Ferrara outshines some bigger-named neighbours. The colourful medieval centre retains the vibe of its heyday as a seat of the Este family (1260–1598) when the town was a dynamic force. Castello Estense remains the imposing landmark in this charming town, though its friendly people are reason enough to visit. The **tourist office** ( ☎ 0532 29 93 03; www.ferraraterraeacqua.it; ☼ 9am-1pm & 2-6pm Mon-Sat, 9.30am-1pm & 2-5.30pm Sun) is inside Castello Estense.

## Sights

The small historic centre encompassing medieval Ferrara lies south of **Castello Estense** ( ☎ info 0532 29 93 03; tickets ☎ 0243 353 522; www.castelloestense.it; Viale Cavour; adult €10, under 18 & over 65 €8.50, reservation €1; ☼ 9am-8pm Mon-Thu, to 10pm Fri-Sun). Complete with moat and drawbridges, the castle was begun by Nicolò II d'Este in 1385. The foreboding atmosphere of its interior isn't mirrored outside, where there's a bustling marketplace.

The pretty pink-and-white-striped **Duomo** dates from the 12th century, with Gothic and Renaissance additions. Its **museum** ( ☎ 0532 76 12 99; Via San Romano 1-9; entry €4.20; ☼ 9am-1pm & 3-8pm Tue-Sun) is worth seeing, with some Renaissance works. The **Palazzo Schifanoia** ( ☎ 0532 20 99 88; Via Scandiana 23; entry €4.20; ☼ 9am-6pm Tue-Sun) is one of the city's earliest major Renaissance buildings and another of the Este palaces. Head for the 'Room of the Months' for Ferrara's finest frescoes.

## Sleeping

You won't need to overnight to see Ferrara's sights, but it's a cheap alternative to Bologna, and a viable base for visiting Venice. It's also small; tourist information can help you find *affittacamere*.

**Albergo Lupa** ( ☎ 0532 76 00 70; Vicolo della Lupa 8; s/d €35/45, with shared bathroom €30/40) This is a fantastic bargain in a quiet street minutes from great nightlife and eating. The rooms are lovely enough, but exceptional at the price.

**Pensione Artisti** ( ☎ 0532 76 10 38; Via Vittoria 66; d €57, s/d with shared bathroom €22/40) A fabulously friendly place on a medieval street, with attentive hosts ensuring the warmest welcome. Clean, bright rooms are secure and comfy. With a good guest kitchen available, this is Ferrara's choicest cheapie.

## Eating & Drinking

**Woodpecker** ( ☎ 0532 20 94 63; Via Saraceno 14; pizzas €7, pastas €8-10; ☼ dinner) The Woodpecker is a popular pizzeria/*ristorante* with a buoyant ambience and crisp, typically Italian décor. The pizzas are fine but try local speciality *cappellacci di zucca*, a hat-shaped pasta filled with pumpkin that is superb, sauced simply with butter, sage and *grana* (parmesan).

**Fusion** ( ☎ 0532 20 14 73; www.viascienze8.it, in Italian; Via Delle Scienze 8/a; ☼ 7.30-1.30am Tue-Sat, 6pm-1.30am Sun & 7.30am-3.30pm Mon) Personal grooming is a contact sport for Ferrara's fashionistas at this slick wine bar. Warm colours, comfy décor and chilled DJ-ing (and occasional live jazz) provide entertainment, but ogling's the real action. There are great snacks, and that inimitable Italian *style*.

**Messisbugo** ( ☎ 0532 76 40 60; www.messisbugo.com; ☼ late Tue-Sun) The cooler big sister to the strutting style warfare at Fusion. Boisterously casual without being raucous, sophisticated without being self-important, Messisbugo is a bar for grown-ups. Unpretentious, friendly staff keep the snacks and wonderful wines coming.

## Getting There & Away

Ferrara is on the Bologna–Venice train line, with regular trains to both (40 minutes to Bologna, 1½ hours to Venice) plus nearby Ravenna. Buses run from the train station to Modena (also in the Emilia-Romagna region).

# BOLOGNA

pop 381,000

Bologna is vibrant, beautiful and *red* – and it's often joked that its politics are reflected in the predominant colour of its buildings. Traditionally well to the Left, Bologna's reputation for spawning fiery rhetoric and socialist sympathies has mutated into a more agreeable one of open-ness and tolerance, reinforced by thousands of progressive-thinking students and teachers who come to study or work at Europe's oldest university, founded here in 1088.

The capital of Emilia-Romagna is further lauded as one of the greatest culinary cities in a great culinary nation. Bologna's traditional nickname was La Grassa ('Fatty'), for the richness of the food, rather than the circumference of its bellies. Besides the eponymous spaghetti bolognese (known as *spaghetti al ragù*), Bologna also gave the world tortellini and lasagne. Wonderful displays fill many a restaurant window – many still hand-cut their pasta under public scrutiny.

Bologna's a beautiful town, fantastic for a few days. Just like the food, however much you have, you'll probably want more.

## Information

**Ambulance** (☎ 118)

**Easy Internet** (☎ 051 23 1074; www.easyInternetcafé .it; Via Rizzoli 9; ⏰ 9am-11pm) The big orange purveyors of Internet access complement Bologna's existing colour scheme.

**Ospedale Maggiore** (☎ 051 647 8111)

**Police station** (Questura; ☎ 051 640 1111; Piazza Galileo 7)

**Post office** (☎ 051 23 0699; Piazza Minghetti 1; ⏰ 8am-6pm Mon-Sat)

**Tourist information** (call centre ☎ 051 24 65 41); Piazza Maggiore 1 (⏰ 9am-7pm Mon-Sat); Train station (⏰ 8.30am-7.30pm Mon-Sat); Airport (⏰ 8am-8pm Mon-Sat, 9am-3pm Sun)

## Sights & Activities

Simply strolling Bologna's porticoes is lovely as there's abundant atmosphere to be absorbed in the architecture.

Begin your exploration in the pedestrianised centre formed by **Piazza Maggiore**, the adjoining **Piazza del Nettuno** and **Fontana del Nettuno** (Neptune's Fountain), sculpted in bronze by Giambologna. Arriving at **Piazza di Porta Ravegnana**, climb the 498 steps up the 97m **Torre Asinelli** (€3; ⏰ 9am-6pm), the larger of Bologna's leaning towers, for wonderful views. The **Basilica di San Petronio** (☎ 051 22 5422; Piazza Maggiore; ⏰ 7.30am-1pm & 2-6pm, free tours 11.30am Tue, Thu & Sat) is dedicated to the city's patron saint, Petronius. Its partially complete state, most detectable in the cracked façade, doesn't diminish its status as the fifth largest basilica in the world. The chapels contain many notable artworks.

The adjacent **Palazzo Comunale** (Town Hall; admission free) combines disparate architectural styles harmoniously. There's a statue of the Bolognese pope, Gregory XIII (creator of the Gregorian calendar), an impressive staircase attributed to Bramante and Bologna's collection of art treasures.

The 16th-century **Basilica di San Domenico** (☎ 051 640 0411; Piazza San Domenico; admission free; ⏰ 8am-1.30pm & 2.30-7.30pm), designed by Nicoló Pisano houses the sarcophagus of St Dominic, namesake of the Dominican order. Its shrine features carvings by a young Michelangelo, and Mozart once played the church's organ.

The **Museo Civico Archeologico** (☎ 051 23 3849; Via dell'Archiginnasio 2; entry adult/concession €4/2; ⏰ 9am-6.30pm Tue-Sat & 10am-6.30pm Sun) houses one of Italy's best Etruscan collections.

## Sleeping

Bologna's budget hotels are in perpetual demand. Finding a room can be nightmarish, especially during the conventions and conferences often held here.

**Ostello Due Torri/San Sisto** (☎ /fax 051 50 1810; Via Viadagola 5; dm/d €13.50/15, sheets €1.50; ⏰ curfew 11pm) Two HI hostels beside each other, so inconveniently located they're nearly redundant. If circumstances necessitate penny-pinching, take bus No 93 (or No 301 Sundays, and 21b daily after 8.30pm) from Via Irnerio to San Sisto. There's nothing notable nearby; bring everything with you.

**Albergo Garisenda** (☎ 051 22 4369, fax 051 22 1007; Via Rizzoli 9, Galleria del Leone 1; s/d/tr with shared bathroom €45/65/90) In the shadow of the two towers, Garisenda has some rooms with a view of Torre Asinelli, as well as buzzing Via Rizzoli. It's conveniently located for pretty much everything, and good value for the unfussy rooms. Small breakfast included.

**Albergo Panorama** (☎ 051 22 1802; www.hotel panoramabologna.it; Via Livraghi 1; s/d/tr/q with shared bathroom €55/75/85/95) Lovely family-run place with spacious, clean rooms, all with TV and phone. You can glimpse the towers from some rooms. It's friendly and inviting – take bus No 25 four stops from the train station.

**Hotel Accademia** (☎ 051 23 2318; www.hotel accademia.it; Via delle Belle Arti 6; s €70-90, with shared bathroom €45-70, d €80-125, with shared bathroom €65-100) Good rooms with satellite TV, phone and decent breakfast make the Accademia great value. There's also uncommonly good disabled access. In the thick of the university quarter, it's great for people watching and close to excellent eating options.

# BOLOGNA

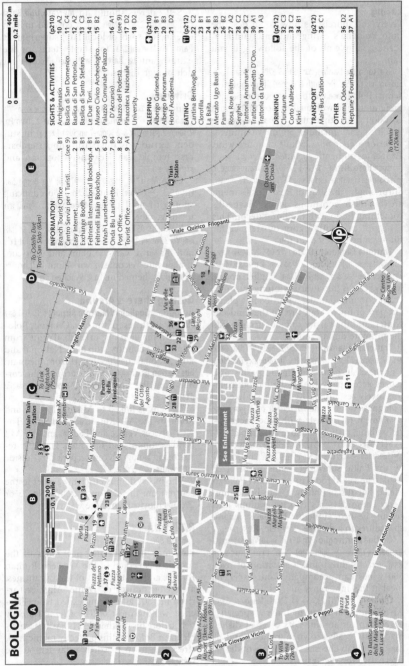

**ITALY**

ITALY

## Eating

Lively and moreish is how you'd describe both Bologna's eating and entertainment scenes. Sample all of the following if you can.

**Trattoria da Danio** ( ☎ 051 55 5202; Via San Felice 50a; menus €11.50; ☺ lunch & dinner) The quintessential Bolognese trattoria; atmospheric, unpretentious and with quality food that would cost double in other cities. The three-course lunch special includes 500ml of mineral water or a *quartino* (250ml) of house wine. Perfect for authentic *tagliatelle al ragu*.

**Rosa Rose Bistro** ( ☎ 051 22 5071; www.rosarose.it, in Italian; Via Clavature 18; lge salad €7; ☺ lunch & dinner) Surprisingly, the stars of Rosa Rose's menu are 'her' lush, enormous salads. Maybe it's something to do with the floral décor. This is a great café with a gorgeous terrace for fine-weather alfresco dining.

**Trattoria Caminetto D'Oro** ( ☎ 051 26 3494; www .caminettodoro.it, in Italian; Via Falegnami 4; mains €14-18; ☺ lunch Thu-Tue & dinner Thu-Mon) Higher up the luxury scale is this award-winning trattoria, cosily ensconced under a portico in a pleasant part of town. Staff fire up the fondo in winter, and the earthy smell of grilling fills the intimate dining rooms.

**Trattoria Annamarie** ( ☎ 051 26 6894; Via delle Belle Arti 17; mains €20-30; ☺ lunch Thu-Tue & dinner Thu-Mon) Unbelievably good handmade pastas and sauces accompany the freshest produce in this lovely restaurant. Keep it basic like the Bolognese do: try the *tortellini alla gorgonzola* (meat-filled pasta with blue cheese) – rich, filling, tasty but, above all, simple.

**Serghei** ( ☎ 051 23 3533; Via Piella 12; mains €15-20; ☺ lunch Mon-Sat & dinner Mon-Fri) Don't be fooled by the Baltic sobriquet – this small place used to be a card room in the former Palazzo Piella, but it's definitely a safe bet dining here. These days it's two generations into serving heaped, authentic Emilia-Romagna specialities to a diverse clientele. Reserve.

**Cantina Bentivoglio** ( ☎ 051 26 54 16; Via Mascarella 4b; mains €12-15; ☺ 8pm-2am) A liberal sauce of live jazz (nightly) and a selection of over 500 wines can accompany your excellent meal at this mid-range marvel.

**Clorofilla** ( ☎ 051 235 53 43; Strada Maggiore 64/c) An uncommon thing in Italy: a specialist vegetarian restaurant! Lots of great dishes made with locally grown ingredients and all manner of fab cheeses. This is a wonderful alternative for vegetarians.

Self caterers should hit **Mercato Ugo Bassi** (Via Ugo Bassi 27; ☺ Mon-Sat), a covered market offering all sorts of local fare, supermarket **Pam** (Via Marconi 28a) for staple items, or the extravagant **La Baita** (Via Pescheria Vecchie) for deluxe ingredients.

## Drinking

**Cluricaune** ( ☎ 051 26 34 19; www.cluricaune.com; Via Zamboni 18/b; ☺ noon-2am Mon-Thu, noon-2.30am Fri, 2.30pm-2.30am Sat & 2.30pm-2am Sun) Deep in student territory is this Irish pub to embarrass Temple Bar. Heavingly popular, and rightly so.

**Corto Maltese** ( ☎ 051 22 97 46; Via Borgo San Pietro 9/2; ☺ till late) Fantastic bar/pub/dancing spot with pool tables, free pasta and an inclusive vibe.

**Kinki** ( ☎ 051 587 5178; www.kinkidisco.com, in Italian; Via Zamboni 1; ☺ 7pm-4am, happy hour 7-9pm) It's hot! It's vinyl! Gays, lesbians and über-cool straights are welcome to work it until all hours at Kinki's themed nights. Wicked fun.

## Getting There & Around

Bologna's **Guglielmo Marconi Airport** ( ☎ 051 647 9615) is northwest of the city. On land, Bologna is a major transport hub. Trains from around the country stop here. National and international coaches depart from the main **bus station** (Piazza XX Settembre) around the corner from the **train station** (Piazza delle Medaglie d'Oro).

The city is linked to Milan, Florence and Rome by the A1 (Autostrada del Sole). The A13 services Venice and Padua, and the A14 handles Rimini and Ravenna. Traffic is restricted in Bologna's centre; park cars outside city walls.

The bus system is efficient. To get to the centre from the station take bus No 25 or 27, or enjoy a 10-minute walk.

## RAVENNA

**pop 139,800**

Ravenna's exquisite mosaics, relics of the time it was capital of the Western Roman Empire and western seat of the Byzantines, are the big drawcards. Dante (Alighieri) arrived in 1302 after being exiled from Florence, writing most of *The Divine Comedy* here before his death in 1321. Easily accessible from Bologna, this perfectly manicured, stress-free town is worth a day trip at the very least.

The **IAT Tourist Information Office** ( ☎ 0544 354 04; Via Salara 12; ☼ 8.30am-7pm Mon-Sat Apr-Sep, to 6pm Mon-Sat Oct-Mar, 10am-4pm Sun year-round) is off Via Cavour. For medical assistance, see **Ospedale Santa Maria delle Croci** ( ☎ 0544 409 111; Via Missiroli 10).

## Sights

You can buy a combination ticket (€8.50) at the tourist office to visit Ravenna's famed mosaics at **Basilica di Sant'Apollinare Nuovo** ( ☼ 9am-7pm; Via di Roma); the **Basilica di San Vitale** ( ☼ 9am-7pm), the oldest of them all; **Mausoleo di Galla Placidia** ( ☼ 9am-7pm); the **Battistero Neoniano** (Via Battistero; ☼ 9am-7pm); and the **Museo Arcivescovile**.

Itself fairly unremarkable, **Dante's tomb** (Via Dante Alighieri 9; admission free; ☼ 9am-7pm) is worth noting for the 'perpetual' lamp – a belated admission from Florence that it had fumbled in exiling the 'father of modern Italian (language)' – which is kept permanently alight in tribute.

## Sleeping & Eating

**Ostello Dante** ( ☎ 0544 42 11 64; Via Aurelio Nicolodi 12; dm with breakfast €12.50, f per person €14) The HI hostel is as neat as a pin. It has friendly staff and good evening meals. You'll find it 1km out of town; take bus No 1 from Viale Pallavacini, by the train station. A taxi costs €6.

**Albergo Al Giaciglio** ( ☎ /fax 0544 394 03; Via Rocca Brancaleone 42; s/d/tr €36/51/65, with shared bathroom €30/42/55) Small family-run hotel near the station with bright blue rooms and a good restaurant (set menus €13).

**Cá de Vén** ( ☎ 0544 301 63; Via Corrado Ricci 24; pastas €6-8, mains €9-14; ☼ Tue-Sun) The best all-round eating option in Ravenna offers good regional dishes and an extensive wine list in monastic surroundings, with a big non-smoking section. Pasta courses are ample for a small meal, but the tempting menu encourages lingering.

## Getting There & Around

Ravenna is accessible by train from Bologna (1½ hours, €7 to €15), sometimes involving a change at Castel Bolognese. Cycling is a popular way to get around; Ravenna's fairly flat. Rental is available from **COOP San Vitale** (Piazza Farini XX; per hr/day €1.20/8) outside the station, or the **tourist office** (free; ☼ spring & summer only).

# THE DOLOMITES

The limestone Dolomites stretch across Trentino–Alto Adige and into the Veneto. Characterised by the reddish glow of the rock formations that jut into the sky like jagged teeth, this spectacular Alpine region is the Italians' favoured area for skiiing and, in summer, hiking.

Information about Trentino–Alto Adige can be obtained in Trent (Trento) at the **APT del Trentino** ( ☎ 0461 83 90 00; www.trentino.to; Via Romagnosi 11); Rome ( ☎ 06 36 09 58 42; Via del Babuino 20); Milan ( ☎ 02 86 46 12 51; apt.milano@trentino.to; Piazza Diaz 5). Bolzano's **tourist office** ( ☎ 0471 30 70 00; www .bolzano-bozen.it; Piazza Walther 8) also has information on the region. The **APT Dolomiti** ( ☎ 0436 32 31/2/3; fax 0436 32 35) at Cortina can provide details on trekking and skiing in the Veneto. An excellent website for planning your trip is www.dolomiti.org, which has comprehensive information, including maps.

## Activities

### SKIING

The Dolomites' many resorts range from posh Cortina d'Ampezzo in the Veneto to more family-oriented resorts in the Val Gardena (Trentino–Alto Adige). Most resorts have helpful tourist offices.

High season (Christmas to early January, and early February to April) costs will hit your pocket hard. Buy a *settimana bianca* (literally 'white week') – a package deal including seven days' worth of accommodation, food and ski passes, available throughout Italy.

Most resort areas also offer their own passes for unlimited use of lifts within nominated periods. Prices vary with resort (six days from €130 to €160). Average cost of ski-plus-boot hire (downhill/cross-country €15/10) is bearable. The **Superski Dolomiti pass** (www.dolomitisuperski.com; high season 3/6 days €100/175) accesses 464 lifts and 1220km of runs in 12 valleys.

### TREKKING

Without doubt, the Dolomites provide the most breathtaking opportunities for walking in the Italian Alps (the season is from the end of June to September) – from basic half-day strolls with the kids to hardcore trekking and mountaineering. Alpine refuges (*rifugi*)

ITALY

usually close around 20 September. Trails are well marked with numbers on red-and-white bands on trees and rocks, or by numbers inside coloured triangles for the four Alte Vie ('High Routes') through the Dolomites.

The best maps are the Tabacco 1:25,000 series, widely available at bookshops throughout the region. Lonely Planet's *Walking in Italy* outlines several treks in detail; the *Italy* guide also suggests hikes.

Recommended hiking areas include:

**Alpe di Siusi** – a vast plateau above the Val Gardena, at the foot of the spectacular Sciliar.

**Cortina area** – featuring the magnificent Parco Naturale di Fanes-Sennes-Braies.

**Pale di San Martino** – accessible from San Martino di Castrozza.

### WARNING

Even in summer the weather is extremely changeable in the Alps; though it may be sweltering when you set off, be prepared for very cold, wet weather on even the shortest walks. Essentials include good-quality, worn-in walking boots, an anorak or wind jacket, lightweight backpack, warm hat and gloves, waterproof poncho, light food and plenty of water.

### Getting There & Away

The region has excellent public transport. The two principal bus companies are **SAD** ( ☎ 800 84 60 409) in Alto Adige and the Veneto, and **Atesina** (www.atesina.it) in Trentino. A network of long-distance buses operated by various companies (eg Lazzi, SITA, Sena, STAT and ATVO) connects major towns and resorts with big cities (Rome, Florence, Venice, Bologna, Milan and Genoa). Information is available from tourist offices and regional *autostazioni* (bus stations). For long-distance travel information, try **Lazzi Express** Rome ( ☎ 06 884 08 40; Via Tagliamento 27b); Florence ( ☎ 055 28 71 18; Piazza Stazione 47r). There is a **SITA office** ( ☎ 055 29 49 55; Via Santa Caterina da Siena 15) in Florence.

### Getting Around

If you're planning an Alpine hike during warmer months, you'll find that hitching is no problem; normal caution should still apply. Areas near major resorts are well serviced by local buses, and tourist offices have information on routes. During winter, most resorts have 'ski bus' shuttle services to the main facilities.

## CORTINA D'AMPEZZO

pop 6570

The ski resort for Italy's elite, Cortina is excruciatingly fashionable with matching prices. It's also one of the best-equipped, most picturesque resorts in the Dolomites. The area is popular for trekking and climbing, with well-marked trails and numerous *rifugi*.

The **main tourist office** ( ☎ 0436 32 31; Piazzetta San Francesco 8) has information on Cortina's accommodation options. **International Camping Olympia** ( ☎ /fax 0436 50 57; per person €8.50, tent & car €9; ☺ year-round) is 3.5km north of Cortina at Fiames. **Casa Tua** ( ☎ 0436 22 78; www .casatuacortina.com; Via Zuel 100; r per person €34-50) in Cortina has season-dependent rates.

SAD buses connect Cortina with Bolzano, via Dobbiaco; ATVO travels to Venice, and Zani to Milan and Bologna.

## CANAZEI

pop 1780

Set in the Fassa Dolomites, Canazei has over 100km of trails and is linked to a challenging network of runs, the **Sella Ronda**. Canazei also offers cross-country and summer skiing on Marmolada (3342m), the highest peak in the Dolomites.

Spend a cheap night at the Marmolada **camping ground** ( ☎ 0462 60 16 60; per person/tent €8/8; ☺ year-round), or contact the **tourist office** ( ☎ 0462 60 11 13; Via Roma 34) for further details on accommodation. The resort is accessible by Atesina bus from Trent and SAD bus from Bolzano.

## VAL GARDENA

A popular area in the Alps, with reasonable prices and top facilities. There are superb walking trails in the Sella Group and the Alpe di Siusi. The Vallunga, behind Selva, is great for family walks and cross-country skiing.

The valley's main towns are Ortisei, Santa Cristina and Selva, all offering plenty of accommodation and easy access to runs. Each town has a **tourist office** (Ortisei ☎ 0471 79 63 28, Santa Cristina ☎ 0471 79 30 46, Selva ☎ 0471 79 51 22) with extensive information on local facilities. Staff speak English and send details on request. The Val Gardena is accessible from Bolzano by SAD bus, and connected to major Italian cities by coach (Lazzi, SITA and STAT).

## SAN MARTINO DI CASTROZZA
pop 700

In a sheltered position beneath the Pale di San Martino, this resort is popular among Italians, offering good skiing and a toboggan run. The **tourist office** ( ☎ 0439 76 88 67) provides lists of accommodation. **Hotel Suisse** ( ☎ 0439 680 87; Via Dolomiti 1; r with breakfast from €33) is a pleasant one-star. Buses travel regularly from Trent, Venice and Padua.

# CENTRAL ITALY

Tuscan light is a thing of unfettered beauty, playing over the rolling green landscapes in a million shades of gorgeous, and the hill towns of Umbria and the Marches (Le Marche) are worth the ankle strain for some of Italy's sweetest vistas. Though you'll be cheek by jowl with the hordes of culture-vultures in buzzing hubs such as Florence – and even some of the smaller towns just hours away – it's still possible to lose yourself down a medieval side street and get a little closer to a sense of Italy's fabled *la dolce vita* ('the good life').

## FLORENCE
pop 375,000

Italy's been successfully selling itself on Florence's appeal for centuries. And although everything they claim is true – that it's a beautiful city with an artistic heritage unrivalled anywhere else in the world – it can also be disheartening. For most of the year, you'll overhear more conversations in English than Italian, and in summer the heat, pollution and crowds are stifling. Griping apart, Florence remains among the most enticing cities in Italy. Cradle of the Renaissance, home of Dante, Machiavelli, Michelangelo, the Medici and Carlo Collodi (who created Pinocchio), the wealth of history, art and culture still overwhelms.

Florence was founded as a colony of the nearby Etruscan city Fiesole around 200 BC, later becoming the strategic Roman settlement of Florentia. In the Middle Ages the city developed a flourishing mercantile economy, sparking a period of building and growth previously unequalled in Italy. But Florence truly flourished under the Medicis (1469–1737), its cultural, artistic and political fecundity culminating in the Renaissance.

The Grand Duchy of the Medici was succeeded in the 18th century by the House of Lorraine (related to the Habsburgs). Following unification, Florence was the capital of the new kingdom of Italy (1865–71). During WWII, parts of the city were destroyed by bombing, including all Florence's bridges except the Ponte Vecchio, and in 1966 a devastating flood destroyed or severely damaged many important works of art.

### Orientation

However you arrive, the main train station Santa Maria Novella is a good reference point. The main thoroughfare to the centre is Via de' Panzani and then Via de' Cerretani – look for the Duomo.

Once at Piazza del Duomo, Florence is easy to negotiate, as most major sights are within comfortable walking distance. Many museums close on Mondays, but you won't waste your time just strolling.

A good map of the city, on sale at newsstands, is *Firenze: Pianta della Città* (€3.50).

### Information
#### BOOKSHOPS

**Feltrinelli International** (Map p218; ☎ 055 21 95 24; Via Cavour 12r) Italy's best foreign-language bookstore has a huge outlet here.

**Paperback Exchange** (Map pp216-7; ☎ 055 247 81 54; Via Fiesolana 31r) Huge range of new and second-hand books.

#### EMERGENCY

**Ambulance & Fire** ( ☎ 118)

**Police station** (Questura; Map pp216-7; general ☎ 055 497 71, lost property ☎ 055 328 39 42, towed vehicles ☎ 055 41 57 81; Via Zara 2) Has a foreigners' office.

#### INTERNET ACCESS

**Internet Train** (www.Internettrain.it, in Italian; from per hr €4) Via Oriuolo (Map p218; ☎ 055 263 89 68); Via Guelfa 24a (Map pp216-7; ☎ 055 21 47 94); Borgo San Jacopo 30r (Map p218; ☎ 055 265 79 35); Stazione Santa Maria Novella (Map pp216-7; ☎ 055 239 97 20) This Internet chain has 15 branches.

**Netgate** (Map p218; ☎ 055 658 02 07; www.thenet gate.it; Via Sant' Egidio 10-20r; ⏰ 10am-10.30pm, free Internet ⏰ 10.30-11am & 2-2.30pm Sat)

#### LAUNDRY

**Wash & Dry** ( ☎ 800 23 11 72; ⏰ 8am-10pm) Via Nazionale 129r (Map pp216-7); Via del Sole 29r (Map p218); Via della Scala 52-54r (Map pp216-7); Via dei Servi 105r (Map pp216-7); Via de' Seragli 87r (Map pp216-7)

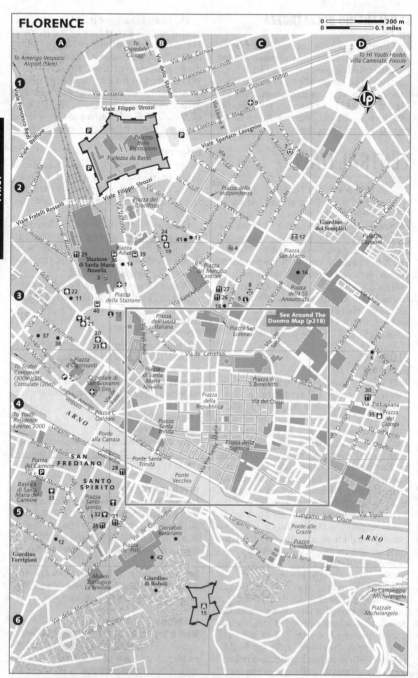

# FLORENCE

0 — 200 m
0 — 0.1 miles

See Around The
Duomo Map (p218)

## MEDICAL SERVICES

**Farmacia Comunale** (Map pp216-7; ☎ 055 28 94 35; Stazione Santa Maria Novella) A late-night pharmacy inside the station.

**Misericordia di Firenze** (Map p218; ☎ 055 21 22 22; Vicolo degli Adimari 1; ☯ 1.30-5pm Mon-Fri) A tourist medical service, just off Piazza Duomo.

**Tourist Medical Service** (Map pp216-7; ☎ 055 47 54 11; Via Lorenzo il Magnifico 59; ☯ 24hr) Has doctors who speak English, French and German.

## MONEY

**American Express** (Map p218; ☎ 055 509 81; Via Dante Alighieri 22r; ☯ 9am-5.30pm Mon-Fri, 9.30am-12.30pm Sat)

**Thomas Cook** (Map p218; ☎ 055 28 97 81; Lungarno degli Acciaiuoli 6r)

## POST

**Main post office** (Map p218; Via Pellicceria 3; ☯ 8.15am-7pm Mon-Fri, to 12.30pm Sat)

## TELEPHONE & FAX

**Telecom office** (Map pp216-7; Via Cavour 21r; ☯ 7am-11pm)

## TOURIST INFORMATION

**Tourist offices** Main office (Map pp216-7; ☎ 055 29 08 32; www.firenzeturismo.it; Via Cavour 1r; ☯ 8.30am-6.30pm Mon-Sat, to 1.30pm Sun); Piazza della Stazione 4 (Map pp216-7; ☎ 055 21 22 45; ☯ 8.30am-7pm Mon-Sat, to 2pm Sun); Borgo Santa Croce 29r (Map p218; ☯ 8.30am-7pm Mon-Sat, to 2pm Sun); Amerigo Vespucci Airport ( ☎ 055 31 58 74; ☯ 7.30am-11.30pm)

## Sights & Activities

Enjoying Florence's sights can be taxing, as lengthy queues stretch patience. Entry to all state museums is half-price for EU passport holders (make sure you have it with you);

if you're a EU passport holder under 18 or over 65 years of age, they're free. You'll still have to wait, though.

But don't despair; call **Firenze Musei** ( ☎ 055 29 48 83; www.firenzemusei.it; fee per museum €3; ☯ 8.30am-6.30pm Mon-Fri, to 12.30pm Sat), which advance books tickets for all state museums, including the Uffizi, Palazzo Pitti, Museo del Bargello, Galleria dell'Accademia and Cappelle Medicee.

Take the city ATAF buses to **Piazzale Michelangelo** or the nearby suburb of **Fiesole**, both offering panoramic views.

## DUOMO

The terracotta-orange roof contrasts dramatically with the red, green and white marble façade of the skyline-dominating cathedral, the **Duomo** (Map p218; ☎ 055 230 28 85; ☯ 10am-5pm Mon-Sat) – among Italy's most beloved monuments, and the world's fourth-largest cathedral. Officially the Cattedrale di Santa Maria del Fiore, the breathtaking structure was begun in 1294 by Sienese architect Arnolfo di Cambio, taking almost 150 years to complete.

Brunelleschi won a competition in 1420 to design the enormous octagonal dome, the first of its kind since antiquity. The interior is decorated with frescoes by Vasari and Zuccari, and the stained-glass windows are by Donatello, Paolo Uccello and Lorenzo Ghiberti. The façade is a 19th-century replacement of the unfinished original, pulled down in the 16th century. For a bird's-eye view of Florence, climb to the top of the **cupola** (admission €6; ☯ 8.30am-6.20pm Mon-Fri, to 5pm Sat).

Giotto designed and began building the graceful 82m **campanile** (Map p218; climb €6; ☯ 8.30am-6.50pm) beside the cathedral in

ITALY

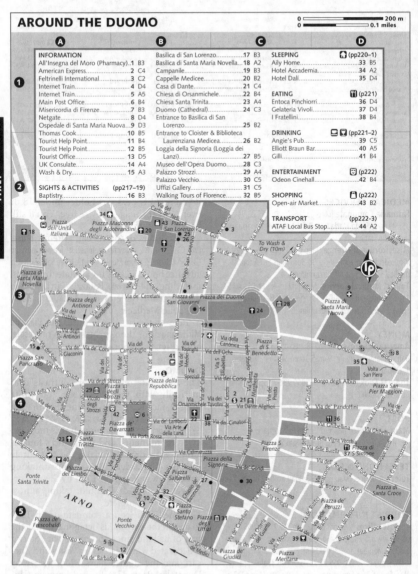

1334, but died before it was completed. The climb to the top yields gorgeous views.

The Romanesque **battistero** (baptistry; Map p218; admission €3; ☼ noon-6.30pm Mon-Sat, 8.30am-1.30pm Sun & holidays), believed built between the 5th and 11th centuries on the site of a Roman temple, is the oldest building in Florence. The infant Dante was baptised here, and it's famous for

its gilded-bronze doors. The celebrated *Gates of Paradise* by Lorenzo Ghiberti face the Duomo to the east. The south door (1336), by Andrea Pisano, is the oldest.

**GALLERIA DEGLI UFFIZI (UFFIZI GALLERY)**
Unless you book ahead (which costs and extra €1.55), you may find yourself waiting

at the end of a very long queue for **Palazzo degli Uffizi** (Map p218; ☎ 055 238 86 51, reservations ☎ 055 294 883; www.uffizi.firenze.it; Piazza degli Uffizi; admission €8; ☑ 8.15am-6.50pm Tue-Sun, ticket office closes 6.05pm) – but it's worthwhile. Begun by Vasari in 1560 and ultimately bequeathed to the city by the Medici family in 1743, it houses the greatest collection of Italian and Florentine art in existence, including many of the world's most recognisable Renaissance paintings.

The gallery's seemingly endless masterpieces include 14th-century gems by Giotto and Cimabue; Botticelli's *Birth of Venus* and *Allegory of Spring* (rooms 10 to 14); plus works by Filippo Lippi, Fra Angelico and Paolo Uccello. *The Annunciation* by Leonardo da Vinci is here (room 15), along with Michelangelo's *Holy Family* (room 25), Titian's *Venus of Urbino* (room 28) and renowned works by Raphael, Andrea del Sarto, Tintoretto and Caravaggio.

## PIAZZA DELLA SIGNORIA & PALAZZO VECCHIO

Designed by Arnolfo di Cambio and built between 1298 and 1340, **Palazzo Vecchio** (Map p218; Piazza della Signoria; adult/child €5.70/4.30; ☑ 9am-7pm Fri-Wed, to 2pm Thu) is the traditional seat of the Florentine government. In the 16th century it became the ducal palace of the Medici (before they occupied the Palazzo Pitti), and was given an interior facelift by Vasari. Visit the Michelozzo courtyard just inside the entrance, and the lavish apartments upstairs.

The **Loggia della Signoria** stands at right angles to the Palazzo Vecchio, displaying sculptures. The statue of *David* is a fine copy of Michelangelo's masterpiece; the original was once here (1504), but is now safely indoors in the Galleria dell'Accademia (p219).

## PONTE VECCHIO

The 14th-century **Ponte Vecchio** (Map p218), lined with gold and silversmiths' shops, was the only one to survive Nazi bombing in WWII. Originally, the shops housed butchers, but when a corridor along the 1st floor was built by the Medici to link the Palazzo Pitti and Palazzo Vecchio, they ordered that goldsmiths rather than noisome butchers should trade on the bridge. The area south of the river after crossing the Ponte Vecchio is the 'Oltrarno' (literally, 'beyond the Arno').

## PALAZZO PITTI

This immense *palazzo* was built for the Pitti family, great rivals of the Medici, who moved in a century later. The **Galleria Palatina** (Palatine Gallery; Map pp216-7; admission before/after 4pm €8.50/4; ☑ 8.15am-6.50pm Tue-Sun) has works by Raphael, Filippo Lippi, Titian and Rubens, hung in lavishly decorated rooms. The gallery and luxuriant decoration of the **royal apartments** are worth seeing. The palace also houses the **Museo degli Argenti** (Silver Museum; Map pp216-7; ☑ 8.15am-4.20pm Tue-Sun, 2nd & 3rd Mon each month), the **Galleria d'Arte Moderna** (Modern Art Gallery; Map pp216-7; admission €5; ☑ 8.15am-1.50pm Tue-Sat) and the **Galleria del Costume** (Costume Gallery; Map pp216-7; admission €5; ☑ 8.15am-1.50pm Tue-Sat).

Don't leave without visiting the Renaissance **Giardino di Boboli** (Boboli Gardens; Map pp216-7; admission €4; ☑ 8.15am-7.30pm Jun-Aug, to 6.30pm Apr-May & Sep, to 5.30pm Mar & Oct, to 4.30pm Nov-Feb), with secluded grottoes, fountains, leafy walkways and panoramic views.

## GALLERIA DELL'ACCADEMIA

Michelangelo's *David,* arguably the most famous sculpture in the Western world, is housed in this **gallery** (Map pp216-7; ☎ 055 238 86 09; Via Ricasoli 60; admission €6.50; ☑ 8.15am-6.50pm Tue-Sun). *David* truly is an amazing work close-up; it's much bigger and more intricately detailed than many might imagine. Be sure you're keen – a two-hour wait is typical, rain or shine.

## BASILICA DI SAN LORENZO & CAPPELLE MEDICEE (MEDICI CHAPELS)

The **Basilica di San Lorenzo** (Map p218; admission €2.50; ☑ 10am-5pm Mon-Sat) was built by Brunelleschi in the 15th century for the Medici and includes his **Sagrestia Vecchia** (Old Sacristy), with sculptural decoration by Donatello. The cloister leads to the **Biblioteca Laurenziana**, the library built to house the Medici collection of some 10,000 manuscripts. Enter via Michelangelo's flowing Mannerist stairway.

The **Cappelle Medicee** (Map p218; ☎ 055 238 86 02; Piazza Madonna degli Aldobrandini; admission €6; ☑ 8.15am-5pm Tue-Sat, 1st, 3rd & 5th Sun of the month, 2nd & 4th Mon of the month) are around the corner. The **Cappella dei Principi** was the principal burial place of the Medici grand dukes. The incomplete **Sagrestia Nuova** was Michelangelo's first architectural effort, and contains his *Medici Madonna, Night & Day* and *Dawn & Dusk* sculptures, which adorn the Medici tombs.

**ITALY**

## Festivals & Events

The **Scoppio del Carro** (Explosion of the Cart) is held in front of the Duomo on Easter Sunday, and involves igniting a cart full of fireworks. Yes – as noisy, colourful and popular as it sounds.

The **Festa di San Giovanni** (Feast of St John), honouring Florence's patron saint, is held on 24 June and includes *calcio storico* ('period football') – soccer matches played in 16th-century costume on the Piazza Santa Croce.

**Maggio Musicale Fiorentino** (April to June) is Italy's longest-running music festival. For information call the **Teatro Comunale** (☎ 800 11 22 11).

## Sleeping

### BUDGET

Budget hotels and *pensioni* are concentrated around Via Nazionale, to the east of the station, and Piazza Santa Maria Novella, to the south. Despite there being over 150 budget hotels in Florence, it's still prudent to book. Arrive by late morning to claim your room.

**Ostello Villa Camerata** (Map pp216-7; ☎ 055 60 14 51; fax 055 61 03 00; Viale Augusto Righi 2-4; dm €15, dinner €8; ⊗ lockout 9am-2pm) This HI hostel, a converted 17th-century villa, is superbly located. If it's not enough being drunk on the sheer beauty of your surrounds, it also has a bar. Take bus No 17 (€1, 30 minutes) from the station. Members only; reservations essential in summer.

**Ostello Archi Rossi** (Map pp216-7; ☎ 055 29 08 04; ostelloarchirossi@hotmail.com; Via Faenza 94r; dm €16-19; ⊗ lockout 9am-2pm; ✗ ❄ 🖳 ) Hugely popular is this fun place, great for meeting other travellers – if privacy and quiet matter, look elsewhere. Good breakfast is included and bright, faux-frescoed décor – three floors of traveller graffiti – adorns the walls. Arrive before 9am to get a bed.

**Campeggio Michelangelo** (Map p218; ☎ 055 681 19 77; Viale Michelangelo 80; per person/tent €8/5) The camping ground closest to town is near Piazzale Michelangelo. Take bus No 13 from the station.

### MID-RANGE

**Albergo Azzi** (Map pp216-7; ⊗ 055 21 38 06; hotel azzi@hotmail.com; Via Faenza 56; bed in shared room €30, s/d with breakfast €60/90, with shared bathroom & breakfast €42/67) One of six basic, comfy and clean hotels operating in the same building; a great bargain option. Upstairs are the very similar Albergo Anna, Paola, Minerva, Merlin and Armonia. Prices flex a bit, so bargain.

**Accademia** (Map p218; ☎ 055 29 34 51; www.hotel accademia.it; Via Faenza 7; s €40-85, d €60-150; ✗ ❄ ) This two-star is in an 18th-century palace, complete with magnificent stained-glass doors, carved wooden ceilings and a grand staircase straight out of a Ziegfield movie. It's a great all-round option with website-only specials, so get surfing.

**La Scala** (Map pp216-7; ☎ 055 21 26 29; Via della Scala; d €85, s with shared bathroom €60; ✗ ❄ ) Gabriele Bini is the charming host of this wonderfully unpretentious place. Rooms are lovely, and value at these prices. There are portions of original frescoes on some ceilings, and the whole place is neat as a pin. Jovial Gabriele may be open to a spot of haggling, so don't hesitate.

**Albergo Margaret** (Map pp216-7; ☎ 055 21 01 38; www.dormireintoscana.it/margaret; Via della Scala 25; d €90, s with shared bathroom €60; ✗ ❄ ) A simple but functional place with pleasantly decorated rooms, serviced by helpful staff. It's possible to negotiate discounts for multi-night stays at this recommended one-star.

**Albergo Montreal** (Map pp216-7; ☎ 055 238 23 31; www.hotelmontreal.com; Via della Scala 43; d €100, s/d with shared bathroom €55/85; 🅿 ✗ ❄ 🖳 ) A well-appointed option, with sound-proofed, air-conditioned rooms featuring TV, phone and fridge. A decent buffet breakfast available.

**Aily Home** (Map p218; ☎ 055 239 65 05; Piazza Santo Stefano 1; s/d with shared bathroom €35/45) A great budget option with disproportionately large rooms overlooking the river. You'll struggle with the tiny lift, but the rooms at the top are worth it.

**Hotel Dalì** (Map p218; ☎ 055 234 07 06; www .hoteldali.com; Via dell'Oriuolo 17; d €75, s/d with shared bathroom €40/60) The only thing melting here will be your heart, as owners Marco and Samanta bend over backwards to ensure a pleasant stay in a city indifferent to some visitors. Rooms are as attractive and relaxing as the charming staff.

### TOP END

**Bencistà** (⊗ 055 591 63; pensionebencista@iol.it; Via Benedetto da Maiano 4; s/d €150/160) A gorgeous villa about 1km from Fiesole in the hills overlooking Florence. It's as close as you'll get to *la dolce vita* without restoring your own ramshackle Tuscan cottage.

**Hotel Aprile/Palazzo del Borgo** (Map pp216-7; ☎ 055 21 62 37; www.hotelaprile.it; Via della Scala 6; s/d €120/180; P ✕ ✕ ☐ ) If you're in the mood to lash out, look no further than this former Medici palace, gorgeously appointed yet disarmingly low-key. Some rooms feature frescoes by Masaccio and Masolino and there's a gorgeous courtyard garden. A worthwhile indulgence.

## Eating

Tuscan cuisine is all about simplicity and quality, exemplified in the staple *fettunta*, crusty bread rubbed with garlic and dripping with virgin olive oil. Other delights include *ribollita*, a heavy soup of vegetables and *canellini* (white beans), and the eponymous, usually enormous, *bistecca alla Fiorentina* (Florentine steak).

You can stock up at the **food market** (Map pp216-7; Piazza San Lorenzo; ☺ 7am-2pm Mon-Sat) or at the **supermarket** (Map pp216-7; Stazione Santa Maria Novella) on the western side of the train station, or the **supermarket** (Map pp216-7; Via Pietrapiana 94) east of Piazza Duomo.

### RESTAURANTS

**Mario's** (Map pp216-7; Via Rosina 2r; pastas & mains €5; ☺ lunch Mon-Sat) Two generations of expertise fuel this cheap-but-great diner perpetually heaving with hungry locals. Delicious authentic pastas can be had for (nearly) a song. Whether you're budgeting or not, Mario's is worth a look for a glimpse of a typical Italian eatery in all its glory – the value's a welcome bonus!

**Borgo Antico** (Map pp216-7; ☎ 055 21 04 37; Piazza Santo Spirito 6r; mains €7-10; ☺ lunch & dinner) Heaping portions may be part of the draw at this great eatery, popular with a hip crowd. It could also be the excellent Tuscan dishes, the prime terrace space on a lovely piazza or the frankly unbelievable prices. Whatever it is, they should bottle it – it's a local favourite.

**Ristorante Beccofino** (Map pp216-7; ☎ 055 29 00 76; Piazza degli Scarlatti 1r; 1st & 2nd course €10-20; ☺ Tue-Sun) In all but quality, chef Francesco Berardinelli always planned to turn Tuscan tradition upside down with Beccofino's modern mojo. From the cyber-toilets to the bold menu, the new kid on Florence's culinary block rocks.

**Trattoria Casalinga** (Map pp216-7; ☎ 055 21 86 24; Via dei Michelozzi 9r; mains €16) The pick of the Piazza Santa Spirito trattorias is rammed with locals for lunch and dinner. There's a bit of a 'hurry-up!' feel to it, but you won't mind being nudged along for food this good at these prices. Fantastic friendly service, flamboyant Florentine clientele, and delicious dishes. Don't miss.

**da Garibardi** (Map pp216-7; ☎ 055 21 22 67; www .garibardi.it; Piazza del Mercato Centrale 38r; mains €15-20; ☺ noon-11pm) A great, authentic trattoria a spit away from more obvious stuff on the piazza. Indulge your Asterix-comic fantasies with *pasta al cinghiale* (wild boar) – a Tuscan speciality – augmented with *alla caccia* (hunter-style) accompaniments: olives, bay leaves, mushrooms and peppercorns. Service is friendly, the dining rooms cobblestone cosy and wood-fired warm.

**Enoteca Pinchiorri** (Map p218; ☎ 055 24 27 77; www.enotecapinchiorri.com; Via Ghibellina 87; mains €80-100) Nothing obvious on Via Ghibellina suggests the presence of possibly Italy's best restaurant, but it's there. Hostess Annie Feolde and sommelier Giorgio Pinchiorri deliver an unparalleled dining experience by combining a daring, innovative menu and jaw-dropping wine list with traditional surrounds and service evocative of fine dining from eras past. Book well ahead, and check online for its latest stunning menu.

### SNACK BARS & GELATI

**Gelateria Vivoli** (Map p218; ☎ 055 29 23 34; Via dell'Isola delle Stinche 7) South of Via Ghibellina, this is widely considered the city's best *gelati*.

**I Fratellini** (Map p218; ☎ 055 239 60 96; Via dei Cimatori 38r; panini €2-3) A Florence institution; for nearly 130 years it's been dishing up the freshest (and quickest!) made-to-order takeaway *panini*. The only place to go if you need a snack to go. Brave the hordes.

## Drinking

Drinking alcohol in Florence can be pricey (from €5). Stick to cocktails or the *aperitivo*/happy hours.

**Gilli** (Map p218; ☎ 055 21 38 96; Piazza della Repubblica 39r; ☺ Wed-Sun) The city's grandest café. Gloriously evocative, Gilli sends you straight back to the *belle époque*.

**Cabiria** (Map pp216-7; ☎ 055 21 53 72; Piazza Santa Spirito 4/r; ☺ late Wed-Mon) Blissful bar with an understated vibe lending itself perfectly to hours

**ITALY**

**THE AUTHOR'S CHOICE**

**Joshua Tree Pub** (Map pp164–5; www.thejosh uatreepub.com; Via della Scala 37r; happy hour pint €2.60; ☺ 4pm-1am, happy hour 4-9pm) Happy hour is actually five, which means plenty of posturing patrons with piercings who know more about how to 'feign sin' than Sinn Fein... Exaggerated gestures and stunt smoking abound, but Florence's coolest little pub still (sham)rocks, more often to the Beta Band or DJ Shadow than U2 or the Pogues, but the Guinness is still great. If you snag a seat, keep it – the Tree is tiny. Chilled owner Massimo is a relaxed sweetie, calm amidst the clamour. Smoky, rowdy and totally addictive.

of languid people watching. Popular for all the right reasons, pulling a diverse crowd.

**La Dolce Vita** (Map pp216–7; ☎ 055 28 45 95; Piazza del Carmine 6/r; ☺ Mon-Thu, to 3am Fri-Sun) Check your style meter – go toe to toe with the fashionistas at this great cocktail bar. Fab décor and swish drinks make a grand night out at this hipster magnet.

**Elliot Braun Bar** (Map pp216–7; ☎ 055 35 23 52; Via Ponte alle Mosse 117r; ☺ 10am-4pm Mon-Fri & 6pm-2am Mon-Sat, aperitivo 6-8pm) An alt-cool mishmash that's a unique treat: art exhibits, cocktails, food, live music and renowned for its *aperitivo*; buy a drink and gorge on the monster buffet at the bar. Anywhere else it would be freeloading – in Italy, it's called 'timing'.

**Angie's Pub** (Map p218; ☎ 055 28 37 64; Via De Neri 35r; snacks €3-5; ☺ noon-1am Mon-Sat, 6pm-1am Sun) One of Florence's better pubs does great on-the-cheap lunches, with a huge *panini* list. There's cold beer to hand, as well as other light meal options and plentiful good cheer.

## Entertainment

*Firenze Spettacolo*, the definitive monthly entertainment guide, is sold at newsstands (€1.75). Concerts, opera and dance are performed year-round at the **Teatro Comunale** ( ☎ 800 11 22 11; Corso Italia 16). Original-language films screen at the **Odeon Cinehall** (Map p218; ☎ 055 21 40 68; www.cinehall.it, in Italian; Piazza Strozzi; tickets €7.20; ☺ Mon, Tue & Thu, other days Italian only).

## Shopping

Shopping is concentrated between the Duomo and the Arno, with boutiques along Via Roma, Via dei Calzaiuoli and Via Por Santa Maria, leading to the goldsmiths lining the Ponte Vecchio.

**Open-air market** (Map p218; Piazza San Lorenzo; ☺ Mon-Sat) Just north of the Duomo and offering leather goods, clothing and jewellery, sometimes of dubious quality.

**Flea market** (Map pp216–7; Piazza dei Ciompi; ☺ daily) Off Borgo Allegri and north of Santa Croce, is better for finding genuine bargains.

## Getting There & Away

Florence is served by two airports. **Amerigo Vespucci** ( ☎ 055 306 15, flight info ☎ 055 306 13 00/02), 5km northwest of the city centre, serves domestic and European flights. **Galileo Galilei** ( ☎ 050 84 92 02) is 50 minutes away, near Pisa, and one of northern Italy's main air-transport hubs.

The **SITA bus station** (Map pp216–7; ☎ 800 37 37 60; Via Santa Caterina da Siena 17) is just west of the train station. Buses leave for Siena, San Gimignano and Volterra. **Lazzi** (Map pp216–7; ☎ 055 35 10 61; Piazza Adua 1), next to the station, runs services to Rome, Prato (€2.20, 45 minutes, every 30 minutes), Pistoia (€2.70, 50 minutes, nine daily), Lucca (€4.70, 1½ hours, 18 daily) and Pisa (€6.20, two hours, hourly).

Florence is on the main Rome–Milan train line; call ☎ 848 88 80 88 for details or visit the **train information office** ( ☎ 7am-9pm) at the station.

Florence is connected by the Autostrada del Sole (A1) to Bologna and Milan in the north and Rome and Naples to the south. The Firenze-Mare motorway (A11) links Florence with Prato, Pistoia, Lucca, Pisa and the Versilia coast, and a *superstrada* (dual carriageway) joins the city to Siena.

## Getting Around
### TO/FROM THE AIRPORT

Regular trains to Pisa airport (1½ hours, 6.45am to 5pm) leave from platform five at Santa Maria Novella station. Check your bags in at the **air terminal** ( ☎ 21 60 73) near platform five at least 15 minutes before train departure time. You can get to Amerigo Vespucci Airport (€4, 25 minutes, every 30 minutes 6am to 11.30pm) by the Vola in Bus shuttle, which departs from the SITA coach depot in Via Santa Caterina da Siena. Tickets can be bought on the bus.

## BUS

ATAF buses service the city centre and Fiesole. The most useful terminal is in a small piazza to the left as you exit the station onto Via Valfonda. Bus No 7 leaves for Fiesole and stops at the Duomo. Tickets (one/three/24 hours €1/1.80/4) must be bought prior to boarding and are sold at most tobacconists and newsstands.

### CAR & MOTORCYCLE

There are several car parks dotted around the city centre. A good choice is **Fortezza da Basso** (per hr €1.10; ☼ 24hr). Further details are available from **Firenze Parcheggi** ( ☎ 055 500 19 94). To rent a car, try **Hertz** ( ☎ 055 239 82 05; Via M Finiguerra 33r) or **Avis** ( ☎ 055 21 36 29; Borgo Ognissanti 128r).

# PISA

**pop 92,000**

Pisa's iconic leaning tower is among Italy's most popular sights, and a godsend to producers of tourist kitsch.

Today an otherwise quiet university town, Pisa was once a maritime power rivalling Genoa and Venice, and the home of Galileo Galilei (1564–1642). Levelled by the Genoese in the 13th century, its history eventually merged with that of Florence, its bigger neighbour up the River Arno. You'd be pressed to find reasons for an extended stay, but the city retains a certain charm.

## Orientation

The Campo dei Miracoli is a 1.5km walk from the train station across the Arno. Bus No 3 will save time. The medieval town centre around Borgo Stretto is 1km or so from the station.

## Information

### INTERNET ACCESS

**Internet Planet** ( ☎ 050 83 07 02; Piazza Cavallotti 3-4; per hr €3.10; ☼ 10am-midnight Mon-Sat, 2pm-midnight Sun)

### LAUNDRY

**Onda Blu** ( ☎ 800 86 13 46; Via San Francesco 8a; 7kg wash/dry €5/5; ☼ 8am-10pm)

### TOURIST INFORMATION

**Tourist offices** Piazza del Duomo ( ☎ 050 56 04 64; ☼ 9am-6pm Mon-Sat, 10.30am-4.30pm Sun); Piazza della Stazione ( ☎ 050 4 22 91; ☼ 9am-7pm Mon-Sat, 9.30am-3.30pm Sun); Airport ( ☎ 050 50 37 00)

## Sights

Pisans claim their **Campo dei Miracoli** (Field of Miracles) is among the most beautiful squares in the world. This is up for debate. While the immaculately manicured lawns provide a gorgeous backdrop for the cathedral, baptistry and bell tower – all leaning – you do have to grit your teeth while making your way through throngs of tat-waving hawkers to approach them. It's a little underwhelming precisely because the square is so spartan – there's nothing going on apart from slanting.

And enchanting. The buildings are gorgeous. The candy-striped **cathedral** (admission €2; ☼ 10am-7.40pm Mon-Sat, 1-7.40pm Sun summer, 10am-12.45pm & 3-4.45pm Sun winter), begun in 1063, has a graceful façade and cavernous interior. The transept's bronze doors, facing the tower, are by Bonanno Pisano, while the 16th-century bronze entrance doors are by Giambologna. The cathedral's cupcake-like **battistero** (baptistry; admission €5; ☼ 8am-7.40pm summer, 9am-4.40pm winter), begun in 1153 (completed 1260), contains a pulpit by Nicola Pisano.

The irony is, Bonnano's biggest mistake ended up being his signature work. The campanile, better known as the **Leaning Tower** (Torre Pendente; www.opapisa.it; admission €15; ☼ 8am-8pm summer, 9am-7pm winter), was wonky immediately; just three of the tower's eventual seven tiers were completed before it started tilting, continuing at a rate of about 1mm per year.

British engineer John Burland was given the task of saving the tower in the early '90s. Burland marvelled at how the tower hadn't fallen; computer models showed the landmark should've toppled once the lean hit 5.4 degrees. In 1990, it was already at 5.5 degrees. But by 2001, 'the old lady of Pisa' was restored to her (secure) 1838 angle by Burland's cunning use of biased weighting and soil drilling, making her sink back into a safer position. In theory, the tower might be in 1990-like peril again in about 300 years. Today it is almost 4.1m off the perpendicular, despite the 11 years of ground-levelling work.

Visits are limited to groups of 30; entry times are staggered and waiting is inevitable. There are many combo-tickets, but admission to the Leaning Tower is always separate.

## Sleeping

**Ostello per la Gioventù** ( ☎ /fax 050 89 06 22; Via Pietrasantina 15; dm €22; ☒ closed 9am-6pm) The youth hostel is basic but friendly and clean. Take bus No 3 from the station, or it's an easy 10-minute walk from the Campo dei Miracoli.

**Hotel di Stefano** ( ☎ 050 55 35 59; www.hoteldistefano .pisa.it; Via Sant'Apollonia 35-37; s/d/tr/q €70/85/110/120, s/d with shared bathroom €45/60) Simply decorated rooms and a lovely breakfast terrace are just two worthy features of this good hotel. It is within walking distance from all sights, in a calm street behind lovely Piazza dei Cavalieri.

**Hotel Francesco** ( ☎ 050 55 54 53; www.hotel francesco.com; Via Santa Maria 129; s/d from €75/110; ☐ ) Fantastic three-star with good disabled access, friendly service and comfortable rooms that feature every imaginable convenience. There's a great buffet breakfast and you're literally down the road from the Campo dei Miracoli. It also hires bikes and scooters; a great way to see Pisa.

**Villa Kinzica** ( ☎ 050 56 04 19; fax 050 55 12 04; Piazza Arcivesovado 2; s/d/tr with breakfast €77/103/123) Lovely refurbished place, souvenir-throwing distance from the tower – some rooms have views of Pisa's centrepiece (ask when you book). Pleasant decorations won't distract from the comforts afforded by the good appointments and polite service.

## Eating

**Antica Trattoria il Campano** ( ☎ 050 58 05 85; Vicolo Santa Margherita; mains €25; ☒ Thu-Tue) Outstanding Tuscan grub in a dungeon-esque, vaulted-ceilinged, medieval atmosphere. If you and a friend are really hungry, kick off with the *Tagliere del Re* ('cut of the king') – a staggering platter of 12 kinds of regional antipasti. You shouldn't need a second course.

**La Tana** ( ☎ 050 58 05 40; Vicolo San Frediano 6; 1st course €4, mains €10-14; ☒ Sat-Thu) Studenty hot spot dishing up voluminous pizza and pasta options. Atmospheric and friendly, with tasty food and fab service. It'll be hard to stay vewy qwiet after sampling its delicious *spaghetti al coniglio* (spaghetti with rabbit).

**Trattoria La Buca** ( ☎ 050 56 06 60; Via Gallit Tussi 6; mains €6-10, pizzas €6; ☒ Sat-Thu) Highly recommended trattoria doing hearty Tuscan fare at reasonable prices. Cheap pizzas are a budget winner, but the whole menu's great. Subdued ambience.

## Getting There & Away

The airport, with domestic and European flights, is minutes away by train, or bus No 3 from the station. **Lazzi** ( ☎ 050 462 88) buses run to Florence via Lucca. Pisa is linked by train to Florence, Rome and Genoa.

## SIENA

### pop 54,350

Don't miss Siena. Despite being surrounded by glamorous neighbours, it's a captivating and beautifully preserved town. Surrounded by mostly intact ramparts, its corkscrew-coiled streets and labyrinthine centre are jam-packed with majestic Gothic buildings in various shades of 'burnt sienna'. It's also usually teeming with visitors.

According to legend, Siena was founded by the sons of Remus (who was one of Rome's founders). In the Middle Ages the city became a free republic. Its dramatic rise – on the back of banking skill – was the cause of political and cultural friction with Florence. Painters of the Sienese School (most notably 13th to 15th centuries) produced significant works of art, and the city was home to St Catherine and St Benedict.

## Orientation

Leaving the train station, cross the concourse to the bus stop opposite for bus No 3, 9 or 10 to central Piazza Gramsci, then walk along Via dei Termini (10 minutes to Piazza del Campo). Visitors' cars aren't permitted in the centre.

## Information

**Ambulance** ( ☎ 118)

**Internet Train** Via di Città 12 (per hr €5); Via di Pantaneto 57 (per hr €5)

**Libreria Senese** ( ☎ 0577 28 08 45; libreria_senese@ libero.it; Via di Citta 62/66) A fantastic bookshop with English books and, more interestingly, a professional-standard language-instruction section.

**Police station** (Questura; ☎ 0577 20 11 11; Via del Castoro 23) Near the Duomo.

**Post office** (Piazza Matteotti 1) North of the centre.

**Tourist office** ( ☎ 0577 28 05 51; www.terresiena.it; Piazza del Campo 56; ☒ 9am-7pm) Can explain the chicanery of the myriad tickets permitting entry to Siena's sights.

**Wash & Dry** (Via di Pantaneto 38; wash/dry €3.50/€3.50; ☒ 8am-10pm)

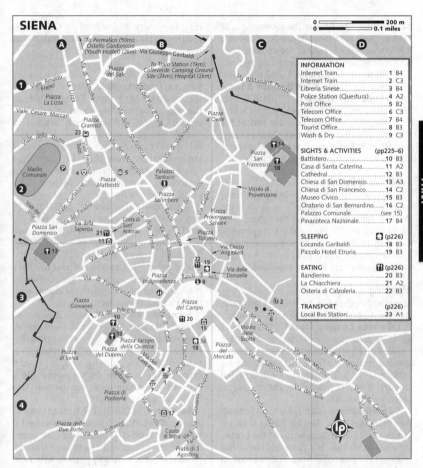

## SIENA

| 0 | 200 m |
| 0 | 0.1 miles |

## Sights & Activities

Siena's uniquely shell-shaped **Piazza del Campo** (simply, Il Campo) has been the city's focus for 700 years. The piazza's base is formed by the nobly proportioned **Palazzo Pubblico** (Town Hall; admission/tower/both €5.50/6.50/9.50; ☼ 10am-7pm mid-Mar–end Oct, to 5.30pm end Nov–mid-Feb, to 6.30pm rest of the year), also known as Palazzo Comunale, which once counted among Italy's most graceful Gothic buildings. Climb the 102m-high **Torre del Mangia** (bell tower) for a pigeon's-eye view of proceedings, as well as those pretty red roofs.

The entirely spectacular **Duomo** (admission free; ☼ 7.30am-7.30pm Mon-Sat, 2-7.30pm Sun mid-Mar–Oct, 7.30am-5pm Mon-Sat, 2-5pm Sun Nov–mid-Mar) is another Gothic masterpiece. Begun in 1196,

extravagant expansion plans were stymied by the niggling arrival of the Black Death in 1348, claiming nearly 70,000 of Siena's 100,000 people. Venice's aside, Siena has the most striking cathedral interior in northern Italy. The green-red-and-white-striped marble of the exterior is, incredibly, maintained throughout – a noteworthy distinction from comparable, or even grander, cathedrals; Florence's Duomo, despite dramatic external decoration, is bland inside.

The Romanesque lower section has carvings by Giovanni Pisano, and the inlaid-marble floor features 56 biblical panels. Other artworks include a bronze of St John the Baptist by Donatello, and statues of St Jerome and Mary Magdalene by Bernini. The

**battistero** (baptistry; Piazza del Duomo; admission €2.50; ⊙9am-7.30pm mid-Mar–Sep, to 6pm Oct, 10am-1pm & 2.30-5pm Nov–mid-Mar) behind the cathedral has a Gothic façade and 15th-century frescoes.

Want to see the preserved head of a saint? Head for the **Chiesa di San Domenico & Santuario di Santa Caterina** (shop ☎ 0577 28 68 48; Piazza San Domenico; free; ⊙7.30am-1pm & 3-6.30pm), where St Catherine's is displayed (plus part of her thumb). The church itself is tranquil and airy, and friendly Federico Muzzi in the souvenir shop sells some funky Christian kitsch.

## Festivals & Events

Siena is divided into 17 *contrade* (districts) and 10 are chosen annually to contest the **Palio**, a tumultuous horse race (and pageant) held in the Piazza del Campo on 2 July and 16 August. Securing accommodation during the Palio will require foresight or luck as it's very heavily touristed.

## Sleeping

It's always advisable to book in advance, but for August and the Palio, it's essential.

**Colleverde Camping Ground** (☎ 0577 28 00 44; Strada di Scacciapensieri 47; per person/tent €8/8; ⊙late Mar-early Nov) Siena's handiest camping ground is 2km north of the historic centre (take bus No 3 from Piazza Gramsci). Tell the driver you're headed for the *campeggio* (cam-*peh*-gee-oh).

**Ostello Guidoriccio** (☎ 0577 522 12; Via Fiorentina; dm with breakfast €16.50) The HI hostel is an inconvenient 2.5km haul north of the centre, up a hill in Stellino. It's clean and bland, but cheap. Take bus No 3 from Piazza Gramsci and tell the driver you're after the *ostello* (hostel). Rooms are quiet, and shutters afford pitch-black rooms, at least ensuring a good night's sleep.

**Piccolo Hotel Etruria** (☎ 0577 28 80 88; fax 0577 28 84 61; Via delle Donzelle 3; s/d/tr/q €44/73/96/119, s with shared bathroom €39) Siena's best all-round value (despite no breakfast); you practically exit onto the Campo! Basic, large rooms are passable, and the 12.30am curfew won't hinder as Siena rarely kicks on that long. Location doesn't get any better than this.

**Locanda Garibaldi** (☎ 0577 28 42 04; Via Giovanni Dupré 18; d/tr/q €70/89/108, menus €15) Fresh from a facelift a few years back, this good option with passable rooms behind the town hall also has a good trattoria. Marcello is an amiable host, flitting fluidly between run-

ning his eatery and managing the accommodation. He'll bargain in nonpeak times, too, so call ahead.

## Eating

**Osteria di Calzoleria** (☎ 0577 28 90 10; Via di Calzoleria 12; mains €15-20; ⊙dinner) Fantastic hole in the wall on a winding street meandering off the Campo, with evocative Tuscan fare and exceptionally good *contorni* (vegetable side dishes); two or three make a great vegetarian meal. A great place to slurp some *ribollita*, a dense vegetable soup, or twirl perfect *pici*, the traditional Sienese thick pasta, round yer fork.

**La Chiacchiera** (The Chatterbox; ☎ 0577 28 06 31; Costa di Sant'Antonio 4; mains €15-20; ⊙lunch & dinner) This rustic place has wooden stools and handwritten menus. An evocative setting for an ideal meal; try the *trippe* (tripe) if you're game – it's a serious threat to offal's bad culinary rep. Served in a garlicky sauce, it's an aeons-old Tuscan traditional dish too few have the audacity to try.

**Permalico** (☎ 0577 411 05; www.permalico.net; Via di Camollia 193; mains €15; ⊙lunch & dinner Mon-Sat) Just north of the centre is this great little medieval cavern/tavern, complete with vaulted ceilings, serving simple Tuscan grub. A fine place to grab a *panini* and a beer, or something more substantial. Also has an excellent wine list.

**Bandierino** (☎ 0577 28 22 17; Piazza del Campo 66; pizza/pasta from €8/10; ⊙lunch & dinner) The best if you must eat on Il Campo. Prices are steepish but the pastas and risotti are excellent, particularly the *ai funghi porcini*, with rich, musty mushrooms; worth opting for over the popular (and cheaper) pizzas. Your politeness will be matched by the brisk staff; just don't slow them down.

## Getting There & Away

Regular Tra-In buses run from Florence to Siena, arriving at Piazza Gramsci. Local buses also go to San Gimignano (€5, 1½ hours, hourly), Volterra (€4.50, 50 minutes, hourly) and other points in Tuscany, and there are daily buses to Rome (€16, three hours, 10 daily). For Perugia (€11, two hours), buses leave infrequently from the train station; inquire at the tourist office. Siena is not on a main train line; from Rome you'll have to change at Chiusi (from Florence, at Empoli).

## SAN GIMIGNANO

pop 7100

In a region famed for its beauty, this tiny hill-top town deep in the Tuscan countryside is still gaspworthy. It's not really the town itself – these days custom-built for tourists – that appeals but some of the incredible vistas available from climbing its steep walkways or remaining towers (of an original 72 built as fortified homes for the town's 11th-century feuding families, 13 remain). The best time to visit is midweek, preferably in deepest winter.

The **Pro Loco tourist office** ( ☎ 0577 94 00 08; Piazza del Duomo 1; ☺ 9am-1pm & 3-7pm, to 6pm in winter) is in the town centre.

Climb San Gimignano's tallest tower, **Torre Grossa**, off Piazza del Duomo, for utterly stunning views of the hills. Entrance is via the **Palazzo del Popolo**, which houses the **Museo Civico** ( ☎ 0577 94 00 08; adult/child €5/4; ☺ 9.30am-7.20pm Mar-Oct, 10am-5.50pm Nov-Feb). The **Duomo**, known also as the Collegiata, has a Romanesque interior, frescoes by Ghirlandaio in the **Cappella di Santa Fina** and a gruesome *Last Judgment* by Taddeo di Bartolo.

### Sleeping

San Gimignano is generally visited from Florence or Siena. Hotels are expensive but there are *affittacamere*, and *agriturismo* is well-organised locally. See the tourist office.

**Foresteria Monastero di San Girolamo** ( ☎ 0577 94 05 73; Via Folgore 26-32; dm with breakfast €23) If budget's the priority and you don't mind moderating your behaviour, the sweet nuns at Girolamo run the best budget option. Mind your Ps & Qs, now.

**Hotel La Cisterna** ( ☎ 0577 94 03 28; www.hotel cisterna.it; Piazza della Cisterna 24; s/d/tr with breakfast €70/90/120; P ✖ ☐ ) If you can afford a splurge, soak up the medieval ambience and awesome views on offer at this excellent hotel. If you've decided to stay, you may as well go the whole hog.

### Eating

For good pasta and decent local wines, stop at **Il Castello** ( ☎ 0577 94 08 78; Via del Castello 20; pastas €5-6), a fine way to punctuate a day's walking, while **Gelateria di Piazza** ( ☎ 0577 94 22 44; Piazza della Cisterna 4; ☺ Mar–mid Nov) provides the obligatory *gelato*.

### Getting There & Away

Regular buses link San Gimignano with Florence and Siena, arriving at Porta San Giovanni.

# UMBRIA & MARCHE

Umbrians consider their hilly region the green heart of Italy. Exemplified in its many medieval hill towns – any of which makes a fantastic excursion – the area's noted for its Romanesque and Gothic architecture. Assisi, Gubbio, Spello, Spoleto, Todi and Orvieto are all accessible from Perugia, the region's sedate but beguiling capital.

Mountainous Marche is more appealing than the mildly grim coastal capital Ancona suggests; nothing can mar the prettiness of its elevated northern villages, particularly the medieval centre of gorgeous Urbino.

## PERUGIA

pop 158,300

Perugia is a well-preserved hill town offering sweeping panoramas at every turn. Best known for its University for Foreigners (established 1925), attracting many international students, the city is also noted for the Umbria Jazz Festival (July) and another excessive indulgence; chocolate.

Highlights, or lowlights, of Perugia's history, bloody even by medieval standards, include the vicious internal feuding of the Baglioni and Oddi families, and the death of a few popes. Art and culture, however, have thrived: painter Perugino and Raphael, his student, both worked here.

### Orientation & Information

Perugia's hub is Corso Vannucci, running north-south from Piazza Italia, through Piazza della Repubblica, ending at Piazza IV Novembre. Get to the centre from the train station with any bus to Piazza Italia, where you then get a **scala mobila** (public escalator; free; ☺ 6.45-1.45am) uphill to the medieval heart.

**InfoUmbria** ( ☎ 075 57 57; Largo Cacciatori delle Alpi 3b) An excellent independent tourist office.

**Internet Train** (Via Ulisse Rocchi 30; per hr €4)

**Post office** (Piazza Matteotti; ☺ 8.10am-6pm Mon-Sat)

**Tourist office** ( ☎ 075 572 33 27; Palazzo Dei Priori, Piazza IV Novembre 3; ☺ 8.30am-1.30pm & 3.30-6.30pm Mon-Sat, 9am-1pm Sun) Opposite the Duomo.

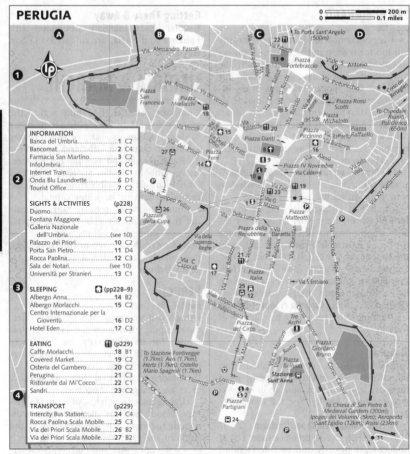

**PERUGIA**

INFORMATION
Banca del Umbria...................1 C2
Bancomat.............................2 C4
Farmacia San Martino............3 C2
InfoUmbria...........................4 C4
Internet Train.......................5 C1
Onda Blu Laundrette..............6 D1
Tourist Office........................7 C2

SIGHTS & ACTIVITIES        (p228)
Duomo.................................8 C2
Fontana Maggiore..................9 C2
Galleria Nazionale
   dell'Umbria....................(see 10)
Palazzo dei Priori.................10 C2
Porta San Pietro...................11 D4
Rocca Paolina......................12 C3
Sala dei Notari..................(see 10)
Università per Stranieri.........13 C1

SLEEPING              (pp228–9)
Albergo Anna......................14 B2
Albergo Morlacchi................15 C2
Centro Internazionale per la
   Gioventù.........................16 D2
Hotel Eden.........................17 C3

EATING                    (p229)
Caffe Morlacchi...................18 B1
Covered Market...................19 C2
Osteria del Gambero.............20 C2
Perugina............................21 C3
Ristorante dal Mi'Cocco.........22 C1
Sandri...............................23 C2

TRANSPORT               (p229)
Intercity Bus Station.............24 C4
Rocca Paolina Scala Mobile....25 C3
Via dei Priori Scala Mobile.....26 B2
Via dei Priori Scala Mobile.....27 B2

## Sights & Activities

Perugia's austere **Duomo** ( ☎ 075 572 38 32; Piazza IV Novembre; admission free; ☑ 8am-noon & 4pm-sunset) has an unfinished two-tone façade. Inside are artworks from the 15th to 18th centuries, as well as the Virgin Mary's wedding ring, unveiled every 30 July. The **Palazzo dei Priori** is a rambling 13th-century palace housing the impressively frescoed **Sala dei Notari** ( ☎ 075 573 03 66; Corso Vanucci 15; admission free; ☑ 9am-1pm & 3-7pm Tue-Sun, daily Jun-Sep) and the **Galleria Nazionale dell'Umbria** ( ☎ 075 572 10 09; www.galleria nazionaledellumbria.it, in Italian; Corso Vanucci 19; adults €6.50, 18-25 yr olds €3.25, EU citizens under 18 & over 65 free; ☑ 8.30am-7.30pm), with works by Perugino and Fra Angelico. The fountain in Piazza IV Novembre is the 13th-century **Fontana Mag-**

**giore**, designed by Fra Bevignate (1278) and carved by Nicola and Giovanni Pisano.

At the other end of Corso Vannucci is the **Rocca Paolina** (Paolina Fortress), the ruins of a massive 16th-century citadel. A series of escalators pass through the underground ruins, sometimes used to host exhibitions. Etruscan remains in Perugia include the **Arco Etrusco** (Etruscan Arch), near the university, and the **Pozzo Etrusco** (Etruscan Well), near the Duomo.

## Sleeping

**Centro Internazionale per la Gioventù** ( ☎ 075 572 28 80; www.ostello.perugia.it; Via Bontempi 13; dm €11.50, sheets €1.50; ☑ from 4pm, midnight curfew, closed Dec-Jan) Possibly Italy's best hostel for value and comfort. The TV room's frescoed ceiling beats anything on the screen, the terrace view's fabulous and there's a guest kitchen. Just don't arrive before 4pm.

**Albergo Anna** ( ☎ 075 573 63 04; www.albergoanna .it; Via dei Priori 48; s/d €40/58, with shared bathroom €30/48) Charming place with delightful rooms off Corso Vannucci, full of character and antiques, and a super-friendly owner (Signora Emma Citti). Great value for this comfort.

**Albergo Morlacchi** ( ☎ 075 572 03 19; Via Leo Tiberi 2; s/d from €38/65, s with shared bathroom from €28; P ☒ ☒ ) A lovely, art-filled place with well-maintained rooms, including phone, TV, antique furnishings, indoor plants and subdued elegance. Pretty and peaceful.

**Hotel Eden** ( ☎ 075 572 81 02; www.hotel eden.191.it; Via Cesare Caporali 9; s/d/tr/q €36/57/77/103; P ☒ ☒ ☒ ) If brightness appeals, the white rooms at Hotel Eden are a perfect place for 'tired starlings' to nest. They're also great value and tended by friendly staff in this 700-year-old building on a quiet street. There are modem points in the rooms for tech-toting travellers, too – rare at this price.

## Eating

**Mercato Coperto** (covered markets; ☒ 7am-1.30pm Mon-Sat) Downstairs from Piazza Matteotti, you can buy fresh vegetables, bread, meat and condiments.

**Caffe Morlacchi** ( ☎ 075 572 17 60; Piazza Morlacchi 8; snacks €7-12; ☒ 8-1am Mon-Sat) THE meeting place in Perugia and kick-off place for many a *festa dell' laurea* (graduation celebration) is also a great spot to grab a light meal. Absolutely packed at peak times, with good reason.

**Ristorante dal Mi'Cocco** ( ☎ 075 573 25 11; Corso Giuseppe Garibaldi 12; mains €6-7, set menus €13; ☒ Tue-Sun) Super place near the university with long communal tables and an *antica taverna* vibe. The set menu (written in local dialect) means you eat what's dished up, and changes weekly, but it's always *dal' cocco* – from the coconut (head) of the creative chef. Luckily it's always tasty – the place is popular, so book.

**Osteria del Gambero** ( ☎ 075 572 19 76; Piazza Danti 16; mains €20-30, set menus €35) Traditional Umbrian dishes are well represented. The land- or sea-themed menus are amazing showcases of the finest ingredients prepared with the best regional know-how. Equally amazing desserts and a cracking wine list.

**Perugina** (Corso Vannucci 101; ☒ 9.30am-7.45pm, closed Mon mornings) Perugina's perfect for handling sublimated desires. Sample its legendary Baci (kisses) chocolates wrapped in romantic quotes.

**Sandri** ( ☎ 075 44 9 41; Corso Vannucci 32; ☒ 8am-11pm Tue-Sun) A Perugian institution, Sandri has the best cakes in town, as well as free chocolate nibbles at the bar.

## Getting There & Away

Perugia is not on the Rome–Florence railway line, but there are trains from both cities. Most services require a change, either at Foligno (from Rome) or Terontola (from Florence). Intercity buses leave from Piazza dei Partigiani (at the bottom of the Rocca Paolina escalators) for Rome, Fiumicino Airport, Florence, Siena and towns throughout Umbria, including Assisi, Gubbio and nearby Lake Trasimeno.

## Getting Around

The train station is way downhill from the historic centre. Catch any bus heading for Piazza Italia. Tickets (€0.80) are available from the ticket office as you leave the station.

The centre is mostly closed to cars; that's a good thing – driving in Perugia frustrates. Park downhill and take the pedestrian escalator up to the centre. There's a supervised **car park** (Piazza dei Partigiani; 1st hr €0.80, per hr thereafter €1.05; ☒ 24hr), from where you can catch the Rocca Paolina escalator to Piazza Italia, and two more car parks beside the Via dei Priori escalator.

## ASSISI

**pop 25,500**

Birthplace and spiritual home of animal-loving St Francis, picturesque Assisi is a major destination for millions of pilgrims wishing to retrace holy footsteps. Somehow this hamlet halfway up Mt Subasio manages to maintain a tranquil air regardless, particularly in the lanes off the central streets.

In September 1997, an earthquake rocked Assisi, causing damage to the upper church of the Basilica di San Francesco (St Francis' Basilica), but nowadays there is little evidence of the destruction.

The **tourist office** ( ☎ 075 81 25 34; info@iat.assisi .pg.it; Via S Croce; ☒ 8am-6.30pm Mon-Sat, 10am-1pm & 2-5pm Sun summer, 8am-2pm & 3-6pm Mon-Sat, 9am-1pm Sun winter) has information.

## Sights

If you're intending to visit the religious sites, look the part, as dress rules are applied rigidly – absolutely no shorts, miniskirts, low-cut dresses or tops allowed.

The **Basilica di San Francesco** ( ☎ 075 81 90 01; Piazza di San Francesco; admission free; ☺ 7am-7pm Apr-Sep, to 5pm Oct-Mar) comprises two churches, one above the other. The lower church is decorated with frescoes by Simone Martini, Cimabue and a pupil of Giotto, and contains the crypt where St Francis is buried. The Italian Gothic upper church has a stone-vaulted roof and decoration by Giotto and Cimabue. The frescoes in the apse and entrance were damaged in the 1997 quake.

The frescoed 13th-century **Basilica di Santa Chiara** (St Clare's Basilica; ☎ 075 81 22 82; Piazza Santa Chiara; admission free; ☺ 7am-noon & 2-7pm) contains the remains of St Clare, friend of St Francis and founder of the Order of Poor Clares. For spectacular valley views, see the massive 14th-century fortress **Rocca Maggiore** ( ☎ 075 81 52 92; Via della Rocca; admission €2.60; ☺ 10am-sunset).

## Sleeping & Eating

Assisi is well geared for tourists. Peak periods are Easter, August, September and the Feast of St Francis (3 to 4 October). The tourist office has extensive *affittacamere* listings and religious information.

**Fontemaggio** ( ☎ 075 81 36 36; Via Eremo delle Carceri 8; dm €18.50) The non-HI hostel also has camping facilities. From Piazza Matteotti, at the far end of town from the basilica, it's a 30-minute uphill walk.

**Pensione La Rocca** ( ☎ /fax 075 81 22 84; Via Porta Perlici 27; s/d €38/45; P ☒ ☒ ☐ ) Tucked away in a quiet corner, with sunny rooms, some with awesome valley views. All have en-suite facilities.

**Pizzeria Flipper** (Via San Francesco 2/d; pizza slice €2; ☺ 9am-7.30pm Thu-Tue) Fab, cheap, convenient *pizze al taglio* and calzone for mobile munching.

**Cantine Di Oddo** (Via San Francesco; mains €7-8; ☺ Thu-Tue) An apt and excellent mostly vegetarian place with mouthwateringly good spinach-and-ricotta ravioli in a basic sauce of butter and lightly fried sage. Even carnivores won't miss the meat.

## Getting There & Away

There are bus services connecting Assisi with Perugia, Foligno and other local towns, leaving from Piazza Matteotti. Buses for Rome and Florence leave from Piazzale dell'Unità d'Italia. Assisi's train station is in the valley, in Santa Maria degli Angeli on the Perugia line; a shuttle bus (€0.60, every 30 minutes) runs between Piazza Matteotti and the station.

## ANCONA

**pop 100,100**

Ancona, a largely industrial port city and capital of the Marches, is worth mentioning mostly because you may find yourself here waiting for onward ferries to Croatia, Greece or Turkey.

Take bus No 1 to get from the train station to the port. The main **tourist office** ( ☎ 071 35 89 91; www.comune.ancona.it, in Italian; Via Thaon de Revel 4; ☺ 9am-2pm & 3-6pm Mon-Fri, 9am-1pm & 3-6pm Sat, to 1pm Sun; limited in winter) is out of the way. Stazione Marittima also has a **tourist office** ( ☎ 071 20 11 83; ☺ 8am-8pm Tue-Sat & 2-8pm Sun & Mon summer). There's a **post office** (Largo XXIV Maggio; ☺ 8.15am-7pm Mon-Sat).

## Sleeping

Many backpackers sleep at the ferry terminal, but Ancona does have cheap hotels.

**Ostello della Gioventú** ( ☎ /fax 071 422 57; Via Lamaticci 7; dm €12) Around 400m from the station, clean, quiet and cheap, with a lift and bathrooms big enough for wheelchair access.

**Hotel della Rosa** ( ☎ 071 413 88; www.hoteldella rosa.it, in Italian; Piazza Rosselli 3; s/d €55/88; P ☒ ☐ ) A recently spruced-up three-star opposite the station and offering comfort in the event of an overnight stay. Rooms are adequate with all mod cons.

## Getting There & Away

Buses depart from Piazza Cavour for towns throughout the Marches. Rome is served by **Marozzi** ( ☎ 071 280 23 98). Ancona is on the Bologna–Lecce train line and easily accessible from major towns. Connect to Rome via Foligno.

Ferry operators have booths at the terminal, off Piazza Kennedy. Companies include **Superfast** ( ☎ 071 207 02 40) to Patra in Greece (€78), **Minoan Lines** ( ☎ 071 20 17 08) to Igoumenitsa and Patra (€68) and **Adriatica** ( ☎ 071 20 49 15) to Durrës in Albania (€86) and Split in Croatia (€47). Prices are one way deck class in high season.

## URBINO

pop 6000

This beautiful medieval town can be tricky to reach, but the 'pride of the Marches' rewards the effort. Birthplace of Raphael and Bramante, university-town Urbino remains a bustling centre of culture and learning. It's small, steep and the streets meander snakily around a gorgeous cobbled core that's been World Heritage listed by Unesco.

The **IAT tourist office** ( ☎ 0722 26 13; Via Puccinoti 3; ⏰ 9am-1pm Mon-Sat, 9am-1pm & 3-6pm Sun & holidays May-Sep) is central. There is a **post office** ( ☎ 0722 37 79 17; Via Bramante 18; ⏰ 8.30am-6.30pm Mon-Sat).

Urbino's centrepiece is the **Palazzo Ducale** ( ☎ 0722 32 90 57; Piazza Duca Federico; adult/child incl Galleria Nazionale €4.15/free; ⏰ 8.30am-7.15pm Tue-Sun, to 2pm Mon), designed by Laurana and completed in 1482. Enter from Piazza Duca Federico and visit the **Galleria Nazionale delle Marche**, within the *palazzo*, which features works by Raphael, Paolo Uccello and Verrocchio.

Visit the **Casa di Raffaello** ( ☎ 0722 32 01 05; Via Rafaello 57; admission €2.60; ⏰ 9am-1pm & 3-7pm Mon-Sat, 10am-1pm Sun spring & summer, morning only Nov-early Mar), where Raphael was born.

### Sleeping & Eating

The tourist office has an *affittacamere* list.

**Albergo Italia** ( ☎ 0722 27 01; www.albergo-italia-urbino.it; Corso Garibaldi 32; s/d €41/62, breakfast €8; P ✗ ✷ ) Good mid-range hotel covering a range of needs from cheap singles to deluxe doubles. Rooms are super-neat and comfortable.

**Gula** ( ☎ 0722 26 94; Corso Garibaldi 23; mains €6-10; ⏰ lunch & dinner) This is a sprawling *birreria/osteria* serving fantastic meals that are cheap, but very good, attracting a broader clientele than just local students.

### Getting There & Away

Trains don't run to Urbino. Instead, buses (running Monday to Friday) will connect to cities including Ancona, Pesaro and Arezzo. There's a bus link to the train station at Fossato di Vico, on the Rome–Ancona line, or to Pesaro on the Bologna–Lecce line. Buses to Rome (€18.10, five hours) run twice daily. Buses arrive at Piazza Mercatale, down Via Mazzini from Piazza della Repubblica.

# SOUTHERN ITALY

While not as wealthy as the north in the traditional sense, you'll be well rewarded by the south's abundant riches. The land of the *mezzogiorno* (midday sun) sizzles with palpable passion, has a rich history and honours deep cultural traditions. Here, the food is magnificent, the people can seem more open and friendly and the varied landscape is resplendently pretty. Campania, Puglia and Basilicata are still under the tourist radar in many parts, and Naples is as unforgettable as your first love.

## NAPLES

pop 1.04 million

Stunningly situated on the Bay of Naples, and lorded over by Mt Vesuvius, Naples has a wily, scrappy and ultimately irresistible charm. The Campania region's capital is edgy, raucous, overwhelming and, above all, fun. Come with your preconceptions – it's hard not to – but expect to be blown away by the disarming energy this city exudes. And yes, the drivers can be reckless and petty thieves are rampant, so look both ways and watch your back.

### Orientation

Naples lazes along the waterfront and is divided into *quartieri* (districts). Both the Stazione Centrale and the main bus terminal are off Piazza Garibaldi, east of Spaccanapoli, the city's ancient heart. Corso Umberto I, the main shopping thoroughfare, heads southwest from Piazza Garibaldi to Piazza Bovio, skirting Spaccanapoli. To the south and west, on the bay, are Santa Lucia and Mergellina, both fashionable and picturesque and a contrast with the chaotic historical centre. In the hills above is the serene and affluent Vomero district, a natural balcony with grand Vesuvian views.

### Information

#### EMERGENCY

**Police station** (Questura; ☎ 081 794 11 11, to report a stolen car ☎ 081 794 14 35; Via Medina 75) Just off Via Armando Diaz.

#### INTERNET ACCESS

**Internetbar** ( ☎ 081 29 52 37; Piazza Belllini 74; per hr €3; ⏰ 9-2am Mon-Sat, from 8pm Sun)

ITALY

**MEDICAL SERVICES**

**Ambulance** ( ☎ 081 752 06 96)

**Guardia Medica** After-hours medical service; phone numbers are listed in *Qui Napoli*.

**Ospedale Loreto-Mare** ( ☎ 081 254 27 01; Via A Vespucci) On the waterfront, near the station.

**Pharmacy** (Stazione Centrale; ☼ 8am-8pm)

**MONEY**

There are plenty of ATMs throughout the city, as well as foreign-exchange booths.

**Every Tour** ( ☎ 081 551 85 64; Piazza Municipio 5-6) Represents American Express, changes money and is a Western Union agent.

**POST**

**Main post office** (Piazza G Matteotti; ☼ 8.15am-7pm Mon-Sat) Off Via Armando Diaz.

**TELEPHONE**

**Telecom office** (Via A Depretis 40; ☼ 9am-1pm & 2-5.30pm Mon-Fri)

**TOURIST INFORMATION**

Ask for *Qui Napoli* (Here Naples), published monthly in English and Italian, listing events in the city, as well as information about transport and other services.

**Tourist offices** Stazione Centrale ( ☎ 081 20 66 66; ☼ 9am-7.30pm Mon-Sat, to 1.30pm Sun) Piazza del Gesù Nuovo ( ☎ 081 552 33 28; ☼ 9am-8pm Mon-Sat, to 3pm Sun) The office at the train station will make hotel bookings.

## Dangers & Annoyances

Although the city's home-grown Mafia, the Camorra, is still a pervasive local force, you're more likely to encounter a thief. The petty-crime rate is very high, and pickpockets, moped bandits and bag-snatchers abound, stealing at any opportunity (including from the car when stopped at a red light). Car theft is also a major problem. Pay attention at night near the station, Piazza Dante, the area west of Via Toledo and as far north as Piazza Carità.

## Sights & Activities

A good investment is the **Campania artecard** ( ☎ 800 600 601; www.napoliartecard.com; €13), giving access to six museums at reduced rates and public transport; purchase at the airport, train and metro stations and selected museums.

Start your sightseeing at Spaccanapoli, the historic centre of Naples. From the station and Corso Umberto I, turn right onto Via Mezzocannone, taking you to Via Benedetto Croce, the bustling main street of the quarter. To the left is spacious Piazza del Gesù Nuovo, with the 15th-century rusticated façade of **Chiesa di Gesù Nuovo** and the 14th-century **Basilicata di Santa Chiara**, restored to its original Gothic-Provençal style after being severely damaged by WWII bombing. The beautifully tiled **Chiostro delle Clarisse** (Nuns' Cloisters; Piazza del Gesù Nuovo; admission €4; ☼ 9.30am-1pm daily & 2.30-5.30pm Mon-Sat) is also worth visiting.

The **Duomo** ( ☎ 081 44 90 97; Via Duomo; ☼ 8am-12.30pm & 4.30-7.30pm Mon-Sat, 8.30am-1pm & 5-8pm Sun) has a 19th-century façade but was built by the Angevin kings at the end of the 13th century on the site of an earlier basilica. Inside is the **Cappella di San Gennaro**, containing the head of St Januarius (the city's patron saint) and two vials of his congealed blood. The saint is said to have saved the city from disasters such as plague and volcanic eruptions.

Turn off Via Duomo onto the very characteristic **Via Tribunali** and head for Piazza Dante, through the 17th-century **Port'Alba**, one of the city's gates. Via Roma, the most fashionable street in old Naples, heads to the left (becoming Via Toledo) and ends at Piazza Trento e Trieste and **Piazza del Plebiscito**.

In the piazza is the **Palazzo Reale** ( ☎ 081 794 40 21; admission €4.50; ☼ 9am-8pm Thu-Tue), the former official residence of the Bourbon and Savoy kings, now a museum. Just off the piazza is the world-renowned **Teatro San Carlo** ( ☎ 081 791 21 11; guided tours €5; Via San Carlo 98), famed for its perfect acoustics and lavish interior and now a ballet school.

The 13th-century **Castel Nuovo** with the **Museo Civico** ( ☎ 081 795 58 77; admission €5; ☼ 9am-7pm Mon-Sat, to 2pm Sun) on the first three floors, overlooks the ferry port. The early Renaissance triumphal arch commemorates the entry of Alfonso I of Aragon into Naples in 1443. Situated southwest along the waterfront, at Santa Lucia, is the **Castel dell'Ovo** ( ☎ 081 764 05 90; Borgo Marinaro; admission free; ☼ 9am-6pm Mon-Fri, to 1pm Sat & Sun), originally a Norman castle, surrounded by **Borgo Marinaro**, a tiny fishing village.

North of Piazza Dante, the **Museo Archeologico Nazionale** ( ☎ 081 44 01 66; Piazza Museo Nazionale; admission €6.50; ☼ 9am-7.30pm Wed-Mon) contains one of the most important collections of

TAMSIN WILSON

Santorini (Thira) Island (p307),
Cyclades, Greece

JOHN ELK III

Street café, Nafplio (Nauplion; p290),
Greece

Mykonos town (p301), Mykonos Island

ADINA TOVY AMSEL

SARA-JANE CLE

Ibiza (p409), Balearic Islands, Spain

The Alhambra (p421),
Granada, Spain

STEVE DAVEY

OLIVER STREWE

Tapas bar, San Sebastián (p394),
Spain

Mallorca (p406), Spain

JON DAVISON

# NAPLES

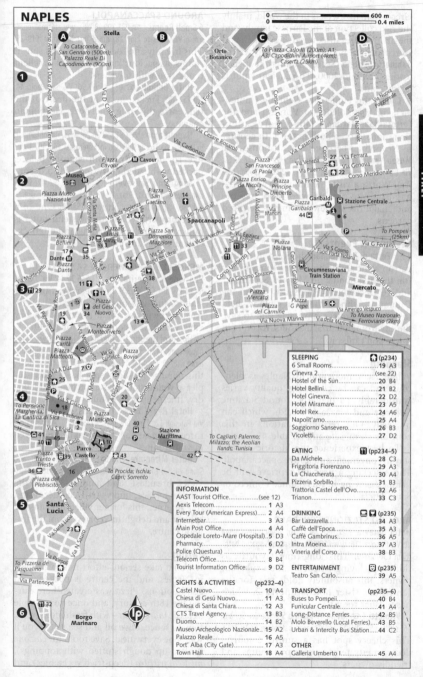

| 0 | 600 m |
| 0 | 0.4 miles |

**ITALY**

**SLEEPING** 🏠 (p234)
6 Small Rooms.................................19 A3
Ginevra 2......................................(see 22)
Hostel of the Sun..........................20 B4
Hotel Bellini.................................21 B2
Hotel Ginevra...............................22 D2
Hotel Miramare.............................23 A5
Hotel Rex.....................................24 A6
Napolit'amo..................................25 A4
Soggiorno Sansevero......................26 B3
Vicoletti......................................27 D2

**EATING** 🍴 (pp234–5)
Da Michele...................................28 C3
Friggitoria Fiorenzano....................29 A4
La Chiacchierata...........................30 A4
Pizzeria Sorbillo..........................31 B3
Trattoria Castel dell'Ovo................32 A6
Trianon.......................................33 C3

**DRINKING** 🍷 (p235)
Bar Lazzarella..............................34 A3
Caffè dell'Epoca...........................35 A3
Caffè Gambrinus...........................36 A5
Intra Moenia................................37 A3
Vineria del Corso.........................38 B3

**ENTERTAINMENT** 🎭 (p235)
Teatro San Carlo..........................39 A5

**TRANSPORT** (pp235–6)
Buses to Pompeii...........................40 B4
Funicular Centrale.........................41 A4
Long-Distance Ferries....................42 B5
Molo Beverello (Local Ferries)........43 B5
Urban & Intercity Bus Station.........44 C2

**OTHER**
Galleria Umberto I........................45 A4

**INFORMATION**
AAST Tourist Office.......................(see 12)
Aexis Telecom..............................1 A3
Every Tour (American Express)........2 A4
Internetbar..................................3 A3
Main Post Office...........................4 A4
Ospedale Loreto-Mare (Hospital)....5 D3
Pharmacy.....................................6 D2
Police (Questura)..........................7 A4
Telecom Office.............................8 B4
Tourist Information Office...............9 D2

**SIGHTS & ACTIVITIES** (pp232–4)
Castel Nuovo...............................10 A4
Chiesa di Gesù Nuovo....................11 A3
Chiesa di Santa Chiara...................12 A3
CTS Travel Agency........................13 B3
Duomo........................................14 B2
Museo Archeologico Nazionale......15 A2
Palazzo Reale...............................16 A5
Port' Alba (City Gate)....................17 A3
Town Hall....................................18 A4

Greco-Roman artefacts in the world, mainly the rich collection of the Farnese family, and the art treasures discovered at Pompeii and Herculaneum. Book a (free) tour to see the **Gabinetto Segreto** (Secret Cabinet), reopened to the public in 2000. The ancient smut is heady stuff!

Catch the Funicolare Centrale (funicular), on Via Toledo, to Vomero and the **Certosa di San Martino**, a 14th-century Carthusian monastery, rebuilt in the 17th century in Neapolitan-baroque style. It houses the **Museo Nazionale di San Martino** (☎ 081 578 17 69; Via Tito Angelini; admission €6; ☉ 8.30am-7.30pm Tue-Sun). Worth a visit, the monastery's church has exquisite marble work and frescoes and magnificent views from the terraced gardens.

## Festivals & Events

The **Festa di San Gennaro** honours the city's patron saint and is held three times a year (on the first Sunday in May, 19 September and 16 December). Thousands swarm the Duomo to witness the saint's blood, held in two vials, liquefy, a miracle said to save the city from potential disasters. If you're in town, don't miss it.

## Sleeping

While accommodation in Naples is plentiful, and can be charming, quality varies considerably, particularly around Stazione Centrale and Piazza Garibaldi, which can be seedy. Our recommendations in this zone are clean, safe and reliable.

To best experience the historic centre, stay in convenient and festive Spaccanapoli. Those seeking a peaceful reprieve will be happiest staying in Mergellina, Vomero or Santa Lucia.

### AROUND STAZIONE CENTRALE

**Hotel Ginevra** (☎ 081 28 32 10; www.hotelginevra .it; Via Genova 116; d/tr €60/100, s/d/tr with shared bathroom €30/50/70) This long-time favourite is tidily and lovingly kept by the exuberant owners; this absolutely holds true for the same-floor sister hotel, Ginevra 2, which has plusher rooms.

**Vicoletti** (☎ 081 56 41 156; Via S Domenico Soriano 46; s/d/tr €55/78/100, with shared bathroom €42/62/90) This cheery spot has a sunny, colourful décor, pretty terrace, spacious rooms and friendly owners.

### AROUND SPACCANAPOLI

**6 Small Rooms** (☎ 081 790 13 78; www.at6smallrooms .com; Via Diodato Lioy 18; dm/d incl breakfast €18/25) This friendly and sociable hostel has sun-lit rooms, a spacious kitchen and an excellent reputation with travellers.

**Hotel Bellini** (☎ 081 45 69 96; Via San Paolo 44; s/d €51/70) Tucked away in the heart of the old centre, this snug hotel oozes Neapolitan charm.

**Napolit'amo** (☎ 081 552 36 26; www.napolitamo.it, in Italian; Via Toledo 148; s/d incl breakfast €65/90) Feel like royalty in this 16th-century palace, packed with faded glory and stylish décor.

**Soggiorno Sansevero** (☎ 081 551 57 42; www .albergosansevero.it; Piazza San Domenico Maggiore 9; s/d €80/100, with shared bathroom €58/68) One of a three-property chain, this tasteful hotel is housed in a historic building and offers excellent value for money.

### MERGELLINA, VOMERO & SANTA LUCIA

**Pensione Margherita** (☎ 081 556 70 44; Via D Cimarosa 29; s/d/tr €35/62/87) Just near the funicular station, this is a no-frills place in a pretty part of town; ask for a room with a bay view, and have a coin handy for the lift.

**Hostel of the Sun** (☎ /fax 081 420 63 93; www.hostel napoli.com; Via Melisurgo 15; d €70, dm/s/d with shared bathroom €18/40/50; ☒ ) Handy for ferry travellers, this popular 7th-floor spot has a ready-to-please young staff, plus a kitchen and laundry. Internet per 30 minutes costs €2.

**Hotel Rex** (☎ 081 764 93 89; www.hotel-rex.it; Via Palepoli 12; d incl breakfast €125; ☒ ) A relaxed three-star near the sea; breakfast is served in your room.

**Hotel Miramare** (☎ 081 764 75 89; Via Nazario Sauro 24; s/d €149/203; ☒ ☐ ) With perfect bay views, breakfast (and hammocks) on the rooftop terrace, funky Art Deco décor and free Internet, this former villa offers an airy splurge and delightful reprieve from the frenetic centre.

## Eating

It would take serious effort not to eat well in Naples, and the centre is packed with good options. Pizza was created here during the 18th century, and once you sample a classic *margherita* – with fresh mozzarella, tomato sauce, olive oil and sea salt – you'll want one every meal. Save room for *calzone* (puffed-up dough stuffed with toppings), *misto di frittura* (deep-fried vegetables) and the excellent local seafood; it's worth sinning for the coffee and cakes. Naples has many good alimentari and food stalls – try **Friggitoria Fiorenzano** (Piazza Montesanto 6) and gorge yourself silly on heavenly fried vegetables at bargain prices.

### CITY CENTRE

**Da Michele** ( ☎ 081 55 39 204; Via Cesare Sersale 1; pizzas €5-7) A top contender for world's best pizza, this unpretentious place draws legions of fans who queue patiently for the masterpieces.

**La Chiacchierata** ( ☎ 081 41 14 65; Piazzetta Matilde Serao 37; mains from €8; ☯ lunch & Fri pm) This Bijou, family-run cosy spot has a loyal local following, simple and delicious fare and an on-view kitchen.

**Trianon** ( ☎ 081 553 94 26; Via P Colletta 46; pizzas €5-10) This local institution, with marble-topped tables and a warm welcome, has been tossing very good pizzas since 1923.

**Pizzeria Sorbillo** ( ☎ 081 44 66 43; Via dei Tribunali; pizzas from €5) A long lineage of talented *pizzaioli* have secured this always-packed place as a shoe-in contender for Naples' No 1 pizza parlour.

### MERGELLINA, VOMERO & SANTA LUCIA

**Pizzeria da Pasqualino** ( ☎ 081 68 15 24; Piazza Sannazaro 79; pizzas €5) Near the Mergellina station, this likeable trattoria has outdoor tables on the busy square; restore your faith in the world with its *margherita* pizza and an *insalata caprese*.

**Cantina di Sica** ( ☎ 081 556 75 20; Via C Bernini 17; mains from €10) This beloved Vomero trattoria (with vaulted ceiling), serves excellent Neapolitan fare; try the *spaghetti alle vongole e pomodorini* (clams and cherry tomatoes).

**Trattoria Castel dell'Ovo** ( ☎ 081 76 46 352; Via Luculliana 28; mains from €8) This unpretentious spot, southwest of Santa Lucia, serves well-priced, delicious seafood at harbour-side tables with lovely views of Borgo Marinaro.

## Drinking
### BARS

There is a handful of lively bars in Piazza Gesù Nuovo.

**Bar Lazzarella** (Calata Trinita Maggiore 7-8) A popular watering hole.

**Vineria del Corso** (Via Paladino 8a) Snug, with a good wine list, welcoming lighting, charming décor and low-key electronica played at a polite volume.

### CAFÉS

**Caffè Gambrinus** ( ☎ 081 41 41 33; Via Chiaia 12) Naples' oldest and most posh café remains a beloved haunt for artists, intellectuals and musicians – including saxophonist and former US president Bill Clinton.

**Intra Moenia** ( ☎ 081 29 07 20; Piazza Bellini 70; salads from €5) Tucked onto a beautiful piazza, this café/bookshop/publishing house hosts the city's intellectual elite; it's arty, literary, left leaning – with excellent salads to boot.

**Caffè dell'Epoca** ( ☎ 081 29 17 22; Via Santa Maria di Constantinopoli 81-82) Serving up Naples' best coffee in a hip way.

## Entertainment

The monthly *Qui Napoli* and local newspapers are the best guides to what's on when. In May the city organises Maggio dei Monumenti, a month of mostly free concerts and cultural events. Ask at the tourist offices for details. **Teatro San Carlo** ( ☎ 081 797 21 11; www.teatrosancarlo.it, in Italian; Via San Carlo 98; tickets from €20) has year-round concerts and performances of opera and ballet.

## Getting There & Away
### AIR

**Capodichino Airport** ( ☎ 081 789 62 59) is about 6km northeast of the city centre and links Naples with most Italian and several European cities. Take an **ANM** ( ☎ 800 63 95 25) city bus No 3S (€0.77, 30 minutes, every 15 minutes) from Piazza Garibaldi or the Alibus airport bus (€3, 20 minutes, at least hourly) from Piazza Municipio. A taxi costs about €30.

### BUS

Buses leave from Piazza Garibaldi, in front of the train station, for nearby destinations, including Salerno, the Amalfi Coast and Caserta, as well as far-flung Bari (€20, three hours), Lecce (€25, 5½ hours) and Brindisi (€23, five hours). Signage is sparse, so check destinations carefully or ask at the information kiosk.

### TRAIN

Naples is the rail hub for the south, and regular trains for most major Italian cities arrive and depart from Stazione Centrale. There are up to 30 trains daily to/from Rome.

## CAR & MOTORCYCLE

If you value your sanity and life, skip driving in Naples. The traffic is constant and chaotic, theft is rife and the street plan does not lend itself to easy navigation. But if you want to tempt fate, the city is easily accessible from Rome on the A1. The Naples–Pompeii–Salerno road (A3) connects with the coastal road to Sorrento and the Amalfi Coast.

## BOAT

Naples is above all a water city, and *traghetti* (ferries), *aliscafi* (hydrofoils) and *navi veloci* (fast ships) leave for Sorrento and the islands of Capri, Ischia and Procida from Molo Beverello, in front of Castel Nuovo. Some hydrofoils leave for the bay islands from Mergellina, and ferries for Ischia and Procida also leave from Pozzuoli. All operators have offices at the various ports from which they leave. Hydrofoils cost around double the price of ferries but take half the time. **Tirrenia** ( ☎ 199 12 31 99) operates ferries to Palermo (€45, 9¾ hours, daily) and Cagliari (€39, 13½ hours, weekly) while **Siremar** ( ☎ 081 580 03 40) services the Aeolian Islands and Milazzo. **SNAV** ( ☎ 081 428 51 11) runs hydrofoils to the islands of Capri (€12, 30 minutes), Procida and Ischia, and a daily Sicilia Jet to Palermo mid-April to September. **Caremar** ( ☎ 081 551 38 82) services Capri (hydrofoil €12, 30 minutes; ferry €6, 1½ hours), Procida and Ischia by ferry and hydrofoil.

## Getting Around

You can make your way around Naples by bus, tram, metro and funicular. City **ANM** ( ☎ 800 63 95 25) buses leave from Piazza Garibaldi for the centre of Naples and Mergellina. You can buy 'Giranapoli' tickets at stations, ANM booths and tobacconists. A ticket costs €0.77 and is valid for 1½ hours of unlimited public transit. A daily ticket is good value at €2.32. Useful buses include No 3S to the airport; the R1 to Piazza Dante; the R3 from Mergellina; and No 110 from Piazza Garibaldi to Piazza Cavour and the archaeological museum. Tram No 1 leaves from east of Stazione Centrale for the city centre. To get to Molo Beverello and the ferry terminal, take bus No R2 or M1.

The metro station is downstairs at the train station. Line one runs north from Piazza Dante, with stops at Piazza Cavour,

Salvator Rosa, Cilea, Piazza Vanvitelli, Piazza Medaglie d'Oro and seven stops beyond. Line two heads west to Mergellina, with stops at Piazza Cavour, Piazza Amedeo and the funicular to Vomero, and on to the Campi Flegrei and Pozzuoli.

The main funicular connecting the city centre with Vomero is located in Piazza Duca d'Aosta, next to Galleria Umberto I, on Via Toledo.

The Ferrovia Circumvesuviana operates trains for Herculaneum, Pompeii and Sorrento. The station is about 400m southwest of Stazione Centrale, in Corso Garibaldi (take the underpass from Stazione Centrale). The Ferrovia Cumana and the Circumflegrea, based at Stazione Cumana in Piazza Montesanto, operate services to Pozzuoli, Baia and Cumae every 20 minutes.

## AROUND NAPLES

From Naples, it's a short jaunt to **Campi Flegrei**, with volcanic lakes and mud baths that provided inspiration for the writings of both Homer and Virgil. Though now an overdeveloped suburb, the area still has tinges of its ancient Greek and Roman past, making it a worthwhile half-day trip. Take metro line two.

In the Greek colony of Cuma, visit the **Cave of the Cumaean Sybil**, home of one of the ancient world's greatest oracles. Nearby are **Lake Avernus**, a crater lake marking the mythical entrance to the underworld (and a nice picnic spot), and **Baia**, once a fashionable and debaucherous Roman resort whose submerged remains are viewable from a glass-bottomed boat.

Reached by CPTC bus (€2.70, every 30 minutes) from Naples' Piazza Garibaldi, or by train from the Stazione Centrale, is the lovely **Palazzo Reale** ( ☎ 0823 44 74 47; admission €6; ☺ 8.30am-7pm Tue-Sun) at Caserta. Built in the 18th century under the Bourbon king Charles III, who wanted his own Versailles, this imposing 1200-room palace is set in elegant gardens.

### Pompeii

In AD 79 Mt Vesuvius blew its top and buried Pompeii under layers of lapilli (burning fragments of pumice stone), killing 2000 in the deluge. The world's most famous volcano disaster left behind fascinating **ruins** ( ☎ 081 857 53 47; www.pompeiisites.org;

admission €10, combined ticket incl Herculaneum & 3 minor sites €18; ⊙ 8.30am-7.30pm Apr-Oct, 8.30-5pm Nov-Mar) that provide insight into the daily life of ancient Romans. Once a resort town for the wealthy, the vast ruins include impressive temples, a forum, an amphitheatre, and streets lined with shops and luxurious homes. Most of the site's original mosaics and frescoes are on view at Naples' Museo Archeologico Nazionale (p232), but those adorning Villa dei Misteri have stayed intact. Many ruins are open to the public and allow about four hours to visit; bring a hat or umbrella, depending on the weather.

There is a **tourist office** ( ☎ 081 850 72 55; Via Sacra 1; ⊙ 8am-3.30pm Mon-Sat Oct-Mar, 8am-7pm Mon-Sat Apr-Sep) in Pompeii town, and another **tourist office** ( ☎ 800 01 33 50; Piazza Porta Marina Inferiore 12; ⊙ 8am-3.30pm Mon-Sat) just outside the excavations at Porta Marina.

Catch the Ferrovia Circumvesuviana train from Naples and get off at the Pompeii Scavi-Villa dei Misteri stop; the Porta Marina entrance is nearby.

# CAPRI
**pop 7270**

Gorgeous Capri has been charming holiday seekers since Emperor Augustus and Tiberius made it their summer play pad around AD 27. Come summer, hordes of chatty day-trippers and swanky jetsetters pack onto the island, less than an hour by boat from Naples and heavily geared towards tourism. Nonetheless, like a deep golden tan, the place never seems to lose its appeal and remains fetchingly beautiful. Famed for its grottoes, Capri also has fantastic walking.

## Information

Online information can be found at www .capri.it and www.capritourism.com.
**Tourist offices** Marina Grande ( ☎ 081 837 06 34; ⊙ 8.30am-8.30pm); Capri town ( ☎ 081 837 06 86; Piazza Umberto I; ⊙ 8.30am-8.30pm); Anacapri ( ☎ 081 837 15 24; Piazza Vittoria 4; ⊙ 8.30am-8.30pm)

## Sights & Activities

Capri's craggy coast is studded with dozens of sea caves, visitable by boat, of which the sparkling **Blue Grotto** (admission €4; ⊙ visits 9am-1hr before sunset) is the most famous. Boats leave to visit the cave from the Marina Grande and a return trip will cost €15.30, including the

return motor boat to the grotto, rowing boat in, admission fee and singing captains; allow an hour for the trip. You'll save little money and spend more time if you catch a bus from either town, as you still have to pay for the rowing boat and admission.

You can walk to most of the interesting points on the island. Close to Capri centre are the commanding **Giardini d'Augusto**. One hour uphill, along Via Tiberio, is **Villa Jovis** (admission €2; ⊙ 9am-1hr before sunset), the ruins of one of Tiberius' villas. It's a gorgeous walk along Via Matrimonia to the **Arco Naturale** – follow the spur trail, marked by splashes of paint, winding up the piny hillside. Near Anacapri, the resplendent **Villa San Michele** ( ☎ 081 837 14 01; Viale Axel Munthe; admission €5; ⊙ 9am-6pm May-Sep, 10.30am-4.30pm Oct-Apr) was the home of Swedish writer and dog-lover Dr Axel Munthe.

## Sleeping & Eating

If you come in spring or autumn, you'll find good off-season rates.

**Albergo Stella Maris** ( ☎ 081 837 04 52; Via Roma 27; s/d €45/80) Right in the noisy heart of town and just off Piazza Umberto I, this place is convenient, with functional but small rooms.

**Hotel La Minerva** ( ☎ 081 837 03 74; www.laminerva capri.com; Via Occhiio Marino; s/d incl breakfast €80/150; ✷ ) This lovely three-star with gorgeous views, bright rooms and sunny tiles everywhere is good value, Capri-style.

**Loreley** ( ☎ 081 837 14 40; fax 081 837 13 99; Via G Orlandi 16; s/d incl breakfast €75/115; ⊙ Mar-Nov) In Anacapri, this above-average hotel has decent rooms, some with views.

**Pulalli Wine Bar** ( ☎ 081 837 4108; Piazza Umberto I; mains from €4) Perched in the clock tower overlooking Capri's main piazza, this great spot serves light meals and good vino.

**La Grottelle** ( ☎ 081 837 57 19; Via Arco Naturale 13; pasta from €8) Tucked inside a couple of small caves near Arco Naturale, this popular spot has simple and tasty dishes.

**Villa Brunella** ( ☎ 081 837 01 22; www.villabrunella .it; Via Tragara 24a; mains from €14) Away from the din, this very pretty restaurant has top service, sea views and some of the best seafood around; the attached **hotel** (d €240; ✷ ⊠ ) is equally elegant, with a nice terrace pool.

**Il Saraceno** ( ☎ 081 837 20 99; Via Trieste e Trento 18; pasta from €7) A pleasant Anacapri spot with tasty *ravioli caprese* and the proprietor's own wine and *limoncello*.

## Getting There & Around

There are hydrofoils and ferries virtually every hour from Naples' Molo Beverello and Mergellina, especially in summer. In Naples, pick up the daily *Il Mattino* for sailing times. Several companies make the trip; see p235. Hydrofoils cost about €12 each way and take about 30 minutes; ferries cost €6 each way and take about 1½ hours.

From Marina Grande, a funicular takes you to Capri, at the top of a hill some 3km from the port up a winding road. Local buses connect the port with Capri, Anacapri and other points around the island, running between the two main towns until past midnight. Tickets for the funicular and buses cost €1.30 per trip or €6.71 per daily ticket.

## SORRENTO

pop 17,450

A shameless resort town, pretty Sorrento gazes out over the Bay of Naples and lures throngs of holiday seekers to its sunny, crowded streets. Still, southern Italian charm goes straight to the soul – come off season or use as a fun, handy pause before heading to Capri and the Amalfi Coast.

## Orientation & Information

The centre of town is Piazza Tasso, a short walk from the train station along Corso Italia. If you arrive by boat at Marina Piccola, walk south along Via Marina Piccola then climb the 200 steps to reach the piazza.

**EMERGENCY**
**Ospedale Civile** ( ☎ 081 533 11 11; Corso Italia 1)
**Police station** (Questura; ☎ 081 807 44 33; Corso Italia 236)

**INTERNET ACCESS**
**Sorrento Info** (Via Tasso 19; per hr €6)

**MONEY**
**Deutsche Bank** (Piazza Angelina Laura) Has an ATM.

**POST**
**Post office** (Corso Italia 210)

**TELEPHONE**
**Telecom office** (Piazza Tasso 37)

**TOURIST INFORMATION**
**Tourist information office** ( ☎ 081 807 40 33; www.sorrentotourism.it; Via Luigi de Maio 35; ⏱ 8.45am-

6.15pm Mon-Sat) An excellent office inside the Circolo dei Forestieri complex.

## Sleeping & Eating

**Nube d'Argento** ( ☎ 081 878 13 44; www.nubedargento.com; Via del Capo 21; per person/tent €9/9.50) This nearby camping ground is tucked into a sea of olive trees and 200m from the beach; head south along Corso Italia, then follow Via Capo.

**Villa Elisa** ( ☎ 081 878 27 92; Piazza S Antonino 2; s/d €70/90) Five pretty rooms surround a courtyard at this convenient, pleasant spot with a sweet rooftop terrace and in-room kitchen facilities.

**Pensione Linda** ( ☎ 081 878 29 16; Via degli Aranci 125; s/d €35/70) This modest hotel has good value, old-fashioned courtesy, spacious rooms and eclectic but attractive furnishings.

**Hotel La Tonnarella** ( ☎ 081 878 11 53; www.latonnarella.com; Via Capo 31; d €140) This elegant roost sports pretty lemon and blue tiles, sweeping sea views and a private lift to the beach.

**Self-Service Angelina Lauro** ( ☎ 081 807 47 08; Piazza Angelina Lauro 39; pastas from €4) An economical snack venue with a nice selection for vegetarians.

**Pizzeria Gastronomia** ( ☎ 081 807 40 97; Via degli Aranci; pizzas from €3) A tasty and cheery spot opposite Pensione Linda.

**Bollicine** ( ☎ 081 878 46 16; Via dell'Accademia 9; glass of wine from €2) This snug wine bar serves good local varietals and light meals.

**La Fenice** ( ☎ 081 878 16 52; Via degli Aranci 11; mains from €8, pizzas from €4) Rightfully popular, this pretty spot serves delicious fresh seafood and good pizzas.

## Getting There & Away

Circumvesuviana trains run every 30 minutes between Sorrento and Naples via Pompeii and Ercolano. At least 12 SITA buses a day leave from outside the train station for the Amalfi Coast (€3). Hydrofoils and ferries leave for Capri (€20 return, 20 minutes), Napoli (€15 return, 35 minutes) and Ischia from the port at Marina Piccola; the tourist office has timetables.

## AMALFI COAST

This 50km of cliff-hugging coastline is some of Europe's most dazzling, luring wealthy holiday seekers who pay skyrockethigh prices in summer. Nonetheless, the natural beauty is dazzling and the lemon-terraced land and aquamarine coves aren't to be missed – save money and patience by visiting in spring or autumn.

There are tourist offices in the individual towns. For itinerary planning, www.amalfi coast.com is useful.

## Getting There & Away

SITA buses head to Sorrento (€2.30, more than 10 daily) via Positano (€1.30), and hourly to Salerno (€1.80), which is a 40-minute train trip from Naples. Buses stop in Amalfi at Piazza Flavio Gioia, from where you can catch a bus to Ravello.

The narrow, spectacular and tortuous coastal road is clogged with traffic in summer – be prepared for delays. Things are quieter at other times. **Sorrento Rentacar** ( ☎ 081 878 13 86; Corso Italia 210a, Sorrento) rents scooters and cars.

Hydrofoils and ferries service the coast between April and mid-September, leaving from Salerno and stopping at Amalfi and Positano. There are also boats between Positano and Capri, and to Naples.

## Positano

pop 3900

With its Moorish flair and colourful houses, Positano is the most photographed, fashionable and expensive town on the coast. The colourful centre is laden with boutiques (selling locally made clothing) and has more steps than streets. The hills behind the town are full of wonderful walks; pick up a hiking map at the **tourist office** ( ☎ 089 87 50 67; Via del Saracino 4; ☉ 8am-2pm & 3.30-8pm Mon-Sat year-round, 3.30-8pm Jul & Aug).

**Villa Nettuno** ( ☎ 089 87 54 01; www.villanettuno positano.it; Via Pasitea 208; s/d €70/80) On the south end of town, this cheery hotel is tucked into a pretty garden and most rooms have balconies.

**Villa Rosa** ( ☎ 089 81 19 55; www.villarosapositano.it; Via C Colombo 127; d incl breakfast €149) This charming family-run villa at the other end of town has very pretty rooms, all with terraces.

**Il Saraceno d'Oro** (Viale Pasitea 254; pizza about €6) A popular eatery with decent pizzas and exceptional profiteroles.

Nearby, the new **2next2** (Via Pasitea 242) bar has a glitterati crowd, while closer to town **Caffè Positano** (Viale Pasitea) has a small terrace ideal for a sunny cappuccino or *aperitivo* under the stars.

### AROUND POSITANO

Hikers will love the classic **Sentiero degli Dei** (Path of the Gods; five to 5½ hours) – ask at the tourist office. For a shorter option, head to **Nocelle**, a tiny village above Positano, accessible by walking track from the stairs near Bar Internazionale. Have lunch at **Trattoria Santa Croce** ( ☎ 089 81 12 60; pastas from €6; ☉ lunch & dinner spring-autumn), with panoramic views. Nocelle is accessible by local bus from Positano via Montepertuso.

Just south of Positano is the town of **Praiano**, less scenic but with the only camping ground on the Amalfi Coast. **La Tranquillità** ( ☎ 089 87 40 84; www.continental.praiano.it; Via Roma 21; 2 people & tent €39, bungalows €90) has many sleeping options, and the SITA bus stops outside.

## Amalfi

pop 5528

A maritime superpower during the 11th century, Amalfi is now a legendary tourist resort. Despite being packed to the gills in summer, the town retains an appealing vibe. In the centre is an impressive **Duomo** ( ☎ 089 87 10 59) and nearby is the **Grotta dello Smeraldo** (admission €5; ☉ 9am-4pm), a rival to Capri's Blue Grotto. This is excellent walking terrain. The **tourist office** ( ☎ 089 87 11 07; Corso Roma 19; ☉ 8.30am-1.30pm & 3-5.30pm Mon-Fri, to 12.30pm Sat) can provide details.

In the hills behind Amalfi is delightful and breezy **Ravello**, accessible by bus and walking paths, with magnificent 11th-century **Villa Rufolo** (admission €4; ☉ 9am-6pm), once the home of popes and later of the German composer Wagner. The 20th-century **Villa Cimbrone**, a Greta Garbo hideaway, is also set in pretty gardens, which end at a terrace offering a spectacular view of the Gulf of Salerno.

There are many walking paths in the hills between Amalfi and Ravello; you can also visit the vineyards surrounding the towns.

### SLEEPING & EATING

**Locanda Costa d'Amalfi** ( ☎ 089 83 19 50; Via G Augustariccio 50; s/d incl breakfast €55/60) This well-priced newcomer, a few kilometres before town, has six well-appointed rooms and a sunny air. You can get there by bus or taxi.

**Hotel Lidomare** ( ☎ 089 87 13 32; www.lidomare.it; Largo Duchi Piccolomini 9; s/d incl breakfast €50/90) This lovely family-run hotel is excellent value – romantic rooms, elegant furnishings and kind service.

**Trattoria San Giuseppe** (Salita Ruggerio II 4; pizza & pasta from €7) A tasty, family-run joint hidden away in Amalfi's maze-like alleyways; follow signs from Via Lorenzo d'Amalfi.

**Pizzeria al Teatro** (Via E Marini 19; pizza & pasta from €7) Good local dishes and a welcoming ambience. Follow the signs to the left from Via Pietro Capuana, the main shopping street.

**Cantina S Nicola** (Salita Marino Sebaste 8) This new wine bar, with vaulted ceilings and a robust by-the-glass list, is excellent for light meals.

The best pastries are at **Pasticceria Andrea Pansa** (Piazza Duomo 40), with luxe charm, and **Casbahr** (Piazza Umberto 1) gets the local vote for friendliest coffee spot.

In Ravello, just off Piazza Duomo, **Hotel Toro** ( ☎ 089 85 72 11; www.hoteltoro.it; s/d incl breakfast €74/105) is exceedingly pleasant with nice rooms and a pretty walled garden. The warm and bustling **Cumpa Cosimo** (Via Roma 44-6; mains from €8) has great food and friendly service, plus everything you eat and drink is from the family farm.

# PAESTUM

One of southern Italy's most lasting images is that of three stark white Greek **temples** ( ☼ 9am-1hr before sunset; admission €4, with museum €6.50) towering in a field of bright red poppies. This majestic trio, just south of Salerno, are among the best-preserved temples of Magna Graecia, a Unesco World Heritage site, and well worth a visit. At the site, there's an informative **tourist office** ( ☎ 0828 81 10 16; ☼ 9am-4pm) and an evocative **museum** ( ☼ 9am-7pm; admission €4, with temples €6.50). Buy a combined entrance ticket (€6.50), covering the temples and museum; separate admissions are €4 each.

Paestum is accessible by **CSTP** ( ☎ 800 01 66 59) and **SCAT** ( ☎ 0974 83 4 15) buses, departing hourly from Salerno's Piazza della Concordia, and by train.

# MATERA

pop 57,315

Unique and ancient Matera delicately balances its peasant-class past with its burgeoning modern face. Its famous *sassi* – stone houses carved into the two ravines that slice through town – were home to half the town's population through the 1950s, when the peasant class was relocated into new government housing just outside of the town. Now a Unesco World Heritage site,

the cave homes still evoke a powerful image of a poverty that's difficult to imagine in a developed European country. Mel Gibson filmed *The Passion of the Christ* in Matera, which has added a new dimension of tourism, and an additional step away from the town's poverty-stricken and malaria-ridden roots. For a refresher course, Francesco Rosi's excellent film *Cristo si é Fermato a Eboli* (Christ Stopped at Eboli), originally a book by Carlo Levi, is a poignant illustration of what life was once like in Basilicata. Today people are returning to live in the *sassi* – but as a trend rather than a necessity.

There's a **tourist office** ( ☎ 0835 33 19 83; Via De Viti De Marco 9; ☼ 9am-1pm Mon-Sat & 4-6.30pm Mon & Thu), off the main Via Romas. It's easy enough to navigate yourself through the *sassi,* particularly with the helpful map *Matera: Percorsi Turistici* (€1.30), with four easy-to-follow itineraries.

## SIGHTS & ACTIVITIES

The two *sassi* areas, **Barisano** and **Caveoso**, had no electricity, running water or sewerage system until well into the 20th century. The oldest *sassi* (dating from medieval times or earlier) are at the top of the ravines, while the dwellings in the lower sections, which appear to be the oldest, were in fact established in the 1920s – as space ran out, the population began moving into hand-hewn or natural caves. The *sassi* zones are accessible from Piazza Vittorio Veneto and Piazza del Duomo in the centre of Matera. Caveoso is the more picturesque and highlights include the rock churches or **Santa Maria d'Idris** and **Santa Lucia alla Malve**, both with well-preserved Byzantine frescoes. The 13th-century Puglian-Romanesque **cathedral**, overlooking Sasso Barisano, also warrants a stop. A couple of *sassi* have been refurnished as they were when the last peasant inhabitants occupied them, of which **Casa-Grotta di Vico Solitario** (admission €1.50) is worth a visit.

## SLEEPING & EATING

**Albergo Roma** ( ☎ /fax 0835 33 39 12; Via Roma 62; s/d €22/32) This very central hotel has basic rooms at unbeatable prices.

**Locanda Di San Martino** ( ☎ /fax 0835 25 66 00; Via San Martino 22; s/d incl breakfast €60/80) This new *sassi* hotel elegantly meshes the past and present; very pretty rooms, balconies and a cave bar.

**Le Botteghe** ( ☎ 0835 34 40 72; Piazza San Pietro Barisano 22; pastas from €6) Tasty local dishes, salads and excellent wines.

**Il Cantuccio** ( ☎ 0835 33 20 90; Via delle Beccherie 33; secondo from €7) Serves creative pastas to a local clientele – try the delicious *cavatelli al frantoio*, a local pasta dish with olives.

**Fresh-produce market** (Via A Persio) Daily market, just south of Piazza Vittoria Veneto.

### GETTING THERE & AWAY
SITA buses connect Matera with Taranto and Metaponto. Matera is on the private Ferrovie Apulo-Lucane train line, connecting with Bari, Altamura and Potenza. There are also three Marozzi buses a day between Rome and Matera (€30). Buy tickets at **Biglietteria Manicone** ( ☎ 0835 332 86 21; Piazza Matteoti 3).

## PUGLIA
The province of Puglia comprises the hardscrabble heel of Italy's boot, bound by the Adriatic and Ionian Seas. Oft dismissed as an impoverished backwater by northerners, the region knows better and seems content to quietly harbour its natural beauty and artistic brilliance. In the past, this coastline was fought over by virtually every major colonial power, from the Greeks to the Spanish, all intent on establishing a strategic foothold in the Mediterranean and leaving their architectural stamp. Today, there's a strong regional pride, the cuisine is exceptional and the area remains relatively untouristed. A helpful source for planning is www.pugliaturismo.com, in Italian.

## Brindisi
**pop 90,020**
Despite its shady reputation, Brindisi is probably more boring than dangerous. The major embarkation point for ferries to Greece, the city swarms with people in transit – and there's little to do here but wait for your boat. Most backpackers gather at the train station or ferry terminal, or in pedestrianised Piazza Cairoli or Piazza del Popolo. The old port is a 10-minute walk from the station, along Corso Umberto I, which leads into Corso Garibaldi; the new port (Costa Morena) is east of town, 7km from the station, with free bus connections linking the two.

Be exceedingly mindful of your possessions at all times, but particularly in the areas around the train station and ports.

There's a helpful **tourist office** ( ☎ 0831 52 30 72; Viale Regina Margherita 44; ☽ 8.30am-2pm & 3.30-7pm Mon-Fri, 8.30am-1pm Sat).

**Carpe Diem** ( ☎ 0831 59 79 54; Via N Brandi 2; dm €14) is a cheery private hostel 2km from town with laundry facilities and offering an evening meal (€7); hop on bus No 3 from Via Cristoforo Colombo near the train station or call for a pick-up.

Tucked off Corso Garibaldi, and a five-minute walk from the port bus stop, the modest **Hotel Altair** ( ☎ 0831 56 22 89; Via Giudea 4; s/d €30/50, with shared bathroom €20/37) with high-ceilinged rooms is ideal for early-morning departures.

The popular **Iaccato** ( ☎ 0831 52 40 84; Via Lenio Flacco 32; mains from €7) has happy owners and terrific seafood specialities.

For boat-trip supplies, hit the morning **market** (Piazza Mercato) or the **supermarket** (Corso Garibaldi 106).

### GETTING THERE & AWAY
#### Boat
Ferries, all of which take vehicles and have snack bars and restaurants, leave Brindisi for Greek destinations, including Corfu (10 to 15 hours), Igoumenitsa (nine to 12 hours) and Patra (15 to 20 hours). Boats also service Albania (daily) and Turkey (seasonal).

Most ferry companies operate only in summer. All have offices at Costa Morena, and the major ones also have offices in town along Corso Garibaldi.

Major ferry companies are **Hellenic Mediterranean Lines** (HML; ☎ 0831 52 85 31; www.hml.gr; Corso Garibaldi 8), **Blue Star Ferries** ( ☎ 0831 56 22 00; www.bluestarferries.com; Corso Garibaldi 65), **Italian Ferries** ( ☎ 0831 59 08 40; www.italianferries.it; Corso Garibaldi 96) and **Med Link Lines** ( ☎ 0831 52 76 67; www.ferries.gr/medlink; Corso Garibaldi 49).

The largest, most expensive and most reliable of the lines, HML also officially accepts Eurail and Inter-Rail passes, entitling you to travel free in deck class (paying a €15 supplement in July and August). If you intend to use your pass, it is best to reserve in advance in summer.

Discounts are available for travellers under 26 years of age and holders of some Italian rail passes. Fares generally increase by up to 40% on peak travel days in July and August, and you might save 20% on a round-trip ticket. At the time of writing, HML's low-/high-season fares for oneway

ITALY

deck-class service to Greece were €30/49; for a car €29/55; and for a motorcycle €12/20.

Look up details of fares and timetables on www.ferries.gr. Be wary of any too-good-to-be-true offers from fly-by-night operators claiming your Eurail and Inter-Rail pass is accepted by them or invalid with anyone else.

The port tax is €6, payable when you buy your ticket. Check in at least two hours before departure or risk losing your reservation. To get to the new port of Costa Morena from the train station take the free Portabagagli bus, departing a handy two hours before boat departures.

### Bus

Marozzi runs four buses daily to Stazione Tiburtina in Rome (€32.55, nine hours), leaving from Viale Arno. **Appia Travel** ( ☎ 0831 52 16 84; Viale Regina Margherita 8-9) sells tickets. There are rail connections to major cities in northern Italy, as well as to Bari, Lecce, Ancona, Naples and Rome, and you can fly to/from Rome, Naples, Milan, Bologna and Pisa from Brindisi's small airport, Papola Casale (BDS).

## Lecce

### pop 97,462

This sparkling little city hosts an astonishing array of baroque architecture and the effect is of a crazy but delightful architect gone a bit mad. Unabashedly opulent, the local style is known to Italians as *barocco leccese* (Lecce baroque), and Lecce is oft referred to as the 'Florence of the South'. The university town exudes a sassy charm and sports a vibrant bar scene at weekends. It's also home to a high population of lawyers, but don't let that discourage you from visiting this elegant surprise.

There is a sleepy **tourist office** ( ☎ 0832 24 80 92; Corso Vittorio Emanuele 24) near Piazza Duomo. The historic centre is a five-minute walk from the station, or take bus No 1, 2 or 4 from the station to Viale Marconi.

### SIGHTS

Lecce's baroque style is most famously on display at the **Basilica della Santa Croce** ( ☎ 0832 24 19 57; Via Umberto I; admission free; ☻ 8am-1pm & 4-7.30pm). A team of artists worked throughout the 16th and 17th centuries to decorate the building and its extraordinarily ornate

façade. In the **Piazza del Duomo** are the 12th-century **cathedral** (admission free; ☻ 6.30am-noon & 5-7.30pm), completely restored in baroque style by Giuseppe Zimbalo, and its 70m-high **bell tower**; the 15th-century **Palazzo Vescovile** (Bishop's Palace); and the **Seminario**, with its elegant façade and baroque well in the courtyard. The piazza is particularly beautiful at night, illuminated by floodlights. In **Piazza Sant'Oronzo** are the remains of a 2nd-century-AD **Roman amphitheatre**.

### SLEEPING & EATING

**Centro Storico Prestige** ( ☎ 0832 24 33 53; www .bbprestige-lecce.it; Via S Maria del Paradiso; per person incl breakfast €40) On the 3rd floor of a 16th-century palazzo, this gem has elegantly furnished and balconied rooms, a roof garden and a hip owner.

**Azzurretta B&B** ( ☎ 338 258 59 58; www.bblecce.it, in Italian; Via Vignes 2; s/d incl breakfast €35/63) On the same floor as the Centro Storico Prestige, and run by the same family; both are excellent city-centre options.

**Hotel Cappello** ( ☎ 0832 30 88 81; Via Montegrappa 4; s/d €30/45) For station convenience, this is your best option.

**Trattoria Casereccia** ( ☎ 0832 24 51 78; Via Colonello Costadura 19; pasta from €6) This family-run favourite serves home cooking at good value.

**Ristorante Da Guido e Figli** ( ☎ 0832 30 58 68; Via XXV Luglio 14; antipasti from €2) Both the formal dining room and take-away area have delicious food; for good value, hit the delicious self-service antipasto buffet.

### ENTERTAINMENT

Seemingly sedate Lecce comes alive on weekend nights, and there are some great little bars in its historic centre. Try **Caffè Letterario** (Via Paladini 46), where you can enjoy wine by the glass in colourful surrounds, **Al di Vino Bicchiere** (Via S Maria del Paradiso 4), an elegant little *enoteca*, **I Merli** (Via Federico D'Aragona), where locals crowd nightly, and **B Lounge** (Via Federico D'Aragona), just across the street.

### GETTING THERE & AWAY

STP buses connect Lecce with towns throughout the Salentine peninsula, leaving from Via Adua. There are frequent trains to Brindisi (€3, 40 minutes), Bari (€8, 2¼ hours), Rome (€40, seven hours), Naples (€30.50, six hours) and Bologna (€42.30, 8½ hours), as well as points throughout Puglia.

# SICILY

Sun-baked Sicily shines with visible layers of its rich and often turbulent history. Afloat in the Mediterranean, Italy's largest island coddles Greek temples, Arab domes, Byzantine mosaics, Norman churches and baroque architecture. Its magnificent landscape is dominated by Mt Etna (3350m) on the east coast, laced with fertile citrus groves, fringed with dazzling coastline, and with a vast plateau at its heart.

With a population of just over five million, Sicily has a mild climate in winter and a relentlessly hot summer. The best times to visit are spring and autumn.

Most ferries from Italy arrive at Sicily's capital, Palermo, which is convenient as a jumping-off point. If you're short on time, spend a day in Palermo and then hit Taormina, Syracuse or Agrigento.

No need to worry about a *Godfather*-style confrontation, though the Mafia does remain a powerful, if crumbling, force. Car thieves and the occasional overly friendly male local are the only safety concerns.

## GETTING THERE & AWAY
### Air
Flights from all over mainland Italy and from major European cities land at Palermo (PMO) and Catania (CTA). For information on flights to/from Sicily, contact **Alitalia** ( ☎ 00 39 06 65 641; www.alitalia.com).

### Boat
Sicily is accessible by ferry from Genoa, Livorno, Naples, Reggio di Calabria and Cagliari, and also from Malta and Tunisia. The main companies servicing the Mediterranean are **Tirrenia** ( ☎ 199 12 31 99; www.tirrenia.it) and **Grimaldi** ( ☎ 091 58 74 04; www.grimaldi.it), which runs Grandi Navi Veloci. **SNAV** (Palermo ☎ 091 58 60 66, Naples ☎ 081 761 23 48; www.snav.com) runs a summer ferry between Naples and Palermo. Prices vary by season and are highest July to September. Timetables can change each year, and it's best to check at a travel agency that takes ferry bookings. Book well in advance during summer, particularly if you have a car.

At the time of writing, high-season fares for a *poltrona* (airline-type seat) were: Genoa to Palermo (€75, 18 hours) and Livorno to Palermo (€80, 19 hours) with Grimaldi's Grandi Navi Veloci; and Naples to Palermo (€45, 9¾ hours) and Cagliari to Palermo (€39, 13½ hours) with Tirrenia.

**Virtu Ferries** (www.virtuferries.com) serves Sicily to Malta March through October.

For information on ferries going from the mainland directly to the Aeolian Islands, see p247.

### Bus
Direct bus services between Rome and Sicily are operated by **SAIS** ( ☎ 091 616 60 28; www.saistrasporti.it, in Italian; Via P Balsamo 20, Palermo) and **Segesta** ( ☎ 091 616 90 39; Via P Balsamo 16, Palermo), departing from Rome's Piazza Tiburtina. Buses service Messina (€27, 9¼ hours), Catania (€30, 11 hours), Palermo (€35, 12 hours) and Syracuse (€32.50, 11½ hours).

### Train
For train information, call ☎ 147 88 80 88 (7am to 9pm) or go to the information office at any station; the ticket cost includes the 3km ferry crossing from Villa San Giovanni (Calabria) to Messina.

## GETTING AROUND
Bus is the most common and convenient mode of public transport in Sicily. There are numerous services between Syracuse, Catania and Palermo, as well as to Agrigento and towns in the interior. The coastal train services between Messina and Palermo and Messina to Syracuse vary from efficient and reliable to delayed and unpredictable, as does the run between Palermo and Agrigento.

## PALERMO
### pop 750,000
Once regarded as Europe's grandest city, Palermo on first glance is more decrepit than dazzling, due to WWII bombing and years of neglect. Look closer and this dignified city's gilded 3000-year history – with stints as an Arab emirate and the seat of a Norman kingdom – shines through the fray. It's a fascinating city, and you'll eat like a king.

### Orientation
Palermo is a large but easily manageable city. The main streets of the historic centre are Via Roma and Via Maqueda, which extend from the central station to Piazza Castelnuovo, a vast square in the modern part of town.

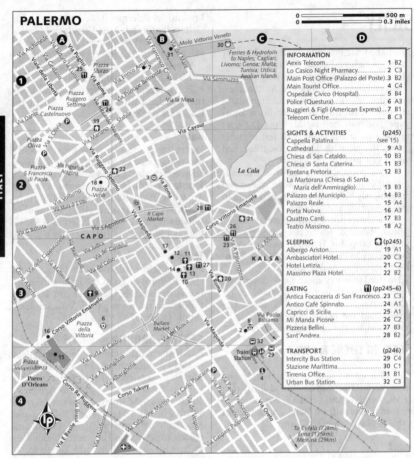

## Information

### EMERGENCY

**Police station** (Questura; theft & lost documents ☎ 091 21 01 11, foreigners office ☎ 091 651 43 30; Piazza della Vittoria; ⏰24hr)

### MEDICAL SERVICES

**Ambulance** (☎ 091 30 66 44)
**Lo Cascio** (☎ 091 616 21 17; Via Roma 1) A late-night pharmacy near the train station.
**Ospedale Civico** (☎ 091 666 11 11; Via Carmelo Lazzaro)

### MONEY

**Exchange offices** Stazione Centrale (⏰8am-8pm); Airport (⏰8am-7pm)
**Ruggieri & Figli** (☎ 091 58 71 44; Via Enrico Amari 40; ⏰9am-1pm & 4-7pm Mon-Fri, to 1pm Sat) Represents

American Express and will cash travellers cheques for cardholders only.

### POST

**Palazzo delle Poste** (Via Roma 322; ⏰8.30am-6.30pm Mon-Fri, to 12.30pm Sat)

### TELEPHONE

**Aexis Telecom** (Via Maqueda 347; Internet per hr €5) Has Internet, fax and phone services.

### TOURIST INFORMATION

**Tourist offices** Piazza Castelnuovo 35 (☎ 091 605 81 11; ⏰8.30am-2pm & 2.30-6pm Mon-Fri, 8.30am-2pm Sat); Stazione Centrale (☎ 091 616 59 14; ⏰8.30am-2pm & 2.30-6pm Mon-Fri, 8.30am-2pm Sat); Airport (☎ 091 59 16 98; ⏰8am-noon) Brochures plus helpful bimonthly *Agenda*.

## Sights & Activities

The intersection of Corso Vittorio Emanuele and Via Maqueda marks the **Quattro Canti**, the ideal and actual centre of historic Palermo. Called *il teatro*, it's marked by four 17th-century Spanish baroque façades, each decorated with a statue. Nearby Piazza Pretoria houses the beautifully ornate **Fontana Pretoria**, created by Florentine sculptors in the 16th century and dubbed the Fountain of Shame because of the cavorting nude statues; despite restoration work, you can still grab a peek. Also in the piazza are the baroque **Chiesa di Santa Caterina** and the **Palazzo del Municipio** (town hall). Around the corner in Piazza Bellini is Palermo's top wedding spot, the famous **La Martorana** ( ☎ 091 616 1692; admission free; ☼ 8am-1pm & 3.30-5.30pm Mon-Sat, to 1pm Sun) church, with a striking Arab-Norman bell tower and stunning Byzantine mosaic interior, and next to the red-domed **Chiesa di San Cataldo**, which meshes Arab and Norman styles.

In Piazza Giuseppe Verdi is the grand neoclassical **Teatro Massimo** ( ☎ 091 605 35 15; www.teatromassimo.it, in Italian; guided tours €3; ☼ 10am-4pm Tue-Sun). Built between 1875 and 1897 to celebrate the unification of Italy, the theatre has become a symbol of the triumph and tragedy of Palermo itself; appropriately, the closing scene of *The Godfather III* was filmed here.

The huge **cathedral** ( ☎ 091 33 43 76; Corso Vittorio Emanuele; admission free; ☼ 7am-7pm Mon-Sat, 8am-1.30pm & 4-7pm Sun & hols), modified often over the centuries, is a good example of Sicily's unique Arab-Norman style. At Piazza Indipendenza is **Palazzo Reale**, also known as the Palazzo dei Normanni, now the seat of the Sicilian parliament. Go downstairs to see the **Cappella Palatina** ( ☎ 091 705 48 79; admission free; ☼ 9am-11.45am & 3-4.45pm Mon-Fri, 9am-11.45am Sat, 9-10am & noon-1pm Sun), a truly jaw-dropping example of Arab-Norman architecture, designed by Roger II in 1130 and lavishly decorated with exquisite mosaics. King Roger's former bedroom, **Sala di Ruggero** ( ☎ 091 705 43 17; admission free; ☼ 9am-noon Mon, Fri & Sat), is adorned with 12th-century mosaics; you can only visit the room with a guide (free).

For a worthy foray, take bus No 389 from Piazza Indipendenza to the nearby town of **Monreale**, 8km southwest of Palermo, to see the gorgeous mosaics in the world-famous 12th-century **Duomo** ( ☎ 091 640 44 13; admission free; ☼ 8am-6pm), plus its **cloisters** (admission €4.50; ☼ 9am-7pm Mon-Sat, 9am-1.30pm Sun).

## Sleeping

**Trinacria** ( ☎ /fax 091 53 05 90; Via Barcarello 25; per person/site €4.10/7.50) The area's best camping is at Sferracavallo, by the sea. Catch bus No 628 from Piazzale Alcide de Gasperi, reached by bus No 101 or 107 from the station.

**Albergo Ariston** ( ☎ 091 33 24 34; Via Marino Stabile; s/d €40/55) Tucked into an unattractive apartment block is Palermo's best lower-priced hotel: great location, sparkling-clean rooms and an exceedingly polite (non-English-speaking) staff.

**Ambasciatori Hotel** ( ☎ 091 610 66 881; Via Roma 111; s/d €47/67; ✖ ) Previously known as the Hotel Azzuro di Lampedusa, this recently revamped hotel resides on the 5th floor of an old *palazzo*; it's friendly, convenient and good value.

**Hotel Letizia** ( ☎ 091 58 91 10; www.hotelletizia.com; Via dei Bottai 30; s/d €78/110; ✖ ) This lovely little hotel off the quaint Piazza Marina has pretty rooms with wood floors, an airy ambience, a cheery reading nook and a breakfast terrace.

**Massimo Plaza Hotel** ( ☎ 091 32 56 57; www.massimoplazahotel.com; Via Maqueda 437; s/d €130/190; P ✖ ) As close as you can stay to the theatre without sleeping on stage, one of Palermo's more intimate luxe hotels is extremely comfortable and boasts impeccable service.

## Eating

Palermo guards its tantalising cuisine with pride, and traditional dishes feature both sweet and spicy flavours reflecting the area's Arab past. A popular Palermitan dish is *pasta con le sarde* (with sardines, fennel, peppers, capers and pine nuts). Locals dine late and restaurants rarely open for dinner before 8.30pm.

**Antico Café Spinnato** ( ☎ 091 58 32 31; Via Principe di Belmonte 107-15) This elegant pastry shop has been serving its loyal clientele since 1860; the cakes are works of art, the *gelato* heavenly and the shaded outdoor tables ideal for a coffee *granita*.

**Antica Focacceria di San Francesco** ( ☎ 091 32 02 64; Via A Paternostro 58; mains €7) A local institution that's popular with workers and families alike, this fast-food spot has a bustling atmosphere and serves delicious calzone, pizza slices and some Palermitan speciality snacks such as *panini* stuffed with ricotta and steaming veal innards.

**Pizzeria Bellini** ( ☎ 091 616 56 91; Piazza Bellini 6) This popular pizzeria has a coveted spot, in the shadow of La Martorana; come at night, when the churches glow with floodlights.

**Mi Manda Picone** ( ☎ 091 616 06 60; Via A Paternostro 59; mains from €10) Nestled in a 13th-century building on Piazza San Francesco, this terrific restaurant serves top-notch contemporary cuisine in an airy arched interior. It doubles as an *enoteca*, where you can opt for generous platters of cheese and salami while sipping Sicilian vino.

**Capricci di Sicilia** ( ☎ 091 32 77 77; Via Instituto Pignatelli 6; secondo from €7) Once a puppet theatre, this cosy restaurant serves typical Sicilian fare, with an excellent selection of antipasto; always whirring with locals, so make a reservation in summer.

**Sant'Andrea** ( ☎ 091 33 49 99; Piazza Sant'Andrea 4; mains from €9) In the heart of the Vucciria market, the chef crafts produce and seafood fresh from the market into superb dishes with innovative twists; the pastas are sublime.

Palermo's best open-air markets are the **Vucciria** ( ☽ Mon-Sat), in the narrow streets around Piazza San Domenico, and Il Ballaro, held in the Albergheria quarter off Via Maqueda; both have excellent offerings and unbeatable local colour.

## Getting There & Away

**Falcone-Borsellino Airport** ( ☎ 091 702 01 11) is at Punta Raisi, 32km west of Palermo. For 24-hour information on domestic flights, ring **Alitalia** ( ☎ 00 39 06 65 641), and for international flights call the airport.

The main intercity bus station is around Via P Balsamo, to the right as you leave the train station. Offices for the various companies are all in this area, including **SAIS Trasporti** ( ☎ 091 617 11 41; www.saistrasporti.it; Via Balsamo 20), **SAIS Autolinee** ( ☎ 091 616 60 28; www.saisautolinee.it, in Italian; Via Balsamo 18) and **Segesta** ( ☎ 091 616 90 39; www.segesta.it, in Italian; Via Balsamo 26).

Regular trains leave from the Stazione Centrale for Milazzo, Messina, Catania, Trapani, Syracuse and Agrigento, as well as for nearby towns such as Cefalù. Direct trains go to Reggio di Calabria, Naples and Rome.

Boats leave from the port (Molo Vittorio Veneto) for Sardinia and the mainland (see p243). The **Tirrenia office** ( ☎ 091 602 11 11) is at the port.

## Getting Around

Taxis to the airport cost about €40. A better option is to hop on one of the blue Prestia e Comande buses, which leave from outside the station every 30 minutes from 5am to 10.45pm. Tickets for the 45-minute trip cost €4.65 and can be purchased on the bus. There's also an hourly train service from the airport to Stazione Centrale (€4.50) between 5.40am and 10.40pm. Most of Palermo's city buses stop outside or near the train station. You must buy tickets before you get on the bus; they cost €0.80 and are valid for two hours, or €2.60 for a day pass.

## AEOLIAN ISLANDS

These seven breezy islands – volcanic spurs strewn in the cobalt sea north of Milazzo – are stunning. Also known as the Liparis, they display an extraordinary range of landscapes, from lush Lipari, a well-honed resort, to tiny and exclusive Panarea, to rugged Vulcano, the gorgeous scenery of Stromboli (with its fiercely active volcano), fertile vineyards of Salina, and tranquil Alicudi and Filicudi, relatively undeveloped. The islands have been inhabited since the Neolithic era, when migrants sought the valuable volcanic glass, obsidian. The Isole Eolie are so named because the ancient Greeks believed they were the home of Aeolus, the god of wind; Homer wrote of their natural beauties in the *Odyssey*. Today they have divine stature among the hordes of summer hedonists – best come in spring or autumn.

## Information

**Tourist information office** ( ☎ 090 988 00 95; www .netnet.it/aasteolie, in Italian; Via Vittorio Emanuele 202, Lipari; ☽ 8am-2pm Mon-Sat & 4.30-7.30pm Mon-Fri). Other offices are open on Vulcano, Salina and Stromboli during summer.

## Sights & Activities

On **Lipari** visit the **citadel** ( ☽ 9am-7pm), with its fabulous **Museo Archeologico Eoliano** ( ☎ 090 988 01 74; admission €4.50; ☽ 9am-1.30pm & 3-7pm Mon-Sat) and museum. There are excellent walks on the island, as well as good snorkelling and scuba diving. The tourist office has information on trails, beaches and excursions.

With its pungent sulphurous odour, **Vulcano** is a short boat trip from Lipari. The main volcano, **Vulcano Fossa**, is still active, although the last recorded period of eruption was 1888–90. You can make the one-hour hike to the crater, or take a bath in the therapeutic hot muds.

On the most spectacular of the islands, **Stromboli**, you can climb the volcano. While recent activity has made it too dangerous to hike to the volcano's 2760-foot summit, you can still hike 1200 feet up the craters with a guide (or 900 feet without) and view the impressive Trail of Fire (Sciara del Fuoco) lava streaming down the side of the volcano. Contact **Magmatrek** ( ☎ 090 98 65 768; www.magmatrek.it) for guided treks to the crater (they only depart if groups are large enough).

## Sleeping & Eating

Camping facilities are available on Lipari, Salina and Vulcano. Most accommodation in summer is booked out well in advance on the smaller islands, particularly on Stromboli, and many places close during winter. Prices skyrocket during summer, but you can find good deals otherwise.

### LIPARI

Lipari has the most options and best range of accommodation. From here the other islands are easily accessible by regular hydrofoil. Don't dismiss outright offers for *affittacamere* (room rentals) by touts when you arrive at the port – they're often genuine.

**Diana Brown** ( ☎ 090 981 25 84; dbrown@netnet.it; Vico Himera 3; s/d €62/68) These comfortable rooms are centrally located and Diana's a font of local expertise; she and her husband also run **Gruppo di Navigazione** (www.navigazioniregina.com), featuring boat tours of all the islands.

**Filippino** ( ☎ 090 981 10 02; Piazza Municipio; mains from €16) Lazing over half the piazza, Lipari's classiest joint has superb seafood and top-notch service; dress to show off your tan and make a reservation. For pizza, hit the rightfully popular **La Piazzetta** ( ☎ 090 981 25 22; pizzas from €5), off Corso Vittorio with piazza-side tables; also recommended is tiny **La Cambusa** ( ☎ 349 476 60 61; Via Garibaldi 72; mains from €12), serving delicious pastas and fish.

### STROMBOLI

**La Sirenetta** ( ☎ 090 98 60 25; lasirenetta@netnet.it; Via Marina 33; s/d €99/212, half-board €132) This serene pad is perfectly located in front of Stròmbolicchio, a towering rock rising out of the sea at San Vincenzo; the panoramic terrace with a great restaurant encourages lingering.

### VULCANO

You'll find good value at **Hotel Torre** ( ☎ /fax 090 985 23 42; Via Favaloro 1; d low/high season €38/75) with its large rooms, kitchens and terraces and close beach access.

### ALICUDI & FILICUDI

If you want seclusion and still-wild beauty, head for Alicudi or Filicudi. The former offers the simple but nice **Ericusa** ( ☎ 090 988 99 02; fax 090 988 96 71; Via Regina Elena; d €62, half-board per person €60), while Filicudi has the truly delightful **La Canna** ( ☎ 090 988 99 56; vianast@tin.it; Via Rosa 43; s/d €40/80). There are good restaurants at both.

## Getting There & Away

Ferries and hydrofoils leave for the islands from Milazzo (easily reached by train from Palermo and Messina) and all ticket offices are along Corso dei Mille at the port. If arriving at Milazzo by train, catch a Giunta bus to the port. **SNAV** ( ☎ 081 428 51 11) and **Siremar** ( ☎ 081 580 03 40) run hydrofoils (€10.10), and the latter also has ferries (€7.50). SNAV also runs hydrofoils between the islands and Palermo (summer only).

You can also travel directly to the islands from the mainland. Siremar runs regular ferries from Naples, and SNAV runs hydrofoils from Naples, Messina and Reggio di Calabria. Occasionally, rough seas cancel sailings.

## Getting Around

Regular hydrofoil and ferry services operate between the islands. Both Siremar and SNAV have booths at Lipari's port, where you can get full timetable information.

## TAORMINA
pop 10,700

Spectacularly located on a mountain terrace, with resplendent views of the glistening sea and Mt Etna, beautiful Taormina has been charming mortals for centuries. Sicily's glitziest resort was long ago discovered by the European jet set, and the chic town is expensive and touristy. But even trinket shops and crowds can't hamper the allure, and its magnificent setting, Greek theatre, medieval centre and great beaches are as seductive now as they were for Goethe and DH Lawrence.

The **tourist office** ( ☎ 0942 2 32 43; www.gate2 taormina.com; Palazzo Corvaja; ✆ 8.30am-2pm & 4-7pm) has extensive information on the town and its wealth of sights.

## Sights & Activities

The **Teatro Greco** ( ☎ 0942 2 32 20; admission €4.50; ✆ 9am-7pm Mon-Sat, 9am-1pm Sun), a perfect horseshoe theatre, was built in the 3rd century BC and later expanded and remodelled by the Romans. Concerts, theatre and festivals are staged here in summer and wonderful views of Mt Etna abound. From the colourful and well-tended gardens of **Villa Comunale** ( ✆ 9am-7pm), there's a panoramic view of the sea. Along Corso Umberto I is **Piazza del Duomo**, with a baroque fountain and Norman-Gothic cathedral. The postcard-perfect local beach is **Isola Bella**, accessible by cable car (€2.70 return, 8am to 1am).

You can organise trips to the volcano Mt Etna (€27) through **CST** ( ☎ 0942 62 60 88; Corso Umberto I 101).

## Sleeping & Eating

The tourist office has a list of *affittacamere* in Taormina.

**Pensione Svizzera** ( ☎ 0942 237 90; svizzera@tao .it; Via Pirandello 26; s/d €70/90; ✆ Feb-Nov) Teetering on the edge of the cliff, this cheery *pensione* is convenient and comfortable. The views and breakfast served in a pretty garden terrace are bonuses.

**Hotel Belvedere** ( ☎ 0942 237 91; www.villa belvedere.it; Via Bagnoli Croce 79; s/d €80/110) One of the first hotels in town, this family-run spot has an enviable location; the high charm, pretty citrus gardens and pool-side lunch service make it a holiday idyll.

**Maffei's** ( ☎ 0942 240 55; Via San Domenico de Guzman 1; mains from €20) With a handful of tables and some of the best seafood in Taormina, this great spot is very popular: book a table and order the evening special.

**Granduca** ( ☎ 0942 249 83; Corso Umberto 172; pizzas from €5) Excellent pizza and a spectacular terrace make this a consistently good choice.

**Arco Rosso** (Via Naumachie 7) This is a good spot for a stiff drink any time.

**DiVino Wine Bar** (Piazza Raggia 4) Has local wines, terrific owners and nice plates of cheese.

**Café Wunderbar** (Piazza IX Aprile) Posers will be well rewarded at this café, sporting Taormina's best view and serving a mean *granita*.

## Getting There & Away

Bus is the easiest way to get to and from Taormina. Interbus services leave for Messina (€2.50, 1½ hours, 12 per day) and Catania (€3.80, 1½ hours, hourly). Taormina is on the main train line between Messina and Catania.

## MT ETNA

Dominating the landscape in eastern Sicily between Taormina and Catania, Mt Etna (3350m) is Europe's largest live volcano and one of the world's most active. Eruptions occur frequently, both from the four live craters at the summit and on the volcano's slopes, littered with fissures and extinct cones.

Recent activity has meant more disruption to services, and visitors should be aware that excursions are at the mercy of volcanic activity. Due to the volcano's unpredictability, you can no longer climb to the craters, although it is still possible to climb one of the peaks in front of the Rifugio Sapienza to get a small taste of the real thing. **Gruppo Guide Alpine Etna Sud** ( ☎ 095 791 47 55) or **Natura e Turismo** ( ☎ 095 33 35 43) organise excursions involving trekking and 4WD vehicles, led by a vulcanologist or alpine guide.

Mt Etna is best approached from Catania by **AST bus** ( ☎ 095 746 10 96), which departs from the car park in front of the main train station at 8.30am, and leaves from Rifugio Sapienza at about 4.45pm (€4.65 return). The private **Ferrovia Circumetnea train line** ( ☎ 095 54 12 50; www.circumetnea.it) circles Mt Etna from Catania to Riposto, a 3½-hour trip. You can reach Riposta from Taormina by train or bus if you want to make the trip from that direction.

**Agora Hostel** ( ☎ 095 723 30 10; agorahostel@hotmail .com; Piazza Curro 6, Catania; dm/d €15.50/40) This classic hostel in Catania is known for its live music, cheap eats and good bar; proximity to La Pescheria market is an added boon.

## SYRACUSE
pop 126,000

Once rivalling Athens in power and prestige, Syracuse is a highlight of a visit to Sicily. Founded in 734 BC by Corinthian settlers, the city became a sultry and dominant Mediterranean power, prompting Athens to attack in 413 BC. Syracuse was the birthplace of Archimedes, Cicero frequented town and Plato attended the court of the tyrant Dionysius, who ruled from 405 BC to 367 BC.

## Orientation & Information

The main sights are on the island of Ortygia and the archaeological park 2km across town.

**Tourist offices** Via San Sebastiano 45 ( ☎ 0931 48 12 00; www.apt-siracusa.it; ⊙ 8.30am-1.30pm & 3.30-6.30pm); Ortygia ( ☎ 0931 46 42 55; Via Maestranza 33; ⊙ 8.30am-2pm & 2.30-5pm Mon-Fri, mornings only Sat) The Via San Sebastiano office has English-speaking staff and a useful city map.

## Sights

### ORTYGIA

The island of Ortygia is the spiritual and physical heart of Syracuse. Despite eye-catching baroque palaces and churches, its Greek essence is everywhere. The **cathedral** (admission free; ⊙ 8am-noon & 4-7pm) was built in the 7th century on top of the Temple of Athena, incorporating most of the original columns in its three-aisled structure. The splendid **Piazza del Duomo** is lined with baroque palaces. Just down the winding street from the cathedral is the **Fontana Aretusa**, a natural freshwater spring. Greek legend has it that the goddess Artemis transformed her handmaiden Aretusa into the spring to protect her from the unwelcome attention of the river-god Alpheus. Undeterred, Alpheus turned himself into the river that feeds the spring.

### NEAPOLIS-PARCO ARCHEOLOGICO

To get to the **Neapolis-Parco Archeologico** ( ☎ 0931 6 62 06; Viale Paradisa; admission €4.50; ⊙ 9am-2hrs before sunset), catch bus No 1 or 2 from Riva della Posta on Ortygia. The main attraction here is the sparkling-white 5th-century-BC **Greek theatre**, entirely hewn out of solid rock and gazing seaward over the city. Nearby is the **Orecchio di Dionisio**, an ear-shaped artificial grotto used by Syracuse's resident tyrant Dionysius to eavesdrop on his prisoners. The impressive 2nd-century **Roman amphitheatre** is well preserved.

The excellent **Museo Archeologico Paolo Orsi** ( ☎ 0931 46 40 22; admission €4.50; ⊙ 9am-1pm Tue-Sat), about 500m east of the archaeological zone, contains Sicily's best-organised and most interesting archaeological collection.

## Sleeping & Eating

**Fontane Bianche** ( ☎ 0931 79 03 33; Via dei Lidi 476; per person/tent €6/4.50; ⊙ May-Sep) About 15km southwest of town, this camping ground is near a beach that teems with active bars come summer; catch bus No 21 or 22 from Corso Umberto.

**B&B Casa Mia** ( ☎ 0931 46 33 49; Corso Umberto 112; s/d €45/75) You'll feel right at home in this comfy old mansion with nicely decorated rooms and a breakfast area designed for lingering.

**Hotel Gutkowski** ( ☎ 0931 46 58 61; www.guthotel.it; Lungomare Vittorini 26; s/d €65/90) This lovely pastel-blue, sea-fronting hotel has an appealing minimalist décor and a helpful entrepreneurial family at the helm, doing its part to help revive the city's crumbling *palazzi*.

There is no shortage of good dining on Ortygia, where all the best eateries are located.

**Trattoria Archimede** ( ☎ 0931 697 01; Via Gemellaro 8; mains from €8) This authentic spot has a daily changing menu featuring excellent seafood and pastas, served smartly in three airy dining rooms.

**Don Camillo** ( ☎ 0931 6 71 33; Via Maestranza 96; mains from €9) Sitting pretty in the old guild quarter, this popular upmarket trattoria serves traditional Sicilian fare matched by excellent wines; it's packed at weekends so book ahead.

For scrumptious Sicilian sweets, head to **Pasticceria Tipica Catanese** (Corso Umberto 46); for good local wines, accompanied by hearty cheese and ham platters, try **Fermento** (Via Crocifisso 44/46), a terrific vaulted wine bar.

## Getting There & Away

Services with **Interbus** ( ☎ 0931 6 67 10) leave from Via Trieste for Catania (€4.60, one hour, Monday to Saturday), Palermo (€14.20, four hours), Enna (€3, one hour) and surrounding towns. The service for Rome (€38, 12 hours) also leaves from here, connecting with the Rome bus at Catania. **AST** ( ☎ 0931 46 48 20) buses service the town and the surrounding area from Riva della Posta. Syracuse is easy to reach by train from Messina (€8.75, three hours) and Catania (€4.70, 1½ hours).

## AGRIGENTO

**pop 55,500**

Founded around 582 BC, Agrigento is today a pleasant (if a little brutish) medieval town, but the Greek temples strewn in the valley below are the reason to visit. Goethe first put Agrigento on the map in the 18th century, which makes it Sicily's oldest tourist site. The Italian novelist and dramatist Luigi Pirandello (1867–1936) was born here, as was the Greek philosopher and scientist Empedocles (c 490–430 BC).

There's a so-so **tourist office** ( ☎ 0922 2 04 54; Via Cesare Battisti 15; ⏱ 8.30am-1.30pm Mon-Fri).

## Sights

Agrigento's **Valley of the Temples** ( ☎ 0922 261 91; admission €2, with museum €6; ⏱ 8.30am-1hr before sunset) is one of the major Greek archaeological sights in the world. Despite its name, the five main Doric temples stand along a ridge, designed to be visible from afar. In varying states of ruin, the 5th-century-BC temples offer a tantalising glimpse of one of the most luxurious cities in Magna Graecia. The only temple to survive relatively intact was **Tempio della Concordia**, transformed into a church. **Tempio di Giunone**, a short walk uphill to the east, has an impressive sacrificial altar. **Tempio di Ercole** is the oldest of the structures. Across the main road that divides the valley is the imposing **Tempio di Giove**, which used to cover an area measuring 112m by 56m, with columns 18m high. *Telamoni*, colossal statues of men, were used in the structure, and the remains of one are in the **Museo Archeologico** ( ☎ 0922 40 15 65; admission €4.50, with temples €6; ⏱ 9am-1.30pm &

---

**TOP TEN ITALY**

- **Top Small Towns** – San Gimignano (p227) and Lecce (p242)
- **Top Festival** – Siena's Il Palio (p224)
- **Top Piazza for a Cocktail** – Campo de'Fiori (p181)
- **Top Ancient Ruins** – the Forum in Rome (p166) and Agrigento, Sicily (p249)
- **Top Coastal Stretch** – Amalfi Coast (p238)
- **Top Sights** – Florence's Duomo (p217) and Sardinia's Grotte di Nettuno (p254)
- **Top Islands** – Aeolian Islands (p246)
- **Top Coffee** – Tazza d'Oro, Rome (p181)
- **Top Alpine Views** – The Dolomites (p213)

---

2-7.30pm Tue-Sat, 9am-1.30pm Sun & Mon), just north of the temples on Via dei Templi. Nearby is the **Tempio di Castore e Polluce**, partly reconstructed in the 19th century.

The temples are beautifully lit up at night. To get to the temples from the town, catch bus No 1, 2 or 3 from the train station.

## Sleeping & Eating

**Bella Napoli** ( ☎ 0922 2 04 35; Piazza Lena 6; s/d/tr €22/54/75) This friendly hotel has clean, comfortable if unremarkable rooms.

**Antica Foresteria Catalana** ( ☎ 0922 204 35; s/d €45/75) With the same owners as Bella Napoli, this has newer rooms that are not necessarily worth the price jump.

**La Corte degli Sfizzi** ( ☎ 0922 59 55 20; Via Atenea 4; pizzas from €5) A popular pizzeria with a pretty garden setting and good value.

**Café Girasole** (Via Atenea 68-70) This is a great little wine bar in the heart of the medieval town.

## Getting There & Away

Intercity buses leave from Piazza Rosselli, just off Piazza Vittorio Emanuele, for Palermo, Catania and surrounding towns.

# SARDINIA

The Mediterranean's second largest island feels like a mini-continent all to itself. Sardinia was colonised by the Phoenicians and Romans, the Pisans and Genoese, and the Spaniards. Despite constant domination, the proud locals (Sardi) have retained a strong sense of identity, far removed from mainland influences. The striking landscape ranges from a wild interior pocked with gorges and valleys, to stunning stretches of unspoiled coastline. The gorgeous island gets overrun with sun seekers in August.

## GETTING THERE & AWAY
### Air

Airports at Cagliari, Olbia, Alghero and Arbatax-Tortoli link Sardinia with major Italian and European cities. Discount airlines, including Air One and Ryanair, are servicing the island more and more.

### Boat

Sardinia is accessible by ferry from Genoa, Livorno, Fiumicino, Civitavecchia, Naples,

Palermo, Trapani, Bonifacio and Porto Vecchio (both Corsica) and Tunis. Departure points in Sardinia are Olbia, Golfo Aranci, Palau, Santa Teresa di Gallura and Porto Torres in the north, Arbatax on the east coast and Cagliari in the south.

The main company, **Tirrenia** (www.tirrenia .com, in Italian), runs a service between Civitavecchia and Olbia, Arbatax or Cagliari, and between Genoa and Porto Torres, Olbia, Arbatax or Cagliari. There are fast ferries between Fiumicino and Golfo Aranci/Arbatax and Civitavecchia and Olbia (both summer only). The national railway, Ferrovie dello Stato (FS), also runs a service between Civitavecchia and Golfo Aranci. **Moby Lines** (www.mobylines.it) and **Sardinia Ferries** (www.sardiniaferries.com), also known as Elba and Corsica Ferries, both operate services from the mainland to Sardinia, as well as to Corsica and Elba. They depart from Genoa, Livorno, Civitavecchia and arrive at Olbia, Cagliari or Golfo Aranci. **Grandi Navi Veloci** (www.gnv.it) runs a service between Genoa and Olbia (June to September) or Porto Torres (year-round). Most Italian travel agencies have brochures on the different services.

Timetables change and prices fluctuate depending on the season. Prices for a *poltrona* (seat) on Tirrenia ferries are: Genoa to Porto Torres or Olbia (€46, 13 hours); Naples to Cagliari (€41, 16¼ hours); Palermo to Cagliari (€39, 13½ hours, weekly); Civitavecchia to Olbia (€25, eight hours); and Civitavecchia to Cagliari (€41, 14½ hours).

The cost of taking a small car from Civitavecchia to Cagliari in the high season is €78. A motorcycle (over 200cc) costs €40 year-round for the same trip.

## GETTING AROUND

The two main bus companies are the state-run **ARST** ( ☎ 0800 86 50 42; www.arst.sardegna .it, in Italian), which operates extensive services throughout the island, and privately owned **PANI** ( ☎ 070 65 23 26), which links main towns.

The main **Trenitalia** (www.trenitalia.it) train lines link Cagliari with Oristano, Sassari and Olbia, and are generally reliable but can be very slow. The private railways that link smaller towns throughout the island can be *very* slow. However, the *Trenino Verde* (Little Green Train), which runs a scenic route from Cagliari to Arbatax through the Barbagia, is a relaxing and lovely way to see part of the interior.

The best way to explore Sardinia properly is by road, and all the major international car-rental agencies are represented at the main airports.

## CAGLIARI

pop 176,000
Sardinia's capital and largest city is an attractive, friendly and cosmopolitan enclave, with a beautifully preserved medieval section, the delightful beach of Poetto and salt lakes that are home to pink flamingos.

### Orientation

The main port, bus and train stations are near Piazza Matteotti, where the useful city tourist office is as well. The main street along the harbour is Via Roma, and the old city stretches up the hill behind it to the castle. There are several hotels and restaurants near the port, normally not a great place in most cities, but perfectly safe and pleasant here.

### Information

#### EMERGENCY
**Police station** (Questura; ☎ 070 49 21 69; Via Amat 9) Tucked behind the imposing law courts.

#### INTERNET ACCESS
**Web Travel Point** ( ☎ 070 65 93 07; Via Maddalena 34; per 30min €2.60)

#### LAUNDRY
**Lavanderia Ghilbi** (Via Sicilia 20; ☽ 8am-10pm; per 6kg €3) Laundrettes are a rarity on the island.

#### MEDICAL SERVICES
**Ospedale San Giovanni di Dio** ( ☎ 070 66 32 37; Via Ospedale)
**Guardia Medica** ( ☎ 070 50 29 31) For after-hour emergencies.

#### POST
**Main post office** ( ☎ 070 6 03 11; Piazza del Carmine 27; ☽ 8.15am-6.40pm Mon-Fri, to 1.20pm Sat)

#### TOURIST INFORMATION
**Main tourist office** ( ☎ 070 66 92 55; Piazza Matteotti 9; ☽ 9am-2pm & 3-6pm Mon-Sat) There are additional information offices at the airport and in the Stazione Marittima.

ITALY

ITALY

# CAGLIARI

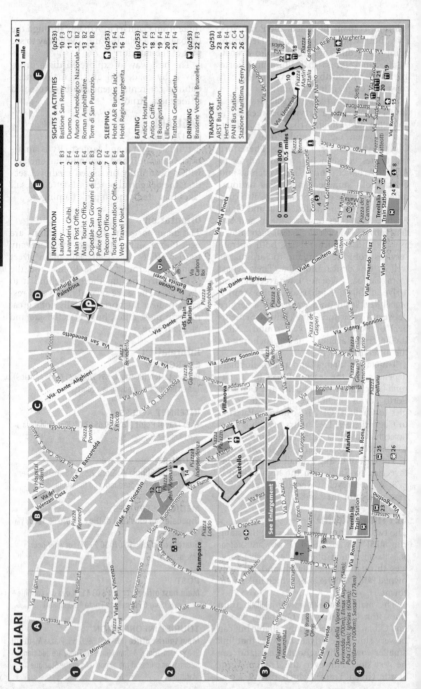

0          1 mile
0          2 km

800 m
0.5 miles

To Grotta della Vipera (600m);
Turin (700m); Elmas Airport (5km);
Pula (32km); Iglesias (60km);
Oristano (100km); Sassari (217km)

## Sights & Activities

In the Citadella dei Musei, the **Museo Archeologico Nazionale** ( ☎ 070 68 40 00; Piazza Arsenale; admission €4; ⏱ 9am-8pm Tue-Sun) has a fascinating collection of Nuraghic bronzes. These bronzes are objects found in stone constructions all over Sardinia (there are about 7000), a legacy of the island's native culture.

It's enjoyable to wander through the medieval quarter. The Pisan-Romanesque **Duomo** (Piazza Palazzo) was built in the 13th century and has an interesting Romanesque pulpit.

There are good sea and city views from **Bastione San Remy** (Piazza Costituzione), in the town's centre. It once formed part of the fortifications of the old city.

The **Torre di San Pancrazio** (Piazza Indipendenza; ⏱ 9am-5pm Tue-Sun) is also worth a look. The **Roman amphitheatre** (Viale Buon Cammino; admission free; ⏱ 9am-5pm Tue-Sun) is considered the most important Roman monument in Sardinia. During summer, opera is performed here.

A day on the **Spiaggia di Poetto**, east of the centre, is a day well spent, and you can wander across the salt lakes to view the flamingos.

## Festivals & Events

The **Festival of Sant'Efisio**, a colourful celebration mixing the secular and the religious, is held annually for four days from 1 May.

## Sleeping & Eating

**Hotel A&R Bundes Jack** ( ☎ /fax 070 66 79 70; Via Roma 75; s/d €47/72, with shared bathroom €40/60) The Marina's choice spot has a warm welcome and high-ceilinged rooms that are spotless and comfortable.

**Hotel Regina Margherita** ( ☎ 070 67 03 42; www .hotelreginamargherita.com; Viale Regina Margherita 44; s/d €128/165) This well-managed hotel has nice views and comfortable, modern rooms.

**Lillicu** ( ☎ 070 65 29 70; Via Sardegna 78; mains from €9) An authentic trattoria that's often packed with happy locals downing good seafood dishes at large communal marble tables.

**Antica Hostaria** ( ☎ 070 66 58 60; Via Cavour 60; mains from €15) Cagliari fine dining at its finest, this antique-laden restaurant has a warm ambience and classic Italian cuisine.

**Il Buongustaio** ( ☎ 070 66 81 24; Via Concezione 7; pasta from €7) This home-spun spot for foodies serves equally good fish and fowl, and the home-made pastas are particularly tasty.

**Trattoria GennarGentu** ( ☎ 070 67 20 21; Via Sardegna 60; pasta from €8) At this welcoming spot, try the Sardinian specialities such as *spaghetti bottarga* (spaghetti with dried tuna roe).

The Marina area is riddled with good little spots to suit all tastes and budgets. Also worth a mention are **Antico Caffè** ( ☎ 070 65 82 96; Piazza Costituzione), Cagliari's most elegant café with a terrace and marble-topped tables, and **Brasserie Vecchia Bruxelles** ( ☎ 070 68 20 37; Via Sulcis 4; ⏱ Mon-Sat), with stone vaults and long comfy sofas, an excellent choice for a beer, snack or nip of whiskey.

## Getting There & Away

Some 8km northwest of the city at Elmas is Cagliari's airport. ARST buses leave regularly from Piazza Matteotti to coincide with flight arrivals and departures. **Alitalia** ( ☎ 070 24 00 79) is at the airport.

Departing from Piazza Matteotti are **ARST** ( ☎ 070 409 83 24) buses servicing nearby towns, the Costa del Sud and the Costa Rei. **PANI** ( ☎ 070 65 23 26) buses leave from Stazione Marittima for towns including Sassari (€15, 3¼ hours), Oristano (€6.10, 1½ hours) and Nuoro (€6.10, 3½ hours).

The main train station is also in Piazza Matteotti, with regular service to Oristano (€4.85, two hours), Sassari (€12.80, 4¼ hours) and Porto Torres via Oristano and Olbia (€13.25, four hours). The private **Ferrovie della Sardegna** (FdS; ☎ 070 49 13 04) train station is in Piazza Repubblica.

Ferries arrive at the port adjacent to Via Roma. Bookings for **Tirrenia** ( ☎ 070 66 60 65) can be made at the Stazione Marittima in the port area. See p251 for details of services.

For rental cars, try **Hertz** ( ☎ 070 66 81 05; Piazza Matteotti 1), which also has a branch at the airport, while **Autonoleggio Cara** ( ☎ 070 66 34 71) can deliver a scooter or bike to your hotel.

## CALA GONONE

pop 1010

This attractive seaside resort makes a good base from which to explore the coves along the Golfo di Orosei's coastline, as well as the Nuraghic sites and rugged terrain inland. Major points are accessible by bus and boat, but you'll need a car to really explore.

## Information

**Coop Ghivine** ( ☎ 0784 9 67 21; www.ghivine.com; Via Montebello 5, Dorgali) Organises excellent guided treks and farm stays in the region from €30 per person. **Tourist office** Cal Gonone ( ☎ 0784 9 36 96; Viale Bue Marino 1a; ☽ 9am-6pm Apr-Oct, to 11pm Jul & Aug); Dorgali ( ☎ 0784 9 62 43; Via Lamarmora 181; ☽ 9am-1pm & 3.30-7pm Mon-Fri) The Cala Gonone office has maps, a list of hotels and plenty of local information.

## Sights & Activities

From Cala Gonone's tiny port, catch a boat to the **Grotta del Bue Marino** (admission €5.50), where a guide will take you on a 1km walk to see vast caves with stalagmites and stalactites. Sardinia's last colony of monk seals once lived here but have not been seen for quite some time. Boats also leave for **Cala Luna**, an isolated beach where you can walk along **Codula di Luna**, a fabulous gorge. The beach is packed with day-tripping tourists in summer. The boat trip to visit the grotto and beach costs around €20.

A **walking track** along the coast links Cala Fuili, about 3.5km south of Cala Gonone, and Cala Luna (about 1½ hours one way). There's also some good mountain biking and diving in the area. Ask at the tourist office for information on outfitters and rentals.

If you want to descend the impressive **Gorropu Gorge**, ask for information from the team of expert guides based in Urzulei – **Società Gorropu** ( ☎ 0782 64 92 82, 0347 775 27 06; francescomurru@virgilio.it) – who also offer a wide range of guided walks in the area. It is necessary to use ropes and harnesses to traverse the Gorropu Gorge.

## Sleeping & Eating

**Camping Gala Gonone** ( ☎ 0784 9 31 65; www.camping calagonone.it; per person €16, 4-bed bungalows up to €135; ☽ Apr-Oct) Along the main road from Dorgali, this camping ground has good-quality and shady sites, plus a pool and restaurant, but gets overrun in August.

**Pop Hotel** ( ☎ 0784 9 31 85; lfancel@box1.tin.it; s/d €59/93) Despite the ugly sign, this terracotta-hued hotel near the port has clean, pleasant rooms and a decent restaurant.

**Hotel Costa Dorada** ( ☎ 0784 9 33 32; www.hotel costadorada.it; Via Lungomare Palmasera 45; d incl breakfast from €74) Has a swatch of beach across the street, flower-laced terraces and lovely rooms.

**Hotel Su Gologone** ( ☎ 0784 28 75 12; www.sugol ogone.it; s/d €80/120; **P** ) If you have your own transport, don't miss the opportunity to stay here, at the base of Sardinia's second-highest peak, about 20 minutes west, near Dorgali. This gorgeous white-washed hacienda has pretty rooms decorated with locally crafted furnishings, walking trails, pool and a fabulous restaurant serving classic Sardinian mountain cuisine.

## Getting There & Away

Catch a PANI bus to Nuoro from Cagliari (€12, 3½ hours), Sassari (€7.20, 2½ hours) or Oristano (€6.20, two hours) and then take an ARST bus to Cala Gonone via Dorgali (€85, 20 minutes). If you are travelling by car, you will need a proper road map of the area.

## ALGHERO

pop 40,600

With a distinctive Spanish flair, this colourful resort town is on the west coast, known as the Coral Riviera. The town makes a good base for exploring the magnificent coastline to the south, and the famed Grotte di Nettuno on the Capo Caccia to the north. The medieval centre, with its sea walls intact, is one of Sardinia's most charming towns. Visit off-season to see pretty Alghero at its peaceful best.

## Orientation & Information

Alghero's historic centre is on a small promontory jutting into the sea, with the new town stretching out behind and along the coast north.

**Main post office** (Via Carducci 35)
**Medical attention** ( ☎ 079 98 71 61)
**Ospedale Civile** ( ☎ 079 99 62 33; Via Don Minzoni)
**Police** ( ☎ 113)
**Public telephones** (Via Vittorio Emanuele)
**Tourist office** ( ☎ 079 97 90 54; www.infoalghero.it, in Italian; Piazza Porta Terra 9; ☽ 8am-8pm Mon-Sat) Near the port and just across the gardens from the bus station, this is an exceedingly helpful office.

## Sights & Activities

The narrow streets of the old city and around the port are lovely. The most interesting church is the **Chiesa di San Francesco** (Via Carlo Alberto; ☽ 7.30am-noon & 5-8.30pm). Although constant remodelling has ruined the cathedral, the **bell tower** (admission €1.50;

⊙ 7am-9.30pm Jun-Sep) remains a fine example of Gothic-Catalan architecture.

Near Alghero at the dramatic cape, **Capo Caccia**, are the **Grotte di Nettuno** ( ☎ 079 94 65 40; admission adult/child €8/4; ⊙ 9am-7pm Apr-Sep, 10am-5pm Oct, 9am-2pm Nov-Mar), an underground fairyland accessible by boat (€10, not including grotto admission, 2½ hours, hourly 8am to 7pm June to September) from the port, or by the FdS bus from Via Catalogna (€3.25 return, 50 minutes, three daily trips June to September).

If you have a car, don't miss the **Nuraghe di Palmavera** ( ☎ 079 95 32 00; admission €2.10; ⊙ 9am-7pm), a ruined palace 10km out of Alghero on the road to Porto Conte.

Rugged cliffs fall down to solitary beaches, and near **Bosa** is one of the last habitats of the griffon vulture. The best way to see the coast is by car or motorcycle. If you want to rent a bicycle (from €9) or motorcycle (from €70) to explore the coast, try **Cicloexpress** ( ☎ 079 98 69 50; Via Garibaldi) at the port.

## Festivals & Events

In summer Alghero stages a music festival in the cloisters of the church of San Francesco. A festival, complete with fireworks display, is held on 15 August for the Feast of the Assumption.

## Sleeping & Eating

It is virtually impossible to find a room in August unless you book in advance. At other times of the year you'll be fine.

**Camping La Mariposa** ( ☎ 079 95 03 60; Via Lido 22; per person/tent €10.50/5, bungalows up to €72; ⊙ Apr-Oct) About 2km north of the centre, this low-key camping ground is on the beach.

**Hotel San Francesco** ( ☎ /fax 079 98 03 30; Via Ambrogio Machin 2; s/d €47/85; P ) In the old town, this hotel exudes charm and is housed in a former convent; the rooms are simple but comfortable, and there's a cloistered courtyard shared with the church of the same name.

**Villa Las Tronas** ( ☎ 079 98 18 18; www.hotelvillalastronas.it; Lungomare Valencia 1; s/d €170/200; P ⌨ ☙ ) On its own private promontory, this former summer residence of the Italian royalty has a pool and very pretty rooms, but an overly formal feel elsewhere. Still, the views are stupendous, the breakfasts enough to cover lunch, and there are mountain bikes for pedalling the coast.

**Trattoria Maristella** ( ☎ 079 97 81 72; Via Fratelli Kennedy 9; mains from €10) This popular spot, with its Mediterranean-splashed décor, offers good value, reliable grub and alfresco dining.

**Da Ninetto** ( ☎ 079 97 80 62; Via Gioberti 4; mains from €12) Locals swear by the lobster served at this unassuming hole-in-the-wall.

**Al Tuguri** ( ☎ 079 97 67 72; Via Maiorca 113; mains from €15) Although this oft-lauded restaurant sometimes rests on its many laurels, and the service can be puffy, the seafood is memorable.

**Focacce Sarde Ripiene** (Via Garibaldi 11; ⊙ until 1.30am) Serves delicious sandwiches, fronts the sea and is always packed with locals.

**Caffè Costantino** (Piazza Civica 30) A classy coffee stop in the historic centre that also serves good wine and tantalising cakes.

## Getting There & Away

Alghero is accessible from Sassari by train (€2.20, 35 minutes) and bus (€2.60, one hour). The main bus station is on Via Catalogna, next to the public park. The **train station** (Via Don Minzoni) is about 1km north of town and is connected to the centre by a regular bus service. **ARST** ( ☎ 079 95 01 79) buses leave for Sassari and Porto Torres. **FdS** ( ☎ 079 95 04 58) buses also service Sassari, Macomer and Bosa. **PANI** ( ☎ 079 23 69 83) buses serve Cagliari, Nuoro and Macomer from Sassari.

# ITALY DIRECTORY

## ACCOMMODATION

Accommodation in Italy ranges from the magnificent to the ridiculous with prices to match. Hotels and *pensioni* make up the bulk of accommodation, with a vast gulf between top-end luxury and budget options that can be pricey and pokey. Fortunately, there's a growing range of good and characterful B&Bs, villa rentals, hostels and *agriturismo* (farm stays) options to fill the void.

Prices fluctuate throughout the country and depend on the season, with Easter and the summer and Christmas holidays being peak tourist times. During low season, prices can be 20% cheaper. Tourist offices have listings for all local accommodation, including prices. In this chapter listings are categorised roughly as budget (under €100), mid-range (€100 to 190) and top end (€190 and up).

## Agriturismo

Farm stays are increasingly popular, particularly in Tuscany and on the islands. For a countrywide directory, contact **Agriturist** ( ☎ 06 685 23 42; www.agriturist.it, in Italian; Corso Vittorio Emanuele II 89, 00186 Rome).

## B&Bs

Bed and breakfast options range from city *palazzi* to seaside bungalows. Prices are typically between €70 and €150.

## Camping

Most camping grounds in Italy have a swimming pool, tennis court and restaurant, and are graded according to a star system. Prices range from €4 to €10 per person and €5 to €12 or more for a site. Lists of sites are available from local tourist offices or can be looked up on the website of **Touring Club Italiano** (TCI; www.touringclub.it).

Independent camping is not permitted in many of the more beautiful parts of Italy but if you choose spots not visible from the road and don't light fires you shouldn't have trouble off season. Always get permission from the landowner if you want to camp on private property.

## Hostels

Hostels in Italy are called *ostelli per la gioventù* and are run by the Associazione Italiana Alberghi per la Gioventù (Italian Youth Hostel Association), affiliated with **Hostelling International** (HI; www.iyhf.org). A valid HI card is required, which you can get in your home country, at the youth hostel in Rome, from CTS offices and from the hostel association offices throughout Italy. The national head office of the **Italian Youth Hostel Association** (Map p167; ☎ 06 487 11 52; www.ostellionline.org; Via Cavour 44, Rome; ☉ 9am-5pm Mon-Fri) has a booklet detailing all Italian hostels.

Accommodation is in segregated dormitories, although some hostels offer higher-priced doubles. Nightly rates, often including breakfast, range from €10 to €20. Lockout times are usually from 9am to 5pm. Check-in is 6pm to 10.30pm and curfews are around midnight.

## Hotels & Pensioni

There is often no difference between a *pensione* and an *albergo*. However, the former will generally be of one- to three-star quality, while the latter can be awarded up to five stars. *Locande* (inns) and *affittacamere* (rooms for rent) are cheaper and not included in the star classification system, although the standard can be very high (particularly on the Aeolian Islands and in the Alps).

Always check on prices before committing to stay in a place. Proprietors have been known to pad bills, so make a complaint to the local tourist office if you believe you're being overcharged.

Prices are higher in northern Italy and highest in major tourist destinations. Rates can soar in the high season. A *camera singola* (single room) costs from €40, and quite a number of establishments do not bother catering to the single traveller; a double room with *camera doppie* (twin beds) or *camera matrimoniale* (double bed) will cost from €55.

## Mountain Refuges

Before hiking in the Alps, Apennines, or other mountains in Italy, obtain information about Italy's wonderful network of *rifugi* from local tourist offices. Refuges are generally open from July to September, and dorm-style accommodation prevails, though some larger ones have double rooms. The price per person for a night with breakfast is around €20, with dinner another €15.

The locations of *rifugi* are marked on good hiking maps. The **Club Alpino Italiano** (CAI; www.cai.it, in Italian) owns and runs many of the refuges. CAI offers discounts to members of associated foreign alpine clubs.

## Rental Accommodation

Finding rental accommodation in the major cities can be difficult, time-consuming and prohibitively costly. Major resort areas, such as the Aeolian Islands, coastal Sardinia and the Alps offer rental accommodation that's more reasonably priced and readily available. Many tourist offices will provide information by mail, fax or email.

**Cuendet & Cie Spa** ( ☎ 0577 57 63 30; www.cuendet .com; Strada di Strove 17, 53035 Monteriggioni, Siena) organises charming (and often pricey) villa rentals throughout Italy.

> **WHERE TO TAKE A DIP**
>
> **Isola Bella** – Taormina's perfect crescent beach is ideal for a dip (p248)
>
> **Spiaggia di Poetto** – Resident flamingos are an added bonus to this Cagliari beach (p253)
>
> **Monterosso Al Mare** – Cinque Terre's main beach is pebbly but pretty (p189)

## ACTIVITIES
### Cycling
Cycling is an excellent way to see Italy's gorgeous countryside. Classic areas include Tuscany and Umbria. Lonely Planet's *Cycling in Italy* is a terrific reference with detailed itineraries.

There is good mountain biking in Sardinia, Sicily and around Maratea. Tourist offices offer information on trails, guided rides and rentals.

### Hiking & Walking
Italy is a walker's paradise with thousands of kilometres of *sentieri* (marked trails). The **Club Alpino Italiano** (CAI; www.cai.it, in Italian) is a useful resource. There are plenty of organised hiking trips, but solo trekkers will find easy-to-follow trails and refuges; the magnificent Dolomites are the most popular area. On Sardinia, head for the coastal gorges between Dorgali and Baunei, and on Sicily for Mt Etna. Coastal walkers will enjoy Liguria and the Amalfi Coast. Check out Lonely Planet's *Walking in Italy* for detailed descriptions of more than 50 walks.

### Skiing
The numerous excellent ski resorts in the Alps and the Apennines offer dramatic scenery and usually good conditions from December to April. See p213 for skiing destinations in the Dolomites.

## BUSINESS HOURS
Hours can vary, but generally shops and businesses are open from 9am to 1pm and 3.30pm to 7.30pm Monday to Saturday, with some also open on Sunday morning. They may close on Saturday afternoon and on Thursday or Monday afternoon.

Restaurants are usually open for lunch from 12.30pm to 3pm. For dinner, opening hours vary from north to south but are generally from 7.30pm to 11.30pm. Restaurants are closed one night a week and for much of August; in seasonal tourist areas, many also close between Christmas and April.

Banks tend to open from 8.30am to 1.30pm and 3.30pm to 4.30pm Monday to Friday. Major post offices open from 8.30am to 6pm Monday to Friday, and until 1pm on Saturday. Most museums are now opening from 9.30am to 7pm, later in summer; many close on Monday.

## CUSTOMS
There is no limit on the amount of euros brought into the country, and duty-free sales within the EU no longer exist. Travellers coming from outside the EU can import, duty-free 200 cigarettes, 1L of spirits, 2L of wine and other goods up to a total value of €175.

## DANGERS & ANNOYANCES
It can require buckets of patience to deal with the Italian concept of service. What for Italians is part of daily life can be horrifying for the foreigner. Long queues are the norm in banks, post offices and any government offices. It definitely pays to remain calm and patient, as a demanding tone can be met with utter indifference.

Theft is the main problem for travellers in Italy, mostly in the form of petty thievery and pickpocketing, especially in the bigger cities. Carry your valuables in a moneybelt and avoid flashing your dough in public. Pickpockets operate in crowded areas, such as markets, and on buses headed for major tourist attractions.

Never leave valuables in a parked car – in fact, try not to leave anything visible in the car if you can help it and it's a good idea to park your car in a supervised car park.

Italy is not a dangerous country for women, but women travelling alone may find themselves plagued by unwanted attention, which can get annoying and old fast. Get used to being ogled and yelled at because it's likely to happen, particularly the further south you travel. It's handy to toss out references to your (real or imagined) *marito* (husband) or *fidanzato* (boyfriend). And if a man's wandering hands find you on the bus, a loud '*Che schifo!*' (How disgusting!) usually does the trick.

## EMBASSIES & CONSULATES
### Italian Embassies & Consulates
Italian diplomatic missions abroad include:

**Australia** Canberra ( ☎ 02-6273 3333; www.ambitalia
.org.au; 12 Grey St, Deakin ACT 2600); Melbourne ( ☎ 03-
9867 5744; itconmel@netlink.com.au; 509 St Kilda Rd VIC
3004); Sydney ( ☎ 02-9392 7900; itconsyd@armadillo
.com.au; Level 43, The Gateway, 1 Macquarie Pl NSW 2000)

**Canada** Ottawa ( ☎ 613-232 2401; www.italyincanada
.com; 21st fl, 275 Slater St, Ontario, K1P 5H9); Vancouver
( ☎ 604-684 7288; consolato@italianconsulate.bc.ca;
Standard Bldg 1100-510 West Hastings St, BC V6B IL8);
Toronto ( ☎ 416-977 1566; consolato.it@toronto.ital
consulate.org; 136 Beverley St, Ontario M5T 1Y5); Montreal
( ☎ 514-849 8351; cgi@italconsul.montreal.qc.ca; 3489
Drummond St, Quebec H3G 1X6)

**France** Paris ( ☎ 01 49 54 03 00; ambasciata@amb-italie
.fr; 7 rue de Varenne 75007); Paris ( ☎ 01 44 30 47 00;
italconsulparigi@mailcity.com; 5 Blvd Emile Augier 75116)

**New Zealand** ( ☎ 04-473 5339; www.italy-embassy
.org.nz; 34 Grant Rd, Thorndon, Wellington )

**UK** London ( ☎ 020-7312 2200; www.embitaly.org.uk; 14
Three Kings Yard, W1Y 4EH); London ( ☎ 020-7235 9371;
38 Eaton Place, SW1X 8AN)

**USA** Washington ( ☎ 202-328 5500; www.italyemb
.org; 1601 Fuller St, NW Washington, DC 20009); New York
( ☎ 212-737 9100; www.italconsulnyc.org; 690 Park Ave,
10021); Los Angeles ( ☎ 310-820 0727; www.italyemb
.org/consolati.htm; ste 300, 12400 Wilshire Blvd, 90025)

### Embassies & Consulates in Italy
The headquarters of most foreign embassies
are in Rome, although there are generally
British and US consulates in other major
cities. The following information is for
Rome unless otherwise stated:

**Australia** ( ☎ 06 85 27 21; Via Alessandria 215, 00198)

**Canada** ( ☎ 06 44 59 81; Via G B de Rossi 27, 00161)

**France** Rome (Map pp170-1; ☎ 06 68 60 11; Piazza
Farnese 67, 00186); Rome (Map pp170-1; ☎ 06 688 02
152; Via Giuila; 251; ☻ 9am-12.30pm Mon-Fri); Florence
(Map pp164-5; ☎ 055 230 25 56; Piazza Ognissanti 2)

**Germany** (Map p167; ☎ 06 49 21 31; Via San Martino
della Battaglia 4, 00185)

**New Zealand** ( ☎ 06 441 71 71; Via Zara 28, 00198)

**UK** Rome ( ☎ 06 42 20 00 01; Via XX Settembre 80a,
00187); Florence (Map p218; ☎ 055 28 41 33; Lungarno
Corsini 2)

**USA** Rome (Map pp172-3; ☎ 06 4 67 41; www.usis
.it; Via Veneto 119a, 00187); Florence ( ☎ 055 239 82 76;
Lungarno Vespucci 38)

For a complete list of all foreign embassies
in Rome and other major cities throughout Italy, look in the local telephone book
under *ambasciate* or *consolati*, or ask for a
list at a tourist office.

## FESTIVALS & EVENTS
Italy's calendar teems with cultural events
ranging from colourful traditional celebrations with a religious and/or historical flavour, to festivals of the performing arts,
including opera, music and theatre. Annual
events worth catching include:

### Late February–Early March
**Carnevale** During the 10 days before Ash Wednesday,
many towns stage carnivals. Venice's is the best known,
but there are others, including at Viareggio in Tuscany and
Ivrea near Turin.

### April
**Holy Week** There are important festivals during this week
countrywide; of note are Sicily's colourful and sombre
traditional festivals and Assisi's rituals, attracting thousands of pilgrims.

**Scoppio del Carro** Literally 'Explosion of the Cart', this
event, held in Florence on Easter Sunday, features the explosion of a cart full of fireworks and dates back to the Crusades.
If all goes well, it is seen as a good omen for the city.

### May
**Corso dei Ceri** One of Italy's strangest festivals is held in
Gubbio on 15 May and features a race run by men carrying
enormous wooden constructions called *ceri*, in honour of
the town's patron saint, Sant'Ubaldo.

### July & August
**Il Palio** On 2 July and 16 August, Siena stages this
extraordinary horse race in the town's main piazza.

### December
**Natale** (Christmas) During the weeks preceding Christ-
mas, there are numerous processions and religious events.
Many churches set up elaborate cribs or nativity scenes –
Naples is famous for these.

## HOLIDAYS
Italy's national public holidays include:
**Epiphany** 6 January
**Easter Monday**
**Liberation Day** 25 April
**Labour Day** 1 May
**Ferragosto** 15 August
**All Saints' Day** 1 November
**Feast of the Immaculate Conception** 8 December
**Christmas Day** 25 December
**Feast of St Stephen** 26 December

Individual towns also have public holidays to celebrate the feasts of their patron saints. These include the Feast of St Mark in Venice on 25 April; the Feast of St John the Baptist on 24 June in Florence, Genoa and Turin; the Feast of St Peter and St Paul in Rome on 29 June; the Feast of St Rosalia in Palermo on 15 July; the Feast of St Januarius in Naples on 19 September; and the Feast of St Ambrose in Milan on 7 December.

## INTERNET RESOURCES

Following are some websites that will be useful planning tools for your trip to Italy:
www.beniculturali.com – museum information and online reservation options
www.cts.it – CTS is Italy's leading student travel organisation
www.italianmade.com or www.deliciousitaly.com – recipes galore
www.parks.it – for nature lovers, information on Italy's national parks
www.vatican.va – all about Vatican City, including virtual tours of the main sights
www.zoomata.com – a close-up on Italy's pop culture

## MONEY

Italy's currency since 2002 is the euro. There is little advantage in bringing foreign cash into Italy. A combination of travellers cheques and credit cards is the best way to take your money. If you buy travellers cheques in euro there should be no commission charged for cashing them. There are exchange offices at all major airports and train stations.

Major credit cards, including Visa, MasterCard and American Express, are widely accepted. They can also be used to get money from ATMs or, if you don't have a PIN, over the counter in major banks. If your credit card is lost, stolen or swallowed by an ATM, you can telephone toll free to have an immediate stop put on its use. For MasterCard the number in Italy is ☎ 800 87 08 66; for Visa ☎ 800 87 72 32; and for American Express, in Rome, call ☎ 06 722 82, which is a 24-hour card-holders' service.

You are not expected to tip in restaurants, but it's common to leave around 10%. In bars, leave small change. Bargaining is common in flea markets, but not in shops.

## POST

Italy's postal system is notoriously unreliable. It can take up to two weeks for mail to arrive in the UK or USA, while a letter to Australia is likely take anywhere up to three weeks. Postcards take even longer. Put them in an envelope and send them as letters.

The most efficient service to use is *posta prioritaria* (priority mail). Registered mail is known as *raccomandato,* insured mail as *assicurato* and express post as *postacelere.* Stamps *(francobolli)* are available at post offices and tobacconists (*tabacchi* – look for the official sign, a big 'T', usually white on black). The cost of sending a letter *via area* (airmail) depends on its weight, destination and method of postage. Information about postal services and rates can be obtained on ☎ 800 22 26 66 or at www.poste.it, in Italian.

## TELEPHONE

Italy's country code is ☎ 39. Area codes are an integral part of the telephone number, even if you're dialling a local number.

Local and long-distance calls can be made from a Telecom office or public phones. Italy's rates, particularly long-distance, are among the highest in Europe. Most public phones accept only *carte/schede telefoniche* (telephone cards), sold at tobacconists and newsstands. Off-peak hours for domestic calls are between 10pm and 8am, and for international calls from 11pm to 8am and Sunday.

To make a reverse-charge (collect) international call from a public phone, dial ☎ 170. For European countries, call ☎ 15. All operators speak English. For international directory inquiries, call ☎ 176. To call Italy from abroad, dial ☎ 39 and then the area code, including the 0.

---

**EMERGENCY NUMBERS**

- Ambulance ☎ 118
- Automobile Club d'Italia (ACI) ☎ 116
- Carabinieri (Police with military and civil duties) ☎ 112
- Fire Brigade ☎ 115
- Police (Questura) ☎ 113

Italy has one of the highest levels of mobile phone penetration in Europe, and there are several companies, including Telecom Italia Mobile, through which you can get a temporary or prepaid account if you already own a GSM, dual- or tri-band cellular phone. You will usually need your passport to open an account.

## VISAS

EU citizens require a national identity card or passport to stay in Italy for as long as they like. Citizens of many other countries, including the USA, Australia, Canada and New Zealand, don't need visas if they are entering as tourists. Visitors are technically obliged to report to a police station if they plan to stay at the same address for more than one week. Tourists staying in hotels or hostels are not required to do this since proprietors need to register guests with the police. A *permesso di soggiorno* is necessary (for non-EU citizens) if you plan to study, work (legally) or live in Italy. Non-EU citizens who want to study at a university or language school in Italy must have a study visa, which can be obtained from your nearest Italian embassy or consulate (see p258).

# TRANSPORT IN ITALY

## GETTING THERE & AWAY

A recent influx of low-cost airlines, and competition this has stirred, means you should be able to track down a decent fare to Italy. If you live in Europe, you can also travel overland by car, bus or train.

### Air

High season in Italy is June to September and bargains are hard to find during this period. Two months either side of this is the shoulder season, with low season officially November to March. Christmas and Easter can also cause fares to spike. The Internet can be the easiest way to locate and book reasonably priced tickets.

Full-time students and those under 26 years are eligible for discounted fares (see p705). Other cheap deals include the ever-expanding no-frills carriers, which sell direct to travellers.

Italy's main intercontinental gateway is the **Leonardo da Vinci Airport** (Fiumicino; ☎ 06

659 51; www.adr.it) in Rome, but regular intercontinental flights also serve Milan's **Linate Airport** ( ☎ 02 748 522 00; www.sea-aeroportimilano.it). Plenty of flights from other European cities also go direct to regional capitals around the country.

Many European and international airlines, as well as discount carriers, compete with the country's national carrier, Alitalia. International airlines flying to/from Italy include:

**Air Canada** (code AC; ☎ 06 55 112, toll free ☎ 91 90 91; www.aircanada.ca)

**Air France** (code AF; ☎ 848 88 44 66; www.airfrance.com)

**Air New Zealand** (code NZ; ☎ 06 48 79 11; www.airnz .co.nz)

**Alitalia** (code AZ; ☎ 06 6 56 41, 848 86 56 41; www .alitalia.it)

**American Airlines** (code AA; Milan ☎ 02 69 68 24 64; Rome ☎ 06 66 05 31 69; www.aa.com)

**British Airways** (code BA; ☎ 199 712 266; www .britishairways.com)

**British Midland** (code BD; ☎ 44-1332 854 000; www .flybmi.com)

**Delta Air Lines** (code DL; ☎ 800-477-999; www.delta .com)

**easyJet** (code U2; ☎ 848 88 77 66; www.easyjet.com)

**KLM** (code KL; ☎ 06 6501 1147; www.klm.com)

**Lufthansa** (code LH; ☎ 06 6568 4004; www.lufthansa .com)

**Meridiana** (code IG; ☎ 199 11 13 33; www.meridiana.it)

**Qantas** (code QF; ☎ 06 529 22 87; www.qantas.com)

**Ryanair** (code FR; ☎ 889 89 98 44; www.ryanair.com)

**Singapore Airlines** (code SQ; ☎ 06 478 55 360; www .singaporeair.com)

**Thai Airways International** (code TG; ☎ 06 47 81 31; www.thaiair.com)

**United Airlines** (code UA; ☎ 02 69 63 37 07; www .ual.com)

**Virgin Express** (code TV; Milan ☎ 02 48 29 60 00, rest of Italy ☎ 800 097 097; www.virgin-express.com)

If you have some patience, and a fast Internet connection, you can find good fares online. An excellent Italian site for low-cost travel is www.volareweb.com, in six different languages and adding new destinations rapidly (such as Warsaw, thanks to the expanding EU).

### Land
#### BUS

A consortium of European coach companies, **Eurolines** (www.eurolines.com), operates across Europe with offices in all major European cities. You can contact it in your own country or in Italy and the multi-language website gives comprehensive details of prices, passes and travel agencies where you can book tickets.

Covering at least 60 European cities and towns, **Busabout** ( ☎ 020 7950 1661; www.busabout.com) offers passes of varying duration, allowing you to use its hop-on hop-off bus network in Western in Central Europe. You can even book onward travel and accommodation on the bus or on the website.

### TRAIN
Trains run from major destinations throughout Europe direct to major Italian cities through **Eurostar** (ES; ☎ 0870 518 6186; www.eurostar.com). On overnight hauls, you can book a couchette for around €25. Travellers can take advantage of a range of passes, including **Inter-Rail** (www.interrailnet.com) and **Eurail** (www.eurail.com) passes (see p730). For prices and purchasing details, visit the websites. You can book local tickets at train stations and most travel agencies. For the latest fare information on journeys to Italy, contact the **Rail Europe Travel Centre** ( ☎ 0870 848 848; www.raileurope.co.uk).

## GETTING AROUND
Italy's extensive network of train and bus services means you can reach almost any destination fairly efficiently; for longer distances there are good domestic air and boat services. Renting a car obviously gives you the most freedom, but be prepared for shockingly expensive petrol and tolls, and you'll likely need a massage (or at least a stiff drink) from the stress of driving and parking in a big Italian city.

### Air
Travelling by plane can be expensive within Italy, but it's becoming more reasonable. The domestic airlines are **Alitalia** (www.alitalia.it), **Meridiana** (www.meridiana.it) and **Air One** (www.flyairone.it). The main airports are in Rome, Pisa, Milan, Bologna, Genoa, Turin, Naples, Catania, Palermo and Cagliari, but there are other, smaller airports throughout Italy. Domestic flights can be booked directly with the airlines or through any travel agency (listed throughout this guide).

---

**WHERE TO TAKE A BOAT RIDE**

**Venice** – Gondolas are pricey but molto romantica (p200)
**Capri** – Take a giro around the island, with a stop at the blue grotto (p237)
**Cala Gonone** – Explore Sardinia's gorgeous Golfo di Orosei (p254)

---

### Bicycle
Bikes are available for rent in many Italian towns (about €10 a day) and can travel in the baggage compartment of some Italian trains (but not on Eurostar or Intercity trains); bikes travel free on ferries.

### Boat
*Navi* (large ferries) service Sicily and Sardinia, and *traghetti* (smaller ferries) and *aliscafi* (hydrofoils) service the smaller islands, including Elba, the Aeolian Islands, Capri and Ischia. The main embarkation points for Sicily and Sardinia are at Genoa, La Spezia, Livorno, Civitavecchia, Fiumicino and Naples. **Tirrenia Navigazione** (www.tirrenia.it) services nearly all the Italian ports and has offices throughout the country. Most long-distance ferries travel overnight.

### Bus
Numerous bus companies operate within Italy. It is usually necessary to make reservations only for long trips, such as Rome–Palermo. Buses can be a cheaper and faster way to get around if your destination is not on major rail lines, such as from Umbria to Rome, and in the interior areas of Sicily and Sardinia. Major companies that run long-haul services include Marozzi (Rome to Brindisi), Interbus (Rome to Sicily) and Lazzi (from Lazio, Tuscany and other regions to the Alps).

### Car & Motorcycle
Roads are generally good throughout the country and there is an excellent network of autostrade. The main north-south link is the Autostrada del Sole, which extends from Milan to Reggio di Calabria (called the A1 from Milan to Naples and the A3 from Naples to Reggio). There's a toll to use most of Italy's autostrade, and you can pay by cash or credit card as you leave it. If you've got time, follow the *strade statali* (state roads),

ITALY

ITALY

toll free and often very scenic; these are designated by an 'S' or 'SS' on maps.

## HIRE

The most competitive multinational car-rental agencies are:

**Autos Abroad** ( ☎ 44-8700 667 788; www.autosabroad .com)

**Avis** ( ☎ 02 754 197 61; www.avis.com)

**Budget** ( ☎ 1-800 472 33 25; www.budget.com)

**Europcar** ( ☎ 06 481 71 62; www.europcar.com)

**Europe by Car** ( ☎ 1-800 223 15 16; www.europebycar .com)

**Hertz** ( ☎ 199 11 22 11; www.hertz.com)

To hire a car or motorcycle, you have to be aged over 21 and have a credit card, along with a valid EU driving licence, an International Driving Permit or your driving licence from your own country. If you're driving your own car, you'll need an international insurance certificate, known as a Carta Verde (Green Card), which can be obtained from your insurer.

Check with your car insurance, and credit cards, to find out what kind of coverage you have internationally. For the best rental rates, book your car before leaving home. The **Automobile Club d'Italia** (ACI; ☎ 06 4 99 81, 24hr info line ☎ 166 66 44 77) can be a helpful source of assistance once in Italy.

You'll have no trouble hiring a small Vespa or moped, with numerous rental agencies in cities, as well as motorcycles for touring (provided you're over 18 years of age).

## ROAD RULES

In Italy people drive on the right-hand side of the road and pass on the left. Unless otherwise indicated, you must give way to cars coming from the right. It is compulsory to wear seat belts if they are fitted to the car. If you are caught not wearing your seat belt, you will be required to pay an on-the-spot fine.

Random breath tests now take place in Italy; the blood-alcohol limit is 0.05%, and the penalities are severe.

Wearing a helmet is compulsory for motorcycle and moped riders and passengers – although you won't necessarily see this.

Some of the Italian cities, including Rome, Bologna, Florence, Milan and Turin, have introduced restricted access to both private and rental cars in their historical centres. The restrictions, however, do not apply to vehicles with foreign registrations. *Motorini* (mopeds) and scooters (such as Vespas) are able to enter the zones without any problems (and park on footpaths).

Speed limits, unless otherwise indicated by local signs, are: on autostrade 130km/h; on non-urban roads 110km/h; on secondary non-urban highways 90km/h; and in built-up areas 50km/h.

Petrol prices are high in Italy. Petrol is called *benzina*, unleaded petrol is *benzina senza piombo* and diesel is *gasolio*.

## Train

The partially privatised state train system that runs most of the services in Italy is **Trenitalia** ( ☎ 848 88 80 88; www.trenitalia.com, Italian only). There are several types of trains. Some stop at all the stations, such as *regionale* or *interregionale*, while faster trains, such as the Intercity (IC) and the fastest Eurostar Italia (ES), stop only at major cities. It is cheaper to buy all local train tickets in the country.

For details on timetables, services and prices, visit www.fs-on-line.com.

There are 1st and 2nd classes on all Italian trains, with the former costing almost double the latter. Intercity and Eurostar trains require a supplement (usually €4 to €16), determined by the distance of travel.

All tickets must be validated – in the yellow machines at the entrance to all train platforms – before you board the train.

Trenitalia offers its own discount passes for travel within Italy, available at major train stations. These include the Carta Verde, which offers a 20% discount for people aged from 12 to 26 years, and the Carta d'Argento offers the same discount to people aged 60 years and over; both cost €26 and are valid for one year.

The new Trenitalia Pass allows for four to 10 days of travel within a two-month period. At the time of writing, passes for 1st/2nd class cost €349/282.

# Greece

CONTENTS

GREECE

Ever popular, Greece has been saying *yasas* (hello) to travellers for thousands of years. Indeed it's been almost 2000 years since the Greek geographer and historian Pausanias penned the first travel guide to Greece. Today, visiting the country's magnificent archaeological sites leads travellers on a journey not only through the landscape but also through time, witnessing the legacy of Europe's greatest ages – the Mycenaean, Minoan, Classical, Hellenistic and Byzantine.

A trip through time isn't the only attraction of Greece – an island-hop around Greece's over 1400 islands is equally popular. Greece has more coastline than any other country in Europe and a breathtaking variety of island experiences await the visitor. You can join the relentless partying on Mykonos, check out the medieval splendour of Rhodes' old town and then recover on fertile Naxos, with its wonderful walks and beaches.

The allure of Greece is also due to less tangible attributes – the dazzling clarity of the light, the floral aromas that permeate the air, the spirit of places – for there is hardly a grove, mountain or stream which is not sacred to a deity, and the ghosts of the past still linger.

Amongst the myriad attractions, travellers to Greece inevitably end up with a favourite location they long to return to – it's just up to you to find yours.

**FAST FACTS**

- **Area** 131,900 sq km
- **Capital** Athens
- **Currency** euro (€); A$1 = €0.58;
  ¥100 = €0.76; NZ$ = €0.54; UK£1 = €1.50;
  US$1 = €0.83
- **Famous for** ancient ruins, beautiful beaches
- **Key Phrases** *yasas* (hello); *andio* (goodbye);
  *parakalo* (please); *efharisto* (thank you); *ne*
  (yes); *ohi* (no)
- **Official Language** Greek
- **Population** 11 million
- **Telephone Codes** country code ☎ 30;
  international access code ☎ 00; area codes
  are part of the 10-digit number within
  Greece – landline prefix ☎ 2, mobiles ☎ 6
- **Visas** visitors from most countries don't
  need a visa

## HIGHLIGHTS

- Explore the most famous monument of the ancient world, the **Acropolis** (p276), which literally towers above all else in the capital, Athens.
- Drink and dine in the gorgeous old Venetian town of **Nafplio** (p290), one of Greece's most romantic destinations.
- Hang out in the submerged caldera of fabulous **Santorini** (p307), regarded as the most spectacular of the Greek Islands.
- Soak in the history of **Rhodes** (p317), built by the Knights of St John and the largest inhabited medieval town in Europe.
- Head to the spectacular beaches of **Skiathos** (p328) – try Banana Beach on the southern coast.

## ITINERARIES

- **One week** Spend a day in Athens seeing its museums and ancient sites, then two days in the Peloponnese visiting Nafplio, Mycenae and Olympia, and four days in the Cyclades.
- **One month** Spend some extra time in both Athens and the Peloponnese, then catch an overnight ferry from Patra to Corfu for a couple of days. Head to Ioannina to explore the Zagoria villages of northern Epiros for two days before travelling back to Athens via Meteora and Delphi over three days. Take a ferry from Piraeus to Chios, then island-hop your way back through the northeastern Aegean Islands, the Dodecanese and the Cyclades over two weeks.

### TOP FIVE BEACHES

- **Little Banana Beach** where bathers go just that wee bit further than at **Big Banana Beach** (p328)
- **Agios Georgios Beach** accessible only by boat and backed by a spectacular 150m cliff (p305)
- **Milopotas Beach** skin-to-skin party mayhem in summer (p306)
- **Perissa Beach** sizzling black-sand beach with smooth lava out under the water (p307)
- **Lambi Beach** a pebble-beach lover's dream come true (p323)

### HOW MUCH?

- **Local telephone call** €0.20
- **Minimum taxi fare** €2
- **Herald Tribune newspaper** €2
- **Coffee** €2.50-3.50
- **Can of soft drink** €0.80

### LONELY PLANET INDEX

- **Litre of petrol** €0.70-0.85
- **Litre of bottled water** €1
- **Bottle of beer** €2
- **Souvenir T-shirt** €12
- **Street snack (gyros)** €1.30

## CLIMATE & WHEN TO GO

Greece's climate is typically Mediterranean with mild, wet winters followed by very hot, dry summers. Spring and autumn are the best times to visit – the weather's fine and there's a relative lack of tourists. Winter is quiet and the islands are in hibernation between late November and early April. The cobwebs are dusted off in time for Easter, and while everything is open the crowds have yet to arrive. From July until mid-September, it's summer madness and if you want to party, this is the time to go. The flipside is that everywhere is packed and rooms can be hard to find.

## HISTORY

Occupying a strategic position at the crossroads of Europe and Asia, Greece has endured a long and turbulent history.

During the Bronze Age (3000 to 1200 BC in Greece), the advanced Cycladic, Minoan and Mycenaean civilisations flourished. The Mycenaeans were swept aside in the 12th century BC and replaced by the Dorians, introducing Greece to the Iron Age. The next 400 years are often referred to as the Dark Ages, a period about which very little is known.

By 800 BC, when Homer's *Odyssey* and *Iliad* were first written down, Greece was undergoing a cultural and military revival with the evolution of the city-states, the most powerful of which were Athens and Sparta. Greater Greece – Magna Graecia –

GREECE

was created, with southern Italy an important component. The unified Greeks repelled the Persians twice, at Marathon (490 BC) and Salamis (480 BC). Victory over Persia was followed by unparalleled growth and prosperity known as the classical (golden) age.

## The Golden Age

During this period, Pericles commissioned the Parthenon, Sophocles wrote *Oedipus the King* and Socrates taught young Athenians to think. The golden age ended with the Peloponnesian War (431–404 BC), when the militaristic Spartans defeated the Athenians. They failed to notice the expansion of Macedonia under King Philip II, who easily conquered the war-weary city-states.

Philip's ambitions were surpassed by those of his son, Alexander the Great, who marched into Asia Minor, Egypt, Persia and what are now parts of Afghanistan and India. In 323 BC he met an untimely death at the age of 33, and his generals divided his empire between themselves.

## Roman Rule & the Byzantine Empire

Roman incursions into Greece began in 205 BC; by 146 BC, Greece and Macedonia had become Roman provinces. After the subdivision of the Roman Empire into eastern and western empires in AD 395, Greece became part of the eastern (Byzantine) Empire, based at Constantinople.

In the centuries that followed, Venetians, Franks, Normans, Slavs, Persians, Arabs and, finally, Turks took turns chipping away at the Byzantine Empire.

## The Ottoman Empire & Independence

After the end of the Byzantine Empire in 1453, when Constantinople fell to the Turks, most of Greece soon became part of the Ottoman Empire. Crete was not captured until 1670, leaving Corfu as the only island never occupied by the Turks. By the 19th century the Ottoman Empire was in decline. The Greeks, seeing nationalism sweep through Europe, fought the War of Independence (1821–32). The great powers – Britain, France and Russia – intervened in 1827, and Ioannis Kapodistrias was elected the first Greek president.

Kapodistrias was assassinated in 1831 and the European powers stepped in once again, declaring that Greece should become a monarchy. In January 1833, Otho of Bavaria was installed as king. His ambition, called the Great Idea, was to unite all the lands of the Greek people to the Greek motherland. In 1862 he was peacefully ousted and the Greeks chose George I, a Danish prince, as king.

During WWI, Prime Minister Venizelos allied Greece with France and Britain. King Constantine (George's son), who was married to the Kaiser's sister Sophia, disputed this and left the country.

## Smyrna & WWII

After the war, Venizelos resurrected the Great Idea. Underestimating the new-found power of Turkey under the leadership of Atatürk, he sent forces to occupy Smyrna (the present-day Turkish port of İzmir), with its large Greek population. The army was heavily defeated and this led to a brutal population exchange between the two countries in 1923.

In 1930 George II, Constantine's son, was reinstated as king and he appointed the dictator General Metaxas as prime minister. Metaxas' grandiose ambition was to combine aspects of Greece's ancient and Byzantine past to create a Third Greek Civilisation. However, his chief claim to fame is his celebrated *ohi* (no) to Mussolini's request to allow Italian troops into Greece in 1940 (see p336).

Greece fell to Germany in 1941 and resistance movements, polarised into royalist and communist factions, staged a bloody civil war lasting until 1949. The civil war was the trigger for a mass exodus that saw almost one million Greeks head off to places such as Australia, Canada and the USA. Entire villages were abandoned as people gambled on a new start in cities such as Melbourne, Toronto, Chicago and New York.

## The Colonels' Coup

Continuing political instability led to the colonels' coup d'etat in 1967. King Constantine (son of King Paul, who succeeded George II) staged an unsuccessful countercoup, and fled the country. The colonels' junta distinguished itself with its brutality, repression and political incompetence. In 1974 they attempted to assassinate Cyprus' leader, Archbishop Makarios, and when he escaped, the junta replaced him with the extremist Nikos Samson, prompting Turkey to occupy North Cyprus. The continued Turkish occupation of Cyprus remains one of the most contentious issues in Greek politics. The junta had little choice but to hand back power to the people. In November 1974 a plebiscite voted against restoration of the monarchy. Greece became a republic with the right-wing New Democracy (ND) party taking power.

## The Socialist 1980s

In 1981 Greece entered the then EC (European Community, now the EU). Andreas Papandreou's Panhellenic Socialist Movement (Pasok) won the next election, giving Greece its first socialist government. Pasok promised the removal of US air bases and withdrawal from NATO, but delivered only rising unemployment and spiralling debt.

Forced to step aside in 1989 during a scandal involving the Bank of Crete, an unprecedented conservative and communist coalition took over. Papandreou and four ministers were ordered to stand trial, and the coalition ordered fresh elections in October 1990.

## The 1990s & Beyond

The elections brought the ND party back to power with a slight majority. Tough economic reforms introduced by Prime Minister Konstantinos Mitsotakis soon made his government unpopular and corruption allegations forced Mitsotakis to call an election in October 1993.

Greeks again turned to Pasok and the ailing Papandreou, who was eventually cleared of all charges. He had little option but to continue with the austerity programme begun by Mitsotakis, quickly making his government equally unpopular.

Papandreou stood down in January 1996 due to ill health and the party abandoned its leftist policies, electing economist and lawyer Costas Simitis as leader. Simitis romped to a comfortable majority at a snap poll called in October 1996.

His government focused strongly on further integration with Europe. In January 2001, the EU agreed that Greece had met the economic requirements for monetary union and Greece duly adopted the euro as its currency in 2002.

Simitis was rewarded with a further four-year mandate in April 2000, but after suffering a serious popularity slump he announced an election as well as his retirement. Andreas Papandreou went to the polls as the prospective new leader in March 2004. The ND party led by Costas Karamanlis soundly defeated Pasok.

## Recent Foreign Policy

Greece's foreign policy is dominated by its sensitive relationship with Turkey. Greece has also had its hands full coping with events to the north precipitated by the break-up of former Yugoslavia and the collapse of the communist regimes in Albania and Romania.

Greece was a somewhat low-key member of the 'coalition of the willing' invasion of Iraq in March 2003. Faced with strong domestic opposition to the war, the government kept the role played by US forces based at Souda Bay in Crete very low key.

## PEOPLE

Greece's population was 10,939,771 according to the 2001 census. About one third of these inhabitants live in the Greater Athens area and more than two thirds of the population live in cities – confirming that Greece is now a primarily urban society. Less than 15% now live on the islands, the most populous being Crete, Evia and Corfu. There are 100,000 foreigners officially living permanently in Greece and an estimated one million living in Greece illegally.

## SPORT

Football (soccer) is by far the most popular spectator sport in Greece – not least since the shock victory of the Greek national team in Euro 2004. The season runs from September to mid-May, and the two most popular domestic teams are Olympiakos of Piraeus and Panathinaikos of Athens. The aforementioned clubs are also the main players in Greece's other main sport, basketball. These teams fare well in European competition, achieving more consistent success than their soccer-playing counterparts.

## RELIGION

About 98% of the Greek population belongs to the Greek Orthodox Church. The remainder are split between the Roman

# GREECE

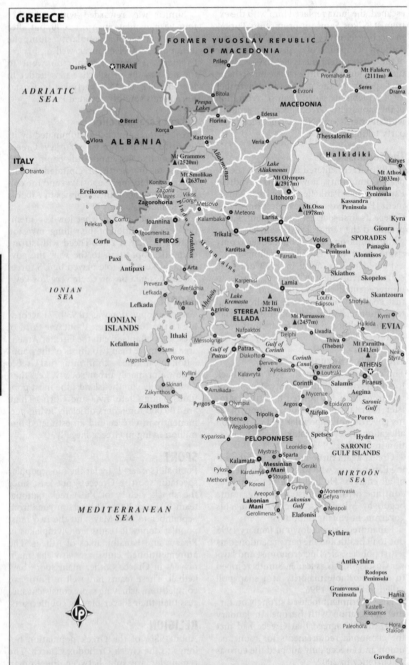

Catholic, Protestant, Evangelist, Jewish and Muslim faiths. While older Greeks and those in rural areas tend to be deeply religious, most young people are decidedly more secular.

## ARTS

The arts have been integral to Greek life since ancient times. Of all the ancient Greek arts, architecture has had the most profound influence. Greek temples, seen throughout history as symbolic of democracy, have been the inspiration for architectural movements such as the Italian Renaissance. While architecture had continuing importance throughout Greece's history, today masses of cheap concrete apartment blocks built in the 20th century in Greece's major cities belie this legacy.

Thankfully, the great works of Greek literature are not as easily besmirched. The first and greatest ancient Greek writer was Homer, author of *Iliad* and *Odyssey*. Little is known of Homer's life; where or when he lived, or whether, as it is alleged, he was blind.

Pindar (c518–438 BC) is regarded as the pre-eminent lyric poet of ancient Greece and was commissioned to recite his odes at the Olympic Games. The great writers of the tradition of love poetry were Sappho (6th century BC) and Alcaeus (5th century BC), both of whom lived on Lesvos. Sappho's poetic descriptions of her affections for women gave rise to the term 'lesbian'.

The Alexandrian, Constantine Cavafy (1863–1933), revolutionised Greek poetry by introducing a personal, conversational style. He is considered to be the TS Eliot of Greek literary verse. Poet George Seferis (1900–71) won the Nobel Prize for literature in 1963, and Odysseus Elytis (1911–96) won the same prize in 1979.

Nikos Kazantzakis, author of *Zorba the Greek* and numerous other novels, plays and poems, is the most famous of 20th-century Greek novelists.

The country's most famous painter was a young Cretan called Domenikos Theotokopoulos, who moved to Spain in 1577 and became known as the great El Greco. Famous painters of the 20th century include Konstantinos, Partenis and, later, George Bouzianis, whose work can be viewed at the National Art Gallery in Athens.

Musical instruments have been an integral part of Greek life since ancient times. In more recent times, the plucked-string sound of the ubiquitous bouzouki provides the background music of a thousand tavernas. The bouzouki is one of the main instruments of Rembetika music – which is in many ways the Greek equivalent of the American blues. Rembetika has its roots in the sufferings of the refugees from Asia Minor in the 1920s and is now enjoying a revival. Alongside the bouzouki, Rembetika music is accompanied by the guitar, violin and accordion. See p283 for where to see live Rembetika music.

Alongside music, dance is an integral part of Greek life. Whether at a wedding, nightclub or a village celebration, traditional dance is still widely practiced. If you don't see folk dancing on your travels, try to catch the Dora Stratou Dance Company (p282), in Athens.

In summer, Greek dramas are staged in the ancient theatres where they were originally performed. Drama continues to feature in domestic arts, but predominantly in Athens and Thessaloniki.

Greek film has for many years been associated with the earnest work of film maker Theo Angelopoulos, who won Cannes' Palme d'Or in 1998 with *An Eternity and One Day*. Since the late '90s, Greek cinema has witnessed a minor renaissance, with films such as *Safe Sex* (2000) luring Greek moviegoers back to the cinema.

Greek TV is dominated by chat shows, sport and foreign movies, only to be interrupted by localised versions of the latest American 'reality TV' hit.

## ENVIRONMENT
### The Land

Greece sits at the southern tip of the Balkan Peninsula and of its 1400 islands, only 169 are inhabited. The land mass is 131,900 sq km and Greek territorial waters cover a further 400,000 sq km.

Around 80% of Greece is mountainous. The Pindos Mountains in Epiros are the southern extension of the Dinaric Alps, which run the length of former Yugoslavia. The range continues down through central Greece and the Peloponnese, and re-emerges in the mountains of Crete. Less than a quarter of the country is suitable for agriculture.

Greece lies in one of the most seismically active regions in the world, recording over 20,000 earthquakes in the last 40 years – most of them very minor. The activity occurs because the eastern Mediterranean lies at the meeting point of three continental plates: the Eurasian, African and Arabian.

## Wildlife

The variety of flora in Greece is unrivalled in Europe. Spectacular wild flowers thrive and the best places to see the dazzling array of flowers are the mountains of Crete and the southern Peloponnese.

You won't encounter many animals in the wild, mainly due to hunting. Wild boar, still found in reasonable numbers in the north, is a favourite target for hunters. Squirrels, rabbits, hares, foxes and weasels are all fairly common on the mainland. Reptiles are well represented by snakes, including several poisonous viper species.

Lake Mikri Prespa in Macedonia has the richest colony of fish-eating birds in Europe, while the Dadia Forest Reserve in Thrace numbers such majestic birds as the golden eagle and the giant black vulture among its residents.

The brown bear, Europe's largest land mammal, still survives in very small numbers in the mountains of northern Greece, as does the grey wolf.

Europe's rarest mammal, the monk seal, was once very common in the Mediterranean Sea, but is now on the brink of extinction in Europe. There are about 400 left in Europe, half of which live in Greece. About 40 frequent the Ionian Sea and the rest are found in the Aegean.

The waters around Zakynthos are home to Europe's last large sea turtle colony, that of the loggerhead turtle *(Careta careta)*. The **Sea Turtle Protection Society of Greece** (☎ /fax 2105 231 342; www.archelon.gr) runs monitoring programmes and is always looking for volunteers.

## National Parks

Visitors who expect Greek national parks to provide facilities on par with those in countries such as Australia and the USA will be disappointed. Although they all have refuges and some have marked hiking trails, facilities are limited.

The most visited parks are Mt Parnitha, just north of Athens, and the Samaria Gorge on Crete. The others are Vikos-Aoös and Prespa national parks in Epiros; Mt Olympus on the border of Thessaly and Macedonia; and Parnassos and Iti national parks in central Greece.

If you want to see wildlife, the place to go is the Dadia Forest Reserve, and there is also a national marine park off the coast of Alonnisos, and another around the Bay of Laganas area off Zakynthos.

## Environmental Issues

Greece is belatedly becoming environmentally conscious but, regrettably, it's too late for some regions. Deforestation and soil erosion are problems that go back thousands of years. Olive cultivation and goats have been the main culprits, but fire-wood gathering, shipbuilding, housing and industry have all taken their toll.

Forest fires are also a major problem, with an estimated 25,000 hectares destroyed every year. Epiros and Macedonia in northern Greece are the only places where extensive forests remain.

General environmental awareness remains at a depressingly low level, especially where litter is concerned. The problem is particularly bad in rural areas, where roadsides are strewn with soft-drink cans and plastic packaging hurled from passing cars. Environmental education has begun in schools, but it will be some time before community attitudes change.

The news from the Aegean Sea is both good and bad. According to EU findings, it is Europe's least-polluted sea – apart from areas surrounding major cities – but like the rest of the Mediterranean, it has been overfished.

## FOOD & DRINK
### Staples & Specialities
#### SNACKS

Greece has a great range of fast-food options. Foremost among them are the *gyros* and the souvlaki. The *gyros* is a giant skewer laden with seasoned meat that grills slowly as it rotates, the meat being steadily trimmed from the outside. Souvlaki are small, individual kebabs (the Turkish name). Both are wrapped in pitta bread with salad and lashings of tzatziki (a yoghurt, cucumber and garlic dip). Other snacks are pretzel rings, *spanakopitta* (spinach and cheese pie) and tyropitta (cheese pie).

### STARTERS

Greece is famous for its appetisers, known as *mezedes* (literally, 'tastes'; *meze* for short). Standards include tzatziki, *melitzanosalata* (aubergine or eggplant dip), taramasalata (fish-roe dip), *dolmades* (stuffed vine leaves), *fasolia* (beans) and *oktapodi* (octopus). A selection of three or four starters represents a good meal and can be a very good option for vegetarians.

### MAIN DISHES

You'll find moussaka (layers of aubergine and mince, topped with béchamel sauce and baked) on every menu, alongside a number of other taverna staples. They include *moschari* (oven-baked veal and potatoes), *keftedes* (meatballs), *stifado* (meat stew), *pastitsio* (baked dish of macaroni with minced meat and béchamel sauce) and *yemista* (either tomatoes or green peppers stuffed with minced meat and rice). Most mains cost between €4 and €8.

The most popular fish are *barbouni* (red mullet) and *sifias* (swordfish) and they tend to be more expensive than meat dishes. Prices start at about €10 a serve. *Kalamaria* (fried squid) is readily available and cheap at about €5.

Fortunately for vegetarians, salad is a mainstay of the Greek diet. The most popular is *horiatiki salata,* normally listed on English-language menus as Greek or country salad. It's a mixed salad comprising cucumbers, peppers, onions, olives, tomatoes and feta cheese.

### DESSERTS

Turkish in origin, most Greek desserts are variations on pastry soaked in honey. Popular ones include baklava (thin layers of pastry filled with honey and nuts) and *kadaïfi* (shredded wheat soaked in honey).

### DRINKS

Bottled mineral water is cheap and available everywhere, as are soft drinks and packaged juices. Greece is traditionally a wine-drinking society. Retsina, wine flavoured with the resin of pine trees, is somewhat of an acquired taste. Fortu-

nately, Greece also produces an increasingly good range of wines from traditional grape varieties.

Mythos, in its distinctive green bottle, is the most common Greek beer, but in many places the choice is either Amstel or Heineken. You can expect to pay about €0.80 in a supermarket, €2 in a restaurant and from €5 in a club. The most popular aperitif is the aniseed-flavoured ouzo, which is mixed with water (turning the drink a milky white) to taste.

## Where to Eat & Drink

There are several varieties of restaurants in Greece. The most common is the taverna, traditionally an extension of the Greek home table. An *Estiatorio* (restaurant) often has the same dishes as a taverna but with higher prices. A *psistaria* specialises in charcoal-grilled dishes while a *psarotaverna* specialises in fish. *Ouzeria* (ouzo bars) often have such a range of *mezedes* that they can be regarded as eating places.

*Kafeneia* are the smoke-filled cafés where men gather to drink 'Greek' coffee, play backgammon and cards, and engage in heated political discussion.

Buying and preparing your own food is easy in Greece – every town of consequence has a supermarket, and there are plenty of fruit-and-vegetable shops.

# ATHENS ΑΘΗΝΑ

pop 3.7 million

Named in honour of Athena, the goddess of wisdom, ancient Athens ranks alongside Rome for its glorious past and its influence on Western civilisation. But it's just as well Athens wasn't named after Eros, the god of love, for it's a city that, until recently, few visitors fell in love with.

Today, however, Athens is undergoing a revival. The 2004 Olympics saw a slew of new public works projects, hotel renovations, new shops and restaurants that have made Athens worthy of more time than most visitors give it.

Still, Athens isn't a Greek goddess in the looks department. The urban sprawl, the appalling traffic congestion and pollution still plague the city. But delve a little deeper and Athens reveals the complexities that

GREECE

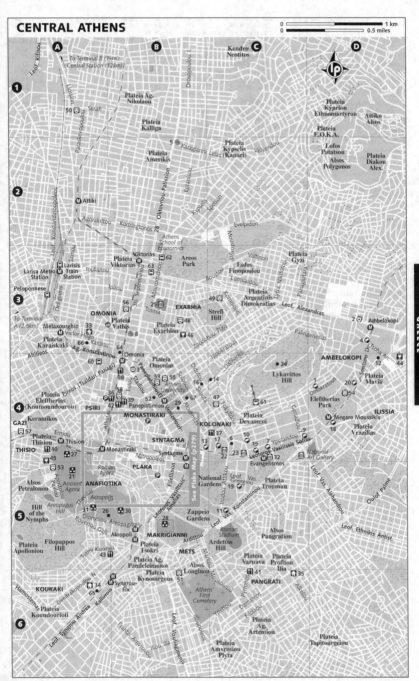

# CENTRAL ATHENS

GREECE

only a city with such a long history can. Traditional tavernas now compete with hip new restaurants; Rembetika is heard alongside DJs playing the latest lounge compilations; and exciting contemporary art can be seen as well as the wonderful Islamic art of the Benaki Museum (p277).

Instead of just relying on the past to attract visitors, Athens has finally started working on its future.

## ORIENTATION

Although Athens is an enormous, sprawling monster of a city, nearly everything of interest to travellers is located within a small area. This part of Athens is bounded by Omonia Sq (Plateia Omonias) to the north, Monastiraki Sq (Plateia Monastirakiou) to the west, Syntagma Sq (Plateia Syntagmatos) to the east and the Plaka district to the south. The city's two major landmarks, the Acropolis and Lykavittos Hill, are able to be seen from just about everywhere in this area.

Syntagma is the heart of modern Athens. Flanked by luxury hotels, banks and fast-food restaurants, the square is dominated by the old royal palace – home of the Greek parliament since 1935.

Once a smart address, Omonia is known today for its prostitutes and pickpockets rather than its position as a central square. All the major streets of central Athens meet here. Panepistimiou (El Venizelou) and Stadiou run parallel southeast to Syntagma, while Athinas leads south to the market district of Monastiraki. Monastiraki is in turn linked to Syntagma by Ermou – home to some of the city's smartest, most stylish shops – and Mitropoleos.

Mitropoleos skirts the northern edge of Plaka, the delightful old quarter of Athens, which was virtually all that existed when Athens was declared the capital of independent Greece. Its labyrinthine streets are nestled on the northeastern slope of the Acropolis, and most of the city's ancient sites are close by.

Streets are clearly signposted in both Greek and English. If you do happen to get lost, it's not at all hard to find help. If people see you glancing at a map, it's often enough to draw an offer of assistance. Anyone you ask will be able to direct you to Syntagma (*syn*-tag-ma).

---

### ATHENS IN TWO DAYS

Rise early and beat the crowds and heat at the **Acropolis** (p276) before retiring to the shade of Byzantino (p281) for lunch or a quick *gyros*. Explore **Plaka** (p283) in the afternoon and have dinner with a view of the Parthenon at **Pil Poul** (p281). On the second day take in the **National Archaeological Museum** (p277) and the **Benaki Museum** (p277) and head to **Plateia Kolonakiou** (p282) for people watching and shopping.

# INFORMATION
## Bookshops
The bigger *periptera* (kiosks) stock a good range of English-language magazines as well as international newspapers.

**Compendium Books** (Map p279; ☎ 2103 221 248; Nikis 28, Plaka) Specialises in English-language books and has a popular second-hand section.

**Eleftheroudakis Books** Syntagma (Map p279; ☎ 2103 314 180; Panepistimiou 17); Plaka (Map p279; ☎ 2103 229 388; Nikis 20) While the Panepistimiou shop is huge, both branches stock a good range of English-language books.

## Cultural Centres
The centres listed here below hold concerts, screen films and have occasional exhibitions. Check the *Kathimerini* section of the *International Herald Tribune* newspaper for listings.

**British Council** (Map pp273-4; ☎ 2103 692 314; www .britishcouncil.gr; Plateia Kolonakiou 17, Kolonaki)

**French Institute of Athens** (Map pp273-4; ☎ 2103 624 301; www.ifa.gr; Sina 31, Kolonaki)

**Hellenic-American Union** (Map pp273-4; ☎ 2103 629 886; Massalias 22) Holds frequent concerts and shows films, exhibitions and the like.

**Goethe Institut** (Map p279; ☎ 2103 608 115; Omirou 14-16, Kolonaki)

## Emergency
**Athens Central Police Station** (Map pp273-4; ☎ 2107 705 701/717; Leof Alexandras 173, Ambelokipi)

**Fire brigade** ( ☎ 199)

**First-aid service** ( ☎ 166)

**Police emergency** ( ☎ 100)

**Tourist police** ( ☎ 2108 707 000; Tsoha7, Ambelokipi; ☻ 24hr)

**Tourist police information service** ( ☎ 171; ☻ 24hr) Offers general tourist information as well as emergency help.

## Internet Access
The following selection of Internet cafés around the city centre charge about €3 per hour.

**Arcade Internet Café** (Map p279; ☎ 2103 210 701; Stadiou 5, Syntagma; ☻ 10am-10pm Mon-Sat, noon-8pm Sun) Has dedicated laptop connections.

**Bits & Bytes Internet Café** Exarhia (Map pp273-4; ☎ 2103 306 590; Akadimias 78; ☻ 24hr); Plaka (Map p279; Kapnikareas 19; ☻ 24hr)

**C@fe4U** (Map pp273-4; ☎ 2103 611 981; Ippocratous 44, Exarhia; ☻ 24hr)

**Plaka Internet World** (Map p279; Pandrosou 29, Monastiraki; ☻ 11am-11pm)

## Laundry
**Plaka Laundrette** (Map p279; Angelou Geronta 10, Plaka; 5kg wash & dry €8; ☻ 10am-6pm Mon-Sat, 10am-2pm Sun)

## Left Luggage
Many hotels store luggage free for guests, but be aware that it is usually nothing more than leaving them unsecured in a hallway. Left-luggage facilities are available at the airport and train station.

## Medical Services
**Duty doctor** ( ☎ 105; ☻ 2pm-7am)

**Duty hospital** ( ☎ 106)

**Duty pharmacy** ( ☎ 107)

**SOS Doctors** ( ☎ 2103 220 046/015; ☻ 24hr) Call-out service with multilingual doctors.

## Money
Most banks have branches around Plateia Syntagmatos. Banks are usually open from 8am to 2pm (from Monday to Thursday) and from 8am to 1.30pm Friday. The following services are useful for travellers:

**Acropole Foreign Exchange** (Map p279; ☎ 2103 312 765; Kydathineon 23, Plaka; ☻ 9am-midnight)

**American Express** (Map p279; ☎ 2103 223 380; Ermou 7, Syntagma; ☻ 8.30am-4pm Mon-Fri, 8.30am-1.30pm Sat)

**Eurochange** Syntagma (Map p279; ☎ 2103 220 155; Karageorgi Servias 4; ☻ 8am-8pm Mon-Fri, 10am-6pm Sat & Sun); Plaka (Map p279; ☎ 2103 243 997; Filellinon 22; ☻ 8am-8pm Mon-Fri, 9am-7pm Sat, 10am-7pm Sun) Exchanges Thomas Cook travellers cheques without commission.

## Post
**Athens' Central Post Office** (Map pp273-4; Eolou 100, Omonia; ☻ 7.30am-8pm Mon-Fri, to 2pm Sat) Unless your mail has specified otherwise, all poste restante will be sent here.

**Parcel post office** (Map p279; Stadiou 4, Syntagma; ☻ 7.30am-2pm Mon-Fri) Parcels over 2kg going abroad must be taken here, unwrapped for inspection. The office is in the arcade.

**Syntagma post office** (Map p279; cnr Mitropoleos & Plateia Syntagmatos; ☻ 7.30am-8pm Mon-Fri, to 2pm Sat, 9am-1pm Sun) If you're staying in Plaka, it's easier to get poste restante sent here.

## Telephone
Public phones are everywhere and only take phonecards – readily available from kiosks. See p338 for card denominations.

GREECE

## Toilets

Public toilets are thin on the ground in Athens, but fast-food outlets around the city have clean toilets that come in handy. You can also try a café, but without buying anything you're testing the hospitality of the tourist-tired Athenians.

## Tourist Information

**EOT Head Office** (Greek National Tourist Organisation; Map pp273-4; ☎ 2108 707 000; www.gnto.gr; Tsoha 7, Ambelokipi; ☺ 9am-4pm Mon-Fri); EOT tourist office (Map p279; ☎ 2103 310 561/562; Amerikis 2; ☺ 9am-4pm Mon-Fri); EOT airport office ( ☎ 2103 530 445; Arrivals Hall, Eleftherios Venizelos International Airport; ☺ 9am-7pm Mon-Fri, 10am-3pm Sat & Sun) Each of these offices stocks a fairly useful map featuring public transport routes around the city.

## DANGERS & ANNOYANCES

Athens has its fair share of problems that are associated with most big cities. Many of Athens' footpaths are marble, so it's important to wear a good pair of shoes and be very careful when these surfaces are wet.

Pickpockets are a major problem in Athens. Be aware on the metro system, the crowded streets around Omonia and the Sunday market on Ermou. Make sure your important documents are not in an outer pocket of a day-pack.

When you get in a taxi, either ensure the driver turns the meter on, negotiate a fair price or wait for another taxi. Be aware that some drivers use that age-old ruse of telling you that the hotel you have directed them to is closed or full. Insist on going where you want.

Several travel agents in the Plaka and Syntagma area employ touts that wander the streets promoting 'cheap' packages to the islands. Slick salespeople at the agency pressure you into buying outrageously overpriced packages.

### Bar Scams

Lonely Planet continues to receive readers' reports warning about bar scams, particularly around Syntagma. The most common ruse runs something like this: friendly Greek approaches solo male traveller and discovers that the traveller knows little about Athens; friendly Greek then reveals that he, too, is from out of town. However, he's found this great little bar and offers

---

**CHEAPER BY THE HALF DOZEN**

The €12 admission charge at the Acropolis buys a collective ticket that also gives entry to all the other significant ancient sites: the ancient agora, the Roman agora, the Keramikos, the Temple of Olympian Zeus and the Theatre of Dionysos. The ticket is valid for 48 hours, otherwise individual site fees apply. If you plan to see them, it's a bargain.

---

to take the visitor for a drink. They order, and the equally friendly owner offers another drink. Women appear, more drinks are provided and the visitor relaxes as he realises that the women are not prostitutes, just friendly Greeks. The crunch comes at the end of the evening when the traveller is presented with an exorbitant bill and the smiles disappear.

## SIGHTS & ACTIVITIES
### The Acropolis

Athens' defining feature is the **Acropolis** (Map p279; ☎ 2103 210 291; sites & museum adult/concession €12/6; ☺ 8am-6.30pm Apr-Oct, 8am-4.30pm Nov-Mar). It's arguably the most important ancient monument in the Western world, a fact not lost on the multitudes of tourists who converge on the Acropolis every day, so it's best to visit first thing in the morning or late in the afternoon.

Pericles commissioned most of the buildings here during the golden age of Athens in the 5th century BC. The site had been cleared for him by the Persians, who destroyed an earlier temple complex on the eve of the Battle of Salamis.

The entrance to the Acropolis is through the **Beule Gate**, a Roman arch that was added in the 3rd century AD. Beyond this is the **Propylaia**, the monumental gate that was the entrance to the city in ancient times. It was damaged in the 17th century when lightning set off a Turkish gunpowder store, but it has since been restored. To the south of the Propylaia is the small, graceful **Temple of Athena Nike**, which is not accessible to visitors.

Standing supreme over the Acropolis is the monument that more than any other epitomises the glory of ancient Greece – the **Parthenon**. Completed in 438 BC, this building is unsurpassed in grace and harmony.

Towards perfect form, its lines were ingeniously curved to counteract optical illusions. The base curves upward slightly towards the ends, and the columns become slightly narrower towards the top, to achieve the overall effect of making them look straight.

Above the columns are the remains of a Doric frieze, which was partly destroyed by Venetian shelling in 1687. The best surviving pieces are the controversial Elgin Marbles, carted off to Britain by Lord Elgin in 1801. The Parthenon, dedicated to Athena, contained an 11m-tall gold-and-ivory statue of the goddess completed in 438 BC by Phidias of Athens (only the statue's foundations exist today).

To the north is the **Erechtheion** and its much-photographed Caryatids, the six maidens who support its southern portico. These are plaster casts – the originals (except for the one taken by Lord Elgin) are in the **Acropolis Museum** (☼ noon-6.30pm Mon, 8am-6.30pm Tue-Sun Apr-Oct, 8am-4.30pm Nov-Mar).

## South of the Acropolis

The importance of theatre in the life of the Athenian city-state can be gauged from the dimensions of the enormous **Theatre of Dionysos** (Map pp273-4; ☎ 2103 224 625; adult/concession €2/1; ☼ 8am-7pm May-Oct, to sunset Nov-Apr), just south of the Acropolis; enter via Dionysiou Areopagitou. Built between 342 and 326 BC on the site of an earlier theatre, in its time it could hold 17,000 people spread over 64 tiers of seats, of which about 20 tiers survive.

The **Stoa of Eumenes**, built as a shelter and promenade for theatre audiences, runs west from the Theatre of Dionysos to the **Theatre of Herodes Atticus**, which was built in Roman times. It is used for performances during the Athens Festival, but is closed at other times.

## Temple of Olympian Zeus

Begun in the 6th century BC, this massive **temple** (Map pp273-4; ☎ 2109 226 330; adult/concession €2/1; ☼ 8.30am-3pm Tue-Sun) took more than 700 years to complete. Emperor Hadrian eventually managed to finish the job in AD 131. It was then the largest temple in Greece, impressive for the sheer size of its 104 Corinthian columns (17m high with a base diameter of 1.7m). The site is just southeast of Plaka, and the 15 remaining columns are a useful landmark.

## Roman Stadium

This **stadium**, east of the Temple of Olympian Zeus, hosted the first modern Olympic Games in 1896. It was originally built in the 4th century BC as a venue for the Panathenaic athletic contests. The seats were rebuilt in Pentelic marble by Herodes Atticus in the 2nd century AD, and faithfully restored in 1895.

## Ancient Agora

The **ancient agora** (Map pp273-4; ☎ 2103 210 185; adult/concession €4/2; ☼ 8.30am-3pm Tue-Sun) was the marketplace of ancient Athens and the focal point of civic and social life. Socrates spent a lot of his time here expounding his philosophy. The main monuments are the well-preserved **Temple of Hephaestus**, the 11th-century **Church of the Holy Apostles** and the reconstructed **Stoa of Attalos**, which houses the site's museum.

## Roman Agora

The Romans built their **agora** (Map pp279; ☎ 2103 245 220; cnr Pelopida Eolou & Markou Aureliou; adult/concession €2/1; ☼ 8.30am-3pm Tue-Sun) just west of its ancient counterpart. Its principal monument is the wonderful **Tower of the Winds**, which was built in the 1st century BC by a Syrian astronomer named Andronicus. Each side represents a point of the compass, and has a relief carving depicting the associated wind.

## National Archaeological Museum

Undoubtedly one of the world's great museums, the **National Archaeological Museum** (Map pp273-4; ☎ 2108 217 717; 28 Oktovriou-Patission 44; www.culture.gr; adult/concession €6/3; ☼ 12.30-7pm Mon, 8am-7pm Tue-Sun Apr-Oct, 10.30am-5pm Mon, 8am-5pm Tue-Sun Nov-Mar) contains important finds from all the major archaeological sites around the country. The crowd-pullers are the magnificent, exquisitely detailed gold artefacts from Mycenae and spectacular Minoan frescoes from Santorini (Thira). There is also a wonderful collection of sculpture, including the superb Cycladic collection of figurines.

## Benaki Museum

The **Benaki Museum** (Map pp273-4; ☎ 2103 671 000; cnr Leof Vasilissis Sofias & Koumbari 1, Kolonaki; adult/concession €6/3; ☼ 9am-5pm Mon, Wed, Fri & Sat, to midnight Thu, to 3pm Sun) houses the sumptuous

GREECE

collection of Antoine Benaki, the son of an Alexandrian cotton magnate named Emmanual Benaki. The collection includes ancient sculpture, Persian, Byzantine and Coptic objects, Chinese ceramics, icons, two El Greco paintings and a superb collection of traditional costumes.

## Goulandris Museum of Cycladic & Ancient Greek Art

This private **museum** (Map pp273-4; ☎ 2108 015 870; Neofytou Douka 4; adult/concession €3.50/2; ☷ 10am-4pm Mon & Wed-Fri, to 3pm Sat) was custom-built to display a fabulous collection of Cycladic art, with an emphasis on the early Bronze Age. Particularly impressive are the beautiful marble figurines.

## Lykavittos Hill

Pine-covered **Lykavittos** (Hill of Wolves; Map pp273-4) is the highest of the eight hills dotted around Athens. From the summit, there are all-embracing views of the city, the Attic basin and the islands of Salamis and Aegina – pollution permitting of course. The open-air Lykavittos Theatre, northeast of the summit, is used for concerts in summer.

GREECE

---

**FREE MUSEUMS**

Athens has nearly 30 museums and the following free museums are interesting and well worth a visit.

**Museum of Greek Popular Instruments** (Map p279; ☎ 2103 254 119; Diogenous 1-3, Plaka; ☷ 10am-2pm Tue & Thu-Sun, noon-6pm Wed) This popular museum has displays and recordings of traditional instruments.

**War Museum** (Map pp273-4; ☎ 2107 290 543/544; cnr Leof Vasilissis Sofias & Rizari 2; ☷ 9am-2pm Tue-Fri, 9.30am-2pm Sat & Sun) An interesting historical record of Greece in war through the ages.

**Theatre Museum** (Map pp273-4; ☎ 2103 629 430; Akadimias 50, Syntagma; ☷ 9am-2pm Mon-Fri) Memorabilia from Greek theatre in the 19th and 20th centuries, including photographs, costumes and props.

**Centre of Folk Arts & Traditions** (Map p279; ☎ 2103 243 987; Hatzimihali Angelikis 6, Plaka; ☷ 9am-1pm daily & 5-9pm Tue-Fri) Good displays of costumes, embroideries, musical instruments and pottery.

---

The main path to the summit starts at the top of Loukianou, or you can take the **funicular railway** (Map pp273-4; one way/return €2/4; ☷ 9.15am-11.45pm), from the top of Ploutarhou.

## Changing of the Guard

Every Sunday at 10.45am a platoon of traditionally costumed *evzones* (guards), accompanied by a band, marches down Vasilissis Sofias to the Tomb of the Unknown Soldier, located in front of the parliament building on Syntagma. The guards also change every hour on the hour – but without the musical accompaniment.

## FESTIVALS & EVENTS

The annual **Hellenic Festival** (www.greekfestival .gr) is the city's most important cultural event, from mid-June to late September. It features a line-up of international music, dance and theatre at the Theatre of Herodes Atticus. The setting is superb, backed by the floodlit Acropolis. Information and tickets are available from the **festival box office** (Map pp273-4; ☎ 2103 221 459; fax 2103 235 172; Stadiou 39, Syntagma; ☷ 8.30am-4pm Mon-Fri, 9am-2.30pm Sat). Tickets are not available for events until three weeks beforehand, but you'll find details of the year's events from February on the festival website.

## SLEEPING

Athens is a late-night and noisy city so we've made an effort to select accommodation that is central to the action, but lets you get some sleep. There's a good range of sleeping options around Plaka, the most popular place to stay due to its proximity to the sights. It fills up quickly in July and August and you should book ahead for this time of year.

## Camping

There are no camping grounds in central Athens, but the EOT has a brochure listing sites in Attica. There are several camping grounds southeast of Athens on the coast road to Cape Sounion.

**Athens Camping** (☎ 2105 814 114; fax 2105 820 353; Leof Athinon 198; per adult/tent €5/3; ☷ year-round) Located 7km west of the city centre on the road to Corinth, this is the closest camping ground to Athens. It has reasonable facilities, but little else going for it.

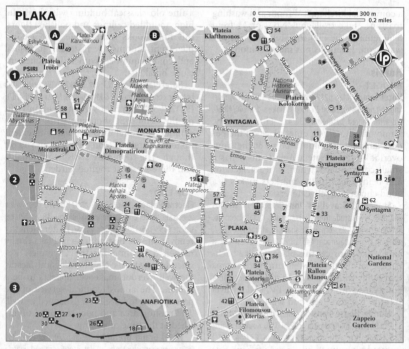

## PLAKA

## Hostels

**Athens International Youth Hostel** (Map pp273-4; ☎ 2105 234 170; fax 2105 234 015; Victor Hugo 16; dm HI members €8.66, dm nonmembers incl joining fee €15, daily stamp €2.50) While it's long been popular with travellers, the HI's dodgy location is a drawback. As long as you're not intimidated by the junkies and prostitutes that inhabit the area, the rooms are good value.

**Youth Hostel No 5** (Map pp273-4; ☎ 2107 519 530; y-hostel@otenet.gr; Damareos 75; dm with shared bathroom €10) The rooms here are basic, but this pleasant hostel is in a quiet neighbourhood. Facilities include coin-operated hot showers, a communal kitchen, TV room and washing machine. Take trolleybus No 2 or 11 from Syntagma to the Filolaou stop on Frinis, or walk from Evangelismos metro station.

## Hotels
### BUDGET

**Hotel Tempi** (Map p279; ☎ 2103 213 175; www.travel ling.gr/tempihotel; Eolou 29, Monastiraki; s/d/tr €40/48/60, s/d with shared bathroom €30/42) This friendly, family-run hotel is a quiet place on the pedestrian part of Eolou. Rooms at the front overlook pretty Plateia Agia Irini. It has a small communal kitchen with refrigerator and being close to the markets makes it a good choice for self-caterers.

**Student & Travellers' Inn** (Map p279; ☎ 2103 244 808; www.studenttravellersinn.com; Kydathineon 16, Plaka; d/tr €60/75, dm with shared bathroom €15-22, s/d with shared bathroom €45/50; ✷ ▯ ) Despite a small hike in prices this place is still a backpacker favourite. It's well-run, with rooms that range widely in size. Facilities include a courtyard with big-screen TV, and a travel service. It's also heated in winter.

**Marble House Pension** (Map pp273-4; ☎ 2109 234 058; www.marblehouse.gr; Zini 35A, Koukaki; s/d/tr €35/43/50, d/tr with shared bathroom €37/44; ✷ ) Located on a quiet cul-de-sac off Zini, this long-standing pension is still one of Athens' better budget hotels. All rooms have a bar fridge, ceiling fans and safety boxes for valuables. Breakfast is an extra €4.

### MID-RANGE

**Acropolis House Pension** (Map p279; ☎ 2103 222 344; fax 2103 244 143; Kodrou 6-8, Plaka; s/d with shared bathroom €64/80/96, s/d with shared bathroom €38.90/51.55; ✷ ) A beautifully preserved 19th-century house, this well-situated pension is a pretty good deal once you get your head around the price structure. There are discounts for longer stays, supplements for the air-conditioning etc. Rooms are heated in winter.

**Hotel Adonis** (Map p279; ☎ 2103 249 737; fax 2103 231 602; Kodrou 3, Plaka; s/d from €44/59; ✷ ) Located opposite the Acropolis House Pension, this comfortable and friendly hotel is one of the best deals around. There are excellent views of the Acropolis from the 4th-floor rooms and the rooftop bar, which doubles as the breakfast room. All rooms have a TV and the price includes breakfast.

**Hotel Cecil** (Map p279; ☎ 2103 217 909; www.cecil .gr; Athinas 39, Monastiraki; s/d/tr €55/80/105; ✷ ) In

a fine old classical building with beautiful high, moulded ceilings and polished floors, this hotel looks immaculate after a complete refit. Rooms are tastefully furnished and come equipped with a TV. Rates include breakfast.

**Hotel Plaka** (Map p279; ☎ 2103 222 096; www.plaka hotel.gr; cnr Kapnikareas 7 & Mitropoleos, Monastiraki; s/d/tr €99/125/145; ✷ ) With its great position right on the Ermou St shopping strip, it's little wonder this hotel is so popular with clued-up tour operators. Don't let that put you off though. The rooms are stylishly minimalist and there's a great rooftop garden.

### TOP END

**Electra Palace** (Map p279; ☎ 2103 370 000; www .electrahotels.gr; Navarchou Nikodimou 18-20, Plaka; s/d/ste €158/186/320; ℗ ✕ ✷ ≋ ) After a lengthy renovation, the best address in Plaka finally reopened in time for the Olympics. Resplendent with its new neoclassical façade, the well-overdue makeover appears to be a winner. The almost comical service of the past appears to have been jettisoned as well. The rooftop area and pool remained unfinished at the time of writing.

**Hotel Grand Bretagne** (Map p279; ☎ 2103 330 000; www.grandebretagne.gr; Vassileos Georgiou 1, Plateia Syntagmatos; s/d from €470/510; ℗ ✕ ✷ ≋ ) Built in 1842 as a residence, this wonderful hotel has a commanding presence – made even more so by its recent renovation. Restored to the opulence of its original transformation to a hotel (in 1874), it has no peer in Athens. Nonsmoking floors, rooms for disabled guests, 24-hour butler service and a gymnasium are just some of the extras on offer. Add to this its prime position off Plateia Syntagmatos and it's a winning combination in this price category.

## EATING

For travellers, eating in Athens has been traditionally associated with a taverna meal in Plaka, yet the past couple of years has seen city eating become both more diversified and sophisticated. While every visitor should experience the traditional taverna meal, there's now some French-influenced fine dining and Asian and fusion food on offer.

## Budget

Athens has plenty of places where you can eat and run. Locals in a hurry grab a coffee and a snack from one of the popular branches of the ubiquitous Flocafé's and a quick bite from a branch of the Everest sandwich shops.

**Savas** (Map p279; ☎ 2103 245 048; Mitropoleos 86; gyros €1.30; ☽ 9pm-3am) One of the best places to try a *gyros* – either pork, beef or chicken, all equally greasy and equally good. Eat in or takeaway.

**O Platanos** (Map p279; ☎ 2103 220 666; Diogenous 4, Plaka; mains €7; ☽ noon-4.30pm & 7.30pm-midnight Mon-Sat, noon-4.30pm Sun) A taverna without touts, O Platanos serves some of the best home cooking around. Try one of the lamb dishes and the barrel retsina that for once is more suited for drinking than stripping the paint off a car. While the service is leisurely, the shady outdoor courtyard is a pleasant and tranquil retreat. No credit cards.

**Noodle House** (Map p279; ☎ 2103 318 585; Apollonos 11, Plaka; mains €8; ☽ 11am-midnight Mon-Sat, from 5pm Sun) The pick of several Asian restaurants around Plaka, Noodle House serves up tasty noodles and soups at honest prices. The menu features a mix of mainly Thai- and Singapore-based dishes and you can order it for takeaway or home delivery.

**Eden Vegetarian Restaurant** (Map p279; ☎ 2103 248 858; Lyssiou 12, Plaka; mains €4.70-8.50; ☽ 11am-midnight Wed-Mon) Eden is the long-standing champion of vegetarian restaurants in Athens, serving up vegetarian versions of Greek classics, such as moussaka (€6.80) and a mushroom *stifado* (cooked in a tomato puree, €8.80). There's also organic wine and beer on offer. No credit cards.

---

**THE AUTHORS CHOICE**

In terms of haute cuisine, honours must go to Spondi (p281), but in the never-ending search for authentic Athenian dining, devoid of the taverna touts and English-language fixed-price touristic menus, **Taverna Papandreou** (Map pp273-4; ☎ 2103 214 970; Aristogeitonos 1; mains €4.50-6.80; ☽ 24hr) fits the bill. Situated in the central meat market – both the location and food are not exactly vegetarian friendly – it attracts the gamut of Athenians, from hungry market workers during the day to bar hoppers at 5am looking for a pre-emptive cure for that hangover. Specialties of the house include *patsa* (tripe soup), but less adventurous taverna fare is also on offer.

## Mid-Range

**Taverna tou Psiri** (Map pp273-4; ☎ 2103 214 923; Eshylou 12, Psiri; meals for 2 people €25; ☽ noon-1am) This taverna is a local favourite, both for its cheerful atmosphere and below-average prices for a Psiri eatery. The daily menu is full of Greek taverna specials – all good stuff. It's tucked away off Plateia Iroön; look for the apt mural of a drunk leaning against a lamppost.

**Eat** (Map pp273-4; ☎ 2103 249 129; Adrianou 91, Plaka; mains €12; ☽ 10-12.30am) A stylish antidote to the endless tavernas of the Plaka eating scene, Eat offers salads, pastas and modern interpretations of some Greek classics, as well as good wines by the glass. Try the *haloumi* salad with balsamic vinaigrette (€8) or just drop in for a coffee and listen to the great music selection.

**Byzantino** (Map p279; ☎ 2103 227 368; Kydathineon 18, Plaka; mains €11; ☽ 9-2am Mon-Sat) One of the better choices for the obligatory Plaka taverna meal, Byzantino offers good-value traditional cuisine. The fish soup and the starters are excellent and it's popular with tourists and locals alike who take an outside table to watch the passing Plaka parade.

**Taverna tou Psara** (Map p279; ☎ 2103 218 734; Eretheos 16, Plaka; mains €5-18; fish from €40 a kg; ☽ 11-1am) This refurbished taverna is one of the best around, serving up fabulous *mezedes* – try the *melizanokeftedes* (eggplant croquettes, €5.30) – and excellent meat or fish grills. Secure a table on the terrace with city views and you've scored one of the best taverna experiences in the city.

## Top End

Here's a small selection from Athens' increasingly impressive fine-dining scene. All accept credit cards, are only open for dinner (keep in mind most Athenians don't arrive before 10pm), and bookings are essential.

**Pil Poul** (Map pp273-4; ☎ 2103 423 665; Apostolou Pavlou 51, Thisio; mains €30; ☽ 8pm-12.30am Mon-Sat) Arguably the best 'great food and great view' combination in Athens. A creative Franco-Mediterranean menu featuring ingredients such as lobster and foie gras, coupled with Acropolis views, makes this an excellent choice for a romantic dinner.

**Spondi** (Map pp273-4; ☎ 2107 520 658; Pyrronos 5, Pag12, Plaka; mains €30; ☽ 8.30pm-12.30am) Perhaps Athens' own temple of gastronomy, Spondi earns its Michelin star for a creative menu combining French technique with fresh ingredients. The starters, such as sea bass with rose petal sauce (€25), are superb, but pace yourself because the desserts are a knock-out. Refreshingly for a restaurant of this pedigree, the staff are friendly and helpful and the atmosphere relaxed.

## Cafés

Athens café society is as strong as ever, despite having some of the highest prices for a coffee in Europe. To best experience the Athens café scene, head to Kolonaki, where a mind-boggling array of cafés run off Plateia Kolonakiou, on Skoufa and Tsakalof Sts. Take whatever free seats you can find and settle in for some slow *frappé* (frothy ice coffee) drinking and plenty of people watching.

## Self-Catering

You'll find the best selection of fresh produce at the **fruit and vegetable market** (Map pp273-4) on Athinas, which is opposite the **meat market** (Map pp273-4). The following are among the main supermarkets in central Athens: **Bazaar Discount Supermarket** (Map pp273-4; Eolou 104, Omonia), **Marinopoulos** (Map pp273-4; Athinas 60, Omonia), **Marinopoulos** (Map p279; Kanari 9, Kolonaki), **Vasilopoulou** (Map pp273-4; Stadiou 19, Syntagma) and **Veropoulos** (Map pp273-4; Parthenos 6, Koukaki).

## DRINKING

Athens has more than its fair share of drinking establishments. There are casual, grungy student hang-outs, pubs for the expats, and bars where you can flash your cash. During the summer months, however, most of the action heads to the islands. Outside summer, the bars of Kolonaki and Psiri are very popular.

**Brettos** (Map p279; ☎ 2103 232 110; Kydathineon 41, Plaka; ☺ 10am-midnight) A distillery and bottle shop by day, at night this old family-run place is a popular stop to imbibe and to check out its eye-catching, back-lit collection of coloured bottles. Right in the heart of Plaka, it's a good stop for a nightcap – just watch those shots of Brettos-brand spirits (€1.50); they're lethal.

**Bee** (Map p279; ☎ 2103 212 624; cnr Miaouli & Themidos, Psiri; ☺ 8pm-1am Tue-Sun, lunch from noon Sat & Sun) A popular bar/restaurant (with good food), Bee attracts a mixed crowd that spills out onto the street when it gets late. Also great for a Sunday-afternoon drink after the markets.

**Mike's Irish Bar** (Map pp273-4; ☎ 2107 776 797; Sinopsis 6, Ambelokipi; ☺ 8pm-4am) For those who can't go too long without a pint of Guinness or Murphy's (both €7), Mike's is where you can satisfy that need. A favourite watering hole of the expat community, you can play darts or listen to live music nightly from 11.30pm.

**Stavlos** (Map pp273-4; ☎ 2103 452 502; Iraklidon 10, Thisio; ☺ 10-4am) One of the originals in Thisio, Stavlos is an arty venue with an internal courtyard and a café/brasserie outside. It has a laid-back, cool vibe during the day, while the DJ sets the mood as the night goes on.

**Wonderbar** (Map pp273-4; ☎ 2103 818 577; Themistokleous 80, Exarhia; ☺ 10-3.30am) Cool by day, packed by night, this café/lounge bar attracts hip young Athenians to the emerging area of Exarhia.

## ENTERTAINMENT

The best source of entertainment information is the weekly *Athenorama*, but it's in Greek only. The *Kathimerini* supplement that accompanies the *International Herald Tribune* has daily event listings and the weekly *Athens News* carries an entertainment guide.

## Cinemas

Most cinemas show recent releases in English and admission prices are €6 to €8. Two of the major cinemas in central Athens are **Apollon** (Map p279; ☎ 2103 236 811; Stadiou 19) and the **Astor** (Map p279; ☎ 2103 231 297; Stadiou 28).

## Classical Music, Opera and Dance

**Dora Stratou Dance Company** (Map p279; ☎ 2109 216 650; Filopappos Hill; tickets €13; ☺ 9.30pm Tue-Sat, 8.15pm Sun May-Sep) A colourful 1½-hour traditional folk dancing show featuring over 75 dancers and musicians.

**Megaron Mousikis** (Athens Concert Hall; Map pp273-4; ☎ 2107 282 333; www.megaron.gr; Leof Vasilissis Sofias, Ambelokipi; ☺ box office 10am-6pm Mon-Fri, to 2pm Sat) An excellent concert venue hosting performances by local and international artists. Tickets generally go on sale three weeks before the performance and range from €10 to €40.

**Olympia Theatre** (Map pp273-4; ☎ 2103 611 516; www.nationalopera.gr; Akadimias 59, Exarhia) The Greek National Opera season runs from November to June, featuring works by artists such as Verdi, Handel and Puccini. Tickets range from €17 for students to €50 for box seats.

## Gay & Lesbian Venues

The greatest concentration of gay bars is to be found around Makrigiann, south of the Temple of Olympian Zeus. Most places don't get moving until midnight. Here's a small selection of the scene:

**Alekos' Island** (Map pp273-4; ☎ 2103 640 249; Tsakalof 42, Kolonaki; ☽ 6pm-late) One of Athens' long-standing gay bars, it attracts an older crowd to its candle-lit interior.

**Aroma Gynekas** (Map pp273-4; ☎ 2103 819 615; Tsamadou 15, Exarhia; ☽ 10.30pm-late) Packed on weekends, this lesbian dance club is one of the busiest in Athens, playing both mainstream and Greek music.

**Kirkis & Lizard** (Map pp273-4; ☎ 2103 466 960; Apostolou Pavlou 31, Thisio; Kirkis ☽ 10–3am, Lizard ☽ 11pm-late Fri-Sun) A popular gay and lesbian hang-out, Kirkis café is busy from late afternoon onwards. Lizard, the club upstairs, is busy over the weekend.

## Live Music

### POP, ROCK & JAZZ

Tickets for concerts are sold at **Ticket House** (Map pp273-4; ☎ 2103 608 366; Panepistimiou 42). Venues include:

**Rodon Club** (Map pp273-4; ☎ 2105 247 427; Marni 24, Omonia; ☽ from 10pm) The city's main rock venue.

**Gagarin 205 Club** (Map pp273-4; ☎ 2108 547 601; Liossion 205; ☽ from 9.30pm) A newer, more intimate live venue.

**Half Note** (Map pp273-4; ☎ 2109 213 310; Trivonianou 17, Mets; ☽ from 10.30pm) The principal jazz venue in Athens.

### REMBETIKA

**Rembetika Stoa Athanaton** (Map pp273-4; ☎ 2103 214 362; Sofokleous 19; ☽ 3-6pm & midnight-6am Mon-Sat Oct-Apr) Located above the meat market, this is *the* place to experience the Greek version of the blues.

## Nightclubs

The clubs don't get busy until midnight, with most people staying at bar-restaurants until then. Expect to pay at least €5 for a beer. A cover charge usually applies, especially later in the week and when there's a guest DJ.

**+ Soda** (Map pp273-4; ☎ 2103 456 187; Ermou 161, Thisio; admission incl one drink €10-20; ☽ midnight-late Sep-May) This multilevel superclub features

international guest DJs and attracts a young group of clubbers who come for progressive and hard-core house and techno.

**Decadence** (Map pp273-4; ☎ 2108 823 544; cnr Pouliherias & Voulgaroktonou 69, Lofos Strefi; admission incl one drink €6-8; ☽ 10.30pm-4am) For indie and alternative music lovers, Decadence has two levels of sonic mayhem, with a quieter bar scene on the lower floor and club upstairs.

## SHOPPING

Athens offers excellent shopping opportunities for Greek jewellery, shoes and clothes, as well as souvenirs. The most concentrated shopping is on Ermou, from Syntagma to Monastiraki, with clothes and shoes being the major attraction. The clothes boutiques are scattered around Kolonaki; designers and jewellers are on Voukourestiou. Plaka and Monastiraki are full of souvenir and gift shops. Here you can pick up common souvenirs such as backgammon sets, olive-wood gift items, key rings, worry beads and silver and gold jewellery.

For folk art and other crafts visit the **National Welfare Organisation** (Map p279; ☎ 2103 218 272; cnr Apollonos & Ipatias, Plaka), which has a great selection of hand-woven carpets, tapestries and tablecloths. Sandal wearers head to **Stavros Melissinos' Store** (Map p279; ☎ 2103 219 247; Aghias Theklas 2, Monastiraki) for some custom Jesus sandals and some poetry from the poet sandal maker. If you're in Athens on a Sunday, it's obligatory to visit the **Sunday market** (Map p279; ☽ 7am-2pm) near the Athens flea market, starting at Plateia Monastiraki and onto Ermou.

## GETTING THERE & AWAY
### Air

Athens is served by **Eleftherios Venizelos International Airport** ( ☎ 2103 530 000; www.aia.gr) at Spata, 27km east of Athens.

Facilities at the new state-of-the-art airport are excellent, with a good selection of reasonably priced cafés and some decent duty free, including local goods and foodstuffs. See p284 for information on getting to/from the airport. International-airline phone numbers in Athens are listed on p329.

The vast majority of domestic flights are handled by Greece's much-maligned national carrier, **Olympic Airways** (toll free ☎ 8011 144 444, flight information ☎ 2109 666 666; www.olympic airways.gr); Koukaki head office (Map pp273-4; ☎ 2103

*GREECE*

569 111; Leof Syngrou Andrea 96); Syntagma (Map p279; ☎ 2109 264 444; Filellinon 15); Omonia (Map pp273-4; ☎ 2109 267 218; Kotopouli Merakas 1).

Crete-based competitor **Aegean Airlines** (reservations ☎ 8011 120 000; www.aegeanair.com) offers flights to many of the same destinations as Olympic. It has a city **sales office** (Map p279; ☎ 2103 315 502; Othonos 10) at Syntagma.

## Bus

Athens has two main intercity bus stations. EOT gives out schedules for both stations detailing departure times, journey times and fares.

**Terminal A** ( ☎ 2105 298 740; Kifissou 100), northwest of Omonia, has buses to the Peloponnese, Ionian Islands and western Greece. To get to Terminal A, take bus No 015 from the junction of Zinonos and Menandrou, near Plateia Omonia.

**Terminal B** ( ☎ 2108 317 096), off Liossion, is north of Omonia and has departures to central and northern Greece, as well as to Evia. To get to Terminal B, take bus No 024 from outside the main gate of the National Gardens on Amalias. Get off the bus at Liossion 260, turn right onto Gousiou and you'll see the terminal at the end of the road.

Buses for Attica leave from the **Mavromateon bus terminal** (Map pp273-4; cnr Alexandras & 28 Oktovriou-Patission). Buses to Rafina and Marathon leave from the bus stops 10m north of Mavromateon.

## Car & Motorcycle

National Rd 1 is the main route north from Athens. It starts at Nea Kifissia. To get there from central Athens, take Vasilissis Sofias from Syntagma and follow the signs. National Rd 8, which begins beyond Dafni, is the road to the Peloponnese; take Agiou Konstantinou from Omonia.

The northern reaches of Syngrou, just south of the Temple of Olympian Zeus, are packed solid with car-rental firms.

## Ferry

See p286 for information on ferries travelling to and from the islands.

## Train

At the time of writing, the city's new Central Station, 12km north of the city at Arharnon, was not yet operational. Access to the station will be by suburban train and all intercity train services will leave from there. Until this opens, trains to central and northern Greece leave from Larisis train station (Map pp273-4), and trains to the Peloponnese leave from the Peloponnese station 200m away.

More information on the services is available from **OSE offices** Omonia (Map pp273-4; ☎ 2105 240 647; Karolou 1; ⏰ 8am-6pm Mon-Fri, to 3pm Sat); Syntagma (Map pp273-4; ☎ 2103 624 402; Sina 6; ⏰ 8am-3.30pm Mon-Fri, to 3pm Sat). Both offices handle advance bookings.

## GETTING AROUND

The new metro system has made getting around central Athens (and to Piraeus) very easy, but Athens' road traffic is still horrendous. Most of Athens' public-transport services were being upgraded for the Olympics at the time of writing. A daily travel pass (€2.90) is valid for all forms of public transport, including a trip to/from the airport.

### To/From the Airport
#### BUS

Bus E94 (25 minutes, every 16 minutes 6am to midnight) operates between the airport and the eastern terminus of metro Line 3 at Ethniki Amyna.

Bus E95 (one to 1½ hours, every 30 minutes) operates between the airport and Plateia Syntagmatos. The bus stop is outside the National Gardens on Amalias on the eastern side of Plateia Syntagmatos.

Bus E96 (one to 1½ hours, every 40 minutes) operates between the airport and Plateia Karaïskaki in Piraeus.

Tickets for all these services cost €2.95, are valid for 24 hours and can be used on all forms of public transport in Athens – buses, trolleybuses and the metro.

#### METRO

Completed just in time for the Olympics, Line 3 of the metro is now linked to the airport via the train system and can take you to the city centre in under 30 minutes.

#### TAXI

Taxi fares vary according to the time of day and level of traffic, but you should expect to pay €20 to €30 from the airport to the city centre, and €20 to €25 from the airport to Piraeus, depending on traffic conditions. Both trips can take anywhere between one and 1½ hours.

## Bus & Trolleybus

Blue-and-white suburban buses operate every 15 minutes from 5am to midnight. Route numbers and destinations, but not the actual routes, are listed on the free EOT map. Timetables can be obtained from the **GNTO** (www.gnto.gr) in EOT tourist offices, or the **Athens Urban Transport Organisation** (OASA; ☎ 8836 076; www.oasa.gr). The EOT map does, however, mark the routes of the yellow trolleybuses, making them easy to use. They also run from 5am to midnight.

There are special buses that operate 24 hours to Piraeus. Bus No 040 leaves from the corner of Syntagma and Filellinon, and No 049 leaves from the Omonia end of Athinas. The buses run every 20 minutes from 6am to midnight, and then hourly until 6am.

Tickets for all these services cost €0.45, and must be purchased before you board – either from a ticket booth or from a *periptero* (kiosk). The same tickets can be used on either buses or trolleybuses and must be validated as soon as you board.

## Metro

The opening of the first phase of the long-awaited new metro system transformed travel around central Athens. Coverage is still largely confined to the city centre, but that's good enough for most visitors. For the latest on the metro, visit www.ametro.gr. The following is a brief outline of the three lines that make up the network:

**Line 1** (Green) This line is the old Kifissia-Piraeus line and is indicated in green on maps and signs. Useful stops include Piraeus (for the port), Monastiraki and Omonia (city centre), Plateia Viktorias (National Archaeological Museum) and Irini (Olympic Stadium). Omonia and Attiki are transfer stations with connections to Line 2; Monastiraki will eventually become a transfer station with connections to Line 3.

**Line 2** (Red) This line runs from Sepolia in the northwest to Dafni in the southeast and is indicated in red on maps and signs. Useful stops include Larisa (for the train stations), Omonia, Panepistimiou and Syntagma (city centre) and Akropoli (Makrigianni). Attiki and Omonia are transfer stations for Line 1, while Syntagma is the transfer station for Line 3.

**Line 3** (Blue) This line runs northeast from Syntagma to Ethniki Amyna. It is indicated in blue on maps and signs. Useful stops are Evangelismos (for the museums on Vasilissis Sofias) and Ethniki Amyna (buses to the airport). Syntagma is the transfer station for Line 2.

Travel on Lines 2 and 3 costs €0.75, while Line 1 is split into three sections: Piraeus–Monastiraki, Monastiraki–Attiki and Attiki–Kifissia. Travel within one section costs €0.60 and a journey covering two or more sections costs €0.75. The same conditions apply everywhere: tickets must be validated at the machines at platform entrances before travelling. The penalty for travelling without a validated ticket is €23.50.

The metro operates from 5am to midnight. Trains run every three minutes during peak periods and every 10 minutes at other times.

## Taxi

Athenian taxis are yellow. The flag fall is €0.75 and there's an extra surcharge of €0.60 from ports and train and bus stations, as well as a €0.90 surcharge from the airport. After that, the day rate (tariff 1 on the meter) is €0.23 per kilometre. The rate doubles between midnight and 5am (tariff 2 on the meter). Baggage is charged at €0.30 per item over 10kg. The minimum fare is €1.50, which covers most journeys in central Athens.

# AROUND ATHENS
## Piraeus Πειραιάς
**pop 175,697**

Greece's main port, and one of the main ports of the Mediterranean, Piraeus is the hub of the Aegean ferry network. Piraeus has been the port of Athens since classical times, but these days it's more like an outer suburb of the space-hungry capital. The streets that most travellers see on their way to a ferry are every bit as traffic-clogged as in Athens, but a trip to tranquil and picturesque Mikrolimano (Small Harbour), with its cafés and fish restaurants, reveals another side to Piraeus.

### ORIENTATION & INFORMATION

Piraeus consists of a peninsula surrounded by harbours. The largest of its three harbours is the Megas Limin (Great Harbour), on the western side, where all the ferries leave from, along with hydrofoil and catamaran services to Aegina and the Cyclades. Zea Marina (Limin Zeas) and Mikrolimano (Small Harbour), on the eastern side of the peninsula, are for private yachts.

An Internet café, **Internet Center** ( ☎ 2104 111 261; Akti Poseidonos 24; ⊙ 10am-11pm) is on the main road, across from the main harbour.

**GREECE**

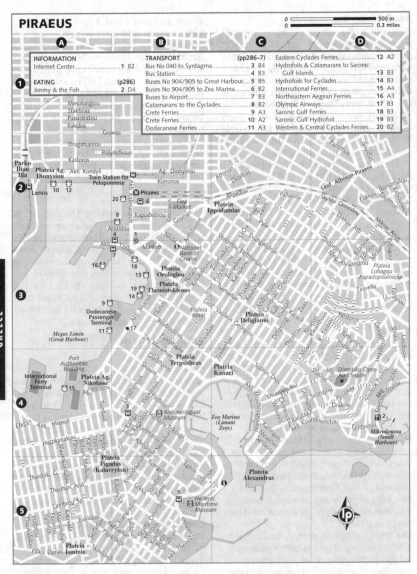

## PIRAEUS

0 — 500 m
0 — 0.3 miles

| INFORMATION | |
|---|---|
| Internet Center | 1 B2 |

| EATING | (p286) |
|---|---|
| Jimmy & the Fish | 2 D4 |

| TRANSPORT | (pp286–7) |
|---|---|
| Bus No 040 to Syntagma | 3 B4 |
| Bus Station | 4 B3 |
| Buses No 904/905 to Great Harbour | 5 B5 |
| Buses No 904/905 to Zea Marina | 6 B2 |
| Buses to Airport | 7 B3 |
| Catamarans to the Cyclades | 8 B2 |
| Crete Ferries | 9 A3 |
| Crete Ferries | 10 A2 |
| Dodacanese Ferries | 11 A3 |

| | |
|---|---|
| Eastern Cyclades Ferries | 12 A2 |
| Hydrofoils & Catamarans to Saronic | |
| Gulf Islands | 13 B3 |
| Hydrofoils for Cyclades | 14 B3 |
| International Ferries | 15 A4 |
| Northeastern Aegean Ferries | 16 A3 |
| Olympic Airways | 17 B3 |
| Saronic Gulf Ferries | 18 B3 |
| Saronic Gulf Hydrofoil | 19 B3 |
| Western & Central Cyclades Ferries | 20 B2 |

## EATING

If you're in Athens for more than a few days, a seafood meal on the harbour at Mikrolimano is a must. **Jimmy & the Fish** ( ☎ 2104 124 417; Koumoundourou 46; mains €16; ⏰ 1pm-1am) is the most reliable of the harbour-front restaurants, serving up excellent seafood in stylish surrounds. There are also a couple of good

cafés along this strip. Trolleybus No 20 runs past the harbour.

## GETTING THERE & AWAY
### Bus

Two 24-hour bus services operate between central Athens and Piraeus. Bus No 049 runs from Omonia to the bus station at the Great Harbour, and bus No 040 runs from Syntagma to the tip of the Piraeus peninsula. No 040 is the service to catch from Athens for Zea Marina – get off at the Hotel Savoy on Iroön Polytehniou – though the trip can take over an hour in bad traffic. The fare is €0.45 for each service. There are no intercity buses to or from Piraeus. The E96 buses to the airport leave from the southern side of Plateia Karaïskaki.

### Metro
The fastest and most convenient link between the Great Harbour and Athens is the metro (€0.60, 20 minutes). The station is close to the ferries, at the northern end of Akti Kalimassioti. There are metro trains every 10 minutes from 5am to midnight.

### Train
At the time of research, all services to the Peloponnese from Athens start and terminate at the Piraeus train station. With the advent of the new Central Station at Arharnon, this is expected to change.

### Ferry
The following information is a guide to departures between June and mid-September. Schedules are similar in April, May and October, but are radically reduced in winter – especially to smaller islands. The main branch of EOT in Athens (see p276) has a reliable schedule, updated weekly. The departure points for the ferry destinations are shown on the map of Piraeus (p285). Check where to find your boat when you buy your ticket. See Getting There & Away sections for each island for more details.

**Crete** There are two boats a day to Hania and Iraklio, a daily service to Rethymno, and three a week to Agios Nikolaos and Sitia.

**Cyclades** There are daily ferries to Amorgos, Folegandros, Ios, Kimolos, Kythnos, Milos, Mykonos, Naxos, Paros, Santorini (Thira), Serifos, Sifnos, Sikinos, Syros and Tinos; two or three ferries a week to Iraklia, Shinoussa, Koufonisi, Donoussa and Anafi; and none to Andros or Kea.

**Dodecanese** There are daily ferries to Kalymnos, Kos, Leros, Patmos and Rhodes; three a week to Karpathos and Kassos; and weekly services to the other islands.

**Northeastern Aegean Islands** Daily ferries sail to Chios, Lesvos (Mytilini), Ikaria and Samos; and two a week to Limnos.

**Saronic Gulf Islands** Daily ferries head to Aegina, Poros, Hydra and Spetses year-round.

### Hydrofoil & Catamaran
The company **Hellas Flying Dolphins** (http://www.dolphins.gr) operate high-speed hydrofoils and catamarans to the Cyclades. These run from early April to the end of October; there are year-round services to the Saronic Gulf Islands. All services to the Cyclades and Aegina leave from Great Harbour. Some services to Poros, Hydra and Spetses also leave from here, but most leave from Zea Marina.

### GETTING AROUND
Local bus Nos 904 and 905 run between the Great Harbour and Zea Marina. They leave from the bus stop beside the metro at Great Harbour, and drop you by the maritime museum at Zea Marina.

# THE PELOPONNESE
# ΠΕΛΟΠΟΝΝΗΣΟΣ

The Peloponnese is a region of outstanding beauty situated at the southern extremity of the rugged Balkan Peninsula. It's linked to the rest of Greece by the narrow Isthmus of Corinth, but technically became an island after the completion of the Corinth Canal across the isthmus in 1893 and is now linked to the mainland by road and rail bridges.

The Peloponnese has played a major role in Greek history, one of the main sites being Olympia, birthplace of the Olympic Games. Other highlights are Mycenae, Epidavros and Corinth in the northeast – all within easy striking distance of the pretty Venetian town of Nafplio.

In the south, Monemvasia is one of the most romantic spots in Greece. The rugged Mani Peninsula is famous for its spectacular wild flowers in spring, as well as for the peculiar tower settlements sprinkled across its landscape.

## PATRA ΠΑΤΡΑ
### pop 160,400
Patra, Greece's third-largest city, is the principal port for ferries to Italy and the Ionian Islands. Despite its long history, stretching back 3000 years, today few travellers hang around any longer than it takes to catch that next connection.

GREECE

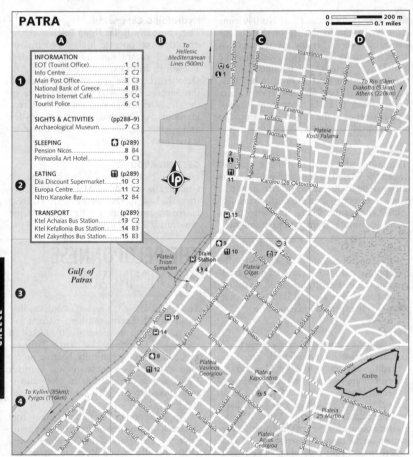

**PATRA**

0 — 200 m
0 — 0.1 miles

| INFORMATION | |
| --- | --- |
| EOT (Tourist Office)................1 | C1 |
| Info Centre............................2 | C2 |
| Main Post Office...................3 | C3 |
| National Bank of Greece.......4 | B3 |
| Netrino Internet Café............5 | C4 |
| Tourist Police.......................6 | C1 |

| SIGHTS & ACTIVITIES | (pp288–9) |
| --- | --- |
| Archaeological Museum.........7 | C3 |

| SLEEPING | (p289) |
| --- | --- |
| Pension Nicos.......................8 | B4 |
| Primarolia Art Hotel..............9 | C3 |

| EATING | (p289) |
| --- | --- |
| Dia Discount Supermarket.....10 | C3 |
| Europa Centre......................11 | C2 |
| Nitro Karaoke Bar................12 | B4 |

| TRANSPORT | (p289) |
| --- | --- |
| Ktel Achaias Bus Station.......13 | C2 |
| Ktel Kefallonia Bus Station...14 | B3 |
| Ktel Zakynthos Bus Station...15 | B3 |

Gulf of Patras

To Hellenic Mediterranean Lines (500m)

To Rio (5km); Diakofto (53km); Athens (220km)

To Kyllini (85km); Pyrgos (116km)

Train Station

Plateia Trion Symahon

Plateia Olgas

Plateia Kosti Palama

Plateia Vasileos Georgiou

Plateia Kapodistrio

Plateia 25 Martiou

Plateia Agios Georgiou

Kastro

## Orientation

The city is easy to negotiate, laid out on a grid stretching uphill from the port to the old *kastro* (castle). Most services of importance to travellers are along the waterfront (Othonos Amalias) in the middle of town, and Iroön Politehniou to the north. The **train station** (Othonos Amalias) is right in the middle of town, and the bus stations are close by.

## Information

**EOT** ( ☎ 2610 620 353; ☙ 7am-8pm) Outside the international arrival terminal.
**Info Centre** ( ☎ 2610 461 740; infopatras@hol.gr; Othonos Amalias 6; ☙ 8am-10pm) Well-organised local information.

**Main post office** (cnr Zaïmi & Mezonos; ☙ 7.30am-8pm Mon-Fri, 7.30am-2pm Sat, 9am-1.30pm Sun)
**National Bank of Greece** (Plateia Trion Symahon; ☙ 8am-2pm Mon-Thu, 8am-1.30pm Fri & 6-8.30pm Mon-Fri) Open weekends 11am-1pm & 6-8.30pm for foreign exchange only.
**Netrino Internet Café** ( ☎ 2610 623 344; Karaïskaki 133; ☙ 10-2am) There are other Internet cafés in the surrounding area.
**Tourist police** ( ☎ 2610 451 833; ☙ 7am-9pm) Upstairs in the embarkation hall at the port.

## Sights & Activities

The city's old **kastro** ( ☙ 8am-7pm Tue-Sun Apr-Oct, 8.30am-5pm Tue-Fri, 8.30am-3pm Sat & Sun Nov-Mar) stands on the site of the acropolis of ancient Patrai. This Byzantine fortress has great views of Zakynthos and Kefallonia. The small **archaeological museum** ( ☎ 2610 275 070; Mezonos 42; ☷ 8.30am-2.30pm Tue-Sun) houses a collection of finds from the Mycenaean, Hellenic and Roma periods. It's well organised and labelled in English.

## Sleeping & Eating

**Pension Nicos** ( ☎ 2610 623 757; cnr Patreos & Agiou Andreou 121; s/d/tr €20/35/45, d/tr with shared bathroom €30/40) The best budget choice in town, with hot water and clean sheets. It's just up from the waterfront.

**Primarolia Art Hotel** ( ☎ 2610 624 900; www.art hotel.gr; Othonos Amalias; d €118-177; ☷ ☐ ) At the opposite end of the accommodation scale, Primarolia is a beautifully designed boutique hotel featuring original Greek art. Prices vary depending on whether you have a sea or city view.

**Europa Centre** ( ☎ 2610 437 006; Othonos Amalias 10; mains €5.50-7; ☷ 7am-midnight) A convenient caféteria-style place close to the international ferry dock, serving up decent taverna fare and vegetarian meals.

**Nitro Karaoke Bar** ( ☎ 2601 279 357; Pantanasis 9; mains €8-10; ☷ 1pm until late) A well set up bar for transitory travellers, offering Internet access and a shower room. You'll find daily specials such as steak-and-kidney pie or shepherd's pie, Sunday roasts and a choice of English beers.

**Dia Discount Supermarket** (Agiou Andreou 29) Ideally located for travellers planning to buy a few provisions and keep moving.

## Getting There & Away

The best way to travel to Athens is by train. Buses may be faster, but they drop you a long way from the city centre at Terminal A on Kifissou. Trains go closer to the centre (five minutes from Syntagma on the metro).

There are nine trains a day to Athens. Four are slow trains (€5.30, five hours) and five are intercity express trains (€10, 3½ hours). Trains also run south to Pyrgos and Kalamata.

**KTEL Achaias bus station** ( ☎ 2610 623 888; Othonos Amalias) has buses to Athens (€12.90, three hours, half-hourly) via Corinth; and 10 buses daily to Pyrgos (for Olympia).

Buses to the Ionian islands of Kefallonia and Lefkada leave from the **Ktel Kefallonia bus station** ( ☎ 2610 277 854; Othonos Amalias). Buses to Zakynthos leave from the **Ktel Zakynthos bus station** ( ☎ 2610 220 219; Othonos Amalias 58). These services travel via the port of Kyllini.

Daily ferries depart for Kefallonia (€11.50, 2½ hours), Ithaki (€11.70, 3¾ hours) and Corfu (€21, seven hours). Ticket agencies line the waterfront.

## DIAKOFTO-KALAVRYTA RAILWAY
ΔΙΑΚΟΦΤΟ-ΚΑΛΑΒΡΥΤΑ

This spectacular rack-and-pinion line climbs up the deep gorge of the Vouraikos River from the small coastal town of Diakofto to the mountain resort of Kalavryta, 22km away. It is a thrilling one-hour journey, with dramatic scenery all the way and it's best viewed from 1st class (€4.40) rather than 2nd (€3.70). There are four trains a day in each direction.

Diakofto is one hour east of Patra on the main train line to Athens.

## CORINTH ΚΟΡΙΝΘΟΣ
**pop 29,787**

Modern Corinth (ko-rin-thoss), 6km west of the Corinth Canal, is an uninspiring town, in part due to the devastating earthquakes it has suffered through its history. It is, however, a convenient base from which to visit nearby ancient Corinth.

About 4km west of town, near the ancient port of Lecheon, the **Blue Dolphin Campground** ( ☎ 2741 025 766; skoupos@otenet.gr; per adult/tent €5.50/4; ☷ ) is a well-organised site with its own stretch of Gulf of Corinth pebble beach. Buses from Corinth to Lecheon can drop you here.

**Hotel Apollon** ( ☎ 2741 022 587; hotapol@otenet .gr; Pirinis 18; s/d €40/50; ☷ ), near the train station, is the best of Corinth's budget hotels. The rooms are equipped with air-con and TV and rooms can go for as low as €25/30, making it good value.

As the name suggests, **Restaurant To 24 Hours** ( ☎ 2741 083 201; Agiou Nikolaou 19; mains €3.25-7.35) is always open. The place consistently turns out an ever-changing selection of taverna favourites.

Buses to Athens (€6, 1½ hours) leave every 30 minutes from the **Ktel Korinthos bus station** ( ☎ 2741 075 424; Dimocratias 4) opposite the train station. This is also the departure point for buses to ancient Corinth (€0.90, 20 minutes, hourly) and Lecheon. Buses to Nafplio leave from the **Argolis bus station** (cnr Ethnikis Antistaseos & Aratou).

GREECE

There are 14 daily trains to Athens, five of which are intercity services. Trains service Kalamata, Nafplio and Patra.

## ANCIENT CORINTH & ACROCORINTH
ΑΡΧΑΙΑ ΚΟΡΙΝΘΟΣ & ΑΚΡΟΚΟΡΙΝΘΟΣ

The ruins of **ancient Corinth** ( ☎ 2741 031 207; site & museum €4; 🕑 8am-7pm Apr-Oct, 8am-5pm Nov-Mar) lie 7km southwest of the modern city. Earthquakes and sacking by a series of invaders have left little standing of the ancient Greek city, which was one of ancient Greece's wealthiest and most wanton cities. The only ancient Greek monument remaining is the imposing **Temple of Apollo**; the others are Roman. Towering over the site is **Acrocorinth**, the ruins of an ancient citadel built on a massive outcrop of limestone.

## NAFPLIO ΝΑΥΠΛΙΟ
**pop 13,822**

Nafplio is one of Greece's prettiest towns. The narrow streets of the old quarter are filled with elegant Venetian houses and neoclassical mansions and the setting is dominated by the towering Palamidi Fortress.

There is a **municipal tourist office** ( ☎ 2752 024 444; 25 Martiou; 🕑 9am-1.30pm & 4-8pm) and **tourist police** ( ☎ 2752 028 131; Kountouridou 16). Good holiday reading can be found at **Odyssey Bookshop** ( ☎ 2752 023 430; Plateia Syntagmatos).

### Sights
There are terrific views of the old town and the surrounding coast from the magnificent hill-top **Palamidi Fortress** ( ☎ 2752 028 036; admission €4; 🕑 8am-6.45pm summer, 8am-5pm at other times), built by the Venetians between 1711 and 1714.

There are also a number of small museums. Contact the tourist office for information.

### Sleeping
The cheapest rooms are in the new part of town along Argous, the road to Argos. Most people prefer to stay in the old town, which is the most interesting place to be. Unfortunately, there is very little budget accommodation here.

**Hotel Economou** ( ☎ 2752 027 721; Argonafton 22; dm €8, d/tr €30/35) This hotel is very accommodating to groups of backpackers, being flexible with sleeping arrangements depending on the number of guests.

**Dimitris Bekas** ( ☎ 2752 024 594; Efthimiopoulou 26; s/d/tr with shared bathroom €16/22/27) This is the only decent budget option in the old town. It offers top value for a great location above the church on the slopes of the Akronafplia, and the rooftop terrace has great views over the old town.

**Pension Marianna** ( ☎ 2752 024 256; www.pensionmarianna.gr; Potamianou 9; s/d/tr €55/60/70; 🖴 ) Tucked beneath the walls of the Akronafplia, at the top of Potamianou, this is the best location in town. All the rooms have wonderful views and the place is spotlessly clean.

### Eating
The streets of Nafplio's old town are filled with restaurants. Staïkopoulou, in particular, is a very busy eat street.

**Taverna Paleo Arhontiko** ( ☎ 2752 022 449; cnr Ypsilandou & Sofroni; mains €4.40-7.65) One of the best tavernas in town and very popular with locals. The food's excellent and there's live music after 10pm in summer. Reservations essential on weekends.

**Taverna O Vassilis** ( ☎ 2752 025 334; Staïkopoulou 20-24; mains €4-8.50) A busy family-run place at the heart of the restaurant strip. It has a large choice of starters and a good selection of main dishes, including a very tasty rabbit *stifado* (€4.85).

### Getting There & Away
The **Ktel Argolis bus station** ( ☎ 2752 027 323; Syngrou 8) has hourly buses to Athens (€9, 2½ hours) via Corinth, as well as services to Argos (for Peloponnese connections), Mycenae and Epidavros.

## EPIDAVROS ΕΠΙΔΑΥΡΟΣ
One of the most renowned of Greece's ancient sites, World Heritage–listed **Epidavros** ( ☎ 2753 022 006; admission €6; 🕑 8am-7pm Apr-Oct, 8am-5pm Nov-Mar) was the sanctuary of Asclepius, the god of medicine. The **theatre** is the star of the show, but don't miss the more peaceful **Sanctuary of Asclepius** nearby, which was once a flourishing spa and healing centre.

You can enjoy the theatre's astounding acoustics first-hand during the annual Hellenic Festival, from July to August.

There are buses to Athens (€8.80, 2½ hours, two daily) and Nafplio (€2, 40 minutes, four daily), which is 30km away.

GREECE

## MYCENAE ΜΥΚΗΝΕΣ

**Ancient Mycenae** ( ☎ 2751 076 585; admission €6; ☻8am-7pm Apr-Oct, 8am-5pm Nov-Mar) was the most powerful influence in Greece from 1600–1200 BC. The rise and fall of Mycenae is shrouded in myth, but the site was settled as early as the sixth millennium BC. Described by Homer as 'rich in gold', Mycenae's entrance, the **Lion Gate**, is Europe's oldest monumental sculpture.

Excavations of **Grave Circle A** by Heinrich Schliemann in the 1870s uncovered magnificent gold treasures (such as the Mask of Agamemnon) that are now on display at the National Archaeological Museum (p277).

Most people visit on day trips from Nafplio, but there are several hotels in the modern village below the site. The **Belle Helene Hotel** ( ☎ 2751 076 225; fax 2751 076 179; Christou Tsounta; s/d €30/45), located on the main street, is where Schliemann stayed during the excavations.

There are three buses daily to Mycenae from Argos (€1.35, 30 minutes) and Nafplio (€2, one hour).

## SPARTA ΣΠΑΡΤΗ

**pop 14,817**

Modern, neat and relaxed, Sparta (*spar*-tee) is in stark contrast to the ancient image of discipline and deprivation. While the Spartans left little in the way of monuments, modern Sparta makes a convenient base from which to visit Mystras.

Sparta's street grid system sees Palaeologou running north-south through the town, and Lykourgou running east-west.

**Cosmos Club Internet Café** ( ☎ 2731 021 500; Palaeologou 34; ☻8.30am-11pm) is on Palaeologou, as is the **National Bank of Greece** (Palaeologou 84). It has an ATM. Tourist information is available from the **municipal tourist office** ( ☎ 2731 024 852; Town Hall, Plateia Kentriki; ☻8am-2.30pm Mon-Fri) and the **tourist police** ( ☎ 2731 020 492; Theodoritou 20) are also helpful. The **post office** (Archidamou 10; ☻7.30am-2pm Mon-Fri) is at Archidamou.

A friendly, camping ground with good facilities is **Camping Paleologou Mystras** ( ☎ 2731 022 724; fax 2731 025 256; per adult/tent €4/3.50; ☻year-round; ☒ ), 2km west of Sparta. It's located on the road to Mystras and buses travelling to Mystras can drop you there.

Most travellers head to the family-run **Hotel Cecil** ( ☎ 2731 024 980; fax 2731 081 318; Palaeologou 125; s/d €35/45; ☒ ) for its clean, comfortable rooms with TV.

**Restaurant Elysse** ( ☎ 2731 029 896; Palaeologou 113; mains €4.50-8.90) is run by a helpful Greek-Canadian family. It offers Lakonian specialties such as chicken *bardouniotiko* (chicken cooked with onions and feta cheese, €4.90).

Sparta's well-organised **Ktel Lakonias bus station** ( ☎ 2731 026 441; cnr Lykourgou & Thivronos) has buses to Athens (€13.30, 3¼ hours, 10 daily); three go to Monemvasia and two to Kalamata. There are also frequent buses to Mystras (€0.90, 30 minutes).

## MYSTRAS ΜΥΣΤΡΑΣ

The magnificent **ruins of Mystras** ( ☎ 2731 083 377; adult/concession €6/3; ☻8am-6pm Apr-Oct, 8am-3.30pm Nov-Mar), 7km from Sparta, were once the shining light of the Byzantine world. The large site needs at least half a day to do it justice. The streets of Mystras are lined with palaces, monasteries and churches, most of them dating from the period between 1271 and 1460, when the town was the effective capital of the Byzantine Empire.

## GEFYRA & MONEMVASIA ΓΕΦΥΡΑ & ΜΟΝΕΜΒΑΣΙΑ

Monemvasia, 99km southeast of Sparta, might no longer be an undiscovered paradise, but tourism hasn't lessened the impact of the first encounter with this extraordinary town – nor the thrill of exploring it.

Separated from mainland Gefyra by an earthquake in AD 375, Monemvasia occupies a great outcrop of rock rising dramatically from the sea. From the causeway, a road curves around the base of the rock for about 1km, then it comes to a narrow L-shaped tunnel in the massive fortifying wall, where you emerge, blinking, into magical Monemvasia.

The cobbled main street is flanked by stairways leading to a complex network of stone houses with tiny walled gardens and courtyards. Signposted steps lead to the ruins of the **fortress** built by the Venetians in the 16th century. The views are amazing, and from here you can explore the Byzantine **Church of Agia Sophia**, perched precariously on the edge of the cliff.

All the practicalities are based in Gefyra. Malvasia Travel, just up from the causeway, acts as the bus stop and the National Bank of Greece and **post office** ( ☻7.30am-2pm Mon-Fri) are opposite.

GREECE

## Sleeping & Eating

There is no budget accommodation in Monemvasia, but there are *domatia* in Gefyra, as well as cheap hotels. However, romantic Monemvasia is certainly one place in Greece worth breaking the budget for.

**Camping Paradise** ( ☎ 2732 061 123; paradise@ otenet .gr; per adult/tent €5/3;  year-round) This pleasant, well-shaded camping ground on the coast 3.5km from Gefyra has its own minimarket, bar and big screen TV.

**Hotel Monemvasia** ( ☎ 2732 061 381; fax 2732 061 707; s/d €30/40) A small, modern hotel 500m north of Gefyra on the road to Molai. It has large balconies looking out to Monemvasia, and prices include breakfast.

**Malvasia Hotel** ( ☎ 2732 061 113; fax 2732 061 722; d €45-78, tr €60, 4-person apt €70-150;  ) This hotel offers a variety of excellent rooms spread around the old town. Prices include an excellent breakfast. The hotel's office is on the main street of the old town.

**Taverna O Botsalo** ( ☎ 2732 061 491; Gefyra; mains €5.90-23.50) Serves up tasty meals overlooking the port in Gefyra.

**Matoula** ( ☎ 2732 061 660; Monemvasia; mains €6-12) Pick of the bunch in the old town, Matoula is on the main street and best if you score a table on the terrace. It's a great place to try the tasty local *barbounia* (red mullet, €10).

## Getting There & Away

Buses leave from outside **Malvasia Travel** ( ☎ 2732 061 752), where you can pick up tickets. Four daily buses travel to Athens (€20, 5½ hours) via Sparta, Tripolis and Corinth.

The **Flying Dolphin** (www.dolphins.gr) hydrofoil service to Monemvasia has been suspended, but this may change.

## GYTHIO ΓΥΘΕΙΟ

**pop 4489**

Once the port of ancient Sparta, Gythio (*yee*-thih-o) is a bustling and attractive fishing town at the head of the Lakonian Gulf. It is the gateway to the rugged Mani Peninsula to the south.

Access the Internet at **Café Mystery** ( ☎ 2733 025 177; cnr Kapsali & Grigoraki;  9am-1pm); there's a **post office** (cnr Ermou & Arhaia Theatrou;  7.30am-2pm Mon-Fri).

## Sights

The main attraction is the picturesque **Marathonisi Islet**, linked to the mainland by a causeway. According to mythology, this islet is ancient Cranae, where Paris (prince of Troy) and Helen (the wife of Menelaus of Sparta) consummated the love affair that sparked the Trojan War. An 18th-century tower on the islet has been turned into the **Museum of Mani History** ( ☎ 2733 024 484; admission €1.50;  9am-7pm).

## Sleeping & Eating

**Camping Meltemi** ( ☎ 2733 022 833; www.camping meltemi.gr; per adult/tent €5/4;  year-round) Situated right behind the beach, 3km south of Gythio, this is the pick of the camp sites along the coast south of town. Buses to Areopoli stop outside.

**Xenia Karlaftis Rooms to Rent** ( ☎ 2733 022 719; s/d/tr €25/35/40) Opposite the causeway to Marathonisi, this is the pick of the budget options, with clean rooms and a communal kitchen.

The waterfront is lined with countless fish tavernas with similar menus. For something completely different, head inland to the tiny **General Store & Wine Bar** ( ☎ 2733 024 113; Vasileos Georgiou 67; mains €3.50-13;  6-11pm Mon-Sat). It has an unusually imaginative menu featuring such dishes as orange-and-pumpkin soup and fillet of pork with black pepper and ouzo.

## Getting There & Away

The **Ktel Lakonias bus station** ( ☎ 2733 022 228; cnr Vasileos Georgios & Evrikleos) has buses to Athens (€16.30, 4¼ hours, five daily) via Sparta (€2.90, one hour), south to Areopoli (€1.80, 30 minutes, four daily), Gerolimenas (€4, 1¼ hours, two daily) and the Diros Caves (€2.50, one hour, one daily).

**ANEN Lines** (www.anen.gr) runs five ferries weekly to Kissamos on Crete (€19.20, seven hours) via Kythira (€8.90, 2½ hours) between June and September. The schedule is subject to constant change, so check with **Rozakis Travel** ( ☎ 2733 022 207; rosakigy@otenet.gr) on the waterfront before coming here to catch a boat.

## THE MANI Η ΜΑΝΗ

The region referred to as the Mani covers the central peninsula in the south of the Peloponnese and is divided into two regions – the Lakonian (inner) Mani in the south and Messinian (outer) Mani in the northwest, below Kalamata.

## Lakonian Mani

The wild and remote Lakonian Mani has a landscape dotted with the striking stone-tower houses that are a feature of the region. The best time to visit is in spring, when the barren countryside briefly bursts into life with a spectacular display of wild flowers.

The region's principal village is **Areopoli**, about 30km southwest of Gythio. There are a number of fine towers on the narrow, cobbled streets of the old town at the lower end of the main street, Kapetan Matepan.

Just south of here are the magnificent **Diros Caves** ( ☎ 2733 052 222; adult/concession €12/6; ⊗ 8am-5.30pm Jun-Sep, 8am-3pm Oct-May), where a subterranean river flows. **Gerolimenas**, 20km further south, is a tranquil fishing village built around a sheltered bay.

Most of the accommodation in the Lakonian Mani is found in Areopoli.

**Tsimova Rooms** ( ☎ 2733 051 301; Kapetan Matepan; s/d €25/40, apt €45) has cosy rooms tucked away behind the Church of Taxiarhes.

**Pyrgos Kapetanakas** ( ☎ 2733 051 233; fax 2733 051 401; s/d/tr €40/60/80; 🛇 ) is an excellent place occupying the tower house built by the powerful Kapetanakas family at the end of the 18th century. It's signposted to the right at the bottom of Kapetan Matepan.

Popular on the central square is **Nicola's Corner Taverna** ( ☎ 2733 051 366; Plateia Athanaton; mains €4-7), with a good choice of tasty taverna staples.

The **bus station** ( ☎ 2733 051 229; Plateia Athanaton) in Areopoli is the focal point of the local bus network. There are buses to Gythio and Sparta, two to Gerolimenas and Itilo, and one to Diros Caves. Crossing to the Messinian Mani involves changing buses at Itilo.

## Messinian Mani

The Messinian Mani runs north along the coast from Itilo to Kalamata. The beaches here are some of the best in Greece, set against the dramatic backdrop of the Taygetos Mountains.

The picturesque coastal village of **Kardamyli**, 37km south of Kalamata, is a favourite destination for trekkers. The walks are well organised and colour-coded, and many incorporate the spectacular **Vyros Gorge**. Kardamyli has a good choice of accommodation to suit all budgets, starting with several *domatia*.

**Olympia Koumounakou rooms** ( ☎ 2721 073 623; s/d €20/28), signposted opposite the post office, is a favourite with budget travellers and has clean, comfortable beds and a communal kitchen.

**Anniska Apartments** ( ☎ 2721 073 600; anniska@otenet.gr; studio/apt €85/90; 🛇 ) has a range of spacious, well-appointed studios and apartments, all with kitchen facilities. The studios sleep two people, while the larger apartments accommodate up to four.

There are several tavernas around the village, the best being **Lela's Taverna** ( ☎ 2721 073 541).

There are two daily buses from Kalamata to Itilo, stopping at Kardamyli and Stoupa.

## OLYMPIA ΟΛΥΜΠΙΑ

pop 1286

The site of ancient Olympia lies 500m beyond the modern town of the same name, surrounded by the foothills of Mt Kronion. The well-organised **municipal tourist office** ( ☎ 2624 023 100; Praxitelous Kondyli; ⊗ 9am-9pm daily Jun-Sep, 8am-2.45pm Mon-Sat Oct-May), on the main street, also changes money.

In ancient times, Olympia was a sacred place of temples, priests' dwellings and public buildings, as well as being the venue for the quadrennial Olympic Games. The first Olympics were staged in 776 BC, reaching the peak of their prestige in the 6th century BC. The city-states were bound by a sacred truce to stop fighting for three months and compete.

**Ancient Olympia** ( ☎ 2624 022 517; adult/concession €6/3, combined site & museum admission €9/5; ⊗ 8am-7pm daily Apr-Oct, 8am-5pm Mon-Fri, 8.30am-3pm Sat & Sun Nov-Mar) is dominated by the immense, ruined **Temple of Zeus**, to whom the games were dedicated. In the **museum** (adult/concession €6/3), which keeps similar hours as the site, don't miss the statue of **Hermes of Praxiteles**, a classical sculpture masterpiece.

**Camping Diana** ( ☎ 2624 022 314; fax 2624 022 425; per adult/tent €5/3.85; ⊗ year-round; 🛇 ), located 250m west of town, is the most convenient of the three camping grounds around Olympia; it has excellent facilities.

The **youth hostel** ( ☎ 2624 022 580; Praxitelous Kondyli 18; dm €8) has free hot showers. There are two more good budget options around the corner on Stefanopoulou: **Pension Achilleys** ( ☎ 2624 022 562; Stefanopoulou 4; s/d/tr €20/30/35), a small, family-run pension (breakfast €5), and **Pension Posidon** ( ☎ 2624 022 567; Stefanopoulou 9; s/d/tr €20/28/36), which is good value with its clean and airy rooms.

**Taverna To Steki tou Vangeli** (Stefanopoulou 13; mains €2.95-6.75) represents better value than most of the tavernas around town.

There are four buses a day to Olympia from Athens (€20, 5½ hours) and regular buses to Pyrgos, 24km away on the coast.

# CENTRAL GREECE
## ΚΕΝΤΡΙΚΗ ΕΛΛΑΔΑ

Central Greece has a dramatic landscape and history, exemplified by its rugged mountains and fertile valleys and the ruins of ancient Delphi, where Alexander the Great sought the advice of the Delphic Oracle. Further to the north, the intriguing rock monasteries of Meteora are another highlight of this less-travelled region.

## DELPHI ΔΕΛΦΟΙ
pop 2373

Like so many of Greece's ancient sites, the setting of Delphi – overlooking the Gulf of Corinth from the slopes of Mt Parnassos – is stunning. Modern Delphi is very much geared towards the number of tourists that come to visit one of Greece's major tourist attractions, but ancient Delphi is still a special place to visit.

The bus station, post office, OTE, National Bank of Greece and **EOT** ( ☎ 2265 082 900; Vasileon Pavlou 44; ☾ 7.30am-2.30pm Mon-Fri) are all on modern Delphi's main street, Vasileon Pavlou.

## Sights
### ANCIENT DELPHI

By the 6th century BC, **ancient Delphi** ( ☎ 2265 082 312; site or museum €6, combined admission €9, EU/non-EU students free/€3, free Sun Nov-Mar; ☾ 7.30am-7pm Apr-Oct, 8.30am-6.45pm Tue-Fri, 8.30am-2.45pm Sat, Sun & holidays Nov-Mar) had become the Sanctuary of Apollo. Thousands of pilgrims would come to consult the oracle, who was always a peasant woman of 50 years or more. She sat at the mouth of a chasm that emitted fumes. These she inhaled, causing her to gasp, writhe and shudder in divine frenzy. After sacrificing a sheep or goat, the pilgrim

would deliver a question, and a priest would translate the oracle's incoherent mumbling. Wars were fought, voyages embarked upon and business transactions undertaken on the strength of these prophecies.

The **Sacred Way** leads up from the entrance of the site to the **Temple of Apollo**. It was here that the oracle supposedly sat, and from here the path continues to the **theatre** and **stadium**. Opposite this sanctuary is the **Sanctuary of Athena** and the much-photographed **Tholos**, a 4th-century-BC columned rotunda of Pentelic marble.

## Sleeping & Eating

There are lots of hotels in the modern town, catering for the many tour groups that stop overnight.

**Apollon Camping** ( ☎ 2265 082 762; apollon4@otenet .gr; per adult/tent €5/3.50; ☒ ) Located 1.5km west of the modern town, first-rate Apollon is the closest camping ground to Delphi. The facilities include a restaurant, minimarket and barbecue.

**Hotel Hermes** ( ☎ 2265 082 318; cnr Vasileon Pavlou & Friderikis 27; s/d €34/40, ste €75; ☒ ) A tastefully furnished and welcoming hotel in the town centre. There are some two-room family suites and many rooms have balcony views. Breakfast included.

**Taverna Vakhos** ( ☎ 2265 083 186; Apollonos 31; mains €4.50-11) This taverna turns out honest and tasty dishes such as lamb in lemon sauce with rice and potatoes (€6.50). Check out the excellent house wine and the great views.

## Getting There & Away

The **bus station** ( ☎ 2266 082 317) sells bus tickets as well as snacks. There are six buses a day to Delphi from Athens (€10.90, three hours).

## METEORA ΜΕΤΕΩΡΑ

The jutting pinnacles of Meteora (meh-*teh*-o-rah), stunning late-14th-century monasteries perched atop, are one of Greece's most extraordinary sights. Meteora is just north of the town of Kalambaka, on the Ioannina–Trikala road. The rocks behind the town are spectacularly floodlit at night. **Kastraki**, which is 2km from Kalambaka, is a charming village of red-tiled houses just west of the monasteries.

There were once monasteries on each of the 24 pinnacles, but only six are still occupied: **Megalou Meteorou** (Grand Meteoron;

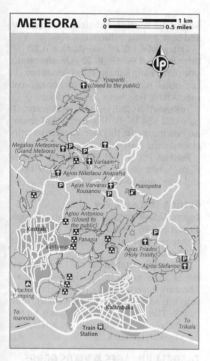

**METEORA**

Ypapanti (closed to the public)

Megalou Meteorou (Grand Meteora)

Varlaam

Agiou Nikolaou Anapafsa

Agias Varvaras Rousanou

Psaropetra

Agiou Antoniou (closed to the public)

Kastraki

Panagia

Bantovas

Agias Triados (Holy Trinity)

Agiou Stefanou

Vrachos Camping

To Ioannina

Kalambaka

To Trikala

Train Station

9am-5pm Wed-Mon), **Varlaam** (  9am-2pm & 3.20-5pm Fri-Wed), **Agiou Stefanou** (  9am-2pm & 3.30-6pm Tue-Sun), **Agias Triados** (Holy Trinity;  9am-12.30pm & 3-5pm Fri-Wed), **Agiou Nikolaou Anapafsa** (  9am-3.30pm Sat-Thu) and **Agias Varvaras Rousanou** (  9am-6pm). Admission is €2 for each monastery; free for Greeks. Bear in mind that they are religious grounds and strict dress codes apply. Women must wear skirts that reach below their knees, men must wear long trousers, and arms must be fully covered.

When looking for somewhere to stay, Kastraki is the best base for visiting Meteora.

**Vrachos Camping** (  2432 022 293; camping-kastraki@kmp.forthnet.gr; per adult & tent €3.50, per car €1;  ) is an excellent camping ground on the edge of the village, with good facilities, including a market, restaurant and a barbecue.

**Dupiani House** (  2432 075 326; dupiani-house@kmp.forthnet.gr; s/d/tr €30/45/55) is a welcoming guesthouse situated only 500m from the town square has spotless rooms with balconies and splendid views from the attractive garden.

Excellent traditional dishes are served at the large and lively **Taverna Paradisos** (  2432 022 723; mains €4-6.50) with its superb views of the Meteora from the large terrace.

Hourly buses travel to Trikala (€1.50, 30 minutes), the region's major transport hub. There are buses to Ioannina (€8.10, three hours, two daily). Local buses shuttle constantly between Kalambaka and Kastraki; five a day continue to Metamorphosis.

From Trikala, there are buses to Athens (€19.10, 5½ hours, eight daily).

From Kalambaka's new station, there are express trains to Athens (€19.10, five hours, two daily). Trains also run to Thessaloniki (€9.50, four hours, two daily) and Volos (€5, 1½ hours, two daily), both changing at Paliofarsalos.

# NORTHERN GREECE
ΒΟΡΕΙΑ ΕΛΛΑΔΑ

Northern Greece rewards those travellers who take the time to explore this vast region. The area comprises Epiros, with its stark and rugged mountains, Macedonia, with its rich archaeological sites and shimmering lakes, and Thrace, where rolling plains front forested mountains laced with meandering rivers. The best reason to visit, however, is that it doesn't take much of an adventure to escape the tourist trail. Your reward is experiencing an aspect of Greece that's noticeably different to other mainland areas and islands of Greece.

## IGOUMENITSA ΗΓΟΥΜΕΝΙΤΣΑ
pop 9104

The west-coast port of Igoumenitsa (ih-goo-meh-*nit*-sah), is generally known as the outpost where you catch ferries to Corfu and Italy. Few people stay here any longer than it takes to buy a ticket out.

If you need to stay the night, you'll find signs for *domatia* around the port. Try the aptly named **Rooms to Let** (  2665 023 612; Xanthou 12; s/d €30/38), which is handy for the ferry and has decent enough rooms.

**Alekos** (  2665 023 708; Ethnikis Andistasis 84; mains €3.50-5.50) is a local favourite eatery 500m north of the Corfu ferry quay. It does a fine moussaka (€3.80) and other taverna favourites.

GREECE

From the **bus station** ( ☎ 2665 022 309; Kyprou 29), there are buses to Ioannina (€6.40, two hours, nine daily) and Athens (€29.80, eight hours, five daily).

Ferries to Corfu (€5.10, 1¾ hours, every hour) operate between 5am and 10pm.

There are international ferry services to the Italian ports of Ancona, Bari, Brindisi, Trieste and Venice. Ticket agencies are opposite the port.

## IOANNINA ΙΩΑΝΝΙΝΑ
### pop 61,629

Ioannina (ih-o-*ah*-nih-nah) is the capital and largest town in Epiros, lying on the western shore of Lake Pamvotis. During Ottoman rule, it became a major commercial and intellectual centre. These days, Ioannina is still a thriving commercial centre and university town.

The town centre is around Plateia Dimokratias where the main streets of the new town meet. All facilities of importance to travellers are nearby; there's Internet access at **The Web** ( ☎ 2651 026 813; Pyrsinella 21; per hr €2.50; ☼ 24hr), regional information at **EOT office** ( ☎ 2651 041 142; Dodonis 39; ☼ 7.30am-2.30pm), and you can find out about treks in the Zagoria region with **Robinson Expeditions** ( ☎ 2651 029 402; www.robinson.gr; Mitropoleos 23).

### Sights

The **old town** juts out into the lake on a small peninsula. Inside the impressive fortifications lies a maze of winding streets flanked by traditional Turkish houses.

The **Nisi** (island) is a serene spot in the middle of the lake, with four monasteries set among the trees. Ferries (€1) to the island leave from just north of the old town. They run half-hourly in summer and hourly in winter.

For information on the decent archaeological museum and Byzantine museum, visit the EOT office.

### Sleeping & Eating

**Limnopoula Camping** ( ☎ 2651 020 541; Kanari 10; per adult/tent €4.40/3; ☼ year-round) An open, breezy camping ground right on the edge of the lake, 2km northwest of town. There's a restaurant and bar and sites are shaded.

**Rooms to Rent** ( ☎ 2651 081 786; Spileou 76, Perama; s/d €22/27) In Perama (take bus No 8), one of many *domatia* in the neighbourhood.

Rooms are smallish but clean and pleasant and have private bathrooms.

**Galaxy Hotel** ( ☎ 2651 025 432; fax 2651 030 724; Plateia Pyrrou; s/d €45/60; **P** ✖ ) On the south side of the main square, it's a pleasant modern hotel with TV and telephone. Most rooms have fine views over the lake.

**To Rembetiko** ( ☎ 2651 075 535; Plataia Georgiou 14; mains €3.50-6.50) While live Rembetika music isn't on the menu, this eatery serves up delicious mixed platters, grills and *mezedes*.

**Presveia** ( ☎ 2651 026 309; Karamanli 17; platters €5-15; ☼ evenings) Serves up over 100 beers and good pub food to boot.

### Getting There & Away

**Aegean Airlines** ( ☎ 2651 064 444) and **Olympic Airways** ( ☎ 2651 026 518) both fly twice a day to Athens, and Olympic has a daily flight to Thessaloniki.

The **main bus station** ( ☎ 2651 026 404; Zossimadon) is 300m north of Plateia Dimokratias. There are buses to Athens (€26, 7½ hours, 10 daily), Igoumenitsa (€6.40, 2½ hours, nine daily), Thessaloniki (€21.45, seven hours, five daily) and Trikala (€10, 3½ hours, two daily) via Kalambaka.

## ZAGORIA VILLAGES & VIKOS GORGE
### ΤΑ ΖΑΓΟΡΟΧΩΡΙΑ & ΧΑΡΑΔΡΑ ΤΟΥ ΒΙΚΟΥ

The Zagoria region covers a large expanse of the Pindos Mountains north of Ioannina. It's a wilderness of raging rivers, crashing waterfalls and deep gorges. Here, snowcapped mountains rise out of dense forests. The remote villages that dot the hillsides are famous for their impressive grey-slate architecture.

The fairy-tale village of **Monodendri** is the starting point for treks through the dramatic **Vikos Gorge**, with its awesome sheer limestone walls. It's a strenuous 7½-hour walk from Monodendri to the twin villages of **Megalo Papingo** and **Mikro Papingo**. The trek is very popular and the path is clearly marked. Ioannina's EOT office has more information.

Other walks start from Tsepelovo, near Monodendri.

There are some wonderful places to stay, but none of them are that cheap. The options in Monodendri include cosy **To Kalderimi** ( ☎ 2653 071 510; d/tr €35/41). For food, **Haradra tou Vikou** ( ☎ 2653 071 559) in Monodendri specialises in fabulous *pittes* (pies).

In Megalo Papingo, you can check out **Xenonas Kalliopi** ( ☎ /fax 2653 041 081; s/d €34/42).

It also has a small restaurant-bar serving meals and *pittes*.

Mikro Papingo has the pleasant **Xenonas Dias** ( ☎ 2653 041 257; www.touristorama.com; s/d €40/54). Its restaurant serves breakfast and excellent meals.

There are buses from Ioannina to Megalo and Mikro Papingo (€3.65, two hours) at 5am and 3pm Monday, Wednesday and Friday, and to Monodendri (€2.50, one hour) at 5.30am and 4.15pm daily.

## THESSALONIKI ΘΕΣΣΑΛΟΝΙΚΗ

**pop 788,551**

Thessaloniki (pronounced thess-ah-lo-*nee*-kih), also known as Salonica, was the second city of Byzantium and that of modern Greece. It's a bustling, sophisticated place with good restaurants and nightlife. While it doesn't possess the monuments of the capital, it has wonderful Byzantine churches, as well as a scattering of Roman ruins.

### Orientation

Thessaloniki is laid out on a grid system. The main thoroughfares (Tsimiski, Egnatia and Agiou Dimitriou) run parallel to Leof Nikis, on the waterfront. Plateias Eleftherias and Aristotelous, both on Leof Nikis, are the main squares. The city's most famous landmark is the White Tower at the eastern end of Nikis.

The train station is on Monastiriou, the westerly continuation of Egnatia beyond Plateia Dimokratias, and the airport is 16km to the southeast.

### Information

**Bianca Laundrette** (Panagias Dexias 3; ⏱ 8am-8.30pm Tue, Thu & Fri, 8.30am-3pm Mon, Wed & Sat; per 6kg load €6)

**Enterprise Internet Café** ( ☎ 2310 211 722; Gounari 52; per hr €2; ⏱ 9-3am)

**First-aid centre** ( ☎ 2310 530 530; Navarhou Koundourioti 10) Near the port.

**Main post office** (Aristotelous 26; ⏱ 7.30am-8pm Mon-Fri, 7.30am-2.15pm Sat, 9am-1.30pm Sun)

**National Bank of Greece** (Tsimiski 11) Open Saturday and Sunday for currency exchange. There are other branches elsewhere.

**Tourist information office** ( ☎ 2310 500 310; passenger terminal Thessaloniki port; ⏱ 7.30am-3pm Mon-Fri, 8am-2pm Sat)

**Tourist police** ( ☎ 2310 554 871; 5th fl, Dodekanisou 4; ⏱ 7.30am-11pm)

### Sights & Activities

The **Archaeological Museum** ( ☎ 2310 830 538; Manoli Andronikou 6; ⏱ 10.30am-5pm Mon, 8.30am-3pm Tue-Sun) lost much of its lustre when the treasures of the Vergina tombs were relocated to Vergina. At the time of research, the museum was being renovated.

The 15th-century **White Tower** ( ☎ 2310 267 832; Lefkos Pyrgos; ⏱ 8am-6pm Tue-Sun) is the city's most prominent landmark – but be aware that it's not white. It was whitewashed after independence as a symbolic gesture, but the whitewash has now been removed.

### Sleeping

**Hotel Acropol** ( ☎ 2310 536 170; fax 2310 528 492; Tandalidou 4; s/d with shared bathroom €18/26) The best budget option in town is on a quiet side street with basic but comfortable rooms.

**Hotel Tourist** ( ☎ 2310 270 501; fax 2310 226 865; Mitropoleos 21; s/d €53/67.50; 🖴 ) Hotel Tourist is a fine old neoclassical hotel, which has comfortable rooms with TV and air-con. Prices include buffet breakfast.

### Eating & Drinking

**Ta Nea Ilysia** ( ☎ 2310 536 996; Leotos Sofou 17; mains €4-6) A popular place with travellers and locals alike, it serves up a good choice of daily specials as well as decent moussaka.

**Zythos** ( ☎ 2310 540 284; Katouni 5; mains €8) This pub-restaurant does a roaring trade, with excellent pub food and pastas and an impressive beer and wine list. It serves a decent pint of Guinness and with its outside tables, it's a great place to settle in for a couple of hours.

**Mylos** ( ☎ 2310 525 968; Andreou Georgiou 56; admission free) This huge old mill, 1km west of town, has been converted into an entertainment complex with an art gallery, restaurant, bar and live-music club (classical and rock). Catch a cab here for €8.

### Getting There & Away

#### AIR

**Olympic Airways** ( ☎ 2310 368 666; Navarhou Koundourioti 1-3) and **Aegean Airlines** ( ☎ 2310 280 050; Venizelou 2) both have several flights a day to Athens (€96). Olympic also has daily flights to Ioannina, Lesvos and Limnos; three weekly to Corfu, Iraklio and Mykonos; and two weekly to Chios, Hania and Samos. Aegean also has two flights a day to Iraklio on Crete, and daily flights to Lesvos, Rhodes and Santorini.

GREECE

# THESSALONIKI

To Yedi (500m)

Eptapyrgio

Kastra (Ana Polis)

Kassándrou

Agíou Dimitríou

University
Campus

Elénikis Amýnis

Gulf of Thessaloniki

Plateía Navarínou

Plateía
Agías
Sofías

Egnatía

Plateía
Eleftherías

Plateía
Aristotélous

Port

See Enlargement

Ladadika

To Panaráma (3km); Bulgaria (113km);
Kavála (160km); Turkey (371km)

To KTEL
Macedonia Bus
Station (3km);
Evzoni (704m);
Edessa (82km)

Train Station

To Mýlos (1km);
National
Road E75 (7km);
Lárisa (150km);
Vólos (214km);
Athens (519km)

To Halkidís
Bus Terminal (1.5km);
Ippokration Hospital (2km)

To Airport (16km);
Agía Triáda (24km);
Epanomí (33km);
Halkidikí

International
Exhibition
Fairground

300 m
0.2 miles

200 m
0.1 mi

## BUS

Most of Thessaloniki's buses depart from the new **main bus station** ( ☎ 2310 595 408; Monastiriou 319). Destinations include Athens (€30.80, 13 daily), Ioannina (€21.45, five daily) and Volos (€12.45, seven daily).

Buses to the Halkidiki Peninsula leave from the smaller **bus terminal** ( ☎ 2310 924 445; Karakasi 68) in the eastern part of the city. To get there, take local bus No 10 from Egnatia to the Botsari stop.

## TRAIN

All domestic trains leave from the **train station** ( ☎ 2310 517 517; Monastiriou). There are four regular trains a day to Athens (€14, 7½ hours) and seven express intercity (IC or ICE) services (€27.60, six hours). There are also five trains to Alexandroupolis, two of which are express services (€16.20, 5½ hours). All international trains from Athens stop at Thessaloniki. You can get more information from the **OSE** ( ☎ 2310 598 120; Aristotelous 18) office or from the train station.

## FERRY & HYDROFOIL

There's a Sunday ferry to Lesvos (€30, 13 hours), Limnos (€20, eight hours) and Chios (€30, 18 hours) throughout the year. In summer there are at least three ferries a week to Iraklio (Crete), stopping in the Sporades and the Cyclades on the way. There are also daily hydrofoils to Skiathos, Skopelos and Alonnisos. **Karaharisis Travel & Shipping Agency** ( ☎ 2310 524 544; fax 2310 532 289; Navarhou Koundourioti 8) handles tickets for both ferries and hydrofoils.

## Getting Around

Bus No 78 plies the airport bus route – slowly. A taxi to the train station through the centre of town from the airport costs about €9 and takes about 20 minutes.

## MT OLYMPUS ΟΛΥΜΠΟΣ ΟΡΟΣ

Greece's highest and mightiest mountain, Mt Olympus was chosen by the ancients as the abode of their gods. Naturally they assumed it to be the exact centre of the earth. Olympus has eight peaks, the highest of which is Mytikas (2918m). The area is popular with trekkers, most of whom use the village of Litohoro as a base. Litohoro is 5km inland from the Athens–Thessaloniki highway.

The **EOS office** ( ☎ 2352 084 544; Plateia Kentriki; ☒ 9.30am-12.30pm & 6-8pm Mon-Sat) has information on the various treks and conditions.

The main route to the top takes two days, with a stay overnight at one of the refuges on the mountain. Good protective clothing is essential, even in summer.

**Olympios Zeus** ( ☎ 2352 022 115; Plaka Litohorou; per adult/tent €4.50/3.20) is one of several good camping grounds with a taverna, snack bar and minimarket.

**Hotel Enipeas** ( ☎ 2352 084 328; fax 2352 081 328; Plateia Kentriki; d/tr €35/40) is bright, breezy and squeaky clean. Rooms have balconies with some of the best views of Olympus in town.

**Psistaria Dias** ( ☎ 2352 082 225; Agiou Nikolaou 36; grills €5-6) attracts hordes of locals who order the popular grills. It gets busy at night, so get in early for a table.

From the **bus station** ( ☎ 2352 081 271) in Litohoro there are buses to Thessaloniki (€6.20, 1½ hours, 10 daily) and Athens (€25.90, 5½ hours).

## HALKIDIKI ΧΑΛΚΙΔΙΚΗ

Halkidiki is a three-pronged peninsula that extends into the Aegean Sea, southeast of Thessaloniki. It's the main resort area of northern Greece, with superb sandy beaches right around its 500km of coastline. **Kassandra**, the southwestern prong of the peninsula, has surrendered irrevocably to mass tourism and is not of much interest to the independent traveller. The **Sithonia Peninsula**, the middle prong, is not as over the top and has some spectacular scenery.

## Mt Athos Άγιος Όρος

Halkidiki's third prong is occupied by the all-male Monastic Republic of Mt Athos (known in Greek as the Holy Mountain), where monasteries full of priceless treasures stand amid an impressive landscape of gorges, wooded mountains and precipitous rocks.

Obtaining a four-day visitor permit involves a bit of work. Only 10 foreign adult males may enter Mt Athos per day and there are long waiting lists in summer. You can start the process from outside Thessaloniki, but you need to travel to Thessaloniki to pick up your reservation.

You must first book a date for your visit with the **Mt Athos Pilgrims' Office** ( ☎ 2310 861 611; fax 2310 861 811; Leoforos Karamanli 14; ☒ 8.30am-1.30pm & 6-8pm Mon, Tue, Thu & Fri), east of the

International Exhibition Fairground in Thessaloniki. Make a telephone booking first. You need to supply a photocopy of your passport details and, if you are Orthodox, a photocopied certificate showing your religion.

You must visit the Pilgrims' Office in person to collect the forms confirming your reservation. You can then proceed from Thessaloniki to the port of Ouranoupolis, which is the departure point for boats to Mt Athos, where you will be given your actual permit.

Armed at last with your permit, you can explore, on foot, the 20 monasteries and dependent religious communities of Mt Athos. You can stay only one night at each monastery.

## ALEXANDROUPOLIS ΑΛΕΞΑΝΔΡΟΥΠΟΛΗ
pop 49,176

While there are few sights in Alexandroupolis, its lively student atmosphere makes for a pleasant stopover on the way to Turkey or Samothraki.

One block north of the bus station, **Hotel Lido** ( ☎ 2551 028 808; fax 2551 025 156; Paleologou 15; s/d €35/43, with shared bathroom €27/35) has comfortable rooms and makes a good budget option.

**Nea Klimataria Restaurant** ( ☎ 2551 026 288; Plateia Polytehniou; mains €5-7) is an attractive dining space with good home-cooked fare and draft wine.

Olympic Airways and Aegean Airlines both have several flights a day to Athens (€75, 55 minutes) from the airport, 7km west of town. Several trains and buses a day travel to Thessaloniki (€20). There's also a daily train and a daily OSE bus to Istanbul. In summer at least two boats a day head to Samothraki, dropping to one boat a day in winter. There are also hydrofoils to Samothraki and Limnos.

# SARONIC GULF ISLANDS
## ΝΗΣΙΑ ΤΟΥ ΣΑΡΩΝΙΚΟΥ

The five Saronic Gulf Islands are the closest island group to Athens. Their proximity to the congested capital makes them a popular escape, so accommodation is scarce between mid-June and September, and at weekends year-round.

## AEGINA ΑΙΓΙΝΑ
pop 13,552

Aegina (*eh*-yee-nah) is the closest island to Athens and a popular destination for day-trippers. The lovely **Temple of Aphaia** ( ☎ 2279 032 398; adult/concession €4/2; ☻ 8am-7pm), a well-preserved Doric temple 12km east of Aegina town, is worth visiting. Buses from Aegina town to the small resort of Agia Marina can drop you at the site.

Most travellers prefer to stay in Aegina town, where the **Hotel Plaza** ( ☎ 2297 025 600; plazainaegina@yahoo.co.uk; s/d €20/25, d with sea-view €30) is a popular choice.

## HYDRA ΥΔΡΑ
pop 2719

Hydra (*ee*-drah) is the most stylish destination of the island group. Its gracious stone mansions are stacked up the rocky hillsides that surround the fine natural harbour. The main attraction is the tranquillity as there are no motorised vehicles – apart from sanitation and construction vehicles.

Accommodation is expensive, but of a high standard. **Pension Erofili** ( ☎ 2298 053 984; www.pensionerofili.gr; Tombazi; s/d/tr €40/50/60; ☒ ) a popular choice, with clean, comfortable rooms, including TV and fridge. It's about 300m from the harbour.

Once the residence of a wealthy Hydriot sea captain, **Hotel Miranda** ( ☎ 2298 052 230; mirhydra@hol.gr; Miaouli; s/d/tr €75/100/150; ☒ ) is a beautifully renovated mansion that has been converted to a very smart hotel.

## SPETSES ΣΠΕΤΣΕΣ
pop 3916

Pine-covered Spetses is perhaps the most beautiful island in the group. Having the best beaches means it's also packed with tourists in summer. The **old harbour** in Spetses town is a delightful place to explore.

**Villa Marina** ( ☎ 2298 072 646; s/d €40/56; ☒ ), located just off Plateia Agios Mamas, beyond the row of restaurants, is a small place with good rooms containing a fridge, and there's a well-equipped communal kitchen.

# CYCLADES ΚΥΚΛΑΔΕΣ

The Cyclades (kih-*klah*-dez), named for the rough circle (*kyklos*) they form around the island of Delos, are what Greek island dreams are made of: rugged outcrops, appealing beaches, azure waters, white cubist buildings and blue-domed Byzantine churches.

Some of the islands, such as Mykonos, Ios and Santorini (Thira), have seized tourism with great enthusiasm, while others are little more than clumps of rock, each with a village, secluded coves and a few curious tourists. Ferry services rarely run in winter, while from July to September the Cyclades are vulnerable to the *meltemi*, a fierce northeasterly wind that can cull ferry schedules.

For detailed information on the islands, check out Lonely Planet's *Greek Islands*.

## History

The Cyclades enjoyed a flourishing Bronze Age civilisation (3000 to 1100 BC), almost concurrent with the Minoan civilisation.

Between the 4th and 7th centuries AD, the islands, like the rest of Greece, suffered a series of invasions and occupations. During the Middle Ages they were raided by pirates – hence the labyrinthine character of their towns, which was meant to confuse attackers. On some islands the whole population would move into the mountainous interior to escape the pirates, while on others they would brave it out on the coast. On some islands the *hora* (main town) is on the coast, and on others it is inland.

The Cyclades became part of independent Greece in 1827. Before the revival of the islands' fortunes by the tourist boom that began in the 1970s, many islanders lived in poverty and many more headed for the mainland or emigrated to America and Australia in search of work.

## MYKONOS ΜΥΚΟΝΟΣ
### pop 9300

The most visited and expensive of the Cyclades, Mykonos survives on tourism, but handles it well. The island has marvellous variety. Sun worshippers will love its beaches, party animals will struggle to escape its bars, shoppers will be trapped by its boutiques, and romantics will savour its sunsets. Add in the nearby sacred island of Delos and the fact that Mykonos is a mecca for gay travellers, and it's clear that the island has something for everybody.

GREECE

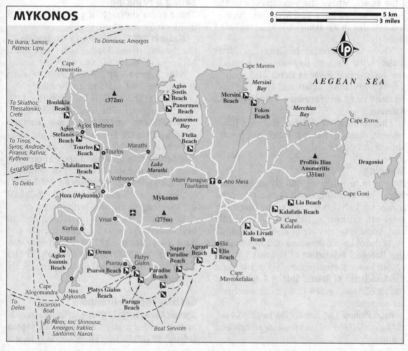

## Orientation

Mykonos town (Hora) has two ferry quays. The old quay, where most of the conventional ferries and some fast ferries dock, is 400m north of the town waterfront. The new quay is 2.5km north of town, where buses meet arriving ferries. When buying outgoing tickets, check which quay the ferry leaves from.

## Information

**Angelo's Internet Café** ( ☎ 2289 024 106; Xenias; per hr €3.50) is on the road between the southern bus station and the windmills. The post office is near the southern bus station. There is no tourist office.

**Island Mykonos Travel** ( ☎ 2289 022 232; www .discovergreece.org; Taxi Sq), where the port road meets the town, is helpful for tourist and travel information.

## Sights & Activities

Summer crowds consume the island's capital and port, shuffling through snaking streets of chic boutiques and blinding white walls with balconies of cascading flowers. **Little Venice**, where the sea laps up to the edge of the buildings, and Mykonos' famous hill-top row of **windmills** should be included in a stroll.

The most popular beaches are **Platys Gialos**, with its wall-to-wall sun lounges, the often-nude **Paradise Beach** and mainly gay **Super Paradise**, **Agrari** and **Elia**. The less-squashy ones are **Panormos**, **Kato Livadi** and **Kalafatis**.

The remarkable World Heritage-listed ancient site on nearby Delos (opposite) should not be missed.

## Sleeping

Rooms in town fill up quickly in high season so it's wise to go with the first *domatia* owner who accosts you. Be aware that room rates can change by the day. Outside July and August, rooms are as cheap as chops.

At the old port, the same building houses the **Hoteliers Association of Mykonos** ( ☎ 2289 024 540; www.mykonosgreece.com; ✆ 9am-11pm) and the **Association of Rooms, Studios & Apartments** ( ☎ 2289 026 860; ✆ 9am-10pm); both can book accommodation.

**Hotel Philippi** ( ☎ 2289 022 294; fax 2289 024 680; 25 Kalogera; s/d €60/75) Has spacious rooms and garden.

**Zorzis Hotel** ( ☎ 2289 022 167; www.zorzishotel.com; 30 Kalogera; s/d €92/115; ⚇ ) An impressive place run by Aussie/Greek owner Jonathan. The rooms are immaculate, and if you turn up outside July/August, a double with bathroom will go for €40.

**Hotel Apollon** ( ☎ 2289 022 223; fax 2289 024 237; Paralia; s/d with shared bathroom €50/65) Upstairs along the waterfront, Apollon has old-world charm.

Mykonos has two camping areas, both on the south coast. Minibuses from both meet the ferries and buses jog regularly into town.

**Paradise Beach Camping** ( ☎ 2289 022 852; www .paradisemykonos.com; per person/tent €8/4) There are lots of options here, including beach cabins and apartments, as well as bars, a swimming pool, games etc. It is skin-to-skin mayhem in summer with a real party atmosphere – and nudity on the beach is not uncommon!

**Mykonos Camping** ( ☎ 2289 024 578; www.my camp.gr; per person/tent €8/4) Near Platys Gialos beach, this place also parties but is a bit more relaxed.

## Eating & Drinking

There is no shortage of places to eat and drink on Mykonos.

**Madupas** ( ☎ 2289 022 224; Paralia; dishes €5-12) On the waterfront, Madupas serves a mean Mykonian sausage for €8.

**Nikos Taverna** ( ☎ 2289 024 320; Porta; dishes €4-13) Dishes out seafood by the kilo.

**Antonini's** ( ☎ 2289 022 319; Taxi Sq; dishes €3.50-12.50) A local hang-out with great Greek food.

**Cavo Paradiso** ( ☎ 2289 027 205; www.cavoparadiso .gr; admission from €20) For those who want to go the whole hog, this club 300m above Paradise Beach picks up around 2pm. There's 24-hour bus to transport clubbers in summer.

In Little Venice, **Katerina's Bar** ( ☎ 2289 023 084; Agion Anargion) and **Verandah Café** ( ☎ 2289 027 400; Agion Anargion) are bars with huge views.

Long feted as a gay travel destination, Mykonos has plenty of gaycentric clubs and hang-outs. **Kastro** ( ☎ 2289 023 072; Agion Anargion), **Diva** ( ☎ 2289 027 271) and **Pierro's** ( ☎ 2289 022 177), just in from Taxi Sq, are particularly popular.

## Getting There & Around

**Olympic Airways** ( ☎ 2289 022 490; Plateia Remezzo) is by the southern bus station, or call **Aegean Airlines** ( ☎ 2289 028 720). There are daily flights

from Mykonos to Athens (€76) and to Santorini (Thira; €65). In summer, there are
flights to and from Rhodes and Thessaloniki.
Daily ferries arrive from Piraeus (€18.20,
six hours). From Mykonos, there are daily
ferries and hydrofoils to most major Cycladic islands, three services weekly to Crete
(€20.50, nine hours), and less-frequent services to the northeastern Aegean Islands and
the Dodecanese. Head to Island Mykonos
Travel (opposite) for details and tickets.

The northern bus station is near the old
port. It serves Agios Stefanos, Elia, Kalafatis
and Ano Mera. The southern bus station,
southeast of the windmills, serves Agios
Ioannis, Psarou, Platys Gialos, Ornos and
Paradise Beach. In summer, *caiques* (small
fishing boats) from Mykonos town and
Platys Gialos putter to Paradise, Super Paradise, Agrari and Elia beaches.

## DELOS ΔΗΛΟΣ

Southeast of Mykonos, the island of **Delos**
( ☎ 2289 022 259; admission €5; ⏲ 9am-3pm Tue-Sun)
is the Cyclades' archaeological jewel, and
the opportunity to clamber among the
ruins shouldn't be missed.

According to mythology, Delos was the
birthplace of Apollo – the god of light,
poetry, music, healing and prophecy. The
island flourished as an important religious
and commercial centre from the 3rd millennium BC, reaching its apex of power in
the 5th century BC.

Ruins include the **Sanctuary of Apollo**, containing temples dedicated to him, and the
**Terrace of the Lions**. These proud beasts were
carved in the early 6th century BC using
marble from Naxos to guard the sacred area.
The original lions are in the island's museum, with replicas on the original site. The
**Sacred Lake** (dry since 1926) is where Leto
supposedly gave birth to Apollo, while the
**Theatre Quarter** is where private houses were
built around the **Theatre of Delos**.

The climb up **Mt Kynthos** (113m), the
island's highest point, is a highlight. The
view of Delos and the surrounding islands
is spectacular, and it's easy to see how the
Cyclades got their name – for the circle
*(kyklos)* they form around Delos.

Numerous companies offer excursion
boats from Mykonos to Delos (€7 return,
30 minutes) between 9am and 12.50pm. The
return boats leave Delos between 12.20pm

and 3pm. To appreciate the site, pick up a
guidebook or take a guided tour. Take a sun-
hat, sunblock, sturdy footwear and water.

## PAROS ΠΑΡΟΣ
### pop 12,850

Paros is an attractive island with good swimming beaches and terraced hills that build
up to Mt Profitis Ilias (770m). It is more
open and laid-back than Mykonos, and
is famous for its pure white marble, from
which the *Venus de Milo* was sculpted.

### Orientation & Information

Paros' main town and port is Parikia, on
the west coast. Agora, known as Market
St, is Parikia's main commercial thoroughfare, running from the main square, Plateia
Mavrogenous (opposite the ferry terminal).

Opposite the ferry quay, to the left, is
**Memphis.net** ( ☎ 2284 022 878; ⏲ 9am-midnight;
per 15min €1), which provides Internet access.
There is no tourist office, but travel agencies
such as **Santorineos Travel** ( ☎ 2284 024 245), on
the waterfront, oblige with information.

Check also the **island website** (www
.parosweb.com).

### Sights & Activities

One of the most notable churches in Greece
is Parikia's **Panagia Ekatontapyliani** (Our Lady of
the Hundred Gates; ☎ 2284 021 243; ⏲ 7.30am-9.30pm)
for its beautiful, ornate interior.

A fantastic option on Paros is to rent a
scooter at one of the many outlets in Parikia
and ride around the island. There are sealed
roads the whole way round, and the opportunity to explore villages such as **Naoussa**,
**Marpissa** and **Aliki**, and swim at beaches such
as **Logaras**, **Pounda** and **Golden Beach**. Naoussa
is a cute little fishing village that is all geared
up to welcome tourists.

Less than 2km from Paros, the small island
of **Antiparos** has fantastic beaches, which have
made it wildly popular. The chief attraction
is its **cave** (admission €3; ⏲ 10.15am-3pm summer),
considered to be one of Europe's best.

### Sleeping

*Domatia* owners come to meet the ferries.
The **Rooms Association** ( ☎ 2284 022 861; ⏲ 9-
1am) has a helpful kiosk on the quay.

**Rooms Mike** ( ☎ 2284 022 856; s/d/tr €25/35/45)
Mike is a brilliant host. Walk 50m left from
the port and it's next to Memphis.net.

## PAROS & ANTIPAROS

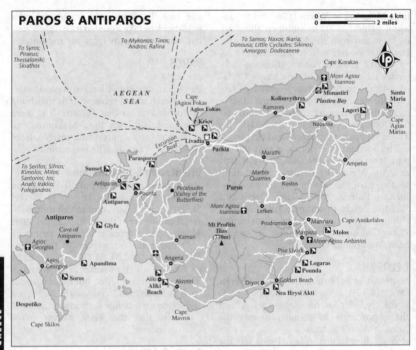

0 — 4 km
0 — 2 miles

Rooms Rena ( ☎ 2284 021 427; Epitropakis; s/d
€25/35) These quiet and well-kept rooms
are excellent value. To get here, turn left
from the pier then turn right at the ancient
cemetery.

Hotel Argonauta ( ☎ 2284 021 440; www.argonauta
.gr; d €60; ☒ ) On the main square, Argonauta
has a more traditional feel.

There's loads of camping around Paros,
with charges of around €6 per person and
€4 per tent. Koula Camping ( ☎ 2284 022 081;
Livadia beach) is about 1km north of Parikia's
waterfront, Naoussa Camping ( ☎ 2284 051 565) is
on the north coast and Alyki Camping ( ☎ 2284
091 303) is on the south coast.

### Eating & Drinking

Zorba's (Plateia Mavrogenous; gyros €1.80) Trust Zorba's *gyros* for a quick fix.

Porphyra ( ☎ 2284 023 410; dishes from €5) Serves
excellent fresh seafood next to the ancient
cemetery.

Happy Green Cows ( ☎ 2284 024 691; dishes from
€5; ☽ 7pm-midnight) Vegetarians should head
to this place behind the main square for a
creative menu.

Pirate ( ☎ 2284 021 114; Market St) Plays great
jazz and blues.

Pebbles Bar ( ☎ 2284 022 283) Perched right
above the waterfront, Pebbles has truly stunning views.

Dubliner ( ☎ 2284 021 113) Houses three bars
in one and is loud and large.

### Getting There & Around

Paros has daily flights to/from Athens
(€72); contact Olympic Airways ( ☎ 2284 021
900; Plateia Mavrogenous, Parikia) for details. Parikia is a major ferry hub with daily connections to Piraeus (€19, five hours) and
frequent ferries and catamarans to Naxos,
Ios, Santorini (Thira) and Mykonos. The
Dodecanese and the northeastern Aegean
Islands are also well serviced from here.
Head to Santorineos Travel (p303) for
tickets.

The bus station, 100m left from the
port, has frequent services to the entire
island. In summer there are hourly excursion boats to Antiparos from Parikia port,
or you can catch a bus to Pounta and ferry
it across.

## NAXOS ΝΑΞΟΣ
### pop 18,200
Naxos is the biggest and greenest of the Cyclades, and enjoys its reputation as a family destination. The island is well worth taking time to explore. It has a fascinating main town, excellent beaches and a striking interior.

### Orientation & Information
Naxos town, on the west coast, is the island's capital and port. Court Sq is also known as Plateia Protodikiou. The island website is www.naxos-greece.net.

**Naxos Tourist Information Centre** (NTIC; ☎ 2285 025 201; www.naxostownhotels.com; ☼ 8am-midnight), a privately owned organisation opposite the port, offers help with accommodation, tours, luggage storage and laundry.

**Zas Travel** (☎ 2285 023 330; ☼ 8am-midnight) is also opposite the port, and sells ferry tickets and offers Internet access for €4 an hour.

### Sights & Activities
Naxos town twists and curves upwards to a crumbling 13th-century **kastro** that looks out over the town. It has a well-stocked **archaeological museum** (☎ 2285 022 725; admission €3; ☼ 8.30am-3pm Tue-Sun).

The beach of **Agios Georgios** is a ten-minute walk from town; turn right from the port. Beyond this spot, wonderful sandy beaches stretch as far south as **Pyrgaki Beach**. **Agia Anna Beach**, 6km from town, and **Plaka Beach**

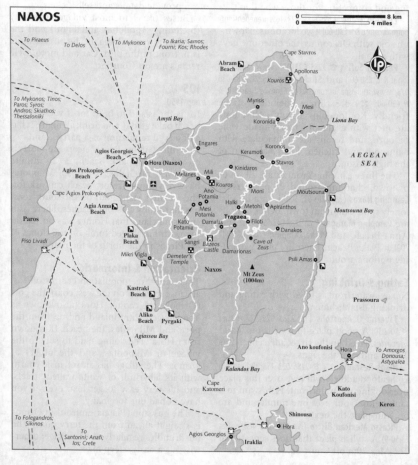

are lined with accommodation and packed in summer.

A rental car or scooter will help reveal Naxos' dramatic landscape. The **Tragea region** has tranquil villages, churches atop rocky crags and huge olive groves. **Filoti**, the largest inland settlement, perches on the slopes of **Mt Zeus** (1004m). It's a tough three-hour trail to the summit.

In Apollonas you'll find the mysterious 10.5m **kouros** (naked male statue), constructed c 7th century, lying abandoned and unfinished in an ancient marble quarry.

### Sleeping

Owners of *domatia* and camping grounds meet ferries, picking up those with a booking and competing for those who don't.

**Pension Irene** ( ☎ 2285 023 169; irenepension@ hotmail.com; d & tr €30-60) Two locations in town – one old with OK rooms, the other one new, with a pool.

**Pension Sofi** ( ☎ 2285 023 077; www.pensionsofi .gr; d & tr €30-60) and **Studios Panos** ( ☎ 2285 026 078; www.studiospanos.com; Agios Georgios Beach; d & tr €30-60; 🔀 ) are run by members of the friendly Koufopoulos family. All guests are met with a glass of family-made wine or ouzo, and rooms are immaculate with bathroom and kitchen. Rates halve out of the high season.

The three camping grounds are all south of town, charging around €5 per person. **Camping Naxos** ( ☎ 2285 023 500) is in a bit of a lonely spot, 2km from town. Better options are **Camping Maragas** ( ☎ 2285 042 552) on Agia Anna Beach, and **Plaka Camping** ( ☎ 2285 042 700) at Plaka Beach. There are plenty of eating options around both.

### Eating & Drinking

Naxos' waterfront is lined with eating and drinking establishments.

**Taverna O Apostolis** ( ☎ 2285 026 777; dishes €1.50-2.50) A good place to try for ouzo and *mezedes*. Head up the street adjacent to Zas Travel and spot the signs.

**Nikos Restaurant** ( ☎ 2285 023 153; dishes from €3) Seafood addicts will rave over this place overlooking the waterfront. Fish swim in a tank before your eyes one minute and are on your plate the next.

**Picasso Mexican Bistro** ( ☎ 2285 025 408; dishes €3.50-9) A stylish place that does sensational Tex-Mex 20m off Court Sq.

Nightlife clusters around the southern end of the waterfront. There's the tropical **Med Bar** and **Caesar's Club**, and if you're up for dancing, the club **Ocean** ( 🌙 from 11pm) goes wild after midnight. **Super Island Dance Club**, on the Grotto Beach waterfront, is also lively.

### Getting There & Around

Naxos has daily flights to Athens (€64); Olympic Airways is represented by **Naxos Travel** ( ☎ 2285 022 095). There are daily ferries to Piraeus (€21.50, six hours) and good ferry and hydrofoil connections to most Cycladic islands. Boats go once a week to Crete, Thessaloniki and Rhodes, and two to three times a week to Samos. Zas Travel (p305) can provide details and sells tickets.

Buses travel to most villages regularly (including Apollonas and Filoti) and the beaches towards Pyrgaki. The bus terminal is in front of the port. Car and motorcycle rentals are off Court Sq.

## IOS ΙΟΣ
### pop 1850

Ios is the island to head for if you want to beach bake all day and drink all night. It has a deserved reputation as a party island.

While Gialos Beach near the port is crowded, Koubara Beach, a 20-minute walk west of Gialos, is less so. Milopotas has everything a resort beach can ask for, and isolated Manganari on the south coast has four sandy crescent beaches. There is an enduring claim that Homer was buried on Ios, with his alleged tomb on the slopes of Mt Pirgos in the north of the island.

### Orientation & Information

There are three population centres on Ios, all close together on the west coast: the port (Ormos); the capital, Hora (also known as 'the village'), 2km inland and up from the port; and Milopotas, the beach 1km down from Hora. The young tend to stay in the village or Milopotas, and the others at Ormos. The village has an intrinsic charm with its labyrinth of white-walled streets, and it's very easy to get lost, even if you haven't had one too many.

The bus stop (Plateia Emirou) in Ormos is straight ahead from the ferry quay. The bus trundles regularly to the village; otherwise it's a nasty, steep hike.

## IOS

Koubara Beach
Gialos Beach
Ormos (Port)
Hora

Milopotas Beach

AEGEAN SEA

Cape Karatza

Plakotos
Homer's Tomb
▲ (417m)
Agia Theodoti Beach
▲ (514m)
Paleokastro Ruins
Psathi Beach
Ios
**See Enlargement**
Ormos (Port)
Hora
Cape Pountas

To Naxos;
Paros; Syros;
Piraeus; Tinos;
Rafina; Mykonos;
Kythnos
▲ (713m)
Moni Kalamou
Plakes Bay
Klima Bay
Kalamos Beach

To Sikinos;
Folegandros;
Sifnos; Kimolos;
Serifos; Milos
Papas Beach
Cape Fidias

To Crete; Santorini;
Amorgos; Anafi
Cape Ahlades
Manganari Beach

There is no tourist office, but **Acteon Travel** ( ☎ 2286 091 343; www.acteon.gr) has four offices in Ormos, the village and Mylopotas to keep busy. Internet access costs around €4 an hour, and is scattered among hotels, cafés, bars and Acteon Travel.

### Sleeping

**Francesco's** ( ☎ 2286 091 223; www.francescos.net; Hora; dm/d €10/50, d with shared bathroom €30; ✦ ) A lively meeting place with superlative views from its terrace bar. All rooms have TV. Very convenient for party going, and the rates halve out of high season.

**Camping Ios** ( ☎ 2286 092 035; www.campingios .com; Ormos; per person €6; ✦ ) Clearly visible just right of the port.

**Far Out Beach Club** ( ☎ 2286 091 468; www.farout club.com; Milopotas; camping per person €7, bungalows €15, r €25-60; ✦ ✦ ) This place has tons of facilities, including bungalows and hotel rooms, and its four pools are open to the public.

**Hotel Nissos Ios** ( ☎ 2286 091 610; www.nissos ioshotel.gr; Milopotas; dm/s/d €25/55/75; ✦ ) Bright, cheerful and right on the beach.

### Eating & Drinking

Milopotas Beach parties hard from noon until midnight with up to 3000 people.

In the village, **Porky's**, just off the main square, is a legend for cheap eats.

**Ali Baba's** ( ☎ 2286 091 558; Hora; dishes €6.50-9) Popular and parties until late. It has huge meals and a funky ambience.

**Fiesta** ( ☎ 2286 091 766; Hora; dishes from €3) A short tumble down the hill from Frances-co's, Fiesta has great wood-oven pizzas.

**Susana** ( ☎ 2286 051 108; Ormos; dishes from €2.50) Hit this spot for an honest feed.

At night, the compact little village erupts with bars to explore and you'll have to elbow your way nicely to the other side. Perennial favourites include **Red Bull** ( ☎ 2286 091 019), **Slammers** ( ☎ 2286 092 119) and **Blue Note** ( ☎ 2286 092 271). Opposite the central car park, **Sweet Irish Dreams** ( ☎ 2286 091 141) is a crowd pleaser with table dancing.

### Getting There & Around

Ios has daily ferry connections to Piraeus (€18.80, seven hours) and there are frequent hydrofoils and ferries to the major Cycladic islands. There are buses every 20 minutes between the port, the village and Milopotas Beach until early morning, and two to three a day to Manganari Beach (45 minutes). Head to Acteon Travel (left) for details and tickets.

## SANTORINI (THIRA) ΣΑΝΤΟΡΙΝΗ (ΘΗΡΑ)
pop 13,400

Stunning Santorini is something special. Visitors cannot help but gaze at the startling sight of the submerged caldera almost encircled by sheer cliffs.

### Orientation & Information

The capital, Fira, perches on top of the caldera on the west coast, with the port of Athinios 10km away by road. The bus station and taxi station are located just south of Fira's main square, Plateia Theotokopoulou.

**Dakoutros Travel** ( ☎ 2286 022 958; www.dakoutros travel.gr; ✆ 8.30am-10pm), opposite the taxi station, is extremely helpful, and there are a batch of other agencies around the square. Internet access is readily available around Fira. **Lava Internet Café** ( ☎ 2286 025 551; 25 Martiou; per 15min €1.50) is funky and just up from the square. The **post office** is one block south of the taxi station.

GREECE

GREECE

### SANTORINI'S BIG BANGS

Santorini, officially known as Thira, is regarded by many as the most spectacular of all the Greek islands. Its violent volcanic past is visible everywhere, and through the centuries eruptions have regularly changed the shape of the island.

First inhabited around 3000 BC, Santorini was circular and known as Strongili (the Round One). About 1650 BC, a massive volcanic explosion – speculated to be the biggest such explosion in recorded history – caused the centre of the island to sink, producing a caldera that the sea quickly filled in. The explosion generated a huge tsunami that caused havoc around the Aegean, and it is widely believed that the catastrophe was responsible for the demise of Crete's powerful Minoan culture.

In 236 BC further volcanic activity separated Thirasia from the main island. The islet of Palia Kameni appeared in the caldera in 197 BC, and in AD 726 a major blast catapulted pumice as far as Asia Minor. The island's south coast collapsed in 1570, while an eruption created the islet of Nea Kameni in 1707.

In 1956 an earthquake measuring 7.8 on the Richter scale pummelled the island, killing scores of people and destroying most of the houses in Fira and Oia.

One thing is for certain – it isn't over yet. Minor tremors are fairly common. Santorini is incomparable when it comes to a sense of impermanence and precariousness.

Those wishing to play in the volcanic wonderland can bake on Santorini's sizzling black-sand beaches, clamber around on volcanic lava on Nea Kameni or swim into the warm sea at Palia Kameni.

On the main street of Perissa, on the southeast coast, **Santosun Travel** ( ☎ 2286 081 456; www.santosun.gr) can book and rent you anything, and has Internet access at €3 per hour.

## Sights & Activities

### FIRA

The shameless commercialism of Fira has not quite reduced its all-pervasive dramatic aura. The best of the town's museums is the exceptional **Museum of Prehistoric Thira** ( ☎ 2286 023 217; admission €3; ☽ 8.30am-3pm Tue-Sun), which has fab displays of artefacts predominantly from ancient Akrotiri. It's two blocks south of the main square. The **Megaron Gyzi Museum** ( ☎ 2286 022 244; admission €3; ☽ 10.30am-1.30pm & 5-8pm Mon-Sat, 10.30am-4.30pm Sun), behind the Catholic cathedral, houses local memorabilia, including photographs of Fira before and after the 1956 earthquake.

### AROUND THE ISLAND

Santorini's **beaches** of black volcanic sand sizzle – beach mats are essential. It's a strange feeling to walk over black sand then out onto smooth lava when going for a dip. **Perissa** and **Kamari** are particularly popular. In Perissa, the **Santorini Dive Centre** ( ☎ 2286 083 190; www.divecenter.gr) can look after divers' needs.

Excavations in 1967 uncovered the remarkably well-preserved Minoan settlement of **Akrotiri** at the south of the island with its remains of two- and three-storey buildings, and evidence of a sophisticated drainage system. It's a popular site for visitors, though it's visually disappointing due to efforts to protect the ruins.

At the north of the island, the flawless village of **Oia** (pronounced ee-ah), famed for its postcard sunsets, is less hectic than Fira and a must-visit. Its caldera-facing tavernas are superb spots for brunch. It's possible to walk from Fira in about three hours along the top of the caldera.

Of the surrounding islets, only **Thirasia** is inhabited. Visitors can clamber around on volcanic lava on **Nea Kameni** then swim into warm springs in the sea at **Palia Kameni**. There are various excursions available to get you there. Also possible is a submarine tour with **Submarine Santorini** ( ☎ 2286 082 577; 1hr tour per person €50), or sea-kayak tours, horse riding and wine-tasting tours. Bookings are possible at most travel agencies.

## Sleeping

Decide where you want to stay before aggressive accommodation owners who meet the boats try to decide things for you. Fira has spectacular views, but is miles from the beaches. Perissa has a great beach but is on the east coast, away from the caldera views. Pick one side of the island and try not to get stuck in the middle.

**Santorini Camping** ( ☎ 2286 022 944; www.santorini camping.gr; Fira; per person €7; P ☺ ) This place, 500m east of the main square, is a bit tired and lacks views, but has a restaurant and swimming pool.

**Pension Petros** ( ☎ 2286 022 573; fax 2286 022 615; Fira; s/d €55/60) Centrally located, 250m east of the square, but without views.

**Maria's Rooms** ( ☎ 2286 025 143; Agiou Mina; d €50; ☺ ) On the southern edge of town, Maria's has small but immaculate rooms, and stunning caldera views from its terrace.

**Hotel Keti** ( ☎ 2286 022 324; www.hotelketi.gr; Agiou Mina; d €70; ☺ ) Just to the north with caldera views to die for.

**Perissa Camping** ( ☎ 2286 081 343; Perissa; per person €7; P ) Right on Perissa's beach.

**Stelio's Place** ( ☎ 2286 081 860; www.steliosplace .com; Perissa; d from €25; P ☺ ☺ ) An excellent option just back from Perissa's beach, with very friendly service and port and airport transfers.

## Eating & Drinking

**Taverna Lava** ( ☎ 2286 081 776; Perissa; dishes €3-8) Along Perissa's waterfront, this island-wide favourite has a mouthwatering menu. Go out to the kitchen and pick what looks good.

**Naoussa** ( ☎ 2286 024 869; Erythrou Stavrou; dishes €3-20) Excellent-value Greek classics.

**Stani Taverna** ( ☎ 2286 023 078; Erythrou Stavrou; dishes €4-15) Has a wide-ranging menu and a rooftop setting.

**Nikolas** ( ☎ 2286 024 550; Erythrou Stavrou; dishes €5-10) Receives rave reviews from diners.

Cheap eateries such as Grill House are in abundance around the square in Fira.

Most of the popular bars and clubs in Fira are clustered along Erythrou Stavrou. **Kira Thira** ( ☎ 2286 022 770) plays smooth jazz. Once things hot up, **Koo Club** ( ☎ 2286 022 025), **Enigma** ( ☎ 2286 022 466) and **Murphys** ( ☎ 2286 022 248) more than meet late-night requirements. In Perissa, the **Full Moon Bar** ( ☎ 2286 081 177; ☺ 9pm-late), on the main street, goes off.

## Getting There & Around

Santorini's international airport has daily flights to Athens (€85), and less regular

GREECE

**SANTORINI (THIRA)**

0 — 4 km
0 — 2 miles

To Ios; Naxos; Paros;
Mykonos; Syros; Tinos;
Piraeus; Skiathos;
Thessaloniki

To Milos;
Folegandros; Kimolos;
Sifnos; Serifos; Kythnos

Paradise Beach
Baxedes
Ammoudi (Port)
Ola
Finikia
Pori Beach
Cape Riva
Armeni Port
Santorini (Thira)
Potamos Beach
Potamos
Manolas
Agrilla
Thirasia
Imerovigli
Vourvoulos
Gialos Beach
Firostefani
Fira
Karterados Beach
Cape Trypiti
Fira Skala (Port)
Monolithos
Monolithos Beach
Karterados
Nea Kameni
Messaria
Hot Springs
Palia Kameni
Vothonas
AEGEAN
SEA
Athinios (Port)
Mesa Gonia
Exo Gonia
Pyrgos
Aspronisi
Megalohori
Kamari
Mt Profitis Ilias (567m)
Kamari Beach
Moni Profiti Ilia
Ancient Thira
Cape Akrotiri
Akrotiri
Ancient Akrotiri
Cape Mesa Vouno (567m)
Perissa
Emporio
Black Beach
White Beach
Red Beach
Perivolos Beach
Vlihada Beach
Agios Georgios Beach
To Crete
To Anafi
Cape Evo Mytis

ones to Rhodes (€90) and Mykonos (€65); call **Olympic Airways** ( ☎ 2286 022 493) or **Aegean Airlines** ( ☎ 2286 028 500) for details.

There are daily ferries to Piraeus (€22.50, nine hours), daily connections in summer to Mykonos, Ios, Naxos, Paros and Iraklio, and ferries to the smaller islands in the Cyclades. Large ferries use Athinios port, where they are met by buses (€1.20) and taxis. Get your tickets from Dakoutros Travel (p307) or Santosun Travel (p308). Small boats use Fira Skala port, where the mode of transport up to Fira is by donkey or cable car (€3); otherwise, it's a clamber up 600 steps.

Buses go frequently to Oia, Kamari, Perissa, Akrotiri, ancient Thira and Monolithos. Port buses usually leave Fira, Kamari and Perissa one to 1½ hours before ferry departures. A rental car or scooter is a great option on Santorini.

# CRETE ΚΡΗΤΗ

Greece's largest and most southerly island, Crete hosts a quarter of all visitors to the country. The island is split by a spectacular chain of mountains that runs east to west. The major towns are on the more hospitable northern coast and it's here that the package-tourism industry thrives. Most of the south coast is too precipitous to support large settlements. The mountainous interior offers rigorous trekking and climbing.

For more detailed information, snap up a copy of Lonely Planet's *Crete*. Good websites on Crete include www.interkriti .org, www.infocrete.com and www.explore crete.com.

## History

Crete was the birthplace of Minoan culture, Europe's first advanced civilisation, which flourished from 2800 to 1450 BC. Very little is known of Minoan civilisation, which came to an abrupt end, possibly destroyed by Santorini's volcanic eruption in around 1650 BC.

Later, Crete passed from the warlike Dorians to the Romans. Then it went to the Genoese, who in turn sold it to the Venetians. Under the Venetians, the island became a refuge for artists, writers and philosophers who fled Constantinople after it fell to the Turks. Their influence inspired the young Cretan painter Domenikos Theotokopoulos, who moved to Spain and there won immortality as the great El Greco.

The Turks conquered Crete in 1670. It then became a British protectorate in 1898 after a series of insurrections and was united with independent Greece in 1913. There was horrendous fighting during WWII when a German airborne invasion defeated the Allied forces in the 10-day Battle of Crete. An active resistance movement drew heavy reprisals from the German occupiers.

CRETE

# IRAKLIO ΗΡΑΚΛΕΙΟ

**pop 133,000**

Iraklio, Crete's capital, is a bustling modern city and the fifth-largest in Greece. It has a lively city centre, an excellent archaeological museum and is close to Knossos, Crete's major tourist attraction.

## Information

The city centre is about 500m west of the port. Banks, a stack of travel agencies and Olympic Airways are on 25 Avgoustou.

**Post office** (Plateia Daskalogiani)

**Skoutelis Travel** ( ☎ 2810 280 808; www.skoutelis.gr; 25 Avgoustou) Handles airline and ferry bookings, and rents cars.

**SportC@fé** (25 Avgoustou; per hr €2; ☼ 24hr) Internet access.

**Tourist police** ( ☎ 2810 283 190; Dikeosynis 10; ☼ 7am-11pm) Helpful with maps and information.

## Sights & Activities

Iraklio's **archaeological museum** ( ☎ 2810 226 092; Xanthoudidou; adult/student €6/3; ☼ 12.30-7pm Mon, 8am-7pm Tue-Sun) has an outstanding Minoan collection, second only to the national museum in Athens. Even a superficial perusal will take half a day.

At the end of the old jetty is the impressive fortress **Rocca al Mare** ( ☎ 2810 246 211; adult/student €2/1; ☼ 8am-6pm Mon-Sat, 10am-3pm Sun), which, like the city walls, was built by the Venetians in the 16th century.

The **Battle of Crete Museum** ( ☎ 2810 346 554; cnr Doukos Beaufort & Hatzidaki; admission free; ☼ 8am-3pm) chronicles the historic WWII battle

with photographs, letters, uniforms and weapons.

## Sleeping

Near the old harbour and bus stations is a cluster of decent mid-range hotels.

**Rent Rooms Hellas** ( ☎ 2810 288 851; Handakos 24; dm/d €10/25) A popular budget choice. It's clean, with packed dorms, a rooftop bar and a bargain breakfast.

**Hotel Kronos** ( ☎ 2810 282 240; www.kronoshotel .gr; Sofokli Venizelou 2; s/d €35/45; ☒ ) This waterfront place has large, airy rooms and includes breakfast.

**Hotel Mirabello** ( ☎ 2810 285 052; www.mirabello hotel.gr; Theotokopoulou 20; s/d €38/50; ☒ ) A pleasant place in the centre of town, run by an ex-sea captain who has travelled the world. Check out the excellent website.

**Hotel Kastro** ( ☎ 2810 284 185; www.kastro-hotel .gr; Theotokopoulou 22; s/d €80/95; ☒ ⌨ ) Next to Mirabello, this upmarket place has large rooms with fridges, TV, phones and ISDN Internet connectivity.

## Eating & Entertainment

There's a congregation of cheap eateries in the Plateia Venizelou and El Greco Park area, as well as a bustling, colourful market all the way along 1866.

**Giakoumis Taverna** ( ☎ 2810 280 277; Theodosaki 5-8; dishes €2.50-8) With a full menu of Cretan specialities, this is the best of a bunch of cheap tavernas in the market area.

**Ippokampos Ouzeri** ( ☎ 2810 280 240; Mitsotaki 2; dishes €3.50-8) On the waterfront, this place serves up a popular, well-priced menu.

**Istioploikos** ( ☎ 2810 228 118; dishes €3-10) In an old warehouse on the harbour, this is perfect for fish lovers.

**Take Five** ( ☎ 2810 226 564; Akroleondos 7) On El Greco Park, this gay-friendly place has low-key music and ambience.

**Jasmin** ( ☎ 2810 288 880; Handakos 45) There's a DJ spinning nightly.

**Guernica** ( ☎ 2810 282 988; Apokoronou Kritis 2) Plays contemporary music.

## Getting There & Around

There are several flights a day to Athens (€76) and, in summer, flights to Thessaloniki and Rhodes. Get tickets from **Olympic Airways** ( ☎ 2810 229 191; 25 Avgoustou 27) and **Aegean Airlines** ( ☎ 2810 344 324; Leof Dimokratias 11). Both also have offices at the airport.

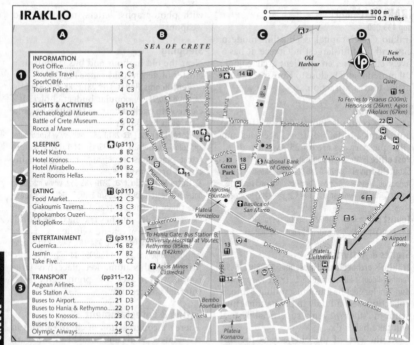

**IRAKLIO**

0 — 300 m
0 — 0.2 miles

| INFORMATION | |
|---|---|
| Post Office | 1 C3 |
| Skoutelis Travel | 2 C1 |
| SportC@fé | 3 C1 |
| Tourist Police | 4 C3 |

| SIGHTS & ACTIVITIES | (p311) |
|---|---|
| Archaeological Museum | 5 D2 |
| Battle of Crete Museum | 6 D2 |
| Rocca al Mare | 7 C1 |

| SLEEPING | (p311) |
|---|---|
| Hotel Kastro | 8 B2 |
| Hotel Kronos | 9 C1 |
| Hotel Mirabello | 10 B2 |
| Rent Rooms Hellas | 11 B2 |

| EATING | (p311) |
|---|---|
| Food Market | 12 C3 |
| Giakoumis Taverna | 13 C3 |
| Ippokambos Ouzeri | 14 C1 |
| Istioploïkos | 15 D1 |

| ENTERTAINMENT | (p311) |
|---|---|
| Guernica | 16 B2 |
| Jasmin | 17 B2 |
| Take Five | 18 C2 |

| TRANSPORT | (pp311–12) |
|---|---|
| Aegean Airlines | 19 D3 |
| Bus Station A | 20 D2 |
| Buses to Airport | 21 D3 |
| Buses to Hania & Rethymno | 22 D1 |
| Buses to Knossos | 23 C2 |
| Buses to Knossos | 24 D2 |
| Olympic Airways | 25 C2 |

SEA OF CRETE

Daily ferries service Piraeus (€29.50, 10 hours), and most days boats go to Santorini (Thira) and continue on to other Cycladic islands. Head to Skoutelis Travel (p311) for schedules and tickets.

Iraklio has two bus stations. Bus Station A, inland from the new harbour, serves eastern Crete (Agios Nikolaos, Ierapetra, Sitia, Malia and the Lasithi Plateau). The Hania and Rethymno terminal is opposite Bus Station A. Bus Station B, 50m beyond the Hania Gate, serves the southern route (Phaestos, Matala and Anogia). Check out www.ktel.org for long-distance bus information.

Bus No 1 travels to and from the airport (€0.70) every 15 minutes from 6am to 1am. It stops at Plateia Eleftherias, across the road from the archaeological museum.

## KNOSSOS ΚΝΩΣΣΟΣ

Five kilometres south of Iraklio, **Knossos** ( ☎ 2810 231 940; admission €6; ⏰ 8am-7pm Apr-Oct, 8am-5pm Nov-Mar) is the most famous of Crete's Minoan sites and is the inspiration for the myth of the Minotaur. According to legend, King Minos of Knossos was given a bull to sacrifice to the god Poseidon, but decided to keep it (as you would). This enraged Poseidon, who punished the king by causing his wife Pasiphae to fall in love with the animal. The result of this odd union was the Minotaur – half-man and half-bull – who lived in a labyrinth beneath the king's palace, munching on youths and maidens.

In 1900, the ruins of Knossos were uncovered by Arthur Evans. Although archaeologists tend to disparage Evans' reconstruction, the buildings – an immense palace, courtyards, private apartments, baths, lively frescoes and more – give a fine idea of what a Minoan palace might have looked like.

A whole day is needed to see the site and a guidebook is essential. Arrive early to avoid the jam. From Iraklio, local bus No 2 goes to Knossos (€0.95) every 10 minutes from Bus Station A; it also stops on 25 Avgoustou.

## PHAESTOS & OTHER MINOAN SITES
ΦΑΙΣΤΟΣ

**Phaestos** (φαιστος; ☎ 2982 042 315; admission €4; ⏰ 8am-7pm May-Oct, 8am-5pm Nov-Apr), 63km from Iraklio, while not as impressive as

Knossos, is Crete's second-most important Minoan site. It's still worth a visit for its stunning views of the surrounding Mesara plain and Mt Ida. Crete's other important Minoan sites are **Malia**, 34km east of Iraklio, where there is a palace complex and adjoining town, and **Zakros**, 40km from Sitia, the smallest and least impressive of the island's palace complexes.

## RETHYMNO PEΘYMNO
**pop 29,000**

Rethymno's gracious old quarter of crumbling Venetian and Turkish buildings is on a peninsula sticking out into the Sea of Crete, with the ferry quay on its eastern side. Incessant hassling from restaurant touts is likely to take some of the enjoyment out of a stroll around the old quarter. El Venizelou is the main strip by the waterfront. Running parallel behind it is Arkadiou, the main commercial street.

The **Venetian fortress** ( ☎ 2831 028 101; Paleokastro Hill; admission €3; ☺ 8am-8pm) affords great views across the town and mountains. **Happy Walker** ( ☎ 2831 052 920; www.happywalker.com; Tombazi 56) runs a programme of daily walks in the countryside (€25 per person).

**Galero Café** ( ☎ 2831 054 345; per hr €4), beside the Rimondi fountain with its spouting lion heads, has Internet access. The **municipal tourist office** ( ☎ 2831 029 148; Eleftheriou Venizelou; ☺ 8.30am-2pm Mon-Fri) is on the beach side of El Venizelou, but is next to useless. **Ellotia Tours** ( ☎ 2831 051 981; www.forthnet.gr/elotia; Arkadiou 155) will answer all transport, accommodation and tour inquiries.

**Elizabeth Camping** ( ☎ 2831 028 694; per person/tent €6.30/4.20) is situated on Mysiria Beach, 4km east of town, and is accessible by the bus that goes to and from Iraklio. **Rethymno Youth hostel** ( ☎ 2831 022 848; www.yhrethymno.com; Tombazi 41; dm €7) is a well-run place with crowded dorms. **Rent Rooms Sea Front** ( ☎ 2831 051 981; www.forthnet.gr/elotia; Arkadiou 159; ☒ ), run by Ellotia Tours, has all sorts of options and is ideally positioned with beach views and spacious rooms.

**Gounakis Restaurant & Bar** ( ☎ 2831 028 816; Koroneou 6; mains from €5) is the place to go for live Cretan music and reasonably priced food. **Restaurant Symposium** ( ☎ 2831 050 538; www.syposium-kriti.gr; dishes from €3.50), near the Rimondi fountain, takes its food seriously but has good prices.

Ferries travel daily from Piraeus to Rethymno (€24, 10 hours). Buses depart regularly to Iraklio (€5.90, 1½ hours), Hania (€5.30, one hour), Agia Galini, Moni Arkadiou and Plakas.

## HANIA XANIA
**pop 53,500**

Hania (often spelt Chania) is Crete's second-largest city and the former capital. The Venetian quarter that surrounds the old harbour lures tourists in droves. The city is a good base for exploring idyllic beaches and a glorious mountain interior.

### Information

**Hotel Manos** (Zambeliou 24; per hr €4) offers Internet access, and there's a **central post office** (Tzanakaki 3). The **tourist information office** ( ☎ 2821 036 155; www.chania.gr; Kydonias 29; ☺ 9am-8pm Mon-Fri, to 2pm Sat), near Plateia 1866, is very helpful.

**Elyros Travel** ( ☎ 2821 074 191; Plateia 1866) can help with schedules and ticketing. There are a stack of other agencies on Halidon, the street leading down to the old harbour.

### Sights & Activities

The **archaeological museum** ( ☎ 2821 090 334; Halidon 21; admission €2; ☺ 8.30am-3pm Tue-Sun) used to be the Venetian Church of San Francesco, until the Turks made it into a mosque.

Hania's spectacular covered **food market** is worth a visit, even if you aren't self-catering. Part of the city wall had to be demolished in 1911 to make way for the cruciform creation.

### Sleeping

There is a swath of sleeping options around the Venetian port.

**Camping Hania** ( ☎ 2821 031 138; per person/tent €5/3.50) Take the Hania–Stalos bus from the southeast corner of Plateia 1866 to get to this place 3km west of town on the beach.

**Pension Fidias** ( ☎ 2821 052 494; Sarpaki 6; dm/d/tr €9/18/27) Behind the Orthodox cathedral, this is still the budget choice.

**Pension Lena** ( ☎ 2821 086 860; www.travelling-crete.com/lena; Ritsou 3; s/d €28/50; ☒ ) A friendly pension in an old Turkish building near the mouth of the old harbour.

**Hotel Manos** ( ☎ 2821 094 156; www.manoshotel.gr; Zambeliou 24; s/d €45/55; ☒ ☐ ) Waterfront Manos has, large airy rooms and its own Internet café.

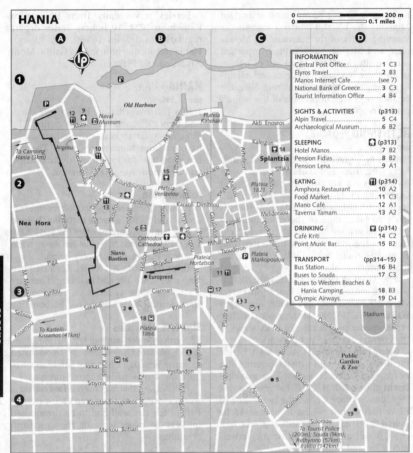

# HANIA

| INFORMATION | |
|---|---|
| Central Post Office | 1 C3 |
| Elyros Travel | 2 B3 |
| Manos Internet Cafe | (see 7) |
| National Bank of Greece | 3 C3 |
| Tourist Information Office | 4 B4 |
| **SIGHTS & ACTIVITIES** | **(p313)** |
| Alpin Travel | 5 C4 |
| Archaeological Museum | 6 B2 |
| **SLEEPING** | **(p313)** |
| Hotel Manos | 7 B2 |
| Pension Fidias | 8 B2 |
| Pension Lena | 9 A1 |
| **EATING** | **(p314)** |
| Amphora Restaurant | 10 A2 |
| Food Market | 11 C3 |
| Mano Café | 12 A1 |
| Taverna Tamam | 13 A2 |
| **DRINKING** | **(p314)** |
| Café Kriti | 14 C2 |
| Point Music Bar | 15 B2 |
| **TRANSPORT** | **(pp314–15)** |
| Bus Station | 16 B4 |
| Buses to Souda | 17 C3 |
| Buses to Western Beaches & | |
| Hania Camping | 18 B3 |
| Olympic Airways | 19 D4 |

## Eating & Drinking

The entire waterfront of the old harbour is lined with restaurants and tavernas. Many of these qualify as tourist traps. Do your best to watch out for touts trying to reel you in.

**Amphora Restaurant** ( ☎ 2821 093 224; Akti Koundourioti 49; mains €4.50-7) Under the hotel of the same name, you'll find this place with excellent pasta dishes and a fine reputation.

**Mano Café** ( ☎ 2821 072 265; Theotokopoulou 62) Next to Pension Lena, this tiny place has good breakfasts and snack food.

**Taverna Tamam** ( ☎ 2821 096 080; Zambeliou 49; mains €4-6.50) A taverna in an old converted Turkish bathhouse that has tasty soups.

**Café Kriti** ( ☎ 2821 058 661; Kalergon 22) The best place to hear live Cretan music while having a drink.

**Point Music Bar** ( ☎ 2821 057 556; Sourmeli 2; ⏱ 9pm-2am) Serves up rock. It has an excellent 1st-floor balcony overlooking the harbour.

## Getting There & Away

There are several flights a day to Athens (€74) and two flights a week to Thessaloniki (€110). Contact **Olympic Airways** ( ☎ 2821 057 701) or **Aegean Airlines** ( ☎ 2821 063 366). Daily ferries to Piraeus (€22) depart from the port of Souda, 7km east of town. Get your tickets at Elyros Travel (p313).

Frequent buses plough daily to Iraklio, Rethymno and Kastelli-Kissamos; buses run less frequently to Paleohora, Omalos, Hora Sfakion and Elafonisi from the main bus station on Kydonias.

Buses for Souda (the port) leave frequently from outside the food market. Buses for the beaches west of Hania leave from the southeastern corner of Plateia 1866.

## SAMARIA GORGE
ΦΑΡΑΓΓΙ ΤΗΣ ΣΑΜΑΡΙΑΣ

**Samaria Gorge** ( ☎ 2825 067 179; admission €5; ☒ 6am-3pm May–mid-Oct) is one of Europe's most spectacular gorges. Walkers should take rugged footwear, food, water and sun protection for this strenuous five- to six-hour trek, which is not recommended for inexperienced walkers.

You can do the walk as part of an excursion tour, or do it independently by taking the Omalos bus from the main bus station in Hania (€4.70, one hour) to the head of the gorge at Xyloskalo (1230m) at 6.15am, 7.30am, 8.30am or 1.45pm. It's a 16.7km walk out to Agia Roumeli on the coast, from where you take a boat to Hora Sfakion (€5, 1¼ hrs, three daily) and then a bus back to Hania (€5.65, two hours, four daily).

There are daily excursions from Hania and other cities that do the whole route, and shorter ones that walk about 4km into the gorge. Check out the travel agencies in Hania and other cities for information.

## LEFKA ORI ΛΕΥΚΑ ΟΡΟΙ
Crete's rugged 'White Mountains' are south of Hania. **Alpine Travel** ( ☎ 2821 053 309; www .alpine.gr; Bouniali 11-19, Hania) offers excellent one- to 15-day trekking programmes from €58 per person, as well as trail advice.

**Trekking Plan** ( ☎ /fax 2821 060 861; www.cycling .gr), based in Agia Marina, 8km west of Hania, next to Santa Marina Hotel, has mountain biking, trekking and mountaineering tours.

## PALEOHORA &
## THE SOUTHWEST COAST ΠΑΛΑΙΟΧΩΡΑ
Paleohora, discovered by hippies back in the 1960s, has a relaxing 'at the end of the line' feel about it. Isolated and a bit hard to get to, the village is on a peninsula with a beach on each side. There's a welcoming **tourist office** ( ☎ 2823 041 507) three blocks south of the bus stop, but don't expect it to be up and running before June. In the main

street, **Notos Rentals/Tsiskakis Travel** ( ☎ 2823 042 110; notosgr@yahoo.gr; Eleftheriou Venizelou) handles everything, including tickets, rental cars/scooters, laundry and Internet access (€4 per hour).

**Camping Paleohora** ( ☎ 2823 041 225; per person/ tent €4/2.50) is 1.5km northeast of town, near the pebble beach. There's also a restaurant and nightclub here.

**Homestay Anonymous** ( ☎ 2823 041 509; Paleohora; s/d €14/18) is a great place for backpackers with its warm service and communal kitchen.

**Poseidon Hotel** ( ☎ 2823 041 374; www.c-v.net/ hotel/paleohora/poseidon; s/d €25/35; ☒ ) is right on the beach. Rooms have kitchen facilities.

*Domatia* and tavernas dot the harbour. Vegetarians rave about the **Third Eye** ( ☎ 2823 041 234; mains €4-6). The special omelette at **Coconuts Cafetaria** ( ☎ 2823 041 523; dishes €3-8) is a winner.

Further east along Crete's southwest coast are **Sougia**, **Agia Roumeli** (at the mouth of the Samaria Gorge), **Loutro** and **Hora Sfakion**. Coastal paths lead from Paleohora to Sougia and from Agia Roumeli to Loutro. Both walks take a hefty six to seven hours. No road links the coastal resorts but daily boats from Paleohora to Elafonisi, Agia Roumeli and Hora Sfakion connect the villages in summer.

There are at least five buses daily between Hania and Paleohora (€5.65, two hours).

## LASITHI PLATEAU ΟΡΟΠΕΔΙΟ ΛΑΣΙΘΙΟΥ
In eastern Crete, the first view of this mountain-fringed plateau, laid out like an immense patchwork quilt, is marvellous. The plateau, 900m above sea level, is a vast flat expanse of orchards and fields, which was once dotted with some 1000 stone windmills with white canvas sails. Now, sadly, there are few of the originals left; most have been replaced by mechanical pumps.

The **Dikteon Cave** ( ☎ 2844 031 316; admission €3; ☒ 8am-4pm) is where, according to mythology, the Titan Rhea hid the newborn Zeus from Cronos, his offspring-gobbling father. The cave is just outside the small village of Psyhro, which is the best place to stay. **Zeus Hotel** ( ☎ 2844 031 284; s/d €23/30) is near the start of the Dikteon Cave road. On the main street, **Stavros** ( ☎ 2844 031 453; dishes €3-5) and **Platanos** ( ☎ 2844 031 668; dishes €3-5) tavernas serve decent food at OK prices.

There are daily buses to the area from Iraklio (€5.15, two hours) and three a week from Agios Nikolaos (€6.30, 2½ hours).

## AGIOS NIKOLAOS ΑΓΙΟΣ ΝΙΚΟΛΑΟΣ
pop 11,000

Agios Nikolaos (*ah*-yee-os nih-*ko*-laos) may be touristy but it is an undeniably pretty former fishing village on Crete's northeast coast that is well worth a visit. The bulk of the action is around the picturesque Voulismeni Lake, about 200m from the main square of Plateia Venizelou. The lake is ringed with cafés and tavernas, and is linked to the sea by a short canal. The ferry port is 150m past the canal.

There are plenty of Internet access options at €4 per hour. The very helpful **municipal tourist office** ( ☎ 2841 022 357; www.aghiosnikolaos.gr; ☼ 8am-9.30pm 1 Apr-15 Nov) is on the north side of the bridge over the canal and does a good job of finding sleeping options. **Mirabello Travel** ( ☎ 2841 022 144; www.mirabellotravelagency.com; 13 M Sfakianakistr) handles ticketing, accommodation and car rentals.

The two nice little beaches in town get a bit crowded in summer. **Almyros Beach**, about 1km south, gets less so. Agios Nikolaos acts as a base for excursion tours to **Spinalonga Island**. The island's massive fortress was built by the Venetians in 1579, but taken by the Turks in 1715. It later became a leper colony, but nowadays is a fascinating place to explore. Tours run for around €20.

For accommodation, **Pergola Hotel** ( ☎ 2841 028 152; Sarolidi 20; s/d €22/32) is a good deal with clean rooms and sea views out near the ferry port. **Afrodite Rooms** ( ☎ 2841 028 058; Korytsas 27; s/d €18/25) is comfortable, but with shared facilities.

Finding a place to eat will not be a problem. **Migomis** ( ☎ 2841 024 353; N Plastira 20; mains €5-10) overlooks the lake from high on the south side, providing great views and ambience. **Itanos** ( ☎ 2841 025 340; Kyprou 1; mains €3-10), tucked away on a back street off the main square, is superb. Head for the kitchen and pick what looks good.

Ferries depart for Rhodes (€25.80, 11 hours) via Kasos and Karpathos three times a week. There are also three weekly ferries to Piraeus (€27, 12 hours). Buses from Iraklio run every 30 minutes (€5) and six times daily to Sitia (€5.25).

## SITIA ΣΗΤΕΙΑ
pop 8750

Sitia is a lovely little town in the northeastern corner of Crete that has escaped much of the package tourism along the north coast. It is on an attractive bay flanked by mountains, and is an easy place to unwind. There are good ferry connections to the Dodecanese islands.

The main square is on the waterfront, in the corner of the bay, recognisable by its palm trees and statue of a dying soldier. The ferry port is about 500m to the north, while the post office is just off the back of the square.

**Porto Belis Travel** ( ☎ 2843 022 370; www.portobelis-crete.gr; Karamanli Aven 34; ☼ 9am-8.30pm), on the waterfront just before the start of the town beach, is a one-stop shop. It handles all – ticketing, rental cars and scooters as well as accommodation bookings in town. In addition it runs **Porto Belis Rooms and Apartments** (d/q €34/57; ✷ ) above the travel agency. These rooms are immaculate, have kitchens and look straight out onto the beach.

**Hotel Arhontiko** ( ☎ 2843 028 172; Kondylaki 16; s/d with shared bathroom €25/30), two streets uphill from the port, is basic but spotless.

**Itanos Hotel** ( ☎ 2843 022 900; www.itanoshotel.com; Karamanli 4; s/d €30/50; ✷ ▣ ) is an upmarket establishment next to the square. It includes breakfast and a drink with dinner if you eat at its excellent **Itanos Taverna** (dishes €3-12), on the waterfront outside the front door.

The lively waterfront is lined with tavernas. Popular with locals is **Gato Negro** ( ☎ 2843 025 873; dishes €3-12), which serves up Cretan specialities. It is the closest taverna to the ferry quay. **Kali Kardia** ( ☎ 2843 022 249; Foundalidou 22; mains €4-6), a couple of streets back from the waterfront, is also just excellent.

Sitia airport has three flights a week to Athens (€75) with **Olympic Airways** ( ☎ 2843 022 270). There are regular ferries from Piraeus to Sitia (€27.50, 14 hours), and three ferries per week via Karpathos to Rhodes (€23, 10 hours). Porto Belis Travel (above) has details and sells tickets.

There are six buses daily to Ierapetra, and five to Iraklio via Agios Nikolaos. In peak season, there are four buses daily to Vaï Beach.

# DODECANESE
## ΔΩΔΕΚΑΝΗΣΑ

Closer to Asia Minor than mainland Greece, the 18 islands of the Dodecanese are strung out along the coast of western Turkey. Due to their strategic position they have suffered a turbulent past of invasions and occupations that has endowed them with a fascinating wealth of diverse archaeological remains.

The islands themselves are verdant and mountainous with appealing beaches – there's something for everyone in the Dodecanese. While Rhodes and Kos host highly developed tourism, the more remote islands await those in search of traditional island life.

## RHODES ΡΟΔΟΣ

Rhodes (*ro-dos* in Greek) is the largest island in the Dodecanese and has a population of nearly 100,000. According to mythology, the sun god Helios chose Rhodes as his bride and bestowed light, warmth and vegetation upon her. The blessing seems to have paid off, for Rhodes produces more flowers and sunny days than most Greek islands.

The ancient sites of Lindos and Kamiros are legacies of Rhodes' importance in antiquity. In 1291, the Knights of St John, having fled Jerusalem, came to Rhodes and established themselves as masters. In 1522,

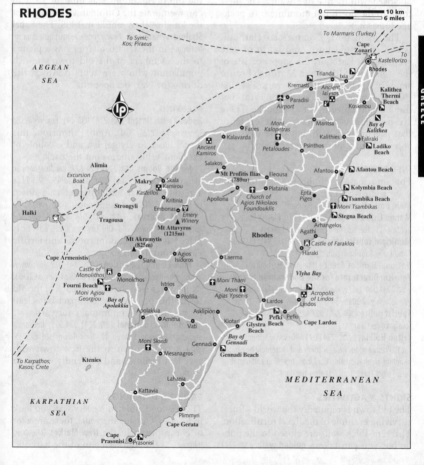

**RHODES**

GREECE

Süleyman I, sultan of the Ottoman Empire, staged a massive attack on the island and took Rhodes City. The island, along with the other Dodecanese islands, then became part of the Ottoman Empire.

In 1912 it was the Italians' turn and in 1944 the Germans took over. The following year Rhodes was liberated by British and Greek commandos. In 1948 the Dodecanese became part of Greece. These days, tourists rule.

## Rhodes City
pop 54,000
Rhodes' capital and port is Rhodes City, on the northern tip of the island. Almost everything of interest lies in the old town, enclosed within massive walls. The new town to the north is a monument to package tourism.

The main port, Commercial Harbour, is east of the old town, and north of here is Mandraki Harbour, the supposed site of the Colossus of Rhodes, a 32m-high bronze statue of Apollo built over 12 years (294–282 BC). The statue stood for a mere 65 years before being toppled by an earthquake. There are no remains and no tangible evidence that it actually existed, but these days you will see it on a lot of souvenir T-shirts.

### INFORMATION
For information about the island, visit www.rodosisland.gr.
**Main post office** (Mandraki Harbour)
**Mango Café Bar** ( ☎ 2241 024 8770; Plateia Dorieos 3; per hr €5) In the old town, with Internet access.
**Municipal tourist office** ( ☎ 2241 035 945; Plateia Rimini; 🕙 8am-8pm summer only)
**National Bank of Greece** (Mandraki Harbour)
**Tourism Directorate for the Dodecanese Islands** ( ☎ 2241 044 335; www.ando.gr/eot; cnr Makariou & Papagou; 🕙 7.30am-3pm Mon-Fri)
**Tourist police** ( ☎ 2241 027 423) Next door to the tourism directorate.
**Triton Holidays** ( ☎ 2241 021 690; www.tritondmc.gr; 1st fl, Plastira 9) In the new town and extremely helpful, handling accommodation bookings, ticketing and rental cars. To get there, turn left after the bank.

### SIGHTS & ACTIVITIES
The old town is reputedly the world's finest surviving example of medieval fortification. The 12m-thick walls are closed to the public but you can take a **guided walk** ( ☎ 2241 023 359; tours €6; 🕙 2.30pm Tue & Sat) along them, starting in the courtyard of the Palace of the Knights.

**Odos Ippoton** (Ave of the Knights) is lined with magnificent medieval buildings, the most imposing of which is the **Palace of the Knights** ( ☎ 2241 023 359; admission €6; 🕙 8.30am-3pm Tue-Sun), which was restored, but never used, as a holiday home for Mussolini.

The 15th-century Knight's Hospital now houses the **archaeological museum** ( ☎ 2241 027 657; Plateia Mousiou; admission €3; 🕙 8am-5.40pm Tue-Sun). The splendid building was restored by the Italians and has an impressive collection that includes the ethereal marble statue *Aphrodite of Rhodes*.

The pink-domed **Mosque of Süleyman** at the top of Sokratous was built in 1522 to commemorate the Ottoman victory against the knights, then rebuilt in 1808. The **Kahal Shalom synagogue** (www.rhodesjewishmuseum.org; Dosiadou) in the Jewish quarter has a plaque to the members of the old town's Jewish population who were sent to Auschwitz during the Nazi occupation.

### SLEEPING
**Rodos Youth Hostel** ( ☎ 2241 030 491; Ergiou 12, Old Town; dm/d €8/25) Off Agio Fanouriou, this hostel has a lovely garden and a couple of excellent-value studios out the back.

**Mango Rooms** ( ☎ 2241 024 877; karelas@hotmail.com; Plateia Dorieos 3, Old Town; s/d €30/45; 💻 ) Has a restaurant, bar and Internet café down below, and six well-kept rooms above.

**Hotel Andreas** ( ☎ 2241 034 156; www.hotelandreas.com; Omirou 28d, Old Town; s/d €50/60) This place has small, pleasant rooms and terrific views from its terrace.

**Pink Elephant Pension** ( ☎ 2241 022 469; www.pinkelephantpension.com; Irodotou 42, Old Town; d €32-53; 🐾 ) Down a side street at the back of the old town, this pension has compact but clean rooms around a communal courtyard.

**Hotel International** ( ☎ 2241 024 595; diethnes@otenet.gr; Ioannou Kazouli 12, New Town; s/d €25/35; 🐾 ) A real bargain in the new town with excellent facilities and a friendly owner in Prokopis.

### EATING & DRINKING
There is food and drink every way you look in Rhodes. Outside the walls, there are a lot of cheap places in the **New Market** (Mandraki Harbour), at the southern end of the harbour.

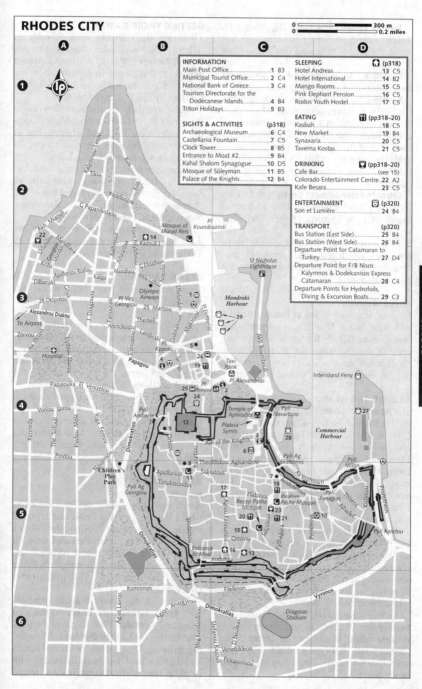

# RHODES CITY

| 0 | 300 m |
| 0 | 0.2 miles |

**INFORMATION**
Main Post Office.........................1 B3
Municipal Tourist Office..............2 C4
National Bank of Greece.............3 C4
Tourism Directorate for the
　Dodecanese Islands................4 B4
Triton Holidays..........................5 B3

**SIGHTS & ACTIVITIES** (p318)
Archaeological Museum...............6 C4
Castellania Fountain...................7 C5
Clock Tower...............................8 B5
Entrance to Moat #2...................9 B4
Kahal Shalom Synagogue...........10 D5
Mosque of Süleyman.................11 B5
Palace of the Knights................12 B4

**SLEEPING** (p318)
Hotel Andreas..........................13 C5
Hotel International.....................14 B2
Mango Rooms...........................15 C5
Pink Elephant Pension...............16 C5
Rodos Youth Hostel...................17 C5

**EATING** (pp318–20)
Kasbah....................................18 C5
New Market..............................19 B4
Synaxaria.................................20 C5
Taverna Kostas.........................21 C5

**DRINKING** (pp318–20)
Cafe Bar...........................(see 15)
Colorado Entertainment Centre..22 A2
Kafe Besara.............................23 C5

**ENTERTAINMENT** (p320)
Son et Lumière.........................24 B4

**TRANSPORT** (p320)
Bus Station (East Side).............25 B4
Bus Station (West Side).............26 B4
Departure Point for Catamaran to
　Turkey.................................27 D4
Departure Point for F/B Nisos
　Kalymnos & Dodekanisos Express
　Catamaran..........................28 C4
Departure Points for Hydrofoils,
　Diving & Excursion Boats........29 C3

GREECE

**Taverna Kostas** ( ☎ 2241 026 217; Pythagora 62, Old Town; mains €5-10) This good-value spot has stood the test of time and can't be beaten on quality.

**Synaxaria** ( ☎ 2241 036 562; Aristofanous 47, Old Town; mains €4-8) A cosy little place.

**Kasbah** ( ☎ 2241 078 633; Platonos 4-8; mains from €10; ☽ dinner) Serves some huge Moroccan-influenced meals in a refined atmosphere.

**Kafe Besara** ( ☎ 2241 030 363; Sofokleous 11, Old Town) One of the Old Town's liveliest bars.

**Mango Café Bar** ( ☎ 2241 024 877; Plateia Dorieos 3, Old Town) Mango claims to have the cheapest drinks.

**Colorado Entertainment Centre** ( ☎ 2241 075 120; cnr Akti Miaouli & Orfanidou) This enormous palace of hype consists of three drinking venues.

In the new town, head to Orfanidou in the city's northwest. The drink-till-you-droppers are there, and there is a bar for every nationality.

### ENTERTAINMENT
Rhodes' impressive **Son et Lumière** (Sound & Light Show; ☎ 2241 021 922; www.hellenicfestival.gr; adult/concession €5/3; ☽ Mon-Sat) is held by the walls of the Old Town off Plateia Rimini. English-language sessions are staggered, but are generally at 9.15pm or 11.15pm.

### AROUND THE ISLAND
The **Acropolis of Lindos** ( ☎ 2244 031 258; admission €6; ☽ 8.30am-6pm Tue-Sun), 47km from Rhodes City, is Rhodes' most important ancient city and is spectacularly perched atop a 116m-high rocky outcrop. Below the site is **Lindos** town, a tangle of streets with elaborately decorated 17th-century houses. It's beautiful but tainted by tourism. The bus to Lindos (€3.40) departs from Rhodes City's east-side station.

The extensive ruins of **Kamiros** (admission €4; ☽ 8am-5pm Tue-Sun), an ancient Doric city on the west coast, are well preserved, with the remains of houses, baths, a cemetery and a temple, but the site should be visited as much for its lovely setting on a gentle hillside overlooking the sea.

Between Rhodes City and Lindos the **beaches** are choked. If you prefer space, venture south to the bay of **Lardos**. Even further south, between Genardi and Plimmyri, you'll find good stretches of deserted sandy beach.

### GETTING THERE & AWAY
There are daily flights from Rhodes to Athens (€90) and Karpathos (€28) with **Olympic Airways** ( ☎ 2241 024 571) and **Aegean Airlines** ( ☎ 2241 024 400). In summer there are regular flights to Iraklio and Kastellorizo. Contact Triton Holidays (p318).

There are daily ferries from Rhodes to Piraeus (€33, 15 to 18 hours). Most sail via the Dodecanese north of Rhodes, but at least three times a week there is a service via Karpathos, Crete and the Cyclades.

Excursion boats (€20 return) and hydrofoils (€12.50 one way) travel daily to Symi. Ferries (€8 one way) travel less often. Similar services also run to Kos, Kalymnos, Nisyros, Tilos, Patmos and Leros.

Between April and October, there are daily boats from Rhodes to Marmaris in Turkey (one way/return €45/60).

### GETTING AROUND
There are frequent buses between the airport and Rhodes City's west-side bus station (€1.70).

Rhodes City has two bus stations. The west-side bus station, next to the New Market, serves the airport, the west coast, Embona and Koskinou; the **east-side bus station** (Plateia Rimini) serves the east coast and the inland southern villages.

Car- and motorcycle-rental outlets compete for business in Rhodes City's new town, on and around 28 Oktovriou. Cars are forbidden in most of the old town but there are small car parks around the periphery.

## KARPATHOS ΚΑΡΠΑΘΟΣ
**pop 6000**
Karpathos is an elongated, mountainous island that lies midway between Crete and Rhodes. It's a scenic, hype-free place with a cosy port, numerous beaches and unspoilt villages. It is a wealthy island, reputedly receiving more money from emigrants living abroad (mostly in the USA) than any other Greek island.

Karpathos has lovely beaches, particularly **Apella**, **Kyra Panagia**, **Lefkos** on the west coast and **Ammoöpi**, 8km south of Pigadia. The northern village of **Olymbos** is like a living museum. Locals wear traditional outfits and the façades of houses are decorated with bright plaster reliefs, though with more and more tourists arriving, the village is becoming less and less 'traditional'. The main port and capital is Pigadia.

**Enter Café** ( ☎ 2245 029 053; 28 Oktovriou; per hr €4; ☯ 9am-2pm & 6pm-1am) has Internet access. For more information on the island, have a squiz – at www.inkarpathos.com and www .karpathos.com.

A booth on the harbour serves as **municipal tourist office** ( ☎ 2245 023 835; ☯ Jul & Aug). **Possi Travel** ( ☎ 2245 022 148; possitvl@hotmail .com) on the waterfront can suggest local tours and handles travel arrangements.

Pigadia accommodation owners usually meet the boats. **Elias Rooms** ( ☎ 2245 022 446; www.eliasroomstripod.com; Dimokratias; s/d €21/25) is a good option. Owner Elias is a mine of information for travellers, and his rooms have great views. **Harry's Rooms** ( ☎ 2245 022 188; Kyprou 21; s/d €20/25) are central and spotless. **Hotel Titania** ( ☎ 2245 022 144; www.titania karpathos.gr; Dimokratias; s/d €35/50; ☒ ) has spacious rooms with fridge, phone and TV.

Head for **Taverna I Orea Karpathos** ( ☎ 2245 022 501; mains €4-6) near the quay for traditional Karpathian dishes. Try the Karpathian goat *stifado* at **To Helliniko** ( ☎ 2245 023 932; dishes €3-8) on the harbour.

Karpathos has daily flights to Rhodes (€29) and five a week to Athens (€75); there is an **Olympic Airways** ( ☎ 2245 022 150) office on the central square in Pigadia. There are three ferries a week to Rhodes (€15.60, four hours) and four to Piraeus (€29, 19 hours) via the Cyclades and Crete. The ferries between Rhodes and Crete stop at Pigadia and the small northern port of Diafani on Karpathos. In summer there are daily excursion boats from Pigadia to Apella and Kyra Panagia beaches. There are also excursions from Pigadia to Diafani that include a bus trip to Olymbos. Local buses drop you at Lefkos and Ammoöpi beaches.

## SYMI ΣΥΜΗ
**pop 2600**

Symi is superb. While the island itself is rocky and dry, the port town of Gialos is a Greek treasure. Pastel-coloured mansions are heaped up the hills surrounding the protective little harbour. The island is swamped by day-trippers from Rhodes; it's worth staying over to enjoy Symi in cruise control. The town is divided into Gialos, the harbour, and the tranquil *horio* (village)

above it, accessible by taxi, bus, or 360 steps from the harbour.

For Internet access head to **Orange & Lemon Café** ( ☎ 2246 071 988; per hr €4) on the waterfront. There is no tourist office or tourist police. The best source of information is the free and widely available monthly English-language **Symi Visitor** (www.symivisitor.com), which includes maps of the town.

**Kalodoukas Holidays** ( ☎ 2246 071 077; www .symi-greece.com) handles accommodation bookings, ticketing and has a book of trails on the island that you can walk independently. **Symi Tours** ( ☎ 2246 071 307; www.symitours.com) runs a trip to Datça in Turkey (€35) on Saturdays.

Budget accommodation is scarce. **Rooms Katerina** ( ☎ 2246 071 813, 6945 130 112; d €25-30) is excellent, but get in quick as there are only three rooms. Each has private bathroom and there is a communal kitchen with breathtaking views. **Pension Catherinettes** ( ☎ 2246 071 671; marina-epe@rho.forthnet.gr; d €55) has airy rooms. It's in the building on the waterfront where the treaty surrendering the Dodecanese to the Allies was signed in 1945. Located back from the excursion boats is **Hotel Albatros** ( ☎ 2246 071 707; www. alba trosymi.gr; d €50), where breakfast is included.

**Bella Napoli** ( ☎ 2246 072 456; pizzas from €5) serves exceptional wood-fired pizzas while, next door, **Vapori Bar** ( ☎ 2246 072 082) is open all day. Drop by to use the Internet or read the free newspapers by day, or for drinks and cruising at night. **Taverna Neraida** ( ☎ 2246 071 841; mains from €5), back from the waterfront by the square, has good food and intriguing old photos of Symi on its walls.

There are frequent ferries and hydrofoils between Rhodes and Kos that also call at Symi, as well as less-frequent services to Tilos, Nisyros, Kalymno, Leros and Patmos. The bus and taxi stop is at the east end of the harbour, past the restaurants. Excursion boats visit inaccessible east-coast beaches daily in summer, including spectacular **Agios Georgious**, backed by a 150m sheer cliff.

## KOS ΚΩΣ
**pop 17,900**

Only 5km from the Turkish peninsula of Bodrum, Kos is a long, narrow island with a mountainous spine. Hippocrates, the father of medicine, was born on Kos, but that's as Greek as this place gets. With its ruins and

GREECE

Turkish buildings on a backdrop of pretty palm-lined streets, neon cafés, pulsing clubs and tourist trains, Kos town, the main town and port, exudes an aura of mini Las Vegas.

## Information
**Café Del Mare** ( ☎ 2242 024 244; Megalou Alexandrou 4; per hr €4) The best-equipped Internet café.

**Municipal tourist office** ( ☎ 2242 024 460; www .hippocrates.gr; Vasileos Georgiou 1; ☼ 8am-8pm Mon-Fri, 8am-3pm Sat May-Oct) On the waterfront directly south of the port, it provides maps and accommodation information.

**Pulia Tours** ( ☎ 2242 026 388; www.laumzis.gr) Handles schedules, ticketing, money exchange, excursions and rental cars.

**Tourist police** ( ☎ 2242 022 444) Housed with the regular police, just opposite the quay.

## Sights & Activities
The focus of the **archaeological museum** ( ☎ 2242 028 326; Plateia Eleftherias; adult/student €3/2; ☼ 8am-2.30pm Tue-Sun) are sculpture from excavations around the island. The **ancient agora**, with the ruins of the **Shrine of Aphrodite** and **Temple of Hercules**, is just off Plateia Eleftherias. It's free but has zero data. North of the agora is the **Hippocrates Plane Tree**, under which the man himself is said to have taught his pupils.

On a pine-clad hill, 4km southwest of Kos town, stand the extensive ruins of the renowned healing centre of **Asklipieion** ( ☎ 2242 028 763; adult/student €4/3; ☼ 8.30am-6pm Tue-Sun), where Hippocrates practised medicine.

At the southern end of Kos is **Kefalos Bay**, a long stretch of beach swamped in sun lounges and rippling with water sports.

## Sleeping
**Pension Alexis** ( ☎ 2242 028 798; fax 2242 025 797; Irodotou 9; s/d €23/29) This convivial place has long been a budget favourite with travellers. It has large rooms, shared facilities and is highly recommended. Try the legendary feta omelette for breakfast. It's back behind Dolphin Sq.

**Hotel Afendoulis** ( ☎ 2242 025 321; afendoulis hotel@kos.forthnet.gr; Evripilou 1; s/d €29/42) Looking for a superior hotel with well-kept rooms in a quieter area? Head south from the ferry quay, walk about 500m to Evripilou and turn right.

**Nitsa Studios** ( ☎ 2242 025 810; Averof 37; d €30-50) North of the harbour and a street back from the beach, Nitsa's rooms have a bathroom, kitchen and balcony.

**Kos Camping** ( ☎ 2242 023 910; per adult/tent €4.50/2.50) This spot, 3km along the eastern waterfront, has good shade and a mini-market. Hop on any of the buses going to Agios Fokas from the harbour.

## Eating & Drinking
Restaurants line the central waterfront, but you might want to hit the backstreets for value. There are a dozen discos and clubs catering to the different music moods of the crowd around the streets of Diakon and Nafklirou, just north of the agora.

**Barbas** ( ☎ 2240 027 856; Evripilou 6; mains €4-7) Opposite Hotel Afendoulis, Barbas specialises in grills and has an excellent chicken souvlaki.

**Taverna Hirodion** ( ☎ 2242 026 634; Artemisias 27; mains €5-8) This place serves good and inexpensive food. Try the pork fillet in brandy sauce.

**Olympiada** ( ☎ 2242 023 031; mains €4-6) Back in the ruins area, Olympiada serves up reliable Greek dishes.

**Fashion Club** ( ☎ 2242 022 592; Kanari 2) Off Dolphin Sq, this monster has three bars.

**Kalua** ( ☎ 2242 024 938; Akti Zouroudi 3) You'll find Kalua by the beach to the north of the harbour. No shortage of bars around that area either.

## Getting There & Around
There are daily flights to Athens (€82) from Kos' international airport with **Olympic Airways** ( ☎ 2242 028 330). The airport is 28km from Kos town.

There are frequent ferries from Rhodes that continue on to Piraeus (€27, 12 to 15 hours) via Kalymnos, Leros and Patmos, and less-frequent connections to Nisyros, Tilos, Symi, Samos and Crete. Daily excursion boats visit Nisyros, Kalymnos, Patmos and Rhodes. In summer, ferries depart daily for Bodrum in Turkey (one way/return €20/34). Get details and tickets at Pulia Tours (left).

Next to the tourist office is a blue mini-train that leaves hourly for Asklipion (€3) and a green mini-train that does city tours (€2).

Buses for Agios Fokas leave from opposite the town hall on the harbour; all other buses (including those to Kefalos Bay) leave from the bus station on Kleopatras, near the ruins at the back of town.

## PATMOS ΠΑΤΜΟΣ

**pop 3050**

Orthodox and Western Christians have long made pilgrimages to Patmos, for it was here that St John wrote his revelations. Not only the religiously motivated will enjoy Patmos, though. It has a mix of qualities that are instantly palatable.

### Information

For information on the island, visit www .patmosweb.gr. The *Patmostimes*, an excellent English-language magazine, is readily available.

**Blue Bay Hotel** (per hr €4), 200m south from the port, has Internet access. The **tourist office** (☎ 2247 031 666; ☼ 8am-6pm Mon-Fri summer only), post office and police station are in the white building at the island's port and capital of Skala. Buses leave regularly for the *hora*, 4.5km inland.

**Apollon Travel** (☎ 2247 031 324; apollon@12net .gr), on the waterfront, handles schedules and ticketing.

### Sights & Activities

The **Cave of the Apocalypse** (☎ 2247 031 234; ☼ 8am-1.30pm daily, 4-6pm Tue, Thu & Sun), where St John wrote the divinely inspired *Book of Revelations*, is halfway between the port and *hora*. Take a bus or make the pilgrimage via the **Byzantine path**: walk up the Skala–Hora road and take the steps to the right 100m beyond the far side of the football field. The path begins opposite the top of the steps.

The **Monastery of St John the Theologian** (☎ 2247 031 223; admission monastery/treasury free/€5; ☼ 8am-1.30pm daily, 4-6pm Tue, Thu & Sun) looks more like a castle than a monastery and crowns the island. It exhibits monastic treasures: early manuscripts, embroidered robes, incredible carvings and an El Greco painting.

Patmos' coastline provides secluded coves, mostly with pebble beaches. The best is **Psili Ammos**, in the south, reached by excursion boat from Skala port. **Lambi Beach**, on the north coast, is a pebble-beach lover's dream come true.

### Sleeping & Eating

There is a cluster of sleeping options about 500m to the north of the port.

**Hotel Australis** (☎ 2247 031 576; www.patmosweb .gr/australis; d incl breakfast €40-60) This place has private facilities, a family church on site and an oasis-like garden that has featured in *Garden Design* magazine. Australis also has apartments in town.

**Villa Knossos** (☎ 2247 032 189; fax 2247 032 284; d €25-50; ☒ ) Next door to Australis, this place has exceptional rooms.

**Blue Bay Hotel** (☎ 2247 031 165; www.bluebay.50g .com; s/d €54/68; ☒ ▣ ) There are great rooms here, 200m south of the port.

**Stefanos Camping** (☎ 2247 031 821; per person/ tent €6/3) On the pleasant tree-shaded Meloi Beach, 2km northeast of Skala, this spot has a minimarket and café-bar.

**Grigoris Taverna** (☎ 2247 031 515; mains €4-8) Opposite the port gate, this is a popular spot.

**Kipos Garden Restaurant** (☎ 2247 031 884; dishes €3-8) Head here for home-grown vegetable dishes such as fried aubergines.

**Aman** (☎ 2247 032 323) Has a tree-shaded patio and relaxing music.

### Getting There & Away

Patmos is well connected, with ferries to Piraeus (€22, eight hours) and to Rhodes (€19, 7½ hours) via Leros, Kalymnos and Kos. In summer, there are daily Flying Dolphin hydrofoils to Leros, Kalymnos, Kos, Rhodes, Fourni, Ikaria, Agathonisi and Samos. Head to Apollon Travel (left) for details and tickets.

# NORTHEASTERN AEGEAN ISLANDS ΤΑ ΝΗΣΙΑ ΤΟΥ ΒΟΡΕΙΟΑΝΑΤΟΛΙΚΟ ΑΙΓΑΙΟΥ

This group consists of seven major islands that are strewn across the northeastern corner of the Aegean, closer to Turkey than mainland Greece. Turkish influence is barely visible, despite the islands being part of the Ottoman Empire until 1912. Though island-hopping can be tricky due to their far-flung nature, these islands remain relatively calm even in the heights of summer and reward exploration with wonderful hiking, crowd-free beaches and unique villages.

## SAMOS ΣΑΜΟΣ

**pop 32,800**

Birthplace of mathematician Pythagoras – remember the triangle man? – and storyteller Aesopus, Samos was an important centre of Hellenic culture. A mountainous island only 3km from Turkey, it is lush and humid with spectacular beaches, a huge variety of flora and fauna, and is worth more than a casual glance.

Samos has two main ports: Vathy (Samos town) in the northeast and Pythagorio on the southeast coast. Those coming from the south generally arrive in Pythagorio. Big ferries use Vathy. Once you're there and have onward tickets, double-check where your boat is leaving from. Buses between the two take 25 minutes. **By Ship Travel** ( ☎ 2273 025 065; www.byshiptravel.gr) has offices at both ports that handle schedules and ticketing.

## Pythagorio Πυθαγόρειο

Pretty Pythagorio, where you'll disembark if you've come from Patmos, is small and attractive. The bus stop is on the main street, about 300m from the waterfront heading inland, on your left.

The cordial **municipal tourist office** ( ☎ 2273 061 389; deap5@otenet.gr; Lykourgou Logotheti; ⏰ 8am-10pm) is two blocks from the waterfront on the main street. By Ship Travel is next door. **Digital World** ( ☎ 2273 062 722; per hr €5; ⏰ 11am-2pm & 5-11pm) provides Internet access across the street.

The **Evpalinos Tunnel** ( ☎ 2273 061 400; adult /student €4/2; ⏰ 8.45am-2.45pm Tue-Sun), built in the 6th century BC, is a 1km tunnel dug by political prisoners and used as an aqueduct to bring water from the springs of Mt Ampelos (1140m). Part of the tunnel can still

be explored. It's a 20-minute walk north of town. If you feel like reminiscing about maths study, there's an excellent **statue of Pythagoras** and his triangle on the waterfront opposite the ferry quay.

**Pension Sydney** ( ☎ 2273 061 733; Pythagora; d €30), a block in from the waterfront, is immaculate with private facilities. **Pension Philoxenia** ( ☎ 2273 061 055; Polykratous; s/d €20/30; ✖ ), on the road to Vathy, but still close, also has private bathrooms, a huge communal kitchen and dining room, and is a good option.

**Iliad Café-Bar** ( ☎ 2273 062 207), on the waterfront and run by Sandy, a Kiwi, is an excellent spot to start or finish the evening. Try the Pythogorian Sunset. Mama's Plate of the Day at **Espirides Garden-Tavern** ( ☎ 2273 061 767; Pythagora; mains from €5) is the stuff legends are made of, while the food at **Poseidonas Neptune Taverna** ( ☎ 2273 062 530; mains from €5), on the small town beach, is superb.

## Vathy (Samos) Βαθύ Σάμος

Busy Vathy, 25 minutes from Pythagorio by bus, is more of a working town. Its **archaeological museum** ( ☎ 2273 027 469; adult/student €3/2; ⏰ 8.30am-3pm Tue-Sun), by the municipal gardens, is first rate. The highlight is a 4.5m male *kouros* statue.

The rarely open, hard-to-find **tourist office** ( ☎ 2273 028 530; ⏰ summer only) is in a side street one block north of the main square, Plateia Pythagorou. **ITSA Travel** ( ☎ 2273 023 605; www .itsatravel.com), opposite the quay, can sort travel enquiries, excursions, accommodation and

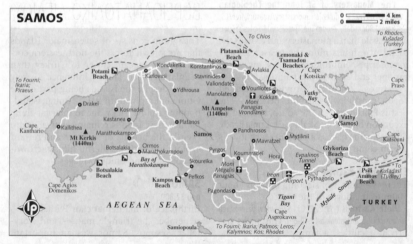

SAMOS

0 _____ 4 km
0 _____ 2 miles

AEGEAN SEA

TURKEY

luggage storage. To get to Vathy's bus station, follow the waterfront and turn left onto Lekati, 250m south of Plateia Pythagorou (just before the police station). **Diavlos NetCafé** ( ☎ 2273 022 469; per hr €3), beside the bus station, offers Internet access.

**Pythagoras Hotel** ( ☎ 2273028601;www.pythagoras hotel.com; Kallistratou; s/d/tr/q €20/26/33/36; ☐ ) is a friendly, great-value place with a convivial atmosphere. There is a restaurant, bar, satellite TV and Internet access on site. Facing inland, the hotel is 500m to the left of the quay. Call ahead for pick up on arrival. **Pension Avli** ( ☎ 2273 022 939; Areos 2; d €28), back up to the left behind the main square, is in a former Roman Catholic convent and built around a lovely courtyard.

**The Garden** ( ☎ 2273 024 033; Manolis Kalomiris; mains €4-9) serves good Greek food in a lovely garden setting up to the left behind the main square. **La Calma** ( ☎ 2273 022 654; Kefalopoulou 7; mains from €6), to the north of the port, has outstanding views. **Ovaga** ( ☎ 2273 025 476; Kefalopoulou 13), near La Calma, serves up tasty cocktails on its stunning terrace by the water.

## Around Samos

**Ireon** ( ☎ 2273 095 277; adult/student €3/2; ⊙ 8.30am-3pm Tue-Sun), the legendary birthplace of the goddess Hera, is 8km west of Pythagorio. The temple at this World Heritage site was enormous – four times the size of the Parthenon – though only one column remains standing.

The captivating villages of **Vourliotes** and **Manolates**, on the slopes of imposing Mt Ampelos, northwest of Vathy, provide excellent walking territory and have many marked pathways.

Choice beaches include **Tsamadu** and **Platanakia** on the north coast, **Botsalakia** in the southwest and **Psili Amos** to the east of Pythagorio.

## Getting There & Around

There are daily flights to Athens (€75) from the airport at Pythagorio, and twice weekly to Thessaloniki (€90) with **Olympic Airways** ( ☎ 2273 027 237).

Ferries leave daily for Piraeus (€24, 13 hours) – most via Paros and Naxos, and some via Mykonos – and Ikaria, but only three a week visit Chios (€10.70, four hours). Daily hydrofoils ski to Patmos

(€13.20, 1¼ hours), carrying on to Leros, Kalymnos and Kos.

There are daily ferries to Kuşadası (for Ephesus) in Turkey (€45 return plus €21 port taxes). Day excursions are also available from April to October.

You can get to most of the island's villages and beaches by bus, except for Manolates. Agios Konstantinos, 4km away, is its closest bus stop. Rental cars and scooters are readily available around the island.

## CHIOS ΧΙΟΣ
pop 54,500

Due to its thriving shipping and mastic industries (mastic produces the resin used in chewing gum) Chios (*hee-os*) has never really bothered much with tourism. The chief attraction lies in exploring its inland villages.

### Information

Chios town is a working port and not really a place to linger. It is, however, a good base for day trips to Turkey.

Slick **Enter Internet Café** ( ☎ 2271 026 108; Leof Aigaiou 48; per hr €3.60) is upstairs on the southern waterfront. The **post office** (Rodokanaki) is one block back from the waterfront.

The **municipal tourist office** ( ☎ 2271 044 389; infochio@otenet.gr; Kanari 18; ⊙ 7am-10pm Apr-Oct, 7am-4pm Nov-Mar) is on the main street that runs from the waterfront to Plateia Vounakiou, the main square. Staff members are extremely helpful and provide information on accommodation, schedules and rentals. The publication *Hiking Routes on Chios* is available at no charge.

**Agean Travel** ( ☎ 2271 041 277; aegeantr@otenet .gr; Leof Aigaiou 14), on the waterfront, handles ticketing.

### Sights & Activities

In Chios town, **Philip Argenti Museum** ( ☎ 2271 023 463; admission €1.50; ⊙ 8am-2pm Mon-Fri, 5-7.30pm Fri, 8am-12.30pm Sat) contains the treasures of the wealthy Argenti family.

World Heritage–listed **Nea Moni** (New Monastery; ⊙ 8am-1pm & 4-8pm) is 14km west of Chios town and reveals some of the finest Byzantine art in the country, with mosaics dating from the 11th century. The mosaics survived, but the resident monks were massacred by the Turks in 1822. Those in the ghost village of **Anavatos**, 10km from Nea

Moni and built on a precipitous cliff, preferred a different fate, hurling themselves off the cliff rather than being taken captive by the Turks. Currently the village is being spruced up in the hope of attracting visitors.

Chios' southern Mastihohoria (mastic villages) were spared in the 1822 massacres thanks to the Turkish fondness for mastic chewing gum. **Pyrgi**, 24km southwest of Chios town, is one of Greece's most unusual villages. The façades of the town's dwellings are decorated with intricate grey and white geometric patterns and motifs. The tiny medieval town of **Mesta**, 10km from Pyrgi and nestled within fortified walls, has four entry gates, two ornate churches and cobbled streets connected by overhead arches.

## Sleeping & Eating

The tourist office gives out a practical accommodation guide for the town and villages.

**Chios Rooms** ( ☎ 2271 020 198; Leoforos Aigaiou 110; s/d/tr with shared bathroom €20/26/35) On the waterfront at the opposite end of the harbour from the ferry dock, Chios Rooms has bright, airy rooms in a building that oozes rustic charm.

**Hotel Kyma** ( ☎ 2271 044 500; kyma@chi.forthnet .gr; Evgenias Chandris 1; s/d incl breakfast €46/60; 🞉 ) Around the corner from Chios Rooms, this place has helpful owners and tons of character.

**To Meliotiko Ouzeri** ( ☎ 2271 040 407; dishes from €3) On the waterfront to the right of the ferry disembarkation point, you'll get huge helpings of Greek classics.

**Taverna Hotzas** ( ☎ 2271 042 787; Kondyli 3; dishes from €3.50) Excellent food and ambience 15 minutes' walk south of the town crush.

## Getting There & Around

There are daily flights from Chios to Athens (€69) with **Olympic Airways** ( ☎ 2271 020 359). Ferries sail daily to Piraeus (€19.50, eight hours) via Lesvos (€12, three hours), and once a week to Thessaloniki (€30, 18 hours) via Lesvos and Limnos. There are three ferries a week to Samos (€10.70, four hours).

Boats to Turkey run all year from Chios, with daily sailings from July to September to Çeşme (one way/return €40/50 plus €9 port tax). For details, check out **Miniotis Lines** ( ☎ 2271 024 670; www.miniotis.gr; Neorion 24).

Chios has two bus stations. Blue buses go regularly to local villages and Karfas and Kontari beaches, and leave from the right side (coming from the waterfront) of Plateia Vounakiou, by the garden. Green long-distance buses to Pyrgi and Mesta leave from the station one block back to the left of Plateia Vounakiou.

## LESVOS (MYTILINI) ΛΕΣΒΟΣ (ΜΥΤΙΛΗΝΗ)

The third largest of the Greek islands, fertile Lesvos has always been a centre of philosophy and artistic achievement and still attracts creative types on sabbatical. Spoil yourself with its prized olive oil, ouzo, sardines and therapeutic hot springs. An excellent source of information on the island is www.greeknet.com.

### Mytilini Μυτιλήνη

pop 27,250

The capital and main port, Mytilini, is a large, dreary working town. **Sponda** ( ☎ 2251 041 007; Komninaki; per hr €2), has impressive Internet access a block back from the waterfront in a pool bar. The **tourist police** ( ☎ 2251 022 776) are at the entrance to the quay. The **tourist office** ( ☎ 2251 042 511; 6 Aristarhou; 🞉 9am-1pm Mon-Fri), 50m up Aristarhou by the quay, offers brochures and maps, but is open limited hours.

**Samiotis Tours** ( ☎ 2251 042 574; samiotistours@ hotmail.com; Kountourioti 43), 400m from the ferry on the waterfront, handles flights, boat schedules, ticketing and runs excursions to Turkey.

### SIGHTS & ACTIVITIES

Mytilini's excellent neoclassical **archaeological museum** ( ☎ 2251 022 087; 8 Noemvriou; adult /senior for both museums €3/2; 🞉 8.30am-7pm Tue-Sun) has a fascinating collection from Neolithic to Roman times. The **new archaeological museum** (8 Noemvriou; 🞉 8.30am-7pm Tue-Sun) displays spectacular mosaics from ancient households. Follow the signposts from the ferry.

**Theophilos Museum** ( ☎ 2251 041 644; admission €2; 🞉 9am-2.30pm & 6-8pm Tue-Sun), 4km south of Mytilini in Varia village, is a shrine to the prolific folk painter Theophilos.

Five kilometres from Mytilini, on the Gulf of Year, are the **Therma hot springs** ( ☎ 2251 024 575; admission €2.50; 🞉 8am-6pm), where you can bathe in a steamy white room overlooking the water and mountains. It's highly recommended.

GREECE

## SLEEPING

**Salina's Rooms** ( ☎ 2251 024 640; cnr Fokeas & Kinikiou; s/d €25/30) Clean rooms, a garden and a kitchen for guest use.

**Pension Thalia** ( ☎ 2251 042 073; Kinikiou 1; s/d €25/30) Virtually next door and run by the same people as Salina's, this pension has clean, bright rooms in a large house. It is about a five-minute walk north of the main square, up Ermou.

**Porto Lesvos Hotel** ( ☎ 2251 022 510; www.porto lesvos.gr; Komninaki 21; s/d €60/90; ✷ ) A newish hotel in a restored building one block back from the waterfront.

## EATING & DRINKING

**Ocean Eleven Bar** (Kountourioti 17) In the corner on the waterfront, this is an excellent place to start or end the evening.

**Restaurant Averof** ( ☎ 2251 022 180; Ermou 52; mains from €4) Hearty Greek staples such as *patsas* are dished up just back from the main square.

**Via Alla Pasta** ( ☎ 2251 037 717; Mitropoleous 22; mains from €7) Top-quality Italian dishes are served in this place behind Ocean Eleven Bar just off the waterfront.

## GETTING THERE & AROUND

There are daily flights to Athens (€78) and to Thessaloniki (€88), five a week to Limnos (€46) and two a week to Chios (€28) with **Olympic Airways** ( ☎ 2251 028 659) and **Aegean Airlines** ( ☎ 2251 061 120).

In summer, there are daily boats to Piraeus (€24, 12 hours), some via Chios, Mykonos and Syros, and one boat a week

to Thessaloniki (€30, 13 hours). There is also one ferry a week to Skiathos (€26) in the Sporades group. There are four ferries a week to Ayvalik in Turkey (one way/return €30/45). Stop by Samiotis Tours (opposite) for ticketing and schedules.

Mytilini has two bus stations. For local buses, walk along the waterfront to the main square, where buses leave regularly for Therma and Varia. For long-distance buses, walk 600m from the ferry along the waterfront to El Venizelou and turn right until you reach Agia Irinis park, which is next to the station. There are regular services in summer to Mithymna, Petra, Agiasos, Skala Eresou, Mantamados and Agia Paraskevi.

## Mithymna Μήθυμνα
### pop 1500

The gracious, preserved town of Mithymna (known by locals as Molyvos) is 62km north of Mytilini. Cobbled streets canopied by flowering vines wind up the hill below the impressive castle. The town is full of cosy tavernas and genteel stone cottages. You'll be tempted never to leave this scenic place.

### ORIENTATION & INFORMATION

There are three Internet cafés along the port road. From the bus stop, walk towards the town for 100m to the helpful **municipal tourist office** ( ☎ 2253 071 347; www.mithymna.gr; ☉ 8am-9pm Mon-Fri, 9am-7pm Sat & Sun), which has good maps. A further 50m on, take the right fork onto 17 Noemvriou, the cobbled main thoroughfare, or continue straight ahead to reach the colourful fishing port.

---

### SAPPHO, LESBIANS AND LESVOS

If you saw *My Big Fat Greek Wedding*, you may remember that Toula's father had a passion for showing how virtually every word in common usage in English today can be traced back to Greek. He even found a way to show that the word *kimono* has Greek origins. One he didn't come up with at the wedding party though was the word lesbian. He would undoubtedly be aware, however, of the word's origins.

One of Greece's great ancient poets, Sappho, was born on the island of Lesvos during the 7th century BC, in the town of Eresos. Her poetry quickly became famous for its lyrically evocative style and richly sumptuous imagery. Most of Sappho's work was devoted to love and desire and the objects of her affection were often female. Owing to this last fact, her name and birthplace have come to be associated with female homosexuality. There is an excellent statue of Sappho taking pride of place in the main square on the waterfront in Mytilini.

These days, Lesvos is visited by many lesbians paying homage to Sappho. The whole island is very gay-friendly, in particular the southwestern beach resort of Skala Eresou, which is built over ancient Eresos, Sappho's birthplace.

**Panatella Holidays** (☎ 2253 071 520; www.Pana
tella-holidays.com), just before the fork, handles
bookings and runs all kinds of local trips,
including Donkey Days (ride a donkey!).

### SIGHTS & ACTIVITIES
The noble **Genoese castle** (☎ 2253 071 803; admission €2; ☼ 8am-7pm Tue-Sun) sits above the town
like a crown and affords tremendous views
out to Turkey.

**Eftalou hot springs** (☎ 2253 071 245; public/private
baths per person €3.50/5; ☼ public baths 10am-2pm &
4-8pm, private baths 9am-4pm), 4km from town on
the beach, is a superb bathhouse complex
with a whitewashed dome and steaming,
pebbled pool. There are also new private
baths where you don't need a bathing suit.

Pebbly **Mithymna Beach** sits below the
town. Don't forget to stroll down to the
harbour.

### SLEEPING & EATING
There are over 50 *domatia* in Mithymna.

**Nassos Guest House** (☎ 2253 071 432; nassos
guesthouse@hotmail.com; Arionis; d/tr €25/30) An
airy, friendly, traditional place with shared
facilities and a communal kitchen. The
views are rapturous. To get here, head up
17 Noemvriou and take the second right
(a sharp switchback).

**Marina's Rooms** (☎ 0253 071 470; d €26-30) On
the main road just short of the port, Marina's has excellent facilities.

**Betty's Restaurant** (☎ 2253 071 421; Agora; mains
from €5) Betty's has superb views and atmosphere in a building that was once a notorious bordello. Ask Betty about the old photos
on the wall.

**Captain's Table** (☎ 2253 071 241; mains from €5)
At the end of the port road, this busy spot
does Greek fare with flair. There is a swath
of bars down at the port.

### GETTING AROUND
In summer, buses go regularly to Petra
Beach and Eftalou. Excursion boats leave
the port daily for Skala Sykaminias. Competitive car- and scooter-hire outlets line
the port road.

## Around the Island
East of Mithymna, the traditional picturesque villages surrounding Mt Lepetymnos
(**Sykaminia**, **Mantamados** and **Agia Paraskevi**)
are worth your time.

Southern Lesvos is dominated by **Mt
Olympus** (968m) and the very pretty day-
trip destination of **Agiasos**, which has good
artisan workshops.

# SPORADES ΣΠΟΡΑΔΕΣ

There are 11 islands in the Sporades group,
four of which are inhabited. Skiathos has
the best beaches and a throbbing tourist
scene, while Skopelos is more relaxed, with
a postcard waterfront, sandy bays and lush
forest trails. Alonnisos is far less visited and
retains more local character. The National
Marine Park of Alonnisos, encompassing
seven islands, is aimed at protecting the
Mediterranean monk seal. It is a welcome
innovation in a country not noted for protecting its fauna.

The main ports for the Sporades are
Volos and Agios Konstantinos on the
mainland.

## SKIATHOS ΣΚΙΑΘΟΣ
pop 6150
Lush and green, Skiathos has a universal
beach-resort feel about it. An international
airport has brought loads of package tourists, but the island still oozes enjoyment.
There are plenty of good beaches awash
with water sports on the south coast, particularly Koukounaries.

## Orientation & Information
Skiathos town's main thoroughfare is Papadiamanti, running inland opposite the
quay. **Internet Zone Café** (☎ 2427 022 767; per hr
€3; ☼ 10.30-1am) is off Papadiamanti, 100m

---

**WHERE TO GET AN ALL-OVER TAN**

Koukounaries Beach on the south coast of
Skiathos has often been touted as Greece's
best beach, but if you're keen for an all-over
tan, a 10-minute stroll over the headland
to the west brings you to Banana Beach.
Named for its curving shape and yellow
sand, Banana Beach is nominally a nudist
beach, when things get too crowded
skinny-dippers tend to abscond to Little
Banana Beach, a tad further north. Gay
and lesbian sunbathers also give it the big
thumbs up.

---

GREECE

up Evangelistrias, on your right just before you reach the post office, and the helpful **tourist police** ( ☎ 2427 023 172; ☷ 8am-9pm).

There's a **tourist information booth** ( ☎ 2427 023 172) to the left as you leave the port, but it opens irregularly.

**Travel Agency Skiathos** ( ☎ 2427 022 209; www .skiathosoe.com; cnr Papadiamantis & waterfront) is flat out with travel schedules and tickets. **Heliotropio Travel** ( ☎ 2427 022 430; helio@skiathos.gr), a few doors right, runs excellent excursions, including one that takes in Skopelos and Alonnisos in a day (€20).

Skiathos has some excellent beaches, particularly on the south coast. **Koukounaries** is popular with families. A short stroll over the headland, **Big Banana Beach** is superb. If you want to tan your whole body, head a tad further on to **Little Banana Beach**, where bathing suits are a rarity.

## Sleeping

The **Rooms to Let** ( ☎ 2427 022 990) bookings kiosk on the waterfront opens when ferries and hydrofoils arrive. *Domatia* owners meet ferries.

**Pension Pandora** ( ☎ 2427 024 357, 6979 156 019; www.skiathosinfo/accommodation/pensionpandora; Paleokastro; s/d/q €30/45/60; ℗ ✻ ) Run by the effervescent Georgina, this superb place is 10 minutes' walk north of the quay. The 14 rooms have TV, kitchens and balconies. Georgina also has two exceptional apartments just off Papadiamanti.

**Apartments Filitsa** ( ☎ 2427 021 185; Metaxa; apt €30-100; ✻ ) In the old part of town near Panagia Theotokos church, these two-bedroom apartments sleep from two to six people, have fully-equipped kitchens and are perfect for a long stay.

**Hotel Marlton** ( ☎ 2427 022 552; fax 2427 022 878; s/d €40/55) This place is friendly and has fresh, pine-furnished rooms. To get there from Papadiamanti, turn right onto Evangelistrias and walk 50m.

**Camping Koukounaries** ( ☎ 2427 049 250; per person/ tent €6/3) A camping ground with minimarket, taverna and good facilities. It's 30 minutes away by bus at Koukounaries Beach.

## Eating & Drinking

Skiathos is brimming with eateries. Nightlife sprawls along Politehniou; to find it, turn left off Papadiamanti at Evangelistrias and walk 100m.

**Taverna Dionysos** ( ☎ 2427 022 675; Panora) Heading up Papadiamanti, turn right opposite the National Bank to find this place, which has tasty three-course menus from €7. Taverna Dionysos presents you with an ouzo before dinner and a *metaxa* with coffee to finish. Bring your appetite.

**Taverna Misogia** ( ☎ 2427 021 440; Grigoriou; mains €3-8) Turn left at the National Bank and walk 150m to get to this taverna, which has great grills of lamb, pork and chicken.

**Psaradiki Ouzeri** ( ☎ 2427 023 412; Paralia; mains €3.50-10) By the fish market at the far end of the old port, this is the seafood winner.

**La Skala Bar** ( ☎ 2427 023 102; Politehniou) Check out Skiathos' low-key gay and lesbian scene above the old port.

**Kahlua Bar** ( ☎ 2427 023 205) On the club strip at the eastern waterfront end of town, Kahlua is popular and pulses with mainstream DJ sets.

## Getting There & Around

In summer, there are daily flights from Athens to Skiathos (€55). There is an **Olympic Airways** ( ☎ 2427 022 200) office at the airport.

There are frequent ferries to the mainland ports of Volos (€11.60) and Agios Konstantinos (€20.80), and frequent hydrofoils each day to Skopelos (€9.10) and Alonnisos (€13). In summer, there are two boats a week to Thessaloniki (€16.80).

Crowded buses ply the south-coast road between Skiathos town and Koukounaries every 20 minutes, stopping at all the beaches along the way. The bus stop is at the eastern end of the harbour.

## SKOPELOS ΣΚΟΠΕΛΟΣ
**pop 4700**

Mountainous and forest-covered Skopelos is less commercialised than Skiathos. Skopelos Town skirts a semicircular bay and clambers in tiers up a hillside, culminating in a ruined fortress.

**Velanio Beach** on the south coast is the island's nudie spot. On the west coast, pebbled **Panormos Beach**, with its sheltered emerald bay surrounded by pine forest, is superb. The 2km stretch of **Milia Beach**, a few kilometres further on, is considered the island's best.

Head 50m up the road opposite the port entrance to find Platanos Sq. Along Doulidi, the street to the left after Gyros.gr, is the **Internet @ Café** (☎ 2424 023 093; 🕓 9am-2.30pm & 5pm-midnight), post office and a stack of popular nightspots. The bus station is next to the port.

There is no tourist office or tourist police, but **Thalpos Leisure & Services** (☎ 2424 022 947; www.holidayislands.com), on the waterfront between the ferry quay and the excursion-boat quay, is handy for accommodation and tours.

*Domatia* owners come to meet the boats. **Pension Sotos** (☎ 2424 022 549; www.skopelos.net/sotos; s/d €25/50), in the middle of the waterfront, has large rooms in an enchanting building. There's also a communal kitchen and courtyard. **Pension Soula** (☎ 2424 022 930; d/tr €25/55), a 10-minute walk out of town, is a welcoming place with airy rooms; you'll awake in rural bliss to donkeys braying and birdsong. To find it, walk left from the port and turn left at Hotel Amalia. Follow the road, bearing right after about 200m; it's on your right. **Hotel Adonis** (☎ 2424 022 231; s/d €50/90) is more upmarket and in a prime spot overlooking the waterfront.

The top spot in town to chill out is under the huge plane tree at **Platanos Jazz Bar** (☎ 2424 023 661), opposite the excursion-boat quay. It's open all day, serves a mean omelette (€3) for breakfast, and plays wicked jazz and blues until the late hours. Next door is **Taverna Ta Kimata** (☎ 2424 022 381; mains from €4), started by the current owner's grandfather in 1928. Try the *yuvetsi* (claypot pasta). **Perivoli Taverna** (☎ 2424 023 758; mains €6-13), 50m inland from Platanos Sq, serves great vegetarian dishes.

**Oionos Blues Bar** (☎ 2424 023 731) offers excellent jazz, blues and soul in a traditional Skopelean house. From the waterfront, turn inland next to Pension Sotos and take the second right. On Doulidi there is a clutch of popular bars, including **Dancing Club Kounos** (☎ 2424 023 623).

In summer, there are daily ferries to Volos (€15.10) and Agios Konstantinos (€28.40) that also call at Skiathos. Flying Dolphin hydrofoils dash several times a day to Skiathos, Alonnisos, Volos and Agios Konstantinos. Most hydrofoils also call in at Loutraki, the port below Glossa on the northwest coast. For schedules and tickets, see **Skopelos Ferry Office** (☎ 2424 022 767), opposite the port. There are frequent buses from Skopelos town to Glossa stopping at all beaches along the way.

## ALONNISOS ΑΛΟΝΝΗΣΟΣ

**pop 2700**

Green, serene Alonnisos is the least visited of the Sporades. The area surrounding the island has been declared a marine park and reputedly has the cleanest waters in the Aegean.

The port village of Patitiri isn't particularly attractive. Its concrete buildings were slapped together in 1965 after an earthquake destroyed the hill-top capital of Alonnisos Town. There are two main thoroughfares; facing inland from the ferry quay, Pelasgon (left) and Ikion Dolopon (far right).

There is no tourist office or tourist police but the post office, police and Internet access at **Il Mondo Café** (☎ 2424 065 834; per hr €4) are on Ikion Dolopon. On the waterfront itself, **Alonnisos Travel** (☎ 2424 065 188; www.alonnisostravel.gr) handles boat scheduling and ticketing. **Ikos Travel** (☎ 2424 065 320; www.ikostravel.com) runs a popular round-the-island excursion. The bus stop is on the corner of Ikion Dolopon and the waterfront.

The tiny *hora,* **Old Alonnisos**, is a few kilometres inland. Its streets sprout a profusion of plant life, alluring villas of eclectic design and dramatic vistas.

Alonnisos is ideal for walking. Waterfront travel agencies offer guided tours or there's an excellent trail guide called *Alonnisos on Foot: A Walking & Swimming Guide* by Bente Keller & Elias Tsoukanas which is available at newsstands for €9.

The **Rooms to Let service** (☎ 2424 066 188; fax 2424 065 577; 🕓 10am-2pm, 6.30-10.30pm), opposite the quay, books accommodation all over the island. **Camping Rocks** (☎ 2424 065 410; per person €5) is a shady, basic site. It is a steep hike about 1.5km from the port; go up Pelasgon and take the first road on your left. **Pension Pleiades** (☎ 2424 065 235; pleiades@Internet.gr; s/d €25/45; 🔀 ) looks out over the harbour and is visible from the quay. The rooms are bright and cheerful. **Illias Rent Rooms** (☎ 2424 065 451; Pelasgon 27; d €25-40) has good-value rooms 300m up Pelasgon.

**To Kamaki Ouzeri** (☎ 2424 065 245; Ikion Dolopon; mains €4-10) is a traditional island eatery. Check the ready-to-eat dishes out in the kitchen. **Café Flisvos** (☎ 2424 065 307; mains from €5) is the pick of the waterfront restaurants, under the canopy opposite the dock. **Symvolo Bar** (☎ 2424 066 156; Ikion Dolopon) plays jazz and

GREECE

blues, while **Club Enigma** ( ☎ 2424 065 307; Pelasgon) rocks once the tourist season kicks in.

Up in the old town, **Fantasia House** ( ☎ 2424 065 186; Plateia Hristou; s/d €30/40) has sweet rooms and a verdant terrace. **Astrofengia** ( ☎ 2424 065 182; mains €5-12), signposted from the bus stop, serves scrumptious alternative fare.

There are daily ferries from Alonnisos to Volos (€15.70) and Agios Konstantinos (€28.40) via Skiathos and Skopelos. Flying Dolphin hydrofoils travel several times a day to Volos and Agios Konstantinos and between the islands.

The local bus (€0.90) runs to the *hora* every hour. Car- and scooter-hire outlets are on Pelasgon and Ikion Dolopon, but only one main road spans the island!

# IONIAN ISLANDS
## ΤΑ ΕΠΤΑΝΗΣΑ

The idyllic Ionian group of islands stretch down the western coast of Greece from Corfu in the north to remote Kythira, off the southern tip of the Peloponnese. These mountainous islands, with their soft light and Italian influence, offer a contrasting experience to other island groups in Greece.

## CORFU ΚΕΡΚΥΡΑ
**pop 109,540**
Corfu is the second-largest and most important island in the group and many consider it to be Greece's most beautiful island.

### Corfu Town
**pop 28,200**
The island's capital is built on a promontory and the old town, wedged between two fortresses, offers up a medley of occupying influences. While the narrow alleyways of high, shuttered tenements are an immediate reminder of the town's long association with Venice, the Liston, a row of arcaded buildings, was based on Paris' Rue de Rivoli.

#### ORIENTATION & INFORMATION
The town's old fortress (Palaio Frourio) stands on an eastern promontory, separated from the town by an area of parks and gardens known as the Spianada. The new fortress (Neo Frourio) lies to the northwest.

Ferries dock at the new port, just west of the new fortress. The **long-distance bus station** (Avrami) is inland from the port.
**National Bank of Greece** (cnr Voulgareos & Theotoki)
**On Line Internet Café** (Kapodistria 28; per hr €4)
**Tourist police** ( ☎ 2661 030 265; 3rd fl, Samartzi 4) A good source of information.

#### SIGHTS
The **Archaeological Museum** ( ☎ 2661 030 680; **P** Vraili 5; admission €3; ☯ 8.30am-3pm Tue-Sun) houses a collection of finds from Mycenaean to classical times. The star attraction is the pediment from the Temple of Artemis, decorated with gorgons.

Corfu's most famous church, the **Church of Agios Spiridon**, has a richly decorated interior. Pride of place is given to the remains of St Spiridon, displayed in a silver casket; four times a year it is paraded around town.

#### SLEEPING & EATING
**Hotel Hermes** ( ☎ 2661 039 268; G Markora 14; s/d with shared bathroom €28/33, s/d €36/44) Hotel Hermes is a tad noisy, has a certain shabby charm and is popular with backpackers.

**Hotel Konstantinoupolis** ( ☎ 2661 048 716; www .konstantinoupolis.com.gr; K Zavitsianou 11; s/d/tr €55/80/96; ✷ ) This renovated hotel has an unbeatable position overlooking the old harbour (ask for a front room). The rooms are spotless, all have TV and there are good discounts off season.

No matter where you choose to eat in Corfu, it's a must to sit on the Liston nursing a *frappé* (€3.50) and indulging in some people watching.

**To Dimarchio** ( ☎ 2661 039 031; Plateia Dimarchio; mains €7-20) Located in a pleasant square, this place serves up the best food in town. The seafood's excellent and there are also some less expensive pasta and salad dishes.

### Around the Island
Hardly anywhere in Corfu hasn't made a play for the tourist dollar, but the north is over the top. The only real attraction there is the view from the summit of **Mt Pantokrator** (906m), Corfu's highest mountain. There's a road to the top from the village of Strinila.

The main resort on the west coast is **Paleokastritsa**, built around a series of pretty bays. Further south, there are good beaches around the small village of **Agios Gordios**.

GREECE

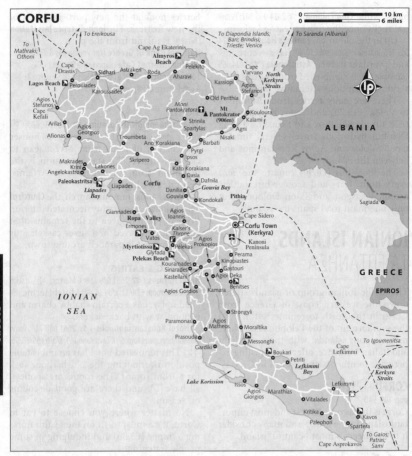

**CORFU**

0      10 km
0      6 miles

To Ereikousa
To Mathraki, Othoni
Cape Drastis
Sidhari
Astrakeri
Roda
Cape Ag Ekaterinis
Almyros Beach
Pelekito
Aharavi
Lagos Beach
Peroulades
Karoussades
Kassiopi
Cape Varvano
North Kerkyra Straits
To Diapondia Islands; Bari; Brindisi; Trieste; Venice
To Saranda (Albania)
Agios Stefanos
Agios Stefanos
Cape Kefali
Arilas
Agios Georgios
Afionas
Troumbeta
Ano Korakiana
Old Perithia
Moni Pantokratora
Mt Pantokrator (906m)
Strinila
Spartylas
Koulour a
Kalami
Agni
Nisaki
Kouloura
ALBANIA
Makrades
Krini
Angelokastro
Lakones
Skripero
Pyrgi
Ipsos
Barbati
Paleokastritsa
Liapades Bay
Liapades
Corfu
Kato Korakiana
Dasia
Dafnila
Danilia
Gouvia
Gouvia Bay
Kondokali
Pithin
Sagiada
Giannades
Ropa Valley
Ermones
Vatos
Kaiser's Throne
Agios Ioannis
Agios Prokopios
Corfu Town (Kerkyra)
Cape Sidero
Myrtiotissa
Pelekas
Glyfada
Pelekas Beach
Kouramades
Sinarades
Kastellani
Kanoni Peninsula
Perama
Kinopiastes
Gastouri
Agioi Deka
Benitses
GREECE
EPIROS
IONIAN SEA
Agios Gordios
Kamara
Paramonas
Agios Matheos
Prasoudo
Gardiki
Strongyli
Moraitika
Messonghi
Boukari
Petriti
Cape Lefkimmi
To Igoumenitsa
Lake Korission
Issos
Agios Giorgios
Marathias
Lefkimmi Bay
Vitalades
Lefkimmi
South Kerkyra Straits
Kritika
Paleohori
Kavos
Spartera
To Gaios; Patras; Sami
Cape Asprokavos

Between Paleokastritsa and Agios Gordios is the hill-top village of **Pelekas**, one of the best places on Corfu to watch the sunset.

### SLEEPING

**Pink Palace** ( ☎ 2661 053 103; www.thepinkpalace .com; A-/B-class room incl breakfast & dinner per person €32/25; ❄ 🖳 ) This huge, garish complex on the main road into Agios Gordios is like a summer camp, with heaps of organised activities such as volleyball, theme parties and water sports. The A-class rooms are hotel-style (including air-con); B-class rooms are hostel-style and sleep up to four people. Long considered an obligatory stop on the European backpacker circuit, it attracts an uninhibited, hard-partying crowd.

**Sunrock** ( ☎ 2661 094 637; www.geocities.com/sun rock_corfu; r per person with shared bathroom €18, r per person with bathroom incl breakfast & dinner €24; 🖳 🖳 ) At the southern end of Pelekas Beach is family-run Sunrock, with facilities and activities that have earned it a place as a firm backpacker favourite. Open year-round, it will arrange for you to be picked up at the port.

### Getting There & Away

Three flights daily to Athens are offered by both **Olympic Airways** ( ☎ 2661 038 694; Polila 11, Corfu town) and **Aegean Airlines** ( ☎ 2661 027 100). Olympic also flies to Thessaloniki three times a week.

There are daily buses to Athens (€29.50, 8½ hours) and Thessaloniki (€28.50, eight hours) from the Avrami terminal in Corfu town. Fares include the ferry to Igoumenitsa.

There are hourly ferries to Igoumenitsa (€5.10, 1½ hours) and a daily ferry to Paxoi. In summer, there are daily services to Patra (€21.50 to €25, six hours) on the international ferries that call at Corfu on their way from Italy.

### Getting Around
Buses for villages close to Corfu town leave from Plateia San Rocco. Services to other destinations leave from the station on Avrami. There's no bus from the airport and a taxi to the old town costs around €9.

## ITHAKI ΙΘΑΚΗ
pop 3080
Ithaki, or ancient Ithaca, was Odysseus' long-lost home in Homer's *Odyssey*. Ithaki doesn't attract large crowds, mainly because of its lack of good beaches, but it's perfect for a quiet holiday. From the main town of Vathy, you can walk to the **Fountain of Arethousa**, the fabled site of Odysseus' meeting with the swineherd Eumaeus on his return to Ithaki.

Ithaki has daily ferries to the mainland ports of Patra and Astakos, as well as daily services to Kefallonia and Lefkada.

## KEFALLONIA ΚΕΦΑΛΛΟΝΙΑ
pop 35,600
After years of relative obscurity, quiet Kefallonia found itself thrust into the international spotlight following the success of the book and film of *Captain Corelli's Mandolin*. Unfortunately for visitors to the island's capital, Sami, the old Venetian streets featured in the movie were as fake as Nicholas Cage's accent – a major earthquake destroyed the original streets in 1953. While Kefallonia is the largest of the Ionians, tourism remains fairly low-key outside the resort areas near the capital and on the beaches in the southwest.

There's an **EOT** ( ☎ 2671 022 248) on the waterfront in Argostoli.

**Karavomilos Beach Camping** ( ☎ 2674 022 480; www.camping-karavomilos.gr; per adult/tent €6/3.50; 🖵 ) is located 800m from Sami. This well-maintained site offers plenty of shade as well as a minimarket, laundry and restaurant.

**Hotel Melissani** ( ☎ 2674 022 464; Sami; d €53; 🔀 ) is a slightly eccentric and pleasant older-style

hotel offering such comforts as TV and fridge. Some rooms have air-con. It's signposted from the eastern end of the waterfront.

**Riviera** ( ☎ 2674 022 777; r €45, mains €3.50-8.50) is a welcoming café-pizzeria on the waterfront with good coffee and light meals. There are also simple rooms available above the café.

There are daily flights to Athens (€65) from the airport, 9km south of Argostoli. Daily ferries operate from Sami to Patra (€11.50, 2½ hours); others depart from Argostoli and the southeastern port of Poros for Kyllini on the Peloponnese. There are also ferry connections to the islands of Ithaki, Lefkada and Zakynthos.

## ZAKYNTHOS ΖΑΚΥΝΘΟΣ
pop 39,020
Zakynthos, or Zante, is a beautiful island resplendent with gorgeous beaches – but during summer it's completely overrun with tourists. Its capital and port, Zakynthos town, is an imposing old Venetian town that has been painstakingly reconstructed after being levelled by an earthquake in 1953.

The area around the huge **Bay of Laganas** in the south has some of the best beaches, but endangered loggerhead turtles come ashore here to lay their eggs in August – at the peak of the tourist invasion. The Greek government has declared this area a national marine park. There are regular ferries between Zakynthos and Kyllini on the Peloponnese.

# GREECE DIRECTORY

## ACCOMMODATION
There is a range of accommodation in Greece to suit every taste and pocket. All accommodation is subject to strict price controls set by the tourist police. By law, a notice must be displayed in every room, stating the category of the room and the seasonal price. If you think you've been ripped off, contact the tourist police. Prices quoted in this book are for the high season, unless otherwise stated. Prices are about 40% cheaper between October and May. It's difficult to generalise about accommodation prices in Greece because of the seasonal variations as well as location.

Greece has almost 350 camping grounds, many of them in great locations. Lots are only open between April and October. Standard facilities include hot showers, kitchens, restaurants and minimarkets and swimming pools. Prices vary according to facilities, but reckon on paying €4.50 to €6 per adult, €3.50 for a small tent and €6 for a large one.

Greece has 55 mountain refuges, which are listed in the booklet *Greece Mountain Refuges & Ski Centres,* available free of charge at EOT and EOS (Ellinikos Orivatikos Syndesmos, the Greek Alpine Club) offices.

You'll find youth hostels in most major towns and on half a dozen islands. The only place affiliated to Hostelling International (HI) is the Athens International Youth Hostel (p279).

Most other hostels throughout Greece are run by the **Greek Youth Hostel Organisation** ( ☎ 210 7519 530; y-hostels@otenet.gr). There are affiliated hostels in Athens, Olympia, Patra and Thessaloniki on the mainland, and on the islands of Crete and Santorini (Thira). Most charge €8 to €10, and you don't have to be a member to stay in any of them.

*Domatia* are the Greek equivalent of a bed and breakfast – minus the breakfast. *Domatia* initially consisted of little more than spare rooms rented out in summer. Nowadays many of these *domatia* are purpose-built appendages to the family house, but can still represent good value. Expect to pay about €25 to €35 for a single and €40 to €50 for a double. Don't worry about finding them – the owners will find you as they greet ferries and buses shouting 'room!'.

Hotels in Greece are classified as deluxe, A, B, C, D or E class. The ratings seldom seem to have much bearing on the price, but expect to pay €18/25 for singles/doubles in D and E class, and anything from €35/45 to €60/80 for singles/doubles with a private bathroom in a decent C-class place.

Some places are classified as pensions and are rated differently. Both are allowed to levy a 10% surcharge for stays of less than three nights, but they seldom do. It normally works the other way – you can bargain a cheaper rate if you're staying more than one night.

## ACTIVITIES
### Diving & Snorkelling
Snorkelling can be enjoyed just about wherever you find coastline in Greece.

Corfu (p331), Mykonos (p301), and Santorini (p307) are just some of the good locations and diving schools operate from these locations as well. Diving outside the organised supervision of a dive school is forbidden in order to protect the many antiquities in the depths of the Aegean. For a complete list of diving possibilities, visit www.isdc.gr.

### Sailing & Yachting
Sailing facilities are generally found at the same locations recommended for windsurfing. Hrysi Akti on Paros and Mylopotas Beach on Ios are two of the best locations. Hire charges for catamarans range from €20 to €25.

Yachting is an excellent way to see the Greek islands. If you have a couple of certified sailors in your group, you can hire a 28-foot bare boat (without crew) that sleeps six for around €1000 per week. Hiring a skipper will nearly double that price. You can find more information at www.yachting.gr.

### Skiing
Greece offers some of the cheapest skiing in Europe with 16 resorts dotted around the mainland, mainly in the north. The resorts are basic and cater mainly to Greek skiers. The season can start late (January) and generally runs through to late March or early April, depending on conditions. The *Greece Mountain Refuges & Ski Centres* brochure is available from EOT offices. Information about snow conditions are available at www.snowreport.gr.

### Trekking
Greece could be a trekkers' paradise if trekking organisations received better funding. Outside the main popular routes, the trails are generally overgrown and poorly marked. A number of companies is run organised treks and the biggest is **Trekking Hellas** (Map p279; ☎ 210 3310 323; www.trekking.gr; Filellinon 7, Athens 105 57).

### Windsurfing
Windsurfing is the most popular water sport in Greece. Sailboards are widely available for hire, priced at €12 to €15 per hour. The top spots for windsurfing are Hrysi Akti on Paros, and Vasiliki on Lefkada, which is a popular place to learn.

## BUSINESS HOURS

Banks are open from 8am to 2pm Monday to Thursday, and 8am to 1.30pm Friday. Some banks in the larger cities and towns are also open from 3.30pm to 6.30pm and on Saturday morning. Post offices are open from 7am to 2pm Monday to Friday; in major cities they're open until 8pm and also open from 7.30am to 2pm on Saturday.

In summer, the usual opening hours for shops are from 8am to 1.30pm and 5.30pm to 8.30pm on Tuesday, Thursday and Friday, and 8am to 2.30pm on Monday, Wednesday and Saturday. Shops generally open 30 minutes later during winter.

Restaurants in tourist areas generally open at 11am and stay open right through to midnight, while normal restaurant hours are 11am to 2pm and from 7pm to midnight or 1am. Cafés tend to open between 9am and 10am and stay open until midnight. Bars open around 8pm and close late; and while discos might open at 10pm, you'll drink alone until midnight. Discos generally close around 4am, but many go through to dawn during summer.

## DANGERS & ANNOYANCES

Greece has the lowest crime rate in Europe. Athens is developing a bad reputation for petty theft and scams, but elsewhere crimes are most likely to be committed by other travellers. See p276 for warnings on the scams in Athens.

## DISABLED TRAVELLERS

If mobility is a problem, the hard fact is that most hotels, museums and ancient sites are not wheelchair accessible. While facilities in Athens are improving (thanks to the 2004 Olympics), elsewhere the uneven terrain is an issue for even able-bodied people.

Useful information on disabled travel is available on the Internet at www.sath.org and www.access-able.com.

## EMBASSIES & CONSULATES
### Greek Embassies

Greek diplomatic missions abroad include:
**Australia** ( ☎ 02-6273 3011; 9 Turrana St, Yarralumla, ACT 2600)
**Canada** ( ☎ 613-238 6271; 76-80 Maclaren St, Ottawa, Ontario K2P 0K6)
**Cyprus** ( ☎ 02-680 670/671; Byron Bvld 8-10, Nicosia)

**France** ( ☎ 01-47 23 72 28; www.amb-grece.fr/presse; 17 Rue Auguste Vaquerie, 75116 Paris)
**Germany** ( ☎ 0228-83010; www.griechische-botschaft .de; Jaegerstrasse 54-55, 10117 Berlin-Mitte)
**Italy** ( ☎ 06-854 9630; Via S Mercadante 36, Rome 3906)
**Japan** ( ☎ 03-3403 0871/2; www.greekemb.jp; 3-16-30 Nishi Azabu, Minato-ku, Tokyo 304-5853)
**New Zealand** ( ☎ 04-473 7775; 5-7 Willeston St, Wellington)
**South Africa** ( ☎ 12-430 7351; 1003 Church St, Hatfield, Pretoria 0028)
**Spain** ( ☎ 01-564 4653; Ave Doctor Arce 24, Madrid 28002)
**Turkey** ( ☎ 312-436 8860; Ziya-ul-Rahman Caddesi 9-11, Gaziosmanpasa 06700, Ankara)
**UK** ( ☎ 020-7229 3850; www.greekembassy.org.uk; 1A Holland Park, London W11 3TP)
**USA** ( ☎ 202-939 1300; www.greekembassy.org; 2221 Massachusetts Ave NW, Washington, DC 20008)

### Embassies in Greece

All foreign embassies in Greece are in Athens and its suburbs.
**Australia** (Map pp273-4; ☎ 2106 450 404; Dimitriou Soutsou 37, 115 21)
**Canada** (Map pp273-4; ☎ 2107 273 400; Genadiou 4, 115 21)
**Cyprus** (Map pp273-4; ☎ 2107 237 883; Irodotou 16, 106 75)
**France** (Map pp273-4; ☎ 2103 611 663; Leof Vasilissis Sofias 7, 106 71)
**Germany** (Map pp273-4; ☎ 2107 285 111; cnr Dimitriou 3 & Karaoli, Kolonaki 106 75)
**Italy** (Map pp273-4; ☎ 2103 617 260; Sekeri 2, 106 74)
**Japan** (Map pp273-4; ☎ 2107 758 101; Athens Tower, Leoforos Messogion 2-4, 115 27)
**New Zealand** (Map pp273-4; ☎ 2106 874 701; Kifissias 268, Halandri)
**South Africa** (Map pp273-4; ☎ 2106 806 645; Kifissias 60, Maroussi, 151 25)
**Turkey** (Map pp273-4; ☎ 2107 245 915; Vasilissis Georgiou 8, 106 74)
**UK** (Map pp273-4; ☎ 2107 236 211; Ploutarhou 1, 106 75)
**USA** (Map pp273-4; ☎ 2107 212 951; Leoforos Vasilissis Sofias 91, 115 21)

## FESTIVALS & EVENTS

In Greece, it's probably easier to list the dates when festivals and events are *not* on! Some are religious, some cultural and others seemingly just an excuse to party. It's worth timing at least one part of your trip to coincide with one as you'll be warmly invited to join in the revelry. The following list is by no means exhaustive and more details can be found at www.cultureguide.gr.

## January
**Epiphany (Blessing of the Waters)** Christ's baptism is celebrated on the 6th when seas, lakes and rivers are blessed. The largest ceremony occurs at Piraeus.

## February
**Carnival Season** The three-week period before the beginning of Lent is celebrated all over Greece with fancy dress, feasting and traditional dance.

## March
**Independence Day** On 25 March, parades and dancing mark the anniversary of the hoisting of the Greek Flag that started the War of Independence.

## April
**Easter** The most important festival of the Greek Orthodox religion. The emphasis is on the Resurrection rather than the Crucifixion so it's a celebratory event. The most significant part of the event is midnight on Easter Saturday when candles are lit (symbolising the Resurrection) and a fireworks and candle-lit procession hits the streets.

## May
**May Day** The celebrations on 1 May see a mass exodus from towns to the country. During picnics, wild flowers are gathered and made into wreaths to decorate just about everything.

## June
**Hellenic Festival** The most important of festivals staged throughout Greece during summer. The Theatre of Herodes Atticus in Athens and the Theatre of Epidavros, near Nafplio, are venues for traditional events.

## July
**Feast of Agia Marina (St Marina)** This feast day is celebrated on 17 July in many parts of Greece, and is a particularly important event on the Dodecanese island of Kasos.

## August
**Feast of the Assumption** Greeks celebrate this day (15 August) with family reunions. There's generally transport chaos on the days before and after the event so it's wise to stay put for a couple of days.

**Samothraki Dance Festival** The northeastern Aegean island of Samothraki plays host to Greece's biggest rave party for a week starting at the end of August.

## September
**Genesis tis Panagias** The birthday of the Virgin Mary is celebrated on 8 September with religious services and feasting.

## October
**Feast of Agios Dimitrios** This feast day, on 26 October, is celebrated in Thessaloniki with much revelry.

**Ohi (No) Day** Metaxas' refusal to allow Mussolini's troops free passage through Greece in WWII is commemorated on 28 October with military parades, folk dancing and feasting.

# GAY & LESBIAN TRAVELLERS
In a country where the church plays a major role in shaping society's views on issues such as sexuality, it should come as no surprise that homosexuality is generally frowned upon. While there is no legislation against homosexual activity, it is wise to be discreet and to avoid open displays of togetherness.

However, Greece is a popular destination for gay travellers. Athens has a busy gay scene – but most people head for the islands. Mykonos (p301) has long been famous for its bars, beaches and hedonism and the town of Eresos (p326) on Lesvos has become something of a pilgrimage for lesbians.

# HOLIDAYS
**New Year's Day** 1 January
**Epiphany** 6 January
**First Sunday in Lent** February
**Greek Independence Day** 25 March
**Good Friday/Easter Sunday** March/April
**Spring Festival/Labour Day** 1 May
**Feast of the Assumption** 15 August
**Ohi Day** 28 October
**Christmas Day** 25 December
**St Stephen's Day** 26 December

# INTERNET ACCESS
Greece was slow to embrace the Internet, but now Internet cafés are springing up everywhere and are listed in this book under Information for cities and islands where available. Charges differ radically – from less than €3.50 per hour in big cities up to €15 per hour on Mykonos.

There has been a huge increase in the number of hotels and businesses using email, and addresses have also been listed in this chapter where available.

# INTERNET RESOURCES
**Culture Guide** (www.cultureguide.gr) Plenty of information about contemporary culture and the arts.
**Greek Ferries** (www.greekferries.org) Get all your ferry information from the source. Covers international and domestic ferries.

**Greek National Tourist Organisation** (www.gnto.gr) Concise tourist information.
**Lonely Planet** (www.lonelyplanet.com) Has postcards from other travellers and the Thorn Tree bulletin board, where you can pose those tricky questions or help answer other travellers' questions on your return.
**Ministry of Culture** (www.culture.gr) Information on ancient sites, art galleries and museums.

## LANGUAGE
Greeks are naturally delighted if you can speak a little of their language, but you don't need Greek to get around. English is almost a second language, especially among younger people. Many Greeks have lived abroad, usually in Australia or the USA, so even in remote villages there are invariably one or two people who can speak English.

## MAPS
Unless you are going to trek or drive, the free maps given out by the tourist offices will probably suffice. The best motoring maps are produced by local company Rd Editions, which also produces a good trekking series.

## MONEY
Banks will exchange all major currencies, in either cash or travellers cheques and also Euro-cheques. Post offices charge less commission than banks, but won't cash travellers cheques.

All major credit cards are accepted, but only in larger establishments. You'll find ATMs everywhere, particularly in tourist areas.

### Costs
Greece is still a cheap destination by northern European standards, but it's no longer dirt-cheap. A rock-bottom daily budget would be €40. This would mean hitching, staying in youth hostels or camping, staying away from bars, and only occasionally eating in restaurants or taking ferries. Allow at least €80 per day if you want your own room and plan to eat out regularly as well as seeing the sights. If you really want a holiday – comfortable rooms and restaurants all the way – you will need closer to €120 per day.

Your money will go a lot further if you travel in the quieter months as accommodation is generally much cheaper outside

the high season. There are fewer tourists around and more opportunities to negotiate even better deals.

### Currency
Greece adopted the euro at the beginning of 2002, and the Greek drachma disappeared after a two-month period of dual circulation.

### Taxes & Refunds
Value-added tax (VAT) varies from 15% to 18%. A tax-rebate scheme applies at a restricted number of shops and stores; look for a Tax Free sign in the window. You must fill in a form at the shop and then present it with the receipt at the airport on departure. A cheque will (hopefully) be sent to your home address.

### Tipping & Bargaining
In restaurants the service charge is included on the bill, but it is the custom to leave a small tip – just round off the bill. Accommodation is nearly always negotiable outside peak season, especially if you are staying more than one night. Souvenir shops will generally bargain. Prices in other shops are normally clearly marked and non-negotiable.

### POST
Post offices *(tahydromia)* are easily identified by the yellow sign outside. Regular post boxes are yellow as well; red post boxes are for express mail only. The postal rate for postcards and airmail letters within the EU is €0.60. To other destinations the rate is €0.65. Post within Europe takes five to eight days and to the USA, Australia and New Zealand, nine to 11 days. Some tourist shops also sell stamps, but with a 10% surcharge.

Mail can be sent poste restante to any main post office and is held for up to one month. Your surname should be underlined and you will need to show your passport when you collect your mail. Parcels are not delivered in Greece – they must be collected from a post office.

### SOLO TRAVELLERS
Greece is a great for solo travellers, particularly in summer when the islands are full of travellers meeting and making friends. Hostels and other backpacker-friendly

accommodation are excellent places to meet other travellers. Solo women are quite safe – which is not to say that problems don't occur, but violent offences are rare.

## TELEPHONE

The Greek telephone service is maintained by the public corporation Organismos Tilepikoinonion Ellados, always referred to by its acronym OTE (*o-teh*). Public phones are easy to use and pressing the 'i' button brings up the operating instructions in English. Public phones are everywhere and all use phonecards.

### Mobile Phones

Mobile phones have become the must-have accessory in Greece. If you have a compatible GSM phone from a country with a global roaming agreement with Greece, you will be able to use your phone in Greece. Make sure you have global roaming activated before you leave your country of residence.

### Phonecards

All public phones use OTE phonecards, sold at OTE offices and *periptera* (street kiosks). These cards are sold in €3, €5, and €9 versions and a local call costs €0.30 for three minutes. There are also discount-card schemes available that give you double the time for your money.

## TIME

Greece is two hours ahead of GMT/UTC and three hours ahead during daylight-saving time, which is in effect from the last Sunday in March until the last Sunday in October.

## TOURIST INFORMATION

Tourist information is handled by the Greek National Tourist Organisation (GNTO), known as EOT in Greece. There is either an EOT office or a local tourist office in almost every town of consequence and on many of the islands. Popular destinations

---

**EMERGENCY NUMBERS**

Ambulance ☎ 166
Fire ☎ 199
Police ☎ 100
Roadside Assistance (ELPA) ☎ 104
Tourist Police ☎ 171

---

have tourist police who can often help in finding accommodation.

### Tourist Offices Abroad

**Australia** Sydney ( ☎ 02-9241 1663/5; hto@tgp.com.au; 51-57 Pitt St, Sydney, NSW 2000)

**Canada** Toronto ( ☎ 416-968 2220; gnto.tor@simpatico .ca; 91 Scollard St, Toronto, Ontario M5R 1G4); Montreal ( ☎ 514-871 1535; 1170 Pl Du Frere Andre, Montreal, Quebec H3B 3C6)

**France** Paris ( ☎ 1-42 60 65 75; eot@club-Internet.fr; 3 Ave de l'Opéra, Paris 75001)

**Germany** Berlin ( ☎ 30-217 6262; Wittenbergplatz 3a, 10789 Berlin 30); Frankfurt ( ☎ 69-236 561; info@gzf-eot .de; Neue Mainzerstrasse 22, 60311 Frankfurt); Hamburg ( ☎ 40-454 498; info-hamburg@gzf-eot.de; Neurer Wall 18, 20254 Hamburg); Munich ( ☎ 89-222 035/6; Pacellistrasse 5, 2W 80333 Munich)

**Italy** Rome ( ☎ 06-474 4249; www.ente-tourismoellenico .com; Via L Bissolati 78-80, Rome 00187); Milan ( ☎ 02-860 470; Piazza Diaz 1, 20123 Milan)

**Japan** Tokyo ( ☎ 03-350 55 917; gnto-jpn@t3.rim.or.jp; Fukuda Bldg West, 5th fl 2-11-3 Akasaka, Minato-ku, Tokyo 107)

**UK** London ( ☎ 020-7734 5997; 4 Conduit St, London W1R 0DJ)

**USA** Chicago ( ☎ 312-782 1084; www.greektourism.com; ste 600, 168 North Michigan Ave, Chicago, IL 60601); Los Angeles ( ☎ 213-626 6696; ste 2198, 611 West 6th St, Los Angeles, CA 92668); New York ( ☎ 212-421 5777; Olympic Tower, 645 5th Ave, New York, NY 10022)

## VISAS

The list of countries whose nationals can stay in Greece for up to three months include Australia, Canada, all EU countries, Iceland, Israel, Japan, New Zealand, Norway, Switzerland and the USA. For the full list, contact a Greek embassy or visit www.lonelyplanet. com/subwwway for updated visa information. For longer stays, apply at a consulate abroad or at least 20 days in advance to the **Aliens Bureau** (Map pp273-4; ☎ 2107 705 711; Leoforos Alexandras 173, Athens; ☉ 8am-1pm Mon-Fri) at the Athens Central Police Station. Elsewhere in Greece, apply to the local police authority.

In the past, Greece has refused entry to those whose passport indicates that they have visited Turkish-occupied North Cyprus. Play it safe and ask the North Cyprus immigration officials to stamp a piece of paper rather than your passport. If you enter North Cyprus from the Greek Republic of Cyprus (only possible for a day visit at present), no exit stamp is put in your passport.

# TRANSPORT IN GREECE

## GETTING THERE & AWAY

### Air

There are no less than 16 international airports in Greece, but most of them handle only summer charter flights to the islands. **Eleftherios Venizelos International Airport** (code ATH; ☎ 2103 530 000; www.aia.gr), near Athens, handles the majority of international flights, including all intercontinental flights, and has regular scheduled flights to all the European capitals. Thessaloniki is also well served by **Macedonia International Airport** (code SKG; ☎ 2310 473 700), and there are scheduled flights to/from Iraklio (Crete) from **Nikos Kazantzakis International Airport** (code HER; ☎ 2810 228 401).

Following is a list of airlines that fly to and from Greece:

**Aegean Airlines** (code A3; www.aegeanair.com)
**Air France** (code AF; ☎ 2103 220 986; www.airfrance .com)
**British Airways** (code BA; ☎ 2108 906 666; www .britishairways.com)
**Delta Airlines** (code DL; ☎ 2103 311 660; www.delta .com)
**easyJet** (code EZY; ☎ 2109 670 000; www.easyjet.com)
**Emirates** (code EK; ☎ 2019 333 400; www.emirates.com)
**Iberia** (code IB; ☎ 2103 234 523; www.iberia.com)
**Japan Airlines** (code JL; ☎ 2103 248 211; www.jal.com)
**KLM** (code WA; ☎ 2103 531 295; www.klm.com)
**Lufthansa** (code IH; ☎ 2106 175 200; www.lufthansa .com)
**Olympic Airways** (code OA; www.olympic-airways.gr)
**Virgin Express** (code TV; ☎ 2106 175 200; www .virgin-express.com)

For details on airlines with services within Greece, see opposite.

### Land

#### NORTHERN EUROPE

Overland travel between northern Europe and Greece is virtually a thing of the past. Buses and trains can't compete with cheap air fares. All bus and train services now go via Italy and take the ferries over to Greece.

Unless you have a Eurail pass (p730), travelling to Greece by train is prohibitively expensive. Greece is part of the Eurail network, and passes are valid on the ferries operated by Adriatica di Navigazione and Hellenic Mediterranean Lines from Brindisi to Corfu, Igoumenitsa and Patra.

#### NEIGHBOURING COUNTRIES

The OSE operates a bus from Athens to Istanbul (€67.50, 22 hours) daily except Wednesday. There are daily trains between Athens and Istanbul (€63, 22 hours) via Thessaloniki (€42.50, 5½ hours).

The crossing points into Turkey are at Kipi and Kastanies, while the crossings into the Former Yugoslav Republic of Macedonia (FYROM) are at Evzoni and Niki, and the Bulgarian crossing is at Promahonas. All are open 24 hours. The crossing points to Albania are at Kakavia and Krystallopigi.

## GETTING AROUND

Greece is an easy destination to travel around thanks to a very comprehensive transport system. On the mainland, buses travel to just about every town on the map and trains offer a good alternative where available. Island-hopping is what most people think of when travelling within Greece and there are myriad ferries that crisscross the Adriatic and Aegean Seas. If you're in a hurry, there's also an extensive and well-priced domestic air network. Timetables are seasonal and change in at least some way every year.

### Air

The vast majority of domestic flights are handled by Greece's much-maligned national carrier, **Olympic Airways** ( ☎ 80 111 444 444; www.olympic-airways.gr).

Crete-based competitor **Aegean Airlines** ( ☎ 8011 120 000; www.aegeanair.com) is the sole survivor of the deregulation of domestic air travel. It offers flights to many of the same destinations as Olympic, and has the same fares, but Aegean often has great discount fares as well as youth and senior discounts.

### Bicycle

Given Greece's hilly terrain, stifling summer heat and rather wayward four-wheeled friends, cycling is not that popular a form of transport. You can hire bicycles at most tourist centres, but these are generally for pedalling around town rather than for serious riding. Prices generally range from €5 to €12 per day. If you wish to do a cycling tour of Greece, bicycles are carried for free on ferries.

## Boat

### CATAMARAN

High-speed catamarans have become an important part of the island travel scene. They are just as fast as hydrofoils, if not faster, and are much more comfortable. They are also much less prone to cancellation in rough weather and the fares are generally the same as hydrofoils. The main players are Hellas Flying Dolphins and Blue Star Ferries.

### FERRY

Every island has a ferry service of some sort, although in winter these are pared back. Services pick up from April, and during July and August Greece's seas are a mass of wake and wash. The ferries come in all shapes and sizes, from the state-of-the-art 'superferries' that run on the major routes to the ageing open ferries that operate local services to outlying islands.

The main ferry companies in Greece include:

**ANEK** ( ☎ 2104 197 420; www.anek.gr)
**Blue Star Ferries** ( ☎ 2108 919 800; www.bluestar ferries.com)
**GA Ferries** ( ☎ 2104 199 100; www.gaferries.com)
**Hellas Flying Dolphins** ( ☎ 2104 199 000; www.dolphins.gr)
**LANE Lines** ( ☎ 2104 274 011; www.lane.gr)
**Minoan Lines** ( ☎ 2104 145 700; www.minoan.gr)
**NEL Lines** ( ☎ 2251 026 299; www.nel.gr)

### Classes

Large ferries usually have four classes: 1st class has air-con cabins and a decent lounge and restaurant; 2nd class has smaller cabins and sometimes a separate lounge; tourist class gives you a berth in a shared four-berth cabin; and the last class, 3rd, is 'deck', which gets you a seat, restaurant, lounge/bar and (drum roll) the deck.

Deck class is an economical way to travel and is the class that most travellers use, while 1st class is almost the same price as the equivalent air fare on some routes. Children under four travel free, while children between four and 10 pay half-fare. Children over 10 pay full fare. When buying tickets you will automatically be given deck class.

### Costs

Fares are fixed by the government. The small differences in price you may find between ticket agencies are the result of some

agencies sacrificing part of their designated commission to qualify as a discount service. The discount offered seldom amounts to much. Tickets can be bought at the last minute from quayside tables set up next to the boats. Prices are the same, contrary to what you will be told by agencies.

### Routes

The hub of the vast ferry network is Piraeus, the main port of Athens. It has ferries to the Cyclades, Crete, the Dodecanese, the Saronic Gulf Islands and the northeastern Aegean Islands. Patra is the main port for ferries to the Ionian Islands, while Volos and Agios Konstantinos are the ports for the group of islands called Sporades.

### HIGH-SPEED FERRY

New high-speed ferries are slashing travel times on some of the longer routes. **NEL Lines** ( ☎ 2251 026 299; www.nel.gr), for example, does Piraeus to Chios in 4½ hours – nearly half the time of a normal ferry and twice the price.

### HYDROFOIL

Hydrofoils offer a faster alternative to ferries on some routes, particularly to islands close to the mainland. They take half the time, but cost twice as much. Most routes operate only during high season. **Hellas Flying Dolphins** ( ☎ 2104 199 000; www.dolphins.gr) travels from Piraeus to the Saronic Gulf Islands and the ports of the eastern Peloponnese, as well as to the Sporades from Agios Konstantinos and Volos.

**Kyriacoulis Hydrofoils** ( ☎ 2241 024 000), based in Rhodes, serves the Dodecanese and provides connections to the northeastern Aegean Islands of Ikaria and Samos as well as other routes.

Tickets for hydrofoils must be bought in advance and there is seat allocation.

## Bus

All long-distance buses on the mainland and the islands are operated by regional collectives known as **KTEL** (Koino Tamio Eispraxeon Leoforion; www.ktel.org). Fares are fixed by the government and service routes can be found on the website.

Greece's buses are comfortable, on time and there are frequent services on all the major routes. The buses are reasonably

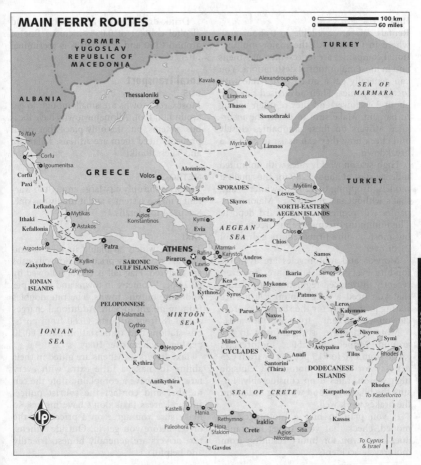

## MAIN FERRY ROUTES

priced, with journeys costing about €4 per 100km. Fares and journey times on a couple of the major routes are Athens–Thessaloniki (€29.40, 7½ hours) and Athens–Patra (€12.25, three hours). Tickets should be bought at least an hour in advance to ensure a seat. Buses don't have toilets and refreshments, but stop around every three hours for those needs.

### Car & Motorcycle

A great way to explore areas in Greece that are off the beaten track is by car. However, it's worth bearing in mind that Greece has the highest road-fatality rate in Europe. The road network has improved dramatically in recent years and places that were little more than a one-lane dirt track masquerading as a road have now been widened and asphalted.

Almost all islands are served by car ferries, but they are expensive. For example, the cost for a small vehicle from Piraeus to Mykonos is €66.60. Petrol in Greece is expensive at around €0.70 per litre in the big cities, but you'll pay €0.90 in remote areas.

The Greek automobile club, ELPA, offers reciprocal services to members of other national motoring associations. If your vehicle breaks down, dial ☎ 104.

You can bring a vehicle into Greece for four months without a carnet – if you have a Green Card (international third-party insurance).

## HIRE

Rentals cars are available just about any-where in Greece. All the major multina-tional companies are represented in Athens and in most major tourist destinations. You can generally get a much better rate with local companies. Their advertised rates are about 25% lower and they're often willing to bargain. Make sure to check the insur-ance waivers on these companies closely and check how they can assist in case of a breakdown.

High-season weekly rates with unlimited mileage start at about €280 for the smallest models, dropping to €200 in winter – and that's without tax and extras. Major com-panies will request a credit card deposit. The minimum driving age in Greece is 18, but most car-hire firms require a driver of 21 or over.

Mopeds and motorcycles are available for hire almost everywhere. There are, however, recently introduced regulations stipulating that you need a valid motorcycle licence stating proficiency for the size of motorcy-cle you wish to rent – from 50cc upwards.

Motorcycles are a cheap way to get around. Mopeds and 50cc motorcycles range from €10 to €15 per day or from €25 per day for a 250cc motorcycle. Outside high season, rates drop considerably. En-sure the bike is in good working order and the brakes work well.

If you plan to hire a motorcycle or moped, check that your travel insurance does cover you for injury resulting from motorcycle accidents.

## ROAD RULES

While it sometimes appears that there aren't any road rules in Greece, you are apparently supposed to drive on the right and overtake on the left. No casual observer would ever guess that it is compulsory to wear seat belts in the front seats of vehicles, and in the back if they are fitted.

The speed limit for cars is 120km/h on toll roads, 90km/h outside built-up areas and 50km/h in built-up areas. For motor-cycles up to 100cc, the speed limit outside built-up areas is 70km/h and for larger motorbikes, 90km/h. Drivers exceeding the speed limit by 20/40% receive a fine of €60/150.

Drink-driving laws are strict; a blood alcohol content of 0.05% incurs a fine of around €150 and over 0.08% is a criminal offence.

## Local Transport

### BUS

Most Greek towns are small enough to get around on foot. All major towns have local bus systems, but the only place that you'll probably need them are Athens, Kalamata and Thessaloniki.

### METRO

Athens is the only city large enough to war-rant a metro system – and it finally has one. See p284 for details.

### TAXI

Taxis are widely available in Greece and they are reasonably priced. Yellow city cabs are metered. Flag fall is €0.75, followed by €0.24 per kilometre in towns and €0.44 per kilometre outside towns. The rate doubles from midnight to 5am. Additional charges are €1.18 from airports, €0.60 from ports, bus stations and train stations, and €0.30 per luggage item over 10kg.

Taxi drivers in Athens are gifted in their ability to make a little extra with every fare. If you have a complaint, note the cab number and contact the tourist police. In rural areas taxis don't have meters, so make sure you agree on a price with the driver before you get in. Outside Athens, taxi drivers are generally honest, friendly and helpful.

## Train

The main problem with train travel in Greece is that there are only two main lines: to Thessaloniki and Alexandroupolis in the north, and to the Peloponnese. In addition there are a number of branch lines, such as the Pyrgos–Olympia line and the spectacu-lar Diakofto–Kalavryta mountain railway. Be aware that there are two distinct levels of service: the painfully slow, dilapidated trains that stop at all stations, and the faster, modern intercity trains.

Inter-Rail and Eurail passes are valid in Greece, but you still need to make a reser-vation. In summer, make reservations at least two days in advance.

# Spain

**SPAIN**

Take a deep breath before setting foot in Spain. The Spaniards' exuberance for life is infectious; there's probably no better place in Europe to work on your tan *and* party like there's no *mañana*.

A mammoth peninsula jutting out from southern Europe, Spain is home to just about every landscape imaginable, from the deserts of Almería to the rugged peaks of the Pyrenees, from the damp green of Galicia to the sunburned plains of Castile. Add then there are the beaches. Glorious swathes of golden sands, rugged coasts and glittering Mediterranean islands make this country a beach loving, sun worshipper's paradise.

Yes, this is the land of flamenco, fiestas and the Costa del Sol but peer past Spain's tourist-brochure image and you'll find a fascinating country rich in history and culture.

*Mudéjar* buildings in Andalucía and the medieval Jewish temples in Toledo are relics of an era when these cultures lived peaceably in Spain. Move on to the breathtakingly beautiful cathedrals for a glimpse of the Church's tremendous power in this historically Catholic country.

Yet not all of Spain's glory lies in the past. The vibrant nightlife in cities such as Madrid and Barcelona are proof of the country's boundless energy, and international success in art, design and cuisine show that Spain's creative flair is undiminished.

**FAST FACTS**

- **Area** 505,000 sq km
- **Capital** Madrid
- **Currency** euro; US$1 = €; UK£1 = €1.50; Aus$1 = €0.58; ¥100 = €0.76; NZ$1 = €0.83
- **Famous for** sunshine, late nights, bullfighting, *jamón serrano* (cured ham), *Don Quixote*, Pedro Almodóvar films
- **Official Languages** Spanish (Castilian or *castellano*), Catalan, Basque, Galecian *(gallego)*
- **Population** 40.2 million
- **Telephone Codes** country code ☎ 34; international access code ☎ 00
- **Visa** EU, Norway and Iceland citizens do not need a visa; nationals of Australia, Canada, Israel, Japan, New Zealand, Switzerland and the USA need no visa for stays of up to 90 days, but must have a passport valid for the whole visit; South Africans are among nationalities that do need a visa

SPAIN

## HIGHLIGHTS

- Behold the wonderfully weird architecture of **Gaudí** (p378) in Barcelona.
- Meet and greet grand dame **San Sebastián** (p392), with her perfect beaches and tasty tapas.
- Sip a glass of chilled gazpacho under the shade of an orange tree in **Andalucía** (p413).
- Experience the beaches, pine forests and laid-back lifestyle of the luminous **Costa de la Luz** (p429).
- Mooch around white-washed, sangria-fuelled and deliciously decadent **Ibiza** Old Town (p409).

## ITINERARIES

- **One week** Start off in easy-to-reach Barcelona, where you spend two days soaking up Modernist architecture and seaside life before zipping up to graze on *pinxos* in San Sebastián. Take a short side trip to Bilbao's Guggenheim, and end your trip testing your endurance on Madrid's legendary night scene.
- **Two weeks** From Madrid, catch the train to Seville before heading south to Tarifa via Cádiz and the Costa de la Luz. Jump on the bus to Granada and visit the Alhambra, then hop on an overnight train to Valencia before boarding a ferry to the Balearics.

## CLIMATE & WHEN TO GO

Most of Spain is drenched with healthy doses of sunshine year-round, though the rainy north and snowcapped Pyrenees don't always comply. Along the coasts, beach weather begins in late May and lasts through September. In the north, the summer season is a little shorter, while Andalucía's summer often lasts longer.

The Mediterranean coast enjoys mild winters, rarely freezing, but central Spain (Madrid, Ávila, Segovia and around) and the Pyrenees get downright cold. The rains and winds along the Atlantic coasts make winters in Galicia, Cantabria, Asturias and the Basque Country occasionally unpleasant. See Climate Charts p703 for more information.

## HISTORY
### Ancient History

The bridge between Africa and Europe, Spain has always been a meeting point for

### HOW MUCH?

- Leg of Jamón Jabugo €225
- Bottle of Torres wine €9
- Bullfighter's suit €2500
- Camper shoes €120
- Ceramic plate from Andalucía €40

### LONELY PLANET INDEX

- Litre of petrol €0.80
- Litre of bottled water €1.50
- Glass of Spanish beer €1.75
- Souvenir T-shirt €16
- Plate of churros €1.50

peoples and cultures, though not necessarily a peaceful one. North African pioneers first began to settle the peninsula around 8000 BC. In the following millennia, Celtic tribes, Phoenician merchants, Greeks and Carthaginians trickled in. The Romans arrived in the 3rd century BC but took 200 years to subdue the peninsula. Peace was short-lived; by AD 419 the Christian Visigoths had established a kingdom that lasted until 711.

### Muslim Spain & the Reconquista

By 714 Muslim armies had occupied nearly the entire peninsula. Muslim dominion was to last almost 800 years in parts of Spain. In Islamic Spain (known as al-Andalus) arts and sciences prospered, new crops and agricultural techniques were introduced and palaces, mosques, schools, public baths and gardens were built.

In 1085 Alfonso VI, king of León and Castilla, took Toledo, the first definitive victory of the Reconquista (the struggle to wrestle Spain into Christian hands). By the mid-13th century, the Christians had taken most of the peninsula, except for the state of Granada.

In the process, the kingdoms of Castilla and Aragón emerged as Christian Spain's two main powers. In 1469 they were united by the marriage of Isabel, princess of Castilla, and Fernando, heir to Aragón's throne. Known as the Catholic Monarchs, they laid the foundations for the Spanish golden age,

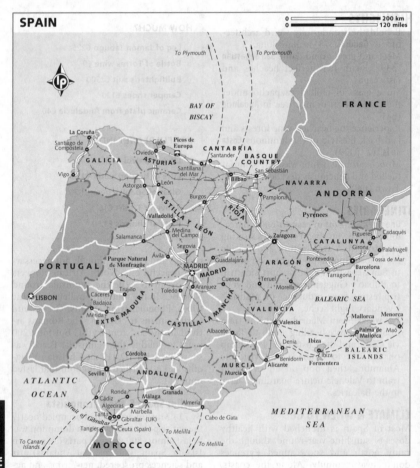

# SPAIN

| 0 | | 200 km |
| 0 | | 120 miles |

To Plymouth    To Portsmouth

*BAY OF BISCAY*

FRANCE

La Coruña
Santiago de Compostela
Vigo
GALICIA
Oviedo
Gijón
Picos de Europa
ASTURIAS
CANTABRIA
Santander
Santillana del Mar
Bilbao
BASQUE COUNTRY
San Sebastián
NAVARRA
Astorga
León
Burgos
Pamplona
ANDORRA
CASTILLA Y LEÓN
Valladolid
Medina del Campo
LA RIOJA
Zaragoza
Pyrenees
Figueres
Cadaqués
CATALUNYA
Girona
Palafrugell
Salamanca
Segovia
Ávila
ARAGÓN
Pontevedra
Tossa de Mar
Barcelona
Parque Natural de Monfragüe
MADRID
Guadalajara
Teruel
Tarragona
PORTUGAL
MADRID
Cuenca
Morella
Cáceres
Trujillo
Toledo
Aranjuez
VALENCIA
BALEARIC SEA
LISBON
Badajoz
Mérida
EXTREMADURA
CASTILLA-LA MANCHA
Valencia
Mallorca
Menorca
Palma de Mallorca
Maó
Albacete
Denia
Ibiza
BALEARIC ISLANDS
Córdoba
Benidorm
Ibiza
Formentera
MURCIA
Alicante
ATLANTIC OCEAN
Seville
ANDALUCÍA
Murcia
Cádiz
Ronda
Granada
Málaga
Almería
MEDITERRANEAN SEA
Algeciras
Marbella
Tarifa
Gibraltar (UK)
Cabo de Gata
Strait of Gibraltar
Tangier
Ceuta (Spain)
To Melilla
To Canary Islands
To Melilla
MOROCCO

but they were also responsible for one of the darkest hours in Spain's history – the Inquisition, a witch-hunt to expel or execute Jews and non-Christians. In 1492 the last Muslim ruler of Granada surrendered to them, marking the end of the Reconquista.

## The Golden Age

Christopher Columbus' so-called discovery of the Americas in 1492 kicked off Spain's golden age. Befuddled Columbus (Colón in Castilian), trying to find a new route to India, stumbled upon the Bahamas, though he never guessed he'd discovered new continents and changed the course of history. His voyages sparked a period of exploration and exploitation that was to yield Spain

enormous wealth, while destroying the ancient American empires. For three centuries, gold and silver from the New World were used to finance the rapid expansion and slow decline of the Spanish empire. By the 18th century, the mighty Spanish empire was on its way out, the life sucked out of it by a series of unwise kings, self-seeking noblemen and unsuccessful wars that left the empire in shambles.

## The 18th & 19th Centuries

The 18th century dawned with a war over the succession to the throne when Carlos II died heirless, but all was soon put right when Felipe V, the first Bourbon king, took control and ushered in a period of stability. Peace would last until the end of the century, when Spain declared war on France and then on Britain and Portugal. The wars proved disastrous, and Spain ultimately lost several colonies and nearly all its sea power.

In 1807–08 Napoleon's forces occupied a weakened Spain, and King Carlos IV abdicated without a fight. In his place Napoleon installed his own brother, Joseph Bonaparte. The Spaniards retaliated with a five-year war of independence, and in 1815 Napoleon was defeated by the Duke of Wellington, who had united with the Portuguese and Spanish troops. A Bourbon, Fernando VII, was restored to the Spanish throne.

Fernando's reign was a disastrous advertisement for monarchy: the Inquisition was re-established, liberals were persecuted, Spain entered a severe recession and the American colonies officially won their independence in 1824. After Fernando's death in 1833 came the First Carlist War (1834–39), which ended with Isabel II, Fernando's daughter, taking the throne. In 1868 the monarchy was overthrown during the Septembrina Revolution and Isabel II was forced to flee from Madrid. The First Republic was declared in 1873, but within 18 months the army had restored the monarchy, with Isabel's son Alfonso XII on the throne. Despite political turmoil, Spain's economy prospered in the second half of the 19th century, fuelled by industrialisation.

The disastrous Spanish-American War of 1898 marked the end of the Spanish empire. Spain was defeated by the USA and lost its last overseas possessions – Cuba, Puerto Rico, Guam and the Philippines.

## The 20th Century

The early 20th century was characterised by growing instability, as anarchists and radicals struggled to overthrow the established order. In 1923, with Spain on the brink of civil war, Miguel Primo de Rivera made himself military dictator, ruling until 1930. In 1931 King Alfonso XIII fled the country and the Second Republic was declared.

Like its predecessor, the Second Republic fell victim to internal conflict. The 1936 elections split the nation in two, with the Popular Front (an uneasy alliance of leftist parties) on one side and the right-wing Nationalists (an alliance of the army, Church and the Fascist-style Falange Party) on the other.

Nationalist plotters in the army rose against the Republican government in July 1936, launching a civil war (1936–39) that would further sink the country in poverty and create bitter wounds that are still healing today. The Nationalists, led by General Francisco Franco, received military support from Nazi Germany and Fascist Italy, while the elected Republican government received support from the Soviet Union and foreign leftists.

The war ended in 1939, with Franco the victor. Some 350,000 Spaniards died in the war, most of them on the battlefield but many others in executions, prison camps or simply from starvation. After the war, thousands of Republicans were executed, jailed or forced into exile, and Franco's 36-year dictatorship began with Spain isolated internationally and crippled by recession. It wasn't until the 1950s and '60s, when the rise in tourism and a treaty with the USA combined to provide much-needed funds, that the country began to recover.

Franco died in 1975, having named Juan Carlos, the grandson of Alfonso XIII, as his successor. Instead of accepting power, King Juan Carlos handed it over to a newly created democratic government, earning the lasting respect of the country. The first elections were held in 1977 and a new constitution was drafted in 1978. Spain joined the European Community (EC) in 1986 and celebrated its return to the world stage in style in 1992, with Expo '92 in Seville and the Olympic Games in Barcelona.

## Spain Today

The modern, forward-thinking Spain of today has long since thrown off the dark cloud of Franco's dictatorship. In 1996 the centre-right Partido Popular (Popular Party; PP), led by José María Aznar, took control of the nation after the long-ruling Socialist party was voted out under accusations of corruption. The PP went on to establish programmes of economic decentralisation and liberalisation, paving the way for economic success.

In 2003 Aznar's government declared its support for the US-led war on Iraq, against

## TOP FIVE SPAIN

■ **Playa Bolonia, Costa de la Luz** – Roman ruins, white sand, windsurfs and chilled out beach bars (p430)

■ **Cabo de Gata, Almeria** – Serene fishing villages, Wild West scenery and soaring temperatures (p424)

■ **L'Estartit, Costa Brava** – Sandy beach with beautiful off-shore islands; wonderful for swimming and scuba diving (p387)

■ **Tarifa, Costa de la Luz** – Bohemian and relaxed, you can see the minarets of Morocco from the Coast of Light (p429)

■ **Formentera, Balearic Islands** – Nudist bathing, bicycling and blissed-out beaches (p411)

the wishes of more than 90% of the Spanish populace. The PP's popularity began to decline, eventually plummeting when it came to light, just days before the 2004 elections, that the PP had misled the Spanish people about the circumstances surrounding the 11 March train bombings in Madrid, leading them to believe ETA was the author of the attack when all along evidence pointed to Al Qaeda. The terrorist bombings killed 200 people.

The Socialist party, led by José Luís Rodríguez Zapatero, was voted into power a few days after the bombings, and newly elected president Zapatero immediately made the call to withdraw Spanish troops from Iraq, a decision applauded by his countrymen. Another plus for Zapatero is the fact that his cabinet is the first in the world to have absolute parity between men and women; there are eight female ministers and eight male ministers.

## PEOPLE

Spain has a population of 40 million, descended from all the many peoples who have settled here over the millennia, among them Iberians, Celts, Romans, Jews, Visigoths, Berbers, Arabs and 20th-century immigrants from across the globe. The biggest cities are Madrid (three million), Barcelona (1.5 million), Valencia (750,000) and Seville (700,000). Each region proudly preserves its

own unique culture, and some – Catalonia and the País Vasco (Basque Country) in particular – display a fiercely independent spirit.

Most Spaniards are economical with etiquette, but this does not signify rudeness. They're gregarious people, on the whole very tolerant and easy-going towards foreigners. It's not easy to give offence. However, obviously disrespectful behaviour, including excessively casual dress in churches and boisterous behaviour in public, won't go down well.

## RELIGION

Only about 20% of Spaniards are regular churchgoers, but Catholicism is deeply ingrained in the culture. As the writer Unamuno said, 'Here in Spain we are all Catholics, even the atheists'.

However, many Spaniards have a deep-seated scepticism about the Church. During the Civil War, anarchists burned churches and shot clerics because they represented repression and corruption. Later, during Franco's rule, church-going was practically obligatory and those who shunned the Church were often treated as outcasts or targeted as delinquents by Franco's police. Understandably, many people began to see the Church as a haven for hypocrites, and the image still hasn't completely worn off.

## ARTS

### Cinema

Classic Spanish directors include Luis Buñuel, whose films include *Un Chien Andalou* (1928), *L'Age d'Or* (1930), *Tierra sin Pan* (Land Without Bread; 1932), Juan Antonio Bardem, who made *Muerte de un Ciclista* (Death of a Cyclist; 1955) and Luis Berlanga, of *Bienvenido Mr Marshall* (Welcome Mr Marshall; 1953) fame.

Modern cinema's best-known director is Pedro Almodóvar, who broke away from the trend that focused only on Franco with humorous films set amid the Movida, the social and artistic revolution of the late 1970s and '80s. Winner of Oscars for *Todo Sobre Mi Madre* (All About My Mother; 1999) and *Habla Con Ella* (Talk to Her; 2002), the wacky, brilliant Almodóvar is Spain's most internationally successful filmmaker.

## Painting

The giants of Spain's golden age (1550–1650) were Toledo-based El Greco (originally from Crete) and Diego Velázquez, perhaps Spain's most revered painter. Both excelled with insightful portraits. The genius of both the 18th and 19th centuries was Francisco Goya, whose versatility ranged from unflattering royal portraits and anguished war scenes to bullfight etchings.

Catalonia was the powerhouse of early-20th-century Spanish art, claiming the hugely prolific Pablo Picasso (although he was born in Andalucía), the colourful symbolist Joan Miró and surrealist Salvador Dalí. Important artists of the late 20th century include Catalan abstract artist Antoni Tàpies and Basque sculptor Eduardo Chillida. Works by these and other major Spanish artists can be found in galleries throughout the country.

## Architecture

Spain's earliest architectural relics are the prehistoric monuments on Menorca. Reminders of Roman times include the ruins of Mérida and Tarragona, and Segovia's amazing aqueduct. The Muslims left behind some of the most splendid buildings in the entire Islamic world, including Granada's Alhambra, Córdoba's awe-inspiring Mezquita and Seville's Alcázar – the latter an example of *Mudéjar* architecture, the name given to Islamic work done throughout Christian-held territory.

The first main Christian architectural movement was Romanesque. Surviving manifestations include countless lovely country churches and several cathedrals, notably that of Santiago de Compostela. Later came the many great Gothic cathedrals (such as Toledo, Barcelona, León, Salamanca and Seville) of the 13th to 16th centuries, as well as Renaissance styles such as the plateresque work so prominent in Salamanca. Spain then followed the usual path to baroque (17th and 18th centuries) and neoclassicism (19th century), before Catalonia produced its startling modernist (roughly Art Nouveau) movement around the turn of the 20th century, of which Antoni Gaudí's Sagrada Família church is the most stunning example.

## Literature

One of the earliest works of Spanish literature is the *Cantar de Mío Cid* (Song of My Cid), an anonymous epic poem describing the life of El Cid, an 11th-century Christian knight buried in the Burgos cathedral. Miguel de Cervantes' novel *Don Quixote de la Mancha* is the masterpiece of the literary flowering of the 16th and 17th centuries, as well as one of the world's great works of fiction. The playwrights Lope de Vega and Pedro Calderón de la Barca were also leading lights of the age.

The next high point, in the early 20th century, grew from crisis: the Spanish-American War that spawned the intellectual Generation of '98. Philosophical essayist Miguel de Unamuno was prominent, but the towering figure was poet and playwright Federico García Lorca, who won international acclaim before he was murdered in the civil war for his Republican sympathies.

Camilo José Cela, author of the civil war–aftermath novel *La Familia de Pascal Duarte* (The Family of Pascal Duarte), won the 1989 Nobel Prize for literature. Contemporary author Juan Goytisolo is one of the country's premier writers; his most approachable work is his autobiography, *Forbidden Territory*. There has been a proliferation of women – particularly feminist writers – during the past 25 years, among whose prominent representatives are Ana María Matute, known for her novels on the civil war, such as *Los Hijos Muertos* (The Lost Children), and Rosa Montero, known for works such as *Historias de Mujeres* (Stories of Women).

## Flamenco

Getting to see real, deeply emotional flamenco can be hard, as it tends to happen semispontaneously in little bars. Andalucía is its traditional home and you'll find plenty of clubs there and elsewhere offering flamenco shows; these are generally aimed at tourists and are expensive, but some are good. Your best chance of catching the real thing is probably at one of the flamenco festivals in the south, usually held in summer. You'll also find quality *tablaos* (flamenco stages) in Madrid and throughout Andalucía.

## ENVIRONMENT

Spain is probably Europe's most geographically diverse country, with landscapes ranging from the near-deserts of Almería to the green, Welsh-like countryside and deep coastal inlets of Galicia, and from the sunbaked plains of Castilla-La Mancha to the rugged mountains of the Pyrenees.

Nearly 5000km of coastline rings the country with even more scenic variety. Spain's shore encompasses the rocky cliffs of the Costa Brava, the endless sandy beaches of the Costa de Luz and the pounding Atlantic waves of the Basque Country.

The country covers 84% of the Iberian Peninsula and spreads over some 505,000 sq km, more than half of which is high tableland (meseta). This is supported and divided by several mountain chains, making Spain Europe's second-hilliest country, after Switzerland. The main mountains are the Pyrenees, along the border with France; the Cordillera Cantábrica, backing the northern coast; the Sistema Ibérico, from the central north towards the middle Mediterranean coast; the Cordillera Central, from north of Madrid towards the Portuguese border; and three east-west chains across Andalucía, one of which is the highest range of all – the Sierra Nevada.

The major rivers are the Ebro, Duero, Tajo (Tagus), Guadiana and Guadalquivir, each draining a different basin between the mountains and all flowing into the Atlantic Ocean (except for the Ebro, which reaches the Mediterranean Sea).

The brown bear, wolf, lynx and wild boar all survive in Spain, although only the boar exists in abundance; farmers delight in shooting and roasting the tasty pest. Spain's high mountains harbour the goat-like chamois and Spanish ibex (the latter is rare) and big birds of prey such as eagles, vultures and the lammergeier. The marshy Ebro delta and Guadalquivir estuary are important for water birds, among them the spectacular greater flamingo. Many of Spain's 5500 seed-bearing plants occur nowhere else in Europe, due to the barrier of the Pyrenees. Spring wild flowers are magnificent in many country and hilly areas.

The conservation picture has improved by leaps and bounds in the past 25 years and Spain now has 25,000 sq km of protected areas, including 10 national parks. However, overgrazing, reservoir creation, tourism, housing developments, agricultural and industrial effluent, fires and hunting all still threaten plant and animal life.

# FOOD & DRINK
## Specialties
It's a good idea to reset your stomach's clock in Spain, unless you want to eat alone or with other tourists. Most Spaniards start the day with a light *desayuno* (breakfast), perhaps coffee with a *tostada* (piece of toast) or *pastel* (pastry). *Churros con chocolate* (long, deep-fried dough with hot chocolate) are a delicious start to the day and unique to Spain.

*Almuerzo* or *la comida* (lunch) is usually the main meal of the day, eaten between about 1.30pm and 3.30pm. The *cena* (evening meal) is usually lighter and may be eaten as late as 10pm or 11pm; meals out with friends may well last until 1am or later. It's common to go to a bar or café for tapas around 11am and again around 7pm or 8pm.

Spain has a huge variety of local cuisines, and each region has its speciality. One of the most characteristic dishes, from the Valencia region, is paella – rice, seafood, the odd vegetable and often chicken or meat, all simmered together and traditionally coloured yellow with saffron. Another dish, of Andalucían origin, is gazpacho, a cold soup made from tomatoes, breadcrumbs, cucumber and green peppers. Tortillas are an inexpensive stand-by snack and come in many varieties. *Jamón serrano* (cured ham) is a delicacy for meat eaters.

## Drinks
Start the day with a strong coffee, either as a *café con leche* (half-coffee, half-milk), *café solo* (short black, espresso-like) or *café cortado* (short black with a little milk.)

The most common way to order a beer *(cerveza)* is to ask for a *caña,* which is a small draught beer. In the Basque country this is called a *zurrito*. A larger beer (about 300mL) is often called a *tubo,* or (in Catalonia) a *jarra*. All these words apply to draught beer *(cerveza de barril)* – if you just ask for a *cerveza* you're likely to get bottled beer, which is more expensive.

*Vino (*wine) comes in *blanco* (white), *tinto* (red) or *rosado* (rosé). Exciting wine regions include Penedès, Priorat and Ribera del Duero. *Tinto de verano,* a kind of wine shandy, is good in summer. There are also plenty of regional grape specialties, such as *jerez* (sherry) in Jerez de la Frontera and *cava* (a sparkling wine) in Catalonia.

SPAIN

### I'LL HAVE FISH WITH THAT....

The Spanish are the most voracious fish eaters in Europe. With nearly 5000km of Atlantic and Mediterranean coastline, it's hardly surprising that seafood features so widely on the menu. Yet even the landlocked citizens of Madrid, more than 300km from the coast, are the most passionate seafood aficionados of them all – so much so that the catch of the day usually hits the Madrid fish markets still flapping.

The Spaniards' annual consumption of seafood clocks in at a staggering 36.6kg per capita, that's more than double the European average. Stroll into any tapas bar or taverna, or even better that seafood-lovers favourite the *marisquería,* and you'll be greeted with a fish and shellfish menu as long as your arm.

All the regions and cities have their own speciality from Malaga's *fritura de pescado* to the fat pink prawns adorning Valencia's famous paella. Among the universal favourites are *boquerones* (fresh anchovies – munched whole); *sardina* (fresh sardines) *gambas* (shrimp or prawns of varying sizes); *lenguado* (sole); *salmonete* (red mullet); *merluza* (hake), *besugo* (red bream); *rodaballo* (turbot); *pez espada* (swordfish); *aguja* (needlefish) and *rape* (monkfish). Not forgetting, of course, those tentacled denizens of the deep the *calamares* (squid) and *pulpo* (octopus). All of them can be grilled, baked, basted and fried like nowhere else in the world. A common boast claims that it is possible to eat fish every day of the year in Spain without ever having the same dish twice.

If trying to decide which of this lot you want on your dinner plate leaves your tastebuds, bewildered, plump for the fish of the day or better still ask the person propping up the bar next to you for advice. The Spaniards' enthusiasm for all things fishy means they are the most courteous guides to their fabulous seafood cuisine.

Sangría, a sweet punch made of red wine, fruit and spirits, is refreshing and very popular with tourists in summer.

*Agua del grifo* (tap water) is usually safe to drink but it may not be very tasty in cities or near the coast. *Agua mineral con gas* (sparkling mineral water) and *agua mineral sin gas* (still mineral water) cost about €1 for a small bottle.

### Where to Eat & Drink

Bars and cafés are open all day, serving coffees, pastries, *bocadillos* (long sandwiches) and usually tapas, which cost around €2. In the evenings these same bars fill with regulars looking for a quick beer or glass of house wine. Groups can order *raciónes,* a large-sized serving of these snacks; a *media ración* is half a *ración.* You can often save 10% to 20% by ordering and eating food at the bar rather than at a table.

Self-caterers will be delighted with Spain's fresh-produce markets, which you'll find near the centre of just about every city and town. Load up on colourful veggies, fresh bread and Spanish cheeses.

Spaniards like to eat out, and restaurants abound even in small towns. At lunch time, most places offer a *menú del dia* – a fixed-price lunch menu and the budget traveller's

best friend. For €7 to €12 you typically get three courses, bread and a drink. The *plato combinado* (combined plate) is a cousin of the *menú* and usually includes a meat dish and a couple of side dishes. Check out the crowd before sitting down; if it's full of locals, that's a good sign. If all the diners speak English, you may want to head elsewhere.

After dinner, you can head to a *bar de copas* (pub), where hard drinks are pretty much the only thing on offer.

### Vegetarian Food

Vegetarians may have to be creative in Spain. Though in larger cities and important student centres there's a growing awareness of vegetarianism, traditional restaurants often offer salads and egg tortillas, but little else for noncarnivores. Even salads may come laden with sausages or tuna. Pasta and pizza are readily available, as is seafood.

# MADRID

**pop 3.09 million**

Madrid's role as the capital of Spain and administrative headquarters of the country requires it to be somewhat austere and serious-faced; yet anyone who's been here

SPAIN

SPAIN

---

**GETTING TO THE COAST FROM MADRID**

**By Train** Renfe trains (www.renfe.es) trains link Madrid's Atocha station with Málaga (for the Costa del Sol, €54, 4½ hours, seven daily), Valencia (for the Costa Blanca, €37, 3½ hours, 13 daily) and Barcelona (for the Costa Brava, €59, 4¾ to 5½ hours, eight daily). Prices given are for oneway, 2nd-class journeys.

**By Bus** There are many bus stations and companies operating in Madrid, offering a number of services to destinations all over the country. However from the Estación Sur de Autobuses you can catch buses to Málaga (Daibus buses, €18.48, six hours, 10 daily), Alicante (ALSA buses, €23.12, 5¼, hours, 8 daily) and Barcelona (ALSA buses, €23.55, seven to eight hours, 15 daily).

**By Car** Madrid is a hub from which most of the country's major roads radiate out to the coast. The N-11 wends its way northeast to Barcelona (621km), the N-1V/A-4 goes south to Andalucía (at Balién, shortly after entering Andalucía, fork south on the N-323/A-44 for Jaén, Granada, Almería or Málaga or keep going southwest on the N-IV/A-4 for Córdoba, Seville, Huelva or Cádiz, from Granada to Málaga take the A-92, A-359 and then N-331/A-45; 544km) and the A-3 goes east to Valencia (352km).

---

on a Friday night knows that few cities let down their hair like Madrid. Plan to check out the anything-goes nightlife, but save energy for visits to the city's amazing art museums and busy historic centre.

## HISTORY

Madrid was little more than a muddy, mediocre village when King Felipe II declared it Spain's capital in 1561. The obvious choice for the capital was nearby Toledo, but Felipe didn't like the fact that the stuck-up clergy already had the upper hand there, so no-name Madrid took the prize.

The city was a squalid grid of unpaved alleys and dirty buildings until the 18th century, when King Carlos III turned his attention to public works. Madrid grew in spurts, and it wasn't until the early 20th century that it began to take on the look of a proper capital.

The post–civil war 1940s and '50s were trying times for the capital, with poverty being a given for many people. Nowhere was Franco's thumb as firmly pressed down as on Madrid, and the city lived under a blanket of fear and forced austerity for nearly four decades. When the dictator died in 1975 the city exploded with creativity and life, giving Madrileños the party-hard reputation they still cherish.

## ORIENTATION

In Spain's case, all roads lead to Madrid and, more specifically, to the Puerta del Sol – kilometre zero – the physical and emotional heart of the city. Radiating out from this harried plaza are the main arteries – Calle Mayor, Calle Arenal, Calle Preciados, Calle Montera and Calle Alcalá – that stretch into the city.

South of Puerta del Sol is the oldest part of the city, with the Plaza Mayor to the southwest and the busy streets of the Huertas district to the southeast. North of the plaza is a modern shopping district and, beyond that, the east-west thoroughfare Gran Vía and the bohemian barrio Chueca. To the east is the stately Palacio Real, while to the west lies the city's green lung, El Retiro.

## INFORMATION
### Bookshops

**La Casa del Libro** (Map pp354-5; ☎ 91 524 19 00; Gran Vía 29; metro Gran Vía; 9.30am-9.30pm Mon-Fri, 11am-9pm Sun) Spain's answer to Barnes & Noble has a large English- and foreign-language literature section.

**Petra's International Bookshop** (Map pp354-5; ☎ 91 541 72 91; Calle Campomanes 13; metro Ópera or Santo Domingo; 11am-9pm Mon-Sat) A lively expat community hosts conversation groups in this English bookshop.

### Emergency

**Ambulance** ☎ 061
**Medical & Fire** ☎ 112
**Police** ☎ 091
**Red Cross** ☎ 91 522 22 22

### Internet Access

**Nets** (Map p356; ☎ 91 522 20 17; Calle Palma 24; noon-1am Mon-Sat, noon-midnight Sun; per hr €1.50; metro Tribunal) To just skim email, you can log on for up to five minutes for free.

**Work Center** (Map pp354-5; ☎ 91 360 13 95; Calle Príncipe 1; ⏱ 24hr; per hr €2; metro Sevilla)

## Laundry
**Lavandería Cervantes** (Map pp354-5; ☎ 91 429 92 16; Calle León 6; ⏱ 9am-9pm; per load €2; metro Antón Martín)

## Medical Services
**Anglo-American Medical Unit** (Map p356; ☎ 91 435 18 23; Calle Conde de Aranda 1; metro Retiro) For medical help in English.
**Farmacia del Globo** (Map pp354-5; ☎ 91 369 20 00; Plaza Antón Martín 46; metro Antón Martín) For help with minor medical problems, ask a pharmacist. This is one of several 24hr pharmacies.

## Money
Large banks such as Caja de Madrid usually have the best rates, but check commissions. Banks usually open from 8.30am to 2pm Monday to Friday and, during winter, to 1pm on Saturday. Using your ATM card will usually give you these same low bank rates, no matter where or what time of day you use it.

If you're desperate, there are plenty of *bureaux de change* around Puerta del Sol and Plaza Mayor, which have the predictable rip-off rates but are often open until midnight.

## Post
**Post Office** (Map p356; ☎ 91 396 24 43; Plaza Cibeles; ⏱ 8.30am-9.30pm Mon-Sat; metro Banco de España) In the gigantic Palacio de Comunicaciones.

---

### MADRID IN TWO DAYS

Start your time in Madrid with breakfast in the **Plaza de Santa Ana** (p360) and then ensure a visit to the **Museo del Prado** (p353). Afterwards, walk around **El Retiro** (p358) but make sure you save energy for the **Palacio Real** (p357), afternoon shopping and mandatory tapas in **Chueca** (p360). At night, catch a **flamenco show** (p362).

On day two, sign up for the tourist office's **walking tour** (p358) of historic Madrid, and then visit either the **Museo Thyssen-Bornemisza** (p357) or the **Reina Sofía** (p357) art museums. At night, head to **Viva Madrid** (p362) for drinks in uniquely *madrileño* style.

---

## Tourist Information
**Municipal tourist office** (Map pp354-5; ☎ 91 366 54 77; www.munimadrid.es; Plaza Mayor 3; ⏱ 10am-8pm Mon-Sat, 10am-3pm Sun; metro Sol)
**Regional tourist office** (Map pp354-5; ☎ 91 429 49 51 or 902 10 00 07; www.madrid.org; Calle Duque Medinaceli 2; ⏱ 9am-7pm Mon-Sat, 9am-3pm Sun; metro Sevilla)

## DANGERS & ANNOYANCES
Madrid is not a dangerous city but you need to constantly be aware of pickpockets, especially in touristy areas like Plaza Mayor (where thieves are astonishingly brash), Huertas and Chueca.

Prostitution (and the slimy clients it attracts) along Calle Montera and in the Casa del Campo park means that you need to exercise extra caution in these areas. Females walking alone should try not to linger here, even if you're just looking at a map, as it could give the wrong idea.

## SIGHTS & ACTIVITIES
Madrid's big three (the outstanding Prado, Reina Sofía and Thyssen-Bornemisza museums) should be the first things on your to-do list. If you still have energy left after soaking up the majestic art on display here, the city's monasteries, palace and luscious gardens promise to keep you busy for days. For information about even more museums and sights, ask at the tourist office (above).

### Museo del Prado
The **Prado** (Map p356; ☎ 91 330 28 00; http://museo prado.mcu.es; Paseo del Prado s/n; metro Banco de España; adult/child €3.01/1.50; ⏱ 9am-7pm Tue-Sun) is not just the best-known museum in Madrid, it's one of the most elite art collections in the world. The main emphasis is on Spanish, Flemish and Italian art from the 15th to 19th centuries, with generous coverage of Spanish greats Goya, Velázquez and El Greco.

Velázquez's masterpiece *Las Meninas* is one of the museum's prized works. This painting depicts maids of honour attending the daughter of King Felipe IV, and Velázquez himself painting portraits of the queen and king (through whose eyes this scene is witnessed).

Virtually the whole southern wing of the 1st floor is given over to Goya. His portraits include the pair *Maja Desnuda* and *Maja*

SPAIN

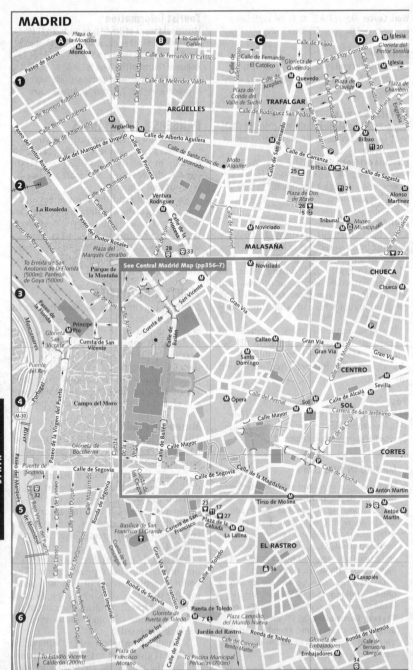

# MADRID

**A** Plaza de la Moncloa
Moncloa

To Galileo Galilei

**B**

**C**

**D** Iglesia
Glorieta del Pintor Sorolla
Iglesia

Paseo de Moret

Calle de Feijoo

Calle de Fernando El Católico

Calle de Fernando El Católico
Glorieta de Quevedo

Calle de Eloy Gonzalo

Calle de Hilarión Eslava

Calle de Guzmán

Calle de Valleherrno

Quevedo

Calle de Juan de Austria

Plaza de Chamberí

**1**

Calle de Meléndez Valdés

Plaza del Conde del Valle de Suchil

Calle de Arapiles

Plaza de Olavide

Calle de Luchana

Calle de Santa Engracia

Calle Romero Robledo

ARGÜELLES

TRAFALGAR

Calle de Cardenal Cisneros

Bilbao

**20**

Calle Benito Gutiérrez

Argüelles

Calle de Alberto Aguilera

Calle de Rodríguez San Pedro

Calle de San Bernardo

Bilbao

Calle de Sagasta

Calle de Altamirano

Calle del Marqués de Urquijo

Calle de Santa Cruz de Marcenado

Moto Alquiler

Calle de Carranza

25

Bilbao

**24**

Calle de Fuencarral

Paseo del Pintor Rosales

Calle Buen Suceso

Calle de la Princesa

**2**

H

**21**

Alonso Martínez

La Rosaleda

Calle de Quintana

Ventura Rodríguez

Plaza de Dos de Mayo

26

**5**

Tribunal

Museo Municipal

Paseo del Rey

Paseo del Pintor Rosales

Calle de Ferraz

Calle de la Princesa

Calle del Tutor

Calle de Amaniel

Noviciado

MALASAÑA

Calle de Hortaleza

**22**

Paseo de la Rosaleda

Plaza del Marqués Cerralbo

28

33

To Ermita de San Antonio de la Florida (500m); Panteón de Goya (500m)

Parque de la Montaña

**See Central Madrid Map (pp356-7)**

Noviciado

CHUECA

Chueca

**3**

Calle de Irún

San Vicente

Gran Vía

Paseo de la Florida

Príncipe Pío

Cuesta de San Vicente

Cuesta de la Vega

Calle de Bailén

Callao

Gran Vía

Gran Vía

Gran Vía

P

Manzanares

Glorieta San Vicente

Cuesta de San Vicente

Santo Domingo

Calle de la Montera

Campo del Moro

Calle del Arenal

CENTRO

**4**

M-30

Portugal

Paseo de la Virgen del Puerto

Ópera

Sol

Sevilla

Calle de Alcalá

River

Glorieta de Boccherini

Calle Mayor

SOL

Carrera de San Jerónimo

Calle de la Cruz

Puente del Rey

Paseo de Marqués

Puente de Segovia

Calle de Segovia

Calle de Bailén

Calle Mayor

CORTES

**32**

Cuesta de la Vega

P

Calle de Atocha

Paseo Bajo Virgen del Puerto

Calle de Segovia

Calle de la Magdalena

Antón Martín

**5**

Calle Linneo

Calle Juan Duque

Ronda de Segovia

Cuesta de los Ciegos

Tirso de Molina

29

Antón Martín

Basílica de San Francisco El Grande

23 17

27

Plaza de la Cebada

La Latina

EL RASTRO

Lavapiés

Calle de Toledo

Gran Vía de San Francisco

Carrera de San Francisco

**36**

Ronda de Segovia

Calle de los Mancebos

Vía Inferior al Paseo Imperial

Paseo Imperial

Glorieta de Puerta de Toledo

Puerta de Toledo

Plaza Campillo del Mundo Nuevo

**6**

Calle Juan Duque

Puerto de Toledo

**7**

Jardín del Rastro

Ronda de Toledo

Glorieta de Embajadores

Ronda de Valencia

Calle de Bernardino Obregón

To Estadio Vicente Calderón (200m)

Plaza de Francisco Morano

Calle del Concejal Benito Martín

To Piscina Municipal Peñuelas (700m)

Embajadores

**34**

SPAIN

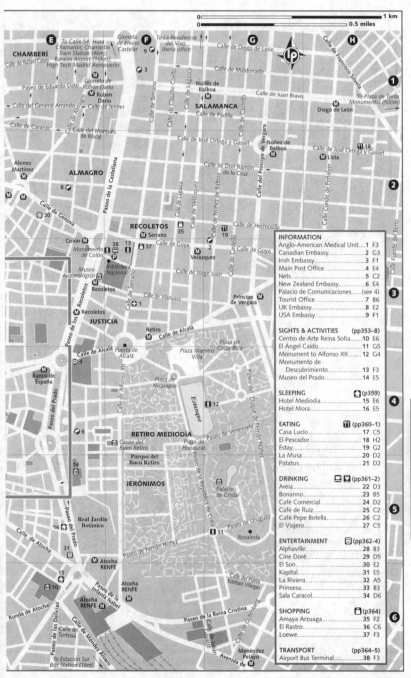

SPAIN

# CENTRAL MADRID

SPAIN

0        300 m
0        0.2 miles

**A** **B** **C** **D** **E** **F**

Jardines de
Ferraz

Jardines de
Sabatini

Calle de Arriaza

Calle del Cadarso

Calle de Ferraz

Plaza de
España

Plaza de
España

Jardines de
las Vistillas

Jardines de
Emir Mohamed I

Parque del
Emir Mohamed I

Plaza del
Alamillo

Plaza de la
Cruz Verde

Cuesta de San Vicente

Calle del Río

Plaza de
la Marina
Española

Calle de la Marina
Española

Calle Princesa

Calle de Isabel
la Católica

Calle Leganitos

Calle del Formento

Plaza de
Mostenses

Calle de la Luna

Calle de San Bernardo

Calle de la Estrella

Plaza de
Santa María
la Soledad

Plaza de
Santo
Domingo

Calle de
Jacometrezo

Calle de Silva

Calle Miguel
Moya

Plaza de
San Roque

Calle del Barco

Calle de la Ballesta

Calle del Pez

Calle Molino
Torrero

Calle San
Onofre

Calle de Valverde

Calle de Fuencarral

Calle de Hernán
Cortés

Calle de Augusto Figueroa

Calle de la Palma

Calle de San Bartolomé

CHUECA

Plaza de
Chueca

Calle de San
Gregorio

Calle de San
Marcos

Calle de la Libertad

Calle de Gravina

Calle Piamonte

Calle de Prim

Calle del Almirante

Calle de Barquillo

Calle de Fortuny

Ministerio
del Ejército

To German Embassy
(900m); Portuguese
Embassy (1.1km); UK
Embassy (1km); French
Embassy (870m); Dutch
Embassy (2.5km)

Ministerio
de Cultura

Calle del Marqués
del Valdeiglesias

Plaza de
Cibeles

Banco de
España

Banco de
España

Banco de
España

Banco de
España

Paseo del Prado

Plaza de
Neptuno
(Cánovas
del Castillo)

Calle del Duque
de Medinaceli

Plaza del
Rey

Calle de las Infantas

Calle del Caballero de Gracia

Gran Vía

Gran Vía

Sevilla

Sevilla

Calle de Alcalá

Calle de Sevilla

Calle de Alcalá

Calle de Arlabán

Carrera de San Jerónimo

Plaza de
las Cortes

Plaza de
Canalejas

Calle del Príncipe

Calle de Cedaceros

Calle de Manuel
Fernández y González

Calle del Prado

CORTES

Plaza de
Santa Ana

Calle de las Huertas

Calle de Jesús

Plaza del
Infante

Calle de Atocha

Calle del Duque
de Medinaceli

Calle de Jovellanos

Calle de Echegaray

Calle de Lope de Vega

Plaza de
Jesús

Calle de Cervantes

Antón
Martín

Calle de las Huertas

Calle del León

Calle de
Relatores

Calle de Atocha

Calle del Doctor
Cortezo

Calle del Conde
de Romanones

Calle de la Colegiata

Calle de
San Sebastián

Calle de la Cruz

Calle de la
Bolsa

Plaza de
Jacinto
Benavente

Plaza
Mayor

Calle Mayor

Calle de Toledo

Calle de los
Cuchilleros

Cava de
San Miguel

Plaza de
San Miguel

Plaza de
San Tomás

Calle de la Concepción
Jerónima

Calle de Esparteros

Sol

Sol

Sol

Puerta del
Sol

Calle del
Correo

Calle Mayor

Calle de Postas

Calle del Arenal

Plaza de
Celenque

Calle de Preciados

Gran Vía

Callao

Plaza del
Callao

Calle de Preciados

Calle del Carmen

Tetuán

Calle de la Montera

Calle de Jardines

Red de
San Luis

Calle de la Abada

Calle de Chinchilla

Callao

Plaza de
San Martín

Calle de la
Aduana

Travesía
Trujillos

Calle de las Hileras

Calle de las Fuentes

Calle del Espejo

Calle de Donados

Plaza de
Herradores

Plaza de la
Encarnación

Jardines
Cabo Noval

Plaza de
Oriente

Jardines del
Cabo Noval

Plaza de
Ramales

Plaza de
Isabel II

Opera

Calle de
Escalinata

Plaza de
San Miguel

Plaza del
Comandante
las Morenas

Calle de
Carlos III

Calle de
Campomanes

Calle de
Torija

Calle del Fomento

Plaza de
la Encarnación

Calle de Bailén

Calle de Requena

Calle del Factor

Calle Mayor

Calle de la Villa

Calle del Sacramento

Plaza del
Conde
de Miranda

Plaza del Conde
de Barajas

Calle de Segovia

Plaza de la
Paja

Calle del Nuncio

Costanilla de San Pedro

Travesía del
Almendro

Calle del
Almendro

Calle de
Bailén

Señores de
Luzón

Plaza de la
Villa

Calle de
la Cruz Verde

Calle de Segovia

Gran Vía

Calle Caballero de Gracia

Plaza de
Oriente

Calle de Bailén

SOL

CENTRO

Calle de la Virgen
de los Peligros

Calle de los
Madrazo

Carrera de San Jerónimo

**1** **2** **3** **4**

| | |
|---|---|
| **INFORMATION** | |
| Farmacia Globo | 1 E4 |
| Internet Centre | 2 E3 |
| La Casa del Libro | 3 D2 |
| Lavandería Cervantes | 4 E4 |
| Municipal Tourist Office | 5 C4 |
| Petra's International Bookshop | 6 B2 |
| Police Station | 7 D3 |
| Police Station | 8 E3 |
| Regional Tourist Office | 9 F4 |
| UK Consulate | 10 F1 |
| Work Center | 11 E3 |
| **SIGHTS & ACTIVITIES** | (pp353–8) |
| Armería Real | 12 A3 |
| Ayuntamiento | 13 B4 |
| Casa de Cisneros | 14 B4 |
| Catedral de Nuestra Señora de la Almudena | 15 A3 |
| Convento de las Trinitarias | 16 E4 |
| Farmacia Real | 17 A3 |
| Iglesia de San Ginés | 18 C3 |
| Iglesia de San Pedro | 19 B4 |
| Monasterio de las Descalzas Reales | 20 C2 |
| Museo Thyssen-Bornemisza | 21 F3 |
| Palacio Real | 22 A3 |
| **SLEEPING** | (pp358–60) |
| Catalonia Moratín | 23 D4 |
| Hostal Aguilar | 24 E3 |
| Hostal Cruz Sol | 25 C3 |
| Hostal Don Juan | 26 E1 |
| Hostal El Catalan | 27 E1 |
| Hostal Internacional La Posada de Huertas | 28 E4 |
| Hostal La Macarena | 29 C4 |
| Hostal La Zona | 30 D1 |
| Hostal Madrid | 31 C3 |
| Hostal María Cristina | 32 D1 |
| Hostal Martín | 33 D4 |
| Hostal Orly | 34 D2 |
| Hostal San Lorenzo | 35 E2 |
| Hostal Triana | 36 D2 |
| Hotel HH Campomanes | (see 40) |
| Hotel Intur Palacio San Martín | 37 C2 |
| Hotel Miau | 38 E4 |
| Hotel Plaza Mayor | 39 C4 |
| Los Amigos Backpackers' Hostel | 40 B2 |
| **EATING** | (pp360–1) |
| Ángel Sierra | 41 E1 |
| Bazaar | 42 E1 |
| Comme Bio | 43 C3 |
| Cuevas El Secreto | 44 D3 |
| La Casa del Abuelo | 45 D3 |
| La Chata | 46 B4 |
| La Finca de Susana | 47 E3 |
| La Gloria de Montera | 48 D2 |
| La Mallorquina | 49 D3 |
| La Trucha | 50 D3 |
| Las Bravas | 51 D4 |
| Lhardy | 52 D3 |
| Mercado de San Miguel | 53 B4 |
| Omertá | 54 E1 |
| Sobrino de Botín | 55 C4 |
| Stop Madrid | 56 D1 |
| Wokcafé | 57 E2 |
| **DRINKING** | (pp361–2) |
| Café del Nuncio | 58 B4 |
| Café del Prado | 59 E4 |
| Casa Alberto | 60 E4 |
| Cervecería Alemana | 61 E4 |
| Chocolatería de San Ginés | 62 C3 |
| Del Diego | 63 E2 |
| Finnegan's | 64 F1 |
| Los Gabrieles | 65 E4 |
| Mamá Inés | 66 E1 |
| Matador | 67 D4 |
| Museo Chicote | 68 E2 |
| Taberna de Dolores | 69 F4 |
| Viva Madrid | 70 E4 |
| Why Not? | 71 E1 |
| **ENTERTAINMENT** | (pp362–4) |
| Café Acuarela | 72 E1 |
| Café Central | 73 D4 |
| Cardamomo | 74 E3 |
| Casa Patas | 75 D4 |
| Cool | 76 B1 |
| Ducados Café | 77 E3 |
| El Sol | 78 D2 |
| Las Tablas | 79 A1 |
| Ohm | 80 C2 |
| Palacio Gaviria | 81 C3 |
| Populart | 82 E4 |
| Teatro Albéniz | 83 D3 |
| Teatro Calderón | 84 D4 |
| Teatro de la Comedia | 85 E3 |
| Teatro de la Zarzuela | 86 E3 |
| Teatro Joy Eslava | 87 C3 |
| Teatro Real | 88 B3 |
| **SHOPPING** | (p364) |
| A Different Life | 89 E1 |
| Divina Providencia | 90 D1 |
| El Corte Inglés Department Store | 91 D3 |
| Gil | 92 D3 |
| José Ramírez | 93 D4 |
| Justo Algaba | 94 D3 |
| Librería Desnivel | 95 E4 |
| Mercado de Fuencarral | 96 D1 |
| **OTHER** | |
| Localidades Galicia | 97 D2 |

*Vestida;* legend has it that the woman depicted here is the Duchess of Alba, Spain's richest woman in Goya's time. Goya was commissioned to paint her portrait by her husband and ended up having an affair with her, so painted an extra portrait for himself. In room 39 are Goya's masterpieces depicting the horrors of the Spanish War of Independence (1808–14). There are more Goya works on the ground floor.

Other well-represented artists include El Greco, the Flemish masters Hieronymus Bosch and Pieter Paul Rubens, and the Italians Tintoretto, Titian and Raphael.

Guided visits are available; ask for details at the ticket booth.

## Centro de Arte Reina Sofía

A fantastic collection of modern, predominantly Spanish art, the **Centro de Arte Reina Sofía** (Map p356; ☎ 91 467 50 62; http://museoreinasofia.mcu.es; Calle Santa Isabel 52; metro Atocha; admission €3.01, free Sat 2.30-9pm & Sun; 10am-9pm Mon-Sat, 10am-2.30pm Sun) showcases Spanish contemporary culture. The exhibition includes Picasso's famous *Guernica,* his protest at the German bombing of the Basque town of Guernica during the Spanish Civil War in 1937.

The museum also contains further works by Picasso, as well as works by surrealist Salvador Dalí and the remarkably simple paintings of Joan Miró.

## Museo Thyssen-Bornemisza

Sitting just opposite the Prado, the **Thyssen-Bornemisza** (Map pp354-5; ☎ 91 369 01 51; Paseo del Prado 8; metro Banco de España; adult/child €4.80/3; 10am-7pm Tue-Sun) is a themeless collection of priceless works, offering one of the most comprehensive art-history lessons you'll ever have. Starting with medieval religious art, it moves on through Titian, El Greco and Rubens to Cézanne, Monet and Van Gogh, then from Miró, Picasso and Gris to Pollock, Dalí and Lichtenstein. Formerly the private collection of the German-Hungarian family of magnates, the Thyssen-Bornemiszas, the collection was purchased by Spain in 1993 for a mere US$300 million.

## Palacio Real

Madrid's 18th-century **Palacio Real** (Map pp354-5; ☎ 91 542 00 59; Calle Bailén s/n; metro Ópera; adult/child €9/3.50; 9.30am-5pm Mon-Sat, 9am-2pm Sun Oct-Mar, 9am-6pm Mon-Sat, 9am-3pm Sun Apr-Sep) is a lesson in what can happen if you give your interior decorators a free hand. You'll see some of the most elaborately decorated walls and ceilings imaginable, including the sublime Throne Room (and other rooms of more dubious merit). This over-the-top palace hasn't been used as a royal residence for some time and today is used only for official receptions and, of course, tourism.

Shuffle through the official tour to see a good selection of Goyas, 215 absurdly ornate clocks from the Royal Clock Collection and five Stradivarius violins, still used for concerts and balls. Most of the tapestries in the palace were made in the Royal Tapestry Factory (10 minutes southeast of the Atocha train station), and all the chandeliers are original and absolutely unique.

Outside the main palace you can also see the **Farmacia Real** (Royal Pharmacy), an unending array of medicine jars and stills for mixing royal concoctions, and the **Armería Real** (Royal Armoury), a shiny collection of mostly 16th- and 17th-century weapons and royal suits of armour.

### Monasterio de las Descalzas Reales

This ornate **monastery** (Convent of the Barefoot Royals; Map pp354–5; ☎ 91 542 00 59; www.patrimonionacional.es; Plaza de las Descalzas; metro Sol; adult/child €5/2.50; ⏱ 10.30am-12.45pm & 4-5.45pm Tue-Thu & Sat, 10.30am-12.45pm Fri, 11am-1.45pm Sun) was founded in 1559 by Juana of Austria, daughter of Spain's King Carlos I, and became one of Spain's richest religious houses thanks to gifts from noblewomen. Much of the wealth came in the form of art; on the obligatory guided tour you'll be confronted by a number of tapestries based on works by Rubens and a wonderful painting entitled *The Voyage of the 11,000 Virgins*.

### Panteón de Goya

Home to Goya's *panteón* (tomb), the **Ermita de San Antonio de la Florida** ( ☎ 91 542 07 22; Glorieta San Antonio de la Florida 5; metro Príncipe Pío; admission free; ⏱ 10am-2pm & 4-8pm Tue-Fri, 10am-2pm Sat & Sun), 500m east of the Príncipe Pío metro, is one of the artist's greatest works. The entire ceiling and dome is beautifully painted with religious scenes. The images on the dome depict the miracle of St Anthony.

### Parque del Buen Retiro

A Sunday stroll in **El Retiro** (Map p356; metro Retiro; ⏱ 7am-midnight summer, 7am-10pm winter) is as much

a Madrid tradition as tapas and *terrazas* (terrace cafés). Time it right and you may even catch a puppet show during summer.

Walk along **Paseo de las Estatuas**, a path lined with statues originally from the Palacio Real. It ends at a lake (Estanque) overlooked by a **statue of Alfonso XII**. There are rowing boats for rent at the northern end. Also search out the **El Ángel Caído** (The Fallen Angel), the first ever statue dedicated to the devil, and gardens such as **La Rosaleda** (rose garden).

### Campo del Moro

This stately **garden** is directly behind the Palacio Real, and the palace is visible through the trees from just about all points. A couple of fountains and statues, a thatch-roofed pagoda and a carriage museum provide artificial diversions, but nature is the real attraction.

## TOURS

The tourist office (p353) organises English-language **walking tours** ( ☎ 902 221 622; adult/child €3/2.50) around the centre of Madrid. You can reserve tickets by telephone or simply show up at the main tourist office on Plaza Mayor 15 minutes before the tour begins. One of the most popular walks is 'Madrid of the Court', a tour of the old quarter starting 10am Saturday. Other tour times vary with the season, so check with the office before you make your plans.

## FESTIVALS & EVENTS

Madrid takes its partying seriously, and festive events are generously sprinkled over the year's calendar. Look out for:

**Día de los Reyes** (Three Kings' Day, Jan 6) The three kings bring gifts to children and a mammoth parade takes over the city centre.

**Fiesta de San Isidro** (May 15) Madrid's patron saint is honoured with nonstop processions, parties and bullfights.

**Fiesta de Otoño** (mid-Oct through mid-Nov) Music, dance and theatre take over Madrid during the fantastically cultural weeks of the Autumn Festival.

## SLEEPING

You're spoiled for choice in Madrid. The city is packed with hotels and *hostales* (cheap hotels) of all shapes and sizes, but booking ahead is always a good idea and may be necessary in summer or during holidays.

Budget accommodation (we mean doubles €50 and under) includes informal youth hostels, cheap *pensiones* (guesthouses) and slightly more upscale *hostales*. Even in this category many places offer private bathrooms and TVs in the rooms. Mid-range (doubles €51 to €90) are more comfortable and usually offer a touch of charm. Top-end hotels (doubles from €91) include everything from business-style three-stars to rooms worthy of royalty.

## Los Austrias & Centro
### BUDGET
**Los Amigos Backpackers' Hostel** (Map pp354-5; ☎ 91 547 17 07; www.losamigoshostel.com; Calle Campomanes 6, 4th fl; metro Oriente; dm with shared bathroom €15; ▣) Clean, friendly and English-speaking, this is one of the city's best budget options. Cheerful, well-kept rooms have four to 10 bunk beds and free lockers.

**Hostal Orly** (Map pp354-5; ☎ 91 531 30 12; 7th fl, Calle Montera 47; metro Gran Vía; s/d/tr with shared bathroom €29/39/51) In a grand 19th-century building, this quiet hostel is excellent value (especially room No 11). Rooms are cheerful, with tall ceilings and wooden floors.

Also recommended:
**Hostal Triana** (Map pp354-5; ☎ 91 532 68 12; www.hostaltriana.com; 1st fl, Calle Salud 13; metro Gran Vía; s/d €35/47; ▣) Tidy rooms with bathroom.
**Hostal Cruz Sol** (Map pp354-5; ☎ 91 532 71 97; www.hostalcruzsol.com; 3rd fl, Plaza Santa Cruz 6; metro Sol; s/d €38/48; ▣) Cheery. Great location.

### MID-RANGE
**Hotel Plaza Mayor** (Map pp354-5; ☎ 91 360 06 06; www.h-plazamayor.com; Calle Atocha 2; metro Sol or Tirso de Molina; s/d €48/70) Original elements of this 150-year-old building have been left intact, while the décor itself is stylish. Great value.

**Hostal La Macarena** (Map pp354-5; ☎ 91 365 92 21; macarena@silserranos.com; Cava San Miguel 8; metro Ópera; s/d €57/70) Near Plaza Mayor, this charming *hostal* is one of the best in the barrio. Rooms are quiet and welcoming.

**Hostal Madrid** (Map pp354-5; ☎ 91 522 00 60; www.hostal-madrid.info; 2nd fl, Calle Esparteros 6; metro Sol; s €50-58, d/tr €70/88; ▣) Rooms here are simple, with rustic décor and fully equipped bathrooms. The owner also rents apartments.

### TOP END
**Hotel HH Campomanes** (Map pp354-5; ☎ 91 548 85 48; www.hhcampomanes.com; Calle Campomanes 4; metro Oriente; s €77-99, d €87-111; ▣▣) The ultimate in minimalism, with black walls and red

lighting in the lobby. Rooms are spacious, with high ceilings and simple furniture.

**Hotel Intur Palacio San Martín** (Map pp354-5; ☎ 91 701 50 00; www.intur.com; Plaza San Martín 5; metro Callao; s €109-165, d €109-204; ▣▣) Set on a picturesque plaza and housed in the former US embassy, this hotel offers simple luxury.

## Sol, Huertas & Atocha
### BUDGET
**Hostal Internacional La Posada de Huertas** (Map pp354-5; ☎ 91 429 35 26; www.posadadehuertas.com; Calle Huertas 21; metro Antón Martín; dm with shared bathroom from €16) This simple youth hostel offers dorm-style rooms with metal beds and lockers. Though the place is clean, with warm blankets and decent (if tiny) bathrooms, it rates a zero on the charm scale.

**Hostal Aguilar** (Map pp354-5; ☎ 91 429 59 26; www.hostalaguilar.com; Carrera San Jerónimo 32, 2nd fl; metro Sol; s/d/tr with shared bathroom €40/47/63; ▣) Tacky décor but pluses include the double-glazed, noise-blocking windows and a computer offering Internet access for €3 per hour.

### MID-RANGE
**Hotel Mediodia** (Map p356; ☎ 91 527 30 60; fax 91 530 70 08; Plaza Emperador Carlos V 8; metro Atocha; s/d/tr €54/64/82; ▣) Just across from Atocha station, this attractive hotel is perfect if you're arriving on a late train.

**Hotel Mora** (Map p356; ☎ 91 420 15 69; Paseo del Prado 32; metro Atocha; s/d €57/75; ▣) Near the main museums, this simple hotel offers great value. Rooms are a bit sparse but some overlook the Real Jardine Botanico (botanical gardens).

**Hostal Martín** (Map pp354-5; ☎ 91 429 95 79; www.hostalmartin.com; Calle Atocha 43; metro Antón Martín; s €36-58, d €45-70; ▣) This fine *hostal* is luminous and sparklingly clean, with a look you'd expect to see in a two- or three-star hotel.

### TOP END
**Hotel Miau** (Map pp354-5; ☎ 91 369 71 20; www.hotelmiau.com; Calle Príncipe 26; metro Sol or Antón Martín; s/d with breakfast €88/98; ▣▣) A boutique hotel overlooking the Plaza Santa Ana. Rooms are airy but can be noisy.

**Catalonia Moratín** (Map pp354-5; ☎ 91 369 71 71; www.hoteles-catalonia.es; Calle Atocha 23; metro Antón Martín; s/d €136/177; ▣▣) Housed in a meticulously restored 18th-century palace, this is a charming place to stay in Madrid. Rooms are rustic-chic, with pretty balconies.

SPAIN

## Malasaña & Chueca

**Hostal Don Juan** (Map pp354-5; ☎ 91 522 77 46; 2nd fl, Plaza Vazquez de Mella 1; metro Gran Vía; s/d €34/48) This elegant *hostal* is filled with art (each room has original works) and antique furniture. Rooms are simple but luminous.

**Hostal La Zona** (Map pp354-5; ☎ 91 521 99 04; www.hostallazona.com; 1st fl, Calle Valverde 7; metro Gran Vía; d €45-65) Catering to gay clientele, rooms are simple but stylish and very well kept. Spacious room 203 is one of the best.

**Hostal San Lorenzo** (Map pp354-5; ☎ 91 521 30 57; www.hostal-lorenzo.com; Calle Clavel 8; metro Gran Vía; s €45-50, d €55-65, tr €75-90; ✹ ) The original stone walls of this 19th-century building have been left exposed, adding unique character. Renovated in 2003, rooms are small but modern.

Also recommended:

**Hostal El Catalan** (Map pp354-5; ☎ 91 532 30 17; Calle Hortaleza 17, 2nd fl; metro Gran Vía; s €27-30, d/tr €42/54) Clean, quiet, good value.

**Hostal Maria Cristina** (Map pp354-5; ☎ 91 531 63 00; www.iespana.es/hostalmariacristina; Calle Fuencarral 20; metro Gran Vía; s/d/tr €32/44/62) Friendly. Lots of light.

## Beyond the Centre

**Husa Chamartín** ( ☎ 91 334 49 00; www.hotelchamartin .com; Calle Augustín de Foxá; metro Chamartín; s €60-111, d €60-130; ✹ ⌨ ) A great option if you're arriving late to the Chamartín train station; rooms have all the comforts.

**High Tech Madrid Aeropuerto** ( ☎ 91 564 59 06; www.hthoteles.com; Calle Galeón 25; metro Aeropuerto; s €100-135, d €120-150; Ⓟ ✹ ⌨ ⊠ ) Within shouting distance of the airport (it provides free airport transport), the High Tech has stylish rooms, free Internet access and an outdoor pool.

**La Residencia del Viso** ( ☎ 91 564 03 70; www.resid enciadelviso.com; Calle Nervión 8; metro Republica Argentina; s €77-103, d €129; ✹ ) Northeast of the centre, this quiet little city oasis has rooms that look rather like a favourite aunt's guest quarters.

## EATING

Madrid's culinary specialties include *cochinillo asad* (roast suckling pig) and *cocido madrileño*, a hearty stew made of beans and various animals' innards (it's tasty, honest). Snacky tapas range from olives and potato chips to sausages, tortillas and grilled meat on a stick. At this point, vegetarians may be questioning what local cuisine has to offer them: not very much, it's true. Look out

for pastas, salads and *bocadillos vegetales* (vegetable sandwiches), which usually have cheese.

Lunch hour runs from about 1.30pm to 3.30pm, and dinner starts at 9pm and lasts until late – any variance in these general opening hours will be stated in reviews. Before meal times, many Madrileños head out for a *caña* and a tapas or two.

## Tapas

Before lunch, before dinner, before the club, after the club...anytime is a good time for tapas! Heading into La Latina, you'll find oodles of tapas bars.

**La Casa del Abuelo** (Map pp354-5; ☎ 91 521 23 19; Calle Victoria 12; metro Sol) Taste the garlicky prawns (€4.35) at this famous bar in the centre of town.

**Las Bravas** (Map pp354-5; ☎ 91 532 26 20; Calle Espoz y Mina 13; metro Sol) Head to this caféteria-style joint known for its patented version of the classic Spanish *salsa brava*, a spicy sauce slathered over fried potatoes, tortillas and even seafood.

**La Chata** (Map pp354-5; ☎ 91 366 14 58; Calle Cava Baja 24; metro La Latina) Enjoy the great cheese plate (€11) and bullfighter-themed décor.

**Angel Sierra** (Map pp354-5; ☎ 91 531 01 26; Calle Gravina 11; metro Chueca) Munchers at this Chueca classic spill onto the Plaza de Chueca with their tapas and drinks.

**Stop Madrid** (Map pp354-5; ☎ 91 521 88 87; Calle Hortaleza 11; metro Gran Vía) Known for its *jamón serrano*.

## Cafés

**Salon del Prado** (Map pp354-5; ☎ 91 429 33 61; Calle Prado 4; metro Antón Martín) Curl up with a tea and a book at the elegant Prado, just off Plaza de Santa Ana.

**Café Comercial** (Map p356; ☎ 91 521 65 55; Glorieta de Bilbao 7; metro Bilbao) You can get a mean coffee and plenty of ambience here.

**Café de Ruiz** (Map p356; ☎ 91 446 12 32; Calle Ruiz 11; metro Bilbao) The cosy Ruiz looks like it was lifted out of a 1930s movie, with marble tables, velvet-covered seats and a welcoming attitude.

**Mamá Inés** (Map pp354-5; ☎ 91 523 23 33; www .mamaines.com; Calle Hortaleza 22; metro Chueca) In Chueca, this romantic place is popular with gay men. By day, get yummy pastries and all the gossip on where that night's hot spot will be.

SPAIN

## Restaurants

### LOS AUSTRIAS & CENTRO

**La Mallorquina** (Map pp354-5; ☎ 91 521 12 01; Puerta del Sol 8; metro Sol; pastries around €1.50) Start the day sweet here, where a throng of white-jacketed waiters serve up pastries, truffles and candies.

**La Gloria de Montera** (Map pp354-5; ☎ 91 523 44 07; Calle Caballero de Gracia 10; metro Gran Vía; menú €6.60) For sit-down fare, there's no beating this place. It's oh-so-stylish, oh-so-cheap and oh-so-popular.

**Sobrino de Botín** (Map pp354-5; ☎ 91 366 42 17; Calle Cuchilleros 17; metro La Latina; mains €11-18) The oldest restaurant in Madrid couldn't be more atmospheric. The delicious speciality is roast suckling pig.

### SOL, HUERTAS & ATOCHA

**Cuevas El Secreto** (Map pp354-5; ☎ 91 531 82 91; Calle Barcelona 2; metro Sol; mains €4-8; ☯ 6.30pm-2am; ☯ 6.30pm-2am;) A tavern serving tasty grilled meat and a few basic tapas. Everything is fresh and served with style, but it's refreshingly cheap.

**La Finca de Susana** (Map pp354-5; ☎ 91 369 35 57; Calle Arlaban 4; metro Sevilla; menú €7) This well-known place is priced right, serving a mix of Spanish and international fare to a professional crowd.

**La Trucha** (Map pp354-5; ☎ 91 532 0890; Calle Núñez de Arce 6) For fish, traditional dishes and tasty tapas, head to this classic.

**Lhardy** (Map pp354-5; ☎ 91 522 22 07; Carrera San Jerónimo 8; metro Sevilla; mains €12-20) Just as emblematic as La Trucha but with a more elegant touch, Lhardy has been in business since 1839.

### LA LATINA & LAVAPIÉS

**Casa Lucio** (Map p356; ☎ 91 365 32 52; Calle Cava Baja 35; metro La Latina; mains €9-18) Popular with politicians, the traditional Casa Lucio is famous for its *huevos rotos*, fried eggs served runny over potatoes.

### MALASAÑA & CHUECA

**Patatus** (Map p356; ☎ 91 532 6129; Calle Fuencarral 98; metro Bilbao; €9-16) Open late and where you go after hours for cheap, filling fare.

**Bazaar** (Map pp354-5; ☎ 91 523 39 05; Calle Libertad 21; metro Chueca; menú €7) For more formal meals, this funky fusion is a great bet for Mediterranean-style dishes with an international flair.

**Omertà** (Map pp354-5; ☎ 91 701 02 42; Calle Gravina 17; metro Chueca; menú €7.50) Bare brick walls and a tall ceiling give Omertà the feel of an old warehouse, though the friendly service and piping-hot square pizzas prove its worth as a pizzeria.

**Wokcafé** (Map pp354-5; ☎ 91 422 90 69; Calle Infantas 44; metro Sevilla; ☯ closed Sun) This chic Chinese-fusion restaurant lives by the motto *sexy y sano* (sexy and healthy). The romantic atmosphere and light dishes live up to the claim.

### SALAMANCA & VENTAS

**Estay** (Map p356; ☎ 91 578 04 70; Calle Hermosilla 46; metro Velázquez; tapas €2-5; ☯ 9-1am) 'Fine dining in miniature' is the claim to fame here. In food terms that means tiny tapas-like dishes of yummy things such as foie gras with raspberry sauce, and zucchini stuffed with shrimp.

**El Pescador** (Map p356; ☎ 91 402 12 90; Calle José Ortega y Gasset 75; metro Núñez de Balboa; mains €10-18) High-end but worth a splurge, this is one of the city's best spots for seafood.

## DRINKING

Bars are something Madrid has plenty of, and finding your favourite shouldn't take long. For traditional style, wander the streets of Huertas. For gay-friendly locales, Chueca is the place. Malasaña caters to a grungy, funky crowd, while La Latina has friendly, no-frills bars that guarantee atmosphere every night of the week. In summer, head to the outdoor cafés in the city's plazas.

Although many bars are open all day, functioning alternately as breakfast cafés, luncheon spots and bars, the night-time crowd starts showing up by 8pm for pre-dinner drinks. The mood really gets rolling around midnight, and the bars all close by about 3am on weekends, or 2am on weekdays.

### LOS AUSTRIAS, CENTRO & LA LATINA

**Café del Nuncio** (Map p356; ☎ 91 366 09 06; Calle Segovia 9; metro La Latina) Straggling down a stairway passage to Calle Segovia, Nuncio has several cosy levels inside and an outdoor *terraza*.

**Chocolatería San Ginés** (Map pp354-5; ☎ 91 365 65 46; Pasadizo San Ginés 5; metro Sol or Ópera) You've got to end the night at this mythic bar at least once – it's famous for its freshly fried *churros* and syrupy hot chocolate.

SPAIN

**El Viajero** (Map p356; ☎ 91 366 90 64; Plaza Cebada 11; metro La Latina) If you wander down and around the Calle Cava Baja there are myriad options such as this one, where you can get an informal dinner downstairs (tapas €3.50 to €8) or head to the bar upstairs, which has a fantastic rooftop terrace.

### SOL, HUERTAS & ATOCHA

**Casa Alberto** (Map pp354-5; ☎ 91 429 93 56; www .casaalberto.es; Calle Huertas 18; metro Antón Martín) Since 1827 Madrileños have been getting their vermouth from the lovely Casa Alberto. Stop by on Sunday for a traditional prelunch apéritif.

**Cervecería Alemana** (Map pp354-5; ☎ 91 429 70 33; Plaza Santa Ana 6; metro Antón Martín or Sol; ⌚ closed Aug) Another classic, this place is renowned for its cold, frothy beers and delicious tapas. It was one of Hemingway's haunts, and the wood-lined bar seemingly hasn't changed since his day.

**Los Gabrieles** (Map pp354-5; ☎ 91 429 62 61; Calle Echegaray 17; metro Sevilla) For a bit of Andalucían flavour, try this tile-covered bar, where you can catch midweek flamenco shows.

**Matador** (Map pp354-5; ☎ 91 531 89 81; Calle Cruz 39; metro Sol) A smoky, dark bar, this is the spot for soulful flamenco music and a totally unpretentious crowd.

**Viva Madrid** (Map pp354-5; ☎ 91 429 36 40; www .barvivamadrid.com; Calle Manuel Fernandez y González 7; metro Sol) Tapas and beer are the staples at this colourful landmark. The beautifully tiled bar is sure to earn oohs and ahs.

### MALASAÑA & CHUECA

One of the liveliest nightlife areas of Madrid, gay-friendly Chueca and let-it-all-hang-loose Malasaña are packed with bars.

**Areia** (Map p356; ☎ 91 310 03 07; www.areiachillout .com; Calle Hortaleza 92; metro Chueca) There's no better place to chill out than this restaurant-cum-bar, where an Arabian vibe dominates the décor and chill-out music drifts up to the rafters.

**Café Pepe Botella** (Map p356; ☎ 91 522 43 09; Calle San Andrés 12; metro Bilbao or Tribunal) This funky bar has cosy velvet benches and marble-topped tables that give it a quirky charm.

**Museo Chicote** (Map pp354-5; ☎ 91 532 67 37; Gran Vía 12; metro Gran Vía) A city classic popular with socialites and film stars, the Museo Chicote has a lounge atmosphere late at night and a stream of famous faces all day.

**Finnegan's** (Map pp354-5; ☎ 91 310 05 21; Plaza Salesas 9; metro Chueca; ⌚ 1pm-2am) The friendliest pub in town, this Irish haven is full of regulars who'll make you feel at home.

## ENTERTAINMENT

The entertainment bible is the *Guía del Ocio*, a weekly magazine sold at newsstands for €1. Highlights are given in English at the back. The best gay guide is *Shanguide*, which you can pick up free in bars around town.

### Cinemas

Several movie theatres are huddled around Gran Vía and Calle Princesa. For a selection of original-version flicks in this area, head to **Princesa** (Map p356; ☎ 91 541 41 00; Calle Princesa 3; metro Plaza España) or **Alphaville** (Map p356; ☎ 91 559 38 36; Calle Martín de los Heros 14; metro Plaza de España).

The National Film Library offers fantastic classic and vanguard films at **Cine Doré** (Map p356; ☎ 91 549 00 11; Calle Santa Isabel 3; metro Antón Martín).

### Gay & Lesbian Venues

Chueca is Madrid's lively, gay-friendly neighbourhood, and you'll find gay and lesbian bars and clubs on nearly every street. Some of the bigger-name gay dance clubs are along Gran Vía.

**Ohm** (Map pp354-5; ☎ 91 541 35 00; Plaza Callao 4; metro Callao) The weekend party hosted by Sala Bash, Ohm is a hit on the gay and straight scenes.

**Cool** (Map pp354-5; ☎ 91 542 34 39; Calle Isabel la Católica 6; metro Santo Domingo) One of Madrid's swankier clubs, Cool guarantees a sexy night for a well-heeled crowd.

**Café Acuarela** (Map pp354-5; ☎ 91 522 21 43; Calle Gravina 10; metro Chueca) For something low-key, head to this quiet bar.

### Live Music

#### FLAMENCO

Madrid is a good place to see professional interpretations of this Andalucían art. Most shows are set up like a dinner theatre and are squarely aimed at tourists, but the quality is generally top-notch.

**Casa Patas** (Map pp354-5; ☎ 91 369 04 96; www .casapatas.com; Calle Cañizares 10; metro Antón Martín; admission about €30; ⌚ noon-5pm & 8pm-3am, shows 10.30pm Mon-Thu, 9pm & midnight Fri & Sat) One of

SPAIN

the best *tablaos* in the city, this is a great place to see passionate dancing and get in a good dinner too.

**Las Tablas** (Map pp354-5; ☎ 91 542 05 20; Plaza España 9; metro España; admission €12-15; ☷ from 7pm, show 10.30pm) Less established (but far cheaper) than other *tablaos*, this intimate spot is nevertheless a great place to see a variety of flamenco styles.

### JAZZ

**Café Central** (Map pp354-5; ☎ 91 369 41 43; www .cafécentralmadrid.com; Plaza del Angel 10; metro Antón Martín; admission €10-12; ☷ 1.30pm-2.30am Sun-Thu, to 3.30am Fri & Sat, shows nightly at 10pm) This Art Deco bar is worth a visit on its own, but the live shows, which range from classic jazz to Latin, fusion or tango-style jazz, are what has made it one of the most popular bars in the city.

**Populart** (Map pp354-5; ☎ 91 429 84 07; www .populart.es; Calle Huertas 22; metro Antón Martín or Sol; admission free; ☷ 6pm-2.30am Mon-Thu, to 3.30am Fri & Sat, shows nightly at 11pm) Get here early if you want a seat because this smoky, atmospheric jazz bar is always packed with fans yearning for some soothing live jazz.

**Calle 54** ( ☎ 91 561 28 32; Paseo de la Habana 3; metro Nuevos Ministerios) Just north of the centre, this has got to be the best Latin jazz in Madrid, an ultra-cool club and restaurant started by film maker Fernando Trueba.

### ROCK

**Sala Caracol** (Map p356; ☎ 91 527 35 94; Calle Bernardino Obregón 18; metro Embajadores) A temple to variety, this club hosts a different style every night of the week.

**Galileo Galilei** ( ☎ 91 534 75 57; Calle Galileo 100; metro Islas Filipinas) This city classic, just north of Argüelles, has been known to stage everything from comedy acts to magic shows, though its strength is up-and-coming bands.

**La Riviera** (Map p356; ☎ 91 365 24 15; Paseo Bajo de la Virgen del Puerto; metro Puerta del Ángel) A club and concert venue all in one, La Riviera has a pretty Art Deco interior and open-air concerts in summer.

### Clubs & Discos

There's no barrio in Madrid without a decent club or disco, but the most popular dance spots are along and around Gran Vía. For some intimate dancing, head to Chueca

or Malasaña, especially the Calle Palma, which is lined with quirky clubs.

Club prices vary wildly, but most charge between €8 and €12, though you can get discounts for arriving early or if you're a girl (sorry guys). Keep your eyes open for discount tickets given out in bars or on the street. Most places, dancing starts at around 1am and lasts until daybreak. Come Thursday through Saturday for the best atmosphere.

**El Sol** (Map pp354-5; ☎ 91 532 64 90; Calle Jardines 3; metro Gran Vía) For guaranteed great dancing on weekends, check out this popular club near Gran Via.

**Palacio Gaviria** (Map pp354-5; ☎ 91 526 60 69; Calle Arenal 9; metro Sol) This palace-turned-club is atmospheric but pricier than most. Thursday is international student night.

**Teatro Joy Eslava** (Map pp354-5; ☎ 91 366 37 33; www.joy-eslava.com; Calle Arenal 11; metro Sol or Ópera) An old theatre that's now got a new lease on life and has become one of Madrid's more popular clubs, this is a great place to meet people.

**El Son** (Map pp354-5; ☎ 91 532 32 83; Calle Victoria 6; metro Sol). Here you'll find the best Latino grooves. There are live shows Monday through Thursday.

**Kapital** (Map p356; ☎ 91 420 29 06; Calle Atocha 125; metro Atocha) If you can't make up your mind about dance styles, this seven-storey mega disco is the place for you. Every floor offers a different mood.

## Sport

### FOOTBALL

Madrid's three major football clubs and accompanying delirious fans are a guarantee that football fever runs high in the city. The mythic Real Madrid plays at the **Santiago Bernabéu Stadium** (Map p356; ☎ 91 398 43 00; www .realmadrid.com; Calle Concha Espina 1; metro Santiago Bernabéu; ☷ 10.30am-6.30pm except day after game), and the also-celebrated Atlético de Madrid plays at the **Vicente Calderón Stadium** (Map p356; ☎ 91 366 47 07; www.at-madrid.com; Calle Virgen del Puerto; metro Pirámides). Though it's no match for these first-division teams, the Rayo Vallecano also plays in the city.

Get tickets (€10 and up) from box offices or through agents such as **Localidades Galicia** (Map pp354-5; ☎ 91 531 27 32 or 629 21 82 91; Plaza Carmen 1; metro Sol; ☷ 9.30am-1pm & 4.30-7pm Tue-Sat).

### BULLFIGHTING

Some of Spain's top *matadores* (bullfighters) swing their capes in **Plaza de Toros de Las Ventas** (Map p356; ☎ 91 356 22 00; www.las-ventas .com; Calle Alcalá 237; metro Ventas), the largest ring in the bullfighting world. You can see them every Sunday afternoon from mid-May through October, when fights are held in the plaza.

Get tickets (from €3.60 in the sun, from €6.60 in the shade) at the plaza box office or at official ticket agents along the Calle Victoria.

## Theatre & Opera

Madrid has a lively cultural scene, with concerts and shows going on throughout the city.

**Teatro Albéniz** (Map pp354-5; ☎ 91 531 83 11; Calle Paz 11; metro Sol) Staging both commercial and vanguard drama, this is just one of Madrid's quality theatres. For more listings, check out the *Guía del Ocio* or local newspapers.

**Teatro Real** (Map pp354-5; ☎ 91 516 06 06; www .teatro-real.com; Plaza Oriente; metro Ópera) Madrid's opulent opera house, this is the city's grandest stage. Here you can see opera, dance or theatre, depending on the offerings.

**Teatro de la Zarzuela** (Map pp354-5; ☎ 91 524 54 00; Calle Jovellanos 4; metro Banco de España) Come here for *zarzuela*, a very Spanish mixture of dance, music and theatre.

## SHOPPING

For artisan goods and typically Spanish items, explore the maze of streets in Huertas and Los Austrias. Alternative, offbeat fashion is found in Chueca; this lively barrio is also a magnet for shoe shops – there are a dozen of them along and around Calle Augusto Figueroa. Roam Calle Fuencarral and Calle Hortaleza for funky clothing stores.

The glitziest shopping district is Salamanca, where all the designer labels show off for drooling window shoppers. This is also the district to find top art, antique and furniture galleries.

**José Ramírez** (Map pp354-5; ☎ 91 531 42 29; Calle Paz 8) Find handmade guitars at this family-run shop. There's a small museum of old guitars in the back.

**Justo Algaba** (Map pp354-5; ☎ 91 523 35 95; Calle Paz 4) The place to buy authentic bullfighters' suits; everything from capes to those sexy pink tights.

**Gil** (Map pp354-5; ☎ 91 521 25 49; Carrera San Jerónimo 2) Spanish shawls and veils are the speciality at this historic shop.

**Divina Providencia** (Map pp354-5; ☎ 91 522 02 65; Calle Fuencarral 45) At Divina you'll find fun clothes for women, with lots of retro and Asian styles.

**Mercado de Fuencarral** (Map pp354-5; ☎ 91 521 41 52; Calle Fuencarral 45) Clubbers should head to this small mall, where at least half the clothes on sale have silver studs or leather accents.

**Loewe** (Map p356; ☎ 91 426 35 88; Calle Serrano 34) One of Spain's classiest fashion labels, Loewe is the place for leather handbags and accessories.

**Amaya Arzuaga** (Map p356; ☎ 91 426 28 15; Calle Lagasca 50) Also top end but rather less austere, this shop has sexy, bold options for women.

**El Rastro** (Map p356; metro La Latina; ⏰ 8am-3pm Sun) The city's main market, El Rastro is a throbbing mass of vendors, browsers, buyers and pickpockets. The madness begins at the Plaza Cascorro and worms its way downhill along the Calle Ribera Curtidores and the streets branching off it.

**El Corte Ingles** (Map pp354-5; ☎ 91 418 88 00) Spain's enormous department store has branches all over the city and sells everything from food and furniture to clothes, appliances and toiletries. It's truly one-stop shopping.

## GETTING THERE & AWAY
### Air

Madrid's international **Barajas Airport** ( ☎ 902 35 35 70), 16km northeast of the city, is a busy place, with flights coming in from all over Europe and beyond.

Most national flights are run by **Iberia** ( ☎ 902 40 05 00; www.iberia.com; Calle Velázquez 130); find the best deals on its website.

### Bus

Though there are several bus stations dotted around the city, most out-of-town buses use the **Estación Sur** ( ☎ 91 468 42 00; Calle Méndez Álvaro; metro Méndez Álvaro). The largest bus company here is **Alsa** ( ☎ 902 42 22 42; www.alsa.es), north of the city.

### Car & Motorcycle

If you arrive by car, be prepared to face gridlocked traffic. The city is surrounded by three ring roads, the M-30, M-40 and brand-new M-50 (still not 100% completed). You'll likely be herded onto one of these, which in turn give access to the city centre.

Car rental companies abound in Madrid; most have offices both at the airport and in town. See p442 for more information.

### Train

**Renfe** ( ☎ 902 24 02 02; www.renfe.es) trains connect Madrid to just about every other point in Spain. The two main rail stations are Atocha, south of the centre; and Chamartín, to the north. Both *cercanías* (regional trains) and long-distance trains pass through these stations. For ticket information, visit the Renfe offices inside the stations.

## GETTING AROUND
### To/From the Airport

The metro (line 8) zips you into the city from the airport's terminal two. The 12-minute trip to the Nuevos Ministerios station costs €1.15; from there, you can easily connect to all other stations.

There's also an airport bus service that makes a run to the Plaza de Colón every 10 minutes. The trip takes 30 minutes and costs €2.50.

A taxi ride to the centre should cost about €20 and the trip takes around 20 minutes.

### Car & Motorcycle

Public transport in Madrid is excellent, so having a car or motorcycle is not usually necessary. If you do have a car, be prepared to face plenty of traffic and high parking prices. Public parking is available in the city centre; a big white 'P' on a blue sign denotes a car park.

Driving around the Plaza Mayor and the centre is especially challenging, as several roads dive underground and following them can be tricky.

### Public Transport

Madrid's extensive **metro** (www.metromadrid .es) can get you to just about any corner of the city. It's quick, clean, relatively safe and runs from 6am until 2am.

The bus system is also good, but working out the maze of bus lines can be a challenge. Contact **EMT** ( ☎ 914 06 88 10; www.emtmadrid.es) for more information.

### Taxi

Madrid's taxis are inexpensive by European standards. They're handy late at night, although in peak hours it's quicker to walk or get the metro. Flag fall is €1.55, after which you are charged by time, so avoid rush hour.

# CASTILLA Y LEÓN

The huge region of Castilla y León is splashed across the Spanish heartland. This is the fabled Spain of castles, knights and strong stone bridges, a hilly landscape that's home to some of the country's most historic towns and prettiest architecture.

## ÁVILA

Its old town huddled behind pristine medieval walls, Ávila is a remarkable, romantic city perfect for simply strolling and soaking up history. The city is most proud of its claim as the birthplace of Santa Teresa, a mystical writer and reformer of the Carmelite order.

### Information

**Cybernet** ( ☎ 92 035 23 52; Ave de Madrid 25; per hr €2.50; ⏲ 11.30am-2.30pm & 4.30pm-1am)
**Post Office** ( ☎ 92 031 35 06; Plaza de la Catedral 2; ⏲ 8.30am-8.30pm Mon-Fri, 9.30am-2pm Sat)
**Tourist Office** ( ☎ 92 021 13 87; www.avilaturismo.com; Plaza de la Catedral 4; ⏲ 9am-2pm & 5-8pm 15 Sep-Jun, 9am-8pm Sun-Thu, 9am-9pm Fri & Sat Jul-Sep 14) In summer, there are also information kiosks set up at the Renfe train station and just outside the Puerta de San Vincente.

### Sights

A walk along the top of Ávila's splendid 12th-century **walls** (murallas; ☎ 92 021 13 87; admission €3.50; ⏲ 11am-5.15pm winter, 10am-7.15pm summer) should be at the top of your list of things to do. More than 1km of wall-top is open to the public, though it's divided into two sections broken up by the cathedral. Made of 2500 turrets and 88 towers, Ávila's walls are some of the best-preserved in Spain.

Embedded into the eastern city walls, the **cathedral** ( ☎ 92 021 16 41; Plaza de la Catedral; admission €3; ⏲ 10am-5pm Mon-Fri, noon-5pm Sat & Sun Nov-Mar, until 7pm Mar-Oct) is the first Gothic church in Spain. It boasts rich walnut choir stalls and a long, narrow central nave that makes the soaring ceilings seem all the more majestic.

SPAIN

Even more beloved by locals than the cathedral is the **Convento de Santa Teresa** ( ☎ 92 021 10 30; Plaza de la Santa; Museum admission €2; museum 10am-2pm & 4-7pm, relic room 9.30am-1.30pm & 3.30-7pm, church 8.30am-1.30pm & 3.30-8.30pm), which was built in 1636 at the birthplace of the 16th-century mystic and ascetic, Saint Theresa. It has a simple interior and a gold-smothered chapel that sits atop Teresa's former bedroom, though more interesting are the relics (including a piece of the saint's ring finger) and the small museum about her life.

## Sleeping

**Pensión Continental** ( ☎ 92 021 15 02; Plaza de la Catedral 6; s €15, d €26-33, tr €39) Modest but offering unbeatable vistas of the cathedral and charming (if aged) décor. Shared bathrooms.

**Hospedería La Sinagoga** ( ☎ 92 035 23 21; www .lasinagoga.com; Calle Reyes Católicos 22; s €48-54, d €66-75; ) More stylish and housed in a 15th-century synagogue.

**Hostería de Bracamonte** ( ☎ 92 025 12 80; Calle Bracamonte 6; s €36, d €50-73) Offers great value and old-world charm at every turn. Rooms boast shiny hardwood floors and antique furniture. The restaurant (below) is top too.

## Eating

**El Fogón de Santa Teresa** ( ☎ 92 021 10 23; Plaza de la Catedral 9; mains €6-15, menú €14) Inside the Palacio Valderrabanos Hotel, with local dishes at reasonable prices and cushy seats perfect for a relaxing meal.

**Hostería de Bracamonte** ( ☎ 92 025 12 80; Calle Bracamonte 6; mains €8-18; closed Tue) One of Ávila's most atmospheric spots for a meal. Old tapestries and photos fill the walls, setting the tone for the traditional Castilian food to come.

**Mesón del Rastro** ( ☎ 92 021 12 18; Plaza del Rastro 4; mains €7-14, menú €14) The spot for simple, tasty home-style cooking. You'll find plenty of local specialties and for noncarnivores there are tortillas and a few veggie dishes.

## Entertainment

There are several good nightlife options just outside the Puerta del Peso de la Harina, along Calle San Segundo; try the **Bodeguito de San Segundo** ( ☎ 92 021 42 47; Calle San Segundo 19; 11am-1am) for a great selection of Spanish wines and tapas.

## Getting There & Away

Renfe trains come and go from Madrid (€5.60 to €7.15, up to two hours, at least 24 daily), León (€15.75 to €23.50, about three hours, seven daily) and other cities.

At least four buses connect Madrid's Estación Sur and Ávila (€6.26, 1½ hours) daily. Contact the **bus station** ( ☎ 92 025 05; Ave de Madrid 2) for more information.

Ávila is an hour's drive from Madrid, off the N-110 highway.

# SALAMANCA

A university town through-and-through, fun, fairy-tale Salamanca is a historic city that's still very much in swing. Sitting on the Tormes River, the old city is a showcase of Spanish building styles, with some of the country's best examples of plateresque, Churrigueresque and Spanish Gothic architecture.

## Information

**Come On** ( ☎ 92 321 56 25; Calle de Palominos 21; per hr €1.50; 10am-midnight)

**Cyberplace** ( ☎ 92 326 42 81; Plaza Mayor 10; per hr €1.20; 10.30am-2pm)

**Municipal tourist office** ( ☎ 92 321 83 42; www .aytosalamanca.es; Plaza Mayor 32; 9am-2pm & 4-6.30pm Mon-Fri, 9am-6.30pm and 9am-2pm Sun)

**Regional tourist office** (Casa de las Conchas; ☎ 92 326 85 71; www.turismocastillayleon.com; Rúa Mayor; 9am-2pm & 5-8pm daily Sep-Jun, 9am-8pm Sun-Thu, 9am-9pm Fri & Sat Jul & Aug)

## Sights & Activities

The spirit of Salamanca isn't found inside museums or churches, it's out in the streets and plazas, where students from all over the globe walk busily and café tables spill onto the footpaths.

Start with a stroll in the harmonious **Plaza Mayor**, designed in 1755 by José Churriguera, founder of the architectural style that carries his name. From here, head up the busy Rúa Mayor to marvel at the **Casa de las Conchas** (House of Shells), a city symbol since it was built in the 15th century and now home to a tourist office and the library.

The **University** ( ☎ 92 329 44 00; Calle Libreros; adult/child €4/2; 9.30am-1.30pm & 4-7pm Mon-Fri, 9.30am-1.30pm & 4-6.30pm Sat, 10am-1pm Sun), which has an ubiquitous presence, is worth a visit. You can peek in the old classrooms

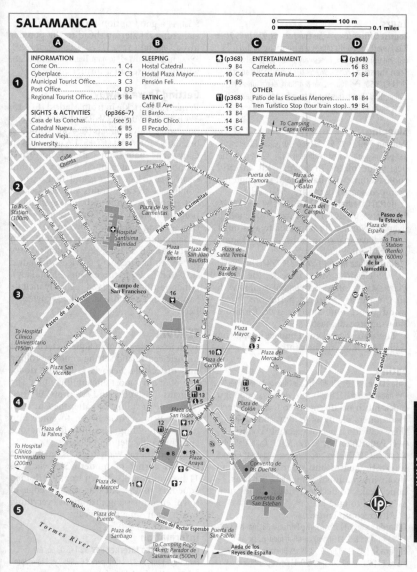

## SALAMANCA

0 — 100 m
0 — 0.1 miles

**INFORMATION**
Come On...........................................1 C4
Cyberplace........................................2 C3
Municipal Tourist Office................3 C3
Post Office.........................................4 D3
Regional Tourist Office..................5 B4

**SIGHTS & ACTIVITIES**     (pp366–7)
Casa de las Conchas................(see 5)
Catedral Nueva...............................6 B5
Catedral Vieja..................................7 B5
University...........................................8 B4

**SLEEPING**     (p368)
Hostal Catedral................................9 B4
Hostal Plaza Mayor.......................10 C4
Pensión Feli.....................................11 B5

**EATING**     (p368)
Café El Ave......................................12 B4
El Bardo............................................13 B4
El Patio Chico.................................14 B4
El Pecado.........................................15 C4

**ENTERTAINMENT**     (p368)
Camelot.............................................16 B3
Peccata Minuta...............................17 B4

**OTHER**
Patio de las Escuelas Menores.........18 B4
Tren Turístico Stop (tour train stop)..19 B4

SPAIN

(complete with torturous-looking original wooden benches), a chapel, a library and a small museum.

Curiously, Salamanca is home to two cathedrals; the new, larger cathedral was built beside the old Romanesque one instead of on top of it, as was the norm. The **Catedral Nueva** (New Cathedral; ☎ 92 321 74 76; Plaza Anaya; 🕑 9am-1pm & 4-6pm Oct-Mar, 9am-2pm & 4-8pm Apr-Sep), completed in 1733, is a Gothic masterpiece that took 220 years to build. From inside, you can head to the **Catedral Vieja** (Old Cathedral; adult/child €3/2.25; 🕑 10am-12.30pm & 4-5.30pm Oct-Mar, 10am-1.30pm & 4-7.30pm Apr-Sep), a 12th-century temple with a stunning altar and several noteworthy chapels.

## Tours

**Tourist Offices** (Casa de las Conchas; ☎ 92 326 85 71; Rúa Mayor) The tourist offices often organise guided tours (€6 and up) of the city. Times vary so ask for details.
**Tren Turística** ( ☎ 64 962 57 03; Plaza Anaya; adult/child €3/1.50; ☾ 10am-2pm & 4-8pm, departures every 30min) Hop aboard this tourist train for an overview of the city's major sights.

## Sleeping

**Pensión Feli** ( ☎ 92 321 60 10; Calle Libreros 58; per person with shared bathroom €12) One of the best-value places in town, with cheerful rooms (some with balconies), although the cramped shared baths are 1960s relics.
**Hostal Catedral** ( ☎ 92 321 14 27; fax 92 327 06 14; Rúa Mayor 46; s/d €30/45) We can't gush enough over this *hostal*. Its immaculate and quiet rooms have sparkling bathrooms and some have cathedral views.
**Hostal Plaza Mayor** ( ☎ 92 321 75 48; Plaza Corrillo 20; s/d/tr €36/60/90) More upscale, the classy Plaza Mayor offers 19 elegant rooms with all the extras. Marbled bathroom, hardwood floors and antique-style furniture show impeccable taste.

There are several good budget *hostales* on Calle Meléndez, in the centre.

## Eating

**Café El Ave** ( ☎ 92 326 45 11; Calle Libreros 24; menú €9.90; ☾ noon-midnight) This bright café is good for a quick lunch or afternoon coffee. The lunch *menú* offers plenty of variety and by night there's a wide range of speciality coffees.
**El Patio Chico** ( ☎ 92 326 51 03; Calle Meléndez 13; mains €5.90-11; ☾ 1-4pm & 8pm-midnight) Good for rustic charm and offering everything (from international standards, such as T-bone steaks, to decidedly local dishes such as 'stewed tongue').

Also recommended:
**El Bardo** ( ☎ 92 325 92 65; Ave Portugal 88; mains €8.40-13; ☾ 1-4pm & 9-11.30pm) Castilian food, rustic air.
**El Pecado** ( ☎ 92 326 65 58; Plaza Poeta Iglesias 12; mains €14-21; ☾ 1.30-3pm & 9-11pm) Upscale and ultra-stylish.

## Entertainment

The student population in Salamanca's ensures that there's always something going on after classes. Wander around the university and the Plaza Mayor for low-key bars; **Peccata Minuta** ( ☎ 92 312 34 47; Calle Francisco Vitoria 3; ☾ 9am-11pm Sun-Thu, 11am-1pm Fri

& Sat) is a good option for drinks and special coffees. Later on, head to the popular disco **Camelot** ( ☎ 92 321 21 84; Calle Bordadores 3; ☾ 8pm-2am Sun-Wed, to 4am Thu, to 6am Fri & Sat), which is housed in a former convent.

## Getting There & Away

Renfe trains trickle in from Madrid (€14.15, 2½ hours, six daily), Valladolid (€5.60, one hour, one daily), Bilbao (€24.50, 5½ hours, one daily) and Ávila (€7.15, 1½ hours, seven daily). The main train station is northwest of the centre (catch bus No 1 or 1B from Gran Vía to get there), and that's where you'll have to catch trains and buy tickets, but incoming trains *only* make an additional stop near the Plaza España, within easy walking distance of the centre.

Salamanca's bus station is about 1km northwest of Plaza Mayor. **AutoRes** (www.auto-res.net) has frequent services to Madrid (€10 to €15, 2½ to three hours, eight daily). Other destinations served regularly include Santiago de Compostela, Ávila, Segovia and León.

# SEGOVIA

With its soaring Roman aqueduct, compact historic centre and setting amid the rolling hills of Castilla, Segovia is without doubt one of Spain's most enchanting cities. The Romans, Visigoths and Muslims all tried their hand at ruling, but after the Christian Reconquista Segovia began to come into its own, building beautiful Romanesque churches and splendid palaces.

The medieval walled city is in the far-western corner of modern Segovia. The 11th-century walls stretch from the Roman aqueduct to the Alcázar on the edge of town, encompassing just about everything worth seeing in a short visit.

## Information

**Cyber Graphika Internet** ( ☎ 92 146 09 66; Ave Fernández Ladreda 12, 1st fl; per hr €1.80; ☾ 11am-2pm & 3-10pm Mon-Fri, 4-10pm Sat)
**Municipal tourist office** ( ☎ 92 146 29 14; www.segoviaturismo.es; Plaza Axoguejo 1; ☾ 10am-8pm)
**Police** ( ☎ 091; Paseo de Ezequiel González 22)
**Post Office** ( ☎ 92 146 16 16; www.correos.es; Plaza Doctor Laguna 5; ☾ 8.30am-8.30pm Mon-Fri, 9am-2pm Sat)
**Regional tourist office** ( ☎ 92 146 03 34 or 902 20 30 30; www.turismocastillayleon.com; Plaza Mayor; ☾ 9am-2pm & 5-8pm)

## Sights

Start your visit at the **Roman aqueduct**, an 894m-long engineering wonder that looks like an enormous comb plunged into the centre of Segovia. It's 28m high and was built without a drop of mortar – just good old Roman know-how.

From here, the lively commercial streets Calle Cervantes and Calle Juan Bravo (together referred to as Calle Real) climb into the innards of Segovia. In the heart of town towers the resplendent **cathedral** ( ☎ 92 146 22 05; Plaza de la Catedral; admission €2, free from 1.30pm Sun; ☺ 10am-2pm & 4-8pm Tue-Fri Sep-July, 10am-8pm Sat & Sun year-round). Completed in 1577, 50 years after its Romanesque predecessor had been destroyed in the revolt of the Comuneros, the cathedral is one of the most homogenous Gothic churches in Spain.

The fortified **Alcázar** ( ☎ 92 146 07 59; www .alcazarsegovia.com; Plaza Reina Victoria Eugenia; admission €3.50; ☺ 10am-6pm Oct-Mar, 10am-7pm Apr-Sep) is a fairy-tale castle perched dramatically on the edge of Segovia. Roman foundations are buried somewhere underneath this splendour, but what we see today is a 13th-century structure that burned down in 1862 and was subsequently rebuilt. Inside is a collection of armour and military gear, but even better are the 360-degree views from its rooftop.

## Sleeping

**Hostal Fornos** ( ☎ 92 146 01 98; Calle Infanta Isabel 13; s €32-38, d €45-51) Hand-painted headboards and wall decorations give this place a cheerful air. Rooms are small but for a bit of extra wiggling room request room Nos 5 or 8.

**Hotel Infanta Isabel** ( ☎ 92 146 13 00; www.hotel infantaisabel.com; Plaza Mayor 12; s €50-73, d €74-108; ☒ ) Sitting right on Plaza Mayor, the utterly charming Infanta Isabel is one of the best in town. Rooms are spacious and full of light.

**Las Sirenas** ( ☎ 92 146 26 63; www.hotelsirenas.com; Calle Juan Bravo 30; s €40-53, d €60-70, tr €80-90; ☒ ) Exuding old-world elegance, Las Sirenas offers simple but sophisticated rooms right off the sunny Plaza Medina del Campo.

## Eating

**Casa Duque** ( ☎ 92 146 24 87; www.restauranteduque .es; Calle Cervantes 12; mains €5.70-21, menú €21; ☺ noon-11pm) A local institution that serves a mean suckling pig, though there is a good range of salads too. Downstairs is the informal

tavern, where you can get tapas and yummy *cazuelas* (stews).

**La Cordorniz** ( ☎ 92 146 38 07; Calle Hermanos Barral 3; mains €9.50-12; ☺ 1.30-4pm & 8-11.30pm) For traditional fare at slightly cheaper prices, head here, where the €9 lunch *menú* is a tasty deal.

**Cueva de San Esteban** ( ☎ 92 146 09 82; Calle Valdelaguila 15; menú €7.70-12.15; ☺ 1pm-11pm) One of the only restaurants in Segovia not pushing suckling pig, this place offers seasonal dishes and an excellent wine list.

## Entertainment

After dark, the action is centred around the Plaza Mayor (especially along Calle Escuderos and Calle Isabel Católica). Some of the best nightspots are **Bar Santana** ( ☎ 92 146 35 64; Calle Infanta Isabel 18; ☺ 10.30-3am, until 4am Fri & Sat) and **El Purgatorio** (Calle Escuderos 26; ☺ 1pm-2am Mon-Fri, 5pm-3.30am Sat, 5pm-2am Sun).

## Getting There & Away

If you're driving, take the A-6 motorway north from Madrid towards the N-603 national highway, which will take you to the city centre. The trip takes about an hour.

Buses (€5.68, 1¼ hours) leave every half-hour from Madrid's Paseo de la Florida bus stop and arrive to Segovia's central **bus station** ( ☎ 92 142 77 07; Paseo Ezequiel González). Renfe trains come in from Madrid (€5.10, two hours, seven daily) and elsewhere.

## LEÓN

León has been called 'the beautiful unknown', and with good reason. This once-mighty city is often overlooked by travellers, but its long boulevards, open squares and historic Barrio Húmedo (Damp District) invite you to pause for a day or two.

## Information

**Cafeteria Santo Domingo** ( ☎ 98 726 13 84; Ave Ordoño II 3; internet per hr €1; ☺ 8am-11pm Mon-Fri, 9am-11pm Sun) At the back of this cafétería is a well-run Internet centre.

**Tourist Office** ( ☎ 98 723 70 82; www.aytoleon.com; Plaza Regla 3; ☺ 9am-2pm & 5-7pm Mon-Fri, 10am-2pm & 5-8pm Sat & Sun)

## Sights & Activities

León's best and most infamous monument is its breathtaking 13th-century **cathedral** ( ☎ 98 787 57 70; www.catedraldeleon.org; admission museum

SPAIN

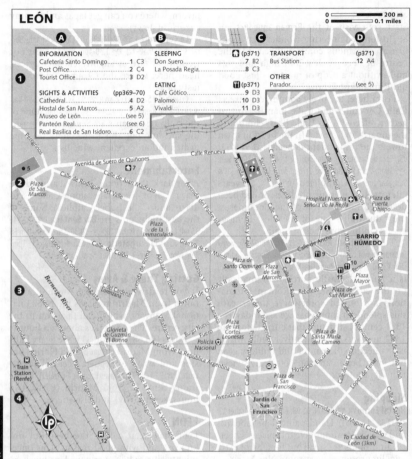

## LEÓN

0 —————— 200 m
0 —————— 0.1 miles

**INFORMATION**
Cafeteria Santo Domingo............1 C3
Post Office.................................2 C4
Tourist Office.............................3 D2

**SIGHTS & ACTIVITIES** (pp369–70)
Cathedral....................................4 D2
Hostal de San Marcos..................5 A2
Museo de León.......................(see 5)
Panteón Real..........................(see 6)
Real Basílica de San Isidoro.........6 C2

**SLEEPING** (p371)
Don Suero...................................7 B2
La Posada Regia..........................8 C3

**EATING** (p371)
Café Gótico................................9 D3
Palomo.....................................10 D3
Vivaldi.....................................11 D3

**TRANSPORT** (p371)
Bus Station...............................12 A4

**OTHER**
Parador................................(see 5)

€3.50; ⏰ cathedral 8.30am-1.30pm & 4-7pm Mon-Sat, 8.30am-2.30pm & 5-7pm Sun Oct-Jun, 8.30am-8pm Mon-Sat, 8.30am-2.30pm & 5-8pm Sun Jul-Sep, museum 9.30am-1.30pm & 4-6.30pm Mon-Fri, 9.30am-1.30pm Sat Oct-May, 9.30am-7.30pm Mon-Fri Jul-Sep). A marvel of Gothic architecture, it has an extraordinarily intricate façade with a rose window, three richly sculptured doorways and two muscular towers. The most outstanding feature, though, is the 128 radiant stained-glass windows (with a surface of 1800 sq metres), which give the place an ethereal quality.

Nearby is the **Real Basílica de San Isidoro** ( ☎ 98 787 61 61; www.sanisidorodeleon.org; admission €3, Thu afternoon free; ⏰ 10am-1.30pm & 4-6.30pm Mon-Sat, 10am-1.30pm Sun Sep-Jun, 9am-8pm Mon-Sat,

9am-2pm Sun Jul & Aug), a simple Romanesque church that houses the interesting **Panteón Real**, where Leonese royalty lie buried beneath a canopy of some of the finest frescoes in all of Spain.

Across town is the equally worthwhile **Hostal de San Marcos**, a former pilgrims' hospital that now houses a luxury parador. The sumptuous interior can only be visited during free **tours** ( ⏰ 1pm & 8.30pm Mon-Thu, 1pm Fri & Sat, 9.30am & 5pm Sun) but the **Museo de León** ( ☎ 98 724 50 61; adult/child €1.20/free, Sun free; ⏰ 10am-2pm & 4-7pm Tue-Sat, 10am-2pm Sun Sep-Jun, 10am-2pm & 5-8pm Tue-Sat, 10am-2pm Sun Jul & Aug), also housed here, gives access to some parts of the building. Don't miss the façade, 100m of ornate golden-hued carvings.

SPAIN

## Sleeping & Eating

**Don Suero** ( ☎ 98 723 06 00; Suero de Quiñones 15; s/d €21.10/40, s with shared bathroom €17.70) A clean, attractive place in the heart of town that could easily pass for a one- or two-star hotel.

**La Posada Regia** ( ☎ 98 721 31 73; www.regialeon .com; Calle Regidores 9-11; s/d with breakfast €55/90) Offering more comfort, this quaint inn has pretty period furniture decorating every room and a great restaurant downstairs.

The Plaza San Martín is packed with bars and restaurants, many with terraces.

**Café Gótico** ( ☎ 98 708 49 56; Calle Varillas 5; menú €8; ☽ noon-midnight Sun-Thu, noon-2am Fri & Sat) Tasty but no-frills, inexpensive fare, including an all-vegetarian daily lunch *menú*.

**Palomo** ( ☎ 98 725 42 25; Calle Escalerilla 8; mains €5.50-14, menú €9-15; ☽ 1.30pm-4pm & 9-midnight, closed Wed & Sun dinner) Cosy, with traditional Castilian dishes.

**Vivaldi** ( ☎ 98 726 00 94; Calle Platerías 4; mains €11-18; ☽ 1-3.30pm, 9-11.30pm Tue-Sat, closed Sun evening & all day Mon) For a treat, head to upscale Vivaldi in the Barrio Húmedo. You'll find seasonal dishes based on local products. There's also a bar area with some great gourmet tapas.

## Getting There & Away

The Renfe train station has regular trains running to and from Madrid (€19.20 to €29, at least four hours, seven daily), Ávila (€15.75 to €23.50, at least 2½ hours, up to nine daily), Burgos (€15.50 to €21, two hours, four daily) and Santiago de Compostela (€24.50, six hours, one daily).

The **bus station** ( ☎ 98 721 10 00; Paseo Ingeniero Saenz de Miera) connects with a myriad of Spanish cities, among them Madrid (€18.31 to €31, at least 3½ hours, up to 12 daily), Burgos (€11.75, two to four hours, three daily) and Ávila (€14.18, 3½ hours, one daily). For more information contact the bus company, **Alsa** (www.alsa.es).

León is on the N-630 highway, 64km north of the A-6 motorway that cuts through the region.

## BURGOS

With its grand riverside promenades and outstanding collection of churches and monasteries, Burgos is one of Spain's hidden gems. Marvel at the gleaming white cathedral (one of Christendom's most splendid) and while away the day strolling the characterful boulevards of the centre.

## Information

**Locutorio Capitanía** ( ☎ 94 726 42 28; Plaza Alonso Martínez 3; per hr €1) Good for Internet access.

**Municipal tourist office** ( ☎ 94 728 88 74; www.ayto burgos.es; Teatro Principal, Paseo Espolón 1; ☽ 10am-2pm & 4.30-7.30pm Mon-Sat, 10am-2pm Sun Oct-Jun, 10am-2pm & 5-8pm Mon-Sat, 10am-2pm Sun Jul-Sep)

**Police** ( ☎ 94 728 88 39 or 091)

## Sights

Burgos' claim to fame is its majestic 1261 Gothic **cathedral** ( ☎ 94 720 47 12; adult/child €3/1, guided tour €1.50; ☽ 10am-1.15pm & 4-6.45pm Sep-Jun, 9.30am-1.15pm & 4-7.15pm Jul & Aug, guided tour 5pm Mon-Fri & 11am Sun), a gleaming-white Gothic masterpiece. On this site, a modest Romanesque church once stood, but today we see ornate spires piercing the skyline, each representing 84m of richly decorated fantasy. Inside, the highlight is the Escalera Dorada (Gilded Staircase) by Diego de Siloé. The famed warrior El Cid lies buried beneath the central dome.

If you have time, visit the **Monasterio de las Huelgas** ( ☎ 94 720 16 30; adult/child €5/2.50; ☽ 10am-1.15pm & 4-5.45pm Tue-Sat, 10.30am-2.15pm Sun), an elegant Cistercian order founded in 1187 by Eleanor of Aquitaine and still home to 35 Cistercian nuns. You can get here by a 30-minute walk west along the southern bank of the Arlanzón River.

## Sleeping & Eating

**Pensión Peña** ( ☎ 94 720 63 23; Calle Puebla 18; s €15-17, d €22-24) You'll pay amazingly low prices for well-kept, cheerful rooms here. All have pretty décor and shared baths.

**Hotel Norte y Londres** ( ☎ 94 726 41 25; www .hotelnorteylondres.com; Plaza Alonso Martínez 10; s €43-49.50, d €61-73.50) Great value and in an unbeatable location, this classy hotel boasts lovely rooms with hardwood floors and fine furnishings. Some rooms have balconies.

**Restaurante La Riojana** ( ☎ 94 720 61 32; Calle Avellanos 10; menú €6; ☽ 1.30-4pm & 8-10.30pm) Home to the cheapest lunch *menú* in town, this no-frills spot has a solid selection of Spanish dishes such as paella and Rioja-style codfish.

**Prego** ( ☎ 94 726 04 47; Huerto del Rey 4; salads & pasta €5-7, pizza €10; ☽ noon-4pm, 8pm-midnight) One of the few good options for vegetarians. It's an elegant Italian restaurant with impressive prices and tasty dishes.

**SPAIN**

**Mesón del Cid** (☎ 94 720 87 15; www.mesondelcid.es; Plaza Santa María 8; mains €11-20; ⏰ 1-4pm & 8.30-11pm) For traditional fare, try the kitschy but atmospheric El Cid, offering roasted meats and waiters in costume.

### Getting There & Away

Trains come and go from cities including Salamanca (€17.50, about three hours, four daily), Madrid (€19.90 to €23, up to five hours, nine daily). The train station is connected to town by bus Nos 3, 5 and 7.

The bus station is just across the river from the cathedral and is home to several companies. One of the largest, **Alsa** (☎ 94 726 63 70; www.alsa.es), makes runs to Salamanca (€13 to €16, four hours, three daily), Valladolid (€7 to €9, two to three hours, three to four daily) and other destinations.

# CASTILLA-LA MANCHA

Best known as the home of Don Quixote, Castilla-La Mancha conjures up images of lonely windmills and bleak, treeless plains giving way to pretty villages and medieval castles.

## TOLEDO

**pop 72,549**

A jumble of narrow, winding streets, perched on a small hill above the Tajo River, Toledo is crammed with museums, churches and other monumental reminders of its splendid and turbulent past. It's also quite expensive and terribly touristy. If you can, try to stay overnight to really appreciate the spark and soul of this remarkable city.

SPAIN

### Information

**Main Tourist Office** (☎ 92 522 08 43; www.jccm.es; Puerta Bisagra; ⏰ 9am-6pm Mon-Sat, 9am-3pm Sun) At the northern end of town.

**Scorpions** (☎ 92 521 25 56; Calle Matías Moreno 10; per hr €2 ⏰ 12.30pm-2am)

**Tourist Office** (☎ 92 525 40 30; ⏰ 10.30am-2.30pm & 4.30-7pm Tue-Sun, 10.30am-2.30pm Mon) Opposite the cathedral and more helpful.

### Sights & Activities

Toledo has lots to see. As well as the historical sights, its tourist shops are fun, many reflecting the city's swashbuckling past with suits of armour and swords for sale. More conventional souvenirs include *damasquinado* (damascene), the Moorish art of inlaying gold thread against matte black steel, available in the form of jewellery, boxes and ornaments. Toledo is also famed for its *mazapán* (marzipan).

You could happily spend an afternoon in Toledo's **cathedral** (☎ 92 522 22 41; Calle Cardenal Cisneros; ⏰ 10.30am-6.30pm Mon-Sat, 2-6pm Sun), admiring the glorious stone architecture, stained-glass windows, tombs of kings in the Capilla Mayor and art by the likes of El Greco, Velázquez and Goya. You have to buy a ticket (€5.50) to enter four areas – the **Coro**, **Sacristía**, **Capilla de la Torre** and **Sala Capitular**, which contain some of the finest art and artisanship.

The **Museo de Santa Cruz** (☎ 92 522 10 36; Calle Cervantes 3; admission free; ⏰ 10am-6.30pm Mon-Sat, 10am-2pm Sun) contains a large collection of furniture, faded tapestries, military and religious paraphernalia, and paintings. Upstairs is an impressive collection of El Greco's works, including the masterpiece *La Asunción* (Assumption of the Virgin).

In the southwestern part of the old city, the queues outside an otherwise unremarkable church, the **Iglesia de Santo Tomé** (☎ 92 525 60 98; Plaza Conde; admission €1.50; ⏰ 10am-6pm Oct-Jun, 10am-7pm Jul-Sep), give away the presence of El Greco's masterpiece *El Entierro del Conde de Orgaz*. The painting depicts the burial of the Count of Orgaz in 1322 by St Stephen and St Augustine, observed by a heavenly entourage.

The **Casa-Museo de El Greco** (☎ 92 522 40 46; Calle Samuel Leví; admission €2.40; ⏰ 10am-2pm & 4-9pm Tue-Sat, 10am-2pm Sun), in Toledo's former Jewish quarter, contains the artist's famous *Vista y Plano de Toledo*, plus about 20 of his minor works. Although El Greco lived in Toledo from 1577 to 1614, it is unlikely he ever lived in this building.

The **Museo Sefardi** (☎ 92 522 36 65; www.museosefardi.net; Calle Samuel Leví s/n; admission €4.50; ⏰ 10am-6pm Tue-Sat, 10am-2pm Sun) is housed in the beautiful 14th century **Sinagoga del Tránsito**. Toledo's other synagogue, **Santa María La Blanca** (☎ 92 522 72 57; Calle Reyes Católicos 4; admission €1.50; ⏰ 10am-6pm), a short way north, dates back to the beginning of the 13th century.

Slightly north is one of the city's most visible sights, **San Juan de los Reyes** (☎ 92 522 38 02; admission €1.50; ⏰ 10am-6pm Oct-Jun, 10am-7pm

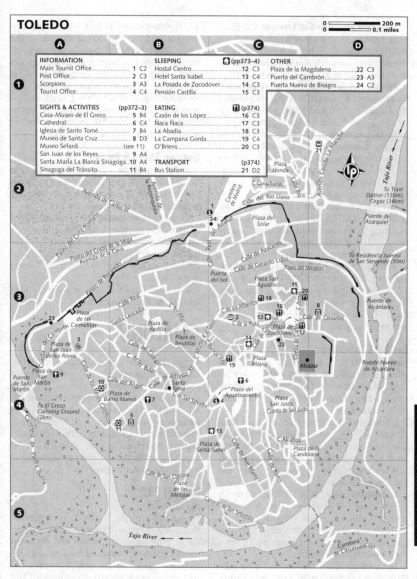

# TOLEDO

| INFORMATION | |
|---|---|
| Main Tourist Office | 1 C2 |
| Post Office | 2 C3 |
| Scorpions | 3 A3 |
| Tourist Office | 4 C4 |

| SIGHTS & ACTIVITIES | (pp372–3) |
|---|---|
| Casa-Museo de El Greco | 5 B4 |
| Cathedral | 6 C4 |
| Iglesia de Santo Tomé | 7 B4 |
| Museo de Santa Cruz | 8 D3 |
| Museo Sefardí | (see 11) |
| San Juan de los Reyes | 9 A4 |
| Santa María La Blanca Sinagoga | 10 A4 |
| Sinagoga del Tránsito | 11 B4 |

| SLEEPING | (pp373–4) |
|---|---|
| Hostal Centro | 12 C3 |
| Hotel Santa Isabel | 13 C4 |
| La Posada de Zocodover | 14 C3 |
| Pensión Castilla | 15 C3 |

| EATING | (p374) |
|---|---|
| Casón de los López | 16 C3 |
| Ñaca Ñaca | 17 C3 |
| La Abadía | 18 C3 |
| La Campana Gorda | 19 C4 |
| O'Briens | 20 C3 |

| TRANSPORT | |
|---|---|
| Bus Station | 21 D2 |

| OTHER | |
|---|---|
| Plaza de la Magdalena | 22 C3 |
| Puerta del Cambrón | 23 A3 |
| Puerta Nueva de Bisagra | 24 C2 |

Jul-Sep), the Franciscan monastery and church founded by Fernando and Isabel. The prevalent late Flemish-Gothic style is tarted up with lavish Isabelline ornamentation and counterbalanced by *Mudéjar* decoration. Outside hang the chains of Christian prisoners freed after the fall of Granada in 1492.

## Sleeping

Cheap accommodation is not easy to come by and is often full, especially from Easter to September.

**Camping El Greco** ( ☎ 92 522 00 90; per person/tent/car €4.75/4.55/4.55; ☼ year-round; ☂ ) The nearest camping ground, well signposted 2.5km southwest of town.

SPAIN

**Residencia Juvenil de San Servando** ( ☎ 92 522 45 54; fax 92 521 39 54; dm 25 yrs & under/26 yrs & over €8.70/11.30) Toledo's HI hostel is beautifully located in the Castillo de San Servando, a castle that started life as a Visigothic monastery.

**Pensión Castilla** ( ☎ 92 525 63 18; Calle Recoletos 6; s/d with shared bathroom €15/25) With its wooden floors, ceiling fans and bright rooms, this is one of Toledo's best budget options.

**Hostal Centro** ( ☎ 92 525 70 91; www.hostalcentro .com; Calle Nueva 13; s/d/tr €30/45/60; 🗱 ) Just off the marvellous social hang-out that is Plaza Zocodover, the *hostal* has wonderful spacious rooms, some with balconies, and a fabulous rooftop terrace.

**La Posada de Zocodover** ( ☎ 92 525 58 14; Calle Condonerias 6; d €37.30; 🗱 ) In an old, narrow building with timbered ceilings, pretty brass beds and tiled floors, the hotel's seven exquisite rooms get snapped up fast.

**Hotel Santa Isabel** ( ☎ 92 525 31 20; www.santa -isabel.com; Calle Santa Isabel 24; s/d €30/45; 🅿 🗱 ) Well placed near the cathedral, this comfortable hotel offers impeccable service in a grand 14th-century building, with rooms around a stunning wooden gallery.

## Eating & Drinking

**Ñaca Ñaca** ( ☎ 92 525 35 59; Plaza Zocodover 7; bocadillos €2-3; 🕑 9am-11pm Mon-Thu, 9-4am Fri, 9am Sat-11pm Sun) For late-night munchies or midday snacks, this place does chunky *bocadillos* (filled rolls) to take-away.

**O'Briens** ( ☎ 92 521 26 65; Calle Cuesta de las Armas 12; mains €4-5; 🕑 noon-2am Sun-Thu, noon-4am Fri & Sat) O'Briens is a friendly Irish pub with good grub, including burgers and hefty club sandwiches (except on Saturday when the kitchen is closed).

**La Campana Gorda** ( ☎ 92 521 01 46; Calle Hombre de Palo 13; mains €9-14; 🕑 9am-11pm) A tavern-style restaurant specialising in roast meats and fish, and football on the telly. It's popular with smartly dressed locals and does a very reasonable €9 *menú*.

**La Abadia** ( ☎ 92 525 07 46; Plaza San Nicolás 3; mains €6-12; 🕑 8am-midnight Sun-Thu, noon-1am Fri & Sat) A popular bar and restaurant, with lots of alcoves and over 30 different types of beer on the menu. Don't leave without trying the *sartén de patatas* (€4), a divine concoction of potatoes, egg, sausage and onion served up in a small frying pan.

**Casón de los López** ( ☎ 92 525 47 74; www.cason toledo.com; Calle Sillería 2; mains €18-21; 🕑 1.30-4pm & 8.30-11.30pm Wed-Sun) Toledo's must-see restaurant and bar is housed in one of the city's most beautiful buildings, with antiques, vaulted ceilings and even a former small chapel with its original baroque altar. There's also an inviting **café** (tapas €2.20; 🕑 noon-midnight), which does a small collection of excellent tapas and a huge variety of wines. The basement **bar** ( 🕑 8pm-1am Wed-Sun) has more than 90 different whiskies.

## Getting There & Away

Toledo's **bus station** ( ☎ 92 521 58 50; Ave Castilla-La Mancha) has buses from about 6am to 10pm to/from Madrid's Estación Sur (€4, 1½ hours, every 30 minutes).

From the **train station** (Calle Paseo Rosa), 400m east of the Puente Azarquiel, trains run to/from Madrid's Atocha station (€5, 1½ hours, five daily). The first train from Madrid departs at 8.30am, the last from Toledo at 6.48pm.

Bus No 5 links the train and bus stations with Plaza Zocodover (€0.80).

# CATALONIA

Forget the Spain of flamenco and bullfights; Catalonia is a proud region that likes to see itself as somewhat independent from the rest of Spain. A smallish triangle in the northeastern corner of the peninsula, Catalonia is a varied region, with both soaring mountain peaks and long, sandy coasts. Its capital, Barcelona is one of Spain's most beautiful cities, but the rest of the region is well worth exploring too.

## BARCELONA

### pop 1.6 million

Sitting right on the Mediterranean, vibrant Barcelona is one of Europe's most exciting cities. With medieval palaces and plazas in the old quarters, fantastical modernist architecture sprinkled throughout L'Eixample district and an innovative contemporary art and design scene, Barcelona won't disappoint. It also boasts great shopping, a lively nightlife and some of the best cuisine in Spain.

Barcelona is a master at reinventing itself. The city has morphed from a wannabe Roman town into a prosperous medieval centre, to a rebellious city during the Spanish Civil War, and finally to its modern cosmopolitan self. In the early 1990s the city underwent a massive cleanup and re-structuring for the 1992 Olympics. Now they're at it again, giving the northern shore (site of the 2004 Forum of Cultures) a major make-over with a new port, new conference centre and new beach.

The effects of so many changes can be seen on the streets. Important splashes of Gothic, Romanesque, modernist and con-temporary works pop up in even the most unexpected corners of the city, haphazardly mixed together like the paellas traditionally eaten for Sunday lunch.

## Orientation

Plaça Catalunya is the heart of Barcelona and the marker between the historic city and the modern one. From here, the long pedestrian Ramblas shoots southeast to the sea, with the busy Gothic quarter and Raval district hugging it on either side. To the northwest of the plaza is L'Eixample, the grid-like district where you'll find shopping areas and the bulk of the city's offices and residences.

## Information

### BOOKSHOPS

**Altair** (Map pp376-7; ☎ 93 342 71 71; Gran Vía 616; metro Plaça Catalunya) All travel books.

**Casa del Llibre** (Map pp379-80; ☎ 93 272 34 80; Passeig de Gràcia 62; metro Passeig de Gràcia) Great English section.

### EMERGENCY

**General Emergencies** ( ☎ 112)

**Guardia Urbana** (City Police; Map pp376-7; ☎ 092; Las Ramblas 43)

### INTERNET ACCESS

**Bigg** (Map pp376-7; ☎ 93 301 40 20; Carrer Comtal 9; per hr €2; ☺ 9am-11pm Mon-Sat, 10am-11pm Sun; metro Plaça Catalunya)

**Cybermundo** (Map pp376-7; ☎ 93 317 71 42; Carrer Bergara 3; per hr €1.20-2.90; ☺ 9am-midnight Mon-Fri, 10am-midnight Sat, 11am-midnight Sun; metro Plaça Catalunya)

### LAUNDRY

**Wash n' Dry** (Map pp379-80; ☎ 93 412 19 53; Carrer Nou de la Rambla 19; €6.61 per load; ☺ 7am-11pm; metro Liceu)

### MEDICAL SERVICES

**24hr pharmacies** (Map pp379-80; Passeig de Gràcia 26 & Las Ramblas 98) You can get help with minor medical problems at these pharmacies.

**Hospital Clinic** (Map pp379-80; ☎ 93 227 54 00; Carrer Villarroel 170; metro Hospital Clinic) Modern hospital with good services for travellers.

### MONEY

The main tourist office (p375) has a money-changing service which is good, or you can also head to banks such as La Caixa or Caixa Catalunya which offer fair rates. Avoid the *casas de cambio* (exchange houses) on Las Ramblas; the rates are exorbitant.

### POST

**Main Post Office** (Map pp376-7; ☎ 93 486 80 50; Plaça Antoni López; ☺ 8.30am-9.30pm Mon-Sat, 9am-2pm Sun; metro Barceloneta)

### TOURIST INFORMATION

**Main Tourist Office** (Map pp376-7; ☎ 80 711 72 22; Plaça Catalunya 17; ☺ 9am-9pm; metro Plaça Catalunya)

## Dangers & Annoyances

You don't need to be concerned about vio-lent crime, but purse snatching and pick-pocketing are a major problem, especially around Plaça Catalunya, Las Ramblas and the Plaça Reial. Classic ploys are fake bird droppings ('I'll help you clean your shirt

SPAIN

---

### BARCELONA IN TWO DAYS

Don't leave Barcelona without seeing architect Antoni Gaudí's masterpieces, **La Sagrada Familia** (p378) and **La Pedrera** (p378), both in L'Eixample. From here, walk down **Passeig de Gràcia** (p385) to reach the **Plaça Catalunya** (p378) and the old quarter. Head down **Las Ramblas** (p378), and duck into the **Barri Gòtic** (p378) to see the cathedral.

On day two, visit the **Museu Picasso** (p380) and the **Basílica de Santa Maria del Mar** (p380), both in El Born district. Stop off here for tapas and wine at **La Vinya del Senyor** (p384) be-fore making your way down to the **waterfront** (p380). End the afternoon with a meal along **La Barceloneta** (p384).

# BARCELONA

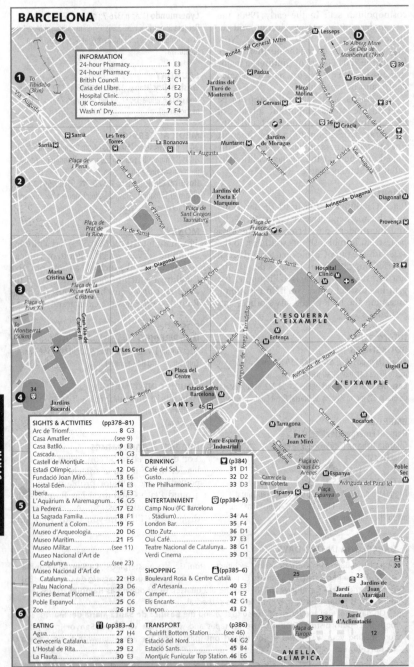

SPAIN

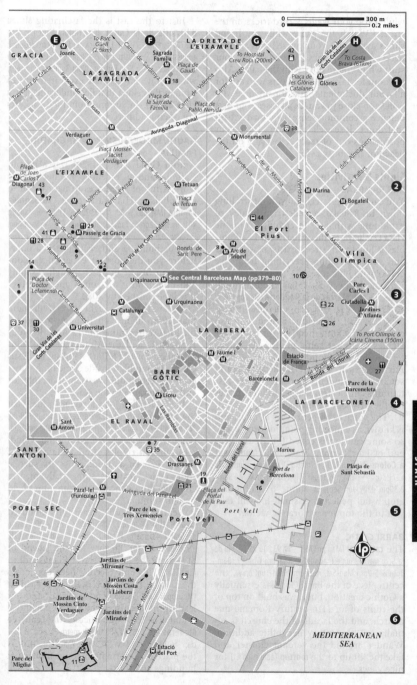

0    300 m
0    0.2 miles

**GRÀCIA**

E Joanic    To Parc
Güell
(2.5km)

F Sagrada
Família    **LA DRETA DE
L'EIXAMPLE**

Carrer de Sardenya    Plaça de
Gaudí    G    To Hospital
Creu Roja (200m)    42    Gran Via de les
Corts Catalanes    H    To Costa
Brava (61km)

**LA SAGRADA
FAMÍLIA**    18    Plaça de
la Sagrada
Família    Carrer de València    Plaça de
les Glòries
Catalanes    Glòries    1

Travessera de Gràcia    Passeig de Sant Joan    Carrer de Pablo Neruda    Carrer d'Aragó

Avinguda Diagonal

Verdaguer    Monumental    38

Plaça Mossèn
Jacint
Verdaguer    Carrer de Sardenya    C. de la Marina    Av. Meridiana    C. dels Almogàvers

Plaça
de Joan
Carlos I    **L'EIXAMPLE**    43    Carrer de València    Carrer d'Aragó    Tetuan    C. de Pallars    2

Diagonal    17    Tetuan    Marina    Bogatell

Passeig de Gràcia    Girona    Plaça
de Tetuan    Carrer de la Marina

28    4    29    **El Fort
Pius**    44    **Vila
Olímpica**

41    Passeig de Gràcia    Passeig de Gràcia    Gran Via de les Corts Catalanes    Ronda de
Sant Pere    8    Arc de
Triomf    Parc
Carles I    3

40    9    15    2    Rambla de Catalunya    10    Parc
Carles I

14    Urquinaona    **See Central Barcelona Map (pp379–80)**    Ciutadella    22    Jardines
d'Atlanta

1    Plaça del
Doctor
Lefamendi    Catalunya    Urquinaona    26    To Port Olímpic &
Icària Cinema (150m)

37    30    Universitat    Carrer de Balmes    Gran Via de les Corts Catalanes    **LA RIBERA**    Estació
de França    Ronda del Litoral    27    la    4

Jaume I    Carrer del Doctor Aiguader    Parc de la
Barconeleta

**BARRI
GÒTIC**    Barceloneta    Barceloneta

Liceu    Les Rambles    **LA BARCELONETA**

Sant
Antoni    **EL RAVAL**

**SANT
ANTONI**    Ronda de Sant Pau    Les Rambles    Marina    Platja de
Sant Sebastià    4

35    7    Drassanes    Ronda del Litoral    Port de
Barcelona    16

Paral·lel
(Funicular)    19    21    Plaça del
Portal de
la Pau

**POBLE SEC**    Avinguda del Paral·lel    Parc de les
Tres Xemeneies    **Port Vell**    Port Vell    5

Jardins de
Miramar    Carretera de Miramar

13    46    Jardins de
Mossèn Costa
i Llobera    **MEDITERRANEAN
SEA**    6

Jardins de
Mossèn Cinto
Verdaguer    Jardins del
Mirador

Parc del
Migdia    11    Estació
del Port    21

**SPAIN**

LP

while I rob your wallet'), card tricks on the street ('Watch the game while my friend slinks away with your purse') and spontaneous football games ('We'll take all your stuff while you're busy with the ball'). Also look out for fake police officers who ask for all your documents, and for anyone who walks too close to you. In all cases your best defence is common sense. Don't carry bags that don't close well, and don't leave your possessions out of reach, especially on the beach or in a busy café.

## Sights & Activities
### LAS RAMBLAS
You can't leave Barcelona without strolling down **Las Ramblas**, a pedestrian boulevard exploding with life. Stretching from the **Plaça Catalunya** to the waterfront, Las Ramblas is lined with street artists, news kiosks and vendors selling everything from live chickens to blue roses.

About halfway down Las Ramblas you'll come to the **Mercat de la Boqueria** (Map pp376-7; ☎ 93 318 25 84; Las Ramblas 91; metro Liceu; ☼ 8am-8.30pm Mon-Sat), Barcelona's premier fresh market and a fantastic place for fruit, vegetables or to get some photos of characteristic Spanish food such as pigs' ears. Further south is the **Plaça Reial**, a grand square surrounded by arcades where restaurants and cafés charge inflated prices for the privilege of sitting here (it's worth it). The square can get rowdy at night and is known as a meeting point for drug users, so some caution is called for. At the very end of Las Ramblas stands the **Monument a Colom** (Map pp379-80; metro Drassanes; adult/child €2/1.30; ☼ 10am-6.30pm Mon-Sat Oct-May, 9am-8.30pm daily Jun-Sep), a statue of Columbus atop a tall pedestal. A small lift will take you to the top for panoramic views.

### BARRI GÒTIC
The **cathedral** (Map pp376-7; ☎ 93 310 25 80; Pla de la Seu; metro Jaume I; admission museum €1; ☼ 10am-1pm & 5-7pm Mon-Sat, museum 10am-1pm only), the centrepiece of the Barri Gòtic, is essentially a Gothic creation, but it was built on top of the ruins of an 11th-century Romanesque church, and the façade of the church is actually a 19th-century neogothic addition. Wander around the verdant cloister and take the lift up to the **rooftop** (admission €1) for nice views.

Just to the east is the fascinating **Museu d'Història de la Ciutat** (City History Museum; Map pp376-7; ☎ 93 315 11 11; Plaça del Rei; metro Jaume I; admission €4; ☼ 10am-2pm & 4-8pm Tue-Sat, 10am-3pm Sun Oct-Apr, 10am-8pm Tue-Sat, 10am-3pm Sun May-Sep), where you can visit an excavated site of Roman Barcelona that lies under the pretty **Plaça del Rei**. In summer, outdoor concerts are often held here.

### GAUDÍ, MODERNISM & LA SAGRADA FAMILIA
Antoni Gaudí (1852–1926) was a devout Catholic and an eccentric architect whose work is full of references to nature and to Catholicism. His masterpiece, **La Sagrada Familia** (Map pp379-80; ☎ 93 207 30 31; Carrer Mallorca 401; metro Sagrada Familia; admission €8; ☼ 9am-6pm Oct-Mar, 9am-8pm Apr-Sep), is Barcelona's most famous building and visiting it is a once-before-you-die sort of experience. Construction began in 1882 though it's only half-built, and it's anyone's guess whether it will be finished by 2082.

Today, there are eight towers, all more than 100m high, with 10 more to come – the total representing the 12 Apostles, four Evangelists and the Mother of God, plus the tallest tower (170m) standing for Jesus Christ. Climb high inside some of the towers for a vertiginous overview of the interior and a panorama to the sea.

For a detailed look at Gaudí's life, visit the museum inside **La Pedrera** (Map pp379-80; ☎ 902 40 09 73; Carrer Provença 261; metro Diagonal; admission €7; ☼ 10am-8pm Mon-Sat), another Gaudí creation that ripples around the corner of Carrer Provença. Don't miss its surreal roof, which features some truly bizarre chimney pots; concerts are sometimes held here in summer.

Nearby is Gaudí's beautifully coloured **Casa Batlló** (Map pp379-80; ☎ 93 216 03 06; Passeig de Gràcia 43; metro Passeig de Gràcia; admission €10; ☼ 9am-8pm), an allegory for the legend of St George the dragon-slayer (Sant Jordi in Catalan). It's only recently been opened to the public. Next door is the **Casa Amatller** (Map pp379-80; Passeig de Gràcia 41), by another leading modernist architect, Josep Puig i Cadafalch. Now the office of the **Centre de Modernisme** ( ☎ 93 488 01 39; metro Passeig de Gràcia; ☼ 10am-7pm Mon-Sat, 10am-2pm Sun), this is the place for information about modernist buildings and tours.

# CENTRAL BARCELONA

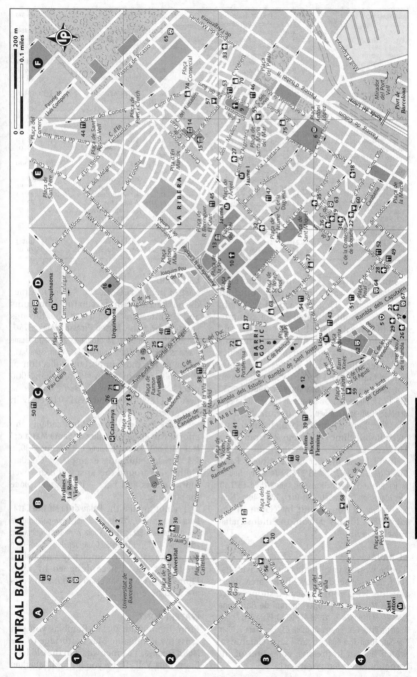

SPAIN

**INFORMATION**
24-hour Pharmacy.....................1 C3
Altair.........................................2 B1
Bigg...........................................3 C2
Cybermundo..............................4 B2
Guardia Urbana.........................5 D4
Main Post Office.......................6 E4
Main Tourist Office....................7 C2
Quera Bookshop........................8 C3

**SIGHTS & ACTIVITIES** (pp378–81)
Basílica de Santa Maria del Mar.....9 F3
Cathedral.................................10 D3
MACBA (Museu d'Art Contemporani
de Barcelona)........................11 B3
Mercat de la Boqueria..............12 C3
Museu d'Història de la Ciutat....13 D2
Museu Picasso.........................14 E2
Museu Tèxtil i d'Indumentària...15 E2
Palau de la Música Catalana.....16 D1
Palau Güell..............................17 D4

**SLEEPING** (pp381–3)
Alberg J New York...................18 E4
Alberg Palau............................19 E4
Gat Raval.................................20 B3
Gat Xino..................................21 B4
Hostal Avinyò...........................22 E4
Hostal Benidorm.......................23 D4
Hostal Fontanella......................24 C1
Hostal Lausanne.......................25 C2

Hostal Morató..........................26 D4
Hotel Banys Orientals...............27 E3
Hotel Barcelona House..............28 D4
Hotel Gaudí..............................29 D4
Hotel Inglaterra........................30 B2
Hotel Pelayo............................31 B2
Hotel Rey Don Jaime I...............32 E3
Park Hotel................................33 F3
Pensión Alamar........................34 E4
Pensión Calella.........................35 E4
Pensión Mari-Luz......................36 E4
Racó del Pi...............................37 D3

**EATING** (pp383–4)
Bagel Shop...............................38 C2
Bar Ra.....................................39 C3
Bar-Bodega Fortuny..................40 D4
Buenas Migas...........................41 C3
Cacao Sampaka........................42 A1
Café de la Òpera......................43 D4
Comerç 24................................44 E1
Comme-Bio..............................45 E2
Coses de Menjar.......................46 F3
El Café de l'Acadèmia...............47 E3
Els Quatre Gats........................48 D2
La Fonda..................................49 D4
Laie Llibreria Café....................50 C1
Les Quinze Nits........................51 D4
Los Caracoles...........................52 D4
Origins 99.9%...........................53 F3
Taller de Tapas.........................54 D3

Venus..................................(see 34)

**DRINKING** (p384)
La Vinya del Senyor..................55 F3
Lletraferit.................................56 A3
Miramelindo.............................57 F2
Muebles Navarro......................58 B4
Rita Blue.................................59 C4
The Philharmonic.....................60 E4

**ENTERTAINMENT** (pp384–5)
Arena Madre............................61 A1
Gran Teatro del Liceu...............62 C4
Harlem Jazz Club......................63 E4
Jamboree.................................64 D4
Magic......................................65 F2
Salvation.................................66 D1
Tablao Cordobés......................67 D4

**SHOPPING** (pp385–6)
Caelum...................................68 D3
Casa Colomina........................69 C3
Custo Barcelona......................70 F3
El Corte Inglés.........................71 C1
El Mercadillo...........................72 C3
La Manual Apargatera..............73 D3
MTX Barcelona........................74 F2
Vila Viniteca...........................75 E3

**TRANSPORT** (p386)
Aerobus Bus Stop....................76 C1

Further afield is Gaudí's **Parc Güell** (☼ 10am-dusk), an enchanting outdoor park in which Dr Seuss would feel right at home. Gaudí designed it as a community that would have houses, schools and shops, but the project flopped, leaving this half-finished playground of tile mosaics and interesting organic shapes. The house where Gaudí lived for 20 years has been converted into the **Casa-Museum Gaudí** ( ☎ 93 219 38 11; metro Lesseps; admission €4; ☼ 10am-6pm Oct-Mar, 10am-8pm Apr-Sep), a museum about his life. Get here by metro (which involves a steep uphill climb) or on bus 24 from Plaça Universitat.

In El Raval district is the moody **Palau Güell** (Map pp376-7; ☎ 93 317 39 74; Carrer Nou de la Rambla 3-5; metro Drassanes; adult/child €3/1.50; ☼ 10am-6pm Mon-Sat Mar-Oct, 10am-4pm Mon-Sat Nov-Feb), a house built by Gaudí in the late 1880s for his patron, the industrialist Eusebi Güell.

### EL RAVAL

To the west of Las Ramblas is El Raval district, a once-seedy, now-funky area overflowing with cool bars and shops. Here is the **Museu d'Art Contemporani de Barcelona** (MACBA; Map pp376-7; ☎ 93 412 08 10; Plaça dels Àngels 1; metro Plaça Catalunya; admission €3; ☼ 11am-7.30pm Tue-Sat, 10am-3pm Sun), near Plaça Catalunya, which has an impressive collection of international contemporary art.

### LA RIBERA

East of the Barri Gòtic, La Ribera is a medieval barrio with fascinating museums and architecture. You'll see the throngs surrounding the **Museu Picasso** (Map pp376-7; ☎ 93 319 63 10; Carrer Montcada 15-21; metro Jaume I; admission €5; ☼ 10am-8pm Tue-Sat, 10am-3pm Sun), home of the most important collection of Picasso's work in Spain – more than 3000 pieces. Most represent Picasso's Barcelona periods (1895–1900 and 1901–04), early in his career.

At the end of Carrer Montcada is the effortlessly elegant **Basílica de Santa Maria del Mar** (Map pp376-7; metro Jaume I; ☼ 9.30am-1.30pm & 4.30-8pm), a stunning example of Catalan Gothic. All around this area you'll discover quirky shops and bars – it's a great place for strolling.

Try not to miss the **Palau de la Música Catalana** (Map pp376-7; ☎ 93 295 72 00; www.palaumusica .org; Carrer Sant Francesc de Paula 2; metro Urquinaona; admission €7; ☼ 10am-3.30pm Sep-Jul, 10am-6pm Aug), an ornate and completely unabashed modernist masterpiece designed by Lluís Domènech i Montaner in 1905. Concerts are held here regularly.

### WATERFRONT

From the bottom of Las Ramblas you can cross the Rambla de Mar footbridge to the **Moll d'Espanya**, a former wharf in the old harbour, Port Vell. There you'll find **L'Aquàrium**

(Map pp379-80; ☎ 93 221 74 74; Moll d'Espanya; metro Drassanes; adult/child €13.50/9.25; ⊙ 9.30am-8pm), one of Europe's best (and more expensive) aquariums. Northeast of Port Vell, on the far side of the fishing-oriented La Barceloneta area, the city **beaches** begin. Along the beachfront, after 1.3km, you'll reach **Vila Olímpica**, site of the 1992 Olympic village, which is fronted by impressive **Port Olímpic**, a large marina with dozens of bars and restaurants. There are some fun nightspots and good restaurants here, but locals are few and far between.

Not far off the water is the **Parc de la Ciutadella** (Map pp379-80; metro Barceloneta; ⊙ 8am-9pm), a large park ideal for strolling or picnics. The small city **zoo** ( ☎ 93 225 67 80; adult/child €12.90/8.20; ⊙ 10am-dusk) is inside the park.

### MONTJUÏC

The Central Park of Barcelona, this hill is the southwestern boundary of the city and is a great place to jog or stroll. There are amazing panoramic views of the city from the top. Public transport in the area is limited; to get here, walk up from Plaça Espanya or wait for bus No 61. A more fun option is take the **funicular railway** (€3.20) from Paral-lel metro station or ride the **cable car** (Transbordador Aeri; €7.50) over from La Barceloneta.

Some interesting attractions on Montjuïc include:

**Museu Nacional d'Art de Catalunya** (Map pp379-80; ☎ 93 622 03 75; Palau Nacional; admission €4.80; ⊙ 10am-7pm Tue-Sat, 10am-2.30pm Sun) Catalan religious art.

**Poble Espanyol** (Spanish Village; Map pp379-80; ☎ 93 508 63 30; Avinguda Marquès de Comillas; admission €7; ⊙ 9am-8pm Mon, 9am-late Tue-Sun) Craft and souvenir shops by day, nightclubs and restaurants by night.

**Fundació Joan Miró** (Map pp379-80; ☎ 93 443 94 70; Parc de Montjuïc; admission €7.20; ⊙ 10am-7pm Tue-Sat, 10am-2.30pm Sun) Fantastic temple to modern art, with many Miró works.

**Castell de Montjuïc** (Map pp379-80; ☎ 93 329 86 13; admission €2.50; ⊙ 9.30am-5.30pm Nov-Mar, 9.30am-8pm Apr-Oct) A small military museum and great views.

### Tours

The **Bus Turístic** ( ☎ 93 423 18 00; adult/child €16/10; ⊙ 9am-9.30pm) service covers two circuits (24 stops), linking virtually all the major tourist sights. Buy tickets on the bus or at the tourist office.

The main tourist office leads **walking tours** (€8) in English and Spanish/Catalan. Ask about times and details in the office.

**Fat Tire Bike Tours** ( ☎ 93 301 36 12; www.fattire biketoursbarcelona.com; metro Liceu; ⊙ tours once daily Mar-Jul, Sep-Dec, twice daily Aug; tours €22-28) is just one of several companies leading two-wheeled tours of the city.

### Festivals & Events

Barcelona's biggest festival is the **La Mercè**, a week-long, city-wide party on the days around 24 September. Another red-letter date on the calendar is **Sant Joan** (St John's Day, 23 July), when days of endless firecrackers welcome summer. In June and July the arts festival **El Grec** fills Barcelona with theatre, dance and music.

### Sleeping

Accommodation in Barcelona is plentiful, but it can be expensive. Most hotels (three-starish) are in L'Eixample; many are huddled near the Plaça Catalunya. Cheaper *pensiones* and *hostales* are in the Barri Gòtic and El Raval, and though you'll pay up to €65 for a double (expensive for Spain), few have much charm to speak of.

#### HOSTELS

**Alberg Palau** (Map pp376-7; ☎ 93 412 50 80; alberg palau@champinet.com; Carrer Palau 6; metro Liceu; dm with shared bathroom €15-20, sheets €2; 🖳 ) Friendly, English-speaking staff run this modest hostel, where dorm-style rooms are cramped but clean. There's a kitchen for your use.

**Alberg J New York** (Map pp376-7; ☎ 93 315 03 04; fax 93 319 53 25; Carrer d'En Cignas 6; metro Liceu; dm with shared bathroom €15-20; 🖳 ) This place is similar to Alberg Palau but has more rooms.

#### HOSTALES & PENSIONES

**Pensión Calella** (Map pp376-7; ☎ 93 317 68 41; Carrer Calella 1; metro Liceu; s €21-26, d €40-46) Calella has just renovated its rooms; now most have baths and all are neat and comfortable, a feat for this price.

**Pensión Avinyò** (Map pp376-7; ☎ 93 318 79 45; www .hostalavinyo.com; Carrer Avinyò 42; metro Liceu; d €38-56, s with shared bathroom €16-26, d with shared bathroom €26-42) Homy rooms all have ceiling fans and many have balconies.

**Pensión Lausanne** (Map pp376-7; ☎ 93 302 11 39; Portal de l'Angel 24; metro Plaça Catalunya; s/d €57/87, s/d without bathroom €40/60) Housed in a pretty,

SPAIN

### HUMAN CASTLES

An element in nearly every Catalan festival is *castellers*, or human castle builders. The tradition – unique to Catalonia – is simple: competing teams try to build the biggest human pyramid possible, and whoever collapses first loses.

The origin of the *castels* is fuzzy; some say it started as a game, others speculate that it was a war technique to enter walled cities. These days, it's serious competition between towns and Barcelona barrios.

Each castle-building attempt begins when the clarinet-like *gralles* play. A tight mass of bodies *(pinya)* forms on the ground, and then the climbers start their work. Four men, their arms tightly interwoven, form the first level, and slowly others climb above them to construct the next levels. Each level has four bodies, their arms linked like the men's below them. The barefoot *castellers* use the hips, shoulders and heads of those below them as steps to make the tower grow ever higher. The top two levels are made by children. The idea is that they are smaller, lighter and have better balance than adults. Also, their bones won't break as easily should they fall, which happens often. The last child, called the *enxaneta* and treated as a local hero, is the most important part of the human castle because he or she is the one who declares the castle complete.

Supporters argue that the sport is less dangerous than a contact sport (it's true that few serious injuries are reported), but eight metres or more off the ground is never the safest place to be.

You can see *castellers* at most major festivals throughout Catalonia. The best teams are usually from the towns of Vilafranca del Penedès and Valls, both southwest of Barcelona. Every two years a huge *casteller* competition is held in early October in Tarragona's bullring. If you're in town then, it's definitely worth a day trip.

old modernist-style building, rooms boast soaring ceilings and attractive tile floors.

**Hostal Morató** (Map pp376-7; ☎ 93 442 36 69; www.hostalmorato.com; Carrer Nou de la Rambla 50; metro Drassanes; s €25-35, d €50-70) This modern *hostal* is excellent value, with spotless rooms that try hard to be stylish. Some have private bathrooms.

**Gat Raval** (Map pp376-7; ☎ 93 481 66 70; www.gataccommodation.com; Carrer Joaquim Costa 44; metro Sant Antoni; d €71, s/d with shared bathroom €39/54; ☐ ) This is by far the coolest *hostal* in town. With well-equipped rooms, neon-green walls and Internet, this place is a hit.

**Gat Xino** (Map pp376-7; Carrer Hospital 149-55) A second branch of Gat Raval, this was about to open at the time of writing.

**Hostal Eden** (Map pp379-80; ☎ 93 452 66 20; www.hostaleden.net; Carrer Balmes 55; metro Passeig de Gràcia; s/d/tr/q €47/72/77/87, s/d with shared bathroom €30/47) In L'Eixample, this *hostal* offers charming but simple rooms; No 11 has a huge Jacuzzi!

Also try:

**Pensión Alamar** (Map pp376-7; ☎ 93 302 50 12; Carrer Comtessa de Sobradiel 1; metro Liceu; s/d with shared bathroom €25/45) Great value, sociable atmosphere.

**Hostal Benidorm** (Map pp376-7; ☎ 93 302 20 54; www.barcelona-on-line.es/benidorm; Las Ramblas 37; metro Liceu; s/d €29/45) Private bathrooms and a superb location.

**Hostal Fontanella** (Map pp376-7; ☎ 93 317 59 43; Via Laietana 71; metro Urquinaona; s €38, d €55-65, s/d with shared bathroom €38/48) Cosy and well kept.

**Pensión Mari-Luz** (Map pp376-7; ☎ 93 317 34 63; Carrer Palau 4; metro Liceu; d with shared bathroom €46-52) Bright and friendly.

### HOTELS

#### Barri Gòtic & Around

**Hotel Barcelona House** (Map pp376-7; ☎ 93 301 82 95; www.hotelbarcelonahouse.com; Carrer Escudellers 19; metro Liceu; s €29-39, d €55-72, tr €85-101) This hotel is two in one, with both a bare-boned, *hostal*-ish area and a newly renovated wing, where rooms (with breakfast) cost a little more. All have bathrooms and the basic comforts.

**Hotel Rey Don Jaime** I (Map pp376-7; ☎ 93 310 62 08; r.d.jaime@atriumhotels.com; Carrer Jaume I 11; metro Jaume I; s €45, d €67-72) The spacious but spartan rooms are good value. Don't be offended by the staff; they're mean to everyone.

**Hotel Banys Orientals** (Map pp376-7; ☎ 93 268 84 61; www.hotelbanysorientals.com; Carrer Argenteria 37; metro Jaume I; s €80, d €90-95) This chic hotel is a great choice, with spiffed-up rooms in an unbeatable location.

Also try:

**Hotel Gaudí** (Map pp376-7; ☎ 93 317 90 32; Carrer Nou de la Rambla 12; metro Drassanes; s/d €95/130) Gaudí-inspired mosaics decorate the lobby.

**Park Hotel** (Map pp376-7; ☎ 93 319 60 00; Avinguda Marquès de l'Argentera 11; metro Barceloneta; s/d €110/145) Breezy, Mediterranean style near the waterfront.

**Racó del Pi** (Map pp376-7; ☎ 93 342 61 90; www .hotelracodelpi.com; Carrer Pi 7; metro Liceu; s/d €145/165) Style and charm near the Plaça del Pi.

### L'Eixample

**Hotel Pelayo** (Map pp376-7; ☎ 93 302 37 27; www .hotelpelayo.com; Carrer Pelai 9; s/d €60/80) Comfortable and great value, the Pelayo has cheery, light-filled rooms, modern bathrooms and a tasty breakfast.

**Hotel Inglaterra** (Map pp376-7; ☎ 93 505 11 00; www.hotel-inglaterra.com; Carrer Pelai 14; metro Plaça Catalunya; s €99-160, d €119-200) With stylish rooms a stone's throw from Plaça Catalunya, this is a great choice.

### APARTMENTS

Several private apartment-rental companies operate in Barcelona. These can often be a better deal than staying in a hotel, especially if you're travelling in a group. Try www .go2barcelona.com, www.inside-bcn.com or www.selfcateringhols.com.

## Eating

Eating in Barcelona is a joy. There's a fantastic selection of regional, international and creative restaurants, ingredients are nearly always fresh, and it's still possible to get a nice meal without blowing your budget.

Typical dishes range from rice and shellfish paella, ubiquitous in the restaurants by the port, to hearty Catalan fare such as pigs' trotters, rabbit with snails and *butifarra* (a tasty local sausage). Lunch is served from 2pm to 3.30pm, and dinner begins at 9pm. In between, you can snack at bars or hunt out the touristy restaurants on Las Ramblas.

### AROUND LAS RAMBLAS
### Budget

**Café de l'Òpera** (Map pp376-7; ☎ 93 317 75 85; Las Ramblas 74; metro Liceu; 8.30-2.45am) A classic spot for breakfast or coffee, this once-high-class café is a little bruised nowadays but that just makes it all the more popular and atmospheric.

**Buenas Migas** (Map pp376-7; ☎ 93 318 37 08; Plaça de Bonsuccés 6; metro Plaça Catalunya; mains €2.20-5; 10am-11pm Sun-Wed, to midnight Thu-Sat) Try the focaccias and awesome desserts at this breezy footpath café.

**Bagel Shop** (Map pp376-7; ☎ 93 302 41 61; Carrer Canuda 25; metro Liceu; mains €3.50-7; 9.30am-9.30pm Mon-Sat, 11am-4pm Sun) For American-style bagels and desserts, there's no better place than this informal café off Las Ramblas.

**Venus** (Map pp376-7; ☎ 93 301 15 85; Carrer Avinyò 25; metro Liceu; menú €8.50; noon-midnight Mon-Sat) Vegetarians will love the salad selection at this grungy-chic café.

Self-caterers can make a beeline for the wildly colourful **Mercat de la Boquería** (p378) for fresh food.

### Mid-Range

**Bar-Bodega Fortuny** (Map pp376-7; ☎ 93 317 98 92; Carrer Pintor Fortuny 31; metro Liceu; mains €4.50-9; 10-2am Tue-Sun) This quirky bar serves salads, couscous and hummus to a largely bohemian group of regulars. At night it's a popular lesbian hang-out.

**Bar Ra** (Map pp376-7; ☎ 93 301 41 63; Plaça Gardunya; metro Liceu; mains €6-9; 9.30-1.30am) For light, international fare alfresco, head to this colourful bar/restaurant just behind the Mercat de la Boquería.

**La Fonda** (Map pp376-7; ☎ 93 301 75 15; Carrer Escudellers 10; metro Drassanes; mains €7-12; 1pm-3.30pm & 8.30-11.30pm) Mediterranean and traditional dishes are served with style at this popular eatery, where you'll almost always have to stand in line before nabbing a table.

**Els Quatre Gats** (Map pp376-7; ☎ 93 302 41 40; Carrer Montsió 3; metro Urquinaona; menú €15-20; 1pm-1am) The legendary modernist café where Picasso had his first exhibit, 'The Four Cats' now serves excellent (though pricey) Catalan dishes.

### Top End

**Los Caracoles** (Map pp376-7; ☎ 93 302 31 85; Carrer Escudellers 14; metro Liceu; mains €11-26; 1pm-midnight) For truly traditional fare, don't miss this raucous Barcelona institution, where grilled meats, seafood and *caracoles* (snails) are the house specialties.

**El Café de l'Acadèmia** (Map pp376-7; ☎ 93 319 82 53; Carrer Lledó 1; metro Jaume I; 1-4pm & 8.45-11.30pm Mon-Fri, closed Aug 15-31) This fine restaurant serves strictly Catalan dishes in a romantic atmosphere. If you're with a group, ask to sit in the downstairs bodega.

**Taller de Tapas** (Map pp376-7; ☎ 93 301 80 20; Plaça Sant Josep Oriol 9; metro Liceu; mains €20-25; 8pm-midnight) This is the place for tapas, Barcelona style. Creativity abounds in every bite.

SPAIN

## LA RIBERA & LA BARCELONETA

**Comme-Bio** (Map pp376-7; ☎ 93 319 89 68; Vía Laietana 28; menú €8.45; ☯ 1-4pm & 8-11pm) At this casual restaurant it's not just vegetarian, it's organic. There's a shop here too.

**Origins 99.9%** (Map pp376-7; ☎ 93 310 75 31; Carrer Vidriera 6-8; menú €12; ☯ 12.30pm-1.30am) Also a shop-restaurant combo, Origins boasts that '99.9%' of everything sold is from Catalonia. The ever-changing daily *menú* features local specialties such as *escalivada* (roasted veggies on bread) and Catalan sausages.

**Coses de Menjar** (Map pp376-7; ☎ 93 310 60 01; Pla de Palau 7; mains €8-16; ☯ 1.30-3.45pm & 9-11.30pm) The wildly creative décor almost outshines the food at this fanciful eatery, where fresh twists are put on old Catalan recipes.

**Comerç 24** (Map pp376-7; ☎ 93 319 21 02; Carrer Comerç 24; metro Jaume; mains €14-20, menú €42; ☯ 11.30am-4pm & 8.30pm-midnight) One of the best seafood choices. Get rice or seafood dishes overlooking the Med.

La Barceloneta is the place to go for seafood. Try one of the many excellent (and pricey) restaurants around the Plaça de Pau Vila or head to the Port Olímpic, where one of the better-priced restaurants is stylish **Agua** (Map pp379-80; ☎ 93 225 12 72; Passeig Marítim Barceloneta 30; metro Ciutadella-Vila Olímpica; mains €12-18).

## L'EIXAMPLE

**Laie Librería Café** (Map pp376-7; ☎ 93 302 73 10; Carrer Pau Claris 85; metro Passeig de Gràcia; mains €5-12; ☯ 1am-1pm Tue-Sat, 1-9pm Mon) The delicious buffet and lunch *menú* is packed with healthy food, local specialties and vegetarian options.

**Cervecería Catalana** (Map pp379-80; ☎ 93 216 03 68; Carrer Mallorca 236; metro Passieg de Gràcia; tapas €2-12, mains €5-14; ☯ 1pm-1am) Arrive early to try the delicious tapas and *flautas* (long 'skinny sandwiches') at this classic tavern off La Rambla de Catalunya.

**La Flauta** (Map pp379-80; ☎ 93 323 70 38; Carrer Aribau 23; metro Universitat; mains €5-14; ☯ 9-1am) Run by the same owners as Cervecería Catalana, La Flauta has the same classic *flautas* and tavern atmosphere.

**L'Hostal de Rita** (Map pp379-80; ☎ 93 487 23 76; Carrer Aribau 279; metro Passeig de Gràcia; mains €6-10, menú €7; ☯ 10am-3.45pm & 8.30-11.30pm) For a bit of style, this popular restaurant does the trick. Be prepared to wait in line for samples of its pastas, seafood and traditional dishes.

**Cacao Sampaka** (Map pp376-7; ☎ 93 272 08 33; Carrer Consell de Cent 292; metro Passeig de Gràcia; snacks €1.50-4; ☯ 9am-8pm Mon-Sat) For dessert, hit this chocolate-lovers' paradise, where you can drool over more than a dozen varieties of chocolate ice cream.

## Drinking

Whether you're in search of a quiet place to chat, drink in hand, or a smoky place with music that doesn't let you think, Barcelona's got an option for you. On weekends, bars stay hopping until 2am and most of the places listed here are open for quiet drinks as early as 8pm.

**Muebles Navarro** (Map pp376-7; ☎ 60 718 80 96; Carrer Riera Alta 4; metro Liceu) Funky and decorated like a furniture flea market. Kick back with a cold one and one of its great cheese plates.

**Lletraferit** (Map pp376-7; ☎ 93 301 19 61; Carrer Joaquim Costa 43; metro Sant Antoni) Just as chill but a bit more sophisticated, this is a book-lovers' café by day and a cocktail bar by night.

**Rita Blue** (Map pp376-7; ☎ 93 342 40 86; Plaça Sant Agustí 3; metro Liceu) Upbeat restaurant and bar where everyone orders the house speciality, a blue margarita.

**Philharmonic** ( ☎ 93 451 11 53; Carrer Mallorca 204; metro Provença) One of Barcelona's most popular pubs. Stop in for all the football matches, some English conversation and a mouthwatering English breakfast.

Head to the Passeig del Born for a great selection of laid-back bars such as **Miramelindo** (Map pp376-7; ☎ 93 319 53 76; Passeig del Born 15; metro Jaume I), a Barcelona favourite, and **La Vinya del Senyor** (Map pp376-7; ☎ 93 310 33 97; Plaça Santa Maria 5; metro Jaume I), a romantic wine bar sitting under the shadow of the Basilica.

The Gràcia district, with its intimate plazas and narrow streets, is the perfect spot for a quiet drink. The **Café del Sol** (Map pp379-80; ☎ 93 415 56 63; Plaça del Sol; metro Fontana) has a fantastic terrace for sipping outdoors, while **Gusto** (Map pp379-80; Carrer Francisco Giner 24; metro Fontana) offers a friendly atmosphere and some of the city's best DJs.

## Entertainment

### CINEMAS

The best original-language cinema is **Verdi** (Map pp379-80; ☎ 93 238 79 90; Carrer Verdi 32; metro Fontana), in Gràcia. Big-budget Hollywood flicks are shown in English at **Icària** ( ☎ 93 221 75 85; Carrer Salvador Espiritu 61; metro Vila Olímpica).

## GAY & LESBIAN VENUES

The gay and lesbian scene is concentrated in the blocks around Carrers Muntaner and Consell de Cent (dubbed Gayxample by the locals). Here you'll find ambience every night of the week in the bars, discos and drag clubs.

**Oui Café** (Map pp379-80; Carrer Consell de Cent 247; metro Universitat) has a sophisticated style and all-white décor reigns. A spiffy clientele comes for low-key drinks.

Party hard at classic gay discos such as **Arena Madre** ( ☎ 93 487 83 42; Carrer Balmes 32; metro Universitat; 🕑 closed Mon) and **Salvation** (Map pp376-7; ☎ 93 318 06 86; Ronda Sant Pere 19-21; metro Universitat; 🕑 Fri-Sun).

The low-key **Bar-Bodega Fortuny** (p383) is a popular lesbian hang-out.

## LIVE MUSIC

**London Bar** (Map pp379-80; ☎ 93 318 52 61; Carrer Nou de la Rambla 34; metro Drassanes) A popular expat hang-out, it hosts concerts most nights. Groups range from jazz to rock to flamenco.

**Harlem Jazz Club** (Map pp376-7; ☎ 93 310 07 55; Carrer Comtessa de Sobradiel 8; metro Liceu) A guaranteed dose of quality jazz and enough smoke to cook a sausage.

**Otto Zutz** (Map pp379-80; ☎ 93 238 07 22; Carrer Lincoln 15; metro Fontana) Often has frontline acts.

**Tablao Cordobés** (Map pp376-7; ☎ 93 317 57 11; Las Ramblas 35; metro Liceu) Though Barcelona is not the best place to see flamenco, you can catch a reasonably authentic show here.

## CLUBS

For discos of every shape, size and variety, head to the Port Olímpic; in summer it's a nonstop party, and winter weekends are fun too.

**Baja Beach Club** ( ☎ 93 225 91 00; Passeig Marítim la Barceloneta 34; metro Ciutadella-Vila Olímpica; 🕑 midnight-6am Thu-Sun) One of Port Olímpic's biggest clubs: being tanned, beautiful and nearly topless seem to be requirements for entry.

**Jamboree** (Map pp376-7; ☎ 93 319 17 89; Plaça Reial 17; 🕑 10.30pm-5am) Jumping with hip-hop music every night of the week, Jamboree is a magnet for foreign students. This could be a draw or a reason to flee, depending on your view.

**Magic** (Map pp376-7; ☎ 93 310 72 67; Passeig Picasso 40; 🕑 11pm-6am Thu-Sun) One of the city's top clubs, with fantastic live music running the gamut between techno and classic rock.

## SPORT

Football fans can see the Fútbol Club Barcelona play at **Camp Nou** (Map pp379-80; ☎ 93 496 36 00; www.fcbarcelona.com; Carrer Arístides Maillol; metro Collblanc). Even if you can't score tickets, stop by for a peek at the **museum** ( ☎ 93 496 36 08; gates 7 & 9; admission €5, tour €9; 🕑 10am-6.30pm Mon-Sat, 10am-2pm Sun).

## THEATRE

Most theatre in the city is in Catalan, but there are quite a few that stage vanguard drama.

**Teatre Nacional de Catalunya** ( ☎ 93 306 57 00; Plaça de les Arts 1; metro Glòries) If you're up for a language lesson, check out the performances at this classy theatre.

**La Fura Dels Baus** (www.lafura.com) Anything performed anywhere by this wild troupe is bound to be funny and energetic and somewhat controversial. They manage to communicate without words, so language isn't a problem.

## Shopping

Shops open Monday through Saturday from 10am until 2pm and again, after a long lunch, from 5pm until 8.30pm. Queen of Barcelona's shopping districts is **Passeig de Gràcia** (metro Passeig de Gràcia), where high-end fashion struts its stuff. Chanel, Hermés and Cartier all have boutiques here, but those without €5000 credit limits don't have to go home empty-handed. For unique clothing and shoes, browse the intimate shops in the mall-like **Boulevard Rosa** (Map pp379-80; ☎ 93 309 06 50; Passeig de Gràcia 53-57). If you like design you'll love gadget-happy **Vinçon** (Map pp379-80; ☎ 93 215 60 50; Passeig de Gràcia 96).

**El Born** (metro Jaume I), the city's original textile centre, is now a hot spot for up-and-coming designers. Try on the funky looks at shops such as **MTX Barcelona** (Map pp376-7; ☎ 93 319 13 98; Carrer Rec 32).

Off Las Ramblas, the **Carrer Portaferrisa** (metro Liceu) has shops selling everything from punk fashion – **El Mercadillo** (Map pp376-7; ☎ 93 301 47 04; Carrer Portaferrisa 17) – to melt-in-your-mouth Spanish *turrón* (nougat) at **Casa Colomina** (Map pp376-7; ☎ 93 412 25 11; Carrer Portaferrisa 8). Nearby, there's a Saturday **art market** (Plaça Sant Josep Oriol) where you'll find prints and originals from local artists, while the connecting Plaça del Pi hosts an **artesan food fair** on alternating weekends.

SPAIN

Bargain hunters love **Els Encants** ( ☎ 93 246 30 30; Carrer Dos de Maig 186; metro Glòries), a free-for-all morning flea market.

## Getting There & Away
### AIR
Barcelona's airport, 14km southwest of the city centre at El Prat de Llobregat, caters to international as well as domestic flights. It's not a European hub, but you can often dig up specials and cheap youth fares. Airlines include Iberia, Air Europa, Spanair and easyJet (p439 for contact details).

### BUS
The terminal for virtually all domestic and international buses is the **Estació del Nord** (Map pp379-80; ☎ 93 265 65 08; Carrer Alí Bei 80; metro Arc de Triomf). Several buses a day go to most main Spanish cities, including Madrid, Zaragoza, Valencia and Granada.

### TRAIN
Virtually all trains travelling to and from destinations within Spain stop at **Estació Sants** (Map pp379-80; metro Sants-Estació Barcelona). Daily trains run to most major cities in Spain. There are seven trains a day to Madrid (six to nine hours), two daily to San Sebastián (eight to 10hrs), 10 daily to Valencia (three hours or more), and one daily to Granada (eight to 10hrs).

Tickets and information are available at the station.

### CAR & MOTORCYCLE
The highways surrounding Barcelona are excellent, though traffic does build up from 8am to 9am, from 7pm to 10pm and on Friday and Saturday afternoons, when everyone hits the high road out of town. The A-7 motorway comes in from the French border, and the A-2 motorway heads toward Zaragoza. Both are toll roads. The N-II is a nontoll alternative, but it's slower and more dangerous.

## Getting Around
### TO/FROM THE AIRPORT
Trains link the airport to Estació Sants and **Catalunya regional train station** (Plaça Catalunya) every half-hour (€2.25, 15 to 20 minutes). The Aerobus (€3.75, 40 minutes) does the run between Plaça Catalunya and the airport every 15 minutes, or every half-hour at

weekends. A taxi from the airport to Plaça Catalunya is around €15 to €20.

### BUS, METRO & TRAIN
Barcelona's metro system spreads its tentacles around the city in such a way that most places of interest are within a 10-minute walk of a station. Buses and suburban trains are needed only for a few destinations. A single metro, bus or suburban train ride costs €1.10, but a T-1 ticket, valid for 10 rides, costs only €6.

### CAR & MOTORCYCLE
Parking a car is difficult and, if you choose a parking garage, quite expensive (€20 per day). It's better to ditch your car and rely on public transport.

### TAXI
Barcelona's black-and-yellow taxis are plentiful, reasonably priced and handy for late-night transport. Flag fall is €1.30.

## MONESTIR DE MONTSERRAT
The prime attraction of Montserrat, 50km northwest of Barcelona, is its incredible setting. The **Benedictine Monastery** of Montserrat sits high on the side of a 1236m-high mountain of weird, bulbous peaks. The monastery was founded in 1025 after a statue of the Virgin Mary was found here. Pilgrims still come from all over Christendom to pay homage to the Black Virgin (La Moreneta), a 12th-century wooden sculpture of Mary, regarded as Catalonia's patroness. The statue stands in the basilica's altar, where the faithful line up to kiss it. Mass is held several times daily; at the 1pm mass Monday to Saturday the monastery boy choir sings.

Montserrat's **information centre** ( ☎ 93 877 77 77; ☼ 10am-6pm) is to the left along the road from the top cable-car station. It has a couple of good free leaflets and maps on the mountain and monastery, as well as information about the **Museu de Montserrat** (admission €5.50; ☼ 10am-7pm Mon-Fri, 9.30am-7.30pm Sat & Sun).

## Sleeping & Eating
There are several accommodation options at the **monastery** (all ☎ 93 877 77 01; www.abadia montserrat.net). The cheapest rooms are in the **Cel.les Abat Olibia** (d from €25), blocks of simple

apartments, with showers, for up to 10 people. Overlooking Plaça Santa Maria is the comfortable and excellent-value **Hotel Abat Cisneros** (s €27-50, d €45-82). The **restaurant** (menú €19) here is miles better than the caféteria down the mountain.

## Getting There & Away

The FGC R5 train runs from Barcelona's Plaça Espanya to both Aeri de Montserrat (one hour, 19 daily), where you can catch a cable car up the mountain, and to Monistrol-Vila, where you can hop on a rack railway to head up. The combined return ticket is €11.40.

## GIRONA & THE COSTA BRAVA

The rocky, rugged scenery of the Costa Brava has made this once-sleepy, now-sizzling area one of Spain's most popular holiday spots. The main jumping-off points for the Costa Brava are the inland towns of Girona (Gerona in Castilian) and Figueres. Along the coast, the most appealing resorts are (from north to south) Cadaqués, L'Escala (La Escala), Tamariu, Llafranc, Calella de Palafrugell and Tossa de Mar.

## Information

**Tourist Office** ( ☺ 10am-1pm & 4-7pm Mon-Sat, 10am-1pm Sun, 9am-9pm daily Jul-Aug); Girona ( ☎ 97 220 84 01; www.costabrava.org; Carrer Emili Grahit 13-15); Figueres ( ☎ 97 250 31 55; www.figueresciutat.com; Plaça del Sol); Palafrugell ( ☎ 97 261 18 20; www.palafrugell.net; Plaça de l'Església)

## Sights & Activities

### COASTAL RESORTS & ISLANDS

The Costa Brava (Rugged Coast) is all about picturesque inlets and coves. Beaches tend to be small and scattered. Some longer beaches at places such as L'Estartit and Empúries are worth visiting off season, but there has been a tendency to build tall buildings wherever engineers think it can be done. Fortunately, in many places it just can't.

**Cadaqués**, at the end of an agonising one hour's drive east of Figueres, at the end of an agonising series of hairpin bends, is perhaps the most picturesque of all Spanish resorts. It's haunted by the memory of former resident Salvador Dalí, whose house is nearby. Beaches here are of the pebbly variety, so people spend a lot of time sitting at waterfront cafés or wandering along the beautiful

coast. Some 10km northeast of Cadaqués is **Cap de Creus**, a rocky mountain park where you can hike and visit a **monastery**.

Further down the coast, past L'Escala and L'Estartit, is Palafrugell. Though the town has little to offer, it's near three gorgeous beach towns that have to be seen to be believed. The most northerly, **Tamariu**, is also the smallest, least crowded and most exclusive. **Llafranc** is the biggest and busiest, and has the longest beach. **Calella de Palafrugell**, with its truly picture-postcard setting, is never overcrowded and always relaxed.

Among the most exciting attractions on the Costa Brava are the **Illes Medes**, off the coast from the package resort of L'Estartit. These seven islets and their surrounding coral reefs have been declared a natural park to protect their extraordinarily diverse flora and fauna. Diving is popular here. Ask at the tourist offices for details.

### OTHER ATTRACTIONS

When you have had enough beach for a while, make sure you put the **Teatre-Museu Dalí** ( ☎ 97 252 28 00; Plaça Gala i Salvador Dalí 5, Figueres; admission €9, incl admission to other Dalí sites; ☺ 10.30am-5.45pm Oct-Jun, 9am-7.45pm Jul-Sep) at the top of your list. This 19th-century theatre was converted by Dalí himself and houses a huge and fascinating collection of his strange creations. You can also visit Dalí's home, now a **museum** ( ☎ 97 225 10 15; Portlligat; admission €8; ☺ 10.30am-6pm Oct-May, 10.30am-9pm Jun-Sep) near Cadaqués.

**Girona** sports a lovely, though tiny, medieval quarter centred on a Gothic cathedral. For a stroll through antiquity, check out the ruins of the Greek and Roman town of **Empúries**, 2km from L'Escala.

## Sleeping & Eating

Most visitors to the Costa Brava rent apartments. If you are interested in renting your own pad for a week or so, contact local tourist offices in advance. Seaside restaurants provide dramatic settings but often at high prices.

### FIGUERES

Avoid sleeping in Figueres' Parc Municipal – people have been attacked here at night.

**Pensión Mallol** ( ☎ 97 250 22 83; Carrer Pep Ventura 9; s/d with shared bathroom €16/28) Simple, no-frills rooms.

**Pensión Isabel II** ( ☎ 97 250 47 35; Carrer Isabel II 16; s/d €22/28) More comfortable and with private bathrooms.

**Restaurant Versalles** ( ☎ 97 250 00 02; Carrer Jonquera 18; mains €5-15) Local cuisine away from the noise and high prices of the main plaza.

### GIRONA

**Alberg de Joventut** ( ☎ 97 221 80 03; www.tujuca .com; Carrer Ciutadans 9; dm with shared bathroom €14-19) Offers standard HI fare.

**Pensión Viladomat** ( ☎ 97 220 31 76; Carrer Ciutadans 5; d with shared bathroom €35) Comfortable rooms.

Dine on Girona's Rambla for good people watching. **Arts Café** (La Rambla 23) offers a low-key atmosphere and cheap, snacky fare.

### CADAQUÉS

**Hostal Marina** ( ☎ 97 225 81 99; Carrer Riera 3; s/d €35/50) Sunny, cheerful rooms.

### AROUND PALAFRUGELL

Hotel and *pensión* rooms are relatively thin on the ground here, as many people come on package deals.

**Hostería del Plancton** ( ☎ 97 261 50 81; Calella de Palafrugell; r from €18; ☒ Jun-Sep) Friendly and one of the best deals on the Costa Brava.

**Hotel Montaña** ( ☎ 97 230 12 91; Carrer Cesàrea 2, Llafranc; r from €78) A good deal, though pricey in summer.

Numerous food stalls and cafés cluster in all three towns.

## Getting There & Away

A few buses run daily from Barcelona to Tossa del Mar, L'Estartit and Cadaqués for a couple of euros, but for the small resorts near Palafrugell you need to get to Girona first. Girona and Figueres are both on the railway connecting Barcelona to France. The dozen or so trains daily from Barcelona to Portbou at the border all stop in Girona (€5.10, 1¼ hours), and most in Figueres (€7.30 to €8.40, one hour and 40 minutes).

## TARRAGONA

Founded in 218 BC, Tarraco was an important Roman centre and the capital of Hispania. Roman structures figure among its most important attractions and the city is fascinating place to visit. Good beaches, a nearby theme park and a large student population keep the city from dwelling too much on its past.

## Orientation & Information

Tarragona's main street is Rambla Nova, which runs northwest from a cliff top overlooking the Mediterranean.

**Café Cantonada** ( ☎ 97 721 35 24; Carrer Fortuny 23; ☒ 10-2am) Internet access.

**Main Tourist Office** ( ☎ 97 725 07 95; Carrer Major 39; ☒ 10am-2pm & 4-7pm Mon-Sat, 10am-2pm Sun) Has maps and accommodation information.

## Sights & Activities

Start at the fascinating **Museu Arqueològic** ( ☎ 97 723 62 09; Plaça del Rei 5; admission €2.40; ☒ 10am-1.30pm & 4-7pm Tue-Sat, 10am-2pm Sun Oct-May, 10am-8pm Tue-Sat, 10am-2pm Sun Jun-Sep), where you'll get an excellent understanding of Roman Spain.

Nearby is the **Museu de la Romanitat**, formed by the **Castell del Rei** ( ☎ 97 724 19 52) and the **Roman Circus**. The Castell once formed part of the city walls. You can head to the top for views and then see the ruins of the Roman Circus, where chariot races were held.

Nearby, and close to the beach, is the well-preserved **Roman amphitheatre**, where gladiators battled each other (or unlucky souls were thrown to wild animals) to the death. On Carrer Lleida, a few blocks west of Rambla Nova, are the remains of a **Roman forum**. The **Passeig Arqueològic** ( ☒ until midnight) is a peaceful walk along a stretch of the old city walls, which are a combination of Roman, Iberian and 17th-century British efforts.

The **cathedral** sits grandly at the highest point of Tarragona, overlooking the old town. Some parts of the building date back to the 12th century. It's open for tourist visits during the week but hours vary with the season (longest in summer). Entrance is through the beautiful cloister with the excellent **Museu Diocesà**.

Clean **Platja del Miracle** is the main city beach; it sits south of the Roman amphitheatre.

### PORT AVENTURA

Some 7km west of Tarragona, near Salou, the **Universal Studios Port Aventura** ( ☎ 97 777 90 90; www.universalmediterranea.com; adult/child €35/28; ☒ 10am-7pm Apr-Oct, summer hrs longer but vary, open weekends only Nov-Mar) is a US-style theme park, fun for the family or the young at heart. Trains run to Port Aventura's own station, about a 1km walk from the site, several times a day from Tarragona and Barcelona.

# TARRAGONA

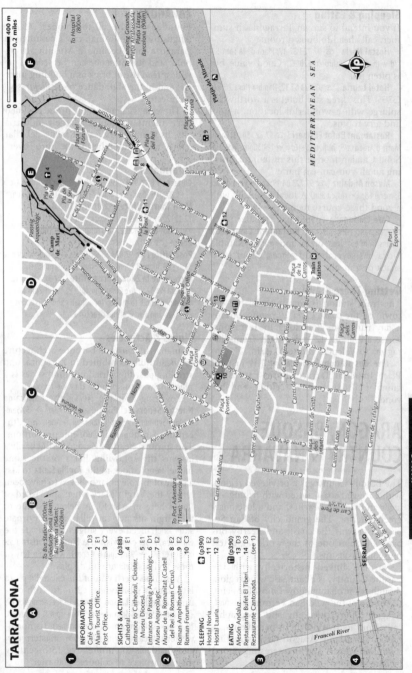

## Sleeping & Eating

If you intend to stay in Tarragona in summer, call ahead to book a room.

**Hostal Noria** ( ☎ 97 723 87 17; Plaça de la Font 53; s/d with shared bathroom €20/32) Good value but is often full.

**Hotel Lauria** ( ☎ 97 723 67 12; Rambla Nova 20; s/d €37/55) This three-star hotel is a worthwhile splurge with a wonderful location, a pool and airy rooms.

**Restaurant Bufet El Tiberi** ( ☎ 97 723 54 03; Carrer Martí d'Ardenya 5; buffet €9-10; ☻ 1-3.30pm Tue-Sun) Solid Catalan food at this restaurant offering an all-you-can-eat buffet.

**Mesón Andaluz** ( ☎ 97 723 84 19; Carrer Pons d'Icart 3; menú €8; ☻ closed Sun) A local favourite with a good three-course menú.

**Café Cantonada** (p388) is a popular place for tapas; next door, **Restaurant Cantonada** (mains from €5) has pizza and pasta. Rambla Nova has several good places, either for a snack or a meal.

## Getting There & Away

The train station is southwest of the old town, on the coast. Over 20 regional trains a day run from Barcelona to Tarragona. There are about 12 trains daily from Tarragona to Valencia and to Madrid.

The **bus station** (Avinguda Roma) is just off Plaça Imperial Tarraco. Buses run to regional cities such as Barcelona, and beyond.

# ARAGÓN, BASQUE COUNTRY & NAVARRA

The Basque Country is a privileged region, with a rugged coast dotted with fishing villages and surfing beaches, and a lusciously green interior. The grand city of San Sebastián crowns the coast, and nearby Bilbao can claim one of the world's greatest museums as its own.

Navarra, linked historically with the Basque Country, is a fantastic wine region, though it's probably known most for being the home of the wild San Fermíne festival. Aragón differs culturally and geographically from its two northern neighbours. A proud, stern land, Aragón has fascinating mountain scenery and an interesting capital in Zaragoza.

## ZARAGOZA

Founded by the all-too-modest Caesar Augustus as the Roman city Caesaragusta, Zaragoza later became a Muslim stronghold, and its influence can be seen in the widespread use of brick as a building material and in the abundance of *Mudéjar*-style architecture.

These days Zaragoza, the proud capital of once-mighty Aragón, is a largely industrial city. Its shining light is the Basílica del Pilar, a fairy-tale creation beside the Ebro River.

## Information

**Conecta-T** ( ☎ 97 620 59 79; Calle Murallas Romanas 4; per hr €1.20; ☻ 10am-11pm Mon-Fri, 11am-11pm Sat & Sun)
**Main Tourist Office** ( ☎ 97 620 12 1200 or 902 20 12 1212; www.turismozaragoza.com; Plaza del Pilar; ☻ 10am-8pm) Housed in a futuristic glass cube.
**Police** ( ☎ 091)
**Post Office** ( ☎ 97 623 68 68; Paseo de la Independencia 33; ☻ 8.30am-8.30pm Mon-Fri, 9.30am-2pm Sat)
**Torreón de la Zuda tourist office** ( ☎ 902 201 212; Glorieta Pío 12 or Ave César Agusto; ☻ 10am-2pm & 4.30-8pm) Climb to the top for a small exhibition about Zaragoza and a view of the river bank.

## Sights & Activities

Roman, *Mudéjar* and baroque architecture are beautifully combined in Zaragoza, and strolling past the varied building styles is a pleasant way to spend a day or two.

Towering over the city is the **Basílica de Nuestra Señora del Pilar** (Plaza del Pilar; ☻ 5.45am-8.30pm Sep-Jun, 5.45am-9.30pm Jul & Aug), a 17th-century baroque basilica of epic proportions. The spiritual heart of Zaragoza, the basilica crowns the sprawling Plaza of the same name. People flock to the **Capilla Santa** to kiss a piece of marble pillar believed to have been left by the Virgin Mary when she visited St James here in AD 40. A beloved statue of the Virgin sits atop the pillar, and her ornate skirt is changed every single day. Inside the Basilica, you can visit the **Museo Pilarista** (admission €1.50, ☻ 9am-2pm & 4-6pm), where a few of these lavish skirts are on display.

At southeastern end of the capital's plaza is Zaragoza's brooding 12th- to 16th-century cathedral, **La Seo** (Plaza de La Seo; admission €2; ☻ 10am-2pm & 4-6pm Tue-Fri, 10am-1pm & 4-6pm Sat, 10am-noon & 4-6pm Sun, 1hr later summer). Its northwestern façade is a *Mudéjar* masterpiece, and inside is an impressive 15th-century main altarpiece in coloured alabaster.

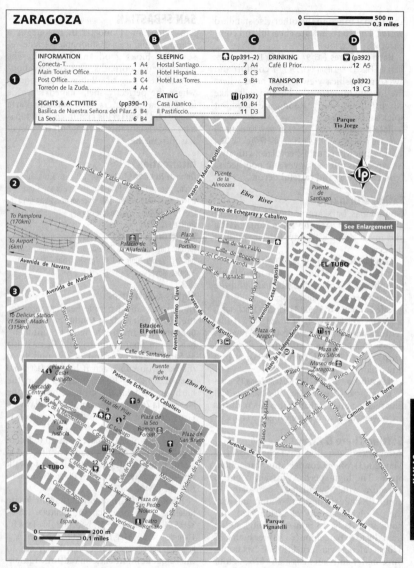

## ZARAGOZA

| | | |
|---|---|---|
| **INFORMATION** | **SLEEPING** (pp391–2) | **DRINKING** (p392) |
| Conecta-T.................................1 A4 | Hostal Santiago.........................7 A4 | Café El Prior.............................12 A5 |
| Main Tourist Office....................2 B4 | Hotel Hispania..........................8 C3 | |
| Post Office................................3 C4 | Hotel Las Torres.......................9 B4 | **TRANSPORT** (p392) |
| Torreón de la Zuda....................4 A4 | | Agreda....................................13 C3 |
| | **EATING** (p392) | |
| **SIGHTS & ACTIVITIES** (pp390–1) | Casa Juanico...........................10 B4 | |
| Basílica de Nuestra Señora del Pilar.5 B4 | il Pastificcio.............................11 D3 | |
| La Seo......................................6 B4 | | |

The odd trapezoid structure in front of La Seo looks like the Louvre, but actually it's the entrance to the **Museo del Foro de Caesaraugusta** ( ☎ 97 639 97 52; Plaza de La Seo; admission €2; 🕑 10am-2pm & 5-8pm Tue-Sat, 10am-2pm Sun), an interesting museum about Roman life. Some 70m below lie the remains of Roman shops, porticoes and a great sewerage system, all brought to life by an audiovisual show.

## Sleeping

Many cheap rooms are found near the Plaza del Pilar.

**Hostal Santiago** ( ☎ 97 639 45 50; Calle Santiago 3-5; s €20-25, d €30-36; 🗙 ) Neon-green walls add an original touch to the otherwise standard *hostal*. The 26 rooms are cheerful and comparatively spacious.

**Hotel Las Torres** ( ☎ 97 639 42 50; torres@able.es; Plaza del Pilar 11; s/d from €41/55) For comfort and awesome basilica views, head here, where the lovely chimes of the basilica will wake you bright and early. Rooms are dated but spick and span.

**Hotel Hispania** ( ☎ 97 628 49 28; www.hotelhispania .com; Ave Augusto 95-103; s €33-47, d €47-70; 🖳 🔄 ) This is a newly refurbished place with stylish, spacious quarters, gym and pool access (you pay extra) and tasteful décor.

## Eating & Drinking

Good tapas bars are scattered around El Tubo, especially around Plaza Santa Marta, and in La Zona, a trendy district south of the centre.

**Casa Juanico** ( ☎ 97 639 72 52; Calle Santa Cruz 21; menú €9) For cheap tapas and a friendly atmosphere, this place can't be beat, and the summer terrace is ideal.

**Café El Prior** ( ☎ 97 620 11 48; Calle Santa Cruz 7; mains €4-8; 🕑 closed Wed) Housed in a 16th-century palace and serving tasty Aragonés dishes such as *ternasco* (lamb's ribs) and *migas* (fried breadcrumbs). Has a pub downstairs.

**Il Pastificcio** ( ☎ 97 623 66 62; Calle Zurita 15; mains €9-10; 🕑 1-4pm & 8pm-midnight) Vegetarians will find plenty at this Italian bistro where dishes are always tasty and big enough to share.

## Getting There & Away

Zaragoza's new station, Las Delicias (opened May 2003) offers connections throughout Spain. The high-speed AVE train connects Zaragoza with Madrid (€43, four daily, 11 non-AVE daily) in under two hours and with the pre-Pyrenean city of Lleida (€24, one hour, four daily, 15 non-AVE daily). Other trains head to Barcelona (€34, three hours, 15 daily), Valencia via Teruel (€16.45, six hours, three daily) and San Sebastián (€26.50, four hours, three daily) via Pamplona.

Though construction is underway on Las Delicias bus terminal, which will one day be the city's one-stop bus stop, currently stations are scattered all over town. **Agreda** ( ☎ 97 622 93 43; www.agredasa.com) runs to most major Spanish cities, including Madrid (€12.09, four hours, 18 daily) from Paseo María Agustín 7.

## SAN SEBASTIÁN

San Sebastián (Donostia in Basque) is a grand old dame, a fashionable seaside resort that looks good and knows it. The clean-swept footpaths and orderly boulevards here hug the Bahía de la Concha, where the perfectly shell-shaped Playa de la Concha shimmers. The buzzing Parte Vieja (Old Quarter) is crammed with tapas bars and restaurants showing off the best of Basque cuisine.

## Information

**Donosti-Net** ( ☎ 94 342 94 97; Calle San Jerónimo 8; internet per hr €3; 🕑 9am-11pm) This is a one-stop travellers' service, with email, office services and even a spot to leave your luggage (per day €9).

**Police** ( ☎ 091)

**Tourist Office** ( ☎ 94 348 11 66; www.sansebastian turismo.com; Calle Reina Regente 3; 🕑 8am-8pm daily Jun-Sep, 9am-1.30pm & 3.30-7pm Mon-Sat, 10am-2pm Sun Oct-May)

## Sights & Activities

In summer, most people head straight for the shore. **Playa de la Concha** and **Playa de Ondarreta** are among the most beautiful city beaches in Spain, and beyond them is **Isla de Santa Clara**, an island in the middle of the bay; you can reach it by **boat** (adult/child return €2.60/1.30; 🕑 10am-8pm Jun-Sep) from the harbour. To beat the crowds, head to the **Playa de la Zurriola** (also known as Playa de Gros), east of the Urumea River, which is popular with surfers.

For views over the bay, head up to **Monte Urgull**, topped by low castle walls and a statue of Christ. It takes 30 minutes to walk up – a stairway starts from Plaza Zuloaga in the old town.

Even better are the views from **Monte Igueldo**. Drive or catch the **funicular** ( ☎ 94 321 05 64; return €1.60; 🕑 11am-6pm Mon, Tue, Thu & Fri, 11am-8pm Sat & Sun Feb, Mar, Nov & Dec, closed Wed, until 8pm daily Apr-Jun & Sep 15-Oct, 10am-10pm Jul-Aug) to the **Parque de Atracciones**, an old-time funfair. At the foot of the hill is Eduardo Chillida's abstract iron sculpture *Peine de los Vientos* (Comb of the Winds).

Kids and adults will have fun at San Sebastián's **aquarium** ( ☎ 943 44 00 99; www.aquariumss .com; Paseo del Muelle 34; admission €9; 🕑 10am-8pm Sep, May & Jun, 10am-7pm Mon-Fri & 11am-8pm Sat & Sun Oct-Apr, 10am-9pm Jul & Aug), which has 10 large tanks teeming with tropical fish, morays,

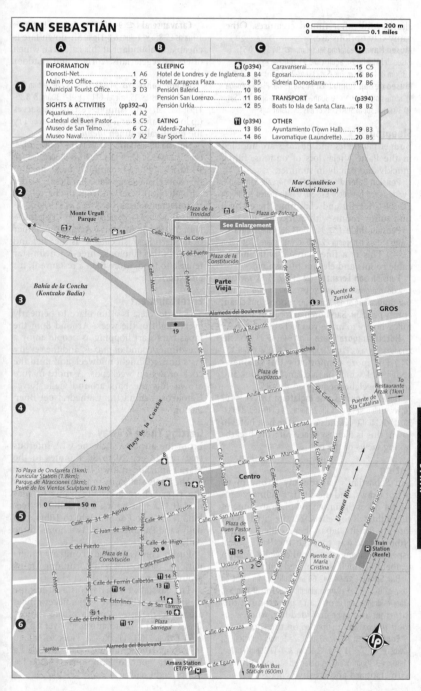

# SAN SEBASTIÁN

| | | |
|---|---|---|
| 0 | | 200 m |
| 0 | | 0.1 miles |

**INFORMATION**
Donosti-Net..........................1 A6
Main Post Office....................2 C5
Municipal Tourist Office.........3 D3

**SIGHTS & ACTIVITIES** (pp392–4)
Aquarium..............................4 A2
Catedral del Buen Pastor........5 C5
Museo de San Telmo..............6 C2
Museo Naval.........................7 A2

**SLEEPING** (p394)
Hotel de Londres y de Inglaterra..8 B4
Hotel Zaragoza Plaza..............9 B5
Pensión Balerid.....................10 B6
Pensión San Lorenzo.............11 B6
Pensión Urkia.......................12 B5

**EATING** (p394)
Alderdi-Zahar.......................13 B6
Bar Sport.............................14 B6

Caravanserai.........................15 C5
Egosari................................16 B6
Sidreria Donostiarra..............17 B6

**TRANSPORT** (p394)
Boats to Isla de Santa Clara....18 B2

**OTHER**
Ayuntamiento (Town Hall).......19 B3
Lavomatique (Laundrette).......20 B5

Mar Cantábrico
(Kantauri Itsasoa)

Monte Urgull
Parque

Plaza de la
Trinidad

Plaza de Zuloaga

Calle de San Juan

*See Enlargement*

Calle Virgen de Coro

C del Puerto

Plaza de la
Constitución

Paseo del Muelle

Calle Mayor

Parte
Vieja

Bahía de la Concha
(Kontxako Badia)

C de Aldamar

Paseo de Salamanca

Puente de
Zurriola

**GROS**

Alameda del Boulevard

Reina Regente

Easo

Peñaflorida Bengoechea

Plaza de
Guipúzcoa

Andía Camino

Sta Catalina

Paseo de la República Argentina

Puente de
Sta Catalina

To
Restaurante
Arzak (1km)

Paseo de Ramón María Lili

Avenida de la Libertad

Playa de la Concha

Calle de San Marcial

Calle de Echaide

Calle de los Fueros

Calle de Vergara

**Centro**

To Playa de Ondarreta (1km);
Funicular Station (1.8km);
Parque de Atracciones (3km);
Peine de los Vientos Sculpture (3.1km)

Calle de Loyola

Calle de Urbieta

Calle de Garibay

Urumea River

Paseo de Francia

| | | |
|---|---|---|
| 0 | | 50 m |

Calle de 31 de Agosto
C de Juan de Bilbao
C del Puerto
Calle de Narrica
Calle de San Vicente
Plaza de la
Constitución
C dela Pescadería
Calle de Íñigo
20
C Mayor
C San Jerónimo
Calle de Fermín Calbetón
16
C de Esterlines
C de San Jeronimo
@ 1
Calle de Embeltrán
17
Plaza
Sarriegui
14
13
11
10
C de San Lorenzo
C de San Juan
Igenteá
Alameda del Boulevard

Calle de 31 de Agosto

Plaza de San Martín

Calle de San Martín

Plaza de
Buen Pastor

C 5

15

Urdaneta
2

Valentín Olano

Puente de
María
Cristina

Calle de Prim

Calle de los Reyes Católicos

Calle de Larramendi

Calle de Moraza

Calle de Guetaria

Paseo de Árbol de Guernica

Train
Station
(Renfe)

Amara Station
(ET/FV)

C de Egana

To Main Bus
Station (600m)

**SPAIN**

sharks and other finned creatures. Other rainy-day options are:

**Museo Naval** (Seafaring Museum; ☎ 94 343 00 51; Paseo del Muelle 24; adult/child €1.20/free; 🕑 10am-1.30pm & 4-7.30pm Tue-Sat, 11am-2pm Sun)

**Museo de San Telmo** ( ☎ 94 348 15 80; Plaza Zuloaga 1; admission free; 🕑 10.30am-1.30pm & 4-8pm Tue-Sat, 10.30am-1.30pm Sun) Lots of Basque paintings.

## Sleeping

Budget *pensiones* and *hostales* are huddled in the Parte Vieja: lots of options, filling quickly and pricily in summer.

**Pensión Balerid** ( ☎ 94 342 68 14; Calle San Juan 1; s with shared bathroom €18-30, d with shared bathroom €35-50) Cheerful and charming, here you'll find sunny rooms with quirky décor.

**Pensión Urkia** ( ☎ 94 342 44 36; Calle Urbieta 12; s with shared bathroom €23-30, d with shared bathroom €33-45) This is a fine *pensión*, with impeccable rooms and elegant furnishings.

**Pensión San Lorenzo** ( ☎ 94 342 55 16; www.info negocio.com/pensionsanlorenzo; Calle San Lorenzo 2; r with shared bathroom €20-45) Another modest but clean, comfy *pensión*, San Lorenzo is run by friendly folk who try to make you feel at home.

**Hotel Zaragoza Plaza** ( ☎ 94 345 21 03; hotel zaragoza@terra.es; Plaza Zaragoza 3; s €48-108, d €60-120; 🔲 ) For more comfort, try this business-style hotel, which has a clean, fresh look and some wheelchair-equipped rooms.

**Hotel de Londres y de Inglaterra** ( ☎ 94 344 07 70; www.hlondres.com; Calle Zubieta 2; s €110-169, d €131-202; 🔲 🔲 🖳 ) Hands down the best hotel in town, this is a classy place offering breathtaking views of the bay.

## Eating

San Sebastián's gastronomy is one of its major draws, and the city is a culinary centre for all of Spain, giving birth to some of the country's top chefs. Yet the city is most known for its tapas, here called *pinxos*. Nibble your way through the Parte Vieja, especially along and around Calle Fermín Calbetón, which is crammed with bars.

**Bar Sport** ( ☎ 94 342 68 88; Calle Fermín Calbetón 10; pinxos €1-5; 🕑 9am-midnight Mon-Fri, 10-1am Sat, 11am-midnight Sun) You can't go wrong at this informal and ever-crowded bar, where seafood *pinxos* are prepared on the spot.

**Egosari** ( ☎ 94 342 82 10; Calle Fermín Calbetón 15; pinxos €1-5; 🕑 11.30am-3.30pm & 7-11.30pm Fri-Tue, 11.30am-3.30pm Wed) Another good choice, with standard and creative *pinxos*.

**Caravanserai** ( ☎ 94 347 54 18; Calle San Bartolome 1; mains €5-8; 🕑 1-4pm & 8-11pm) Sit-down fare is cheap and abundant at this caféteria, which offers a 'vegetarians' corner' and outdoor dining.

**Alderdi-Zahar** ( ☎ 94 342 52 54; Calle Fermín Calbetón 9; mains €9-15, menú €11; 🕑 1-3.30pm & 8.30-11pm Tue-Sat) This simple restaurant serves up local seafood and hardy Basque fare. Try the good-value lunch *menú*.

**Sidreria Donostiarra** ( ☎ 94 342 04 21; Calle Embeltran 5; mains €5.50-17; 🕑 1-3.30pm & 8-10.30pm Tue-Sat, 1-3.30pm Sun) For a memorable meal, head to this homely tavern, where hard cider (cider with alcohol) is served from the barrel.

**Restaurante Arzak** ( ☎ 94 327 84 65; Alto de Miracruz 21; mains €44-59, menú €99; 🕑 1.30-4pm & 9-11pm Wed-Sun) Juan Maria Arzak, the 'father of modern Spanish cuisine' is the chef and owner of this fabulous, three-Michelin-star temple to food. More than a restaurant, it's an experience.

## Entertainment

The Parte Vieja is a fun place to be nearly every night of the week. Around 8pm the tapas bars start hopping as people enjoy a pre-dinner round of *pinxos*, and the revelry lasts until midnight midweek and until the cock crows on weekends. A more mature crowd fills the bars around Calle Reyes Católicos, behind the Cathedral del Buen Pastor.

## Getting There & Away

From the airport, catch the CIA Interbus that runs every 20 to 30 minutes to the Plaza Gipuzkoa in town (€1.40).

The **Renfe station** (Paseo de Francia) is across the river. There are daily trains to Madrid (€33, eight hours, four daily), Barcelona (€33.50 to €42.50, eight to 10hrs, two daily) and Pamplona (€16, two hours, three daily).

Eusko Tren is a private company (international passes not valid) running trains around the region.

The **bus station** (Plaza Pío XII) is a 20-minute walk south of the Parte Vieja; ticket offices are along the streets north of the station. Buses leave for destinations all over Spain. **PESA** ( ☎ 90 210 12 10) has services to Bilbao (€7.75, up to one hour, 27 daily), while La Roncalesa goes to Pamplona (€5.60, 1¼ hours, eight daily).

# BILBAO

Straddling the Ría Bilbao and surrounded by green mountains on all sides, Bilbao is a spirited city in the midst of the beautiful Basque countryside. Most people who come here limit their visit to the Guggenheim Museum, Frank Gehry's masterpiece of modern architecture and one of the best modern-art museums in the world. But this evocative city has a lot more to offer. The Casco Viejo (Old Quarter) is full of funky shops and traditional cafés, and smaller museums scattered about town are worth visiting too.

## Information

**Police** ( ☎ 092 or 94 420 50 00; Calle Luis Briñas 14)
**Postal Transfer** ( ☎ 94 415 30 42; Calle Santa Maria 5; per hr €1.50; ☙ 10am-11pm Mon-Fri, 11am-midnight Sat, noon-11pm Sun) Run by the state post office, this is the place to come to send packages, receive faxes or connect cheaply to the Internet.
**Tourist Office** Teatro Arriaga ( ☎ 94 479 57 60; www .bilbao.net; Teatro Arriaga, Paseo del Arenal; ☙ 9.30am-2pm & 4-7.30pm Mon-Sat, 9.30am-2pm Sun); Guggenheim (Calle Alameda Mazarredo; ☙ 11am-2.30pm & 3.30-6pm Mon-Fri, 11am-3pm & 4-7pm Sat, 11am-2pm Sun)

## Sights

Frank Gehry designed, the spectacular **Guggenheim Museum** ( ☎ 94 435 90 00; www.guggenheim -bilbao.es; Abandoibarra Et 2; admission €10, kids under 12 free; ☙ 10am-8pm Tue-Sun year-round, open Mon Jul & Aug) is an experience not soon forgotten. The building itself, undulating forms covered in titanium scales, was inspired by ships and fish, two of Bilbao's traditional industries. Inside, the guts of the building are exposed, with few columns, ugly support beams or, for that matter, floors and walls, obstructing the view. Many credit this creation with revitalising modern architecture and creating a new standard in vanguard design.

To dig further into the local culture, head to the **Euskal Museoa** (Basque Museum; ☎ 94 415 54 23; http://euskal-museoa.org; Plaza Miguel de Unamuno 4; adult/child €3/free; ☙ 11am-5pm Tue-Sat, 11am-2pm Sun), a museum documenting the history and lifestyle of the Basque people.

## Sleeping & Eating

**Hostal-Residencia La Estrella** ( ☎ 94 416 40 66; Calle María Muñoz 6; s €30-39, d €48-57) The grand spiral staircase prepares you for grandeur, and the sparkling *hostal* doesn't disappoint, with spotless, freshly painted rooms.

**Iturrienea Ostatua** ( ☎ 94 416 15 00; Calle Santa María 14; s €45, d €54-60) Unbeatable charm at a B&B decorated with museum-worthy Basque artefacts and rustic elegance.

**Rio-Oja** ( ☎ 94 415 08 71; Calle Perro 4; mains €4-12; ☙ noon-11pm Tue-Sun) Codfish and local stews are the star dishes in Bilbao. Try some of both at this great spot for wallet-friendly fare. Just don't pay close attention to the unappetising English translations, such as 'beef face stew' or 'lamb insides stew'.

**Harrobia** ( ☎ 94 679 00 90; Calle Perro 2; mains €15-20, menú €9.90; ☙ 1-4pm & 8.30-11pm) A sleek restaurant that's pricey at night but has a great-value lunch menú. Specialties are local seafood and, in season, game dishes.

**Zuretzat** ( ☎ 94 424 85 05; Calle Iparraguirre 7; menú €8.50; ☙ 1-11pm) Near the Guggenheim, with *pinxos* or, downstairs, a tasty, fixed-price *menú*.

## Getting There & Away

From the airport, bus No 3247 leaves every half-hour from 6.30am until 10.30pm and drops you off in the Plaza Moyúa, in the centre of Bilbao, where there's a metro stop.

Bilbao is served by two train stations and two rail companies, Renfe and Feve, both beside the river. Renfe offers services to Madrid (€30 to €38, six to eight hours, two daily) and Barcelona (€34.50, seven hours, two daily).

**Feve** (www.feve.es), the national narrow-gauge railway line, has trains heading westward to Cantabria and beyond. Often these bumpy rides take considerably longer than the bus trip to the same destinations.

The main bus station (Termibús) is west of town but sits just next to the San Mamés metro stop, a five-minute ride from the centre. Regular buses come and go from San Sebastián (€7.75, one hour, up to 27 daily), Santander (€5.40 to €9.65, 1½ hours, up to 27 daily) and Zaragoza (€16.14 to €26.75, three to four hours, up to 10 daily).

Bilbao has an outstanding public transport system, with an easy-to-follow web of metros, trams and buses crisscrossing the city and heading into the countryside.

# PAMPLONA

Immortalized by Ernest Hemingway in *The Sun Also Rises*, the busy pre-Pyrenean city of Pamplona (Iruña in Basque) is, the home of the wild San Fermíne (aka Encierro or

SPAIN

Running of the Bulls) festival, but it's also an extremely walkable city that's managed to mix the charm of old plazas and buildings with modern shops and lively nightlife.

This is the capital of Navarra, but there are few noteworthy sights in town, which means you can party all night and not feel guilty for whiling the day away in the street cafés. Make an exception for the **cathedral** ( ☎ 94 821 08 27; adult/child €3.85/2.25; ☼ 10am-1.30pm & 4-7pm Mon-Fri, 10am-1.30pm Sat), a 14th-century Gothic creation with a neoclassical façade.

## Information

**Kuria.net** ( ☎ 94 822 30 77; Calle Curia 15; per hr €3; ☼ 10am-10pm Mon-Sat, noon-10pm Sun)
**Police** ( ☎ 092)
**Tourist Office** ( ☎ 94 842 04 20; www.navarra.es; Calle Eslava 1; ☼ 10am-2pm & 4-6pm Mon-Sat, 10am-2pm Sun Sep-Jun, 9am-8pm Mon-Sat, 10am-2pm Sun Jul & Aug, during San Fermíne 8am-8pm daily) Don't expect this otherwise-helpful office to provide much guidance during San Fermíne.

## Sleeping

Accommodation is expensive and hard to come by during San Fermíne; you'll need to book months in advance. Prices below don't reflect the huge (up to 300%) mark-up you'll find in mid-July.

**Camping Ezcaba** ( ☎ 94 833 03 15; N-125; per person/car €7/3.85) The nearest camping ground, 7km north of the city. Regular buses head to Pamplona.

**La Viña** ( ☎ 94 821 32 50; Calle Jarauta 8; s/d with shared bathroom from €15/25) Cheerful rooms with sky-blue walls and clean bathrooms.

**Hotel Europa** ( ☎ 94 822 18 00; www.hreuropa.com; Calle Espoz y Mina 11; s €61-68, d €65-74) Comfortable,

and stylish, this family-run hotel offers class and value. The swish **restaurant** (mains €18-25) is great for a splurge.

## Eating & Drinking

Central streets such as Calle San Nicolás and Calle Estafeta are lined with tapas bars, many of which morph into nightspots on weekends.

**Café Iruña** ( ☎ 94 822 20 64; Plaza Castillo 44; menú €10-21) This old Hemingway haunt was mentioned 14 times in *The Sun Also Rises*. This grand old café is great for coffee, breakfast or a quick meal.

Get great tapas at **Bar Baserri** ( ☎ 94 822 20 21; www.restaurantebaserri.com; Calle San Nicolás 32; pinxo menú €17) and **Cervecería La Estafeta** ( ☎ 94 822 79 77; Calle Estafeta 54).

For sit-down local fare, **La Chistera** ( ☎ 94 821 05 12; Calle San Nicolás 40-42; mains €15) serves great grilled meats and Basque seafood, while **Restaurant Saraste** ( ☎ 94 822 57 27; Calle San Nicolás 19-21; menú €10 or €16) caters to vegetarians.

## Getting There & Away

Up to four trains arrive daily from Madrid (four hours). Bus No 9 connects the station with the centre.

Several companies operate out of Pamplona's central bus station near Plaza Castilla. **Conda** ( ☎ 94 822 10 26) runs up to seven daily buses each way between Madrid and Pamplona. Up to 10 buses come and go daily from Zaragoza.

# CANTABRIA, ASTURIAS & GALICIA

Green Spain has little in common with the dry, sun-baked regions of the rest of the country and provides a fascinating contrast to the rest of Spain. You'll think you're in Scotland with the lush green hills and powerfully wet Atlantic climate.

## SANTANDER

Stylish Santander has a pretty old town, but it's most known for its upscale beach, **El Sardinero**. Many beachside shops, restaurants and hotels are open in summer only, but surfers abound year-round, braving the cold to ride winter's powerful waves.

---

### SURVIVING SAN FERMÍNE

The madcap San Fermíne festival runs from 6–14 July, when the city is overrun with thrill-seekers, curious onlookers and, oh yeah, bulls. The Encierro (Running of the Bulls) begins at 8am daily, when bulls are let loose from the Corralillos Santo Domingo. The race lasts just three minutes, so don't be late. The safest place to watch the Encierro is on TV. If that's too tame for you, try to sweet-talk your way onto a balcony or book a room in a hotel with views.

Near Santander is the fascinating **Cueva de Altamira** ( ☎ 94 281 80 05; www.cultura.mecd .es; ⊙ 9.30am-7.30pm Tue-Sat, to 3pm Sun Jun-Sep, 9.30am-5pm Tue-Sat, to 3pm Sun Oct-May), a cave full of prehistoric paintings that's been dubbed the Sistine Chapel of the prehistoric world. The 270m-long cave is 2km southwest of Santillana de Mar. The waiting list to get into the cave itself is years long, but you can visit an excellent on-site **museum** (admission €2.40) with replicas of the cave art.

### Information
**Municipal tourist office** ( ☎ 94 220 30 00; www .ayto-santander.es; Jardines de Pereda; ⊙ 9.30am-1.30pm & 4-7pm Mon-Fri, 9am-1.30pm Sat) Very helpful.

### Sleeping & Eating
**Pensión La Corza** ( ☎ 94 221 29 50; Calle Hernán Cortés 25; s €20-30, d €35-50) La Corza offers the best value in town, with spotless, colour-coordinated rooms, some with their own tidy bathrooms.

**Pensión Picos de Europa** ( ☎ 94 222 53 74; Calderón Barca 5; s with shared bathroom €20-25, d with shared bathroom €28-36) The quirky rooms are packed with antique furniture, knick-knacks and ornate touches, and are beyond comfortable. Try to book room No 3.

Old Santander is full of traditional-style *mesones* (inns) and bodegas that serve as both pubs and sit-down restaurants. One of the better priced is **Cervecería Apsy** ( ☎ 94 231 45 95; Calle Hernán Cortés 22; mains €5.40-13), with a lot of seafood dishes on the *menú*.

### Getting There & Away
Santander is loaded with public transport options. Its ferry port is one of Spain's largest, and regular ferries arrive here from the UK. Trains come from Madrid (from €23.75, six hours, four daily) and Valladolid (€12.80 to €22.50, three to four hours, six daily). The jostling **Feve** (www.feve.es) trains are usually slower than the bus, but this is a scenic way to get to and from Bilbao (€6.25, 2½ hours, three daily).

The excellent **bus station** ( ☎ 94 221 19 95; Plaza Estaciones) is home to a half-dozen companies offering service to destinations throughout Cantabria and further afield.

## SANTIAGO DE COMPOSTELA
The supposed burial place of Saint James (Santiago in Castilian), this beautiful city is the end of the Camino de Santiago and one of the Christian world's most important pilgrimage sites. Santiago's compact old town is a work of art, and a walk around the cathedral will take you through some of its most inviting squares.

### Information
**Camino de Santiago information** (Xacobeo; ☎ 98 157 20 04; www.xacobeo.es; Ave Coruña 6; ⊙ 8.30am-2.30pm & 4.30-6.30pm Mon-Fri) Just west of town.
**Cyber Nova 50** ( ☎ 98 157 51 88; Rúa Nova 50; per hr €1.20; ⊙ 9am-1am Mon-Sat, 10am-1am Sun)
**Municipal tourist office** ( ☎ 98 155 51 29; Rúa Vilar 63; ⊙ 10am-3pm & 5-8pm Oct-May, 9am-9pm Jun-Sep)
**Police** ( ☎ 092; Rua Trindade)
**Post Office** ( ☎ 98 158 12 52; Travesía Fonesca; ⊙ 8.30am-8.30pm Mon-Fri, 9.30am-2pm Sat)

### Sights & Activities
The **cathedral** ( ☎ 98 156 05 27; Plaza Obradoiro; ⊙ museum 10am-1.30pm & 4-6.30pm Mon-Sat, 10am-1.30pm Sun, mass noon & 6pm daily), a superb Romanesque creation of the 11th to 13th centuries, is the heart and soul of Santiago. It's said that St James' remains were buried here in the 1st century AD and rediscovered in 813. Today, visitors line up to kiss his statue, which sits behind the main altar.

To get a grasp on local culture, visit the **Museo do Pobo Galego** ( ☎ 98 158 36 20; www.museo dopobo.es; San Domingos de Bonaval; admission free; ⊙ 10am-2pm & 4-8pm Tue-Sat), which has exhibits on everything from boating and fishing to music and pottery.

The **Museo das Peregrinacións** ( ☎ 98 158 15 58; www.mdperegrinacions.com; Rúa San Miguel 4; adult/child €2.40/free; ⊙ 10am-8pm Tue-Fri, 10.30am-1.30pm & 5-8pm Sat) explores the pilgrim culture that has so shaped Santiago.

Santiago's university is one of Spain's oldest and most emblematic. The 16th-century **Colexio de Fonesca** (Fonesca College; ☎ 98 156 31 00; Plaza Fonesca; ⊙ 11am-2pm & 5-8.30pm Tue-Sat, 11am-2pm Sun) is one of the prettiest university buildings and now houses the university library. There are usually exhibits held in the two ornate rooms at the front.

### Tours
The **Tren Turístico** (adult/child €3.60/1.80; ⊙ 10am-8pm Mar-Oct, 10am-1.30pm Nov-Feb) loops around the city, starting and finishing on the Rúa San Francisco, by the Plaza Obrero.

SPAIN

## SANTIAGO DE COMPOSTELA

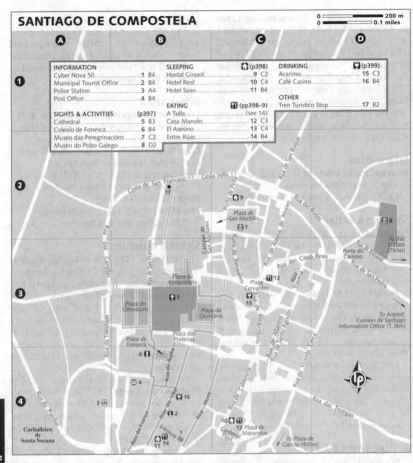

```
0                    200 m
0                    0.1 miles
```

| INFORMATION | | |
| --- | --- | --- |
| Cyber Nova 50 | 1 | B4 |
| Municipal Tourist Office | 2 | B4 |
| Police Station | 3 | A4 |
| Post Office | 4 | B4 |

| SIGHTS & ACTIVITIES | (p397) | |
| --- | --- | --- |
| Cathedral | 5 | B3 |
| Colexio de Fonseca | 6 | B4 |
| Museo das Peregrinacións | 7 | C2 |
| Museo do Pobo Galego | 8 | D2 |

| SLEEPING | (p398) | |
| --- | --- | --- |
| Hostal Girasol | 9 | C2 |
| Hotel Real | 10 | C4 |
| Hotel Suso | 11 | B4 |

| EATING | (pp398–9) | |
| --- | --- | --- |
| A Tulla | (see 14) | |
| Casa Manolo | 12 | C3 |
| El Asesino | 13 | C4 |
| Entre Rúas | 14 | B4 |

| DRINKING | (p399) | |
| --- | --- | --- |
| Acarimo | 15 | C3 |
| Café Casino | 16 | B4 |

| OTHER | | |
| --- | --- | --- |
| Tren Turístico Stop | 17 | B2 |

Walking tours ( ☎ 98 156 98 90; Plaza Platerías; adult/child €8/free; ☺ noon Oct-Mar, noon & 6pm Apr-Sep) are also interesting.

## Sleeping

**Hostal Girasol** ( ☎ 98 156 62 87; www.hgirasol.com; Porta de Pena 4; d €33-39, s with shared bathroom €15-20, d with shared bathroom €26-32) With wrought-iron beds, wooden floors and a country charm, the clean, bright Girasol is a great choice.

**Hostal Suso** ( ☎ 98 158 66 11; Rúa Vilar 65; s €15-18, d €30-36) Excellent value, the Suso boasts fashionable décor, parquet floors and rooms with small balconies.

**Hotel Real** ( ☎ 98 156 92 90; Rúa Caldererría 49; s €41-45, d €58-66, tr €69-80) A great find in the old city, with all the comforts (though loud rooms).

## Eating & Drinking

Seafood is the local speciality, and you'll find tasty delights from the ocean just about everywhere, especially along central streets such as Calle Franco and Calle Raiña.

**Casa Manolo** ( ☎ 98 158 29 50; Plaza Cervantes; menú €6; ☺ 1pm-4pm & 8pm-11pm Mon-Sat, 1pm-4pm Sun) Everything is served as part of a super-cheap fixed-price *menú*.

**El Asesino** (The Killer; ☎ 98 158 15 68; Plaza Universidad 16; mains €8-12, menú €12-15; ☺ 1pm-3.30pm & 8pm-11pm Mon-Sat) Homy and has been serving local specialties for 127 years.

**Entre-Ruas** ( ☎ 98 158 61 08; Callejón Entre-Rúas 2; raciones €2.50-8, menú €8; ☺ 1pm-4pm & 8.30pm-midnight Mon-Sat) Have seafood alfresco at Entre-Ruas, which sits on a tiny plaza in the middle of the thinnest street in all Santiago.

**A Tulla** ( ☎ 98 158 0889; Callejon Entre-Rúas 1; menú €8.50-10.50; ☽ 1-4pm & 8-11pm Mon-Sat) Next door to Entre-Ruas, with a vegetarian *menú*.

The old quarter is home to atmospheric bars and pubs popular with the city's large student population. Some of the best spots are around the Rúa da Congo, the Rúa San Paio de Antealtares and the Plaza Cervantes. At **Acarimo** (Calle Preguntoiro 2; ☽ 8-2.30am) you'll find a laid-back atmosphere, and at classy **Café Casino** ( ☎ 98 157 75 03; Rúa Villar 35; ☽ 8am-midnight Sun-Thu, 8am-1am Fri & Sat) live piano music starts nightly at 8.30pm.

### Getting There & Around
From the airport, regular **Freire** ( ☎ 98 154 24 16) buses run to the bus station and to República de El Salvador about once an hour.

Two trains come in from Madrid (€38.50, eight hours). It's a 15-minute walk from the station to central Plaza de Galicia.

From the **bus station** ( ☎ 98 158 77 00; Calle San Caetano) you can hop on bus No 10 to get to Plaza de Galicia. Buses come in from León (€22.52, 6½ hours, one daily) and Oviedo (€22.18, five hours, three daily).

# VALENCIA & MURCIA

Best known for the package resorts of the Costa Blanca, this region also includes the lively cities of Valencia and Alicante, and some rare undiscovered secrets if you go inland. South of Valencia, the province of Murcia has fertile plains blessed by some of the Mediterranean's warmest waters.

## VALENCIA
pop 746,610

Exuberant, friendly and appealingly chaotic, Valencia is Spain's third-largest city. Its old quarter brims with gracious baroque-fronted houses and its streets buzz with life until the early hours. Kick back with a meal of paella washed down with a jar of *agua de Valencia* (orange juice and sparkling wine) to really get into the spirit of things.

### Orientation
The part of the city where there is most action is oval, bounded by the dried-up Turia river bed (now a park) and the sickle-shaped inner ring road of Calles Colón, Játiva and Guillem de Castro. These trace the old city walls, demolished in 1865 as – believe it or not – a job-creation project.

### Information
Grab a copy of the freebie mag *24/7 Valencia*, a fantastic guide (in English) to Valencia's bars, clubs, restaurants and music venues.

**Ono** ( ☎ 96 328 19 02; Calle San Vicente 22; per hr €2; ☽ 9-1am) Internet access just off Plaza Ayuntamiento.

**Tourist Offices** Main office ( ☎ 96 398 64 22; www .turisvalencia.es; Calle Paz 48; ☽ 10am-6.30pm Mon-Fri, 10am-2pm Sat); Train station ( ☎ 96 352 85 73) Teatro Principal ( ☎ 96 351 49 07); Plaza Reina ( ☎ 96 352 54 78, ext 1739; ☽ 9am-7pm Mon-Sat, 10am-2pm Sun)

### Sights & Activities
One of Spain's prettiest markets, Valencia's **Mercado Central** (Plaza Mercado; ☽ 8am-2.30pm) is a feast of colours and smells, with nearly 1000 stallholders crammed under the market's modernist glass domes.

Valencia's **cathedral** ( ☽ 7.30am-1pm & 5-8.30pm) boasts three magnificent portals – one Romanesque, one Gothic and one baroque – the only Holy Grail recognised (albeit tentatively) by the Vatican, a fantastic Goya and the withered left arm of St Vincent. Climb the **Miguelete bell tower** (admission €1.50; ☽ 10.30am-12.30pm & 4.30-6.30pm Tue-Fri, 10.30am-1pm Sat-Mon) for sweeping views of the city.

The aesthetically stunning **Ciudad de las Artes y las Ciencias** ( ☎ 902 100 031; adult/child €10.50/8; ☽ 10am-9pm) includes the Hemisfèric (a planetarium, IMAX cinema and laser show), interactive science museum, aquarium and open-air auditorium.

Among Valencia's art galleries, the two unmissables are the **Museo de Bellas Artes** ( ☎ 96 360 57 93; Calle San Pío V 9; admission free; ☽ 10am-2.15pm & 4-7.30pm Tue-Sat, 10am-7.30pm Sun) and the **Instituto Valenciano de Arte Moderno** ( ☎ 96 386 30 00; Calle Guillem de Castro 118; adult/student €2/1, free Sun).

Don't miss the extravagantly sculpted façade of the rococo-fabulous **Palacio del Marqués de Dos Aguas** (Calle Poeta Querol).

### Sleeping
A wide range of accommodation is available in Valencia.

**Devesa Gardens** ( ☎ /fax 961 61 11 36; www.devesa gardens.com; per person/tent/car €4.50/4.50/4.50; ☒ ) The city's nearest camping ground is 13km

SPAIN

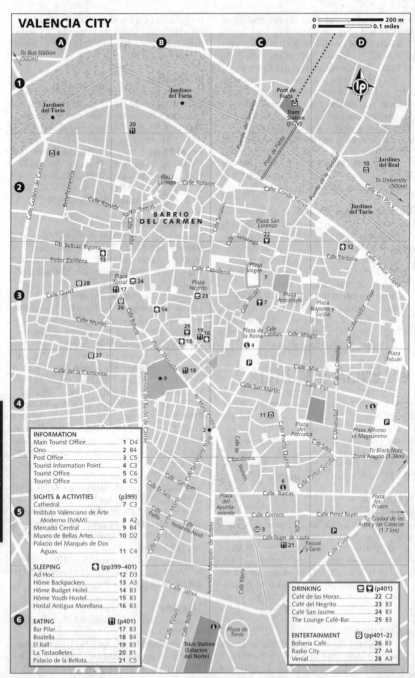

# VALENCIA CITY

| 0 | 200 m |
| 0 | 0.1 miles |

To Bus Station (500m)

Jardines del Turia

Jardines del Turia

Pont de Fusta

Tram Station (FGV)

**20**

Calle Guillem de Castro

Beneficencia

**8**

Calle Ripalda

Calle Alta

Santo Tomas

Plaza Carmen — Calle Roteros

**BARRIO DEL CARMEN**

Calle Serranos

Calle Conde Trénor

Puente de Serranos

Pont de Fusta

Puente de la Trinidad

Jardines del Real

**10**

To University (500m)

Jardines del Turia

Calle San Pío V

Dr. Beltrán Bigorra

Pintor Zariñena

**13**

**28**

Calle Quart

Plaza Tossal

**24**

**17**

**26**

Calle Murillo

Calle Bolsería

Plaza Negrito

**23**

Calle Caballeros

Plaza San Lorenzo

**22**

Calle Samaniego

Plaza Virgen

**7**

Plaza Arzobispo

Calle Trinitanos

**12**

Calle Pintor López

Calle Gobernador Viejo

Calle Micalet

**7**

Plaza Nápoles y Sicilia

Plaza Tetuán

**14**

**25**

**19 16**

**15**

**27**

Calle de la Carniceros

Avenida del Barón de Cárcer

Plaza Mercado

**9**

**18**

Plaza de la Reina

**4**

Calle Cabillars

Calle Milagro

Calle Mar

Calle de las Comedias

Calle San Martín

Calle Paz

**11**

Plaza del Patriarca

**2**

C de Salvà

C Universidad

Plaza Alfonso el Magnánimo

**1**

Plaza los Pinazo

To Black Note; Zona Aragón (1.3km)

Calle Poeta Querol

Calle Pintor Sorolla

Av Maria Cristina

Calle San Vicente Mártir

C Barcelonina

Calle Moratín

Plaza del Ayuntamiento

**6**

Calle Barcas

Calle Correos

Calle Pérez Bayer

To Ciudad de las Artes y las Ciencias (1.7 km)

Calle Roger de Lauria

Pascual y Gens

**3**

**21**

Calle Ribera

Calle Colón

Calle En Sanz

Calle Garrigues

Calle Padilla

Calle San Vicente Mártir

Calle Periodista Azzati

Avenida Marqués de Sotelo

Calle Pelayo

Calle Bailén

Calle Játiva

**5**

Plaza de Toros

Train Station (Estación del Norte)

---

## INFORMATION

Main Tourist Office............................ **1** D4
Ono................................................ **2** B4
Post Office...................................... **3** C5
Tourist Information Point.................... **4** C3
Tourist Office.................................. **5** C6
Tourist Office.................................. **6** C5

## SIGHTS & ACTIVITIES (p399)

Cathedral........................................ **7** C3
Instituto Valenciano de Arte
Moderno (IVAM)............................. **8** A2
Mercado Central............................... **9** B4
Museo de Bellas Artes....................... **10** D2
Palacio del Marqués de Dos
Aguas.......................................... **11** C4

## SLEEPING (pp399–401)

Ad Hoc........................................... **12** D3
Hôme Backpackers........................... **13** A3
Hôme Budget Hotel.......................... **14** B3
Hôme Youth Hostel........................... **15** B3
Hostal Antigua Morellana................... **16** B3

## EATING (p401)

Bar Pilar........................................ **17** B3
Boatella......................................... **18** B4
El Rall........................................... **19** B3
La Tastaolletes................................. **20** B1
Palacio de la Bellota......................... **21** C5

## DRINKING (p401)

Café de las Horas............................. **22** C2
Café del Negrito............................... **23** B3
Café San Jaume................................ **24** B3
The Lounge Café-Bar......................... **25** B3

## ENTERTAINMENT (pp401–2)

Bolsería Café................................... **26** B3
Radio City...................................... **27** A4
Venial............................................ **28** A3

SPAIN

**BURN BABY BURN**

In mid-March, Valencia hosts what has become one of Europe's wildest street parties: **Las Fallas de San José**. For one week the city is engulfed by an anarchic swirl of fireworks, music, festive bonfires and all-night partying. On the final night, giant *niñots* (effigies), many of political and social personages, are torched in the main plaza.

If you're not around then, see the *niñots* saved from the flames by popular vote at the **Museo Fallero** ( ☎ 96 352 54 78; Plaza Monteolivete 4; adult/child €2/0.60; ❤ 9.15am-2pm & 4.30-8pm Tue-Sat, 9.15am-2pm Sun)

south of Valencia, near El Saler beach. The complex includes restaurants, tennis courts and even a mini zoo.

**Hôme Youth Hostel** ( ☎ 96 391 62 29; www.like athome.net; Calle Lonja 4; dm/s/d with shared bathroom €14/21/32; 🖳 ) With its brightly painted rooms, big kitchen, healthy DVD stash and even laundry facilities, this place is pure backpacking heaven.

**Hôme Backpackers** ( ☎ 963913797; www.likeathome .net; Plaza Vicente Iborra; dm €12-14, d/tr/q with shared bathroom €32/48/64; 🖳 ) Valencia's latest addition to the budget travel scene has 100 beds (some bunks) and friendly, multilingual young staff.

**Hôme Budget Hotel** ( ☎ 96 392 40 63; www.like athome.net; Calle Cadirers 11; d with breakfast €40) The individually designed rooms come complete with king-sized beds and private stereos. Perfect for flashpackers.

**Hostal Antigua Morellana** ( ☎ 96 391 57 73; info@hostalam.com; Calle En Bou 2; s/d €33/48; 🐱 ) In an elegant renovated 18th-century building, this helpful hotel has cosy, good-sized rooms with satellite TV and balconies.

**Ad Hoc** ( ☎ 96 391 91 40; www.adhochoteles.com; Calle Boix 4; s/d €87/115; 🐱 ) This charming boutique hotel has stencilled ceilings, pretty balconies and fabulous colour schemes.

## Eating

Lots of cheap (generally fishy) eats can be found near the market. For authentic paella, head for Las Arenas, just north of the port, where a strip of restaurants serves up the real stuff from €6.60 per person.

**Boatella** (Plaza Mercado 33; tapas €3; ❤ 8am-1.30pm) Crammed with locals chucking down

glasses of beer and platefuls of fried fish and seafood.

**Bar Pilar** (Calle Moro Zeit 13; tapas €1.50; ❤ noon-midnight) This Valencian classic is where folks come to eat mussels, chucking the shells into the plastic buckets on the floor.

**Palacio de la Bellota** ( ☎ 96 351 49 94; Calle Mosén Femades 7; raciones €7; ❤ 1-4pm & 8pm-midnight) The cured ham (*jamón*), which hangs from the ceilings, is absolutely divine but this place is also famous for its Valencian eel stew (*all i pebre*).

**La Tastaolletes** ( ☎ 96 392 18 62; Calle Salvador Giner 6; mains €7; ❤ 2-4pm & 8pm-midnight Tue-Sat, 2-4pm Sun) An excellent vegetarian restaurant in a colourful setting. It is good at salads and the vegetable lasagne is to die for.

**El Rall** ( ☎ 96 392 20 90; Calle Tundidores 2; mains €8; ❤ 2-4.30pm & 9pm-midnight) A firm favourite, El Rall serves up paellas, meat dishes and great desserts in a funky setting and has a good outside terrace.

## Drinking

Much of the action centres on Barrio del Carmen, which caters for every taste from grunge to glam.

**Café San Jaume** (Calle Caballeros 51; ❤ noon-1am) A stalwart of Carmen's café/bar scene, with lots of room upstairs and a particularly fine terrace for eyeing up the characters on Calle Caballeros.

**Café de las Horas** (Calle Conde de Almodóvar 1; ❤ 4pm-1am Mon-Thu, 4pm-3.30am Fri & Sat) With its deep-red walls, theatrical drapes and frescoes, this bar/café has the feel of an 18th-century boudoir. The best *agua de Valencia* in town.

**The Lounge Café-Bar** ( ☎ 96 391 80 94; Calle Estamiñería Vieja 2; ❤ 11-1am) This popular international hang-out has comfy sofas and free Internet. Good snacks too.

**Café del Negrito** ( ☎ 96 391 42 33; Plaza Negrito; ❤ 3pm-3.30am) On a kicking little plaza, this bar/café is generally packed with lots of liberal, arty 30-somethings.

## Entertainment

**Radio City** ( ☎ 96 391 41 51; Santa Teresa 19; ❤ 11pm-late) Everyone goes here for post-bar dancing to salsa, house and cheesy pop. It also has a live flamenco show at 11pm Tuesday.

**Bolsería Café** ( ☎ 96 391 89 03; Calle Bolsería 41; ❤ 11pm-4am) A fashionable place that plays house music upstairs and has bizarre toilets with glass walls.

SPAIN

**Venial** ( ☎ 96 391 73 56; Quart 26; ⊙ 12.30-8am) Valencia's oldest gay club is always jumping with theme parties throughout the year, and fashion shows and male strippers in summer. It has a big open-plan dance floor and chill-out zone. Mixed crowd.

**The Black Note** ( ☎ 96 393 36 63; Polo y Peyrolón 15; ⊙ from 11.30pm) Jazz cats and live music junkies should head here, in the Zona Aragón.

Younger groovers head for the university, 2km east (€3.50 by taxi from the centre). Along Ave Blasco Ibáñez and particularly around Plaza Xuquer there are scores of dusk-to-dawn bars and discos.

### Getting There & Away

From the **bus station** ( ☎ 96 349 72 22; Ave Menéndez Pidal), services go to/from Madrid (€21, four hours, 10 daily), Barcelona (€22, five hours, 12 daily) and Alicante (€15, 2¼ hours, 11 daily).

From Valencia's **Estación del Norte** (Calle Jativa), trains go to/from Madrid (€37, 3½ hours, 10 daily), Barcelona (€29, 3½ hours, 14 daily) and Alicante (€20.50, two hours, 10 daily).

Regular car and passenger ferries go to the Balearic Islands (p406).

### Getting Around

**EMT** ( ☎ 96 352 83 99) buses run until about 10pm, with night services continuing on seven routes until around 1am. Bus No 8 connects the bus station with Plaza Ayuntamiento.

The smart high-speed tram leaves from the FGV tram station, 500m north of the cathedral, at the Pont de Fusta. It's a pleasant way to get to the beach, the paella restaurants of Las Arenas and the port (€1). Metro lines primarily serve the outer suburbs.

## INLAND VALENCIA

### Morella

pop 2720

Perched on a hill top, crowned by a castle and completely enclosed by a wall over 2km long, the fairy-tale town of Morella, in the north of the Valencia region, is one of Spain's oldest continually inhabited towns. The **tourist office** ( ☎ 96 417 30 32; morella@touristinfo.net; ⊙ 10am-2pm & 4-7pm Tue-Sat, 10am-2pm Sun) is just behind the Torres de San Miguel (the twin 14th century towers which flank the main entrance to the town).

The old town itself is easily explored on foot. Morella's **castle** ( ☎ 96 417 31 28; admission €1.20; ⊙ 10am-7.30pm), although in ruins, remains imposing and gives breathtaking views of the town and surrounding countryside.

Friendly **Fonda Moreno** ( ☎ 96 416 01 05; Calle San Nicolás 12; d with shared bathroom €21) has six quaint doubles. **Hotel El Cid** ( ☎ 96 416 01 25; www .hotelelcidmorella.com; Puerta San Mateo 2; s/d with breakfast €26/37) has spruced-up rooms with bathrooms and good views. Occupying a 16th-century cardinal's palace, **Hotel Cardenal Ram** ( ☎ 96 417 30 85; hotelcardenalram@ctv.es; Cuesta Suñer 1; s/d €42.80/64.20) has rooms with all facilities.

For excellent tapas, plus a *menú* that is rich in local dishes, check out **Restaurante Vinatea** ( ☎ 96 416 07 44; Calle Blasco de Alagón 17; menú €6; ⊙ 1-4pm & 8-11.30pm Tue-Sun).

**Autos Mediterráneo** ( ☎ 96 422 05 36) runs two buses daily from Monday to Saturday to/from Castellón (€7, 2½ hours) and Vinarós (€7, 2½ hours).

## ALICANTE

pop 299,977

There's an endearingly faded grandeur about Alicante, particularly around the old quarter, overlooked by its majestic limestone cathedral. The nightlife is also equal to that of any self-respecting Andalucían city, particularly during the Fiesta de Sant Joan (24 June), when Alicante stages its own version of Las Fallas (p401).

Alicante has five tourist offices but the most central is the **main tourist office** ( ☎ 96 520 00 00; www.landofvalencia.com; Rambla Méndez Núñez 23; ⊙ 10am-7.30pm Mon-Fri, 10am-2pm Sat). You can connect to the Internet at **Up Internet** (www .upInternet.es; Angel Lozano 10; per hr €2.95; ⊙ 10-2am).

### Sights & Activities

The **Castillo de Santa Bárbara** ( ☎ 96 526 31 31; Monte Benacantil; admission free; ⊙ 10am-8pm Apr-Sep, 9am-7pm Oct-Mar), a 16th-century fortress, overlooks the city. You can either walk up or take the lift (€2.40 return), reached by a footbridge opposite Playa del Postiguet.

The **Museo de la Asegurada** ( ☎ 96 514 07 68; Plaza Santa María 3; admission free; ⊙ 10am-2pm & 4-8pm Tue-Sat, 10.30am-2.30pm Sun) hosts exhibitions by contemporary artists. On the same square, the **Iglesia de Santa María** ( ⊙ 10.30am-1pm & 6-7.30pm) dates from the 14th century and incorporates a variety of styles from the stunning baroque façade to the Gothic nave.

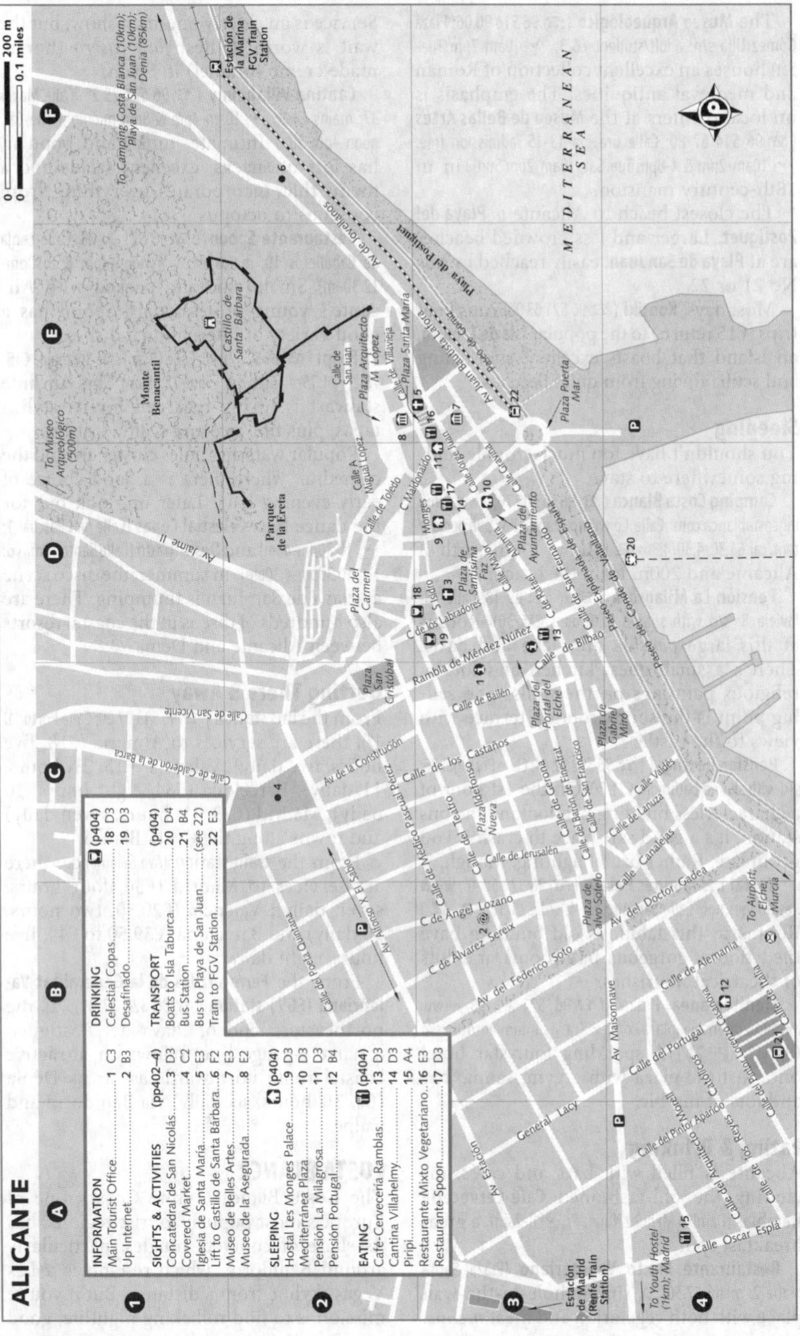

# ALICANTE

To Camping Costa Blanca (10km);
Playa de San Juan (10km);
Denia (85km)

Estación de
La Marina
FGV Train
Station

MEDITERRANEAN SEA

Av de Conde

Av de Villavieja

Plaza Puerta Mar

To Museo
Arqueológico
(500m)

Castillo de
Santa Bárbara

Monte
Benacantil

Parque
de la Ereta

Av Jaime II

Plaza del
Carmen

Calle de San Vicente

Calle de Calderón de la Barca

Av de la Construcción

Calle de los Castaños

Rambla de Méndez Núñez

Plaza
San Cristóbal

Calle de Bailén

Plaza del
Portal de
Elche

Av Alfonso X - El Sabio

C de Angel Lozano

C de Álvarez Sereix

Av de Federico Soto

General Lacy

Av Estación

Estación
de Madrid
(Renfe Train
Station)

To Youth Hostel
(1km); Madrid

To Airport;
Elche;
Murcia

SPAIN

0      200 m
0      0.1 miles

The **Museo Arqueológico** ( ☎ 96 514 90 06; Plaza Gómez Ulla s/n; adult/student €6/3; ☺ 10am-7pm Tue-Sat) houses an excellent collection of Roman and medieval antiquities. The emphasis is on local painters at the **Museo de Bellas Artes** ( ☎ 96 514 67 80; Calle Gravina 13-15; admission free; ☺ 10am-2pm & 4-8pm Tue-Sat, 10am-2pm Sun), in an 18th-century mansion.

The closest beach to Alicante is **Playa del Postiguet**. Larger and less crowded beaches are at **Playa de San Juan**, easily reached by bus No 21 or 22.

Most days, **Kontiki** ( ☎ 96 521 63 96) runs boat trips (€15 return) to the popular **Isla de Tabarca**, an island that boasts excellent snorkelling and scuba diving from quiet beaches.

## Sleeping

You shouldn't have too much trouble finding somewhere to stay.

**Camping Costa Blanca** ( ☎ 96 563 06 70; www.camp ingcostablanca.com; Calle Convento, Campello; per person/tent/car €4.30/4.30/4.30; ☒ ) About 10km north of Alicante and 200m from the beach.

**Pensión La Milagrosa** ( ☎ 96 521 69 18; Calle Villavieja 8; s/d with shared bathroom €15/30) Rooms at this large *pensión* are clean and basic. There's a small guest kitchen and lots of religious paintings on the walls. The selling point is the sunny rooftop terrace with views to the castle.

**Pensión Portugal** ( ☎ 96 592 92 44; Calle Portugal 26; s/d with shared bathroom €21/30) On the 1st floor of a characterless building overlooking the bus station, it's a good safe place to crash if you get in late. Rather brutal lighting, though.

**Hostal Les Monges Palace** ( ☎ 96 521 50 46; www .lesmonges.net; Calle San Agustín 4; s/d €25/37; Ⓟ ☒ ) Rooms in this fabulous old building have tiled floors, gorgeous bathrooms and lots of theatrical flourishes.

**Mediterránea Plaza** ( ☎ 96 521 01 88; www .hotelmediterraneaplaza.com; Plaza Ayuntamiento 6; s/d €96/110; Ⓟ ☒ ) A sparkling four-star hotel on a historic plaza with a gym, sauna, bar and lots of marble.

## Eating & Drinking

Alicante is filled with bars and cafés, including the old-fashioned **Café-Cervecería Ramblas** (Rambla Mendez Nuñez 7; ☺ 8-2am), a great breakfast spot.

**Restaurante Mixto Vegetariano** (Plaza Santa María 2; menú €7.50) A simple hole-in-the-wall place with both vegetarian and meat *menús*.

Service is an elderly one-man show, but the wait is worth it. Best *flan casero* (homemade crème caramel) in Spain.

**Cantina Villahelmy** ( ☎ 96 521 25 29; Calle Mayor 37; mains €4-8; ☺ 10am-4pm & 8pm-midnight Tue-Sat, noon-4pm Sun) Intimate, funky and popular, has lots of snacks, excellent salads and a menu that incorporates everything from couscous to octopus.

**Restaurante Spoon** ( ☎ 96 521 90 28; Calle Lonja de Caballeros 10; mains €12 ☺ noon-4pm & 8.30pm-12.30am) Small, chic and packed with Alicante's young professionals, Spoon has a good variety of international dishes.

**Piripi** ( ☎ 96 522 79 40; Calle Oscar Esplá 30; mains €15-18; ☺ 1.15-4.15pm & 8.15pm-12.15am) This Alicante stalwart is highly regarded for its stylish tapas, plus fine rice and seafood dishes.

Popular watering holes cluster around the cathedral, where there is a good choice of early-evening bars. Later on, look out for the dance bars **Celestial Copas** (Calle San Pascual 1; ☺ 10.30pm-4am) and **Desafinado** (Calle Santo Tomas 6; ☺ 10.30pm-4.30am). In summer, the disco scene at Playa de San Juan is thumping. There are also hundreds of discos in the coastal resorts between Alicante and Dénia.

## Getting There & Away

From the **bus station** ( ☎ 96 513 07 00; Calle Portugal 17), there are services to Almería (€18, five hours, five daily), Valencia (€15, 2¼ hours, 11 daily), Barcelona (€34, eight hours, 10 daily), Madrid (€23, 4½ hours, seven daily) and towns along the Costa Blanca.

From the **train station** (Ave Salamanca), there are services to Madrid (€36, four hours, seven daily), Valencia (€20.50, two hours, 10 daily) and Barcelona (€39.50 to €44, five hours, eight daily).

From the **Ferrocarriles de la Generalitat Valenciana (FGV) station** ( ☎ 96 526 27 31), at the northeastern end of Playa del Postiguet, a narrow-gauge line follows an attractive coastal route northwards as far as Dénia (€7, 2¼ hours, six daily) via Benidorm and Calpe.

## COSTA BLANCA

The Costa Blanca (White Coast), one of Europe's most popular tourist regions, has its share of concrete jungles, particularly around Benidorm, which resembles a Las Vegas skyline from a distance. But if you're mission is to find rollicking nightlife, good beaches and a suntan, you won't be disappointed. Accommodation is almost impossible to find during the coach-tour months of July and August.

## Xàbia
**pop 28,493**

More than two-thirds of annual visitors to Xàbia (Jávea) are foreigners, so it's not the greatest place to brush up on your Spanish. This laid-back resort is in three parts: the old town (3km inland), the port and the beach zone of El Arenal, lined with pleasant bar-restaurants.

**Camping Jávea** ( ☎ 96 579 10 70; www.camping-javea .com; per person €4.50, per tent & car €11.60; ⌘ ) is just over 1km from El Arenal. The port area is pleasant and has some reasonably priced *pensiones*. In the old town, **Hostal Levante** ( ☎ 96 579 15 91; Calle Maestro Alonso 5; d with shower/bathroom €40/43, s/d with shared bathroom €25/34) has basic rooms.

## Calpe

Calpe is dominated by the Gibraltaresque **Peñon de Ifach** (332m), a giant molar-like rock protruding from the sea. The climb towards the summit is popular – while you're up there, enjoy the seascape and decide which of Calpe's two long sandy beaches you want to laze on.

**Camping Ifach** ( ☎ 96 583 04 77; per person/tent/car €4.50/4/4.50) and **Camping Levante** ( ☎ 96 583 22 72; per person/tent/car €4.60/4.40/4.60), both on Ave Marina, are a short walk from Playa Levante.

**Pensión Céntrica** ( ☎ 96 583 55 28; Plaza Ilfach; s/d with shared bathroom €12/24) just off Ave Gabriel Miró, is squeaky clean.

## MURCIA & THE COSTA CALÍDA

Murcia is one of the most conservative of Spain's provinces. The capital, also called Murcia, has a traditional Spanish appeal, liberally sprinkled with plazas and some gorgeous architecture. It's also foodie heaven; Murcia's elegant citizens are pros when it comes to fine cuisine.

Both the **municipal tourist office** ( ☎ 96 835 87 49; www.murciaciudad.com; Plaza Cardinal Belluga; ⌚ 10am-2pm & 5-9pm Mon-Sat, 10am-2pm Sun) and **regional tourist office** ( ☎ 902 10 10 70; Plaza Romea 4; ⌚ 9.30am-1.30pm & 5-7pm Mon-Fri) are helpful.

### Sights & Activities

Murcia's opulent **cathedral** (Plaza Cardinal Belluga; ⌚ 10am-1pm & 5-7pm) took four centuries to build. The 23 chapels and a 92m-high tower cover a dizzying range of styles. But it is the façade, dripping in cherubs, that is the real jaw-dropper. The city's sumptuous 19th-century **casino** ( ☎ 96 821 22 55; admission €1.20; ⌚ 10am-9pm) features an Arabian patio and a magnificent ballroom.

The main draw of Murcia's Costa Calída (Warm Coast) is the **Mar Menor**, a vast saltwater lagoon separated from the sea by a 22km sliver of land known as **La Manga**. The water here is so warm that you can swim year-round.

### Sleeping & Eating

Accommodation in Murcia city is limited and not really geared towards tourists.

**Pensión Murcia** ( ☎ 96 821 99 63; Calle Vinadel 6; s/d with shared bathroom €18/38) Family-run, with cosy rooms with ceiling fans.

**La Huertanica** ( ☎ 96 821 76 68; Calle Infante 3; s/d/tr €44/57/71; P ⌘ ) Modern and comfortable; rooms with balconies.

Murcia is a gourmet's delight. Don't leave without trying the tapas.

**Señorío de Jomelsu** ( ☎ 96 821 21 33; Calle Isidoro de la Cierva 3; tapas from €1.20; ⌚ 10am-4.30pm & 8pm-2.30am) Does a mean *sobrasada* (chorizo pâté).

**La Barra del Rincón de Pepe** ( ☎ 96 821 22 39; Calle Apóstoles 34; menú €12; ⌚ 1.30-4pm & 8pm-midnight) Something of a local institution, serving up delicious Murcian fare.

### Getting There & Away

From Murcia, buses serve Madrid (€21, five hours, nine daily), Alicante (€5, one hour, every two hours), Almería (€11, three hours, five daily) and towns on the Costa Calída, including La Manga (€4, 1½ hours, three daily). Trains go from Murcia to Alicante (€13.50, 1¼ hours, five daily) and Madrid (€35.50, five hours, five daily).

# BALEARIC ISLANDS

**pop 916,968**

The Balearic Islands of Mallorca, Menorca, Ibiza and Formentera are a surprising mix of cultural wealth and mass tourism, set against a backdrop of stunning natural beauty. Although they all have a distinctly Mediterranean feel, each island also closely guards its own identity.

SPAIN

For those searching the simple pleasures of sun, sea and sand, the gorgeous beaches will happily oblige, but the heart of the Balearics lies away from its resorts. Beyond the bars and beaches, you'll discover Gothic cathedrals, Stone Age ruins and Moorish remains, as well as simple fishing villages, endless olive groves and orange orchards.

Most place names and addresses are given in Catalan. High-season prices are quoted here but out of season, you will usually find things are much cheaper.

## Getting There & Away

### AIR

Scheduled flights from the major cities on the Spanish mainland are operated by several airlines, including Iberia, Air Europa and Spanair.

Return fares from Barcelona to Palma de Mallorca can be had for as little as €66, though standard oneway fares generally hover around €45.

Interisland flights are expensive (given the flying times involved), with Palma to Maó or Ibiza costing €77/147 one way/ return.

### BOAT

The major ferry company for the islands is **Trasmediterránea** ( ☎ 902 45 46 45; www.trasmedit erranea.es) with offices in Barcelona ( ☎ 93 295 90 00), Valencia ( ☎ 96 367 65 12), Palma de Mallorca ( ☎ 97 140 50 14), Maó ( ☎ 97 136 60 50) and Ibiza city ( ☎ 97 131 51 00).

The duration of the services varies dramatically, depending on the type of ferry. The maximum times are given here, but always check whether there is a faster ferry (such as a catamaran) available. Scheduled services are: between Barcelona and Palma (seven hours, 12 services weekly); Palma and Maó (5½ hours, one service a week on Sunday); Valencia and Palma (seven hours, two services daily); Barcelona and Ibiza (nine hours, four services weekly); Palma and Ibiza (four hours, eight weekly). Prices quoted below are the oneway fares during summer; low- and mid-season fares may be cheaper.

Fares from the mainland to any of the islands are €49.55 for a *butaca turista* (seat) and €68.90 for the same class on a catamaran. Taking a small car costs €126, or there are economy packages (*paquete ahorro*) available.

Interisland services between Palma and Ibiza city cost €44.20 and Palma and Maó cost €26.70 for a *butaca turista*. A small car is another €74.26. Ask, too, about economy packages.

Another company, **Balearia** ( ☎ 902 16 01 80; www.balearia.com), operates fast ferries from Dénia (on the coast between Valencia and Alicante) to Palma (€48, five hours, two daily) via Ibiza (from €48, two hours). There are services between Valencia and Palma (€48, six hours, two daily), Valencia and Ibiza (€48, 3¾ hours, two daily) and between Ibiza and Palma (€32, four hours, two daily). There are also services between Ibiza and Formentera (€10, one hour, 12 daily) and between Port d'Alcúdia on Mallorca and Cituadella on Menorca (€32, one hour, two daily).

**Iscomar** ( ☎ 902 11 91 28; www.iscomarferrys.com) has from one to four daily car ferries (depending on the season) between Ciutadella and Port d'Alcúdia, and between Palma and Dénia via Ibiza. **Cape Balear** ( ☎ 902 10 04 44) operates fast ferries to Ciutadella from Cala Ratjada in Mallorca (€45, one hour, three daily).

# MALLORCA

Mallorca's capital city of Palma, with its tangle of narrow backstreets and towering Gothic cathedral, is a joy to explore. Inland, you can happily lose yourself in the mountains before stumbling across a hilltop village seemingly unchanged for centuries. And then there are the beaches… It's hardly surprising that so many great artists and writers decided to make this beguiling Mediterranean island their home.

## Orientation & Information

Palma is on the southern side of the island, on a bay famous for its brilliant sunsets. The Serra de Tramuntana mountain range, which runs parallel with the northwestern coastline, is trekkers' heaven. Mallorca's best beaches are along the northern and eastern coasts, along with most of the big tourist resorts.

All the major resorts have at least one tourist office.

**Big Byte** ( ☎ 97 171 17 54; Carrer Apuntadores 6; per hr €2.75; ☺ 10am-10pm Mon-Thu, 10am-6pm Fri, 11am-7pm Sat & Sun)

**Tourist Offices** Main office ( ☎ 97 171 22 16; www.a-palma .es; Plaça Reina 2; ☺ 9am-8pm Mon-Fri, 9am-2.30pm Sat); Parc de les Estacions ( ☎ 97 175 43 29); Carrer Sant Domingo 11 ( ☎ 97 172 40 90); Airport ( ☎ 97 178 95 56)

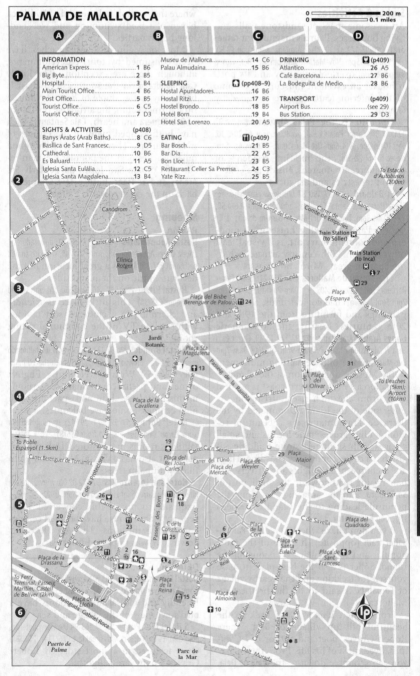

# PALMA DE MALLORCA

| | 0 | 200 m |
| 0 | | 0.1 miles |

**INFORMATION**
American Express.............................**1** B6
Big Byte.............................................**2** B5
Hospital.............................................**3** B4
Main Tourist Office..........................**4** B6
Post Office........................................**5** B5
Tourist Office..................................**6** C5
Tourist Office..................................**7** D3

**SIGHTS & ACTIVITIES**               (p408)
Banys Árabs (Arab Baths)................**8** C6
Basílica de Sant Francesc.................**9** D5
Cathedral........................................**10** B6
Es Baluard.......................................**11** A5
Iglesia Santa Eulália......................**12** C5
Iglesia Santa Magdalena...............**13** B4

Museu de Mallorca.......................**14** C6
Palau Almudaina...........................**15** B6

**SLEEPING**                          (pp408–9)
Hostal Apuntadores......................**16** B6
Hostal Ritzi....................................**17** B6
Hostel Brondo...............................**18** B5
Hotel Born.....................................**19** B4
Hotel San Lorenzo........................**20** A5

**EATING**                               (p409)
Bar Bosch........................................**21** B5
Bar Dia............................................**22** A5
Bon Lloc.........................................**23** B5
Restaurant Celler Sa Premsa..........**24** C3
Yate Rizz.........................................**25** B5

**DRINKING**                            (p409)
Atlantico.........................................**26** A5
Café Barcelona..............................**27** B6
La Bodeguita de Medio.................**28** B6

**TRANSPORT**                          (p409)
Airport Bus...............................(see 29)
Bus Station.....................................**29** D3

SPAIN

## Sights & Activities

An awesome mass of sandstone walls and flying buttresses, Palma's magnificent **cathedral** ( ☎ 97 172 31 30; Plaça Almoina; admission €3.50; ☽ 10am-3.15pm Nov-Mar, 10am-6pm Apr-Oct, closed Sat pm & Sun) overlooks the city and its port. It houses an excellent museum, and some of the interior features were designed by Gaudí.

Opposite is the **Palau Almudaina** ( ☎ 97 121 41 34; Carrer Palau Reial; adult/student €3.20/2.30; ☽ 10am-2pm & 4-6pm Oct-Mar, 10am-6.30pm Apr-Sep, closed Sat pm & Sun), the one-time residence of the Mallorcan monarchs. Inside is a collection of tapestries and artworks.

**Es Baluard** ( ☎ 97 190 82 00; www.esbaluard.org; Plaça Porta de Santa Catalina; adult/student €6/4.50; ☽ 10am-8pm Tue-Sun Oct-May, 10am-midnight daily Jun-Sep), Palma's striking museum of modern and contemporary art, is a visual feast of works from 20th-century artists, including Spanish greats Miró and Picasso.

The **Museu de Mallorca** ( ☎ 97 171 75 40; Carrer Portella 5; admission €2.40; ☽ 10am-7pm Tue-Sat, 10am-2pm Sun) has archaeological finds, as well as paintings and furniture from the 19th and 20th centuries. Nearby, the atmospheric **Banys Àrabs** (Arab Baths; ☎ 97 172 15 49; Carrer Ca'n Sera 7; admission €1.50; ☽ 9am-9pm Apr-Nov, 9am-7pm Dec-Mar) are the only remaining monument to the Muslim domination of the island.

Mallorca's northwestern coast is a world away from the high-rise tourism on the other side of the island. Dominated by the Serra de Tramuntana, it's a beautiful region of olive groves, pine forests and small villages with shuttered stone buildings; it also has a rugged and rocky coastline. There are a couple of highlights for drivers: the hair-raising road down to the small port of **Sa Calobra**, and the amazing trip along the peninsula leading to the island's northern tip, **Cap Formentor**.

If you don't have wheels, take the **Palma–Sóller train** (opposite). It's one of the most popular and spectacular excursions on the island. Sóller is also the best place to base yourself for trekking and the nearby village of **Fornalutx** is said to be the prettiest on Mallorca.

From Sóller, it is a 10km walk to the beautiful hill-top village of **Deià**, where Robert Graves, poet and author of *I Claudius*, lived most of his life. From the village, you can scramble down to the **Cala de Deià**,

where the small shingle beach is a laid-back haven of naked swimming and weekend-long beach parties.

Most of Mallorca's best beaches have been consumed by tourist developments, although there are exceptions. The lovely **Cala Mondragó** on the southeastern coast is backed by just a couple of *hostales* while, a little further south, the attractive port town of **Cala Figuera** and nearby **Cala Santanyi** beach have both escaped many of the ravages of mass tourism. There are also some good quiet beaches near the popular German resort of Colonia San Jordi, particularly **Ses Arenes** and **Es Trenc**, both a few kilometres back up the coast towards Palma.

## Sleeping

### PALMA

**Hostal Apuntadores** ( ☎ 97 171 34 91; apuntadores@ ctv.es; Carrer Apuntadores 8; dm/d €17/45, s/d with shared bathroom €27/35) It has a great location but the décor is a little on the bland side.

**Hostal Ritzi** ( ☎ 97 171 46 10; d €50, s/d with shared bathroom €25/38) This little place is friendly and charming in a cluttered sort of way, with satellite TV in the communal sitting room.

**Hostal Brondo** ( ☎ 97 171 90 43; www.hostalbrondo .net; Carrer C'an Brondo 1; d €60, s/d/tr with shared bathroom €30/45/55) With a welcoming English owner and pretty communal areas, rooms in this *hostal* are clean and spacious, with high ceilings. Some have balconies.

**Hotel Born** ( ☎ 97 171 29 42; www.hotelborn .com; Carrer Sant Jaume 3; s/d from €56/81; ⧉ ) With fabulous rooms in a restored 18th-century palace, it also has a classic Mallorcan patio filled with palm trees.

**Hotel San Lorenzo** ( ☎ 97 172 82 00; www.hotelsan lorenzo.com; Carrer Sant Llorenç 14; r from €140; ⧉ ⧉ ) Exquisite rooms in this converted 17th-century manor house have beamed ceilings and tiled bathrooms. The Art Deco bar downstairs was imported from Paris.

### DEIÀ

**Hostal Miramar** ( ☎ 97 163 90 84; www.pensionmiramar .com; Can Oliver s/n; s/d/tr with breakfast €31/60/82; ⧉ ) Friendly and old-fashioned, rooms have a bird's-eye view of the village and sea.

**S'Hotel D'es Puig** ( ☎ 97 163 94 09; www.hoteldes puig.com; Es Puig 4; s/d with breakfast €76/114; ⧉ ⧉ ) Once featured in a short story by Robert Graves. Rooms are delightful.

**SÓLLER & FORNALUTX**

**Hostal Nadal** ( ☎ 97 163 11 80; Carrer Romaguera 29, Sóller; s/d/tr €22/34/44; s/d/tr with shared bathroom €18/26/35) This place has simple rooms but it's clean and airy and there is a small patio and bar downstairs.

**Cán Verdera** ( ☎ 97 163 82 03; www.canverdera .com; Carrer Toros 1, Fornalutx; s/d €89/105.30; 🔀 🌊 🖹 ) An old stone building with original beams, pool and great views.

**EAST COAST**

**Hostal Cán Jordi** ( ☎ 97 164 50 35; Carrer Virgen del Carmen 58, Cala Figuera; s/d with shared bathroom €28/41) This place is justifiably popular, with wonderful views over the inlet.

**Hostal Playa Mondragó** ( ☎ 97 165 77 52; Cala Mondragó; s/d €32/64; 🏵 May-Oct; 🔀 🌊 ) Five storeys high, this small beach resort overlooks one of the island's best (and least developed) sandy beaches.

## Eating & Drinking

For Palma's best range of eateries, wander through the maze of streets between Plaça de la Reina and the port. Carrer Apuntadores is lined with bars and restaurants, including seafood, Italian and an inexpensive take-away **Bar Dia** (Carrer Apuntadores 18).

**Yate Rizz** (Passeig des Born 2; menú €5.30; 🏵 1-3.30pm Mon-Sat) This place serves up the cheapest three-course meals (with wine) in town to a happy mix of locals and tourists crammed shoulder-to-shoulder over red-checked tablecloths.

**Bar Bosch** ( ☎ 97 172 11 31; Plaça Rei Joan Carlos; coffee & croissant €2.35; 🏵 7-1am) In a prime people-watching spot, Bar Bosch is good for breakfast, sandwiches and snacks.

**Restaurant Celler Sa Premsa** ( ☎ 97 172 35 29; www.cellersapremsa.com; Plaça Bisbe Berenguer de Palou 8; mains €7-8; 🏵 noon-4pm & 7.30-11.30pm Mon-Sat) This local institution is the size of a warehouse, serving enormous portions of classic Mallorcan fare.

**Bon Lloc** ( ☎ 97 171 86 17; Carrer San Feliu 7; menú €11; 🏵 1-4pm Mon-Sat; 🍴 ) Popular with Palma's young professionals, it serves up tasty vegetarian dishes.

Good late-night drinking dens include **Atlantico** (Carrer Sant Feliu 12; 🏵 8pm-4am), with its unique combination of knock-out cocktails and grunge; **Café Barcelona** (Carrer Apuntadores 5; 🏵 8.30pm-1am Sun-Thu & 8.30pm-3am Fri & Sat), an intimate jazz club; and the fiery **La Bodeguita**

**de Medio** (Carrer Vallseca 18; 🏵 8pm-1am Mon-Thu & 8pm-3am Fri & Sat), blaring out salsa to a *mojito*-fuelled crowd.

## Getting Around

Bus No 25 runs between the airport and Plaça Espanya in central Palma (€1.80, 20 minutes, every 20 minutes). A taxi will cost around €14.

Most parts of the island are accessible by bus from Palma. Buses generally depart from or near the bus station at Plaça Espanya. Mallorca's two train lines also start from Plaça Espanya. One goes to the inland town of Inca (€1.80, 30 minutes, every 30 minutes) and the other goes to Sóller (€2.50, one hour, five daily), both highly picturesque jaunts.

The best way to get around the island is by car – it's worth renting one just for the drive along the northwestern coast. There are about 30 rental agencies in Palma (and all the big companies have reps at the airport). If you want to compare prices, check the many harbourside offices along Passeig Marítim.

# IBIZA

From the bohemian atmosphere of Ibiza's old town to the hedonistic, foam-soaked fun of its world-famous clubs, Ibiza (Eivissa in Catalan) has a unique spirit, which can't fail to captivate.

Away from the remarkable clubbing scene, particularly in the rural villages in the south, you'll find an island that dashes any preconceived notions of Ibiza. Here the women wear long black skirts and wide straw hats and – forget the nudist beaches – the only traffic stoppers are the goatherds.

## Orientation & Information

The capital, Ibiza city, is on the southeastern side of the island. This is where most travellers arrive (by ferry or air; the airport is to the south) and it's also the best base. The next largest towns are Santa Eulària des Riu, on the eastern coast, and Sant Antoni de Portmany, on the western coast (the latter best avoided unless you are seriously into discos and getting drunk). Other big resorts are scattered around the island.

**Tourist Office** ( ☎ 97 130 19 00; oitport@cief.es; Carrer Antoni Riquer 2; 🏵 9.30am-1.30pm & 5-7.30pm Mon-Fri, 10.30am-1pm Sat Apr-Oct, 8.30am-3pm Mon-Fri, 10.30am-1pm Sat Nov-Mar) Opposite the Estación Marítima.

**SPAIN**

**Wash and Dry.Com** ( ☎ 97 139 48 22; Avinguda Espanya 53; ☉ 10am-8.30pm Mon-Sat) There are numerous cafés where you can go online but not many where you can do a cheap load of washing as well as access the Internet.

## Sights & Activities

Shopping is a major pastime in Ibiza city. The port area of **Sa Penya** is crammed with funky and trashy clothes boutiques and arty-crafty market stalls. From here, you can wander up into **D'Alt Vila**, the atmospheric old walled town, with its upmarket restaurants, galleries and the **Museu d'Art Contemporani** ( ☎ 97 130 27 23; Ronda Narcís Puget; admission free; ☉ 10am-1.30pm & 4-6pm Tue-Fri, 10am-6pm Sat & Sun Oct-Apr, 10am-1.30pm & 5-8pm Tue-Fri, 10am-1.30pm Sat & Sun May-Sep). There are fine views from the walls and from the **cathedral** (Plaça Catedral; ☉ 10am-1pm Tue-Sat) at the top, and the **Museu Arqueològic** ( ☎ 97 130 12 31; Plaça Catedral 3; admission €2.40; ☉ 10am-2pm & 6-8pm Mon-Sat, 10am-2pm Sun Apr-Sep, 9am-3pm Mon-Sat, 10am-2pm Sun Oct-Mar) is worth a visit.

The heavily developed **Platja de ses Figueretes** beach is a 20-minute walk south of Sa Penya – you'd be better off heading south to the beaches at **Ses Salines**, a half-hour ride on bus No 11 (€1.50).

Ibiza has numerous unspoiled and relatively undeveloped beaches. On the northeastern coast, **Cala de Boix** is the only black-sand beach on the island, while further north are the lovely beaches of **S'Aigua Blanca**. On the northern coast near Portinatx, **Cala Xarraca** is in a picturesque, secluded bay and near Port de Sant Miquel is the attractive **Cala Benirras**. On the southwestern coast, **Cala d'Hort** has a spectacular setting overlooking two rugged rock-islets, Es Verda and Es Verdranell.

## Sleeping

### IBIZA CITY

There are several *hostales* in the streets around the port, although in midsummer cheap beds are scarce.

**Casa de Huéspedes Navarro** ( ☎ 97 131 07 71; Carrer sa Creu 20; d/tr with shared bathroom €38/50; ☉ Apr-Oct) With 10 rooms at the top of a long flight of stairs, this place is in a good central location, with a sunny rooftop terrace.

**Casa de Huéspedes Vara de Rey** ( ☎ 97 130 13 76; hibiza@wanadoo.es; Passeig Vara de Rey 7; s/d with shared bathroom €36/72; ☉ Mar-Dec), Friendly, charming and eclectic, it has 11 rooms, all with washbasins and old-fashioned ceiling fans.

**Hostal-Restaurante La Marina** ( ☎ 97 131 01 72; reservas@hostal-lamarina.com; Carrer Barcelona 7; s/d €62/77; ☒ ) On the waterfront, La Marina has immaculate rooms in cool colours and lots of wrought-iron furniture.

**Hostal Parque** ( ☎ 97 130 13 58; info@hostalparque .com; Plaça Parque 4; d €100, s/d with shared bathroom €48/72; ☒ ) Sleek, modern and minimalist, this place is on one of Ibiza's liveliest squares.

### OTHER AREAS

**Camping Cala Nova** ( ☎ 97 133 17 74; per person/tent/car €5.40/4.60/4.60) Close to a good beach and 500m north of the resort town of Cala Nova, this is one of Ibiza's best camping grounds.

**Hostal Cala Boix** ( ☎ 97 133 52 24; s/d incl breakfast & shared bathroom €24.50/49; ☒ ) By the black-sand beach at Cala Boix, this place is in a cliff-top location.

**Pensión Sa Plana** ( ☎ 97 133 50 73; d incl breakfast & shared bathroom €58; ☒ ☒ ) Near the S'Aigua Blanca beaches, with a poolside bar and barbecue.

**Can Curreu** ( ☎ 97 133 52 80; www.cancurreu .com; d €240; ☒ ☒ ☒ ) This is the place for a fabulous splurge. It's a beautifully restored Ibizan farmhouse, with a pool, sauna, gymnasium and open fireplaces in the rooms.

## Eating & Drinking

Start your evening with a drink and some people-watching (this island is stacked with poseurs) at one of the bars lining the lively Plaça Parque, such as **Herry's Bar** ( ☎ 97 139 11 52; Plaça Parque 2; ☉ 11.30am-midnight), which does the best *mojitos* this side of the Atlantic, or **Café Madagascar** (Plaça Parque 3; sandwiches €3.60; ☉ 9-2am), with fresh juices and tasty sandwiches, as well as the usual alcoholic fare.

**Croissant Show** ( ☎ 97 131 76 65; Plaça Constitució s/n; ☉ 7am-3pm) This is where everyone comes for post-clubbing munchies. The pastries are as good as any in Paris.

**Comidas-Bar San Juan** ( ☎ 97 131 16 03; Carrer Guillem de Montgri 8; mains €4-7; ☉ 1-3.30pm & 8.30-11pm) A popular, noisy place where diners share tables. The food is hearty and extremely good value for money. The fresh fish of the day comes highly recommended.

**La Oliva** ( ☎ 97 130 57 52; Calle Santa Cruz; mains €12-14; ☉ 1-4pm & 8-11.30pm Mon-Sat) With its pretty patio and Andalucían-style fare, La Oliva has maintained its good reputation. The fish soup is excellent.

**Teatro Pereyra** ( ☎ 97 119 14 68; Carrer Conde Roselló 3; ⏰ 8-4am) In an old theatre, this is the place for jazz, blues and soul. Expect lots of atmosphere and live music every night. Entrance is free but the price of drinks shoots up once the music starts.

**KM5** ( ☎ 97 139 63 49; www.km5-lounge.com; Carretera San José 5; ⏰ 8pm-1.30am May-Oct) On the road to San Josep, 5km from Ibiza city, KM5 is a glam bar, lounge and garden hang-out.

## Entertainment

Ibiza's summer nightlife is renowned. At night, wander the fashion catwalk of cobbled streets where designer-chic couples and seriously studded swingers dodge the outrageous PR performers hired by the discos to attract dusk-to-dawn clubbers. Dozens of bars keep Ibiza city's port area jumping until the early hours – particularly on Carrer Barcelona and Carrer Garijo Cipriano. After they wind down, you can continue on to one of the island's world-famous discos – if you can afford the €40 entry, that is. There's a handy Discobus service that operates nightly from midnight until 6am doing circuits between the major discos, the bars and hotels in Ibiza city, Platja d'en Bossa, San Rafael and San Antonio. The big names are **Pacha** (www.pacha .net), on the northern side of Ibiza city's port; **Privilege** (www.privilege.es) and **Amnesia** (www.amnesia -ibiza.com), both 6km out on the road to Sant Antoni; **El Divino** (www.eldivino-ibiza.com), across the water from the town centre (hop on one of its boats); and **Space** (www.space-ibiza.es), south of Ibiza city in Platja d'En Bossa.

## Getting Around

Buses run between the airport and Ibiza city hourly (€1, 15 minutes); a taxi costs around €10. Buses to other parts of the island leave from the series of bus stops along Avinguda d'Isidoro Macabich. Pick up a timetable from the tourist office.

If you want to get to some of the more secluded beaches you will need to rent wheels. In Ibiza city, **Autos Isla Blanca** ( ☎ 97 131 54 07; Carrer Antoni Jaume s/n) will hire out a Renault Twingo for €103 for three days, all-inclusive.

# FORMENTERA

A short boat ride south of Ibiza, Formentera is the smallest, least developed of the four main Balearic Islands and mostly it's still possible to spread a towel out on the beach without kicking sand over your neighbour. The island is also famously flat and fantastic for cycling with some excellent trails.

## Orientation & Information

Formentera is about 20km from east to west. Ferries arrive at La Savina on the northwestern coast; the **tourist office** ( ☎ 97 132 20 57; www .formentera.es; ⏰ 10am-2pm & 5-7pm Mon-Fri, 10am-2pm Sat) is behind the rental agencies you'll see when you disembark. Three kilometres south is the island's pretty capital, Sant Francesc Xavier, where you'll find a pharmacy, several banks and a good-sized supermarket for your picnic supplies. From here, the main road runs along the middle of the island before climbing to the highest point (192m). At the eastern end of the island is the Sa Mola lighthouse. Es Pujols is 3km east of La Savina and is the main tourist resort, with most of the *hostales* located here (and the only place with any nightlife to speak of).

## Sights & Activities

Some of the island's best and most popular beaches are the beautiful white strips of sand along the narrow promontory that stretches north towards Ibiza. A 2km walking trail leads from the La Savina–Es Pujols road past the divine **Platja de Ses Illetes** to the far end of the promontory, from where you can wade (carefully) across a narrow strait to **S'Espalmador**, a privately owned uninhabited islet with beautiful, quiet beaches. If you don't fancy the paddle, there are regular boat rides. Along Formentera's southern coast, **Platja de Migjorn** is made up of numerous coves and beaches. Tracks lead down to these from the main road. On the western coast is the lovely **Cala Saona** beach.

The tourist office's *Green Tours* brochure outlines 19 excellent walking and cycling trails in five languages that take you through some of the island's most scenic areas.

## Sleeping & Eating

Camping is not allowed on Formentera. Sadly, the coastal accommodation places mainly cater to German and British package-tour agencies and are overpriced and/ or booked out in summer.

There are some fantastic seafood restaurants on the island and, thanks to a particularly large Argentine community, some excellent places to get grilled meat.

SPAIN

**Hostal Capri** ( ☎ 97 132 83 52; Es Pujols; s/d with breakfast €46/60; ☾ May-Sep) This place has whitewashed rooms with ceiling fans and balconies. Downstairs is a lovely shaded terrace restaurant specialising in paella.

**Hostal Bellavista** ( ☎ 97 132 22 55; La Savina; s/d €80/120; ☒ ) The Bellavista has port views, a handy terrace bar, spotless rooms and parrots in the lobby.

**Casa de Huéspedes Miramar** ( ☎ 97 132 70 60; Es Caló; s/d with shared bathroom €30/40; ☾ Apr-Oct) This family-run place has small rooms.

**Fonda Rafalet** ( ☎ 97 132 70 16; s/d €55/73; ☾ Apr-Oct) The quiet Rafalet has rooms with balconies overlooking the sea.

**Hostal Pepe** ( ☎ 97 132 80 33; Sant Ferrán de Ses Roques; s/d with breakfast €28/46) This popular *hostal* is run by a very chatty landlady. The restaurant here also has an excellent reputation. From this place, Es Pujols is an easy cycle or walk along a 1.5km dusty (but pretty) track.

**S'Avaradero** ( ☎ 97 132 90 43; Ave Miramar 32-36, Es Pujols; mains €10-15; ☾ 1-4pm & 8-11.30pm) On the seafront and serving great seafood and Argentine-style meat dishes.

**Pizza Art** ( ☎ 97 132 90 94; Edificio Sa Varadeors; mains €5-7; ☾ 7pm-2am) Among the plethora of pizzerias, this place is better than most.

Wind up the evening with a blast of good music at the **Blue Bar** ( ☎ 97 118 70 11; Playa Mitjorn km 8; ☾ 8pm-4am) or, for tapas and local wine, **Bar Sa Barraca** ( ☎ 97 132 80 27; Ave Miramar, Es Pujols) is great.

### Getting There & Around

There are 20 to 25 ferries daily between Ibiza city and Formentera. The trip takes around 30 minutes and prices between the various companies are fiercely competitive, but cost around €10 one way.

A string of rental agencies lines the harbour in La Savina. Bikes start at €5 a day (€7 for a mountain bike) and scooters start at €20. A regular bus service connects all the main towns.

## MENORCA

Menorca, the least overrun of the Balearic Islands, is a popular destination for families. Famed for its undeveloped beaches, archaeological sites and environmental areas, such as the Albufera d'es Grau wetlands, the island was declared a Biosphere Reserve by Unesco in 1993.

### Orientation & Information

The capital, Maó (Mahón in Castilian), is at the eastern end of the island. Its busy port is the arrival point for most ferries and Menorca's airport is 7km southwest. The main road runs down the middle of the island to Ciutadella, Menorca's second-largest town, with secondary roads leading north and south to the resorts and beaches.

**Post Offices** Maó (Carrer Bon Aire); Ciutadella (Carrer Pío VI 4)

**Tourist Offices** Main office ( ☎ 97 136 37 90; infomenorcamao@cime.es; Carrer Sa Rovellada de Dalt 24, Maó; ☾ 9.30am-3pm & 5-7pm Mon-Fri, 9am-1pm Sat); Ciutadella ( ☎ 97 138 26 93; Plaça la Catedral 5; ☾ 9.30am-1.30pm & 5-7pm Mon-Fri, 9am-1pm Sat) During summer there is also an office at the airport.

### Sights & Activities

Maó and Ciutadella are both harbour towns, and from either place you'll have to commute to the beaches. Maó absorbs most of the tourist traffic. While you're here, you can take a boat cruise around its impressive harbour and sample the local gin at the **Xoriguer distillery** ( ☎ 97 136 21 97; Moll de Ponent 93; ☾ 8am-7pm Mon-Fri, 9am-1pm Sat).

Ciutadella, with its smaller harbour and historic buildings, has a more distinctly Spanish feel about it. Follow the shopping baskets to the colourful **market** (Plaça Llibertat), surrounded by lively tapas bars.

In the centre of the island, the 357m-high **Monte Toro** has great views of the whole island and, on a clear day, you can see as far as Mallorca.

With your own transport and a bit of footwork, you'll be able to discover some of Menorca's off-the-beaten-track beaches. North of Maó, a drive across a lunar landscape leads to the lighthouse at **Cabo de Favàritx**. If you park just before the gate to the lighthouse and climb up the rocks behind you, you'll see a couple of the eight beaches that are just waiting for scramblers such as yourself to explore.

On the northern coast, the picturesque town of **Fornells** is on a large bay popular with windsurfers. Further west, at the beach of Binimella, you can continue to the unspoilt **Cala Pregonda**, which is a good 20-minute walk from the nearest parking spot.

North of Ciutadella is **La Vall** (€5 per car; ☾ 10am-7pm), another stretch of untouched beach backed by a private nature park. On

SPAIN

the southern coast are two good beaches either side of the Santa Galdana resort: **Cala Mitjana** to the east and **Macarella** to the west.

Menorca's beaches aren't its only attractions. The interior of the island is liberally sprinkled with reminders of its rich and ancient heritage. Pick up a copy of the tourist office's *Archaeological Guide to Menorca*.

## Sleeping

Menorca's two camping grounds are **Camping S'atalaia** ( ☎ 971 37 30 95; per person/tent/car €5.50/4.50/3; 🕑 Apr-Oct), near the resorts of Santa Galdana, about 4km south of Ferreries, and **Camping Son Bou** (971 37 27 27; www .campingsonbou.com; per person/tent/car €6.20/3.45/4.15; 🕑 Apr-Oct), near Son Bou, south of Alaior.

**Posada Orsi** ( ☎ 97 136 47 51; posadaorsi@hotmail .com; Carrer Infanta 19, Maó; s/d with shared bathroom €23/38) A riot of acid colours and stripy sofas, Orsi is bright, clean and well located. Tent-like mosquito nets add to the exotic air.

**Hotel del Almirante** ( ☎ 97 136 27 00; www.hotel delalmirante.com; Carreterra Maó–Es Castel; s/d €63/89.50; Ⓟ 🛏 🕑 ) A magnificent Georgian-style mansion and a former residence of Nelson's second-in-command at Trafalgar, this place is a haven of terraces, lovely gardens, a pool and tennis court.

**Hostal Oasis** ( ☎ 97 138 21 97; Carrer Sant Isidre 33, Ciutadella; d with breakfast & shared bathroom €46; 🕑 Apr-Oct) Run by an elderly couple, it has homy rooms around a central courtyard.

## Eating & Drinking

Both Maó and Ciutadella's ports are lined with restaurants and you won't have any trouble finding somewhere to eat.

### MAÓ

**La Bombilla** ( ☎ 97 136 45 76; Plaça Bastión; bocadillos €2.70; 🕑 10.30am-11.30pm Tue-Sun) Noisy and smoky but an excellent no-nonsense choice for cheap snacks and tapas.

**Casanova** ( ☎ 97 135 41 69; Andén Poniente 15; pizzas €7; 🕑 1-4pm & 7.30-11.30pm) A popular pizzeria with a wood-burning oven.

**Es Fosquet** ( ☎ 97 135 00 58; Moll Llevant 256; mains €9-12; 🕑 1-4pm & 8-11.30pm Thu-Sun) A tiny but chic hole-in-the-wall place, serving up freshly caught fish and shellfish.

**Latitud 40** ( ☎ 97 136 41 76; Moll Llevant 265, Maó; 🕑 7pm-1am) A hip little bar-restaurant popular with yachties.

### CIUTADELLA

There are lots of good drinking holes near the port.

**La Guitarra** (%97 138 13 55; Carrer Dolores 1; mains €12; h12.30-3.30pm & 7.30-11.30pm Mon-Sat) A classy place for a local meal, La Guitarra has a charming cellar-like setting with stone vaulted ceilings. The speciality is pato a la menorquina (Menorcan duck).

## Getting Around

From the airport, a taxi into Maó costs around €10; there are no buses.

**TMSA** ( ☎ 97 136 04 75) runs six buses a day between Maó and Ciutadella (€3.75), with connections to the major resorts on the southern coast. In summer there are also daily bus services to most of the coastal towns from both Maó and Ciutadella.

If you're planning to hire a car, rates vary seasonally from around €28 to €48 a day; during summer, minimum hire periods sometimes apply. In Maó, places worth trying include **Autos Valls** ( ☎ 97 136 84 65; Plaça Espanya 13) and **Autos Isla** ( ☎ 97 136 65 69; Avinguda Josep Maria Quadrado 28).

# ANDALUCÍA

Life is sweet and simple in Andalucía. Whether you are soaking up the rays on a beach, exploring all the little alleyways of some historic barrio or simply sipping a glass of chilled gazpacho in a leafy plaza, pleasures here are plenty.

The stronghold of the Muslims in Spain for nearly eight centuries, Andalucía is peppered with Moorish reminders of the past: the magnificent Alhambra in Granada, the timeless elegance of Córdoba's Mezquita and the whitewashed villages nestling in ochre hills. The regional capital, Seville, is one of the country's most enticing cities.

Away from the cities and resorts, Andalucía is relatively untainted by tourists. Its scenery ranges from semideserts to lush river valleys to gorge-riddled mountains. Its long coastline stretches from the remote beaches of Cabo de Gata, past the crowds of the Costa del Sol, to come within 14km of Africa at Tarifa, before opening up to the Atlantic Ocean with the long sandy beaches of the Costa de la Luz.

SPAIN

**FLAMENCO FUSION**

Flamenco has become much more than the traditional signature music of southern Spain. It was once exclusively the music of the Gitanos (Roma people), however in recent years flamenco has also morphed into a modern fusion of different rhythms and styles. Since the 1970s, bands have experimented with blues, rock, Latin, jazz and even punk to create cool new sounds as well as a new fan base of young Spaniards. This is so much the case that these days you are as likely to hear flamenco hip-hop blasting out of a souped-up car on a Friday night as to catch it at a tourist show.

Bands that first broke the ground in this new wave of flamenco include the bluesy-style Pata Negra, Ketama (African, Cuban and Brazilian rhythms) and Radio Tarifa (North African and medieval mix). In recent years Chambao has hit the mark with its flamenco chill and Mala Rodriguez has put flamenco hip into hip-hop.

# SEVILLE

**pop 709,975**

An impossibly sexy and intoxicating city, Seville seduces all the senses. From its jumble of cobbled alleys and bright plazas to the spontaneous bursts of flamenco in the bars and the passion of its festivals, this is the most *andaluz* of Spain's cities. Even once you've left, Seville's memory lingers on.

If this wasn't enough, there is the marvellous exuberance and elegance of its people. Seville's air of contentment is well founded. It was an important and prosperous centre in Muslim times and, later, in the 16th and 17th centuries.

Seville is an expensive place, so it's worth planning your visit carefully. In July and August, the city is stiflingly hot. The best time to come is during the unforgettable Easter week and April *feria* (fair), although rooms then (if you can get one) cost close to double the regular rates.

## Orientation

The Guadalquivir River cuts through Seville, with most places of interest on the river's eastern side. The centre is a confusion of small plazas and winding streets, except for the broad, straight Ave Consitución. Most of the city's major monuments, including the cathedral, the Giralda and the Alcázar are just east of Ave Constitución. Further east, the Barrio de Santa Cruz is an appealing tangle of streets with most of Seville's budget accommodation.

## Information

**Internet Multimedia Center** (☎ 95 450 25 43; Calle Adriano 7; per hr €2; 🕑 10am-10pm Mon-Fri, 5-10pm Sat & Sun) One of Seville's many Internet places.

**Lavandería Roma** (Calle Castelar 2C; 🕑 9.30am-1.30pm & 5-8.30pm Mon-Fri, 9am-2pm Sat) Will wash, dry and fold a load of washing for €6.

**Librería Beta** (☎ 95 456 28 17; Ave Constitución 9; 🕑 10am-8pm Mon-Sat) Has guidebooks and novels in English.

**Tourist offices** Main office (☎ 95 422 14 04; otsevilla@andalucia.org; Ave Constitución 21; 🕑 9am-7pm Mon-Fri, 10am-2pm & 3-7pm Sat, 10am-2pm Sun); Paseo de las Delicias 9 (☎ 95 423 44 65; 🕑 8.30am-2.45pm Mon-Fri); Calle de Arjona 28 (☎ 95 450 56 00; 🕑 8am-8.45pm Mon-Fri, 8.30am-2.30pm Sat & Sun)

## Sights & Activities

### CATHEDRAL & LA GIRALDA

Seville's towering **cathedral** (☎ 95 421 49 71; Calle Alemanes; adult/student €7/1.50, free Sun; 🕑 11am-5pm Mon-Sat, 2.30-6pm Sun), one of the biggest in the world, was built on the site of Muslim Seville's main mosque between 1401 and 1507. The structure is primarily Gothic, though most of the internal decoration is in later styles. The adjoining tower, La Giralda, was the mosque's minaret and dates from the 12th century. The exhausting climb to the top is worth it for the stunning panoramic views of the city. One highlight of the cathedral's lavish interior is Christopher Columbus' supposed tomb inside the southern door (although recent research has revealed that Columbus was most likely laid to rest in the Caribbean and the remains here are in fact those of his lesser-known son Diego). The four crowned sepulchre-bearers represent the four kingdoms of Spain that existed at the time of Columbus' sailing to the Americas. The entrance to the cathedral and La Giralda is the Puerta del Perdón on Calle Alemanes.

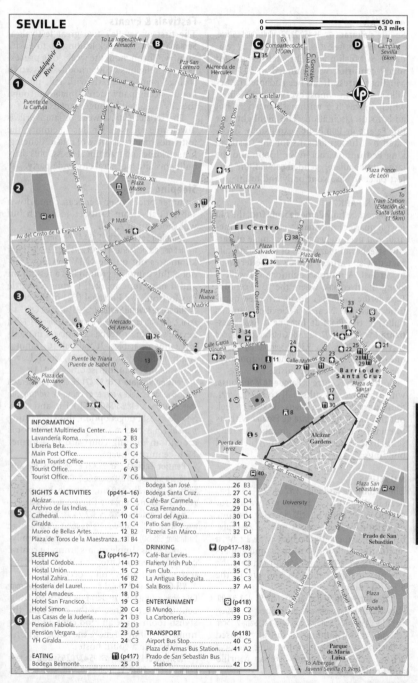

# SEVILLE

0 — 500 m
0 — 0.3 miles

SPAIN

## INFORMATION

| | | |
|---|---|---|
| Internet Multimedia Center | 1 | B4 |
| Lavandería Roma | 2 | B3 |
| Librería Beta | 3 | C3 |
| Main Post Office | 4 | C4 |
| Main Tourist Office | 5 | C4 |
| Tourist Office | 6 | A3 |
| Tourist Office | 7 | C6 |

## SIGHTS & ACTIVITIES (pp414–16)

| | | |
|---|---|---|
| Alcázar | 8 | C4 |
| Archivo de las Indias | 9 | C4 |
| Cathedral | 10 | C4 |
| Giralda | 11 | C4 |
| Museo de Bellas Artes | 12 | B2 |
| Plaza de Toros de la Maestranza | 13 | B4 |

## SLEEPING (pp416–17)

| | | |
|---|---|---|
| Hostal Córdoba | 14 | D3 |
| Hostal Unión | 15 | C2 |
| Hostal Zahira | 16 | B2 |
| Hostería del Laurel | 17 | D4 |
| Hotel Amadeus | 18 | D3 |
| Hotel San Francisco | 19 | C3 |
| Hotel Simon | 20 | C4 |
| Las Casas de la Judería | 21 | D3 |
| Pensión Fabiola | 22 | D3 |
| Pensión Vergara | 23 | D4 |
| YH Giralda | 24 | C3 |

## EATING (p417)

| | | |
|---|---|---|
| Bodega Belmonte | 25 | D3 |
| Bodega San José | 26 | B3 |
| Bodega Santa Cruz | 27 | C4 |
| Café-Bar Carmela | 28 | D4 |
| Casa Fernando | 29 | D4 |
| Corral del Agua | 30 | D4 |
| Patio San Eloy | 31 | B2 |
| Pizzeria San Marco | 32 | D4 |

## DRINKING (pp417–18)

| | | |
|---|---|---|
| Café-Bar Levies | 33 | D3 |
| Flaherty Irish Pub | 34 | C3 |
| Fun Club | 35 | C1 |
| La Antigua Bodeguita | 36 | C3 |
| Sala Boss | 37 | A4 |

## ENTERTAINMENT (p418)

| | | |
|---|---|---|
| El Mundo | 38 | C2 |
| La Carbonería | 39 | D3 |

## TRANSPORT (p418)

| | | |
|---|---|---|
| Airport Bus Stop | 40 | C5 |
| Plaza de Armas Bus Station | 41 | A2 |
| Prado de San Sebastián Bus Station | 42 | D5 |

### ALCÁZAR

Seville's **alcázar** ( ☎ 95 450 23 23; adult/child €5/free; 🕙 9.30am-7pm Tue-Sat, 9.30am-5pm Sun), a residence of Muslim and Christian royalty for many centuries, was founded in 913 as a Muslim fortress. It has been adapted by Seville's rulers in almost every century since, which makes it a mishmash of styles but adds to its fascination. The highlights are the **Palacio de Don Pedro**, exquisitely decorated by Muslim artisans for the Castilian king Pedro the Cruel in the 1360s, and the large, immaculately tended **gardens**, the perfect place to ease your body and brain.

### WALKS & PARKS

To appreciate fully **Barrio de Santa Cruz**, the old Jewish quarter immediately east of the cathedral, you need to head for the tangle of narrow streets and plazas east of the main Calle Mateus Gago artery. There's no better place to get lost. A more straightforward walk is along the **riverbank**, where the 13th-century **Torre del Oro** contains a small, crowded maritime museum. Nearby is Seville's famous bullring, the **Plaza de Toros de la Real Maestranza** ( ☎ 95 422 45 77; Paseo de Cristóbal Colón; guided tours €4; 🕙 9.30am-7pm, 9.30am-3pm bullfight days), one of the oldest in Spain. The (compulsory) tour is in English and Spanish.

South of the centre is **Parque de María Luisa**, with its maze of paths, tall trees, flowers, fountains and shaded lawns. Be sure to seek out the magnificent **Plaza de España** with its fountains, canal and a simply dazzling semicircle of *azulejo* (ceramic tile) clad buildings.

### MUSEUMS

The **Archivo de las Indias** ( ☎ 95 421 12 34) has been undergoing exhaustive renovation for several years, and was still closed at the time of writing. When it does open (hopefully by 2005), expect to be blown away by a fascinating collection of maps and papers dating from 1492 and documenting the conquest of the Americas and life in the Spanish colonies.

The **Museo de Bellas Artes** ( ☎ 95 422 07 90; Plaza Museo 9; admission non-EU/EU citizens €1.50/free; 🕙 2.30-8.15pm Tue, 9am-8.15pm Wed-Sat, 9am-2.15pm Sun) has an outstanding, beautifully housed collection of Spanish art, focusing on local artists such as Bartolemé Esteban Murillo and Francisco Zurbarán.

## Festivals & Events

The first of Seville's two great festivals is **Semana Santa**, the week leading up to Easter Sunday. Throughout the week, long processions of religious brotherhoods, dressed in strange penitents' garb with tall, pointed hoods, accompany sacred images through the city, watched by huge crowds.

The **Feria de Abril**, a week in late April, is a welcome release after this solemnity: the festivities involve six days of music, dancing, horse-riding and traditional dress, plus daily bullfights and a general city-wide party.

## Sleeping

Summer prices given here can come down substantially from October to March but will shoot up in April.

**Camping Sevilla** ( ☎ 95 451 43 79; campingsevilla@ turinet.net; per person/tent/car €3.25/3.25/3.25; 🏊 ) Six kilometres out on the N-IV towards Córdoba, this camping ground has a restaurant and a mini supermarket; it runs a shuttle bus to/from Ave Portugal (€2) in the city.

**Albergue Juvenil Sevilla** ( ☎ 95 505 65 00; Calle Isaac Peral 2; dm with breakfast 25 & under/26 & over €13/17.50) Seville's youth hostel has 277 places in modern twins or triples. It's about 10 minutes south of the city by bus No 34, which leaves opposite the main tourist office (p414).

**Pensión Vergara** ( ☎ 95 421 56 68; pensionvergara sevilla@yahoo.es; Calle Ximenez de Enciso 11; s/d/tr/q with shared bathroom €18/36/54/72; 🖳 ) Far and away Seville's best budget option, this enchanting *pensión* has twelve very pretty, airy rooms around an inviting courtyard in a former 15th-century convent.

**Pensión Fabiola** ( ☎ 95 421 83 46; Calle Fabiola 16; d €46, s/d with shared bathroom €20/40) A quiet place with a friendly *señora*, Fabiola has pretty rooms around a plant-filled courtyard.

**Hostal Córdoba** ( ☎ 95 422 74 98; hostalcordoba@ mixmail.com; Calle Farnesio 12; s/d €40/60, s/d with shared bathroom €35/50) This very welcoming, family-run place has simple rooms around a central courtyard where Otto, the West Highland terrier, keeps an eye on proceedings.

**YH Giralda** ( ☎ 95 422 83 24; www.yh-hoteles.com; Calle Abades 30; d €55; 🅿 😵 ) Formerly an 18th-century palace, close to the cathedral, the stylish rooms have all mod cons and lovely timbered ceilings. Ignore the name – it isn't anything like a youth hostel.

**Hostería del Laurel** ( ☎ 95 422 02 95; www.hosteria dellaurel.com; Plaza Venerables 5; s/d with breakfast

€67/97; ⛤ ) With its enviable location on one of Barrio de Santa Cruz's prettiest plazas, this place is great if you get an attack of the munchies, as there's a busy bar and restaurant downstairs. The rooms are a little lacking in pazzazz for the price, though.

**Hotel Simon** ( ☎ 95 422 66 60; www.hotelsimonsevilla.com; Calle Garcia de Vinuesa 19; s/d €50/75; ⛤ ) The internal courtyard is perfect for chilling out with the papers. Rooms are spacious and airy and most are decked with pretty tiles.

**Hotel Amadeus** ( ☎ 95 450 14 43; Calle Farnesio 6; s/d €63/76; P ⛤ 🖳 ) Filled with pianos and other musical instruments, this place is excellent value for money and the individually designed rooms are dazzling.

**Las Casas de la Judería** ( ☎ 95 441 51 50; www .casasypalacios.com; Callejón Dos Hermanas 7; s/d from €101/156; ⛤ ) Rooms here are in small Andalucían-style houses set around patios and fountains. Worth every penny.

Away from the Barrio de Santa Cruz, you could try **Hostal Zahira** ( ☎ 95 422 10 61; Calle San Eloy 43; s/d/tr €30/45/60) on an attractive pedestrian shopping street or helpful **Hostal Union** ( ☎ 95 421 17 90; Calle Tarifa 4; s/d €30/42, s/d with shared bathroom €21/30), with big old-fashioned rooms. **Hotel San Francisco** ( ☎ 95 450 15 41; Calle Alvarez Quintero 38; s/d from €55/68; ⛤ ) is bright and cheery.

## Eating

The Barrio de Santa Cruz provides a wonderful setting for restaurants, although you can expect to pay slightly inflated prices.

**Bodega Santa Cruz** (Calle Mateos Gago; tapas €1.40; ☻ 8am-midnight) Among the tapas bars in the Barrio de Santa Cruz, this joint buzzes with tourists and locals. The crowd spills out onto the footpath.

**Bodega Belmonte** ( ☎ 95 421 40 14; Calle Mateos Gago 24; tapas €1.50; ☻ 9-1am) Has stuffed bull's heads on the walls and an impressive selection of wines. It also does a fine sangría.

**Patio San Eloy** ( ☎ 95 422 11 48; Calle San Eloy 9; tapas & montaditos €1.50; ☻ 11.30am-5pm & 7.30pm-midnight) Bright and busy, this bar is famed for its *fino* (sherry) bar and *montaditos* (multi-tiered sandwiches); madly popular with locals of all ages.

**Bodega San Jose** ( ☎ 95 422 41 05; Calle Adriano 10; tapas €1.50; ☻ 8am-11.30pm) This ancient, dishevelled bar, filled with rickety wooden tables, beer crates and peeling posters of '50s football stars, is known for its fried prawns and it's superb tortilla.

**Pizzeria San Marco** ( ☎ 95 456 43 90; Calle Mesón del Moro 6; mains €6; ☻ 1.15-4.30pm & 8.15pm-midnight Tue-Sun) In what was once a Moorish bathhouse, San Marco has plenty of atmosphere and does highly popular pizzas and pastas.

**Corral del Agua** ( ☎ 95 422 48 42; Callejon Agua 6; mains €12-16; ☻ 1-4pm & 8.30pm-midnight Mon-Sat) The cool courtyard of this place makes it an ideal summer spot for enjoying excellent fish dishes. It's a good idea to make a reservation.

Calle Santa María La Blanca has several simple places with outdoor tables doing generous set-lunch *menús* for about €7. Two of the best are **Casa Fernando** ( ☎ 95 442 26 60; Calle Santa Maria la Blanca 10; menú €7; ☻ 11am-4pm & 7-11pm Mon-Sat) and the trendier **Café-Bar Carmela** ( ☎ 95 454 05 90; Calle Santa Maria la Blanca 6; menú €7; ☻ 9-1am), with some excellent vegetarian options on the menu, including a divine raspberry gazpacho.

## Drinking

On fine nights throngs of people block the streets outside popular bars, leaning against their scooters and eyeing up the crowd.

**Café-Bar Levies** ( ☎ 95 421 53 08; Calle San José 15; ☻ 8-3am) Heaving at various times throughout the day and night with American students and locals knocking back €1 glasses of beer, this is a good place to meet fellow travellers as well as a cheap source of snacks and tapas (from €1.50).

Until 1am, Plaza Salvador has several popular watering holes, including **La Antigua Bodeguita** (Plaza Salvador 6; ☻ 11-2am), with outdoor barrel tables for checking out the crowd.

There are some hugely popular bars around the cathedral, including **Flaherty Irish Pub** ( ☎ 95 421 04 51; Calle Alemanes 7; ☻ 11-3am) with regular live Celtic music.

From about 1am things start building up in the busy music bars around Calle Adriano, west of Ave Constitución. Nearby, on Calle García Vinuesa and Calle Dos de Mayo, are some quieter bodegas, some with good tapas, that attract an older crowd.

The Alameda de Hercules area, a former red-light district north of the city centre, is another buzzing place with lots of offbeat bars. Some have live music, including the **Fun Club** ( ☎ 95 438 93 29; Alameda de Hércules 86; live music about €5; ☻ 10pm-6am Thu-Sat), a small dance warehouse where rock, pop and indie bands play live. Several good pub-like bars line the same street a little further north.

SPAIN

SPAIN

---

**DEATH IN THE AFTERNOON**

Seville's bullfight season runs from Easter to October, with fights about 6.30pm most Sundays, and every day during the Feria de Abril and the preceding week. Tickets start at around €10 or €20, depending on who's fighting. *Sol* (sun) seats are cheaper than *sombra* (shadow) seats. If you get a particularly good matador, the atmosphere in the ring can be electrifying. Tickets can be purchased in advance from any of the official kiosks on streets near the bullring.

---

In summer there's a lively scene along the eastern bank of the Guadalquivir River, which is dotted with temporary bars. On Calle Betis, on the far bank, you'll find some good dance bars/discos, including **Sala Boss** ( ☎ 95 428 19 93; www.discotecaboss.com; Calle Betis 67; admission free; ☼ 10.30pm-6am), Seville's biggest nightclub. You have to dress up and look at least 24 years old to get in.

## Entertainment

Seville is arguably Spain's flamenco capital and you're most likely to catch a spontaneous atmosphere (of varied quality) in one of the bars staging regular nights of flamenco with no admission fee. These include the sprawling **La Carbonería** ( ☎ 95 421 44 60; Calle Levíes 18; ☼ 9pm-4am), thronged every night with tourists and locals (flamenco kicks off at about 11pm), and **El Mundo** (www.elmundotrobar .com; Calle Siete Revueltas 5; ☼ 11pm-late), which has flamenco at 11pm most Tuesday nights.

## Getting There & Away

### AIR

There's a range of domestic and international flights at **Seville airport** ( ☎ 95 444 90 00).

### BUS

Buses from **Plaza de Armas bus station** ( ☎ 95 490 80 40) run to/from Madrid (€16, six hours, hourly), to/from Lisbon (€25, 6¼ hours, three weekly) and Andalucían towns west of Seville, and to Extremadura.

Buses to other parts of Andalucía and eastern Spain use **Prado de San Sebastián bus station** ( ☎ 95 441 71 11), with services to/from Córdoba (€9, 1¾ hours, 10 daily), Granada (€16, three hours, 10 daily) and Málaga (€12, 2½ hours, seven daily).

### TRAIN

From Seville's **Eastación Santa Justa** (Ave Kansas City), 1.5km northeast of the centre, there are both super fast AVE trains and regular trains to/from Madrid (€51.50 to €65, 2½ to 3¼ hours, hourly) and Córdoba (€7 to €20, 45 minutes to 1¼ hours, hourly).

Other trains travel to/from Cádiz (€8.40, 1¾ hours, 10 daily), Granada (€17.65, 3¼ hours, four daily), Málaga (€14, 2½ hours, five daily) and Mérida (€11, 4¾ hours, one a day).

## Getting Around

The airport is 7km from the centre, off the N-IV Córdoba road. **Amarillos Tour** ( ☎ 902 21 03 17) runs half-hourly buses to/from Puerta Jerez in the city (€2.30). Bus No C1, in front of Santa Justa train station, follows a clockwise circuit via Ave Carlos V, close to Prado de San Sebastián bus station and the city centre; bus No C2 does the same route anticlockwise. Bus No C4, south down Calle Arjona from Plaza Armas bus station, goes to Puerta Jerez in the centre; returning, take No C3.

# CÓRDOBA

**pop 318,628**

There can't be many more enjoyable ways to explore the soul of Andalucía than to lose yourself in Cordoba's old quarter, a maze of winding, cobbled alleyways, pretty plazas and lovely flower-filled patios.

The city is a testament to its Moorish past, when Córdoba became the effective Islamic capital on the peninsula following the Muslim invasion in AD 711, a position it held for nearly 300 years. Muslim Córdoba at its peak was the most splendid city in Europe and its Mezquita (mosque) is one of the most magnificent of all Islamic buildings.

## Orientation

Immediately north of the Guadalquivir River is the old city, a warren of narrow streets surrounding the Mezquita. Around 500m north of here is Plaza Tendillas, the main square of the modern city.

## Information

**Navegaweb** (Plaza Judá Leví s/n; per hr €1.50; ☼ 10am-10pm) Internet access.
**Regional tourist office** ( ☎ 95 747 12 35; Calle Torrijos 10; ☼ 9.30am-6pm Mon-Fri, 10am-7pm Sat,

10am-2pm Sun Mar-Oct, until 6pm Mon-Fri Nov-Feb)
Officious service; facing the Mezquita. There are more
helpful **municipal tourist office kiosks** (h10am-2pm
& 4.30-7.30pm) at Plaza Tendillas, Campo Santos Mártires,
Plaza Posada del Potro and at the train station.

## Sights & Activities

The inside of the famous **Mezquita** ( ☎ 95
747 05 12; adult/child €6.50/3.25;  10am-7pm Mon-Sat,
2-6.30pm Sun Mar-Oct, 10am-5.30pm Mon-Sat, 2-6.30pm
Sun Jan, Feb, Nov & Dec), which was begun by
emir Abd ar-Rahman I in 785 and enlarged
by subsequent generations, is a mesmerising sequence of two-tier arches amid a
thicket of columns. From 1236, the mosque
was used as a church and in the 16th century a cathedral was built right in its centre – somewhat wrecking the effect of the
original Muslim building, in many people's
opinion.

The **Judería**, Córdoba's medieval Jewish quarter northwest of the Mezquita, is
an intriguing maze of narrow streets and
small plazas. Don't miss the beautiful lit-
tle **Sinagoga** ( ☎ 95 720 29 28; Calle Judíos; admission
non-EU/EU citizens €0.30/free;  10am-7pm Tue-Sun),
one of Spain's very few surviving medieval
synagogues. The **Museo Taurino** (Bullfighting Museum; ☎ 95 720 10 56; Plaza Maimónides; admission €3;
 10am-2pm & 5.30-7.30pm Tue-Sat, 9.30am-2.30pm
Sun) celebrates Córdoba's legendary mata-
dors such as El Cordobés and Manolete.

Southwest of the Mezquita stands the **Al-
cázar de los Reyes Cristianos** (Fortress of the Christian
Monarchs; ☎ 95 742 01 51; admission €2;  10am-2pm
& 5.30-7.30pm Tue-Sat, 9.30am-2.30pm Sun), with
large and lovely gardens.

On the southern side of the river,
across the Puente Romano, is the **Torre de
la Calahorra** ( ☎ 95 729 39 29; adult/student €4/2.50;
 10am-2pm & 4.30-8.30pm), with a museum
highlighting the intellectual achievements
of Islamic Córdoba, and featuring excellent models of the Mezquita and Granada's
Alhambra.

It is well worth the 8km trip west of Córdoba to the intriguing **Medina Azahara** ( ☎ 95
732 91 30; Carretera Palma del Río, km 5.5; admission non-
EU/EU citizens €1.50/free;  10am-6.30pm Tue-Sat, 10am-
2pm Sun), a mighty Muslim city-palace in the
10th century. If you don't have your own
wheels, catch the tourist bus (€5), which
leaves from Ave Alcázar at 11am and returns two hours later. Tickets can be bought
from the tourist office.

## Sleeping

Most lodgings are close to the Mezquita
and nearly all are built around lovely cool
patios. High-season prices are given below
but many places drop their rates from November to mid-March and in the hot summer months of July and August.

**Albergue Juvenil Córdoba** ( ☎ 95 729 01 66; Plaza
Judá Leví s/n; dm with breakfast 25yrs & under/26yrs & over
€13.35/18.35) Córdoba's excellent youth hostel
is perfectly positioned on a pretty and central plaza. It has no curfew.

**Huéspedes Martínez Rücker** ( ☎ 95 747 67 97;
Calle Martínez Rücker 14; s/d/tr with shared bathroom
€12.50/25/37.50) Some rooms in this chaotic,
leafy haven have gorgeous old beds and are
dotted with antiques. All are fairly basic
though and it can get nippy in winter.

**Hostal Osio** ( ☎ 95 748 51 65; Calle Osio 6; s/d with
shared bathroom €25/40;  P  ) One of Cordoba's
prettiest *hostales*, the Osio has pine furnishings, patios and good views – try for room
No 10 overlooking the adjacent convent.

**Hostal Séneca** ( ☎ 95 747 32 34; hostalseneca@
eresmas.com; Calle Conde y Luque 7; s/d €34/46, s/d with
shared bathroom €22/39) This charming place has
welcoming owners and rooms around an
enchanting patio and little bar. It's popular
so phone ahead. Breakfast included.

**Hotel Maestre** ( ☎ 95 747 24 10; www.hotelmaestre
.com; Calle Romero Barros 4; s/d €29/47;  P  ) This
small, bright hotel has a dash of Spanish
chic in a good location northeast of the
Mezquita.

Other recommendations:

**Hostal La Fuente** ( ☎ 95 748 78 27; Calle San
Fernando 51; s/d €24/42) Large patio and roof terrace.

**Hostal Deanes** ( ☎ 95 729 37 44; Calle Deanes 6; d with
shared bathroom €31) Friendly, central but noisy; its patio
doubles as a tapas bar.

**Hostal Portillo** ( ☎ 95 747 20 91; Calle Cabezas 2;
s/d/tr with shared bathroom €18/30/45) Housed in an
ancient, atmospheric building.

**Hotel Lola** ( ☎ 95 720 03 05; www.hotelconencantolola
.com; Calle Romero 3; d €115,  ) *Típico* Córdoban décor,
fabulous original tiled floors and beamed ceilings.

## Eating

**Bar Estupendo** ( ☎ 95 747 04 94; Calle San Fernando 39;
mains €4-5, incl drinks menu €7.50;  1pm-4pm & 8pm-
11pm Tue-Sat, 1pm-4pm Sun) It may not be much
to look at, with its plastic furniture and
gloomy interior, but this bar does a roaring
trade serving up hearty three-course *menús*
to hungry Córdobans.

SPAIN

# CÓRDOBA

0 _____ 200 m
0 _____ 0.1 miles

| INFORMATION | |
| --- | --- |
| Main Post Office | 1 B2 |
| Navegaweb | 2 B5 |
| Regional Tourist Office | 3 C5 |
| Tourist Office Kiosk (Campo Santos Mártires) | 4 B6 |
| Tourist Office Kiosk (Plaza de las Tendillas) | 5 C3 |
| Tourist Office Kiosk (Plaza Posada del Potro) | 6 D4 |

| SIGHTS & ACTIVITIES | (p419) |
| --- | --- |
| Alcázar de los Reyes Cristianos | 7 B6 |
| Mezquita | 8 C5 |

| | |
| --- | --- |
| Museo Taurino | 9 B5 |
| Sinagoga | 10 B5 |
| Torre de la Calahorra | 11 D6 |

| SLEEPING | (p419) |
| --- | --- |
| Albergue Juvenil Córdoba | 12 B5 |
| Hostal Deanes | 13 B5 |
| Hostal La Fuente | 14 D4 |
| Hostal Osio | 15 C4 |
| Hostal Portillo | 16 D4 |
| Hostal Séneca | 17 B5 |
| Hotel Lola | 18 B5 |
| Hotel Maestre | 19 D4 |
| Huéspedes Martínez Rücker | 20 C5 |

| EATING | (pp419–21) |
| --- | --- |
| Bar Estupendo | 21 D4 |
| Bar Santos | 22 C5 |
| Casa Pepe de la Judería | 23 B5 |
| Comedor Arabe-Andalussi | 24 C5 |
| Meson Pilar Cafeteria | 25 C5 |
| Taberna Plateros | 26 D4 |

| DRINKING | (p421) |
| --- | --- |
| Soul | 27 C3 |
| Velvet Bar | 28 C2 |

| TRANSPORT | (p421) |
| --- | --- |
| Tourist Bus to the Medina Azahara | 29 B6 |

To Train Station & Bus Station (400m)

Jardines de la Agricultura

Jardines Diego de Rivas

Jardines de la Victoria

Avenida de Cervantes
Avenida del Gran Capitán
Avenida de la Victoria
República Argentina
Paseo de la Victoria

Calle Alonso de Burgos
Calle Córdoba de Veracruz
Calle José Cruz Conde
C Robledo
Calle Góngora
Calle Morería
Calle Concepción
C Conde de Gondomar
Felipe II
R Sánchez
C Lope de Hoces
Calle Barroso

Plaza San Miguel
Calle de Alfonso XIII
Plaza de las Tendillas
Calle Claudio Marcelo
Calle Ambrosio Morales
Jesús María
C Juan Valera

C Carbonell y Morand
Calle Altziros
Calle Santa Marta
C Conde de Arenales
Calle de San Pablo
Villalones

Calle de Córdoba
R Marin
Calle Pedro López
Plaza de la Corredera

Calle Maese Luis C Tarrillo
Plaza del Potro
Calle de San Fernando
Calle de San Francisco
R Barros
Calle de Lucano
Torres
Calle de los Lineros

Plaza de Jerónimo Páez
Calle de Rey Heredia
Calle Velázquez Bosco
C Buen Pastor
C Conde y Luque
Plaza Angel Torres
Calle Fernández
Calle Almanzor Calle Romero
Cúchos
Puerta de Almodóvar
Judería
C Deanes
C Céspedes
C Blanco-Belmonte
Cardenal Herrero
Encarnación
C Magistral González
Calle Corregidor
Calle Oso
C M Rücker
Luis de Cerda

Patio de los Naranjos
C Medina y Corella
Plaza de Maimónides
Plaza de Judá Leví
Campo Santos Mártires
C corregidor

Avenida Conde de Vallellano
Avenida Conde de Vallellano
Calle Doctor Barraquer
Calle Doctor Fleming
C Amador de los Ríos
Ronda de Isasa
Guadalquivir River
Acera Mira al Río
Puente Romano

To N-IV (East)
Paseo de la Ribera

Jardines del Alcázar
To Granada, & Seville
Calle San Basilio

Calle del Santo Crispo
Plaza Santa Teresa

**Comedor Arabe-Andalussi** ( ☎ 95 747 51 62; Plaza Abades 4; mains €3.50-5; ☻ noon-4pm & 7-11pm Tue-Sun) Set on a pretty plaza, this Arabian-style eatery has a wonderfully exotic setting of oriental carpets and low, candle-lit tables. The lamb kebab, in particular, is superb but vegetarians will also love the fantastic salads and falafel.

**Taberna Platerors** ( ☎ 95 747 00 42; Calle San Francisco 6; raciónes €4-6; ☻ 1-4pm & 8pm-midnight) This large patio tavern is noisy and slightly peeling around the edges but the solid Córdoban fare is fabulous. Try the *berenjenas fritas*, a large plate of aubergines fried in batter and better than French fries!

**Casa Pepe de la Judería** ( ☎ 95 720 07 44; Calle Romero 1; mains €10-15; ☻ 1-4pm & 8.30-11.30pm) This local classic is always hopping and even though it's a bit pricey, it's Córdoban food at its best.

Good tapas bars include **Bar Santos** (Calle Magistral González Francés 3; tapas €1.20; ☻ 12.30-4pm & 7pm-midnight), famed for its tortilla, while **Meson Pilar Cafeteria** (Calle Cardenal González 66; breakfast from €1.70; ☻ 8am-10.30pm) is *the* place for breakfast.

## Drinking

Córdoba's livelier bars are scattered around the north and west of town.

**Velvet Bar** (Calle Alfaros 29; ☻ 5pm-4am) With wicked flower-power décor over two floors, it pulls in a gay and mixed crowd.

**Soul** ( ☎ 95 749 15 80; Calle Alfonso XIII 3; ☻ 10-3am Mon-Fri, 5pm-4am Sat & Sun) Attracts student/arty types and has live music.

## Getting There & Away

From the **bus station** ( ☎ 95 740 40 40; Plaza Tres Culturas), about 1km northwest of Plaza Tendillas, buses run to/from Seville (€9, 1¾ hours, 10 daily), Granada (€13, 2½ hours, eight daily), Madrid (€11, 4¾ hours, seven daily) and Málaga (€11, three hours, five daily), among many other destinations.

From the **train station** (Ave América), services run to/from Seville (€7 to €20, 45 minutes to 1¼ hours, 20 daily) and Madrid (€48, 1¾ hours to 2¼ hours, every 30 minutes). There are also trains to/from Málaga (€16, 2¼ hours, nine daily) and Algeciras (€26.50, four hours, two daily).

## GRANADA

pop 237,663

You can't help falling in love with Granada. This engaging city, popular with travellers, students and street artists, enjoys one of

Europe's finest settings beneath the snowy peaks of Andalucía's Sierra Nevada.

From the 13th to 15th centuries, Granada was capital of the last Muslim kingdom in Spain. Today it has the greatest Muslim legacy in the country and one of the most magnificent buildings on the continent – the Alhambra.

## Information

**Navegaweb** (Calle Reyes Católicos 55; per hr €1; ☻ 10am-11pm daily) Internet access.

**Tourist Offices** Main office ( ☎ 95 824 71 28; www .turismogranada.org; Plaza Mariana Pineda 10; ☻ 9am-8pm Mon-Fri, 10am-7pm Sat, 10am-3pm Sun); Plaza Santa Ana ( ☎ 95 822 59 90; ☻ 9am-8pm Mon-Fri, 9am-6pm Sat, 9am-2pm Sun)

## Sights & Activities

### ALHAMBRA

One of the greatest accomplishments of Islamic art and architecture, the **Alhambra** ( ☎ 902 44 12 21; admission €10; ☻ 8.30am-8pm Apr-Oct, 8.30am-6pm Nov-Mar) is breathtaking. Much has been written about the Alhambra's fortress, palace, patios and gardens, but nothing can really prepare you for what you will see.

The **Alcazaba** is the Alhambra's fortress, dating from the 11th to the 13th centuries. There are spectacular, heady views from the tops of the towers. The **Palacio Nazaries** (Nasrid Palace), built for Granada's Muslim rulers in their 13th- to 15th-century heyday, is the centrepiece of the Alhambra. The beauty of its patios and intricacy of its stucco and woodwork, epitomised by the Patio de los Leones (Patio of the Lions) and Sala de las Dos Hermanas (Hall of the Two Sisters), are stunning. Don't miss the **Generalife**, the soul-soothing palace gardens – a great spot to relax and contemplate the Alhambra from a little distance.

> ### ALHAMBRA TICKETS
>
> It is becoming increasingly essential to book tickets to the Alhambra in advance. You can reserve via any branch of the Banco Bilbao Viscaya (BBV), including the Granada branch on Plaza Isabel la Católica, or by calling ☎ 902 22 44 60 from within Spain ( ☎ 00 34 91 537 91 78 from abroad) or paying by credit card on the website www.alhambra tickets.com.

SPAIN

# GRANADA

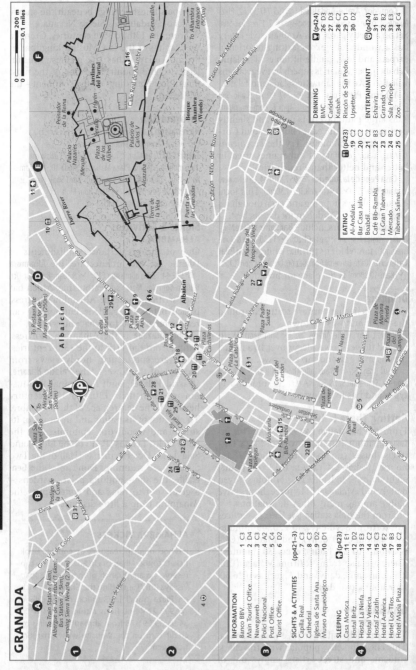

0                200 m
0                0.1 miles

To Train Station (1km);
Albergue de Juventud (1.6km);
Bus Station (2.5km);
Camping Sierra Nevada (2.7km)

**Albaicín**

To Mirador de
Magayma (250m)

To Restaurante
Mirador de
Morayma (250m)

To Mirador
San Nicolás
(800m)

To Generalife

To Alhambra
Entrance
(500m)

Jardines
del Partal

Bosque
Alhambra
(Woods)

Peinador
de la Reina

Palacio
Nazaries

Palacio de
Carlos V

Plaza de
los Aljibes

Mexuar

Alcazaba

Torre de
la Vela

Puerta de
las Granadas

Paseo de los Mártires

Antequeruela Baja

Callejón · Niño del Royo

Campo
del Príncipe

Calle Real de Alhambra

Calle San Matías

Plaza de
Mariana
Pineda

Calle de las Navas

Calle Ángel Ganivet

Acera del Casino

Acera del Darro

Calle de los Reyes Católicos

Puente
Real

Calle Pescadería

Calle de los Mesones

Plaza de la
Trinidad

Gran Vía de Colón

Calle de Elvira

Plaza San
Miguel Bajo

**Albaicín**

Plaza
Santa Ana

Plaza
Nueva

Plaza
Cuchilleros

Plaza Isabel
La Católica

Plaza
Nueva

Plaza del
Campillo

Plaza
del
Carmen

Corral del
Carbón

Calle Calderería

Cuesta del Chapiz

Carrera del Darro

Darro River

Paseo de los Tristes

Placeta del
Hospicio Viejo

Cuesta Rodrigo del Campo

Cuesta Padre
Suárez

Calle San Matías

C Mesón de Hierro

Postigo de
la Cuna

C San Agustín

Gran Vía de Colón

C Calderería Vieja

C Cetti Merién

Puente de la
Escuela

Plaza de la
Romanilla

Alcaicería

Calle Reyes Católicos

Calle Matilde Pineda

Calle San
Sebastián

Calle Fundación

SPAIN

## OTHER ATTRACTIONS

Explore the narrow, hilly streets of the **Albaicín**, the old Moorish quarter across the river from the Alhambra, and head uphill for the **Mirador de San Nicolas** – a viewpoint with breathtaking vistas and a relaxed, hippy scene. On your way down, stop by the **Museo Arqueológico** ( ☎ 95 822 56 40; Carrera Darro; admission non-EU/EU citizen €1.50/free; ☺ 9am-8pm Wed-Sat, 3-8pm Tue, 9am-2.30pm Sun), at the foot of the Albaicín.

Another enjoyable area for strolling is around **Plaza de Bib-Rambla**, looking in at the **Capilla Real** (Royal Chapel; ☎ 95 822 92 39; Calle Oficios; admission €3; ☺ 10.30am-1pm & 4.30-7pm), in which Fernando and Isabel, the Christian conquerors of Granada in 1492, are buried. Next door to the chapel is Granada's **cathedral** ( ☎ 95 822 29 59; admission €3; ☺ 10.45am-1.30pm & 4-8pm Mon-Sat, 4-8pm Sun), dating from the early 16th century.

## Sleeping

Things can get very booked up year-round, so it's a good idea to phone ahead. Good budget options can be found around the social hub of Plaza Nueva.

**Camping Sierra Nevada** ( ☎ 95 815 00 62; Ave Madrid 107; per person/tent €4.50/4.50; ☒ ) Two hundred metres from the Estación de Autobuses, this is the closest camping ground to the centre and is open year-round.

**Albergue de Juventud** ( ☎ 95 827 26 38 or ☎ 95 800 29 00; Calle Ramón y Cajal 2; dm 25yrs & under/26yrs & over €12/18.50) Granada's modern youth hostel is 1.7km southwest of the centre and a 600m walk southwest of the train station.

**Hostal Venecia** ( ☎ 95 822 39 87; Cuesta Gomérez 2; s/d/tr with shared bathroom €15/28/41) A fabulous, if tiny, place, whose friendly owners bring you herbal tea in the morning.

**Hostal Britz** ( ☎ 95 822 36 52; Cuesta Gomérez 1; s/d with shared bathroom €19/29) With saggy beds and big, old-fashioned rooms, this budget travellers' classic can get noisy at times.

**Hostal Zacatín** ( ☎ 95 822 11 55; hostalzacatin@ hotmail.com; Calle Ermita 11; d €38, s/d with shared bathroom €17/28) Hidden away up a narrow alleyway off the pretty Plaza de Bib-Rambla, this place is a little gem, with clean simple rooms.

**Hostal La Ninfa** ( ☎ 95 822 26 61; Campo Príncipe s/n; s/d €45/52; ☒ ) This enchanting, eclectic *hostal* is covered in ceramic designs. Rooms have pretty beamed ceilings and tiled floors.

**Hotel Los Tilos** ( ☎ 95 826 67 12; Plaza Bib-Rambla; s/d from €41/55; ☒ ) Overlooking a daily flower market, there are superb views from its 4th-floor terrace and rooms are comfortable.

**Hotel Macía Plaza** ( ☎ 95 822 75; www.macia hoteles.com; Plaza Nueva 4; s/d €49/73; ☒ ) A well-located, modernised hotel with very pleasant rooms overlooking Plaza Nueva.

**Casa Morisca** ( ☎ 95 822 11 00; www.hotelcasa morisca.com; Cuesta Victoria 9; d from €111; ☒ ) This place has Alhambra views and fabulous Moorish-inspired décor with central patio, wooden ceilings and rich tile work.

**Hotel América** ( ☎ 95 822 74 71; www.hotelamerica granada.com; Calle Real de Alhambra 53; s/d €68/107; ☺ Mar-Oct; ⓟ ☒ ) Occupying a magical position within the walls of the Alhambra; you need to reserve well ahead.

## Eating

Plaza Nueva and the surrounding streets are the best places for good eats.

**Café Bib-Rambla** (Plaza Bib-Rambla; ☺ 8am-midnight) This café has been going for nearly a century and is great for a breakfast of chocolate and *churros*.

**Al-Andalus** ( ☎ 95 822 67 30; Calle Elivira; filled pittas €2; ☺ 11-3am) The place for divine Arabian food, either to take-away or to eat at the outside tables. Vegetarians will adore the pitta and felafel. Great for those 2am munchies.

**Bar Casa Julio** (Calle Hermosa s/n; ☺ 10.30am-4.30pm & 8.30pm-midnight) A no-nonsense bar renowned for its traditional tapas, especially the fried fresh anchovies (*boquerones fritos*). Wildly popular.

**Restaurante Mirador de Morayma** ( ☎ 95 822 82 90; Calle Pianista Garcia Carrillo 2; mains €10-15; ☺ 1.30-3.30pm & 8.30-11.30pm) In the Albaicín, this restaurant has fabulous views of the Alhambra, a very pretty terrace and excellent dishes such as *remojón* (orange and bacalao; €6.40). There's live flamenco at 11pm Tuesday.

For fresh fruit and veggies, there is the large covered **market** (Calle San Agustín).

Other good options around Plaza Nueva:

**Taberna Salinas** ( ☎ 95 822 14 11; Calle Elvira 13; mains €7-15; ☺ 1.30-4pm & 8pm-midnight) Busy with great grilled seafood and meat.

**Boabdil** ( ☎ 95 822 81 36; Calle Hospital de Peregrines 2; mains €4-5; ☺ 1.30-4pm & 8-11.30pm Tue-Sun) A kitchen sink–informal restaurant.

**La Gran Taberna** ( ☎ 95 822 88 46; Plaza Nueva 12; tapas €1.50) Traditional-style bodega with inexpensive tapas; good for breakfast.

**SPAIN**

**TEA-TASTIC**

Granada's Moorish legacy lives on in the city's fabulous Arabian-style *teterías* (tea-houses). One of the best is **Kasbah** ( ☎ 95 822 79 36; Calle Calderería Nueva 4; teas €2; ⏰ 12.30pm-12.30am), a candle-lit den filled with Persian rugs and secret alcoves. It serves up a staggering number of varieties: nearly 100 different types of tea.

## Drinking

Nightlife in the Albaicín centres on Carrera Darro, with several bars and clubs within a few doors of each other, including **Rincón de San Pedro** (Carrera Darro 12) and the late-night reggae bar **Upsetter** (Carrera Darro 7; ⏰ from 11pm).

Further east, the Realejo barrio is another up-and-coming scene stacked with bars, including **BMC** (Calle Escolástica 15; ⏰ 10pm-3am), pumping out dance music to a young crowd on the pull, and the mellower **Candela** (Calle Escolástica 1; ⏰ 8pm-1am).

## Entertainment

**Eshavira** (Postigo Cuna 2; ⏰ 8.30pm-3am) Live jazz and flamenco.

**Granada 10** (Calle Cárcel Baja; admission €6; ⏰ midnight-dawn) This disco has salsa on Sunday night.

**Sala Principe** (Campo Principe 7; admission €6; ⏰ 11pm-8am Thu-Sun) House music in an old cinema (no sportswear).

**Zoo** (Plaza Campillo; admission €6; ⏰ 2-8am Thu-Sun) A good gay/mixed dance club.

## Getting There & Away

Granada's **bus station** ( ☎ 95 818 54 80; Carretera Jáen) is 3km northwest of the centre. Catch bus No 3 or 33 to reach the centre. Buses serve Madrid (€13, five hours, 10 daily), Málaga (€8, two hours, hourly), Seville (€16, three hours, 10 daily) and Córdoba (€10, 2¾ hours, 11 daily).

The **train station** (Ave de Andaluces) is about 1.5km southwest of the centre. There are trains to Madrid (€28.50, six hours, two daily) and Seville (€18, three hours, four daily). For Málaga (€19) and Córdoba (€19), passengers have to change trains in Bobadilla. There is one overnight train to Valencia (€41, 7½ hours) and Barcelona (€50, 11½ hours).

## COSTA DE ALMERÍA

The coast east of Almería in eastern Andalucía is perhaps the last section of Spain's Mediterranean coast where you can have a beach to yourself. This is Spain's sunniest region – even in late March it can be warm enough to strip off and take in the rays.

## Information

**Tourist Offices** Almería ( ☎ 95 062 11 17); San José ( ☎ 95 038 02 99); Mojácar ( ☎ 95 047 51 62).

## Sights & Activities

The **alcazaba** ( ☎ 95 027 16 17; Calle Almanzor; admission non-EU/EU citizens €1.50/free; ⏰ 9am-8.30pm Tue-Sun Apr-Sep, 9am-6.30pm Tue-Sun Nov-Mar), an enormous 10th-century Muslim fortress, is the highlight of Almería city.

The best thing about the region is the wonderful coastline and semidesert scenery of the **Cabo de Gata** promontory. All along the 50km coast from El Cabo de Gata village to Agua Amarga, some of the most beautiful and empty beaches on the Mediterranean alternate with precipitous cliffs and scattered villages. Roads or paths run along or close to this whole coastline, a protected area. The main village is laid-back **San José**, with excellent beaches nearby, such as **Playa de los Genoveses** and **Playa de Mónsul**. **Mojácar Pueblo**, 30km north of Agua Amarga and 2km inland from the coast, is a white hill-top town of Muslim origin. It's fun to wander the town's maze-like streets or just take in the spectacular views.

## Sleeping & Eating

### ALMERÍA

**Hostal Americano** ( ☎ 95 028 10 15; Ave Estación 6; s/d with shared bathroom from €18.50/32) Clean and popular with backpackers, it's well located between the city centre and the bus station.

**La Perla** ( ☎ 95 023 88 77; fax 95 027 58 16; Plaza Carmen 7; d €49; 🄿 🖳 ) The oldest hotel in town, still exuding a certain old-world charm.

**Taberna Torreluz** ( ☎ 95 023 43 99; Plaza Flores 3; raciónes €8; ⏰ noon-4pm & 7.30pm-12.30am) Everyone goes for the fabulous *raciónes* at this cosy wood-panelled bar.

### CABO DE GATA

In San José there is **Camping Tau** ( ☎ 95 038 01 66; ⏰ Apr-Sep) and the friendly non-HI hostel **Albergue Juvenil de San José** ( ☎ 95 038 03 53; Calle Montemar; dm €10; ⏰ Apr-Sep).

**Hostal Bahía** ( ☎ 95 038 03 07; Calle Correo; s/d €32/45) Attractive, whitewashed rooms with bathroom.

**Restaurante Azulón** (Calle Correos 2; mains €5-8, menu €9; ☽ noon-4.30pm & 8pm-midnight) For Mediterranean food, including fish and pizza, the Azulón does an excellent *menú*.

**Casa Emilio** ( ☎ 95 038 97 61; s/d from €35/40) In the quiet village of Los Escullos, a few kilometres up the coast, with clean, simple rooms with balconies and a bar/restaurant downstairs.

### MOJÁCAR

**Hostal La Esquinica** ( ☎ 95 047 50 09; Calle Cano 1; s/d with shared bathroom €20/25) Tiny and covered in climbing plants, this *hostal* has sweet but simple rooms with wooden beds, and a small bar.

**Hostal Mamabel's** ( ☎ 95 047 24 48; www.mamabels .com; Calle Embajadores 5; d €65; ☒ ) Eight big rooms with sea views and an excellent **restaurant** (menú €18; ☽ 1-4pm & 8-11.30pm).

### Getting There & Away

From Almería's **bus station** ( ☎ 95 026 20 98; Plaza Barcelona), buses go to/from Madrid, Granada, Seville, Málaga, Valencia and Barcelona and also to San José and Mojácar.

From the **train station** (Plaza Estación) there are services to/from Madrid (€31, seven hours, two daily), to/from Granada (€11.80, 2½ hours, four daily) and to/from Seville (€28.25, 5¾ hours, four daily).

## MÁLAGA
pop 547,105

From Moorish monuments to arguably the best fried fish in Spain, Málaga has *andaluz* charm in spades. This exuberant port city is an enticing mix of tangled streets and a rollicking nightlife. There's plenty to see and savour here.

### Orientation

Málaga is situated at the mouth of the Guadalmedina River. The central thoroughfare is the Alameda Principal, which continues eastward as the tree-lined Paseo del Parque and westward as Ave Andalucía.

The historic core of the city lies around the cathedral: a web of narrow, cobbled streets lined with faded, ochre-coloured buildings, interspersed with small squares, tapas bars, old-fashioned shops and cafés.

### Information

**Internet Meeting Point** (Plaza Merced 20; per hr €1; ☽ 10-12.30am) Coffee and Internet access.

**Main Tourist Office** ( ☎ 95 221 34 45; www.malaga turismo.com, in Spanish; Pasaje Chinitas 4; ☽ 8.30am-8pm Mon-Fri, 10am-2pm Sat & Sun) In the city's historic centre.

**Municipal tourist office** ( ☎ 95 213 47 30; Ave Cervantes 1; ☽ 8am-2.30pm & 4-7pm Mon-Fri, 9.30am-1.30pm Sat) Near the park. There are additional information kiosks near the train station and in the centre.

### Sights & Activities

The city's history is colourfully diverse. The **Alcazaba** ( ☎ 95 222 72 30; Calle Alcazabilla; admission €1.80; ☽ 8.30am-7pm Tue-Sun) fortress and palace dates from the 8th century. A **Roman amphitheatre**, currently being restored, is in plain view near the Alcazaba's main entrance.

The hill-top **Castillo Gibralfaro** (admission €1.80; ☽ 9am-6pm), a Moorish castle, commands spectacular views across the city and sea. The **cathedral** ( ☎ 95 221 59 17; Calle Molina Larios s/n; admission €3; ☽ 10am-6.45pm Mon-Sat) has a peculiar lopsided look (the south tower was never completed) and a magnificent 18th-century baroque façade. Check it out from one of the footpath cafés across the way.

Whatever you do, don't leave Málaga without visiting the fabulous **Museo Picasso Málaga** ( ☎ 95 260 27 31; www.museopicassomalaga.org; Calle San Augustín; adult/student €6/3; ☽ 10am-8pm Tue-Sun). Set in the contemplative setting of the lovely 16th-century Palacio de Buenavista, the museum is stacked with over 200 of Picasso's works, covering the length and breadth of his astonishing career.

### Sleeping

Málaga is short on accommodation, so book ahead. Prices tend to shoot up in August and during Easter week. Regular rates are listed below.

**Albergue Juvenil Málaga** ( ☎ 95 230 85 00; Plaza Pío XII 6; dm 25 & under/26 & over €11.65/17.20) The city's HI hostel is 1.5km west of the city centre. Take bus No 14 or 31 from the Alameda Principal.

**Pensión Rosa** ( ☎ 95 221 27 16; Calle Martinez 10; s/d with shared bathroom €25/35) The pretty courtyard entrance is filled with colourful potted plants and rooms are simple but bright.

**Hostel Victoria** ( ☎ 95 222 42 24; Calle Sancha de Lara 3; s/d €25/50; ☒ ) In a good central location, the Victoria has comfortable rooms.

SPAIN

**Hotel Venecía** ( ☎ 95 221 36 36; Alameda Principal 9; s/d €58/72; ❷ ) This small, secure and picturesque hotel has charming rooms, some with balconies.

**Hostal Madrid** ( ☎ 95 222 45 92; Calle Marin Garcia 4; s/d with shared bathroom €20/30) This sociable option is another good budget choice, but it's often full with long-term residents.

Also try:

**Hostal Mundial** ( ☎ 95 221 06 18; Calle Hoyo de Esparteros 1; s/d with shared bathroom €18/34) Has plenty of spartan, dog-eared rooms.

**Hotel Don Curro** ( ☎ 95 222 72 00; Calle Sancha de Lara 7; s/d €70/99; ❷ ) A central three-star.

## Eating

Málaga's tapas bars are particularly good. Drop by the wonderful **Bar Logueno** ( ☎ 95 222 30 48; Calle Marín García 9; tapas from €1.50; ☯ 1-4.30pm & 8pm-midnight), something of a local institution, with 75-plus varieties of tapas to choose from.

**La Dehesa** ( ☎ 95 221 21 32; Calle La Bolsa 3; mains €6-7; ☯ 12.30pm-midnight Mon-Sat) Cosy and rustic, La Dehesa is a great place for stews, salads and paellas, all tasty home-cooked fare.

**La Vegetariano de la Alcazabilla** ( ☎ 95 221 48 58; Calle Pozo del Rey 5; mains €6-8; ☯ 1.30-4pm & 9-11.30pm Mon-Sat) The décor may be basic but the vegetarian portions are generous. It also does a particularly good cheese fondue.

**La Posada de Antonio** ( ☎ 95 221 70 69; Calle Granada 33; mains €6-12; ☯ 1-4.30 & 8pm-midnight) With its high ceilings and chunky wooden tables, this restaurant serves up tasty meat dishes cooked on an open grill.

**El Chinitas** ( ☎ 95 221 09 72; Calle Moreno Monroy 4; mains €8-14; ☯ 1.30-4.30pm & 8-11.30pm) Serving up consistently good malagueño meat and fish dishes to noisy tables of locals and tourists, El Chinitas has an extraordinary setting under timber beams and garish oil paintings of flamenco dancers and bullfighters.

---

**FISHY BUSINESS**

Look out for frituna de pescado, a typical malagueño dish of fried squid and fish served with wedges of lemon. The best place to eat this is in any one of the excellent fish restaurants in the Pedregalejo area, 4.5km east of the centre. All have sunny terraces facing the beach.

---

## Drinking

Serious party time kicks off at about midnight around Calle Granada and Plaza Merced.

**ZZ Pub** (Calle Tejón y Rodriguez 6) Grungy, with live music on Monday and Thursday.

**Doctor Funk** (Calle José Denis Belgrano 19) Just off Calle Granada is this heaving reggae/funk club shoehorned into a small smoky space.

**O'Neills Irish Pub** (Calle Luis de Velazquez 3) Appeals enormously to young malagueños.

**Liceo** (Calle Beatas 21) A bar/disco popular with students and travellers.

**Sodoma** (Calle Juan de Padilla 15; ☯ Thu-Sat) A gay/mixed disco with house music.

## Getting There & Away

Málaga's **airport** ( ☎ 95 204 88 04) has a good range of domestic as well as international flights. Trains and buses run every half-hour from the airport to the city centre (€0.95). The bus and train stations are around the corner from each other, 1km west of the city centre.

From the **bus station** ( ☎ 95 235 00 61; Paseo Tilos), buses go to Madrid (€17, six hours, seven daily), Granada (€8, two hours, hourly), Marbella (€4, one hour, hourly), Ronda (€7.50, two hours, 10 daily) and Algeciras (€10, 2½ hours, 12 daily).

From the **train station** (Esplanada Estación), there are services to/from Madrid (€54, 4¼ hours, eight daily), Seville (€14.15, 2½ hours, five daily) and Córdoba (€16, 2¼ hours, nine daily).

## TORREMOLINOS

pop 50,649

Torremolinos is trying hard to shed its image as a spam-and-chips resort by pumping money into landscaping and more-upmarket tourist facilities. Attractions around town include an equestrian show, birds-of-prey exhibition, a water park and various sea sports. Surprisingly, there is still a relatively untainted old part of town with local bars frequented by old men who play dominoes and drink anís (aniseed liqueur).

Nearby, **Tivoli World** ( ☎ 95 257 70 16; Arroyo Miel, Benalmadena; admission €4.50; ☯ 11am-9pm Nov-Mar, 4pm-1am Apr, May, Sep & Oct, 6pm-3am Jun-Aug) is the Costa del Sol's biggest theme park.

In the old part of town, **Hostal Castilla** ( ☎ 95 238 10 50; Calle Manila 3; s/d with breakfast & shared bathroom €32/44) is small and friendly. Nearer to the beach, **Hotel Cabello** ( ☎ 95 238 45 05; Calle Chiriva; s/d €60/75) is located in the former fishing village of La Carihuela. The best seafood restaurants are here, too, including **El Roqueo** ( ☎ 95 238 49 46; Calle Carmen 35; ☉ closed Tue) – owned by a former fisherman.

Trains to/from Málaga and Fuengirola run every 30 minutes from 6am to 10.30pm, stopping at the airport. The bus station is on Calle Hoyo and there are services to all the major Costa del Sol resorts, as well as to Ronda, Cádiz and Granada, several times a day.

## FUENGIROLA
pop 57,133
In spite of the annual tide of tourists who come here to flop on the beach, Fuengirola remains essentially a Spanish working town. It's not pretty, having suffered from greedy developers and political corruption, but there's a nice beach; a vast choice of shops, restaurants and bars; and bargain hunters will enjoy rooting through the Saturday-morning **flea market** at the fairground.

Fuengirola's **fair** at the beginning of October is one of the biggest and best on the Costa del Sol. Aside from then, accommodation is plentiful, although the faceless high-rise hotels on the beachfront tend to be block-booked in advance by tour companies. *Hostales* include the spick-and-span **Hostal Italia** ( ☎ 95 247 41 93; fax 95 247 11 40; Calle Cruz 1; s/d €36/61), near the main plaza. There are plenty of budget restaurants and bars here.

Half-hourly trains run to/from Málaga, with stops including Torremolinos and the airport. There are also regular buses to Marbella, Mijas and major Andalucían cities leaving the main bus station on Calle Alfonso XIII.

## MARBELLA
pop 116,234
Marbella is this coast's classiest resort. The inherent wealth glitters most brightly along the Golden Mile, a tiara of star-studded clubs, restaurants and hotels that stretches from Marbella to Puerto Banus, where black-windowed Mercs slide along a quayside of jaw-dropping luxury yachts.

## Information
**Neotel** (Plaza Puente de Ronda 6; per hr €2; ☉ 10am-midnight) Internet access.

**Tourist Offices** Main office ( ☎ 95 277 14 42; Glorieta Fontanilla; ☉ 9.30am-9pm Mon-Fri, 10am-2pm Sat); Plaza Naranjos ( ☎ 95 282 35 50; ☉ 9am-9pm Mon-Fri, 9am-2pm Sat)

## Sights & Activities
The old part of Marbella around the Plaza Naranjos is very pretty, duly reflected by the drink prices at the outdoor cafés.

The **Museo del Grabado Español Contemporáneo** ( ☎ 95 276 57 41; Calle Hospital Bazán s/n; admission €2.50; ☉ 10am-2pm & 5.30-8.30pm Mon-Sat) houses works by Picasso, Miró and Dalí. The only **Bonsai Museum** ( ☎ 95 286 29 26; adult/child €3/1.50; ☉ 10.30am-1.30pm & 4-7pm) in Spain is in Parque de la Represa.

## Sleeping & Eating
The old town has several reasonable *hostales* to stay at.

**Hostal del Pilar** ( ☎ 95 282 99 36; www.hostel-marbella.com; Calle Mesoncillo 4; s/d with shared bathroom €15/30; ✘ ) This classic backpackers' hangout has crowded rooms and a pool table downstairs.

**Hostal La Luna** ( ☎ 95 282 57 78; Calle Luna 7; s/d/tr from €30/42/60) Near the beach, La Luna has balconied rooms, a charming patio and simply lovely owners.

**Hotel Linda Marbella** ( ☎ 95 285 71 71; lindamarbellasl@terra.es; Calle Ancha 21; s/d/tr from €40/55/85; ✘ ) Set on a pretty street in the old part of town, this place has very comfortable rooms.

**Bodega La Venecia** ( ☎ 95 285 79 13; Ave Miguel Cano 15; raciones €5-8; ☉ 1-4.30pm & 8pm-1am) Wildly popular with all ages, La Venecia serves excellent tapas and *raciones* in nice woody surroundings.

**Sociedad de Pesca Deportiva Marbella** ( ☎ 95 277 54 38; Club Maritimo Loc 5; Puerto Deportivo; mains €8-12; ☉ 12.30-5pm & 8pm-1am Tue-Sun) It looks nothing special from outside but this restaurant serves up the best fried fish in town.

## Getting There & Away
The **bus station** ( ☎ 95 276 44 00; Calle Trapiche) is a good 30-minute hike from the hub of town. Bus No 7 connects the terminal with the centre (€1). Buses from the station run regularly to Málaga (€4, 1¼ hours, 15 daily), Fuengirola (€2, one hour, every 20 minutes), Algeciras (€5, 1½ hours, 15 daily), Cádiz (€14, 4¾ hours, six daily), Seville (€13, 3¾ hours, two daily) and Ronda (€4, 1½ hours, six daily).

SPAIN

# RONDA

**pop 35,137**

One of Andalucía's prettiest towns, Ronda is split in two by the savagely deep El Tajo gorge, at the heart of some lovely hill country.

The **municipal tourist office** ( ☎ 95 218 71 19; www.turismoderonda.es; Paseo Blas Infante s/n; ☯ 9.30am-7pm Mon-Fri, 10am-2pm & 3.30-6.30pm Sat & Sun) is helpful but can get overrun.

## Sights & Activities

Ronda is a pleasure to explore, but during the day you'll have to contend with bus-loads of day-trippers from the coast.

The **Plaza de Toros** (1785), considered the home of bullfighting, is a mecca for aficionados; inside is the small but fascinating **Museo Taurino** (Bullfighting Museum; ☎ 95 287 41 32; adult/student €5/3; ☯ 10am-7pm). Vertiginous cliff-top views open out from the nearby **Alameda del Tajo** park.

The 18th-century **Puente Nuevo** (New Bridge), an amazing feat of engineering, crosses the 100m-deep gorge to the originally Muslim old town (La Ciudad), which is littered with ancient churches, monuments and palaces. At the **Casa del Rey Moro** ( ☎ 95 218 72 00; Calle Santo Domingo 17; adult/child €4/2; ☯ 10am-8pm), you can climb down La Mina, a Muslim-era stairway cut inside the rock, right to the bottom of the gorge. Try not to miss the **Iglesia de Santa María la Mayor** (Plaza Duquesa de Parcent; admission €2; ☯ 10am-7pm), whose tower was once the minaret of a mosque, or the beautiful 13th-century **Baños Arabes** (Arab Baths; Barrio Padre Jesus; adult/child €2/free; ☯ 10am-7pm Mon-Fri, 10am-3pm Sat & Sun).

## Sleeping & Eating

There are a couple of budget *pensiones* on Calle Almendre, including the dark, old-fashioned **Hostal Biarritz** ( ☎ 95 287 29 10; Calle Almendre 7; s/d with shared bathroom €11/17).

**Hotel Morales** ( ☎ 95 287 15 38; Calle Sevilla 51; s/d €21/45) Friendly, with decorative rooms.

**Alavera de los Baños** ( ☎ 95 287 91 43; alavera@ctv .es; Calle San Miguel s/n; d with breakfast €76; ☼ ) This small hotel next to the Arab baths is rustic and romantic, with heavy beamed ceilings, and away from the tourist hordes. But it is one helluva climb back into town – luckily it has its own good **restaurant** (mains €15).

**Relax Vegetariano Café-Bar** ( ☎ 95 287 72 07; Calle Los Remedios 27; mains €5; ☯ noon-4pm & 7-11pm)

This British-owned café has bright red walls, rustic wooden tables and fabulous vegetarian food. It does big mugs of English tea, too.

**Marisquería Paco** (Plaza Socorro 9; mains €10; ☯ 10am-10pm) Tiny, but a popular seafood place.

## Getting There & Away

From the **bus station** ( ☎ 95 287 26 57; Plaza Concepción García Redondo), services run to/from Seville (€9, 2½ hours, five daily), Málaga (€7.50, two hours, 10 daily) and Cádiz (€7.50; three hours, four daily).

From the **train station** (Ave Andalucía), trains run to/from Granada (€11, three hours, three daily), Algeciras (€6, 1½ hours, four daily) and Madrid (€32, 4½ hours, two daily).

# ALGECIRAS

**pop 105,070**

Algeciras, an unattractive industrial and fishing town between Tarifa and Gibraltar, is the major port linking Spain with Morocco. Keep your wits about you, and ignore offers from the legions of money-changers, drug-pushers and ticket-hawkers. If you need a room, there's loads of budget accommodation in the streets behind the port. The **tourist office** ( ☎ 95 657 26 36; Calle Juan Cierva; ☯ 9am-2pm Mon-Fri) is near the port.

## Getting There & Away

### BOAT

Frequent ferries to/from Tangier, in Morocco, and Ceuta, the Spanish enclave on the Moroccan coast, are operated by **Trasmediterránea** ( ☎ 902 45 46 45), **EuroFerrys** ( ☎ 95 665 11 78) and other companies. Usually at least 20 ferries daily go to Tangier (€28, 2½ hours) and more to Ceuta (€22, 1½ hours). From late June to September there are ferries almost around the clock. Buy your ticket in the port or at agencies on Ave Marina – prices are the same. **Buquebus** ( ☎ 902 41 42 42) makes a fast crossing to Ceuta (€38.50, 30 minutes).

### BUS

About 400m inland from the port, **Comes** ( ☎ 95 665 34 56; Calle San Bernardo) runs frequent buses to/from La Línea, and several daily to/from Tarifa, Cádiz and Seville. **Portillo** (Ave Virgen del Carmen 15), 200m north of the port, runs buses to/from Málaga, the Costa del Sol and Granada. **Bacoma**, inside the port, runs buses to/from Barcelona, Valencia, France, Germany and Holland.

**TRAIN**
From the **station** (Calle Agustín Bálsamo 12), services run to/from Madrid (€35 to €52, six hours, two daily), Córdoba (€26.50, four hours, two daily), Ronda (€6, 1½ hours, four daily) and Granada (€15.75, 4¾ hours, three daily).

# CÁDIZ

The historic port of Cádiz is a beautiful city with a well-aged atmosphere and winding streets flanked by magnificent, if dishevelled, 18th-century buildings. All around is the Atlantic Ocean, beating against the city's sea defences. The best time to visit is during the February *carnaval*, close to Rio in terms of outrageous exuberance.

## Information
**EnRed** ( ☎ 95 621 45 22; Calle Sacramento 36; per hr €1.50 🕒 11am-11pm Mon-Sat) Internet access.
**Municipal tourist office** ( ☎ 95 624 10 01; Plaza San Juan de Dios 11; 🕒 9.30am-1.30pm & 4-7pm Mon-Fri) Helpful staff.

## Sights & Activities
The yellow-domed soaring 18th-century **cathedral** (Plaza de la Catedral; adult/child €4/2.50; 🕒 10am-1.30pm & 4.30-8pm Tue-Fri, 10am-2pm Sat, 11am-1pm Sun) is the city's most striking landmark.

Get your bearings by climbing up the baroque **Torre Tavira** ( ☎ 95 621 29 10; Calle Marqués del Real Tesoro; admission €3.50; 🕒 10am-6pm), the highest of Cádiz's old watchtowers, with a camera obscura and sweeping views of the city.

The **Museo de Cádiz** ( ☎ 95 621 22 81; Plaza Mina; non-EU/EU citizens €1.50/free; 🕒 2.30-8pm Tue, 9am-8pm Wed-Sat, 9.30am-2.30pm Sun) has a magnificent collection of archaeological remains, as well as a fine art collection. The city's lively **central market** (Plaza de las Flores) is on the site of a former Phoenician temple.

## Sleeping & Eating
Accommodation can get quite booked up at weekends so it's worth phoning ahead.

**Quo Qádis** ( ☎ /fax 95 622 19 39; Calle Diego Arias 1; dm/d €9/42, d with shared bathroom €36) Cádiz's excellent independent hostel is colourful and quirky. You can rent bikes for €6 a day, or tuck into a vegetarian supper for just €2. Prices drop significantly from October to June.

**Hostal Bahía** ( ☎ 95 625 90 61; Calle Plocia 5; s/d €47/64) Just off the bustling main square, this *hostal* is a winner.

**Hotel Francia y Paris** ( ☎ 95 621 23 18; www.hotelfrancia.com; Plaza San Francisco 2; s/d €61/77; 🖳 ) More luxurious and overlooking a pretty plaza; the spacious carpeted rooms have a faded '70s feel.

**Restaurante Parissien** ( ☎ 95 622 36 77; Plaza San Francisco 1; mains €6-8; 🕒 9am-11.30pm) With lots of outside tables on a pretty cobbled plaza, this place does excellent fried fish and a succulent *carne estofada* (beef stew).

It's a pleasure to graze your way through Cádiz's superb *marisquerías* (seafood bars). Kick off with a fishy tapa at the **Cervecería Aurelio** ( ☎ 95 622 10 31; Calle Zorrilla 1; tapas/raciones €1.50/5; 🕒 12.30-5pm & 8.30pm-1am).

People go out late in Cádiz and the city's streets and plazas throng until the early hours. **Woodstock Bar** ( ☎ 95 621 21 63; Calle Canovas del Castillo 25; 🕒 4pm-2am Sun-Thu, 4pm-4am Fri & Sat) is a fashionable late-night hang-out.

## Getting There & Away
From the **bus station** ( ☎ 95 680 70 59; Plaza Hispanidad), there are buses to/from Algeciras (€9, 2¾ hours, 10 daily), Seville (€9.50, 1½ hours, hourly), Cordoba (€18, 4½ hours, two daily), Málaga (€18, five hours, six daily), Ronda (€12, three hours, three daily) and Tarifa (€7, 1¼ hours, five daily).

From the **train station** (Plaza Sevilla), services go to/from Seville (€8.40, 1¾ hours, 10 daily), Córdoba (€31, three hours, four daily) and Madrid (€56, five hours, twice daily).

# TARIFA & THE COSTA DE LA LUZ

Windy, laid-back Tarifa, perched at continental Europe's most southerly point, is so close to Africa that you can see the sunlight flashing on Morocco's minarets. The town is a bohemian haven of cafés and crumbling Moorish ruins. There is also a lively windsurfing and kite-surfing scene.

Stretching west from Tarifa are the long, sandy (and largely deserted) beaches of the Costa de la Luz (Coast of Light), backed by cool pine forests and green hills.

Tarifa's **tourist office** ( ☎ 95 668 09 93; www.tarifaweb.com; Plaza Alameda; 🕒 9am-9pm Jun-Sep, 9am-3pm Oct-May) has lots of information on the area. Internet access is pricey, but your best bet is **Planet** (www.planet-up.com; per hr €3; 🕒 10.30am-2.30pm & 6-10pm), run by friendly German owners.

SPAIN

## SURF WARS

Tarifa remained relatively unknown until windsurfers started to flock here in the mid-1980s, lured by the notorious winds of the Strait of Gibraltar that provided perfect conditions for their sport.

In recent years, the new craze of kite-surfing has taken off (it involves surfing and jumping across waves, attached to a large kite).

Needless to say, Tarifa's windsurfers aren't thrilled by the arrival of the kiters, whose lines get easily tangled on their masts, causing all sorts of mischief. The rivalry between the two camps is fierce, so much so that there have been recent attempts to divide Tarifa's beaches into separate zones for the different sports.

## Sights & Activities

Enjoy exploring Tarifa's winding old streets and visit the castle, **Castillo de Guzmán** ( ☎ 95 668 46 89; Calle Guzmán El Bueno; adult/child €1.80/0.60; ☾ 11am-2pm & 5-7pm), dating from the 10th century.

The waters of the Algeciras Bay are prime whale and dolphin watching territory. **Whale Watch España** ( ☎ 95 662 70 13; www.whalewatch tarifa.com; Ave Constitución 6; per person €27) runs daily boat excursions (1½ to two hours).

The tiny, protected **Playa Chica**, just southeast of the centre, is best for swimming. **Playa de los Lances**, the 10km-long beach beloved of wind- and kite surfers, stretches northwest from Tarifa. For windsurf and kite-surf rental and classes, try places along Calle Batalla de Salado. **Big Fish** ( ☎ 95 668 02 19; El Recreo III, Local 16, Calle Batalla de Salado) rents out surfboards for €20 a day and offers three-day (four hours a day) kite- and windsurfing courses for €180. This strip is also a great place to stock up on surfer-chic clothing and accessories.

If you have your own wheels, head west to the Costa de la Luz. Don't miss out on the Roman ruins of **Baelo Claudia** (admission non-EU/EU citizens €1.50/free; ☾ 10am-6pm Tue-Sat, 10am-2pm Sun) at Bolonia and the magical laid-back villages of **Zahara de los Atunes** and **Los Caños de Meca**.

## Sleeping

**Pensión Correo** ( ☎ 95 668 02 06; Calle Coronel Moscardó 8; r €40-50, r with shared bathroom €25-35) Run by a charming Italian, the Correo has fabulous, if fairly basic, rooms with high beamed ceilings, archways and a ramshackle air.

**Hostal Facundo** ( ☎ 95 668 42 98; h.facundo@terra .es; Calle Batalla del Salado 47; dm Aug only €12, d €36, s/d with shared bathroom €15/22) Long established and popular with windsurfers.

**Casa Amarilla** ( ☎ 95 668 19 93; www.lacasaamarilla .net; Calle Sancho IV El Bravo 9; d €40-60, tr €53-80, q €66-99) Right in the thick of things, with exquisite, quirky apartment rooms with kitchenette.

## Eating & Drinking

Tarifa has no shortage of places to hang out, people watch, and wait for the right sort of wind to pick up. The legendary **Café Central** ( ☎ 95 668 05 90; Calle Sancho IV El Bravo; ☾ 9-1am) is at the heart of it all, with a daily wind report posted on its walls and the best cooked breakfasts in town.

**Café Continental** ( ☎ 95 668 47 76; Paseo Alameda; ☾ 9-1am) People play chess and board games over coffee in this dark, woody café.

**La Vaca Loca** (Calle Alcantarillo s/n; mains €8-12; ☾ 6pm-1am) This tiny cave-like place, with surf videos running on the TV, serves up amazing barbecued food in huge portions on a handful of tables on the plaza outside.

**Mesón Perulero** ( ☎ 95 668 19 97; Plaza San Hiscio; tapas €1.50; ☾ 12.30-4pm & 6pm-midnight) In a gorgeous building with an airy patio, this place does some excellent fishy tapas; try the sea *ortigas de mar* (anemones). Regular live flamenco here in summer.

## Getting There & Away

**Comes** ( ☎ 95 668 40 38; Batalla del Salado s/n) runs buses to/from Algeciras (€1.50, 30 minutes, 17 daily), La Línea (€3, one hour, seven daily), Cádiz (€7, 1¼ hours, seven daily) and Seville (€14, three hours, four daily).

**FRS** ( ☎ 95 668 18 30; Estación Marítima) runs ferries between Tarifa and Tangier (adult/car €24.50/73, 1½ hours, five daily).

# GIBRALTAR

pop 27,776

The British colony of Gibraltar is like 1960s Britain on a sunny day. It is both old-fashioned and safe, attracting coachloads of day-trippers from the Costa del Sol who come here to be reassured by the helmet-wearing policemen, the double-decker buses and Marks & Spencer.

Occupying a huge lump of limestone, almost 5km long and over 1km wide, near the mouth of the Mediterranean, Gibraltar has certainly had a rocky history: it was the bridgehead for the Muslim invasion of Spain in AD 711. Castilla finally wrested it from the Muslims in 1462. In 1704 an Anglo-Dutch fleet captured Gibraltar. Spain gave up military attempts to regain it from Britain after the failure of the Great Siege of 1779–83, but after 300 years of concentrated Britishness, both Britain and Spain are now talking about joint Anglo-Spanish sovereignty – much to the ire of the Gibraltarians.

## Information

To enter Gibraltar you need a passport or EU national identity card. EU, US, Canadian, Australian, New Zealand, Israeli, South African and Singaporean passport holders are among those who do *not* need visitors' visas for Gibraltar, though anyone who needs a visa for Spain should have at least a double-entry Spanish visa if they intend to return to Spain from Gibraltar.

The currency is the Gibraltar pound or pound sterling. Change any unspent Gibraltar pounds before you leave. You can always use euros.

To phone Gibraltar from Spain, the telephone code is ☎ 9567; from other countries dial the international access code, then ☎ 350 and the local number.

**Tourist Offices** Main office ( ☎ 45000; www.gibraltar .gov.gi; Duke of Kent House, Cathedral Sq; ✆ 9am-5.30pm Mon-Fri); Casemates Sq ( ☎ 74982; ✆ 9am-5.30pm Mon-Fri, 10am-3pm Sat, 10am-1pm Sun)

## Sights & Activities

Central Gibraltar can get crowded and claustrophobic but the **Gibraltar Museum** ( ☎ 74289; Bomb House Lane; adult/child £2/1; ✆ 10am-6pm Mon-Fri, 10am-2pm Sat), with its interesting historical collection and Muslim-era bathhouse, is worth a peek. Wander into the **Alameda Botanical Gardens** (Red Sands Rd; ✆ 8am-sunset) for some chill-out time.

The large **Upper Rock Nature Reserve** ( ☎ 74950; adult/child/vehicle £7/4/1.50; ✆ 9.30am-7pm), covering most of the upper rock, has spectacular views and several interesting spots to visit.

The rock's most famous inhabitants are its colony of Barbary macaques, the only wild primates in Europe. Some of these hang around the **Apes' Den** near the middle cable-car station; others can often be seen at the top station or Great Siege Tunnels.

Other attractions include **St Michael's Cave**, a large natural grotto renowned for its stalagmites and stalactites and the **Great Siege Tunnels**, a series of galleries hewn from the rock by the British during the Great Siege to provide new gun emplacements. Worth a stop on the way down to the town from here are the **Gibraltar, a City under Siege** exhibition and the **Tower of Homage**, part of Gibraltar's 14th-century Muslim castle.

A **cable car** (adult/child return £6.50/3; ✆ 10am-6pm Mon-Sat) leaves its lower station on Red Sands Rd every few minutes. For the Apes' Den, disembark at the middle station.

## Sleeping

Compared to Spain, expect to pay through the nose.

**Emile Youth Hostel** ( ☎ 51106; Montagu Bastion, Line Wall Rd; dm with breakfast £15) The cheapest place is this privately run hostel with fairly soulless dorms.

**Cannon Hotel** ( ☎ 51711; www.cannonhotel.gi; 9 Cannon Lane; d £45, s/d with shared bathroom £24.50/36.50) This friendly hotel is in the heart of town with a bar, pretty patio and airy rooms. Rates include an English breakfast.

**Queen's Hotel** ( ☎ 74000; www.queenshotel.gi; 1 Boyd St; s/d/tr with English breakfast £40/50/75; P ✗ ) Queen's is just outside the city walls, a big peach-coloured mansion, with a decidedly '70s feel. You'll pay more for sea views but students get a 20% discount.

## Eating & Drinking

Brace yourself for British food at British prices: pub grub, all day fry-ups, curries and ale by the pint.

**Lord Nelson** ( ☎ 50009; 10 Casemates Sq; mains £5-8; ✆ 10-2am) Decked out as Nelson's ship, with painted clouds on a ceiling crossed with sails, this brasserie is a great choice. The mussels in white wine, garlic and cream are particularly good. Live music at weekends.

Other recommendations:

**Sacarello's** ( ☎ 70625; 57 Irish Town; mains £6-7; ✆ 9am-7.30pm Mon-Fri, 9am-3pm Sat) Low, beamed ceilings and delicious soups, salads and afternoon tea.

**Star Bar** ( ☎ 75924; Parliament Lane; mains £6-7; ✆ 7am-11pm) Gibraltar's oldest pub.

**Clipper** ( ☎ 79791; Irish Town; mains £3-5; ✆ 9.30am-11pm) Sport on the TV, friendly waiters, great English breakfast.

SPAIN

## Getting There & Away

**GB Airways** ( ☎ 79300, UK 0345-222111) flies daily to/from London. Return fares range from around £175 to £400, depending on the season. **Monarch Airlines** ( ☎ 47477, UK 08700-406300; www.flymonarch.com) flies from London's Luton; return fares start at about £96.

There are no regular buses to Gibraltar, but La Línea bus station is only a five-minute walk from the border.

To take a car into Gibraltar, you need an insurance certificate, registration document, nationality plate and driving licence. You do *not* have to pay any fee, despite what con artists might try to tell you.

# EXTREMADURA

A sparsely populated land of vast skies and open plains, Extremadura is far enough from most beaten tourist trails to give you a genuine sense of exploration, something for which *extremeños* themselves have a flair. Many epic 16th-century conquistadors, including Francisco Pizarro (who conquered the Incas), sprang from this land.

The mountains and valleys of northeast Extremadura are perfect for hiking and the remarkable old towns of Trujillo and Cáceres are so perfectly preserved that they are often used as film sets. In Mérida, some of Spain's most spectacular and complete Roman ruins scatter the city.

## TRUJILLO

pop 9564

Trujillo is a delightful little town that can't be much bigger now than in 1529, when its most famous son, Francisco Pizarro, set off with his three brothers and a few local buddies for an expedition that culminated in the bloody conquest of the Incan empire.

From the broad, fine Plaza Mayor a remarkably preserved town rises, stacked with ancient buildings seeping history. There is a **tourist office** ( ☎ 92 732 26 77; ofitur@ayto-trujillo.com; Plaza Mayor; ☿ 9.30am-2pm & 4.30-7.30pm) and you can connect to the Internet at **Ciberalia** (Calle Tiendas 18; per hr €2; ☿ 10.30-2am) for €2 an hour.

## Sights & Activities

A **statue of Pizarro**, by American Charles Rumsey, dominates the Plaza Mayor. On the plaza's southern side, the **Palacio de la Conquista** (closed to visitors) sports the carved images of Francisco Pizarro and the Inca princess Inés Yupanqui.

Two noble mansions are the 16th-century **Palacio de los Duques de San Carlos** (Plaza Mayor; admission €1.30; ☿ 9.30am-1pm & 4.30-6.30pm Mon-Sat, 10am-12.30pm Sun) and **Palacio de Juan-Pizarro de Orellana** (admission free; ☿ 10am-1pm & 4-6pm Mon-Fri, 11am-2pm & 4.30-7pm Sat & Sun), through the alley in the plaza's southwestern corner.

Up the hill, the **Iglesia de Santa María la Mayor** (admission €1.20; ☿ 10am-2pm & 4.30-8pm) is a hotch-potch of 13th- to 16th-century styles, with fine paintings by Fernando Gallego of the Flemish school. Higher up, the **Casa-Museo de Pizarro** (admission €1.30; ☿ 10am-2pm & 4-7pm) has displays (in Spanish) on the Pizarro family. At the top of the hill, Trujillo's **castillo** (admission €1.30; ☿ 10am-2pm & 4.30-7.30pm) is an impressive structure, primarily of Moorish origin with a hermitage within.

## Sleeping & Eating

**Pension Roque** ( ☎ 92 732 23 13; Calle Domingo de Ramos 30; d €24, d with shared bathroom €18) Quiet, with lots of communal space.

**Hostal La Cadena** ( ☎ 92 732 14 63; Plaza Mayor 8; d €37.30; ❊ ) In a tastefully restored 16th-century building, with a handy tapas bar and restaurant.

**Parador de Trujillo** ( ☎ 92 732 13 50; trujillo@parador .es; Calle Santa Beatriz de Silva 1; d €97; P ❊ ) Positioned around a central courtyard with fountains, arches and pillars, this converted convent dates from the 16th century. King Juan Carlos apparently enjoys the stewed lamb tails served in the restaurant here.

**Restaurante La Troya** ( ☎ 92 723 13 64; Plaza Mayor 10; menú €17) Carnivores shouldn't miss out on this place. The food isn't cheap, but portions are gigantic and it will save you from eating much else for the next few days. There are great tapas, too.

## Getting There & Away

From the **bus station** ( ☎ 92 732 12 02; Carretera Mérida), 500m south of Plaza Mayor, buses run to/from Cáceres (€3, 45 minutes, eight daily), Mérida (€7.50, 1¼ hours, four daily) and Madrid (€17, four hours, 10 daily).

## CÁCERES

pop 87,088

Cáceres' *ciudad monumental* (old town), built in the 15th and 16th centuries, is so perfectly preserved it can seem lifeless at times. Then you gaze skywards and see the vast colony of storks that perch on every worthwhile vertical protuberance. The *ciudad monumental* is worth two visits – one by day to look around and one by night to soak up the atmosphere of the accumulated ages.

There is a **tourist office** (☎ 92 701 08 34; otcaceres@eco.juntaex.es; Plaza Mayor 3; 🕙 9am-2pm & 4-6pm Mon-Fri, 9.30am-2pm Sat & Sun Oct-May, 9am-2pm & 5-7pm, 9.30am-2pm Sat & Sun Jun-Sep). At **Ciberjust** (Calle Diego Maria Crehuet 7; per hr €2; 🕙 10am-2.30pm & 4.30pm-midnight Mon-Sat, 5pm-midnight Sun) you can connect to the Internet.

## Sights

The *ciudad monumental* is surrounded by walls and towers raised by the Almohads in the 12th century. Entering it from Plaza Mayor, you'll see the fine 15th-century **Con-catedral de Santa María** (🕙 10am-1pm) ahead.

Many of the old city's churches and imposing medieval mansions can be admired only from outside, but you can climb up the **Torre de Bujaco** (🕙 10am-2pm & 4.30-7.30pm Tue-Sun) and enter the good **Museo Provincial de Cáceres** (☎ 92 724 72 34; Plaza Veletas; admission non-EU/EU citizens €2/free; 🕙 9.30am-2.30pm & 4-7pm Tue-Sat, 10.15am-2.30pm Sun), housed in a 16th-century mansion built over a 12th-century Moorish *aljibe* (cistern), the museum's prize exhibit.

## Sleeping

The best area to stay is around the pretty, pedestrianised Plaza Mayor.

**Albergue Turístico Las Veletas** (☎ 92 721 12 10; www.alberguesturisticos.com; Calle Margallo 36; dm with breakfast €20) This charming, privately run hostel has sparkling, bright and airy rooms in a recently restored mansion.

**Pensión Carretera** (☎ 927247482; pens_carretero@yahoo.es; Plaza Mayor 22; s/d with shared bathroom €13/22) Rooms in this early-20th-century building overlooking the Plaza have high ceilings and an old-fashioned, crumbling air. The bathrooms are a bit dog-eared.

**Hotel Iberia** (☎ 92 724 76 34; www.iberiahotel.com; Calle Pintores 2; s/d €45/55) In a sumptuous former palace, this hotel is amazing value for money and rooms are blissfully comfortable.

## Eating & Drinking

The bars and cafés on Plaza Mayor are perfect for watching the world go by over a coffee or beer, but the food is overpriced and not terribly good. Your best bet is to go up one of the side streets off the plaza for a bite to eat.

**Croissanterie** (Calle Pintores 4; bocadillos €1.50; 🕙 10am-11pm) A hole-in-the-wall with an amazing range of freshly baked, filled baguettes, croissants and *paninis*.

**Café-Bar Adarve** (☎ 92 724 48 74; Calle Sánchez Garrido 4; raciones €6-8; 🕙 7.30-1am) This place does a roaring trade with locals who come here to eat €6 platefuls of *riñones* (kidneys) and the bar's famous *gambas rebozadas* (deep-fried battered prawns – €7.50). Lots of noisy banter between the waiters.

**El Figón de Eustaquio** (☎ 92 724 43 62; Plaza San Juan 14; mains €10-15, menú €17.50; 🕙 1-4pm & 8-11.30pm) Serving up excellent traditional *extremeño* food in an attractive wood-panelled setting, this restaurant is always busy.

**El Corral de las Cigüeñas** (Cuesta Aldana; breakfast/milkshakes/cocktails €2/3/5; 🕙 8-3am) In the heart of the *ciudad monumental*, the fabulous ivy-clad courtyard of this bar is filled with cool young things. It hosts regular live gigs of pop, rock and funk.

## Getting There & Away

From the **bus station** (☎ 92 723 25 50; Carretera Gijón–Sevilla), 1.5km southwest of Plaza Mayor, services run to/from Trujillo (€3, 45 minutes, eight daily), Mérida (€6, 1¼ hours, six daily), Madrid (€16, 3½ hours, eight daily) and Seville (€27, four hours, six daily).

From the **train station** (Ave Alemania s/n), services run to/from Madrid (€22.50, 3½ to five hours, five daily), Mérida (€3.30 to €11.50, one hour, four daily). The single daily train to Lisbon (€35, 5¼ hours) leaves at 3am.

## MÉRIDA

pop 52,110

Once the biggest city in Roman Spain, Mérida is home to more ruins of that age than anywhere else in the country. The **tourist office** (☎ 92 400 97 30; otmerida@eco.juntaex.es; Ave José Álvarez Saenz de Buruaga s/n; 🕙 9am-2pm & 4-6.30pm Mon-Sat, 9.30am-2pm Sun) is by the gates to the Roman theatre. **Cibersala** (Calle Camilo Cela 28; per hr €1.50; 🕙 10am-2pm & 5pm-midnight) is a dingy Internet hang-out.

## Sights

The awesome ruins of Mérida's **Teatro Romano & Anfiteatro** (☎ 92 431 25 30; admission €5.50) shouldn't be missed. The theatre was built in 15 BC and the gladiators' ring, or Anfiteatro, seven years later. Combined they could hold 20,000 spectators. Other monuments of interest are the **Casa del Anfiteatro** ( ☎ 92 431 85 09; admission €2.80), the **Casa Romana del Mithraeo** ( ☎ 92 430 15 04; admission €3.50) the **Alcazaba** ( ☎ 92 431 73 09; admission €2.80), the **Basílica de Santa Eulalia** ( ☎ 92 430 34 07; admission €2.80) and the **Arqueológica de Moreria** (admission €2.80).

The opening hours for all of these sights are 9.30am to 1.45pm and 4pm to 6.15pm October to May, and 9.30am to 1.45pm and 5pm to 7.15pm June to September. You can buy a combined ticket for entry into all of them for €8/4 per adult/concession.

Various other reminders of imperial days are scattered about town, including the **Puente Romano**, at 792m one of the longest bridges the Romans ever built.

### Sleeping & Eating

**Hostal Nueva España** ( ☎ 92 431 33 56; Ave Extremadura 6; s/d €23/35) A modern building a short walk from the centre and near the train station with friendly young owners. Rooms have TV and phone but gloomy overhead lighting.

**Hostal El Alfarero** ( ☎ 92 430 31 83; www.hostalelalfarero.com; Calle Sagasta 40; d €40) Owned by a family of potters, this *hostal* has bright, quirky rooms with hand-painted washbasins and a lovely patio.

**Casa Benito** ( ☎ 92 433 07 69; Calle San Francisco 3; tapas/raciones €1.50/8.50; ☼ 8-1am) A great old-style, wood-panelled bar and restaurant, decked with bullfighting memorabilia, serves local fare at reasonable prices.

**Bar-Restaurante Briz** ( ☎ 92 431 93 07; Calle Felix Valverde Lillo 7; menú €9.60; ☼ 7am-midnight) Walk through the busy tapas bar at the front to get to the glaringly lit, windowless *comedor* (dining room). Don't let the décor put you off – this place is fabulous value for money and serves huge portions (the steak is particularly divine). There are gooey bits (brains and tripe) on the menu, so choose wisely.

### Getting There & Away

From the **bus station** ( ☎ 92 437 14 04; Ave Libertad), buses run to/from Seville (€10, three hours, seven daily), Madrid (€20, four hours, seven daily), Cáceres (€6, 1¼ hours, four daily) and Trujillo (€7.50, 1¼ hours, four daily).

From the **train station** (Calle Cardero), services run to/from Cáceres (€3.30, one hour, four daily), Seville (€11, 4¾ hours, one daily) and Madrid (€19.20, six hours, four daily).

# SPAIN DIRECTORY

## ACCOMMODATION

Spain's camping grounds vary enormously and grounds are officially rated from 1st class to 3rd class. You can expect to pay around €4 for each person, car and tent. Quite a few close from around October to Easter. With certain exceptions (such as many beaches and environmentally protected areas) it is legal to camp outside camping grounds. You'll need permission to camp on private land.

Youth hostels (*albergues juveniles*) are often the cheapest place to stay for lone travellers. Prices often depend on whether you're aged under 26; typically you pay €12 or more. Many hostels have curfews and are often heavily booked by school groups. Most are members of the country's Hostelling International (HI) organisation **Red Española de Albergues Juveniles** (REAJ; ☎ 91 522 70 07; www.reaj.com). Some hostels require HI membership; others may charge more if you're not a member. You can buy HI cards for €11 at virtually all hostels.

Officially, other establishments are either hotels (from one to five stars), *hostales* (one to two stars) or *pensiones*. In practice, there are all sorts of overlapping categories, especially at the budget end of the market. In broad terms, the cheapest are usually *fondas* and *casas de huéspedes*, followed by *pensiones*. All these normally have shared bathrooms and singles for €10 to €20, doubles for €15 to €30. Some *hostales* and *hostal-residencias* come in the same price range, but others have rooms with private bathrooms costing anywhere up to €60 or so. A double in a three-star hotel will run over €90. The luxurious state-run paradors, often converted historic buildings, cost upwards of €100.

Always check room charges before putting down your bags and remember that prices can and do change with time. The price of any type of accommodation varies with the season and accommodation prices listed in this book are a guide only.

Virtually all accommodation prices are subject to IVA, the Spanish version of value-added tax, which is 7%. This may or may not be included in the price. To check, ask: *Está incluido el IVA?* (Is IVA included?). In some cases you will be charged the IVA only if you ask for a receipt.

## ACTIVITIES
### Surfing, Windsurfing & Kite Surfing
The País Vasco has good surf spots, including San Sebastián, Zarauz and the legendary left at Mundaca. Tarifa, with its long, empty beaches and ceaseless wind, is generally considered to be the windsurfing capital of Europe. It has also recently seen a rise in the sport of kite surfing.

### Skiing
Skiing is cheap, and facilities and conditions are good, but queuing at lifts can be a mad scramble. The season runs from December to May. The most accessible resorts are in the Sierra Nevada, close to Granada, and the Pyrenees, north of Barcelona. Contact tourist offices in these cities for information. Affordable day trips can be booked through travel agents.

### Cycling
Bike touring isn't as common as in other parts of Europe because of deterrents such as the often-mountainous terrain and summer heat. It's a more viable option on the Balearic Islands than on much of the mainland, although plenty of people get on their bikes in spring and autumn in the south. Mountain biking is increasingly popular, and areas such as Andalucía and Catalonia have many good tracks.

### Walking
Spain is a trekker's paradise, so much so that Lonely Planet has published a guide to some of the best treks in the country, *Walking in Spain*. Walking country roads and paths between settlements can also be highly enjoyable and a great way to meet the locals.

Useful for hiking and exploring some areas are the *Guía Cartográfica* and *Guía Excursionista y Turística* series published by Editorial Alpina. The series combines information booklets in Spanish (or sometimes Catalan) with detailed maps at scales ranging from 1:25,000 to 1:50,000, and well worth the price (around €8). If you fancy a really long walk, there's the Camino de Santiago. This route, which has been followed by Christian pilgrims for centuries, can be commenced at various places in France. It then crosses the Pyrenees and runs via Pamplona, Logroño and León all the way to the cathedral in Santiago de Compostela.

There are numerous guidebooks explaining the route, and the best map is published by CNIG for €6 (p437).

## BUSINESS HOURS
Generally, people work Monday to Friday from 9am to 2pm and then again from 4.30pm or 5pm to about 8pm, with a siesta in the middle of the afternoon. Shops and travel agencies are usually open these hours on Saturday too, though some may skip the evening session. Museums all have their own unique opening hours; major ones tend to open for something like normal business hours (with or without the afternoon break), but often have their weekly closing day on Monday.

## COURSES
The best place to take a language course in Spain is generally at a university. There are also hundreds of private language colleges throughout the country; the **Instituto Cervantes** (www.cervantes.es); UK ( ☎ 020-7235 0353; 102 Eaton Sq, London SW1 W9AN); Spain ( ☎ 91 436 76 00; Palacio de la Trinidad, Calle Francisco Silvela 82, 28028 Madrid) can send you lists of these and of universities that run courses. Have a look at the excellent website www.spanish-in-spain.biz.

## EMBASSIES & CONSULATES
### Spanish Embassies & Consulates
**Australia** Canberra ( ☎ 02-6273 3555; embespau@mail.mae.es; 15 Arkana St, Yarralumla, Canberra ACT 2600); Melbourne ( ☎ 03-9347 1966); Sydney ( ☎ 02-9261 2433)
**Canada** Ottawa ( ☎ 613-747 2252; embespca@mail.mae.es; 74 Stanley Ave, Ottawa, Ontario K1M 1P4); Montreal ( ☎ 514-935 5235); Toronto ( ☎ 416-977 1661)
**France** Paris ( ☎ 01 44 43 18 00; ambespfr@mail.mae.es; 22 Ave Marceau, 75381 Paris, Cedex 08)
**Germany** Berlin ( ☎ 030-254 0070; embespde@correo.mae.es; Lichtensteinallee 1, 10787 Berlin)
**Ireland** Dublin ( ☎ 269 16 40; embespie@mail.mae.es; 17A Merlyn Park, Ballsbridge, Dublin 4)
**Portugal** Lisbon ( ☎ 01-347 2381; embesppt@mail.mae.es; Rua do Salitre 1, 1250 Lisbon)
**Netherlands** The Hague ( ☎ 302 49 99; ambassade.spanje@worldonline.nl; Lange Voorhout 50, The Hague 2514EG)
**UK** London ( ☎ 020-7235 5555; embespuk@mail.mae.es; 39 Chesham Pl, London SW1X 8SB); Edinburgh ( ☎ 0131 220 1843); Manchester ( ☎ 0161 236 1262)
**USA** Washington DC ( ☎ 202-452 0100; embespus@mail.mae.es; 2375 Pennsylvania Ave NW, Washington DC 20037); Boston ( ☎ 617-536 2506); Chicago ( ☎ 312-782 4588); Houston ( ☎ 713-783 6200); Los Angeles ( ☎ 323-938 0158);

SPAIN

Miami ( ☎ 305-446 5511); New Orleans ( ☎ 504-525 4951); New York ( ☎ 212-355 4080); San Francisco ( ☎ 415-922 2995)

## Embassies & Consulates in Spain

Some 70 countries have embassies in Madrid, including:

**Australia** ( ☎ 91 441 93 00; Plaza del Descubridor Diego de Ordás 3-28003, Edificio Santa Engrácia 120)

**Canada** (Map p356; ☎ 91 431 43 00; Calle Núñez de Balboa 35)

**France** ( ☎ 91 423 89 00; Calle Salustiano Olózaga 9)

**Germany** ( ☎ 91 557 90 00; Calle Fortuny 8)

**Ireland** (Map p356; ☎ 91 576 35 00; Paseo Castellana 36)

**Netherlands** ( ☎ 91 535 75 00; Ave Comandante Franco 32)

**New Zealand** (Map p356; ☎ 91 523 02 26; Plaza Lealtad 3)

**Portugal** ( ☎ 91 782 49 60; Calle Pinar 1); Consulate ( ☎ 91 577 35 85; Calle Martínez Campos 11)

**UK** (Map p356; ☎ 91 700 82 00; Calle Fernando el Santo 16); Consulate (Map pp354-5; ☎ 91 308 52 01; Edificio Colón, Calle Marqués Ensenada 16) Consulate in Barcelona (Map pp379-80; ☎ 93 366 62 00; www.ukinspain.com; Ave Diagonal 477; ⏱ 9.30am-2pm Mon-Fri)

**USA** (Map p356; ☎ 91 587 22 00; Calle Serrano 75) Consulate in Barcelona ( ☎ 93 280 22 27; http://barcelona. usconsulate.gov; Paseo Reina Elisenda de Montcada 23; ⏱ 9am-1pm Mon-Fri)

## FESTIVALS & EVENTS

Spaniards indulge their love of colour, noise, crowds and partying at local fiestas and *ferias* (fairs), many based on religion. Local tourist offices can supply detailed information. Following is a list of festivals to look out for:

### January

**La Tamborada** Held in San Sebastián on 20 January; the whole town dresses up and goes berserk.

### February–March

**Carnaval** A time of fancy-dress parades and merrymaking celebrated around the country about seven weeks before Easter (wildest in Cádiz and Sitges).

**Las Fallas de San José** Valencia's week-long mid-March party, with all-night dancing and drinking, first-class fireworks and processions.

### April

**Semana Santa** Parades of holy images and huge crowds, notably in Seville, during Easter week.

**Feria de Abril** A week-long party held in Seville in late April, a kind of counterbalance to the religious peak of Easter.

### July

**San Fermíne** Combines with the running of the bulls, in Pamplona.

### August

**Semana Grande** A week of heavy drinking and hangovers all along the northern coast during the first half of August.

### September

**Festes de la Mercè** Barcelona's week-long party, held around 24 September.

## HOLIDAYS

Spain has at least 14 official holidays a year, some observed nationwide, some very local. When a holiday falls close to a weekend, Spaniards like to make a *puente* (bridge), taking the intervening day off, too. The holidays listed following are observed virtually everywhere.

**New Year's Day** 1 January

**Epiphany** or **Three Kings' Day** (when children receive presents) 6 January

**Good Friday** before Easter Sunday

**Labour Day** 1 May

**Feast of the Assumption** 15 August

**National Day** 12 October

**All Saints' Day** 1 November

**Feast of the Immaculate Conception** 8 December

**Christmas** 25 December

The two main periods when Spaniards go on holiday are Semana Santa (the week leading up to Easter Sunday) and in August. At these times accommodation in resorts can be scarce and transport heavily booked, but other cities are often half-empty.

## LANGUAGE

Spanish, or Castilian (*castellano*) as it is more precisely called, is spoken throughout Spain, but there are also three important regional languages: Catalan (*catalá*; another Romance language with close ties to French) is spoken in Catalonia, the Balearic Islands and Valencia; Galician (*gallego*), similar to Portuguese, is spoken in Galicia; and Basque (*euskara*; of obscure, non-Latin origin) is spoken in the Basque Country and Navarra.

## LEGAL MATTERS

Spaniards no longer enjoy liberal drug laws. No matter what anyone tells you, it is not legal to smoke dope in public bars. There is a reasonable degree of tolerance when it comes to people having a smoke in their own home, but not in hotel rooms or guesthouses.

If arrested in Spain, you have the right to an attorney and to know the reason you are being held. You are also entitled to make a phone call.

## MAPS

If you're driving around Spain, consider investing in the *Michelin Spain and Portugal Touring and Motoring Atlas* (€18.90). It's a handy atlas with detailed road maps as well as maps of all the main towns and cities. Most travel stores and petrol stations stock it.

Two organizations publish detailed maps of small parts of Spain. The CNIG covers most of the country in 1:25,000 sheets. The CNIG and the Servicio Geográfico del Ejército (SGE; Army Geographic Service) each publish a 1:50,000 series.

## MEDIA
### Magazines

US current-affairs magazines such as *Time* and *Newsweek* can be easily found in major cities. Among Spain's numerous magazine titles, the most popular are the glossy and gossipy *¡Hola!* and the slightly more serious (but still celebrity-obsessed) *Semana*.

### Newspapers

The major daily newspapers in Spain are the solidly liberal *El País*, the conservative *ABC* and *El Mundo*, which specialises in breaking political scandals. There's also a welter of regional dailies, some of the best coming out of Barcelona, the Basque Country (País Vasco) and Andalucía.

International press, such as the *International Herald Tribune*, and daily papers from Western European countries reach major cities and tourist areas on the day of publication.

### Radio

Numerous radio stations occupy the FM band. You'll hear a substantial proportion of British and US music. The national pop/rock station, RNE 3, has well-varied programming.

### TV

Spaniards are Europe's greatest TV watchers after the British, but they do a lot of this watching in bars and cafés, which makes it more of a social activity. Most TVs receive six channels: two state-run (TVE1 and La2), three privately run (Antena 3, Tele 5 and Canal Plus) and one regional channel. Apart from news, TV seems to consist mostly of chat shows, sports, soap operas, sitcoms and English-language films dubbed into Spanish.

## MONEY

Spain's currency is the euro (€). Banks mostly open 8.30am to 2pm Monday to Friday and 8.30am to 1pm Saturday, and tend to give better exchange rates than do currency-exchange offices. Travellers cheques attract a slightly better rate than cash. ATMs accepting a wide variety of cards are common.

### Costs

Spain is one of Western Europe's more affordable countries. If you are particularly frugal, it's possible to scrape by on as little as €30 a day. This would involve staying in the cheapest possible accommodation, avoiding eating in restaurants or going to museums or bars, and not moving around too much. Places such as Madrid, Barcelona, Seville and San Sebastián will place a greater strain on your moneybelt.

A more reasonable budget would be €60 a day. This would allow you €25 for accommodation, €20 for meals, €2 for public transport and €5 for entry fees to museums, sights and entertainment…and a bit left over for intercity travel and a drink or two.

Students (and sometimes seniors) are entitled to discounts of up to 50% on admission fees and about 30% on transport.

### Taxes & Refunds

In Spain, VAT (value-added tax) is known as *impuesto sobre el valor añadido* (IVA). On accommodation and restaurant prices, there's a flat IVA of 7%, which is usually, but not always, included in quoted prices.

On such items as retail goods, alcohol and electrical appliances, IVA is 16%. Visitors are entitled to a refund of IVA on any item costing more than €90 that they are taking out of the EU. Ask for a Europe Tax-Free Shopping Cheque when you buy, then present the goods and cheque to customs when you leave. If the shop can't offer a cheque, get an official receipt with the business' address and a description of the item purchased. Customs stamps the cheque and you then cash it at a booth with the 'Cash Refund' sign. There are booths at all main Spanish airports; at the border crossings at Algeciras, Gibraltar and Andorra; and at similar points throughout the EU.

## Tipping & Bargaining

In restaurants, prices include a service charge, and tipping is a matter of personal choice – most people leave some small change; 5% is plenty. It's common to leave small change in bars and cafés. The only places in Spain where you are likely to bargain are markets and, occasionally, cheap hotels, particularly if you're staying for a few days.

## POST

Main post offices in provincial capitals are usually open from 8.30am to 8.30pm Monday to Friday and from about 9am to 1.30pm Saturday. Stamps are also sold at *estancos* (tobacco shops with the Tabacos sign in yellow letters on a maroon background). A standard airmail letter or card costs €0.27 within Spain, €0.50 to the rest of Europe and €0.77 to the rest of the world.

Mail to/from Europe normally takes up to a week, and to North America, Australia or New Zealand around 10 days, but there may be some long, unaccountable delays.

Poste-restante mail can be addressed to you at either *poste restante* or *lista de correos,* the Spanish name for it, at the city in question. It's a fairly reliable system, although mail may well arrive late.

## TELEPHONE & FAX

Blue public payphones are common and easy to use. They accept coins, phonecards and, in some cases, credit cards.

A three-minute call from a pay phone costs about €0.15 within a local area, €0.35 to other places in the same province, €0.45 to other provinces, or €1 to another EU country or the USA. A three-minute call to Australia and Asia is about €4.50.

Provincial and interprovincial calls, except those to mobile phones, are around 50% cheaper between 8pm and 8am weekdays and all day Saturday and Sunday. Local and international calls are around 10% cheaper between 6pm and 8am and all day Saturday and Sunday.

---

> **EMERGENCY NUMBERS**
>
> ■ Police ☎ 092
>
> ■ Fire Department ☎ 112
>
> ■ Medical ☎ 061

---

International reverse-charge (collect) calls are simple to make: from a pay phone or private phone dial ☎ 900 99 00 followed by ☎ 61 for Australia, ☎ 44 for the UK, ☎ 64 for New Zealand, ☎ 15 for Canada, and for the USA ☎ 11 (AT&T) or ☎ 14 (MCI).

## Fax

Most main post offices have a fax service, but you'll often find cheaper rates at shops or offices with Fax Público signs.

## Mobile Phones

Mobile phone numbers in Spain start with the number 6. Calls to mobiles vary but a three-minute call should cost about €1.20.

## Phone Cards

Phonecards *(tarjetas telefónicas)* come in denominations of €6 and €12 and are available at main post offices and *estancos.*

## Phone Codes

Area codes in Spain are an integral part of the phone number. All numbers are nine digits and you just dial that nine-digit number, wherever in the country you are calling from. All numbers prefixed with ☎ 900 are toll-free numbers.

## TIME

Spain is one hour ahead of GMT/UTC during winter, and two hours ahead from the last Sunday in March to the last Sunday in September. See p735 for a map of world time zones.

## TOURIST INFORMATION

Most towns and large villages of any interest have an *oficina de turismo* (tourist office). These will supply you with a map and brochures with basic information on local sights, attractions, accommodation, history etc. Staff are generally helpful and often speak some English. A **nationwide phone line** ( ☎ 901 30 06 00; ☉ 8am-10pm) offers basic information in English.

## Tourist Offices Abroad

Spain has tourist information centres in 29 countries, including:

**Canada** ( ☎ 416-961 3131; toronto@tourspain.es; 34th fl, 2 Bloor St W, Toronto, Ontario M4W 3E2)

**France** ( ☎ 01-45 03 82 57; paris@tourspain.es; 43 Rue Decamps, 75784 Paris, Cedex 16)

**Germany** ( ☎ 030-882 6543; berlin@tourspain.es; Kurfürstendamm 63, 10707 Berlin)

**Portugal** ( ☎ 01-21 354 1992; lisboa@tourspain.es; Ave Sidónio Pais 28 3 Dto, 1050-215 Lisbon)

**UK** ( ☎ 020-7486 8077, brochure request 090-6364 0630 at £0.60 per min; londres@tourspain.es; 22-23 Manchester Sq, London W1M 5AP)

**USA** ( ☎ 212-265 8822; oetny@tourspain.es; 35th fl, 666 Fifth Ave, New York, NY 10103)

## VISAS

Citizens of EU countries can enter Spain with their national identity card or passport. Citizens of the UK must have a full passport, not just a British visitor passport. Non-EU nationals must take their passport.

EU, Norway and Iceland citizens do not need a visa. Nationals of Australia, Canada, Israel, Japan, New Zealand, Switzerland and the USA need no visa for stays of up to 90 days but must have a passport valid for the whole visit. This 90-day limit applies throughout the EU. South Africans are among nationalities that do need a visa.

It's best to obtain the visa in your country of residence. Single-entry visas are available in flavours of 30-day and 90-day, and there's a 90-day multiple-entry visa, too, though if you apply in a country where you're not resident, the 90-day option may not be available. Multiple-entry visas will save you a lot of time and trouble if you plan to leave Spain (say to Gibraltar or Morocco), then re-enter it.

Spain is one of the Schengen countries; the others are Portugal, Italy, France, Germany, Austria, the Netherlands, Belgium, Luxembourg, Sweden, Finland, Denmark and Greece. A visa for one Schengen country is valid for the others. Compare validity, prices and permitted entries before applying. Schengen countries theoretically have done away with passport control on travel between them.

EU, Norway and Iceland nationals planning to stay in Spain more than 90 days are supposed to apply for a residence card during their first month in the country. This is a lengthy, complicated procedure; if you intend to subject yourself to it, consult a Spanish consulate before you go to Spain, as you'll need to take certain documents with you.

Other nationalities on a Schengen visa are flat out of luck when it comes to extensions. For stays of longer than 90 days you're supposed to get a residence card. This is a nightmarish process, starting with a residence visa issued by a Spanish consulate in your country of residence; start the process well in advance.

## WORK

EU, Norway and Iceland nationals are allowed to work in Spain without a visa, but if they plan to stay more than three months they are supposed to apply within the first month for a residence card (left). Virtually everyone else is supposed to obtain (from a Spanish consulate in their country of residence) a work permit and, if they plan to stay more than 90 days, a residence visa. These procedures can be difficult and time-consuming.

That said, quite a few people do manage to work in Spain one way or another – although with Spain's unemployment rate running at around 15%, don't rely on it. Teaching English is an obvious option. A TEFL certificate will be a big help. Another possibility is gaining summer work in a bar or restaurant in a tourist resort, many of which are run by foreigners.

# TRANSPORT IN SPAIN

## GETTING THERE & AWAY
### Air

Spain has many international airports, including:

**Alicante** ( ☎ 96 691 90 00)

**Almería** ( ☎ 95 021 37 15)

**Barcelona** ( ☎ 93 298 38 38; www.barcelona-airport.com)

**Bilbao** ( ☎ 94 486 93 00)

**Ibiza** ( ☎ 97 180 90 00)

**Madrid** ( ☎ 91 393 60 60; www.madrid-mad.com)

**Málaga** ( ☎ 95 204 84 84)

**Maó** ( ☎ 97 115 70 00)

**Palma de Mallorca** ( ☎ 97 178 90 00)

**Santiago de Compostela** ( ☎ 98 154 75 00)

**Seville** ( ☎ 95 444 90 00)

**Valencia** ( ☎ 96 159 85 15)

SPAIN

In general, the cheapest destinations are Má-laga, the Balearic Islands, Bilbao, Barcelona and Madrid. Departure taxes on flights out of Spain, which vary, are factored directly into tickets. There are many international airlines that fly to and from Spain.

**Aer Lingus** (code EI; www.aerlingus.com; ☎ 902 502 737)

**Air Europa** (code UX; www.aireuropa.com; ☎ 902 401 501)

**Air France** (code AF; www.airfrance.com; ☎ 901 11 22 66)

**Alitalia** (code AZ; www.alitalia.com; ☎ 902 10 03 23)

**American Airlines** (code AA; www.aa.com; ☎ 902 11 55 70)

**BMI Baby** (code WW; www.bmibaby.com; ☎ 902 10 07 37)

**BMI British Midland** (code BD; www.flybmi.com; ☎ 91 393 72 53)

**British Airways** (code BA; www.britishairways.com; ☎ 902 111 333)

**easyJet** (code EZY; www.easyjet.com; ☎ 902 29 99 92)

**Iberia** (code IB; www.iberia.com; ☎ 902 40 04 33)

**KLM** (code KL; www.klm.com; ☎ 902 22 27 47)

**Lufthansa** (code LH; www.lufthansa.com; ☎ 902 22 01 01)

**Monarch Airlines** (code ZB; www.flymonarch.com; ☎ 902 50 27 37)

**Ryanair** (code FR; www.ryanair.com; ☎ 972 18 67 34)

**SAS** (code SK; www.sas.se; ☎ 902 11 71 92)

**Spanair** (code JK; www.spanair.com; ☎ 902 13 14 15)

**Swiss Air** (code LX; www.swiss.com; ☎ 901 11 67 12)

**Virgin Express** (code TV; www.virgin-express.com; ☎ 902 88 84 59)

## Land
### BUS

There are regular bus services to Spain from all major centres in Europe, including Lisbon, London and Paris. In London, **Eurolines** ( ☎ 08705-143219; www.eurolines.com) has services at least three times a week to Barcelona (£65/95 one way/return, 26hrs), Madrid (£92/122, at least 27hrs) and Málaga (£96/128, 35hrs). Tickets are sold by major travel agencies and if you book in advance you can get good discounts of up to one-third. People aged under 26 and senior citizens qualify for a 10% discount.

### CAR & MOTORCYCLE

If you're driving or riding to Spain from England, you'll have to choose between going through France (check visa requirements) or taking a direct ferry from England to Spain (p440). The cheapest way is to take one of the shorter ferries from England to France, then a quick drive down through France.

### TRAIN

Reaching Spain by train is more expensive than by bus, unless you have a rail pass, though fares for those under 26 come close to the bus price. Return fares from London (using the Eurostar) to Madrid (via Paris) can be had for as little as UK£137 provided you book well in advance. For more details, contact the **Rail Europe Travel Centre** ( ☎ 08705-848848; www.raileurope.co.uk) in London or a travel agent. See p730 for more on rail passes and train travel through Europe.

## Sea
### THE UK

**Brittany Ferries** (UK ☎ 08705-360360; www.brittany ferries.com) runs Plymouth–Santander ferries (24hrs) twice weekly from about mid-March to mid-November, and usually once a week in other months. Oneway passenger fares range from about UK£61 in winter to UK£100 in summer; a two-berth cabin is an extra UK£67; a car and driver costs from UK£245 to UK£473.

**P&O European Ferries** (UK ☎ 08702-424999; www .poportsmouth.com) runs Portsmouth–Bilbao ferries (35hrs) twice-weekly, on Tuesday and Saturday, year-round. Oneway/return prices with a berth start at UK£114/214 in winter and £166/262 in summer.

### MOROCCO

Ferry services between Spain and Morocco include those between Algeciras–Tangier, Algeciras–Ceuta, Gibraltar–Tangier, Tarifa–Tangier, Málaga–Melilla, Almería–Melilla and Almería–Nador. Those to and from Algeciras are the fastest, cheapest and most frequent, with over 20 ferries a day to Ceuta (€22, 1½ hours) and 14 to Tangier (€28, 2½ hours). Hydrofoils make the same trip in half the time for about 75% more. Taking a car to Ceuta/Tangier costs €62/73.

Don't buy Moroccan currency until you reach Morocco, as you will get ripped off in Algeciras.

## GETTING AROUND

Students and seniors are eligible for discounts of 30% to 50% on almost all types of transport within Spain. The travel agency **TIVE** ( ☎ 91 543 74 12; tive.juventud@madrid.org; Calle

Fernando El Católico 88, Madrid) has offices in major cities throughout Spain. It specialises in discounted tickets and travel arrangements for students and young people.

## Air

Spain has three main domestic airlines: **Iberia** ( ☎ 902 40 05 00; www.iberia.com), **Air Europa** ( ☎ 902 40 15 01; www.aireuropa.com) and **Spanair** ( ☎ 902 13 14 15; www.spanair.com). They, and a couple of smaller airlines, compete to produce some fares that can make flying worthwhile if you're in a hurry, especially for longer trips. A single fare from Madrid to Barcelona, Palma de Mallorca, Santiago de Compostela or Málaga starts at about €85.

There are some useful deals if you're under 26 (or, in some cases, over 63).

## Bicycle

Finding bikes to rent in Spain is a hit-and-miss affair, so it's best to bring your own. However, the Spanish do enjoy recreational cycling, so getting hold of spare parts shouldn't be a problem. Cyclists should be aware that quiet roads may suddenly merge into fast *autopistas* without much warning.

Spain's high-speed AVE and Talgo trains will not allow bicycles on board unless boxed, but slower regional trains will. Provided there's room, buses will take bikes in their lower luggage hold (you'll probably have to remove the front wheel).

## Boat

Regular ferries connect the Spanish mainland with the Balearic Islands. In bad weather or rough seas, services are restricted. For destinations, schedules and prices see p406. The main companies are:
**Balearia** ( ☎ 902 16 01 80; www.balearia.com)
**Cape Balear** ( ☎ 902 10 04 44)
**Iscomar** ( ☎ 902 11 91 28; www.iscomarferrys.com)
**Trasmediterránea** ( ☎ 902 45 46 45; www.trasmedi terranea.es)

## Bus

Spain's bus network is operated by dozens of independent companies and is more extensive than its train system, serving remote towns and villages as well as the major routes. The choice between bus and train depends on the particular trip you're taking. for the best value, compare fares, journey times and frequencies each time you move.

Many towns and cities have one main bus station where most buses arrive and depart, and these usually have an information desk giving information on all services. Tourist offices can also help with information.

Spain's has dozens of local and regional bus companies. The best known national service is run by **ALSA** ( ☎ 902 42 22 42; www.alsa.es).

### COSTS

Buses to and from Madrid are often cheaper than (or not that much different) from cross-country routes. For instance the three-hour Seville–Granada trip costs €16, the same price as the much longer Seville–Madrid trip.

### RESERVATIONS

It is not necessary, and often not possible, to make advance reservations for local bus journeys. It is, however, a good idea to turn up at least 30 minutes before the bus is due to leave to guarantee a seat.

For longer trips (eg, Madrid–Seville) it's a good idea to buy your ticket in advance.

## Car & Motorcycle

Spain's roads vary but are generally quite good. Fastest are the *autopistas* (multilane freeways between major cities). On those in the north, you have to pay hefty tolls (from the French border to Barcelona, for example, it's about €12). Minor routes can be slow going but are usually more scenic. Trying to find a parking spot in larger towns and cities can be a nightmare. Spanish drivers park anywhere to save themselves the hassle of a half-hour search, but *grúas* (tow trucks) will tow your car, given half a chance. The cost of bailing out a car can be as high as €100.

Spanish cities do not have US-style parking meters at every spot. Instead, if you park in a blue zone from around 8am to 8pm, you have to obtain a ticket from a street-side meter, which may be several blocks away. You then display the ticket from your dashboard until your time runs out (expiration time is written on the ticket).

If you are bringing your own vehicle into Spain, remember to always carry your proof of ownership (or Vehicle Registration Document) at all times.

### AUTOMOBILE ASSOCIATIONS

The Spanish automobile club is **Real Automovil Club de España** (RACE; ☎ 91 434 11 22;

SPAIN

www.race.es; Ave Ciudad de Barcelona 132, Madrid). For the RACE's 24hr, nationwide, on-road emergency service, call ☎ 900 11 22 22.

## DRIVING LICENCE

All EU member states' driving licences (pink or pink and green) are recognised. Other foreign licences should be accompanied by an International Driving Permit. These are available from automobile clubs in your country and valid for 12 months.

## FUEL & SPARE PARTS

*Gasolina* (petrol) is expensive, at around €0.87 for a litre of unleaded *(sin plomo)*. Diesel *(gasóleo)* costs about €0.73 per litre. Petrol stations *(gasolineras)* are everywhere and finding labour and spare parts isn't a problem.

## HIRE

Rates vary widely from place to place. The best deals tend to be in major tourist areas, including airports. At Málaga airport you can rent a small car for under €110 a week. More generally, you're looking at about €50 a day with unlimited kilometres, plus insurance, damage waiver and taxes. Hiring for several days can bring the average daily cost down a lot – a small car for a week might cost under €140. Local companies often have better rates than the big firms.

## INSURANCE

Third-party motor insurance is a minimum requirement and it is compulsory to have a Green Card, an internationally recognised proof of insurance, which can be obtained from your insurer.

## ROAD RULES

Driving in Spain is not too bad. Locals respect road rules but do have a tendency to tailgate. Speed limits are 120km/h on the *autopistas*, 90km/h or 100km/h on other country roads and 50km/h in built-up areas. The maximum allowable blood-alcohol level is 0.05%. Seat belts must be worn, and motorcyclists must always wear a helmet and keep headlights on day and night.

## Train

Trains are mostly modern and comfortable, and late arrivals are now the exception rather than the rule.

**Renfe** ( ☎ 902 24 02 02; www.renfe.es), the national railway company, runs numerous types of train, and travel times can vary a lot on the same route. So can fares, which may depend not just on the type of train but also the day of the week and time of day. Renfe's website is a great resource for schedule and fare information.

*Regionales* are all-stops trains (think cheap and slow). *Cercanías* provide regular services from major cities to the surrounding suburbs and hinterland, sometimes even crossing regional boundaries.

Among long-distance trains, the standard daytime train is the *diurno* (its nighttime equivalent is the *estrella*). Quicker is the InterCity (mainly because it makes fewer stops), while Talgo is fastest and dearest.

Best of all is the AVE high-speed service that links Madrid and Seville in just 2½ hours. The *Talgo 200* uses part of this line to speed down to Málaga from Madrid. The *Euromed* is an AVE-style train that speeds south from Barcelona to Valencia and Alicante. A *Tren Hotel* is a 1st-class sleeper-only express.

There's also a bewildering range of accommodation types, especially on overnight trains (fares quoted in this chapter are typically 2nd-class seat fares). The cheapest sleeper option is usually a *litera*, a bunk in a six-berth 2nd-class compartment.

You can buy tickets and make reservations at stations, Renfe offices in many city centres and travel agencies that display the Renfe logo.

## TRAIN PASSES

Rail passes are valid for all Renfe trains, but Inter-Rail users have to pay €9.50 supplements on Talgo and InterCity services, and on the high-speed AVE service (Madrid–Seville). All passholders making reservations for long-distance trains pay a fee of about €5.

Renfe's Tarjeta Turística (also known as the Spain Flexipass) is a rail pass valid for three to 10 days' travel in a two-month period. (Spanish residents are not eligible). In 2nd class, three days costs US$155, and 10 days is US$365. It can be purchased from agents outside Europe, or at a few main train stations and Renfe offices in Spain.

# Portugal

CONTENTS

Portugal's reserve, especially when compared with its exuberant neighbour, Spain, conceals a quiet confidence. Things are pretty good for the country right now: EU funding has brought the infrastructure up to speed and several recent big-time international events have led to some well-deserved showing off.

One of Europe's smallest capitals, Lisbon is a hussy of a city: easy on the eye with an upbeat atmosphere and is appealingly rough around the edges. Nearby beach resorts, like Cascais and Estoril are a taster for all that endless fun-in-the-sun entertainment down south. Although the Algarve's holiday combo of sunbeds, sand and sea equals the inevitable egg-carton-style hotels and holiday homes, it's easy to escape the concrete and coach loads by heading away from the major resorts, and visiting out of season. Inland is also surprisingly unspoilt; in many places you're more likely to be surrounded by goats than folk, and may still need the lingo to order a beer.

PORTUGAL

**FAST FACTS**

- **Area** 92,389 sq km
- **Capital** Lisbon
- **Currency** euro; A$1 = €0.58; ¥100 = €0.76; NZ$1 = €0.54; UK£1 = €1.50; US$1 = €0.83
- **Famous for** port wine, *fado* music, Algarve beaches, *azulejo* tiles, Manueline architecture
- **Official Language** Portuguese
- **Population** 10 million
- **Telephone Codes** country code ☎ 351; international access code ☎ 00; reverse-charge call ☎ 171; area codes are always dialled in Portugal and are listed with all numbers
- **Visas** EU nationals don't need a visa; most other nationalities can stay for up to 90 days in any half-year without a visa

## HIGHLIGHTS

- Sample some of the local tipple at a **port lodge** (p469) in Vila Nova de Gaia, across the water from Porto.
- Indulge the taste buds on a classic fishy **Algarve** dish – Cataplana (seafood cooked in a *cataplana*, or copper pan).
- Saunter around the fabulous palaces, villas and pampered gardens of **Sintra** (p458), a wooded hilltop retreat and seductive must-see on everyone's itinerary.
- Check out other-worldly grottoes and rock formations by taking one of the boat trips from Lagos in the **Algarve** (p462).
- Visit Lisbon's fascinating **Alfama district** (p452), a medieval tangle of narrow alleys and steep streets with an earthy lived-in feel.

## ITINERARIES

- **One week** Start big with two days (and nights) in Portugal's grand-slam city of Lisbon, followed by a day's jaunt to romantic Sintra. Stay here overnight to appreciate the tranquil beauty of the place after the coach tours have left. Try a morning's beach stroll in Cascais before hitting the road to the Algarve. Hot spots here are Silves for its castle and atmosphere, Faro for its lively feel – albeit summer crowds – and pretty Tavira with its rambling old town and kick-back cafés and bars.

- **Two weeks** Spend one day exploring Lisbon's Alfama, topped by the castle with its panoramic views; then the evening bar hopping at nail-bitingly trendy Alcântara. Next day take in the Baixa, Chiado winding up at Bairro Alto, with its cool nightlife. On day three wander around Europe's largest Oceanarium, followed by lunch and a monastery gawp at Belém. Day four sidestep to Sintra (see 'One Week'). Beach it at Cascais on the fifth day, have a flutter at Estoril's casino and next day hightail it to untouristy Setúbal for a slug of real Portugal and overnight stay. Spend week two in the Algarve (see 'One Week') but taking in the additional hotspots of Lagos (some of the finest beaches), Monchique (charming and tranquil) and dramatic Sagres where you can perfect your windsurfing skills at Europe's most southwestern point.

## HISTORY

Portugal is a holiday-brochure 'land of contrasts' cliché and has enjoyed a similarly chequered history, stretching back to 700 BC when the Celts arrived on the Iberian Peninsula, followed by the Phoenicians, Greeks, Romans and Visigoths.

In the 8th century the Moors conquered Portugal. Their influence lingers in the culture, architecture and dark features of the people, particularly in the Algarve where the Moors established their capital in Silves (p463). After the Christian conquest, new trade routes were discovered in the 15th century, creating an empire that extended to four continents and launched Lisbon as the wealthiest city in Europe. Portugal's exuberant Gothic-style Manueline architecture dates from this time. This period of opulence was short-lived; in 1580 Spain occupied the Portuguese throne and, although the Portuguese regained it within 90 years, their imperial momentum had been lost forever.

In 1755 a massive earthquake tragically destroyed most of Lisbon followed, around 50 years later, by Napoleon's thwarted invasion, which further weakened and destabilised the country. A period of civil war and political mayhem followed, culminating in the abolition of the monarchy in 1910 and the founding of a democratic republic.

In 1926 a military coup set the stage for the dictatorship of António de Oliveira Salazar, who clung to power until his death in 1970. General dissatisfaction with his regime and a ruinous colonial war in Africa led to a peaceful military coup on 25 April 1974.

The subsequent granting of independence to Portugal's African colonies produced a flood of nearly a million refugees into the country. Today, the influence of these distant worlds, particularly Brazil, Cape Verde and Mozambique, are reflected in the music and food, especially in Lisbon and Porto.

The 1970s and early 1980s saw extreme swings between political right and left, and strikes over state versus private ownership. Portugal's entry into the EU in 1986 secured a measure of stability, although the 1990s remained consistently troubled by recession and rising unemployment.

---

### GO, GO, GO

- **Where to take a boat trip** Speed boats from Lagos marina, boat trips along the cast departing Sagres

- **Where to go fishing** Deep sea fishing from Lagos. Freshwater fishing in the reservoirs and rivers, notably the Guadiana.

- **Where to go hiking** The Costa Vicentina, Serra de Monchique and the Serra do Caldeirão all offer unspoilt surroundings for striding out.

---

### HOW MUCH?

- **Loaf of bread** €0.65
- **Ice-cream** €1
- **Beach towel** €6
- **Gin and tonic** (or similar) €3.50
- **Underground parking** €1 per hour

### LONELY PLANET INDEX

- **Litre of petrol** €0.97
- **Litre of bottled water** €0.40
- **Beer** €1
- **Souvenir T-shirt** €10
- **Street snack (sandwich)** €1.75

---

Expo '98 gave the country an essential boost, triggered vast transport and communications' projects and launched Portugal into a new era of economic success. This was further advanced by Porto's status as a European Capital of Culture in 2001, followed in 2004 by Portugal playing host to the Euro 2004 football championships. The ensuing high international profile contributed further to a vast injection of funds into the country's infrastructure, including a Porto metro, 10 new/refurbished stadia and plans for a second international airline terminal to be built northwest of Lisbon in 2010.

## PEOPLE

Portugal's population of 10.3 million excludes the estimated three million Portuguese living abroad, but includes the considerable number of African and Brazilian immigrants. There has also been an influx of new immigrants post-May 2004 when the European community embraced 10 new member countries.

## RELIGION

Portugal is 98% Roman Catholic, with around 120,000 Protestants, of which a large percentage are evangelical Protestants from Brazil. There are approximately 5000 Jews.

## ARTS
### Music

The best-known form of Portuguese music is the melancholy, nostalgic songs called

# PORTUGAL

0 ——— 100 km
0 ——— 60 miles

**ATLANTIC OCEAN**

Valença do Minho
Arcos de Valdevez
Viana do Castelo
Ponte de Lima
*Lima River*
**MINHO**
Barcelos
Braga
Guimarães
Parque Natural da Peneda Gerês
Montalegre
Caldas do Gerês
Parque Natural do Alvão
Parque Natural de Montesinho
Verin
Bragança
E82
Chaves
Mirandela
Miranda do Douro
**TRÁS-OS-MONTES**
Amarante
Vila Real
Parque Natural do Douro Internacional
A3-IP1
Porto
A4
**DOURO**
Peso da Régua
*Douro River*
Lamego
Pocinho
A1-IP1-E01
**BEIRA ALTA**
**SPAIN**
Aveiro
Viseu
Vilar Formoso
Guarda
E80
Buçaco Forest
Luso
Gouveia
Seia
Manteigas
**BEIRA LITORAL**
Pampilhosa
Torre (1993m)
Penhas da Saúde
Covilhã
Figueira da Foz
Coimbra
Serra da Estrela
Parque Natural da Serra da Estrela
Lousã
**BEIRA BAIXA**
Monsanto
Leiria
Nazaré
Batalha
Fátima
Tomar
Castelo Branco
Parque Natural do Tejo Internacional
Parque Natural das Serras de Aire e Candeeiros
Alcobaça
Entroncamento
*(Rio Tejo)*
A1-IP1-E80
*Tagus River*
Castelo de Vide
Peniche
Óbidos
Santarém
**RIBATEJO**
Portalegre
Marvão
Parque Natural da Serra de São Mamede
A8
Parque Natural de Sintra-Cascais
Ericeira
Mafra
Sintra
Vila Franca de Xira
**ESTREMADURA**
**ALTO ALENTEJO**
Estremoz
E90
Badajoz
Queluz
Cascais
Estoril
**LISBON**
Arraiolos
Vila Viçosa
A2
A6-IP7-E90
Parque Natural da Arrábida
Setúbal
Évora
Monsaraz
Reguengos de Monsaraz
Reserva Natural do Estuário do Sado
IP2
IP8
Beja
Sines
A2-IP1-EO1
Serpa
**BAIXO**
**ALENTEJO**
IC1
Parque Natural do Vale do Guadiana
**SPAIN**
**ATLANTIC OCEAN**
Parque Natural do Sudoeste Alentejano e Costa Vicentina
Monchique
Silves
**ALGARVE**
N125
A22-IP1-EO1
Vila Real de Santo António
Sagres
Lagos
Albufeira
Faro
Tavira

**PORTUGAL**

*fado* (fate), popularly considered to have originated from the Portuguese sailors expressing the swell of the seamen's emotions on the high seas. They sang of loneliness, danger, nostalgia, the joy of survival; and, although their accounts could be graphic and literal, the voyage was also a metaphor for the greater passage of life. The late Amália Rodrigues was the Edith Piaf of Portuguese *fado*. Today it is Mariza who has captured the public's imagination with her heart-wrenching voice, passionate recordings and blonde cornrows of hair contrasting with her dramatic dark colouring. Lisbon's Alfama district has plenty of *fado* houses (p452), ranging from the grandiose and tourist-conscious to small family affairs; the tourist office can supply you with a list.

## Literature

Two of Portugal's finest writers of the 20th century are poet–dramatist Fernando Pessoa (1888–1935), author of the 1934 *Message;* and the 1998 Nobel Prize–winning novelist José Saramago, whose novels (notably *Baltasar and Blimunda* and *The Year of the Death of Ricardo Reis*) weave together the real and imaginary. Others to try are Eça de Queiroz *(The Maias)* and Fernando Namora *(Mountain Doctor)*. A contemporary Portuguese 'whodunnit', close to the political bone, is *The Ballad of Dog's Beach* by José Cardoso Pires.

## Architecture

Unique to Portugal is Manueline architecture, named after its patron King Manuel I (1495–1521). It symbolises the zest for discovery of that era and is hugely flamboyant, characterised by fantastically spiralling columns and elaborate carving and ornamentation.

## Visual Arts

The most striking Portuguese visual art is pottery, with superb examples of the decorative blue-and-white *azulejo* tiles based on traditional Moorish designs of the 15th century. Lisbon has its own *azulejo* museum (p453).

# ENVIRONMENT
## The Land

Portugal stretches 560km from north to south and 220km at its widest east–west point. The country is bordered on the north and east by Spain and on the south and west by the Atlantic.

## National Parks

Portugal has one international-standard national park (70,290-hectare Peneda-Gerês), 12 *parques naturais* (natural parks), nine nature reserves and several other protected areas. The government's **Instituto da Conservação Wasteels** (ICN; Information Division ☎ 213 523 317; Rua Ferreira Lapa 29-A, Lisbon) manages these, though information is best sourced from each park's headquarters. There are 12 **World Heritage Sites** in Portugal, including the Monastery of Batalha, the historic centre of Évora, and Sintra. For a complete list check http://whc.unesco.org/pg.cfm?cid=30.

## Environmental Issues

Portugal's most heated environmental issue concerns the Alqueva dam that opened in February 2002 as Europe's largest artificial lake. Over a million trees were cut down to create the dam, and some 160 rocks covered with Stone Age drawings were submerged. Environmentalists also voiced concern at the inevitable destruction of rare species, including kites, wild boars and the Iberian lynx.

On a more positive note, Portugal has fast come up to speed in the recycling department with colour-coded receptacles in every town and city.

# FOOD & DRINK

In the larger towns and cities, restaurants in this chapter are divided into budget (€2 to €7), mid-range (€8 to €12), and top end (€13 to €20) for the average price of a main dish.

## Staples & Specialities

Seafood offers exceptional value, especially *caldeirada* (seafood stew), *sardinhas assadas* (grilled sardines) and *bacalhau* (dried cod) reputedly prepared in some 365 ways.

---

**PIRI PIRI**

All over the Algarve, particularly around Monchique, restaurants you'll find frango piri-piri on the menu. This spicy, hot condiment has plenty of the wow factor and originates in Africa. It is particularly popular when cooked with that all-time Portuguese favourite: roast chicken.

Meat dishes can be a letdown; among the safer bets are local *presunto* (ham), *borrego* (roast lamb) and *cabrito* (kid). Main-dish prices start around €6.

Diet-defying cafés and *pastelarias* (pastry shops) are everywhere in Portugal and offer splendid desserts and cakes. Try a delicious – and addictive – *pastel de nata* (custard tart).

Portuguese coffee is always good, in even the grungiest bar. In Lisbon, a small black espresso is known as a *bica*, and elsewhere simply as a *café*. Half-and-half coffee and milk is *café com leite*. Local beers *(cerveja)* include Sagres in the south and Super Bock in the north.

Portuguese wine *(vinho)* offers great value in all varieties: red *(tinto)*, white *(branco)* and semi-sparkling young *(vinho verde)*, which is usually white. Restaurants often have *vinho da casa* (house wine) for as little as €2.50 per 350ml jug, although sometimes it would be better suited for pickling onions. Port, synonymous with Portugal, is produced in the Douro Valley east of Porto and drunk in three forms: ruby, tawny and white.

### Where to Eat & Drink

The line between snacks and meals is blurred. Bars and cafés offer snacks or even a small menu. For full meals try a *casa do pasto* (a simple, cheap eatery), *restaurante, cervejaria* (bar-restaurant) or *marisqueira* (seafood restaurant). Lunch time typically lasts from noon to 3pm, and evening meals from 7pm to 10.30pm.

The *prato do dia* (dish of the day) is often a bargain at around €6; the *ementa turística* (tourist menu) rarely is. A full portion or *dose* is ample for two decent appetites; a *meia dose* (half-portion) is a quarter to a third cheaper. The *couvert* – the bread, cheese, butter, olives and other titbits at the start of a meal – costs extra, sometimes a considerable sum. You can send it back without causing offence, although you should do this right away, rather than wait until the end of the meal! All restaurants in this chapter are open daily for lunch (noon to 3pm) and dinner (7pm to 10pm) unless otherwise noted.

### Vegetarians & Vegans

The typical Portuguese menu does not cater to vegetarians, although the ubiquitous *sopa de legumes* (vegetable soup) is often included as a starter, together with the inevitable

**NIBBLING AT THE BANK BALANCE**

Be warned that those tasty nibbles that are routinely plonked on your table as soon as you sit down cost extra. At one rip-off Lisbon restaurant this author paid €8 for a measly plate of paper thin slices of cheese and ham. Even if you don't eat any of the tidbits, you will still be charged for them so, if you are not interested, send them back straight away.

*salada* (salad). Generally the only other option (for vegetarians) is an *omeleta simple* (plain omelette) or the marginally more exciting *omeleta com queijo* (cheese omelette). Vegans have an even tougher time, although larger cities and the Algarve have a handful of vegetarian restaurants. Chinese restaurants are more common and always have plenty of vegetarian (and vegan) options.

# LISBON

**pop 720,000**

Lisbon is one of Europe's smallest and most beguiling capitals; a life-affirming, lung-busting city of hills offering views over the sparkling Tagus River (Rio Tejo). The narrow streets and alleys of this once-great port city exude a sense of history with traditional shops and cafés, and ancient street trams that rattle up the steep gradients. Away from the centre are great stroll-around districts, like Moorish Alfama with its crumbling pastel-coloured houses packed into a steep shoulder of the city between the river and the castle.

Aside from the spoilt-for-choice nightlife, restaurants and entertainment, Lisbon has been busy playing host to the 2004 European Football Championships with preparations including a spanking new stadium and a general scrub-and-brush-up throughout town.

## HISTORY

The history of lisbon is a roller coaster of power and poverty. Until the 1755 earthquake destroyed most of the centre – and killed some 40,000 people – the capital was one of Europe's most prosperous port cities with thriving trade routes to India, Africa and Brazil. Post-quake there was the inevitable backlash of political upheaval and suffering. Only in the last couple of decades has Lisbon begun to flex its muscles on the international power front, most noticeably in its recognition as the European City of Culture in 1994 and as the venue for the 1998 Expo and the 2004 European Football Championships.

## ORIENTATION

Baixa is the heart of the modern city with its grid of wide streets and huge square, Praça do Comércio, to the south on the river's edge. To the north stands its second main square, Praça Dom Pedro IV, better known as Rossio and the commercial hub of the city, surrounded by cafés, bars and shops.

The Chiado and Bairro Alto districts lie above the Baixa, to the west. The Chiado is the affluent quarter with sophisticated shops, restaurants and cafés, while the Bairro Alto, the upper town, is famed for its wonderful nightlife and narrow 17th-century streets.

Alfama, northeast of the Baixa, is the oldest part of Lisbon with its warren of medieval streets plunging from the castle to the river and its animated, traditional life.

Belem, a peaceful suburb 6km west of Rossio, is home to Lisbon's finest monument, the Mosteiro dos Jerónimos, and several other historical sights.

Saldanha district is around a kilometre northeast of Marquês de Pombal; it has a couple of great museums (p452) and a metro stop, but not much else.

### Maps

**Instituto Português de Cartográfia e Cadastro** (Map pp450–1; ☎ 213 819 600; ipcc@ipcc.pt; Rua Artilharia Um 107) Publishes and sells topographic maps.

---

**LISBON IN TWO DAYS**

Start at **Rossio**, then walk to **Alfama** (above) and the heady castle views there. Tram it back and on to the suburb of **Belém** (p452) and the **Mosteiro dos Jerónimos** (p452). Duck into **Confeitaria de Belém** (p456) for a custard tart (or three) and return via the **Museu de Arte Antiga** (p453).

Explore the **Bairro Alto** and **Chiado**, popping into the **Solar do Vinho do Porto** (above) for a port pick-me-up. Return to Baixa via the **Elevador da Glória** then bus or metro it to the **Museu Calouste Gulbenkian** (p452) and Centro de Arte Moderna (p452) for the rest of the day.

---

## INFORMATION
### Bookshops

**The English Bookshop** (Map pp454–5; ☎ 213 428 472; Rua do S. Marçal 83) Has a vast choice of English books ranging from blockbusters to the classics.

**Livraria Buchholz** (Map pp450–1; Rua Duque de Palmela 4) Has multilingual literature, including English, French and German.

### Internet Access

**Great Western** (Map pp454–5; ☎ 213 431 004; Rua das Portas de Santo Antão 54; ⏰ 9am–10pm Mon–Fri, 10am–7pm Sat & Sun)

**Lisboa Welcome Center** (Map pp454–5; ☎ 210 312 810; 2nd fl Praça do Comércio; ⏰ 9am–8pm)

**Web Café** (Map pp454–5; ☎ 213 421 181; Rua do Diário de Notícias 126; ⏰ 4pm–2am)

### Medical Services

**British Hospital** (Map pp450–1; ☎ 213 955 067; Rua Saraiva de Carvalho 49) English-speaking staff.

### Money

**Cota Câmbios** (Map pp454–5; ☎ 213 220 470; Rossio 41; ⏰ 8am–10pm) One of the best exchange rates in town, hence the queue.

**Top Atlântico** (Map pp450–1; ☎ 213 108 800; Avenida Duque de Loulé 108; ⏰ 9am–8pm Mon–Fri) Commission-free currency exchange for AMEX cardholders, help with lost cards or cheques.

### Post

**Main post office** (Map pp454–5; Praça do Comércio; ⏰ 8.30am–6.30pm Mon–Fri, 9am–noon Sat) Handles poste restante collection.

**Post office** (Map pp454–5; Praça dos Restauradores; ⏰ 8am–8pm Mon–Fri, 9am–noon Sat) This second branch is opposite the ICEP tourist office.

### Telephone

**Portugal Telecom** (Map pp454–5; Rossio 68; ⏰ 8am–11pm) Telephone booths and phonecards for sale.

### Tourist Information

**Ask Me Lisboa kiosks** Palácio Foz (Map pp454–5; ☎ 213 463 314); Santa Apolónia train station (Map pp450–1; ☎ 218 821 606); Belém (Map pp450–1; ☎ 213 658 435); Lisbon airport (Map pp450–1; ☎ 218 450 660; ⏰ 6am–midnight). All kiosks have free maps, the bimonthly guide *Follow Me Lisboa* and sell the Lisboa Card (see the boxed text p452).

**Gay & Lesbian Community Center** (Centro Comunitário Gay e Lésbico de Lisboa; Map pp454–5; ☎ 218 873 918; Rua de São Lazaro 88; ⏰ 5–9pm) Has gay-friendly info on bars, restaurants and clubs. Also check websites: www.ilga-portugal.org and www.portugalgay.pt.

# LISBON

**A**     **B**     **C**     **D**

**1**

To Torres
Vedras (40km);
Caldas da Rainha
(88km)

IC1

Campo
Grande Ⓜ

Pontinha Ⓜ

Carnide Ⓜ

Avenida General Norton de Matos

**2**

Colégio
Militar-Luz
38 Ⓜ

Alameda da
Universidade

Av Lusíada

Alto dos
Moinhos Ⓜ

To Queluz (5km);
Almornos (20km);
Sintra (28km)

Cidade
Universitária Ⓜ

Laranjeiras Ⓜ

IC19

Avenida das Forças Armadas

**3**

Aqueduto das Águas Livres

Jardim
Zoológico Ⓜ

14

Parque
Florestal
de Monsanto

Praça de Espanha Ⓜ

17
15

São Sebastião Ⓜ

N117

Campolide

**4**

27

CRIL-IC17

A5-IC15

9

Av Eng Duarte Pacheco

37

Mãe
d'Água

To Estoril (23km);
Cascais (26km)

Estrada do Alvito

Estrada do Penedo

Rato Ⓜ

26

5

13

Av da Ponte

Av de Ceuta

11

10

**5**

Av das Descobertas

Restelo

Alcântara

Estrela

7

Av da Ilha da Madeira

Rua do Alto
do Duque

Lapa

Ajuda

20

Calçada da Ajuda

To Cruz
Quebrada (3km);
Oeiras (9km);
Estoril (20km);
Cascais (23km)

Av do Restelo

Alcântara-Mar
Train Station

34

35

Doca de Alcântara

Belém

16

30

42

**6**

18

Rua da Junqueira

19

29

Av de Brasília

Av da Índia

Ponte 25
de Abril

North South
Railway Line

25

To Trafaria
(3km)

To Porto
Brandão (1km)

To Setúbal (47km)

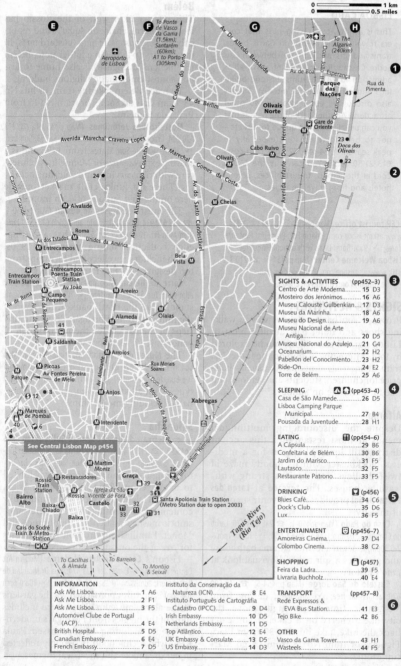

| 0 | 1 km |
| 0 | 0.5 miles |

To Ponte de Vasco da Gama (1.5km); Santarém (60km); A1 to Porto (305km)

Aeroporto de Lisboa

Av D. Alfredo Bensaúde

Av de Boa

To The Algarve (240km)

Parque das Nações

Rua da Pimenta

Av de Berlim

Olivais Norte

Gare do Oriente

Cabo Ruivo

Doca dos Olivais

Avenida Marechal Craveiro Lopes

Av Marechal Gomes da Costa

Olivais

Chelas

Alvalade

Roma

Unidos da América

Av dos Estados

Entrecampos

Bela Vista

Entrecampos Train Station

Entrecampos Poente Train Station

Av João

Campo Pequeno

Areeiro

Alameda

Olaias

Saldanha

Arroios

Picoas

Rua Morais Soares

Parque

Av Fontes Pereira de Melo

Anjos

Xabregas

Marquês de Pombal

Intendente

**See Central Lisbon Map p454**

Martim Moniz

Graça

Rossio Train Station

Restauradores

Igreja de São Vicente de Fora

Bairro Alto

Rossio

Baixa-Chiado

Castelo

Baixa

Santa Apolónia Train Station (Metro Station due to open 2003)

Cais do Sodré Train & Metro Station

Tagus River (Rio Tejo)

To Cacilhas & Almada

To Barreiro

To Montijo & Seixal

### SIGHTS & ACTIVITIES (pp452–3)
| | |
|---|---|
| Centro de Arte Moderna | 15 D3 |
| Mosteiro dos Jerónimos | 16 A6 |
| Museu Calouste Gulbenkian | 17 D3 |
| Museu da Marinha | 18 A6 |
| Museu do Design | 19 A6 |
| Museu Nacional de Arte Antiga | 20 D5 |
| Museu Nacional do Azulejo | 21 G4 |
| Oceanarium | 22 H2 |
| Pabellón del Conocimiento | 23 H2 |
| Ride-On | 24 E2 |
| Torre de Belém | 25 A6 |

### SLEEPING (pp453–4)
| | |
|---|---|
| Casa de São Mamede | 26 D5 |
| Lisboa Camping Parque Municipal | 27 B4 |
| Pousada da Juventude | 28 H1 |

### EATING (pp454–6)
| | |
|---|---|
| A Cápsula | 29 B6 |
| Confeitaria de Belém | 30 B6 |
| Jardim do Marisco | 31 F5 |
| Lautasco | 32 F5 |
| Restaurante Patrono | 33 F5 |

### DRINKING (p456)
| | |
|---|---|
| Blues Café | 34 C6 |
| Dock's Club | 35 D6 |
| Lux | 36 F5 |

### ENTERTAINMENT (pp456–7)
| | |
|---|---|
| Amoreiras Cinema | 37 D4 |
| Colombo Cinema | 38 C2 |

### SHOPPING (p457)
| | |
|---|---|
| Feira da Ladra | 39 F5 |
| Livraria Buchholz | 40 E4 |

### TRANSPORT (pp457–8)
| | |
|---|---|
| Rede Expressos & EVA Bus Station | 41 E3 |
| Tejo Bike | 42 B6 |

### OTHER
| | |
|---|---|
| Vasco da Gama Tower | 43 H1 |
| Wasteels | 44 F5 |

### INFORMATION
| | |
|---|---|
| Ask Me Lisboa | 1 A6 |
| Ask Me Lisboa | 2 F1 |
| Ask Me Lisboa | 3 F5 |
| Automóvel Clube de Portugal (ACP) | 4 E4 |
| British Hospital | 5 D5 |
| Canadian Embassy | 6 E4 |
| French Embassy | 7 D5 |
| Instituto da Conservação da Natureza (ICN) | 8 E4 |
| Instituto Português de Cartográfia Cadastro (IPCC) | 9 D4 |
| Irish Embassy | 10 D5 |
| Netherland Embassy | 11 D5 |
| Top Atlántico | 12 E4 |
| UK Embassy & Consulate | 13 D5 |
| US Embassy | 14 D3 |

**LISBOA CARD**

This is a nifty, cost-saving pass that covers travel on the metro, on Carris buses, trams and lifts, and on trains between Cais Sodre, Cascais, Rossio and Sintra, as well as admission to 28 museums, historic buildings and other places of interest. There's also discounted entry to about 40 other attractions. Another perk of the pass is that you can usually skip the queue for tickets – not to be underestimated, especially in peak season. A 24-/48-/72 hour card costs €13/21.50/26.55. You can buy the *Lisboa Card* at the airport, tourist offices, several hotels and from travel agencies.

**ICEP tourist office** (Map pp454-5; ☎ 213 463 314; www.askmelisboa.com; Palácio Foz, Praça dos Restauradores; ☽ 9am-8pm) Deals with national inquiries.
**Lisboa Welcome Center** (Map pp454-5; ☎ 210 312 810; www.visitlisboa.com; Praça do Comércio; ☽ 9am-8pm) Concentrates on Lisbon.

## SIGHTS & ACTIVITIES

Provided you have a pair of sturdy walking shoes and don't balk at hills, most of Lisbon's grand-slam sights can be explored by foot. Alternatively, hop on the funicular, tram or metro. Admission is usually half-price for children, students and seniors, and free for everyone on Sundays.

### Alfama

Despite the discouraging multilingual menus at most restaurants, this ancient district still looks like a set for a medieval blockbuster with its moody maze of twisted alleys and ancient strung-with-washing houses. The terrace at **Largo das Portas do Sol** provides *the* souvenir snapshot of the city.

**Casa do Fado** (Map pp450-1; ☎ 218 823 470; Largo do Chafariz de Dentro 1; admission €2.50; ☽ 10am-1pm & 2-5.30pm) is set in a former Alfama bathhouse and provides a spirited audiovisual look at *fado*'s history.

**Castelo de São Jorge** (Map pp454-5; ☎ 218 800 620; admission free; ☽ 9am-6pm), dating from Visigothic times, sits high above the city like a cherry on a cake. If you can't hack the hike, take bus No 37 from Plaça Figueira or tram No 28 from Largo Martim Moniz.

### Belém

This quarter 6km west of the Rossio has loads of charm, chairs on squares and reputedly the best *pasteis de nata* (custard tarts) in the country (p456). On a loftier note, Belém (Bethlehem in English) is also home to Lisbon's most emblematic religious building.

To reach Belém take the train, or bus No 43, from Cais do Sodré, or tram No 15 from Praça da Figueira.

**Mosteiro dos Jerónimos** (Map pp450-1; ☎ 213 620 034; Praça do Império; admission Tue-Sat €3, Sun free; ☽ 10am-5pm Tue-Sun) dates from 1496 and is a soaring extravaganza of Manueline architecture with rich carvings and stunning *azuelejos*. There's a funky craft market outside here on the first Sunday of each month.

The must-see **Museu do design** (Map pp450-1; ☎ 213 612 934; Praça do Império; admission €3; ☽ 11am-8pm Mon-Fri, 10am-7pm Sat & Sun) has a cutting-edge collection dating from the 1930s, which includes jewellery and furniture from top design gurus like Philippe Starck.

**Torre de Belém** (Map pp450-1; ☎ 213 620 034; admission Tue-Sat €3, Sun free; ☽ 10am-5pm Tue-Sun), standing on the north bank of the river, is *the* tourist icon of Portugal. Brave the tiny steps of the turrets for the natural high of panoramic views from the top.

The **Museu da Marinha** (Maritime Museum; Map pp450-1; ☎ 213 620 019; admission €3; ☽ 10am-6pm Tue-Sun, to 5pm winter) is a winner for nautical types, with all kinds of seafaring paraphernalia, including model ships.

### Saldanha

The celebrated **Museu Calouste Gulbenkian** (Map pp450-1; ☎ 217 823 461; Ave de Berna 45; admission Tue-Sat €3, Sun free; ☽ 10am-6pm Tue-Sun) has an astounding collection that formerly belonged to an oil tycoon. There are Egyptian, Asian, Greek and Islamic artefacts and wonderfully contemplative paintings by such beret-and-smock masters as Renoir, Rembrandt and Monet. Families can drop off their kiddies for *free* at the on-site childcare centre.

Lisbon's **Centro de Arte Moderna** (Modern Art Centre; Map pp450-1; ☎ 217 823 474; Rua Dr Nicaulau de Bettencourt; admission Tue-Sat €3, Sun free; ☽ 10am-6pm Tue-Sun) is prettily approached via the gardens of the above museum. The centre includes most of the biggies from Portugal's modern-art scene, including London-based Paula Rego whose childhood is strongly reflected in her dreamlike and theatrical themes.

PORTUGAL

## Museums

The following two museums are away from the centre, but well worth the detour time.

The **Museu Nacional do Azulejo** (Map pp450-1; ☎ 218 100 340; Rua Madre de Deus 4; admission €2.50, Sun free; ⊙ 10am-6pm Wed-Sun, 2-6pm Tue) has an evocative 17th-century convent setting, plus magnificent display of tiles, including a 36m panel of Lisbon dating from 1730.

The **Museu Nacional de Arte Antiga** (Ancient Art Museum; Map pp450-1; ☎ 213 962 825; Rua das Janelas Verdes; admission €3, 10am-2pm Sun free; ⊙ 10am-5pm Wed-Sun, 2-6pm Tue) houses a beautifully displayed collection of works by Portuguese painters.

## Parque das Nações

The former Expo '98 site, a revitalised 2km-long waterfront area in the northeast, has a range of attractions, including Europe's biggest **Oceanarium** (Map pp450-1; ☎ 218 917 002; adult/child €9/4.50; ⊙ 10am-7pm) and a **Pabellón del Conocimiento** (Living Science Centre; Map pp450-1; ☎ 218 917 100; adult/child €5/2.50; ⊙ 10am-7pm) with over 300 interactive exhibits for kids of all ages. Take the metro to Oriente station – an equally impressive Expo project.

## Alcântara

The old wharves have been slickly revamped into a swanky strip of bars and restaurants with tables sprawling out onto the promenade. After your blow-out brunch, enjoy the half-hour waterfront stroll to Belém.

## TOURS

**Carris** (Map pp454-5; ☎ 966 298 558; Praça da Figueira; adult/child from €13/6.50) offers various bus, tram and walking tours. **Transtejo** (Map pp454-5; Terreiro do Paço ferry terminal; ☎ 218 820 348; adult/child €15/8; ⊙ Mar-Oct) runs cruises on the Tagus. There are great views of the city from this watery perspective.

## FESTIVALS

The **Festa do Santo António** (Festival of Saint Anthony) fills the streets of Lisbon on 13 June.

## SLEEPING
### Budget

**Lisboa Camping Parque Municipal** (Map pp450-1; ☎ 217 623 100; Parque Florestal de Monsanto; camp sites €5) This is a well-treed spot 6km northwest of town. Take bus No 43 from Cais do Sodré.

**Pensão Tomar** (Map pp454-5; ☎ 218 888 484; Poço do Borraté; s/d €20/30) High ceilings, large rooms and chandeliers equal swish surrounds for a bargain-basement price.

**Pensão Globo** (Map pp454-5; ☎ 213 462 279; www .pglobo.com; Rua do Teixeira 37; d from €30) No-frills with a range of prices, although you need a mountaineering degree to reach the best rooms at the top with their vast windows overlooking the leafy street.

**Pousada da Juventude** (Map pp450-1; ☎ 218 920 890; Via de Moscavide; dm/d €13/35) Pick-of-the-hostel bunch with a welcoming vibe and well-maintained rooms.

**Pensão Prata** (Map pp454-5; ☎ 213 468 908; 3rd fl Rua da Prata 71; s/d €20/35) Bland and institutional but very central if all you're looking for is a cheap sleep.

**Pensão Imperial** (Map pp454-5; ☎ 213 420 166; 4th fl Praça dos Restauradores 78; d €35) Charismatic owner and spotless comfortably worn rooms overlooking the city's main square.

Also recommended is **Pensão Norte** (Map pp454-5; ☎ 218 878 941; 2nd fl, Rua dos Douradores 159; d €35).

### Mid-Range

**Residencial Florescente** (Map pp454-5; ☎ 213 463 517; www.residencialflorescente.com; Rua Portas de Santo Antão 99; s/d €45/55; 🖳 ) Comfortable hotel on pedestrian cobbles a short suitcase trundle from the Praça dos Restauradores underground car park. Rooms are light and bright.

**Pensão Residencial Gerês** (Map pp454-5; ☎ 218 810 497; www.pensaogeres.web.pt; Calçada do Garcia 6; s/d €50/60) Religious pics, traditional tiles and carpeted comfy rooms. Go for corner room number 104 with its five-star view.

**Pensão Londres** (Map pp454-5; ☎ 213 462 203; Rua Dom Pedro V 53; s/d €50/65) Old-fashioned appeal with high-ceilinged and large, carpeted rooms that have small balconies with neck-craning views of this bustling tree-lined street.

**Sé Guest House** (Map pp454-5; ☎ 218 864 400; 2nd fl Rua São João da Praça 97; s/d €40/70) Owner Luis is a traveller and cultural buff, hence the intriguing clutter of global artefacts and antiques throughout this historic, homy lodging.

### Top End

**Casa de São Mamede** (Map pp450-1; ☎ 213 963 166; fax 213 951 896; Rua Escola Politécnica 159; s/d €75/80; 🖳 ) A soothing stay in 18th-century surroundings; this former magistrate's house has gorgeous original tiles and antique-clad rooms.

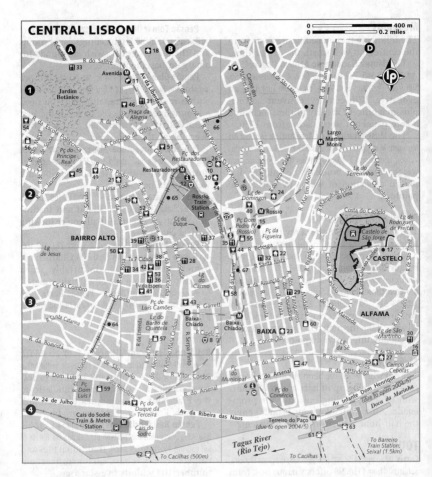

**CENTRAL LISBON**

**Hotel Britania**, (Map pp454-5; ☎ 213 155 016; www.heritage.pt; Rua Rodrigues Sampaio 17; s/d €146/156; 🗙 💻 Ⓟ) Classic Art Deco touches and massive luxury rooms in this go-for-the-splurge hotel a short walk from the centre.

## EATING

All ages and incomes socialise over food in Lisbon. Watch out for tourist rip-offs like some of the energetic stretch of restaurants on Baixa's Correeiros (that *is* how it is spelt). Seafood is widely available and locals have an insatiable appetite for all things Brazilian including *feijoada* (bean stew) – and the daily dose of soap operas. The Bairro Alto has good-value eateries while the Alfama has some of the most characterful

restaurants, but can be touristy on the main castle route. The main market, Mercado da Ribeira, is near Cais do Sodré station and a good central supermarket is **Pingo Doce** (Rua de Dezembro 73), with the Celeira Health Shop right next door.

### Baixa & Alfama

**Restaurante O Sol** (Map pp454-5; ☎ 213 471 944; Calçada do Duque 23; mains €4; 🕑 closed Sun) A rare fast-food vegetarian restaurant featuring outside seating, heady views and takeaways like soy burgers, pasties and seaweed-cannelloni.

**Gingvinga** (Map pp450-1; ☎ 218 850 377; Rua das Canastras 14; mains €6) Chow down on spicy African fare typical of Madagascar at this funky swing-a-cat-size restaurant with its suitably soul-searching surrounds.

**Nilo** (Map pp454-5; ☎ 213 467 014; Rua dos Correeiros 217; mains €6) No-frills Nilo is one of the better-priced eateries on this restaurant strip. The pork with spicy *piri-piri* is recommended.

**Restaurante Patrono** (Map pp450-1; ☎ 218 868 887; Largo Chafariz de Dentro 20; mains €7) Ideally situated for a spot of refuelling, this is one of the cheapest restaurants in the nucleus of eateries in the winding backstreets of Alfama. It's usually packed with cheerful locals feasting on such specialities as hearty *aroz detamboril* (stew of monkfish and rice).

**Gandhi Palace** (Map pp454-5; ☎ 218 873 839; Rua dos Douradores 214-216; mains €9) Good central choice for those suffering from curry-house withdrawal, and popular with intrepid Portuguese. If you like it hot, ask – local tastes are mild.

**Lautasco** (Map pp450-1; Beco do Azinhal 7-7A; mains €9; ☼ closed Sun; ☒) Full points for atmosphere with seating on a secluded square in the shade of a magnificent rubber tree. All the usual suspects are on the menu, including cod fritters and the ubiquitous *bacalhau*.

**Jardim do Marisco** (Map pp450-1; ☎ 218 824 242; Avenida Infante Dom Henrique, Doca Jardim do Tobaco; mains €10; ☒) A large, airy warehouse in a slick dock development on the river. The Spoilt-for-choice menu includes grilled meats, seafood and pasta, plus cut-price kiddie choices.

## Avenida de Liberdade

**Os Tibetanos** (Map pp454-5; ☎ 213 142 038; Rua do Salitre 117; mains from €6; ☼ closed Sat & Sun; ☒ ☒ ) Doubles as a Tibetan Buddhist school with Zen-style surroundings, leafy patio and diverse meatless menu; try the Japanese mushrooms with seaweed and tofu.

**La Caffé** (Map pp454-5; ☎ 213 256 736; Ave de Liberdade 129B; mains €8; ☼ 12.30-3.30pm & 8pm-11pm Tue-Sun; ☒) Upbeat décor plus free Internet, giant fashion TV screens and a creative twist on Med cuisine, like cream of parsnip soup with green apple, Roquefort and walnuts, and black spaghetti with smoked salmon.

## Bairro Alto & Saldanha

**Restaurante a Primavera** (Map pp454-5; ☎ 213 420 477; Travessa da Espera 34; mains from €6; ☒ ) Hugely popular with a homey informality. Try the clams in garlic and coriander followed by a girth-expanding creamy dessert.

**Cervejaria da Trindade** (Map pp454-5; ☎ 213 423 506; Rua Nova da Trindade 20-C; mains €7) This vaulted restaurant in a former convent has nothing-fancy food, but the setting, in a former convent with dazzling pictorial tilework, provides serious food for thought.

**Stravaganza** (Map pp454-5; ☎ 213 468 868; Rua do Grémio Lusitano 18; mains €7-10; ☒ ) A stylish Italian restaurant serving a better class of pizza and pasta, including seven vegetarian pasta choices. The goldfish bowls suspended on the wall are serious double-take stuff.

**Restaurante Sinal Vermelho** (Map pp454-5; ☎ 213 461 252; Rua das Gáveas 89; mains €8.50-11.50;

PORTUGAL

☺ closed Sat lunch & Sun; ☒ ) Elegant restaurant decorated with breezy-blue *azulejos* and shelves of dusty bottles. Menu is reassuringly traditional and generous with groaning plates of seafood, rice (and the like).

**Pap 'Acorda** (Map pp454-5; ☎ 213 464 811; Rua da Atalaia 57-59; mains €12-15; ☒ ) Lisbon luvvies lord it up in this former bakery now hung with thick curtains and chandeliers. The house speciality is various takes on *acorda*, a type of puree with lots of coriander and garlic.

## Belém

**Confeitaria de Belém** (Map pp450-1; ☎ 213 637 423; Rua de Belém 86-88) A classic tiled warren with reputedly the best *pasteis de nata* (custard tarts) in Portugal. Delicious!

**A Cápsula** (Map pp450-1; ☎ 213 648 768; Rua Vieira Portuense 72; mains €8; ☺ Wed-Sun) This popular meeting-and-greeting place serves simple calorie-stoking food including Brazilian steak with rice and beans.

## DRINKING

Lisbon is great if you suffer a perpetual sugar low with fabulous Art-Deco cafés particularly around Bairro Alto and Rossio. The Alcântara and Oriente area bars attract a well-heeled set while Alfama has plenty of gluggable choices, including moody low-lit places for locked-eyes-over-cocktails types. Gay and lesbian bars are mainly concentrated around the Príncipe Real area.

**Café Nicola** (Map pp454-5; ☎ 213 460 579; Rossio 24; ☺ closed Sat pm & Sun) This sumptuous Art Deco café is past winner of the Café of the Year award.

**Martinho da Arcada** (Map pp454-5; ☎ 218 879 259; Praça do Comércio 3; ☺ closed Sun) Former haunt of writer Pessoa; grab a coffee and head for an outdoor table under the arches.

**Café a Brasileira** (Map pp454-5; ☎ 213 469 547; Rua Garrett 120) Another historic watering hole for Lisbon's 19th-century greats with warm wooden innards and a busy counter serving daytime coffees and pints at night.

**A Ginjinha** (Map pp454-5; Largo de Domingos) Titchy, crusty local specialising in powerful *ginjinha* (cherry brandy).

**Solar do Vinho do Porto** (Map pp454-5; ☎ 213 475 707; Rua de São Pedro de Alcântara 45; ☺ closed Sun) While away an evening in soft chairs with a lengthy list of white and red ports.

**Pavilhão Chines** (Map pp454-5; ☎ 213 424 729; Rua Dom Pedro V 89) A global mishmash of bizarre ornaments, including a roomful of war helmets, and legendary cocktails.

## ENTERTAINMENT

Pick up the free monthly *Follow me Lisboa, Agenda Cultural Lisboa* or quarterly *Lisboa Step By Step* from the tourist office for what's on listings. Also, check out www.visitlisboa.com (Lisbon tourist office website), www.lisboacultural.pt (cultural events) and www.ticketline.pt (concert info and reservations).

## Live Music

**Adega Machado** (Map pp454-5; ☎ 213 224 640; Rua do Norte 91; ☺ 8pm-3am, closed Mon) Earthy and authentic, run by Rita, goddaughter of the legendary Amalia Rodrigues; the walls are papered with signed photos of *fado* enthusiasts – including Kirk Douglas.

**Adega do Ribatejo** (Map pp454-5; ☎ 213 468 343; Rua Diário de Notícias 23; ☺ 8pm-2am) High on atmosphere with nightly *fado*.

**Hot Clube de Portugal** (Map pp454-5; ☎ 213 467 369; Praça da Alegria 39; ☺ 10pm-2am, closed Sun & Mon) Hot, sweaty and packed with nightly gigs and raw new jazz sounds.

**Ó Gilíns Irish Pub** (Map pp454-5; ☎ 213 421 899; Rua dos Remolares 8-10; ☺ 11am-2am) Predictable blarney atmosphere with live music on Friday and Saturday evenings.

**Tertúlia** (Map pp454-5; ☎ 213 462 704; Rua do Dia'rio de Noticias 60; ☺ 8pm-2am Mon-Sun) Low-lit bar with newspapers, live jazz, exhibitions and – for those who can't resist a tinkle – a piano for customer use.

## Nightclubs

**Lux** (Map pp450-1; ☎ 218 820 890; Armazém A, Cais da Pedra; ☺ midnight-5am) Part-owned by John Malkovich, it's a trendy beat-happy club with towering ceilings, river-side terraces and dance floors.

**Dock's Club** (Map pp450-1; ☎ 213 950 856; Rua da Cintura do Porto de Lisboa 226; ☺ 11pm-6am Tue-Sat) Another river-side dance temple attracting a voguish clientele.

**Blues Café** (Map pp450-1; ☎ 213 957 085; Rua da Cintura do Porto; ☺ 11pm-6am Tue-Sat) Jazz, blues and club nights, plus dock-side drinking in cool warehouse development.

**Ritz Club** (Map pp454-5; ☎ 213 425 140; Rua da Glória 57; ☺ 9pm-3am) The city's largest African club, it's an atmospheric place with pulsating music and a friendly vibe.

## Gay & Lesbian Venues

Lisbon has a relaxed yet flourishing gay scene, with an annual Gay Pride Festival at the end of June.

**Portas Largas** (Map pp454-5; ☎ 218 461 379; Rua da Atalaia 105) A tiled bar with barn-size doors attracting a mainly gay crowd with its giant carafes of sangria.

**Trumps** (Map pp454-5; Rua da Imprensa Nacional 104B) Not much elbow space in these two bars; one has a dance floor to get jiggy.

**Finalmente** (Map pp454-5; Rua da Palmeira 38) A heaving dance floor and nightly drag shows.

## Cinemas

Lisbon has dozens of cinemas, including the multiscreen **Amoreiras** (Map pp450-1; ☎ 213 878 752) and **Colombo** (Map pp450-1; ☎ 217 113 222), both located within shopping centres.

## Sport

Lisbon's football teams are Benfica, Belenenses and Sporting. Preparations for Euro 2004 led to the upgrading of the 65,000-seat Esta'dio da Luz and the construction of a new 54,000-seat Estadio Nacional. Bullfights are staged at Campo Pequeno between April and October. Tickets for both are available at **ABEP ticket agency** (Map pp454-5; Praça dos Restauradores). The tourist office can help with transport and locations of the city's stadia.

## SHOPPING

One of the delights of shopping in Lisbon is exploring the idiosyncratic small shops. Many have remained in the same family for generations (personalised service). In contrast, the shopping malls are packed with glossy new boutiques, familiar chains and snack bars for those shopping on the go. Antique shops are mainly in the Barro Alto district. Hand-painted ceramics are found around Baixa and Chiado. Don't miss the flea market **Feira da Ladra** (Map pp450-1; Campo de Santa Clara; ☼ Tue & Sat). For designer boutiques take a high-heeled strut down swanky Rua Garrett.

**Grandes Armazens do Chiado** (Map pp454-5; Rua do Carmo) is artfully concealed behind the restored façade of the historic main department store. FNAC is good for electronic items, music and booking concert tickets.

**Fabrica Sant'Ana** (Map pp454-5; Rua do Alecrim 95) and **Santos Ofícios** (Map pp454-5; Rua da Madalena 87) are touristy but have an eclectic range of Portuguese folk art.

## GETTING THERE & AWAY

### Air

Lisbon is connected by daily flights to Porto, Faro and many European centres. For arrival and departure information call ☎ 218 413 700.

### Bus

A dozen companies, including **Renex** (☎ 222 003 395), operate from Gare do Oriente. The Arco do Cego terminal is the base for **Rede Expressos** (☎ 707 223 344) and **EVA** (☎ 213 147 710), whose networks cover the whole country.

### Train

**Santa Apolónia station** (Map pp450-1; ☎ 218 816 121) is the terminus for northern and central Portugal, and for all international services (trains also stop en route at the better connected Gare do Oriente). Cais do Sodré station is for Belém, Cascais and Estoril. Rossio station serves Sintra.

Barreiro station, which is across the river, is the terminus for southern Portugal; connecting ferries leave frequently from the pier at Terréiro do Paço.

The north–south railway line, over the Ponte de 25 Abril, goes to suburban areas and will eventually carry on further to southern Portugal.

For more detailed information on all above modes of transport see p478.

## GETTING AROUND

### To/From the Airport

The AeroBus runs every 20 minutes from 7.45am to 8.45pm, taking 30 to 45 minutes between the airport and Cais do Sodré, including a stop by the ICEP tourist office. A €2.35/5.50 ticket is good for one/three days on all buses, trams and funiculars. Local bus Nos 44 and 45 also run near the ICEP tourist office; No 44 links the airport with Gare do Oriente too. A taxi into town is about €10, plus €1.50 for luggage.

### Bicycle

**Tejo Bike** (Map pp450-1; ☎ 218 871 976), 300m east of Belém, rents out bicycles for €5 an hour to ride along the waterfront.

### Car & Motorcycle

Car rental companies at Lisbon airport include **Avis** (☎ 800 201 002; www.avis.com), **Europcar** (☎ 218 410 163; www.europcar.com) or the nearby (and cheaper) **Ride-On** ( ☎ 218 452 811; Rua Reinaldo Ferreira 29; ride_on@netcabo.pt). The most central underground car park is at Praça dos Restauradores, costing around €0.75 an hour. There are cheaper (or free) car parks near Parque das Nações or Belém, from where you can catch a bus or tram to the centre.

## Public Transport

### BUS & TRAM
Two-journey bus or tram tickets are €0.93 from Carris kiosks, most conveniently at Praça da Figueira and the Santa Justa Elevador, or €0.90 per ride from the driver. A one-/four-/seven-day Passe Turístico, valid for trams, buses and the metro, costs €2.55/9.25/13.10. The Lisboa Card enables unlimited travel on city transport (see p452).

Buses and trams run from 6am to 1am, with some night services. Pick up a transport map from tourist offices or Carris kiosks.

### FERRY
Cais da Alfândega is the terminal for several ferries, including to Cacilhas (€0.60), a transfer point for some buses to Setúbal. A car (and bike) ferry runs from Cais do Sodré terminal.

### METRO
The metro is useful for hops across town and to the Parque das Nações. Individual tickets cost €0.65; a caderneta of 10 tickets is €6. A return ticket (allé et retour) is €1.20. The metro operates from 6.30am to 1am.

## Taxi
Lisbon's taxis are metered and best hired from taxi ranks. Confusingly, when the green light is on, it means the taxi is already occupied. Some at the airport are less than scrupulous. From the Rossio to Belém is around €6 and to the castle about €4.50.

## AROUND LISBON

### Sintra
pop 20,000

This hilltop town, less than an hour west of Lisbon, has traditionally been the holiday home for royalty, the rich and the famous. With stunning palaces and manors surrounded by lush green countryside it is a captivating camera-clicking place. Word is out, so visit out of season if you can.

The **tourist office** ( ☎ 219 231 157; www.cm-sintra.pt; Praça da República 23; � 9am-7pm) sells tourist passes and has a list of accommodation. Check your emails at the **Internet Lounge** ( ☎ 219 109 078; Rua Dr Alfredo da Costa 76; � 10.30am-midnight Mon-Fri, 11.30am-11pm Sat, 12.30am-10pm Sun) near the centre.

### SIGHTS
Although the whole town resembles a historical theme park, there are several compulsory eye-catching sights. Most are free or discounted with the Lisboa Card (see boxed text p452); pensioners, students and children pay half-price.

The **Palácio Nacional de Sintra** ( ☎ 219 106 840; admission €3; � 10am-5.30pm Thu-Tue) is a dizzy mix of Moorish and Gothic architecture with twin chimneys that dominate the town.

The **Museu do Brinquedo** ( ☎ 219 242 172; Rua Visconde de Monserrate; admission €3; � 10am-6pm Tue-Sun) offers serious playtime stuff with 20,000 toys from all over the world.

An energetic 3km greenery-flanked hike from the centre, the 8th-century ruined ramparts of **Castelo dos Mouros** ( ☎ 219 237 300; admission €3; � 9am-7pm) provide fine views.

Trudge on for 20 minutes more to the exuberantly kitsch **Palácio da Pena** ( ☎ 219 105 340; admission €6; � 10am-5.30pm Tue-Sun). Alternatively take the cop-out bus No 434 (€3.20) from the station, via the tourist office.

**Monserrate Gardens** ( ☎ 219 237 116; admission €3; � 9am-7pm) are fabulously lush botanical gardens 4km from town.

En route to the gardens is **Quinta da Regaleira** ( ☎ 219 106 650; admission €10; � 10am-6pm, to 3.30pm winter), a World Heritage site. Visits to this extraordinary mansion must be pre-arranged.

### SLEEPING
**Residencial Adelaide** ( ☎ 219 230 873; Rua Guilherme Gomes Fernandes 11; d from €25) Some paint could do wonders for this great-value accommodation, 10-minutes from the centre, with its pretty garden and large, well-worn rooms.

**Estrada Velha** ( ☎ 219 234 355; Consiglieri Pedroso 16; s/d €40/50; ⚒ ) Just five meticulously decorated rooms with wood-panelling and wrought-iron beds; the downstairs bar-restaurant is excellent for light tasty fare like sweet and savoury crepes.

**Lawrence's Hotel** ( ☎ 219 105 500; www.lawrenceshotel.com; Rua Consiglieri Pedroso 38-40; s/d €180/235; P ⚒ ▯ ) Shift your credit card into overdrive to stay at Iberia's oldest hotel, certainly vintage enough to have bedded Lord Byron and William Beckford, and more recently revamped to five-star luxury by its Dutch owners.

### EATING
**Xentra** ( ☎ 219 240 759; Rua Consiglieri Pedroso 2-A; mains €6) Has a beamed cavernous bar and restaurant, rock music on Sunday nights and karaoke on Mondays.

**Tulhas** ( ☎ 219 232 378; Rua Gil Vicente 4-6; mains €7) Typically full of happily chomping locals, it dishes up comfort food like *bacalhau* with cream and at least one vegetarian dish in rustic surrounds.

### GETTING THERE & AWAY
The Lisbon–Sintra railway terminates in Estefânia, 1.5km northeast of the town's historic centre. Sintra's bus station, and another train station, are a further 1km east in the new-town district of Portela de Sintra. Frequent shuttle buses run to the historic centre from the bus station.

Trains run every 15 minutes from Lisbon's Rossio station (€1.30, 45 minutes). Buses run hourly from Sintra to Estoril (€2.50, 40 minutes) and Cascais (€2.50, 45 minutes).

### GETTING AROUND
A taxi to Pena or Monserrate costs around €10 return. Horse-drawn carriages are a spoil-her-rotten alternative: expect €55 to get to Monserrate and back. Old trams run from Ribeira de Sintra (1.5km from the centre) to Praia das Maças, 12km to the west.

## Cascais
**pop 30,000**
Cascais has grown from a fishing village into a sunbed-and-sandcastle resort that is packed in summer. The **tourist office** ( ☎ 214 868 204; www.estorilcoast-tourism.com; Rua Visconde de Luz 14; ☼ 9am-7pm Mon-Fri Sep-Jun, 9am-8pm Mon-Fri Jul-Aug, 10am-6pm Sat & Sun year-round) has accommodation lists and bus timetables; there's also a **tourist police post** ( ☎ 214 863 929). You can slurp a soft drink while checking your emails at **Golfinho** ( ☎ 214 840 150; Sebastião Carvalho e Melo 17; ☼ 10am-midnight Mon-Sat May-Sep, 10am-8pm Mon-Sat Oct-Apr).

### SIGHTS & ACTIVITIES
**Estoril** is an old-fashioned resort 2km east of Cascais with a superb sandy beach and

Europe's largest **casino** ( ☎ 214 667 700; www.casino-estoril.pt, in Portuguese; ☼ 3pm-3am, fl show 11pm).

**Praia Tamariz** has an ocean swimming pool. The sea roars into the coast at **Boca do Inferno** (Hell's Mouth) 2km west of Cascais. Spectacular **Cabo da Roca**, Europe's westernmost point, is 16km from Cascais and Sintra (served by buses from both towns). Wild **Guincho** beach, 3km from Cascais, is a popular surfing venue.

### SLEEPING & EATING
**Residencial Avenida** ( ☎ 214 864 417; Rua da Palmeira 14; d €30) This sparkling clean, well-placed accommodation efficiently run by English-speaking owners.

**Casa da Pergola** ( ☎ 214 840 040; www.ciberguia .pt/casa-da-pergola; Avenida Valbom 13; d €99; ☒ ) Well worth the splurge, this elegant 19th-century home is tastefully done up with expensive art and antiques. Enjoy breakfast and birdsong in the pretty garden.

**Dom Grelhas** ( ☎ 214 839 963; Rua Sebastião J C Melo 35, Casa da Guia; mains €8) On the way to Guincho, Casa da Guia is a fashionable small complex of edgy boutiques, art galleries, bars and restaurants, including this one with healthy salad and seafood choices accompanied by seamless sea views.

### GETTING THERE & AROUND
Trains run frequently to Cascais, via Estoril (€1.30, 30 minutes) from Cais do Sodré station in Lisbon. **Transrent** ( ☎ 214 864 566; www .transrent.pt; Centro Commercial Cisne, Avenida Marginal) rents cars, bicycles and motorcycles.

## Setúbal
**pop 110,500**
Portugal's third-largest port has a stunning church, a spectacular castle and a largely pedestrianised centre packed with good-looking shops and cafés. Pity about the in-your-face piped music over the city sound system. The municipal **tourist office** ( ☎ /fax 265 534 402; Praça do Quebedo; ☼ 9am-7pm) is a five-minute walk east from the **bus station** (Avenida 5 de Outubro). There's also a **regional tourist office** ( ☎ 265 539 130; www.mun-setubal.pt; Travessa Frei Gaspar 10) with the oddity of a Roman fish-preserving factory under its glass floor. The **Instituto Português da Juventude** (IPJ; ☎ 265 534 431; Largo José Afonso) has free Internet access for limited periods on weekdays.

PORTUGAL

## SIGHTS & ACTIVITIES

Portugal's first Manueline building, the stunning **Igreja de Jesus** (Praça Miguel Bombarda) has maritime motifs and twisted pillars that resemble coiled ropes. The **Galeria da Pintura Quinhentista** (admission free; ⊙ 9am-noon & 2-5pm Tue-Sat), around the corner, has a renowned collection of 16th-century paintings.

Good **beaches** west of town include Praia da Figuerinha (accessible by bus in summer). Across the estuary at Tróia is a more developed beach, plus the ruins of a Roman settlement. On the ferry trip across you may see some of the estuary's 30 or so bottlenosed dolphins.

**SAL** ( ☎ 265 227 685; www.sal.pt, in Portuguese; ⊙ Sat) organises walks from €5 per person. For jeep safaris, hiking and biking in the Serra da Arrábida, or canoe trips through the Reserva Natural do Estuário do Sado, contact **Planeta Terra** ( ☎ 919 471 871; Praça General Luís Domingues 9). **Vertigem Azul** ( ☎ 265 238 000; www.vertigemazul.com; Avenida Luísa Todi 375) offers canoe and dolphin-spotting excursions.

## SLEEPING

**Pousada da Juventude** ( ☎ 265 534 431; setubal@movijovem.pt; Largo José Afonso; dm/d €11/35) Well-equipped hostel with a buzzy vibe.

**Pensão Bom Regresso** ( ☎ 265 229 812; Praça de Bocage 48; d €40) Overlooks the main square; about as close to church as you can get without attending confession. Rooms are clean but monastically basic.

**Bom Amigo** ( ☎ 265 526 290; Rua do Concelho 7; s/d €36/48) Pristine, down to the freshly dusted plastic flowers. Room 4 has great contemplative views of the plaza.

## EATING

**O Beco** ( ☎ 265 524 617; Largo da Misericordia 24; mains €10) Locals rate this restaurant as one of the city's best. Go for one of the cockle dishes for that special seafood moment.

**Peregrina** ( ☎ 265 230 602; Rua dos Almocreves 74; mains €10) One of three vegetarian restaurants in town, although all close at an unsociable 6pm. Quiche, *seitan* (wheat gluten), nut rissoles and more salads than you can shake a carrot stick at.

**Xica Bia** ( ☎ 265 522 559; Ave Luisa Todi 131; mains from €10) Dinner-for-two setting with barrel-vault brick ceiling, candles and a wallet-slimming menu of dishes. Try the *arroz de marisco* (shellfish rice).

## GETTING THERE & AWAY

Buses leave every half-hour from Lisbon's Praça de Espanha (€3.10, one hour). Ferries shuttle across the estuary to Tróia roughly every 45 minutes (€1.10, 15 minutes).

# THE ALGARVE

The Algarve is popular not only as a sun-and-sea holiday resort, but also for an increasing number of permanent residents, particularly from Germany and the UK. While this may sound depressing, the good news is that away from the coastal strip (and the golf courses) you are back in Portugal again with attractions that include the forested slopes of Monchique, the fortified village of Silves and windswept, historic Sagres. Faro is the regional capital.

## Getting There & Around

**Air Portugal** (TAP; ☎ 707 205 700; www.tap.pt) has daily Lisbon–Faro flights (under an hour) year-round.

There is no direct rail link from Lisbon to the Algarve. There are some regional services but these are generally slower than the long-distance buses. For drivers a speedy 235km toll road (around €20) links Lisbon with the Algarve.

**EVA** ( ☎ 289 899 740) and **Rede Expressos** ( ☎ 289 899 760) operate frequent and efficient bus services between Lisbon and major cities and various Algarve resorts. The IP1/EO1 super highway runs the length of the coast.

Bicycles, scooters and motorcycles can be rented everywhere; see town listings or check the nearest tourist office.

## FARO

pop 45,000

Aside from midsummer when it is heaving, with no towel space on the beach, Faro is

---

### WINES OF THE ALGARVE

The Algarve has long been a prime wine-making area with about 40,000 vineyards at last count. The sunshine, rich soil and high-quality vines produce full-bodied excellent wines. The whites are traditionally very dry, the reds light and young. The best known wines come from the Lagoa area.

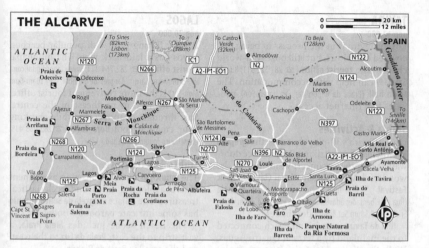

**THE ALGARVE**

pleasantly low-key, as well as being the main transport hub and commercial centre

## Information
Expat-oriented, English-language newspapers with entertainment information include the *Algarve Good Life* and *The Resident*.

Go online at the good, central **Self-Service Internet** (☎ 289 873 731; Largo Pé da Cruz 1; closed Sun).

The central **tourist office** (☎ 289 803 604; www.rtalgarve.pt; Rua da Misericórdia) has informative leaflets and maps.

## Sights & Activities
The palm-clad **waterfront** around Praça de Dom Francisco Gomes has kick-back cafés. Faro's beach, **Praia de Faro** (Ilha de Faro), is 6km southwest of the city; take bus No 16 from opposite the bus station. Less crowded, unspoilt **Ilha Desserta** is in the nature park **Parque Natural da Ria Formosa** (☎ 917 811 856); ask about lagoon tours. Access is by ferry from June to mid-September from Cais da Porta Nova.

At Estói, 12km north of Faro, the romantically ruined **Estói Palace** has a surreal garden of statues, balustrades and *azulejos*. It's earmarked for a government-run pousada so visit soon.

## Sleeping & Eating
Avoid midsummer when many of the hotels are block-booked by tour groups.

**Pousada da Juventude** (☎ 289 826 521; Rua da Polícia de Segurança Pública 1; dm/d €12/25) This is

welcoming low-key accommodation if you're euro economising.

**Pensão Residencial Central** (☎ 289 807 291; Largo Terreiro do Bispo 10; s/d €30/40) Squeaky clean if characterless, aside from its position overlooking the jacaranda-fringed square.

**Residencial Adelaide** (☎ 289 802 383; fax 289 826 870; Rua Cruz dos Mestres 7; d €45) Lots of clinical white with large rooms, balconies, rooftop terrace and chatty owner. Disabled unit.

**Sol e Jardim** (☎ 289 820 030; Praça Ferreira de Almeida 22; mains €9) This is an atmospheric seafood restaurant decorated with nets, jolly murals and aquariums. Try the seafood spaghetti.

**Velha Casa** (☎ 289 824 719; Rua do Pé da Cruz 33, mains €7) Solidly reliable traditional fare, including mixed kebabs, pork with pineapple and creamy, gut-sticking rice pud.

## Getting There & Away
Faro airport has both domestic and international flights (p478).

From the bus station, just west of the centre, there are at least six daily express coaches to Lisbon (€14, four hours) and frequent buses to other coastal towns.

The train station is a few minutes' walk west of the bus station. Four trains run daily to Lisbon (€10, five hours).

## Getting Around
The airport is 6km from the centre. Bus Nos 14 and 16 run into town until 9pm. A taxi costs about €12.

**PORTUGAL**

## TAVIRA

pop 12,000

Lovely Tavira is in the process of being discovered by visitors, but still oozes old-world charm. The **tourist office** ( ☎ 281 322 511; Rua da Galeria 9) can help with accommodation. The **town hall** (Praça da Republica; ⊙ closed Sun) provides free Internet access.

### Sights & Activities

One of Tavira's 30-plus churches, the **Igreja da Misericórdia**, has a striking Renaissance doorway. It becomes a concert venue during the wonderful **Algarve International Classical Music Festival** ( ⊙ May-July). The town's ruined **castle** (Rua da Liberdade; admission free; ⊙ 8am-4.30pm Mon-Fri, 10am-5.30pm Sat & Sun) dominates.

**Ilha da Tavira** is an island beach connected to the mainland by a ferry at Quatro Águas. Walk the 2km or take the (summer only) bus from the bus station.

Try pedal power: rent a bike from **Casa Abilio** ( ☎ 281 323 467). For walking or biking trips call **Exploratio** ( ☎ 919 338 226). To sail contact **Clube Náutico** ( ☎ 281 326 858). Jose Salvador Rocha organises **diving trips** ( ☎ 939 017 329).

### Sleeping & Eating

**Camping ground** ( ☎ 281 324 455; camp sites €9) A summer-only budget option.

**Pensão Residencial Lagoas** ( ☎ 281 322 252; Almirante Cândido dos Reis 24; d €40) Pretty handy for self-catering, across the road from a supermarket. Rooms are dingy but clean.

**Residencial Imperial** ( ☎ 281 322 234; José Pires Padinha 24; d €40) Plain, no-nonsense pensão with balconies and a downstairs restaurant overlooking the river.

**Marés** ( ☎ 281 325 815; José Pires Padinha 134; s/d €40/60; ⊠ ) Snazzy modern rooms with balconies and CNN. The restaurant is good.

**Restaurante Bica** ( ☎ 281 332 483; below Residencial Lagoas; mains €7; ⊠ ) Has delicious specials such as sole with orange followed by own-made almond cake.

**Patio** ( ☎ 281 323 008; António Cabreira 30; mains €8-10; ⊠ ) Fatten your credit card at the town's most famous restaurant dishing up traditional cuisine like octopus-studded rice. Terrace with panoramic views and vegetarian dishes.

### Getting There & Away

Some 15 trains and at least six express buses run daily between Faro and Tavira (€1.80, 45 minutes).

## LAGOS

pop 20,000

A busy fishing port with popular beaches, Lagos has a laid-back vibe. The municipal **tourist office** ( ☎ 282 764 111; www.lagosdigital.com, in Portuguese; Largo Marquês de Pombal; ⊙ 10am-6pm Mon-Sat) is the more convenient tourist office; the other is 1km northeast of the centre. Surf through a cappuccino while checking your email at cool **Bora Café** ( ☎ 282 083 438; Conselheiro Joaquim Machado 17).

### Sights & Activities

The **municipal museum** houses an assortment of archaeological finds and ecclesiastical treasures. The adjacent **Igreja de Santo António** has some intricate baroque woodwork.

The beach scene includes **Meia Praia**, a vast strip to the east; **Praia da Luz** to the west; and the smaller **Praia do Pinhão**.

**Blue Ocean** ( ☎ 282 782 718; www.blue-ocean-divers .de) organises diving, kayaking and snorkelling safaris. On the seaside promenade, fishermen offer motorboat jaunts to nearby grottoes. For horse riding in the Algarve interior ring **Tiffany's** ( ☎ 282 697 395).

### Sleeping

**Campismo da Trindade** ( ☎ 282 763 893; camp sites €4) Not much tent-peg space in summer at this camping ground 200m south of town.

**Pensão Caravaela** ( ☎ 289 763 361; 25 de Abril 16; d from €32) Plain comfy rooms on a busy pedestrian street; you may need earplugs on a Saturday night.

**Pousada da Juventude** ( ☎ 282 761 970; Rua Lançarote de Freitas 50; dm/d €16/44) Up there with the best, the rooms are light and airy and there's a cosy kitchen and garden.

---

**TOP ALGARVE BEACHES**

- **Watersports** Wind/kite surfing: Mareta, Martinhal (Sagres); surfing: Amado (Carrapateira), Monte Clérigo (Aljezur) Odeciexe; scuba-diving: Burgau (Luz), water and jet-skiing: Galé (Albufeira)

- **Spectacular Settings & Coves** Don Ana (Lagos), Beliche (Sagres), Rocha (Portimão), Centianes (Carvoeiro)

- **Sweeping Stretches** Meia Prai (Lagos), Barril (Ilha de Tavira), Faro, Ilha da Culatra (Olhão)

PORTUGAL

## Eating & Drinking

**Maharaja de Lagos** ( ☎ 282 761 507; Dr Jose Formozinho; mains €7) High above the old town with all those spicy stand-bys like baltis, biryanis and *bhunas*.

**Taberna de Lagos** ( ☎ 282 084 250; 25 de Abril; mains €7) Former warehouse equals a roomy grand space with beams and arches, serving pizzas, pastas salads and veggie dishes.

**Lounge www.Cocktail** ( ☎ 963 821 067; Sr da Graç 2; snacks €3) Funky English-run bar with chicken tikka, quiche and piled-high nachos. DJs weekend nights.

## Getting There & Away

Bus and train services depart frequently for other Algarve towns and around six times daily to Lisbon (€14, four hours).

## Getting Around

You can rent bicycles, mopeds and motorcycles from **Motoride** ( ☎ 289 761 720; Rua José Afonso 23; per day from €5) or agents in town.

# MONCHIQUE

pop 6840

The rural B-side to the clamour and crowds of the coast, pretty Monchique is surrounded by the forested Serra de Monchique. The **tourist office** ( ☎ 282 911 189; ☼ 9.30am-1pm & 2-5.30pm Mon-Fri, 9.30am-noon Sat) is on the square.

## Sights & Activities

**Igreja Matriz** has a stunning Manueline portal, its stone seemingly tied in knots. Follow the brown pedestrian signs up from the bus station, around the old town's narrow streets.

**Caldas de Monchique**, 6km south, is a mildly heritaged yet still quaint hot-spring hamlet. Some 8km west is the Algarve's 'rooftop', the 902m **Fóia** peak atop the Serra de Monchique, with heady views through a forest of radio masts.

**Alternativtour** ( ☎ 282 420 800; from €25) organises bike and walking tours.

## Sleeping & Eating

**Residencial Estrela de Monchique** ( ☎ 282 913 111; Rua do Porto Fundo 46; s/d €20/35) Small scrubbed pine rooms with homy views of neighbouring gardens.

**Restaurante A Charrete** ( ☎ 282 912 142; Rua Dr Samora Gil 30; mains €7.50) Worth the climb; try the beans with cabbage followed by rice-and-honey pudding.

## Getting There & Away

Over a dozen buses run daily from Lagos to Portimão. From here there are five to nine services that run daily (€2.30, 45 minutes) to Monchique.

# SILVES

pop 10,500

It's hard to believe that this small, genteel town was once capital of Moorish Algarve. Take a deep breath and climb up to the fairy-tale castle on the hill. The **tourist office** ( ☎ 289 442 255; Rua 25 de Abril; ☼ Mon-Fri & Sat am) can help with accommodation. The main **post office** (Rua do Correio) has a Netpost (Internet) kiosk.

## Sleeping & Eating

**Residencial Sousa** ( ☎ 282 442 502; Rua Samoura Barros 17; s/d €15/30) Plain, no-frills rooms in the centre of town.

**Residencial Ponte Romana** ( ☎ 282 443 275; d €30) Ace location beside the Roman bridge with castle views, Sky TV, good-size rooms and a cavernous bar-restaurant that packs them in at weekends.

**Café Ingles** ( ☎ 282 442 585; mains €8) Just below castle entrance, this English-owned funky place has vegetarian dishes, home-made soups, pasta and wood-fired pizza, plus live music at weekends, including sultry Brazilian café music on Sunday summer afternoons.

**Restaurante Rui** ( ☎ 282 442 682; Rua C Vilarinho 27; mains from €9) Push the boat out at this superb fish restaurant with everything from spider crab to cockles on the menu.

## Getting There & Away

Silves train station is 2km from town; trains from Lagos (€1.50, 35 minutes) stop nine times daily (from Faro, change at Tunes), to be met by local buses. Six buses run daily to Silves from Albufeira (€2.75, 40 minutes).

# SAGRES

pop 2500

Tucked away in Portugal's southwestern corner, Sagres is all drama and history with its evocative albeit bleak fort perched high above the thundering surf. There is a central **tourist office** ( ☎ 282 624 873; Rua Comandante Matoso; ☼ 10am-1.30pm & 2.30-6pm Mon-Fri, 10am-1.30pm Sat) plus **Turinfo** ( ☎ 282 620 003; Praça da República), which rents cars and bikes, books hotels and arranges jeep and fishing trips.

PORTUGAL

## Sights & Activities

The **fort** (admission €3; ☼ 10am-6.30pm Mon-Sat, to 8.30pm Sun) has a 12-minute historical slide show; Henry the Navigator established his navigation school here to prime the explorers who later founded the Portuguese empire.

This coast is ideal for the surfing set; hire windsurfers at sand-dune fringed **Praia do Martinhal**.

**Surfcamp** (Mestre António Galhardo; from €30) organises canoeing trips plus surfing and body-board classes.

Visit Europe's southwestern-most point, the **Cabo de São Vicente** (Cape St Vincent), 6km to the west. A solitary lighthouse stands on this barren cape.

## Sleeping & Eating

**Parque de Campismo Sagres** ( ☎ 282 624 351; camp sites €5) This is 2km from town, off the Vila do Bispo road.

**Mar à Vista** ( ☎ 282 624 247; Praia da Mareta; mains €8) Sea-and-surf views from the terrace. Med cuisine includes pasta with lobster and eight different salads.

## Getting There & Away

Frequent buses run daily to Sagres from Lagos (€2.50, 50 minutes), with fewer on Sunday. Three continue out to Cabo de São Vicente on weekdays.

# CENTRAL PORTUGAL

The central slice of Portugal has a raw beauty with tumbling rivers, dense forests and stuck-in-a-time-warp stone villages where local women still carry their shopping on their head. The coast, too, has more sunbed space than further south; the energetic can enjoy hiking and skiing in the dramatic Beiras region. History is everywhere, with castles, fortresses and even Roman temples, while the more modern gourmet can enjoy the fine local wines from the Dão region.

## ÉVORA

pop 50,000

A Unesco World Heritage Site, Évora is walled and medieval with cobblestones, narrow alleys and arches, blockbuster mansions and palaces. Hugely atmospheric and popular, it's well worth a stroll around, despite its mild overdose of souvenir shops. The **tourist**

**office** ( ☎ 266 702 671; www.cm-evora.pt, in Portuguese; Praça do Giraldo 73; ☼ 9am-7pm Mon-Sat) has an excellent city map. Log on at the **Cyber Center** ( ☎ 266 746 923; Rua dos Mercadores 42; ☼ 9am-2am).

## Sights & Activities

**Sé** (Largo do Marquês de Marialva; admission €2.25; ☼ 9am-noon & 2-5pm), Évora's cathedral, has fabulous cloisters and a museum jam-packed with ecclesiastical treasures.

The **Temple of Diana** with its graceful Corinthian columns is definitely worth seeing. At the time of research, the museum opposite was closed for renovations.

**Capela dos Ossos** ( ☎ 266 744 307; Largo Conde de Vila Flor; admission €2; ☼ 9am-1pm & 2.30-6pm) was discovered in 1958 during restoration work. This ghoulish Chapel of Bones is constructed from the bones and skulls of several thousand people; not for the faint-hearted.

**Turaventur** ( ☎ 266 743 134; www.evora.net/turaventur; Qta Serrado, Sr Aflitos) offers a range of adrenaline-fuelled activities – canoeing (half-day, €60), mountain biking (four hours, €35) and 4WD safari tours (full day, €60).

## Sleeping

**Pousada da Juventude** ( ☎ 266 744 848; Rua Miguel Bombarda 40; dm/d €14/35) Recently renovated with a bright imaginative interior, providing excellent cut-price accommodation.

**Residencial O Alentejo** ( ☎ 266 702 903; Rua Serpa Pinto 74; s/d €30/35) Nothing fancy but with a certain charm thanks to the folksy painted furniture and courtyard with cats.

**Pensão Policarpo** ( ☎ 266 702 424; www.localnet.pt/residencialpolicarpo; Rua da Freiria de Baixo 16; s/d €30/40; ⛄ ) Hats off for the setting: a 17th-century manor house complete with Roman columns and part of the original city wall in the foyer. Large pleasant rooms with views.

**Solar Monfalim** ( ☎ 266 750 000; www.monfalimtur.pt/monfalim/ingles; Largo da Misericórdia 1; s/d €70/80; P ⛄ 🖥 ) An exquisitely renovated, 16th-century nobleman's house with an arched gallery overlooking the cobbles. Rooms are top dollar in elegance and style.

## Eating

**Sopas da Terra** ( ☎ 266 744 703; Rua da Moeda 5; snacks €3) You'll have to queue at this young-vibe café-restaurant with its belly-warming soups, doorstops and *salgados* (savoury pasties).

**Café Restaurant O Cruz** ( ☎ 266 747 228; Praça 1 de Maio 20; mains €6) Earthy and inexpensive for a

## ÉVORA

| | | |
|---|---|---|
| **INFORMATION** | | |
| Cyber Centre | 1 | B3 |
| Hospital | 2 | D3 |
| Post & Telephone Office | 3 | B2 |
| Tourist Office | 4 | B3 |
| | | |
| **SIGHTS & ACTIVITIES** | | (p464) |
| Capela dos Ossos | 5 | B3 |
| Policarpo | 6 | B3 |
| Sé | 7 | C3 |
| Temple of Diana | 8 | C2 |
| | | |
| **SLEEPING** | | (p464) |
| Pensão Policarpo | 9 | C3 |
| Pousada da Juventude | 10 | C3 |
| Residencial O Alentejo | 11 | A3 |
| Solar Monfalim | 12 | C3 |
| | | |
| **EATING** | | (pp464–5) |
| Botequim da Mouraria | 13 | B2 |
| Café Restaurante O Cruz | 14 | B3 |
| Pane & Vino | 15 | C3 |
| Sopas de Terr | 16 | B3 |
| | | |
| **DRINKING** | | (p465) |
| Club Dezasseis | 17 | A2 |
| Diplomata Pub | 18 | A2 |
| Pub O Trovador | 19 | B2 |

spot of refuelling with plain filling fare like *acorda com bacalhau e ovo escalfado* (bread soup with codfish and egg).

**Pane & Vino** ( ☎ 266 746 960; Páteo do Salema 22; mains €7; closed Mon) Sunny colours, cheery staff and a vast menu including pizzas, swanky salad bar and creamy tiramisu.

**Botequim da Mouraria** ( ☎ 266 746 775; Rua da Mouraria 16a; mains €8; closed Sun) A real insider's place; there are just a dozen bar-stool places and a nightly set menu of creations by master chef-cum-barman-cum-owner. Get here early to grab a pew.

## Entertainment

**Club Dezasseis** ( ☎ 266 706 559; Rua do Escrivão da Câmara 16) Attracts a mix of suits and scruffs.

**Diplomata Pub** ( ☎ 266 705 675; Rua do Apóstolo 4) Live music and a frazzled bar staff.

**Pub O Trovador** ( ☎ 266 707 370; Rua da Mostardeira 4) A chilled-out setting for a smarter crowd.

## Getting There & Away

Évora has six buses to Lisbon (€9.50, 1½ hours) Monday to Friday and two to Faro (€11.50, four hours), departing from the station off Avenida Túlio Espanca (700m southwest of the centre). Three daily trains run from Lisbon (€7.10, 2½ hours).

## Getting Around

**Bike Lab** ( ☎ 266 735 500; summer only) rents out bicycles. **Policarpo** ( ☎ 266 746 970; www.policarpo

-viagens.pt, in Portuguese; Rua 5 de Outubro 63) does jaunts to megaliths and nearby attractions.

# NAZARÉ
pop 16,000

A real seaside resort, it's impossible to park here in summer. Locals wear national dress to charm the tourists and the restaurants use tiresome hassle techniques to lure in diners. On the plus side, the beach is sweeping and sandy and the seafood is some of the best on the coast. The **tourist office** ( ☎ 262 561 194; ☼ 10am-8pm May-Sep, 10am-1pm & 3-7pm Oct-Apr) is at the end of Avenida da República.

## Sights & Activities

The **beaches** are the main attraction, although swimmers should beware of dangerous currents. Climb or take the funicular to the cliff-top **Sítio** with its cluster of fisherman's cottages and great view.

Two of Portugal's big-time architectural masterpieces are close by. Follow the signs to **Alcobaça** where, right in the centre of town, is the immense **Mosteiro de Santa Maria de Alcobaça** ( ☎ 262 505 120; admission €3, church free; ☼ 9am-7pm, to 5pm winter) dating from 1178; don't miss the colossal former kitchen!

Batalha's Gothic **Mosteiro de Santa Maria de Vitória** ( ☎ 244 765 497; admission Cloisters & Unfinished Chapels €3; ☼ 9am-6pm, to 5pm winter) from 1388, is home to Henry the Navigator's tomb.

## Sleeping & Eating

Many townspeople rent out rooms; doubles start from €35.

**Vale Paraíso** ( ☎ 262 561 800; camp sites €3.50) A well-equipped camping ground with bikes to hire.

**Ribamar** ( ☎ 262 551 158; fax 262 562 224; Rua Gomes Freire 9; d €45; ✂ ) A sunny yellow-and-white frontage a towel's throw from the beach, this 25-room hotel has sea-view balconies and spacious bijou rooms.

**Casa Marques** ( ☎ 262 551 680; Rua Gil Vicente 37; mains €5) Kitchen-sink informal with reliably good traditional dishes. There are kebab and pizza takeaways on the same street – fussy families take note.

**Nova Casa Caçao** ( ☎ 262 551 035; Rua das Caldeiras 1; mains €7) In a small square away from the main strip, choose from 40-plus seafood dishes, including black clams, lobster and sea bass.

## Getting There & Away

The nearest train station, 6km away at Valado, is connected to Nazaré by frequent buses. Nazaré has numerous bus connections to Lisbon (€7, two hours).

# TOMAR
pop 17,000

A town with history, charm – and a rare thing, the vegetarian restaurant. Tomar reached dizzy historical heights as the headquarters of the Knights Templar. It's home to the outstanding Unesco-listed **Convento de Cristo**. Cradling the monastery's southern walls is the awesome 17th-century **Aqueduto de Pegões** (aquaduct), beyond which is the dense greenery of the **Mata Nacional dos Sete Montes** (Seven Hills National Forest). Tomar's **tourist office** ( ☎ 249 329 000; www.rttemplarios.pt, in Portuguese; Serpa Pinto) can provide town and forest maps.

## Sleeping & Eating

**Pensão Residencial União** ( ☎ 249 323 161; Rua Serpa Pinto 94; d €35) Within a reasonable baggage-lug from the main car park, this gracious older home has dark wood furnishing, creaky floor boards and old-fashioned bathrooms.

**Estalagem de Santa Iria** ( ☎ 249 313 326; Mouchão Parque; s/d €65/85; ℗ ✂ ) Boutique hotel with just 13 large sunny rooms with balconies overlooking the park and river beyond.

**Gaia** ( ☎ 249 311 109; Rua dos Moínhos 75; mains €6; ☼ 9am-8pm Mon-Fri, to 2pm Sat) A few tables and dishes that can include *seitan* stew, tofu burgers or *feijada* (Brazilian bean stew).

**Casinha d'Avó Bia** ( ☎ 249 323 828; Rua Dr Joaquim Jacinto 16; mains €8) The quality is good. Try the seafood *açorda* (fish and bread stew).

## Getting There & Away

There are at least four express buses daily to Lisbon (€6.20, two hours) and even more frequent trains (€5.60, two hours).

# COIMBRA
pop 150,000

Coimbra has a lively young vibe thanks to the student life centred on the magnificent 13th-century university. It is a handsome, eclectic city with elegant shopping streets, ancient stone walls and narrow cobbled backstreets. Coimbra played a key role in the country's history and was the birth and burial place of Portugal's first king.

## Information

### INTERNET ACCESS

**Esp@çoInternet** (Praça 8 de Maio; ⏰ 10am-8pm Mon-Fri, to 10pm Sat & Sun) has free Internet access for 30 minutes.

### TOURIST INFORMATION

The **regional tourist office** ( ☎ 239 855 930; www .turismo-centro.pt; Largo da Portagem) has pamphlets and cultural-events information, but a **municipal tourist office** ( ☎ 239 832 591; Praça Dom Dinis) and another **tourist office** ( ☎ 239 833 202; Praça da República) are more useful.

## Sights & Activities

**Mosteiro de Santa Cruz** ( ☎ 239 822 941; Rua Visconde da Luz; admission €1; ⏰ 9am-noon & 2-5pm) has a fabulous ornate pulpit and medieval royal tombs. Located at the bottom of the hill in the old town, you can reach the monastery via the **elevator** (€1; ⏰ daily) by the market; tickets are available from the booth or kiosks.

**University Velha** ( ☎ 239 822 941; www.uc.pt/sri; admission €3; ⏰ 10am-noon & 2-5pm) is unmissable in its grandeur. You can visit the library with its gorgeous book-lined hallways and the Manueline chapel dating back to 1517.

**Machado de Castro Museum** ( ☎ 239 823 727; Largo Dr José Rodrigues; admission €3; ⏰ 9.30am-12.30pm & 2-5.30pm) has a diverse collection of sculpture and paintings, and the 12th-century building is itself a work of art.

**Conimbriga**, 16km south of Coimbra, is the site of the well-preserved ruins of a **Roman town** ( ⏰ 9am-8pm summer, 10am-6pm winter), including mosaic floors, baths and fountains. There's a good **site museum** (admission €3; ⏰ 9am-8pm summer, 10am-6pm winter) with restaurant. Frequent buses run to Condeixa, 2km from the site; direct buses depart at 9.05am and 9.35am (only 9.35am at weekends) from the **AVIC terminal** (Rua João de Ruão 18) returning at 1pm and 6pm (only 6pm at weekends).

## Festivals & Events

Coimbra's annual highlight is **Queima das Fitas**, a boozy week of *fado* and revelry that begins on the first Thursday in May when students celebrate the end of the academic year.

## Sleeping

**Pousada da Juventude** ( ☎ 239 822 955; coimbra@ movijovem.pt; Rua António Henriques Seco 12-14; dm/ d €12/29) Solid, efficiently run hostel; take bus No 7 from outside the Astoria hotel on Avenida Emíidio Navarro 50m south of Coimbra A train station.

**Pensão Santa Cruz** ( ☎ 239 826 197; Praça 8 de Maio; d €32) Threadbare, large rooms in this old building in a great position, overlooking one of the city's most dynamic squares.

**Pensão Flôr de Coimbra** ( ☎ 239 823 865; fax 239 821 545; Rua do Poço 5; d from €35) Loads of *fin de siècle* atmosphere in this renovated family home run by sons; the restaurant has a small daily vegetarian menu.

**Casa Pombal Guesthouse** ( ☎ 239 835 175; www .casa.pombal@oninet.pt; Rua das Flores 18; d from €38) Has pretty rooms painted in pastel colours with roof-top views. The Dutch owner includes a blowout breakfast in the price.

**Residência Coimbra** ( ☎ 239 837 996; fax 239 838 124; Rua das Azeiteiras 55; s/d €35/45) Freshly redecorated carpeted rooms with shiny-white bathrooms, satellite TV and fridges.

## Eating

Head to the lanes west of Praça do Comércio, especially Rua das Azeiteiras, for cheap eats.

**O Cantinho das Escadas** ( ☎ 239 820 578; Rua dos Gato 29; mains €4) House wine would be better for pickling onions, but the stews (fish, pork and veal) are excellent value at this brightly lit caf.

**Restaurante Democrática** ( ☎ 239 823 784; Travessa da Rua Nova; mains €6) Barrel-lined rustic restaurant dishing up stoking chow like *caldo verde* (potato soup with cabbage and sausage) in a low-key chummy atmosphere.

**Restaurante Jardim da Manga** ( ☎ 239 829 156; Rua Olímpio Nicolau Rui Fernanda; mains €7; ⏰ closed Sat) A better breed of self-service restaurant at the back of the Mosteiro de Santa Cruz. Vegetarian dishes are available.

**Café Santa Cruz** ( ☎ 239 833 617; Praçca Maio) Former chapel that has been resurrected into one of Portugal's most atmospheric cafés.

**Zé Carioca** ( ☎ 239 835 450; Avenida Sá da Bandeira 89; mains €9-15). Chow down on fruity Brazilian dishes at this mellow restaurant northwest of Praça da República.

## Entertainment

Coimbra-style *fado* is more cerebral than the Lisbon variety, and its adherents staunchly protective. **Bar Diligência** ( ☎ 239 827 667; Rua Nova 30) and **Boémia Bar** ( ☎ 239 834 547; Rua do Cabido 6) are popular *casas de fado*.

**Á Capella** ( ☎ 239 833 985; Capela de Nossa Senhora de Victoria, Rua Corpo de Deus, Largo da Victoria;

10.30pm Thu-Sat) is a fabulous new *fado* place attracting a groovy young crowd with nightly shows in a former chapel.

**Vinyl** ( ☎ 239 404 047; Avenida Afonso Henriques 43) and **Via Latina** ( ☎ 239 833 034; Rua Almeida Garrett 1) are a couple of popular discos for the bump and grinders.

### Getting There & Away

At least a dozen buses and as many trains run daily from Lisbon (€9.20, 2½ hours) and Porto (€8.50, 1½ hours), plus frequent express buses from Faro and Évora, via Lisbon. The main long-distance train stations are Coimbra B, 2km northwest of the centre, and central Coimbra A (on timetables this is called just 'Coimbra'). Most long-distance trains call at both. Other useful connections are to Figueira da Foz and eight daily buses to Luso/Buçaco (from Coimbra A).

## LUSO & THE BUÇACO FOREST

pop 2000

This region has an other-worldly appeal: dense forest of century-old trees surrounded by an impressionist-style landscape dappled with heather, wild flowers and leafy ferns. Buçaco was chosen as a retreat by 16th-century monks and surrounds the pretty spa town of Luso.

The **tourist office** ( ☎ /fax 231 939 133; Avenida Emídio Navarro; 9.30am-12.30pm & 2-6pm) has maps and leaflets about the forest and trails, as well as free Internet access. The **Termas** (thermal baths; ☎ 231 937 910; Avenida Emídio Navarro; May-Oct) offers a range of treatments.

### Sleeping & Eating

The Luso tourist office has a list of pensãos with an average cost of €30.

**Astória** ( ☎ 231 939 182; Avenida Emídio Navarro; s/d €20/30) Dark wood and beams equal cosy surroundings at this well-situated pensão near the baths.

---

> **THE AUTHOR'S CHOICE**
>
> **Zé Manel** ( ☎ 239 823 790; Beco do Forno 12; mains €5; Mon-Fri, lunch Sat) Great food, huge servings and a zany atmosphere with walls papered with diners' comments, cartoons and poems. There's just a few tables so arrive before 8pm to beat the crowds. Vegetarian choices include meatless bean stew.

---

**Palace Hotel do Buçaco** ( ☎ 231 930 101; www.almeidahotels.com; s/d from €145/185) If this is a hunting lodge – bring on the palace!, truly sumptuous with gargoyles, Manueline extravagance, an ornamental garden and Edwardian-style gracious rooms. The equally elegant restaurant offers set menus for €40.

**Restaurante O Cesteiro** ( ☎ 231 939 360; EN 234; mains €7) Large dining room with extensive menu of confident traditional dishes. The grilled chicken is a winner.

### Getting There & Away

There are three buses daily Monday to Friday, two on Saturdays and one on Sundays from Coimbra (€2.50, 50 minutes). Just one train, departing around 10.30am from Coimbra B (€1.30, 30 minutes) provides enough time to take a day trip.

# THE NORTH

Portugal's northern Minho region is a colourful patchwork of rolling country, dense forests and dramatic mountains. This is also *vinho verde* country, that wholly addictive young green wine, while its capital Porto is named after another tipple and is a fascinating mix of the medieval and modern. Also here are two more must-see historical cities: Braga, the country's religious heart, and the finely situated Viana do Castelo.

## PORTO

pop 305,000

Portugal's second-largest city, Porto has real charm. It combines a slick commercial hub with the charmingly dilapidated river-frontage district – a World Heritage Site. Across the water is Vila Nova de Gaia, the headquarters of a thriving port trade since a 1703 agreement with England. Porto's role as one of the prime venues for the Euro 2004 football championships equalled a healthy boost to the economy and infrastructure.

### Orientation

Porto centre is small enough to cover mainly by foot. The city clings to the north bank of the Rio Douro, spanned by five bridges across from Vila Nova de Gaia, home to the port wine lodges.

Central Porto's axis is Avenida dos Aliados. Major shopping areas are eastward around the Bolhão Market and Rua Santa Catarina, home to the glassy shopping complex Via Catarina, and westward along Rua dos Clérigos. South on Avenida dos Aliados, Praça da Liberdade and São Bento train station are major local bus hubs. Another is Jardim da Cordoaria (called Jardim de João Chagas on some maps), about 400m west.

The picturesque Ribeira district lies along the waterfront, in the shadow of the great Ponte de Dom Luís I bridge.

## Information

### INTERNET ACCESS
**Portweb** ( ☎ 222 005 922; Praça General Humberto Delgado 291; ⌚ 10-2am Mon-Sat, 3pm-2am Sun) Central, cheap Internet access.

### MEDICAL SERVICES
**Santo António Hospital** ( ☎ 222 077 500; Largo Prof Abel Salazar) Has English-speaking staff.

### MONEY
**Intercontinental** (Rua de Ramalho Ortigão 8) Exchange facilities.
**Portocâmbios** (Rua Rodrigues Sampaio 193)
**Top Atlântico** ( ☎ 222 074 020; trinidade@topatlantico .com; Rua Alferes Malheiro 96) Doubles as an Amex representative.

### POST
**Main post office** (Praça General Humberto Delgado) Across from the main tourist office.
**Telephone office** (Praça da Liberdade 62; ⌚ 10am-10pm) Where faxes also can be sent.

### TOURIST INFORMATION
**ICEP tourist office** ( ☎ 222 057 514; fax 222 053 212; Praça Dom João I 43; ⌚ 9am-7pm Mon-Fri, 9.30am-3.30pm Sat & Sun) The national tourist office.
**Municipal tourist office** ( ☎ 223 393 472; www.porto turismo.pt; Rua Clube dos Fenianos 25; ⌚ 9am-5.30pm Mon-Fri, 9.30am-4.30pm Sat & Sun Oct-Jun, 9am-7pm daily Jul-Sep) Next door to the tourist police office.
**Tourist office** ( ☎ 222 009 770; Rua Infante Don Henrique 63; ⌚ 9am-5.30pm Mon-Fri)

### TRAVEL AGENCIES
**Montes d'Aventura** ( ☎ 228 305 157; Alameda Dr Antonio Macedo 19) Organises walking, cycling and canoeing trips.
**Tagus** ( ☎ 226 094 146; fax 226 094 141; Rua Campo Alegre 261) Youth-oriented agency.
**Top Atlântico** ( ☎ 222 074 020; trinidade@topatlantico .com; Rua Alferes Malheiro 96)

**Trilhos** ( ☎ /fax 225 020 740; www.trilhos.pt, in Portuguese; Rua de Belém 94) Another option for canoe and hydrospeed excursions.
**Wasteels** ( ☎ 225 194 230; fax 225 194 239; Rua Pinto Bessa 27/29) Near Campanhã station and also youth oriented.

## Sights & Activities
Head for the river-front Ribeira district for a stroll, checking out the gritty local bars, restaurants and river cruises. For most museums and attractions, admission is half-price for children, students and seniors, and free for everyone on Sundays.

**Torre dos Clérigos** (Rua dos Clérigos; admission €1; ⌚ 10am-noon & 2-5pm) rewards the 225 steep steps with the best panorama of the city.

**Sé** ( ☎ 222 059 028; Terreiro da Sé; cloisters €2; ⌚ 9am-12.30pm & 2.30-7pm Apr-Oct, to 6pm rest of the year, closed Sun morning) dominates Porto. The cathedral is worth a visit for its mixture of architectural styles and vast ornate interior.

Many port-wine lodges (Vila Nova de Gaia) offer daily tours and tastings, including **Croft** ( ☎ 223 742 800; www.croftport.com; admission €3) and **Osborne** ( ☎ 223 757 517; www.osborne .es, in Spanish; admission free).

**Museum of Contemporary Art** ( ☎ 226 156 571; www.serralves.pt, in Portuguese; Rua Dom João de Castro 210; admission €5; ⌚ 10am-7pm Tue-Fri, 10am-8pm Sat & Sun Apr-Sep, 10am-7pm Oct-Mar) is enclosed by pretty gardens and has works by contemporary Portuguese artists.

**Museu do Vinho** (Wine Museum; ☎ 222 076 300; museuvinhoporto@cm-porto.pt; Rua de Monchique 45-52; admission free; ⌚ 11am-7pm Tue-Sun), The newest museum here, traces the history of wine- and port-making with an informative short film, models and exhibits, plus tastings.

**Soares dos Reis National Museum** ( ☎ 223 393 770; Rua Dom Manuel II 44; admission €3; ⌚ 10am-6pm Wed-Sun) has masterpieces of 19th- and 20th-century Portuguese painting and sculpture. Take bus No 78 from Praça da Liberdade.

## Festivals & Events
Porto's big festivals are the **Festa de São João** (St John's Festival) in June and the international film festival **Fantasporto** in February. Also worth catching are the **Celtic music festival** in April/May, and the **rock festival** in August.

## Sleeping
### BUDGET
**Campismo Salgueiros** ( ☎ 227 810 500; fax 227 718 239; Praia de Salgueiros; camp sites €2.50) One of

three camping grounds near the sea; all get packed in summer. Note that the coast here is too rocky and polluted for swimming.

**Camping da Prelada** ( ☎ 228 312 616; Rua Monte dos Burgos; camp sites €3.50) Basic, big and open year-round, 4km northwest of the centre. Take bus No 6 from Praça de Liberdade or bus No 54 from Jardim da Cordoaria.

**Pousada da Juventude** ( ☎ 226 177 257; porto@ movijovem.pt; Rua Paulo da Gama 551; dm/d €18/35) is a tastefully spruced-up hostel 4km west of the centre. Reservations are essential. Take bus No 35 from Praça da Liberdade or No 1 from São Bento station.

**Residencial União** ( ☎ 222 003 078; Rua Conde de Vizela 62; d from €25) Faded large rooms; the approach is via a gloomy backstreet, which could be dodgy after dark.

**Pensão Astória** ( ☎ 222 008 175; Rua Arnaldo Gama 56; d €35) Next to a handy car park or approach via the steep steps from the river front. Elegant old doubles, some with river views.

**Pensão Mira Norte** ( ☎ 222 001 118; Rua de Santa Catarina 969; d €30) Basic rooms, well placed for shopaholics, but not so good at siesta time.

**Pensão Santa Luzia** ( ☎ 222 001 119; Rua da Alegria; d €35; 🍴 ) Very pleasant, spotless rooms run by an elderly senhora who is still charging escuda-era rates.

Also recommended is **Pensão Porto Rico** ( ☎ 223 394 690; Rua do Almada 237; d €30; 🍴 ).

**MID-RANGE**

**Pensão Residencial Paulista** ( ☎ 222 054 692; Avenida dos Aliados 214; s/d €40/50; 🍴 ) Small wooden rooms with balconies overlooking a treed avenue crowned by the majestic city hall.

**Pensão Sã Marino** ( ☎ 223 325 499; Praça Carlos Alberto 59; s/d €38/45; 🍴 ) Seductive 19th-century building overlooking the square (airport bus stops outside). Carpeted good-sized rooms.

Also recommended is **Pensão Estoril** ( ☎ 222 002 751; fax 222 082 468; Rua de Cedofeita 193; d €40; 🍴 ).

**TOP END**

**Pensão Pão de Açucar** ( ☎ 222 002 425; Rua do Almada 262; d €75; 🅿 🍴 ) Upbeat Art-Nouveau décor. Go for the top floor with rooms opening onto the palm-fringed terrace.

**Pestana Porto Carlton** ( ☎ 223 402 300; www.resid encialpaodeacucar.com, in Portuguese; Praça da Ribeira 1; s/d €118/140; 🅿 ✗ 🍴 🖵 ) Red-carpet service in a gorgeous 16th-century setting. Rooms have city or river views and sleek glossy furnishings with all the extras.

## Eating
### RESTAURANTS

**Restaurante Romão** ( ☎ 222 005 639; Praça Carlos Alberto 100; mains €7) Agreeable little space with northern specialities such as tripe and roast kid. Leave room for *torta de noz* (walnut tart).

**Geometria** ( ☎ 222 030 398; Infante D Henrique 133; mains €9; ⏱ closed Mon) Dress-for-dinner style place with two candlelit dining rooms overlooking the river. Reasonably priced pizza and pasta dishes and classy downstairs bar.

**Casa Filha da Mãe Preta** ( ☎ 222 055 515; Cais da Ribeira 40; mains €10; ⏱ closed Sun) Don't confuse this place with the same-name but less salubrious caf one street back! Head upstairs for Douro views from the *azulejo*-lined dining room. Simple fish and meat dishes served with veggies, rice and boiled potatoes.

### CAFÉS, QUICK EATS & SELF-CATERING

**Café Majestic** ( ☎ 222 003 887; Rua Santa Catarina 112; ⏱ closed Sun) An extravagant Art Nouveau relic where powdered ladies enjoy afternoon teas.

**Confeitaria Império** (149 Rua Santa Catarina; snacks €2.50) Brilliant bites like delicious *pasteis de carne* (meat and veggie filled pasties) and custard tarts.

**Café Ancôra Douro** ( ☎ 222 003 749; Praça de Parada Leitão 49; snacks €3) Heaving with peckish students, the vast menu includes veggie burgers, hotdogs and crepes.

**Bolhão market** (Rua Formosa; ⏱ closed Sun) Sells fruit and veggies in season, plus cheese and deli goodies.

## Drinking

**Solar do Vinho do Porto** ( ☎ 226 094 749; Rua Entre Quintas 220; ⏱ 11am-midnight Mon-Sat) Laid-back yet elegant setting for tasting the port made just across the river.

**La Maison des Porto** ( ☎ 936 057 340; Rua São Joã 46; ⏱ closed Sun) French-owned vinotheque where you can taste and be educated about port by the charming multilingual owner.

**Ryan's Irish Pub** ( ☎ 222 005 366; Rua Infante Dom Henrique 18) Has the usual range of gluggable beer in blarney surroundings.

## Entertainment

**Academia** ( ☎ 222 005 737; Rua São João 80) Stylishly hip and smoky disco-bar.

**Taverna do Infante** ( ☎ 205 49 86; Rua da Alfándega 13) Atmospheric macho den with Brazilian dancers.

# PORTO

PORTUGAL

| EATING | (p470) |
|---|---|
| Café Âncora Douro | 27 D3 |
| Café Majestic | 28 E3 |
| Casa Filha da Mãe Preta | 29 D4 |
| Confeitaria Império | 30 E3 |
| Geometria | 31 D4 |
| O Muro | 32 D4 |
| Restaurante Romão | 33 D3 |

| DRINKING | (p470) |
|---|---|
| Academia | 34 D4 |
| Club Mau-Mau | 35 B3 |
| La Maison des Porto | 36 D4 |
| Maré Alta | 37 A3 |
| Mexcal | 38 B3 |
| Ryan's Irish Pub | 39 D4 |
| Solar do Vinho do Porto | 40 B3 |
| Taverna do Infante | 41 D4 |

| SHOPPING | (p472) |
|---|---|
| Arte Facto | 42 D4 |
| Bolhão Market | 43 E2 |
| Casa Januário | 44 E2 |
| Casa Oriental | 45 D3 |
| Garrafeira do Carmo | 46 C3 |
| Via Catarina Shopping Centre | 47 E2 |

| TRANSPORT | (pp472-3) |
|---|---|
| AV Minho Tickets & Buses | (see 51) |
| Carlos Soares Tickets & Buses | (see 51) |
| Cordoaria Bus Stop | 48 C3 |
| Intermorte Tickets and Buses | 49 B2 |
| Rede Expressos Bus Station | 50 E3 |
| REDM | 51 D1 |
| Renex Tickets and Buses | 52 D3 |
| Rodonorte Bus Station | 53 E3 |
| Tram Terminus | 54 D4 |

| OTHER | |
|---|---|
| STCP Kiosk | 55 D3 |
| STCP Kiosk | 56 A1 |
| STCP Kiosk | (see 43) |
| Town Hall | 57 D2 |

| SLEEPING | (pp469-70) |
|---|---|
| Pensão Astória | 17 E4 |
| Pensão Estoril | 18 C2 |
| Pensão Mira Norte | 19 E1 |
| Pensão Pão de Açúcar | 20 D3 |
| Pensão Paulista | 21 D3 |
| Pensão Porto Rico | 22 D3 |
| Pensão Residencial Santa Luzia | 23 E2 |
| Pensão Sã Marino | 24 D3 |
| Pestana Porto Carlton | 25 D4 |
| Residencial União | 26 D3 |

| INFORMATION | |
|---|---|
| ICEP Tourist Office | 1 E3 |
| Intercontinental | 2 D2 |
| Main Post Office | 3 D2 |
| Municipal Tourist Office | 4 D2 |
| Portocâmbios Exchange | 5 D3 |
| Portweb | 6 D2 |
| Santo António Hospital | 7 C3 |
| Spanish Embassy | 8 E2 |
| Tagus | 9 A2 |
| Telephone Office | 10 D3 |
| Tourism Police | 11 D4 |

| SIGHTS & ACTIVITIES | (p469) |
|---|---|
| Museu do Vinho | 12 B3 |
| Sé | 13 D4 |
| Soares dos Reis National Museum | 14 C3 |
| Top Atlântico & American Express | 15 D2 |
| Torre dos Clérigos | 16 D3 |

To French Embassy & Consulate (1km); Fez do Douro (5km)

To Airport (10km); (900m)

To Braga (55km)

To Mortes d'Aventura (1km)

To Camping da Prelada (1.6km)

To Museum of Contemporary Art (1.5km)

To Pousada da Juventude (1.8km)

To Vila Nova de Gaia (Port Wine Lodges, 500m)

To Coimbra (123km); Lisbon (320km)

To Campismo Salgueiros

Douro River

Ponte de Dom Luís I

0    400 m
0    0.2 miles

---

**THE AUTHOR'S CHOICE**

**O Muro** ( ☎ 222 083 426; Muro dos Bacalhoeiros 88; mains €7; ⏰ noon-2am) Top-notch, well-priced restaurant with five-star river views. The charismatic owner is an ex-professional soccer player who, together with his Mozambican wife, prepares delicious, filling food, including several wacky vegetarian choices. Delightful wacky décor ranges from dried *bacalhau* to Che Guevara; ask to see the guest book!

---

**Mexcal** ( ☎ 226 009 188; Rua da Restauração 39) Latino music for late-night hip-swinging.

**Club Mau-Mau** ( ☎ 226 076 660; Rua do Outeiro 4) A dodging-elbows disco with live music on Thursday nights.

**Maré Alta** ( ☎ 226 162 540; Alameda Basilio Teles) Nail-bitingly trendy. Occasional live gigs.

## Shopping

The best central shopping mall is **Via Catarina Shopping Centre** (Rua Santa Catarina) in a tasteful building. Port is naturally a popular purchase in this town; shops with a broad selection include knowledgeable **Garrafeira do Carmo** (Rua do Carmo 17), the deli **Casa Januário** (Rua do Bonjardim 352) and **Casa Oriental** (Campo dos Mártires de Pátria 111). Other good buys are shoes and gold-filigree jewellery. For handicrafts visit **Arte Facto** (Rua da Reboleira 37; ⏰ Tue-Sun) in the Ribeira.

## Getting There & Away

### AIR

Porto is connected by daily flights from Lisbon and London, and almost-daily direct links from other European centres (p478). For flight information call ☎ 229 413 260.

### BUS

Porto has a baffling number of private bus companies; the main tourist office has a transport department which can assist with timetables and fares. Generally for Lisbon and the Algarve the choice is **Renex** ( ☎ 222 003 395; Rua das Carmelitas 32) or **Rede Expressos** ( ☎ 222 052 459). Three companies operate from or near Praceto Régulo Magauanha, off Rua Dr Alfredo Magalhães: **REDM** ( ☎ 222 003 152) goes to Braga; **AV Minho** ( ☎ 222 006 121) to Viana do Castelo; and **Carlos Soares** ( ☎ 222 051 383) to Guimarães. **Rodonorte** ( ☎ 222 004 398; Rua Ateneu Comércial do Porto 19) departs from its own terminal, mainly to Vila Real and Bragança.

Northern Portugal's main international carrier is **Internorte** ( ☎ 226 093 220; www.internorte.com, in Portuguese; Praça da Galiza 96) whose coaches depart from its booking office.

### TRAIN

Porto is a northern Portugal rail hub with three stations. Most international trains, and all intercity links, start at Campanhã, 2km east of the centre. Inter-regional and regional services depart from either Campanhã or the central **São Bento station** ( ☎ 225 364 141; ⏰ 8am-11pm); bus Nos 34 and 35 run frequently between these two.

At São Bento station you can book tickets to any destination from any Porto station.

## Getting Around

### TO/FROM THE AIRPORT

The **AeroBus** ( ☎ 808 200 166; www.stcp.pt; €2.60; ⏰ 7.30am to 7pm) runs every half-hour between Avenida dos Aliados and the airport via Boavista. The ticket, purchased on the bus, also serves as a free bus pass until midnight of the day you buy it.

City buses 56 and 87 run about every half-hour until 8.30pm to/from Jardim da Cordoaria, and until about 12.30am to/from Praça da Liberdade.

A taxi costs around €12.50 plus a possible €1.50 baggage charge.

### BUS

Central hubs of Porto's extensive bus system include Jardim da Cordoaria, Praça da Liberdade and São Bento station (Praça Almeida Garrett). Tickets are cheapest from STCP kiosks (eg opposite São Bento station, beside Bolhão market and at Boavista) and many newsagents and tobacconists: €0.70 for a short hop, €0.90 to outlying areas or €2.05 for an airport return trip. Tickets bought on the bus are always €1.20. There's also a €2.10 day pass available.

### TRAM

Porto has one remaining tram, the No 1E, trundling daily from the Ribeira to the coast at Foz do Douro.

### METRO

Work is well away on Porto's **metro** (1-2 zones €0.80, 3 zones €1), which is utilisng a combination of upgraded new track that will reach Campanhã, Vila Nova de Gaia and several coastal resorts to the north. The Blue Line was due to open mid-2005 (from Trindade to Gondomar) and already runs from Trindade to Sr Matosinhos in the northwest.

### TAXI
To cross town, expect to pay about €5. An additional charge is made to leave the city limits, including across the Ponte Dom Luís I to Vila Nova de Gaia.

## ALONG THE DOURO
Portugal's rural heartland of the Douro Valley stretches some 200km to the Spanish border. In the upper reaches, port-wine vineyards wrap around every hillside punctuated by wonderfully remote stone villages and, in spring, splashes of dazzling white almond blossom.

The Douro River, tamed by eight dams and locks since the late 1980s, is navigable across Portugal. Highly recommended is the train journey from Porto to Peso da Régua (about a dozen trains daily, 2½ hours), the last 50km on the river's edge; four trains continue daily to Pocinho (4½ hours). **Douro Azul** ( ☎ 223 393 950; www.douroazul.com) and other companies run one- and two-day river cruises, mostly from March to October. Cyclists and drivers can choose river-hugging roads along either bank, although they're crowded at weekends.

The elegant, detailed colour map *Rio Douro* (€3) is available from Porto bookshops.

## VIANA DO CASTELO
pop 18,000

A gracious and historic port town with some striking 16th-century buildings, regarded as the region's folk capital specialising in the traditional embroidered costumes. The **tourist office** ( ☎ 258 822 620; www.rtam.pt; Rua Hospital Velho; ☯ 9am-12.30pm & 2.30-6pm Mon-Fri, 9am-1pm Sat) has information on festivals and the region in general. In August Viana hosts the **Festas de Nossa Senhora da Agonia** (p477).

### Sights
The stately heart of town is Praça da República, with its fountain and elegant buildings, including the 16th-century **Misericórdia**.

Atop Santa Luzia Hill, the **Templo do Sagrado Coração de Jesus** offers a grand panorama across the river. The funicular railway was temporarily closed at the time of re-

search. Check at the tourist office for an update – or prepare for a 5km uphill climb.

### Sleeping
**Pousada da Juventude** ( ☎ 258 800 260; vianacastelo @movijovem.pt; Rua da Argaçosa; dm/d €13/35) A friendly clean place about a kilometre east of the town centre.

**Residencial Magalhães** ( ☎ 258 823 293; Avenida Combatentes da G. Guerra 215; s/d €30/38) One of a best of a handful of inexpensive pensãos on this street. Good-size rooms with wardrobes and lacy curtains.

**Residencial Viana Mar** ( ☎ 258 828 962; Avenida Combatentes da G Guerra 215) Well positioned with comfortable chintzy rooms and a sunken bar that dates from the sixties when it was Viana's first nightclub; the décor remains captivatingly unchanged.

### Eating
**A Gruta Snack Bar** ( ☎ 258 820 214; Rua Grande 87; mains €5) Canteen-style surrounds with light lunches including a good salad choice.

**Dolce Vita** ( ☎ 258 820 214; Rua do Poço 44; mains €6) Wood-fired pizza and pasta sauces make this *the* refuelling spot in town.

**O Grelhador** ( ☎ 258 825 219; Rua do Anjinho 17; mains €7) There's not much elbowroom at this small bar-restaurant but its speciality – crêpes – makes a change if you're suffering from *bacalau* burn out.

**O Pipo** ( ☎ 258 825 097; Rua Prior do Crato 68; mains €9) Octopus-studded rice, veal in green sauce and almond cake are just some of the traditional goodies available at this earthy restaurant in the centre of town.

### Getting There & Away
Six express coaches daily go to Porto (€6.20, two hours) and Lisbon (€14, 5½ hours) Monday to Friday, with fewer at weekends.

## BRAGA
pop 80,000

It's a pity about the brash new McDonald's stuck in the middle of Braga's most beautiful square; otherwise the religious capital of Portugal is monolithic in its ecclesiastical architecture with a contemporary contrast of pedestrian streets flanked with classy cafés, shops and boutiques. The **tourist office** ( ☎ 253 262 550; Praça da República; ☯ 9am-7pm Mon-Fri, 9am-12.30pm & 2-5.30pm Sat) can help with accommodation and maps.

## Sights & Activities

In the centre of Braga is the **Sé** (museum & chapels €2; 8.30am-5.30pm), an elegant cathedral complex.

At Bom Jesus do Monte, a hilltop pilgrimage site 5km from Braga, is an extraordinary stairway, the **Escadaria do Bom Jesus**, with allegorical fountains, chapels and a superb view. Buses run frequently from Braga to the site where you can climb the steps (pilgrims sometimes do this on their knees) or ascend by funicular railway (€1).

It's an easy day trip to **Guimarães**, considered the cradle of the Portuguese nation, with a medieval town centre and a palace of the dukes of Bragança.

## Sleeping

**Pousada da Juventude** ( ☎ 253 616 163; braga@ movijovem.pt; Rua de Santa Margarida 6; dm/d €10/26) This bright and cheerful hostel is a 10-minute walk from the city centre.

**Hotel Francfort** ( ☎ 253 262 648; Avenida Central 7; d €35) Large rooms, lofty ceilings, antiques and an extremely elderly owner equal the mildly threadbare state of the place.

**Grande Residência Avenida** ( ☎ 253 609 020; fax 253 609 028; Avenida da Liberdade 738; d €50; ) Had a glossy makeover with shiny white bathrooms and good-sized plushly carpeted rooms.

## Eating & Drinking

**Restaurante Pópulo** ( ☎ 253 215 147; Praça Conde de Agrolongo 116; mains €11) Heavy on regional classics including duck, veal and pork dishes. Ask for the daily specials when the chef likes to indulge in a little nouvelle innovation.

**D. Diogo** ( ☎ 253 262 297; RD Diogo de Sousa 81-83; mains €15) Go for the splurge at this classy candlelit restaurant with its limited menu of refined fish, meat and rice dishes.

**Café Vianna** ( ☎ 253 262 336; Praça da República) A classic 19th-century café. Great breakfast.

## Getting There & Away

The motorway from Porto puts Braga within easy day-trip reach. Intercidade trains arrive twice daily from Lisbon (€15, five hours), Coimbra (€10, three hours) and Porto (€2, 1¾ hours), and there are daily connections north to Viana do Castelo. Daily bus services link Braga to Porto (€3.80, 1½ hours) and Lisbon (€14.20, five hours).

# PARQUE NACIONAL DA PENEDA-GERÊS

This magnificent park, northeast of Braga, has some of the most stunning scenery as well as being a popular holiday spot for Portugal's happy campers, appeals to hikers with its wilder northern region around Serra de Peneda. The area has an ancient history with dolmens, stone circles and standing stones; most are marked on tourist maps.

The park's main centre is at **Caldas do Gerês**, a sleepy, hot-spring village.

## Orientation & Information

Gerês' **tourist office** ( ☎ 253 391 133; fax 253 391 282) is in the colonnade at the upper end of the village and can provide information on activities and accommodation.

Other park offices are at Arcos de Valdevez, Montalegre. All have a map of the park (€3) with some roads and tracks marked but no trails, and a free English-language booklet on the park's features.

## Activities

### HIKING

There are trails and footpaths through the park, some between villages with accommodation. Leaflets detailing these are available from the park offices.

Day hikes around Gerês are popular. An adventurous option is the old Roman road from Mata do Albergaria (10km up-valley from Gerês by taxi or hitching), past the **Vilarinho das Furnas** reservoir to Campo do Gerês. More distant are **Ermida** and **Cabril**, both with simple cafés and accommodation.

### CYCLING

Mountain bikes can be hired from **Incentivos Outdoors** ( ☎ 914 863 353) or the German-run **Pensão Carvalho Araújo** ( ☎ 253 391 185; May-Sep).

### HORSE RIDING

The national park operates **horse riding facilities** ( ☎ 253 390 110) from beside its Vidoeiro camping ground, near Gerês. Incentivos Outdoors also has horses for hire.

### WATER SPORTS

Rio Caldo, 8km south of Gerês, is the base for water sports on the Caniçada reservoir. **Agua Montanha Lazer** ( ☎ 253 391 779; www.aguamontanha.com) rents out canoes and boats. For paddling the Salamonde reservoir, Trote-Gerês rents canoes from its campsite at Cabril.

## Sleeping

Gerês has plenty of pensões, although many are completely booked by groups of spa patients in summer.

**Pousada da Juventude** (Campo do Gerês; ☎ /fax 253 351 339; dm/d €10/24) A former dam workers' camp equals comfy, sprawling accommodation.

**Cerdeira Camping Ground** (Campo do Gerês; ☎ 253 351 005; fax 253 353 315; camp sites €4) Has shady camp sites, a laundry and mini-supermarket.

**Vidoeiro Camping Ground** (Gerês; ☎ 253 391 289; camp sites €4) Open year-round, just out of town on the river.

**Pensão Adelaide** ( ☎ 253 390 020; fax 253 390 029; d €40; ) Bit of a hike from the centre but the views are a suitable reward. Rooms are clean and bright.

**Hotel Universal** ( ☎ 253 390 020; ehgeres@netc.pt; s/d €58/70; ) A leafy inner patio lends an air of elegance to this main-street hotel with its comfortable carpeted rooms and energetic swimming pool and tennis court extras.

## Eating

Most of Gerês pensões serve hearty meals to guests and nonguests. There are several restaurants, plus shops in the main street for picnic provisions. The Cerdeira Camping Ground at Campo do Gerês has a cheap okay-standard restaurant.

## Getting There & Away

From Braga, at least six coaches daily run to Rio Caldo and Gerês, and seven to Campo do Gerês (fewer at weekends). Coming from Lisbon or Porto, change at Braga.

# PORTUGAL DIRECTORY

## ACCOMMODATION

Most tourist offices have lists of accommodation to suit a range of budgets, and can help you find and book it. Although the government uses stars to grade some types of accommodation, criteria seem erratic. In this chapter the Budget category is up to €35, Mid-Range is between €36 and €70 and Top End is over €71. The cheapest accommodation is listed first.

## Camping

If you're economising, camping's always the cheapest option although some grounds close out of season. The multilingual, yearly updated *Roteiro Campista* (€5), sold in larger bookshops, contains details of nearly all Portugal's camping grounds.

## Youth Hostels

Portugal has 41 *pousadas da juventude* (youth hostels), all part of the Hostelling International (HI) system. You can reserve in advance for a €1.50 fee by contacting their central reservations office: **Movijovem** ( ☎ 213 524 072; reservas@movijovem.pt; Avenida Duque d'Ávila 137, Lisbon).

If you don't already have a card from your national hostel association, you can pay a €2 supplement per night (and have a one-night, six-night or year-long 'guest card').

Another cheaper option is a private room *(quarto particular)*, usually in a private house, with shared facilities. Homeowners may approach you at the bus or train station; otherwise watch for 'quartos' signs or ask at tourist offices. Rooms are usually clean and cheap (€25 to €50 for a double in summer). You may be able to bargain in the low season.

## Guesthouses

The most common types of guesthouse, the Portuguese equivalent of B&Bs, are the *residencial* and the *pensão*. Both are graded from one to three stars, and the best are often cheaper and better run than some hotels. High-season pensão rates for a double start from around €35; a residencial, where breakfast is normally included, is a bit more. Many have cheaper rooms with shared bath.

## Hotels

The government grades hotels with one to five stars. For a high-season double expect to pay €60 up to as much as €250. *Estalagem* and *albergaria* refer to upmarket inns. Prices drop considerably in low season. Breakfast is usually included.

## Pousadas

Pousadas are government-run former castles, monasteries or palaces, often in spectacular locations. For details contact tourist offices, or **Pousadas de Portugal** ( ☎ 218 442 001; www.pousadasjuventude.pt; Avenida Santa Joana Princesa 10, 1749 Lisbon).

PORTUGAL

Private counterparts are operated under a scheme called Turismo de Habitação and a number of smaller schemes (often collectively called 'Turihab'), which allow you to stay in anything from a farmhouse to a manor house; some also have self-catering cottages. The tourist offices can tell you about local Turihab properties.

## ACTIVITIES

Off-road cycling (BTT; *bicyclete tudo terrano*, all-terrain bicycle) is booming in Portugal, with bike trips on offer at many tourist destinations (see Tavira p462, Setúbal p459, Évora p464 and Parque Nacional da Peneda-Gerês p474).

Despite some fine rambling country, walking is not a Portuguese passion. Some parks are establishing trails, though, and some adventure travel agencies offer walking tours (see p453, p460, p463, p469 and p474).

Popular water sports include surfing, windsurfing, canoeing, white-water rafting and water-skiing. For information on some local specialists see Lagos (p462), Sagres (p464), Évora (p464), Tavira (p462), and Parque Nacional da Peneda-Gerês (p474).

The **Instituto Português da Juventude** ( ☎ 218 920 800; www.sej.pt, in Portuguese; Rua de Moscavide 47, Lisbon) offers holiday programs for 16- to 30-year-olds (visitors too), including BTT, canoeing and rock climbing.

## BUSINESS HOURS

Banks are open 8.30am to 3pm weekdays. Museums and tourist attractions are open 10am to 5pm Tuesday to Friday, but are often closed at lunch time. Shopping hours generally extend from 9am to 7pm on weekdays, and 9am to 1pm on Saturday. Lunch is given lingering and serious attention between noon and 3pm.

## DANGERS & ANNOYANCES

Petty theft is the main problem in Portugal. Be wary of anyone asking you directions or the time, which may just be a distraction while an accomplice snatches your bag.

### Scams

A common scam takes place predominantly at supermarket (or similar) car parks. After you have deposited your shopping in the trunk of the car and your bag on the passenger seat, someone will approach and inform you that you have a puncture in your back tyre. When you get out to investigate, the accomplice opens the passenger door and swipes your bag.

Despite all the adverse publicity and warnings from local tourist offices, timeshare touts on the Algarve continue to convince tourists that *their* scratch card is the one-in-a-hundred/thousand/million winner. And the prize (usually a bottle of cheap champagne) can, of course, only be collected in person from the resort – after several hours of being on the hard-sell receiving end. If you do end up there, don't sign anything until a week's 'cooling off' period and leave your credit cards at home.

## EMBASSIES & CONSULATES
### Portuguese Embassies & Consulates
Portuguese embassies abroad include:

**Australia** Canberra ( ☎ 026-2901 733; 23 Culgoa Circuit, O'Malley, ACT 2606)
**Canada** Ottawa ( ☎ 613-7290 883; 645 Island Park Dr, Ont K1Y 0B8)
**France** Paris ( ☎ 01 47 27 35 29; 3 Rue de Noisiel, 75116)
**Germany** Berlin ( ☎ 030-590 063 500; Zimmerstrasse 56, 10117)
**Ireland** Dublin ( ☎ 012-894 46; Knocksinna House, Foxrock, Dublin 18)
**New Zealand** Auckland ( ☎ 09-309 1454; PO Box 305, 33 Garfield St, Parnell)
**Spain** Madrid ( ☎ 915 617 800; Calle Castello 128, 28006)
**Netherlands** The Hague ( ☎ 070-363 02 17; Bazarstraat 21, 2518)
**UK** London ( ☎ 0207-235 5331; 11 Belgrave Square SW1X 8PP)
**USA** Washington ( ☎ 202-328 8610; 2125 Kalorama Rd NW, DC 20008)

### Embassies & Consulates in Portugal
The following are embassies unless otherwise stated:

**Canada** Lisbon (Map pp450-1; ☎ 213 164 600; Avenida da Liberdade 196) Faro ( ☎ 289 521 120; Rua Frei Lourenço de Santa Maria 1)
**France** Lisbon (Map pp450-1; ☎ 226 939 292; Calçada a Marques de Abrantes 123) Porto ( ☎ 226 094 805; Rua Eugénio de Castro 352)
**Germany** Lisbon (Map pp454-5; ☎ 213 810 210; Campo dos Mártires da Pátria 38)
**Ireland** Lisbon (Map pp450-1; ☎ 213 929 440; Rua da Imprensa à Estrela 1)

**Spain** Lisbon (Map pp454-5; Consulate ☎ 213 472 792; Rua do Salitre 1) Porto (Map p471; ☎ 225 101 685; Rua de Dom João IV 341) Vila Real de Santo António ( ☎ 281 544 888; Avenida Ministro Duarte Pacheco)

**Netherlands** Lisbon ( ☎ 213 914 900; Avenida Infante Santo 43) Porto (Consulate ☎ 222 080 061; Rua da Reboleira 7)

**UK** Lisbon (Map pp450-1; ☎ 213 924 000; Rua de São Bernardo 33) Porto ( ☎ 226 184 789; Avenida da Boavista 3072) Portimão ( ☎ 282 417 800; Largo Francisco a Maurício 7) The UK consulate also oversees consular matters for New Zealand.

**USA** Lisbon (Map pp450-1; ☎ 217 273 300; Avenida das Forças Armadas)

## FESTIVALS & EVENTS

**Holy Week Festival** Easter week in Braga features colourful processions, including Ecce Homo, with barefoot penitents carrying torches.

**Festas das Cruzes** Held in Barcelos in May, the Festival of the Crosses is known for processions, folk music and dance, and regional handicrafts.

**Feira Nacional da Agricultura** In June, Santarém hosts the National Agricultural Fair, with bullfighting, folk singing and dancing.

**Festa do Santo António** The Festival of Saint Anthony fills the streets of Lisbon on 13 June.

**Festas de São João** Porto's big street bash is the St John's Festival, from 16 to 24 June.

**Festas da Nossa Senhora da Agonia** Viana do Castelo's Our Lady of Suffering Festival runs for three days, including the weekend nearest to 20 August, and is famed for its folk arts, parades and fireworks.

## HOLIDAYS

**New Year's Day** 1 January
**Carnival** Shrove Tuesday; February/March
**Good Friday and the following Saturday** March/April
**Liberty Day** 25 April (commemorating the 1975 Revolution)
**Labour Day** 1 May
**Corpus Christi** May/June (the ninth Thursday after Easter)
**National Day** 10 June
**Feast of the Assumption** 15 August
**Republic Day** 5 October
**All Saints' Day** 1 November
**Independence Day** 1 December (celebrating independence from Spain in 1640)
**Immaculate Conception** 8 December
**Christmas Day** 25 December

## MONEY
### ATMs

There are dozens of banks with ATMs throughout Portugal. However, some only accept credit (rather than debit) cards.

## Credit Cards

Credit cards are increasingly accepted in hotels, restaurants and shops, however, you will normally be asked to provide some form of photo identification (ie passport).

## Moneychangers

Exchange bureaux are common throughout Portugal, located near to or even within the same building as the tourist offices. They often offer a better rate of exchange for cash and travellers cheques than the banks.

## POST

Post offices *(correios)* are open Monday to Friday 8.30am to 6pm. In Lisbon and Porto they're also open on Saturday mornings. Stamps can be bought at the counter or from a dispensing machine *(Correio de Portugal – Selos)*. Depending on the size of the city/town, there are usually several in and near the centre. A letter within Europe costs €0.56, or €0.72 to anywhere else. An increasing number of post offices also have a Netpost Internet kiosk (€5.50 for three hours).

## TELEPHONE
### Mobile Phones

Mobile phone numbers within Portugal have nine digits and begin with ☎ 9.

### Phone Codes

All Portuguese phone numbers have nine digits. These include area codes which always need to be dialled. For general information dial ☎ 118, for international inquiries dial ☎ 179, and for reverse-charge (collect) calls dial ☎ 120.

### Phonecards

Phonecards are the most reliable and cheap way of making a phone call from a telephone booth. They are sold at post offices, newsagents and tobacconists in denominations of €5 and €10.

## VISAS

EU nationals need a valid passport or identity card for entry to Portugal, and may stay indefinitely. Citizens of Australia, Canada,

---

**EMERGENCY NUMBERS**
Ambulance, fire, police ☎ 112

New Zealand and the United States can stay for up to 90 days in any half-year without a visa. Check out www.travisa.com/visa1.htm for more visa information.

# TRANSPORT IN PORTUGAL

## GETTING THERE & AWAY
### Air

Portugal's main gateway is the **Aeroporto Portela** ( ☎ 218 413 700) in Lisbon approximately 8km north of the city centre.

Porto's Aeroporto **Francisco Sá Carneiro** ( ☎ 229 432 400) handles international flights, as does the **Aeroporto de Faro** ( ☎ 229 800 801) in the Algarve, with the largest number of charter flights. The website for all three airports is www.ana-aeroportos.pt (it's in Portuguese).

**Air Portugal** (TAP; ☎ 289 800 218; www.tap.pt, in Portuguese) is the main international airline. **Portugália Airlines** (PGA; ☎ 218 425 559; www.pga.pt, in Portuguese) is primarily a domestic airline, but is increasingly opening up international routes including to/from Manchester, Brussels, Nice and Lyon. Both airlines have an excellent safety record.

Following is a list of the major carriers serving Portugal, along with the airports they use – Lisbon, Porto or Faro. For details of carriers to/from outside Mediterranean Europe see the Transport chapter (p717):

**Air France** (code AF; ☎ 218 482 177; www.airfrance.com;) Lisbon, Porto.

**Air Portugal** (code TAP; ☎ 289 800 218; www.tap.pt) Lisbon, Porto, Faro.

**British Airways** (code BA; ☎ 214 154 151; www.ba.com;) Lisbon, Porto, Faro.

**British Midlands/bmibaby** (code WW; UK ☎ 0870 264 2229; www.bmibaby.com) Lisbon, Porto, Faro.

**EasyJet** (code EZY; UK ☎ 0870 600 000; www.easyjet.com) Lisbon, Faro.

**Iberia** (code IB; ☎ 808 261 261; www.iberia.com, in Spanish) Lisbon, Porto.

**Lufthansa** (code IH; London ☎ 020-8750 3460; www.lufthansa.com, in German) Lisbon, Porto.

**Monarch Airlines** (code ZB; ☎ 289 889 475; www.fly-monarch.com) Faro.

**Portugália Airlines** (code PGA; ☎ 218 425 559; www.pga.pt, in Portuguese) Lisbon, Porto, Faro.

**Spanair** (code JK; ☎ 218 4998 578; www.spanair.com) Lisbon.

There are scheduled year-round flights from the UK to Lisbon, Porto and Faro with BA, PGA and TAP and from Frankfurt (Germany) with Lufthansa.

TAP and Continental Airlines both have a daily flight from New York to Lisbon with connections to Faro and Porto. Air France has multiple daily non-stop Paris–Lisbon and Paris–Porto connections, while PGA has a daily flight from Paris to Porto. From neighbouring Spain, TAP, Iberia and Spanair have daily Madrid–Lisbon flights. Elsewhere in Europe, KLM and TAP flies to Lisbon and Porto daily from Amsterdam, while PGA has regular direct flights to Lisbon from Berlin, Stuttgart, Cologne and Hamburg.

There are no direct flights from Australia/New Zealand to Portugal, but dozens of indirect routes via third countries. Tap has regular routes to Lisbon from South America, including Rio and Recife (Brazil) and Caracas (Venezuela).

Among the cheaper scheduled options using the UK as a base or transfer is no-frills Easyjet with flights from London, Stanstead, Bristol and East Midland to Faro starting as low as UK£100 return. British Midland's bmibaby also has inexpensive flights from the East Midlands to Faro, and Monarch Airlines flies from Luton and Manchester.

### Land
#### BUS
#### From the UK & France

**Eurolines** (UK ☎ 08705-143 219; www.eurolines.co.uk) operated by National Express, offers departures once a week to Portugal with several stops including Lisbon (42hrs) and Porto (40hrs). Buses go from Victoria coach station via the Channel ferry, with a 7½-hour stopover and change of coach in Paris. The current return fare London–Lisbon is UK£145.

**Busabout** (UK ☎ 020 7950 1661; www.busabout.com) is a Europe-wide hop-on–hop-off coach network with passes that let you travel as much as you want within a set period. Its stops in Portugal are in Lisbon and Lagos. The current eight-day under-26 Flexipass costs UK£249.

**IASA** (Paris ☎ 014 353 9082; fax 014 353 4957) have several different routes within Portugal departing from Paris. The current return fare Paris–Lisbon is €135, with discounts for seniors and students.

### From Spain
**Eurolines** (Madrid ☎ 915 063 360; www.eurolines.es, in Spanish) operates several services from Spain to Portugal, including Madrid–Lisbon (€38, eight hours), Madrid–Porto (€38, seven hours), Seville–Lisbon (€35, four hours) and Barcelona–Lisbon (€74, 16hrs), all going at least three times weekly.

**ALSA** (Madrid ☎ 902 422 242) has twice-daily Madrid–Lisbon services, while **Damas** (Huelva ☎ 959 256 900) runs twice daily Monday to Saturday from Seville to Faro and Lagos via Huelva, jointly with the Algarve line EVA.

### CAR & MOTORCYCLE
There is no border control in Portugal. For more information about driving in Portugal see p480.

### TRAIN
### From the UK & France
In general, it's only worth taking the train from the UK if you can use under-26 rail passes such as **Inter-Rail**. See p730.

All services from London to Portugal go via Paris, where you change trains (and stations) for the *TGV Atlantique* to Irún in Spain (change trains again). From Irún there are two standard routes: the *Sud-Expresso* across Spain to Coimbra in Portugal, where you can continue to Lisbon or change for Porto; and an express service to Madrid, changing there to the overnight *Lusitânia* to Lisbon. Change at Lisbon for the south of Portugal.

Buying a one way, 2nd-class, adult/youth London–Lisbon ticket (seat only) for the cheapest route, via the channel ferry, costs around UK£120; allow at least 24hrs. Tickets for this route are available from bigger train stations or from **Trains Europe** (UK ☎ 01354-660 222; www.trainseurope.co.uk). The Eurostar service to Paris via the Channel Tunnel cuts several hours off the trip but bumps up the cost. Contact **Rail Europe** (UK ☎ 08705-848 848; www.raileurope.co.uk) for details.

### From Spain
**Renfe** (Spain ☎ 902 240 202; www.renfe.es, in Spanish; return ticket €118) has a nightly sleeper service between Madrid and Lisbon. Badajoz–Elvas–Lisbon is slow and there is only one regional service daily, but the scenery is stunning. There are no direct southern trains: from Seville you can ride to Huelva

(three daily), catch a bus for Ayamonte, change buses to cross the border to Vila Real de Santo António then catch one of the frequent trains to Faro and Lagos.

## Sea
### From the UK
There are no ferries from the UK to Portugal, but you can travel to northern Spain with the following operators and then hit the road to Portugal.

**P&O Ferries** (UK ☎ 0870 520 2020; www.poef.com; adult one way from UK£125) operates the Portsmouth–Bilbao route (30hrs) with crossings twice weekly throughout the year except for three weeks in January.

**Brittany Ferries** (UK ☎ 0870 366 5333; www.brittanyferries.com; from UK£110/per adult one way) operates between Plymouth and Santander twice weekly. The 24-hour crossing can be rough.

## GETTING AROUND
## Air
### AIRLINES IN PORTUGAL
Flights within Portugal are poor value unless you have a youth/student card.

**Portugália Airlines** (PGA; Lisbon ☎ 218 425 559; www.pga.pt) and **TAP** (Lisbon ☎ 808 205 700; www.tap.pt) both have multiple daily Lisbon–Porto and Lisbon–Faro links for around €105. Portugália has a 50% youth discount. TAP has a daily Lisbon–Faro service connecting with its international arrivals and departures at Lisbon. Portugal's domestic departure tax is €7 and is generally included in the ticket price.

Both airlines have good safety records, marred only by a 1977 TAP accident in Madeira when there were 131 fatalities.

## Bicycle
Mountain biking is popular and a great way to explore Portugal, although given the Portuguese penchant for overtaking on blind corners, it can be dangerous on lesser roads. Bicycle lanes are rare, aside from in the natural parks: Veteran pedallers recommend the Parque Nacional da Peneda-Gare (p474). A growing number of towns have bike-rental outfits (around €10 a day). If you're bringing your own machine, pack plenty of spares. Bicycles can no longer be taken with you on trains, although most bus lines will accept them as accompanied baggage, subject to space and sometimes for an extra fee.

PORTUGAL

## Boat

Portugal is not big on waterborne transport, other than river cruises along the Douro River from Porto (p473), Lisbon's river trips (p453) and commuter ferries.

## Bus

Portugal's buses are generally modern and comfortable. However, there is a baffling number of privatised bus companies operating across the country. In Porto alone there are at least 18 bus companies, most based at different terminals.

Unless you're a local or speak fluent Portuguese, the only company really worth worrying about is the national network **Rede Expressos** ( ☎ 969 502 050; www.rede-expressos.pt, in Portuguese), which has a fleet of 100 buses, a comprehensive website and provides connections to 300 locations throughout the country. Portugal's main Eurolines agents are **Internorte** (Porto ☎ 226 052 420), **Intercentro** (Lisbon ☎ 213 571 745) and **Intersul** (Faro ☎ 289 899 770), serving north, central and southern Portugal, respectively.

### CLASSES

There are three classes of bus service: *Expressos* are comfortable, fast, direct buses between major cities. *Rápidas* are fast regional buses. *Carreiras* stop at every crossroad. *Expressos* are generally the best cheap way to get around (particularly for long trips, where per-kilometre costs are lowest). An under-26 card should get you a discount of around 20%, at least on the long-distance services.

### COSTS

Travelling by bus in Portugal is comparatively inexpensive – especially when compared with the UK. Refer to the Getting There & Away section of the respective city or town you are travelling to or from for more information, including fares.

### RESERVATIONS

Advance reservations are only necessary on the longer routes of the *expresso* service.

## Car & Motorcycle

### AUTOMOBILE ASSOCIATIONS

**ACP** (Automóvel Clube de Portugal; head office ☎ 213 180 100; emergency help number for the south ☎ 219 429 103;

emergency help number for the north ☎ 228 340 001; www .acp.pt, in Portuguese; Rua Rosa Araújo 24, Lisbon) has a reciprocal arrangement with many of the better-known foreign automobile clubs, including AA and RAC. ACP provides medical, legal and breakdown assistance.

### FUEL & SPARE PARTS

Fuel costs around €0.97 for a litre of 95-octane *sem chumbo* (unleaded petrol) and €0.71 for a *gasóleo* (diesel). There are lots of self-service stations; some have garages that can replace batteries, repair punctures and do minor mechanical repairs, as well as carry some spare parts. Alternatively, they can direct you to the nearest car workshop.

### HIRE

To hire a car in Portugal you must be at least 25 and have held your home licence for over a year (some companies allow younger drivers at higher rates). To hire a scooter of up to 50cc you must be over 18 years old and have a valid driving licence. For more powerful scooters and motorbikes you must have a valid driving licence covering these vehicles from your home country.

### INSURANCE

Although most car insurance companies within the EU will cover your car in Portugal, it is prudent to consider extra cover for assistance in case your car breaks down. The minimum insurance required is third party.

**ACP Insurance** ( ☎ 217 991 200; www.acp.pt, in Portuguese) can advise members on car and motorcycle insurance.

### ROAD RULES

Driving is on the right. Speed limits for cars and motorcycles are 50km/h in cities and public centres, 90km/h on normal roads and 120km/h on motorways (but 50, 70 and 100km/h for motorcycles with sidecars). Drivers and front passengers in cars must wear seat belts. Motorcyclists and passengers must wear helmets; motorcycles must have headlights on day and night. Using a mobile phone while driving could result in a fine.

Drink-driving laws are strict here with a maximum legal blood-alcohol level of 0.05%.

# Croatia

## CONTENTS

Croatia is the Mediterranean's best-kept secret. Its lush islands, unspoiled fishing villages, beaches, lakes, waterfalls and walled cities were the star attraction of the former Yugoslavia before it split apart in 1991. The essential fabulousness of the country was forgotten as the region descended into war, but travellers are once again discovering its many treasures.

With 6000km of coastline winding around innumerable bays and almost 1100 offshore islands, there's a dream spot for every taste. The magnificent walled city of Dubrovnik, on the country's southern tip, is Croatia's crown jewel; lovely Hvar and Korčula islands are within easy reach. Istria, on the north coast, is famous for its delicious food, rocky beaches and relaxed, Italian-influenced lifestyle. Austrian influence is most pronounced in Croatia's capital, Zagreb, a calm and gracious city. Yet, wherever you go, you'll find easy-going, tolerant people, accustomed to welcoming visitors and proud of the country they fought so hard to establish.

This chapter focuses on Croatia's Mediterranean highlights but if you want to learn more about the country then check out Lonely Planet's guide to *Eastern Europe*.

## FAST FACTS

- **Area** 56,538 sq km
- **Capital** Zagreb
- **Currency** kuna (KN); €1=7.70KN; US$1=6.41KN; UK£1=11.49KN; A$1=4.48KN; ¥17.50=1KN; NZ$1=3.90KN
- **Famous For** neckties, war, Tito
- **Key Phrases** *bog* (hello); *doviđenja* (good-bye); *hvala* (thanks); *pardon* (sorry)
- **Official Language** Croatian
- **Population** 4,496,869
- **Telephone codes** country code ☎ 385; international access code ☎ 00
- **Visas** unnecessary for citizens of the EU, USA, Australia and Canada

## HIGHLIGHTS

- Admire the luminous marble streets, finely ornamented buildings and heavy stone walls of **Dubrovnik** (p525).
- Check out the nightlife that throbs within the old palaces of **Hvar town** (p520) while the pine-covered island sleeps.
- Feel the excitement of a *moreška* sword dance in **Korčula** (p522).
- Relish the untamed natural beauty of **Mljet** (p523) and its lakes, coves and island monastery.
- Wander the cobbled streets and unspoiled fishing port of **Rovinj** (p500).

## ITINERARIES

- **One week** After a day in Zagreb head down to Split. Spend a day exploring Diocletian's Palace and Solin before taking ferries to Hvar and Korčula. End with three days in Dubrovnik, taking a day trip to Mljet.
- **Two weeks** After two days in Zagreb, head to Pula for a three-day stay, taking day trips to Rovinj and Poreč. Head south to Zadar for a night and then go on to Split for a two-night stay. Take ferries to Hvar and Korčula before ending with three days in Dubrovnik and a day trip to Mljet.

## CLIMATE & WHEN TO GO

The climate varies from Mediterranean along the Adriatic coast, with hot, dry summers and mild, rainy winters, to continental inland, with cold winters and warm summers. You can swim in the sea from mid-June until late September. Coastal temperatures are slightly warmer south of Split. The peak tourist season runs from mid-July to the end of August. Prices are highest and accommodation scarcest during this period. See the Climate Charts on p703 for more.

The best time to be in Croatia is June. The weather is beautiful, the boats and excursions are running often and it's not yet too crowded. The end of May and the beginning of September are also good, especially if you're interested in hiking.

## HISTORY

In 229 BC the Romans began their conquest of the indigenous Illyrians by establishing a colony at Solin (Salona), close to Split in Dalmatia. Emperor Augustus then extended the empire and created the provinces of Illyricum (Dalmatia and Bosnia) and Pannonia (Croatia). In AD 285 Emperor Diocletian decided to retire to his palace fortress in Split, today the greatest Roman ruin in Eastern Europe. When the empire was divided in 395, what are now known as Slovenia, Croatia and Bosnia and Hercegovina stayed with the Western Roman

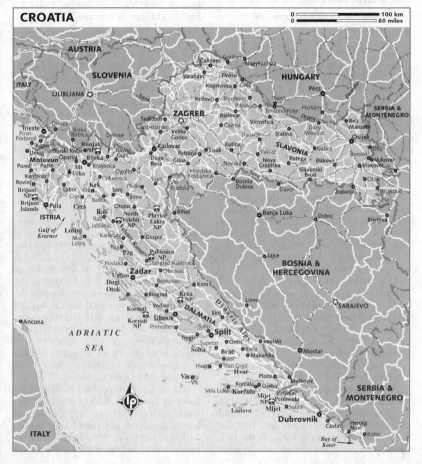

**CROATIA**

**HOW MUCH?**

- **Bottle of house white** 20KN
- **Litre of milk** 7KN
- **Loaf of bread** 3KN
- **Newspaper** 5KN
- **Short taxi ride** 35KN

**LONELY PLANET INDEX**

- **Litre of petrol** 8KN
- **Litre of bottled water** 5KN
- **Beer – bottle of Karlovačko (33cl)** 10KN
- **Souvenir T-shirt** 75KN
- **Street snack – slice of burek** 7KN

Empire, while present Serbia, Kosovo and Macedonia went to the Eastern Roman Empire, later known as the Byzantine Empire.

Around 625, Slavic tribes migrated from present-day Poland. The Serbian tribe settled in the region that is now southwestern Serbia. The Croatian tribe moved into what is now Croatia and occupied two former Roman provinces: Dalmatian Croatia along the Adriatic, and Pannonian Croatia to the north.

By the early part of the 9th century both settlements had accepted Christianity but the northern Croats fell under Frankish domination while Dalmatian Croats came under the nominal control of the Byzantine Empire. The Dalmatian duke Tomislav united the two groups in 925 in a single kingdom that prospered for nearly 200 years.

Late in the 11th century the throne fell vacant and a series of power struggles weakened central authority and split the kingdom. The northern Croats, unable to agree upon a ruler, united with Hungary in 1102 for protection against the Orthodox Byzantine Empire.

In the 14th century the Turks began pushing into the Balkans, defeating the Serbs in 1389 and the Hungarians in 1526. Northern Croatia turned to the Habsburgs of Austria for protection against the Turks in 1527 and remained part of their empire until 1918. To form a buffer against the Turks, in the 16th century the Austrians invited Serbs to settle

the Vojna Krajina (Military Frontier) north of Zadar. The Serbs in the borderlands had an autonomous administration under Austrian control; these areas were reincorporated into Croatia in 1881.

The Adriatic coast fell under Venetian influence as early as the 12th century, although Hungary continued to struggle for control of the region. Some Dalmatian cities changed hands repeatedly until Venice imposed its rule on the Adriatic coast in the early 15th century and occupied it for nearly four centuries. Only the Republic of Ragusa (Dubrovnik) maintained its independence.

After Venice was shattered by Napoleonic France in 1797, the French occupied southern Croatia, abolishing the Republic of Ragusa in 1808. Napoleon merged Dalmatia, Istria and Slovenia into the 'Illyrian Provinces', but following his defeat at Waterloo in 1815, Austria-Hungary moved in to pick up the pieces along the coast.

A revival of Croatian cultural and political life began in 1835, and with the defeat of the Austro-Hungarian empire in WWI, Croatia became part of the Kingdom of Serbs, Croats and Slovenes (called Yugoslavia after 1929), with a centralised government in Belgrade. Italy had been promised control of the Adriatic coast as an incentive to join the war against Austria-Hungary in 1915 and it held much of northern Dalmatia from 1918 to 1943, which explains the strong Italian influence along the coast.

After the German invasion of Yugoslavia in March 1941, a puppet government dominated by the fascist Ustaša movement was set up in Croatia and Bosnia and Hercegovina under Ante Pavelić (who fled to Argentina after WWII). At first the Ustaša tried to expel all Serbs from Croatia to Serbia. But when the Germans stopped this because of the problems it was causing, the Ustaša launched an extermination campaign that rivalled the Nazis in its brutality. Although there is much controversy over the number of victims, estimates indicate that from 60,000 to 600,000 ethnic Serbs, Jews and Roma were murdered.

Not all Croats supported these policies, however. Josip Broz, known as Maršal Tito, was himself of Croat-Slovene parentage and tens of thousands of Croats fought bravely with his partisans. Massacres of Croats conducted by Serbian Četniks in southern

Croatia and Bosnia forced almost all anti-fascist Croats into the communist ranks, where they joined the numerous Serbs trying to defend themselves from the Ustaša. In all, about a million people died violently in a war that was fought mostly in Croatia and Bosnia and Hercegovina.

## Recent History

After the war, Maršal Tito became the prime minister of the new Yugoslav Federation. He divided it into five republics: Croatia, Serbia, Slovenia, Bosnia and Hercegovina and Macedonia. Even with a Stalin-style system of state planning, Croatia and Slovenia moved far ahead of the southern republics economically, leading to demands by reformers, intellectuals and students for greater autonomy. The 'Croatian Spring' of 1971 caused a backlash and purge of reformers, who were jailed or expelled from the Communist Party.

Tito's habit of borrowing from abroad to flood the country with cheap consumer goods produced an economic crisis after his death in 1980. The sinking economy provoked greater tension among Yugoslavia's ethnic groups, which came to a head when Serbian politician Slobodan Milošević whipped Serbs into a nationalistic frenzy over the aspirations of the Albanian majority in the province of Kosovo.

Fearing a renewal of Serbian hegemony, many Croats felt the time had come to end more than four decades of communist rule and attain complete autonomy into the bargain. In the free elections of April 1990 Franjo Tudjman's Hrvatska Demokratska Zajednica (HDZ; Croatian Democratic Union) easily defeated the old Communist Party. On 22 December 1990 a new Croatian constitution was promulgated, changing the status of Serbs in Croatia to a national minority.

The constitution's failure to guarantee minority rights, and mass dismissals of Serbs from the public service, led the 600,000-strong ethnic Serb community to demand autonomy. When Croatia declared independence from Yugoslavia on 25 June 1991, the Serbian enclave of Krajina proclaimed its independence from Croatia.

Heavy fighting broke out in Krajina (the area around Knin, north of Split), Baranja (the area north of the Drava River opposite Osijek) and Slavonia (the region west of the Danube). The 180,000-member, 2000-tank Yugoslav People's Army, dominated by Serbian communists, began to intervene on its own authority in support of Serbian irregulars, under the pretext of halting ethnic violence.

In the three months following 25 June, a quarter of Croatia fell to Serbian militias and the federal army. In September the Croatian government ordered a blockade of 32 federal military installations in the republic, gaining much-needed military equipment. In response, the Yugoslav navy blockaded the Adriatic coast and laid siege to the strategic town of Vukovar on the Danube.

In early October 1991 the federal army and Montenegrin militia moved against Dubrovnik to protest against the ongoing blockade of their garrisons in Croatia. On 7 October the presidential palace in Zagreb was hit by rockets fired from Yugoslav airforce jets in an unsuccessful assassination attempt against President Tudjman. Heroic Vukovar finally fell on 19 November when the Yugoslav army ended a bloody three-month siege by concentrating 600 tanks and 30,000 soldiers there. During the six months of fighting in Croatia 10,000 people died, hundreds of thousands fled and tens of thousands of homes were deliberately destroyed.

## Independence

After the Croatian parliament amended its constitution to protect minority and human rights the European Community (EC), succumbing to strong pressure from Germany, recognised Croatia in January 1992. This was followed three months later by US recognition and in May 1992 Croatia was admitted to the UN.

In January 1993 the Croatian army suddenly launched an offensive in southern Krajina, pushing the Serbs back as much as 24km in some areas and recapturing strategic points. The Krajina Serbs vowed never to accept rule from Zagreb and in June 1993 they voted overwhelmingly to join the Bosnian Serbs (and eventually Greater Serbia).

The self-proclaimed 'Republic of Serbian Krajina' held elections in December 1993, which no international body recognised as legitimate or fair. Continued 'ethnic cleansing' left only about 900 Croats in Krajina out of an original population of 44,000.

On 1 May 1995 the Croatian army and police entered and occupied western Slavonia, east of Zagreb, causing some 15,000 Serbs to flee the region. At dawn on 4 August 1995 the military launched a massive assault on the rebel Serb capital of Knin. Outnumbered by two to one, the Serb army fled to northern Bosnia, along with about 150,000 civilians whose roots in the Krajina stretched back centuries. The military operation lasted just days, but was followed by months of terror. Widespread looting and burning of Serb villages, as well as attacks on the few remaining elderly Serbs, seemed designed to ensure the permanence of this massive population shift.

The Dayton Agreement, signed in Paris in December 1995, recognised Croatia's traditional borders and provided for the return of eastern Slavonia, a transition that was finally completed in January 1998.

Croatia's first president, Franjo Tudjman, died in 1999 after presiding over a regime notable for corruption, cronyism and suppression of dissent. The centre-left coalition that took power in 2000 swiftly made known their desire to enter the European mainstream but failed to make a dent in Croatia's serious economic problems. The road to privatisation has been bumpy, unemployment remains at a stubbornly high 22%, inflation is at 5.4% and the average monthly salary is only 5411KN (about €730). In the elections of 2003 Tudjman's reformed HDZ party was returned to power on a promise to reduce the detested Value Added Tax (VAT) from 22% to 20%. Ivo Sanader, called 'the grey man', was named prime minister but the HDZ parliamentary majority remains weak.

In April 2004 the European Commission recommended that negotiations be opened with a view to admitting Croatia to the EU. A major sticking point remains the return of Serbs who fled during the war. In many cases their homes have been reoccupied by Croats and no legal mechanism is in place to give back or provide new housing for the returning refugees. Croatia is also expected to comply with the International Criminal Tribunal for the former Yugoslavia (ICTY) by handing over accused war criminals.

## PEOPLE

Croatia has a population of roughly 4.5 million people. Before the war Croatia had a population of nearly five million, of which 78% were Croats and 12% were Serbs. Bos-

nians, Hungarians, Italians, Czechs, Roma and Albanians made up the remaining 10%. Today Croats constitute 89% of the population, as there was a large influx of Croats from other parts of the former Yugoslavia after the war. Now, slightly less than 5% of the populations are Serb, followed by 0.5% Bosnians and about 0.4% each of Hungarians and Italians. Small communities of Czechs, Roma and Albanians complete the mosaic. Most Serbs live in eastern Croatia (Slavonia) where ethnic tensions between the Serbs and Croats run highest. The largest cities in Croatia are Zagreb (780,000), Split (188,700), Rijeka (144,000), Osijek (114,600) and Zadar (72,700).

Croats are united by a common religion, Catholicism, and a common sense of themselves as European. If you ask a Croat what distinguishes Croatian culture from Bosnian or Serbian culture, the answer is likely to be a variant of 'We are Western and they are Eastern'. Even Croats who bear no particular ill will towards other ethnicities will nonetheless note that their former compatriots in Bosnia and Hercegovina, Macedonia and Serbia and Montenegro eat different food, listen to different music, have different customs and, of course, go to different churches.

Although the shelling of Dubrovnik and the atrocities committed in eastern Slavonia and the Krajina have left a bitter taste in those regions, many Croatians are increasingly open to questioning the conduct of the 'Homeland War'. Self-examining books and articles are a staple of the country's intellectual life but the extradition to the Hague of Croatian generals accused of war crimes remains highly controversial.

## RELIGION

Croats are overwhelmingly Roman Catholic, while virtually all Serbs belong to the Eastern Orthodox Church. In addition to doctrinal differences, Orthodox Christians venerate icons, allow priests to marry and do not accept the authority of the Roman Catholic pope. Long suppressed under communism, Catholicism is undergoing a strong resurgence in Croatia and churches have good attendance on Sunday. The Pope has visited Croatia several times and religious holidays are scrupulously observed. Muslims make up 1.2% of the population and Protestants 0.4%, with a tiny Jewish population in Zagreb.

CROATIA

## ARTS

The exhibition pavilion (p491) in Zagreb is a good place to keep up with the latest developments in Croatian art.

### Painting

Vlaho Bukovac (1855–1922) was the most notable Croatian painter in the late 19th century. Important early-20th-century painters include Miroslav Kraljević (1885–1913) and Josip Račić (1885–1908). Post-WWII artists experimented with abstract expressionism but this period is best remembered for the naive art that was typified by Ivan Generalić (1914–92). Recent trends have included minimalism, conceptual art and pop art. Contemporary artists that are attracting notice include Jasna Barišić of Zadar, Andrea Musa of Split, and Višeslav Aralica and Ivana Ožetski of Zagreb.

### Sculpture

The work of sculptor Ivan Meštrović (1883–1962) is seen in town squares throughout Croatia. Besides creating public monuments, Meštrović designed imposing buildings, such as the circular Croatian History Museum (p491)in Zagreb. Both his sculptures and architecture display the powerful classical restraint he learnt from Auguste Rodin. Meštrović's studio in Zagreb (p491) and his retirement home at Split (p516) have been made into galleries of his work.

### Music & Dance

Croatian folk music has many influences. The *kolo*, a lively Slavic round dance where men and women alternate in the circle, is accompanied by Roma-style violinists or players of the *tambura*, a three- or five-string mandolin popular throughout the country. The measured guitar-playing and rhythmic accordions of Dalmatia have a gentle Italian air.

A recommended recording available locally on CD is *Narodne Pjesme i Plesovi Sjeverne Hrvatske* (Northern Croatian Folk Songs and Dances) by the Croatian folkloric ensemble Lado. The 22 tracks on this album represent nine regions, with everything from haunting Balkan voices reminiscent of Bulgaria to lively Mediterranean dance rhythms. Traditional Croatian music has influenced other musicians, most notable the Croatian-American jazz singer Helen Merrill who recorded Croatian melodies on her album, *Jelena Ana Milcetic a.k.a. Helen Merrill*.

On the radio, you're likely to hear a lot of 'turbofolk', a charged up version of folk music that is widely popular throughout former Yugoslavia. Split-born Severina Vuckovic enjoys tremendous popularity, probably enhanced by a compromising video circulating on the Internet. Also popular are Doris Dragović and Mirakul Gibonni.

## ENVIRONMENT
### The Land

Croatia is half the size of present-day Serbia and Montenegro in area and population. The republic swings around like a boomerang from the Pannonian plains of Slavonia between the Sava, Drava and Danube Rivers, across hilly central Croatia to the Istrian Peninsula, then south through Dalmatia along the rugged Adriatic coast.

The narrow Croatian coastal belt at the foot of the Dinaric Alps is only about 600km long as the crow flies, but it's so indented that the actual length is 1778km. If the 4012km of coastline around the offshore islands is added to the total, the length becomes 5790km. Most of the 'beaches' along this jagged coast consist of slabs of rock sprinkled with naturists. Don't come expecting to find sand, but the waters are sparkling clean, even around large towns.

Croatia's offshore islands are every bit as beautiful as those off the coast of Greece. There are 1185 islands and islets along the tectonically submerged Adriatic coastline, 66 inhabited. The largest are Cres, Krk, Lošinj, Pag and Rab in the north; Dugi Otok in the middle; and Brač, Hvar, Korčula, Mljet and Vis in the south. Most are barren and elongated from northwest to southeast, with high mountains that drop right into the sea.

---

## TOP FIVE WALKS

■ **Dubrovnik** – along the walls (p525)

■ **Opatija** – promenading the Lungomare (p508)

■ **Mljet** – on the shores of the lakes (p524)

■ **Rovinj** – around the harbour (p500)

■ **Baška beach** – down the long stretch of sand (p509)

## National Parks

When the Yugoslav Federation collapsed, eight of its finest national parks ended up in Croatia, occupying nearly 10% of the country. Brijuni near Pula is the most carefully cultivated park, with well-preserved Mediterranean holm oak forests. The mountainous Risnjak National Park near Delnice, east of Rijeka, is named after one of its inhabitants – the *ris* (lynx).

Dense forests of beech and black pine in the Paklenica National Park near Zadar are home to a number of endemic insects, reptiles and birds. The abundant plant and animal life, including bears, wolves and deer, in the Plitvice Lakes National Park between Zagreb and Zadar has warranted its inclusion on Unesco's list of World Natural Heritage Sites. Both Plitvice Lakes and Krka National Parks (near Šibenik) feature a dramatic series of cascades and incredible turquoise lakes.

The 101 stark and rocky islands of the Kornati Archipelago and National Park make it the largest in the Mediterranean. The island of Mljet near Korčula also contains a forested national park, and the North Velebit National Park includes Croatia's longest mountain range.

## Environmental Issues

The lack of heavy industry in Croatia has left the country largely free of industrial pollution, but its forests are under threat from acid rain from neighbouring countries. The dry summers and brisk *maestral* winds pose substantial fire hazards along the coast. The sea along the Adriatic coast is among the world's cleanest especially throughout Istria and the southern Adriatic. Waste disposal is a pressing problem in Croatia, with insufficient and poorly regulated disposal sites.

## FOOD & DRINK

A restaurant *(restauracija)* or pub may also be called a *gostionica* and a café is known as a *kavana*. Self-service caféterias are quick, easy and cheap, though the quality of the food tends to vary. Better restaurants aren't that much more expensive if you choose carefully. The cheapest dishes are pasta and risotto, which can be filling meals. Fish dishes are often charged by weight (from 280KN to 320KN per kilogram), which makes it difficult to know how much a dish will cost but an average portion is about 250g. Some restaurants tack on a 10% cover charge, which is *supposed* to be mentioned on the menu.

Breakfast is included in the price of the hotels mentioned in this chapter and usually includes a juice drink, bread, cheese, yogurt, cereal and cold cuts, as well as coffee and tea. No restaurants serve breakfast.

A load of fruit and vegetables from the local market can make a healthy, cheap picnic lunch. There are plenty of supermarkets in Croatia; cheese, cold cuts, bread, wine and milk are readily available and fairly cheap. The person behind the meat counter at supermarkets will make a big cheese or bologna sandwich for you upon request and you only pay the price of the ingredients.

## Staples & Specialities

Croatian meals often start with a dish of locally smoked ham or Pag cheese with olives. A Zagreb speciality is *štrukli* (boiled cheesecake), served either plain as a starter or sugared as a dessert. In the north you also might begin with a hearty *Zagorska juha od krumpira* (potato soup Zagorje style) or *manistra od bobića* (beans and fresh maize soup), while coastal folk follow the Italian habit of beginning with a serving of spaghetti or risotto. *Risotto neri* (black risotto) made from squid in its own ink is a particular delicacy.

---

**MYSTERIOUS FLAVOURS**

No Croatian cook could do without it yet it is almost unknown outside former Yugoslavia. It's the secret ingredient in nearly every fish, vegetable or meat dish yet it's hard to describe what it actually contains. What is it ? It's 'Vegeta', sold by the kilo in nearly every grocery store. We know that there's salt, sugar, corn starch and various dehydrated vegetables plus 'flavour enhancers' that end in –ate in there. There are also 'spices' of indeterminate composition. We don't know how it works its magic in Croatian dishes, but even the simplest sauces are imbued with subtle flavours. Pick up a package and add a tablespoon or so to your favourite tomato sauce. *Dobar tek!* (Bon appetit!)

For a main meal, the Adriatic coast excels in seafood, including scampi (look for *scampi bouzzara*), *prstaci* (shellfish), *lignje* (calamari) and Dalmatian *brodet* (fish stew served with polenta). Istria is known for its *tartufe* (truffles), which frequently appear in risotto or pasta dishes or flavouring meat. The season is from September to January; any other time the chef is using preserved truffles. In Zagreb and in the north you'll find exquisite spit-roasted goose, duck and lamb. Turkey with *mlinci* (baked noodles) is another Zagrebian wonder.

For fast food you can usually snack on *čevapčići* (spicy beef or pork meatballs), *ražnjiči* (shish kebab), *burek* (a greasy layered pie made with meat) or *sira* (cheese), which is cut on a huge metal tray.

It's customary to have a small glass of brandy before a meal and to accompany the food with one of Croatia's fine wines – there are about 700 to choose from! Croatians often mix their wine with water, calling it *bevanda*. Croatia is also famous for its *šljivovica* (plum brandies), *travarica* (herbal brandies), *vinjak* (cognacs) and liqueurs, such as maraschino (a cherry liqueur made in Zadar) or herbal *pelinkovac*. Italian-style espresso is popular in Croatia.

Zagreb's Ožujsko *pivo* (beer) is very good but Karlovačko *pivo* from Karlovac is even better. You'll probably want to practise saying *živjeli!* (cheers!).

## Vegetarians & Vegans

Outside of Zagreb, vegetarian restaurants are few and far between but Croatia's vegetables are usually locally grown and quite tasty. *Blitva* (swiss chard) is a nutritious side dish often served with potatoes. Pasta, risotto and pizza are often made from scratch and lacto-ovo vegetarians will appreciate Croatia's wide variety of cheese. Look for the sharp lamb's-milk cheese from the island of Pag.

# ZAGREB

☎ 01 / pop 780,000

Zagreb is finally coming into its own as an intriguing combination of Eastern and Western Europe. The sober Austro-Hungarian architecture in the town centre houses newly opened boutiques displaying the latest fashions from France and Italy. Bohemian cafés and sleek cocktail bars enliven the medieval streets of the old Kaptol and Gradec neighbourhoods. The Croatian appreciation of food is divided between its traditional hearty meat and potatoes restaurants and a new smattering of more worldly flavours.

Spreading up from the Sava River, Zagreb sits on the southern slopes of Mt Medvednica and throbs with the energy you would expect from a capital city, but the bustle of business life is interrupted by the long, refreshing stretch of park that bisects the town centre. With simmering nightlife and a wealth of outdoor cafés, packed from the first hint of mild weather, there's no shortage of diversions. Plus, there's an assortment of museums and galleries to explore and a regular concert schedule for the culturally minded.

## HISTORY

Medieval Zagreb developed from the 11th to the 13th centuries in the twin villages of Kaptol and Gradec, which make up the city's hilly Old Town. Kaptol grew around St Stephen's Cathedral (now renamed the Cathedral of the Assumption of the Blessed Virgin Mary) and Gradec centred on St Mark's Church. The two hill-top administrations were bitter and often warring rivals until a common threat in the form of Turkish invaders emerged in the 15th century. The two communities merged and became Zagreb, capital of the small portion of Croatia that hadn't fallen to the Turks in the 16th century. As the Turkish threat receded in the 18th century, the town expanded and the population grew. It was the centre of intellectual and political life under the Austro-Hungarian empire and became capital of the Independent State of Croatia in 1941 after the German invasion. The 'independent state' was in fact a Nazi puppet regime in the hands of Ante Pavelić and the Ustaša movement, even though most Zagrebians supported Tito's partisans.

In postwar Yugoslavia Zagreb took second place to Belgrade but continued expanding. The area south of the Sava River developed into a new district, Novi Zagreb, replete with the glum residential blocks that were a hallmark of postwar Eastern European architecture. Zagreb has been capital of Croatia since 1991 when the country became independent.

## ORIENTATION

The city is divided into Lower Zagreb, where most shops, restaurants and businesses are located, and Upper Zagreb, defined by the two hills of Kaptol and Gradec. As you come out of the train station, you'll see a series of parks and pavilions directly in front of you and the twin neo-Gothic towers of the cathedral in Kaptol in the distance. Trg Jelačića, beyond the northern end of the parks, is the main city square of Lower Zagreb. The bus station is 1km east of the train station. Tram Nos 2 and 6 run from the bus station to the train station, with No 6 continuing to Trg Jelačića.

## INFORMATION

### Bookshops

**Algoritam** (Gajeva; Hotel Dubrovnik) Off Trg Jelačića, Algoritam has a wide selection of books and magazines to choose from in English, French, German, Italian and Croatian.

### Emergency

**Police station** ( ☎ 45 63 311; Petrinjska 30) Assists foreigners with visa problems.

### Internet Access

**Art Net Club** ( ☎ 45 58 471; Preradovićeva 25; per hr 20KN; ☼ 9am-11pm) Zagreb's flashiest Internet café, it frequently hosts concerts and performances.

**Sublink** ( ☎ 48 11 329; Teslina 12; per hr 20KN; ☼ 9am-10pm Mon-Sat, 3-10pm Sun) It was here first and has a comfortable set up.

### Laundry

If you're staying in private accommodation you can usually arrange with the owner to do your laundry, which would be cheaper than the two options listed below. Five kilograms of laundry will cost about 60KN.

**Petecin** (Kaptol 11; ☼ 8am-8pm Mon-Fri)

**Predom** (Draškovićeva 31; ☼ 7am-7pm Mon-Fri)

## Left Luggage

**Garderoba** (per day 10KN; ☼ 24hr) In the train station.

**Garderoba** (per hr 1.20KN; ☼ 5am-10pm Mon-Sat, 6am-10pm Sun) In the bus station.

## Medical Services

**Dental Emergency** ( ☎ 48 28 488; Perkovčeva 3; ☼ 24hr)

**KBC Rebro** ( ☎ 23 88 888; Kišpatićeva 12; ☼ 24hr) East of the city, it provides emergency aid.

**Pharmacy** ( ☎ 48 48 450; Ilica 43; ☼ 24hr)

## Money

There are ATMs at the bus and train stations and the airport as well as numerous locations around town. Exchange offices at the bus and train stations change money at the bank rate with 1.5% commission. Both the banks in the train station (open 7am to 9pm) and the bus station (open 6am to 8pm) accept travellers cheques.

**Atlas travel agency** ( ☎ 48 13 933; Zrinjevac 17) The Amex representative in Zagreb.

## Post

**Main Post Office** (Branimirova 4; ☼ 24hr Mon-Sat, 1pm-midnight Sun) Holds poste-restante mail. This post office is also the best place to make long-distance telephone calls and send packages.

## Tourist Information

**Main tourist office** ( ☎ 48 14 051; www.zagreb-tourist info.hr; Trg Jelačića 11; ☼ 8.30am-8pm Mon-Fri, 9am-5pm Sat, 10am-4pm Sun) Distributes city maps and free leaflets. It also sells the Zagreb Card, which costs 60KN and includes 72 hours of free transport and a 50% discount on museums.

**Marko Polo** ( ☎ 48 15 216; Masarykova 24) Handles information and ticketing for Jadrolinija's coastal ferries.

**National Park Information Office** ( ☎ 46 13 586; Trg Tomislava 19; ☼ 8am-4pm Mon-Fri) Has details on Croatia's national parks.

**Tourist office annex** ( ☎ 49 21 645; Trg Nikole Šubića Zrinjskog 14; ☼ 9am-6pm Mon-Fri) Same services as the main tourist office, but stocks fewer publications.

---

### ZAGREB IN TWO DAYS

From Trg Jelačića, take a stroll through Kaptol and Gradec, stopping to admire the **Cathedral** (p491), the **Archiepiscopal Palace** (p491), the **Dolac vegetable market** (p491), the **Stone Gate** (p491), **St Mark's Church** (p491) and the **Banski Dvori Palace** (p491) for the changing of the guard. Visit the **Museum of the City of Zagreb** (p491) and the **Meštrović Studio** (p491). Have a drink at **Indy's** (p476) and dine at **Baltazar** (p476) or **Kaptolska Klet** (p475). On day two, explore the lower town. Visit the **Museum Mimara** (p494), the **Strossmayer Gallery of Old Masters** (p491) and the **Archaeological Museum** (p491). Take a break in the park along Zrinjskog. Head to **Boban** (p495) for lunch and **Konoba Čiho** (p496) for dinner.

**Zagreb County Tourist Association** ( ☎ 48 73 665; www.tzzz.hr; Preradovićeva 42; ☺ 8am-4pm Mon-Fri) Has information about attractions in the region outside Zagreb.

## Travel Agencies

**Dali Travel** ( ☎ 48 47 472; hfhs-cms@zg.htnet.hr; Dežmanova 9; ☺ 9am-5pm Mon-Fri) The travel branch of the Croatian YHA. Can provide information on HI hostels throughout Croatia and make advance bookings.

## SIGHTS & ACTIVITIES
### Kaptol

Zagreb's colourful **Dolac vegetable market** ( ☺ 7am-2pm) is just up the steps from Trg Jelačića and continues north along Opatovina. The twin neo-Gothic spires of the 1899 **Cathedral of the Assumption of the Blessed Virgin Mary** (formerly known as St Stephen's Cathedral) are nearby. Elements of the medieval cathedral on this site, destroyed by an earthquake in 1880, can be seen inside, including 13th-century frescoes, Renaissance pews, marble altars and a baroque pulpit. The baroque **Archiepiscopal Palace** surrounds the cathedral, as do 16th-century fortifications constructed when Zagreb was threatened by the Turks.

### Gradec

From ul Radićeva 5, off Trg Jelačića, a pedestrian walkway called stube Ivana Zakmardija leads to the **Lotrščak Tower** ( ☎ 48 51 768; admission 5KN; ☺ 11am-7pm Tue-Sun) and a **funicular railway** (one way 3KN; ☺ 6.30am-9pm) built in 1888, which connects the lower and upper towns. The tower has a sweeping 360-degree view of the city. To the east is the baroque **St Catherine's Church**, with Jezuitski trg beyond. The **Galerija Klovićevi Dvori** ( ☎ 48 51 926; Jezuitski trg 4; adult/student 20/10KN; ☺ 11am-7pm Tue-Sun) is Zagreb's premier exhibition hall where superb art shows are staged. Further north and to the east is the 13th-century **Stone Gate**, with a painting of the Virgin, which escaped the devastating fire of 1731.

Gothic **St Mark's Church** ( ☎ 48 51 611; Markovićev trg; ☺ 11am-4pm & 5.30-7pm) marks the centre of Gradec. Inside are works by Ivan Meštrović, Croatia's most famous modern sculptor. On the eastern side of St Mark's is the **Sabor** (1908), Croatia's National Assembly.

West of the church is the 18th-century **Banski Dvori Palace**, the presidential palace, with guards at the door in red ceremonial uniform. Between April and September there is a changing of the guard ceremony at noon at the weekend.

Not far from the palace is the former **Meštrović Studio** ( ☎ 48 51 123; Mletačka 8; adult/concession 20/10KN; ☺ 10am-6pm Tue-Fri, 10am-2pm Sat), now housing an excellent collection of some 100 sculptures, drawings, lithographs and furniture created by the artist. Other museums nearby include the less-than-gripping **Croatian History Museum** ( ☎ 48 51 900; Matoševa 9; temporary exhibitions adult/concession 10/5KN; ☺ 10am-5pm Mon-Fri, 10am-1pm Sat & Sun); the lively and colourful **Croatian Naive Art Museum** ( ☎ 48 51 911; Čirilometodska 3; adult/concession 10/5KN; ☺ 10am-6pm Tue-Fri, 10am-1pm Sat & Sun); and also the **Croatian Natural History Museum** ( ☎ 48 51 700; Demetrova 1; adult/concession 15/7KN; ☺ 10am-5pm Tue-Fri, 10am-1pm Sat & Sun) which has a collection of prehistoric tools and bones plus exhibits on the evolution of plant and animal life in Croatia. The best is the **Museum of the City of Zagreb** ( ☎ 48 51 364; Opatička 20; adult/concession 20/10KN; ☺ 10am-6pm Tue-Fri, 10am-1pm Sat & Sun), with a scale model of old Gradec, atmospheric background music, and interactive exhibits that fascinate kids. Summaries in English and German are in each room of the museum, which is in the former Convent of St Claire (1650).

### Lower Town

Zagreb really is a city of museums. There are four in the parks between the train station and Trg Jelačića. The yellow **exhibition pavilion** (1897) across the park from the station presents changing contemporary art exhibitions. The second building north, also in the park, houses the **Strossmayer Gallery of Old Masters** ( ☎ 48 95 115; adult/concession 20/15KN; ☺ 10am-1pm & 5-7pm Tue, 10am-1pm Wed-Sun). When it's closed you can still enter the interior courtyard to see the Baška Slab (1102) from the island of Krk, one of the oldest inscriptions in the Croatian language.

The fascinating **Archaeological Museum** ( ☎ 48 73 101; Trg Nikole Šubića Zrinjskog 19; adult/concession 20/10KN; ☺ 10am-5pm Tue-Fri, 10am-1pm Sat & Sun) has a wide-ranging display of artefacts from prehistoric times through to the medieval period. The ambient sounds and light put you in a contemplative mood. Behind the museum is a garden of Roman sculpture that is turned into a pleasant open-air café in the summer.

CROATIA

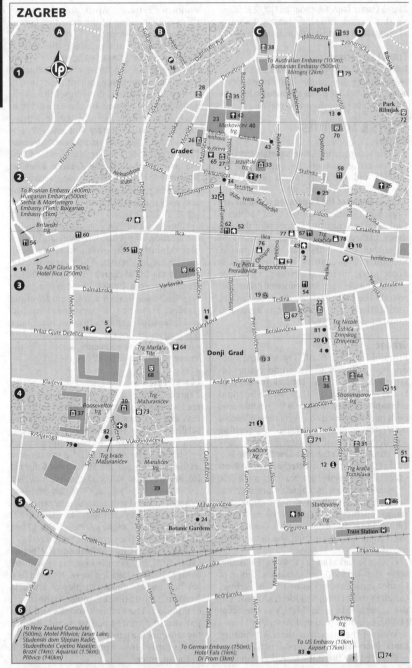

# ZAGREB

To Australian Embassy (100m);
Romanian Embassy (500m);
Mirogoj (2km)

Kaptol

Park
Ribnjak

Gradec

Jezuitski
trg

Markovićev
trg

To Bosnian Embassy (400m);
Hungarian Embassy (500m);
Serbia & Montenegro
Embassy (1km); Bulgarian
Embassy (1km)

Britanski
trg

Trg
Jelačića

To ADP Gloria (50m);
Hotel Ilica (250m)

Ilica

Trg Petra
Preradovića

Donji Grad

Trg Maršala
Tita

Trg Nicole
Šubića
Zrinskog
(Zrinjevac)

Roosveltov
trg

Trg
Mažuranićev

Strossmajerov
trg

Trg braće
Mažuranićev

Marulićev
trg

Trg kralja
Tomislava

Botanic Gardens

Starčevićev
trg

Train Station

To New Zealand Consulate
(500m); Motel Plitvice; Jarun Lake;
Studenski dom Stjepan Radić;
Studenthotel Cvjetno Naselje;
Brazil (1km); Aquarius (1.5km);
Plitvice (140km)

Padićev
trg

To German Embassy (150m);
Hotel Fala (1km);
Di Prom (3km)

To US Embassy (10km);
Airport (17km)

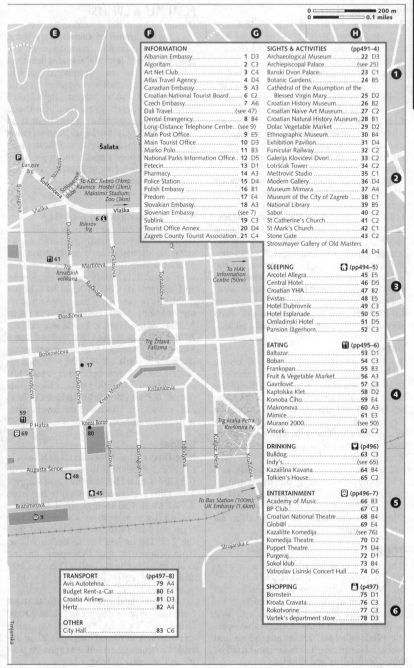

| 0 | 200 m |
| 0 | 0.1 miles |

**INFORMATION**
| Albanian Embassy | 1 D3 |
| Algoritam | 2 C3 |
| Art Net Club | 3 C4 |
| Atlas Travel Agency | 4 D4 |
| Canadian Embassy | 5 A3 |
| Croatian National Tourist Board | 6 E2 |
| Czech Embassy | 7 A6 |
| Dali Travel | (see 47) |
| Dental Emergency | 8 B4 |
| Long-Distance Telephone Centre | (see 9) |
| Main Post Office | 9 E5 |
| Main Tourist Office | 10 D3 |
| Marko Polo | 11 B3 |
| National Parks Information Office | 12 D5 |
| Petecin | 13 D1 |
| Pharmacy | 14 A3 |
| Police Station | 15 D4 |
| Polish Embassy | 16 B1 |
| Predom | 17 E4 |
| Slovakian Embassy | 18 A3 |
| Slovenian Embassy | (see 7) |
| Sublink | 19 C3 |
| Tourist Office Annex | 20 D4 |
| Zagreb County Tourist Association | 21 C4 |

**SIGHTS & ACTIVITIES** (pp491–4)
| Archaeological Museum | 22 D3 |
| Archiepiscopal Palace | (see 25) |
| Banski Dvori Palace | 23 C1 |
| Botanic Gardens | 24 B5 |
| Cathedral of the Assumption of the Blessed Virgin Mary | 25 D2 |
| Croatian History Museum | 26 B2 |
| Croatian Naive Art Museum | 27 C2 |
| Croatian Natural History Museum | 28 B1 |
| Dolac Vegetable Market | 29 D2 |
| Ethnographic Museum | 30 B4 |
| Exhibition Pavilion | 31 D4 |
| Funicular Railway | 32 C2 |
| Galerija Klovićevi Dvori | 33 C2 |
| Lotršćak Tower | 34 C2 |
| Meštrović Studio | 35 C1 |
| Modern Gallery | 36 D4 |
| Museum Mimara | 37 A4 |
| Museum of the City of Zagreb | 38 C1 |
| National Library | 39 B5 |
| Sabor | 40 C2 |
| St Catherine's Church | 41 C2 |
| St Mark's Church | 42 C1 |
| Stone Gate | 43 C2 |
| Strossmayer Gallery of Old Masters | 44 D4 |

**SLEEPING** (pp494–5)
| Arcotel Allegra | 45 E5 |
| Central Hotel | 46 D5 |
| Croatian YHA | 47 B2 |
| Evistas | 48 E5 |
| Hotel Dubrovnik | 49 C3 |
| Hotel Esplanade | 50 C5 |
| Omladinski Hotel | 51 D5 |
| Pansion Jägerhorn | 52 C3 |

**EATING** (pp495–6)
| Baltazar | 53 D1 |
| Boban | 54 C3 |
| Frankopan | 55 B3 |
| Fruit & Vegetable Market | 56 A3 |
| Gavrilović | 57 C3 |
| Kaptolska Klet | 58 D2 |
| Konoba Čiho | 59 E4 |
| Makronova | 60 A3 |
| Mimice | 61 E3 |
| Murano 2000 | (see 50) |
| Vincek | 62 C2 |

**DRINKING** (p496)
| Bulldog | 63 C3 |
| Indy's | (see 65) |
| Kazališna Kavana | 64 B4 |
| Tolkien's House | 65 C2 |

**ENTERTAINMENT** (pp496–7)
| Academy of Music | 66 B3 |
| BP Club | 67 C3 |
| Croatian National Theatre | 68 B4 |
| Glob@l | 69 E4 |
| Kazalište Komedija | (see 76) |
| Komedija Theatre | 70 D2 |
| Puppet Theatre | 71 D4 |
| Purgeraj | 72 D1 |
| Sokol klub | 73 B4 |
| Vatroslav Lisinski Concert Hall | 74 D6 |

**SHOPPING** (p497)
| Bornstein | 75 D1 |
| Kroata Cravata | 76 C3 |
| Rokotvorine | 77 C3 |
| Vartek's department store | 78 D3 |

**TRANSPORT** (pp497–8)
| Avis Autotehna | 79 A4 |
| Budget Rent-a-Car | 80 E4 |
| Croatia Airlines | 81 D3 |
| Hertz | 82 A4 |

**OTHER**
| City Hall | 83 C6 |

Šalata

To KBC Rebro (1km);
Ravnice Hostel (2km);
Maksimir Stadium;
Zoo (3km)

Langov trg

Vlaška

Iblerov trg

Trg hrvatskih velikana

To HAK Information Centre (50m)

Đorđićeva

Trg žrtava Fašizma

Boškovićeva

Križanićeva

Trg kralja Petra Krešimira IV

P Hatza

Augusta Šenoe

To Bus Station (100m);
UK Embassy (1.6km)

Branimirova

Strojarska c

Tkalčićeva

## West of the Centre

The **Museum Mimara** ( ☎ 48 28 100; Rooseveltov trg 5; adult/concession 20/15KN; ☼ 10am-5pm Tue, Wed, Fri & Sat, 10am-7pm Thu, 10am-2pm Sun) houses a diverse collection amassed by Ante Topić Mimara and donated to Croatia. Housed in a neo-Renaissance palace, the collection includes icons, glassware, sculpture, Oriental art and works by renowned painters such as Rembrandt, Velázquez, Raphael and Degas. The **Modern Gallery** ( ☎ 49 22 368; A Hebrangova 1) presents temporary exhibitions that offer an excellent chance to catch up with the latest in Croatian painting.

The neobaroque **Croatian National Theatre** (Trg Maršala Tita 15) dates from 1895 and has Ivan Meštrović's sculpture *Fountain of Life* (1905) in front. The **Ethnographic Museum** ( ☎ 48 26 220; Trg Mažuranićev 14; adult/concession 15/10KN; ☼ 10am-6pm Tue-Thu, 10am-1pm Fri-Sun) has a large collection of Croatian folk costumes, accompanied by English captions. To the south is the Art-Nouveau **National Library** (1907). The **Botanical Gardens** (Mihanovićeva; admission free; ☼ 9am-7pm Tue-Sun) is attractive for its plants and landscaping, as well as its restful corners, perfect for a family picnic.

## Out of town

A 20-minute ride north of the city centre on bus No 106 from the cathedral takes you to **Mirogoj** (Medvednica; ☼ 6am-10pm), one of the most beautiful cemeteries in Europe. The sculptured and artfully designed tombs lie beyond a majestic arcade topped by a string of cupolas. Don't miss the flower-bedecked tomb of Croatia's last president-dictator, Franjo Tudjman. Some Croats were very sad at his death, some were slightly sad, and some wondered if the international community would have paid Croatia as much for his extradition to the war crimes tribunal at the Hague as they paid Serbia for Milošević.

## TOURS

The main tourist office sells tickets for two-hour walking tours (95KN), which operate Monday afternoon and Tuesday and Thursday mornings leaving from in front of the tourist office on Trg Jelačića, as well as three-hour bus tours (150KN) that operate Wednesday and Friday afternoons and weekend mornings. Tours are conducted by noted journalists and novelists.

## FESTIVALS & EVENTS

During odd-numbered years in April there's the **Zagreb Biennial of Contemporary Music**, Croatia's most important music event. Zagreb also hosts a **festival of animated films** (www .animafest.hr) during even-numbered years in June and a **film festival** (www.zagrebfilmfestival.com) in October. Croatia's largest international fairs are the Zagreb spring (mid-April) and autumn (mid-September) grand trade fairs. In July and August the **Zagreb Summer Festival** presents a cycle of concerts and theatre performances on open stages in the upper town. For a complete listing of Zagreb events, see www.zagreb-convention.hr.

## SLEEPING

Budget accommodation is in short supply in Zagreb. An early arrival is recommended, since private room–finding agencies are an attractive alternative and usually refuse telephone bookings. Prices for private rooms run from about 170/220KN per single/double, and apartments cost at least 300KN per night. There's usually a surcharge for staying only one night. **Evistas** ( ☎ 48 39 554; fax 48 39 543; evistas@zg.htnet.hr; Augusta Šenoe 28; s 172-227KN, d 234-314KN, apt 364-835KN; ☼ 9am-1.30pm & 3-8pm Mon-Fri, 9.30am-5pm Sat) is closest to the train station. **ADP Gloria** ( ☎ 48 23 567; www.adp-glorija .com, in Croatian; Britanski trg 5; ☼ closed Sun), just west of here, is another option for private rooms. **Di Prom** ( ☎ 65 50 039; fax 65 50 233; Trnsko 25a; ☼ closed Sun) is south of the town centre with rooms in Novi Zagreb.

### Budget

**Motel Plitvice** ( ☎ 65 30 444; fax 65 30 445) It's not in Plitvice at all but near the town of Lučko on the Obilazinica Hwy southwest of Zagreb. The motel sometimes runs a minibus from Savski Most. Call to find out if and when the service is operating. Otherwise, take tram No 7 or 14 to Savski Most and then the 125, 165 or 168 bus to Lučko village, from where the motel/camping ground is about a 20-minute walk. There's a lake and sports centre nearby and it's open year-round.

**Omladinski Hotel** ( ☎ 48 41 261; fax 48 41 269; Petrinjska 77; per person in 6/3-bed dm 73/83KN, d 211KN) Some say it's a dump. We prefer to call it an auditory and visual challenge with maintenance issues. Checkout is at 9am. At least it's in the centre of town.

**Ravnice Hostel** ( ☎ /fax 23 32 325; www.ravnice-youth
-hostel.hr; Ravnice 38d; dm 99KN; ☐ ) This is really
a delightful option, designed and run by an
Australian woman. Comfortable, clean rooms
have two, four or 10 beds. Solo female travellers would be most comfortable here. Tram
Nos 4, 7, 11 and 12 will take you there.

**Studentski dom Stjepan Radić** ( ☎ 36 34 255;
Jarunska 3; dm 125KN) This student dorm is near
Jarun Lake and its nightlife in the southwest
of the city. Take tram No 5 or 17.

**Studenthotel Cvjetno Naselje** ( ☎ 61 91 239; dm
210KN; ☼ mid-Jul–Sep) Off Slavonska avenija in
the south of the city, this dormitory has good
rooms each with a bathroom. Take tram No
4, 5, 14, 16 or 17 southwest on Savska cesta
to 'Vjesnik'.

## Mid-Range
**Hotel Ilica** ( ☎ 37 77 522; www.hotel-ilica.hr, in Croatian;
Ilica 102; s/d/tw/apt 349/449/549/749KN; **P** ⚡ ) For
a small hotel, you can't do better than this
stylish joint just west of town with comfortable rooms and friendly service. Tram
Nos 6, 11 and 12 stop right outside the
entrance.

**Hotel Fala** ( ☎ /fax 61 94 498; www.hotel-fala-zg.hr;
Trnjanske ledine 18; s/d 350/470KN; **P** ⚡ ) The small
rooms have no frills but the price is right
and you're not too terribly far from the town
centre.

**Central Hotel** ( ☎ 48 41 122; www.hotel-central.hr;
Branimirova 3; s/d 520/680KN; ⚡ ) Entirely renovated with modern, plush rooms, this hotel
represents good value for money, especially
given its location across from the train station. The service is coldly efficient.

**Pansion Jägerhorn** ( ☎ 48 33 877; fax 48 33 573;
Ilica 14; s/d/apt 550/750/900KN; ⚡ ) The downstairs
restaurant is known for serving wild game
but there's no wildness in the civilised rooms
here. Everything is up to date and well
maintained.

**Hotel Dubrovnik** ( ☎ 48 73 555; www.hotel-dubrovnik
.htnet.hr; Gajeva 1; s/d from 650/850KN; ⚡ ) Business
travellers love this modern hotel right in the
centre of town. Services, rooms and facilities
are all first-rate.

## Top End
**Arcotel Allegra** ( ☎ 46 96 000; www.arcotel.at/allegra;
Branimirova 29; r 680-2410KN; **P** ⚡ ⚡ ☐ ) Billing
itself as Zagreb's first 'lifestyle hotel', it's clear
that the style of life is quite high here. Your
lifestyle, should you choose to accept it, will

include ultracontemporary Mediterranean-
inspired décor, and a fitness centre, plus
rooms and accoutrements for your business
meetings. The hotel is gay friendly.

**Hotel Esplanade** ( ☎ 45 66 666; esplanade@esplanade
.hr; Mihanovićeva 1; s/d 1875/2025KN; **P** ⚡ ⚡ ☐ )
This six-storey, 215-room hotel, built in
1924, is an Art-Nouveau masterpiece with
marble-panelled halls and stately rooms
equipped with every comfort. There's also an
in-house restaurant (p496). It was built next
to the train station for the Agatha Christie
crowd when simply everyone took the Orient Express, darling.

## EATING
As befits an up-and-coming international
city, Zagreb presents a fairly wide array of
culinary styles. Exotic spices are not part of
the Croatian gastronomic vocabulary, but
you can't go wrong with fish, pizza, pasta
and roasted meats.

**Mimice** ( ☎ no phone; Jurišićeva 21; mains 12-30KN;
☼ closed Sun) It's a local favourite and deservedly so. The fish is sure to be fresh because
turnover is high, especially at noontime
when workers in the offices around Trg
Jelačića turn out in droves for their lunch.

**Boban** ( ☎ 48 11 549; Gajeva 9; mains 30-50KN) This
Italian restaurant/bar/café offers sophisticated food at good prices. It has an outdoor
terrace and an indoor lounge and terrace
that is popular with Zagreb yuppies. Try the
gnocchi made from squid ink and topped
with salmon sauce.

**Kaptolska Klet** ( ☎ 48 14 838; Kaptol 5; mains 55-
70KN) This huge and inviting space is comfortable for everyone from solo diners to
groups of noisy backpackers. Although
famous for its Zagreb specialities such as
grilled meats, spit-roasted lamb, duck, pork
and veal as well as home-made sausages, it
turns out a nice platter of grilled vegetables
and a vegetable loaf.

**Makronova** ( ☎ 48 47 115; Ilica 72; mains 70KN;
☼ closed Sun) All very Zen, purely macrobi-
otic and more than welcome for those of the
vegan persuasion. There's also shiatsu treatment, yoga classes and feng shui courses.

**Frankopan** ( ☎ 48 48 547; Frankopanska 8; mains
35-85KN) It's a gilt trip with chubby cherubs
frolicking on the ceiling while you munch
on relatively adventurous dishes. The prices
are good because meals are prepared by a
hostelry school.

**STREET NAMES**

In Zagreb, you may notice a discrepancy between the names used in this book and the names you'll actually see on the street. In Croatian, a street name can be rendered either in the nominative or possessive case. The difference is apparent in the name's ending. Thus, Ulica Ljedevita Gaja (street of Ljudevita Gaja) becomes Gajeva ulica (Gaja's street). The latter version is the one most commonly seen on the street sign and used in everyday conversation. The same principle applies to a square *(trg)* which can be rendered as Trg Petra Preradovića or Preradovićev trg. Some of the more common names are: Trg svetog Marka (Markov trg), Trg Josipa Jurja Strossmayera (Strossmayerov trg), Ulica Andrije Hebranga (Hebrangova), Ulica Pavla Radića (Radićeva), Ulica Augusta Šenoe (Šenoina), Ulica Ivana Tkalčića (Tkalčićeva) and Ulica Nikole Tesle (Teslina). Be aware also that Trg Nikole Šubića Zrinjskog is almost always called Zrinjevac.

**Konoba Čiho** ( ☎ 48 17 060; Hatza 15; mains from 55KN; ☺ closed Sun) Tucked away downstairs, this cosy restaurant turns out a startling assortment of fish and seafood, grilled, fried and combined in delicious stews.

**Baltazar** ( ☎ 46 66 824; Nova Ves 4; mains from 70KN; ☺ closed Sun) Duck, lamb, pork, beef and turkey are cooked to perfection here, served with a good choice of local wines.

**Murano 2000** ( ☎ 456 66 66; Mihanovićeva 1; mains 90-200KN; ☺ closed Sun) Here are the tastiest, most creative dishes in town served with polish in the dining room of the Hotel Esplanade, a world-class hotel.

There's a **fruit and vegetable market** (Britanski trg; ☺ 7am-3pm) and you can pick up yummy fresh produce at Dolac (p491), and local cheese, smoked meat and cold cuts at nearby **Gavrilović** ( ☺ closed Sun). Slurp up dessert at **Vincek** ( ☎ 45 50 834; Ilica 18), famous for its ice cream.

## DRINKING

The architecture may be sober but the nightlife definitely is not, especially as the weather warms up and Zagrebians take to the streets. Wander along Tkalčićeva in the upper town or around along bar-lined Bogovićeva, just south of Trg Jelačića, which turns into prime meet-and-greet territory each evening. Tkalčićeva attracts a slightly funkier crowd. The places listed below open around noon for café society and turn into bars around dinner time.

**Bulldog** ( ☎ 48 17 393; Bogovićeva 6) Belgian beer loosens up a crowd of young execs, sales reps, minor politicos and expats.

**Tolkien's House** ( ☎ 48 51 776; Vranicanijeva 8) Decorated in the style of JRR Tolkien's books, it's very Frodo.

**Indy's** ( ☎ 48 52 053; Vranicanijeva 4) A dazzling assortment of juicy and fruity cocktails are presented at this friendly bar on an outdoor terrace.

**Brazil** ( ☎ 091 200 24 81; Veslačka bb) Parked on the Sava River, this bar on a boat refreshes a throng of thirsty revellers and offers occasional live music.

**Kazališna Kavana** ( ☎ 48 55 851; Trg Maršala Tita) Everyone seems to wind up at this café, known as Kav Kaz, at one time or another, even though it's beyond pretentious.

## ENTERTAINMENT

Zagreb is a happening city. Its theatres and concert halls present a marvellous variety of programmes throughout the year. Many (but by no means all) are listed in the monthly brochure *Zagreb Events & Performances,* which is available from the tourist office. Otherwise, drop in at Art Net Club (p490) and peruse the many flyers announcing breaking developments on the music scene.

### Discos & Clubs

The dress code is relaxed in most Zagreb clubs but neatness counts. The cover usually runs to 30KN and the action doesn't heat up until near midnight.

**Aquarius** ( ☎ 36 40 231; Ljubeka bb) On Lake Jarun, this is the night temple of choice for Zagrebians of all ages and styles. The design cleverly includes an open-air terrace on the lake and the sound is usually house. Take tram No 17 to the Jarun stop.

**Purgeraj** ( ☎ 48 14 734; Park Ribnjak) A funky, relaxed space to listen to live rock, blues, rock-blues, blues-rock, country rock. You get the idea.

**Glob@l** ( ☎ 48 76 146; Hatza 14) Gays and lesbians are more than welcome to take in the friendly, tolerant vibes.

**Sokol klub** ( ☎ 48 28 510; Trg Maršala Tita 6) Across the street from the Ethnographic Museum, Sokol is fashionable without being snooty and the dance floor is always packed.

**BP Club** ( ☎ 48 14 444; Nikole Tesle 7; ⏰ 5pm-1am) Famous for its high-quality musicians and occasional jam sessions, this is one of Zagreb's classic addresses.

## Sport

Basketball is popular in Zagreb, and from October to April games take place in a variety of venues around town, usually at the weekend. The tourist office has the schedule.

Football (soccer) games are held every Sunday afternoon at the **Maksimir Stadium** (Maksimirska 128), on the eastern side of Zagreb; catch tram No 4, 7, 11 or 12 to Bukovačka. If you arrive too early for the game, Zagreb's zoo is just across the street.

## Theatre

It's worth making the rounds of the theatres in person to check their programmes. Tickets are usually available for performances, even for the best shows. A small office marked 'Kazalište Komedija' (look out for the posters) also sells theatre tickets; it's in the Oktogon, a passage connecting Trg Petra Preradovića to Ilica 3.

**Croatian National Theatre** ( ☎ 48 28 532; Trg Maršala Tita 15; box office ⏰ 10am-1pm & 5-7.30pm Mon-Fri, 10am-1pm Sat, 30 min before performances Sun) This neobaroque theatre was established in 1895. It stages opera and ballet performances.

**Komedija Theatre** ( ☎ 48 14 566; Kaptol 9) Near the cathedral, the Komedija Theatre stages operettas and musicals.

**Vatroslav Lisinski Concert Hall** (ticket office ☎ 61 21 166; Trg Stjepana Radica 4; ⏰ 9am-8pm Mon-Fri, 9am-2pm Sat) Just south of the train station, this concert hall is a prestigious venue. There are symphony concerts held here on a regular basis.

Concerts also take place at the **Academy of Music** ( ☎ 48 30 822; Gundulićeva 6a) off Ilica. Another entertainment option is the **Puppet Theatre** (Baruna Trenka 3; performances 5pm Sat, noon Sun).

## SHOPPING

Ilica is Zagreb's main shopping street.

**Vartek's department store** (Trg Jelačića) You can get in touch with true Croatian consumerism at this new store.

**Kroata Cravata** (Oktogon) Croatia is the birthplace of the necktie (cravat); Kroata Cravata has locally made silk neckties at prices that run from 175KN to 380KN.

**Rokotvorine** (Trg Jelačića 7) This place sells traditional Croatian handicrafts, such as red-and-white embroidered tablecloths, dolls and pottery.

**Bornstein** ( ☎ 48 12 361; Kaptol 19) If Croatia's wine and spirits have gone to your head, get your fix at Bornstein, which presents an astonishing collection of brandy, wine and gourmet products.

## GETTING THERE & AWAY
### Air

For information about the flights to and from Zagreb, see p535 and p537.

### Bus

Zagreb's big, modern **bus station** ( ☎ 61 57 983; www.akz.hr, in Croatian) has a large, enclosed waiting room and a number of shops, including grocery stores. You can buy most international tickets at windows No 17 to 20.

Buses depart from Zagreb for most parts of Croatia, Slovenia and places beyond. Buy an advance ticket at the station if you're planning to travel far.

The following domestic buses depart from Zagreb:

| destination | cost | duration | frequency |
| --- | --- | --- | --- |
| Dubrovnik | 205-410KN | 11hr | 7 daily |
| Korčula | 195KN | 12hr | 1 daily |
| Krk | 136KN | 4-5hr | 4 daily |
| Ljubljana | 115KN | 2½hr | 2 daily |
| Osijek | 88KN | 4hr | 8 daily |
| Plitvice | 50KN | 2½hr | 19 daily |
| Poreč | 123KN | 5hr | 6 daily |
| Pula | 114-161KN | 4-6hr | 13 daily |
| Rab | 144KN | 4½-5hr | 2 daily |
| Rijeka | 75-129KN | 2½-3hr | 21 daily |
| Rovinj | 132KN | 5-8hr | 8 daily |
| Split | 112-143KN | 6-9hr | 27 daily |
| Varaždin | 51KN | 1¾hr | 20 daily |
| Zadar | 97-157KN | 4-5hr | 20 daily |

For international bus connections see p536.

**CROATIA**

## Train

The following domestic trains depart from **Zagreb train station** ( ☎ 060 33 34 44):

| destination | cost | duration | frequency |
| --- | --- | --- | --- |
| Osijek | 117KN | 4½hr | 4 daily |
| Pula | 123KN | 5½hr | 2 daily |
| Rijeka | 102KN | 5hr | 5 daily |
| Split | 138KN | 6½-9hr | 6 daily |
| Varaždin | 47KN | 3hr | 13 daily |
| Zadar | 134N | 8hr | 4 daily |

All daily trains to Zadar stop at Knin. Reservations are required on fast InterCity (IC) trains and there's a supplement of 5KN to 15KN for fast or express trains.

For international train connections see p536.

## GETTING AROUND

Zagreb is fairly easy to navigate, whether by car or public transport. Traffic isn't bad, there's sufficient parking, and the efficient tram system should be a model for other polluted, traffic-clogged European capitals.

### To/From the Airport

The Croatia Airlines bus to Zagreb airport, 17km southeast of the city, leaves from the bus station every half-hour or hour from about 5.30am to 7.30pm, depending on flights, and returns from the airport on about the same schedule (25KN). A taxi would cost about 250KN.

### Car

Of the major car-rental companies, you could try **Budget Rent-a-Car** ( ☎ 45 54 936) in the Hotel Sheraton, **Avis Autotehna** ( ☎ 48 36 006) at the Hotel Opera and **Hertz** ( ☎ 48 46 777; Vukotinovićeva 1). Prices start at 300KN per day. Zagreb is relatively easy to navigate by car but remember that the streets around Trg Jelačića and up through Kaptol and Gradec are pedestrian only. Watch out for trams sneaking up on you.

**Croatian Auto Club (HAK) Information Centre** ( ☎ 46 40 800; Derenčinova 20) Helps motorists in need.

### Public Transport

Public transport is based on an efficient but overcrowded network of trams, though the city centre is compact enough to make them unnecessary. Tram Nos 3 and 8 don't run at weekends. Buy tickets at newspaper kiosks for 6.50KN or from the driver for 8KN. Each ticket must be stamped when you board. You can use your ticket for transfers within 90 minutes but only in one direction.

A *dnevna karta* (day ticket), valid on all public transport until 4am the next morning, is 18KN at most Vjesnik or Tisak news outlets. (See p490 for details of the Zagreb Card.) Controls are frequent on the tram system with fines for not having the proper ticket starting at €30.

### Taxi

Zagreb's taxis ring up 8KN per kilometre after a whopping flag fall of 25KN. On Sunday and from 10pm to 5am there's a 20% surcharge.

# ISTRIA

Istria (Istra to Croatians) is the heart-shaped 3600-sq-km peninsula just south of Trieste, Italy, that retains a pronounced Italian influence. Sometimes called the 'new Tuscany', the Istrian interior is a peaceful landscape of green rolling hills, drowned valleys and fertile plains. The rugged and indented coastline is enormously popular with Italian tourists, comfortable with the excellent pasta and seafood on the menus and the fact that Italian is a second language for most Istrians.

Perhaps they dream of the days when the string of Istrian resorts was a part of Italy. Italy seized Istria from Austria-Hungary in 1918, was allowed to keep it in 1920, then had to give it to Yugoslavia in 1947. Tito wanted Trieste (Trst) as part of Yugoslavia too, but in 1954 the Anglo-American occupiers returned the city to Italy so that it wouldn't fall into the hands of the 'communists'. Today the Koper to Piran strip belongs to Slovenia while the rest is held by Croatia. Visit Piran quickly, then move south to Pula, a perfect base from which to explore Poreč and Rovinj.

## POREČ

☎ 052 / pop 10,450

Poreč (Parenzo in Italian) sits on a low, narrow peninsula halfway down the western coast of Istria. The town is the centre of a region dotted with sprawling tourist resorts, but vestiges of earlier times and a quiet, small-town atmosphere (at least in the low season) make it well worth a stop. There are the magnificent mosaics in the Euphrasian Basilica, and places to swim off the rocks north of the old town.

## History

The Romans called the town Parentium and made it an important administrative base, leaving their mark on the rectangular street plan, which still is evident. After the fall of Rome, Poreč came under the rule of the Byzantines and constructed the famous Euphrasian Basilica, now a World Heritage Site. It was later ruled by Venice, then Austria.

## Orientation

The compact old town is squeezed into the peninsula and packed with thousands of shops. The ancient Roman Dekumanus (a Roman longitudinal road) with its polished stones is still the main street, bisected by the latitudinal Cardo. Hotels, travel agencies and excursion boats are on the quay, Obala Maršala Tita, which runs from the small-boat harbour to the tip of the peninsula. The bus station is directly opposite the small-boat harbour just outside the old town.

## Information

### INTERNET ACCESS
**Internet Centre** ( ☎ 427 075; Grahalića 1; per hr 42KN) A full service Internet and computer centre.

### LEFT LUGGAGE
**Garderoba** ( ☉ 6am-8pm Mon-Sat, 6am-5pm Sun)

### MONEY
You can change money at any travel agency. **Istarska Banka** (A Negrija 6) Has an ATM.

### POST
**Main post office** (Trg Slobode 14) Has a telephone centre.

### TOURIST INFORMATION
**Tourist Office** ( ☎ 451 293; www.istra.com/porec; Zagrebačka 11; ☉ 8am-10pm Mon-Sat year-round, 9am-1pm & 6-10pm Sun Jul & Aug)

### TRAVEL AGENCIES
**Atlas travel agency** ( ☎ 434 983; Eufrazijeva 63) Represents Amex.

**Di Tours** ( ☎ 432 100, 452 018; www.di-tours.hr; Prvomajska 2) Finds private accommodation.
**Fiore tours** ( ☎ /fax 431 397; fiore@pu.htnet.hr; Mate Vašića 6) Also handles private accommodation.
**Istra-Line** ( ☎ 451 067; Setaliste 2) If you follow Nikole Tesle until it becomes Kalčića you'll come to Mate Vašića, where you'll find this agency in a pink building.
**Sunny Way agency** ( ☎ 452 021; Negrija 1) Has information about boat connections to Italy.

## Sights

The main reason to visit Poreč is to visit the 6th-century **Euphrasian Basilica** ( ☎ 431 635; admission free; ☉ 7.30am-8pm, to 7pm Oct-Mar), which features some wonderfully preserved Byzantine gold mosaics. The sculpture and architecture of the basilica are remarkable survivors of that distant period. For 10KN you may visit the 4th-century mosaic floor of the adjacent early Christian basilica or visit the baptistry and climb the bell tower for a spectacular view of the region.

The numerous historic sites in the old town include the ruins of two **Roman temples**, between Trg Marafor and the western end of the peninsula. Archaeology and history are featured in the **Regional Museum** ( ☎ 431 585; Dekumanus 9; adult/concession 10/5KN; ☉ 10am-1pm & 5-9pm Jul-Aug, 10am-1pm rest of year) in an old baroque palace. The captions are in German and Italian but there's an explanatory leaflet in English.

From May to mid-October there are passenger boats (20KN return) every half-hour to **Sveti Nikola**, the small island opposite Poreč Harbour, for some wonderful swimming. The boats depart from the wharf on Obala Maršala Tita.

## Festivals & Events

Annual events in Poreč include the day-long **Folk Festival** (June) and the **Musical Summer** (May to September). Ask about these at the tourist office.

## Sleeping

All of the travel agencies listed on p499 find private accommodation. Expect to pay from 165/240KN for a room with shared/private bathroom in the high season, plus a 30% surcharge for stays less than three nights. There are a limited number of rooms available in the old town and it's wise to reserve far in advance for the July to August period.

CROATIA

## BUDGET

Camping grounds are large, well-organised little cities with plenty of activities. Take the 'Zelena Laguna' resort tourist train (20KN), which runs half-hourly or hourly from the town centre between April and October, or the boat shuttle. Prices in high season: about 50KN per person and 60KN for a site.

**Autocamp Zelena Laguna** ( ☎ 410 541) Well-equipped for sports, this autocamp can house up to 2700.

**Autocamp Bijela Uvala** ( ☎ 410 551) Housing up to 6000, the camping ground can be crowded.

### MID-RANGE

**Hotel Poreč** ( ☎ 451 811; www.hotelporec.com; s/d 445/678KN; ✂ ) Near the bus station and an easy walk from the old town, you'll find freshly renovated and comfortable rooms in this hotel.

**Hotel Neptun** ( ☎ 400 800; fax 431 531; Obala Maršala Tita 15; s/d 436/685KN; P ✂ ) This is the best hotel in the town centre, which is an advantage if you want to be in the centre of the action, but it also means being in the centre of a traffic snarl in peak season. The front rooms with harbour view are unbeatable.

**Hotel Hostin** ( ☎ 432 112; www.hostin.hr; Rade Končara 4; per person 556KN; P ✂ ✂ ▯ ▯ ) One of the newer entries on the hotel scene, this sparkling place is in verdant parkland just behind the bus station. An indoor swimming pool, fitness room and sauna are nice little extras plus the hotel is only 70m from a pebble beach. The price includes obligatory half-board.

## Eating

**Barilla** ( ☎ 452 742; Eufrazijeva 26; mains 50-90KN) This authentic Italian restaurant serves delicious pasta and pizza as well as more sophisticated Italian dishes on two outdoor terraces.

**Konoba Ulixes** ( ☎ 451 132; Dekumanus 2; mains 40-100KN) Truffles are one of Istria's most precious products and you can taste them here in pasta, with beef or fresh tuna.

There is a large supermarket and department store next to Hotel Poreč, near the bus station.

## Getting There & Away

From the **bus station** ( ☎ 432 153; Karla Hugesa 2), buses depart for Rovinj (23KN, one hour, seven daily), Zagreb (123KN to 155KN, five hours, six daily) and Rijeka (55KN, 5½ hours, eight daily), and Pula (33KN, 1¼ hours, 12 daily). Between Poreč and Rovinj the bus runs along the Lim Channel, a drowned valley. To see it clearly, sit on the right-hand side if you're southbound, or the left if you're northbound.

The nearest train station is at Pazin, 30km east (five buses daily from Poreč).

For information about bus and boat connections to Italy and Slovenia see p535.

# ROVINJ

☎ 052 / pop 14,200

Yes, it is touristy and residents are developing a sharp eye for maximising their profits but Rovinj (Rovigno in Italian) is one of the last of the true Mediterranean fishing ports. Fishermen haul their catch into the harbour in the early morning, followed by a horde of squawking gulls, and mend their nets before lunch. Prayers for a good catch are sent forth at the massive Cathedral of St Euphemia, whose 60m tower punctuates the peninsula. Wooded hills and low-rise luxury hotels surround a town webbed by steep, cobbled streets. The 13 green, offshore islands of the Rovinj archipelago make for pleasant, varied views and you can swim from the rocks in the sparkling water below Hotel Rovinj.

## Orientation & Information

The bus station is in the southeastern corner of the old town and there's an ATM next to the entrance, as well as the Autotrans Travel Agency, which will change money.

### INTERNET ACCESS

**Planet Tourist Agency** ( ☎ 840 494; Sv Križ 1; per hr 30KN) The most convenient Internet access in Rovinj has a couple of computers.

### LAUNDRY

**Lavanderie Galax** ( ☎ 814 059; M Benussi; per 5kg 5KN) It may be pricey but at least you can get your clothes washed.

### LEFT LUGGAGE

**Garderoba** ( ◷ 8am-9pm daily Jun-Sep, 8am-3pm Mon-Fri, 8am-2pm Sat Oct-May) At the bus station.

### POST

**Main post office** (M Benussi 4) Situated across from the bus station, you can make phone calls here.

## TOURIST INFORMATION

**Tourist office** ( ☎ 811 566; fax 816 007; www.tzgrovinj
.hr; Obala Pina Budicina 12; ☹ 8am-9pm Mon-Sat,
9am-1pm Sun Jun-Sep, 8am-3pm Mon-Fri, 8am-noon Sat
Oct-May) Just off Trg Maršala Tita, this office is less than a
fountain of information; more of a trickle.

## TRAVEL AGENCIES

**Eurostar Travel** ( ☎ 813 144; Obala Pina Budicina 1)
Has schedules and tickets for boats to Italy.
**Futura Travel** ( ☎ 817 281; futura-travel@pu.htnet.hr;
M Benussi 2)
**Marco Polo** ( ☎ 816 616; www.marcopolo.hr; Istarska 2)
**Planet Tourist Agency** ( ☎ 840 494; Sv Križ 1)

## Sights

The **Cathedral of St Euphemia** ( ☹ 10am-noon
& 2-5pm), which completely dominates the
town from its hill-top location, was built
in 1736 and is the largest baroque building
in Istria. It reflects the period during the
18th century when Rovinj was the most
populous town in Istria, an important fishing centre and the bulwark of the Venetian
fleet.

Inside the cathedral, don't miss the tomb
of St Euphemia (martyred in AD 304) behind the right-hand altar. The saint's remains
were brought from Constantinople in 800.
On the anniversary of her martyrdom (16
September) devotees congregate here. A copper statue of her tops the cathedral's mighty
tower.

Take a wander along the winding narrow backstreets below the cathedral, such as
**ul Grisia**, where local artists sell their work.
Each year in August Rovinj's painters stage
a big open-air art show in town.

The Rovinj **Regional Museum** ( ☎ 816 720; Trg
Maršala Tita; adult/concession 10/8KN; ☹ 9am-12.30pm
& 6-9pm Mon-Sat mid-Jun–mid-Sep, 10am-1pm Tue-Sat
rest of year) contains an unexciting collection
of paintings and a few Etruscan artefacts
that have been found in Istria; it's probably only worth a visit when the weather
turns bad. Captions are only in Croatian
and Italian.

When you've seen enough of the town,
follow the waterfront south past Hotel Park
to **Punta Corrente Forest Park**, which was established in 1890 by Baron Hütterodt, an
Austrian admiral who kept a villa on Crveni
otok (Red Island). Here you can swim off
the rocks, climb a cliff or just sit and admire
the offshore islands.

## Tours

**Delfin Agency** ( ☎ 813 383), near the ferry dock
for Crveni otok, runs half-day scenic cruises
to the Lim Channel for 130KN per person,
or you can go with one of the independent
operators at the end of Alzo Rismondo that
run half-day and full-day boat trips around
the region. There's an hourly ferry to the
lovely and wooded Crveni otok (20KN return) and a frequent ferry to nearby Katarina Island (10KN return) from the same
landing. Get tickets on the boat or at the
nearby kiosk. These boats operate only
from May to mid-October.

## Festivals & Events

The city's annual events include the **Rovinj-
Pesaro Regatta** (early May), **Rovinj Summer**
concert series (July and August) and the
**Grisia Art Market** on the 2nd Sunday of August. The tourist office has full details.

## Sleeping

Private rooms with two beds cost 200KN in
high season with a small discount for single
occupancy. The surcharge for a stay of less
than three nights is 50% and guests who stay
only one night are punished with a 100% surcharge, but you should be able to bargain the
surcharge away outside of July and August.
You can book directly from www.inforovinj
.com or consult one of the travel agencies
listed on p501. There are almost no rooms at
all available in the old town however.

**Polari Camping** ( ☎ 800 376; per person/camp sites
55/30KN) This spot is about 5km southeast
of town and is much larger than Porton
Biondi, but it also has more facilities.

**Porton Biondi** ( ☎ 813 557; per person/camp sites for
55/35KN) Less than a 1km from the town (on
the Monsena bus route).

**Hotel Monte Mulin** ( ☎ 811 512; mulin@jadran.tdr
.hr; s/d 241/410KN; ℗ ) On the wooded hillside
overlooking the bay just beyond Hotel Park,
it's about a 15-minute walk to this hotel,
heading south of the bus station. Rooms are
bland but perfectly serviceable.

**Hotel Rovinj** ( ☎ 811 288; fax 840 757; Sv Križ; s/d
from 380/640KN; ☒ ) This hotel has a splendid
location overlooking the sea and is undergoing renovation which may make it more
expensive.

**Vila Lili** ( ☎ 840 940; www.cel.hr/vilalili; Mohorovicica
16; s/d 410/750KN; ☒ ) This small hotel provides an excellent level of comfort, which

includes satellite TV, a sauna and bright, modern rooms. It's just a short walk out of town past the marina.

**Hotel Villa Angelo D'Oro** ( ☎ 840 502; hotel.angelo@ vip.hr; Via Svalba 38-42; s/d 823/1455KN; 🔀 ) This new luxury hotel in a renovated Venetian building has plush, lavishly decorated rooms with satellite TV, minibar, and a free sauna and Jacuzzi room.

## Eating

Most of the fish and spaghetti places along the harbour cater to the more upmarket crowd.

**Cantinon** ( ☎ 811 970; Alzo Rismondo 18; fish mains from 40KN) This welcoming restaurant is becoming touristy but locals still come here for the variety of well-prepared fresh fish.

**Veli Jože** ( ☎ 816 337; Sv Križ 1; mains 30-140KN) In an interior crammed with knick-knacks or at tables outside, you can feast on a wide assortment of Istrian delicacies.

Picnickers can buy supplies at the supermarket only about 25m downhill from the bus station or in one of the kiosks selling *burek* near the vegetable market.

## Getting There & Away

From the **bus station** ( ☎ 811 453; Trg na Lokvi 6), there's a bus from Rovinj to Pula, which sometimes continues on to Poreč (23KN to 40KN, one hour), eight buses daily to Rijeka (73KN, 3½ hours), nine daily to Zagreb

(132KN to 146KN, five to eight hours), one daily each to Koper (79KN, three hours) and Split (295KN, 11¼ hours), and one daily each to Dubrovnik (379KN, 17½ hours) and Ljubljana (155KN, 5½ hours, July and August). Prices and durations vary between different companies and routes.

The closest train station is Kanfanar, 19km away on the Pula–Divača line.

## PULA

☎ 052 / pop 62,400

Pula (the ancient Polensium) is a large regional centre with a wealth of Roman ruins to explore. Its star attraction is a remarkably well-preserved amphitheatre that dominates the town centre and is often the scene of concerts and shows. Despite its busy commercial life, Pula retains an easy-going small-town appeal. Nearby are some rocky wooded peninsulas overlooking the clear Adriatic waters, which explain the many resort hotels and camping grounds circling the city. Most residents head out to Verudela Peninsula for the nightlife and swimming coves.

## Orientation

The bus station is 500m northeast of the town centre. The centre of town is Giardini, while the harbour is west of the bus station. The train station is near the water, about 500m north of town.

---

**MAGIC MUSHROOMS?**

The truffle trade is less like a business than a highly profitable cult. It revolves around an expensive, malodorous fungus endowed with semimagical powers, which is collected by shadowy characters who deal in cash and smuggle their booty across borders. Devotees claim that once you've tasted this small, nut-shaped delicacy, all other flavours seem insipid.

Although France, Spain and Italy are the traditional truffle-producing countries, Istrian truffles are rapidly gaining a foothold in the marketplace. Even at 14KN per gram, the price is significantly cheaper than other European truffles and the taste is said to be at least as good as their more expensive counterparts. In fact, there have been unconfirmed reports that certain nefarious parties are collecting Istrian truffles and packaging them as Italian truffles.

The truffle-hunting season lasts from October to January, during which time at least 3000 people and 9000 to 12,000 dogs are wandering around Istrian forests. The Motovun region is especially rich in truffles, but they are also found on the slopes of Mt Učka and in the Labin region. Truffle hunters are so determined to remain underground (for obvious tax reasons) that they will never admit to truffle hunting, no matter how unmistakable the evidence.

Some people believe truffles are an aphrodisiac, though scientific research has failed to uncover any basis for this claim. Conduct your own experiment: get a truffle and mix a few shavings into scrambled eggs or sprinkle them on top of a risotto. Turn the lights way down low, put on some nice music and see what happens.

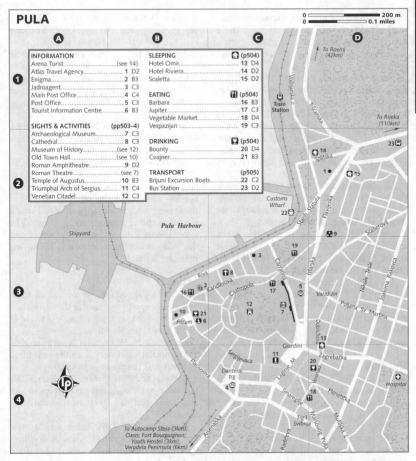

**PULA**

| | | |
|---|---|---|
| **INFORMATION** | | |
| Arena Turist | (see 14) | |
| Atlas Travel Agency | **1** D2 | |
| Enigma | **2** B3 | |
| Jadroagent | **3** C3 | |
| Main Post Office | **4** C4 | |
| Post Office | **5** C3 | |
| Tourist Information Centre | **6** B3 | |
| | | |
| **SIGHTS & ACTIVITIES** | (pp503–4) | |
| Archaeological Museum | **7** C3 | |
| Cathedral | **8** C3 | |
| Museum of History | (see 12) | |
| Old Town Hall | (see 10) | |
| Roman Amphitheatre | **9** D2 | |
| Roman Theatre | (see 7) | |
| Temple of Augustus | **10** B3 | |
| Triumphal Arch of Sergius | **11** C4 | |
| Venetian Citadel | **12** C3 | |

| | |
|---|---|
| **SLEEPING** | (p504) |
| Hotel Omir | **13** D4 |
| Hotel Riviera | **14** D2 |
| Scaletta | **15** D2 |
| | |
| **EATING** | (p504) |
| Barbara | **16** B3 |
| Jupiter | **17** C3 |
| Vegetable Market | **18** D4 |
| Vespazijan | **19** C3 |
| | |
| **DRINKING** | (p504) |
| Bounty | **20** D4 |
| Cvajner | **21** B3 |
| | |
| **TRANSPORT** | (p505) |
| Brijuni Excursion Boats | **22** C2 |
| Bus Station | **23** D2 |

## Information

You can exchange money in travel agencies or at either of the post offices where there is an ATM.

**Arena Turist** ( ☎ 529 400; fax 529 401; www.arena turist.hr; Splitska 1a) In the Hotel Riviera, Arena Turist finds private accommodation.

**Atlas travel agency** ( ☎ 393 040; atlas.pula@atlas .hr; Starih Statuta 1) Finds private accommodation and organises tours.

**Enigma** ( ☎ 381 615; Kandlerova 19; per hr 20KN) Internet access.

**Jadroagent** ( ☎ 210 431; jadroagent-pula@pu.htnet .hr; Riva 14) Has schedules and tickets for boats connecting Istria with Italy and the islands.

**Main post office** (Danteov trg 4; ☆ 7am-8pm) You can make long distance calls.

**Tourist Information Centre** ( ☎ 219 197; fax 211 955; www.pulainfo.hr; Forum 2; ☆ 9am-8pm Mon-Sat, 10am-6pm Sun) With knowledgeable and friendly staff, this centre provides maps, brochures and schedules of upcoming events in Pula and around Istria.

## Sights & Activities

Pula's imposing sight is the 1st-century **Roman amphitheatre** ( ☎ 219 028; Flavijevska; adult/concession 16/8KN; ☆ 8am-9pm Jun-Sep, 8.30am-4.30pm Oct-May) overlooking the harbour and northeast of the old town. Built entirely from local limestone, the amphitheatre was designed to host gladiatorial contests and could accommodate up to 20,000 spectators. The 30m-high outer wall is almost intact and contains two rows of 72 arches.

Around the end of July a Croatian film festival is held in the amphitheatre, and there are pop, jazz and classical events, often with major international stars, throughout summer.

The **Archaeological Museum** (☎ 218 603; Cararina 3; adult/concession 12/6KN; ◷ 9am-7pm Mon-Sat, 10am-3pm Sun Jun-Sep, 9am-3pm Mon-Fri Oct-May) is uphill from the town centre. Even if you don't visit the museum be sure to visit the large sculpture garden around it, and the **Roman theatre** behind the museum. The garden is entered through 2nd-century twin gates.

Along Istarska are **Roman walls** that mark the eastern boundary of old Pula. Follow these walls south and continue down Giardini to the **Triumphal Arch of Sergius** (27 BC). The street beyond the arch winds right around old Pula, changing names several times. Follow it to the ancient **Temple of Augustus** and the **old town hall** (1296).

The 17th-century **Venetian Citadel**, on a high hill in the centre of the old town, is worth the climb for the view if not for the meagre exhibits in the tiny **Museum of History** (Kaštel; admission 7KN; ◷ 8am-7pm daily Jun-Sep, 9am-5pm Mon-Fri Oct-May) inside.

## Sleeping

The tip of the Verudela Peninsula, about 6km southwest of the city centre, is a vast tourist complex with plenty of sprawling hotels that you can book through Arena Turist (p503).

The travel agencies listed on p503 find private accommodation but there is little available in the town centre. Count on paying from 110KN per person for a double room and up to 430KN for an apartment.

**Autocamp Stoja** (☎ 387 144; fax 387 748; per person/camp site & car 50/110KN; ◷ Apr-Oct) Three kilometres southwest of the city centre, Autocamp Stoja is on a shady promontory, with swimming possible off the rocks. There are more camping grounds at Medulin and Premantura, which are coastal resorts southeast of Pula (take the buses heading southeast from town).

**Youth Hostel** (☎ 391 133; pula@hfhs.hr; camp sites/B&B/half-board 72/110/142KN) Only 3km south of central Pula, this hostel overlooks a beach and is near one of the region's largest discos. Take the No 2 or 7 Verudela bus to the 'Piramida' stop, walk back to the first street,

then turn left and look for the sign. The rate for camping includes breakfast. You can rent tents for 10.50KN, year round.

**Scaletta** (☎ 541 599; www.hotel-scaletta.com; Flavijeska 26; s/d 410/535KN; P ✖ ) This hotel offers beautifully decorated and thoughtfully arranged rooms with every comfort accounted for. The hotel restaurant is also first-rate.

**Hotel Omir** (☎ 210 614; fax 213 944; Dobricheva 6; s/d 424/550KN) Rooms are small but comfortable here. Prices stay the same year-round.

**Hotel Riviera** (☎ 211 166; fax 211 166; Splitska 1; s/d 437/715KN) Neither the service nor the comfort quite justifies the price (which eases in the low season) in this one-star hotel, but there is an undeniably appealing old-world elegance and the rooms are spacious. The front rooms have a view of the water and the wide shady hotel terrace is a relaxing place for a drink.

## Eating

The best local restaurants are out of town but the cheapest places are in the centre and the eating isn't bad. You'll have a number of choices along Kandlerova.

**Jupiter** (☎ 214 333; Castropola 38; mains from 25KN) This popular place serves up the best pizza in town and the pasta is good too.

**Barbara** (☎ 219 317; Kandlerova 5; mains from 25KN) It's your basic calamari and čevapčići but well done and in a great people-watching location.

**Vespazijan** (☎ 210 016; Amfiteatarska 11; mains from 30KN) This unpretentious spot conjures up yummy risottos and a variety of seafood dishes.

Self-caterers can pick up vegetables, cold cuts and local cheese at the morning vegetable market.

## Drinking & Entertainment

The streets of Flanatička, Kandlerova and Sergijevaca are lively people-watching spots, and the Forum has several outdoor cafés that fill up in the early evening.

**Cvajner** (Forum) The trendiest café/gallery in town, with a stunning, art-filled interior.

**Bounty** (☎ 218 088; Veronska 8) Irish beer and cheer are served up in liberal doses here.

Posters around Pula advertise live performances at the amphitheatre or details of rave parties at two venues in Verudela: Oasis and Fort Bourguignon.

## Getting There & Away

### BOAT
For information about ferries to Italy, see Getting There & Away (p537).

### BUS
The buses that travel to Rijeka (48KN, 2½ hours, 20 daily) are sometimes crowded, especially the eight that continue to Zagreb, so be sure to reserve a seat in advance. Going from Pula to Rijeka, be sure to sit on the right-hand side of the bus for a stunning view of the Gulf of Kvarner.

Other destinations you can reach from the **bus station** ( ☎ 502 997; Istarske Brigade bb) include: Rovinj (23KN, 40 minutes, 18 daily); Poreč (32KN, one hour, 12 daily); Zagreb (124KN to 147KN, five hours, 11 daily); Zadar (161KN, seven hours, four daily); Split (215KN to 278KN, 10 hours, four daily); and Dubrovnik (366KN, 15 hours, one daily).

### TRAIN
There are two daily trains to Ljubljana (115KN, four hours) and two to Zagreb (123KN, 6½ hours), but you must board a bus for part of the trip.

## Getting Around
The only city buses of use to visitors are bus No 1, which runs to the camping ground at Stoja, and bus Nos 2 and 7 to Verudela, which pass the youth hostel. Frequency varies from every 15 minutes to every 30 minutes, with service from 5am to 11.30pm daily. Tickets are sold at newsstands for 10KN and are good for two trips.

## Around Pula

### BRIJUNI ISLANDS
The Brijuni (Brioni in Italian) island group consists of two main pine-covered islands and 12 islets just northwest of Pula. Notable as the summer residence of Maršal Tito, the Brijuni islands are now a highly groomed and scrupulously maintained national park. Some 680 species of plants grow on the islands, including many exotic subtropical species, which were planted at Tito's request. Tito's former private hunting grounds are now a safari park where elephants, zebras and antelope roam.

You may only visit Brijuni National Park with a group. Instead of booking an excursion with one of the travel agencies in Pula, Rovinj or Poreč, which costs 340KN, you could take a public bus from Pula to Fažana (8km), then sign up for a tour (180KN) at the **Brijuni Tourist Service** ( ☎ 525 883) office near the wharf. It's best to book in advance, especially in summer.

Also check along the Pula waterfront for excursion boats to Brijuni. The five-hour boat trips from Pula to Brijuni (60KN) may not actually visit the islands but only sail around them. Still, it makes a nice day out.

# GULF OF KVARNER

The Gulf of Kvarner (Quarnero in Italian) covers 3300 sq km between Rijeka and Pag island in the south. Protected by the Velebit range in the northeast, the Gorski Kotar in the north and the Ucka massif in the east, the climate is gentle and the range of vegetation wide.

The largest city is the busy commercial port of Rijeka, only a few kilometres from the aristocratic Opatija riviera. The large islands of Krk, Cres, Lošinj and Rab also have their share of admirers, who come for the luxuriant slopes dipping down to the sea.

## RIJEKA
☎ 051  /  pop 144,000
As Croatia's largest port, Rijeka (Fiume in Italian) is full of boats, cargo, fumes, cranes and the bustling sense of purpose that characterises most port cities. All of the buses, trains and ferries that form the network connecting Istria and Dalmatia with Zagreb and points beyond seem to pass through Rijeka, making the town almost impossible to avoid. Since Rijeka is hardly one of the 'must-see' destinations, the café-lined boulevard Korzo is refreshingly tourist free, and few visitors make the trek up to Trsat Castle for the views over the gulf. With stately 19th-century buildings, a tree-lined promenade along the harbour and a smattering of museums and restaurants, you won't regret spending a day here.

## Orientation
The **bus station** ( ☎ 060 333 444; Trg Žabica) is south of the Capuchin Church in the centre of town. The **train station** (ul Krešimirova) is a seven-minute walk west of the bus station.

The Jadrolinija ferry wharf (no left-luggage section) is a few minutes east of the bus station. Korzo runs easterly through the centre towards the fast-moving Rječina River.

## Information

### INTERNET ACCESS
**Hotel Continental** (Andrije Kašića Miočica; per hr 10-15KN) This hotel east of town has a full bank of modern computers.

### LAUNDRY
**Blitz** (Krešimirova 3a; 7am-8pm Mon-Fri, 7am-1pm Sat) Situated between the bus and train stations, Blitz will do a small load of laundry for 60KN.

### LEFT LUGGAGE
**Garderoba** (per day 10KN; 5.30am-10.30pm) In the bus station.
**Garderoba** (per day 10KN; 24hr) In the train station.

### MONEY
There's no ATM at the train station, but the exchange offices adjacent to the train and bus stations keep long hours. There are a number of ATMs along Korzo and an exchange counter in the main post office.

### POST
**Main post office** (Korzo) Opposite the old City Tower, the post office also houses a telephone centre.

### TOURIST INFORMATION
**Hostelling International** ( 264 176; Korzo 22) Sells HI cards and is a good source of information about Croatian hostels.
**Tourist Information Centre** ( 335 882; www.tz -rijeka.hr; Korzo 33) Distributes *Rijeka Tourist Route,* a walking-tour guide that is so well produced it makes you actually want to stay and look around.

## Sights & Activities
Rijeka's main orientation point is the **City Tower** (Korzo), which was originally one of the main gates to the city, and is one of the few monuments to have survived the earthquake of 1750.

The **Modern Art Gallery** ( 334 280; Dolac 1; adult/concession 10/5KN; 10am-1pm & 5-9pm Tue-Sun) is in the upstairs scientific library opposite Hotel Bonavia. The **Naval and Historical Museum** ( 213 578; Muzejski trg 1; adult/student 10/1KN; 9am-1pm Tue-Sat) traces the development of sailing, with models

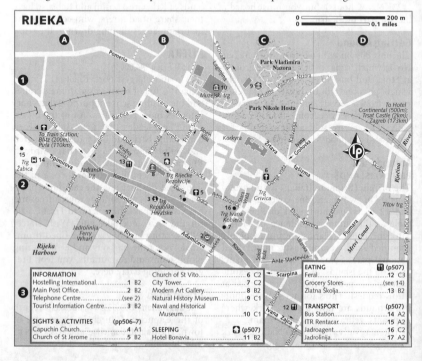

**RIJEKA**

0 — 200 m
0 — 0.1 miles

and paintings of ships and portraits of the captains. The **Natural History Museum** ( ☎ 334 988; Lorenzov prolaz 1; adult/student 10/5KN; ⏱ 9am-7pm Mon-Fri, 9am-2pm Sat) is devoted to regional geology and botany.

Also worth a visit is the 13th-century **Trsat Castle** (admission 15KN; ⏱ 9am-11pm Tue-Sun Apr-Nov, 9am-3pm Tue-Sun Dec-Mar), which is on a high ridge overlooking Rijeka, and the canyon of the Rječina River. If you have some more time to kill, stroll into some of Rijeka's churches, such as **Church of St Vito** (Trg Grivica 11), **Church of St Jerome** (Trg Riječke Rezolucije) or the ornate **Capuchin Church** (Trg Žabica), all open for mass only.

## Sleeping

The tourist office can direct you to the few options for private accommodation, most of which are a few kilometres out of town on the road to Opatija. It's just as easy to go on to Opatija, where there are more and better choices for hotels and private accommodation (for details on getting to/from Opatija see p508).

**Hotel Continental** ( ☎ 372 008; www.jadran-hoteli .hr, in Croatian; Andrije Kašića Miočića; s/d 376/425KN; P 🖳) This old building, to the northeast of the town centre, has spacious rooms that could probably use an overhaul. At least you're close to Internet access (see opposite).

**Hotel Bonavia** ( ☎ 333 744; www.bonavia.hr; Dolac 4; s/d from 830/980KN; P ✕ 🛏 🖳 🍴) The four-star Bonavia is the only hotel in the centre of town and it has all of the niceties that businesspeople on generous expense accounts find indispensable.

## Eating

If you get hungry on Sunday, you'll have to head to one of the hotel restaurants, since nearly every restaurant in town will be closed.

**Feral** ( ☎ 212 274; Matije Gupca 5B; mains from 60KN) The marine theme runs strong here with slightly cheaper seafood than Zlatna Školja, but its still beautifully prepared.

**Zlatna Školja** ( ☎ 213 782; Kružna 12; mains 100KN) The fetching maritime décor puts you in the mood to savour the astonishingly creative seafood dishes here. The wine list is also notable.

There are several 24-hour grocery stores in and around the bus station.

## Getting There & Away

### CAR
Close to the bus station, **ITR Rent a Car** ( ☎ 337 544; Riva 20) has rental cars for about 300KN per day.

### BOAT
Croatia's national boat line, **Jadrolinija** ( ☎ 211 444; www.jadrolinija.hr; Riva 16), has tickets for the large coastal ferries that run all year between Rijeka and Dubrovnik. For fares, see p537. For information on all boats to Croatia contact **Jadroagent** ( ☎ 211 276; Trg Ivana Koblera 2).

### BUS
There are 13 buses daily between Rijeka and Krk (33KN, 1½ hours), via the huge Krk Bridge. Buses to Krk are overcrowded and a ticket in no way guarantees a seat. Don't worry – the bus from Rijeka to Krk empties fast so you won't be standing for long.

Other buses departing from Rijeka include:

| destination | cost | duration | frequency |
| --- | --- | --- | --- |
| Baška | | | |
| (Krk Island) | 42KN | 2hr | 1 daily |
| Dubrovnik | 205-309KN | 13hr | 2 daily |
| Poreč | 55KN | 4½hr | 5 daily |
| Pula | 48KN | 2½hr | 17 daily |
| Rab | 87KN | 3½hr | 2 daily |
| Rovinj | 73KN | 3½hr | 10 daily |
| Split | 161-231KN | 8½hr | 11 daily |
| Trieste | 62KN | 2-3hr | 3 daily |
| Zadar | 115KN | 5hr | 12 daily |
| Zagreb | 75-129KN | 2½-3hr | 21 daily |

For international connections see p536.

### TRAIN
Four trains run daily to Zagreb (102KN, five hours). There's also a daily direct train to Osijek (162KN, eight hours) and a daily train to Split that changes at Ogulin where you wait for two hours (142KN, 10 hours). Several of the seven daily services to Ljubljana (86KN, three hours) require a change of trains at the Slovenian border and again at Bifka or Bistrica in Slovenia, but there are also two direct trains. Reservations are compulsory on some *poslovni* (express) trains.

CROATIA

# OPATIJA

☎ 051 / pop 12,719

Opatija, just a few kilometres due west of Rijeka, was where fashionable 19th-century aristocrats came to 'take the waters'. The Lungomare, a shady waterfront promenade that stretches for 12km along the Gulf of Kvarner, offers genteel exercise and a calming view of the mountainous coast. The nightlife is decidedly uncalming; there's far more going on here than in Rijeka. And to rest your weary head, there's a wide choice of hotels with baroque exteriors and high-ceilinged plush interiors that offer good value for money.

## Information

There's no left-luggage facility at **Opatija bus station** (Trg Vladimira Gortana), which is in the town centre, but Autotrans Agency at the station will usually watch luggage.

**Atlas travel agency** ( ☎ 271 032; Maršala Tita 116) Accommodation and excursions.

**Da Riva** ( ☎ 272 482; www.da-riva.hr; Maršala Tita 162) Finds private accommodation and organises group transfers to regional airports.

**GIT travel agency** ( ☎ /fax 271 967; gi-trade@ri.htnet .hr; Maršala Tita 65) Finds private accommodation.

**Internet Café** ( ☎ 271 511; Maršala Tita 85; per hr 20KN) Offers Internet access in a comfortable environment.

**Main post office** (Eugena Kumičića 2; ✆ 8am-7pm Mon-Sat) Behind the market.

**Tourist office** ( ☎ 271 310; www.opatija-tourism.hr; Maršala Tita 101; ✆ 8am-7pm Mon-Sat & 2-6pm Sun Jun-Sep, 9am-noon & 2-4.30pm Mon-Sat Oct-May) Has some information on local events.

## Activities

Opatija is not a museum/gallery kind of place. Come for the swimming in the coves along the Lungomare or just stroll the great seaside promenade. There's also hiking up Mt Učka. Head to the tourist office (p508) for details.

## Sleeping & Eating

Private rooms are abundant and reasonably priced. The travel agencies listed above (p508) have rooms starting at 150KN to 210KN, depending on the amenities.

The hotel scene is competitive and offers good value for money, especially outside of July and August. Most hotels are handled by **Liburnia Hotels** ( ☎ 710 300; www.liburnia.hr).

**Camping Opatija** ( ☎ 704 387; fax 704 112; Liburnjska 46, Ičići; per person/camp sites 30/50KN; ✆ May-Sep) Right on the sea and only 5km south of town.

**Hotel Residenz** ( ☎ 271 399; residenz@liburnia.hr; Maršala Tita 133; s/d from 325/550KN) This place has stodgy but decent rooms in a classic building. You can use the swimming pool at the neighbouring Hotel Kristol and the Residenz is right on the sea. More expensive rooms with balconies are available.

**Hotel Kvarner** ( ☎ 271 233; kvarner@liburnia.hr; s/d from 410/580KN; P ✸ ) This genteel 19th-century establishment has an indoor and outdoor swimming pool and easy access to the sea. It oozes elegance and has more expensive rooms with sea views and balconies.

Maršala Tita is lined with a number of decent restaurants offering pizza, grilled meat and fish. For a special meal, the best choice is **Bevanda** ( ☎ 712 769; Zert 8; mains from 70KN), located on the port, which has the freshest fish and a good wine list.

## Entertainment

An **open air-cinema** (Park Angiolina) screens films and presents occasional concerts nightly at 9.30pm from May to September. There's a boisterous bar scene centred around the harbour, plus the ever-popular Caffé Harbour or Hemingways.

## Getting There & Away

Bus No 32 stops in front of the train station in Rijeka (11KN, 30 minutes) and runs right along the Opatija Riviera, west of Rijeka, every 20 minutes until late in the evening. If you're looking for accommodation, it's easiest to get off at the first stop and walk downhill, passing hotels and other agencies on the way to the bus station.

# KRK ISLAND

☎ 051 / pop 18,000

The comparatively barren and rocky Krk (Veglia in Italian) is Croatia's largest island, connected to the mainland in 1980 by the enormous Krk Bridge. The northern part of the island is the site of Rijeka airport, which was a boon to the island economy at the cost of rapid overdevelopment. Real estate was quickly snapped up leaving few areas untouched. Still, the main town (also called Krk) is rather picturesque, and the popular resort of Baška at the island's southern end has a 2km-long pebbly beach set below a high ridge.

## Krk Town

Tiny Krk town has a compact medieval centre that opens onto a scenic port. From the 12th to 15th centuries, Krk town and the surrounding region remained semi-independent under the Frankopan Dukes of Krk, an indigenous Croatian dynasty, at a time when much of the Adriatic was controlled by Venice. This history explains the various medieval sights in Krk town, the ducal seat.

The bus from Baška and Rijeka stops by the harbour, a few minutes' walk from the old town of Krk. There's no left-luggage facility at Krk bus station. The **Turistička Zajednica** ( ☎ /fax 221 414; www.tz-krk.hr, in Croatian; Velika Placa 1; ☼ 8am-3pm Mon-Fri) is in the city wall's Guard Tower. You can change money at any travel agency and there's an ATM in the shopping centre near the bus station.

The lovely 14th-century **Frankopan Castle** and 12th-century Romanesque **cathedral** are in the lower town near the harbour. In the upper part of Krk town are three old **monastic churches**. The narrow streets of Krk are worth exploring.

### SLEEPING & EATING

There is a range of accommodation in and around Krk, but many places only open during summertime. Private rooms can be organised through **Autotrans** ( ☎ 221 172; www .autotrans.hr) at the bus station. You can expect to pay from about 140/160KN for a single/double.

**Autocamp Ježevac** ( ☎ 221 081; per person/camp sites 40/40KN; ☼ mid-Apr–mid-Oct) On the coast, a 10-minute walk southwest of Krk town, is this camping ground with easy sea access and merciful shade.

**Veli Jože** ( ☎ /fax 220 212; damir.dugandzija@sb .htnet.hr; Vitezića 32; dm incl breakfast 145KN) This relatively new hostel is located in a spruced-up older building and is open year-round. Rooms have three, four or six beds.

**Hotel Marina** ( ☎ 221 128; Obala Hrvatske Mornarice 6; www.hotelikrk.com; s/d 435/625KN) It's really nothing special, but this is the only hotel right in the town centre.

There are a number of restaurants around the harbour, but for something different, try **Konobo Nono** (Krčkih iseljenika 8; mains from 65KN) which offers *šurlice* (homemade noodles topped with goulash), as well as grilled fish and meat dishes.

## Baška

At the southern end of Krk Island, Baška is popular for its 2km-long pebbly beach set below a dramatic, barren range of mountains. Although crowded in summer, the old town and harbour make a pleasant stroll and there's always that splendid beach. The bus from Krk stops at the top of a hill on the edge of the old town, between the beach and the harbour.

The main street of Baška is Zvonimirova, overlooking the harbour, and the beach begins at the western end of the harbour, continuing southwards past a big sprawling hotel complex. The town's **tourist office** ( ☎ 856 544; www.tz-baska.hr; Zvonimirova 114; ☼ 8am-8pm daily mid-Jun–Sep, 8am-3pm Mon-Fri Oct–mid-Jun) is just down the street from the bus stop. To arrange hotels or camping, contact **Hoteli Baška** ( ☎ 656 801; www.hotelibaska.hr). For private accommodation, there's **Gulliver** ( ☎ 586 004; pdm-baska@ri.htnet.hr; Zvonimirova 98).

### GETTING THERE & AWAY

About 14 buses a day travel between Rijeka and Krk town (32KN, 1½ hours), of which six continue on to Baška (16KN, up to one hour). One of the Rijeka buses is to/from Zagreb (90KN, four hours). To go from Krk to Zadar, take one of the many buses to Kraljevica and then change to a southbound bus.

# DALMATIA

Roman ruins, spectacular beaches, old fishing ports, medieval architecture and unspoilt offshore islands make a trip to Dalmatia (Dalmacija) unforgettable. Occupying the central 375km of Croatia's Adriatic coast, Dalmatia offers a matchless combination of hedonism and historical discovery. The jagged coast is speckled with lush offshore islands and dotted with historic cities.

Split is the largest city in the region and a hub for bus and boat connections along the Adriatic, as well as home to the late Roman Diocletian's Palace. Nearby are the early Roman ruins in Solin. Zadar has yet more Roman ruins and a wealth of churches. The architecture of Hvar and Korčula recalls the days when these places were outposts of the Venetian empire. None can rival majestic Dubrovnik, a cultural and aesthetic jewel.

The dramatic coastal scenery is due to the rugged Dinaric Alps, which form a 1500m-long barrier that separates Dalmatia from Bosnia and Hercegovina. After the last Ice Age part of the coastal mountains were flooded, creating the sort of long, high islands seen in the Gulf of Kvarner. The deep, protected passages between these islands are a paradise for sailors and cruisers.

# ZADAR

☎ 023 / pop 72,700

Zadar (ancient Zara), the main city of northern Dalmatia, is one of Croatia's more underrated destinations. The marble, traffic-free streets of the old town are replete with Roman ruins, medieval churches and several fascinating museums. Massive 16th-century fortifications still shield the city on the landward side, with high walls running along the harbour. The tree-lined promenade along Obala kralja Petra Krešimira IV is perfect for a lazy stroll or a picnic, and there are several small beaches east of the old town. More beaches lie to the northwest at Borik as well as on the islands of Ugljan and Dugi Otok, both within easy reach of the town.

## History

In the past 2000 years Zadar has escaped few wars. Its strategic position on the Adriatic coast made Zadar a target for the Romans, the Byzantine, Venetian and Austro-Hungarian empires, and Italy. Although it was damaged by Allied bombing raids in 1943–44 and Yugoslav rockets in 1991, this resilient city has been rebuilt and restored, retaining much of its old flavour. Don't forget to sample Zadar's famous maraschino cherry liqueur.

## Orientation

The train station and the **bus station** ( ☎ 211 035) are adjacent and are 1km southeast of the harbour and old town. From the stations, Zrinsko-Frankopanska ul leads northwest past the main post office to the harbour. Buses marked 'Poluotok' run from the bus station to the harbour. Narodni trg is the heart of Zadar.

## Information

### INTERNET ACCESS

**Multi-net** ( ☎ 302 207; Stomorica 8; per hr 30KN)

### LEFT LUGGAGE

**Garderoba** (per day 10KN; 24hr) At the train station.
**Garderoba** (per day 10KN; 7am-9pm Mon-Fri) At the bus station.
**Garderoba** (per day 10KN; 7am-8pm Mon-Fri, 7am-3pm Sat) At the Jadrolinija dock.

### POST

**Main post office** (Poljana Pape Aleksandra III) You can make phone calls here.

### TOURIST INFORMATION

**Tourist office** ( ☎ 316 166; tzg-zadar@zd.htnet.hr; Mihe Klaića 5; 8am-8pm Mon-Sat, 8am-1pm Sun Jun-Sep, 8am-6pm Mon-Sat Oct-May)

### TRAVEL AGENCIES

**Aquarius Travel Agency** ( ☎ /fax 212 919; juresko@zd .htnet.hr; Nova Vrata bb) Accommodation and excursions.
**Atlas travel agency** ( ☎ 235 850; atlas@zadar.net; Branimirova Obala 12) Across the footbridge over the harbour, and just northeast of Narodni trg, Atlas finds private accommodation and runs excursions.
**Miatours** ( ☎ /fax 212 788; miatrade@zd.htnet.hr; Vrata Sveti Krševana) Accommodation and excursions.

## Sights & Activities

Most attractions are near **St Donatus Church** (Šimuna Kožičića Benje; admission 5KN; 9.30am-2pm & 4-6pm Mar-Oct), a circular 9th-century Byzantine structure built over the Roman forum. Slabs for the ancient forum are visible in the church and there is a pillar from the Roman era on the northwestern side. In summer ask about the musical evenings here (featuring Renaissance and early baroque music). The outstanding **Museum of Church Art** (Trg Opatice Čike bb; adult/student 20/10KN; 10am-12.30pm daily, 6-8pm Mon-Sat), in the Benedictine monastery opposite St Donatus, offers three floors of elaborate gold and silver reliquaries, religious paintings, icons and local lacework.

The 13th-century Romanesque **Cathedral of St Anastasia** (Trg Svete Stošije; only for Mass) has some fine Venetian carvings in the 15th-century choir stalls. The **Franciscan Monastery** (Zadarscog mira 1358; admission free; 7.30am-noon & 4.30-6pm) is the oldest Gothic church in Dalmatia (consecrated in 1280), with lovely interior Renaissance features and a large Romanesque cross in the treasury.

The most interesting museum is the **Archaeological Museum** (Trg Opatice Čike 1; adult/student 10/5KN; 9am-1pm & 6-9pm Mon-Fri, 9am-1pm Sat), across from St Donatus, with an extensive

CROATIA

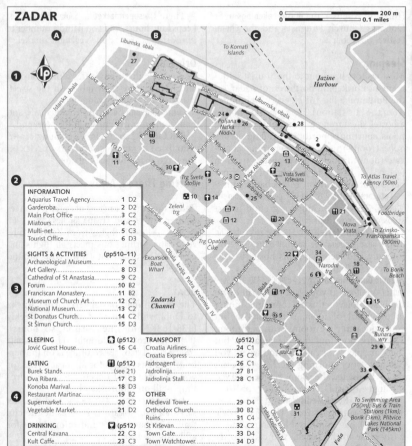

**ZADAR**

0 — 200 m
0 — 0.1 miles

collection of artefacts, from the Neolithic period through the Roman occupation to the development of Croatian culture under the Byzantines. Some captions are in English and you are handed a leaflet in English when you buy your ticket.

Less interesting is the **National Museum** (Poljana Pape Aleksandra III; admission 5KN; 🕒 9am-noon & 5-8pm Mon-Fri), just inside the sea gate, featuring photos of Zadar from different periods, and old paintings and engravings of many coastal cities. The same admission ticket will get you into the **art gallery** (Smiljanića; 🕒 9am-noon & 5-8pm Mon-Fri, 9am-1pm Sat). One church worth a visit is **St Šimun Church** (Šime Budinica; 🕒 8am-noon & 6-8pm Jun-Sep), which has a 14th-century gold chest.

There's a swimming area with diving boards, a small park and a café on the coastal promenade off Zvonimira. Bordered by pine trees and parks, the promenade takes you to a beach in front of Hotel Kolovare. It winds on for about a kilometre up the coast.

## Tours

Any of the many travel agencies around town can supply information on tourist cruises to the beautiful Kornati Islands, river-rafting and half-day excursions to the Krka waterfalls.

## Festivals & Events

Major annual events include the **town fair** (July and August), the **Dalmatian Song Festival**

(July and August), the **musical evenings** in St Donatus Church (August) and the **Choral Festival** (October).

## Sleeping

Most visitors head out to the 'tourist settlement' at Borik, 3km northwest of Zadar, on the Puntamika bus (6KN, every 20 minutes from the bus station). Here there are hotels, a hostel, a camping ground, big swimming pools, sporting opportunities and numerous '*sobe*' (rooms) signs; you can arrange a private room through a travel agency in town (see p510). Expect to pay about 140KN per person for a nice room with a bathroom.

**Autocamp Borik** ( ☎ 332 074; per person/camp site 30/60KN) This large camping ground is just steps away from Borik beach.

**Borik Youth Hostel** ( ☎ 331 145; zadar@hfhs.hr; Obala Kneza Trpimira 76; B&B/half-board 90/120KN) Friendly and well-kept, this hostel is near the beach at Borik.

**Jović Guest House** ( ☎ 214 098, 098 330 958; Šime Ljubića 4a; d 300KN) If you want to stay in town, the best choice is this 12-room guesthouse in the heart of town, with smallish but cool and attractive rooms with bathroom. The price does not include breakfast but there are plenty of cafés around where you can have your morning meal. If you can't reach the owner, the rooms can be reserved through Aquarius Travel Agency (p510).

In Borik, **Hotel Mediteran** ( ☎ 337 500; www .hotelmediteran-zd.hr; M Gupca 19; s/d 380/495KN; P ✖ 🖳 ) has comfortable rooms and is fairly close to the beach. You can also try the **Hotel President** ( ☎ 333 464; www.hotel-presi dent.hr; Vladana Desnice 16; rooms 835KN; P ✖ 🖳 ) for the full first-class treatment, also near the beach.

## Eating

**Dva Ribara** (Blaža Jurjeva 1; mains from 40KN) With a wide range of food and an outdoor terrace, Dva Ribara is justifiably popular with the local crowd.

**Konoba Marival** ( ☎ 213 239; Don Ive Prodana 3; mains from 45KN) If your mama married a fisherman, she'd probably dream up the kinds of dishes that are served here. The ambience is also homy and intimate.

**Restaurant Martinac** (Papavije 7; mains from 55KN) The secluded backyard terrace behind this restaurant provides a relaxed atmosphere in which to sample delicious risotto and fish.

There's a **supermarket** (cnr Široka & Sabora) that keeps long hours, and you'll find a number of *burek* stands around the vegetable market.

## Drinking

In summer the many cafés along Varoška and Klaića place their tables on the street; it's great for people-watching.

**Central Kavana** (Široka) A spacious café and hang-out with live music at the weekend.

**Kult Caffe** (Stomarica) Draws a young crowd who listen to rap music indoors or relax on the large shady terrace outside.

## Getting There & Away

### AIR

Zadar's airport, 12km east of the city, receives charter flights and **Croatia Airlines** ( ☎ 250 101; Poljana Natka Nodila 7) flights from Zagreb daily. A Croatia Airlines bus meets all flights and costs 15KN; a taxi into town costs around 175KN.

### BOAT

The Jadrolinija coastal ferry from Rijeka to Dubrovnik calls at Zadar twice weekly (138/168KN low/high season, six hours). It arrives around midnight. The **Jadrolinija** ( ☎ 254 800; Liburnska obala 7) office is on the harbour and has tickets for all local ferries, or you can buy ferry tickets from the Jadrolinija stall on Liburnska obala.

**Jadroagent** ( ☎ 211 447; jadroagent-zadar@zd.htnet .hr; Poljana Natka Nodila 4) is just inside the city walls and has tickets and information for all boats.

For information on boat connections to Italy see p357.

### BUS & TRAIN

Zadar is on the coastal route that goes from Rijeka down to Split and Dubrovnik. There are four daily trains to Zagreb (84KN, 9¾ hours) that change at Knin, but the bus to Zagreb is quicker and stops at Plitvice Lakes National Park (32KN, three hours).

**Croatia Express** ( ☎ 250 502; croatiae@zd.htnet.hr; Široka) sells bus tickets to many German cities. See p536.

## Around Zadar

### PLITVICE LAKES

**Plitvice Lakes National Park** (admission Oct-May/ Jun-Sep 75/95KN, students 45/55KN) lies midway between Zagreb and Zadar. The 19.5 hectares of wooded hills enclose 16 turquoise lakes, which are connected by a series of waterfalls and cascades. The mineral-rich waters carve new paths through the rock, depositing tufa (new porous rock) in continually changing formations. Wooden footbridges follow the lakes and streams over, under and across the rumbling water for an exhilaratingly damp 18km. Swimming is not allowed. Your park admission is valid for the entire stay and also includes the boats and buses you need to use to see the lakes. There is accommodation on site, as well as private accommodation nearby. Check the options with the National Park information office in Zagreb (see p490).

### Getting There & Away

All buses from Zadar to Zagreb stop at Plitvice (32KN, three hours). It is possible to visit Plitvice for the day on the way to or from the coast but be awa re that if they are full buses will not pick up passengers at Plitvice. Luggage can be left at the **tourist information centre** ( ☎ 053-751 015; www.np-plitvice .com; ☽ 7am-8pm), located at the first entrance to the park.

## SPLIT

☎ 021 / pop 188,700

Split (Spalato in Italian), the largest Croatian city on the Adriatic coast, is a major industrial city ringed with apartment-block housing of stupefying ugliness, but the remarkable Diocletian's Palace (which is a now World Heritage Site) makes a visit to the city worthwhile – and a visit is indispensable if you'll be visiting one of the many islands within reach of Split. In the centre of town, within the ancient walls of Diocletian's Palace, rises the majestic cathedral surrounded by a tangle of marble streets containing shops and businesses. The entire western end of town is a vast, wooded mountain park with beaches below and pathways above. A refurbished harbourside promenade lined with cafés makes for a pleasant stroll, and the high coastal mountains set against the blue Adriatic provide a striking frame, best appreciated as your ferry heads into or out of the port.

### History

Split achieved fame when Roman emperor Diocletian (AD 245-313), who was noted for his persecution of the early Christians, had his retirement palace built here from 295 to 305. After his death the great stone palace continued to be used as a retreat by Roman rulers. When the neighbouring colony of Salona was abandoned in the 7th century, many of the Romanised inhabitants fled to Split and barricaded themselves behind the high palace walls, where their descendants continue to live to this day.

The town was hard-hit economically (although not militarily) when the former Yugoslavia split up, and is still struggling to regains its footing. It's clearly less prosperous than Zagreb or Dubrovnik, which helps explain why so many residents flock to the bus station and port to hawk their extra rooms to disembarking tourists.

## Orientation

The bus, train and ferry terminals are adjacent on the eastern side of the harbour, a short walk from the old town. Obala hrvatskog narodnog preporoda, the waterfront promenade, is your best central reference point in Split.

## Information

### BOOKSHOPS

**Algoritam** (Map p515; Bajamontijeva 2) A good English-language bookshop.

### INTERNET ACCESS

**Mriža** (Map p515; ☎ 321 320; Kružićeva 3; per hr 20KN)

### LEFT LUGGAGE

**Garderoba** ( ☽ 6am-10pm) At the bus station.
**Garderoba** (Obala Kneza Domagoja 6; ☽ 7am-9pm) The train station's left luggage office is about 50m north of the station.

### MONEY

Change money at travel agencies or the post office. You'll find ATMs around the bus and train stations.

### POST

**Main post office** (Map p515; Kralja Tomislava 9) There's also a telephone centre ( ☽ 7am-9pm Mon-Sat) here.

### TOURIST INFORMATION

**Internet Games & Books** (Map p515; ☎ 338 548; Obala Kneza Domagoja 3) Luggage storage, information for backpackers, used books and an Internet connection for 35KN per hour.

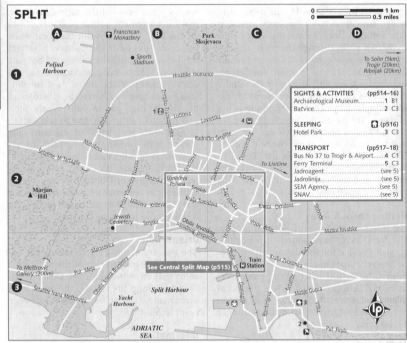

**SPLIT**

SIGHTS & ACTIVITIES (pp514–16)
Archaeological Museum.............1 B1
Bačvice.................................2 C3

SLEEPING (p516)
Hotel Park...............................3 C3

TRANSPORT (pp517–18)
Bus No 37 to Trogir & Airport......4 C1
Ferry Terminal...........................5 C3
Jadroagent..........................(see 5)
Jadrolinija...........................(see 5)
SEM Agency.........................(see 5)
SNAV.................................(see 5)

See Central Split Map (p515)

---

**Turist Biro** (Map opposite; ☎ /fax 342 142; turist-biro
-split@st.htnet.hr; Obala hrvatskog narodnog preporoda 12)
Arranges private accommodation and sells guidebooks and
the Split Card.
**Turistička Zajednica** (Map opposite; ☎ /fax 342 606;
www.visitsplit.com; Peristyle; ☼ 9am-8.30pm Mon-Sat,
8am-1pm Sun) Has information on Split; sells the Split
Card for 60KN, offering free and discounted admission to
Split attractions.

### TRAVEL AGENCIES
**Atlas travel agency** (Map opposite; ☎ 343 055;
Nepotova 4) The town's Amex representative.
**Daluma Travel** (Map opposite; ☎ /fax 338 484; daluma
-st@st.htnet.hr; Obala Kneza Domagoja 1) Finds private
accommodation.

## Sights & Activities
### DIOCLETIAN'S PALACE          Map opposite
The old town is a vast open-air museum and
the new information signs at the important
sights explain a great deal of Split's history.
**Diocletian's Palace** (entrance: Obala hrvatskog narodnog
preporoda 22), facing the harbour, is one of the
most imposing Roman ruins in existence.
It was built as a strong rectangular fortress,

with walls measuring 215m from east to
west, 181m wide at the southernmost point
and reinforced by square corner towers.
The imperial residence, mausoleum and
temples were south of the main street, now
called Krešlmirova, connecting the east and
west palace gates.

Enter through the central ground floor
of the palace. On the left are the excavated
**basement halls** (adult/concession 6/3KN; ☼ 10am-
6pm), which are empty but still impressive.
Go through the passage to the **peristyle**, a
picturesque colonnaded square, with a
neo-Romanesque cathedral tower rising
above. The **vestibule**, an open dome above
the ground-floor passageway at the southern end of the peristyle, is overpoweringly
grand and cavernous. A lane off the peristyle opposite the cathedral leads to the **Temple of Jupiter**, which is now a baptistry.

On the eastern side of the peristyle is
the **cathedral**, originally Diocletian's mausoleum. The only reminder of Diocletian
in the cathedral is a sculpture of his head
in a circular stone wreath, below the dome
which is directly above the baroque white-

marble altar. The Romanesque wooden doors (1214) and stone pulpit are notable. For a small fee you can climb the tower.

In the Middle Ages the nobility and rich merchants built their residences within the old palace walls; the Papalic Palace is now the **town museum** ( ☎ 341 240; Papalićeva ul 5; adult/concession 10/5KN; ⏱ 9am-noon & 5-8pm Tue-Fri, 10am-noon Sat & Sun Jun-Sep, 10am-5pm Tue-Fri, 10am-noon Sat & Sun Oct-May). It has a tidy collection of artefacts, paintings, furniture and clothes from Split; captions are in Croatian.

**OUTSIDE THE PALACE WALLS** Map below
The east palace gate leads into the market area. The west palace gate opens onto medieval Narodni trg, dominated by the

15th-century Venetian Gothic **old town hall**. The **Ethnographic Museum** ( ☎ 344 164; Narodni trg; adult/student 10/5KN; ⏱ 10am-1pm Tue-Fri Jun-Sep, 10am-4pm Tue-Fri, 10am-1pm Sat & Sun Oct-May) has a mildly interesting collection of photos of old Split, traditional costumes and memorabilia of important citizens, but captions are in Croatian.

Trg Braće Radića, between Narodni trg and the harbour, contains the surviving north tower of the 15th-century Venetian garrison castle, which once extended to the water's edge.

Go through the north palace gate to see Ivan Meštrović's powerful 1929 **statue of Gregorius of Nin**, a 10th-century Slavic religious leader who fought for the right to perform

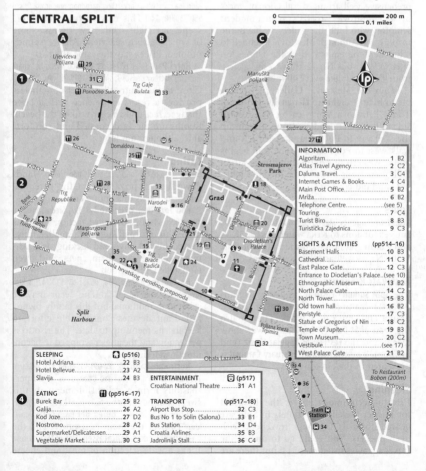

**CENTRAL SPLIT**

0 — 200 m
0 — 0.1 miles

Mass in Croatian. Notice that his big toe has been polished to a shine; it's said that touching it brings good luck.

**OUTSIDE CENTRAL SPLIT**                Map p514
The **archaeological museum** ( ☎ 318 720; Zrinjsko-Frankopanska 25; adult/student 10/5KN; ☼ 9am-noon & 5-8pm Tue-Fri, 9am-noon Sat & Sun), north of town, is a fascinating supplement to your walk around Diocletian's Palace and to the site of ancient Salona. The history of Split is traced from Illyrian times to the Middle Ages, in chronological order, with explanations in English.

The finest art museum in Split is **Meštrović Gallery** ( ☎ 358 450; Šetalište Ivana Meštrovića 46; adult/student 15/10KN; ☼ 9am-9pm Tue-Sun Jun-Sep, 9am-4pm Tue-Sat, 10am-3pm Sun Oct-May). You'll see a comprehensive, well-arranged collection of works by Ivan Meštrović, Croatia's premier modern sculptor, who built the gallery as his home in 1931–39. Although Meštrović intended to retire here, he emigrated to the USA soon after WWII. Bus No 12 runs to the gallery from Trg Republike every 40 minutes.

From the Meštrović Gallery it's possible to hike straight up **Marjan Hill**. Go up ul Tonća Petrasova Marovića on the western side of the gallery and continue straight up the stairway to Put Meja ul. Turn left and walk west to Put Meja 76. The trail begins on the western side of this building. Marjan Hill offers trails through the forest to lookouts and old chapels.

## Tours
**Atlas travel agency** (Map p515; ☎ 343 055; Nepotova 4) runs excursions to Krka waterfalls (225KN) and Zlatni Rat beach on the island of Brač (140KN), as well as other excursions.

## Festivals & Events
The **Split Summer Festival** (mid-July to mid-August) features open-air opera, ballet, drama and musical concerts. There's also the **Feast of St Dujo** (7 May), a flower show (May) and the **Festival of Popular Music** (end of June). The traditional **February Carnival** is presented in the old town.

## Sleeping
Private accommodation is the best bet for budget travellers, as hotels in Split are geared towards business travellers with deep pockets. You could go to one of the travel agencies listed on p514, but there are usually packs of women at the bus, train and ferry terminals ready to propose rooms to travellers. Prices rarely exceed 100KN for a room but you'll be sharing the bathroom with the proprietor.

**Slavija** (Map p515; ☎ 347 053; fax 344 062; Buvinova 3; r with/without bath 450/350KN) Has a great location in the old town but somewhat noisy rooms.

**Hotel Bellevue** (Map p515; ☎ 347 499; fax 362 383; www.hotel-bellevue-split.hr; bana Josipa Jelačića 2; s/d 490/682KN) The Bellevue is an old classic that has seen better days. Rooms on the street side can be noisy but the location's good and rooms are well tended. A taxi from the port will mean a long, meandering ride as the driver navigates the many one way streets.

**Hotel Adriana** (Map p515; ☎ 340 000; info@hotel-adriana.com; Obala hrvatskog narodnog preporoda 9; s/d 550/750KN; ﷯) This new entry on the hotel scene has eight fresh new rooms, some of which have a sea view. All are soundproofed. Prices stay the same all year.

**Hotel Park** (Map p514; ☎ 406 400; www.hotelpark -split.hr; Hatzeov perivoj 3; s/d 795/1015KN; ﷯ ﷯ ﷯) Close to the centre, this hotel nonetheless provides a resort experience with a large shady terrace and an easy walk to the beach. Rooms are nicely decorated and comfortable, although not large.

## Eating
**Galija** (Map p515; Tončićeva; pizzas from 26KN) Hands down the best pizza in town, this perennial favourite packs in a young crowd.

**Kod Joze** (Map p515; ☎ 347 397; Sredmanuška 4; mains from 40KN) A die-hard faction of locals keeps this informal *konoba* (a small, family-owned bistro) alive and kicking. It's Dalmatian all the way – ham, cheese and green tagliatelle with seafood.

**Restaurant Boban** (Map p515; ☎ 510 142; Hektorovićeva 49; mains from 60KN) The décor may be sober and traditional but this family-owned restaurant devotes considerable effort to keeping its menu up to date. The risotto is perfection and the angler wrapped in bacon, mouth watering.

**Nostromo** (Map p515; ☎ 091 405 66 66; Kraj Sv Marije 10; mains from 65KN) Marine creatures of all persuasions form a delightful menu in this sweet spot next to the fish market.

There's a spiffy **Burek Bar** (Map p515; Domaldova 13) near the main post office, and the vast **supermarket/delicatessen** (Map p515; Svačićeva 1) has a wide selection of meat and cheese for sandwiches. The vegetable market has a wide array of fresh local produce.

## Entertainment

In summer everyone starts the evening at one of the cafés along Obala hrvatskog narodnog preporoda and then heads towards the Bačvice (Map p514) complex on the beach. These former public baths offer restaurants, cafés, discos and venues for live rock and salsa. During winter, opera and ballet are presented at the **Croatian National Theatre** (Trg Gaje Bulata; best seats about 60KN); tickets for the same night are usually available. Erected in 1891, the theatre was fully restored in 1979 in the original style; it's worth attending a performance for the architecture alone.

## Getting There & Away

### AIR

The country's national air carrier, **Croatia Airlines** (Map p515; ☎ 362 997; Obala hrvatskog narodnog preporoda 8), operates flights between Zagreb and Split up to four times every day (475KN, one hour). Rates are lower if you book in advance.

---

### WHERE TO TAKE A BOAT RIDE

**Mljet** – From Dubrovnik or Korčula, there are photo-ready views of the old towns from on board (p523)

**Brijuni Islands** – Give me a home where the antelopes roam, sang Tito on his island (p505)

**Lokrum** – The greenery is a startling change from marble-paved Dubrovnik (p527)

**Crveni Otok** – Secluded coves for secluded activities (p501)

**Jerolim & Stipanska** – Take it all off, but put it back on before returning to Hvar (p524)

---

### BOAT

You can buy tickets for passenger ferries at the **Jadrolinija stall** (Map p515; Obala Kneza Domagoja). There are also several agents in the large ferry terminal opposite the bus station that can assist with boat trips from Split: **Jadroagent** (Map p514; ☎ 338 335) represents Adriatica Navigazione for its connections between Split and Ancona; **Jadrolinija** (Map p514; ☎ 338 333) handles all car ferry services that depart

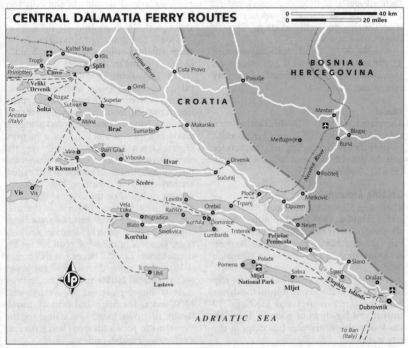

**CENTRAL DALMATIA FERRY ROUTES**

from the docks around the ferry terminal; **SEM agency** (Map p514; ☎ 338 292) handles tickets between Ancona, Split and Hvar; and **SNAV** (Map p514; ☎ 322 252) has a four-hour connection to Ancona and Pescara.

For more details on connections to/from Italy see p537.

### BUS

Advance bus tickets with seat reservations are recommended. There are buses from the main **bus station** (Map p515; ☎ 060 327 327; www .ak-split.hr, in Croatian) beside the harbour to:

| destination | cost | duration | frequency |
| --- | --- | --- | --- |
| Dubrovnik | 72-111KN | 4½hr | 12 daily |
| Ljubljana | 230KN | 10hr | 1 daily |
| Međugorje | 54-89KN | 3hr | 4 daily |
| Mostar | 54-65KN | 2-4hr | 4 daily |
| Pula | 215-278KN | 10hr | 3 daily |
| Rijeka | 161-231KN | 8hr | 14 daily |
| Sarajevo | 93-128KN | 7hr | 11 daily |
| Zadar | 66-89KN | 3hr | 26 daily |
| Zagreb | 112-143KN | 6-9hr | 27 daily |

**Touring** (Map p515; ☎ 338 503; Obala Kneza Domagojeva 10), near the bus station, represents Deutsche Touring and sells tickets to German cities.

Bus No 37 to Solin, Split airport and Trogir leaves from a local bus station on Domovinskog, 1km northeast of the city centre (see Map p514).

### TRAIN

There are four trains daily that run between Split and Zagreb (90KN to 131KN, eight to nine hours depending on the service and the time of day), and Split and Šibenik (33KN, 90 minutes).

## Getting Around

There's an airport bus stop on Obala Lazareta 3. The bus (30KN, 30 minutes) leaves about 90 minutes before flight times, or you can take bus No 37 from the bus station on Domovinskog (9.50KN for a two-zone ticket).

A one-zone ticket costs 7KN for one trip in Central Split if you buy it from the driver but 11KN for two trips and 55KN for 10 trips if you buy it from a kiosk. There's a kiosk that also distributes bus maps at the city bus stop.

# SOLIN (SALONA)

The ruins of the ancient city of Solin (known as Salona by the Romans), among the vineyards at the foot of mountains 5km northeast of Split, are the most interesting archaeological site in Croatia. Today surrounded by noisy highways and industry, Salona was the capital of the Roman province of Dalmatia from the time Julius Caesar elevated it to the status of colony. Salona held out against the barbarians and was only evacuated in AD 614 when the inhabitants fled to Split and neighbouring islands in the face of Avar and Slav attacks.

## Sights & Activities

A good place to begin your visit is at the main entrance, near Caffe Bar Salona. There's a small **museum and information centre** (admission 10KN; ☺ 9am-6pm Mon-Sat Jun-Sep, 9am-1pm Mon-Sat Oct-May) at the entrance, which also provides a helpful map and some literature about the complex.

**Manastirine**, the fenced area behind the car park, was a burial place for early Christian martyrs before the legalisation of Christianity. Excavated remains of the cemetery and the 5th-century basilica are highlights, although this area was outside the ancient city itself. Overlooking Manastirine is **Tusculum** with interesting sculptures embedded in the walls and in the garden.

The Manastirine-Tusculum complex is a part of an archaeological reserve which can be freely entered. A path bordered by cypress trees runs south towards the northern **city wall** of Salona. Note the **covered aqueduct** along the inside base of the wall. The ruins in front of you as you stand on the wall were the early Christian cult centre, which include the three-aisled, 5th-century **cathedral** and a small **baptistry** with inner columns. **Public baths** adjoin the cathedral on the eastern side.

Southwest of the cathedral is the 1st-century east city gate, **Porta Caesarea**, later engulfed by the growth of Salona in all directions. Grooves in the stone road left by ancient chariots can still be seen at this gate.

Walk west along the city wall for about 500m to **Kapljuč Basilica** on the right, another martyrs' burial place. At the western end of Salona is the huge 2nd-century **amphitheatre**, destroyed in the 17th century by the Venetians to prevent it from being used as a refuge by Turkish raiders.

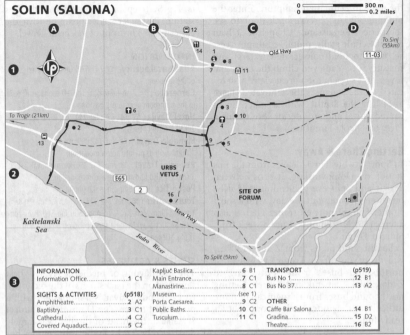

**SOLIN (SALONA)**

To Sinj (55km)

To Trogir (21km)

Kaštelanski Sea

URBS VETUS

SITE OF FORUM

New Hwy

Judro River

To Split (5km)

| INFORMATION | | SIGHTS & ACTIVITIES | (p518) | Kapljuč Basilica | 6 B1 | TRANSPORT | (p519) |
|---|---|---|---|---|---|---|---|
| Information Office | 1 C1 | Amphitheatre | 2 A2 | Main Entrance | 7 C1 | Bus No 1 | 12 B1 |
| | | Baptistry | 3 C1 | Manastirine | 8 C1 | Bus No 37 | 13 A2 |
| | | Cathedral | 4 C2 | Museum | (see 1) | | |
| | | Covered Aquaduct | 5 C2 | Porta Caesarea | 9 C2 | OTHER | |
| | | | | Public Baths | 10 C1 | Caffe Bar Salona | 14 B1 |
| | | | | Tusculum | 11 C1 | Gradina | 15 D2 |
| | | | | | | Theatre | 16 B2 |

## Getting There & Away

The ruins are easily accessible on Split city bus No 1 direct to Solin every half-hour from the city bus stop at Trg Gaje Bulata.

From the amphitheatre at Solin it's easy to continue to Trogir by catching a westbound bus No 37 from the nearby stop on the adjacent new highway. If, on the other hand, you want to return to Split, use the underpass to cross the highway and catch an eastbound bus No 37 (buy a four-zone ticket in Split if you plan to do this).

Alternatively, you can catch most Sinj-bound buses (5KN, 10 daily) from Split's main bus station to take you to Solin.

## TROGIR

☎ 021 / pop 600

Trogir (formerly Trau) occupies a tiny island in the narrow channel lying between Čiovo Island and the mainland, and is just off the coastal highway. The profusion of Romanesque and Renaissance architectural styles within 15th-century walls, as well as the magnificent cathedral at the town centre, inspired Unesco to name the town a World Heritage Site. A day trip to Trogir from Split can easily be combined with a visit to the Roman ruins of Solin. If you're coming by car and in high season, try to get there early in the morning to find a place to park.

## Orientation & Information

The heart of the old town is a few minutes' walk from the bus station. After crossing the small bridge near the station, go through the north gate. Trogir's finest sights are around Narodni trg to the southeast.

A private tourist office, **Čipiko Tourist Office** ( ☎ 881 554; ⏰ 9am-12.30pm & 2.30-5pm Mon-Fri Sep-Jun, 9am-8pm Mon-Sat Jul-Aug), opposite the cathedral, sells a map of the area and arranges private accommodation. There's no left-luggage office in Trogir bus station, so you may end up toting your bags around town.

## Sights

The glory of the three-nave Venetian **Cathedral of St Lovro** (Trg Ivana Pavla II; ⏰ 9.30am-noon year-round & 4.30-7pm daily during summer) is the Romanesque portal of *Adam and Eve* (1240) by Master Radovan, the earliest example of the nude in Dalmatian sculpture. Enter the building via an obscure back door to see the perfect Renaissance Chapel of St Ivan and the choir stalls, pulpit, ciborium (vessel used to hold consecrated wafers) and treasury. You can even climb the cathedral tower, if it's open, for a great view. Also located on the square is the renovated **Church of St John the Baptist** with a magnificent carved portal and an interior showcasing a *Pietá* by Nicola Firentinac.

## Getting There & Away

In Split, city bus No 37 leaves from the bus station on Domovinskog. It runs between Trogir and Split every 20 minutes (15KN, one hour) throughout the day, with a short stop at Split airport en route. There's also a ferry (35KN, 2½hours) once a week from Split to Trogir.

Southbound buses from Zadar (130km) will drop you off in Trogir, as will most northbound buses from Split going to Zadar, Rijeka, Šibenik and Zagreb. Getting northbound buses from Trogir can be more difficult, as they often arrive from Split already full.

# HVAR ISLAND

☎ 021 / pop 12,600

Rapidly becoming the island of choice for a swanky international crowd, Hvar deserves the honour, for it is the sunniest and greenest of the Croatian islands. Called the 'Croatian Madeira', Hvar receives 2724 hours of sunshine each year. The stunning interior is a panorama of lavender fields, peaceful villages and pine-covered slopes.

## Hvar Town

Within the 13th-century walls of medieval Hvar lie beautifully ornamented Gothic palaces and traffic-free marble streets. A long seaside promenade, dotted with small rocky beaches, stretches from each end of the harbour. A few tasteful bars and cafés along the harbour are relaxing spots for people-watching. For more activity, hop on a launch to the Pakleni islands, famous for nude sunbathing.

### ORIENTATION

Car ferries from Split drop you in Stari Grad but in summer local buses meet most ferries for the trip to Hvar town. The town centre

is Trg Sv Stjepana, 100m west of the bus station. Passenger ferries tie up on Riva, the eastern quay, in front of Pelegrini Travel.

### INFORMATION

**Atlas travel agency** ( ☎ 741 670) On the western side of the harbour.

**Garderoba** ( 🕙 7am-midnight) The left luggage office is in the bathroom next to the bus station.

**Hotel Slavija** ( ☎ 741 820; fax 741 147; Riva; per hr 20KN) Internet access.

**Mengola Travel** ( ☎ /fax 742 099; megola-hvar@st .htnet.hr) Finds private accommodation.

**Pelegrini Travel** ( ☎ /fax 742 250; kuzma.novak@st .htnet.hr) Also finds private accommodation.

**Post office** (Riva) You can make phone calls here.

**Tourist office** ( ☎ /fax 742 977; www.hvar.hr; 🕙 8am-1pm & 5-9pm Mon-Sat, 9am-noon Sun Jun-Sep, 8am-2pm Mon-Sat Oct-May) In the arsenal building on the corner of Trg Sv Stjepana.

### SIGHTS & ACTIVITIES

The full flavour of medieval Hvar is best savoured on the backstreets of the old town. At each end of Hvar is a monastery with a prominent tower. The Dominican **Church of St Marko** at the head of the bay was largely destroyed by Turks in the 16th century but you can visit the local **archaeological museum** (admission 10KN; 🕙 10am-noon Jun-Sep) in the ruins. If it is closed you'll still get a good view of the ruins from the road just above, which leads up to a stone cross on a hill top offering a picture-postcard view of Hvar.

At the southeastern end of Hvar you'll find the 15th-century Renaissance **Franciscan Monastery** ( 🕙 10am-noon & 5-7pm Jun-Sep & Christmas week & Holy Week), with a wonderful collection of Venetian paintings in the church and adjacent **museum** (admission 10KN; 🕙 10am-noon & 5-7pm Mon-Sat Jun-Sep), including *The Last Supper* by Matteo Ingoli.

Smack in the middle of Hvar is the imposing Gothic **arsenal**, its great arch visible from afar. The local commune's war galley was once kept here. Upstairs off the arsenal terrace is Hvar's prize; the first **municipal theatre** (admission 10KN; 🕙 10am-noon & 5-7pm) in Europe (1612), rebuilt in the 19th century. Hours can vary and you enter through the adjoining **Gallery of Contemporary Croatian Art** (arsenal; admission 10KN; 🕙 10am-noon & 7-11pm Jun-Sep & Christmas week & Holy Week, 10am-noon low season).

On the hill high above Hvar town is a **Venetian fortress** (1551), and it's worth the climb

Lagos (p462), The Algarve

CARLOS COSTA

Kotor (p548), Montenegro

Carrapateira, north of Sagres (p463), The Algarve

PAUL BERNHARDT

PATRICK HORTON

Kotor Fjord (p548), Montenegro

PATRICK HORTON

Southern Dalmatian coast (p509), Croatia

Franciscan Monastery tower (p526),
Dubrovnik, Croatia

Plitvice Lakes National Park (p512),
Dalmatia, Croatia

Lake Bled and Bled Island,
Slovenia (p541)

for the sweeping panoramic views. The fort was built to defend Hvar from the Turks, who sacked the town in 1539 and 1571.

There is a small town beach next to the Franciscan Monastery, but the best beach is in front of the Hotel Amphora, around the western corner of the cove. Most people take a launch to the offshore islands that include the naturist Pakleni islands of Jerolim and Stipanska and lovely Palmižana.

In front of the Hotel Amphora, **Diving Centar Jurgovan** ( ☎ 742 490) is a large operation that offers a certification course, dives (€40 with equipment) and all sorts of water sports (banana boating, snorkelling, water-skiing), as well as hotel packages.

### SLEEPING

Accommodation in Hvar is extremely tight in July and August: a reservation is highly recommended. For private accommodation, try Mengola Travel or Pelegrini (p520). Expect to pay from 160/280KN per single/double with bathroom in the town centre.

**Mala Milna** ( ☎ 745 027; per person/camp sites 40/30KN) This restful camping ground is the closest, only 2km southeast of town.

**Jagoda & Ante Bracanović Guesthouse** ( ☎ 741 416; 091 520 37 96; virgilye@yahoo.com; Poviše Škole; s 100-120KN, d 190-220KN) This friendly place is close to the town centre and offers six spacious rooms, each with a bathroom, balcony and kitchen access.

**Hotel Slavija** ( ☎ 741 820; fax 741 147; Riva; s/d 533/840KN; 🖳 ) The great thing here is that you step off the passenger boat from Split and into hotel reception. The location on the harbour is the main selling point and the rooms are more than acceptable. Reservations for this and the other large hotels in and around the old town are handled by **Sunčani Hvar** ( ☎ 741 026; www.suncanihvar.hr).

**Hotel Podstine** ( ☎ 741 118; www.podstine.com; s/d 659/1147KN; 🔀 ) Just 2km southwest of the town centre on the secluded Podstine cove lies this beautifully restored and romantic hotel with its own private beach.

### EATING

The pizzerias along the harbour offer predictable but inexpensive eating.

**Konoba Menego** ( ☎ 742 036; mains 40KN) Located on the stairway over the Benedictine convent, this eatery is a good choice.

**Bounty** ( ☎ 742 565; mains from 60KN) Next to Mengola travel agency, this place is a long-time favourite for its succulent fish, pasta and meat dishes at reasonable prices.

**Macondo** ( ☎ 741 851; mains from 60KN) Head upstairs from the northern side of Trg Sv Stjepana for mouth-watering seafood.

The **grocery store** (Trg Sv Stjepana) is a viable restaurant alternative and there's a morning market next to the bus station.

### DRINKING

Hvar has some of the best nightlife on the Adriatic coast, mostly centred around the harbour.

**Carpe Diem** ( ☎ 742 369; Riva) From a groggy breakfast to late-night cocktails, there is no time of day when this swanky place is dull. The music is smooth, the drinks fruity and expensive, and the sofas more than welcoming.

**Nautika** (Fabrika) With cocktails called 'Sex on the Beach' and nonstop dance music, from techno to hip-hop, this place is ground zero for Hvar's explosive nightlife. Just up the street is Kiva Bar, where you can chill out and talk between dance numbers.

### GETTING THERE & AWAY

The Jadrolinija ferries between Rijeka and Dubrovnik stop in Stari Grad before continuing to Korčula. The **Jadrolinija agency** ( ☎ 741 132; Riva) sells boat tickets.

Car ferries from Split call at Stari Grad (32KN, one hour) three times daily (five daily in July and August) and there's an afternoon passenger boat from Split to Hvar town (23KN, 50 minutes) that goes on to Vela Luka on Korčula Island (22KN, one hour). See p537 for information on international connections. Buses meet most ferries that dock at Stari Grad in July and August. If you come in winter, it's best to check with one of the travel agencies to make sure the bus is running. A taxi costs about 100KN.

It's possible to visit Hvar on a (hectic) day trip from Split by catching the morning Jadrolinija ferry to Stari Grad, a bus to Hvar town, then the last ferry from Stari Grad directly back to Split.

## KORČULA ISLAND

☎ 020 / pop 16,200

Rich in vineyards and olive trees, Korčula was named Korkyra Melaina (Black Korčula) by the original Greek settlers because of its dense woods and plant life. As the largest island in an archipelago of 48 islands, it provides plenty of opportunities for scenic drives, particularly along the southern coast. Swimming opportunities abound in the many quiet coves and secluded beaches, while the interior produces some of Croatia's finest wine, especially dessert wines made from the *grk* grape cultivated around Lumbarda. Local olive oil is another product worth seeking out.

## Korčula Town

On a hilly peninsula jutting into the Adriatic sits Korčula Town, a striking walled town of round defensive towers and red-roofed houses. Resembling a miniature Dubrovnik, the gated, walled Old Town is crisscrossed by narrow stone streets designed to protect its inhabitants from the winds swirling around the peninsula. Korčula Island was controlled by Venice from the 14th to the 18th centuries, as is evident from the Venetian coats of arms adorning the official buildings. If you don't stop in Korčula, one look at this unique town from the Jadrolinija ferry will make you regret it.

### ORIENTATION

The big Jadrolinija car ferry drops you off either in the west harbour next to the Hotel Korčula or the east harbour next to Marko Polo Tours. The Old Town lies between the two harbours. The large hotels and main beach lie south of the east harbour, and the residential neighbourhood Sveti Nikola (with a smaller beach) is southwest of the west harbour. The town bus station is 100m south of the Old Town centre.

### INFORMATION

There are ATMs in town at Splitska Banka and Dubrovačka Banka. You can change money there, at the post office, or at any of the travel agencies.

**Atlas travel agency** ( ☎ 711 231) Represents Amex, runs excursions and finds private accommodation.

**Jadrolinija office** ( ☎ 715 410) About 25m up from the west harbour.

**Marko Polo Tours** ( ☎ 715 400; marko-polo-tours@du .htnet.hr; east harbour) Finds private accommodation and organises excursions.

**Post office** Hidden next to the stairway up to the Old Town, the post office also has telephones.

**Tino's Internet** ( ☎ 091 509 11 82; Ul Tri Sulara; per hr 25KN) Tino's other outlet is at the ACI Marina; both are open long hours.

**Tourist office** ( ☎ 715 701; www.korcula.net; Obala Franje Tudjmana bb; ☼ 8am-3pm & 5-9pm Mon-Sat, 8am-3pm Sun Jun-Sep, 8am-1pm & 5-9pm Mon-Sat Oct-May) An excellent source of information, located on the west harbour.

### SIGHTS

Other than following the circuit of the former city walls or walking along the shore, sightseeing in Korčula centres on Cathedral Square. The Gothic **Cathedral of St Mark** ( ☼ 10am-noon, 5-7pm Jul & Aug, off season Mass only) features two paintings by Tintoretto (*Three Saints* on the altar and *Annunciation* to one side).

The **treasury** ( ☎ 711 049; Trg Sv Marka Statuta; admission 10KN; ☼ 9am-7pm Jun-Aug) in the 14th-century Abbey Palace next to the cathedral is worth a look, as is the **Town Museum** ( ☎ 711 420; Trg Sv Marka Statuta; admission 10KN; ☼ 9am-1.30pm Mon-Sat Jun-Aug) in the 15th-century Gabriellis Palace opposite. The exhibits (Greek pottery, Roman ceramics, home furnishings) have English captions. It's said that Marco Polo was born in Korčula in 1254; climb the **tower** (admission 5KN; ☼ 10am-1pm & 5-7pm Mon-Sat Jul & Aug) of what is believed to have been his house.

There's also an **Icon Museum** (Trg Svih Svetih; admission 8KN; ☼ 10am-1pm Mon-Sat) in the Old Town. It isn't much of a museum, but visitors are let into the beautiful old **Church of All Saints**.

In the high summer season water taxis at the east harbour collect passengers to visit various points on the island, as well as Badija Island, which features a 15th-century Franciscan monastery (now a dormitory), plus Orebić and the nearby village of Lumbarda, which both have sandy beaches.

### TOURS

Both **Atlas travel agency** ( ☎ 711 231) and **Marko Polo Tours** ( ☎ 715 400; fax 715 800; marko-polo -tours@du.htnet.hr) offer a variety of boat tours and island excursions.

### SLEEPING

The big hotels in Korčula are overpriced, but there are a wealth of guesthouses that offer clean, attractive rooms and friendly service. Atlas and Marko Polo Tours arrange private rooms, charging from 200KN to 220KN for a room with a bathroom, and with apartments starting at about 400KN. Or, you could try one of the following options.

**Autocamp Kalac** ( ☎ 711 182; fax 711 146; per person/camp sites 40/50KN) This attractive camping ground is behind Hotel Bon Repos in a dense pine grove near the beach.

**Depolo** ( ☎ /fax 711 621; tereza.depolo@du.htnet .hr; d with/without sea view 240/200KN; 🏠 ) Close to the Old Town in the residential neighbourhood of Sveti Nikola and 100m west of the bus station, this guesthouse has spiffy and modern rooms.

**Tarle** ( ☎ 711 712; fax 711 243; Stalište Frana Kršinića; d with/without kitchen 270/210KN) Next to the Hotel Marko Polo, about 500m southeast of the bus station, this place has a pretty enclosed garden and attractive rooms with balconies.

Other guesthouses nearby for about the same price include **Peručić** ( ☎ /fax 711 458), with great balconies, and the homy **Ojdanić** ( ☎ /fax 711 708; roko-taxi@du.htnet.hr). Ratko Ojdanić also has a water taxi and a lot of experience with fishing trips around the island.

### EATING

**Planjak** ( ☎ 711 015; Plokata 19 Travnja; mains from 50KN) This restaurant-grill, between the supermarket and the Jadrolinija office in town, is popular with a local crowd who appreciate the fresh, Dalmatian dishes as much as the low prices.

**Gradski Podrum** (Kaparova; mains from 65KN) Serves up local specialities, such as Korčula-style fish boiled with potatoes and topped with tomato sauce.

**Adio Mare** ( ☎ 711 253; Ulica Sveti Roka; mains 80KN) The charming, maritime décor here puts you in the mood for fish.

There's a supermarket next to Marko Polo Tours.

### ENTERTAINMENT

Between May and September there's **moreška sword dancing** (tickets 60KN; 🕘 9pm Thu) by the Old Town gate; performances are more frequent during July and August. The clash of swords and the graceful movements of the dancers/fighters make an exciting show. Atlas, the tourist office or Marko Polo Tours sell tickets.

### GETTING THERE & AWAY

Transport connections to Korčula are good. There's one bus every day to Dubrovnik (80KN, three hours), one to Zagreb (195KN, 12 hours), and one a week to Sarajevo (152KN, eight hours).

A regular afternoon car ferry between Split and Vela Luka (35KN, three hours), on the island's western end, stops at Hvar most days. Six daily buses link Korčula town to Vela Luka (24KN, one hour), but services from Vela Luka are reduced at the weekend.

From Orebić, look for the passenger launch (15KN, 15 minutes, at least four times daily year-round), which will drop you off near Hotel Korčula right below the Old Town's towers. There's also a car ferry to Dominče (10KN, 15 minutes) which stops near the Hotel Bon Repos, where you can pick up the bus from Lumbarda or take a water taxi to Korčula town (10KN). For international connections see p535.

## OREBIĆ

Orebić, on the southern coast of the Pelješac Peninsula between Korčula and Ploče, offers better beaches than those found at Korčula, 2.5km across the water. The easy access by ferry from Korčula makes it the perfect place to go for the day. The best beach in Orebić is Trstenica cove, a 15-minute walk east along the shore from the port.

### Getting There & Away

The Orebić ferry terminal and bus station are adjacent to each other. Korčula buses to Dubrovnik, Zagreb and Sarajevo stop at Orebić. See the Korčula section (p523) for additional bus and ferry information.

## MLJET ISLAND

☎ 020 / pop 1111

Of all the Adriatic islands, Mljet (Meleda in Italian) may be the most seductive. Over 72% of the island is covered by forests and the rest is dotted by fields, vineyards and small villages. Created in 1960, **Mljet National Park** occupies the western third of the island and surrounds two saltwater lakes, Malo Jezero and Veliko Jezero. Most people visit the island on excursions from Korčula or Dubrovnik, but it is now possible to take a passenger boat from Dubrovnik or come on the regular ferry from Dubrovnik and stay a few days for hiking, cycling and boating.

### Orientation & Information

Tour boats arrive at Pomena wharf at Mljet's western end. Jadrolinija ferries arrive at Sobra on the eastern end and they are met by a local bus for the 1½-hour ride to Pomena and Polače. The *Nikolina* passenger boat from Dubrovnik docks at Sobra and then the little town of Polače, about 5km from Pomena. You can enter the National Park from either Pomena or Polače. The **tourist office** ( ☎ 744 186; np-mljet@np-mljet.hr; ⏲ 8am-1pm & 5-8pm Mon-Fri Oct-May, 8am-8pm Mon-Sat & 8am-1pm Sun Jun-Sep) is in Polače, and the only ATM on the island is at the Odisej hotel in Pomena. The admission price for the national park is 65/45KN adult/concession during July and August, 45/30KN from September to June. The price includes a bus and boat transfer to the **Benedictine monastery** and there is no park admission price if you stay overnight on the island.

## Sights & Activities

From Pomena it's a 15-minute walk to a jetty on **Veliko Jezero**, the larger of the two lakes. Here you can board a boat to a small lake islet and have lunch at a 12th-century **Benedictine monastery**, which is now a restaurant.

Those who don't want to spend the rest of the afternoon swimming and sunbathing on the monastery island can catch an early boat back to the main island and spend a couple of hours walking along the shore of the lake before taking the late-afternoon excursion boat back to Korčula or Dubrovnik. There's a small landing on the main island opposite the monastery where the boat operator drops off passengers upon request. It's not possible to walk right around Veliko Jezero because there's no bridge over the channel that connects the lakes to the sea.

Mljet is good for cycling; several restaurants along the dock in Polače and the Odisej hotel in Pomena rent bicycles (90KN per half day). If you plan to cycle between Pomena and Polače be aware that the two towns are separated by a steep mountain. The bike path along Veliko Jezero is an easier pedal but it doesn't link the two towns.

## Tours

See p522 and p527 in Korčula and Dubrovnik respectively for agencies offering excursions to Mljet. The tour lasts from 8.30am to 6pm and includes the park entry fee. The boat trip from Korčula to Pomena takes at least two hours, less by hydrofoil; from Dubrovnik it takes longer. Lunch isn't included in the tour price and the opportunities for self-catering are limited.

## Sleeping

The Polače **tourist office** ( ☎ 744 186; np-mljet@np-mljet.hr; ⏲ 8am-1pm & 5-8pm Mon-Fri Oct-May, 8am-8pm Mon-Sat & 8am-1pm Sun Jun-Sep) arranges private accommodation at 200KN per double room in summer but it is essential to make arrangements before arrival in peak season. There are more *sobe* (private rooms) signs around Pomena than Polače, but practically none at all in Sobra.

There's no camping permitted inside the national park but there are two grounds outside it.

**Marina** ( ☎ 745 071; per person/camp sites 25/25KN; ⏲ Jun-Sep) This a small camping ground is in Ropa, about 1km from the park.

**Camping Mungos** ( ☎ 745 300; Babino Poje; per person/camp sites 47/30KN; ⏲ May-Sep) Not very shady, but well located, this new camping ground is not far from the beach and the lovely grotto of Odysseus.

The only hotel option available on the island is the **Odisej** ( ☎ 744 022; www.hotelodisej.hr; d from 335KN; ❄ ) in Pomena, which has decent enough rooms and offers a range of activities.

## Eating

**Nine** ( ☎ 744 037; Pomena; mains from 80KN) The Nine, opposite hotel Odisej, is by the sea and, though touristy in high season, turns out succulent seafood.

## Getting There & Away

It is possible to make a quick visit to Mljet by a regular morning ferry (32KN, two hours) from Dubrovnik in the months of July and August. The rest of the year the ferry leaves Dubrovnik in the mid-afternoon Monday to Saturday, or Sunday evening. The ferry docks in Sobra where it is met by a bus. The big Jadrolinija coastal ferries also stop at Mljet twice a week in summer and once a week during the rest of the year. The *Nikolina* is a small boat that makes a 2¾-hour run to and from Dubrovnik to Polače three times a week, leaving in the morning and returning in late afternoon (45KN). You'll be able to buy tickets in the **Turistička Zajednica** (Map pp526-7; ☎ 417 983; Gruška obala bb) in Gruž, at **Atlantagent** (Map pp526-7; ☎ 419 044; obala Stjepana Radića 26; ⏲ 10am-4pm) in Dubrovnik, or on board, but it's wise to buy in advance as the boat fills up quickly.

# DUBROVNIK

☎ 020 / pop 43,770

Whether you call it 'paradise on earth' (George Bernard Shaw) or merely 'the pearl of the Adriatic' (Lord Byron), Dubrovnik is clearly special. Enclosed in a curtain of stone walls, the town centre is radiant with the light reflected from its white marble paving stones. The main pedestrian thoroughfare, Placa, is a melange of cafés and shops with outstanding monuments at either end. Churches, monasteries and museums ornamented with finely carved stone recall an eventful history, and the vibrant artistic tradition is continued with regular concerts and plays. Beyond the walls stretch the crystal-blue waters of the southern Adriatic, sprinkled with tiny islands for the hedonistically inclined.

## History

Founded 1300 years ago by refugees from Epidaurus in Greece, medieval Dubrovnik (Ragusa until 1918) shook off Venetian control in the 14th century, becoming an independent republic and one of Venice's more important maritime rivals, trading with Egypt, Syria, Sicily, Spain, France and later Turkey. The double blow of an earthquake in 1667 and the opening of new trade routes to the east sent Ragusa into a slow decline, ending with Napoleon's conquest of the town in 1806.

The deliberate and militarily pointless shelling of Dubrovnik by the Yugoslav army in 1991 sent shockwaves through the international community but, when the smoke cleared in 1992, traumatised residents cleared the rubble and set about repairing the damage. With a substantial amount of international aid, the famous monuments were rebuilt and resculpted, the streets sealed and the clay roofs retiled. The reconstruction has been extraordinarily skilful but you will notice different shades of rose-tiled roofs as you walk around the city walls.

After a steep postwar decline in tourism, visitors are once again flocking to Dubrovnik. It has become a main port of call for Mediterranean cruise ships, whose passengers are sometimes elbow-to-elbow in peak season. Come in June or September if you can but whatever the time of year the interlay of light and stone is enchanting. Don't miss it.

## Orientation

The Jadrolinija ferry terminal and the bus station are a few hundred metres apart at Gruž, several kilometres northwest of the Old Town (closed to cars). The main street in the Old Town is Placa (also called Stradun). Most accommodation is on the leafy Lapad Peninsula, west of the bus station.

## Information

### BOOKSHOPS
**Algoritam** (Map p528; Placa) Has a good selection of English-language books, including guidebooks.

### INTERNET ACCESS
**Dubrovnik Internet Centar** (Map p528; ☎ 311 017; Starčevića 7; ☺ 9am-9pm; per hr 20KN)

### LEFT LUGGAGE
**Garderoba** (Map pp526-7; ☺ 5.30am-9pm) At the bus station.

### MONEY
You can change money at any travel agency or post office. There are numerous ATMs in town, near the bus station and near the ferry terminal.

### POST
**Main post office** (Map p528; cnr Široka & Od Puča)
**Lapad post office** (Map pp526-7; Šetalište Kralja Zvonimira 21)

### TOURIST INFORMATION
**Tourist Information Centar** (Map p528; ☎ 323 350; fax 323 351; Placa 1) Across from the Franciscan monastery in the Old Town, it's privately run and moderately helpful.
**Turistička Zajednica** (www.tzdubrovnik.hr) outside Pile gate (Map pp526-7; ☎ 427 591; Ante Starčevića 7; ☺ 8am-8pm Mon-Sat, 9am-noon Sun Jun-Sep, 9am-7pm Mon-Fri, 9am-1pm Sat Oct-May); Old Town (Map p528; ☎ 321 561; Placa bb); at the harbour (Map pp526-7; ☎ 417 983; Gruška obala bb) Offers maps and the indispensable Dubrovnik Riviera guide. The harbour branch has limited information.

### TRAVEL AGENCIES
**Atlas travel agency** outside Pile gate (Map p528; ☎ 442 574; Sv Đurđa 1); Old Town (Map p528; ☎ 323 609; Lučarica 1); at the harbour (Map pp526-7; ☎ 418 001; Gruška obala) In convenient locations, this agency is extremely helpful for general information as well as finding private accommodation. All excursions are run by Atlas.
**Dubrovnikturist** (Map pp526-7; ☎ 356 959; fax 356 885; dubrovnikturist@net.hr; Put Republike 7) The option

# DUBROVNIK

ADRIATIC SEA

closest to the bus station for finding private accommodation, renting cars etc.

**Gulliver** (Map above; ☎ 313 300; fax 419 119; Obala Stjepana Radića 32) Near the Jadrolinija dock, Gulliver finds private accommodation, changes money and rents cars and scooters.

## Sights & Activities

### OLD TOWN                                     Map p528

You will probably begin your visit at the city bus stop outside **Pile Gate**. As you enter the city Dubrovnik's wonderful pedestrian promenade, Placa, extends before you all the way to the **clock tower** at the other end of town.

Just inside Pile Gate is the huge Onofrio Fountain (1438) and **Franciscan monastery** (☉ 9am-5pm) with a splendid cloister and the third-oldest functioning **pharmacy** (☉ 9am-5pm) in Europe; it's been operating since 1391. The **church** (☉ 7am-7pm) has recently undergone a long and expensive restoration to startling effect. The **monastery museum** (adult/concession 10/5KN; ☉ 9am-5pm) has a collection of liturgical objects, paintings and pharmacy equipment.

In front of the clock tower at the eastern end of Placa, is the **Orlando Column** (1419) – a favourite meeting place. On opposite sides of Orlando are the 16th-century **Sponza Palace** (originally a customs house, then later a bank), which now houses the **State Archives** (☎ 321 032; admission free; ☉ 8am-3pm Mon-Fri, 8am-1pm Sat), and **St Blaise's Church**, a lovely Italian baroque building built in 1715 to replace an earlier church destroyed in the 1667 earthquake. At the end of Pred Dvorom, the wide street beside St Blaise, is the baroque **Cathedral of the Assumption of the Virgin**. Located between the two churches, the 1441 Gothic **Rector's Palace** (adult/concession 15/7KN; ☉ 9am-2pm Mon-Sat Oct-May, 9am-5pm daily Jun-Sep) houses a museum with furnished rooms, baroque paintings and historical exhibits. The elected rector was not permitted to leave the building during his one-month term without the permission of the senate. The narrow street opposite opens onto Gundulićeva Poljana, a bustling morning market. Up the stairs at the southern end of the square is the **Jesuit monastery** (1725).

As you proceed up Placa, make a detour to the **Museum of the Orthodox Church** (adult/

ENTERTAINMENT 🖵 (p529)
Latino Club Fuego.....................(see 7)
Open-air Cinema.....................**21** C1

TRANSPORT (p530)
Boat to Mljet.....................**22** D1
Bus Station.....................**23** D2
Jadroagent.....................**24** D1
Jadrolinija Ferry Terminal &
Office.....................**25** D1

OTHER
Fort Lovrjenac.....................**26** E3
Hotel Kompas.....................**27** B2

free; 🕙 10am-1pm Mon-Fri) near the clock tower, which is the second oldest synagogue in Europe. The uppermost streets of the Old Town below the north and south walls are pleasant to wander along.

### BEACHES

**Ploče** (Map left), the closest beach to the old city, is just beyond the 17th-century **Lazareti** (Map left; a former quarantine station) outside Ploče Gate. There are also hotel beaches along the **Lapad Peninsula** (Map left), which you are able to use without a problem. The largest is outside the Hotel Kompas.

An even better option is to take the ferry that shuttles half-hourly in summer to lush **Lokrum Island** (35KN return), a national park with a rocky nudist beach (marked FKK), a botanical garden and the ruins of a medieval Benedictine monastery.

### Tours

Atlas travel agency (p525) offers full-day tours to Mostar (240KN), Međugorje (220KN), the Elafiti Islands (240KN) and Mljet (350KN), among other destinations. Its tour to Montenegro (310KN) is a good alternative to taking the morning bus to Montenegro, since the bus schedules make a day trip there impractical.

### Festivals & Events

The **Dubrovnik Summer Festival** (mid-July to mid-August) is a major cultural event: over 100 performances at different venues in the Old Town. The **Feast of St Blaise** (3 February) and **carnival** (February) are also celebrated.

### Sleeping

concession 10/5KN; 🕙 9am-1pm Mon-Fri) for a look at a fascinating collection of 15th- to 19th-century icons.

By this time you'll be ready for a leisurely walk around the **city walls** (adult/concession 30/10KN; 🕙 9am-7pm), which has entrances just inside Pile Gate, across from the Dominican monastery and near Fort St John. Built between the 13th and 16th centuries and still intact, these powerful walls are the finest in the world and Dubrovnik's main claim to fame. They enclose the entire city in a protective veil over 2km long and up to 25m high, with two round towers, 14 square towers, two corner fortifications and a large fortress. The views over the town and sea are great – this walk could be the high point of your visit.

Whichever way you go, you'll notice the 14th-century **Dominican monastery** (adult/concession 10/5KN; 🕙 9am-6pm) in the northeastern corner of the city, whose forbidding fortress-like exterior shelters a rich trove of paintings from Dubrovnik's finest 15th- and 16th-century artists.

Dubrovnik has many other sights, such as the unmarked **synagogue** (ul Žudioska 5; admission

Private accommodation is generally the best option in Dubrovnik, but beware the scramble of private owners at the bus station or Jadrolinija wharf. Some offer what they say, others are rip-off artists. Be aware that most accommodation in the Old Town involves sharing with the owner's family. Apartments Silva Kusjanović, Begović Boarding House and Apartments van Bloemen (p528) are reputable and can often refer you to other places if they are full. All will meet you at the station if you call in advance. Otherwise head to any of the travel agencies or the Turistička Zajednica. Expect to pay about 200KN to 220KN a room in high season.

# DUBROVNIK – OLD TOWN

0 — 100 m
0 — 0.1 miles

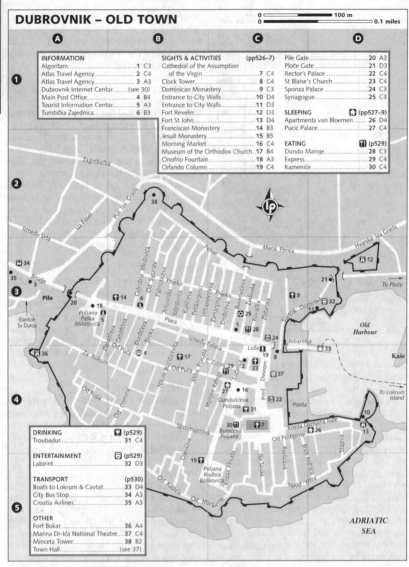

| INFORMATION | |
|---|---|
| Algoritam | 1 C3 |
| Atlas Travel Agency | 2 C4 |
| Atlas Travel Agency | 3 A3 |
| Dubrovnik Internet Centar | (see 30) |
| Main Post Office | 4 B4 |
| Tourist Information Centar | 5 A3 |
| Turistička Zajednica | 6 B3 |

| SIGHTS & ACTIVITIES | (pp526–7) |
|---|---|
| Cathedral of the Assumption | |
| of the Virgin | 7 C4 |
| Clock Tower | 8 C4 |
| Dominican Monastery | 9 C3 |
| Entrance to City Walls | 10 D4 |
| Entrance to City Walls | 11 D3 |
| Fort Revelin | 12 D3 |
| Fort St John | 13 D4 |
| Franciscan Monastery | 14 B3 |
| Jesuit Monastery | 15 B5 |
| Morning Market | 16 C4 |
| Museum of the Orthodox Church | 17 B4 |
| Onofrio Fountain | 18 A3 |
| Orlando Column | 19 C4 |

| | |
|---|---|
| Pile Gate | 20 A3 |
| Ploče Gate | 21 D3 |
| Rector's Palace | 22 C4 |
| St Blaise's Church | 23 C4 |
| Sponza Palace | 24 C3 |
| Synagogue | 25 C3 |

| SLEEPING | (pp527–9) |
|---|---|
| Apartments van Bloemen | 26 D4 |
| Pucić Palace | 27 C4 |

| EATING | (p529) |
|---|---|
| Dundo Maroje | 28 C3 |
| Express | 29 C4 |
| Kamenice | 30 C4 |

| DRINKING | (p529) |
|---|---|
| Troubadur | 31 C4 |

| ENTERTAINMENT | (p529) |
|---|---|
| Labirint | 32 D3 |

| TRANSPORT | (p530) |
|---|---|
| Boats to Lokrum & Cavtat | 33 D4 |
| City Bus Stop | 34 A3 |
| Croatia Airlines | 35 A3 |

| OTHER | |
|---|---|
| Fort Bokar | 36 A4 |
| Marina Dr-Iča National Theatre | 37 C4 |
| Minceta Tower | 38 B2 |
| Town Hall | (see 37) |

## OLD TOWN
Map above

### Budget

**Apartments van Bloemen** ( ☎ 323 433, 091 33 24 106; www.karmendu.tk; Bandureva 1; apt 750KN; ✂ ) Dubrovnik's most personal, original accommodation, with a great location in the Old Town. All apartments are decorated with original art; three sleep three people comfortably.

### Top End

**Pucić Palace** ( ☎ 324 111; www.thepucicpalace.com; Od Puča 1; s/d 2200/4000KN; P ✂ ) Right in the heart of the Old Town, these palatial digs have been designed and decorated to the cutting edge of fashion. Warm and cosy it's not but the countesses and moguls that stay here probably don't care.

## OUTSIDE THE OLD TOWN · Map pp526-7
### Budget
**Solitudo** ( ☎ 448 200; Iva Dulčića 39; per person/camp sites 32/60KN) This pretty and renovated camping ground is within walking distance of the beach.

**YHA hostel** ( ☎ 423 241; dubrovnik@hfhs.hr; Vinka Sagrestana 3; B&B/half-board 95/140KN) It's not exactly restful here, but you'll have a lot of fun.

**Apartments Silva Kusjanović** ( ☎ 435 071, 098 244 639; antonia_du@hotmail.com; Kardinala Stepinća 62; per person 100KN) Sweet Silva has four large apartments that can hold four to eight beds. All have terraces with gorgeous views and it's possible to barbecue.

**Begović Boarding House** ( ☎ 435 191; fax 452 752; Primorska 17; per person 110KN) A long-time favourite with our readers, this friendly place in Lapad has three rooms with shared bathroom and three apartments. There's a terrace out the back with a good view. Breakfast is an additional 30KN.

### Mid-Range
**Hotel Sumratin** ( ☎ 436 333; hot-sumratin@du.htnet.hr; Šetalište Kralja Zvonimira 31; s/d 355/600KN; P ) About 200m from the water, this calm hotel offers good value for money.

**Hotel Petka** ( ☎ 410 500; www.hotelpetka.com; Obala Stjepana Radića 38; s/d from 510/690KN; P ☒ ) Situated opposite the Jadrolinija ferry landing, Hotel Petka won't bowl you over with charm but the location is great for getting back and forth to the ferry.

**Hotel Lapad** ( ☎ 432 922; www.hotel-lapad.hr; Lapadska Obala 37; s/d 600/775KN; ☒ ☒ ) This hotel is a solid, old limestone structure with simple but cheerful rooms and an outdoor swimming pool.

## Eating
### OLD TOWN · Map opposite
There are dozens of places to chow down in the Old Town but there's not a great deal of variety. Pizza, pasta, pasta, pizza. Yawn.

**Express** ( ☎ 329 994; Marojice Kaboge 1; mains from 16KN) It's self-service here, but the soups, salads, vegetables and desserts are freshly prepared and vegetarians will have an easy time assembling a meal.

**Kamenice** ( ☎ 421 499; Gundulićeva poljana 8; mains from 40KN) Portions are huge at this convivial hang-out known for its mussels. Plus, its outdoor terrace is on one of Dubrovnik's more scenic squares.

**Dundo Maroje** ( ☎ 321 445; Kovaćka; mains from 55KN) Nothing adventurous here, but everything is cooked exactly as it should be. The menu is wide ranging with an accent on seafood.

### LAPAD · Map ppp526-7
The better dining is in Lapad.

**Atlantic** ( ☎ 098 185 96 25; Kardinala Stepinca 42; mains from 40KN) The homemade pasta and vegetarian lasagne are outstanding here, even if the ambience is not terribly atmospheric.

**Levenat** ( ☎ 435 352; Šetalište Nika i Meda Pucića 15; mains 45-120KN) The interior at this eatery is classic and the outdoor terrace has a smashing view. The food is superb and there's even a vegetarian plate.

**Pergola** ( ☎ 436 848; Kralja Tomislava 1; mains from 50KN) This is another consistently satisfying place with an outdoor terrace and good seafood.

**Eden** ( ☎ 435 133; Kardinala Stepinca 54; mains 55-90KN) The leafy terrace upstairs is an agreeable spot to enjoy meat, pasta or fish dishes.

## Drinking
Bars have sprung up like mushrooms on Bana Josipa Jelačića near the youth hostel but these days thirsty young singles fill the cafés and terraces on Bunićeva in the Old Town. **Troubadur** (Map opposite; ☎ 412 154; Gundulićeva Poljana) is a long-time favourite for jazz; the ambience is joyous, especially when the owner, Marko, plays.

## Entertainment
The summer months are chock-full of concerts and folk dancing. The tourist office has the full schedule.

**Latino Club Fuego** (Map pp526-7; Starčevića 2) Despite the name, at this disco you'll find a gamut of dance music that includes techno and pop.

**Open-air cinema** (Map pp526-7; Kumičića) In Lapad, this spot allows you to watch movies, shown in their original language, by starlight.

**Labirint** (Map p528; ☎ 322 222; Svetog Dominika 2) A vast restaurant, nightclub, disco and cabaret complex that caters to high rollers. It can chew through your wallet pretty quickly unless you just come for a romantic cocktail on the roof terrace.

## Getting There & Away

### AIR

Daily flights to/from Zagreb are operated by **Croatia Airlines** (Map p528; ☎ 413 777; Brsalje 9). The fare runs about 400KN one way, higher in peak season; the trip takes about an hour.

There are also nonstop flights to Rome, London and Manchester from April to October.

### BOAT

In addition to the **Jadrolinija** (Map pp526-7; ☎ 418 000; Gruž) coastal ferry north to Hvar, Split, Zadar and Rijeka, there's a local ferry that leaves Dubrovnik for Sobra on Mljet Island (26KN to 32KN, 2½ hours) throughout the year. In summer there are two ferries a day. There are several ferries a day year-round to the outlying islands of Šipanska, Sugjuraj, Lopud and Koločep. See also the Central Dalmatia Ferry Routes map on p517.

**Jadroagent** (Map pp526-7; ☎ 419 009; fax 419 029; Radića 32) handles ticketing for most international boats from Croatia.

For information on international connections see p535.

### BUS

Buses from Dubrovnik include:

| destination | cost | duration | frequency |
| --- | --- | --- | --- |
| Korčula | 80KN | 3hr | 1 daily |
| Mostar | 77KN | 3hr | 2 daily |
| Orebić | 80KN | 2½hr | 1 daily |
| Rijeka | 295-309KN | 12hr | 4 daily |
| Sarajevo | 160KN | 5hr | 1 daily |
| Split | 72-111KN | 4½hr | 14 daily |
| Zadar | 160-190KN | 8hr | 7 daily |
| Zagreb | 205-401KN | 11hr | 7 daily |

There's a daily 11am bus to the Montenegrin border, from where a Montenegro bus takes you to Herceg Novi (60KN, two hours) and on to Kotor (100KN, 2½ hours) and Bar (130KN, three hours). In a busy summer season and at weekends buses out of Dubrovnik can be crowded, so book a ticket well before the scheduled departure time.

## Getting Around

Čilipi international airport is 24km southeast of Dubrovnik. The Croatia Airlines airport buses (25KN, 45 minutes) leave from the main **bus station** (Map pp526-7; ☎ 357 088)

1½ hours before flight times. A taxi costs around 200KN).

Dubrovnik's buses run frequently and generally on time. The fare is 10KN if you buy from the driver but only 8KN if you buy a ticket at a kiosk.

## Around Dubrovnik

**Cavtat** is a small town that curves around an attractive harbour bordered by nice beaches. Although it does not have as many interesting sights as Dubrovnik, Cavtat does make a good alternative place to stay if Dubrovnik is fully booked out or the summer crowds become overwhelming. Don't miss the memorial chapel to the Račič family designed by Ivan Meštrović.

A day trip can be made from Dubrovnik to this resort town, just to the southeast. Bus No 10 to Cavtat runs often from Dubrovnik's bus station and there are three daily boats during the summer (40KN).

# CROATIA DIRECTORY

## ACCOMMODATION

Accommodation listings in this guide have been ordered by pricing from cheapest to most expensive (ie budget to top end).

Along the Croatian coast accommodation is priced according to three seasons, which tend to vary from place to place. Generally October to May are the cheapest months, June and September are mid-priced, but count on paying top price for the peak season, which runs for a six-week period in July and August. Prices quoted in this chapter are for the peak period and do not include 'residence tax', which runs from about 4KN to 7.50KN depending on the location and season. Deduct about 25% if you come in June, the beginning of July and September, about 35% for May and October and about 50% for all other times. Note that prices for rooms in Zagreb are pretty much constant all year and that many hotels on the coast close in winter. Some places offer half-board which is bed and two meals a day, usually breakfast and one other meal. It can be good value if you're not too fussy about what you eat.

### Camping

Nearly 100 camping grounds are scattered along the Croatian coast. Opening times of campgrounds generally run from mid-April to September, give or take a few weeks. The exact times change from year to year so it's wise to call in advance if you're arriving at either end of the season.

Many camping grounds, especially in Istria, are gigantic 'autocamps' with restaurants, shops and row upon row of caravans. Expect to pay up to 100KN for the camp site at some of the larger establishments but half that at most other camping grounds, in addition to 38KN to 48KN per person.

**Nudist camping grounds** (marked FKK) are among the best because their secluded locations ensure peace and quiet. However, bear in mind that freelance camping is officially prohibited. A good site for camping information and links is www.camping.hr.

## Hostels

The **Croatian YHA** ( ☎ 01-48 47 472; www.hfhs.hr; Dežmanova 9, Zagreb) operates youth hostels in Dubrovnik, Zadar, Zagreb and Pula. Nonmembers pay an additional 10KN per person daily for a stamp on a welcome card; six stamps entitles you to a membership. Prices in this chapter are for high season during July and August; prices fall the rest of the year. The Croatian YHA can also provide information about private youth hostels in Krk, Zadar, Dubrovnik and Zagreb.

## Private Rooms

Private rooms or apartments are the best accommodation in Croatia. Service is excellent and the rooms are usually extremely well kept. You may very well be greeted by offers of *sobe* as you step off your bus and boat but rooms are most often arranged by travel agencies or the local tourist office. Booking through an agency is somewhat more expensive but at least you'll know who to complain to if things go wrong.

The most expensive rooms are three star and have private bathrooms, in establishments resembling small guesthouses. Some of the better ones are listed in this chapter. It's best to call in advance as the owners will often meet you at the bus station or ferry dock. In a two-star room, the bathroom is shared with one other room; in a one-star room, the bathroom is shared with two other rooms or with the owner who is usually an elderly widow. Breakfast is usually not included but can sometimes

be arranged for an additional 30KN; be sure to clarify whether the price agreed upon is per person or per room. If you're travelling in a small group it may be worthwhile to get a small apartment with cooking facilities, which are widely available along the coast.

It makes little sense to price-shop from agency to agency since prices are fixed by the local tourist association. Whether you deal with the owner directly or book through an agency, you'll pay a 30% surcharge for stays of less than four nights and sometimes 50% or even 100% more for a one-night stay, although you may be able to get them to waive the surcharge if you arrive in the low season. Prices for private rooms in this chapter are for a four-night stay in peak season.

## Hotels

Hotels are ranked from one to five stars with the most in the two- and three-star range. Features, such as satellite TV, direct-dial phones, hi-tech bathrooms, minibars and air-con, are standard in four- and five-star hotels and one-star hotels have at least a bathroom in the room. Many two- and three-star hotels offer satellite TV but you'll find better décor in the higher categories. Unfortunately the country is saddled with too many 1970s, concrete-block hotels, built to warehouse package tourists, but there are more and more options for those looking for smaller and more personal establishments. Prices for hotels in this chapter are for the pricey six-week period that begins in mid-July and lasts until the end of August. During this period some hotels may demand a surcharge for stays of less than four nights but this surcharge is usually waived during the rest of the year, when prices drop steeply. In Zagreb prices are the same all year.

Breakfast is included in hotel prices quoted in this chapter, unless stated otherwise.

## ACTIVITIES
### Kayaking

There are countless possibilities for anyone carrying a folding sea kayak, especially among the Elafiti and Kornati Islands. Lopud makes a good launch point from which to explore the Elafiti Islands – there's a daily ferry from Dubrovnik. Sali on Dugi Otok is close to the Kornati Islands and is connected by daily ferry to Zadar.

CROATIA

## Hiking

Risnjak National Park at Crni Lug, 12km west of Delnice between Zagreb and Rijeka, is a good hiking area in summer. Hiking is advisable only from late spring to early autumn. The steep gorges and beech forests of Paklenica National Park, 40km northeast of Zadar, also offer excellent hiking.

## Diving

The clear waters and varied underwater life of the Adriatic have led to a flourishing dive industry along the coast. Cave diving is the real speciality in Croatia; night diving and wreck diving are also offered and there are coral reefs in some places, but they are in rather deep water. You must get a permit for a boat dive: go to the harbour captain in any port with your passport, certification card and 100KN. Permission is valid for a year. If you dive with a dive centre, they will take care of the paperwork. Most of the coastal resorts mentioned in this chapter have dive shops. See **Diving Croatia** (www.diving -hrs.hr) for contact information.

## BOOKS

Lonely Planet's *Croatia* is a comprehensive guide to the country. There's also Zoë Brân's *After Yugoslavia,* part of the Lonely Planet Journeys series, which recounts the author's return to a troubled region.

As Croatia emerges from the shadow of the former Yugoslavia, several writers of Croatian origin have taken the opportunity to rediscover their roots. *Plum Brandy: Croatian Journeys* by Josip Novakovich is a sensitive exploration of his family's Croatian background. *Croatia: Travels in Undiscovered Country* by Tony Fabijancic recounts the life of rural folks in a new Croatia. For a comprehensive account of the personalities and events surrounding the collapse of the former Yugoslavia it would be hard to go past *Yugoslavia: Death of a Nation* by Laura Silber and Allan Little, based on the 1995 BBC TV series of the same name. Richard Holbrooke's *To End a War* is a riveting look at the people and events surrounding the Dayton Agreement. *Café Europa* is a series of essays by a Croatian journalist, Slavenka Drakulić, which provides an inside look at life in the country since independence. Rebecca West's travel classic, *Black Lamb & Grey*

*Falcon,* contains a long section on Croatia as part of her trip through Yugoslavia in 1937. Marcus Tanner's *Croatia: A Nation Forged in War* provides an excellent overview of Croatia's history.

## BUSINESS HOURS

Banking and post office hours are 7.30am to 7pm on weekdays and 8am to noon on Saturday. Many shops are open 8am to 7pm on weekdays and until 2pm on Saturday. Along the coast life is more relaxed; shops and offices frequently close around noon for an afternoon break and reopen around 4pm. Restaurants are open long hours, often noon to midnight, with Sunday closings outside of peak season. Cafés are generally open from 10am to midnight, bars from 9pm to 2am. Internet cafés are also open long hours, usually seven days a week.

## CUSTOMS

Travellers can bring their personal effects into the country, along with 1L of liquor, 1L of wine, 500g of coffee, 200 cigarettes and 50mL of perfume. The import or export of kuna is limited to 15,000KN per person.

## DISABLED TRAVELLERS

Because of the number of wounded war veterans, more attention is being paid to the needs of disabled travellers. Public toilets at bus stations, train stations, airports and large public venues are usually wheelchair accessible. Large hotels are wheelchair accessible but very little private accommodation is. The bus and train stations in Zagreb, Zadar, Rijeka, Split and Dubrovnik are wheelchair accessible but the local Jadrolinija ferries are not. For further information, get in touch with **Savez Organizacija Invalida Hrvatske** ( ☎ /fax 01-48 29 394; Savska cesta 3; 10000 Zagreb).

---

### DANGERS & ANNOYANCES

Personal security, including theft, is not really a problem in Croatia, but the former confrontation line between Croat and federal Yugoslav forces is still undergoing de-mining operations. The hills behind Dubrovnik still contain some mines so don't go wandering off on your own before checking with a local.

# EMBASSIES & CONSULATES
## Croatian Embassies & Consulates

Croatian embassies and consulates abroad include:

**Australia** ( ☎ 02-6286 6988; 14 Jindalee Cres, O'Malley, ACT 2601)

**Canada** ( ☎ 613-562 7820; 229 Chapel St, Ottawa, Ontario K1N 7Y6)

**France** ( ☎ 01 5370 0287; 2 rue de Lubeck, Paris)

**Germany** Berlin ( ☎ 030-219 15 514; Ahornstrasse 4, Berlin 10787); Bonn ( ☎ 022-895 29 20; Rolandstrasse 52, Bonn 53179)

**Ireland** ( ☎ 1 4767 181; Adelaide Chambers, Peter St, Dublin)

**Netherlands** ( ☎ 70 362 36 38; Amaliastraat 16; The Hague)

**New Zealand** ( ☎ 09-836 5581; 131 Lincoln Rd, Henderson, Box 83200, Edmonton, Auckland)

**South Africa** ( ☎ 012-342 1206; 1160 Church St, 0083 Colbyn, Pretoria)

**UK** ( ☎ 020-7387 2022; 21 Conway St, London W1P 5HL)

**USA** ( ☎ 202-588 5899; www.croatiaemb.org; 2343 Massachusetts Ave NW, Washington, DC 20008)

## Embassies & Consulates in Croatia

The following addresses are in Zagreb (area code ☎ 01):

**Albania** ( ☎ 48 10 679; Jurišićeva 2a)

**Australia** ( ☎ 48 91 200; www.auembassy.hr; Kaptol Centar, Nova Ves 11)

**Bosnia and Hercegovina** ( ☎ 46 83 761; Torbarova 9)

**Bulgaria** ( ☎ 48 23 336; Novi Goljak 25)

**Canada** ( ☎ 48 81 200; zagreb@dfait-maeci.gc.ca; Prilaz Gjure Deželića 4)

**Czech Republic** ( ☎ 61 77 239; Savska 41)

**France** (48 93 680; consulat@ambafrance.hr; Hebrangova 2)

**Germany** ( ☎ 61 58 105; www.deutschebotschaft-zagreb .hr, in German; avenija grada Vukovara 64)

**Hungary** ( ☎ 48 22 051; Pantovčak 128/I)

**Ireland** ( ☎ 48 77 900; Zrinskog 5)

**Netherlands** ( ☎ 46 84 880; nlgovzag@zg.htnet.hr; Medveščak 56)

**New Zealand** ( ☎ 65 20 888; avenija Dubrovnik 15)

**Poland** ( ☎ 48 99 444; Krležin Gvozd 3)

**Romania** ( ☎ 45 77 550; roamb@zg.htnet.hr; Mlinarska ul 43)

**Serbia & Montenegro** ( ☎ 01 45 79 067; Pantovčak 245)

**Slovakia** ( ☎ 48 48 941; Prilaz Gjure Deželića 10)

**Slovenia** ( ☎ 63 11 000; Savska 41)

**UK** ( ☎ 60 09 100; I Lučića 4)

**USA** ( ☎ 66 12 200; www.usembassy.hr; Ul Thomasa Jeffersona 2)

# FESTIVALS & EVENTS

In July and August there are **summer festivals** in Dubrovnik, Split, Pula and Zagreb.

Dubrovnik's summer music festival emphasises classical music with concerts in churches around town, while Pula hosts a variety of pop and classical stars in the Roman amphitheatre and also hosts a **film festival**. **Mardi Gras** celebrations have recently been revived in many towns with attendant parades and festivities, but nowhere is it celebrated with more verve than in Rijeka.

# HOLIDAYS

**New Year's Day** 1 January
**Epiphany** 6 January
**Easter Monday** March/April
**Labour Day** 1 May
**Corpus Christi** 10 June
**Day of Antifascist Resistance** 22 June; marks the outbreak of resistance in 1941
**Statehood Day** 25 June
**Victory Day and National Thanksgiving Day** 5 August
**Feast of the Assumption** 15 August
**Independence Day** 8 October
**All Saints' Day** 1 November
**Christmas** 25 & 26 December

# INTERNET ACCESS

Internet cafés are springing up everywhere. The going rate is about 20KN per hour, and connections are usually good. They can be busy, especially with kids playing online games.

# INTERNET RESOURCES

**Croatia Homepage** (www.hr.hr) Hundreds of links to everything you want to know about Croatia.

**Dalmatia Travel Guide** (www.dalmacija.net) All about Dalmatia, including reservations for private accommodation.

**Find Croatia** (www.findcroatia.com) More Croatia links, with an emphasis on tourism and outdoor activities.

**Visit Croatia** (www.visit-croatia.co.uk) Easy to navigate with updated travel and tourist information.

# MEDIA
## Newspapers & Magazines

The most respected daily in Croatia is *Vjesnik*, but the most daring is the satirical news weekly *Feral Tribune*. Its investigative articles and sly graphics keep Croatian politicians and businesspeople edgy. The English-language *Croatia Monthly* covers optimistic social, political and cultural developments. American, British and French newspapers and magazines are available in most destinations in this chapter.

## Radio & TV

The three national TV stations fill a lot of their air time with foreign programming, generally American, and always in the original language. For local news, residents of Zadar, Split, Vinkovci and Osijek turn to their regional stations. Croatian Radio broadcasts news in English four times daily (8am, 10am, 2pm and 11pm) on FM frequencies 88.9, 91.3 and 99.3.

## MONEY
### Changing Money

Exchange offices may deduct a commission of 1% to change cash or travellers cheques, but some banks do not. Hungarian currency is difficult to change in Croatia and Croatian currency can be difficult to exchange in some neighbouring countries.

### Costs

Accommodation takes the largest chunk of a travel budget, and costs vary widely depending on the season. If you travel in March you'll quite easily find a private room for 100KN per person, but prices climb upward to double that in July and August. Count on 30KN for a meal at a self-service restaurant and 35KN to 50KN for an average intercity bus fare.

### Credit Cards

Amex, MasterCard, Visa and Diners Club cards are widely accepted in large hotels, stores and many restaurants, but don't count on cards to pay for private accommodation or meals in small restaurants. ATMs accepting MasterCard, Maestro, Cirrus, Plus and Visa are available in most bus and train stations, airports, all major cities and most small towns. Many branches of Privredna Banka have ATMs that allow cash withdrawals on an Amex card.

### Currency

The currency is the kuna. Banknotes are in denominations of 500, 200, 100, 50, 20, 10 and 5. Each kuna is divided into 100 lipa in coins of 50, 20 and 10. Many places exchange money, all with similar rates.

### Tipping

If you're served well at a restaurant, you should round up the bill, but a service charge is always included. (Don't leave money on the table.) Bar bills and taxi fares can also be rounded up. Tour guides on day excursions expect to be tipped.

### Tax

A 22% VAT is usually imposed upon most purchases and services, and is included in the price. If your purchases exceed 500KN in one shop you can claim a refund upon leaving the country. Ask the merchant for the paperwork, but don't be surprised if they don't have it.

## POST

Mail sent to Poste Restante, 10000 Zagreb, Croatia, is held at the **main post office** (Branimirova 4; ⊙ 24hr Mon-Sat, 1pm-midnight Sun) next to the Zagreb train station. A good coastal address to use is c/o Poste Restante, Main Post Office, 21000 Split, Croatia. If you have an Amex card, most Atlas travel agencies will hold your mail.

## TELEPHONE
### Mobile Phones

Croatia uses GSM 900/1800 and the two mobile networks are Cronet and VIP. If your mobile is compatible, SIM cards are widely available and cost about 300KN.

### Phone Codes

To call Croatia from abroad, dial your international access code, ☎ 385 (Croatia's country code), the area code (without the initial zero) and the local number. When calling from one region to another within Croatia, use the initial zero. Phone numbers with the prefix 060 are free of charge and numbers that begin with 09 are mobile numbers which are billed at a much higher rate – figure on about 6KN a minute. When in Croatia, dial ☎ 00 to speak to the international operator.

---

**EMERGENCY NUMBERS**

- ∎ Police ☎ 92
- ∎ Fire Brigade ☎ 93
- ∎ Ambulance ☎ 94
- ∎ Roadside Assistance ☎ 987
- ∎ Tourist Information (Croatian Angels) ☎ 062 999 999 (April to October)

## Phonecards

To make a phone call from Croatia, go to the town's main post office. You'll need a phonecard to use public telephones, but calls using a phonecard are about 50% more expensive. Phonecards are sold according to *impulsa* (units), and you can buy cards of 25 (15KN), 50 (30KN), 100 (50KN) and 200 (100KN) units. These can be purchased at any post office and most tobacco shops and newspaper kiosks.

## TOURIST INFORMATION

The **Croatian National Tourist Board** ( ☎ 45 56 455; www.htz.hr; Iblerov trg 10, Importanne Gallerija, 10000 Zagreb) is a good source of information. There are regional tourist offices which supervise tourist development, and municipal tourist offices which have free brochures and good information on local events. Some arrange private accommodation.

Tourist information is also dispensed by commercial travel agencies such as **Atlas** (http://atlas-croatia.com), Croatia Express, Generalturist and Kompas, which also arrange private rooms, sightseeing tours and so on. Ask for the schedule for coastal ferries.

Croatian tourist offices abroad include:
**UK** ( ☎ 020-8563 7979; info@cnto.freeserve.co.uk; Croatian National Tourist Office, 2 Lanchesters, 162-64 Fulham Palace Rd, London W6 9ER)
**USA** ( ☎ 212-279 8672; cntony@earthlink.net; Croatian National Tourist Office, Suite 4003, 350 Fifth Ave, New York, NY 10118)

## TOURS

An interesting option for sailing enthusiasts is **Katarina Line** ( ☎ 051-272 110; www.katarina-line.hr; Tita 75, Opatija), which offers week-long cruises from Opatija to Krk, Rab, Dugi Otok, Lošinj and Cres, or cruises from Split to Dubrovnik that pass the Kornati Islands. Prices run from €250 to €480 a week per person depending on the season and cabin class and include half-board. For specific tours in individual regions, see Tours in the destination sections.

## VISAS

Visitors from Australia, Canada, New Zealand, the EU and the USA do not require a visa for stays of less than 90 days. For other nationalities, visas are issued free of charge at Croatian consulates. Croatian authorities require all foreigners to register with the local police when they first arrive in a new area of the country, but this is a routine matter that is normally handled by your hotel, hostel or camping ground, or the agency that organises your private accommodation.

# TRANSPORT IN CROATIA

## GETTING THERE & AWAY
### Air

The major airports in the country are as follows:
**Dubrovnik** ( ☎ 020-773 377; www.airport-dubrovnik.hr)
**Pula** ( ☎ 052-530 105; www.airport-pula.com)
**Rijeka** ( ☎ 051-842 132)
**Split** ( ☎ 021-203 506; www.split-airport.hr)
**Zadar** ( ☎ 023-313 311; www.zadar-airport.hr)
**Zagreb** ( ☎ 01-62 65 222; www.zagreb-airport.hr)

In addition to domestic connections to Zagreb, Rijeka has a direct flight to London (Heathrow), Pula has a direct flight to Manchester, and Split has direct flights to Manchester, London (Gatwick), Prague and Rome (Fiumicino).

Dubrovnik has direct flights to Manchester, London (Gatwick), Glasgow, and Vienna as well as flights to Zagreb and Split.

Zagreb is connected domestically to Dubrovnik, Split, Pula, Rijeka and Zadar and internationally to all European capitals plus Munich, Frankfurt, Istanbul, and Damascus.

Zadar receives domestic flights from Zagreb only.

The following are the major airlines flying into the country:
**Adria Airways** (code JD; www.adria-airways.com; ☎ 01-48 10 011)
**Aeroflot** (code SU; www.aeroflot.ru; ☎ 01-48 72 055)
**Air Canada** (code AC; www.aircanada.ca; ☎ 01-48 22 033)
**Air France** (code AF; www.airfrance.com; ☎ 01-48 37 100)
**Alitalia** (code AZ; www.alitalia.it; ☎ 01-48 10 413)
**Austrian Airlines** (code OS; www.aua.com; ☎ 062 65 900)
**British Airways** (code BA; www.british-airways.com)
**Croatia Airlines** (code OU; ☎ 01-48 19 633; www.croatiaairlines.hr; Zrinjevac 17, Zagreb) Croatia's national carrier has recently stepped up its service.
**ČSA** (code OK; www.csa.cz; ☎ 01-48 73 301)

**Delta Airlines** (code DL; www.delta.com; ☎ 01-48 78 760)

**KLM-Northwest** (code KL; www.klm.com; ☎ 01-48 78 601)

**Lot** (code LO; www.lot.com; ☎ 01 48 37 500)

**Lufthansa** (code LH; www.lufthansa.com; ☎ 01-48 73 121)

**Malev Hungarian Airlines** (code MA; www.malev.hu; ☎ 01-48 36 935)

**Turkish Airlines** (code TK; www.turkishairlines.com; ☎ 01-49 21 854)

## Land

### BUS

#### Austria
Eurolines runs buses from Vienna to Zagreb (€32, six hours, two daily), Rijeka (€47, 8¼ hours), Split (€51, 15 hours) and Zadar (€43, 13 hours).

#### Bosnia & Hercegovina
There are daily connections from Sarajevo (€22, five hours, daily) and Mostar (€10.65, three hours) to Dubrovnik; from Sarajevo to Split (€14 to €16, seven hours, five daily), which stop at Mostar; and from Sarajevo to Zagreb (€28, eight hours) and Rijeka (€34, 10 hours).

#### Italy
Trieste is well connected with the Istrian coast. There are around six buses a day to Rijeka (€7.50, two to three hours), plus buses to Rovinj (€10.50, 3½ hours, three daily) Poreč (€8.50, 2¼ hours, three daily) and Pula (€14, 3¾ hours, four daily). There are fewer buses on Sunday. To Dalmatia there's a daily bus that leaves at 5.30pm and stops at Rijeka, Zadar (€32, 7½ hours), Split (€35.60, 10½ hours) and Dubrovnik (€64, 15 hours).

There's also a bus from Venice, Monday to Saturday, that stops in Poreč (€19, 2½ hours), Rovinj (€21, three hours) and Pula (€24, 3¼ hours). For schedules, see www.saf.ud.it. There's also a weekly bus in the summer from Milan to Poreč, Rovinj and Pula (€49, 8½ hours).

#### Serbia & Montenegro
There's one bus each morning from Zagreb to Belgrade (€25.50, six hours). At Bajakovo on the border, a Yugoslav bus takes you on to Belgrade. The border between Serbia and Montenegro and Croatia is open to visitors, allowing Americans, Australians, Canadians and Brits to enter visa-free. There's a daily bus from Kotor to Dubrovnik (100KN, 2½ hours, daily) that starts at Bar and stops at Herceg Novi.

#### Slovenia
Slovenia is also well connected with the Istrian coast. There is one weekday bus between Rovinj and Koper (€11, three hours) and Poreč and Portorož (€5.50, 1½ hours), as well as a daily bus in summer from Rovinj to Ljubljana (5050SIT, 5½ hours) and Piran (2020SIT, 2½ hours).

There are also buses from Ljubljana to Zagreb (3070SIT, three hours, two daily), Rijeka (2280SIT, 2½ hours, one daily) and Split (6550SIT, 10½ hours, one daily).

### CAR & MOTORCYCLE
The main highway entry/exit points between Croatia and Hungary are Goričan (between Nagykanisza and Varaždin), Gola (23km east of Koprivnica), Terezino Polje (opposite Barcs) and Donji Miholjac (7km south of Harkány). There are dozens of crossing points to/from Slovenia, too many to list here. There are 23 border crossings into Bosnia and Hercegovina and 10 into Serbia and Montenegro, including the main Zagreb to Belgrade highway. Major destinations in Bosnia and Hercegovina, like Sarajevo, Mostar and Međugorje, are accessible from Zagreb, Split and Dubrovnik.

Motorists require vehicle registration papers and the green insurance card to enter Croatia. Bear in mind that if you rent a car in Italy, many insurance companies will not insure you for a trip into Croatia. Border officials know this and may refuse you entry unless permission to drive into Croatia is clearly marked on the insurance documents. Most car rental companies in Trieste and Venice are familiar with this requirement and will furnish you with the correct stamp. Otherwise, you must make specific inquiries.

See p539 for road rules and further information.

### TRAIN

#### Austria
The *Ljubljana* express travels daily from Vienna to Rijeka (€65.50, 11½ hours, two

daily) through Ljubljana, and the EuroCity *Croatia* travels from Vienna to Zagreb (€60.50, 6½ hours). Both travel via Maribor, Slovenia.

### Hungary
The four daily trains from Zagreb to Budapest (€30, 6½ hours) also stop in Nagykanisza, the first main junction inside Hungary (€11, two hours).

### Italy
Between Venice and Zagreb (€41, eight hours) there's a daily connection via Ljubljana.

### Serbia & Montenegro
Five trains daily connect Zagreb with Belgrade (€17.50, six hours).

### Slovenia
There are up to eleven trains daily between Zagreb and Ljubljana (€23, 2¼ hours) and four between Rijeka and Ljubljana (€25, three hours).

## Sea
Regular boats from several companies connect Croatia with Italy and Slovenia. All of the boat-company offices in Split are located inside the ferry terminal.

**Jadrolinija** (www.jadrolinija.hr; Rijeka ☎ 051-211 444; Riva 16; Ancona ☎ 071-20 71 465; Bari ☎ 080-52 75 439), Croatia's national boat line, runs car ferries from Ancona to Split (€44, 10 hours) and Zadar (€41, seven hours), and a line from Bari to Dubrovnik (€49, eight hours).

**Lošinska Plovidba** (Rijeka ☎ 051-352 200; www .losinjska-plovidba.hr) runs boats connecting Koper, Slovenia, with Pula (€9, 4½ hours) and Zadar (€23, 13½ hours).

**SEM** (www.sem-marina.hr; Split ☎ 021-338 292; Gat Sv Duje; Ancona ☎ 071-20 40 90) connects Ancona with Zadar and Split, continuing on to Stari Grad (Hvar).

**SNAV** (www.snav.com; Ancona ☎ 071-20 76 116; Naples ☎ 081-76 12 348; Split ☎ 021-322 252) has a fast car ferry that links Pescara and Ancona with Split (€73, 4½ hours) and Pescara with Hvar (€80, 3½ hours), as well as a passenger boat that connects Civitanova and Ancona with Zadar (€70, 3¼ hours).

**Adriatica Navigazione** (www.adriatica.it, in Italian; Venice ☎ 041-781 611; Ancona ☎ 071-20 74 334) con-

**DEPARTURE TAX**

There is an embarkment tax of €3 from Italian ports.

nects Ancona and Split and runs between Trieste and Rovinj (€15.49, 3½ hours).

**Venezia Lines** ( ☎ 041-52 22 568; www.venezialines .com; Santa Croce 518/A, Venice 30135) runs passenger boats from Venice to the following destinations once, twice or three times weekly, depending on the season: Pula (€45, three hours), Rovinj, (€45, 3¾ hours) and Poreč (€45 2½ hours) as well as from Trieste to Rovinj (€45, 2¼ hours) and Poreč (€45, 1¼ hours).

**Archibugi** (Ravena ☎ 0544-422 682; archibugi@tin .it; Via Magazzini anteriori 27, Ravenna; Rijeka 051-325 540; travel.rijeka@transagent.hr; Verdijeva 6 Rijeka) runs a daily ferry from July to mid-September connecting Ravenna to Rijeka (€40, eight hours).

In Croatia, contact **Jadroagent** ( ☎ 052-210 431; jadroagent-pula@pu.htnet.hr; Riva 14) in Pula and **Istra Line** ( ☎ 052-451 067; Partizansko 2) in Poreč for information and tickets on boats between Italy and Croatia.

## GETTING AROUND
### Air
Croatia Airlines is the one and only carrier for flights within Croatia. The price of flights depends on the season and you get better deals if you book ahead. Seniors and people aged under 26 get discounts. There are daily flights between Zagreb and Dubrovnik (549KN, one hour), Pula (170KN, 45 minutes), Split (207KN, 45 minutes) and Zadar (341KN, 40 minutes).

### Bicycle
Cycling is a great way to see the islands and bikes are fairly easy to rent in most tourist spots. Many tourist offices have helpful maps of cycling routes. Bike lanes are nearly unknown in Croatia, however; you'll need to exercise extreme caution on the many narrow two-lane roads.

### Boat
Year-round Jadrolinija car ferries operate along the Bari–Rijeka–Dubrovnik coastal route, stopping at Zadar, Split, and the islands of Hvar, Korčula and Mljet. Services

are less frequent in winter. The most scenic section is Split to Dubrovnik, which all Jadrolinija ferries cover during the day. The ferries are considerably more comfortable than buses, though somewhat more expensive. From Rijeka to Dubrovnik the deck fare is €21/25 low/high season with high season running from about the end of June to the end of August; there's a 20% reduction on the return portion of a return ticket. With a through ticket, deck passengers can stop at any port for up to a week, provided they notify the purser beforehand and have their ticket validated. This is much cheaper than buying individual sector tickets but is only good for one stopover. Cabins should be booked a week ahead, but deck space is usually available on all sailings.

Deck passage on Jadrolinija is just that: *poltrone* (reclining seats) are about €4 extra and four-berth cabins (if available) begin at €37/44 low/high season (Rijeka to Dubrovnik). Cabins can be arranged at the reservation counter aboard ship, but advance bookings are recommended if you want to be sure of a place. You must buy tickets in advance at an agency or Jadrolinija office since they are not sold on board. Bringing a car means checking in two hours in advance.

Local ferries connect the bigger offshore islands with each other and the mainland. Some of the ferries operate only a couple of times a day and, once the vehicular capacity is reached, the remaining motorists must wait for the next available service. During summer the lines of waiting cars can be long, so it's important to arrive early.

Foot passengers and cyclists should have no problem getting on but you must buy your tickets at an agency before boarding since they are not sold on board. You should bear in mind that taking a bicycle on these services will incur an extra charge, which depends on the distance.

## Bus

Bus services are excellent and relatively inexpensive. There are often a number of different companies handling each route so prices can vary substantially, but the prices in this book should give you an idea of costs (and unless otherwise noted, all bus prices are for one way fares). Following are some prices for the most popular routes:

| destination | cost | duration | frequency |
| --- | --- | --- | --- |
| Zagreb-Dubrovnik | 205-401KN | 11hr | 7 daily |
| Zagreb-Korčula | 195KN | 12hr | 1 daily |
| Zagreb-Pula | 114-161KN | 4-6hr | 13 daily |
| Zagreb-Split | 112-143KN | 6-9hr | 27 daily |
| Dubrovnik-Rijeka | 300-309KN | 12hr | 4 daily |
| Dubrovnik-Split | 100-111KN | 4½hr | 14 daily |
| Dubrovnik-Zadar | 160-190KN | 8hr | 7 daily |

It's generally best to call or visit the bus station to get the complete schedule but the following companies are among the largest:

**Autotrans** ( ☎ 051-66 03 60; www.autotrans.hr) Based in Rijeka with connections to Istria, Zagreb, Varaždin and Kvarner.

**Brioni Pula** ( ☎ 052-502 997; www.brioni.hr, in Croatian) Based in Pula with connections to Istria, Trieste, Padua, Split and Zagreb.

**Contus** ( ☎ 023-315 315; www.contus.hr) Based in Zadar with connections to Split and Zagreb.

At large stations bus tickets must be purchased at the office. It's a good idea to book ahead to be sure of a seat. Tickets for buses that arrive from somewhere else are usually purchased from the conductor. Buy a one way ticket only or you'll be locked into one company's schedule for the return. Most intercity buses are air-conditioned and make rest stops every two hours or so. Some of the more expensive companies charge extra for a video system that allows you to watch Croatian soap operas during your trip...unmissable. If you plan to catch a nap, bring earplugs since there's bound to be music playing. Luggage stowed in the baggage compartment under the bus costs extra (7KN a piece, including insurance).

On schedules, *vozi svaki dan* means 'every day' and *ne vozi nedjeljom ni praznikom* means 'not Sunday and public holidays'. Check www.akz.hr, in Croatian, for information on schedules and fares to and from Zagreb.

## Car & Motorcycle

Any valid driving licence is sufficient to legally drive and rent a car; an international driving licence is not necessary. **Hrvatski Autoklub** (HAK; Croatian Auto Club) offers help and advice, plus there's the nationwide **HAK road assistance** (vučna služba; ☎ 987).

Petrol stations are generally open 7am to 7pm and often until 10pm in summer. Petrol is Eurosuper 95, Super 98, normal or diesel. See www.ina.hr for up-to-date fuel prices.

You have to pay tolls on the motorways around Zagreb, to use the Učka tunnel between Rijeka and Istria, the bridge to Krk Island, as well as the road from Rijeka to Delnice. The long-awaited motorway connecting Zagreb and Split is scheduled to open in 2005. and will cut the travel time to the coast to about five hours. For general news on Croatia's motorways and tolls, see www.hac.hr.

### ROAD RULES

Unless otherwise posted, the speed limits for cars and motorcycles are 50km/h in the built-up areas, 80km/h on main highways and 130km/h on motorways. On any of Croatia's winding two-lane highways, it's illegal to pass either long military convoys or a line of cars caught behind a slow-moving truck. The maximum permitted amount of alcohol in the blood is – none whatsoever! It is also forbidden to use a mobile phone while driving. Drive defensively, as some local drivers lack discipline, to put it mildly.

### RENTAL

The large car-rental chains represented in Croatia are Avis, Budget, Europcar and Hertz. Throughout Croatia, Avis is allied with the Autotehna company, while Hertz is often represented by Kompas.

Independent local companies are often much cheaper than the international chains, but Avis, Budget, Europcar and Hertz have the big advantage of offering one way rentals that allow you to drop the car off at any one of their many stations in Croatia free of charge.

Prices at local companies begin at around 350KN a day with unlimited kilometres. Shop around as deals vary widely and 'special' discounts and weekend rates

are often available. Third-party public liability insurance is included by law, but make sure your quoted price includes full collision insurance, called collision damage waiver (CDW). Otherwise your responsibility for damage done to the vehicle is usually determined as a percentage of the car's value. Full CDW begins at 40KN a day extra (compulsory for those aged under 25), theft insurance is 15KN a day and personal accident insurance another 40KN a day.

Sometimes you can get a lower car-rental rate by booking the car from abroad. Tour companies in Western Europe often have fly-drive packages that include a flight to Croatia and a car (two-person minimum).

## Hitching

Hitching is never entirely safe, and we don't recommend it. Hitchhiking in Croatia is unreliable. You'll have better luck on the islands, but in the interior cars are small and usually full.

## Local Transport

Zagreb has a well-developed tram system as well as local buses, but in the rest of the country you'll only find buses. In major cities such as Rijeka, Split, Zadar and Dubrovnik buses run about every 20 minutes, and less often on Sunday. Small medieval towns along the coast are generally closed to traffic and have infrequent links to outlying suburbs.

Taxis are available in all cities and towns, but must be called or boarded at a taxi stand. Prices are high (meters start at 25KN).

## Train

Train travel is about 15% cheaper than bus travel and often more comfortable, although slower. The main lines run from Zagreb to Rijeka, Zadar and Split and east to Osijek. There are no trains along the coast. Local trains usually have only unreserved 2nd-class seats. Reservations may be required on express trains. 'Executive' trains have only 1st-class seats and are 40% more expensive than local trains.

On posted timetables in Croatia, the word for arrivals is *dolazak* and for departures it's *odlazak* or *polazak*. For train information check out **Croatian Railway** (www.hznet.hr, in Croatian).

# A SLOVENIAN SOJOURN

## FAST FACTS

- **Area** 20,256 sq km
- **Capital** Ljubljana
- **Currency** tolar (SIT); €1 = 238SIT; US$1 = 198SIT; UK£1 = 358SIT; A$1 = 139SIT; ¥100 = 1.73SIT; NZ$1 = 123SIT
- **Famous For** mountain sports, Lipizzaner horses; plonky Ljutomer Riesling

- **Official Language** Slovene; English, Italian and German are widely understood
- **Key Phrases** *živijo* (hello); *dober dan* (g'day); *nasvidenje* (goodbye); *hvala* (thanks); *oprostite* (sorry)
- **Telephone codes** national ☎ 386; mobile ☎ 030, 031, 040, 041; ☎ toll free 080
- **Visas** not required by most visitors

Few countries pack in as many delights per square kilometre as loveable little Slovenia (Slovenija). Imagine: a patchwork of emerald Alpine meadows crisscrossed by idyllically quiet yet well-paved rural lanes; picture-book villages crowned with baroque churches, reminiscent of unspoilt Austria; soaring grey peaks fringed with forests and wild valleys, offering affordable adrenaline rushes for extreme-sports fanatics; lowland hills covered with vines and riddled with breathtaking caves. The short, developed coastline has no real beaches, but there's a trio of quaint old Venetian ports. From the most perfect of these, Piran, you can scuba dive to WWII wrecks. Ljubljana is a 'mini Prague', with stylishly atmospheric street cafés and impressive galleries.

Safe, clean and not yet overrun by Austrian caravanners, Slovenia isn't the cheapest place in Eastern Europe, but it's fabulously good value.

## Highlights

- Romance the Venetian minicity of **Piran**
- Enact fairytale lakeland scenes around **Bled**
- Glimpse dramatic mountain scenery at **Bovec**, as you slither down waterfalls or jump off mountains

- See graffiti art and unpredictable entertainment in the daunting but inspirational venues of **Metelkova**, lovely Ljubljana's alter ego
- Discover the dizzying underground gorge within the **Škocjan Caves**

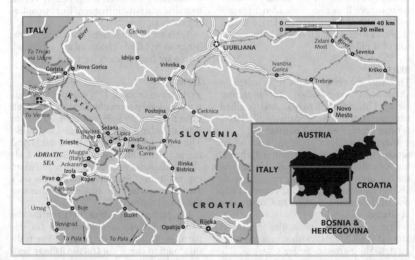

## Planning

Lake Bled freezes over in winter, but the short coastline has a contrastingly mild, typically Mediterranean climate. April is often wet, but this means accommodation is cheaper and the vivid blossom-dappled forests are at their scenic best. May and June are warmer, but during these months hotel prices start to rise, peaking in August, when rooms can be hard to find at any price. September days are calm and ideal for hiking and climbing, while October can be damp.

## Coastal Routes

Slovenia acts as a gateway between Italy and Croatia and the most popular travel routes are along the coast, where those heading north and south cross paths. From Dubrovnik or Split in Croatia, north-bound travellers often stop off at Zadar, RIjeka and Istria (the heart-shaped peninsula just south of Trieste) before heading up to Piran. Those starting their journeys in Trieste, Italy, often do the same trip in reverse.

## Information

The super-helpful **Slovenian Tourist Board** (www.slovenia-tourism.org.si) has dozens of information centres (TICs) in Slovenia and branches abroad; see the website for details.

Accommodation varies in standard and price but guesthouses *(penzion, gostišče,* or *prenočišča)* are often cosy and better value than full-blown hotels some of which are ugly if well renovated Communist-era Frankensteins. Nonetheless, it can be pretty hard to find a double room for under €50. Camping grounds generally charge per person, whether you're camping or caravanning. Rates usually include hot showers. Almost all sites close November to April. Camping 'rough' is illegal, and this is enforced especially around Bled.

Until 2007 Slovenia's legal currency remains the tolar (SIT) but Euros are already very widely accepted. Exchanging cash is simple at banks, major post offices, travel agencies and *menjalnica* (exchange bureaux). Travellers' cheques are less convenient. Major credit and debit cards are accepted almost everywhere and ATMs are astonishingly ubiquitous.

## Getting There & Around

Slovenia's only international airport is **Brnik** (www.lju-airport.si; code LJU) near Kranj, some 23km north of Ljubljana. From here the national carrier, **Adria Airways** (code ADR; ☎ 01-239 1010; www .adria-airways.com), serves up to 20 European destinations. **EasyJet** (code EZY; ☎ 04-206 1677; www .easyjet.com) also flies to Slovenia from London Stansted and Berlin Shönefeld.

Before you book your flight, look closely at a map. There are four alternative airports just beyond Slovenia's borders, all offering low-cost flights to and from London Stansted on **Ryanair** (www.ryanair.com), plus a variety of other destinations.

**Trieste Airport** (www.aeroporto.fvg.it) may be in Italy but it's much closer to Koper, Piran and the Soča valley than Brnik. From the airport terminal there are direct if infrequent buses (€2.20, 15 minutes) to the border towns of Gorizia and Novo Gorica.

**Treviso Airport** (www.trevisoairport.it), often misdescribed as Venice-Treviso, is also handy for western Slovenia. Bus No 6 (€0.80 if prepaid) from outside the terminal barn goes to Treviso Centrale; from here trains (€6.90, two hours) whisk you to Gorizia. That's quicker and cheaper than coming from Ljubljana.

## Bus & Train

International bus destinations from Ljubljana include Sarajevo (8250SIT, 10 hours, 7.15pm Monday, Wednesday and Friday), Split (6550SIT, 10½ hours, 7.40pm daily) via Rijeka (2280SIT, 2½ hours), and Zagreb (3070SIT, three hours, 2.30am, 7.30am and 8.40am) via attractive Novo Mesto.

There are regular, if very slow, Koper–Trieste buses, plus one direct Ljubljana–Trieste service (2360SIT, 6.25am Monday to Saturday).

Daily Ljubljana–Vienna trains (12,979SIT, 6¼ hours) via Graz (6761SIT) are expensive. Save money by going first to Maribor (1380SIT): buy a Maribor–Graz ticket (2665SIT, 1¼ hours, six daily) then continue on domestic tickets from Graz to Vienna (€13.50, 2¾ hours). Similar savings apply via Jesenice and Villach and/or Klagenfurt.

Ljubljana–Trieste–Venice trains (7945SIT) depart at 2.50am or 10.30am. It's vastly cheaper to go first to Novo Gorica (1570SIT), walk to Gorizia then take an Italian train to Venice (€7.90, 2¼ hours).

For Zagreb (Croatia) there are two direct trains daily from both Maribor (3331SIT, 2¾ hours) and Ljubljana (2739SIT, 2½ hours). Several trains serve Rijeka (Croatian coast) from Ljubljana (2665SIT, 2½ hours) via Postojna. The 9.05pm train to Thessaloniki (Greece, 19,912SIT, 25 hours) goes via Belgrade (9450SIT, nine hours).

Seat reservations, often compulsory, cost 800SIT extra.

**Slovenske Železnice** (Slovenian Railways; www.slo-zeleznice.si) has a useful online timetable that's in Slovene but easy to use. Buy tickets before boarding or you'll incur a 200SIT supplement. Beware that IC (InterCity) trains include a 320SIT surcharge on top of standard quoted fares.

### Sea

From Venice, **Venezia Lines** (Atlas Express agency ☎ 05-6745 6772; www.venezialines.com) catamarans sail to Piran (one way/return €42/65, 2¼ hours, mid-April to late September). The **Prince of Venice** (Kompas; ☎ 05-617 8000; portoroz@kompas.si) catamaran from nearby Izola also serves Venice (10,800SIT to 14,000SIT, 2¼ hours, March to October). Both operate between once and four times a week, generally returning the same evening. The **Marina** (jadroagent-zadar@zd.htnet.hr) sails weekly from Koper to Zadar in Croatia (5500SIT, 14 hours, mid-June to early September).

# Albania

ALBANIA

Both sandy *and* pebbly beaches stretch along the Adriatic and Ionian coasts, giving Albania a real Medditerranean feel, from Tirana's cafés on wide, shady boulevards, to the long sandy beach at Durrës that's perfect for relaxing on. You can dip your feet in at any number of places, from the bustling town of Vlora, where urban life abuts the sea, to quiet Himara and its long crescent of beach. The virgin beach at Drymades is ideal for drinking at beach bars and sleeping under the stars. Fresh fish abounds, as well as meat- and vegetable-laden traditional dishes, which will keep visitors happy.

Yet, visiting Albania remains an experience only for the 'adventurous' and many people associate it with its former isolation, peppered with stories of corruption and poverty. In reality, you'll find a warm and sincerely hospitable country with fantastic natural attractions, from breathtaking mountain landscapes to long white beaches and the clear blue sea.

This chapter focuses on Albania's Mediterranean highlights but if you want to learn more about the country then check out Lonely Planet's *Eastern Europe*.

---

**FAST FACTS**

- **Area** 28, 748 sq km
- **Capital** Tirana
- **Currency** lekë; Aus$1 = 76 lekë; €1 = 130 lekë; Ÿ100 = 95 lekë; NZ$1 = 70 lekë; UK£1 = 190 lekë; US$ = 105 lekë
- **Famous for** Mother Teresa
- **Official Languages** Albanian (TOSK)
- **Population** 3.5 million
- **Telephone Codes** country code ☎ 355, international access code ☎ 00, domestic directory assistance ☎ 124, international directory assistance ☎ 122
- **Visas** No visa needed for citizens of EU, Australia, New Zealand, the US, and Canada. Everyone pays €10 entrance fee at airports, ports, or border crossings.

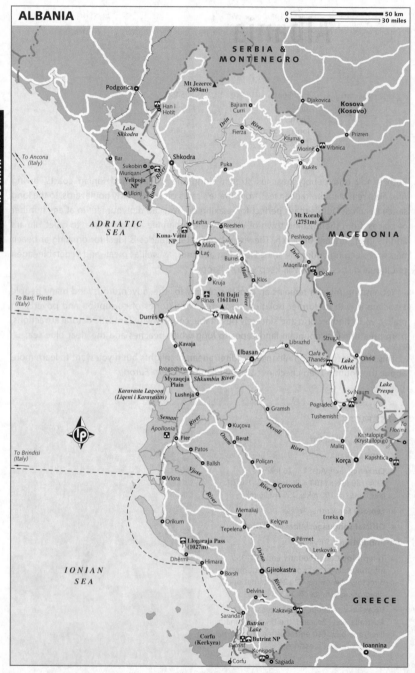

# ALBANIA

To Ancona (Italy)

To Bari; Trieste (Italy)

To Brindisi (Italy)

To Florina

SERBIA & MONTENEGRO

Kosova (Kosovo)

MACEDONIA

GREECE

ADRIATIC SEA

IONIAN SEA

Lake Shkodra

Lake Ohrid

Lake Prespa

Mt Jezerce (2694m)

Mt Korab (2751m)

Mt Dajti (1611m)

Drin River

Drin River

Mati River

Seman River

Osum River

Devoll River

Vjose River

Drino River

Shkumbin River

Buna River

Podgorica

Han i Hotit

Bajram Curri

Djakovica

Fierza

Kruma

Prizren

Vrbnica

Morine

Shkodra

Kukës

Bar

Sukobin

Muriqani

Velipoja NP

Ulcinj

Puka

Lezha

Rreshen

Peshkopi

Kuna-Vaini NP

Milot

Laç

Burrel

Maqellare

Debar

Klos

Kruja

Rinas

TIRANA

Durrës

Kavaja

Librazhd

Struga

Elbasan

Qafa e Thanës

Ohrid

Rrogozhina

Myzaqeja Plain

Sv Naum

Karavasta Lagoon (Liqeni i Karavastas)

Lushnja

Gramsh

Pogradec

Tushemisht

Apollonia

Kuçova

Berat

Kristalopigi (Krystallopigi)

Fier

Maliq

Korça

Kapshtica

Patos

Poliçan

Ballsh

Çorovoda

Vlora

Memaliaj

Kelçyra

Erseka

Orikum

Tepelena

Përmet

Leskoviku

Llogaraja Pass (1027m)

Dhërmi

Himara

Gjirokastra

Borsh

Delvina

GREECE

Saranda

Kakavija

Butrint Lake

Corfu (Kerkyra)

Butrint NP

Butrint

Konispoli

Corfu

Sagiada

Ioannina

0   50 km
0   30 miles

# HIGHLIGHTS

- Immerse yourself in the café culture of **Tirana** (below), the capital.
- Walk down the sandy beach at **Durrës** (right) and watch families at play.
- Witness the magical meeting of the Adriatic and Ionian Seas at **Vlora** (p546).
- Look out over the clear blue sea on the gorgeous beaches at **Dhërmi** (p546) and **Drymades** (p546).
- Enjoy the bobbing boats and relaxing walks of **Saranda** (p546).

## TIRANA

Tirana is a city of dusty streets, shaded boulevards with elegant 1930s Italian architecture, street markets, trendy bars, parks, beautiful mosques, rows of moneychangers, remnants of socialist-realist art and fun nightlife. You may well be surprised to see how different one street is from the next and to discover a small lake and a lush park at the city's edge.

For Internet access go to **F@stech** ( ☎ 251 947; Rruga Brigada e VIII, 1st fl; ☽ 8.30am-11pm), with high stools bringing you up to your walled-in screen. If you need a doctor go to **ABC Clinic** ( ☎ 234 105; 360 Rruga Qemal Stafa; ☽ 8am-4pm Mon-Fri). While there are plenty of banks in Tirana, there were no international ATMs at the time of writing. The **main Post Office** ( ☎ 228 262; Sheshi Çameria; ☽ 8am-8pm Mon-Fri) and telephone centre

---

**HOW MUCH?**

- **Shot of mulberry raki** 100 lekë
- **Souvenir bunker-shaped ashtray** 500 lekë
- **Short taxi ride** 300 lekë
- **Loaf of bread** 50 lekë
- **Meal of Fërgesë Tiranë (traditional Tirana dish)** 300 lekë

**LONELY PLANET INDEX**

- **Litre of petrol** 100 lekë
- **Litre of bottled water** 50 lekë
- **Bottle of beer** 150 lekë
- **Souvenir T-shirt** 800 lekë
- **Street snack (byrek)** 30 lekë

---

are adjacent on a street jutting west from Skanderbeg Square.

Stay at **Hotel Lugano** ( ☎ /fax 222 023; Rruga Mihal Duri 34; s US$50, d US$70) where the newly renovated rooms have heavy red drapes on the windows, good beds, and some, though not all, have kitsch faux-marble bathrooms that may give you a shock in the morning.

Lick your fingers after trying tasty Albanian dishes for carnivores and vegetarians at **Villa Ambassador** (mobile/cell ☎ 038-202 4293; Rruga Themistokli Gërmenji; mains 500 lekë; ☽ noon-11.30pm); it has a homey atmosphere and fantastic service. This former embassy is among Tirana's best eating options.

Stay up till dawn partying at **Living Room bar** ( ☎ 242 481; Bulevardi Zhan d'Ark, Pall. Italiane 1; ☽ 24hr), one of the hippest places to drink and dance in Tirana, with an eclectic DJ on weekends and a good crowd.

## DURRËS

Durrës, an ancient city and Albania's old capital, is a city under construction with a long 10km built-up beach stretching south where families play football, people stroll and cool down in the shallow waters of the Adriatic. Unfortunately, cars also drive on the beach, which makes sunbathing something of a risky sport. Ancient remains, an interesting museum and good bus and train connections make Durrës a great base for archaeological exploration of places like Apollonia and Butrint, and a quieter alternative to the capital.

The **Savings Bank of Albania** ( ☽ 8am-2pm Mon-Fri), across the bus station parking lot from the train station, changes travellers cheques and offers MasterCard advances for a 1% commission. The Post Office and telephone centre are one block west of the train and bus stations. For email go to **Galaxy Internet Cafe** ( ☎ 038-213 5637; Rruga Taulantia; 200 lekë).

Let waves lull you to sleep at **Hotel Besani** ( ☎ 068-203 5781; Skëmbi i Kavajës; s US$20, d US$40), one of the best choices among dozens of beach hotels. Seaview rooms are clean and comfortable. It's 1km south of the NATO base.

**Bunker Blue** (per plate 350 lekë) is the best food option in Durrës. Not actually a bunker, although it is blue, this taverna right on the beach 1km south of the harbour has fresh and cheap seafood.

**ALBANIA**

# IONIAN COAST

## Vlora

One of Albania's major cities, the Mediterranen port of Vlora is where the Adriatic and Ionian Seas meet and form a blue line across the clear waters.

Sleep at **Palma** ( ☎ 29 320; Uji i Ftohtë beach; per person €8), seated on top of a hill with views of the Bay of Vlora to die for. This magnificent former workers' camp still gives off a whiff of socialist idealism. Basic double and triple rooms have run-down bathrooms.

## Dhërmi & Drymades Beaches

Immaculate white crescent-shaped beaches and azure waters will lure you to Dhërmi. A half-hour walk through some olive groves brings you to Drymades, with a pristine white beach stretched before you.

To get to Drymades, turn off the asphalt road going down into Dhërmi, at the sign indicating that it's 1200m to Drymades beach.

Sitting right on the beach, all rooms look onto the sea at **Dhërmi Hotel** ( ☎ 068-224 68 05; s 3000 lekë, d 5000 lekë).

A constellation of bungalows makes up **Drymades Hotel** ( ☎ 068-228 56 37; per bungalow 4000 lekë). It's under the shade of pine trees, a step away from the blue sea.

## Himara

This is a sleepy, dusty small town with a lovely beach that comes alive in the summer months with holiday-makers strolling down the promenade.

You can make yourself quite at home in **Likoka** ( ☎ 2745/068-226 36 08; per person €20), a white, circular hotel halfway down the beach with spacious rooms and light balconies for alfresco breakfasts overlooking the sea.

## Saranda (Sarandë)

Horseshoe-shaped Saranda is a stone's throw from Corfu (38km) in Greece and a good point to cross into Albania from Greece. Its houses descend from the hillsides, small boats bob on the blue sea, and the town boasts around 290 sunny days per year.

For great seaviews from bed, go to **Kaonia** ( ☎ 26 00/26 08; Rruga 1 Maji; s 2000 lekë, d 3000 lekë), a lovely small hotel on the seafront with great beds, power showers, TVs and sea views.

# TRANSPORT

## Air

**Albanian Airlines** (code LV; www.flyalbanian.com; ☎ 35 162/33 494) and **Alitalia** (code AZ; www.alitalia .it; ☎ 311 86 02) serve Maria Teresa airport from various destinations. There is no public transport to and from Maria Teresa airport. A taxi should cost about €30 from Tirana.

## Boat & Hydrofoil

The Italian company of **Adriatica di Navigazione** operates ferry services to Durrës from Bari in Italy (€60, 8½ hours) daily and from Ancona in Italy (€85, 19 hours) four times a week. A daily ferry and hydrofoil service plies between Saranda and Corfu (€14 one way). Call **Finikas Lines** ( ☎ 30-9-4485 3228) in Corfu for schedules from Corfu. The hydrofoil normally leaves Saranda at 10am.

Vlora is connected to Brindisi in Italy by ferry daily during the summer leaving each side at 10pm and docking at 7am. You can book through **Skenderbeg Lines** ( ☎ /fax 0831 525 448/562 662; Corso Garibaldi 100, Brindisi; per person €36) in Brindisi.

Possibly the best and certainly the most comfortable way to see the coast is by hydrofoil linking Corfu with Saranda, Himara and Vlora. This operates only in the summer months, on Wednesdays and Saturdays, but daily in August. Contact **Colombo Agency** ( ☎ 033-23 578/27 659) in Vlora for details.

## Bus

Getting to Vlora from Tirana and Durrës is easy, with buses and minibuses whizzing back and forth in the morning. The bus fare is 300 lekë and the journey lasts around three hours. In Vlora, the bus station is easily spotted – look for the Muradi Mosque, which makes an excellent landmark.

Buses go regularly between Vlora and Himara and Vlora and Saranda and stop at Dhërmi on the way. Buses run from 7am between Saranda, Himara and Vlora, and minibuses go from Himara itself, from the seafront at the end of the promenade.

## Train

The train station is at the northern end of Tirana's Bulevardi Zogu I. Trains go to Durrës (55 lekë, one hour, eight daily) and Vlora (210 lekë, 5½ hours, two daily).

# Montenegro

From an interior of alpine scenery with giddy-deep canyons, to a sparsely vegetated and limestone mountain range plummeting to an azure Adriatic Sea replete with fjords, this 13,812-sq-km republic has got the lot. Montenegro (Crna Gora) is a very popular holiday spot with locals and holiday-makers, who appreciate the chance to tan by the calm waters of the Adriatic by day and party under the stars by night.

Montenegro has been a stalwart of several Yugoslav federations and is now in a 'suck it and see' union with Serbia that may last no longer than the 2006 referendum.

This chapter focuses on Montenegro's Mediterranean highlights but if you want to learn more about the country then check out the Serbia & Montenegro chapter of Lonely Planet's *Eastern Europe*.

## FAST FACTS

- **Area** 102,350 sq km (Serbia & **Montenegro**)
- **Capital** Podgorica
- **Currency** euro; A$1 = €0.59; ¥100 = €0.78; NZ$ = €0.52; UK£1 = €1.44; US$1 = €0.86
- **Famous for** Basketball players
- **Official Language** Serbian
- **Population** 7.5 million (Serbia & Montenegro)
- **Telephone Codes** country code ☎ 381; international access code ☎ 99
- **Visas** Not required by most Europeans, Australian, New Zealand, US and Canadian citizens

## BUDVA
☎ 086 / pop 11,700

Budva is Serbia & Montenegro's top beach resort. A series of fine beaches punctuate the coastline all the way to Sveti Stefan, with high barren coastal mountains forming a magnificent backdrop. Budva's big tourist-puller is its old **walled town**. Levelled by earthquakes in 1979, it's been completely rebuilt as a tourist attraction – so picturesque it seems almost contrived. The old town has plenty of cafés, restaurants and bars to entice visitors edging through the narrow streets.

The best beaches are either side of the town.

**JAMB travel** ( ☎ 452 992; www.jamb-travel.com; Mediteranska 23; r €5.90-14, 2-/5-person apt €16-80; ✆ 8am-3pm Mon-Fri Nov-May, 8am-8pm Jun-Oct) books accommodation and organises day tours to interesting parts of Montenegro. Half-board/full board is available for €9/13 extra.

**Restaurant Jadran** ( ☎ 451 028; Slovenska Obala 10; dishes €5-10; ✆ 8am-late) is probably the best restaurant in Budva, with luxury lobster at €60 per kg or substantial soup or čevapčići (meat rolls) for €2.

## ADRIATIC COAST
### Bar
☎ 085 / pop 37,000

Surrounded by precipitous mountains, modern Bar is a doorway to the coast. Stari Bar (Old Bar), about 4km northeast of the modern town, comprises some 240 ruins dating back 1000 years.

**Montenegro Express** ( ☎ /fax 312 589; Obala 13 Jula bb; r €7-20, hotels €30-100; ✆ 8am-8pm Mon-Sat Jul-Aug, 8am-2pm Mon-Sat Sep-Jun), opposite the ferry terminal, books accommodation along the coast.

## Ulcinj

☎ 085 / pop 24,000

This town heads a series of sandy beaches from Mala Plaža (Small Beach) below the old town to Velika Plaža (Great Beach), a famous 12km-long beach stretching eastwards towards Albania. In July and August, Ulcinj bulges with tens of thousands of holiday-makers, parasols dotting the white sands.

**Real Estate Tourist Agency** ( ☎ 421 612; www .realestate.cg.yu; 26 Novembar bb; r €10, hotels from €16, 2-/3-/4-person apt €27/36/43; 8am-9pm) has accommodation in private rooms, hotels and apartments without board.

**Bazar** ( ☎ 421 639; 26 Novembar bb; mains €5-8; 8am-late) is an upstairs restaurant that's an ideal place to escape summer crowds and feast on a plate of fried *lignje na žaru* (calamari), the restaurant's speciality.

## Kotor

☎ 082 / pop 22,500

Picturesque Kotor, with its walled town nestled at the head of southern Europe's deepest fjord, has Montenegro's most dramatic setting. Cobbled laneways form a labyrinth connecting small squares with ancient churches and former aristocratic mansions.

**Meridian Travel Agency** ( ☎ 322 968; travel@cg.yu; private rooms €8-15, apt €30-55, hotel s €25-44, d €41-63; 9am-2pm & 6-7pm Mon-Fri, 9am-2pm Sat) has staff that can help you find accommodation. It's in a small lane behind the clock tower.

---

**HOW MUCH?**

- Short taxi ride €2
- Internet access per hour €1
- Coffee €1
- Bottle of plum brandy €7

**LONELY PLANET INDEX**

- Litre of petrol €0.88
- Litre of bottled water €1
- Bottle of beer €1
- Street snack €0.50

---

**Pizzeria Giardino** ( ☎ 323 324; Stari Grad; meals €4-5; 9am-late) is probably the best-value restaurant within the old town. Their pizza marinara is among Montenegro's best.

## TRANSPORT

JAT Airways (the Serbian airline) and Montenegro Airlines have regional services. **Mecur** ( ☎ 313 617; www.mercuradriatica.com; Obala 13 Jula bb; 8am-8pm Mon-Fri, 9am-2pm Sat) books Adriatica ferries to Ancona (€51/61/82 for passage only/deck seat/cabin bed, 16 hours, 5.30pm Thursday).

**Barska Plovidba** ( ☎ 312 336; mlinesagency@cg.yu; Obala 13 Jula bb; 8am-10pm) are the agents for Montenegro Lines sailing between Bar and Bari (Italy). For times and prices check the website at www.montenegrolines.net.

Four trains travel daily between Belgrade and bar. Eight buses run between Budva and Belgrade (€15, 12 hours). For general tourist information, as well as transport and accommodation info, check the **Montenegro Tourist Organisation** (www.visit-montenegro.cg.yu).

# Cyprus

## FAST FACTS

- **Area** 9250 sq km – about four Luxembourgs
- **Capital** Lefkosia for the Republic; Lefkoşa in the north
- **Currency** Cyprus Pound CY£ in south; Turkish Lira TL in the north (prices are in euros); A$1 = CY£0.33, €0.59; ¥100 = CY£0.44, €0.78; NZ$1 = CY£0.32, €0.52; UK£1 = CY£1.17, €1.44; US$1 = CY£0.48, €0.86
- **Famous for** beaches, icons and mezes
- **Official Languages** Greek in the south, Turkish in the north
- **Telephone Codes** country code for the south ☎ 357, for the north ☎ 90 392; to call from south to north ☎ 0139, to call north to south dial ☎ 0123.
- **Visas** none required for most nationalities

The third-largest island in the Mediterranean, Cyprus is a famous destination for package tours, but there's plenty here for the independent traveller. Cyprus is the legendary birth-place of Aphrodite (Goddess of Love), who blessed the island with golden beaches, great food and a laid-back, Mediterranean way of doing things.

Where you go in Cyprus depends on whether you are a sun-worshipper or a culture vulture. For sun, sand and surf, you have the choice of the tourist beaches at Pafos, Protaras and Ayia Napa, or wild, empty beaches in the Akamas and Karpas peninsulas.

History buffs swoon at the mention of Cyprus – you can't go more than a few miles in any direction without hitting a Roman ruin or Byzantine monastery. The south is packed with Graeco-Roman and Byzantine relics, while in the North there are ruined Frankish cathedrals and castles on every other hilltop.

Cyprus has seen its share of troubles and the north part of the island has been occupied by Turkey since 1974. However, each year seems to bring the situation a little closer to resolution and the attractions speak for themselves. If you want a holiday with history, just follow in the footsteps of empire builders from Athens to Istanbul.

## HIGHLIGHTS

- Let the crowded **Pafos** mosaics (p561) take your breath away – Cyprus is full of Graeco-Roman ruins.
- Sample every dish in Cyprus in one sitting with a bottomless meze dinner at **Zanettos restaurant** (p564) in Lefkosia.
- Bask in the glory of Byzantine frescoes and World Heritage-listed churches in the gorgeous **Troodos Mountains** (p560).
- Be king of your own castle at remote Kantara Castle, on the edge of the **Karpas Peninsula** (p566)
- Barely see a soul on the blissful beaches of the unspoiled **Akamas** peninsula (p562).

## ITINERARIES

- **One week** With just a week in Cyprus, fly into the south and head for Polis and the wild walking country of the Akamas peninsula. Stop in on ancient ruins at Pafos and Lemesos and tour the Byzantine monasteries in the Troodos mountains. Drop down into Lefkosia for fine food and wonderful museums and day trip over to Girne in North Cyprus for the harbour views.
- **Two weeks** With time to kill, you can see more of the south and the north. Rent a car and visit some of the smaller villages inland from Polis and higher up in the Troodos. Visit Larnaka to see the final resting place of Lazaros and spend a party

| HOW MUCH? |
| --- |
| ■ **Meze meal** CY£7 in the Republic; €4.30 in the North |
| ■ **Budget hotel room** CY£15-18/ €5.40-16.00 |
| ■ **Intercity bus ride** CY£2-3/€1.10-1.60 |
| ■ **Museum admission** CY£0.75-1.50/ €2.40-4.80 |
| ■ **2kg bag of oranges** CY£1/€1.10 |

| LP INDEX |
| --- |
| ■ **Litre of petrol** CY£0.46 in the south, €0.80 in the north |
| ■ **Litre of bottled water** CY£0.50/€0.55 |
| ■ **Beer** CY£2/€1.60 |
| ■ **Souvenir T-shirt** CY£6/€10 |
| ■ **Snack kebab** CY£2/€1.60 |

night in touristy Ayia Napa. In the north, tour the Frankish ruins in Gazimağusa and drive up the wild and wonderful Karpas peninsula via Kantara castle.

## CLIMATE & WHEN TO GO

Cyprus has a typical Mediterranean climate, cool and dry in winter, hot and dry in summer. The peak season is from June

## TOP FIVE

■ **Superb Sight** Archangelos church in Pedoulas

■ **Finest Festival** Kataklysmos Festival, 50 days after Easter in coastal towns

■ **Blondest Beach** Altinkum Beach in the Karpas

■ **Coolest Club** the Castle Club in Ayia Napa

■ **Wildest Walk** Gorgeous (ahem) Avakas Gorge in the Akamas

to August, but the island really cooks and you can go from pasty white to lobster red in minutes. April to May and September to October offer warm sunny days and pleasantly balmy nights – perfect for outdoor dining and walking in the hills.

## HISTORY

Blessed with natural resources but cursed by a strategic location, Cyprus has been a pawn in the games of empires since ancient times. The island was settled around 8500 BC, but Greek culture arrived in 1400 BC with the Mycenaeans. Over the next 2000 years, Cyprus was dominated by various Mediterranean empires, most importantly the Romans, who introduced Christianity and expanded the ancient Greek cities at Pafos, Salamis, Kition and Kourion.

As Roman influence declined, Cyprus was incorporated into the Byzantine Empire, a nd Orthodox churches and monasteries were constructed all over the island. The English king, Richard the Lionheart, annexed Cyprus on his way to the Third Crusade in 1191 and sold the island on to the fanatical Knights Templar – most of the castles in Cyprus date from this turbulent period in history.

In 1192, the Crusaders sold Cyprus to Guy de Lusignan, the deposed king of Jerusalem, who suppressed the Greek Orthodox church and erected Roman Catholic cathedrals in Lefkosia and Famagusta. The Frankish period lasted until 1489, and Cyprus passed to the Venetians, who built huge city walls around Lefkosia and Famagusta to protect them from Arab marauders. This failed to stop the Ottomans, who

invaded in 1570 and dominated Cyprus for the next 300 years.

In 1878, Turkey sold Cyprus to Britain in exchange for protection from Russia, but the majority Greek Cypriot population demanded *enosis:* independence from British and Turkish rule and union with Greece. The British government declared in 1954 that Cyprus would never gain independence, and the National Organisation of Freedom Fighters (EOKA) launched a guerrilla war against the colonial administration and the mainly Turkish Cypriot colonial police force.

In 1958, Turkish agitators detonated a bomb at the Turkish embassy in Lefkosia. This triggered riots in which several Greek Cypriots were killed. A wave of intercommunal violence ensued sweeping across the island, spearheaded by EOKA and the Turkish Defence Organisation (TMT). TMT's aim was to divide the Greek and Turkish Cypriot populations as a stepping stone towards *taksim* – the partition of Cyprus.

Britain finally granted independence to Cyprus in August 1960, but the constitution proved unworkable and the violence continued. From 1963 to 1967, the island teetered on the brink of civil war, to the great alarm of Britain and America, who regarded Cyprus as an essential base for monitoring the Soviet Union during the Cold War.

On 15 July 1974, forces from mainland Greece launched a coup against the government of Archbishop Makarios III, killing many Turkish Cypriots. In response, Turkish forces occupied the northern third of the island, driving 180,000 Greek Cypriots from their homes and killing thousands more. Some 65,000 Turkish Cypriots were displaced in the opposite direction before the island was partitioned into Greek and Turkish states.

Over the following decades, all traces of Greek culture were removed from the north. The area was flooded with settlers from mainland Turkey and hundreds of churches, monasteries and archaeological sites were plundered of their treasures.

Despite a series of international resolutions, Cyprus remains a divided island. The Turkish Republic of Northern Cyprus, created by Turkish Cypriot leader Rauf Denktash in 1983, is currently recognised only by Turkey.

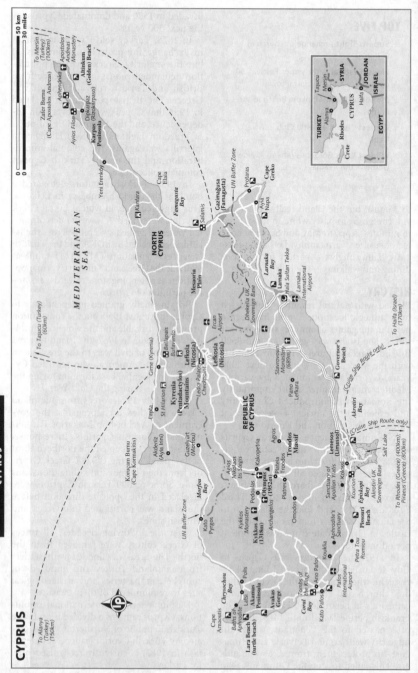

CYPRUS

ANDERS BLOMQVIST

Blue Mosque (p606), Istanbul, Turkey

*Gulet* (traditional wooden boat),
Marmaris (p622), Turkey

IZZET KERIBAR

GREG ELMS

Kebab restaurant, Turkey

MICHAEL GEBICKI

Senglea, Valletta (p578), Malta

SARA-JANE CLE

Berber acrobats, Djemaa el-Fna square (p677), Marrakesh

PAUL DAVID HELLANDER

Kantara Castle (p566),
Karpas Peninsula, Cyprus

Chellah (p667), Rabat

FRANCES LINZEE GOR

Banquet, Marrakesh (p680), Morocco

CATHERINE HANGER

**WHERE TO EXPLORE ANCIENT HISTORY**

Cyprus is drenched in history – here's a quick guide to the best historical sites:

■ For Greek and Roman ruins, head to the Pafos Mosaics and the Tombs of the Kings in Pafos, Kourion and the Sanctuary of Apollon Ylatis near Lemesos, or Salamis near Gazimağusa.

■ Craving castles? Head to Kolossi and Lemesos in the south or St Hilarion, Bufavento and Kantara in the north.

■ Witness Byzantine brilliance at the Church of St Lazaros in Larnaka and the fresco-covered monasteries in Pedoulas and Kakopetria in the Troodos mountains.

■ Lefkoşa and Gazimağusa are packed with Frankish churches and stately Ottoman mosques.

■ Amazing museums include the Cyprus Museum and Byzantine Museum in Lefkosia, the Pierides Museum in Larnaka and the Kykkos Monastery museum in the Troodos.

In recent years, there has been a growing acceptance that reunification is the only way forward for the economically starved northern state. As a gesture of goodwill, the border was opened in 2003 to allow refugees from both sides to revisit their homes.

In 2004, the two communities were presented with a UN proposal for reunification in a referendum, but the agreement allowed Turkish settlers and troops to remain in Cyprus, and limited the right of return for Greek Cypriot refugees – it was accepted by 65% of Turkish Cypriots and rejected by 75% of Greek Cypriots.

As a result, the southern Republic of Cyprus entered the EU alone in May 2004, with no resolution currently in sight for the Cyprus problem.

## PEOPLE

According to the last official census, the total population of Cyprus is 922,500. Since partition, the vast majority of Greek Cypriots live in the Republic, but a few hundred Greek Cypriot farmers still live in the remote Karpas peninsula.

In the north, the Turkish Cypriot population is now heavily outnumbered by Anatolian settlers from the Turkish mainland and the occupied area is culturally closer to mainland Turkey than pre-1974 Cyprus.

Cypriots on both sides of the line are friendly, honest and law-abiding, if nationalistic. Family life, marriage and children still play a central role in society, as does religion. The population of the Republic has recently become much more diverse with the arrival of large numbers of migrant workers from Asia.

## RELIGION

More than 99% of the North Cyprus population is Sunni Muslim, while the south is 94% Greek Orthodox, with Maronite, Roman Catholic and Muslim minorities. You should wear clothing that covers the legs and shoulders when visiting churches and monasteries, and remove your shoes before entering mosques.

## ARTS

The definitive art of Cyprus is the production of icons – the paintings of saints that grace Greek Orthodox churches. You can see examples dating back to the Byzantine period in many churches and monasteries.

Performing arts have been big in Cyprus since ancient times and several Roman amphitheatres are still used for performances. In recent years, the Eurovision Song Contest has become a major forum for Cypriot performers.

Relics of Cyprus' architectural heritage can be seen all over the island, from stone age settlements to vast Roman cities and Frankish cathedrals.

## ENVIRONMENT

Cyprus is divided by two mountain ranges: the Kyrenia (Pentadactylos) Mountains in North Cyprus and the Troodos Massif in the centre of the Republic, separated by the flat Mesaoria Plain. The most important nature reserves in the Republic are the Troodos National Forest Park and Akamas Peninsula. The north has just one reserve in the Karpas.

On both sides of the divide, the construction of tourist villas is putting a huge strain

CYPRUS

on natural resources – as long as expats continue to buy holiday homes, the cement trucks will keep rolling. Tourism is the big polluter, but urbanisation and hunting are affecting wildlife populations, including the rare mouflon (wild sheep).

## FOOD & DRINK

Cypriot food is a combination of Greek and Turkish cuisines, based primarily on meat, salad and bread. Popular Cypriot dishes include *souvlakia* (pork kebabs), *seftalia* (pork rissoles), *kleftiko ofto* (lamb baked in a sealed oven), *afelia* (pork stew with wine and coriander), *stifado* (beef and onion stew), *koupepia* (stuffed vine leaves) and *yemista* (vegetables stuffed with rice and mince). These dishes are often served together in a huge meal known as a *meze*.

The north relies on Anatolian cuisine, including the omnipresent doner kebab. For a quick picnic anywhere in Cyprus, grab some bread, *haloumi* (squeaky cheese), *lountza* (smoked ham) and fresh tomatoes.

The wine from the Troodos mountains is excellent – sweet *komandaria* is the traditional wine, while *zivania* (a strong spirit distilled from grape pressings) is the local firewater. Kykkos monastery in the Republic is one of the biggest distillers on the island.

# THE REPUBLIC OF CYPRUS

The Republic of Cyprus covers the southern 63% of the island and includes many of the most important historical sites and finest beaches. Over-development has reduced the charm of some seaside resorts, but the Troodos Mountains and Akamas peninsula are still wonderfully unspoiled. To see the best of the Republic hire a car and head into the mountains.

## LEFKOSIA (LEUKWSIA, NICOSIA)
pop 208,900

The Greek Cypriot capital was enclosed by a star-shaped city wall in the 16th century but the boundaries of the modern city are dictated by the UN-patrolled Green Line, which separates the Republic from Northern Cyprus. Despite its troubles, Lefkosia remains a friendly, laid-back place, with

good restaurants and museums, a lively art scene, and a more genuinely Cypriot atmosphere than anywhere on the coast.

## Orientation

The city centre is Plateia Eleftherias (Eleftheria Square) on the southern edge of the city wall. Pedestrian Lidras St runs north from the square to the Green Line and most of the tourist attractions are tucked away in the nearby alleys of Laiki Yeitonia or around the old Famagusta gate.

## Information

### EMERGENCY
**Police, fire & ambulance** ☎ 199 or ☎ 112
**Police station** ( ☎ 2267 1434; Lidras) In the Old Town is at the top of Lidras, by the barrier.
**General hospital** ( ☎ 2280 1400; Leoforos Nechrou). Dial ☎ 1402 for recorded information, in English, about late-night pharmacies.

### INTERNET ACCESS
**Cyberia** ( ☎ 2245 9911; Kostaki Pantelidi; 10 per hour CY£1; 🕑 9.15am-1pm Mon-Sat, 2-6pm Mon, Tue, Thu, 2-8pm Fri)
**Kennedy Call Centre** ( ☎ 2245 1020; Regina 60; per hour CY£1; 🕑 9am-10pm)

### MONEY
Banks with foreign exchange desks and ATMs are around Plateia Eleftherias, open weekday mornings and Monday afternoon.
**Holiday Inn** (Rigainis) Has a foreign exchange office open outside banking hours.

### POST
**Main Post Office** (Leoforos Konstantinou Palaiologou; 🕑 7.30am-1.30pm Mon-Fri, 3-5.30pm Thu) On top of D'Avila Bastion, near Plateia Eleftherias.

### TELEPHONE
There are payphones and kiosks that sell phonecards on Plateia Eleftherias.
**CYTA office** (cnr Leoforos Mouseiou & Leoforos Aigyptou; 🕑 7.30am-5.15pm, to 3.30pm Wed, to 1pm Sat) Near Pafos Gate.

### TOURIST INFORMATION
**Cyprus Tourist Organisation** (CTO; ☎ 2267 4264; cytour@cto.org.cy; Aristokyprou; 🕑 8.30am-4pm Mon-Fri, to 2pm Sat) Close to Plateia Eleftherias in Laiki Yeitonia, they have free maps for the whole of the Republic. Free walking tours of the city leave the office at 10am on Monday, Thursday and Friday – call ahead to book a place.

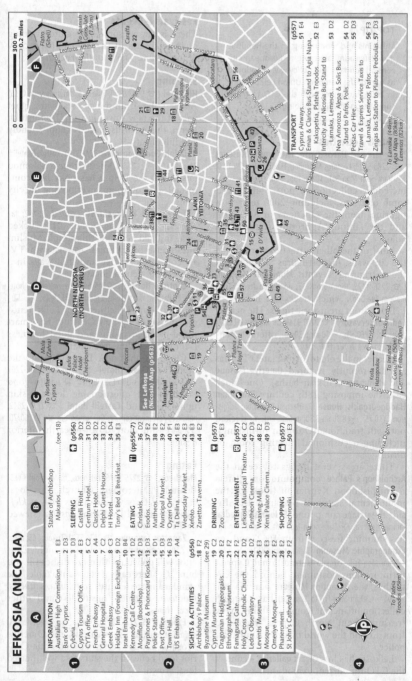

---

**TOP TIP**

Museums and monuments in the Republic now offer admission free to European citizens on Sundays. The policy was introduced as part of the European Union celebrations in 2004, but check with the CTO to make sure the goodwill is ongoing.

---

## Sights & Activities

Near the old Pafos Gate, the **Cyprus Museum** ( ☎ 2286 5888; Leoforos Mouseiou 1; admission CY£1.50; ☼ 9am-5pm Mon-Sat, 10am-1pm Sun) houses an incredible collection of pots, statues and tomb offerings, including 2000 terracotta figurines from the sanctuary of Ayia Irini and the famous Aphrodite statue from Soloi.

Most of the other attractions are inside the city walls. Just off Lidras St you'll find the intriguing **Leventis Municipal Museum** ( ☎ 2266 1475; Ippokratous 17; admission free; 10am-4.30pm Tue-Sun), which traces the history of Lefkosia from prehistoric times. The nearby **Ledra Observatory** ( ☎ 2267 9369; cnr Arsinois & Lidras; admission CY£0.50; ☼ 10am-6.30pm), offers stupendous views over the city.

Deeper in the old town on Plateia Tillirias are the recently restored **Omeriye Mosque** and **Hammam** (Turkish baths). One block east, the imposing 18th century **Dragoman Hadjigeorgakis House** (Patriachou Grigoriou; admission CY£0.75; ☼ 8.30am-3.30pm Mon-Fri), is decked out with traditional Ottoman furnishings, including a cushioned meeting room or *divan*.

There are several things to see in the **Archbishop's Palace** compound on Plateia Archiepiskopou Kyprianou (look for the monumental statue of Makarios III). Inside the palace compound, **St John's Cathedral** (admission free; ☼ 9am-noon Mon-Sat, 2-4pm Mon-Fri) has stunning frescoes from 1662, and the **Ethnographic Museum** (admission CY£1; ☼ 9am-1.30pm Mon-Fri), displays traditional Cypriot furniture and costumes. Behind the cathedral, the **Byzantine Museum** (admission CY£1; ☼ 9am-4.30pm Mon-Fri, to 1pm Sat) has a superb collection of ancient icons, including many treasures from North Cyprus, recovered from around the world by international art police.

Lefkosia has lots of **art galleries** – contact the CTO for current exhibitions.

## Festivals & Events

There is always something cultural going on in Lefkosia – ask the CTO for a free copy of the *Nicosia This Month* brochure.

## Sleeping

**HI Hostel** ( ☎ 9943 8360; Tefkrou 5; dm per person CY£5) About 1.5km from the city walls in a quiet part of the new town, just off Themistokli Dervi, this no-frills place is calm, friendly and full of cats.

**Delphi Guest House** ( ☎ 2266 5211; Kostaki Pantelidi 24; s/d CY£12/15; 🔀 ) Close to Plateia Solomou bus stand, the Delphi has poky but comfortable air-con rooms overlooking the city walls.

**Tony's Bed & Breakfast** ( ☎ 2266 6752; fax 2266 2225; Solonos 13; s/d CY£18/28; 🔀 ). Tucked away in Laiki Yeitonia, this simple Muslim guesthouse offers small rooms with TV, air-con, kettle, fridge and thin walls in a convenient, central location.

**Centrum Hotel** ( ☎ 2245 6444; www.centrumhotel .net; 15 Pasikratous; s/d with breakfast CY£35/45; 🔀 🖵 ) Close to Plateia Eleftherias in Laiki Yeitonia, the spanking-new Centrum has smart wood-panelled rooms and good business facilities, including free email.

Close together near Pafos Gate are the upmarket **Classic Hotel** ( ☎ 2266 4006; fax 2267 0072; Rigainis 94; s/d CY£38/48; 🔀 🖵 ) with good facilities but questionable leopard-skin upholstery, and **Castelli Hotel** ( ☎ 2271 2812; hinnicres@cytanent.com.cy; Ouzounian 38; s/d CY£60/70; 🔀 🖵 ) with more down-to-earth interior design.

## Eating

**Mattheos** ( ☎ 2275 5846; Lefkonos; mains from CY£3) Behind Phaneromeni Church, this local café serves tasty village dishes such as *kleftiko ofto* (baked lamb) and *fasolia* (stewed haricot beans).

**Zanettos Taverna** ( ☎ 2276 5501; Trikoupi 65; meze CY£7.50) Packed with locals every night, Zanettos will ply you with meze dishes till you burst. Get here early if you want a table. The standard meze features *souvlakia*, *seftalias*, *haloumi*, *keftedes* (meatballs) and other local treats.

**Erodos** ( ☎ 2275 2250; Patriachou Gregoriou 1; mains CY£3-7) On the square by the Omeriye Mosque, Erodos serves up authentic Cypriot food beneath the stars to a well-heeled local crowd.

**Xefoto** ( ☎ 2266 6567; Aeschylou 6; mains from CY£4-8) This touristy pavement restaurant in Laiki Yeitonia serves tasty Cypriot food – including *meze* meals – but the live bouzouki music is an acquired taste.

**Oyzeri Orfeas** ( ☎ 2243 0524; Leoforos Athinas 23; mains from CY£3-6) Locals congregate upstairs in this old townhouse near Famagusta Gate for top-notch village-style food.

Several rustic workers' cafés sell cheap and tasty seftalias (pork rissoles) and souvlakia (kebabs) for less than CY£3 – try **Christakis** ( ☎ 2266 8537; Plateia Solomou; ⏱ closed Sun) by the bus stand or **Ta Deilina** ( ☎ 2275 8287; Thermopylon; ⏱ evenings only, closed Sun) just off Xanthis Xenierou.

Every Wednesday there's a fantastic fruit and veg **market** in the Constanza bastion, or you can drop in on the daily **municipal market** (Plateia Dimarchias) in the old town. The best stocked supermarket is **Woolworths** (Lidras St).

## Entertainment

There are several cinemas that show international films, including **Zena Palace** ( ☎ 2267 4128; Theodotou 28) and **Pantheon** ( ☎ 2267 5787; Diogorou 29) – the *Cyprus Mail* has movie listings. Art-house movies with English subtitles are shown at the recommended **Weaving Mill** ( ☎ 2276 2275; Lefkonos 67-71) in the old town.

The main venue for theatre is the **Lefkosia Municipal Theatre** ( ☎ 2266 4028; Leoforos Mouseiou). Contact the CTO for information on theatre performances around town.

Lefkosia has a handful of energetic nightclubs – the modernist **Zoo** ( ☎ 2245 8811; cnr Afroditis & Leoforos Stasinou), just outside the walls, pulls in a young party crowd at weekends.

## Shopping

Laiki Yeitonia is full of touristy souvenir shops – **Diachroniki** ( ☎ 2268 0257; Aristokyprou 2B) sells reproductions of old maps and woodcuts of Cyprus. The best stocked bookshop in town is **Moufflon** ( ☎ 2266 5155; Sofouli 1), just south of Plateia Solomou.

## Getting There & Away

Buses leave from several stands around the old city walls, but there are no Sunday services. **Intercity** ( ☎ 2266 5814; Plateia Solomou) has seven daily buses to Lemesos (CY£2, 1½ hours) and six to Larnaka (CY£2, one hour). **Nea Amoroza** ( ☎ 2693 6822; Plateia Solomou) and **Alepa** ( ☎ 2266 4636; Tripolis Bastion) both

operate at least one daily bus to Pafos (CY£3 to CY£4.50, 2½ hours).

**Solis** ( ☎ 2266 6388) and **Lysos** ( ☎ 9941 4777) have a daily bus from Tripolis Bastion to Polis (CY£1.70, 3½ hours), leaving at noon, while **Eman** ( ☎ 2372 1321; Constanza Bastion) goes to Ayia Napa (CY£3, 1½ hours) at 3pm.

For towns in the Troodos, **Clarios** ( ☎ 2275 3234; Constanza Bastion) has around 10 daily buses to Kakopetria (CY£1.30, one hour) – the 10.20am weekday service continues to Plateia Troodos (CY£1.70, 1½ hours). **Zingas** ( ☎ 2295 2437; Leonidou 34) has a 12.30pm bus on weekdays to Platres (CY£2.50, two hours) via Pedoulas – the depot is just south of Plateia Solomou. There is also a noon bus from Tripolis Bastion to Kykkos Monastery (CY£3, two hours).The return service leaves Kyykkos at 6am.

Close to Podocataro Bastion, **Travel & Express** ( ☎ 7777 7474; Municipal Parking Space, Leoforos Salaminos) has half-hourly service-taxis to Larnaka (CY£3.05, one hour) and Lemesos (CY£4.10, one hour).

## Getting Around

Buses to the suburbs, **Nicosia Buses** ( ☎ 2266 5814), leave from the Plateia Solomou bus stand (no services inside the city walls.)

Private taxis loiter around Plateia Eleftherias. For car hire, try **Petsas** ( ☎ 2266 2650; Kostaki Pantelidi 24; per day from CY£20) near Plateia Solomou.

## LARNAKA

pop 73,200

Built over the ruins of ancient Kition, Larnaka is the final resting place of two religious celebrities – Hala Sultan, the foster-aunt of the prophet Mohammed and Agios Lazaros, who rose from the dead in the Bible. It's now a busy little resort with a waterfront hotel strip and a quieter old town and Turkish district.

The **Central Cyprus Tourist Office** (CTO; ☎ 2465 4322; Plateia Vasileos Pavlou; ⏱ 8.15am-2.30pm & 3-6.15pm Mon-Fri, closed Wed afternoon, to 1.15pm Sat) is at the northern end of town and has the usual maps and brochures. There are free walking tours of the city at 10am on Wednesday (from the CTO) and Friday (from the Fort) – call ahead to book a place.

There are several **banks** around the church, and **Alto Café** ( ☎ 2465 9625; Grigoriou Afxentiou; per hour CY£2; ⏱ 10-2am) offers Internet access.

CYPRUS

## Sights

The most famous sight is the ornate Byzantine **Church of St Lazaros** (Agiou Lazarou; 8am-
12.30pm & 3.30-6.30pm), which contains fabulous
icons and the bones of the esteemed Lazaros. There's also a small **museum** ( 2465
2498; admission CY£0.50; 8.30am-1pm & 3-5.30pm Sun-
Tue, Thu & Fri) with Byzantine relics. Down on
the waterfront, **Larnaka Fort** (admission CY£0.75;
8am-6pm Mon-Fri) contains a small museum
and an open-air stage used for theatrical
performances.

Close to the tourist office, the excellent
**Pierides Museum** ( 2481 4555; Zenonos Kitieos 4;
admission CY£1; 9am-4pm Mon-Thu, to 1pm Fri-Sat), has
an amazing collection of artefacts amassed by
several generations of the Pierides family.

Islamic monuments include the **Büyük
Mosque** (Büyük Cami) in old Larnaka and the
**Hala Sultan Tekke** near the airport, containing
the mausoleum of Hala Sultan. Larnaka's
promenade beach is no Waikiki, but there
is a decent strip of sand at **Makenzy Beach**,
about 2km south. Both of these places are
open daylight hours providing the attendants are awake (they don't get many visitors
outside of Friday or after work prayers).

About 30km west of Larnaka, the monas-
tery of **Stavrovouni** (admission free; 3-6pm, closed
to women) is perched atop a 688m buttress
with panoramic views over the island – you
need a hire car to get here.

## Sleeping & Eating

**HI hostel** ( 9993 5583; Nikolaou Rossou 27; dm/r
CY£5/10) Attached to the Bekir Pasa mosque,
this simple HI hostel isn't bad for the
money, with single-sex dorms and family
rooms that sleep four.

**Onisillos Hotel** ( 2465 1100; onisillos@cytanet
.com.cy; Onisillos 17; s/d incl breakfast CY£25/30; )
About 500m west of the fort in a quiet residential area, this friendly two-star offers
tidy rooms with bath and air-con.

**Militzis Restaurant** ( 2465 5867; Piale Pasia 42;
mains from CY£4) Packed with locals and tourists, Militzis offers fabulous *kleftiko ofto*
(baked lamb) fresh from the clay oven.

**Art Café 1900** ( 2465 3027; Stasinou 6; mains from
CY£4; from 6pm, closed Tue) Near the CTO, this
trendy place is a bookshop, gallery and restaurant, and it serves up some of the best
Cypriot food in town.

For self-caterers, the municipal market is
at the north end of Nikolaou Rossou.

## Getting There & Away

The bus stop is on the waterfront opposite
the Four Lanterns Hotel. **Eman** ( 2372 1321)
has daily buses to Ayia Napa (CY£1.80, 40
minutes, hourly). From Monday to Saturday, **Intercity** ( 2462 3492) has four daily
buses to Lefkosia (CY£2, one hour) and
six daily buses to Lemesos (CY£2.50, one
hour).

**Travel & Express** ( 7777 7474) operates
service-taxis every half hour to Lemesos
(CY£3.60, one hour) and Lefkosia (CY£3,
one hour) – call ahead for a pick up.

### TO/FROM AIRPORT

From the airport to central Larnaka, you
have the choice of a taxi (CY£5, 20 minutes)
or the local buses (Nos 22 and 24; CY£0.60,
30 minutes). There are also shuttle buses
that connect with Intercity bus services to
Lefkosia and Lemesos. In the opposite direction, local buses stop on Erimou, near
the junction with Vasilou Evagorou.

# AYIA NAPA (AGIA NAPA)

Once a peaceful fishing village, Ayia Napa
has grown into Cyprus' busiest beach resort. The clubs and bars attract big name
DJs from June to August but Ayia Napa is
famous for British people behaving badly –
if public drunkenness leaves you cold, give
it a miss!

As well as the busy beach, there's a **monastery** and a **Tourist Office** ( 2372 1796; Kyrou Nerou
12; 8.30am-2.30pm & 3.15-6pm Mon-Fri, 8.30am-
1.30pm every other Sat, closed Wed afternoon). Various
**watersports** are available on the beach, and
rocky **Cape Greko** has attractive blue bays and
good snorkelling. You can find more package holiday resorts at **Protaras** on the other
side of the cape.

There are loads of holiday apartments
for rent – **Eligonia Hotel Apartments** ( 2381
9292; Kyro Nero Ave 1; studio/1-bed/2-bed apt CY£28/32;
) has spic-and-span self-catering
apartments arranged around a pool and
sun-lounging deck.

**Leros Hotel** ( 2372 1126; lerosyiannis@hotmail
.com; Archiepiskopou Makarios III 41; s/d with air-con
CY£17.50/28; ) Close to the beach, Leros
has a pretty good set of facilities and caters
to walk-ins as well as package tourists.

Most restaurants specialise in roast beef
and Yorkshire pudding, but a handful of
places serve Cypriot food.

**Limelight Taverna** ( ☎ 2372 1650; Dionysiou Solomou 10; mains from CY£5) Limelight cooks up authentic Cypriot dishes like *seftalias* (pork rissoles) – a refreshing change from Yorkshire pud and fish and chips.

Ayia Napa is packed with bars and clubs – the over-the-top **Castle Club** ( ☎ 2372 2286; www .thecastleclub.com; Grigoriou Afxentiou) is a favourite with people who like to party all night. Other popular nightspots include **Abyss** ( ☎ 2372 5066; Ayios Mavris 9) and **P'zazz** ( ☎ 2372 2276; Kriou Nerou 10).

From Monday to Saturday, **Eman** ( ☎ 2372 1321; Archiepiskopou Makarios III) has hourly buses to Larnaka (CY£1.80, one hour) and buses every 20 minutes to Protaras (CY£0.50, 20 minutes, also Sunday in season). There's also an 8am bus to Lefkosia (CY£3, 1½ hours).

## LEMESOS (LEMESOS, LIMASSOL)
pop 163,400
The Republic's second city, Lemesos is a major holiday resort and also the location of the main port. Richard the Lionheart married Berengaria of Navarre here in 1191 on his way to the Third Crusade. As with many coastal towns, Lemesos has a historic and interesting old town centred on the old port, and a bland tourist strip running east along the waterfront.

### Orientation & Information
The main shopping street is Agiou Andreou, one street back from the waterfront near the old port, but most of the tourist developments are along Spyros Araouzou. The new port, 2km west of the centre, is mainly used by freight and cruise ships.

The main **CTO** ( ☎ 2536 2756; cnr Spyros Araouzou & Dimitriou Nikolaidi; ⏲ 8.15am-2.30pm & 3-6.15pm Mon-Fri, to 1.30pm Sat, closed Wed afternoon) is on the waterfront, a few blocks east of the old harbour.

There are banks all over town and there's a **Main Post Office** (Archiepiskopou Kyprianos). Your best bet for Internet-access in the old town is **Travellers Tales** ( ☎ 2587 8340; Ayiou Andreou 4; per hour CY£1.50) – there are more cybercafés on the tourist strip.

### Sights
Just back from the waterfront near the old port, the solid-looking **Lemesos Castle Medieval Museum** ( ☎ 2253 0419; Eirinis; admission CY£1; ⏲ 9am-5pm Mon-Sat, 10am-1pm Sun) displays Crusader gravestones, armour and old pots.

On the same square, the hi-tech **Time Elevator** ( ☎ 2576 2828; Evagoras Lanitis Centre, Vasilissis 1; adult/child CY£7/5; hourly shows 9am-7pm) offers a virtual tour through the history of Cyprus from 8500 BC to 1974.

In the same area are the **Jami Kebir mosque** (Genethliou Mitella) and the restored **Turkish baths** (2 Loutron St; steam bath and massage from £5; ⏲ 2-10pm) where you can get a traditional scrub and rub.

Just west of Lemesos are the extensive Graeco-Roman ruins of **Kourion** (Curium; admission CY£1; ⏲ 8am-5.45pm) with Roman baths, an *agora* (public forum) and a famous amphitheatre backed by the setting sun. Get here before 10am to avoid the crowds. There are several beach **cafés** on the popular stony beach in front of the ruins, but watch out for the surf.

Nearby are the partly-restored remains of the **Sanctuary of Apollon Ylatis** (admission CY£0.75; ⏲ 9am-6pm), sacred to a cult of Apollo worshippers in Graeco-Roman times. A few kilometres closer to Lemesos is the stocky **Kolossi Castle** (admission CY£0.75; ⏲ 9am-6pm), built in Crusader times.

About 26km towards Pafos, **Petra tou Romiou** is the legendary birthplace of Aphrodite. It's a scenic spot with huge white marble boulders on a pebble beach with great skimming stones, but tourists flock here. Nearby **Pissouri Beach** is nicer and less developed than the main tourist beach at Lemesos, but you need your own vehicle to get here.

### Sleeping & Eating
There are a few old-fashioned guest-houses on Agiou Andreou in the old port area.

**Luxor Guest House** ( ☎ 2536 2265; Agiou Andreou 101; s CY£6-10, d CY£12) This reliable cheapy has friendly, eccentric staff and clean rooms of various shapes and sizes.

**Continental Hotel** ( ☎ 2536 2530; fax 2537 3030; Spyros Araouzou 115; s/d inlc breakfast CY£14/24) One of the cheapest seafront places, the Continental has perfectly respectable two-star rooms with sea views.

**Kalymnos Beach Camping Site** ( ☎ 2563 2878; per person CY£1, per tent/caravan CY£1.50) About 20km east at Governors Beach, this place has shady plots for tents and caravans, a good restaurant and a black-sand beach.

**Apollo Garden Café** ( ☎ 2536 2890; Ifigenias 14D; snack meals from CY£1.50) Offers inexpensive sandwiches and snacks in a peaceful atrium just off Ifigenias.

**Rizitiko** ( ☎ 6534 8769; Tzami 4; mains £3-7) It's worth paying a bit more for the excellent food at this intimate Cypriot taverna – wash the *afelia* (pork in wine) or *stifado* (beef stew) down with a glass of village wine.

## Getting There & Around

Local and long-distance buses run from near the market on Georgiou Gennadiou, except on Sunday. From Monday to Friday, **Troodos Mountain Bus** ( ☎ 2555 2220) has a 9.30am service to Platres (two hours) and Plateia Troodos (CY£2.50, two hours, 20 mins). **Intercity** ( ☎ 2266 5814) has hourly buses to Lefkosia (CY£2, 1½ hours) and four daily buses from the old port roundabout to Larnaka (CY£2.50, one hour).

The daily **Alepa** ( ☎ 9962 5027) bus between Nicosia and Pafos stops near the Maltese Consulate on Spyros Amaouzou – the fare from Lemesos to Pafos is CY£2 (1½ hours). Otherwise, **Travel & Express** ( ☎ 7777 7474) has regular service taxis to Pafos (CY£3.30), Lefkosia (CY£4.10, 1½ hours) and Larnaka (CY£3.60, one hour).

Local buses charge a flat fare of CY£0.65 – the No 6 bus runs from the old port along the hotel strip. There are also buses to the ruins and beach at Kourion (CY£1.20, 30 minutes) from Lemesos castle. For Governors Beach (CY£2.50, 30 minutes), a bus leaves from near the CTO at 9.50am, returning at 4.30pm.

You can rent cars and mopeds all along the tourist strip.

## TROODOS MASSIF (TROODOS)

The last great wilderness in the Republic, the Troodos mountains are rich in wildlife and provide fantastic country for walking. Dotted among the pine trees are small winemaking villages and a number of World Heritage–listed Byzantine monasteries. The highest point is Mt Olympus (1952m), crowned by NATO radar beacons.

## Orientation & Information

Most of the interesting villages are clustered around Plateia Troodos (Troodos Square), the former summer home of the British colonial government. The main accommodation centre is Platres, about 7km south.

There are banks, a post office and **CTO** ( ☎ 2542 1316; ☽ 8.30am-4.30pm Mon-Fri, to 2.30pm Sat) in Platres.

Plateia Troodos has the **Troodos Visitor Centre** ( ☎ 2542 0144; admission CY£0.50; ☽ 10am-4pm) with a nature museum, video show and information leaflets. For skiing information, contact the **Cyprus Ski Club** ( ☎ 2267 5340; PO Box 22185, Lefkosia).

## Sights & Activities

The famous monastery of **Kykkos**, 20km west of Pedoulas, dates from the 12th century, but the mosaics and frescoes are much more recent. The fascinating **museum** ( ☎ 2294 2736; CY£1.50; ☽ 10am-4pm) is full of intriguing religious paraphernalia. Archbishop Makarios III is buried in a guarded mausoleum about 2km above the monastery. You can stay at the **monastery** ( ☎ 2294 2435; donation requested) but book in advance.

Nearby Pedoulas has a small **icon museum** (admission by donation CY£1; ☽ 9.30am-1pm & 2-6pm) and the tiny stone **Church of Archangelos**, with stunning frescoes from 1474 – the key to the church is at a nearby house (signposted). Don't confuse this place with the red-and-white church on the main road through Pedoulas. Another World Heritage–listed church is **Agios Nikolaos tis Stegis** (admission by donation; ☽ 9am-4pm Tue-Sat), near Kakopetria, which has amazing frescoes dating from the 12th century.

About 30km south of Pedoulas on the Lemesos road, **Omodos** has a gorgeous village square, dominated by the **Timios Stavros Monastery** (admission by donation; ☽ 8am-4pm). Several local wine-makers sell *komandaria* (traditional sweet wine), including the 500-year-old **House of Socrates** (Linou; ☽ 9am-8pm), which has been converted into a free wine-making museum.

Walkers can pick up walking trail brochures from the Troodos Visitors Centre.

## Sleeping & Eating

Platres and Plateia Troodos are the most popular places to stay, but book ahead in July and August.

**Village Restaurant** ( ☎ 2542 1741; Leoforos Makariou; half-board with shared bathroom per person CY£10; meals CY£3-7) In Platres, the cheapest option is to rent a room from the Village Restaurant, which also serves the best Cypriot food in town.

**Minerva Hotel** ( ☎ 2542 1731; Kaledonia 36; s/d CY£18/28) A 10-minute walk uphill on the old Platres to Pedoulas road, the Minerva is tastefully decorated with Turkmen carpets and is set in a shady garden.

**Petit Palais** ( ☎ 2542 2723; Faneromenis; s/d CY£16/28) Done up like a Swiss chalet, Petit Palais has neat rooms with TV, bathroom and little balconies – rooms at the back look out over the forest.

**Pigasos** ( ☎ 2542 1744; Faneromenis; light meals CY£1-3) Popular for snack lunches, Pigasos has good *lamajun* (pitta bread stuffed with mince) and *haloumi* and *lountza* sandwiches.

**Skylight** ( ☎ 2542 2244; Faneromenis; mains CY£4-9) On the main road in Platres, Skylight has a swimming pool for diners and sundeck for lounging, plus tasty home-cooked Cypriot food.

**Jubilee Hotel** ( ☎ 2542 0107; jubilee@cytanet.com .cy; s/d CY£18/30; 🕃 ) This is an old-fashioned two-star place on the Plateia Troodos to Kykkos road that is fine for the money and has forest views.

Plateia Troodos is being redeveloped so the youth hostel and hotel are now closed, but you can camp at the **Troodos camping ground** ( ☎ 2542 0205; per tent/caravan CY£2/2.50), a few kilometres below town on the road to Lefkosia.

There are several anglicised cafés on the main road in Plateia Troodos.

## Getting There & Around

Villages in the Troodos are widely spaced so a rental-car's the best way to get around. From Lemesos, **Troodos Mountain Bus** ( ☎ 2555 2220) has a daily service that leaves for Platres and Plateia Troodos (CY£2.50, two hours), except on Sunday. The return service leaves Platres at 8am. See under Lefkosia for information on buses from the capital.

The Jubilee Hotel in Plateia Troodos (p561) rents out **mountain bikes**.

Rural taxis in Platres can ferry you around the monasteries. A taxi from Lemesos to Platres will cost around CY£25.

## PAFOS

pop 48,300

The former capital of Cyprus, Pafos is divided into laid-back Ano Pafos on the hillside and tacky Kato Pafos down on the waterfront. Because of the international airport, Pafos is very touristy, but the historical treasures make up for a lot.

The **CTO** ( ☎ 2693 2841; Gladstonos 3; 🕒 8.15am-2.30pm & 3-6pm Mon-Fri, to 1.30pm Sat, closed Wed afternoon) is just down from Pafos' main square, and there's a second office on Poseidonos in Kato Pafos.

There are banks and post offices in Ano Pafos and on the tourist strip. The most convenient Internet café is **Maroushia Internet** ( ☎ 2694 7240; Platia Kennedy 6; per hour CY£2) above the Hellenic Bank in Ano Pafos.

## Sights

Pafos is packed with historical sights. Tourists crowd the famous **Pafos Mosaics** ( ☎ 2694 0217; admission CY£1.50; 🕒 8am-5pm) but the Roman mosaic floors are amazing. Quite a few feature the rambunctious exploits of Dionysos, the uninhibited god of wine. Within the same compound are the ruins of a castle and amphitheatre.

There's another **castle** on the harbour and more Roman ruins in the grounds of the **Chrysopolitissa church** (Agias Kriakis).

For a quieter historical experience, visit the 3rd century BC **Tombs of the Kings** ( ☎ 2694 0295; admission CY£0.75; 🕒 8.30am-7.30pm ) about 2km north of Kato Pafos. You can really envision the regal burial ceremonies that must have taken place here.

Pafos is a good base for exploring the **Akamas Peninsula**. You can follow the dirt road as far as Lara (p562) in a conventional car.

## Sleeping & Eating

**HI Hostel** ( ☎ 2693 2588; Eleftheriou Venizelou 45; dm CY£4-5) This humble hostel is in a converted private house off Evagora Pallikaridi, quite a long walk north of central Ano Pafos.

**Trianon Hotel** ( ☎ 2693 2193; Archiepiskopou Makariou III 99; s/d CY£5/12) Right on the main shopping street, the Trianon has cheap simple rooms but the shared bathroom is off the kitchen and the toilet is off the lounge.

**Axiothea Hotel** ( ☎ 2693 2866; axiothea_hotel@ hotmail.com; Eves Malioti 2; s/d with bath CY£23/32; 🕃 ) Near the park in Ano Pafos, the Axiothea has a jolly owner and tidy rooms with balconies and cracking views over the coast.

**Kiniras Hotel** ( ☎ 2624 1604; www.kiniras.cy.net; Archiepiskopou Makariou III 91; s/d with bath CY£38/60; 🕃 🖳 ) Close to the Trianon, this uplifting midrange place has a shady plant-filled courtyard and well-tended rooms with balconies.

The best places to eat are inland from the seafront.

**Nikos Tyrimos Fish Tavern** ( ☎ 2694 2846; Agapinoros 71; fish dishes CY£4-8) About 500m inland from the tourist strip, Tyrimos cooks up fantastic fish, caught daily and served fresh to a mainly local clientele.

**Argo** ( ☎ 2693 3327; Pafias Afroditis 21; mains CY£4-7) A few streets back from the tourist strip, Argo has a good reputation for its *mousakka* (layered mince and aubergines with béchamel sauce), *kleftiko* (baked lamb) and stews.

The waterfront restaurants by the harbour in Kato Pafos serve decent Cypriot and Western European food but these places positively heave with tourists in summer.

## Getting There & Around

From Monday to Saturday, **Alepa** ( ☎ 2693 4410; Nikodimou Mylona) runs one morning bus to Lefkosia (CY£3, 2½) via Lemesos (CY£2, 1½) at 8.30am (8am on Wednesday and Saturday). Alepa also has local buses every few minutes to Kato Pafos (CY£0.50, 15 minutes). **Nea Amaroza Co** ( ☎ 2693 6822; Evagora Pallikaridi 79) operates hourly buses to Polis (CY£1.60, 45 minutes).

For Lemesos, you are probably better off taking a **Travel & Express** ( ☎ 7777 7474; Evagora Pallikaridi) service-taxi (CY£3.30, 40 minutes, half-hourly). A private taxi to the airport will cost around CY£10.

Just off the Tombs of the Kings road, **Antoniades** ( ☎ 2622 1125; Parmenionos 4; bike/moped/motorbike hire per day CY£2/3/5) rents out bikes, mopeds and motorbikes. All the big car-hire companies have offices at the airport and along Apostolou Pavlou in Kato Pafos.

## POLIS

pop 1800

The most unspoiled of the Republic's coastal towns, Polis is built over the ruins of the ancient Greek city of Marion. It retains much of the laid-back charm that first attracted holiday-makers to Cyprus, and there's a good beach and a pretty village square.

Pedestrianised Griva Digeni is the main street and the beach is a 15-minute walk downhill along Verginas. The **CTO** ( ☎ 2632 2468; Vasileos Stasioikou 2; ⏱ 8.30am-4pm Mon-Fri) is on the road to Prodromi. There are several banks and a post office around Griva Digeni.

## Sights

Polis has a small sandy **beach** and an interesting **museum** ( ☎ 2632 2955; Makariou III; admission CY£75; ⏱ 8am-2pm Mon-Fri, 9am-5pm Sat) with treasures excavated from Marion.

Heading west along the coast, **Laikki** has a decent beach and several beach cafés. About 5km on are the **Baths of Aphrodite**, a natural spring where the goddess is said to have bathed to restore her virginity. You can't try this out for yourself, but the baths are a great starting point for hikes into the **Akamas Peninsula**. This wonderful, wild area is protected as a national park and the hills are criss-crossed by dirt tracks and walking trails – pick up the CTO's *Nature Trails* brochure. The **Avakas Gorge** on the west side of the cape is a particularly rewarding hike.

There are also some wonderful isolated beaches – gorgeous **Lara beach** has a turtle research station operating from June to September.

## Sleeping & Eating

There are numerous self-catering apartments for rent in town.

**Lemon Garden** ( ☎ 2632 1443; Makariou III 12; s/d CY£15/28; 🕸 🛋 ) Near the museum, it has a gregarious owner, spacious apartments hidden away in a shady garden and a pool.

**C&A Tourist Apartments** ( ☎ 2632 1881; Apostolou Andrea; apt from CY£25; 🕸 🛋 ) Homy and disabled-friendly, C&A has tidy apartments arranged around a pool. Transport can be organised for wheelchair users.

**Bougainvillea Hotel Apartments** ( ☎ 2681 2250; Verginas 13; apt from CY£25; 🕸 🛋 ) On the beach road, Bougainvillea is another good choice. The apartments get plenty of loving care and there's a large pool.

**Polis camping ground** ( ☎ 2681 5080; per tent CY£2.50, per person CY£1.50) Hidden in a grove of eucalyptus trees down on the beach, it has a beach café for day-trippers.

**Alekos** ( ☎ 2632 3381; Makariou III; mains CY£2-7) Near the museum, this old-fashioned taverna serves home-style Cypriot cuisine.

The main square is thoroughly packed with pavement cafés serving Cypriot and international food – just wander down and see which places are pulling in the diners.

## Getting There & Around

Hourly **Nea Amaroza** ( ☎ 2632 1114; Kyproleontos) buses between Polis and Pafos (CY£1.60, not Sunday, 45 minutes) leave from near the CTO, except on Sunday. There are also three buses every weekday to the Baths of Aphrodite (CY£1, 15 minutes).

You can rent mountain bikes, motorbikes and cars from **Petrides Motors** ( ☎ 2632 1541; Georgiou Stylianou; mountain bike/motorbike hire per day CY£3/6, car hire from CY£18).

# NORTH CYPRUS

The Turkish Republic of Northern Cyprus (TRNC) occupies the northern 37% of the island. The north is impressively unspoiled by tourism and people are friendly, but the ruined churches are a sad reminder of the events of 1974. You can get some kind of hint of what Cyprus used to be like in the remote Karpas peninsula. This area also has some of the best beaches on the island.

## LEFKOŞA (NICOSIA)
pop 46,600

The capital of North Cyprus occupies the northern half of divided Lefkosia. The pace of life is refreshingly unhurried and there are some interesting Frankish ruins, but it's more a place to day-trip from than to stay in. The only legal route between the north and south is the checkpoint by the Ledra Palace Hotel, on the western edge of the city wall.

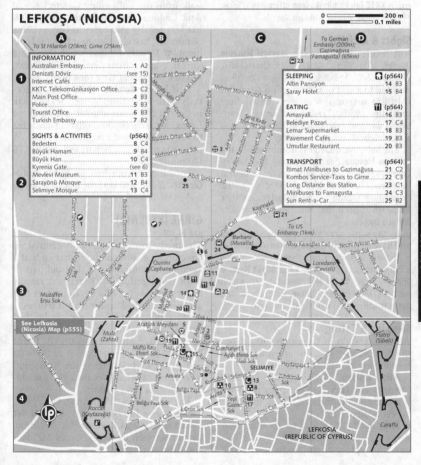

## Information & Orientation

The well-preserved Kyrenia Gate on the north side of the city wall contains the **main Tourist Office** ( ☎ 227 2994;  9am-3.30pm Mon-Fri, 10am-1pm Sat & Sun). From here, Girne Caddesi runs south to Atatürk Meydani (the main square) and on to the historic Selimiye quarter, where you'll find most of the interesting sights.

For foreign exchange, try the **banks** on Girne Caddesi or the **Denizati Döviz** ( ☎ 228 2623; Girne Caddesi 17) exchange office by the Saray Hotel. There's a **Post Office** ( 7.30am-2pm, 3.30-6pm Mon) on Sarayönü Sokak and slow 24-hour cybercafés on Mediciye Sokak.

For phone calls, the private *telefon* offices in the centre are more useful than the main **KKTC Telekomünikasyon office** (Kizilay Sokak;  8am-1.30pm Mon-Fri, 3.30-5pm Mon).

## Sights & Activities

Just inside the walls, the **Mevlevi Museum** (Mevlevi Tekke Müzesi; ☎ 227 1283; Girne Caddesi; admission €2.40;  9am-1pm & 2-4.45pm Mon-Fri) is devoted to a sect of whirling Sufi dervishes (Muslim mystics) who were based here until the 1950s. Traditional *sema* (devotional dances) take place during the Shebu Arus celebrations in December.

The Selimiye quarter is dominated by the **Selimiye Mosque** (San Sophia Mosque, Agios Nikolaos Cathedral; Selimiye Sokak) built as a cathedral between 1209 and 1326. Next door is the crumbling façade of the **Bedesten**, another Frankish church that functioned as an Ottoman bazaar.

In the same area you can buy souvenirs and have a coffee in the **Büyük Han** (Arasta Sokak), a historic Ottoman inn that now contains a crafts market. Nearby is the **Büyük Hamam** (Irfan Bey Sokak; ☎ 228 4462; steam bath with/without massage €17/8.5;  7am-10.30pm) where you can get a traditional Turkish steam bath.

## Sleeping & Eating

Accommodation in Lefkoşa is limited and the few budget options are not recommended for lone female travellers.

**Altin Pansiyon** ( ☎ 228 5049; Girne Caddesi 63; r per person €16) There are inexpensive rooms here right in the thick of things, but don't expect luxury.

**Saray Hotel** ( ☎ 228 3115; fax 228 4808; Atatürk Meydani; s/d with air-con €38.70/63.40; P  ) This upmarket option offers tasteful rooms with deep-pile carpets you sink into, right on the main square.

Foodwise, you pretty much have a choice of kebabs or kebabs. On Girne Caddesi you'll find good fare at reasonable prices: **Amasyali** ( ☎ 228 3294; Girne Caddesi 186; doner kebabs €0.80) and **Umutlar Restaurant** ( ☎ 227 3236; Girne Caddesi 51; mains from €0.80). It also serves stews.

Alternatively, there are several pavement cafés on Atatürk Meydani.

Self-caterers should head to the **Lemar Supermarket** (Girne Caddesi) or the Belediye Pazari covered market, just south of the Selimiye Mosque.

## Getting There & Away

The **long-distance bus station** is a 15-minute walk from the walls along Gazeteci Kemal Aşik Caddesi. **Girneliler Seyahat** ( ☎ 228 1018) has very regular minibuses to Girne (€0.80, 30 minutes) that also stop near Kyrenia Gate. **İtimat** ( ☎ 227 1617) minibuses to Gazimağusa leave half-hourly from Kaymakli Yolu Sokak, just east of Kyrenia Gate (one hour).

Half-hourly **Kombos** ( ☎ 227 2929) service-taxis to Girne run from Mevlevi Tekke Sokak in the old city. Taxis also loiter around the Ledra Palace checkpoint, offering day tours to Girne (€60) and Gazimağusa (€80). A private taxi to Ercan airport will cost €10.75 (40 minutes).

For car hire, your best bet is **Sun Rent-a-Car** ( ☎ 227 2303; Abdi Ipekci Ave 10; car/jeep hire per day from €30/43).

## GIRNE (KYRENIA)

pop 19,300

The pretty town of Kyrenia is centred on a picturesque stone harbour that ends at a looming Byzantine castle. The old part of town is delightful, but Kyrenia is rapidly being engulfed by villa developments that are being knocked up for British retirees.

Most things in Girne are sandwiched between the harbour and Ramadan Cemil Meydani, the main roundabout. The **Tourist Office** ( ☎ 815 2145;  9am-5pm) is at the west end of the harbour. There are banks and foreign exchange offices near the roundabout on Ziya Rifki Caddesi.

The post office is on Mustafa Çağatay Caddesi. For Internet-access, try **Café Net** ( ☎ 815 9259; Efeler Sokak; per hour €1.10;  9am-7pm Mon-Sat) between Ramadan Cemil Meydani and the waterfront.

## Sights & Activities

The main attraction in Girne is the **Kyrenia Castle & Shipwreck Museum** (Girne Kalesi; ☎ 815 2142; admission €4.80; ⏰ 9am-7pm), which has some sinister dungeons and the remains of Cyprus' oldest shipwreck – thought to have sunk in a storm around 3000 BC.

A €2.15 taxi ride from Girne gets you to the late Byzantine abbey ruins at **Bellapais**, the setting for Lawrence Durrell's *Bitter Lemons*. Local minibuses run from the main roundabout to the pretty hill village of **Lapta**, a popular retirement spot for British expats.

Clinging to a rocky spur on the highest ridge above Kyrenia, **St Hilarion Castle** (admission €2.40; ⏰ 9am-5pm) offers stupendous views over the coast, but it sits in the middle of an army base so you need a hire car to get here. On a 4WD track off the Girne–Gazimağusa road, the remote Crusader castle of **Bufavento** offers more breathtaking views.

Various **adventure activities** are possible at the harbour, including diving, paragliding and boating – half-day boat trips cost €30 per person including a barbecue lunch.

## Sleeping & Eating

Most of the budget and mid-range accommodation is between the harbour and the roundabout.

**Bingöl Guest House** ( ☎ 815 2749; Efeler Sokak; r per person €5.40) Down a quiet alley below the main roundabout, this place is cheap, but you get what you pay for – a tiny room with a tiny bathroom.

**Erkenekon Hotel** ( ☎ 815 4677; fax 815 6010; s/d with air-con €16/27; ❄ ) The family-run Erkenekon stands at the west end of the harbour and offers sea views that won't break the bank.

**Bristol Hotel** ( ☎ 815 6570; fax 815 7364; Ziya Rizki Caddesi; s/d €19/30; ❄ ) On the main shopping street, this recently renovated place has cheerful, chintzy rooms with fluffy carpets, fridges and pink TVs.

**Girne Serhat Restaurant** ( ☎ 815 8947; Gösku Sokak; mains from €2) Inland from the waterfront near the Limani Casino, Serhat serves sizzling Anatolian kebabs and *pide* (Turkish bread with mince) till late.

Light-lunchers have the choice of the expensive waterfront restaurants on the harbour or the finger-licking kebab houses around Ramadan Cemil Meydani.

For a romantic dinner, whisk your date into the alleys behind the harbour. **Set Restorante Italiano** ( ☎ 815 6008; Aga Cafér Sokak; mains from €7) serves authentic Italian food in a gorgeous stone courtyard, while **Brasserie** ( ☎ 815 9481; Efeler Sokak; mains from €10) serves Cypriot and French delicacies in a stylish colonial mansion.

## Getting There & Away

Buses and service-taxis stop near the main roundabout. **Girneliler Seyahat** ( ☎ 866 1068) minibuses to Lefkoşa (€0.80, 30 minutes) depart every few minutes from Mustafa Çağatay Caddesi. Hourly **Göçmen** ( ☎ 815 7287) minibuses to Gazimağusa (€1.60, one hour) leave from Ecevit Caddesi.

**Kombos** ( ☎ 815 1872; Ramadan Cemil Meydani) has service-taxis to Lefkoşa (€1.10, 30 minutes, half-hourly) and Gazimağusa (€2.15, one hour, hourly).

The ferry terminal is a €2.70 taxi ride from town – see p571 for information on boats to Turkey. **Akgünler** ( ☎ 815 3510) has an office on Ramadan Cemil Meydani.

## GAZIMAĞUSA (FAMAGUSTA, AMMACHOUSTOS)

pop 36,400

The sleepy town of Gazimağusa dozes inside vast Venetian walls on the edge of the Mesaoria plain. The city was one of the last places to fall in the Ottoman invasion and the old town is dotted with Frankish and Venetian ruins. Ferries leave from here to Mersin in mainland Turkey.

There are three entrances through the city walls. Two are by the waterfront and there's one near the main roundabout with the monument to Kemal Atatürk. From the inland gate, Istiklal Caddesi runs down to Kemal Meydani (the main square) where you'll find shops, banks and foreign exchange offices. The **Tourist Office** ( ☎ 366 2864; ⏰ 7.30am-2pm Mon-Fri, 3.30-6pm Mon, 9am-6pm Sat & Sun) is outside the walls, just east of the main roundabout.

## Sights

Several of Gazimağusa's Frankish churches have been converted into mosques, including **Lala Mustafa Paşa** (St Nicholas Cathedral; Kemal Meydani) where the Lusignan kings were crowned – it's probably the finest example of Gothic architecture in Cyprus.

CYPRUS

On the shore side of the city walls is **Othello's Tower** (Othello Kalesi; admission €3.20; ⏰ 10am-6pm ), where the Venetian governor Cristofo Moro is said to have killed his wife Desdemona in a fit of jealous rage. The incident inspired Shakespeare to write Othello, but the bard mixed up the governor's name with his race, adding some eastern spice to the story.

About 9km north of Famagusta are the rather unkempt Graeco-Roman ruins of **Salamis** (admission €3.20; ⏰ 7.30am-7.30pm). You can see mosaics, columns and a huge amphitheatre, and there's a popular sandy beach – a return taxi from Famagusta will cost €10.75.

Nearby, the **Monastery of St Barnabas** has been opened as an icon museum, but most of the valuable treasures from the area vanished after 1974.

### Sleeping & Eating

There are a few places to stay inside the city walls.

**Altun Tabya Hotel** ( ☎ cnr Altun Tabya & Kizilkule Sokak; s/d €14/22) Tucked inside the city walls, this family-owned place has simple, tidy rooms. To get here, turn right after you pass through the inland gate.

**Golden Set Pansiyon** ( ☎ 0536 469 1771; Yeşil Deniz Sokak; s/d with air-con €14/22; ✖ ) Close to Othello's Tower, this old arched house has chintzy but comfortable apartment-style rooms with cooking facilities.

The camping ground near the ruins at Salamis is intermittently open to tourists – check with the tourist office.

**Viyana** ( ☎ 366 6037; Liman Yolu 19; kebabs from €3-6) This old-fashioned garden restaurant beside the mosque offers inexpensive and authentic Turkish Cypriot food.

**Petek** ( ☎ 366 7104; Yeşil Deniz Sokak 1; snacks & sweets from €2) This Aladdin's Cave of a cake shop offers sweet and savoury pastries, Turkish delight, and strong, sweet Turkish coffee.

For a break from kebabs, there are several pavement restaurants on Kemal Meydani that serve pizzas, burgers and other Anglo-American meals.

### Getting There & Away

**İtimat** ( ☎ 366 6666) minibuses to Lefkoşa (€1.30, one hour) leave every half-hour from the main roundabout.

**Göçmen** ( ☎ 366 4313) minibuses to Girne (€1.60, one hour) leave hourly from Gazi Mustafa Kemal Bulvari.

**Kombos** ( ☎ 365 2623) share-taxis to Girne (€2.15, one hour) leave hourly from Eşref Bitlis Caddesi, about 500m northwest of the city walls.

The ferry terminal is about 500m southeast of the centre – see p571 for information on ferries to Turkey. **Cyprus Turkish Shipping** ( ☎ 366 5786) has an office on Ecevit Bulvari.

### Karpas Peninsula

For a taste of what Cyprus was like before partition, hire a car and head to the remote Karpas peninsula. This wild area has barely been touched by tourism, though there is a tiny **Tourist Office** ( ☎ 374 4984; ⏰ 9am-1pm & 2-5pm) in the post office in Yeni Erenköy.

The enclaved Greek Cypriot population was able to protect some of the churches and monasteries and you can see ancient icons in the slightly forlorn-looking monastery of **Apostolos Andreas** at the tip of the peninsula.

At the west end of the Karpas on the edge of the Kyrenia Mountains, the romantic Crusader-era castle of **Kantara** (admission €2.40; ⏰ 10am-6pm) floats above the Mesaoria plain. Access is via a slow, winding, bumpy road, so you may well have this spectacular fortress to yourself.

Glorious **Altinkum beach** (Golden Beach) on the south coast is the site of nesting turtles from June to August. It also has a handful of simple cafés that rent out wooden cabins. On the north coast, there's another nice beach and a ruined Byzantine basilica at **Ayios Filon**, and more Byzantine ruins at **Aphendrika**.

Ayios Filon has the friendly **Oasis** ( ☎ 824 4952; www.ayfilon.com; d with breakfast from €25), that provides a small restaurant and tasteful rooms with an immaculate shared bathroom, right on the water.

# CYPRUS DIRECTORY

## ACCOMMODATION

Prices for a single/double room in a hotel or guesthouse start at CY£15/28 in the Republic and €14/21 in the north, though cheaper rooms are sometimes available. There are Hostelling International (HI) affiliated hostels in Lefkosia, Pafos and Larnaka, but none in Northern Cyprus. Monasteries in the south sometimes accept overnight guests for a donation.

The Republic has six licensed camping grounds, including good sites at Polis, Plateia Troodos and Governor's Beach (near Lemesos) – expect to pay CY£3.50 to CY£6 for two people and a tent. The North has four official camping grounds but wild camping is popular in the Karpas.

## ACTIVITIES
All the seaside resorts offer watersports like banana boat rides, scuba dives, boat trips and paragliding. The Akamas peninsula and Troodos mountains in the south and the Karpas peninsula in the North offer fantastic opportunities for hiking – pick up the *Nature Trails* brochure from any CTO office or pop into the visitor centre in Plateia Troodos.

See p571 for information on mountain biking in Cyprus.

## BOOKS
Lonely Planet's *Cyprus* covers the whole island. To understand the glory that was undivided Cyprus, read Colin Thubron's *Journey into Cyprus* or Lawrence Durrell's *Bitter Lemons*, which is set around Bellapais. Brendan O'Malley and Ian Craig's *The Cyprus Conspiracy* explores American collusion in the partition of Cyprus.

## BUSINESS HOURS
As a general guide, banks are open from 8.30am to 12.30pm on weekdays, plus 3.15pm to 4.45pm Monday afternoon. Government offices are open from 7.30am to 2.30pm on weekdays and 3pm to 6pm Thursday afternoon (or Monday afternoon in the north). Shops close early on Wednesday and Saturday and many places close at lunchtime in summer. Almost all restaurants are open for lunch and dinner daily, but smaller places close on Sunday.

## CUSTOMS
The Republic joined the EU in 2004 so duty-free allowances are being phased out. In Northern Cyprus you can bring in 500g of tobacco or 400 cigarettes, and 1.5L of spirits or wine and 100mL of perfume duty-free.

## DISABLED TRAVELLERS
Any of the Cyprus Tourist Organisation offices can post out the *What the Disabled Visitor Needs to Know about Cyprus* fact sheet, which lists some useful organisations. **Paraquip** ( ☎ 2632 1881; www.paraquip.com .cy) offers transport for wheelchair users, and disabled-friendly accommodation in Polis. In Northern Cyprus there aren't many facilities for the disabled visitor.

## ELECTRICITY
The electricity supply in Cyprus is 240 volts at 50Hz. Most places, both in north and south Cyprus, use mainly British three-pin plugs.

## EMBASSIES & CONSULATES
The Republic of Cyprus is represented worldwide while North Cyprus has just a few overseas offices. Take a look at p570 for visa information.

### Cypriot Embassies & Consulates
Diplomatic offices for the Republic of Cyprus include:

**Australia** ( ☎ 61-2-6281 0832; 30 Beale Crescent, Deakin ACT 2600, Canberra)
**France** ( ☎ 33-1 4720 8628; 23 Rue Galilèe, 75116 Paris)
**Germany** ( ☎ 49-30 308 6830; Wallstrasse 27, D-10179 Berlin)
**Greece** ( ☎ 30-21 0723 2727; Irodotou 16, 10675 Athens)
**Ireland** ( ☎ 35-31 676 3060; 71 Lower Leeson St, Dublin 2)
**Israel** ( ☎ 97-23 525 0212; 4th Floor, Top Tower, 50 Dizengoff St, Dizengoff Centre, 64332 Tel Aviv)
**Netherlands** ( ☎ 31-70 346 6499; 15 Surinamestraat, 2585 GG Den Haag)
**Spain** ( ☎ 34-91 578 3114; C/Serrano 23 (2D), 28001 Madrid)
**UK** ( ☎ 44-20 7499 8272; 93 Park St, London W1K 7ET)
**USA** ( ☎ 1-202 462 5772; 2211 R St Northwest, Washington DC 20008-4082)

In other countries, you can contact the Turkish embassies for information. The Turkish Republic of Northern Cyprus has offices in:

**Belgium** ( ☎ 32-26 484 756; Avenue Louise 207, BTE-8, 1050 Brussels)
**Turkey** ( ☎ 90 312-446 2920; Rabat Sokak 20, Gaziosmanpaşa, 06700 Ankara)
**UK** ( ☎ 44-20 7631 1920; 29 Bedford Square, London, WC1B 3EG)
**USA** ( ☎ 1-212 687 2350; 821 United Nations Plaza, 6th Floor, New York, NY-10017)

CYPRUS

### Embassies & Consulates in Cyprus

Countries with diplomatic representation in the Republic of Cyprus include:

**Australia** ( ☎ 2275 3001/3; Leoforos Stasinou & Annis Komninis 4, 2nd Floor, CY 1060 Lefkosia)

**France** ( ☎ 2277 9910/1; Ploutarchou 12, 2406 Egkomi, CY 1512 Lefkosia)

**Germany** ( ☎ 2245 1145; Nikitara 10, 1080 Lefkosia, CY 1311 Lefkosia)

**Greece** ( ☎ 2268 0670; Leoforos Vyronos 8-10, CY 1513 Lefkosia)

**Ireland** ( ☎ 2281 8183; Aiantas 7, Agiou Omologites, 1082 Lefkosia)

**Israel** ( ☎ 2236 9500; I Grypari 4, CY 1307 Lefkosia)

**Spain** ( ☎ 2245 0410; Leoforos Strovolou 32, CY 2093 Strovolos)

**UK** ( ☎ 2286 1100; Alexandrou Palli, CY 1587 Lefkosia)

**USA** ( ☎ 2277 6400; Gonia Metochiou & Ploutarchou, Egkomi, 2407 Lefkosia)

Countries with diplomatic representation in Northern Cyprus include:

**Australia** ( ☎ 227 7332; Güner Türkmen Sokak 20, Lefkoşa)

**Germany** ( ☎ 227 5161; 28 Kasım Sokak 15, Lefkoşa)

**Turkey** ( ☎ 227 2314; Bedreddin Demirel Caddesi, Lefkoşa)

**UK** ( ☎ 227 4938; Mehmet Akif Caddesi 23, Lefkoşa)

**USA** ( ☎ 227 8295; Saran Sokak 6, K. Kaymakli, Lefkoşa)

## FESTIVALS & EVENTS

The Republic has numerous festivals, and Christian feast days are celebrated with aplomb – the useful *List of Events* brochure is available from Cyprus Tourist Organisation offices. The main celebrations in the North are linked to Muslim holidays – see p568. Events held every year include the following.

### January

**Epiphany** (6 January) Priests bless houses with holy water, villagers throw sausages on the roof to appease demons and a sacred cross is thrown into the sea by the Archbishop and retrieved by local youths.

### February

**Apokreo** (2nd week of February) Two weeks of pre-Lent feasting all over Cyprus and a big carnival in Lemesos.

### March/April

**Easter** (March/April) Huge Holy Week celebrations with special meals, religious processions and bonfires for the symbolic burning of Judas.

### May

**Kataklysmos** (50 days after Easter) Coastal towns celebrate the Biblical flood by throwing water around, feasting and singing improvised songs.

**International Bellapais Music Festival** (May) – One month of live classical music performances in Bellapais abbey.

### June to September

**Gazimağusa International Festival** (June) Three weeks of live music and arts events in Gazimağusa.

**Paphia Festival** (June to September) Annual music, theatre and dance festival in Pafos.

**Lemesos Festival** (July) Lemesos municipal festival with live music, dance and theatre.

**Larnaka** (July) One month festival of music, theatre and arts in Larnaka.

**Ancient Greek Drama Festival** (July/August) Open-air performances of Greek dramas at Kourion and other amphitheatres.

**Lemesos Wine Festival** (August/September) Twelve-day festival with free wine and open air dining in Lemesos.

**Cyprus Rally** (see www.cyprusrally.org.cy for dates) This annual road rally follows a gruelling course around the island.

The main celebrations in the north are linked to Muslim holidays – see later in the Holidays section.

## GAY & LESBIAN TRAVELLERS

Homosexuality is illegal in North Cyprus, but legal for people over 18 in the Republic. There are a few gay-friendly bars in Lemesos, Ayia Napa and Pafos – the website www.gay-cyprus.com has useful information.

## HOLIDAYS

Holidays in the Republic are the same as those in Greece (p336), with the addition of: **Greek Cypriot Day** (1 April) and **Cyprus Independence Day** (1 October).

North Cyprus has a three-day holiday to celebrate the end of Ramazan, starting on 14 November in 2004, 2 November in 2005 and 22 October in 2006. There is also a four-day holiday for the Muslim festival of Kurban, starting on 20 January in 2005, 9 January in 2006 and 29 December in 2007. Annual holidays include:

**National Sovereignty/Children's Day** (23 April)

**Labour Day** 1 May

**Youth & Sport Day** 19 May

**Peace & Freedom Day** 20 July

**TMT Day** 1 August

**Victory Day** 30 August

**Turkish Republic Day** 29 October

**Proclamation of the Turkish Republic of Northern Cyprus Day** 15 November

## INTERNET RESOURCES

As well as the official tourist department sites, useful web resources on Cyprus include:

**www.traveltocyprus.com.cy** Reliable site on the Republic with digital city maps.

**www.kypros.org** Extensive Republic site with tourism information and news.

**www.cypnet.co.uk/cyradise/index.html** Long-established site on North Cyprus.

**www.northcyprus.net** Site with good information on historic sites in the north.

## LANGUAGE

Cypriots on both sides of the divide usually speak some English, but settlers in the North tend to speak only Turkish – see the Turkish and Greek language sections (p752 and 741) at the back of the book for useful words and phrases.

## MAPS

The free maps available from tourist offices are more than sufficient for most needs. A good overall map of the island is the 1:200,00 *Cyprus Travel Map* by Insight (UK£5).

## MEDIA

Republic English-language newspapers include **Cyprus Weekly** (www.cyprusweekly.com.cy) and **Cyprus Mail** (www.cyprus-mail.com). **Cyprus Today** and the **Turkish Daily News** (www.turkishdailynews.com) are the English-language newspapers in the North. The Republic's main radio and TV broadcaster is the **Cyprus Broadcasting Corporation** (www.cybc.com.cy) – you can see English TV news on CYBC2 at 9pm daily. CYBC radio 2 broadcasts in English from 6pm to midnight, with an extra English newscast at 1.30pm. **BFBS** (www.ssvc.com/bfbs/radio/cyprus) broadcasts from the British sovereign bases and has English music, soccer and news. On the Turkish side, **Bayrak International** (www.brt.gov.nc.tr) has mainly English-language radio shows. See the websites for all frequencies.

## MONEY

The Republic's currency is the Cyprus pound (CY£). Foreign exchange is mainly handled by banks, except in the coastal resorts. Most currencies of cash and travellers cheques are accepted and almost all banks have ATMs that take international cards.

The unit of currency in Northern Cyprus is the Turkish lira (TL) but UK pounds, euros and Cyprus pounds are widely accepted. The value of the lira fluctuates widely so prices in this guide are given in euros. Banks have exchange facilities and international ATMs but do not give cash advances on credit cards over the counter. Private foreign exchange offices can be found in all towns.

## POST

There are post offices in most towns in Cyprus. For post restante, stick to the main post offices in south and north Lefkosia. Mail to the North must be addressed Mersin 10, Turkey, *not* North Cyprus.

From the Republic, postcards cost CY£0.26 to all countries and letters cost CY£0.31 to Europe and CY£0.41 to Australia or the United States. From the north, postcards cost €0.27 to Europe and €0.32 to Australia or the USA; letters cost €0.32 and €0.38.

## TELEPHONE

In the Republic, phone booths use **CYTA** (www.cytawebshop.cyta.com.cy) phonecards, which are available from shops – a three-minute call to Europe or the USA will cost around CY£0.60. The Republic's country code is ☎ 357.

In Northern Cyprus, payphones take KKTC Telekomünikasyon phonecards, available from shops – calls cost €0.30 per minute to Europe and €0.60 to the USA. To call North Cyprus from abroad, dial ☎ 90 (Turkey), the regional code ☎ 392, and then the number.

Roaming GSM phones can be used all over Cyprus. Prepaid SIM packs for mobile phonesavailable from shops and phone offices. The main mobile companies are **CYTAGSM** (www.soeasy.cyta.com.cy) in the Republic and **Telsim** (www.kktctelsim.com) in the north.

To call the North from the Republic, dial the UN switchboard on ☎ 0139 followed by the local number. To call the South from

---

**EMERGENCY NUMBERS**

- In the north, dial ☎ 155 for the police and ☎ 122 for an ambulance.
- In the Republic dial ☎ 199 or ☎ 112 for the police, fire service or an ambulance.

the North, call ☎ 0123 followed by the local number. Regional area codes form part of the phone number throughout Cyprus.

## TIME
Cyprus is two hours ahead of GMT/UTC – noon in Lefkosia is 10am in London, 5am in New York and 8pm in Sydney. Clocks gain an hour on the last weekend in March and lose an hour on the last weekend in October.

## TOURIST INFORMATION
The **Cyprus Tourism Organisation** (CTO; www.visit cyprus.org.cy) has offices at Larnaka and Pafos airport and in all major towns in the Republic, with excellent maps and information leaflets.

**North Cyprus Tourism** (www.holidayinnorthcyprus. com) has offices in Lefkoşa, Gazimağusa, Girne and Yeni Erenköy in the Karpas, with limited brochures and information, plus desks at Ercan airport and the Ledra Palace checkpoint in Lefkoşa.

## VISAS
Nationals of Australia, New Zealand, USA, Canada, Japan and all European Economic Area countries can enter and stay in either the Republic or North Cyprus for up to three months without a visa. However, citizens of Greece, the Republic of Cyprus and Armenia need a visa for the North and Turkish citizens need a visa for the Republic.

Tourists are allowed to day trip across the border, but overnight stays are not permitted – see the boxed text Crossing the Green Line (right) for more information. When entering the north, get immigration to stamp a separate piece of paper instead of your passport to avoid future problems entering the south.

## WORK
Throughout Cyprus, work permits can only be obtained through a prospective employer applying on your behalf. You may be able to pick up casual work on the sly at the tourist resorts in exchange for room and board. The best place to look for jobs is in the *Cyprus Weekly*. Private schools sometimes need TEFL teachers to teach English to recently arrived migrant workers – try searching on www.google.com for 'TEFL' and 'Cyprus'.

# TRANSPORT IN CYPRUS

Cyprus is a convenient gateway between Europe and the Middle East. There are air connections to major cities in Europe and the Middle Eastern cities; and ferries between North Cyprus and Turkey. Day trips are possible between the Republic of Cyprus and North Cyprus but you must enter and leave Cyprus from the same side you arrived on. See the boxed text Crossing the Green Line, below, for more information.

## GETTING THERE & AWAY
Ferry services to the Republic are currently suspended so almost all travellers arrive by air. Flights and ferries to North Cyprus all originate in Turkey, so you have to travel there first. Departure tax varies with the destination and is always included in the ticket price.

### Air
The Republic's international airports are at Larnaka and Pafos. There are scheduled and charter flights from major cities in Europe and the Middle East with Cyprus Airways and other carriers – It's around UK£150 from London to Cyprus. Heading on from Cyprus, oneway fares include CY£31 to Rhodes or Heraklion, CY£36 to Athens, CY£54 to Damascus and CY£60 to Cairo, Amman, Tel Aviv or Beirut.

Flights to Ercan airport in North Cyprus start in Turkey so you must fly there first – Cyprus Turkish Airlines and Turkish Airlines are the main carriers. Fares from

---

**CROSSING THE GREEN LINE**

Depending on prevailing diplomatic relations, you are usually allowed to cross from the Republic into Northern Cyprus for a day trip via the Ledra Palace checkpoint in Lefkosia – European citizens only can also do a day trip in the opposite direction. You must show your passport and if you enter the north, you must get a Turkish entry stamp on a separate piece of paper – the border is open from 7am to midnight daily. The border situation is highly volatile so check with the CTO before you cross.

London to Ercan (via Istanbul) start at UK£400. A return ticket to Ercan from Istanbul costs around US$100.

Airlines flying to the Republic include:

**British Airways** (code BA; ☎ 2276 1166; www.british airways.com)

**Cyprus Airways** (code CY; www.cyprusairways.com; ☎ 2266 3054)

**Egypt Air** (code MS; ☎ 2276 3777; www.egyptair.com .eg)

**El Al Israel Airlines** (code LY; ☎ 2557 4180; www .elal.co.il)

**Emirates** (code EK; ☎ 2237 4010; www.emirates.com)

**Gulf Air** (code GF; ☎ 2237 4064; www.gulfairco.com)

**Helios Airways** (code HCY; ☎ 2481 5700; www.helios -airways.com)

**KLM Royal Dutch Airlines** (code KL; ☎ 2267 1616; www.klm.com)

**Lufthansa German Airlines** (code LH; ☎ 2287 3330; www.lufthansa.com)

**Middle East Airlines** (code ME; ☎ 2267 0444; www .mea.com.lb)

**Olympic Airways** (code OA; ☎ 2271 6500; www .olympicairlines.com)

**Royal Jordanian Airlines** (code RJ; ☎ 2237 5360; www.rja.com.jo)

**Syrian Airlines** (code RB; ☎ 2237 6552; www.syrian -airlines.com)

Airlines flying to North Cyprus are:

**Cyprus Turkish Airlines** (code YK; ☎ 227 3820; www .kthy.net)

**Turkish Airlines** (code TK; ☎ 227 1061; www .turkishairlines.com)

## Sea

Passenger services to the Republic's main port at Lemesos are currently suspended. You should check with **Salamis Cruise Lines** ( ☎ 2586 0000), **Paradise Cruises** ( ☎ 2535 7604) or **Louis Cruise Centre** ( ☎ 2557 0000) to see if any of the cruise ships to Greece, Israel and Egypt are carrying passengers to and from Cyprus again.

From North Cyprus there are several ferry routes to mainland Turkey. **Cyprus Turkish Shipping** ( ☎ 366 5786) sails from Gazimağusa to Mersin (€31, 12 hours) on Tuesday, Thursday and Sunday, returning the following day.

**Fergün** ( ☎ 815 4993) and **Akgünler** ( ☎ 815 3510) both have daily fast passenger ferries and slow car ferries from Girne to Taşucu (€21.50, two to five hours). During the summer there's also a twice-weekly ferry

between Girne and Alanya (€19, four to five hours).

# GETTING AROUND
## Bicycle

Cyprus has loads of quiet back roads for cyclists and there are occasional cycle lanes in the Republic. The CTO produces the occasionally inaccurate *Cycling Routes* booklet or you can contact the **Cyprus Cycling Federation** ( ☎ 2266 3344; PO Box 24572, Lefkosia) for information.

Mountain bikes can be rented in Plateia Troodos and Polis and in many coastal resorts. **Bike Trek Cyprus** (www.biketrekcyprus.com) is one of several companies offering custom mountain bike tours of the Republic.

## Bus

Inexpensive buses and minibuses are operated by various private companies on both sides of the Green Line – contact details for bus companies are listed under individual towns. Buses link all major cities and many villages and fares are under CY£5 for most journeys. The last daily service on most routes leaves around 5pm and there are few Sunday buses.

## Car & Motorcycle

You can rent cars and motorbikes in most towns and rates start at around CY£20 per day for cars and CY£4 to CY£8 per day for mopeds and motorcycles. Most car and motorcycle licenses are valid in the Republic, but only British and international licenses are accepted in the north. The minimum age for renting a car is 21, drivers under 25 pay insurance fee. You must be 17 or over to ride a motorcycle (18 or over for engines bigger than 50cc).

Car hire fees include insurance, but you can pay an additional fee for zero liability. Cars hired in the Republic are not insured for North Cyprus and vice versa, but temporary insurance for private cars can be arranged at the border. If you bring your car to Cyprus on the ferry from Turkey, you are then eligible to obtain a three-month duty waiver and local insurance on arrival.

Cypriots drive on the left and seatbelts are compulsory for all passengers. Driving while using a mobile phone is prohibited and the blood-alcohol limit for driving is 90mg per 100ml. The speed limit across the island is 100km on main highways, 80km on minor roads and 50km or lower in built-up areas. Inexpensive parking meters and municipal car parks are found in main towns. Petrol costs around CY£0.45 in the south and €0.80 in the north.

For more information contact the **Cyprus Automobile Association** ( ☎ 2231 3233; Christou Mylona 12, Lefkosia).

## Taxi
Service taxis, which take up to eight people, cost about the same as buses and offer similar routes. All service-taxis in the Republic are run by **Travel & Express** ( ☎ 7777 7474) – you can go directly to the depots or call ahead to arrange a pick-up. In the north, **Kombos** ( ☎ 227 2929) connects Lefkoşa, Girne and Gazimağusa.

There are urban taxis in all large towns and rural taxis connect rural villages.

# Malta

**CONTENTS**

---

## FAST FACTS

- **Area** 316 sq km
- **Capital** Valletta
- **Currency** Maltese lira (Lm), Lm1 = 100c; US$1 = Lm0.34, €1 = Lm0.42
- **Famous for** prehistoric temples, the Knights of the Order of St John, the unique language, birthplace of Edward de Bono
- **Official Languages** Malti, English
- **Population** 400,000
- **Telephone Codes** country code ☎ 356; international access code ☎ 00
- **Visas** not needed for most visitors for stays of up to three months

The diminutive island nation of Malta (all 316 sq km of it, comprising the islands of Malta, Gozo and Comino) may look like a tiny speck on the map south of Sicily, but you'll be amazed by how much it has to offer. Strategically placed in the Mediterranean, it has been occupied by several civilisations and has proved a tempting target for explorers and invaders. This tug of war has left Malta with an eclectic mix of influences and yet it has managed to retain a certain individuality.

Its warm climate, scenic coastline and reasonable prices have earned Malta a package-holiday reputation, but look beyond the beaches and there's a 5000-year history to explore. From prehistoric temples to baroque architecture you're never short of sights to pique your interest.

Despite much development (especially in the tourism sector), Malta has kept a traditional outlook. The sense of family is still very strong and community spirit is at its best during *festa* (feast day) season, when whole towns and villages join to pay homage to their patron saint.

The Maltese are warm and friendly people and you'll feel at home in no time. Get caught up in the hustle and bustle of the modern-day Mediterranean lifestyle, delve into a fascinating history, chill out on a beach, enjoy some of Europe's best diving, or escape to the quiet recesses of rural life on Gozo. Malta proves that good things do come in small packages!

## HIGHLIGHTS

- See the capital, **Valletta** (p574), a magnificent fortified city built in the 16th century by the Knights of the Order of St John.
- Take a trip to the **Blue Lagoon** (p588) on tiny Comino and swim and snorkel in exquisitely clear water.
- Wander the silent streets of the old capital, **Mdina** (p585), which exudes an air of aristocratic elegance.
- Celebrate a **festa** (p590) with the locals – a party to celebrate a patron saint, always accompanied by music, food and fireworks.
- Get off the beaten track on **Gozo** (p586); smaller, greener and quieter that Malta, it has good walking, superb coastal sites and excellent scuba-diving.

## ITINERARIES

- **Three days** On your first day check out the sights of Valletta: wander the streets, enjoy the views, visit the museums. On the second day head to the Hypogeum (remember to prebook) before lunching in Marsaxlokk and visiting Haġar Qim and Mnajdra temples in the afternoon. On the third day make a trip to Mdina and Rabat, then escape to a beach in the northwest.

- **One week** As above, then on the fourth day take a boat trip to Comino, spend a couple of days on Gozo and laze away your final day on a beach.
- **Two weeks** Spend a week seeing the sights of Malta and a week unwinding on Gozo (possibly with some diving thrown in). Consider spending a night or two on Comino.

## CLIMATE & WHEN TO GO

Malta is a year-round destination. The peak season is June to September, but you should try to avoid July and August, when it can get unbearably hot (35ºC) and Malta is overrun with tourists. The best time to visit is in spring (April to June) and autumn (September and October). From October to May most hotels offer discounted rates (up to 50% below high-season prices). Winter weather is mild, but the Christmas and New Year period is busy, with room prices rising to peak-season rates.

## HISTORY

Malta has a fascinating history and is crowded with physical and cultural reminders of its past. The megalithic temples built between 3600 BC and 2500 BC are the oldest surviving freestanding structures in

## TOP FIVE MALTA

- **Best beach** A tough choice between the Blue Lagoon on Comino, Golden Bay in Malta's northwest or Ramla Bay on Gozo

- **Views to die for** The magnificent panorama from the Upper Barrakka Gardens in Valletta

- **Hidden cove** Join the locals for a dip at Għar Lapsi in the island's southwest

- **Historic towns** Valletta and Mdina, great places for aimless wandering and soaking up history

- **Nightlife** Paceville – where the locals and holiday-makers come to play

the world, predating the Pyramids by over 500 years. The best places to view these prehistoric marvels are on the south coast (p586) and at Xagħra on Gozo (p587).

From around 800 BC to 218 BC, Malta was colonised by the Phoenicians and, for the last 250 years of this period, by Phoenicia's principal North African colony, Carthage. The Maltese language (Malti) is Semitic in origin and is believed to be based on Phoenician. With watchful eyes painted on the prow, the colourful Maltese fishing boats are scarcely changed from the Phoenician trading vessels that once plied the Mediterranean (check them out at Marsaxlokk harbour, p586).

The Punic Wars saw the defeat of Carthage in 208 BC, and Malta became part of the Roman Empire. In AD 60, St Paul – a prisoner en route to Rome – was shipwrecked on the island. According to local folklore he converted the islanders to Christianity.

Arabs from North Africa arrived in AD 870 and tolerated the local Christians. They brought citrus fruits and cotton and had an impact on Maltese customs and language. The Arabs were expelled in 1090 by the Norman King Roger of Sicily. For the next 400 years, Malta's history was linked to Sicily, and its rulers were a succession of Normans, Angevins (French), Aragónese and Castilians (Spanish). The relatively small population of downtrodden islanders paid their taxes by trading, slaving and piracy, and were harassed by marauding North Africans (Berbers and Arabs) and Turks.

In 1530, the islands were given to the Knights of the Order of St John of Jerusalem by Charles V, Emperor of Spain; the local inhabitants were given no say in the matter.

The Order of St John was founded during the crusades to protect Christian pilgrims travelling to and from the Holy Land, and to care for the sick. The Knights were drawn from the younger male members of Europe's aristocratic families (those who were not the principal heirs). The order comprised eight nationalities or *langues*. In order to preserve their identities, the *langues* built palaces, called *auberges*. The eight *langues* – Italy, Germany, France, Provence, Castile, Aragón, Auvergne and England – correspond to the eight points of the Maltese Cross. It was a religious order, with the Knights taking vows of celibacy, poverty and obedience, and handing over their patrimonies. The Order of St John became extremely prestigious, wealthy and powerful as a military and maritime force, and as a charitable organisation that founded and operated several hospitals.

As soon as they arrived in Malta, the Knights began to fortify the harbour and to skirmish with infidels. In May 1565, a huge Ottoman fleet carrying more than 30,000 men laid siege to the island. The 700 Knights and 8000 Maltese and mercenary troops were commanded by a 70-year-old Grand Master, Jean Parisot de la Valette. The Great Siege lasted for more than three months, with continuous and unbelievably ferocious fighting. After enormous bloodshed on both sides, help finally arrived from Sicily and the Turks withdrew.

The Knights were hailed as the saviours of Europe. Money and honours were heaped upon them by grateful monarchs, and the construction of the new city of Valletta (named after the hero of the siege) and its enormous fortifications began. Malta was never again seriously threatened by the Turks.

Although the order continued to embellish Valletta, the Knights sank into corrupt and ostentatious ways, largely supported by piracy. In 1798 Napoleon arrived, seeking to counter the British influence in the Mediterranean, and the Knights, who were mostly French, surrendered to him without a fight.

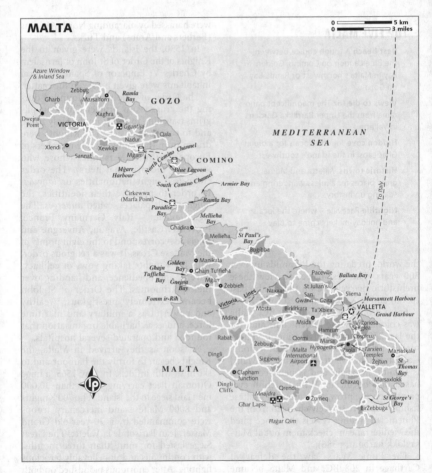

# MALTA

| | |
| 0 | 5 km |
| 0 | 3 miles |

**GOZO**

Azure Window & Inland Sea

Zebbug · Marsalforn · Ramla Bay

Gharb

Dwejra Point

**VICTORIA** · Ġgantija

Xaghra

Nadur · Qala

Xlendi · Sannat · Xewkija

Mġarr

Mġarr Harbour

North Comino Channel

Blue Lagoon

**COMINO**

South Comino Channel · Armier Bay

Ċirkewwa (Marfa Point) · Ramla Bay

Paradise Bay

Mellieħa Bay

Ghadira · Mellieħa · St Paul's Bay

Bugibba

**MEDITERRANEAN SEA**

To Italy

Golden Bay · Manikata

Għajn Tuffieħa Bay · Għajn Tuffieħa

Għajn Tuffieħa Bay · Gnejna Bay · Mġarr · Żebbieħ

Paceville · Balluta Bay

St Julian's · Sliema

Marsamxett Harbour

Fomm ir-Riħ

Naxxar · San Gwann · Gzira · Ta'Xbiex · **VALLETTA**

Victoria Lines · Mosta · Birkirkara · Grand Harbour

Mdina · Lija · Msida · Vittoriosa · Senglea · Cospicua

Rabat · Qormi · Hamrun · Marsa · Marsaskala

Zebbug · Malta Hypogeum · Paola · Tarxien Temples · Żejtun

Dingli · Siggiewi · Malta International Airport · St Thomas Bay

Clapham Junction · Qrendi · Ghaxaq · Marsaxlokk

Dingli Cliffs

Mnajdra · Żurrieq · St George's Bay

Ghar Lapsi · Hagar Qim · BirŻebbuga

**MALTA**

---

The Maltese defeated the French in 1800 with the assistance of the British, and in 1814 Malta officially became part of the British Empire. The British decided to develop Malta into a major naval base. In WWII, Malta once again found itself under siege. Considered a linchpin in the battle for the Mediterranean, Malta was subjected to a blockade. In 1942 it suffered five months of day-and-night bombing raids, which left 40,000 homes destroyed and the population on the brink of starvation. Visit the National War Museum (p578) in Valletta for more information on this period.

In 1947 the devastated island was given a measure of self-government. The country gained independence in 1964, and became a republic in 1974. In 1979 links with Britain were further reduced when the British armed services were expelled.

From 1987 to 2002 the issue of whether Malta should apply for membership of the European Union (EU) was a political hot potato, and elections were like a seesaw between the pro-EU Nationalist Party and anti-EU Labour Party. Malta was formally invited to join the EU in 2002. In March 2003 the population had its say in a referendum on the matter; just over 53% voted in favour of EU membership. This pro-EU result was confirmed when the Nationalist Party won a general election one month later. Malta became a member of the EU on 1 May 2004.

**HOW MUCH?**

■ **Room in guesthouse** Lm 6-8 per person

■ **Postage stamp** local Lm0.07, airmail Lm0.16-0.27

■ **Harbour cruise** Lm6.50

■ **Bus trip** Lm0.15-0.20

■ **Cup of coffee** Lm0.50

**LONELY PLANET INDEX**

■ **Litre of petrol** Lm0.36

■ **Litre of bottled water** Lm0.40

■ **Beer in bar** Lm0.40

■ **Souvenir T-shirt** Lm4

■ **Street snack (pastizzi, pastry filled with ricotta or mushy peas)** Lm0.10

## PEOPLE

Malta's population is around 400,000, with most people living in the satellite towns around Valletta, Sliema and the Grand Harbour. Approximately 30,000 live on Gozo, while Comino has a mere handful of farmers (and a couple of hundred tourists in summer). More than 95% of the population is Maltese-born.

## RELIGION

Despite an easy blend of Mediterranean and British culture throughout the islands, there's still a strong feeling of tradition. The people are fairly conservative in outlook and family values are highly regarded. Around 98% of the population are members of the Roman Catholic Church, and the Church is still influential in many people's lives. This is most noticeable on Sundays when many shops and businesses are closed. Abortion and divorce are illegal.

## ARTS

Lace-making is thought to have been introduced to the island in the 16th century when the Knights arrived. There are plenty of stalls and shops selling traditional tablecloths and other such souvenirs in the more touristy areas. Look out, too, for beautiful, intricate silver filigree – the art is thought to have been brought over to Malta from Sicily in the 17th century. The Maltese glassblowing

industry has enjoyed increasing success and many pieces are exported internationally.

## ENVIRONMENT
### Environmental Issues

Malta's small surface area has been subjected to pressures of population, land use and development, a lack of protection for natural areas and, more recently, a significant increase in pollution. There is also a severe shortage of fresh water. Hunting and trapping of birds remains a part of the Maltese way of life.

### The Land

The Maltese archipelago consists of three inhabited islands: Malta (246 sq km), Gozo (67 sq km) and Comino (2.7 sq km). They lie in the middle of the Mediterranean, 93km south of Sicily, east of Tunisia and north of Libya.

The densely populated islands are formed of soft limestone: the golden building material used in all constructions. There are some low ridges and outcrops, but no major hills. The soil is generally thin and rocky, although in some valleys it is terraced and farmed intensively. There are few trees and, for most of the year, little greenery to soften the sun-bleached landscape; in turn, the sparse vegetation supports little in the way of wildlife. (The notable exception is Buskett Gardens, south of Rabat, a lush valley of trees and orange groves protected by the imposing southern Dingli Cliffs.) There is virtually no surface water and there are no permanent creeks or rivers. The water table is the main source of fresh water, but it is supplemented by several desalination plants.

## FOOD & DRINK

Like the Maltese language, the cuisine demonstrates the influences of the many foreign cultures that have ruled the country. The food is rustic and meals are based on seasonal produce and the fisherman's catch.

**COVER UP!**

Beachwear is for beaches – don't wear bathing suits in public areas in Malta. Females should cover up modestly in places of worship and men should opt for long trousers rather than shorts.

MALTA

Malta is not known as a destination for gourmets, but the food is generally good and cheap. Most restaurants offer inexpensive pizzas and pastas and there is often a variety of vegetarian options on most menus. The national dish is *fenek* (rabbit), and it can be fried in olive oil, roasted, stewed, served with spaghetti or baked in a pie. Make sure you also try the locally caught fish and seafood.

Look out for *pastizzi*, favourite local snacks. These small parcels of flaky pastry are filled with ricotta cheese or mushy peas, and a couple of *pastizzi* make for a tasty breakfast or afternoon filler. You'll pay around Lm0.10 for one, so they're also great for budget travellers. A main dish you're sure to encounter is *braġioli* – prepared by wrapping a thin slice of beef around a stuffing of breadcrumbs, chopped bacon, hard-boiled egg and parsley, then braising these 'beef olives' in a red wine sauce.

Local beers are good, particularly Cisk (pronounced chisk). The range of locally produced wine is surprisingly good, and the quality is improving all the time. Imported beers, wines and spirits can be bought everywhere.

# VALLETTA

Valletta, city of the Knights of the Order of St John, is steeped in history and renowned for its architectural excellence. Commercial activity bustles around Triq ir-Repubblika (Republic St) but the quiet back streets are where you'll get a feel for everyday life. The city overlooks the impressive Grand Harbour to the southeast and Marsamxett Harbour to the northwest. Across Grand Harbour, the fortified peninsulas of Vittoriosa and Senglea, as well as Cospicua, are collectively known as the Three Cities.

## ORIENTATION

Valletta is a compact town barely a kilometre long and 600m wide, with a regular grid of narrow streets within the massive medieval fortifications. The main street, known as Triq ir-Repubblika, runs in a straight line northeast from City Gate (adjacent to City Gate bus terminus) to Fort St Elmo.

## INFORMATION

**Bank of Valletta** (cnr Triq ir-Repubblika & Triq San Ġwann) Foreign exchange machine and ATMs.
**Main Post Office** (Pjazza Kastilja; ☺ 8.15am-4.30pm Mon-Fri, 8.15am-12.30pm Sat)
**MelitaNet** (28 Triq Melita; per hour Lm1) Internet café.
**Police Station** ( ☎ 21 225 495; Triq Nofs in-Nhar)
**St Luke's Hospital** ( ☎ 21 241 251; Gwardamanġa Hill, Gwardamanġa) Malta's public hospital, near Pietà (about 3km southwest of Valletta); take bus No 75.
**Tourist Information Office** Misraħ il-Helsien ( ☎ 21 237 747 or 21 255 844; ☺ 9am-5.30pm Mon-Sat, 9am-12.30pm Sun, closed public holidays); Malta International Airport ( ☎ 23 696 073/4; ☺ 10am-10pm) Main office is in the City Arcade immediately on the right as you enter through City Gate.
**Travelex** (20 Triq ir-Repubblika) Currency exchange bureau.
**Ziffa** (194 Triq id-Dejqa) Internet access, and good rates for international phone calls.

## SIGHTS & ACTIVITIES

A walk around the city walls is a good way to get your bearings. The views are spectacular and you'll get to see many of the city's highlights along the way. Be sure to stop at the **Upper Barrakka Gardens** in the southwest to take in the view that puts the grand in Grand Harbour.

**St John's Co-Cathedral** ( ☎ 21 225 639; entrance on Triq ir-Repubblika; adult/child Lm1/free; ☺ 9.30am-12.30pm & 1.30-4.15pm Mon-Fri, 9.30am-12.30pm Sat, closed Sun, public holidays & during services), built in the 1570s, dominates the centre of town with its grave exterior. Its baroque interior is breathtaking and the floor is covered with marble tombstones, marking the resting place of Knights and dignitaries. Inside the cathedral is the entry to the **Cathedral Museum** ( ☎ 21 220 536; entrance incl in ticket price; ☺ 9.30am-12.30pm & 1.30-4.15pm Mon-Fri, 9.30am-12.30pm Sat, closed Sun, public holidays & during services), which houses two magnificent works by the Italian painter, Caravaggio.

The 16th-century **Grand Master's Palace** (Pjazza San Ġorġ) is now the seat of the Maltese parliament. From the public entrance on Triq il-Merkanti, it is possible to visit the **Armoury** ( ☎ 21 249 349; adult/child Lm1/free; ☺ 7.45am-2pm mid-Jun–Sep, 8.15am-5pm Mon-Sat & 8.15am-4pm Sun Oct–mid-Jun) and **State Apartments** ( ☎ 21 221 221; adult/child Lm1/free; ☺ 7.45am-2pm mid-Jun–Sep, 8.15am-5pm Mon-Sat & 8.15am-4pm Sun Oct–mid-Jun). The corridors of the State Apartments are lined with paintings of the Grand Masters and there is an exquisite fresco depicting the Great Siege of 1565; however, this area is closed when official state visits are taking place.

At the **National Museum of Archaeology** ( ☎ 21 221 623; Triq ir-Repubblika; adult/child Lm1/free; ☑ 7.45am–2pm mid-Jun–Sep, 8.15am–5pm Mon-Sat & 8.15am-4pm Sun Oct–mid-Jun) you can admire beautiful objects that have been found at Malta's prehistoric sites – check out the female figurines found at Ħaġar Qim, the so-called 'fat ladies'. Best of all is the *Sleeping Lady*, found at the Hypogeum and dating from around 3000 BC.

At the furthest point of Valletta is **Fort St Elmo**, built in 1552 by the Knights of the Order of St John. Its strategic location and design were vital to the islands' defence. Today the fort is only open to the public for historical re-enactments, such as **In Guardia** ( ☎ 21 237 747; adult/child Lm1.50/0.50; ☑ 11am 1st & 3rd Sun of month Sep-Jun), a colourful military pageant in 16th-century costume.

Next to Fort St Elmo, the **National War Museum** ( ☎ 21 222 430; entrance on Triq il-Fontana; adult/child Lm1/free; ☑ 7.45am-2pm mid-Jun–Sep, 8.15am-5pm Mon-Sat & 8.15am Sun Oct–mid-Jun), informatively commemorates Malta's involvement in WWII.

The beautiful **Manoel Theatre** ( ☎ 21 246 389; www.teatrumanoel.com; 115 Triq it-Teatru l-Antik; theatre tours Lm1.65; tours ☑ 10.30am, 11.30am & 5.15pm Mon-Fri, 11.30am & 12.30pm Sat), built in 1731, is one of the oldest theatres in Europe. There is a varied programme of events from October to May (drama, concerts, opera, ballet), or you can take a guided tour to see the restored baroque auditorium.

The St James' Cavalier has undergone a transformation from a 16th-century fortification into a bright, modern arts centre. The **St James' Cavalier Centre for Creativity** ( ☎ 21 223 200; www.sjcav.org; entrance on Triq Nofs in-Nhar; admission free; ☑ 10am-9.30pm) houses a couple of exhibition spaces, a theatre for live performances, and an art-house cinema. Stop by to check out the interior and grab a programme of what's on.

Multimedia audiovisual experiences have sprung up all over Valletta but some are better than others. The **Malta Experience** ( ☎ 21 243 776; Triq il-Mediterran; adult/child Lm3/1.75; ☑ 11am-4pm Mon-Fri, 11am-1pm Sat & Sun) provides a good introduction to the country's history and culture. Shows start every hour on the hour during opening times. The **Wartime Experience** ( ☎ 21 222 225; Embassy Cinema, Triq Santa Luċija; adult/child Lm2/1.50; screenings ☑ 10am, 11am, noon & 1pm)

### VALLETTA IN TWO DAYS

Wake yourself up with coffee at **Caffe Cordina** (p580) then take in the **Malta Experience** (right) for some historical background. Spend a few hours wandering Valletta's streets, stopping to admire the beautiful architecture and take in the magnificent views, especially from the **Upper Barrakka Gardens** (p578) over Grand Harbour. Afterwards, take in a show or a tour at the **Manoel Theatre** (this page) and sample some local wine at the atmospheric **Castille Wine Vaults** (p581). On the second day, spend the morning visiting **St John's Co-Cathedral** (p578), the **Grand Master's Palace** (p578) and the **National Museum of Archaeology** (right), before taking a tour of the **Hypogeum** (p581) (be sure to prebook). Finish by enjoying dinner at one of Valletta's fine restaurants.

is a poignant 45-minute film presentation depicting Malta's struggle against the odds during WWII.

## SLEEPING

**Asti Guesthouse** ( ☎ 21 239 506; http://mol.net.mt/asti; 18 Triq Sant'Orsla; B&B per person Lm5.50) This classy guesthouse offers the best-value accommodation in Valletta. There is a charming host; simple, spacious rooms (each with handbasin); and spotless shared bathrooms. Breakfast (included in the price) is served in a vaulted dining room complete with a huge chandelier.

**British Hotel** ( ☎ 21 224 730; www.britishhotel.com; 40 Triq il-Batterija; s/d Lm12/18, with sea view Lm16/22) You can enjoy excellent views over Grand Harbour with your breakfast at this affordable, well-located hotel. It's a bit of a rabbit warren, however, and the rooms, although clean, are basic and rather lacking in charm. It's worth paying extra for a balcony and view.

**Osborne Hotel** ( ☎ 21 243 656/7; www.osbornehotel.com; 50 Triq Nofs in-Nhar; s/d Lm19/28; ☒ ☒ ) The pick of the mid-range options, this former Knight's palace has an inviting lobby, restaurant and lounge, but the smallish rooms don't quite live up to this high standard. Still, they're well equipped, with air-con and satellite TV (try for a room on the higher floors to ensure a view). On the 6th floor there's a roof terrace with a small pool.

**MALTA**

# VALLETTA

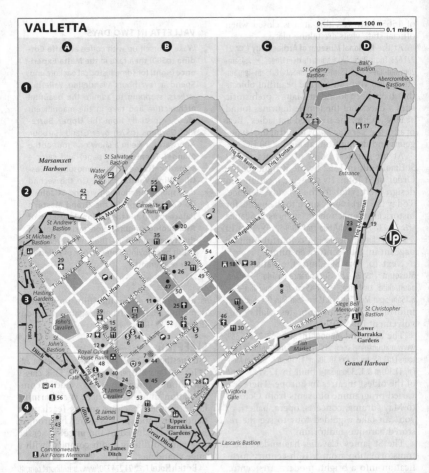

## EATING

**Caffe Cordina** ( ☎ 21 234 385; 244 Triq ir-Repubblika; snacks & meals Lm0.70-3.60) The prime people-watching spot in Valletta is Misrah ir-Repubblika, and the oldest option here is Caffe Cordina, established in 1837 and perfect for savoury pastries and decadent sweets. You have the choice of tables on the square or inside, or join the locals at the counter for a quick caffeine hit. And be sure to look up (the ceiling is exquisitely painted).

**Café Jubilee** ( ☎ 21 252 332; 125 Triq Santa Lućija; snacks & meals Lm0.90-3; ☼ 8-1am) This is the kind of place you can drop in to anytime, for a breakfast of coffee and some *pastizzi*, a lunchtime baguette, or a dinner of salad, pasta or risotto. It's a continental-style

bistro, with low lighting, cosy nooks and poster-plastered walls. It's also a great spot for a night-time drink.

**Rubino** ( ☎ 21 224 656; 53 Triq L-Ifran; mains Lm4-6; ☼ lunch Mon-Fri, dinner Tue & Fri) Ranking among Malta's finest restaurants, this place earns rave reviews for reinventing traditional Maltese cuisine while staying true to its roots. There's no menu, just a selection of dishes depending on seasonal produce and local tradition. Tuesday night is usually rabbit night. Bookings are advised.

**Agius Pastizzerija** (273 Triq San Pawl; pastries from Lm0.7) Search out this friendly hole-in-the-wall place for traditional snacks. There are both sweet and savoury and you can take away, at bargain prices.

MALTA

**Wembley Stores** (305 Triq ir-Repubblika; ☼ 7.15am-7pm Mon-Sat) has a wide selection of groceries and there is a **fresh produce market** (Triq il-Merkanti; ☼ 7am-1pm Mon-Sat) behind the Grand Master's Palace, where you can buy fruit and vegetables, fish, meat etc.

## DRINKING

For years Valletta seemed half dead after 8pm and those seeking nightlife automatically headed to Paceville (p584). But there seems to have been a revival of late, and Valletta is now home to a few café-bars where you can eat and drink among in-the-know locals. Venues worth seeking out include Castille Wine Vaults and Café Jubilee (see Eating for details), plus **Maestro e Fresco** ( ☎ 21 233 801; Triq Nofs in-Nhar) and **Tra Buxu** ( ☎ 21 223 036; Triq Nofs in-Nhar). Both open at around 5.30pm nightly; there's often live music at Maestro e Fresco (especially later in the week).

---

### AUTHOR'S CHOICE

**Castille Wine Vaults** ( ☎ 21 237 707; Pjazza Kastilja; light meals Lm1.50-3) This fabulously situated café-bar is underneath the stock exchange building, accessed by steps and a long passageway. Here you can sate your hunger with light meals including *panini* and platters (of antipasto, cheese, seafood or dips), plus learn about and sample some good local wine (Lm2 for four wines). After 10pm Friday and Saturday this is a popular nightspot, playing ambient tunes by candlelight.

---

Raise a glass in memory of the late Oliver Reed in his favourite drinking spot, simply named the **Pub** ( ☎ 21 237 525; 136 Triq l-Arċisqof; ☼ 10am-4.30pm year-round, also Thu-Sat evenings in low season).

## ENTERTAINMENT

See p579 for information on theatres in Valletta.

## GETTING THERE & AWAY

The City Gate bus terminus has services to all parts of the island (p593). Bus No 8 runs between the City Gate terminus and Malta's airport (Lm0.15) approximately every half-hour. On the return trip, the bus leaves from outside the departures hall. To do the airport–Valletta trip by taxi, book and pay at the designated booth in the arrivals hall. The official rate is Lm6. Ferries from Italy dock southwest of Valletta at Pinto Wharf in Grand Harbour (p592).

## AROUND VALLETTA

The town of Paola, about 4km south of Valletta, is home to the magnificent **Hal Saflieni Hypogeum** ( ☎ 21 805 019, 21 825 579; entry on Triq iċ-Ċimiterju; adult/child Lm3/1; ☼ 5-7 tours conducted daily: 8.30am-12.30pm mid-Jun–Sep, 8.30am-3.30pm Mon-Sat & 8.30am-2.30pm Sun Oct–mid-Jun), a complex of underground burial chambers thought to date from 3600 BC to 3000 BC. Excellent 50-minute tours of the complex are available, but the number of visitors has been restricted in order to preserve this fragile Unesco National World Heritage site. Prebooking is therefore essential (usually at least 10 days before you wish to visit); tickets are available in person from the Hypogeum and the Museum of Archaeology in Valletta (p579), or on line at www.heritagemalta.org.

More than a dozen buses pass through Paola, including Nos 1, 2, 3, 4 and 6. Get off at the main square, Pjazza Paola – the Hypogeum is a five-minute walk south (signposted).

# AROUND VALLETTA

## SLIEMA, ST JULIAN'S & PACEVILLE

The modern, fashionable areas of Sliema, St Julian's and Paceville lie to the north of Valletta. Constantly being developed, they are crammed with high-rise hotels, apartment blocks, shops, restaurants, bars and nightclubs. This is where the locals come to promenade, eat, drink, shop and play, and where many tourists base themselves.

## Information

**American Express** ( ☎ 21 334 051; Airways House, Triq il-Kbira, Sliema) Cashes travellers cheques and provides travel services.

**Magic Kiosk** (cnr Triq ix-Xatt & Triq it-Torri, Sliema) Internet access plus good rates for international calls.

**MelitaNet** (Triq Ball, Paceville; ☼ 24hr) Large Internet café inside Tropicana Hotel. Also offers good-value rates for international calls.

**Police Station** ( ☎ 21 330 502; cnr Triq Manwel Dimech & Triq Rudolfu, Sliema)

**Post Office** (Triq Manwel Dimech, Sliema)

**Tourist Information Office** ( ☎ 21 381 392; Palazzo Spinola, enter from Triq Ross, Paceville; generally ☼ 8am-12.30pm & 1.30-5pm Mon-Fri)

## Sights & Activities

There's not a lot to see in Sliema itself, but there are good views of Valletta from Triq ix-Xatt (The Strand) and Tigné Point, especially at dusk as the floodlights are switched on. Triq ix-Xatt and Triq it-Torri (Tower Rd) make for a pleasant waterfront stroll, with plenty of bars and cafés in which to quench a thirst. **Beaches** in the area are mostly shelves of bare rock, and clambering in and out of the sea can be a bit awkward. There are better facilities at the many private **lidos** along the coast, including swimming pools, sun lounges, bars and watersports; admission costs around Lm2 to Lm3 per day.

**Captain Morgan Cruises** ( ☎ 21 343 373; www.captainmorgan.com.mt), at the Ferries in Sliema, has a boat trip for every traveller's taste and pocket. There's a popular short tour of Grand Harbour (Lm6.25), or an all-day cruise around Malta and Comino (Lm15). Other options include day trips to the Blue Lagoon, a sunset cruise, a sailing cruise on a catamaran or an 'underwater safari' on a glass-bottom boat. Tickets can be purchased at any of the travel agencies on the waterfront.

## Sleeping

**Hibernia Residence & Hostel** ( ☎ 21 333 859; hibernia@nsts.org; Triq Mons G Depiro, Sliema; dm/s/d/tr low season Lm2.15/8.85/8.40/10.35, high season Lm3.45/15/17.80/20.55; ▣ ) Hibernia has self-catering studios in a residence (popular with English-language students) and dorm beds in a hostel area. It has good facilities, including helpful staff, Internet access, rooftop sun terrace, kitchens, laundry and caféteria (breakfast is an additional Lm1). To get here from Valletta, take bus No 62 or 67 to Balluta Bay and walk up Triq Manwel Dimech for 300m – Triq Mons G Depiro is on the left.

**Pinto Guesthouse** ( ☎ 21 313 897; www.pintohotel.com; Triq il-Qalb Imqaddsa, St Julian's; s/d/tr low season Lm5.50/8/11, high season Lm8.50/14/15) A steep walk up from Balluta Bay, but worth the hike for the warm welcome, bargain prices, clean, spacious rooms and excellent view (better than walking is to take bus No 42 from Valletta, which passes nearby). About half the rooms have *en-suite* bathrooms, some have sun terraces, and there's a TV lounge and small communal kitchen. Three-night minimum stay.

**Imperial Hotel** ( ☎ 21 344 093; www.imperialhotelmalta.com; Triq Rudolfu, Sliema; s/d low season Lm11/16, high season Lm18/30; ▨ ▩ ) The Imperial is tucked away in the heart of Sliema, and once inside you'll be impressed with the grand decor in the lobby. The rooms don't quite live up to the high standards set downstairs, but they're clean, comfortable and well-equipped (you'll pay more for a garden/pool view and a balcony). Extras include pool, courtyard garden and restaurant. There's good wheelchair access.

**Carlton Hotel** ( ☎ 21 315 764; Triq it-Torri, Sliema; s/d low season Lm10/15, high season Lm19/26; ▨ ▣ ▩ ) At the western edge of Sliema, not far from the restaurants of Balluta Bay, the Carlton has good-value rooms, small but neat and

# VALLETTA, SLIEMA, ST JULIAN'S & FLORIANA

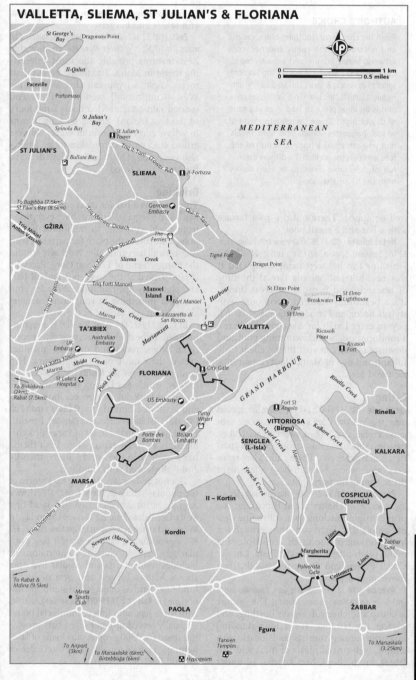

**MALTA**

**AUTHOR'S CHOICE**

From the chic décor (soothing blues, greens and neutrals) to the comfy couches, cool artwork, water feature and smooth tunes, **Café Juliani** ( ☎ 21 377 888; 12 Triq San Ġorġ, Spinola Bay; snacks & meals Lm1.60-3.50; ✢ until midnight Sun-Thu, until 2am Fri & Sat) oozes style and is an ideal place to stop in at any time of day or night. There's a modern menu of wraps, baguettes, salads and light meals, and you can enjoy a huge selection of coffees and teas (or cocktails), a display cabinet full of delectable desserts, or even dainty high tea of an afternoon.

well-equipped. There's also a roof terrace with a bar and a small pool.

**Hotel Juliani** ( ☎ 21 380 000; www.hoteljuliani.com; 12 Triq San Ġorġ, Spinola Bay; r from Lm55; ✖ ☐ ☎ ) Finishing touches were being completed at this new hotel at Spinola Bay at the time of research, and it promises great things. It's a beautifully restored townhouse with stylish décor and modern facilities (you'll pay an extra Lm10 for a sea view). There's a rooftop sundeck and swimming pool, and downstairs you can visit the excellent Café Juliani, and two of Malta's best restaurants, Zest and Mezè.

## Eating

**Cara's Café** ( ☎ 21 343 432; 249 Triq it-Torri, Sliema; snacks under Lm1; ✢ 9-1am) Cara's is a popular café with good coffee and lots of sweet treats (cakes, pastries, sundaes), plus savoury snacks (*pastizzi*, sandwiches etc). There's also a large outdoor area, where you can have a late-night drink among the fairy lights.

**Papparazzi** ( ☎ 21 374 966; Triq San Ġorġ, Spinola Bay; mains Lm3-4) The terrace at Papparazzi is a prime people-watching spot, with a fine view of Spinola Bay. Fight your way through the huge portions on the kitsch, crowd-pleasing menu (with titles like Fork It Pasta, Cheeky Chick Burger and Octopussy Salad), then move on to dessert.

**Avenue** ( ☎ 21 311 753; Triq Gort, Paceville; mains Lm1-5; ✢ lunch Mon-Sat, dinner nightly) The Avenue is cheap and cheerful, always bustling, and perfect for families. It's a long-standing favourite among tourists and locals, with simple, well-priced meals of meat and fish (steak, lamb chops, beef kebabs, all under

Lm5) plus huge portions of pizza and pasta, and salads and burgers.

**Zest** ( ☎ 21 387 600; 12 Triq San Ġorġ, Spinola Bay; mains Lm3-7.50; ✢ dinner Mon-Sat) Fashionable Zest features possibly the most interesting menu in Malta. The theme here is 'East meets West', so you can choose from the West (Continental) section of the menu (seared salmon, pan-fried duck, lamb loin), or the East (Asian) section: try king prawns in yellow curry and coconut sauce, Balinese grilled chicken or curry laksa soup. There's also a selection of sushi, and fabulous desserts. Bookings are advised.

## Drinking

This area has a bar for everyone. The St Julian's and Sliema waterfronts have everything from posh wine bars to traditional British pubs. Paceville is the place for partying, with wall-to-wall bars and clubs, especially around the northern end of Triq San Ġorġ. Paceville is jam-packed at the weekends and all bars and clubs stay open until late. Wander until you find something to your taste (or quiet enough that you can get in the door).

**BJ's** ( ☎ 21 337 642; Triq Ball, Paceville) is a recommended offbeat club featuring live music (jazz, blues, rock) and drawing an older crowd than most of its neighbours. Hip young things opt for **Misfits** ( ☎ 21 361 766; Triq Paceville), which has DJs on weekends but is more laid-back during the week, hosting jazz and art-house film nights. **O'Casey's Irish Pub** ( ☎ 21 373 900; Triq ix-Xatt San Ġorġ, Paceville), beneath Hotel Bernard in the heart of Paceville's clubland, is as you'd expect of an Irish theme bar anywhere in the world – lively, friendly and well stocked with Guinness.

Get hot and sweaty dancing up a storm at the popular salsa bar, **Fuego** ( ☎ 21 373 211; www .fuego.com.mt; Triq Santu Wistin, Paceville) – head first to its free salsa dancing classes (Monday to Wednesday from 8.30pm). **Pips Club** ( ☎ 21 373 957; www.pips.com.mt; Triq Wilga, Paceville) is a popular gay bar and club, and entertainment includes resident DJs and regular live drag shows. Malta's biggest and best nightclub (and one that has managed to stand the test of time) is **Axis** ( ☎ 21 318 078; Triq San Ġorġ, Paceville) with three separate clubs (commercial house is usually served up) and seven bars providing space for 3500 people, plus loads of laser lighting. There's usually an entrance fee of around Lm2.50.

## Getting There & Away

Bus Nos 62, 64 and 67 run regularly between Valletta and Sliema, St Julian's and Paceville. The useful **Marsamxetto ferry service** ( ☎ 21 338 981) crosses frequently between Sliema and Valletta, taking five minutes and costing Lm0.35 each way. Boats operate from 8am to 6pm. Arrival and departure points are at the Strand in Sliema and at the end of Triq San Marku in northwest Valletta.

## MDINA & RABAT

Elegant, aristocratic Mdina, once the capital of Malta, is perched on a rocky outcrop in the southwest of Malta. Thanks to its geographical attributes, it has been a fortified city for over 3000 years and was the island's political centre before the Knights arrived and chose to settle around Grand Harbour. You can spend hours wandering around the quiet, narrow streets of the affectionately nicknamed Silent City. Despite the small honeypots of tourist bustle that have inevitably developed, the city has retained its historical charm.

The name Mdina comes from the Arabic term for 'walled city'. Rabat is the sprawling town settlement outside the walls to Mdina's south.

### Sights

Mdina's main square is dominated by **St Paul's Cathedral** (Pjazza San Pawl; admission free, donations welcome; ✆ 9.30-11.45am & 2-5pm Mon-Sat, 3-4.30pm Sun). It's not as impressive as St John's in Valletta but still worth visiting to see the marble tombstones covering the floor and the huge fresco of St Paul's Shipwreck. The **Cathedral Museum** ( ☎ 21 454 697; Pjazza San Pawl; adult/child Lm1/free; ✆ 10am-5.15pm Mon-Fri, 10am-3.15pm Sat), opposite, is housed in a baroque 18th-century palace originally used as a seminary. It contains collections of coins, silver, vestments, manuscripts and religious paintings.

The **Mdina Experience** ( ☎ 21 454 322; Misrah Mesquita; adult/child Lm1.60/0.80; ✆ 10.30am-4pm Mon-Fri, 10.30am-2pm Sat) is a worthwhile 25-minute audiovisual show encompassing the history of Mdina.

Head south from Mdina to Rabat, where you can visit **St Paul's Church** and **St Paul's Grotto** (Misrah il Parroċċa; admission free, donations welcome; ✆ 10am-5pm Mon-Sat). The grotto is a cave where St Paul is said to have preached during his stay on the island. Further down

the road you'll come across **St Paul's Catacombs**, a series of rock-cut tombs thought to date back to the 3rd century. Far more interesting are the nearby **St Agatha's Crypt & Catacombs** ( ☎ 21 454 503; Triq Sant'Agata; adult/child Lm0.75/free; ✆ 9am-5pm Mon-Fri, 9am-1pm Sat Jul-Sep, 9am-noon & 1-4.30pm Mon-Fri, 9am-12.30pm Sat Oct-Jun), an underground complex of burial chambers boasting some amazing Byzantine frescoes. Wait by the entrance to the museum for the next guided tour.

### Sleeping & Eating

**University Residence** ( ☎ 21 436 168, 21 430 360; www.university-residence.com.mt; Triq R M Bonnici, Lija; dm low/high season from Lm3.20/5.50; 🖳 🖭 ) The official student residence for the University of Malta is in Lija, about 5km northeast of Rabat. It's a well-equipped and well-run facility, and a good place to meet travellers and students. There's a swimming pool, large grounds, a mini-market, café and laundrette. There's a three-night minimum on stays, and a variety of accommodation available (including hotel-standard rooms; see the website). To get here, catch bus No 40 from Valletta.

**Point de Vue Guesthouse & Restaurant** ( ☎ 21 454 117; http://mol.net.mt/point; 5 Is-Saqqajja; B&B per person Lm7-8) Just outside Mdina's Main Gate is this affordable guesthouse, with simple but comfortable rooms (with private bath). Book ahead.

**Fontanella Tea Gardens** ( ☎ 21 454 264; Triq is-Sur; snacks & meals Lm0.50-3; ✆ 10am-7pm winter, 10am-11pm summer) Enjoy a relaxing lunch or afternoon drink at this wonderful setting on top of the city walls. Fontanella serves home-baked cakes (Lm0.70 per piece), sandwiches and light meals, and you'll have ample time to admire the sweeping views from its terrace. Service is ordinary.

**Medina** ( ☎ 21 454 004; 7 Triq is-Salib Imqaddes; mains Lm3-8; ✆ dinner Mon-Sat) One of Malta's most romantic venues – a medieval townhouse with vaulted ceilings and fireplaces for cooler evenings, and an attractive garden-courtyard for alfresco dining in warmer months. The menu offers a mix of Maltese, Italian and French dishes, with good vegetarian selections.

### Getting There & Away

From Valletta, take bus No 80 or 81 to reach Rabat; from Sliema and St Julian's No 65.

The bus terminus in Rabat is on Is-Saqqajja, 150m south of Mdina's Main Gate.

## SOUTHWEST COAST

The views are fantastic from the top of **Dingli Cliffs**, south of Rabat. While you're here, stop by **Bobbyland Restaurant** ( ☎ 21 452 895; mains Lm4-7; ✆ closed lunch Sat, dinner Sun & all day Mon), a favourite weekend venue for locals. It's regularly crowded with diners munching contentedly on house specialities like rabbit or lamb.

To the southeast, you'll find the village of Qrendi and the nearby prehistoric temples of **Ħaġar Qim** ( ☎ 21 424 231; adult/child Lm1/free; ✆ 7.45am-2pm mid-Jun–Sep, 8.15am-5pm Mon-Sat & 8.15am-4pm Sun Oct–mid-Jun) and **Mnajdra** (adult/child Lm1/free; ✆ 7.45am-2pm mid-Jun–Sep, 8.15am-5pm Mon-Sat & 8.15am-4pm Sun Oct–mid-Jun). Built between 3600 BC and 3000 BC, these are perhaps the best preserved and most evocative of Malta's prehistoric sites. Bus Nos 38 and 138 run from Valletta to the temples (Lm0.40).

While you're out this way, call in to **Għar Lapsi**, a cove in the low cliffs that's a popular spot among locals for bathing and picnicking. To sate a swimmer's hunger, there are two restaurants above the cove. No buses run to Għar Lapsi.

## SOUTHEAST COAST

**Marsaxlokk** is a small fishing village and a charming place to spend a couple of hours. The harbour is crammed with colourful fishing boats and there are many good fish restaurants where you can sample the local fare. Bus No 27 runs every half-hour from Valletta to Marsaxlokk from around 6.30am to 9pm (services are more frequent on Sunday morning for the weekly fish market). Tickets cost Lm0.15. Bus No 627 runs hourly until 3pm from Buġibba via Sliema to Marsaxlokk (Lm0.40).

## NORTH COAST

**Buġibba** in the northeast is Malta's largest resort but it could just as easily be called 'Package Resort Central'. Crammed full of hotels, bars and restaurants, it gets bombarded by tourists in summer. It's fine if you want a couple of weeks of pure hedonism, but there are nicer places to plump for with lots more to offer. Bus Nos 49 and 58 run frequently between Valletta and Buġibba (Lm0.15).

The north is also home to a handful of excellent beaches. Beachbums should make a beeline for **Mellieħa Bay** if you like your facilities and watersports laid on thick, or **Għajn Tuffieħa Bay** or **Għejna Bay** if you're after something more low-key. **Golden Bay** offers a choice midway between those two extremes. Bus No 47 from Valletta runs to Golden Bay and Għajn Tuffieħa Bay (Lm0.15).

# GOZO

The island of Gozo is much smaller and quieter than Malta and life slips by here at a slower pace. Fewer tourists venture over to Gozo and if they do, it is often on a day trip. The sights can be packed into one day but we recommend spending several days here – traipse round the sights, visit the beaches, take a boat trip, or simply relax.

Gozo is an excellent place for diving (p588) and there are several dive operators dotted around the island. You can also take a cruise from resorts such as Marsalforn and Xlendi; this is the best way to enjoy the breathtaking coastline and see features such as the Azure Window and the Inland Sea at Dwejra on the west coast.

## VICTORIA (RABAT)

Victoria, also known as Rabat, is the chief town of Gozo and sits in the centre of the island, 6km from the ferry terminal at Mġarr. Victoria's main attraction is the compact and photogenic Citadel, with its cathedral and museums.

### Information

**Bank of Valletta** (Triq ir-Repubblika)
**Internet House** (44 Triq L'Assunta) Internet access plus printing and scanning facilities.
**Police Station** ( ☎ 21 562 040; Triq ir-Repubblika)
**Post Office** (Triq ir-Repubblika)
**Tourist Information Office** ( ☎ 21 561 419; Tigrija Palazz; cnr Triq ir-Reppublika & Triq Putirjal; ✆ 9am-12.30pm & 1-5pm Mon-Sat, 9am-12.30pm Sun & public holidays) On the ground floor of a shopping arcade, not far from the bus station.
**Travelex** (cnr Triq ir-Repubblika & Telgħa Tal-Belt) Currency exchange bureau.

### Sights

**Pjazza Indipendenza**, the main square of Victoria, is a hive of activity with open-air cafés, treasure-trove craft shops and traders peddling their fresh produce.

Victoria is built on a hill, crowned by the **Citadel** (also known as Il-Kastell, or Citadella), a miniature version of Malta's Mdina. A stroll around the Citadel offers breathtaking views across the island. The **Cathedral of the Assumption** (Misraħ il-Katidral; Lm0.25; 9am-4.30pm Mon-Sat) was built between 1697 and 1711. Its elegant design is marred only by the fact that funds ran out before completion and the structure remained flat-topped. This cannot be detected from inside due to an elaborate trompe l'oeil painted on the ceiling. The illusion is impressive.

The handful of small **museums** inside the Citadel display reasonable collections, but if you're pushed for time, don't feel like you've missed out – the museums in Valletta are much better. But make time to stop in at **Ta'Ricardo** ( 21 555 953; 4 Triq il-Fossos; 10am-6pm), where you can pick up souvenirs as well as flavoursome local produce. Take a seat and order a platter (Lm3 for two people), which includes cheese, bread, tomatoes, capers and olives. Wash it all down with a glass or two of Gozitan wine.

## Getting There & Away

See p592 for details of ferry services between Malta and Gozo.

Gozo's central bus station is on Triq Putirjal in Victoria, just south of Triq ir-Repubblika and about 10 minutes' walk from the Citadel. All the island's bus routes are circular, starting and finishing at Victoria; the flat fare is Lm0.15.

## MARSALFORN

Marsalforn is built around a cove and, with its good facilities, is the favoured choice for tourists in the summer months. There is nothing to see in the town itself. At the head of the bay is a tiny scrap of sand; better swimming and sunbathing can be found on the rocks out to the west. Hike eastward over the hill to Ramla Bay in about 45 minutes.

### Sleeping & Eating

**Calypso Hotel** ( 21 562 000; www.hotelcalypsogozo.com; Triq il-Port; s/d low season from Lm15/21, high season from Lm23/33; ) After closing for two years for renovations and refurbishment, the Calypso now boasts fresh, stylish décor and modernised facilities. Guests can take ad-

**AUTHOR'S CHOICE**

**Maria-Giovanna Hostel** ( 21 553 630; www.gozohostels.com; Triq ir-Rabat; B&B per person low/high season Lm4/7) The pick of the budget accommodation on Gozo is this small guesthouse just back from the beach in Marsalforn. There are five rooms (two with *en-suite*) with pretty, rustic décor, plus a living room and guest kitchen. Advance bookings are suggested, especially for the high season.

vantage of two excellent on-site restaurants and a cool café, plus a pool, bar and sun terrace on the roof. Sea-view rooms cost an additional Lm3 per person.

**Il-Kartell** ( 21 556 918; Triq il-Port; mains Lm4-5.50; lunch & dinner Thu-Tue) Sit by the water or inside the atmospheric dining area at this laid-back place, housed in a couple of old boathouses in the southwest corner of the bay. The menu includes pasta dishes around the Lm2 mark, along with fresh fish, traditional dishes and daily specials.

**Ritz** ( 21 558 392; Triq il-Wied) is a cheap-and-cheerful café-bar selling snacks and sandwiches to quickly settle a rumbling tum. Fashionable **Caffino**, at the Calypso Hotel, is actually a far ritzier option, with savoury snacks and mouthwatering cakes (Lm0.60 to Lm0.95 each).

### Getting There & Away

Marsalforn is a 4km walk from Victoria, or you can catch bus No 21.

## XAGĦRA

The early-19th-century **Church of Our Lady of Victory** looks down on the tree-lined village square of Xagħra, where old men sit and chat in the shade of the oleanders.

Close by are the megalithic temples of **Ġgantija** ( 21 553 194; access from Triq L-Imqades; adult/child Lm1/free; 8.30am-4.30pm Mon-Sat, 8.30am-3pm Sun), with a splendid view over most of southern Gozo and beyond. As the name implies (*ġgantija*, pronounced dje-*gant*-ee-ya, means giantess), these are the largest of the megalithic temples found in the Maltese Islands – the walls stand over 6m high, and together the two temples are 40m wide.

It's not far from here to one of the best beaches on Gozo. **Ramla Bay** has a beautiful

MALTA

sandy beach that is perfect for sunbathing. It gets crowded in summer so you'll need to get here early to get a good spot. Follow the signposts from town.

### Sleeping & Eating

**Xagħra Lodge** ( ☎ 21 562 362; www.gozo.com/xaghra lodge; Triq Dun Gorġ Preca; s/d low season Lm16/21, high season Lm19/25; ✗ ➜ ) This is a cosy guesthouse run by a friendly English couple. There are excellent facilities for the price, including air-con, *en-suite*, balcony and cable TV in all rooms, plus swimming pool, terrace and an adjacent bar and Chinese restaurant. It's a five-minute walk east of the town square.

**Oleander** ( ☎ 21 557 230; Pjazza Vittorija; mains Lm3.50-6; ✆ lunch & dinner Tue-Sun) On the pretty village square, the popular Oleander has a menu of well-prepared local favourites (pastas, *braġioli*, rabbit, fresh fish, local lamb) and regulars rave over the rabbit dishes. It's a pleasant place to while away an evening.

### Getting There & Away

Bus Nos 64 and 65 run between Victoria and Xagħra.

# COMINO

While visiting Malta or Gozo, hop across to the neighbouring island of Comino, once reportedly the hideout of pirates and smugglers but now host to boatloads of bikini-clad invaders. Being only 2.5km by 1.5km in size it is impossible to get lost here; you can hike around the whole of Comino in an hour or two.

The island's biggest attraction is the **Blue Lagoon**, a sheltered, photogenic cove between the west end of the island and the uninhabited islet of Cominotto, with a white-sand sea-bed and clear turquoise waters. In summer the bay is inundated with people, and there is excellent swimming and snorkelling. Take care in the summer heat – there is no shade, and most sunbathing is done on the rocky ledges surrounding the cove, so bring a hat and heavy-duty sunscreen. There are public toilets, and a few kiosks selling drinks and snacks.

**Comino Hotel & Bungalows** ( ☎ 21 529 821; www .cominohotels.com; half-board per person Lm17-28; ✆ Apr-Oct; ✗ 🖵 ➜ ) is the only place to stay on the island, with bright but simply furnished

rooms, a restaurant, café and bar, private beach, swimming pools and tennis courts. Guests can also pay for bike rental, boat excursions, water-skiing, dive instruction and other watersports facilities.

The Comino Hotel runs its own ferry service, with around seven crossings a day from Ċirkewwa in Malta and Mġarr in Gozo. The ferry can be used by nonresidents of the hotel at a cost of Lm3.50 return (the boats don't run from November to March when the hotel is closed). You can also make a day trip to the Blue Lagoon from tourist areas like Sliema and Buġibba in Malta, and Xlendi in Gozo.

# MALTA DIRECTORY

## ACCOMMODATION

Accommodation in Malta is plentiful and the **Malta Tourism Authority** (www.visitmalta.com) can provide listings. Camping is not permitted.

The **National Student Travel Service** (NSTS; ☎ 21 244 983; www.nsts.org; 220 Triq San Pawl, Valletta) is an associate member of Hostelling International (HI). It runs a few hostels in Malta and also has agreements with certain guesthouses to provide cheap accommodation to hostellers. An HI-membership card is required in order to stay at any of these hostels; cards can be obtained from the NSTS or from the main hostel, Hibernia Residence & Hostel (p582). The NSTS also offers a special week-long hostelling package, which includes airport welcome and transfers, seven overnight stays (with breakfast) and a week's bus pass, for €140 (approx Lm60) per person from October to June, and €170 (approx Lm72) from July to September. These prices are for accommodation in dorms (extra charges apply for rooms with two beds).

Hotels in Malta range from crumbling but characterful old townhouses to modern gilt-and-chrome palaces of five-star luxury overlooking a private marina. Most places offer significantly reduced rates during off-peak periods for stays of more than one night. The high season is generally June to September, as well as the Christmas–New Year period.

## ACTIVITIES

The website of the **Malta Tourism Authority** (www .visitmalta.com) has information on the different activities possible in Malta, and organisations that can help you pursue them. Click onto the 'What to Do' pages.

## Diving

Water babies are well catered for in Malta. Diving conditions are excellent: visibility often exceeds 30m and there's a huge variety of marine life. The warm temperatures of the Mediterranean (with highs of 25°C in summer, falling only to 14°C in the winter) mean that diving is possible year-round. Favourite dive spots include Ċirkewwa on Malta and Dwejra on Gozo.

There are more than 30 diving schools to choose from. The majority are members of the **Professional Diving Schools Association** (PDSA; www.digigate.net/divers; 1 Msida Court, 61 ix-Xatt Ta-Msida, Msida). See also www.visitmalta.com/en /diving for comprehensive details of dive sites, regulations and operators.

Most schools offer a 'taster course' or 'beginner's dive' costing around Lm15. A so-called 'resort course' gives you shore-based instruction plus four to six open water dives accompanied by an instructor, and costs around Lm40 to Lm70. A course that will give you an entry-level diving qualification (CMAS One-Star Diver, PADI Open Water Diver, BSAC Ocean Diver) should take four or five days and cost around Lm130.

All divers must provide a medical certificate from either their own doctor or a local doctor (Lm3 to Lm5, arranged through dive centres). The minimum age for diving is 14 years. If you plan to dive, make sure your travel insurance covers this – some policies specifically exclude 'dangerous activities', which can include scuba-diving.

### Swimming & Sunbathing

The best sandy beaches on Malta are Ġnejna Bay; Għajn Tuffieħa Bay and Golden Bay, all in Malta's northwest (bus No 47 from Valletta, Nos 51 and 652 from Buġibba, and No 652 from Sliema), and Mellieħa Bay in the north (bus Nos 44, 45 and 48). The best sandy beaches on Gozo are Ramla Bay (bus No 42) and Xlendi Bay (bus No 87).

There are also some excellent rocky swimming spots on Comino (the Blue Lagoon) and in Malta's south (Għar Lapsi and Peter's Pool near Marsaxlokk). Gozo has some good rocky sites too, including Dwejra in the west, Wied il-Għasri in the north and San Blas in the northeast. Don't expect to have any

of these to yourself in high season – and remember the sunscreen and snorkel!

## BUSINESS HOURS

Banks are generally open from 8.30am to 12.30pm Monday to Friday and from 8.30am to 11.30am Saturday; they have slightly longer hours from June to September.

Government museums in Malta open from 8.15am to 5pm Monday to Saturday, 8.15am to 4.15pm Sunday 1 October to 15 June; and 7.45am to 2pm daily from 16 June to 30 September (closed public holidays). Government museums in Gozo open from 8.30am to 4.30pm Monday to Saturday, and 8.30am to 3pm Sunday (closed public holidays).

Restaurants generally open from noon to 3pm and 7pm to 11pm

Shops generally open from 9am to 1pm and 4pm to 7pm Monday to Saturday (sometimes all day during summer, especially in tourist areas). Shops are closed Sundays and public holidays.

## COURSES

Malta is one of the few places where people wanting to learn or improve their English can combine a language course with a Mediterranean holiday. There are around 40 English-language schools, and together they cater to around 40,000 students a year. Sliema and St Julian's have the greatest concentration of schools. Full details of courses can be obtained from the **Malta Tourism Authority** (www.visitmalta.com); the website has loads of information in various languages and a full list of schools.

## CUSTOMS

Items for personal use are not subject to duty. The duty-free allowance per person is 1L of spirits, 1L of wine and 200 cigarettes. Duty will be charged on any gifts over Lm50 intended for local residents.

## DANGERS & ANNOYANCES

Malta is pretty much crime-free but normal precautions should be taken.

Taxi drivers will often try and overcharge unsuspecting tourists so make sure you agree on a reasonable price before you get into the vehicle. On arrival at the airport, ignore any taxi driver that tells you that the bus stop is miles away – they're just touting for business.

**MALTA**

Most towns and villages are well served by buses and are only a short (and cheap) ride from one another. If you're driving around, you'll notice that much of the road network is badly in need of repair, and rules of the road are rarely observed – take care!

If you go walking in the countryside, beware of the national obsession with shooting and trapping birds – the little stone shacks that pepper the clifftops are shooters' hides. You will hear the popping of shotguns before you see the shooters (and they are not welcoming).

## ELECTRICITY

Unlike most of Mediterranean Europe, Malta's electricity supply is 240V/50Hz and the plugs have three flat pins as in the UK. Continental European appliances (plugs with two round pins) will need an adaptor.

## EMBASSIES & CONSULATES
### Maltese Embassies & Consulates

Diplomatic representation abroad includes:

**Australia** ( ☎ 02-6290 1724; maltahc@bigpond.com; 38 Culgoa Circuit, O'Malley ACT 2606)

**France** ( ☎ 01 56 59 75 90; fax 01 45 62 00 36; 92 Ave des Champs Elysées, 75008 Paris)

**Germany** ( ☎ 030-26 39 110; maltaembgrm@ndh.net; Tiergarten Dreieck, Block 4, Klingelhöferstrasse 7, 10785 Berlin)

**Italy** ( ☎ 06-687 99 90; maltaembassy.rome@gov.mt; 12 Lungotevere Marzio, 00186 Rome)

**Netherlands** ( ☎ 070-356 1252; malta.embassy@planet.nl; 2 Scheveningensweg, 2517 KT, The Hague)

**Tunisia** ( ☎ 071-847 048; ambassade.malte@planet.tn; 5 Rue Achart, Nord Hilton, 1082 Tunis)

**UK** ( ☎ 020-7292 4800; maltahighcommission.london@gov.mt; Malta House, 36-38 Piccadilly, London W1J 0LE)

**USA** ( ☎ 202-462 3611/2; malta_embassy@compuserve.com; 2017 Connecticut Ave NW, Washington DC 20008)

### Embassies & Consulates in Malta

Countries with representation in Malta include:

**Australia** ( ☎ 21 338 201; Villa Fiorentina, Rampa Ta'Xbiex, Ta'Xbiex)

**Canada** ( ☎ 21 233 121; 103 Triq I-Arċisqof, Valletta)

**France** ( ☎ 21 233 430; 130 Triq Melita, Valletta)

**Germany** ( ☎ 21 336 531; Il-Piazzetta, Entrance B, 1st fl, Triq it-Torri, Sliema)

**Italy** ( ☎ 21 233 157/8/9; 1 Triq Vilhena, Floriana)

**Netherlands** ( ☎ 25 691 790; 19 Triq San Zakkarija, Valletta)

**Tunisia** ( ☎ 21 417 171; Valletta Rd, Attard)

**UK** ( ☎ 23 230 000; Whitehall Mansions, Xatt Ta'Xbiex, Ta'Xbiex)

**USA** ( ☎ 21 235 960; 3rd fl, Development House, Triq Sant'Anna, Floriana)

## FESTIVALS & EVENTS

Each village has a *festa* (feast day) honouring their patron saint. You can't avoid getting caught up in the excitement as the whole community gets involved in the celebrations. Religious enthusiasm is apparent in the days leading up to and during the *festa* as families flock to the churches to give thanks. The streets are illuminated with thousands of lights and the festivities culminate in a huge procession. There are fireworks, marching brass bands and the villagers pay homage to a life-size statue of their patron saint. *Festa* season runs from June to September; the local tourist offices should be able to tell you when and where festas are being held during your stay, or a good idea is to download info before your travel – go to www.maltachurch.org.mt, then click on Feast Days.

But *festas* aren't the only excuse to throw a party in Malta, and the website of the **Malta Tourism Authority** (www.visitmalta.com/en/whats_on) has a comprehensive list of what's on, where and when.

## GAY & LESBIAN TRAVELLERS

Homosexual sex was legalised in Malta in 1973. Attitudes towards homosexuality are much the same as in most of southern Europe; remember that this is a Catholic country, and public displays of affection are generally frowned upon. Still, although Malta is not a very 'out' destination, it is gay-friendly. Find out more about the local scene by checking these websites: www.gaymalta.org, www.maltagayrights.org and www.gayroom.co.uk.

## HOLIDAYS

**New Year's Day** 1 January
**St Paul's Shipwreck** 10 February
**St Joseph's Day** 19 March
**Good Friday** March/April
**Freedom Day** 31 March
**Labour Day** 1 May
**Commemoration of 1919 independence riots** 7 June
**Feast of Sts Peter and Paul (L-Imnarja Festival)** 29 June
**Feast of the Assumption** 15 August
**Victory Day** 8 September

**Independence Day** 21 September
**Feast of the Immaculate Conception** 8 December
**Republic Day** 13 December
**Christmas Day** 25 December

## INTERNET ACCESS

Malta is a well-wired destination. There are numerous Internet cafés and more are springing up, while many hotels have at least one computer available for guest use. Rates vary, but typical hourly charges for Internet access are Lm1 to Lm1.50. Many computers belong to the **MelitaNet** (www.melita.net) or **Yellow Blue** (www.yellowblue.net) networks of machines for public use – if you purchase a voucher for one network, you receive a password allowing the voucher to be used at any of their computers throughout Malta. The websites for each network list computer locations.

## INTERNET RESOURCES

**About Malta** (www.aboutmalta.com) Directory of Malta sites.
**Gozo** (www.gozo.com) Gozo-specific travel information.
**Malta Tourism Authority** (www.visitmalta.com) Huge official site.
**Maltese Islands** (www.malteseislands.com) Extensive travel information.
**Search Malta** (www.searchmalta.com) Directory of links to Malta-related websites.
**StarWeb Malta** (www.starwebmalta.com) Malta's 'first on-line concierge' with great listings.

## MONEY

The Maltese lira (Lm), plural liri, is divided into 100 cents (c). The currency is often referred to as the pound, and a £ symbol is sometimes used.

Banks usually offer better rates of exchange than hotels. There is a 24-hour exchange bureau at the airport. Travellers arriving by ferry should note that there are no exchange facilities at the port. ATMs can be found in most towns and tourist areas.

Restaurants and taxis expect a 10% tip. Shops have fixed prices, but hotels and car-hire agencies offer reduced rates in the low season (October to May).

## TELEPHONE

Public telephones (mostly card-operated) are widely available. You can buy phonecards at many kiosks, post offices and souvenir shops. Local calls cost Lm0.10. International calls are discounted between 6pm and 8am weekdays and all day Saturday and Sunday. For local telephone inquiries, call ☎ 1182; for overseas inquiries, call ☎ 1152.

The international direct dialling code is ☎ 00. To call Malta from abroad, dial the international access code, ☎ 356 (the country code for Malta) and the eight-digit number (there are no area codes in Malta). Some 70% of Malta's population has a mobile (cell) phone, and mobile phone numbers begin with either 79 or 99.

## TOURIST INFORMATION

Your best source of planning information is the comprehensive website of the **Malta Tourism Authority** (www.visitmalta.com). There are local tourist information offices at Valletta, Malta International Airport, St Julian's, Victoria on Gozo and Mġarr Harbour, Gozo (where the ferry from Malta docks).

## VISAS

Visas are not needed for visits of up to three months by nationals of most Commonwealth countries (excluding South Africa, India and Pakistan), most European countries, the USA and Japan. A list of countries whose nationals don't need a visa is at www.foreign.gov.mt/service/visa/reqs4foreigners.htm.

Other nationalities must apply for a visa; details (and application forms) are on the website of Malta's **Ministry of Foreign Affairs** (www.foreign.gov.mt/service/visa).

## WOMEN TRAVELLERS

Malta remains a conservative society by Western standards. Men are friendly towards female travellers and rarely threatening or imposing. Normal caution should be observed but problems are unlikely.

# TRANSPORT IN MALTA

## GETTING THERE & AWAY

### Air

Malta is well connected to Europe and North Africa. Pick up a cheap charter flight from the UK. All flights arrive at and depart from **Malta International Airport** (code MLA; ☎ 21 249 600; www.maltairport.com) at Luqa, 8km south of Valletta. The airport has good facilities, including ATMs and

**DEPARTURE TAX**

All passengers leaving Malta by sea are required to pay a Lm6 departure tax, which should be added by the travel agent when you buy your ticket.

currency exchange, a tourist office, left luggage, and a cheap bus service to and from Valletta. Gozo has a **heliport** (code GAM; ☎ 21 557 905) with a helicopter link to Luqa (p593).

The Maltese national airline is **Air Malta** (code KM; ☎ 21 662 211; www.airmalta.com; Misrah il-Helsien, near the tourist information office), with a good safety record (no crashes or fatalities) and numerous overseas offices.

Airlines flying to and from Malta include:

**Aeroflot** (code SU; ☎ 21 314 134; www.aeroflotmalta .com) Hub in Moscow.

**Alitalia** (code AZ; ☎ 21 237 115; www.alitalia.com) Hub in Rome.

**British Airways** (code BA; ☎ 21 242 233; www.ba.com) Hub in London.

**Egyptair** (code MS; ☎ 21 322 256; www.egyptair.com .eg) Hub in Cairo.

**Emirates** (code EK; ☎ 23 696 455; www.emirates.com) Hub in Dubai.

**JAT Yugoslav Airlines** (code JU; ☎ 21 332 814; www .jat.com) Hub in Belgrade.

**KLM Royal Dutch Airlines** (code KL; ☎ 21 342 472; www.klm.com) Hub in Amsterdam.

**Libyan Arab Airlines** (code LN; ☎ 21 222 735) Hub in Tripoli.

**Lufthansa** (code LH; ☎ 21 252 020; www.lufthansa .com) Hub in Frankfurt.

**Snowflake** (code SK; www.flysnowflake.com) Hubs in Stockholm & Copenhagen.

**Swiss International Air Lines** (code LX; ☎ 21 802 777; www.swiss.com) Hub in Geneva/Zürich.

**Tuninter** (code UG; ☎ 21 320 732) Hub in Tunis.

## Sea

Malta has regular sea links with Sicily (Pozzallo and Catania), southern Italy (Reggio di Calabria and Salerno) and northern Italy (Genoa). Cars may be brought by ferry and may be imported for up to three months. Malta's ferry terminal is on Pinto Wharf in Floriana, southwest of Valletta.

The Italy–Malta ferry schedules change frequently, so it's best to confirm information with a travel agent such as **SMS Travel & Tourism** ( ☎ 21 232 211; www.smstravel.net; 311 Triq ir-Repubblika, Valletta).

**Virtu Ferries** (www.virtuferries.com; Malta ☎ 21 318 854; Catania ☎ 095-535 711; Pozzallo ☎ 0932-954 062) offer the shortest and fastest Malta–Italy crossing with its catamaran service (carrying cars and passengers) to/from Pozzallo and Catania (in Sicily). The Pozzallo–Malta crossing takes only 90 minutes and operates year-round. Fares one way/return from Pozzallo are €70/86, one way/return from Malta Lm24/36.

**Ma.Re.Si Shipping** ( ☎ 21 233 129; www.sms.com .mt/maresi.htm) has a ferry making weekly trips year-round between Catania and Malta (Lm20/35 one way/return, 12 hours) and also between Malta and Reggio di Calabria (Lm25/45 one way/return, 15 hours).

**Grimaldi Ferries** ( ☎ 21 226 873; www.grimaldi -ferries.com) operate a weekly service year-round between Malta and Salerno, south of Naples (cabin berth from €93, 19 hours). From Salerno, it is possible to sail on to Valencia in southern Spain. **Grandi Navi Veloci** ( ☎ 21 334 023; www.gnv.it/tunisia.asp) has a twice-weekly service between Genoa and Tunis that calls in at Malta. You can sail directly from Tunis to Malta, but there is no direct service from Malta to Tunis.

It is important to note that ferries do not have exchange facilities and there are none at Malta's ferry terminal in Floriana. Nor is there any public transport the 500m from the ferry terminal on Pinto Quay up to the city of Valletta – you can either catch a taxi or make the steep 15-minute climb; if you decide to walk it's best to follow the waterfront northeast, under the Lascaris Bastion, then veer left and climb the steps up at Victoria Gate.

## Tours

There are lots of companies offering tours around the islands. Half-day tours cost around Lm5 but prices vary so shop around. If you're pushed for time they can be a good way to see the highlights but itineraries can often be rushed with little or no free time. Day trips to Gozo and Comino are also available.

**Captain Morgan Cruises** ( ☎ 21 343 373; www .captainmorgan.com.mt) runs a range of sailing trips, cruises and jeep safaris, primarily out of Sliema. See p582 for information on harbour tours.

**Virtu Ferries** ( ☎ 21 318 854; www.virtuferries.com) operate day trips to Sicily, travelling on its catamaran services to Pozzallo or Catania then by bus to a few of Sicily's east-coast attractions. The cost is Lm37; you can book a trip through most hotels and travel agents.

# GETTING AROUND
## Bicycle
Cycling on Maltese roads can be nerve-racking. The roads are often narrow and potholed, and drivers show little consideration for cyclists. Things are much better on Gozo – the roads are still rough, but there's far less traffic. You can rent bikes from **Victoria Garage** ( ☎ 21 556 414, 21 553 741; Triq Putirjal, Victoria; bike hire per day Lm1.50-2) on Gozo.

## Boat
**Gozo Channel Company** (www.gozochannel.com; Ċirkewwa ☎ 21 580 435; Mġarr ☎ 21 561 622) runs the regular car ferry services between Ċirkewwa (Malta) and Mġarr (Gozo), with crossings every 45 to 60 minutes from 6am to around 11pm (and every two hours throughout the night from July to September). The journey takes 25 minutes, and the return fare for an adult/child is Lm1.75/0.50, and car/bicycle Lm4/0.50. Bus No 45 runs regularly from Valletta to Ċirkewwa to connect with the ferry to Gozo. Bus No 25 runs between Victoria and Mġarr on Gozo.

There is also a ferry service between Valletta and Sliema (p584).

If you want to explore Malta's coastline at a slower pace, one interesting option is to charter a yacht from **Captain Morgan Yacht Charter** ( ☎ 21 343 373; www.yachtcharter.com.mt).

## Bus
Malta and Gozo are served by a network of buses run by the **Malta Public Transport Authority** (ATP; ☎ 21 250 007/8/9; www.atp.com.mt). Most of Malta's services originate from the chaotic City Gate terminus, just outside Valletta's city gates. The buses are bright yellow and many of them are relics of the 1950s. Fares are inexpensive, ranging from Lm0.15 to Lm0.50 (make sure you have small change for your ticket at the time you're boarding). Services are regular and the more popular routes run until 11pm. Ask at the tourist office or an ATP kiosk for a free timetable.

On Gozo, the bus terminus is in Victoria, just south of Triq ir-Repubblika. All services depart from here and cost Lm0.15.

## Car & Motorcycle
Considering the low rental rates in Malta it may make economic sense to hire a car, but unless you're a pretty confident driver it might not be worth the aggravation. Road rules are often ignored, roads are confusingly signposted and parking can be difficult in some areas. Distance isn't a problem, however – the longest distance on Malta is 27km, and the widest point is around 15km. On Gozo it's half that!

You'll find all the major international car-hire companies at the airport. In addition there are dozens of local agencies. It makes sense to shop around – rates depend on season, length of rental period and the size and make of car. Daily rates for the smallest vehicles start from around Lm6 a day (for rental of seven days or longer), and the next size up starts at Lm8. The age limit for rental drivers is generally 21 to 70, but drivers between 21 and 25 may be asked to pay a supplement.

### ROAD RULES
The Maltese drive on the lefthand side of the road. Speed limits are 80km/h on highways and 50km/h in urban areas, but they are rarely observed. The wearing of seat belts is compulsory for the driver and front-seat passenger. The maximum blood-alcohol concentration level allowed in drivers is 0.08%.

Road conditions are invariably poor with lots of potholes and inadequate markings. There are no right-of-way rules at roundabouts and at intersections priority is given to whoever gets there first. Any accidents must be reported to the nearest police station (and to the rental company if the car is hired) – don't move your vehicle until the police have arrived, otherwise your insurance may be nullified.

## Helicopter
Malta's only internal air service is the regular helicopter link between Malta International Airport and the heliport on Gozo. It's operated by **Malta Aircharter** (MAC; ☎ 21 557 905; mac@airmalta.com.mt; one way/return Lm18/27), and concessions are available.

## Hitching
Hitching is unusual in Malta and is frowned upon.

## Taxi

Official Maltese taxis are white (with a taxi sign on top) and are fitted with meters, though these are rarely switched on. Fares are expensive, and you should establish a price in advance.

Black taxis (no sign on top) are owned by private companies and usually offer cheaper rates than official taxis. To order a taxi by phone, ask at your hotel's reception or try **Wembley Motors** ( ☎ 21 374 141), for 24-hour service.

# Turkey

CONTENTS

Given Turkey's unique position, bridging the vast physical and cultural gap between Europe and Islamic Asia, it's hardly surprising that a unique culture has developed here.

In fact, without Turkey, East might never have met West in the first place – for centuries Istanbul was the seat of Roman, Byzantine and Ottoman empires, exerting influence as far afield as Iran and the Balkans, and a host of familiar figures, from Achilles to St Paul, once strode through these very lands. Hundreds of ancient sites illustrate the triumphs and defeats of some truly epoch-making generations.

Modern Turkey somehow manages to have its cake and eat it, effortlessly handling its many contradictions: secular but Muslim, Mediterranean but not European, rich but under-producing, traditional but ever-modernising. Even sticking to the tourist-swamped riviera regions you'll encounter many different sides to the country, from paragliding one moment to prayer the next, headscarves mingling with halter tops.

Of course, the best way to get to know Turkey is to dive in and make the most of everything it has to offer – swim, sunbathe, sightsee, snorkel, explore, discuss, test, taste and above all, enjoy. Your experiences as a traveller may vary wildly from town to town, but it takes a hard heart to resist the charms of this legendary country and its genuinely friendly people. Take some time and you'll quickly understand why so many visitors never go home…

## FAST FACTS

- **Area** 788,695 sq km
- **Capital** Ankara
- **Currency** Turkish Lira; US$1 = TRL1.4 million, €1 = TRL1.7 million
- **Famous for** delight, baths, ruins, resorts, moustaches
- **Official Language** Turkish
- **Key Phrases** *merhaba* (hello), *tamam* (OK), *teşekkürler* (thank you), *bu akşam olmaz* (not tonight, thanks)
- **Population** 69 million
- **Telephone Codes** country code ☎ 90; Istanbul ☎ 0212, ☎ 0216; international access code ☎ 00
- **Visa** available on entry

TURKEY

## HOW MUCH?

- **Budget hotel room** €9
- **Two-course meal** €5
- **Loaf of bread** €0.10
- **Double rakı** €1.75
- **Nargileh (water-pipe)** €3

## LONELY PLANET INDEX

- **Litre of petrol** €1
- **Litre of bottled water** €0.45
- **Beer – 0.5l of Efes** €1.50
- **Souvenir T-shirt** €5
- **Street snack – döner kebap** €0.90

## HIGHLIGHTS

- Get intimate with **Istanbul** (p603) and discover the irresistible mystique of the old Ottoman capital.
- Go blue cruising: jump aboard and sail the Med from **Fethiye** (p625) to Olympos, or Marmaris, or wherever…
- Bed down in **Selçuk** (p617) for the best pensions on the coast, with some of the best Roman ruins down the road.
- Explore fairy chimneys, underground chambers and cave houses in **Cappadocia** (p637), Turkey's top natural attraction.
- Give the beaten track a miss and head for the neglected coast around **Antakya** (p629), former Syrian outpost in the east.

## ITINERARIES

- **One week** Spend a couple of days exploring Istanbul, then head down the Aegean coast towards Bodrum, making sure you stop at the Gallipoli battlefields, Bergama and the ruins of Ephesus.
- **Two weeks** Continue east along the Mediterranean to Antalya, visiting Fethiye and Olympos along the way, then return to Istanbul via Konya and Cappadocia. If you can fit it in, a boat trip along the coast is a must.

## CLIMATE & WHEN TO GO

The Aegean and Mediterranean coasts have mild, rainy winters and hot, dry summers. In Istanbul, summer temperatures average around 28°C to 30°C; winters are chilly but usually above freezing, with rain and perhaps a dusting of snow. The Anatolian plateau can be boiling hot (although less humid than the coast) in summer and freezing in winter.

In general, spring (April/May) and autumn (September/October) are the most pleasant times of year. The heat and crowds of July and August can be unbearable, especially in Istanbul.

## HISTORY

The sheer weight and depth of history in Turkey is overwhelming – the Anatolian plateau features in various guises in both the *Iliad* and the Bible; it has produced some of the world's longest-lasting empires, controlled much of Europe and the Middle East for centuries, and still holds the most strategic position on two continents. Just look at the ruins that litter the coast to get a glimpse of the country's former glories.

By 7000 BC a Neolithic city, one of the oldest ever recorded, was established at Çatal Höyük, near Konya. The greatest of the early civilisations of Anatolia (Asian Turkey) was that of the Hittites, a force to be reckoned with from 2000 to 1200 BC with their capital at Hattuşa, east of Ankara – traces of their existence can still be seen throughout central Turkey.

After the collapse of the Hittite empire, Anatolia splintered into several small states and it wasn't until the Greco-Roman period that parts of the country were reunited. Later, Christianity spread through Anatolia, carried by the apostle Paul, a native of Tarsus (near Adana).

### Byzantine Empire & the Crusades

In AD 330 the Roman emperor Constantine founded a new imperial city at Byzantium (modern Istanbul). Renamed Constantinople, this strategic city became the capital of the Eastern Roman Empire and was the centre of the Byzantine Empire for 1000 years. During the European Dark Ages, the Byzantine Empire kept alive the flame of Western culture although it was occasionally threatened by the empires of the East (Persians, Arabs, Turks) and West (the Christian powers of Europe).

The Byzantine Empire's decline came with the arrival of the Seljuk Turks and their defeat of the Byzantine forces in August 1071. Seljuks overran most of Anatolia, and

TURKEY

# TURKEY

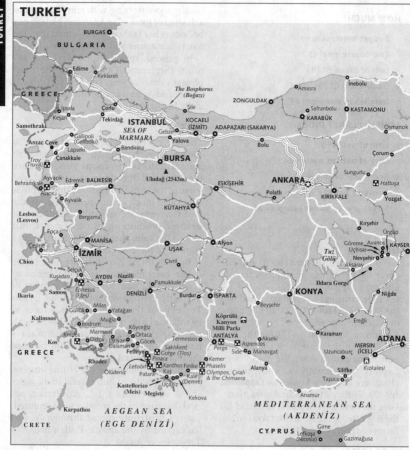

established a provincial capital at Konya, ruling over domains that included today's Turkey, Iran and Iraq.

With significantly reduced territory, the Byzantines endeavoured to protect their capital and reclaim Anatolia but the Fourth Crusade (1202–04) proved disastrous for them when a combined Venetian and crusader force took and plundered Constantinople. They eventually regained the ravaged city in 1261.

## Ottoman Empire

A Mongol invasion of the late 1200s put an end to Seljuk power, but new small Turkish states soon arose in western Anatolia. One, headed by Gazi Osman (1258–1326), grew

into the Ottoman Empire, and in 1453 Constantinople finally fell to the Ottoman sultan Mehmet II (the Conqueror), replacing Bursa as the capital of the dynasty.

A century later, under Süleyman the Magnificent, the Ottoman Empire reached the peak of its power, spreading deep into Europe, Asia and North Africa. Ottoman success was based on military expansion. When their march westwards was stalled at Vienna in 1683, the rot set in and by the 19th century the great European powers had begun to covet the sultan's vast domains.

Nationalist ideas swept through Europe after the French Revolution. In 1829 the Greeks won their independence, followed by the Serbs, the Romanians and the Bulgarians.

In the ensuing territorial scrambles, Italy took Tripolitania (now Libya) in North Africa from Turkey, and in 1913 the Ottomans lost both Albania and Macedonia.

Having sided with the Axis powers in 1914, the Turks emerged from WWI stripped of their last non-Turkish provinces: Syria, Palestine, Mesopotamia (Iraq) and the Arabian peninsula. Most of Anatolia itself was to be parcelled out to the victorious Europeans, leaving the Turks virtually nothing.

### Mustafa Kemal Atatürk

At this low point, Mustafa Kemal, the father of modern Turkey, took over (around 1920). Atatürk, as he was later called, had made his name by repelling the Anzacs in their heroic but futile attempt to capture the strategic Dardanelles strait at Gallipoli during WWI.

Rallying the remnants of the Turkish army during the Turkish War of Independence that followed WWI, Kemal pushed the last of the weak Ottoman rulers aside and out-manoeuvred the Allied forces. The Turks finally won in 1922 by repelling the invading Greeks at Smyrna (present-day İzmir). In the ensuing population exchange. over a million Greeks left Turkey and nearly half a million Turks moved in; many towns and cities on the coast still have noticeable numbers of Greek-style buildings left from the brief occupation.

After the renegotiation of the WWI treaties, a new Turkish republic, reduced to

Anatolia and part of Thrace, was born. Atatürk then embarked on a rapid modernisation programme: establishing a secular democracy, introducing the Latin script and European dress, and adopting equal rights for women (at least in theory). The capital was also moved from Istanbul to Ankara. Such sweeping changes did not come easily, and some of the disputes from that period have never been fully resolved.

Relations with Greece improved in the 1930s (the Greek president even nominated Atatürk for the Nobel Peace Prize in 1934) but soured again after WWII by the conflict over Cyprus, particularly after the Greek-led anti-Makarios coup and the subsequent Turkish invasion in 1974. (For more information see Cyprus, p551).

### Modern Turkey

After Atatürk's death on 10 November 1938, Turkey experienced three military coups and a lot of political turbulence – no fewer than 60 different governments have held office since independence. During the 1980s and '90s the country was also wracked by the conflict with the PKK (Kurdistan Workers Party), led by Abdullah Öcalan, who wanted the creation of a Kurdish state in Turkey's southeastern corner. This conflict led to an estimated 35,000 deaths and huge population shifts inside the country. In 1999 Öcalan was sentenced to death, a controversial decision which caught the attention of the international community and was referred to the European Court of Human Rights.

In 1999 an unlikely coalition government made up of representatives of the right-wing MHP (National Unity Party), the right-of-centre ANAP (Motherland Party) and the left-wing DSP (Democratic Socialist Party) came to power. To most people's amazement it managed to stay in office despite presiding over the worst economic disaster in the Republic's history in 2001.

In February that year the Turkish economy collapsed in spectacular fashion. Over a million people lost their jobs, and the value of the Turkish lira slumped from TRL650,000 for US$1 to TRL1.6 million. One of the few sectors to stay in shape was tourism, which was then knocked for six by the events of 11 September 2001 and the ensuing wariness about travel. By late 2001 the IMF was pumping in funds to refloat the economy.

### Current Events

Ill health prevented elderly prime minister Bülent Ecevit from working effectively later on in his tenure, and he was finally forced to call elections for November 2002. The newly formed AKP (Islamic Justice and Development Party), a religious party dominated by one-time Istanbul mayor Recep Tayyip Erdoğan, won an unprecedented victory, becoming the first non-coalition government in 15 years and ousting 90% of the existing members of parliament. Only one other party won any seats at all.

With Erdoğan's dubious past (he was once jailed for inciting religious hatred, and was still banned from sitting in parliament at the time his party came to power), many people feared the AKP would bring an inrush of hardline Islamism to national politics. So far, however, the new regime has proved reassuringly moderate, concentrating on stabilising the economy and strengthening the country's bid to join the EU.

Terrorism and the increasing polarisation of East and West have reinforced Turkey's unique position as a US ally and NATO member, and joining Europe remains a key priority. The death penalty has been abolished to meet EU criteria (incidentally reprieving PKK leader Öcalan), and the Kurdish minority have been granted greater rights and freedoms. Britain and Germany have both given cautious assurances of support in the future, but with human rights still an issue and many member countries ambivalent, it will surely be quite some time before accession talks begin.

Arguments about the place of religion in Turkey's secular society continue to be a key talking point, in particular state occasions. The situation has been further fuelled by a wave of bomb attacks on government and tourist areas in Istanbul and Ankara, apparently terrorist reactions to the occupation of Iraq. As Turkey is seen as a 'soft' pro-Western target on account of its secular system, religious polarisation seems certain to remain a major issue for years to come.

## PEOPLE

Turkey's population is predominantly Turks (69 million), with a big Kurdish minority (perhaps 12 million) and much smaller groups of Laz, Hemsin, Arabs, Jews, Greeks and Armenians. The Laz and Hemsin people

**TURKEY**

**RESPONSIBLE TRAVEL**

Respecting Muslim sensibilities should be a point of principle, even when you're surrounded by half-naked sunseekers. Women should keep their legs, upper arms and neckline covered, except on the beach. When entering a mosque, women should cover their heads and shoulders, while everyone should cover their legs and remove their shoes.

Equally, though, there's no need to go overboard: obvious non-Muslims wearing headscarves and the like will probably attract just as much curious attention as those without!

are natives of the northeastern corner of Turkey on the Black Sea coast, while Arab influence is strongest in the Hatay area abutting Syria. Southeastern Turkey is pretty solidly Kurdish, although the problems of the last 20 years have led many to head west in search of a better life.

As a result of Atatürk's reforms, republican Turkey has largely adapted to a modern Westernised lifestyle, at least on the surface. In the big cities and coastal resorts you will not feel much need to adapt to fit in. In smaller towns and villages, however, you may find people warier and more conservative.

One stereotype you'll find confirmed is the potency of the Turkish moustache. Almost two thirds of adult men sport a 'tash, and in a recent survey 30% of the population said they thought it was a sign of virility. Unfortunately, in the same survey almost 70% of women under 40 found facial hair unattractive. Could the moustache be the next casualty of modernisation?

## RELIGION

Turkey is 99% Muslim, overwhelmingly of the Sunni variety, with small groups of Shiites and larger groups of Alevis (around 20%), mainly in the east. Most Turks are fairly relaxed about their religion; many women uncover their heads and many men drink alcohol (although almost no one touches pork). However, there is also a small but growing group of 'born-again' Muslims who may make you feel uncomfortable, especially about alcohol, dress and anything pertaining to religion.

## ARTS

As with all else, Atatürk changed Turkey's cultural picture, encouraging painting, sculpture, Western music (he loved opera), dance and drama. Today's arts scene is a vibrant, if at times discordant, mix of the traditional, the innovative and the painfully modern.

The source of most traditional influences is, of course, the Ottoman Empire. Islam discourages images of humans or animals, so the Ottomans produced little sculpture or portraiture. Instead artists concentrated on calligraphy, architecture, tiles, jewellery, carpet-making, textiles and glass-making, with geometric motifs dominating most forms. More obscure arts like paper-marbling and Karagöz shadow-puppetry have also been enjoying a resurgence, seen as crafts worthy of preservation. It goes without saying that carpet-weaving continues to be a Turkish passion.

Ottoman court music was mostly religious and can sound pompous and turgid to Western ears. Folk music was rather livelier, however, and has since undergone a major revival. Some modern Turkish pop music draws on folk traditions, though most is very much of its time, with scantily clad dancers, hirsute men in tight trousers and Turkish-language cover versions of anything from Gloria Gaynor to Will Smith. Big names in recent years have included Gülben Ergen, Deniz Arcak, Sezen Aksu, Haluk Levent, Tarkan and Nilüfer.

Despite the popularity of Western music in cities and tourist areas, Turkish music still reigns supreme here; artists generally make no effort to break into English-speaking markets, and the national MTV counterpart, Kral TV, only shows Turkish videos. Turkey did, however, host the Eurovision Song Contest in 2004 after winning it for the first time in 2003 with a song in English.

Turkish TV is mostly limited to incomprehensible soap operas in the American daytime mould, but in 2002 the small screen fostered a genuine smash hit in *Asmalı Konak* (Grapevine House), a drama series about the effects on a wealthy Turkish family when their sons return from America. The runaway success of the show has sent fans flocking to see the locations used in Cappadocia, and also spawned a feature film in 2004.

## SPORT

Turks are fanatical lovers of football (soccer), and if you can get to a match involving one of the big Istanbul three – Galatasaray, Fenerbahçe and Beşiktaş – you're guaranteed to have a good time. Try to make sure you're cheering for the right side!

The other main spectator sport here is *yağı güreş* (oil wrestling), where burly men in leather shorts lather themselves up with olive oil and go at it. Basketball comes in a distant third.

## ENVIRONMENT

The Dardanelles, the Sea of Marmara and the Bosphorus strait divide Turkey into Asian and European parts, but Eastern Thrace (European Turkey) makes up only 3% of the land area. The remaining 97% is Anatolia, a vast plateau rising eastward towards the Caucasus Mountains. Turkey's 6000km coastline is almost entirely given over to tourism, except where the mountains come right down to the sea.

The country is home to a variety of plant and animal life; the most noted *cause célèbre* is the loggerhead turtle *(caretta caretta),* whose beach nesting grounds have long been endangered by tourism and development. Various national and international schemes are underway to protect these areas during the breeding season – look out for signs telling you when to avoid which stretches.

Turkey also has a network of national parks preserving some of its most spectacular scenery and, with it, the bird and animal life. Sadly, rapid development is effectively eliminating all the remaining fauna outside these reserves; you'll see many more birds, for example, in eastern Turkey than in the west, and on a short visit you may well not see any wildlife at all.

Despite the success of the turtle projects, Turkey's embryonic environmental movement is making slow progress, and you may well be shocked by the amount of discarded litter and the number of half-built properties fouling the landscape.

Recently, the biggest environmental rows have been over Turkey's programme for building large dams. One such scheme that would have drowned the historic town of Hasankeyf in southeastern Turkey seems to have been derailed, but Allianoi, near Bergama, and much of the Çoruh River area in northeastern Turkey look likely to vanish for the sake of hydroelectric schemes.

## FOOD & DRINK

The infamous *döner kebap* (doner kebab) is the mainstay of the Turkish diet, and you'll find a range of lamb and chicken kebabs in street stalls and *lokantas* (restaurants) almost everywhere. Even the unadventurous should branch out a bit and try the *dürüm kebap,* sliced lamb rolled up in flatbread, or the *İskender kebap,* a bed of bread covered with lamb slices, yoghurt and tomato purée, all drizzled with melted butter. A popular alternative to kebabs is *köfte,* minced meat formed into flattened meatballs.

The cheapest, quickest options in most restaurants and cafeterias are *pide,* a kind of oval Turkish pizza topped with cheese and/or meat; *lahmacun,* wafer-thin Arabic-style pizza smeared with tomato sauce and minced lamb; and *gözleme,* thin bread pancakes filled with cheese or meat. *Mantı,* the Turkish version of ravioli, is also a good bet.

For vegetarians, a meal of *mezes* (hors d'oeuvres) can be an excellent way to avoid meat while ensuring a varied diet. Most restaurants will be able to rustle up at least *beyaz peynir* (white sheep's milk cheese), *börek* (flaky pastry stuffed with white cheese and parsley), *kuru fasulye* (fried beans), *dolma* (stuffed vegetables) and *patlıcan tava* (fried aubergine). *Çorba* (soup) of various shades is also a reliable fixture on most menus, though many are made with meat stock.

It's impossible to go a day in Turkey without being offered *çay* (tea), grown on the eastern Black Sea coast and served in tiny tulip-shaped glasses with copious quantities of sugar. The milder but wholly chemical *elma çay* (apple tea) is a travellers' favourite and more or less unique to Turkey. Traditional Turkish *kahve* (coffee) is drunk like espresso; order it *sade* (no sugar), *orta* (medium-sweet) or *çok şekerli* (very sweet) and take care not to swig the grains.

The Turkish liquor of choice is *rakı,* a fiery aniseed drink resembling Greek *ouzo;* it's traditionally cut by half with water and drunk to accompany *mezes.* Turkish wine, both red and white, is worth the occasional blowout. You can buy Efes and Tuborg beers everywhere, although outside the resorts you may need to find a *tekel bayii* (off-licence) store to buy wine.

# ISTANBUL

☎ 0212 / pop 12 million

You'll quickly see what a sprawling monster of a city the former Ottoman capital is. Straddling the Bosphorus with a foot in both Europe and Asia, it embodies the head-on collision of ancient and modern, exotic and prosaic. Minarets jostle for space with banks and housing developments, Western chic competes with Oriental kitsch, Starbucks and sex shops rub up against carpet traders, and the beer flows as freely as the *çay*. Istanbul's tourist sites may emphasise tradition, but its inhabitants are on the cutting edge of everything that is modern Turkey.

## HISTORY

Late in the 2nd century AD, the Roman Empire conquered the small city-state of Byzantium, which was renamed Constantinople in AD 330 after Emperor Constantine moved his capital there. The city walls kept out barbarians for centuries while the western part of the Roman Empire collapsed. When Constantinople fell for the first time in 1204, it was ransacked by the loot-hungry Europeans of the misguided Fourth Crusade.

Istanbul only regained its former glory after 1453, when it was captured by Mehmet the Conqueror and made capital of the Ottoman Empire. During the glittering reign of Süleyman the Magnificent (1520–66) the city was graced with many beautiful new buildings, and retained much of its charm even during the empire's long decline.

Occupied by Allied forces after WWI, the city came to be thought of as the decadent playpen of the sultans, notorious for its extravagant lifestyle and insidious spy games. As a result, when the Turkish Republic was proclaimed in 1923, Ankara became the new capital, in an attempt to wipe the slate clean. Nevertheless, Istanbul remains a commercial and financial centre, and is still Turkey's number one city in all but name.

Perhaps because of this reputation and its conspicuous Westernisation, Istanbul was the target for terrorist attacks in 2003, when car bombs exploded near the British Consulate and the headquarters of the British-owned HSBC bank and in 2004, when simultaneous explosions hit hotels in Laleli and Sultanahmet.

## ORIENTATION

The Bosphorus strait, between the Black and Marmara Seas, divides European Istanbul from its Asian half. The European side is divided by the Haliç (Golden Horn) estuary into the 'newer' quarter of Beyoğlu in the north and Old Istanbul in the south; the Galata Bridge spans the two. Istanbul's *otogar* (bus terminal) is at Esenler, about 10km west of the city.

Sultanahmet, the heart of Old Istanbul, has the bulk of the tourist sites, exchange offices, cheap hotels and restaurants. Divan Yolu runs west through Sultanahmet past the Grand Bazaar to Aksaray, a major transport intersection.

Eminönü, at the southern end of Galata Bridge, is the terminus for a tram line as well as many buses and ferries. Sirkeci train station is 100m east.

Karaköy, on the other side of the bridge, is another ferry terminus. Up the hill is the southern end of Beyoğlu's pedestrian shopping strip, İstiklal Caddesi; at its northern end is Taksim Square, heart of 'modern' Istanbul.

## INFORMATION

### Bookshops

**Robinson Crusoe** (Map pp604-5; ☎ 293 6968; İstiklal Caddesi 389)

**Homer** (Map pp604-5; ☎ 249 5902; Yeni Çarşı Caddesi 28)

### Emergency

**Tourist Police** (Map p607; ☎ 527 4503; Yerebatan Caddesi 6, Sultanahmet)

### Internet Access

**Café Turka** (Map p607; ☎ 514 6551; Divan Yolu 22/2, Sultanahmet; per hr €1.50)

**Otantik** (Map p607; ☎ 513 2676; Alayköskü Caddesi 2B; per hr US$2)

---

### ISTANBUL IN TWO DAYS

Starting in Sultanahmet, **Topkapı Palace** (p606) could easily occupy you for your first day; try and fit in **Aya Sofya** (p606) and the **Blue Mosque** (p606) as well. In the evening, head to a *hammam* or grab a kebab.

For the second day, spend the morning in the controlled chaos of the **Grand Bazaar** (p608), then head over the river to **Beyoğlu** (p608) for a glimpse of modern Istanbul.

TURKEY

# ISTANBUL

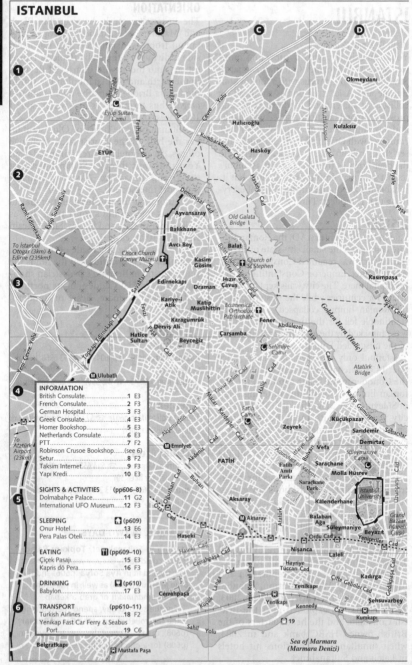

**SKM** (Map p607; ☎ 518 1075; Şehit Mehmetpaşa Sokak 21, Sultanahmet; per hr €1.25)

**Taksim Internet** (Map pp604-5; ☎ 243 9567; Zombak Sokak 10, Taksim; per hr €0.60-0.75)

## Internet Resources

**www.biletix.com** Entertainment listings and tickets.
**www.istanbulgay.com**
**www.istanbulguide.net**
**www.istanbullife.org**

## Medical Services

**American Hospital** (Map pp604-5; ☎ 231 4050; Güzelbahçe Sokak 20, Nişantaşı)
**German Hospital** (Map pp604-5; Alman Hastanesi; ☎ 293 2150; Sıraselviler Caddesi 119, Taksim)

## Money

There are banks, ATMs and exchange offices all over Istanbul.

## Post

**PTT** Sirkeci (Map p607; Büyük Postane Caddesi, Eminönü)
Taksim (Map p607; Cumhuriyet Caddesi)

## Telephone

Istanbul has two area codes: 0212 for the European side, 0216 for the Asian zone. All numbers here use the 0212 code unless otherwise indicated.

## Tourist Information

**Atatürk Airport** ( ☎ 573 4136; international arrivals)
**Eminönü** (Map p607; ☎ 511 5888; Sirkeci station)
**Sultanahmet** (Map p607; ☎ 518 8754; Divan Yolu)

## Travel Agencies

**Backpackers Travel** (Map p607; ☎ 638 6343; www .backpackerstravel.net; Yeni Akbıyık Caddesi 22)
**Fez Travel** (Map p607; ☎ 516 9024; www.feztravel.com; Akbıyık Caddesi 15, Sultanahmet)
**Setur** (Map pp604-5; ☎ 230 0336; www.setur.com.tr; Cumhuriyet Caddesi 107, Elmadağ)

## SIGHTS & ACTIVITIES
### Old Istanbul

Sultanahmet is the first place to head to, with all the major sights arranged around the Hippodrome.

### AYA SOFYA (CHURCH OF HOLY WISDOM)

When the Emperor Justinian ordered work to start on **Sancta Sofya** (Hagia Sofia; Map p607; ☎ 522 0989; Aya Sofya Meydanı; admission €9; ☿ 9am-5pm Tue-Sun) in AD 532, he meant to create the grandest church in the world, and it's certainly hard to miss the result. For 1000 years it was Christendom's largest place of worship, and despite the scaffolding, the interior is still impressive.

Climb up to the **gallery** to see temporary exhibitions and the splendid mosaics surviving from the Christian period. When the church was captured by the Ottomans and converted into a mosque, the mosaics were actually plastered over, as strict Islam prohibits images of living creatures. They were only revealed in the 1930s, when Atatürk declared Aya Sofya a museum.

### BLUE MOSQUE

Equally hard to overlook, the **Mosque of Sultan Ahmet I** (Map p607; ☿ all times except during prayer) is just south of Aya Sofya. Built between 1609 and 1619, it's light and delicate compared with its squat ancient neighbour, and looks particularly good lit up at night. The nickname comes from the luminous blue impression created by the tiled walls and painted dome of the interior. Make a small donation and leave your shoes outside.

Rents from the *arasta* (row of shops) to the east provide support for the Blue Mosque's upkeep. Nearby is the entrance to the **Great Palace Mosaic Museum** (Büyüksaray Mozaik Müzesi; Map p607; adult/concession €2.50/1.25; ☿ 9am-4.30pm Tue-Sun), a spectacular stretch of ancient Byzantine pavement featuring hunting scenes.

### TOPKAPI PALACE

Just northeast of Aya Sofya, the sprawling **Topkapı Sarayı** (Map p607; ☎ 512 0480; Soğukçeşme Sokak; admission €9; palace ☿ 9am-4pm Wed-Mon) was the opulent seat of the sultans from 1462 until they moved to Dolmabahçe Palace in the 19th century. It's not just a single palace but a massive collection of courtyards, houses and libraries, with an intriguing 400-room harem.

In the vast First Court is the **Aya Irini** (Church of Divine Peace), dating from around AD 540. Within the Second Court are exhibits of priceless porcelain, silverware, crystal, weaponry and calligraphy. Right beside the Imperial Council Chamber (Kubbealtı) is the entrance to the **harem** (admission €9; ☿ 9.30am-noon & 1-3.30pm), a succession of sumptuously decorated rooms that served as the sultan's family quarters (yes, 'family' does include concubines).

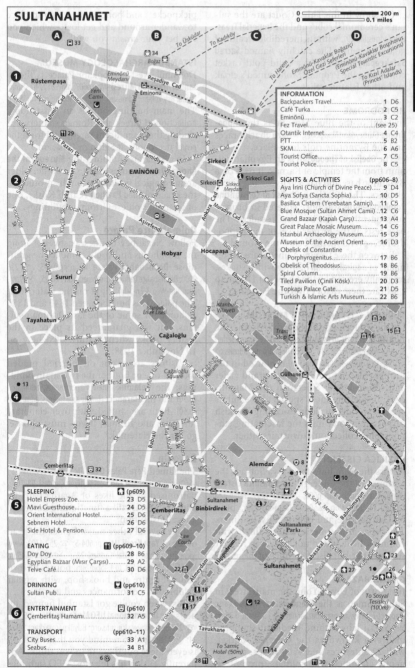

# SULTANAHMET

| | 0 | 200 m |
| | 0 | 0.1 miles |

**INFORMATION**
| | | |
|---|---|---|
| Backpackers Travel | 1 | D6 |
| Café Turka | 2 | C5 |
| Eminönü | 3 | C2 |
| Fez Travel | (see 25) | |
| Otantik Internet | 4 | C4 |
| PTT | 5 | B2 |
| SKM | 6 | A6 |
| Tourist Office | 7 | C5 |
| Tourist Police | 8 | C5 |

**SIGHTS & ACTIVITIES** (pp606–8)
| | | |
|---|---|---|
| Aya Irini (Church of Divine Peace) | 9 | D4 |
| Aya Sofya (Sancta Sophia) | 10 | D5 |
| Basilica Cistern (Yerebatan Sarnıçı) | 11 | C5 |
| Blue Mosque (Sultan Ahmet Camii) | 12 | C6 |
| Grand Bazaar (Kapalı Çarşı) | 13 | A4 |
| Great Palace Mosaic Museum | 14 | C6 |
| Istanbul Archaeology Museum | 15 | D3 |
| Museum of the Ancient Orient | 16 | D3 |
| Obelisk of Constantine Porphyrogenitus | 17 | B6 |
| Obelisk of Theodosius | 18 | B6 |
| Spiral Column | 19 | B6 |
| Tiled Pavilion (Çinili Köşk) | 20 | D3 |
| Topkapı Palace Gate | 21 | D5 |
| Turkish & Islamic Arts Museum | 22 | B6 |

**SLEEPING** (p609)
| | | |
|---|---|---|
| Hotel Empress Zoe | 23 | D5 |
| Mavi Guesthouse | 24 | D5 |
| Orient International Hostel | 25 | D6 |
| Sebnem Hotel | 26 | D6 |
| Side Hotel & Pension | 27 | D6 |

**EATING** (pp609–10)
| | | |
|---|---|---|
| Doy Doy | 28 | B6 |
| Egyptian Bazaar (Mısır Çarşısı) | 29 | A2 |
| Telve Café | 30 | D6 |

**DRINKING** (pp610)
| | | |
|---|---|---|
| Sultan Pub | 31 | C5 |

**ENTERTAINMENT** (p610)
| | | |
|---|---|---|
| Çemberlitaş Hamamı | 32 | A5 |

**TRANSPORT** (pp610–11)
| | | |
|---|---|---|
| City Buses | 33 | A1 |
| Seabus | 34 | B1 |

On show in the Third Court are the sultan's ceremonial robes and the **Imperial Treasury** (admission €9), with its incredible wealth of gold and gems. The catchily named **Sacred Safekeeping Rooms** hold a solid gold casket containing the Prophet Mohammed's cloak and other Islamic relics.

### HIPPODROME

In front of the Blue Mosque is the **Hippodrome** (Atmeydanı; Map p607), where chariot races and the Byzantine riots took place.

The **Obelisk of Theodosius** is an Egyptian column from the temple of Karnak. It rests on a Byzantine base and has 3500-year-old hieroglyphics. The 10m-high **Obelisk of Constantine Porphyrogenitus** was once covered in bronze, subsequently stolen by the Crusaders. The base rests at the former level of the Hippodrome, several metres below the ground.

Between these two monuments are the remains of a **spiral column** of intertwined snakes, originally erected by the Greeks at Delphi to celebrate their victory over the Persians.

### TURKISH & ISLAMIC ARTS MUSEUM

On the western side of the Hippodrome, the **Turkish & Islamic Arts Museum** (Türk ve İslam Eserleri Müzesi; Map p607; ☎ 518 1805; Hippodrome; admission €1.75; 9.30am-4.30pm Tue-Sun) is housed in the former palace of İbrahim Paşa, grand vizier and son-in-law of Süleyman the Magnificent. Inside, the most spectacular exhibits are the wonderful floor-to-ceiling Turkish carpets, but don't miss the fascinating ethnographic collection downstairs either.

### BASILICA CISTERN

Across the tram lines from Aya Sofya is the entrance to the underground **Basilica Cistern** (Yerebatan Sarnıçı; Map p607; ☎ 522 1259; Yerebatan Caddesi 13; admission €2.50; 9am-5.30pm), built by Constantine and enlarged by Justinian. This vast, atmospheric cistern filled with columns held water not only for regular summer use but also for times of siege.

### GRAND BAZAAR

Just north of Divan Yolu, the main street in Sultanahmet, is the **Grand Bazaar** (Kapalı Çarşı; Map p607; www.mygrandbazaar.net; 8.30am-6.30pm Mon-Sat), a labyrinthine medieval shopping mall also known as the Covered Market, with 22 entrances and 4500 shops, permanently crammed with punters, promoters,

pickpockets and policemen. It's a fun place to wander around and get lost – which you can bet your *arasta* you will!

### ISTANBUL ARCHAEOLOGY MUSEUM

Downhill, west of Topkapı Palace is the **Istanbul Arkeoloji Müzesi** (Map p607; ☎ 520 7740; Osman Hamdi Bey Yokuşu; admission €3; 9.30am-5pm Tue-Sun). The main building houses an outstanding collection of Greek and Roman statuary, including the magnificent sarcophagi from the royal necropolis at Sidon in Lebanon.

In a separate building, the **Museum of the Ancient Orient** houses Hittite and other older archaeological finds. Also on the grounds is the graceful **Tiled Pavilion** (Çinili Köşk), one of Istanbul's oldest Ottoman buildings.

## Dolmabahçe Palace

Follow Necatibey Caddesi eastwards along the Bosphorus and you'll come to the grandiose **Dolmabahçe Palace** (Map pp604–5; ☎ 236 9000; Dolmabahçe Caddesi; combined ticket €6.25; 9am-3pm Tue-Wed & Fri-Sun), right on the waterfront. The palace was built between 1843 and 1856 as home for some of the last Ottoman sultans, but was guaranteed its place in the history books when Atatürk died here on 10 November 1938.

Visitors are taken on hurried guided tours of one or both of the two main buildings: the **Selamlik** (men's apartments; admission €3.50) and the **Haremlik** (family apartments; admission €3.50). Both are stuffed with over-elaborate furniture and fittings; if you must choose, go for the Haremlik.

## Beyoğlu

The famed **Pera Palas Oteli** (Map pp604–5; ☎ 251 4560; www.perapalas.com; Meşrutiyet Caddesi 98-100), patronised by the likes of Agatha Christie and Atatürk, is still a functioning hotel and a local institution.

Like several other major banks, the head office of **Yapı Kredi** (Map pp604–5; ☎ 252 4700; www.ykykultur.com.tr; İstiklal Caddesi 285; 10am-6.45pm Mon-Fri, to 5.45pm Sat, to 1.45pm Sun) houses its own cultural centre and bookshop, with regular exhibitions, performances and events.

Just when you've got Istanbul figured, up pops the **International UFO Museum** (Map pp604–5; ☎ 252 8646; www.siriusufo.org; Büyükparmakkapı Sokak 14; 11am-8pm) to remind you that the truth is even more out there than you think. Apparently Turkey has the most UFO sightings in the Middle East, although the overfamiliar Roswell displays here won't do much to convince unbelievers.

### The Bosphorus

In summer there's no finer way to soak up the city than a ferry ride up the Bosphorus. Organised excursion ferries depart from Eminönü daily, stopping at Beşiktaş, Kanlıca, Yeniköy, Sarıyer, Rumeli Kavağı and Anadolu Kavağı (1¾ hours). Extra trips are added on Sunday and holidays. The weekday return fare is €4.

## SLEEPING

The big international hotels generally favour Beyoğlu, but the best place to head for accommodation to suit all budgets is the Sultanahmet/Cankurtaran district.

### Budget

**Orient International Hostel** (Map p607; ☎ 518 0789; www.orienthostel.com; Akbıyık Caddesi 13; dm €7-9, s/d €16.50/19, deluxe €35; 🖵 ) The best-frequented of the many Sultanahmet hostels, a top-floor café overlooks the Bosphorus. A basement bar features belly dancers and *nargileh* (hookah) pipes. Newer rooms are best.

**Mavi Guesthouse** (Map p607; ☎ 516 5878; www.maviguesthouse.com; Kutluğün Sokak 3; dm €6, s/d €10.75/15.50; 🖵 ) A good alternative to the hostels, with competitive prices, a family atmosphere and no-one pushing travel services.

### Mid-Range

**Side Hotel & Pension** (Map p607; ☎ 517 6590; www.sidehotel.com; Utangaç Sokak 20; s/d from US$20/25; 🗷 🖵 ) Friendly and comfortable, the Side is grown-up enough to appeal to the whole spectrum of independent travellers without losing all the sociable element of the 'youth' backpacker places.

**Onur Hotel** (Map p607; ☎ 458 0690; www.onurhotel.com; Aksakal Sokak 28; s/d/tr €22/33/44; 🗷 🖵 ) A more upmarket but still good-value venture from the former owner of the Mavi Guesthouse. With just six rooms, early booking is probably a good idea.

**Sebnem Hotel** (Map p607; ☎ 517 6623; www.sebnemhotel.com; Akbıyık Caddesi; s/d €35/55; 🗷 ) Head to this smart little house for a spot of Ottoman colour – paintings, dashes of silk and four-poster beds all add to the charm.

**Hotel Empress Zoe** (Map p607; ☎ 518 2504; www.emzoe.com; Adliye Sokak 10; s €65, d €70-100, ste €100-150; 🗷 ) Climb the spiral staircase to enter some of the most civilised bedrooms in Sultanahmet, with massive beds, stone fittings and a lovely garden terrace, including pet cats.

**Sarnıç Hotel** (Map p607; ☎ 518 2323; www.sarnichotel.com; Küçük Ayasofya Caddesi 26; s/d US$80/95; 🗷 🖵 ) The classical façade isn't quite echoed by the floral prints inside, but the services here are top-notch: massages, babysitting, even a house doctor! Oh, and there's a Byzantine cistern under the building. Substantial discounts for online booking or cash payment.

## EATING
### Restaurants

**Sosyal Tesisleri** (Map p607; ☎ 458 5414; Ahırkapı Sokak 1; mains €1.50-3.25) Enter the small walled park in Cankurtaran to find a low-key café and restaurant run by Eminönü town hall, with Marmara views and outdoor seating.

**Doy Doy** (Map p607; ☎ 517 1588; Şifa Hamamı Sokak 13; mains €2-4.75; ⏱ 8am-11pm) Look at the fading photos upstairs to see just how long this pide and kebab place has been a travellers' favourite – bizarrely, the display also seems to include a shot of Whitney Houston leaving prison. Luckily none of this has put off the regular local diners.

**Telve Café** (Map p607; ☎ 516 7995; Ak Cad 96-98, Akbıyık Caddesi; mains €2.50-6) At the far western end of the main backpacker strip, this vaguely authentic-looking patio restaurant serves up traditional meals and nargilehs (€4.25), away from the crowds.

**Kapris dö Pera** (Map pp604-5; ☎ 292 0747; Abdullah Sokak 9; mains €1.25-4.75; ⏱ 11am-midnight) A recent addition to the off-İstiklal scene, the Kapris aims to resurrect 1920s Istanbul cuisine, bringing in the long-lost Armenian, Asian, Mediterranean and French influences that rewrote the Ottoman cookbook. The biggest plus, though, is the almost historic prices.

In the Kumkapı neighbourhood, **Tiyatro Caddesi** boasts dozens of good seafood restaurants; always check prices before ordering. On the breadline, €1 buys you a fish sandwich straight from the boat on **Eminönü waterfront**.

Beyoğlu is the place to go for maximum choice – just saunter along **İstiklal Caddesi** and take your pick, from takeaway *döner* windows to fully Westernised bar-bistros. **Çiçek Pasajı** (Flower Passage; Map pp604-5; ⏱ 10am-midnight) hosts a good assortment of fish 'n' beer restaurants offering a fun night out.

## Self Catering

Every Wednesday you can pick up what you need at the Akbıyık Caddesi street market. Further north, the **Egyptian Bazaar** (Map p607; ⊗ 8.30am-6.30pm Mon-Sat) and surrounding streets sell dried fruit, pulses, fish and more.

## DRINKING

The Sultanahmet bar scene is concentrated on Akbıyık Caddesi, catering mainly to the denizens of the surrounding hostels. Dedicated clubgoers should head to the sidestreets of Beyoğlu, where the flashier local hipsters groove to cutting-edge electronic music. There are also plenty of more traditional *meyhanes* and Turkish bars off İstiklal Caddesi. Opening times vary completely, anywhere from 9am at places which serve food to 8pm at booze-only bars. Most bars close between midnight and 2am, clubs around 4am.

Beyoğlu can be pretty seedy. Ignore the 'friendly' locals who try to lure you into trouble with promises of free drinks and so on.

**Babylon** (Map pp604-5; ☎ 292 7368; www.babylon .com.tr; ⊗ from 9pm Tue-Thu, from 10pm Fri & Sat; Şehbender Sokak 3, Beyoğlu) An essential stop on the Taksim circuit, with regular film screenings and more than its fair share of big-name DJs and bands.

**Sultan Pub** (Map p607; ☎ 528 1719; Divan Yolu 2, Sultanahmet; ⊗ 9am-midnight) Popular pub-restaurant opposite Sultanahmet Meydanı, with a less rowdy atmosphere than some of the backpacker bars.

The biggest and brightest clubs of the moment are **Crystal** (Map pp604-5; ☎ 261 1988; Muallim Naci Caddesi 111, Ortaköy; ⊗ 8pm-4am) and **2C** (Map pp604-5; ☎ 235 6197; Abdülhakhamit Caddesi 19, Taksim; ⊗ 10pm-4am Sun-Thu, 10pm-5am Fri & Sat).

## ENTERTAINMENT

Check *Time Out Istanbul* (€1.50) for monthly listings on every aspect of the city's cultural scene. *The Guide Istanbul* (€2.50) is less hip but has more tourist information, and appears every two months.

## Turkish Baths

Istanbul's most interesting historical *hammams* (Turkish baths) are pretty touristy, with prices to reflect their non-Turkish clientele.

**Çemberlitaş Hamamı** (Map p607; ☎ 522 7974; Vezirhan Caddesi 8; wash & massage €18; ⊗ 6am-midnight)

The best choice for first-timers, with separate baths for men and women in a building possibly designed by the great Ottoman architect Mimar Sinan. Prices would be outrageous anywhere else in Turkey but service is experienced and hassle-free.

## GETTING THERE & AWAY
### Air

Most people fly into Istanbul's Atatürk International Airport, Turkey's international flight hub. Most foreign airlines have their offices near Taksim, or north of it, along Cumhuriyet Caddesi.

Turkish Airlines and its new rival Onur Air cover most domestic destinations with at least one daily flight each.

### Bus

At Esenler, Istanbul Otogar is a monster, with 168 ticket offices and buses leaving for all parts of Turkey and beyond. Buses depart for Ankara (€12 to €28, six hours) about every 15 minutes, day and night; buses for most other cities depart at least every hour.

Coming from or heading to Anatolia, you could also use the smaller Harem Otogar on the Asian shore, which is accessible by ferry (€0.60) and saves you crossing town twice.

### Train

The station for services to Edirne, Greece and Eastern Europe is Sirkeci. The nightly *Bosfor Expresi* goes to Bucharest (€26, 15½ hours) and Budapest (€95, 32 hours).

On the Asian shore, Haydarpaşa is the terminus for trains to Anatolia, Syria and Iran. Seven express trains a day run to Ankara (€10 to €28, seven to 10 hours), the fastest being sleeper only.

### Boat

For information on car ferries to İzmir, see p645.

Yenikapı, south of Aksaray Square, is the dock for *hızlı feribot* (fast car-ferries) across the Sea of Marmara.

## GETTING AROUND
### To/From the Airport

The Aksaray Metro serves both the airport and the *otogar*; change at Aksaray and board the tram from Yusufpaşa for Sultanahmet and Eminönü (€1.25, up to 80 minutes).

The fastest way into town is by taxi. During the day (*gündüz*) it costs around €10 to Sultanahmet (20 minutes), €12 to Taksim (30 minutes) and €8 to the *otogar* (20 minutes).

Several shuttle buses also operate, including the Havaş airport bus (€4.50, 35 minutes to one hour, every 30 minutes), which goes to Taksim Square via Aksaray. Sultanahmet travel agencies and hostels book minibuses in the other direction for around €3 a head.

### Boat

The cheapest and nicest way to travel any distance in Istanbul is by ferry. Short ferry hops cost €0.60, longer ones €1.20. The main ferry docks are located at the mouth of the Golden Horn (Eminönü, Sirkeci and Karaköy) and at Kabataş, just before Dolmabahçe Palace.

### Bus

City buses are crowded but can be useful. On most routes you must have a ticket (€0.60) before boarding; stock up from the white booths near major stops, or nearby shops.

### Taxi

Istanbul has 60,000 yellow taxis, all of them with meters (although not every driver wants to run them, and we still hear stories of rigged machines). A trip from Sultanahmet to Taksim costs around €5.

### Train

To get to Sirkeci station, take the *tramvay* (tram) from Aksaray or Sultanahmet, or any bus for Eminönü. Haydarpaşa station is connected by ferry to Karaköy (€0.60, at least every 30 minutes).

Suburban trains from Sirkeci (€0.60) run along the southern walls of Old Istanbul and the Marmara shore at least twice an hour.

### Tram

The useful *hızlı tramvay* (fast tram) or Metro network has three lines. The first runs between Eminönü and Aksaray via Divan Yolu and Sultanahmet; the second runs west from Aksaray to the airport, and the third line from Taksim to 4 Levent. A separate restored tram also trundles along İstiklal Caddesi to Taksim. All tram tickets cost €0.60.

### Underground

The Tünel, Istanbul's ancient underground train, mounts the hill from Karaköy to Tünel Meydanı and İstiklal Caddesi (€0.60, 7am to 9pm).

## AROUND ISTANBUL

Since Istanbul is such a vast city, few places are within easy day-trip reach. However, if you make an early start it's possible to see Edirne in Thrace (Trakya), the only bit of Turkey that is geographically within Europe. The fast ferry link means that you can also just about make Bursa and back in a day, although it's much better to plan an overnight stay.

### Edirne

☎ 0284 / pop 115,000

Edirne is a surprisingly pleasant, undervisited town with several fine old mosques. If you're passing through, have a look at the **Üçşerefeli Cami**, the **Eski Cami** and especially the **Selimiye Camii**, the finest work of master architect Sinan.

It's also worth sparing a little time to visit the impressive **Beyazıt II Camii complex** (admission €1.75; ⏰9am-6pm), on the outskirts of town. The award-winning **Health Museum** inside provides a fascinating glimpse of Ottoman medicine, while the **Museum of Contemporary Painting and Sculpture** does exactly what it says on the tin.

Buses to Istanbul run up to every 20 minutes (€7, three hours). There's also an hourly direct service to Çanakkale (€6.50, 3½ hours).

### Bursa

☎ 0224 / pop 1.2 million

Sprawling at the base of Uludağ, Turkey's biggest winter sports centre, Bursa was the original centre of the Ottoman empire. It retains several fine mosques from those days, as well as some popular thermal springs in the suburb of **Çekirge**. Bursa's great covered market makes a good visitor-friendly alternative to Istanbul's efforts; the local tradition of shadow puppet theatre, known as Karagöz, is another unique selling point.

#### ORIENTATION

The city centre is along Atatürk Caddesi, with the Ulu Cami (Grand Mosque) to the west and the main square, Cumhuriyet

Alanı (commonly called Heykel), to the east. The *otogar* is 10km north of the centre. Çekirge is about 6km west of Heykel.

### INFORMATION

**Internet House Rock Café** (Sanatçılar Sokak 10; per hr €1.75)

**Karagöz Travel** ( ☎ 221 8727; www.karagoztravel.com; Eski Aynalı Çarşı 4) Travel agency and puppet shop.

**Tourist Office** ( ☎ 251 1834; Orhangazi Altgeçidi subway, Ulu Cami Parkı)

### SIGHTS & ACTIVITIES

The largest of Bursa's lovely mosques is the 20-domed **Ulu Cami** (Grand Mosque; Atatürk Caddesi), built in 1399 in the traditional Seljuk style.

Northeast of Ulu Cami is the **bedesten** or covered bazaar, the heart of Bursa's browsing scene, which buzzes with little shops and keen local shoppers. The **Koza Han** (Silk Cocoon Market) here is worth wandering through, too.

On the western side of town, Timurtaş Paşa Park holds the **tombs** ( 8.30am-noon & 1-5pm) of Osman Gazi and his son Orhan Gazi, the founders of the Ottoman empire, as well as one of those 'distance to everywhere' signs which slightly undermines the gravitas of the monuments (denizens of Tiffin, Ohio, are doubtless thrilled to learn they're 9600km from home).

The new **City Museum** (Kent Müzesi; Heykel; adult/concession €0.60/0.30; 9.30am-5pm) opened in 2004 and has some interesting interactive exhibits on local history, including a recreation of a traditional English handicrafts bazaar, though the lack of English signage is a pain.

East of Heykel, the **Yeşil Cami** (Green Mosque; Emir Sultan Caddesi) is widely considered Bursa's finest building, marking the transition from Seljuk to true Ottoman architecture.

### SLEEPING

The centre of town has a motley bunch of places to stay. You're better off forking out a bit more and staying in Çekirge where you'll also get free mineral baths.

**Hotel Çeşmeli** ( ☎ 224 1511; Gümüşçeken Caddesi 6; s/d €20.75/35.50) Sliding up the scale a bit, worn carpets are the worst thing you have to worry about in this comfortable tourist-class hotel.

**Hotel Efehan** ( ☎ 225 2260; Gümüşçeken Caddesi 34; s/d €23.50/38.25) If it's a touch of class you're after, the Efehan is about the smartest

good-value option in town, and looks to have upgraded its fixtures recently.

**Kervansaray Termal Hotel** ( ☎ 233 9300; Çekirge Meydanı, Çekirge; s/d US$65/90; P ) This vast five-star complex has just about every facility you'd expect in a small town, from the five inhouse restaurants to its own hairdressers and market. Thermal bath included.

### EATING

Bursa was the birthplace of the *İskender kebab*, and shops all over town still dole out large portions on a daily basis. For an evening of seafood and drinks, head straight for Sakarya Caddesi, off Altıparmak Caddesi.

**Turan** ( ☎ 221 2025; Sönmez İş Sarayı 120; cakes from €0.60) Those with sweet teeth should sink them into the perfect profiteroles at this long-running *pastane* (patisserie).

**Çınar Izgara** ( ☎ 221 6767; Atatürk Caddesi, Ulucami Yanı; mains €1.25-4) The former toilet block of the Ulu Cami has pictures of old Bursa on the walls to distract you from its past function. Service is attentive and the food is tasty.

**Çiçek Izgara** (Belediye Caddesi 15; mains €1.25-6.50) While outdoor seating would be better, the first-floor restaurant here is great for catching the flower market action on the street.

### GETTING THERE & AROUND

If you time it right, the fastest way to get to Istanbul is to take the hourly bus to Yalova (€3, one hour), then a catamaran or fast car-ferry to Istanbul's Yenikapı docks (€4.25, one hour, at least seven a day). Get a bus at least 1½ hours before the scheduled boat departure.

There are also regular direct buses to Istanbul (€6); those designated *feribot ile* (by ferry) are quicker and much more pleasant than the *karayolu ile* (by road) services.

There are no *servis* buses between the *otogar* and the centre; take a normal bus (€0.30, 45 minutes).

# THE AEGEAN COAST

While the coastal scenery of the Aegean Coast is not as spectacular as that of the Mediterranean, this is the part of Turkey that was once Asia Minor and it is studded with fantastic historic sites, including the ruins of Troy, Ephesus and Pergamum (Bergama). This is also where you come to see the battlefield sites at Gallipoli.

# GALLIPOLI

To most Europeans Gallipoli (Gelibolo) is little more than a footnote in WWI events, but to generations of Australians, New Zealanders and Turks the battle for the Dardanelles represents one of the most poignant moments in their history. On 25 April 1915 the first Anzac (Australia and New Zealand Army Corps) and British troops landed on the Gallipoli peninsula, hoping for a quick victory against inferior Turkish defences. However, strategic blunders turned the operation into a protracted stalemate, and after nine months of horrendous casualties the Allied forces withdrew.

The Turkish officer responsible for the defence of Gallipoli was none other than Mustafa Kemal, later Atatürk, and his success is commemorated in Turkey on 18 March. The big draw for visitors, though, is Anzac Day on 25 April, when a dawn service commemorates the anniversary of the Allied landings, attracting thousands of travellers from Down Under and beyond.

The scenic peninsula is now a national park, scattered with moving memorials to the dead of the various nations that fought here. If time is tight, the easiest way to see the sights is on a minibus tour from Çanakkale with **Hassle Free Tours** ( ☎ 213 5969) or **Troyanzac Tours** ( ☎ 217 5849) for about €20 per person. If you're less pressed, it's cheaper to take a ferry from Çanakkale to Eceabat and a *dolmuş* to Kabatepe, then follow the heritage trail.

You could also stay at Eceabat, on the Thracian (European) side of the strait. **TJs Hostel** ( ☎ 814 3122; www.anzacgallipolitours.com; Cumhuriyet Caddesi 5; dm €4, s/d €7.50/11.50; 🖳 ) gets fond reviews from its guests, and also runs its own highly rated tours.

Hourly car ferries cross the strait from Çanakkale to Eceabat and from Lapseki to Gallipoli (€0.60).

# TROY

Ask any classicist: Troy is one of the most evocative names in legend, conjuring up images from Homer's great saga of the Trojan War. According to the *Odyssey*, the Greeks besieged Troy for 10 years trying to win back King Menelaus' wife Helen, who had been lured away by the charms of Prince Paris. Eventually victory was secured when the Greeks pretended to retreat and hid soldiers inside a wooden horse; the Trojans fell for it, wheeled the horse inside the city and were duly defeated.

However, even hardcore Homer (or Brad Pitt) fans may be disappointed at the actual **site** (admission €6; ☑ 8.30am-5pm Nov-May, 8am-7.30pm Jun-Oct), as there's not much dramatic here apart from the playground-style 'reconstruction' Trojan Horse.

Excavations illustrate parts of nine successive cities built on this site: Troy I goes right back to the Bronze Age; legendary Troy could be Troy VI or VII; and most of the visible ruins are Roman ones from Troy IX. Unless you're well up on archaeological matters, it's worth taking a guided tour from Çanakkale (around €15) to get the most out of a visit here.

In summer, frequent *dolmuşes* run from Çanakkale (€1.25).

# ÇANAKKALE

☎ 0286 / pop 60,000

While it's mainly used as a base for excursions to Gallipoli and Troy, there's enough to the town of Çanakkale itself to keep you busy in between tours, although it can get pretty crowded at peak times, principally around Anzac Day. The slightly touristy centre is close to the ferry pier, around the small clock tower.

## Information

**Tourist Information** ( ☎ 217 1187; Rıhtım Caddesi)
**Uğur Internet** ( ☎ 214 0634; Kemalyeri Sokak; per hr €0.50)

## Sights

Built by Sultan Mehmet the Conqueror in 1452, the **Ottoman castle** at the southern end of the waterfront now houses a **Naval Museum** (adult/student €1.25/0.50; ☑ 9am-noon & 1.30-5pm Tue-Wed & Fri-Sun). Just over 2km south of the ferry pier, on the road to Troy, the **Archaeological Museum** (admission €1.25; ☑ 9am-5pm) holds artefacts found at Troy and Assos.

## Sleeping

Except on Anzac Day, Çanakkale has accommodation to fit all pockets. Unfortunately the stresses and strains of 25 April result in more complaints from readers about Çanakkale hotels than about anywhere else in the country. Do yourself a favour and check prices carefully before settling in.

**Anzac House** ( ☎ 213 5969; www.anzachouse.com; Cumhuriyet Bulvarı; dm €4, s/d €7.50/11.75; 🖳 ) Not to be confused with the smarter Anzac Hotel round the corner, Anzac House is the first place most backpackers head for, because it's big, cheap and is the base for Hassle Free tours. Unfortunately many of the rooms are not much more than cupboards.

**Yellow Rose Pension** ( ☎ 217 3343; www.yellow rose.4mg.com; Yeni Sokak 5; dm €4, s/d €9/14.75; 🖳 ) Increasingly popular with travellers, this attractive guesthouse has a quiet location and lots of extras, from laundry and book exchange to a video library. It's the local agent for TJs tours.

**Sera Palas Pansiyon** ( ☎ 217 4240; Çimenlik Kalesi Karşısı; s/d €11.75/14.75) If you want to dodge the big Anzac groups, skip east from the museum to grab one of the unexpectedly spacious family-run rooms here. The showers aren't great and you'll probably have to communicate with hand gestures, but it's worth the money.

**Hotel Helen** ( ☎ 212 1818; www.helenhotel.com; Cumhuriyet Meydanı 57; s/d US$45/60) All the usual Western-style hotel comforts are on offer at this smart new establishment, including minibars, lifts and nice big beds.

## Eating & Drinking

Central Çanakkale's range of restaurants includes a couple of Western-style bars and clubs (complete with vomit-spattered pavements at weekends). The harbour area is full of tea gardens and more expensive eateries.

**Mantı Evi** (Rıhtım Caddesi 13; mains €0.60-1.75) Maintaining the Turkish lunchtime tradition, you'll often see headscarved women rolling out the ravioli in the window of this tiny café.

**L&N Pizza** ( ☎ 217 5517; Rıhtım Caddesi; mains €0.60-2.50) Settle in for incomprehensible TV and some popular pizzas, burgers and set meals (€1.50 to €2.75).

**Pier** ( ☎ 213 9638; Kayserili Ahmet Paşa Caddesi; mains €3-7) This lively, hip café-bar-restaurant wouldn't look out of place in fashionable Istanbul, and neither would many of the bright young clientele.

## Getting There & Away

There are hourly buses to Istanbul (US$11, six hours) and İzmir (US$8, five hours).

## BEHRAMKALE (ASSOS)

☎ 0286 / pop 500

Behramkale, 19km southwest of Ayvacık, is a beautiful hilltop village with a rare pre-Ottoman **mosque** (without minaret) and the ruins of a **Temple of Athena** (admission €3; ☼ 8am-5pm Tue-Sun) looking across the water to Lesvos in Greece. Two kilometres further on, on the other side of the hill, is a small *iskele* (port), packed with waterfront restaurants and several camp sites. Both get overcrowded in summer, especially at weekends, so visit in low season if possible.

With freshly spruced-up decking and solar power, **Tekin Pension** ( ☎ 721 7099; s/d €9/18) is among the best of the many cheap options on the hillside. **Old Bridge House** ( ☎ 721 7426; www.oldbridgehouse.com; s/d €17.75/30; 🅿 ⚙ 🖳 ), at the bottom of the hill, and **Eris Pansiyon** ( ☎ 721 7080; www.assos.de/eris; Köyü 6; s/d €30/45), further up, are run by expats from opposite sides of the Atlantic, offering extra comfort and a more personal touch.

Infrequent *dolmuşes* come here from Ayvacık (€1.75), which is linked by bus to Çanakkale and Ayvalık.

## AYVALIK

☎ 0266 / pop 30,000

Inhabited by Ottoman Greeks until 1923, this small fishing port and beach resort is the departure point for ferries to Lesvos. Also offshore is **Alibey Island** (Cunda), lined with open-air fish restaurants and linked to the mainland by ferries and a causeway. The *otogar* is 1.5km north of the town centre, the **tourist office** ( ☎ 312 2122) 1km south, opposite the marina.

## Sleeping & Eating

**Taksiyarhis Pansiyon** ( ☎ 312 1494; www.taksiyarhis .com; Mareşal Çakmak Caddesi 71; r €9 per person) A rare bargain opportunity to stay in a renovated Ottoman house. It's five minutes' walk east of the main street, behind the former Taxi-arkhis church, and is often full in summer. Breakfast not included.

**Bonjour Pansiyon** ( ☎ 312 8085; Çeşme Sokak 5; s/d €12/20; ☼ May-Sep) This fine, restored house once accommodated a French ambassador to the sultan (take a peek at the grand salon) and now caters for more humble travellers, with an excellent local breakfast.

**Ayvalık Palas** ( ☎ 312 1064; Gümrük Meydanı; s/d/ ste €11.75/23.50/47) If you need to stay in the centre of town to catch an early boat, this is a reasonable choice, despite the seemingly arbitrary colour scheme.

**Deniziçi Cafeteria** (mains €0.75-3.50) At the far end of the restaurant-filled quay area, there are no surprises here but the corner terrace occupies a good spot.

**Hüsnü Baba'nin Yeri** (Tenekeciler Sokağı 16; mains €1-4) Head off İnönü Caddesi for some excellent *mezes* to soak up the *rakı*.

### Getting There & Away

There are frequent direct buses from İzmir to Ayvalık (€3, three hours). Coming from Çanakkale (€4, 3½ hours), buses drop you off at the OPET station on the main highway to take a *servis* or hitch to the centre.

Boats to Lesvos (€40/50 one way/return) operate at least three times a week year-round.

## BERGAMA

☎ 0232 / pop 50,000

From the 3rd century BC to the 1st century AD, Bergama (formerly Pergamum) was a powerful and cultured kingdom. A line of rulers beginning with one of Alexander the Great's generals reigned over this small but wealthy kingdom, leaving the extensive ruins that have made the site famous. The old centre is now a charming, old-fashioned town, deceptively isolated from the growing urban sprawl around it.

The **tourist office** (☎ 633 1862; İzmir Caddesi 57) is midway between the *otogar* and the market.

### Sights

The **Acropolis** (admission €6; ☼ 8.30am-5pm), a windswept hilltop site 6km from the city centre, is the part everyone comes to see, with its commanding location, reconstructed columns and spectacular sloping amphitheatre. You can follow the pretty path marked by dots down through the ruins to get back to town. The **Asclepion** (Temple of Asclepios; admission €6; ☼ 8.30am-5pm), 3.5km from the city centre, is the remains of a famous medical school with a library that rivalled that of Alexandria in Egypt. In the centre itself, the **Red Basilica** (admission €3; ☼ 8.30am-5pm) is the crumbling remains of a vast temple mentioned in both the *Iliad* and the Bible.

The excellent **Archaeology Museum** (admission €2.50; ☼ 8.30am-5pm) contains finds from all these sites, though the stunning Altar of Zeus

was whisked away to Berlin by the German excavators so you can only see pictures of it.

Taxis charge €5 to the Acropolis, or €23.50 for a full tour of the sights, including waiting time.

### Sleeping & Eating

**Pension Athena** ( ☎ 633 3420; www.athenapension.8m .com; İmam Çıkmazı 5; s/d €4.50/9, with shower €6/12) At the Acropolis end of town, this old Ottoman house is arguably the best place in town. Breakfast is extra (but worth it).

**Anıl Hotel** ( ☎ 631 3031; Hatuniye Caddesi 4; s/d €43/60; ✷ ) The cheerful modern rooms and convenient central location make this a good bet for short stays; the pink building is also nice and easy to spot. Ask for a quieter room at the back.

**Meydan Restaurant** (İstiklal Meydanı; mains €1-3) Near the Basilica, Meydan's vine-shaded terrace is an engaging setting for a leisurely meal.

### Getting There & Away

Buses run between Bergama and İzmir at least every hour (€3.50, two hours). Fairly frequent buses and *dolmuşes* also connect Bergama with Ayvalık (€3, one hour).

## İZMIR

☎ 0232 / pop 2.5 million

Turkey's third-largest city, İzmir (once Smyrna) carpets the hills around the Bay of İzmir like concrete mould, with buildings as far as you can see in all directions. The city was the birthplace of Homer in about 700 BC, saw the final battle of Turkey's war of independence in 1922, and is now the main transport hub for the Aegean coast, but its sites are relatively minor and few people stick around here unless they have some spare time or crave some riviera sophistication.

### Orientation

Central İzmir is a confusing web of plazas, boulevards and side streets; get hold of a map pronto if you want to explore at all.

The key landmark of the inner centre is the Dokuz Eylül Meydanı roundabout, near Basmane train station. Southwest, Anafartalar Caddesi winds through the bazaar to the upscale waterfront at Konak. The Kordon (Atatürk Caddesi) runs northeast along the waterfront past Cumhuriyet

Meydanı, the main PTT and plenty of luxury hotels. At the northern end is the Alsancak harbour district.

İzmir's flashy new *otogar* is 6km northeast of the town centre.

## Information

**İpeksan Internet** (857 Sokak 6; per hr €0.90)
**Tourist Information** ( ☎ 484 2147; Gaziosmanpaşa Bulvarı 1/C)
**Türk Telekom** ( ☎ 425 6408; 857 Sokak 6/C)

## Sights

Since most of old İzmir was destroyed by earthquakes there's little to see here. Those who do stick around could check out the ruins of the extensive 2nd-century AD Roman **agora** (admission €1.25; 8.30am–noon & 1–5pm), 'built before Jesus', on the eastern edge of the chaotic, atmospheric **bazaar**. It's also worth taking a bus to the hilltop **Kadifekale** fortress, where women still weave traditional *kilims* (rugs) on horizontal looms.

The **Archaeology** and **Ethnography museums** (admission €2.50; 8am–noon & 1–5pm Tue–Sun), above the leafy Turgutreis Parkı, both contain some interesting displays.

## Sleeping

İzmir's not short on hotels, but make sure you have a look around – many of the places with nice lobbies don't actually have much upstairs. For the cheapest rooms, walk up Anafartalar Caddesi, the busy area near Basmane station.

**Hotel Alav** ( ☎ 484 9925; Anafartalar Caddesi 749; s/d €4.25/8.50, with shower & TV €12/15) Favoured by Turkish businessmen, the Alav is not as dubious as some of its budget counterparts.

**Alican Otel** ( ☎ 484 2768; Favzi Paşa Bulvarı 157; s/d €18/30; ) In the thick of the hotel quarter around Dokuz Eylül Meydanı, this is a good bet in value-for-money terms, despite some street noise. The unfancy house restaurant is also worth a try.

**Hotel Baylan** ( ☎ 483 1426; 1299 Sokak No 8; s/d US$55/65; P ) Tucked away near the station, the Baylan positively showers guests with little extras, from hairdryers and slippers to minibars. Advertised prices shouldn't apply unless it's busy. The hotel also has another, more modern location at Gaziler Caddesi 290 ( ☎ 458 2580), east of the centre.

**Otel Antik Han** ( ☎ 489 2750; Anafartalar Caddesi 600; s/d US$50/70; P ) A restored 19th-century house near the bazaar provides a pleasant change from the bland mid-range. Rooms have TVs, fans and plenty of character, but nearby music bars can be noisy.

## Eating & Drinking

For bargain basement meals, especially in the middle of the day, head down Anafartalar Caddesi towards the bazaar and take your pick of what's cooking. The Kordon is home to the city's swisher restaurants and bars, while Kıbrısşehitleri Caddesi in trendy Alsancak has dozens of varied eateries.

**Gönlübol** (Anafartalar Caddesi 878; mains €1–1.75) Near the station, this is a good spot for kebabs, *pide* and all the usuals.

**Park Köftecisi** ( ☎ 482 2120; Akdeniz Caddesi 6; mains €1.25–2.50) One of the new breed of smart bistro-style fast food joints, off Cumhuriyet Bulvarı.

**Pepe Rosso** ( ☎ 464 9663; Atatürk Caddesi 202B; mains €3.25–7.75) A modest Italian by normal standards, a real find in Turkish terms – the excellent menu here brings a touch of authentic mid-Med cuisine into play, with added treats like milkshakes, tiramisu and flavoured coffees.

## Getting There & Away

### AIR

Onur Air and Turkish Airlines provide frequent nonstop flights to Istanbul (from €53, one hour); THY also flies to Ankara (€76, 70 minutes, twice daily).

### BOAT

Ferry services operate to Istanbul in summer (see p645).

### BUS

There are plenty of bus companies that have ticket offices around Dokuz Eylül Meydanı or Gaziosmanpaşa Bulvarı. They usually provide a *servis* (free minibus) to the *otogar*. From İzmir there are frequent buses to Istanbul (€17.75, eight hours), Çeşme (€3.50, 1¼ hours), Selçuk (€4.40, one hour), Çanakkale (€7, five hours) and many other destinations.

### TRAIN

The evening *Mavi Tren* hauls sleeping cars from Basmane train station to Ankara (€14, 14 hours); or you can take the *İzmir Express* for €9.50.

## Getting Around
### TO/FROM THE AIRPORT
A Havaş bus (€4.50, 30 minutes) departs for Adnan Menderes airport from outside the Turkish Airlines office 1½ hours before every Turkish Airlines' departure.

Hourly trains run from Alsancak train station to the airport (€0.50). A taxi can cost up to €30.

### BUS
There is a local bus terminal at Konak Meydanı. Local bus tickets cost €0.60 and must be bought before boarding. Catch bus No 33 to Kadifekale or bus Nos 601, 603 and 605 to the *otogar*.

## ÇEŞME
☎ 0232 / pop 100,000
Popular with French tourists and İzmir families, Çeşme is very much a seasonal tourist town, though it's mainly used as a stopping-off point between Chios (Greece) and Turkey. If you're staying, it has a small **Genoese fortress**, a 16th-century **caravanserai** (now a hotel) and a choice of **boat excursions**. There's a decent beach 6km away at **Ilıca**.

## Sleeping & Eating
Çeşme has plenty of hotels clustered north and south of the main square, but most close out of season. There's a booking and information booth by the İzmir bus stop.

**Barınak Pansiyon** (☎ 712 6670; 3052 Sokak 58; s/d €10.50/17.75), up the hill past the marina, is a good simple choice with light rooms, roof terrace and shared fridge, TV and sewing machine.

On the main square itself, **Rıdvan Otel** (☎ 712 6336; Cumhuriyet Meydanı 11; s/d €20.75/30.50; ✗) has benefited from a major refit and looks immaculate, as well as giving a vague nod at wheelchair access.

Tourist restaurants cluster around the main square; the multilingual set menus at **Star Restaurant** (Cumhuriyet Meydanı; mains €4.50-5) are good value.

## Getting There & Away
Buses to İzmir (€3, 1¼ hours) often stop at Üçkuyular rather than the main İzmir *otogar*; take bus No 605 into the centre.

Ferries run between Çeşme and Chios (one way/return €35/50) six days a week in summer, once or twice weekly in winter.

## SELÇUK
☎ 0232 / pop 23,100
Selçuk is a pleasant, generally easy-going town best known for its population of storks and for the splendid Roman ruins of Ephesus (Efes), once Rome's capital in the province of Asia. In its heyday only Athens was more magnificent, and the site is one of Turkey's major attractions.

While Selçuk is undeniably touristy, most bus tours skip the town itself and you're spared the resort mentality you'll find elsewhere, making it a popular backpacker destination.

## Orientation & Information
The western side of Atatürk Caddesi, behind the museum, is the quieter part of town and contains some of the best pensions; the eastern side holds the *otogar* and plenty of shops and restaurants.

The **tourist office** (☎ 892 1328) is in the park across from the *otogar*. The PTT (Cengiz Topel Caddesi) will change money as well as providing postal services. The **police station** (2002 Sokak) is near the train station.

## Sights & Activities
The city of **Ephesus** (admission €9; ☉ 8am-5pm, to 7pm in summer) first flourished as a centre for worship of the Anatolian goddess later identified with Diana/Artemis, and quickly became an important port, though the harbour has long since silted up. Wandering down the former main street, you'll see the well-preserved (or restored) remains of structures such as the Temple of Hadrian, Marble Way (where the rich folk lived) and the Fountain of Trajan. The real photo opps, though, are the reconstructed façade of the monumental Library of Celsus and the immense Great Theatre, which could hold 24,000 people. An audio guide with brain-addling amounts of information can be hired for €3 (€1.25 for students). Ephesus is a 3km, 35-minute walk west of Selçuk. Frequent *dolmuşes* to Pamucak and Kuşadası pass the turn-off (€0.90, five minutes).

In Selçuk, the main attraction is the excellent **Ephesus Museum** (admission €2.50; Uğur Mumcu Caddesi; ☉ 8.30am-noon & 12.30-4.30pm), with its priceless collection of artefacts from the Roman period. On the hill above Atatürk Caddesi, the **Basilica of St John** (admission €2.50; ☉ 8am-6pm) is said to be built over the

TURKEY

## SELÇUK

| INFORMATION | |
|---|---|
| Police | 1 C1 |
| PTT | 2 C2 |
| Tourist Office | 3 A3 |

| SIGHTS & ACTIVITIES | (pp617–18) |
|---|---|
| Basilica of St John | 4 A1 |
| Ephesus Museum | 5 A3 |
| Mosque | 6 C2 |
| Temple of Artemis | 7 A3 |

| SLEEPING | (p618) |
|---|---|
| Artemis Guest House | 8 C2 |
| Australia & New Zealand Pension | 9 A2 |
| Homeros Pension | 10 A2 |
| Hotel Nilya | 11 A2 |

| EATING | pp618–19) |
|---|---|
| Kurkıca Şaraplan | 12 B2 |
| Tat | 13 C2 |
| Zefk'ü Sefa | 14 A3 |

| TRANSPORT | (p619) |
|---|---|
| Otogar | 15 B3 |

| OTHER | |
|---|---|
| Toilets | 16 B2 |

apostle's tomb, and is another common coach party stop. Between Ephesus and Selçuk, the foundations and one solitary pillar of the **Temple of Artemis** ( 8.30am-5.30pm) are all that remain of one of the Seven Wonders of the Ancient World.

On Saturdays a lively and mostly untouristy **market** is held on the main square.

## Sleeping

Hospitality is a serious business in Selçuk, with dozens of small pensions competing for backpacker trade; as a result standards and services are pretty high, and the best places put a lot of effort into making sure you won't want to leave (even if you've just come to look round). In summer you can often camp or sleep outside.

**Artemis Guest House** ( 892 6191; www.artemisguesthouse.com; 1012 Sokak 2; dm €6, s/d €9/15.25; ) On the more modern eastern side of town, 'Jimmy's Place' is paradise for frill-seekers, with everything from balconies and satellite TV to Turkish nights, wall paintings and swimming pool. Deluxe rooms also available (€30).

**Australia & New Zealand Guesthouse** ( 892 6050; www.anzguesthouse.com; 1064 Sokak 12; dm €6, r €9 per person; ) This sociable multilevel backpacker favourite has plenty of communal terrace and lounging space, plus a room with Jacuzzi (€30) for those who fancy a soak.

**Homeros Pension** ( 892 3995; homerospension@yahoo.com; Asmali Sokak 17; s €7.50-10.25, d €14.75-20.75; ) A consistent standard-setter, you'll be showered with extras here: free transfers, free bike hire and free homemade wine. The superb rooms display the owner's carpentry skills to great effect, and ambitious expansion plans are in the offing, including a swimming pool.

**Hotel Nilya** ( 0892 9081; 1051 Sokak 7; s/d €30/50; ) Individually decorated rooms and a great collection of random objects give guests plenty to look at in this small, smart pension. Sadly it's closed out of season.

## Eating

**Tat** (Cengiz Topel Caddesi 19; mains €0.75-2.50) Offers reliable standard sit-down food, with owners and staff who are always keen to chew the fat in English.

**Zefk'ü Sefa** ( ☎ 892 9443; 1066 Sokak 1; mains €2.50-5.25) Below the town's chamber of commerce, you'll find a decent menu and friendly service here, plus a great rear courtyard set away from the central hubbub.

**Kurkıca Şaraplan** ( ☎ 892 9797; Atatürk Bulvarı 3) If you're planning a picnic or just bored with beer, pop into this great wine store and choose from the range of local reds, whites and fruit brews. Bottles start around €2.75.

There's no shortage of cheap restaurants in Selçuk; those at the eastern end of Cengiz Topel Caddesi have neat views of the town's Byzantine aqueduct. When it's open, the **Belediye Restaurant** at the municipal swimming pool is a local favourite – ask for directions.

## Getting There & Away

Buses from İzmir (€4.50, one hour) usually drop you on the main highway nearby. Frequent minibuses head for Kuşadası (€1.25, 30 minutes) and the excellent beach at Pamucak (€0.90, 10 minutes).

## KUŞADASI

☎ 0256 / pop 50,000

Kuşadası is an unabashed resort town, with everything that entails, and is effectively the start of Turkey's coastal package holiday strip – many independent travellers just dash through to catch a boat out to Samos (Greece). If you're up for a big, messy night out, though, you can practically guarantee it on Bar St here.

## Information

**Kismet Internet** (Liman Caddesi 1; per hr €1.75)
**Meander Travel** ( ☎ 614 3859; www.meandertravel.com; Kıbrıs Caddesi 1A)
**Tourist Office** ( ☎ 614 1103; İskele Meydanı)

## Sights & Activities

The 16th-century **castle** on the island in the harbour aside, Kuşadası is short on sights,

---

| **TOP FIVE WALKS & BEACHES** |
| :--- |
| ▪ **Pamucak beach** (p617), Selçuk |
| ▪ **Lycian Way** (p640), Fethiye-Antalya |
| ▪ **Patara beach** (p626), Patara |
| ▪ **Ölüdeniz lagoon** (p625), Fethiye |
| ▪ **Ihlara Gorge** (p639), Cappadocia |

---

although it does make a good base for visits to the ancient cities of **Priene, Miletus** ( ☼ 8am-7.30pm May-Oct, 8.30am-5.30pm Oct-Apr) and **Didyma** ( ☼ 9am-7pm May-Sep, 8am-5.30pm Oct-Apr) to the south. Admission to each site is US$1. If you're pushed for time a tour of the ancient cities from the *otogar* costs around US$20.

Locals also recommend **Dilek National Park**, known as the Milliparkı, a lovely peaceful forest area a short drive from town. A *dolmuş* here costs €1.25 (45 minutes). For more watery action, try the **Adaland Aquapark** ( ☎ 618 1252; www.adaland.com; Çamlımanı Mevkii; adult/child €15/9), off the Selçuk road.

## Sleeping

Coming from the harbour, walk up Barbaros Hayrettin Caddesi, turn right and take Yıldırım Caddesi or Aslanlar Caddesi to reach most of the *pensions* and cheap hotels.

**Hotel Sammy's Palace** ( ☎ 612 2588; www.hotel sammyspalace.com; Belediye Çarsisi 17; dm €5, s/d/tr €12/18/24; ✖ ) An old favourite in a new location, Sammy's has been a staple of the backpacker scene since forever, and can still pull them in. Breakfast not included.

**Hotel Liman** ( ☎ 614 7770; Buyral Sokak 4; dm €5, s/d €14.75/20.75; ✖ ☐ ) 'Mr Happy's' could hardly be handier for the ferry to Samos, and offers good comfortable rooms of varying sizes. The nickname comes from the owner, Hasan, who worked Bar Street for years and must count as one of the most hilarious guys you'll ever meet.

**Stella Travellers Inn** ( ☎ 614 1632; www.stella hostel.com; Bezirgan Sokak 44; dm €9, s/d/tr €20/30/36; ☐ ☒ ) Once a standard package-tour high rise, Stella's is now a big backpackers den with balconies, great sea views and unusual extras like a basketball court.

**Club Caravanserail** ( ☎ 614 4115; Öküz Mehmet Paşa Kervansarayı; s US$50-65, d US$80-110; ✖ ☐ ) The imposing former caravanserai opposite the harbour houses Kuşadası's premier hotel, maintaining Ottoman flair and staging regular Turkish nights in the house nightclub.

## Eating & Drinking

If you don't fancy paying €10 for fish'n'chips or roast beef and Yorkshires, there are plenty of cheaper Turkish options in the Kaleiçi district, behind the harbour. Seafood places around the harbour itself charge €15 to €25 for a fish dinner, depending on the fish and the season.

**Ismail Usta** ( ☎ 612 9454; Cephane Sokak 1/1; mains €1.50-3.50) Off the main drag just before the harbour, this smart new restaurant caters more to locals than tourists, and staff even seem to care about whether you enjoy the food or not.

**Pizza Meetza** (Liman Caddesi 1; mains €3-4; 🖳 ) Other Italians in town may offer a bit more variety and service, but the third-storey sea views here more than compensate.

Bar St (Barlar Sokak) is Kuşadası's tourist bar strip, crammed with the kind of crass noisy dives you wouldn't be seen dead in back home. Chances are you'll end up in Jimmy's Irish Pub at some point; if you can escape, head for Kaleiçi, where you'll find several charming café-bars and proper Turkish clubs such as **Le Meyhane** (Sakarya Sokak).

### Getting There & Away

Kuşadası's *otogar* is 1.5km southeast of the centre. Out of season you'll probably have to change at İzmir (€5, 1½ hours) or Söke (€1.25, 30 minutes) for most destinations. In summer there are frequent buses to Bodrum (€6, two hours) and Denizli (for Pamukkale; €7, three hours). For Selçuk (€1.25, 30 minutes) and Söke, pick up a minibus on Adnan Menderes Bulvarı.

In summer three boats daily sail to Samos (same day/open return US$35/55). In winter there may be only one or two boats a week.

## PAMUKKALE

☎ 0258 / pop 4000

Renowned for its brilliant white ledges and pools (travertines), the Pamukkale plateau can disappoint as much as it delights – in recent years the water supply has dried up, you can no longer swim in most of the pools, and rumour has it some of the famous calcium ridges have been touched up with whitewash. It's still an impressive site, however, and if you're not convinced there's the added bonus of the extensive Hierapolis ruins.

### Sights & Activities

As you climb the hill above Pamukkale village you pay to enter the **travertines** and **Hierapolis** (admission €2.50; valid 9am-10am next day). The ruins of Hierapolis, including a theatre, a colonnaded street with public toilet and a vast necropolis, are very spread out; allow at least half a day to do them justice.

Afterwards, swim amid sunken Roman columns at **Pamukkale Termal** (€9.50), on top of the ridge, and visit **Hierapolis Archaeology Museum** (admission €1; admission 🕑 9am-noon & 1-5pm Tue-Sun), which contains some spectacular sarcophagi and friezes from Hierapolis and the nearby ruins of Afrodisias.

### Sleeping & Eating

Over 60 pensions and hotels lurk below the travertines in Pamukkale village. Eating at your accommodation is usually the best idea – most places have poolside terraces.

**Kervansaray Pension** ( ☎ 272 2209; kervansaray2@ hotmail.com; İnönü Caddesi; s/d €12/18; 🔀 🖳 ) This popular travellers' hangout has a good reputation for cheerful service and decent rooms. It's hard to miss the fuschia-and-yellow exterior.

**Hotel Dört Mevsim** ( ☎ 272 2009; www.hoteldort mevsim.com; Hasan Tahsin Caddesi; r US$6.50 per person; 🅿 🖳 🐾 ) The 'Four Seasons' may not bear much resemblance to its illustrious counterparts but it's a good stopover for mere mortals. Meals here are well rated.

**Venüs Hotel** ( ☎ 272 2152; Hasan Tahsin Caddesi; s/d €25/35; 🅿 🔀 🖳 🐾 ) Pink and vaguely rustic, Venüs offers plenty of amenities for your money, and also allows camping in the large garden in summer.

**Koray Otel** ( ☎ 272 2300; Fevzi Çakmak Caddesi 27; s/d €35/45; 🅿 🔀 🐾 ) Another traveller-friendly establishment in much the same mould. Rooms here are nicer and tour services are available.

Of Pamukkale's restaurants, **Han** (mains €2-5), on the main square, probably offers best value for money.

### Getting There & Away

Frequent buses run from local hub Denizli to İzmir (€4, four hours) and Konya (€10, seven hours); a full-day tour will cost around €30 from most Aegean towns.

Buses and *dolmuşes* shuttle between Denizli and Pamukkale every half-hour (€0.50, 30 minutes).

## BODRUM

☎ 0252 / pop 30,000

Once known as Halicarnassus, Bodrum has gone through various incarnations in its long history but is now hardcore resort territory, rammed with (mainly British) tourists every summer. Luckily the town has resisted rampant modernisation and retains charm in the winding streets of its old town and bazaar area; only the pricey restaurants and the persistent bass beats from water-front clubs belie the illusion of a fishing village lifestyle.

## Orientation

The Adliye Camii, a small mosque on the castle promontory, marks the centre, separating the town's two main bays. The *otogar* is 500m inland, along Cevat Sakir Caddesi.

## Information

**Doğuş Internet** (Türkuyusu Caddesi 175A; per hr €0.90)
**Mola Internet** (Menekşe Çık 2/1; per hr €1.25)
**PTT** ( ☎ 316 1212; Cevat Sakir Caddesi)
**Tourist Information** ( ☎ 316 1091; Kale Meydanı 48)

## Sights

You'll see the **Castle of St Peter** on just about every brochure, postcard and flyer in Bod-rum, and it's still an essential stop as well as a scenic asset. Built in 1402 and rebuilt in 1522 by the Crusaders, the castle houses the **Museum of Underwater Archaeology** (admission €6; ☺ 9am-noon & 1-5pm Tue-Sun), containing finds from the oldest Mediterranean shipwreck ever discovered, and a model of a Carian princess's **tomb** (admission €1.75). Just ignore the poor excuse for a 'Trojan horse' in the courtyard.

Westward past the marina and over the hill, **Gümbet** has a nicer beach than Bod-rum but is solid package-holiday territory. You'll probably prefer the less-developed **Ortakent**. To the west of the Bodrum penin-sula, **Gümüşlük** is the least spoilt of the many smaller villages nearby. Hourly *dolmuşes* run there (€1).

Sadly there's little left of the **Mausoleum** (admission €2.50; ☺ 8am-4pm), the monumental tomb of King Mausolus, which made the city famous and was once among the Seven Wonders of the Ancient World. The gar-dens and excavations do merit a wander if you're interested in the period.

Bodrum is a popular **diving** centre – **Crystal Divers** ( ☎ 313 0732; www.crystaltours.com) offers courses for disabled swimmers as well as the usual PADI training. Land-lubbers can work out their aggression with a spot of **paintballing** ( ☎ 394 3777; rifatormen@d-daypaintball club.com).

## Sleeping

The narrow streets around the harbour have plenty of pensions, though few places stay open out of season, and breakfast, air con and other 'extras' are seldom included in the price. The western bay tends to be quieter, as it's further from the main bars and clubs.

**Bodrum Backpacker** ( ☎ 313 2762; www.bodrum backpackers.com; Atatürk Caddesi 31/B; dm €3; ☐ ) If you've been through Selçuk the standards here may come as a rude awakening, but it's the cheapest option in town by quite a margin. Roof space is available in summer, with special deals for Brits.

**Sevin Pansiyon** ( ☎ 3167682; www.sevinpansiyon.com; Türkkuyusu Sokak 5; s/d €9/12, with air con & TV €12/17.75; ☒ ☐ ) The Sevin's extras are a bit perfunc-tory but the rooms are a decent size and it's well placed for just about everything.

**Emiko Pension** ( ☎ 316 5560; Uslu Sokak 11; s/d €9/18) This Japanese-run guesthouse just off Atatürk Caddesi has simple rooms with paved floors and a leafy courtyard setting – not exactly feng shui, but it works.

**Baraz Hotel** ( ☎ 316 1857; Cumhuriyet Caddesi 70; s €26.50-32.50, d €44.25-53; ☒ ) The modern tourist-block building is a bit of a travesty amid the low bazaar shops, but comes with a small stretch of private beach and the usual tourist-class comforts. Best visited out of season.

**Su Otel** ( ☎ 316 6906; www.suhotel.net; 1201 Sokak; s/d/ste €35/70/90; ☒ ☒ ) Indisputably the best place in town. Decked out in bright primary colours and local crafts, this is a friendly, comfy home from home, with a new wing under construction and two holiday cot-tages (€100 and €150) sleeping up to eight people. Book in advance.

## Eating & Drinking

The small streets east of the Adliye Camii harbour several cheap eateries where you can grab a *döner* for less than €2. Otherwise, continue east to Kilise Meydanı, a plaza filled with open-air restaurants. More substantial soirées can be had at lively Meyhaneler Sokak (Taverna St), off İskele Caddesi, or among the many fish restaurants lining the eastern bay. Check all prices before ordering.

**Nazik Ana** (Eskihükümet Sokak 7; mains €0.90-1.75) Vegetarians should sample the self-service lunches at this engaging little café.

**Mantı Evi** ( ☎ 316 7925; Sanatokulu Caddesi 14; mains €1.50-2.50; ☺ dinner only) Family-run and convincingly traditional, nip off Atatürk

Caddesi for a proper dose of homemade *mantı* (Turkish ravioli).

**Liman Köftecisi** (Neyzen Tevfik Caddesi 172; mains €1.90-7) On the western food strip, this is Bodrum's trendiest spot for meatballs, attracting streams of loyal clientele at mealtimes. Turn up early.

**Mor & Jazz** ( ☎ 313 3716; Usla Sokak 8; mains €6-10) OK, so jazz isn't exactly a Turkish art form, but if you crave Western syncopation with your food you can't go far wrong here.

*Nargileh* fans should try the **Old Café** (Cumhuriyet Caddesi) for a post-prandial puff, while no dedicated clubber should miss out on the mighty **Halikarnas Disco** ( ☎ 316 8000; www.halikarnas.com.tr; Cumhuriyet Caddesi 178; ☻ from 10pm), still dominating the eastern end of the bay with its overpowered sound system and open-air dancefloor.

### Getting There & Away

Bodrum airport is actually nearer to Milas; Havaş buses run there and back according to departure times (€6.50, 45 minutes). The taxi fare is around €30.

There are frequent bus services from Bodrum to Antalya (€14.75, eight hours), Fethiye (€6, 4½ hours), İzmir (€7.75, four hours), Kuşadası and Selçuk (€6, two hours) and Marmaris (€6, three hours).

In summer daily hydrofoils and boats link Bodrum with Kos (€20, one hour); in winter services are cut to three times weekly, but prices fall accordingly. Summer boats also run to Datça, Knidos, Marmaris and Rhodes; check with the ferry offices near the castle.

# THE MEDITERRANEAN COAST

Turkey's Mediterranean coastline winds eastward for more than 1200km from Marmaris to Antakya on the Syrian border. From Marmaris to Fethiye the gorgeous 'Turquoise Coast' is perfect for boat excursions, with many secluded coves for swimming. The rugged peninsula between Fethiye and Antalya, and the Taurus Mountains east of Antalya, are wild and beautiful. Further east you pass through fewer resorts and more workaday cities. The entire coast is liberally sprinkled with impressive ruins.

## MARMARIS

☎ 0252 / pop 22,700

A firm favourite with UK and Dutch package companies, Marmaris has suffered from some haphazard town planning and lacks the endearing qualities of Bodrum, despite a very similar setting. However, if you steer clear of the tackier Brit-swamped parts you'll find the atmosphere isn't actually all bad, and it's a good place to board a boat or have a few beers.

### Orientation

İskele Meydanı, the main square, is by the ferry pier northeast of the castle; Hacı Mustafa Sokak, known as Bar St for instantly obvious reasons, runs east from here. The *otogar* is 2km north of town, off the road to Bodrum.

### Information

**Digital Internet** (42 Sokak 26/7; per hr €1.25)
**Galaxie Internet** ( ☎ 413 4082; 44 Sokak 30/1; per hr €1.25)
**PTT** ( ☎ 412 1212; Fevzipaşa Caddesi 14)
**Tourist Information** ( ☎ 412 1035; İskele Meydanı)

### Sights & Activities

Wooden boats along the waterfront offer **tours** of outlying beaches and islands. Check carefully exactly what you pay and what you get for it before agreeing to anything. A day's outing usually costs around €20 per person.

The most popular excursions are to **Dalyan** and **Kaunos** or to the bays around Marmaris, but you can also take longer, more serious trips to **Datça** and the ruins at **Knidos**. It's also worth asking about boats heading for **Cleopatra's Island**, which offers silky-soft sand and water as warm as a Jacuzzi.

The small **castle** ( ☎ 412 1459; admission €0.75; ☻ 8.30am-noon & 1-5.30pm Tue-Sun) has a few unexciting exhibition rooms but offers fine views of Marmaris.

Down on the harbour, you might also notice a **statue** resembling an old-fashioned diver – it actually depicts an astronaut, in honour of NASA man James Reilly, who took the Turkish flag into space in 1998.

### Sleeping

Unlike Kuşadası and Bodrum, Marmaris lacks a network of small, welcoming *pensions*. Indeed, almost all the budget places have been squeezed out by the package-holiday market, and the survivors are often noisy and uninspiring. For the cheapest accommodation stroll along the waterfront and turn inland just past Abdi İpekçi Park.

**Interyouth Hostel** ( ☎ 412 7823; interyouth@turk .net; 42 Sokak 45; dm/r €6/15; ☐ ) In the depths of the bazaar, the local HI outpost can be sociable when it's full but is little more than functional out of season.

**Barış Motel** ( ☎ 413 0652; www.barismotel.com; 66 Sokak 10; s/d €9/12, with shower €18/23.50) There's no attempt at flashiness in this family-run establishment, but the rooms are a pristine shade of whiter-than-white and the staff are utterly obliging.

**Hotel Begonya** ( ☎ 412 4095; Hacı Mustafa Sokak 71; s/d €35/50) If it wasn't right on Bar St this walled pension would be a perfect rustic retreat. As it is, you'll need the earplugs on offer to sleep, but the plant-crammed courtyard is perfect for al fresco lazing during the day.

**Ayçe Otel** ( ☎ 412 3136; 64 Sokak 11; s/d US$45/75; ☒ ☒ ☒ ) Don't be put off (or otherwise influenced) by the topless sunbather in the brochure – the Ayçe is a thoroughly respectable and family-friendly modern hotel with plenty of facilities and nice, if compact, rooms.

**Club Sediz** ( ☎ 413 3452; Gen. Mustafa Muğlalı Caddesi 15; s/d/tr US$60/75/90; ☐ ☒ ☐ ) A mainstay of the self-catering package trade, all the apartment-rooms here have kitchens and full resort amenities.

## Eating & Drinking

Marmaris has literally hundreds of restaurants. For the cheapest fare, head for the bazaar and the streets around it. The many waterfront restaurants around the harbour and the Netsel marina have pleasant outdoor dining areas, but prices are often unjustifiably high. Self-caterers can stock up in the huge **Tansaş shopping centre** ( ☎ 413 9100; Ulusal Egemenlık Bulvarı).

**Azmakbası Restaurant** (Hacı Mustafa Sokak; mains €1.50-9) At the eastern end of Bar St, opposite the marina, this deceptively smart place serves up cheap *mantı* and *gözleme* as well as the tourist standards.

**Ney Restaurant** ( ☎ 412 0212; 26 Sokak 24; mains €3-9) The discreet roof terrace is the perfect place to sample *mezes* and home-style Turkish dishes from an authentic family institution.

**Pineapple** ( ☎ 412 0976; Netsel Marina; mains €3.50-16) A rare chance to dabble in non-Turkish

food: Pineapple serves up an ambitious selection of pan-Asian and international dishes, as well as a stout range of all-day breakfasts (€4.50 to €7.50).

**Bedesten Café** ( ☎ 412 8838; Çeşme Meydanı) To escape some of the streetside bustle, try the town's former covered market, now an atmospheric courtyard serving up drinks, snacks and *nargilehs*.

## Getting There & Away

The nearest airports are Bodrum (see p622) and Dalaman, which has up to 10 weekly flights from Istanbul in summer. The Havaş shuttle to Dalaman costs €11.75.

Frequent buses and minibuses serve Fethiye (€4.75, three hours, hourly), Bodrum (€6, three hours) and Dalyan (via Ortaca; €4, two hours), plus several daily services to Antalya (€13, seven hours).

Car ferries run to Rhodes daily in summer, less frequently in winter (same day/open return €40/65).

## DATÇA

☎ 0252 / pop 6100

Once you've had enough of Brit-spotting and drunk-dodging in Marmaris, it's worth considering a side trip to Datça, a little harbour town that has embraced tourism without being consumed by it. You'll notice the difference in atmosphere the second you step off the bus.

Datça has no specific sights, but there's a nice outdoor **cinema** by the harbour, two narrow **beaches** bordering the centre, a **park** with playground and an army barracks that looks more resorty than any of the hotels. In summer you can take boat trips to Knidos or the Greek islands of Rhodes and Symi.

**Eski Datça** or Old Datça, a picturesque hamlet of cobbled streets and old stone houses on the eastern outskirts, is an even quieter place to stay.

## Information

**Datça Diving** ( ☎ 712 3759; www.datcadiving.com)
**Knidos Yachting** ( ☎ 712 9464; Yalı Caddesi 17)
**Sun Internet** ( ☎ 712 3656; İskele Caddesi 10; per hr €1)

## Sleeping & Eating

**Tunç Pansiyon** ( ☎ 712 3036; Buxerolles Caddesi; s/d €7.50/14.75) Off the main street, the Tunç has neat and thoroughly serviceable rooms. Bring a device you can plug in – it almost

TURKEY

seems a shame to waste the many power points provided.

**Villa Tokur** ( ☎ 712 8728; www.hotel-tokur.com; s/d €30/40; 🍴 🏊 ) On the far side of the harbour, this has a good claim to be Datça's best boutique hotel. A four-bed apartment is also available (€57).

**Çınar Köfte** (İskele Caddesi; mains €0.60-2.75) Go the caféteria route for a good cheap meatball lunch; the range of grills exceeds most other rock-bottom snack joints.

**Papatya Restaurant** (Kargı Yolu Caddesi 4; mains €5-10) You can't miss the brightly coloured terrace here, occupying a fantastic spot above the harbour bay. The taverna-style food is equally well chosen.

### Getting There & Away

Regular buses shuttle to/from Marmaris (€4, 1¾ hours). Minibuses from Datça to Karaköy pass the junction to Old Datça regularly (€0.30). It's a five-minute walk into the village.

In summer you can catch boats to Bodrum (€9) up to twice daily and hydrofoils to Rhodes (one way/return €40/45) via Symi (€30) three times weekly.

## KÖYCEĞIZ

☎ 0252 / pop 7600

Earning its name from the tranquil lake that laps its shore, Köyceğiz takes the yearly influxes of German and Dutch tourists well in its stride and still gives the impression of a town where life doesn't stop out of season, with a thriving agricultural community. Many people prefer it to Dalyan as a base for visiting Kaunos and İztuzu beach.

### Sleeping & Eating

**Flora Hotel** ( ☎ 262 4976; www.florahotel.info; Kordon Boyu 96; s/d €9/18; 🖥 ) One of several backpacker-oriented pensions in town, offering a range of services and excursions. Dutch spoken.

**Hotel Alila** ( ☎ 262 1150; Emeksiz Caddesi; s/d €15/21; 🍴 🏊 ) Rejoicing in a superb lakefront location, complete with well-liked restaurant, this boutique hotel is excellent value and seldom disappoints.

**Panorama Plaza** ( ☎ 262 3773; www.panorama-plaza .de; Cengiz Topel Caddesi 69; s/d €22/44; P 🍴 🏊 ) 'Holydays for the pretentious'? Maybe it's better in German. Either way, the Plaza is Köyceğiz's top hotel, featured and tricked out in marble. Check for promotions.

The best places to eat are around the main square and the adjacent lakeside park. **Çiçek Restaurant** (mains €2-5) is good for people-watching, while the **Atapark** (drinks €0.5-1) is a pleasant tea garden by the Atatürk statue.

### Getting There & Away

Hourly buses run to Ortaca (€0.90, 25 minutes) from the *otogar*, 2km up the main road.

## DALYAN

☎ 0252 / pop 4000

Independent travellers may have trouble knowing what to make of Dalyan – in summer the crowds, facilities and coloured lights (even on the mosque) virtually scream 'tourist trap'. However, the setting, right on the Dalyan River and overlooked by Lycian rock tombs, is so perfect it's hard to write it off completely.

In any case, the main activity here is boating out of town, with a range of excursions on offer. The most popular jaunt takes you to **İztuzu beach**, a short paddle away. It's a gorgeous place to sun yourself as well as being one of the few remaining nesting grounds of the endangered sea turtle *(caretta caretta)*. The same trips (€5) usually take in a visit to the ruined city of **Kaunos** (admission €1.75; 🕑 8.30am-5.30pm) and the **Sultaniye hot springs** (admission €0.60) on the shores of Köyceğiz Lake, possibly with a mud bath thrown in.

### Sleeping & Eating

**Dalyan Camping** ( ☎ 0532-700 6565; per tent/caravan €7/14.75, bungalows s/d €11.75/17.75) Tucked away amid the many pensions around the southern reaches of Maraş Caddesi, this is a passable camping ground with few facilities.

**Kristal Pansiyon** ( ☎ 284 2263; Erkul Sokak; s/d €12/18; 🍴 🏊 ) The roof terrace and swimming pool set this family-run guesthouse apart from many of its counterparts, though the lack of river frontage is a major minus.

**Metin Hotel** ( ☎ 284 2040; Erkul Sokak 14; s/d UK£20/26; 🍴 🏊 ) One of Dalyan's swisher options, spread over three buildings with big rooms and plenty of trimmings. Prices come down outside July and August.

**Fırat Restaurant** (mains €1.75-7.50) The *pide* here is probably the cheapest bite in town, and certainly better value than the larger grills. It's down the small street just opposite the town hall.

**Bistro Clou** ( ☎ 284 3452; mains €3-7) Just north of the market and the *dolmuş* stand, this friendly place, lit by atmospheric gourd lanterns, is a notch above the bog-standard tourist fare elsewhere.

## Getting There & Away
To get anywhere from Dalyan you have to take a minibus to Ortaca (€0.75, 30 minutes) and change. Ortaca to Fethiye costs €2.50 (one hour).

## FETHIYE
☎ 0252 / pop 48,200

Thanks to the popular 'blue cruises' that leave from here, Fethiye is much more geared towards independent travellers than wholesale resort towns such as Marmaris, although it still gets very hot and crowded in summer. The picture-perfect harbour and mountain backdrop are pretty irresistible at any time, and the town also makes a good base for visiting the beautiful **Saklıkent Gorge** and the ruins of **Tlos** and **Pınara**.

The beach at **Çalış**, 5km northeast of the centre, is many kilometres long, and backed by hotels.

## Orientation
Fethiye's *otogar* is 2km east of the centre. Karagözler *dolmuşes* ply up and down the main street, taking you past the government buildings, the PTT and several banks, before skirting the bazaar district, curving around the bay and cutting up by the marina on the western side of the town.

## Information
**Madlife Travel** ( ☎ 612 1564; www.blueyachtcruise
.com; Atatürk Caddesi; 🖳 )
**Tourist Office** ( ☎ 614 1527; İskele Meydanı)
**Trend Internet** (İshane Caddesi; per hr €2)

## Sights & Activities
In Fethiye itself, little remains of the original town of Telmessos: the ruins of a Roman **theatre** and several Lycian sarcophagi dating from about 400 BC. The cliff backdrops hold several picturesque Lycian tombs, including the **Tomb of Amyntas** (admission €1.75; 117 Sokak; 🕑 8am-7pm), ideal for gazing out over the harbour and thinking about ancient times.

Fethiye is also the starting (or finishing) point for the 500km **Lycian Way** (see p640), a superb scenic walking trail along the coast.

Most people succumb to, and enjoy, the well-promoted **12 Island boat tours**, a populist mix of swimming, cruising and sightseeing. Prices are typically around €15 per person, or UK£75 for a three-day, two-night trip.

*Dolmuşes* run to the nearby evocative Ottoman Greek 'ghost town' of **Kayaköy** (admission €1.75), abandoned after the population exchange of 1923.

## Ölüdeniz
Over the mountains south of Fethiye, lovely Ölüdeniz (Dead Sea) is a textbook example of a good thing marred by progress, with over 50 hotels nudging the small, secluded beach. Still, the famous **lagoon** (adult/student €1.25/0.60; 🕑 8am-8pm) remains tranquility incarnate, especially out of season, and the various camping grounds provide a welcome alternative to the concrete jungle.

Popular activities are **paragliding** and **parasailing** – tandem canopies swoop over the bay most days in summer. You can also catch a boat to the beautiful **Butterfly Valley** here (€8 return), or take the free shuttle to **Suara Beach**.

Frequent *dolmuşes* to Ölüdeniz (€1.25, 45 minutes) run from behind Fethiye's Yeni Cami, passing through the odious tourist zone of Hisarönü.

## Sleeping
Most of the nicer pensions are uphill from the marina, off Fevzi Çakmak Caddesi.
**Ferah Pension** ( ☎ 614 2816; www.ferahpension.com; Ordu Caddesi 2; dm €6, d €14.75-17.75; 🖳 ) 'Monica's

---

### WHERE TO TAKE A BOAT RIDE
Fethiye is the hub of Turkey's cruising scene, dispatching dozens of yachts on a daily basis in summer. The most popular voyage is the 'Blue Cruise' to Kale (near Olympos), a three- to four-day route that attracts more than its share of young party animals. You can also continue as far as Antalya, or head in the opposite direction towards Marmaris – many people argue this is actually a finer stretch of coast.

For more ambitious trips you can charter the whole boat yourself, with or without crew, and set off wherever the fancy takes you. Fethiye, Kaş and Marmaris are all good starting points.

Place' is well-known locally and consistently popular with backpackers. The shady terrace is a real plus in a hot summer.

**İrem Hotel** ( ☎ 614 3006; Fevzi Çakmak Caddesi 38; s/d €17.75/23.50; ⚡ ⚑ ) Mod cons and sea views pitch this somewhere between the resort hotels and the family pensions. It also operates the simpler **İrem Pansiyon** ( ☎ 614 3985; s/d €11.75/20.75) across the road.

**Hotel Ivy** ( ☎ 612 5807; www.hotelivy.com; Ordu Caddesi 66; s/d €14.75/29.50; ⚡ ⚑ ) You can't fault the light, clean rooms at this new modern hotel. It was being extended at the time of writing.

**Villa Daffodil** ( ☎ 614 9595; www.villadaffodil.com; Fevzi Çakmak Caddesi 115; s/d €23.50/35.50; ⚡ ⚑ ) Named in tribute to Wordsworth's famous poem, the green surrounds of this charming villa-pension may not include daffodils but definitely adds to the relaxed atmosphere.

### Eating

**İslam Usta Börekcisi** ( ☎ 614 4413) A double portion of *börek* (filled pastry) costs €2 in this tiny outlet, part of the busy covered market.

**Şark Sofrası** ( ☎ 612 0233; Çarşı Caddesi; mains €0.90-3) Dig into the usual prosaic grill fare here, near the bazaar, or try the intriguing 'sensitive meatball'.

**Café Oley** (Eski Meğri Sokak 4; mains €2-6; 🖳 ) A homesick traveller's paradise, offering sandwiches, cakes, muffins, Thai curry and other rare handmade treats in inviting, comfy surrounds.

**Meğri Restaurant** ( ☎ 614 4046; Geçidi Likya Sokak 8/9; mains €4-10) This perennial favourite is as reliable as the summer sun, serving up good Turkish food and fish dishes in a lovely garden. Also on Çarşı Caddesi.

### Getting There & Away

Heading for Antalya, the *yayla* (inland) bus route (€6, four hours) is shorter and cheaper, though less scenic, than the *sahil* (coastal) route (€8, seven hours), which also serves Patara (€1.75, 1½ hours) and Kaş (€3, 2½ hours). Minibuses to local destinations leave from behind the Yeni Cami in the centre.

A summer hydrofoil service links Rhodes (Greece) and Fethiye on Tuesday and Thursday (€50).

The 'blue cruise' (see boxed text, p625) has become a travellers' institution, and is still the nicest way to get between Fethiye

and Olympos or Marmaris – you travel on a *gület* (wooden yacht), calling in at bays along the way for swimming, sunbathing and variable amounts of boozing. Prices for three-day cruises start around UK£99.

## PATARA
☎ 0242

Patara's main claim to fame is its superb 20km-long **beach**, one of Turkey's best – it's also a turtle breeding ground, so most of the sandy expanse is out of bounds between 8pm and 8am in summer. A secondary attraction is the extensive but overgrown **ruined city** (admission €6; ☯ 8.30am-7pm May-Oct, 9am-5.30pm Nov-Apr), good for a scramble.

Patara is also a good base for visiting two of Turkey's Unesco-listed World Heritage Sites, both of them atmospheric ruins. The **Letoön** (admission €1.75), off the Fethiye–Antalya highway near Kumluova, boasts excellent mosaics, a good amphitheatre and a sacred pool used in the worship of the goddess Leto. A few kilometres southeast, **Xanthos** (admission €1.75), with its Roman theatre and Lycian pillar tombs, is among the most impressive sites along this part of the coast, even though many of its best sculptures are now in the British Museum in London.

### Sleeping & Eating

All Patara's amenities are in Gelemiş village, 1.5km inland from the beach.

**St Nicholas Pension** ( ☎ 843 5154; s/d €7/14) One of several competing family pensions around the main beach access road. The terrace restaurant is a real plus.

**Apollon Hotel** ( ☎ 843 5048; www.hotelapollon.com; s/d €25/50; ⚡ ⚑ ) Check out the famed underwear collection at this mid-range hotel on the road heading west of town.

**Jimmy's** (mains €0.90-3) The 'Harrods of Patara' claims to sell everything, as well as serving food on a roadside terrace – try testing them.

### Getting There & Away

Midibuses plying the Fethiye–Antalya main road will drop you 2km from Gelemiş.

## KALKAN
☎ 0242 / pop 1500

Kalkan is the kind of quaint, picturesque fishing village that looks great on postcards, resulting in mass influxes of tourists and property-buying expats. That's not to say that it's lost all its charm, and the major upside of this development is that Kalkan is now one of the best places to eat on the coast, with dozens of competing restaurants.

## Sleeping & Eating

**Patara Stone House** ( ☎ 844 3076; Atatürk Caddesi; s/d €15/28) A wonderful old-fashioned villa right on the waterfront, almost hidden beneath a veil of bougainvillea. The Fish Terrace restaurant on the roof is an expat favourite.

**Caretta Caretta** ( ☎ 844 3435; Yalibolu Mahallesi; s/d UK£20/25; 🖳 ) This apartment-style pension has a good bar-restaurant and its own 'beach platforms' overhanging the sea.

**Daphne Pansiyon** ( ☎ 844 3547; Posta Kutusu 14; s/d €33/46; 🖳 ) German-Turkish collaboration seems to be working well here: not only are the rooms very pleasant, but the owners now run two restaurants in town as well as the pension's own terrace.

**Korsan Restaurant** ( ☎ 844 3622; Kocakaya Caddesi; mains €4-10) One of Kalkan's top-rated dining spots, operated by the same firm as the Stone House.

## Getting There & Away

Hourly buses connect Kalkan with Kaş (€1.25, 35 mins) and Patara (€0.50, 25 mins).

# KAŞ

☎ 0242 / pop 8000

Of all Turkey's popular coastal towns, Kaş has perhaps the most convincing small-town feel to it, with some wonderful winding streets in its old quarter and a waterfront area that retains enough character to be charming even at the height of the tourist season. The drive here is a treat, strewn with mountain views all the way from Fethiye.

## Information

**Bougainville Travel** ( ☎ 836 3737; www.bougainville -turkey.com; İbrahim Selin Caddesi 10)

**Nethouse Internet** ( ☎ 836 2845; Çukurbağlı Sokak 16; per hr €0.90)

**PTT** (İbrahim Serin Caddesi)

**Tourist Office** ( ☎ 836 1238; Cumhuriyet Meydanı)

## Sights & Activities

Apart from enjoying the town's ambience, the Sunday **market** and the small pebble **beaches**, you can also walk west a few hun-

dred metres to the well-preserved Roman **theatre**. Lycian **sarcophagi** are dotted about the streets, and the **tombs** cut into the cliffs above the town are beautifully lit at night.

There are dozens of travel and tour outfits in Kaş just waiting to whisk you off diving, trekking, sailing and so on. Boat trips are the most popular excursions here: common routes head round **Kekova island** and out to beautiful **Kaleköy** (Simena), passing over Lycian ruins beneath the sea. You'll pay around €10 per person in a glass-bottomed boat.

Land-based day trips may take in Patara, Xanthos or the wonderful 18km-long **Saklıkent Gorge**, where you can eat trout on platforms over an ice-cold river.

## Sleeping

Kaş's quietest places to stay are all found on the western side of town, rising in quality the nearer you get to the sea. Yenicami Caddesi, just south of the *otogar*, has lots of small, family-run pensions.

**Kaş Camping** ( ☎ 836 1050; Hastane Caddesi; tent €5) A popular and pleasant site in an olive grove west of town.

**Anı Motel** ( ☎ 836 1791; www.motelani.com; Recep Bilgin Caddesi 12; s €6, d €11.75-14.75; 🖳 🖳 ) Some effort has actually been put into the décor at this backpacker haunt, which boasts spacious rooms, nice windows and a large roof terrace, complete with hammocks.

**Otel Sardunya** ( ☎ 836 3080; www.sardunyaotel .com; Hastane Caddesi; s/d €35.50/47; 🖳 ) Not only do you get immaculate rooms, balconies and sea views here, but prices include half board at the excellent seafront Sardunya Paşabahçesi restaurant, just opposite. There are substantial discounts out of season.

**Hera Hotel** ( ☎ 836 3063; Küçükçakıl Mevkii; s/d €30/60; 🖳 🖳 ) Big, flash and quite spectacularly over the top, even the balconies at this four-star theme resort have classical columns. Luckily the copious facilities make up for the abuses of antiquity.

## Eating

**Türkmen Sofrası** (PTT Caddesi; mains €1.50-3) It's not the most atmospheric place in town, but the Türkmen's set menus (€3.25 to €5) are top value. The outside seating faces the park.

**Hanimeli** (mains €0.90-4) More bargain set meals, this time €10 for four courses of good old-fashioned Turkish cooking, on a big terrace near the PTT.

**İkbal** (Süleyman Sandıklı Sokak; mains €4.75-10.75) If you're going to dine out at any of the touristy restaurants in town, the stepped stone terrace here must be the coolest setting around.

**Chez Evy** (Terzy Sokak; mains €14.75-16.50; ☺ dinner only) Finding such an upmarket French restaurant in the heart of the Turkish riviera comes as a shock, but it's the food that will make you go *ooh la la*. Try the wild boar.

### Getting There & Away

Midibuses depart from Kaş's convenient central *otogar* for all local destinations. Regular services include Fethiye (€3, 2½ hours), Kale (€1.25, one hour), Olympos (€4.25, 2½ hours) and Antalya (€4.25, four hours).

## KALE (DEMRE)

☎ 0242 / pop 13,600

Set on an alluvial plain covered in greenhouses, Kale (ancient Myra) is famous for a certain generous 4th-century bishop who, according to legend, gave anonymous gifts to dowryless girls, thus enabling them to marry. He was later canonised as St Nicholas – yes, the original, pre–Coca Cola Father Christmas (Noel Baba in Turkish). The restored 3rd-century **Church of St Nicholas** (admission €4; ☺ 8am-5.30pm) supposedly holds his tomb but is more interesting for the remains of Byzantine frescoes and mosaic floors.

About 2km inland from the church is a rock face honeycombed with ancient **Lycian tombs**, right next to a large **Roman theatre** (admission €7; ☺ 8am-5.30pm).

Frequent midibuses ply up and down the coastal road, connecting Kale with Kaş and the turn-off for Olympos.

## OLYMPOS

☎ 0242

After climbing into the mountains, the switchback coastal road reaches a turn-off marked for Olympos. From here it's just over 8km down a winding unpaved road to the village and a further 3.5km along an ever-worsening road to **ancient Olympos** (adult/concession €6/1.75; ☺ 8am-7pm). Once a major port city; now it's a fantastically wild, abandoned place beloved of hippies and New Age types, with ruins peeking out from copses, outcrops and riverbanks. You also have to pay the admission fee to reach the extensive **beach**, although your ticket should be valid for at least two days.

## Chimaera

According to legend, the natural eternal flame of the **Chimaera** (Yanartaş) was the hot breath of a subterranean monster with the head of a lion, the body of a goat and a snake's tail, descended from the earth goddess Gaia. Easily sighted by mariners in ancient times, it is now a mere glimmer of its former fiery self, but no less exotic – don't let jaded camp staff talk you out of having a look.

To find the Chimaera, follow the signs 3km east down a neighbouring valley. A half-hour climb leads to the flames.

### Sleeping & Eating

Most visitors come here to stay in the treehouse camps, a motley assortment of wooden huts, restaurants and bars lining the 3.5km road from the beach to Olympos village. If that's not your thing, there are normal pensions and hotels at neighbouring Çıralı. All prices here are half-board – as meals are provided, few people choose to eat elsewhere.

**Türkmen** ( ☎ 892 1249; www.olymposturkmen.com; dm US$8, r per person US$10-14; 🖥 ) A good example of a successful, popular camp, with real treehouses (as opposed to the low huts elsewhere) and the full range of facilities.

**Bayram's** ( ☎ 892 1243; www.bayrams.com; r per person €10-15; 🅿 🖥 ) More relaxed and grown-up than some of the competition, Bayram's makes the most of its orange grove setting. It claims to be wheelchair-friendly, though it's hard to see how.

**Kadir's** ( ☎ 892 1250; dm €9, r per person €11.75-18; 🔀 🖥 ) The place that started it all is still a good bet, daubed colourfully throughout and staffed by a range of seasoned Antipodeans. The bar-disco is throbbing in every sense, but it's the furthest camp from the beach.

**Olympos Lodge** ( ☎ 825 7171; Çıralı Köyu 38, Çıralı; s/d €140/175, deluxe r €200; 🔀 ) Right at the opposite end of the elegance scale, the luxury bungalows here dispose of a grand four-acre setting between the beach and the ruins. If you're going to splash out, this is a fine place to do it.

### Getting There & Away

Fethiye–Antalya buses will drop you at the highway turn-off, where *dolmuşes* wait to run you down to Olympos village and the camps (€1.50). To get to Çıralı you may need to ring a *pension* to collect you, or take a taxi.

The nicest way to get from Olympos to Fethiye is on a cruise (see p626).

## ANTALYA

☎ 0242 / pop 509,000

A bustling, modern town, Antalya's unspectacular beaches are pure tourist zones but the city itself has much more to it. **Kaleiçi**, the restored Ottoman old town, is a charming hillful of winding lanes, characterful buildings and souvenir shops, while cliffside vantage points on either side of the harbour provide superb views over a beautiful marina and the sea-facing Karaalioğlu Parkı.

### Orientation

The *otogar* is 4km north of the centre; a minibus into town costs €0.45. The city centre is at Kalekapısı, a major intersection marked by a landmark clock tower. To get into Kaleiçi, head south down the hill.

Pebbly **Konyaaltı** beach spreads out to the west of town, sandy **Lara** beach to the east. Both are solidly back dropped with package-holiday hotels.

### Information

**Natural Internet** ( ☎ 243 8763; Tophane Parkı; per hr €0.75)
**Onur Air** ( ☎ 330 3432; Cumhuriyet Caddesi 91)
**Owl Bookshop** ( ☎ 243 5718; Akarçeşme Sokak 21)
**PTT** (Güllük Caddesi)

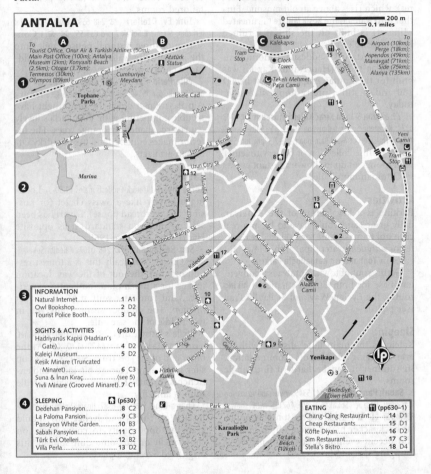

### ANTALYA

| INFORMATION | |
|---|---|
| Natural Internet | 1 A1 |
| Owl Bookshop | 2 D2 |
| Tourist Police Booth | 3 D4 |

| SIGHTS & ACTIVITIES | (p630) |
|---|---|
| Hadriyanüs Kapisi (Hadrian's Gate) | 4 D2 |
| Kaleiçi Museum | 5 D2 |
| Kesik Minare (Truncated Minaret) | 6 C3 |
| Suna & İnan Kıraç | (see 5) |
| Yivli Minare (Grooved Minaret) | 7 C1 |

| SLEEPING | (p630) |
|---|---|
| Dedehan Pansiyon | 8 C2 |
| La Paloma Pansion | 9 C3 |
| Pansiyon White Garden | 10 B3 |
| Sabah Pansyion | 11 C3 |
| Türk Evi Otelleri | 12 B2 |
| Villa Perla | 13 D2 |

| EATING | (pp630–1) |
|---|---|
| Chang-Qing Restaurant | 14 D1 |
| Cheap Restaurants | 15 D1 |
| Köfte Diyarı | 16 D2 |
| Sim Restaurant | 17 C3 |
| Stella's Bistro | 18 D4 |

**Tourist Office** ( ☎ 241 1747; Cumhuriyet Caddesi 91)
**Tourist police booth** (Park Sokak)

## Sights

### ANTALYA MUSEUM
**Antalya Müzesi** (Cumhuriyet Caddesi; admission €6; ☯ 9am-6pm Tue-Sun) is about 2km from the centre but houses spectacular finds from nearby Perge, Aspendos and Side, as well as a wonderful ethnographical collection. Look out for the 12 Labours of Hercules relief. The *tramvay* (tram; €0.50) takes you to the Müze stop.

### KALEIÇI
Heading down from the clock tower you'll pass the elegant **Yivli Minare** (Grooved Minaret), which rises above an old mosque. Further into Kaleiçi, the **Kesik Minare** (Truncated Minaret) is built on the site of a ruined Roman temple.

Just off Atatürk Caddesi, the monumental **Hadrian's Gate** (Hadriyanüs Kapısı) was built for the Roman emperor's visit in AD 130 and is still a pretty impressive sight today.

The **Suna & İnan Kıraç Kaleiçi Museum** ( ☎ 243 4274; Kocatepe Sokak; admission €0.90; ☯ 9am-noon & 1-6pm Thu-Tue Oct-May, 9am-noon & 2-7.30pm Jun-Sep) houses a fine collection of pottery together with rooms set up to show important events in Ottoman family life.

## Activities
Parklife is a key feature of the Antalyan daily grind, and you'd have to be in a real rush not to make time for a relaxed tea, coffee or *nargileh* (water pipe) at the viewpoint cafés in **Tophane** or **Karaalioğlu Parkı**.

Getting out of town, Antalya is a convenient base for both Turkey's national **hiking** routes, the Lycian Way and St Paul's Trail (see p640).

## Sleeping
Kaleiçi is the main hotel district, with an ever-changing selection of accommodation. In summer it can be hard to find single rooms.

**Sabah Pansiyon** ( ☎ 247 5345; www.sabahpansiyon .8m.com; Hesapçı Sokak 60; s/d €6/12, with shower €9/14.75; ☢ ▢ ) Antalya's most highly popular backpacker haven offers tours, car hire and decent evening meals, with plenty of lounging space to boot.

**Pansiyon White Garden** ( ☎ 241 9115; Hesapçı Geçidi 9; s/d €9/14.75; ☢ ) Floral motifs and spotless rooms give the Garden a dash of homely charm, and the shady rear courtyard is a real selling point.

**Dedehan Pansiyon** ( ☎ 248 3787; Mescit Sokak 29; s/d €17.75/20; ▣ ☢ ) How can you dislike a place with heart-shaped pillows? The décor isn't exactly urban chic but this is another good family place.

**La Paloma Pansion** ( ☎ 244 8497; www.lapaloma pansion.com; Tabakhane Sokak 3; s/d €25/40; ☢ ☣ ) It may be situated at the grottier end of its street, but La Paloma is a real delight and an absolute bargain. Some genuine charm lies in the details here, from the separate children's pool to the perfectly tailored rooms.

**Türk Evi Otelleri** ( ☎ 248 6591; www.turkeviotel leri.com; Mermerli Sokak 2; s/d €35/55; ☢ ☣ ) Consisting of three restored houses built onto the ancient city walls, this is a smart midrange choice with plenty of character.

**Villa Perla** ( ☎ 248 9793; www.villaperla.com; Hesapçı Sokak 26; r US$40-70; ☢ ☣ ) Even the luxury Alp Paşa Hotel down the road might have trouble competing with Villa Perla's lovely courtyard, shaded by orange trees. The interior makes equally good use of quirky Ottoman artefacts.

## Eating
**Köfte Diyarı** (Atatürk Caddesi; mains €1.50-3) Looking bizarrely like a Swiss chalet (or possibly a gingerbread house), Diyarı has been serving up good standard grills opposite Hadrian's Gate since 1965.

**Sim Restaurant** ( ☎ 248 0107; Kaledibi Sokak 7; mains €1.75-6) Technically this is a tourist restaurant, but the out-of-the-way location makes for a much more 'authentic' experience, and you can't sniff at €5.50 for *filet mignon*. The outdoor seating puts you in the middle of the streetlife.

**Stella's Bistro** ( ☎ 243 3931; www.stellasbistro.net; Fevzi Çakmak Caddesi 3; mains €4.70-11.40; ☢ ) At the other end of the spectrum, Stella's dishes up slick international fare to hip locals and entrenched expats. The white chocolate trifle sounds amazing.

**Chang-Qing** ( ☎ 247 6587; İmaret Sokak; mains €4-17.50) Wok chicks and lychee lads should grab the opportunity to chow down on chow mein or do some dim sum at this bright red Szechuan place.

A covered passage close to the junction of Cumhuriyet and Atatürk Caddesis, **Eski Sebzeciler İçi Sokak** is lined with streetside restaurants, where a *tandır kebap* (mutton cooked in earthenware), salad and drink can cost as little as €4. The bazaar's also a good starting point, but avoid the rip-off kebab shops without marked prices around the clock tower.

### Getting There & Away

Turkish Airlines and Onur Air offer frequent flights to Istanbul from €53; THY also flies to Ankara (€64, one hour, twice daily). The airport is 10km east of the city centre; the Havaş bus costs €4.50 (30 minutes), a taxi about €10.

From the *otogar*, regular buses head for Olympos (€2, 1½ hours), Manavgat/Side (€2.50, 1¾ hours), Alanya (€4, 2½ hours), Konya (€10.50, six hours), Göreme (€10.50, 10 hours) and most of the other major destinations.

## AROUND ANTALYA

Between Antalya and Alanya there are several spectacular Graeco-Roman ruins. **Perge** (admission €9), east of Antalya near Aksu, boasts a 12,000-seat stadium and a 15,000-seat theatre. **Aspendos** (admission €9), 47km east of Antalya, has Turkey's best preserved ancient theatre, dating from the 2nd century AD and still used for performances during the Aspendos Festival every June/July. **Termessos** (admission €0.70), high in the mountains off the Korkuteli road to the west of Antalya, has a spectacular setting but demands some vigorous walking and climbing.

The **Köprülü Kanyon**, 96km northeast of Antalya, is a deservedly popular spot for white-water rafting. **MedRaft** (☎ 0242-312 5770; www.medraft.com) can fix you up from around US$60 per person.

## SIDE

☎ 0242 / pop 18,000

Set on a distinctive promontory, Side is one of those unfortunate seaside towns that have been completely spoilt by tourism, with coach-party crowds and the cult of the fast buck wiping out any charm it might have had in high season. If you can time it right, though, the attractions here are worth a look outside peak periods.

Side's impressive ancient structures include two sets of **Roman baths**, one of which houses the town **museum** (adult/student €3/1.25; ☼ 8.30am-5.30pm); the old **city walls**; a huge **amphitheatre** (adult/student €6/1.75; ☼ 8am-5pm), used for events during the Aspendos Festival; and seaside **temples** to Apollo and Athena. The sandy **beaches** here are understandably popular.

### Sleeping & Eating

The village is packed with pensions and hotels, which fill up quickly in summer.

**Piknik Garden Pansiyon** (☎ 753 3712; Zambak Sokak; s €9, d €14.75-17.75) One of the more bizarre options in town, offering beds in peculiar triangular huts – imagine sleeping in a wooden Toblerone.

**Hotel Sevil** (☎ 753 2041; Zambak Sokak Köyiçi; s/d €11.75/23.50; ✷) For a normal night's rest, the Sevil has decent rooms with a few extra services like books and table tennis.

**Soundwaves Restaurant** (☎ 753 1607; Barbaros Caddesi; mains €3.25-11.25) The Beach House Hotel's house restaurant is set slightly away from the central tourist action and has some good lunch deals (€2 to 3.50). The giant TV shows mainly sports.

### Getting There & Away

Frequent minibuses connect Side with Manavgat *otogar* (€0.60), 4km north, where there are onward buses to Antalya (€2.50, 1¾ hours) and Alanya (€2.50, one hour).

## ALANYA

☎ 0242 / pop 110,100

In 1427 Alanya was sold, in its entirety, for 5000 gold coins. The amount of development since then should have added at least a few doubloons to its value – with hundreds of tourist hotels and restaurants, the package holiday industry practically owns the city, and independent travellers are a rarity. The main reason to stop by is to take in the ruins of the magnificent Seljuk castle.

### Orientation

The long-distance *otogar* is 3km west of the centre; to get into town take a *dolmuş* (€0.45) to the central stop by the covered Grand Bazaar. Downhill lies the old bazaar and waterfront area, with trendy shops and good food.

## Information

**Active Divers** ( ☎ 512 8811; www.activedivers.com; Tophane Caddesi)
**Fergün Shipping** ( ☎ 511 5565; İskele Caddesi)
**Tourist Office** ( ☎ 513 1240; Kalearkası Caddesi)
**Turkuaz Internet** (Kural Sokak 4; per hr €0.60)

## Sights & Activities

Perched high above the frolicking sun-seekers, Alanya's Seljuk **castle** (admission €9; ⊙ 8am-7pm) was built in 1226 under the reign of Alaeddin Keykubad I and still has some functioning buildings inside the massive walls. Take a bus or taxi up and then stroll back down to take advantage of the views. Several natural **caves** in the hill below can also be visited; the humidity is reputedly good for asthma sufferers. A few unofficial 'guides' may hang around the road up to the castle – ignore them, they're rubbish!

The octagonal **Kızıl Kule** (Red Tower; admission €1.75; ⊙ 8am-noon & 1.30-5.30pm Tue-Sun), down by the harbour, was also built in the year 1226.

There are good **beaches** to the east and west but they're solidly backed with high-rise hotels.

## Sleeping

Sadly, most of Alanya's cheap pensions have given way to package resorts, and only a couple of places linger on in noise-ridden İskele Caddesi, above the harbour. On the plus side, in the tourist hotels you might pay as little as half the advertised prices out of season.

**Hotel Temiz** ( ☎ 513 1016; İskele Caddesi 12; s/d €14.75/23.50; ❄ ) A viable budget-ish option, with at least a modicum of comfort to compensate for the lack of alternatives.

**Grand Bali Hotel** ( ☎ 511 0453; www.grandbali .com; Damlataş Caddesi; s €20, d €40-50; ❄ ⓢ ) This freshly opened four-star block looks to be good value while it's finding its feet (expect prices to rocket within a couple of years). In-house *hammam*, sauna, games room and entertainment liven things up a bit.

**Hotel Kaptan** ( ☎ 513 4899; www.kaptanhotels.com; İskele Caddesi 80; s €37-53, d €50-70; ❄ ⓢ ) Three-star comfort in fine style marks out this local chain establishment, and the terraced pool gives it an edge over the newer Seaport Hotel next door.

## Eating & Drinking

For a cheap bite you'll have to head inland, towards the bazaar. Otherwise, the densely packed waterfront restaurants have the best range of evening meals.

Damlataş Caddesi has plenty of options, including **Mangal** (mains €0.75-5), for cheap (German is spoken) *döners* and fish, and **Old House** ( ☎ 511 6054; mains €5.50-10), for Turkish classics in a leafy garden setting.

There's no shortage of bars and clubs amid the seafront restaurants. **Atlantis** (Gazipaşa Caddesi), in the park just back from the water, has the most interesting (read weirdest) design.

## Getting There & Away

There are frequent buses west via Antalya (€4, 2½ hours) and east to Adana (€11.75, 10 hours) and Antakya (€16.25, 13½ hours, four daily). Minibuses from the central stop serve Manavgat (€2.50, one hour) and other local destinations.

## THE EASTERN COAST

After Alanya holiday traffic starts to thin out, and by the time you reach the Syrian border there's barely a resort in sight. If you want to get the best of the summer Med without the crowds, this is a great stretch of coast to trawl along, with some of Turkey's lesser-known sights (particularly castles) and cities providing stops along the way.

### Anamur

There's nothing special about the service town of Anamur – the attraction here is the ruined Byzantine city of **Anemurium** (admission €1.25), 8.5km west of the town, where a number of buildings are still identifiable and the occasional fragmented mosaic pokes through the topsoil. About 7km out the other side of town is a wonderful 13th-century **castle** right on the beach, with pensions and camping grounds nearby.

A bus from Alanya will cost you €6 (three hours).

### Silifke

Larger than Anamur but just as unassuming, Silifke is in the throes of some extensive development. Stop over here to visit the medieval **fortress** (admission free), with its gateless walls and ancient rock-carved cistern, and the ruined Roman **temple of Jupi-**

ter (admission free). The stone **bridge** over the Göksu River holds an interesting place in local folklore, worth investigating for fans of the bizarre.

A bus from Alanya costs €10 (6½ hours), travelling via Anamur (€6, 3½ hours). From **Taşucu**, 11km southwest, boats and hydrofoils depart for Girne (Kyrenia) in Northern Cyprus (see p644).

## Kızkalesi

'Maiden's Castle' is a growing holiday resort named for the striking **Byzantine castle** offshore. Unless you're up to swimming 150m, you'll need to take a boat (€2.50) to get out and see it. The ruins of a **twin castle** (admission €2.50) are just opposite, on the shore itself; the two were once linked by a causeway, a very unusual defensive ploy.

## Tarsus

The birthplace of St Paul doesn't offer much for budding pilgrims, though everything from churches to bars are named after him. You may find other features nearby more interesting: the stretch of Roman road in the **Old City**, the medieval **Eski Cami** (Old Mosque), and the lovely **waterfall** on the Cydnus River (accessible by *dolmuş* from the Eski Cami).

## ADANA

☎ 0322 / pop 1.1 million

Turkey's fourth-largest city is not the kind of place you visit for fun. Lacking the mystique of Istanbul and the sophistication of İzmir, it's useful as a transport hub connecting the eastern Mediterranean with the west coast and Anatolia. If you end up with some time to kill here, it's worth having a look at the extravagant **Sabancı Merkez Cami**, built by legendary tycoon Sakip Sabancı (see boxed text), and the two city **museums**.

### Sleeping & Eating

**Akdeniz Oteli** ( ☎ 363 1510; İnönü Caddesi 22; s/d €24/40; ✖ ) A comfortable alternative to the cheap hotels opposite, with good spacious rooms.

**Otel Seyhan** ( ☎ 457 5810; www.otelseyhan.com.tr; Turhan Cemal Beriker Bulvarı 18; s/d US$85/100; P ✖ ⌨ ) Adana's top-end edifice is prominent enough to attract big performers like Gülben Ergen to amuse its wealthy conference clientele. The accommodation, too, is up to international business-travel standards.

**Tarihi Ocakbaşı Mesut** ( ☎ 453 6970; Valiyolu Caddesi; mains €1-5) On the smarter northern side of town, this classical-themed restaurant

---

**IF YOU'RE SABANCI AND YOU KNOW IT**

Sakip Sabancı, the wealthiest man in Turkey, died on 10 April 2004, leaving a giant Sabancı-shaped hole not only in national industry but also in the hearts of many ordinary Turkish people. Born in 1933, the dynamic businessman had become one of the best-known figures on the national scene, and his death was greeted with unprecedented outbreaks of countrywide mourning.

In a typical riches-to-even-more-riches story, the young Sabancı initially eschewed his father's flour and textile factories in favour of working as a clerk in the local bank. By the 1960s, however, he had rejoined the family business and helped make it a serious regional concern, moving its headquarters from Adana to Istanbul; by the 1980s he was CEO of Turkey's most powerful conglomerate, controlling a network of over 60 major companies (including his old employer Akbank) and numerous international partnerships.

By this time, however, Sabancı's main concern was not his vast fortune (estimated at US$3.2 billion at the time of his death) but his social conscience. His acts of philanthropy had a huge impact on many aspects of life in Turkey: the Sabancı University in Istanbul has become one of the most respected institutions in the region; the family mansion was converted into a major art and calligraphy museum; and Vaksa, the charitable organisation he founded in association with Sabancı Holdings, is the largest of its kind, running over 100 health and education centres around the country.

Amid all this conspicuous charity, Sabancı managed to retain a common touch which endeared him to the ordinary people of Turkey, exaggerating his provincial Kayseri accent and never shying from expressing his often forthright views on politics and bureaucracy. Despite amassing wealth beyond the wildest dreams of working-class Turks, he remained a hugely popular figure right up until his death, and few people disputed that his state funeral was an honour richly deserved.

is a cut above the many kebab shops on nearby Atatürk Caddesi.

## Getting There & Away

Şakirpaşa airport is just 4km from the centre. Onur Air and Turkish Airlines fly daily to Istanbul (from €53, 80 minutes).

Adana's *otogar*, 2km beyond the airport, serves destinations throughout Turkey, including Antakya (€6, 3½ hours), Konya (€11.75, six hours), Ankara (€10.75, 10 hours) and Istanbul (€17.75, 15 hours). Most bus companies have *servis* buses from their town centre offices.

## ANTAKYA (HATAY)

☎ 0326 / pop 141,000

Part of Syria until 1939, you might recognise Antakya from its biblical name, Antioch – the city was vilified as the Roman empire's most depraved outpost, a claim that the local tourist board keeps strangely quiet about. Sadly present-day Antakya isn't nearly that exciting, though it's a thoroughly amenable modern town with distinct Arabic influences and worth a wander even if you're not heading for the border.

The magnificent Roman and Byzantine mosaics in the **Archaeology Museum** (adult/concession €3/1.25; ☾ 8.30am-noon & 1.30-5pm Tue-Sun) more than justify a trip here, with some extraordinary examples from nearby Daphne (Harbiye) and Tarsus. You can also visit the ancient **St Peter Church** (St Pierre Kilisesi; admission €3; ☾ 8.30am-noon & 1.30-4.30pm Tue-Sun), in a cave 3km east of the centre, where St Pete dropped by to do his bit in the war on debauchery.

## Information

**Al-Tel Internet** ( ☎ 213 0893; Gündüz Caddesi 2; per hr €0.60)

**Ferah Kitabevi** ( ☎ 215 1899; Hürriyet Caddesi 17/D-E) Books, newspapers and magazines.

**Tourist Office** ( ☎ 216 0610; Şehit Nevrez Caddesi)

## Sleeping & Eating

You'll find just about everything you need on the main street, İstiklal Caddesi, though it's more fun to wander off into the extensive bazaar area. Prices are considerably lower than most coastal cities.

**Hotel Şeker Palas** ( ☎ 215 1603; İstiklal Caddesi 79; s/d €4.75/9; ☒ ) Obviously you can't expect too much from rooms this cheap, but the hotel is very close to the *otogar* and it's not a total dive.

**Grand Kavak Otel** ( ☎ 212 7171; www.kavakotel .com; İstiklal Caddesi 16; s €14.75, d €20.75-23.50; ☒ ) Considerably more upmarket, a pink/red theme runs through the understated décor here. You'll have to ask them what the 'Otantic Sheep' is.

**Sultan Sofrası** ( ☎ 213 8759; İstiklal Caddesi 18; mains €0.60-3.50) Friendly and pristine, Middle Eastern touches (lots of mint) make the steam-tray lunches and grills here go down very nicely. The cashier's screensaver is an exercise in food photography.

## Getting There & Away

All buses heading west into Turkey go via Adana (€6, 3½ hours, every 30 minutes). Daily direct buses also head to Syria and Saudi Arabia.

# CENTRAL ANATOLIA

Istanbul may be exotic and intriguing, the coast's pretty and relaxing, but it's the Anatolian plateau which is Turkey's heartland, as Atatürk acknowledged when he moved the capital to Ankara in 1923.

## ANKARA

☎ 0312 / pop 4 million

Ankara has never enjoyed a great reputation either as a tourist hotspot or a dynamic capital, but it's a much more manageable size than Istanbul and no less cosmopolitan in its outlook. With its key position at the heart of the country, transport links here are unbeatable, and it's worth checking out the citadel area and the city's excellent museum before you hop aboard.

## Orientation

Ankara's *hisar* (citadel) crowns a hill 1km east of Ulus Meydanı (Ulus Square), the heart of Old Ankara. Modern Ankara lies further south, around Kızılay Meydanı (Kızılay Square) and Kavaklıdere.

Atatürk Bulvarı is the city's main north–south axis, running right the way through town. Ankara's mammoth *otogar* is 6.5km southwest of Ulus Meydanı. Ankara Garı (train station) is 1.4km southwest of Ulus Meydanı.

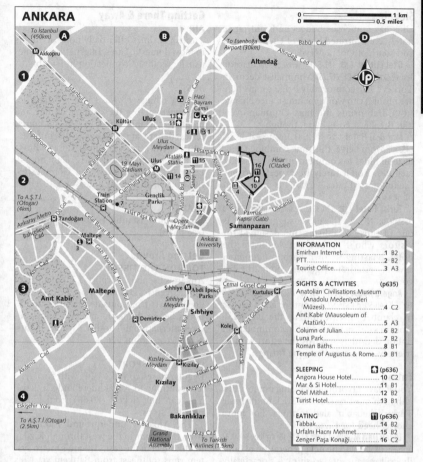

## ANKARA

INFORMATION
Emirhan Internet..................1 B2
PTT.................................2 B2
Tourist Office.....................3 A3

SIGHTS & ACTIVITIES          (p635)
Anatolian Civilisations Museum
  (Anadolu Medeniyetleri
  Müzesi)..........................4 C2
Anıt Kabir (Mausoleum of
  Atatürk)..........................5 A3
Column of Julian..................6 B2
Luna Park.........................7 B2
Roman Baths......................8 B1
Temple of Augustus & Rome......9 B1

SLEEPING                     (p636)
Angora House Hotel...............10 C2
Mar & Si Hotel...................11 B1
Otel Mithat.......................12 B2
Turist Hotel......................13 B1

EATING                       (p636)
Tabbak...........................14 B2
Urfalı Hacı Mehmet...............15 B2
Zenger Paşa Konağı...............16 C2

## Information

**Emirhan Internet** ( ☎ 311 5771; Rüzgarlı Plevni Sokak 9/1; per hr €0.90)

**PTT** (Atatürk Bulvarı)

**Tourist Office** ( ☎ 231 5572; Gazi Mustafa Kemal Bulvarı 121)

## Sights & Activities

Next to the citadel, the **Anatolian Civilisations Museum** (Anadolu Medeniyetleri Müzesi; ☎ 329 3160; Hisarparkı Caddesi; admission €4.75; ⌚ 8.30am-5pm Tue-Sun) is home to the world's richest collection of Hittite artefacts, and so becomes an essential supplement to visiting central Turkey's various Hittite sites. However museum-fatigued you're feeling, this place is a must, and provides a perfect excuse

to wander around the living streets of the citadel itself.

The **Anıt Kabir** (Mausoleum of Atatürk; ⌚ 9am-5pm), 2km west of Kızılay Meydanı, is the monumental tomb of modern Turkey's founder and tantamount to a place of pilgrimage for many Turks.

Various Roman ruins are scattered around town, including the **Column of Julian**, erected in AD 363, and the **Temple of Augustus & Rome**. Nearby are remains of the **Roman Baths** (admission €1.25; ⌚ 8.30am-12.30pm & 1.30-5.30pm).

After all this antiquity, take a break and see the lighter side of Ankara life by eating, drinking or swanning around the boating lake in **Gençlik Parkı** and nipping into the **Luna Park** (€0.15) funfair.

## Sleeping

Ulus has numerous budget and mid-range hotels, concentrated north of Ulus Meydanı and south of Opera Meydanı.

**Otel Mithat** ( ☎ 311 5410; www.otelmithat.com.tr; Tavus Sokak 2; s/d €13/17.75) Minimalist décor in Turkey? The comfortably beige rooms here are proof it can work, making a nice change from drab prints and faux-Ottoman overkill. Breakfast costs extra, though.

**Mar & Si Hotel** ( ☎ 310 8383; Eşdost Sokak 10; s/d €45/56) More beige, this time combined with tasteful blues to complement the three-star facilities. You'll rarely be expected to pay the full posted rates – €18/24 is normal out of season.

**Turist Hotel** ( ☎ 310 3980; Çankırı Caddesi 37; s/d US$50/70; ⚡ ) As the name suggests, this is one of those establishments designed for visitors who'll probably never leave the hotel, boasting its own barber, *hammam*, several restaurants, games room...the list goes on.

**Angora House Hotel** ( ☎ 309 8380; Kalekapısı Sokak 16; s US$40-50, d US$60-75) Another good excuse to clamber up the hill to the citadel – Ankara's most individual accommodation option definitely rewards the effort with its friendly service and antique fittings.

## Eating

You'll have no problems eating out in Ulus, although most restaurants stick to the basic Turkish kebab'n'salad formula. For more choice, head for Kızılay.

**Urfalı Hacı Mehmet** ( ☎ 311 2636; Kızılbey Sokak 3/A; mains €0.60-3.50) The next generation of family grill restaurants, so shiny it's practically space age. The descriptions may not appeal – 'compacted sliced meat' anyone? – but the special Urfa kebabs (€5.75 to €22.50) will feed up to eight people.

**Tabbak** ( ☎ 310 1555; İstiklal Caddesi 1/A; mains €1.25-4.75) 'The New Bistro' is the central branch of an expanding local chain, now with branches in Istanbul. The above-average menu includes European pub standards like cordon bleu and, for Germanists, '*şinitzel*'.

**Zenger Paşa Konağı** ( ☎ 311 7070; www.zenger pasa.com; Doyran Sokak 13; mains €1.75-6; ⚡ ) One of several atmospheric (if slightly touristy) restaurants up in the citadel, wonderful ethnographic displays liven up this restored old house.

## Getting There & Away

### AIR

Turkish Airlines offer daily nonstop flights to most domestic cities. International routes usually require a connection in Istanbul.

### BUS

Ankara's huge *otogar* (AŞTİ) dispatches passengers across the country all day and night. For Istanbul (€12 to €28, six hours) buses depart at least every 15 minutes. Other useful services include those yo Bursa (€11, 5½ hours), Antalya (€12, eight hours), İzmir (€12, nine hours) and Göreme (€9, five hours), all at least hourly.

### TRAIN

Trains run to Istanbul (see p610) and İzmir (see p616).

## Getting Around

### TO/FROM THE AIRPORT

Ankara's Esenboğa airport is 33km north of the city centre. Havaş buses (€4.75, 45 minutes) depart from outside Ankara Garı 1½ hours before domestic and two hours before international Turkish Airlines flights. A taxi costs about €26.

### LOCAL TRANSPORT

Regular buses connect Ulus with Kızılay; a few continue to Kavaklıdere and Çankaya. You can buy tickets (€0.60) from kiosks near the stops.

The Ankaray underground train runs from the *otogar* in the west through Kızılay to Dikimevi in the east. Ankara's metro system runs southeast from Batıkent via Ulus and Maltepe, connecting with the underground at Kızılay. Tickets cost €0.60 on both.

A taxi between the *otogar* and the train station or the centre costs around €3.

## SAFRANBOLU

☎ 0370 pop / 32,500

A real treat for architecture fans, Safranbolu's beautifully preserved old Ottoman quarter, **Çarşı**, is full of half-timbered houses, earning it a place on the Unesco World Heritage List. The antique atmosphere and sprawling bazaar lend themselves perfectly to a day or two's relaxed pottering, particularly if you've come for a break from the disparate pleasures of the coast.

The **tourist office** ( ☎ 712 3863; www.safranbolu .gov.tr, in Turkish) is on the main square.

The best way to appreciate Safranbolu is to stay in one of the many restored Ottoman houses, all furnished and run in keeping with their colourful heritage. **Selvili Köşk** ( ☎ 712 8646; www.selvilikosk.com, in Turkish; Mescit Sokak 23; s/d €23.50/35.50) is among the best, with some great communal areas, while **Havuzlu Asmazlar Konağı** ( ☎ 725 2883; s €26.50, s/d €53-60), off the main road just outside Çarşı, has tons of space and a beautiful traditional pool room (not for swimming).

### Getting There & Around

Direct bus services to Ankara cost €3 (four hours, five daily), to Istanbul €6 (five hours, four daily).

The new *otogar* is 2.5km out of town; take a *servis* to Kıranköy, the modern centre, and a bus or *dolmuş* on to Çarşı (€0.50).

## KONYA

☎ 0332 / pop 680,000

An important Muslim town with a lingering reputation for conservatism, Konya was the capital of the Seljuk Turks and showcases some excellent Seljuk architecture. It was here that the 13th-century poet Mevlana Rumi founded the whirling dervishes, one of Islam's most important mystical orders. Their successors still perform during the **Mevlana Festival** every December.

### Orientation

The centre of town stretches from Alaettin Tepesi (Aladdin Hill) along Alaettin Caddesi and Mevlana Caddesi to the Mevlana Museum. The *otogar* is 10km northwest of the centre; minibuses run you into town, or you can catch the tram as far as Alaettin Tepesi (€0.30).

### Information

**PTT** (Hükümet Meydanı)
**Selale Internet** ( ☎ 350 1061; Başaralı Caddesi; per hr €0.45)
**Tourist Office** ( ☎ 351 1074; Mevlana Caddesi 67)

### Sights

The **Mevlana museum** (Mevlana Müsezi; adult/ concession €2.50/1.25; ☼ 10am-5.30pm Mon, 9am-5.30pm Tue-Sun) holds the mortal remains of the great Sufi saint and many other important figures in the dervish order, all in

coffins topped with turbans, as well as a casket supposedly containing Mohammed's beard. It's very popular with pilgrims, and visitors should definitely show due respect here. The distinctive turquoise tower is an unofficial symbol of the city.

If you don't feel like paying admission prices, just exploring the town centre is effectively a crash course in Seljuk architecture, with some spectacular specimens on show. Start at Alaettin Tepesi and wander at will.

### Sleeping & Eating

**Hotel Ulusan** ( ☎ 351 5004; Kurşuncular Sokak 2; s/d €11.75/13.50, with shower €16.50/19; ▯ ) Tucked away behind the PTT, this impeccably renovated gem is as good as many twice the price, with that all-important dash of character (teddy bears!).

**Yeni Kök & Esra Otel** ( ☎ 352 0671; Kadılar Sokak 28; s/tw/d €17.75/26.50/29.50; ℗ ⊠ ▯ ) A bizarre subterranean tunnel links two separate buildings here, each with small but well-equipped rooms.

**Şifa Restaurant** ( ☎ 352 0519; Mevlana Caddesi 56; mains €1.25-4.50) Regional speciality *tandır kebap* (lamb baked in earthenware) tops the bill of standards at Şifa. Service can be pretty rushed when it's busy.

### Getting There & Away

There are frequent buses from Konya to Cappadocia, via Nevşehir (€9, three hours), Ankara (€9, three hours) and Pamukkale (€10, seven hours).

# CAPPADOCIA

Kapadokya (Cappadocia), the central region between Ankara and Kayseri, is famous for its unique scenery, strewn with fantastic natural rock formations, cave houses and the historical remnants of a semi-troglodyte population. Highlights include the Göreme valleys, Ihlara Gorge and some extraordinary underground cities.

Cappadocia was also historically a key stretch of the **Silk Road**, the long route from Turkey to China that allowed trade to flourish under the various great empires of the region. There's no trace of the original caravan trails left, but plenty of Seljuk caravanserais survive between the major towns here and can be visited with a minimum of effort.

# GÖREME

☎ 0384 / pop 2000

The Göreme landscape is one of Turkey's most amazing sights. Over the centuries a thick layer of volcanic tufa has been eroded into fantastic, eerie shapes, dubbed fairy chimneys by the locals. Early Christians carved chambers and vaults into the chimneys for use as churches, stables and homes. For the best possible bird's-eye views, blow your budget and take in the drama from above in a hot-air balloon.

## Information

**Flintstones Internet** ( ☎ 271 2825; Belediye Caddesi; per hr €1.75)

**Göreme Balloons** ( ☎ 341 5662; www.goremeballoons .com; Elgin Sokak 2)

**Middle Earth Travel** ( ☎ 271 2559; www.middleearth travel.com; Cevizler Sokak 20)

**Ötüken Voyage** ( ☎ 271 2588; www.otukentravel.8m .com; Avanos Yolu 9)

**Zemi Tours** ( ☎ 271 2576; Kayseri Caddesi 28)

## Sights

Ditch your bags on arrival and leg it straight to the **Göreme Open Air Museum** (adult/ concession €7/1.75; ⏱ 8.30am-5.30pm), Cappadocia's finest collection of rock-hewn cave churches, complete with medieval frescoes. The churches are tiny, so try and get in between the many bus tours – you can have your photo taken on a camel while you wait. Don't miss the **Tokalı Church**, one of the largest here, or the **Dark Church** (Karanlık Kilise; admission €3), which has some of the most colourful frescoes.

## Organised Tours

Göreme is the main base for **tours** of Cappadocia's most popular sites (one-day trips from €30), though every travel agent within 200km runs similar excursions. Stops usually include nearby Pigeon Valley, Ihlara Gorge, Ürgüp or Avanos, a convenient caravanserai, the **rock citadel** (admission €1.25; ⏱ 8am to sunset) at Uçhisar, and one of the fascinating underground cities at **Kaymaklı** or **Derinkuyu** (adult/concession €6/1.75; ⏱ 8am-5pm), excavated over years to provide shelter for the indigent population during Hittite invasions. Many companies also offer trips

further afield, around central Anatolia and into eastern Turkey.

Unless you're really pressed for time, avoid taking a tour here from Istanbul, as the overnight journey won't do much for your appreciation of the sights next morning.

## Sleeping

Clustered on the hilly southern side of town are dozens of charismatic pensions, many offering rooms carved out of the natural rock itself. A small information office in the *otogar* displays details of most options.

You can camp at **Dilek** or **Berlin camping grounds** (per tent €5.50), on the road leading to the open-air museum.

**ShoeString Cave Pension** ( ☎ 271 2450; shoestring@ superonline.com; dm US$4, r per person US$5-7; 🖳 ) On the eastern side of Göreme's central hill, the ShoeString tempts shoestringers with simple cave rooms set around a pleasant courtyard.

**Köse Pension** ( ☎ 271 2294; www.kosepension.com; Ragıp Üner Caddesi; dm €3, r €18; 🖳 🎮 ) Staying in a modern building instead of a cave may seem dull, but you'll really appreciate the difference in winter. In summer the lovely pool and home-cooked food make this a popular choice.

**Elif Star Caves** ( ☎ 271 2479; www.elifstar.com.tr.tc; Uzundere Caddesi; dm €6, r per person €10.75) The latest expat operation to enter the fray offers excellent cave rooms with bathroom and a family-friendly atmosphere.

**Kelebek Pension** ( ☎ 271 2531; www.kelebekhotel .com; r €40-60) Luxury-lovers are assured of something to write home about here – Göreme's top option is built around two fairy chimneys and includes plenty of mod cons, right down to the Jacuzzi in the honeymoon suite.

## Eating

Most of Göreme's eating options are lined up on the main street, though there are some good 'uns further afield.

**Fırın Express** (Cami Sokak; mains €0.60-2.50) Seek out this little local place for excellent *pide* at rock-bottom (sorry) prices.

**Orient** (Adnan Menderes Caddesi; mains €2.50-8.50) Harder to find but widely regarded as the best in town, the Orient does a good line in steaks as well as the Turkish staples.

**A La Turca** (Müze Caddesi; mains €3.50-10) The fanciest new arrival in town yet – Istanbul chic meets Ottoman décor in this upmarket Turkish brasserie, with appropriately tasty (and popular) results.

### Getting There & Away

As well as regular services to Ankara (€9, five hours) and Konya (€9, 3½ hours), overnight buses run to Istanbul (€17.75, 11 hours) and Antalya (€10.50, 10 hours). Half-hourly *dolmuşes* connect Göreme with Nevşehir (€0.60, 30 minutes), a bigger town and the region's principal transport hub. There are also regular buses to Avanos and Ürgüp.

## AVANOS

☎ 0384 / pop 12,000

On the northern bank of the sweeping Kızılırmak (Red River), Avanos is known for its pottery. You can visit any of the little workshops around town for a demonstration; tours stop at the bigger, more commercial factory shops on the outskirts.

**Kirkit Pension** ( ☎ 511 3148; www.kirkit.com; r per person €14.75) Wood and stone combine to good effect in this charming old house. Brush up on your French for best results.

**Sofa Hotel** ( ☎ 511 5186; www.sofa-hotel.com; s/d €23.50/35.50) Amazingly, the Sofa used to be 10 separate houses and a stretch of street, now artfully cobbled together to make a smart, friendly institution with full traditional trimmings.

Two buses an hour link Avanos with Nevşehir (€0.60).

## ÜRGÜP

☎ 0384 / pop 13,500

Lacking the spectacular setting of Göreme, Ürgüp used to be a quieter alternative base but now attracts huge numbers of Turkish visitors thanks to the massive popularity of the *Asmalı Konak* TV series (see p601), which was filmed here and in nearby Mustafapaşa. Even if you're not a fan, it's worth a visit to see the restored sandstone houses and try some local wine.

The helpful **tourist office** ( ☎ 341 4059; Kayseri Caddesi) is in the park.

### Sleeping & Eating

**Hotel Elvan** ( ☎ 341 4191; Barbaros Hayrettin Sokak 11; s/d US$15/25) Vaulted stone rooms, big beds and small bathrooms all contribute to the charm of this family-run pension/hotel. The roof terrace is a particular bonus.

**Melis Hotel** ( ☎ 341 2495; www.melishotel.com; İstiklal Caddesi 35; s/d US$30/50; ☐ ☒ ) Set around a fantastic courtyard, you can take your pick from a range of excellent rooms here, from plainer Greek style to caves and vaulted Ottoman stone.

**Hotel Cappadocia Palace** ( ☎ 341 2510; www .hotel-cappadocia.com; Mestan Sokak 2; s/d €20/30, cave rooms €45-75) From the outside it looks like you're entering prison, but first impressions couldn't be more wrong: 'inmates' here get treated to arched ceilings, Ottoman touches and cave rooms with Jacuzzis.

**Sömine Restaurant** (mains €3-8) With most of Ürgüp's best eateries set around the main square, Sömine goes one better and occupies the square itself. Ürgüp-style kebabs, baked on tiles, are a speciality.

### Getting There & Away

Buses run hourly to Nevşehir (€0.80) and every two hours to Göreme (€0.60).

## IHLARA GORGE

☎ 0382

A beautiful canyon full of rock-cut churches dating back to Byzantine times, Ihlara is now a mainstay of the excursions run out of Göreme. With time on your hands, you might be better off staying and walking the entire 16km length of the gorge.

There are four main entrances to the gorge; admission costs €3. The most inviting camp sites and restaurants are in the gorge itself, near the village of Belisırma.

Several daily buses connect Ihlara with Aksaray (€0.60), where you can pick up buses to the rest of the region.

## KAYSERI

☎ 0352 / pop 425,000

Despite its rapid modernisation, the former capital of Cappadocia still boasts many ancient buildings – don't listen to locals elsewhere who tell you to avoid the place completely. If nothing else, it's worth a stop to feast your eyes on the broadside views of Mt Erciyes, a major winter ski centre.

### Information

**Gülveren Internet** ( ☎ 233 1762; Sivas Caddesi 17; per hr €0.40)
**Tourist Office** ( ☎ 222 3903; Seyyıd Burhaneddin Caddesi)

## Sights & Activities

The beautiful **Hunat Hatun** mosque, tomb and seminary is Kayseri's centrepiece, occupying most of the main square with its imposing bulk. Opposite, behind the massive 6th-century city walls, are the **Ulu Cami** (Great Mosque), begun by the Seljuks in 1136, and the venerable **Vezirhanı**, once a caravanserai. The beautifully decorated **Güpgüpoğlu Konağı**, an 18th-century mansion, now houses the city's interesting **Ethnographic Museum** (admission €1.25; ☻ 8am-5pm Tue-Sun).

## Sleeping & Eating

**Hotel Sur** ( ☎ 222 4080; Talas Caddesi 12; s/d €14.75/23.50; **P** ) Right behind the city walls, the big Sur has prison-style corridors but decent mod cons amid its marble staircases.

**Hotel Kadioğlu** ( ☎ 231 6320; Kiçikapı Serdar Caddesi 45; s/d €22.50/37) You can't beat the uninterrupted views of the mountain from this small but nicely formed hotel, especially from the rooftop restaurant.

The areas around Düvenönü Meydanı (the large central roundabout), Sivas Caddesi (running east from the main square) and Millet Caddesi (south of the city walls) all have more than enough restaurants to keep you fed and watered. **Sultan Sofrası** ( ☎ 232 6425; Düvenönü Park Caddesi 16/A; mains €0.90-4.50) does a good line in Kayseri *mantı* (ravioli with garlic-yoghurt sauce).

## Getting There & Away

Buses serve all local destinations, including Ürgüp (€3, 1¼ hours) and Göreme (€4, 1½ hours). Turkish Airlines and Onur Air both fly to Istanbul (from €53, 70 minutes).

# TURKEY DIRECTORY

## ACCOMMODATION

Camping grounds are dotted around Turkey, though not as frequently as you might hope. Some hotels and pensions will also let you camp on their grounds for a small fee (€2 to €4).

HI-type hostels are a rarity in Turkey, although Istanbul and other tourist areas have a few backpacker-oriented institutions with dorms (from €3) and extensive services. Otherwise, small family-run pensions take in most of the traveller traffic and

generally offer excellent value for money; singles and doubles with shared bathroom start at €6 and €9 respectively.

There are also plenty of budget hotels, but the very cheapest are very basic and not really suitable for lone women. On the other hand, TVs, phones and air conditioning can crop up even in one-star places. Rack rates are fixed by local authorities – if you're not offered a cheaper price straight away it's often worth bargaining, particularly out of season. Singles and doubles with bathroom should cost from €9 and €12.

Note that virtually nowhere in Turkey is far from a mosque – light sleepers may well find themselves woken at ungodly hours by the morning call to prayer.

## ACTIVITIES

Hiking and trekking, particularly in national parks, are a great way to get to grips with the country. So far Turkey has two waymarked national routes, the Lycian Way (Fethiye to Antalya) and St Paul's Trail (Perge/Aspendos to Lake Egirdir), both around 500km long. **Middle Earth Travel** (www .middleearthtravel.com), which set up the trails, has full information.

Water sports from diving to kayaking are available in all the Aegean and Mediterranean resorts, with more 'extreme' pursuits like paragliding gaining popularity. Those of a lazier (or drunker) disposition can take an extended boat trip along the coast (see p625), stopping off to swim in bays along the way.

Skiing is another growth sport; keen powder monkeys can find the best facilities at Uludağ, near Bursa, and Mt Erciyes, near Kayseri.

For an essential taste of Turkey visit a *hammam* (Turkish bath), where you can get yourself scrubbed and massaged without lifting a finger. In traditional baths the sexes are always segregated, but in tourist areas mixed bathing has become the norm, along with inflated prices.

## BUSINESS HOURS

Most banks, businesses and offices are open 8.30am to noon and 1pm to 5pm Monday to Friday, with Saturday opening common in cities. Many museums close on Mondays. In tourist areas food and

---

**QUIRKY TURKEY**

▪ **International UFO Museum** (p608), Istanbul

▪ **Mohammed's beard** (p367), Konya

▪ **NASA statue** (p622), Marmaris

▪ **Health Museum** (p611), Edirne

---

souvenir shops are often open virtually around the clock.

As a rule, restaurants are open roughly 9am or 10am to 10pm or 11pm, depending on size and clientele. Bars usually start serving between 5pm and 8pm, though in tourist areas they might be open all day as well.

## CUSTOMS

Duty-free items can be bought both on arrival and departure from Turkey's international airports.

It's strictly illegal to buy, sell or export antiquities – anything over 200 years old falls into this category. Customs officers spot-check luggage and will want proof that you have permission before letting you leave with an antique carpet.

## DANGERS & ANNOYANCES

Like most of Europe, Turkey counts as a relatively safe destination, but tourists are not exempt from hassle. Wear a moneybelt under your clothing, be wary in crowded places and when using ATMs, and remember that a Western passport can be a valuable commodity.

In Istanbul, single men are sometimes lured to bars by new Turkish 'friends', then made to pay an outrageous bill. Drugging is also a serious risk. Be a tad wary who you befriend, especially when you're new to the country.

You may also encounter the old ruse of someone asking you the time in Turkish, then saying 'sorry, I thought you were Turkish' and launching into conversation. The intentions behind it can be anything from selling carpets to full-scale rip-offs; it's probably easier chatting than telling them to get stuffed straight off, but don't let yourself be steered anywhere you're not comfortable.

After the 2004 bomb attacks in Istanbul, visitors (especially travellers who are British and American citizens) should be aware of the risk of terrorism. Even with security stepped up at major hotels, metro and bus stations and tourist sites, a repeat can't be discounted.

## DISABLED TRAVELLERS

Turkey is a real nightmare for physically disabled travellers, not just because of a lack of facilities. Obstacles lurk everywhere, properly equipped toilets are almost unheard-of, and crossing the road is tough even for the fully mobile. Plan your trip very carefully and budget to patronise mostly luxury hotels, restaurants and transport.

## EMBASSIES & CONSULATES
### Turkish Embassies & Consulates

Turkey has embassies in the following countries:

**Australia** ( ☎ 02-6295 0227; 60 Mugga Way, Red Hill ACT 2603)

**Canada** ( ☎ 613-789 4044; 197 Wurtemburg St, Ottawa, Ontario KIN 8L9)

**France** ( ☎ 01-539 271;16 Ave de Lamballe, 75016 Paris)

**Germany** ( ☎ 030-275 850; Rungestrasse 9, 10179 Berlin)

**Ireland** ( ☎ 01-668 5240; 11 Clyde Rd, Ballsbridge, Dublin 4)

**Netherlands** ( ☎ 070-360 4912; Jan Evenstraat 2514 BS, The Hague)

**New Zealand** ( ☎ 04-472 1290; 15-17 Murphy St, Level 8, Wellington)

**UK** ( ☎ 020-7393 0202; 43 Belgrave Square, London SW1X 8PA)

**USA** ( ☎ 202-659 8200; 1714 Massachusetts Ave, NW Washington, DC 20036)

### Consulates in Turkey

Most embassies are in Ankara. Countries with consulates in Istanbul (code ☎ 0212) include:

**Australia** ( ☎ 257 7050; Tepecik Yolu 58, Etiler)

**Canada** ( ☎ 251 9838; İstiklal Caddesi 373-5, Beyoğlu)

**France** (Map pp604–5; ☎ 334 8730; İstiklal Caddesi 8, Taksim)

**Germany** (Map pp604–5; ☎ 334 6100; İsmet İnönü Caddesi 16-18, Taksim)

**Greece** (Map pp604–5; ☎ 245 0597; Turnacıbaşı Sokak 32, Beyoğlu)

**Ireland** ( ☎ 246 6025; Cumhuriyet Caddesi 26/A, Harbiye)

**Netherlands** (☎ 393 2121; İstiklal Caddesi 393, Beyoğlu)
**New Zealand** (☎ 327 2211; Yeşilgimen Sokak 75, Ihlamur)
**UK** (Map pp604-5; ☎ 334 6400; Meşrutiyet Caddesi 34, Beyoğlu)
**USA** (☎ 335 9000; Kaplıcalar Mevkii 2, İstinye)

## FESTIVALS & EVENTS
### April
**Istanbul International Film Festival**
**Anzac Day** Held at Gallipoli.

### May
**Phonem Electronic Music Platform** International club festival, held in Istanbul.

### June–July
**Oil-wrestling Championships** Held at Kırkpınar, near Edirne.
**International Istanbul Music Festival**
**Aspendos Festival** Held in Aspendos and Side.

### December
**Mevlana Festival** Held in Konya.

## GAY & LESBIAN TRAVELLERS
Although not uncommon in a culture that traditionally separates men and women, overt homosexuality is not socially acceptable except in a few small pockets of Istanbul and some resorts. Laws prohibiting 'lewd behaviour' can be turned against homosexuals, so it's best to be discreet. Some *hammams* are known to be gay meeting places.

For more information, contact Turkey's gay and lesbian support group, **Lambda Istanbul** (www.lambdaistanbul.org).

## HOLIDAYS
Public holidays in Turkey include:
**New Year's Day** 1 January
**Children's Day** 23 April
**Youth & Sports Day** 19 May
**Victory Day** 30 August
**Republic Day** 29 October
**Atatürk's Death** 10 November

Turkey also celebrates all of the main Islamic holidays, the most important of which are the month-long **Ramazan** and, two months later, **Kurban Bayramı**. Due to the fact that these holidays are celebrated according to the Muslim lunar calendar, they take place around 11 days earlier each year.

## INTERNET ACCESS
Some post offices and Türk Telekom branches offer Internet access. Generally you're better off using one of the ubiquitous Internet cafés, which provide fast, cheap connections, though they're often packed with schoolboys playing Counter Strike.

## INTERNET RESOURCES
**www.about-turkey.com** Information and links.
**www.letsgoturkey.com** Information and travel resources.
**www.mymerhaba.com** Information site aimed at foreign expats.
**www.neredennereye.com** Public transport timetables.
**www.turkey.org** News, arts, upcoming events and links.
**www.turkeytravelplanner.com** Regularly updated travel information.
**www.turkishdailynews.com** Newspaper home page.

## MONEY
As the Turkish lira (TRL) remains unstable, prices here are given in euros, except where they are quoted in another hard currency (US$ or UK£) by the establishment concerned.

The lira comes in coins of 25,000, 50,000, 100,000 and 250,000 lira, and notes (bills) of 100,000, 250,000, 500,000, one million, five million, 10 million and 20 million lira.

### Cash & Credit Cards
It's easy to change major currencies in most exchange offices, post offices (PTTs), shops and hotels. Foreign currencies are widely accepted in the main tourist areas, and prices are increasingly being quoted in euros as the US dollar loses favour. Exchange rates fluctuate daily – check shortly before your visit.

A surprising number of places take plastic, from kebab shacks to carpet emporia; Visa and MasterCard are the most widely recognised. Widespread ATMs dispense cash for most international credit and debit cards: **Yapı Kredi** machines seem best; **İş Bankası** least good because they let you remove so little at a time.

### Taxes & Refunds
Value-added tax (KDV) is included in the price of most items and services. If you buy

an expensive item, ask the shopkeeper for a *KDV iade özel fatura* (special VAT-refund receipt). Get it stamped as you clear customs, then try and get a refund at a bank in the departure lounge.

## Tipping & Bargaining

Waiters and bath attendants expect around 10% of the bill. You can also round up taxi fares if you wish. Hotel, food and transport prices may or may not be negotiable, but you should always bargain for souvenirs, even if prices are 'fixed'.

## Travellers Cheques

Changing travellers cheques is harder than changing cash (try post offices in tourist areas), and the exchange rate is usually worse. Places that don't charge commission generally offer poor rates.

## POST

The Turkish postal service is known as the PTT. *Postanes* (post offices) are indicated by black-on-yellow 'PTT' signs.

## STUDYING

Most opportunities for study are in Istanbul. **Dilmer** ( ☎ 252 5154; www.dilmer.com) offers one-and two-month Turkish language courses (morning, afternoon and evening) at a variety of levels. **International House** ( ☎ 282 9064; www.ihlstanbul.com) runs similar courses on a monthly basis.

## TELEPHONE

Phoning home from Turkey is surprisingly expensive, mainly due to taxes. The cheapest rates are at night and on Sunday. Wherever possible, try to make reverse charge (collect) calls.

Almost all public telephones require phonecards, which can be bought from telephone centres, shops and street vendors. If you're only going to make one call, it's easier to look for signs saying *köntörlü telefon*, where the cost of your call will be metered. Post offices often have the best rates.

To call the international operator in Turkey, dial ☎ 115.

### Mobile Phones

The Turks just love mobile *(cep)* phones – the main operators are Turkcell, Telsim

---

**EMERGENCY NUMBERS**

- Ambulance ☎ 112
- Doctor (after hours) ☎ 141
- Fire ☎ 110
- Jandarma (Gendarmerie) ☎ 156
- Police ☎ 155

Most services only have Turkish-speaking operators, so find an English-speaking local to help.

---

and Aria-Aycell. Numbers begin with the ☎ 05 prefix; note that calling a mobile costs roughly three times more than a land line.

Turkcell and Telsim have international roaming agreements with many major providers. At the time of writing, though, standard American GSM1900 mobile phones couldn't be used in Turkey.

## TOURIST INFORMATION

Local tourist offices can rarely do more than hand out glossy brochures and sketch maps. That said, some staff have a genuine interest in their region and may make a real effort to help you with any specific queries.

## TOURS

Most independent travellers find tours around Turkey expensive, especially since many bundle you into carpet shops and other high-commission outlets. In general, it's faster and cheaper to make your own travel arrangements. Be particularly careful if booking a tour out of Istanbul, as many are ludicrously expensive compared with doing it yourself.

Areas where an organised tour makes sense, particularly on limited time, include Troy and the Gallipoli battlefields (see p613) and Cappadocia (see p638).

Another useful service is the **Fez Bus** ( ☎ 516 9024; www.fezbus.com) run by Fez Travel, a sociable 'hop-on, hop-off' bus service linking the main resorts of the Aegean and Mediterranean with Istanbul and Cappadocia. The Turkish Delight pass, covering the full circuit, costs €187 (student/under 26 €174), with various other options and extras available.

## VISAS

Nationals of the following countries don't need a visa to visit Turkey for up to three months: Denmark, Finland, France, Germany, Greece, Israel, Japan, New Zealand, Sweden and Switzerland.

Although nationals of Australia, Austria, Belgium, Canada, Ireland, Italy, Malta, the Netherlands, Norway, Portugal, Spain, the UK and the USA need a visa, this is just a sticker which you buy on arrival; join the queue before passport control. Prices depend on nationality: British citizens pay UK£10, Australians, Canadians and Americans US$20, and Irish nationals US$10, payable in hard currency cash.

The standard visa is valid for three months and allows for multiple entries.

## WOMEN TRAVELLERS

Things may be changing but Turkish society is still basically sexually segregated, especially once you get away from the big cities and tourist resorts. Although younger Turks are questioning the old ways and women do hold positions of authority (there's even been a female prime minister), foreign women still find themselves being routinely hassled, supposedly because Turkish men are unaccustomed to brazen Western ways. It's mostly just catcalls and dubious remarks, but serious assaults do occasionally occur.

Travelling with companions usually improves matters, and it's worth remembering that Turkish women ignore men who speak to them in the street. Dressing appropriately (see boxed text, p601) should also reduce unwanted attention.

## WORK

The most lucrative work (up to €200 a week) involves nannying for the wealthy city elite, a job mainly offered to English-speaking women who must be prepared for long hours and demanding employers. Otherwise there is some work available for qualified teachers of English (whose employers should be able to arrange a work permit).

Most travellers who want to work end up grafting illegally for subsistence wages in pensions, bars and carpet shops, leaving the country every three months to renew their visas.

# TRANSPORT IN TURKEY

## GETTING THERE & AWAY

### Air

The cheapest air fares are almost always to Istanbul's **Atatürk International airport** ( ☎ 0212-663 2550; www.ataturkairport.com). To reach other Turkish airports, even Ankara, you usually have to transit at Istanbul.

Turkish Airlines (THY) and European carriers fly to Istanbul from all the European capitals. If you're planning a longer stay, it's also worth inquiring about charter flights.

Airlines flying to and from Turkey:
**Air France** (www.airfrance.com; AF; ☎ 0212-310 1919)
**Alitalia** (www.alitalia.com; AZ; ☎ 0212-315 1900)
**British Airways** (www.britishairways.com; BA; ☎ 0212-234 1300)
**Cyprus Turkish Airlines** (www.kthy.net; YK; ☎ 0212-663 0759)
**Iberia** (www.iberia.com; IB; ☎ 0212-468 8018)
**KLM** (www.klm.com; KL; ☎ 0212-368 3333)
**Lufthansa** (www.lufthansa.com; LH; ☎ 0212-315 3434)
**Onur Air** (www.onurair.com.tr; OH; ☎ 0212-662 9797)
**Royal Air Maroc** (www.royalairmaroc.com; AT; ☎ 0212-231 8021)
**Turkish Airlines** Head office (www.turkishairlines.com; TK; ☎ 0212-444 0849) Antalya ( ☎ 243 4383; Cumhuriyet Caddesi 91) Ankara ( ☎ 428 0200; Atatürk Bulvarı 154, Kavaklıdere) Istanbul (Map pp604-5; ☎ 225 0556; Cumhuriyet Caddesi 199-201, Taksim) In İzmir ( ☎ 489 2881; Akdeniz Caddesi 14) Bodrum ( ☎ 317 1203; Oasis Centre, Kıbrıs Şehitler Caddesi 8217/2) Marmaris ( ☎ 412 3750; Atatürk Caddesi 26-B)

### Sea

**Turkish Maritime Lines** (TML; ☎ 0212-251 9025; www.tdi.com.tr, in Turkish) runs weekly car ferries from Çeşme to the Italian ports of Brindisi (€110 to €330, 36 hours, May to September) and Ancona (€170 to €500, 2½ days, April to November).

Private ferries link Turkey's Aegean coast and the Greek islands, which are in turn linked by air or boat to Athens. In summer, you can expect daily boats connecting Lesvos–Ayvalık, Chios–Çeşme, Kos–Bodrum, Rhodes–Bodrum and Rhodes–Fethiye. The cheapest and most frequent ferries serve the Samos–Kuşadası and Rhodes–Marmaris routes. **Aegean Tour Travel** (www.aegean.com.tr) has comprehensive information.

There are daily ferry/catamaran services between the northern Turkish sector of Cyprus and Taşucu, near Silifke (€26.50/29.50, four to five hours). Less frequent boats also run from Alanya to Cyprus.

## Land

Despite the aesthetic appeal of international train journeys, getting to Turkey overland is usually cheaper, faster and easier by bus. Major Turkish bus companies such as Ulusoy, Varan and Bosfor offer reliable, comfortable services between Istanbul and major European cities like Athens, Zagreb, Vienna, Milan, Frankfurt and Paris for less than €150 one way. Services which travel via Greece and Italy avoid any potential hassle at the Bulgarian border.

## GETTING AROUND
### Air

Turkish Airlines links all the country's major cities, with increasing competition from cheaper rival Onur Air. Domestic flights can fill up rapidly so try to book in advance.

One way tickets from Istanbul start at €53; only THY flies to Ankara (€76, one hour, 15 daily).

### Bicycle

Hiring a bike can be a good way of exploring, especially in backpacker areas, where many pensions lend them out for free. You may even come across the odd cycle path in towns like Alanya. Road surfaces are acceptable, if a bit rough, though many Turkish drivers regard cyclists as a curiosity and/or a nuisance.

### Boat

TML operates a car ferry service between Istanbul and İzmir from May to October (€20 to €170, 28 hours).

### Bus

The Turkish bus network is a very pleasant surprise: coaches go just about everywhere, they're cheap and comfortable, smoking isn't permitted, drinks and snacks are often provided, regular toilet stops are built into longer routes, and drivers even use the breaks to wash down their vehicles! It certainly puts the rail company (and many a European transport system) to shame.

The premium companies have nationwide networks offering greater speed and comfort for slightly higher fares. They also have the best safety records. Departures on popular routes can be as frequent as every 15 minutes, with hourly services the norm from major cities. Costs vary according to distance and popularity of the route; short trips with local companies can start from as little as €0.60, going up to €30 for a luxury long-haul service.

A town's *otogar* (bus terminal) is often on the outskirts, but most bus companies will have free *servis* minibuses to ferry you into the centre and back again.

Main nationwide bus companies:
**Kamil Koç** (www.kamilkoc.com.tr, in Turkish; ☎ 444 0562)
**Metro** (www.metroturizm.com.tr; ☎ 444 3455)
**Pamukkale** (www.pamukkaleturizm.com.tr, in Turkish; ☎ 444 3535)
**Ulusoy** (www.ulusoy.com.tr, in Turkish; ☎ 444 1888)
**Varan** (www.varan.com.tr; ☎ 0212-551 5000)

### Car & Motorcycle

The **Turkish Touring & Automobile Association** (Türkiye Turing ve Otomobil Kurumu, TTOK; ☎ 0212-282 8140; www.turing.org.tr) can help with questions and problems.

Carnets (permits to import cars) are not required for stays of less than three months, but details of your car are stamped in your passport to ensure it leaves the country with you. An International Driving Permit is handy if your licence is from a country likely to seem obscure to a Turkish police officer.

Car mechanical services are easy to find, reasonably competent and cheap. The most common and so most easily serviced models are Fiat, Renault, Mercedes, Volkswagen and Toyota.

All the main car rental companies are represented in Istanbul, Ankara, İzmir and other tourist area; Avis in particular has an extensive national network. However, car hire in Turkey is pricey (budget around €40 a day) and driving is hazardous.

Turkey has a very high motor-vehicle accident rate, so always drive defensively and avoid driving at night. In the major cities, plan to park your car and use public transport – traffic is terrible and parking almost impossible.

Note that speed limits for motorcycles are considerably lower than for cars:

TURKEY

80km/h instead of 120km/h on motorways, 70km/h instead of 90km/h on major roads. There's a 10% tolerance policy and many police officers will only enforce the higher car limits, but don't count on this.

## Hitching

Hitching is possible but not common in Turkey, and works better over short distances. Commercial vehicles are most likely to pick you up, but will often expect payment. Women should never hitchhike alone.

## Local Transport

Short-distance and local routes are usually served by medium-sized 'midibuses' or smaller *dolmuşes* (minibuses), run by private operators. Most towns have an internal bus network funded by the council; this may be supplemented by underground, tram, train and even ferry services in the largest cities.

## Train

Trains have a hard time competing with the long-distance buses: the **Turkish State Railways** (TCDD; www.tcdd.gov.tr, in Turkish) trains are usually marginally cheaper, but only special express services, such as the *Fatih* and *Başkent* lines, are faster. With *yolcu* and *posta* trains you'd probably be quicker jogging.

The sleeper trains linking Istanbul, İzmir and Ankara are essentially the only services offering vaguely good value.

# Morocco

**MOROCCO**

648

Red baked-mud kasbahs beneath the towering High Atlas. Seething *souqs* in dusty towns. Breezy beach haunts under massive skies. Nowhere is as fascinating as Morocco – a country full of contrasting images, colourful sights, stirring smells and exotic experiences.

Serried mountains carve up the country from the Mediterranean Rif to the High Atlas. Icy snowcapped peaks hoard the moisture, leaving the Western Sahara gasping in the torrid heat. Such geographical diversity has engendered cultures as varied as the views, from pale-skinned Berber tribes to urban Islamists and southern nomads.

From as early as the Phoenecians and the Romans, cultural and historical ties have bound Morocco to its European neighbours across the Mediterranean. Great civilisations such as the Almohads and Almoravids took their refined Islamic aesthetic north into Andalucía, while lucrative caravans built the great imperial cities of Fès, Meknès and Marrakesh, shipping their produce north through Portuguese entrepôts at Tangier, Casablanca and Essaouira.

Morocco is a destination of infinite possibility, where you can swelter in the heat of the market place or ramble through Roman ruins, and in the space of a day find yourself trekking through a cool Atlas village or surfing the rolling breakers of the Atlantic. And while the Maghreb does not immediately spring to mind as a Mediterranean destination, it is in fact only 35 minutes by ferry from mainland Spain.

This chapter concentrates on the Mediterranean and the Rif, the Atlantic coast, and the imperial cities in the interior. For full coverage of the country, check out the latest edition of Lonely Planet's *Morocco*.

**FAST FACTS**

- **Area** 446,550 sq km
- **Capital** Rabat
- **Currency** dirham (Dh); A$1 = Dh6.30; €1 = Dh10.99; ¥100 = Dh8.26; NZ$1 = Dh5.64; UK£1 = Dh16.69; US$1 = Dh9.12
- **Famous for** hashish, Humphrey Bogart
- **Official Languages** Arabic, French, Berber
- **Population** 30.7 million
- **Telephone Codes** country code ☎ 212; international access code ☎ 00
- **Visas** most visitors to Morocco do not require visas and are allowed to remain in the country for 90 days on entry. Exceptions to this include nationals of Israel, South Africa and Zimbabwe.

# HIGHLIGHTS

- Admire the mural-painted walls and windswept beaches of picture-perfect **Asilah** (p666).
- Follow in the footsteps of a generation of artists and writers who found their inspiration in **Tangier** (p653).
- Dip into fishing's most fashionable port, **Essaouira** (p675), with its movie moghuls and maverick surf crowd.
- Soak up centuries of history in one of Morocco's imperial cities – **Marrakesh** (p676), **Fès** (p682), **Meknès** (p687) or **Rabat** (p667).
- Chill out in Chefchaouen (p662) or heading into the hills of the Rif Mountains.

# ITINERARIES

- **One week** From Tangier, explore the Mediterranean coast and the Rif, especially the beaches near Hispanic Tetouan or the mountains around chilled-out Chefchaouen. Make your way back up the Atlantic coast, stopping at cosmopolitan Casablanca, imperial Rabat or artsy Asilah on the way.
- **Two weeks** Follow the itinerary above, but head further inland. Spend time wandering the Fès medina and the Roman ruins at Volubilis, then take the train south to Marrakesh to haggle in the *souqs*. Continue on to laid-back Essaouira to recoup at the beach before heading back up the coast as outlined above.

# CLIMATE & WHEN TO GO

The most pleasant time to explore Morocco is spring (March to May), when the country is lush and green, and autumn (September to October), after the worst of the summer heat. Summer months (June to August) are best for sun and surf. In August, beaches get crowded with holiday-makers.

Bear in mind that during Ramadan, the traditional month of fasting and purification, some restaurants and cafés close during the day and general business hours are reduced. Ramadan is the ninth month of the Muslim calendar, which is based on the lunar calendar, so the dates fluctuate from year to year. In 2005, Ramadan is estimated to occur from October 4 to November 2, and the dates move forward by approximately 11 days in each subsequent year (eg September 23 to October 22 in 2006).

---

**HOW MUCH?**

- **Dorm bed** Dh45
- **Pot of mint tea** Dh4-5
- **Museum entry** Dh10
- **Hammam** Dh10
- **Petit-taxi ride** Dh5-10
- **Babouches (traditional hand-made slippers)** Dh100

**LONELY PLANET INDEX**

- **Litre of petrol** Dh9
- **Litre of bottled water** Dh5
- **Bottled beer (Flag)** Dh5
- **Souvenir T-shirt** Dh100
- **Grilled brochette (kebab)** Dh35

---

# HISTORY

Most modern Moroccans are descendents of indigenous tribes that have inhabited the Maghreb hills for thousands of years. When the Romans arrived in North Africa in the 2nd century BC, they called the natives 'Berbers' (similar to the term 'Barbarian' ascribed to the northern European tribes) because of their incomprehensible tongue.

In the second half of the 7th century, the inspired soldiers of the prophet Mohammed set forth from the Arabian Peninsula and overwhelmed the peoples of the Middle East. Before long, nearly all Berber tribes were embracing Islam, although local tribes developed their own brand of Islamic Shi'ism, which sparked rebellion against the eastern Arabs.

By 829 local elites had established an Idrissid state with its capital at Fès, dominating all of Morocco. Thus commenced a cycle of rising and falling dynasties, which included: the Almoravids (1062–1147), who built their capital at Marrakesh; the Almohads (1147–1269), famous for building the Koutoubia Mosque; the Merenids (1269–1465), known for their exquisite mosques and *medersas*, especially in Fès; the Saadians (1524–1659), responsible for the Palais el-Badi; and the Alawites (1659–present), who still rule today. The Koutoubia Mosque and Palais el-Badi are in Marrakesh (visitors can still see them there).

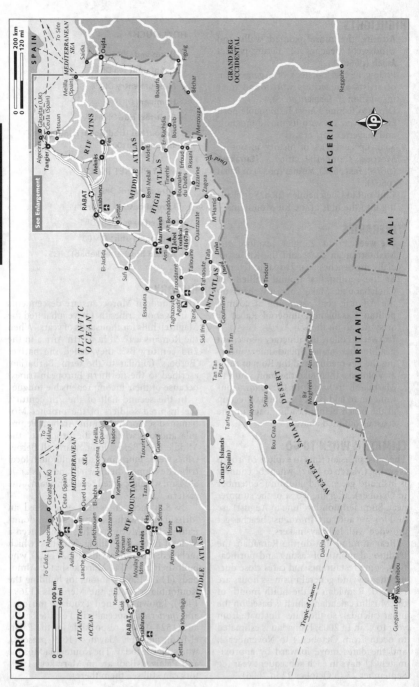

MOROCCO

## TOP FIVE SPOTS FOR SUN & SAND

With its Atlantic coastline and white-sand beaches, Morocco is as popular with surfers as it is with beach bums.

- **Cap Spartel** sun spot of the rich and famous (p658)

- **Essaouira** windsurfers' and fishermen's delight (p675)

- **Oued Laou** tiny fishing village tucked into the Rif (p664)

- **Paradise Beach** pristine stretch south of Asilah that lives up to its name (p666)

- **Temara Beach** the first of the good surfing spots south of Rabat (p670)

France took control in 1912, making its capital at Rabat and handing Spain a token zone in the north. Opposition from Berber mountain tribes was crushed, but Moroccan resistance moved into political channels with the development of the Istiqlal (independence) party.

Independence was finally granted in 1956. The Spanish also withdrew, retaining the coastal enclaves of Ceuta and Melilla. Sultan Mohammed V became king, succeeded by his son in 1961. Despite moves towards democracy and several coup attempts, Hassan II retained all effective power until his death in 1999.

The new king, Mohammed VI, has adopted a reformist agenda, especially in the area of social policy and women's rights. His Western-looking policies are controversial, feeding a small but growing Islamic fundamentalist movement.

## PEOPLE

Morocco's population is made up of Berbers and Arabs (almost 50% each), although the distinction is not well defined. Arabs have mixed with the indigenous Berbers, who in turn have been Arabised.

Morocco's population is mainly rural (about 60%) and young (70% are under 30 years). With a growth rate of 2.2%, the population threatens to destabilise this country, where a rift separates the well-off minority from the legions of unemployed youth.

## RELIGION

Ninety-nine percent of Moroccans are Muslim. Muslims share their roots with Jews and Christians and respect these groups as *Ahl al-Kteb*, People of the Book. Fundamentalism is mostly discouraged but its existence is not surprising in light of religion's role in Muslim countries: Islam cannot be separated from daily life and politics; it governs both secular and spiritual life.

That said, it is only fair to note that the majority of Muslims do not favour such development and that the popularity of fundamentalism is not as great as Westerners imagine. The groups' success is less about religious fervour and more a reflection of frustration in countries grappling with severe economic difficulties.

## ARTS
### Architecture

Moroccan religious buildings are adorned with hand-carved detailing, gilded accents, chiselled mosaics etc. A mosque consists of a courtyard, arcaded portico, and main prayer hall facing Mecca. Great examples

### TOURS

Many companies offer package tours for activity-based or theme holidays.

**Best of Morocco** ( ☎ 01380-828533; www .morocco-travel.com) With over 30 years' experience this is one of the best-established tour operators for Morocco. Tailormade tours and holidays include everything from camel trekking and skiing to cultural tours and beach holidays.

**Heritage Tours** ( ☎ 800-378 4555, www.heritage toursonline.com) Customised travel with a real emphasis on culture and the arts. Fantastic city tours and classic itineraries.

**Marrakesh Voyage** ( ☎ 1-888-990 2999; www .onlymorocco.com) Extensive list of itineraries including a New Year's Rave and Atlas Caravan Adventure as well as Jewish Heritage tours. Customised tours based on golfing and music.

**Naturally Morocco** ( ☎ /fax 0709-2343879; www.naturallymorocco.co.uk) Sustainable, ecotourism deeply involved in local communities. The centre in Taroudannt is also an educational organisation, Centre Environmental et Culturel Marocain (CECU).

MOROCCO

**THE EVIL EYE**

The power of the evil eye is a potent force in the minds of many Moroccans. A symbolic means of warding it off is to show the open palm of the hand, fingers pointing upwards. This 'hand of Fatima' (the Prophet's daughter) can frequently be spotted on stickers, painted on doors or as jewellery.

In the spice markets you may come across another force enlisted to avert the evil eye: the *al-boua* (chameleon). Many believe that these harmless insect-eaters possess considerable magical powers. To restore the fidelity of a straying husband, a wife may conceal chameleon meat or bones in his food. If Moroccans feel they've been struck by misfortune from a spiritual source beyond their control, one option is to throw a chameleon into a small, wood-fired oven and walk around it three times. If the chameleon explodes, the evil has been averted, but if it just melts down to goo, they're still in trouble. Not that either outcome is any consolation to the hapless chameleon.

include the 9th century Kairaouine Mosque in Fès and the colossal Hassan II Mosque in Casablanca. While most mosques are closed to non-Muslims, the *medersas* (Qur'anic schools) that bejewel major Moroccan cities are open for visits.

The street façade of the Moroccan town house *(riad* or *dar)* is usually just a plain wall, and the only opening is the entrance door. The inner courtyard allows light to penetrate during the day, and cool air to settle at night. Many classy guesthouses – especially in Marrakesh and Fès – occupy beautifully rennovated traditional *riads*.

## Music

Berber tribes have long had their own music, later enhanced by Arab instruments and styles. The most famous Berber group is the Master Musicians of Joujouka, introduced to Western audiences by Brian Jones of the Rolling Stones. Gnawa music is a blend of Berber and Arabic influences with roots in sub-Saharan Africa. Raï, originally from Algeria, is one of the strongest influences on Moroccan contemporary music, incorporating elements of jazz, hip-hop and rap. A popular artist is Cheb Mami, famous for vocals on Sting's 'Desert Rose'. The music can be heard around the country, especially at the Gnawa and World Music Festival in Essaouira and the Fès Festival of World Sacred Music.

## ENVIRONMENT

Morocco's awesome fusion of rock, sand, and sea presents the most varied topography in North Africa. In the north, the Rif Mountains form an arc of impenetrable limestone and sandstone, which shoots steeply back from the Mediterranean. The Middle Atlas mountains run northeast to southwest from the Rif. The low hills east of Agadir rise to form the High Atlas. Towering over the villages of Marrakesh at 4167m is Jebel Toubkal, North Africa's highest summit. Lastly, further south, the low and calloused Anti Atlas drops down into the arid wastes of the Sahara. Morocco's coastline stretches across the Mediterranean and down the Atlantic.

Pollution, desertification, overgrazing, deforestation: together these form a glimpse of Morocco's urgent environmental troubles. To combat these problems, a few initiatives are under way, including plantation programmes and public education on rubbish disposal and water pollution. However, the situation remains grave.

Worried about the increasing loss of habitat and the resulting disappearance of plant and animal species, Morocco has distinguished certain areas for protection. So far, a mere 0.01% of Morocco's land is protected territory; other parks in the Atlas Mountains and the Moroccan Sahara are expected in the next few years – particularly to combat threats to argan and thuya trees.

## FOOD & DRINK

Influenced by Berber, Arabic and Mediterranean traditions, Moroccan cuisine features a sublime use of spices and fresh produce. The most typical Moroccan dish is *tajine*, a meat and vegetable stew cooked slowly in an earthenware dish. Couscous is fluffy steamed semolina served with tender meat and vegetables. Brochettes (skewered meat barbecued over hot coals) or roast chicken are other staples, served with crispy french fries. Fish dishes also make an excellent choice in coastal areas.

*Harira* is a thick soup made from lamb stock, lentils, chickpeas, onions, tomatoes, fresh herbs and spices. In a cheap restaurant a bowl costs around Dh5. *Pastilla,* a speciality of Fès, includes poultry (chicken or pigeon), almonds, cinnamon, saffron and sugar, encased in layer upon layer of very fine pastry.

Vegetarians shouldn't have any problems – fresh fruit and vegetables are widely available, as well as lentils and chickpeas. Salads are ubiquitous in Morocco, particularly the traditional *salade marocaine* made from diced green peppers, tomatoes and red onion. Ask for your couscous or *tajine sans viande* (without meat).

For dessert, Moroccan patisseries concoct excellent French and Moroccan sweets. Café culture is alive and well in Morocco. Many of these *grands cafés* are serious, all-male preserves – female travellers may prefer to patronise the patisseries.

Mint tea, the legendary 'Moroccan whisky', is made with Chinese gunpowder tea, fresh mint and copious sugar. It usually comes in elegant teapots, served with much ritual. Fruit juices, especially freshly squeezed orange juice, are the country's greatest bargain (only Dh2.50 on the Djemaa al-Fna in Marrakesh). It's not advisable to drink tap water in Morocco, and water from mountain streams should be purified. Beer's easy to find in the *villes nouvelles* (new towns) – local brands include

Stork or Flag. Decent Moroccan wines are available in upscale restaurants and in liquor shops.

If you're on a tight budget, you can eat well for as little as Dh50 per day. A three-course meal in a medium-priced restaurant will cost Dh80 to Dh120 (without drinks); if you want to treat yourself in a traditional Moroccan palace restaurant or a smart French joint, expect to pay anywhere from Dh150 to Dh600 per person.

# THE MEDITERRANEAN COAST & THE RIF

On the northern coast of Morocco, the waves of the Mediterranean Sea crash against the red, rocky cliffs of the Rif Mountains, which form the coastline for 300km from Ceuta to Melilla. For the most part, this coastline is breathtakingly beautiful and wildly savage.

The region retains a noticeable Andalucían flavour, and not only because of the enclaves of Ceuta and Melilla, which remain in Spanish hands. Language, cuisine and culture still reflects the influence of the neighbours to the north, lending the Mediterranean Coast and the Rif an atmosphere that is noticeably different than the rest of Morocco.

## TANGIER

In the days author William Burroughs called Interzone (when Tangier was officially an 'international zone') home, every kind of questionable activity took place here. As such, it was a haven for artists and writers in search of cheap drugs and artistic inspiration, and one of the Mediterranean's most fashionable resorts, renowned for its high-profile gay scene. Although it's not quite so hedonistic, the traces of past decadence linger on.

The *Brigade Touristique* (tourist police) has cracked down on Tangier's legendary hustlers, but the city is not altogether hassle free. If you take it head on and learn to handle the hustlers, you'll find it a likable, lively place. The nightlife is vibrant; the population is cosmopolitan; and the cultural vibe – which has attracted artists from Henri Matisse to Paul Bowles to the Rolling Stones – is infamous.

---

**RESPONSIBLE TRAVEL**

Despite extensive Westernisation, Morocco remains a largely conservative Muslim society. As a rule, a high degree of modesty is demanded of both sexes. Women are advised to keep their shoulders and upper arms covered and to opt for long skirts or trousers. All mosques, cemeteries and religious buildings in active use are off limits to non-Muslims.

If invited into a Moroccan home, it is customary to remove your shoes before stepping onto the carpet. Food is served in common dishes and eaten with the right hand – the left hand is used for personal hygiene and should not be used to eat with or to touch any common source of food or water, or to hand over money or presents.

MOROCCO

## Orientation

Tangier is divided between the tangled web of the old medina and the wide, ordered boulevards of the ville nouvelle (new town). Most of the restaurants and better hotels are in the ville nouvelle, while the medina has markets, craft shops and cheaper hotels. The large square known as the Grand Socco marks the meeting point of new and old.

## Information

### EMERGENCY

**Emergency service** ( ☎ 039 373737; ☻ 24hr)

### INTERNET ACCESS

**Cyber Café Adam** ( ☎ 039 948397; Rue ibn Rochd; per hour Dh10; ☻ 9.30am-3.30am) Besides computers, offers coffee, tea and other refreshments.

**Espace Net** (16 Ave Mexique; per hour Dh10; ☻ 9.30am-midnight)

### LEFT LUGGAGE

**Consigne** (cnr Rue DarDbagh & Rue du Portugal) The 'consignment office', a convenient place to leave your luggage for the day is this place at the southeast entrance to the medina.

### MEDICAL SERVICES

**Clinique du Croissant Rouge** (Red Cross Clinic; ☎ 039 946976; 6 Rue al-Mansour Dahabi)

**Pharmacy El Yousr** (Blvd Mohammed V)

### MONEY

Plenty of banks with ATMs are along Blvd Pasteur and Blvd Mohammed V in the ville nouvelle.

**Banque Marocaine du Commerce Extérieur** (BMCE; Blvd Pasteur; ☻ 9am-1pm & 3pm-7pm Mon-Fri, 10am-1pm & 4pm-7pm Sat & Sun)

### POST

**Main Post Office** (Blvd Mohammed V)

### TOURIST INFORMATION

**Délégation Régionale du Tourisme** ( ☎ 039 948050; 29 Blvd Pasteur; ☻ 8.30am-noon & 2.30-6.30pm Mon-Fri)

## Dangers & Annoyances

Despite improvements in recent years, Tangier is home to some of the most persistent hustlers and adept pickpockets in the country. Don't dally around the port, which is a hotspot for *faux guides* in search of 'clients'. Problems with a shopkeeper, unofficial guide or anyone else – contact the **Brigade Touristique** (Tourist Police; Ave des FAR, Tangier Port).

---

**TANGIER IN ONE DAY**

In the morning, check out the **American Legation Museum** (p654) or the **Musée de la Fondation Lorin** (p654). Have lunch at **Restaurant Populaire Saveur** (p657) before heading into the depths of the medina to haggle over carpets and explore the **kasbah** (p654). Catch the sunset over the Straits from **Café Hafa** (p657).

---

## Sights & Activities

Heading north from the Petit Socco, Rue des Almohades takes you to the **Kasbah**, built on the highest point of the city. Enter from Bab el-Assa (at the end of Rue ben Raissouli) into a large courtyard leading to the 17th-century **Dar el-Makhzen** ( ☎ 039 932097; admission Dh10; ☻ 9am-12.30pm & 3pm-5.30pm Wed-Mon, closed Fri afternoon), the former sultan's palace. It's now a museum devoted to Moroccan arts.

In the southwest corner of the medina, the **American Legation Museum** ( ☎ 039 935317; 8 Rue d'Amerique; admission free, donations welcome; ☻ 10am-1pm & 3pm-5pm Mon-Fri) houses a fascinating collection of antique maps, furniture and 17th- to 20th-century paintings, prints and drawings by various artists who either lived in or passed through Tangier.

Housed in a former synagogue, the **Musée de la Fondation Lorin** ( ☎ 039 930306; lorin@wanadoo.net.ma; 44 Rue Touahine; admission free, donations appreciated; ☻ 11am-1pm & 3.30pm-7.30pm Sun-Fri) contains an engaging collection of photographs, posters and prints of Tangier from 1890 to 1960.

## Sleeping

### BUDGET

**Youth Hostel** ( ☎ 039 946127; 8 Rue al-Antaki; dm with/without HI card Dh30/40, hot showers Dh5; ☻ 8am-10am, noon-3pm & 6-11pm) Tangier's youth hostel is just off Ave d'Espagne in a rough-and-tumble part of town.

**Camping Miramonte** ( ☎ 039 937133; camp sites per adult/child Dh20/15, plus Dh20/15/25 per tent/car/caravan, hot showers Dh10, electricity Dh10; ℗ ☙ ) The most convenient camping ground is on a hillside in lush gardens 2km from the city centre. The facility is pleasant but isolated.

**Pension Hollanda** ( ☎ 039 937838; 139 Rue de Hollande; s/d Dh80/150; ℗ ) This friendly pension is clean and quiet. Double rooms have private showers, and Western toilets.

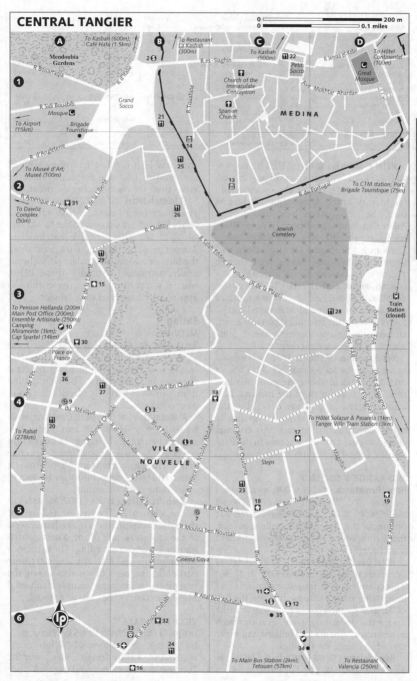

# CENTRAL TANGIER

0 ——————— 200 m
0 ——————— 0.1 miles

**MOROCCO**

To Kasbah (600m);
Café Hafa (1.5km)

To Restaurant
La Kasbah
(300m)

To Kasbah
(500m)

To Hôtel
Continental
(100m)

**A** Mendoubia
Gardens

R Bouarraqia

2 🛈

R es-Siaghin

R Jemaa el-Kebir

22

Petit
Socco

Ave Mokhtar Ahardan

Great
Mosque

**1**

R d'Italie

Grand
Socco

Church of the
Immaculate
Conception

R Touahine

**MEDINA**

R Sidi Bouabib
Mosque 🛈

Spanish
Church

To Airport
(15km)

Brigade
Touristique

21

14

To Museé d'Art;
Museé (100m)

25

R d'Angleterre

6

**2**

R Amérique du Sud 31

R de la Liberté

13

R du Portugal

To CTM station; Port;
Brigade Touristique (75m)

To Dawliz
Complex
(50m)

26

R Oualilis

R Salah Eddine el-Ayoubi (R de la Plage)

Jewish
Cemetery

29

**3**

R de la Liberté

15

To Pension Hollanda (200m);
Main Post Office (200m);
Ensemble Artisinale (250m);
Camping
Miramonte (3km);
Cap Spartel (14km)

10

28

Ave des FAR

Train
Station
(closed)

30

Place de
France

Ave des FAR

Ave d'Espagne

36

27

R Khalid Ibn Oualid

38

**4**

9
R du Méxique

3

Blvd Pasteur

17

To Hôtel Solazur & Pasarela (1km);
Tanger Ville Train Station (3km)

Ave de Fès

20

To Rabat
(278km)

R Ahmed Chaouki

R el-Moutanabi

8

R el-Jebha el-Ouatania

R Magellan

**VILLE**

**NOUVELLE**

Steps

Ave du Prince Héritier

R Omar Ibn al-Âhas

R de la Croix

R du Prince Moulay Abdallah

23

18

R Ibn Jubair

19

**5**

7
R Ibn Rochd

R Moussaï ben Noussair

R Sorolla

Cinéma Goya

Blvd Mohammed V

R Allal ben Abdallah

11

1 🛈

12

**6**

33

32

R al-Mansour Dahabi

35

4

5 ✚

24

34

16

To Main Bus Station (2km);
Tetouan (57km)

To Restaurant
Valencia (250m)

**Hôtel el-Muniria** ( ☎ 039 935337; 1 Rue Magellan; s/d Dh130/150) El-Muniria is showing its age, but remains an excellent choice, especially for literary buffs. A nostalgic air lingers from the 1950s, when Jack Kerouac and Allen Ginsberg stayed here. William Burroughs supposedly wrote *The Naked Lunch* in room No 9. Rooms are large, clean and slightly shabby; some have private shower and/or toilet (same price as shared).

**Hotel Andalucia** ( ☎ 039 941334; 14-16 Rue Vermeer; s/d Dh190/230, s/d Dh225/250; P ) Set just south of the centre off of Rue al-Mansour Dahabi, this is possibly the friendliest place in town, and usually requires booking ahead. Simple, clean rooms are excellent value.

**Hôtel Continental** ( ☎ 039 931024; hcontinental@ am.net.ma; 36 Rue Dar el-Baroud; s/d Dh275/325, s/d Dh335/385) Perched above the port, this historic hotel is the pick of the medina. It is a little ragged around the edges, but the rooms and common areas are gradually being redecorated. Fun fact: this colonial classic was used for some scenes in the Paul Bowles' film, *The Sheltering Sky*.

### MID-RANGE & TOP END

**Hôtel Rembrandt** ( ☎ 039 937870; www.hotel-rem brandt.com; Blvd Mohammed V; s/d Dh387/474, s/d Dh487/574; P 🍴 🍷 ) A dependable three-star option in the heart of the ville nouvelle, the Rembrandt offers stylish rooms and friendly, efficient service.

**Hôtel Dawliz** ( ☎ 039 333151; fax 039 370661; 42 Rue Hollande; s/d Dh519/678, s/d Dh659/808; P 🍴 🍷 ) This complex offers four-star comforts and unbeatable views of the medina and the Bay of Tangier – which goes a long way to make up for the unexciting décor. Features such as an arcade, cinema and billiard hall make this a top choice for families.

**Hôtel Solazur** ( ☎ 039 940164; fax 039 945286; Ave des FAR; s/d Dh642/774; 🍴 ) The Solazur offers

comfortable, if nondescript, rooms with all the standard four-star amenities. Fantastic views from the rooms facing the ocean.

**El-Minzah Hôtel** ( ☎ 039 935885; fax 039 934546; www.elminzah.com; 85 Rue de la Liberté; s/d with breakfast from Dh1200/1500, s/d with breakfast from Dh1500/1800; P 🍴 🍷 🍷 ) The only five-star hotel in Tangier proper is this landmark, built along the lines of a Moroccan palace. It's a beautifully maintained reminder of the 1930s, when it was patronised by anyone who was anyone who happened into Tangier.

## Eating
### MEDINA

**Restaurant La Kasbah** ( ☎ 067 118847; 7 Rue Gzenaya; menus Dh40-80; ⏰ 11am-10pm) This hole-in-the-wall is one of the more pleasant cheapies in the medina. The simple tiled dining-room is perfectly placed for a noon or evening snack.

**Al Mountazah** ( ☎ 039 934816; Grand Socco; breakfast Dh12; ⏰ 7am-10pm) You can't beat this rooftop perch for observing the activity on the Grand Socco – sip your morning coffee and watch the square come alive. This is a wonderful (rare) opportunity for women to enjoy some outdoor seating.

**Marhaba Palace** ( ☎ 039 937927; Rue de la Kasbah; meals from Dh120) The newest and best of the palace restaurants is immediately west of the kasbah in one of the oldest garden houses in Tangier's medina.-The luxurious surroundings and folkloric show are only part of the fun here; this is also among the best places in Tangier to sample traditional Moroccan fare as the sultans enjoyed.

### VILLE NOUVELLE

**La Giralda** ( ☎ 039 370407; 1st fl, 5 Blvd Pasteur; breakfast from Dh12; ⏰ 6am-10pm; 🍴 ) While enormous windows give fantastic views over the Terrasse des Paresseux and beyond, they are double-plated to keep out the noise of the street, lending an air of calm elegance. Young, rich and beautiful Tangerines adore this chic café.

**Agadir** ( ☎ 068 827696; 21 Ave du Prince Héritier; mains Dh32-40, set menu Dh48) It may not look like much, but this tiny, family-run place offers top-value local fare with a French twist. The freshly cooked, succulent *tajines* are served with a cold beer or a Spanish *rioja*.

**Restaurant Valencia** ( ☎ 039 945146; 6 Ave Youssef ben Tachfine; mains Dh50-70; ☽ closed Tue) This waterfront spot deserves its reputation for excellent seafood. Big mirrors and brasswork hint at the captain's cabin, lending a nautical ambience to your dinner of fresh fish.

**Casa de España** ( ☎ 039 947359; 11 Rue el-Jebha el-Ouatania; mains from Dh50, lunch set menu Dh60) Buzzing with Spanish expats, local businessmen and the occasional tourist, this Spanish joint is as lively as they come – an excellent choice for lunch or a drink.

**Restaurant Populaire Saveur** ( ☎ 039 336326; 2 Escalier Waller; set menus Dh100-150; ☽ closed Fri) This attractive and welcoming little fish restaurant down the steps from Rue de la Liberté serves excellent, filling set menus. Four courses might include steaming fish soup, spicy shrimp *pil-pil* and grilled fish. Dessert is often sticky, sweet *seffa* (sweet couscous).

Also recommended are: **Casa della Pizza** ( ☎ 039 324817; 3 Rue Quevada; pizzas from Dh40; ☽ noon-1am) and **Africa** (83 Rue Salah Eddine el-Ayoubi; mains from Dh35; ☽ 10am-11pm), one of two adjacent places down near the port.

## Drinking

As you'd expect from its colourful past, Tangier has its fair share of drinking establishments. Most are typically male oriented.

**Café Hafa** (Ave Mohammed Tazi; ☽ 10am-8pm) Set in shaded, terraced gardens, this is a simple but delightful place. It used to be a favourite of artists and writers – including Paul Bowles and the Rolling Stones – who came here to smoke hashish and watch the sun set over the Straits.

**London's Pub** ( ☎ 039 942094; 15 Rue al-Mansour Dahabi; draught beer from Dh20; ☽ 6.30-1am) Tangier's interpretation of an English pub is a civilised place for a drink – for everyone.

Classic pubs that remain from the Interzone years include **Dean's Bar** ( ☎ 039 931671; 2 Rue Amérique du Sud; ☽ 9am-11pm) and **Tanger Inn** ( ☎ 039 935337; 1 Rue Magellan, Hôtel el-Muniria; bottle

of beer Dh10; ☽ 10.30-1am, to 3am weekends) – the latter can be dodgy after dark. Of the many coffee-drinking establishments along Blvd Pasteur, **Café de Paris** ( ☎ 039 938444; Place de France; ☽ 6am-11pm) is the most famous.

## Entertainment

By night, Tangier rocks, especially in summer, when Europeans descend on the city and party all night. Entry for most nightclubs is around Dh100 (not always applied to tourists); drinks usually cost Dh40 to Dh50. Popular clubs include **Regine's** ( ☎ 039 340238; 8 Rue al-Mansour Dahabi; ☽ 11.30pm-3am Mon-Sat) and **Pasarela** ( ☎ 039 945246; Ave des FAR; ☽ 8pm-3am Mon-Sat), where happy hour takes place between 8pm and 11pm from September to June.

## Shopping

Tangier is not the best place for souvenir hunting. The choice is quite wide, the quality variable and prices inflated to catch the hordes of unwary day-trippers. As in all Moroccan towns, the best bargains are to be found in the medina – spend some time looking around and be prepared to haggle hard. For comparison sake, check out the **Ensemble Artisanal** ( ☎ 039 933100; cnr Rue Belgique & Rue Lamsalla; ☽ 8.30am-noon & 2.30pm-7pm).

---

### WHERE TO TAKE A HAMMAM

Besides the ubiquitous public *hammam*, a few fancy facilities cater to foreigners and guests. These places have gorgeous, floor-to-ceiling tile *hammams* and other spa facilities.

■ **El Minzah Wellness** ( ☎ 039 935885; www.elminzah.com; 85 Rue de la Liberté, Tangier; admission Dh150) Luxury spa that also offers exercise facilities, sauna and jacuzzi, as well as a whole range of massage and therapeutic treatments.

■ **Hammam Ziani** ( ☎ 022 319695; www.hammamziani.ma; 59 Rue Abou Rakrak, Casablanca; Mon-Fri/Sat & Sun Dh30/40; ☽ 7am-10pm) Clean and modern *hammam* with whirlpool, massage and juice bar.

■ **Hammam Hilton** ( ☎ 044 493129; 230 Targa Rd, Marrakesh; admission Dh30; ☽ 6am-10pm) Featuring an exquisite marble Turkish bath.

MOROCCO

## Getting There & Away

### AIR

Flights by **Royal Air Maroc** (RAM; ☎ 039 379503; fax 039 932681; 1 Place de France) from Tangier go via Casablanca (return Dh1089, 50 minutes).

### BUS

The **CTM station** ( ☎ 039 931172) is beside the port gate, serving Casablanca (Dh115, six hours), Rabat (Dh78, 4½ hours), Marrakesh (Dh170, 10 hours), Fès (Dh85, six hours), Asilah (Dh15, one hour), Meknès (Dh70, five hours) and Chefchaouen (Dh33, three hours). Cheaper bus companies operate from the **Main Bus Station** (Gare routière; ☎ 039 946928; Place Jamia el-Arabia), about 2km to the south of the city centre.

### CAR

Tangier car rental agencies include **Amine Car** ( ☎ 039 944050; fax 039 325835; 43 Blvd Mohammed V) and **Cady Loc** ( ☎ 039 322207; fax 039 322209; 3 Rue Allal ben Abdallah).

### TAXI

You can get grands taxis to places outside Tangier from a lot next to the main bus station. The most common destinations are Asilah (Dh12) and Fnideq (Dh25) on the Ceuta border.

### TRAIN

Four trains depart daily from Tanger Ville, the new station 3km southeast of the centre. Two services go to Casa-Voyageurs in Casablanca (Dh117, 5½ hours); one travels via Meknès (Dh80, four hours) to Fès (Dh96, five hours); and a night service (with couchettes) goes all the way to Marrakesh (1st/2nd class Dh281/182).

## Getting Around

Distinguishable by their ultramarine colour with a yellow stripe down the side, petits taxis do standard journeys around town for Dh6 to Dh8 (50% higher at night). Taxis to **Boukhalef Airport** ( ☎ 039 393720), 15km southwest of the city in the district of Ibn Batouta, are about Dh70.

## AROUND TANGIER

Just 14km west of Tangier lies **Cap Spartel**, the northwestern extremity of Africa's Atlantic coast. It is a great place for watching flocks of birds migrating in spring and autumn.

Below Cap Spartel, the beach **Plage Robinson** stretches to the south. Five kilometres along here you reach the **Grottes d'Hercule** (admission Dh10), next to the Mirage hotel. Mythically, these caves were the dwelling place for Hercules when he mightily separated Europe from Africa.

## CEUTA (SEBTA)

Jutting out into the Mediterranean, the 20 sq km peninsula that is Ceuta has been a Spanish enclave since 1640. As soon as the border is crossed, there's no question that Ceuta is a small corner of Mediterranean Europe in Africa. The place has an Andalucían atmosphere, and it remains, officially, part of that Spanish province.

The African influence is, nonetheless, undeniable. One-third of the population is 'Spanish Muslim'. Most people are Rif Berber, with few cultural ties to Spain or Arab Morocco. This results in a rich Iberian–African mix – sometimes a source of tension but more often a fascinating example of the interplay of cultures.

## Information

To phone Ceuta from outside Spain, dial ☎ 0034. Also remember that Ceuta is on Spanish time and uses the euro.

**Main Post Office** (correos y telégrafos; Plaza de España; ☽ 8.30am-8.30pm Mon-Fri, 9.30am-2pm Sat)
**Indy Net Café** (6 Isabel Cabral; per hour € 3; ☽ 10am-10pm)
**Tourist Office** (www.turiceuta.com); Avenida Muelle Cañonero Dato ( ☎ 956 501401; fax 956 507746; ☽ 9am-3pm Mon-Fri); Ferry Terminal ( ☎ 956 506275; ☽ 9am-9pm) Plaza de Africa ( ☎ 956 528146; ☽ 9am-9pm Mon-Fri, 10am-2pm & 5-7pm Sat & Sun)

## Sights

The impressive remnants of the **city walls** ( ☎ 956 511770; Avenida González Tablas; admission free; ☽ 10am-2pm & 5-8pm) and the navigable, walled **moat of Foso de San Felipe** remain from the Hispano-Portuguese period in the 16th century. They have been almost completely restored for visitors to explore.

The most intriguing museum is the **Museo de la Legión** ( ☎ 606 733566; Paseo de Colón; admission free, donations appreciated; ☽ 10am-1.30pm & 4pm-6pm Mon-Fri, 4pm-6pm Sat & Sun). It is dedicated to and run by the Spanish Legion, an army unit set up in 1920 that played a pivotal role in

Franco's republican army at the beginning of the Spanish Civil War.

The **Parque Marítimo del Mediterráneo** (Maritime Park; ☎ 956 517742; adult/child high season €6/3; ⏰ 11am-8pm & 9pm-1am) is a huge complex on the seafront, complete with manufactured beach, landscaped pools and waterfalls, bridges, sculptures and even a mock castle. It is a great stop for families with children.

## Sleeping

**Pensión Charito** ( ☎ 956 513982; pcharito@terra.es; 1st fl, 5 Calle Arrabal; s/d shared bath €15/20) The cheapest option in town is a 2km walk along the waterfront from the ferry terminal. Don't be put off by the exterior: inside it's clean and homy, with hot showers and a small, well-equipped kitchen.

**Pensión La Bohemia** ( ☎ 956 510615; 16 Paseo de Revellín; r shared bath €25) You'll find the best deals in town is on the 1st floor above the shopping arcade. The place is charming – potted plants, shiny tile floors and smiling staff.

**Hostal Central** ( ☎ 956 516716; Paseo del Revellín; s/d €36/48) This well-priced two-star hotel is efficiently managed and centrally located. Bright rooms with private bathrooms are small but spotless.

**Hostal Plaza Ruiz** ( ☎ 956 516733; 3 Plaza Ruiz; s/d €30/40) This place is similar in style and service to its sister, the Hostal Central. It is smaller, but equally accommodating and convenient. Again, bathrooms and TV are standard; prices increase in summer.

**Parador-Hotel La Muralla** ( ☎ 956 514940; fax 956 514947; www.parador.es; 15 Plaza de Africa; r €107; Ⓟ ✕ ☒ ☒ ⓔ ) Ceuta's top address is this luxurious, four-star hotel on the main square. Balconies overlook a garden overflowing with palm trees.

## Eating

**La Mar Chica** ( ☎ 956 517240; 8 Plaza Rafael Gilbert; mains €3-4; ⏰ 8am-7pm Mon-Fri, 8am-5pm Sat) This cheap local bar has reasonable lunchtime paella and fish dishes, plus a few Moroccan staples such as *tajine* and couscous.

**La Tasca de Pedro** ( ☎ 956 510473; 3 Avenida Alcalde Sánchez Prados; mains €5-10) Small, friendly and popular with the locals, this restaurant specialises in straightforward meals prepared with fresh ingredients and simple techniques.

**La Marina** ( ☎ 956 514007; 1 Alférez Bayton; mains €10-12, set menu €7) This smart, friendly restaurant is often crowded at lunchtime. It specialises in fish dishes, but also does a reasonable three-course set menu of the chicken/fish and chips variety.

The best place to stock up on goodies before heading to Morocco is the giant **Supersol supermarket** (Avenida Muelle Cañonero Dato).

## Getting There & Away
### MOROCCO

Bus No 7 runs up to the *frontera* (border) every 10 minutes or so from Plaza de la Constitución (€0.50). Once in Morocco, the most frequent destination for grands taxis is Tetouan (per person Dh15), although there are occasional departures for Chefchaouen (Dh70) and Tangier (Dh25).

### MAINLAND SPAIN

The **estación marítima** (ferry terminal; Calle Muelle Cañonero Dato) is west of the town centre. There are frequent high-speed ferries to Algeciras. You can purchase train tickets to European destinations at the **Renfe office** ( ☎ 956 511317; www.renfe.es; 17 Plaza Rafael Gilbert).

# TETOUAN

Tetouan owes its Hispano-Moroccan atmosphere to its role as the destination for emigrants from Granada in the 15th and 16th centuries, and to its more than 40 years (1912–1956) as the capital of the Spanish protectorate. The medina, a conglomeration of whitewashed and tiled buildings set against the brooding Rif Mountains, shows off this Andalucían heritage. The Spaniards added the new part of town, where even now you can buy a *bocadillo* and as many people speak Spanish as French as their second language.

## Orientation

The ville nouvelle is centred on Place Moulay el-Mehdi and the pedestrian stretch of Ave Mohammed V, which runs east to the vast Place Hassan II. The entrance to the medina is off the grand Place Hassan II, flanked on the north side by the Royal Palace.

## Information

**BMCE** (Place Moulay el-Mehdi) Convenient bank with ATM.
**Cyber Primo** ( ☎ 039 963271; 1st fl, 6 Place Moulay el-Mehdi; per hour Dh10; ⏰ 9am-11pm)

MOROCCO

# TETOUAN

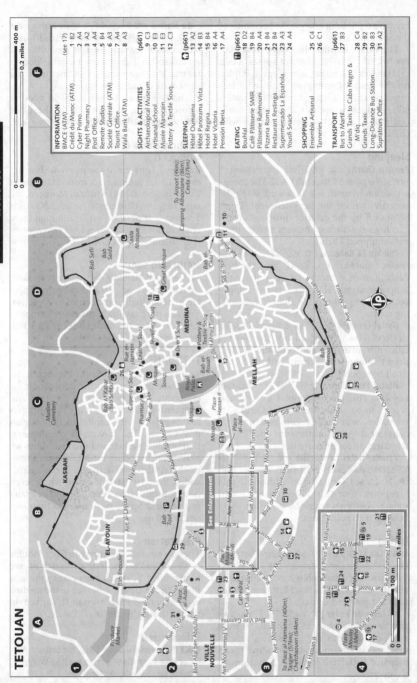

| INFORMATION | |
|---|---|
| BMCE (ATM)........................... | (see 17) |
| Crédit du Maroc (ATM)........... | 1 B2 |
| Cyber Primo........................... | 2 A4 |
| Night Pharmacy..................... | 3 A2 |
| Post Office............................ | 4 A4 |
| Remote Studios..................... | 5 B4 |
| Société Generale (ATM).......... | 6 A3 |
| Tourist Office....................... | 7 A4 |
| Wafa Bank (ATM).................. | 8 A3 |

| SIGHTS & ACTIVITIES | (pp661) |
|---|---|
| Archaeological Museum.......... | 9 C3 |
| Artisanal School.................... | 10 E3 |
| Musée Marocain.................... | 11 E3 |
| Pottery & Textile Souq.......... | 12 C3 |

| SLEEPING | (pp661) |
|---|---|
| Hotel Oumaima..................... | 13 A2 |
| Hôtel Panorama Vista............. | 14 B3 |
| Hotel Regina........................ | 15 B4 |
| Hotel Victoria...................... | 16 A4 |
| Pension Iberia...................... | 17 A4 |

| EATING | (pp661) |
|---|---|
| Bouhlal............................... | 18 D2 |
| Café Pâtisserie SMIR.............. | 19 B4 |
| Pâtisserie Rahmouni.............. | 20 A4 |
| Pizzeria Roma....................... | 21 B4 |
| Restaurant Restinga.............. | 22 B4 |
| Supermercado La Española...... | 23 A3 |
| Yousfi Snack......................... | 24 A4 |

| SHOPPING | |
|---|---|
| Ensemble Artisanal................ | 25 C4 |
| Tanneries............................ | 26 C1 |

| TRANSPORT | |
|---|---|
| Bus to Martil........................ | 27 B3 |
| Grands Taxis to Cabo Negro & | |
| M'diq................................ | 28 C4 |
| Grands Taxis........................ | 29 B2 |
| Long-Distance Bus Station...... | 30 B3 |
| Supratours Office.................. | 31 A2 |

**Délégation Régionale du Tourisme** ( ☎ 039 961915; fax 039 961914; 30 Ave Mohammed V; ☺ 8.30am-noon & 2.30pm-6.30pm Mon-Thu, 8.30pm-11am & 3pm-6.30pm Fri) Medina tours available (per half-day Dh200).
**Post Office** (Place Moulay el-Mehdi)
**Remote Studios** ( ☎ 039 711172; 13 Ave Mohammed V; ☺ 24hr) Internet café.

## Sights & Activities

The bustling Unesco World Heritage-listed **medina** opens through its main gate, Bab er-Rouah, onto Place Hassan II, Tetouan's grand main square. Nearby, the small but fascinating **archaeology museum** (Ave al-Jazaer; admission Dh10; ☺ 8.30am-noon & 2.30pm-6.30pm Mon-Fri) is filled with relics from the Roman ruins of Lixus on the Atlantic Coast.

At the opposite end of the medina, the **Musée Marocaine** (Musée Ethnographique; admission Dh10; ☺ 9.30am-noon & 3.30-6.30pm Mon-Fri) is housed inside the bastion in the town wall. Across the street, children learn traditional arts and crafts at the **artisanal school** ( ☎ 039 972721; admission Dh10; ☺ 8am-noon & 2.30-5.30pm Mon-Thu & Sat).

## Sleeping

**Hôtel Panorama Vista** ( ☎ 039 964970; www.panorama vista.ma; Ave Moulay Abbas; s/d with breakfast from Dh236/322; ☒ ☺ ) New in 2003, this classy three-star fills a void in the mid-range accommodation options in Tetouan. All rooms are spotless, tastefully decorated and fully equipped with TV, telephone and bathroom. The *salon de thé* on the 1st floor is pleasant and popular.

Cheaper options include:
**Pensión Iberia** ( ☎ 039 963679; 5 Place Moulay el-Mehdi; s/d/tr Dh50/80/120, hot showers Dh7) Small, spick-and-span pension above the BMCE.
**Hotel Victoria** ( ☎ 039 965015; 23 Ave Mohammed V; s/d/tr Dh50/80/120) Well-scrubbed, family-run place.
**Hotel Regina** ( ☎ 039 962113; 8 Rue Sidi Mandri; s/d Dh145/168) Good-value rooms with orange-and-brown 1970s décor.
**Hôtel Oumaima** ( ☎ 039 963473; 10 Rue 10 Mai; s/d Dh205/246) Aged two-star; the best of the budget options.

The nearest camping ground is **Camping Alboustane** ( ☎ 688822) on the beach at Martil, 8km away.

## Eating

**Yousfi Snack** (Rue Youseff ben Tachfine; sandwiches from Dh16; ☺ till midnight) Yousef sure knows how to make a sandwich, stuffing various meats and salads into a baguette.

**Pizzeria Roma** ( ☎ 039 713140; 8 Rue Mohammed ben Larbi Torres; pizzas Dh18-45) Fresh salads and pizza hot from the oven, as well as sandwiches and pasta, will sate any hungry traveller (including vegetarians).

**Restaurant Restinga** (21 Ave Mohammed V; mains Dh35-45; ☺ noon-2.30pm & 7pm-9.30pm) Outside of hotels, the top spot for dining in Tetouan is the vine-covered courtyard of this charming seafood restaurant. Service is not particularly friendly, but it is professional.

**Bouhlal** ( ☎ 039 998797; 48 Jamaa Kebir; menu Dh100; ☺ 10am-4pm) This sumptuous palace restaurant is tucked away in the north of the medina. Follow the lane north around the Great Mosque and look for signs directing you down a tiny alley.

For breakfast, head to **Café Pâtisserie SMIR** ( ☎ 039 961734; 17 Ave Mohammed V; ☺ 5am-10pm) or **Pâtisserie Rahmouni** (10 Youssef ben Tachfine; ☺ 6am-10pm).

## Getting There & Away

**CTM** ( ☎ 039 961688) has buses to Tangier (Dh15, 1¼ hours, one daily); Casablanca (Dh100, six to seven hours, two daily) via Rabat (Dh80, four to five hours); and Chefchaouen (Dh18, 1½ hours, three daily).

Grands taxis for Fnideq (Dh15), Martil (Dh5), Cabo Negro and M'diq leave from Ave Hassan II, southeast of the bus station. Taxis to Chefchaouen (Dh30) and Tangier (Dh25) depart the rank on Place al-Hamama, 400m from town towards Tangier.

## AROUND TETOUAN

About 8km northeast of Tetouan is the beach town of **Martil**. Once Tetouan's port and home to pirates, it's altogether quieter now, especially out of season. The pleasant beach lined with waterfront cafés comes to life in July and August.

About 5km up the coast from Martil, the headland of **Cabo Negro** (Ras Aswad in Arabic) juts out into the Mediterranean. Tucked in the lee of its north side is the small fishing port of **M'diq**. Fishing is the lifeblood of this small community: the hassles are few and the pace of life is slow. The port, with its boat building, fishing fleet and hordes of expectant cats, makes for an interesting (if smelly) visit. The nice stretch of beach to the north is now dominated by the sprawling tourist resorts of Restinga-Smir, complete with discos, bars, restaurants and all the rest.

## CHEFCHAOUEN (CHAOUEN, XAOUEN)

Set on a wide valley in the Rif Mountains, charming Chefchaouen has long been a favourite with travellers. The air is cool and clear; the medina is small and manageable; and there's more *kif* (marijuana) than you can poke a pipe at. Once the exclusive domain of bleary-eyed backpackers, Chefchaouen now attracts all types of tourists.

### Orientation

The medina occupies the eastern half of the town centre, with its main entrance on its western side at Bab el-Ain. From here, Ave Hassan II stretches west to Plaza Mohammed V, comprising the principal route of the ville nouvelle. The majority of hotels and restaurants are in the medina, while the bus station is a 1km hike southwest of the town centre (Dh15 by petit taxi) in the ville nouvelle.

### Information

**Banque Populaire** ville nouvelle (Ave Hassan II); medina (Plaza Uta el-Hammam; ⏰ 9.30am-1pm & 3.30pm-9pm)
**Echo Web** ( ☎ 039 883110; Ave ibn Rochd; per hour Dh10; ⏰ 10am-1pm & 3pm-9pm)
**Hospital Mohammed V** ( ☎ 039 986228; Ave al-Massira al-Khadra)
**Institut Raouachid pour l'Information et le Commerce** (IRIC; Ave Hassan II; per hour Dh10; ⏰ 9am-midnight) Internet café.
**Pharmacie Chefchaouen** (Ave Moulay Driss)
**Post Office** (Ave Hassan II)

### Sights & Activities

The main square of the charming medina is the shady, cobbled **Plaza Uta el-Hammam**, dominated by the red-hued walls of the kasbah and the striking **Great Mosque**. Inside the kasbah is a peaceful, blooming garden and a modest **ethnographic museum** ( ☎ 039 986343; admission Dh10; ⏰ 9am-1pm & 3-6.30pm Wed-Mon).

For information on excellent trekking opportunities in the Rif, contact the **Association des Guides du Tourisme** ( ☎ 062 113917; guide5@caramail.com) for information.

### Sleeping

**Camping Azilan** ( ☎ 039 986979; camp sites per adult Dh10, plus per small tent/large tent/car/camper Dh13/18/13/20, hot shower Dh10) A well-maintained, shady setting on the hillside behind the Hotel Azilan makes this place popular, but facilities are pretty basic. The rough-and-tumble **Youth Hostel** ( ☎ 039 986979; dm Dh20) is nearby.

**Pensión La Castellana** ( ☎ 039 986295; 4 Sidi el Bouhali; r with shared bath per person Dh40) This hangout has a welcoming atmosphere, fantastic roof terrace and convenient kitchen.

**Hotel Andaluz** ( ☎ 039 986034; 1 Rue Sidi Salem; r with shared bath per person Dh40) Similar to La Castellana, this hostel is equally inviting and equally popular.

**Hotel Madrid** ( ☎ 039 987496; Ave Hassan II; s/d/tr Dh184/264/368) The best on this strip below the medina walls, Hotel Madrid offers a strangely mixed European–Moroccan décor: floral seems to be the operative word. All the rooms are colourfully decorated and fully equipped with bathrooms etc.

**Dar Terrae** ( ☎ 070 465370, 061 758687; darterrae@hotmail.com; Ave Hassan I; r with breakfast Dh250-450) Each individually decorated room has its own unique style (not to mention its own fireplace). If you tire of your cosy room, catch some rays on one of three sunny terraces.

**Hotel Parador** ( ☎ 039 986324; parador@iam.net.ma; Place el-Majzen; s/d Dh369/476, s/d Dh438/538; P X ⏰ ) This ageing four-star hotel inside the medina remains a faithful stand-by. It's popular with tour groups.

**Casa Hassan** ( ☎ 039 986153; fax 039 988196; 22 Rue Targui; s with half-board Dh450-650, d with half-board Dh500-800) The discerning upmarket choice for over 20 years. Each room in this charming guesthouse is individually decorated with carved wooden doors, beds tucked into alcoves, colourfully tiled bathrooms and locally woven rugs.

### Eating

For self-caterers, the market off Ave Hassan II is the place to stock up on fresh produce and fresh goat's cheese (a local speciality). The cluster of small restaurants and cafés on Plaza Uta el-Hammam all feature Moroccan and Spanish dishes for about Dh25.

**Restaurant Assada** (Calle Abi Jancha; tajines Dh20, set menu Dh40) This friendly, family-run place has mastered the art of doing simple things well. It draws a mostly local crowd, which is always a good sign.

**Restaurant Les Raisins** ( ☎ 039 988641; 7 Rue Sidi Sifri; tajines Dh20, set menu from Dh40; ⏰ 7am-9pm) Although it's a bit out of the loop in the ville nouvelle, this simple restaurant has been pleasing the palates of locals and tourists alike for 25 years. The couscous especially receives rave reviews, but the menu offers all the local standards.

# CHEFCHAOUEN

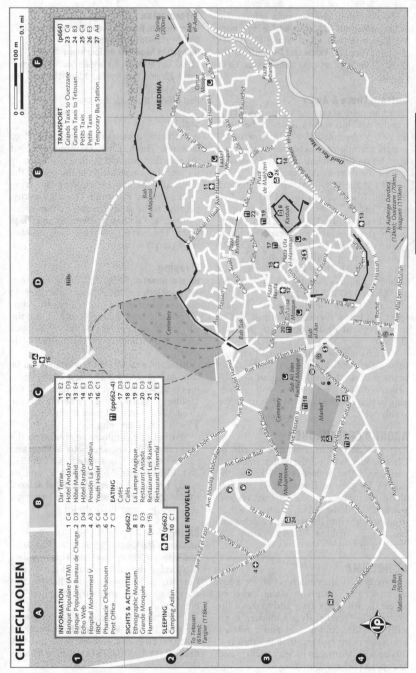

MOROCCO

Two excellent choices for a splurge are **La Lampe Magique** ( ☎ 065 406464; Rue Targui; mains from Dh45, menu Dh75), overlooking Plaza Uta el-Hammam, and **Restaurant Tissemlal** ( ☎ 039 986153; 22 Rue Targui; set menu Dh60), inside Casa Hassan.

### Getting There & Away
One kilometre southwest of the town centre, the new bus station is down the slope on Ave Mohammed V. At the time of research, a temporary bus terminal in the vast open lot on Rue Mohammed Abdou was in use for the foreseeable future.

**CTM** ( ☎ 039 988769) has services passing through Chefchaouen to Fès (Dh60, five hours) and to Tangier (Dh36, three hours) via Tetouan (Dh18, 1½ hours). Other companies run a number of cheaper services, including buses to Tetouan (Dh15, 1½ hours), Fnideq (Dh20, 2½ hours), and Tangier (Dh27, three hours), Casablanca (Dh65, six hours), Rabat (Dh50, five hours) and Meknès (Dh45, five hours).

Grands taxis heading north depart from just below Plaza Mohammed V. The most frequent destination is to Tetouan (Dh30).

Chefchaouen is generally small enough to walk around, but there is a stand for petits taxis south of the market on Ave Abdelkrim el-Kattabi – useful if you are lugging baggage to the bus station or up to the youth hostel.

## AROUND CHEFCHAOUEN
The Mediterranean coastline north of Chefchaouen is far off the beaten track and stunning. Between **Oued Laou**, 44km southeast of Tetouan, to **El-Jebha**, 87km further along, the mountain road S608 weaves and winds around the rocky coastline, which drops straight into the sea. Tiny black-sand beaches and fishing villages occupy any break in the cliffs.

## AL-HOCEIMA
Picturesque Al-Hoceima is set above a bay at one of the rare points along the coast where the Rif drops away and makes a little room for beaches. It is a modern town with an active fishing port and a relaxed beach resort atmosphere. In high summer it fills up with Moroccan holiday-makers and European package tourists.

### Information
**Cyber Club On-line** (103 Blvd Mohammed V; per hour Dh8; ☯ 10am-2pm & 4pm-midnight)
**Délégation Régionale du Tourisme** ( ☎ 039 981185; fax 039 985476; Ave Tariq ibn Ziad; ☯ 8.30am-noon & 2.30pm-6.30pm Mon-Thu, 8.30am-11.30am & 3pm-6.30pm Fri)
**Post Office** (Calle Moulay Idriss Alkbar)

### Sights
A pretty bay protects the town beach, **Plage Quemado**. The beach is clean enough, but the seaside resort atmosphere is marred by the ongoing construction at the port to the north and the massive buildings towering on the cliffs to the south. Outside the city, pristine, white sandy beaches lie 5km south of town at **Cala Bonita**, **Plage Isly** and **Plage Asfiha**. The best way to reach these beaches is by grands taxi.

### Sleeping
**Hôtel al-Hana** ( ☎ 039 981642; 17 Calle Imzouren; s/d/tr with shared bathroom Dh50/60/75, hot showers Dh10) At the lower end of the price range, this simple but immaculate hotel is tucked into the tiny streets east of Place du Rif. All facilities are shared, including the clean, squat-style toilets.

**Hôtel Etoile du Rif** ( ☎ 039 840848; Place du Rif; s/d/tr Dh159/185/239; **P** ) The best of the cheapies is this curious Art Deco building in the middle of Place du Rif. Considering that the clean, tiled rooms all have bathrooms and TVs, it's excellent value.

Two reliably comfortable options in the mid-range bracket are **Hôtel al-Khouzama** ( ☎ /fax 039 985669; Calle al-Andalous; s/d Dh264/333; **P** ), just off Blvd Mohammed V, and its newly renovated sister hotel, **Hôtel National** ( ☎ 039 982681; fax 039 981123; 23 Rue Tetouan; s/d Dh264/333; **P** ), near Place du Rif.

### Eating
**Restaurant Marhabata** ( ☎ 071 655081; Place du Rif; salad/sardines Dh5/15; ☯ 8am-11pm) This tiny dive is typical of the eateries around the square. Catering to the bus station clientele, it's cheap and filling, small on atmosphere but big on portions.

Two excellent seafood restaurants near the port include **Restaurant Escorpio** ( ☎ 039 984410; Port d'Al-Hoceima; meals around Dh70) and **Club Nautique** ( ☎ 039 981461; Port d'Al-Hoceima; fish mains Dh60-90).

## Getting There & Away

**BOAT**

Trasmediterranea runs daily ferries from Al-Hoceima to Almería and Málaga. This service commenced in 2003, and at the time of research was operating only during June to August.

**BUS**

All the bus companies have offices situated around Place du Rif. **CTM** ( ☎ 039 982273) operates buses to Tetouan (Dh68, seven hours) via Chefchaouen (Dh50, five hours) and to Casablanca (Dh150, 11½ hours) via Fès (Dh85, six hours), Meknès (Dh100, 7½ hours) and Rabat (Dh130, 10 hours). Several small companies also serve the aforementioned destinations.

## MELILLA

With roughly a third of its inhabitants Muslims of Rif Berber origin, Melilla is smaller and less affluent than its Spanish sister to the west, Ceuta. However, the town centre, with its palm trees, well-tended gardens and restored Spanish-era façades, has more immediate appeal than Ceuta.

## Information

To phone Melilla from Morocco, dial ☎ 0034. Also remember that Melilla is two hours ahead of Morocco during summer and one hour ahead at other times. The unit of currency here is the euro.

**Cajamar** (Plaza de España; ☒ 8.30am-2pm Mon-Fri)

**Main Post Office** (correos y telégrafos; Calle Pablo Vallescá; ☒ 8.30am-8.30pm Mon-Fri, 9.30am-1pm Sat)

**Officiana du Turismo** ( ☎ 956 675444; www .melilla500.com; 21 Calle Fortuny, Palicio de Congresos y Exposiciones; ☒ 8am-2.45pm & 4.30om-8.30pm Mon-Fri)

**Telefonica** (Calle General Aizpuru; per hour €1.50; ☒ 9am-2.15pm & 4-11pm) Internet access.

## Sights

Perched over the Mediterranean, Melilla la Vieja is a prime example of the fortress strongholds that the Portuguese and (in this case) the Spaniards built along the Moroccan littoral during the 16th and 17th centuries. Much of it has been painstakingly restored in recent years. Sights include **Aljibes de las Peñuelas** (admission €1.20; ☒ 10am-2pm & 5pm-9.30pm Tue-Sat, 10am-2pm Sun Apr-Sep, 10am-2pm & 4.30pm-8.30pm Tue-Sat, 10am-2pm Sun Oct-Mar), which is a pair of 15th-century water cisterns.

**Museo de Arqueología e Historia de Melilla** ( ☎ 952 681339; Plaza Pedro de Estopiñán; admission free; ☒ 10am-1.30pm & 4-8.30pm Tue-Sat, 10am-2pm Sun) It's worth visiting for the fantastic views overlooking the city, not to mention its collection of archaeological finds.

**Las Cuevas del Conventico** ( ☎ 952 680929; admission €1.20; ☒ 10.30am-1.30pm & 4.30-8pm Tue-Sat, 10.30am-2pm Sun) are caves and tunnels underneath the Iglesia de la Concepción.

## Sleeping

**Hostal Residencia Parque** ( ☎ 956 682143; 15 Calle General Marina; s/d €20/40) A popular pension overlooking the park. Bright, tidy rooms all have a TV and bathroom. Service is friendly and efficient.

**Hostal Residencia Cazaza** ( ☎ 956 684648; 6 Calle Primo de Rivera; s/d €23/35) If the Parque is full, this excellent alternative is just down the street and similar in style and service. Eleven smallish but comfortable rooms have TVs, bathtubs and balconies.

**Hotel Rusadir** ( ☎ 956 681240; hotelrusadir@wana doo.es; 5 Calle Pablo Vallescá; s/d with breakfast €65/81; ☒ ) Stylish rooms are fully equipped with satellite TV, minibar and balcony. The restaurant, recommended for its buffet breakfast, puts out a pretty impressive spread.

**Parador de Melilla** ( ☎ 956 684940; www.paradores .es; Avenida Cándido Lobera; r €97; P ☒ ☒ ) The best of the lot offers incredible views over the Mediterranean from its perch above the valley. Guests enjoy subtly elegant rooms, a private garden and top-notch seafood.

## Eating

**Cafetería Nuevo California** (11 Avenida de Juan Carlos I Rey; mains €2am -5; ☒ 7am-2am Mon-Sat) A popular meeting place for young and old alike, this modern cafeteria has a pleasant outdoor terrace and friendly wait staff.

**Antony Pizza Factory** ( ☎ 956 684320; Avenida de la Democracia; pizza €4-6, burgers €2-3) This factory works overtime, churning out hot and spicy pizzas loaded with toppings, as well as other simple fare like pasta and sandwiches.

## Getting There & Away

At least six ferries a week run to/from Málaga and Almería from the **estación marítima** ( ☎ 956 681633).

On the Moroccan side of the border, the No 19 bus (Dh2.50, hourly) and grands taxis (Dh4) go to Nador, which is a large

MOROCCO

transport hub. To get to the border, the No 2 local bus (marked 'Aforos') runs between Plaza de España and the Beni–Enzar border post (€0.60).

# ATLANTIC COAST

From Tangier to the Mauritanian border, Morocco boasts an Atlantic seaboard of some 2500km, including the still-disputed territory of the Western Sahara. Morocco has debated over this territory with Spain, Algeria and Mauritania, although Spain dropped its claim in 1975. Also (most notably), the indigenous Saharawi people (complete with guerilla movement) have made claims for independence with support (at various times) from Libya, Algeria and Mauritania.

Most of Morocco's coastal towns and cities were occupied, or even founded, by European powers. Rabat and Casablanca, the political and economic capitals respectively since the French installed their protectorate in 1912, are cosmopolitan centres at the heart of modern Morocco. They are flanked up and down the coast by towns that at one time or another served as bridgeheads for European merchant empires. What remains is a curious combination of European and Moroccan fortifications, ancient medinas and modern colonial-built cities.

## ASILAH

The port of Asilah, 46km south of Tangier, has found its niche as a bijou resort town. Affluent Moroccans and Europeans – as well as the Moroccan government – have poured money into gentrifying houses within the whitewashed and mural-painted city walls. Galleries line the narrow streets, which host the sophisticated annual International Cultural Festival.

The impressive 15th-century Portuguese ramparts are largely intact, partly as a result of modern restoration work. Of the two prongs that jut out into the ocean, only the southwestern is open for great views and photographic opportunities. There is no better seat from which to catch a sunset. It also offers a peek into the nearby **Koubba of Sidi Mamsur** (which is otherwise closed to non-Muslims) and the **Mujaheddin Graveyard**.

A revolving exhibition of international painting and sculpture is housed in the **Centre de Hassan II** ( ☎ 039 417065; admission free;  ⏰ 8.30am-12.30pm & 2.30pm-7pm) and in the nearby **El-Kamra Tower**, a renovated Portuguese fortification on Place Abdellah Guennoun.

While the beaches north of town are not bad, sun worshippers and bathing beauties are advised to head 3km south of Asilah to **Paradise Beach**, a gorgeous, pristine spot that really does live up to its name.

### Sleeping
**Hôtel Sahara** ( ☎ 039 417185; 9 Rue Tarfaya; s/d with shared bathrooms Dh70/100, Dh100/128, hot showers Dh5) This well-maintained hotel is an excellent budget option. The pretty, tiled entrance is adorned with plants. Rooms are small, but facilities are spotless.

**Hôtel Azayla** ( ☎ 039 416717; fax 039 417600; 20 Rue ibn Rouchd; s/d Dh186/226, Dh226/286) This spic-and-span hotel still feels new, with its bright rooms and modern private bathrooms. There are also some family-style rooms for up to five people.

**Hôtel Patio de la Luna** ( ☎ 039 416074; 12 Place Zellaka; s/d Dh250/400) Set around a leafy patio, this intimate Spanish-run guesthouse is the only place in town that retains some local flavour. Seven rooms are decorated with wooden furniture and woven blankets, and equipped with tiled bathrooms.

**Hôtel Zelis** ( ☎ 039 417069; fax 039 417098; 10 Ave Mansour Eddahabi; s/d Dh364/439, high season Dh474/549; ✷ ⊜ ) This big, brash, modern place is more reminiscent of a city hotel. It is European in style and service.

For campers, a number of well-equipped camping grounds are along the beach north of town. The first two – a few hundred metres north of town – are among the best. They are **Camping as-Saada** ( ☎ 039 417317; camp sites per person Dh12, plus per tent/car/caravan/camper Dh10/10/20/20, electricity Dh15, r low/high season Dh100/120) and **Camping Echrigui** ( ☎ 039 417182; r low/high season Dh100/200), which has facilities including a café and market.

### Eating
For main meals, about the cheapest option is the string of restaurants and cafés by the medina wall on Ave Hassan II.

**La Symphonie des Douceurs II** ( ☎ 039 416633; 26 Place Zellaka) Women will appreciate this new French patisserie, which specialises in delicious pastries and ice cream in a very civilised décor.

**Restaurant de la Place** ( ☎ 039 417326; 7 Ave Moulay Hassan ben el-Mehdi; mains Dh40-60) For fine dining, the strip of restaurants opposite Bab Kasbah represents the best Asilah has to offer. This place marries the best of two worlds, offering a wide range of seafood and classic Moroccan fare.

## Getting There & Away
Your best bet for getting to and from Asilah is the bus. Services run to Tangier (Dh10 to Dh15, one hour), Fès (Dh55) via Meknès, Casablanca (Dh70, four hours) via Rabat (Dh50, three hours).

# RABAT
The great walls of Rabat enclose a largely modern city with wide boulevards and bureaucratic-looking buildings. But several quarters recall Rabat's rich past, including the ancient Kasbah des Oudaias and white-washed Salé, home to the colourful corsairs. Besides being historically rich, Rabat is the modern capital, and thus houses monuments and museums of national importance.

## Orientation
All the main administrative buildings and many of the hotels lie just off the city's main thoroughfare, the wide, palm-lined Ave Mohammed V. The entrance to the medina is at the northern end of the avenue, while the train station Rabat Ville is at the southern end.

## Information
**English Bookshop** ( ☎ 037 706593; 7 Rue al-Yamama) Stocks second-hand English-language novels.
**Main Post Office** (cnr Rue Soékarno & Ave Mohammed V)
**Menara Internet** (Rue Soékarno; per hour Dh12; ⏱ 9am-8pm Mon-Sat)
**Office National Marocain du Tourisme** (ONMT; ☎ 037 673756; visitmorocco@onmt.org.ma; cnr Rue Oued El Makhazine & Rue Zalaka, Agdal; ⏱ 8.30am-noon & 3-6.30pm Mon-Fri) Take bus No 3 from the train station or take a taxi; the office is opposite the 'Belle Vue' swimming pool.

## Sights & Activities
### MEDINA
Dating from the 17th century, the walled medina is slightly sanitised compared to the older medinas in the interior. Which isn't to say that it won't pique the senses with its fresh foodstuffs and souvenir stalls.

Head north along the Rue des Consuls to the **Kasbah des Oudaias**, high up on the bluff overlooking the Oued Bou Regreg.

The southern corner of the kasbah houses the **Andalucían Gardens** ( ⏱ sunrise-sunset), laid out by the French during the colonial period. The centrepiece is the grand 17th-century palace containing the **Musée des Oudaia** ( ☎ 037 731537; admission Dh10; ⏱ 9am-noon & 3pm-5pm, till 6pm in summer).

### TOUR HASSAN & MAUSOLEUM
In 1195, the Almohad sultan Yacoub al-Mansour begain constructing an enormous minaret, intending to make it the highest in the Muslim world, but he died before the project was completed. What remains is Rabat's most famous landmark, **La Tour Hassan** (Hassan Tower); the adjacent mosque was all but destroyed by an earthquake in 1755. On the same site is the cool marble **Mausoleum of Mohammed V** (admission free; ⏱ sunrise-sunset), where the present king's grandfather and father (the late Hassan II) are laid to rest.

### ARCHAEOLOGICAL SITES
One of Rabat's most peaceful corners is the site of the ancient Roman city of **Sala Colonia** and the Merenid necropolis of **Chellah** (cnr Ave Yacoub al-Mansour & Blvd ad-Douster; admission adults/children Dh10/3; ⏱ 9am-5.30pm) south of the centre.

Many of the relics from Sala Colonia and other highlights of Morocco's ancient history are on display at the **Archaeology Museum** ( ☎ 037 701919; 23 Rue al-Brihi Parent; admission Dh10; ⏱ 9am-11.30am & 2.30pm-5.30pm Wed-Mon).

### SURFING
Above the breakers of the Atlantic coast, the modern building between the kasbah and the lighthouse is the **Oudayas Surf Club** ( ☎ 037 260683; fax 037 260684; 3 Plage des Oudayas; 1½-hr lesson Dh90, insurance Dh50), a school for surfing and body boarding.

### GOLF
The best and most modern of Morocco's courses is the **Royal Dar es-Salaam Golf Course** ( ☎ 037 755864; fax 037 757671; Ave Imam Malik); which has two 18-hole courses and one nine-whole course. It hosts the annual Hassan II Challenge Cup (as well as flocks of wild ducks and pink flamingos). This course is 10km out of town along the road to the Forest of Zaer.

MOROCCO

MOROCCO

# CENTRAL RABAT

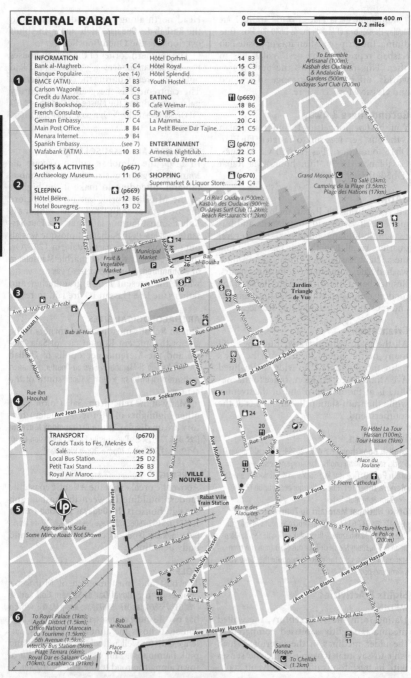

0 — 400 m
0 — 0.2 miles

**INFORMATION**
Bank al-Maghreb.........................1 C4
Banque Populaire..................(see 14)
BMCE (ATM)..............................2 B3
Carlson Wagonlit.......................3 C4
Credit du Maroc.........................4 C3
English Bookshop.......................5 B6
French Consulate.......................6 C5
German Embassy........................7 C4
Main Post Office........................8 B4
Menara Internet.........................9 B4
Spanish Embassy...................(see 7)
Wafabank (ATM).......................10 B3

**SIGHTS & ACTIVITIES** (p667)
Archaeology Museum................11 D6

**SLEEPING** (p669)
Hôtel Bélère..............................12 B6
Hotel Bouregreg.......................13 D2

Hôtel Dorhmi............................14 B3
Hôtel Royal..............................15 C3
Hôtel Splendid.........................16 B3
Youth Hostel............................17 A2

**EATING** (p669)
Café Weimar............................18 B6
City VIPS.................................19 C5
La Mamma...............................20 C4
La Petit Beure Dar Tajine..........21 C5

**ENTERTAINMENT** (p670)
Amnesia Nightclub...................22 C3
Cinéma du 7ème Art.................23 C4

**SHOPPING** (p670)
Supermarket & Liquor Store.......24 C4

To Ensemble
Artisanal (100m);
Kasbah des Oudaias
& Andalucian
Gardens (500m);
Oudayas Surf Club (700m)

Rue des Consuls

Rue Souika

Grand Mosque
To Salé (3km);
Camping de la Plage (3.5km);
Plage des Nations (17km)

To Riad Oudaya (500m);
Kasbah des Oudaias (900m);
Oudayas Surf Club (1.2km);
Beach Restaurants (1.2km)

Ave de l'Egypte

17

Rue Souk Semara

Ave Mohammed V

Municipal Market
Fruit & Vegetable Market

Bab
el-Bouiba

26

Ave Hassan II

Rue Yougoslavia

Jardins
Triangle
de Vue

Ave al-Maghrib al-Arabi

Ave Hassan II

Bab al-Had

Rue de Beyrouth

Rue Ghazza

Rue de Monastir

Ammane

Rue de l'Abdali

Rue Jeddah

Rue Damiate Halab

Rue al-Mansourad-Dahbi

Rue Chariai

Rue Soekarno

Rue Moulay Rachid

Rue ibn
Haouhal

Ave Jean Jaurès

Rue al-Kahira

To Hôtel La Tour
Hassan (100m);
Tour Hassan (1km)

Ave Pasteur

**TRANSPORT** (p670)
Grands Taxis to Fès, Meknès &
Salé................................(see 25)
Local Bus Station......................25 D2
Petit Taxi Stand........................26 B3
Royal Air Maroc........................27 C5

Rue Tanta

Ave Mohammed V

Rue Raoul Marc

Rue Damas

Rue Moulay Abdallah

Allal ben Abdallah

Rue Marchand

Place du
Joulane

St Pierre Cathedral

Rue al-Forat

Approximate Scale
Some Minor Roads Not Shown

Ave ibn Toumrette

VILLE
NOUVELLE

Rabat Ville
Train Station

Place des
Alaouites

Rue Zahla

Rue Abou Faris al-Marini

To Préfecture
de Police
(200m)

Rue de Bagdad

Rue de Berghaz

19

6

Rue Tessa

Ave Moulay Hassan

Rue Moulay Youssef

Rue Hatim

Rue al-Khalil

(Ave Urbain Blanc)

Rue al-Bah Ferri

Rue Berthelot

Rue al-Yamama

5

12

Sana'a

Rue al-Maubua

18

Rue Moulay Abdel Aziz

To Royal Palace (1km);
Agdal District (1.5km);
Office National Marocain
du Tourisme (1.5km);
5th Avenue (1.5km);
Intercity Bus Station (5km);
Plage Temara (6km);
Royal Dar es-Salaam Golf
(10km); Casablanca (91km)

Bab
ar-Rouah

Place
an-Nasr

Ave Moulay Hassan

Sunna
Mosque

To Chellah
(1.2km)

11

## Sleeping

### BUDGET

**Youth Hostel** ( ☎ 037 725769; 43 Rue Marassa; dm HI members/nonmembers Dh30/35, hot showers Dh7.50; ⏰ 8am-10.30pm, closed 10am-noon & 3pm-6pm Oct-Apr) Opposite the walls of the medina, the youth hostel is a pleasant place with an attractive and verdant courtyard. Lock your bags and don't leave valuables in the dorms.

**Hôtel Dorhmi** ( ☎ 037 723898; 313 Ave Mohammed V; s/d with shared bath Dh80/120, hot showers Dh10) This small, family-run hotel above the Banque Populaire is worth seeking out for its immaculate rooms and homy atmosphere. Fresh paint and a bit of sunlight make this the most welcoming option at this price.

**Hôtel Splendid** ( ☎ 037 723283; 8 Rue Ghazza; s/d Dh160/185) The Hôtel Splendid is set around a tranquil garden courtyard with an exquisite *zelij*-tiled entry. Wood furniture and linoleum floors outfit the cheery rooms. Rooms with shared bathroom are cheaper.

**Hôtel Royal** ( ☎ 037 721171; royalhotel@mtds.com; 1 Rue Jeddah Ammane; s/d Dh230/270) Renovated in 2004, the Royal provides excellent value. Its spacious, comfortable rooms are equipped with polished-wood furniture and modern, marble bathrooms.

**Camping de la Plage** (camp sites adult/child under 12 Dh15/8, plus per small tent/large tent/car/camper/bus Dh15/22/12/30/50, power & water Dh15, hot showers Dh10) The nearest camping ground is in from the beach at Salé.

### MID-RANGE & TOP END

**Hôtel Bélère** ( ☎ 037 709689; fax 037 709801; 33 Ave Moulay Youssef; s/d Dh674/882; P ⓧ ⓧ ⓛ ⓡ ) Steps from Rabat Ville train station, the Bélère features small but plush rooms with all the amenities of a four-star hotel. Rooms are wheelchair accessible.

**Le Dawliz Rabat-Salé** ( ☎ 037 883277; ledawliz@iam .net.ma; Ave du Prince Héritier Sidi Mohamed, Salé; s/d Dh674/898; P ⓧ ⓧ ⓡ ) Complete with movie theatre, bowling, billiards and arcade, this is the place to stay if you are travelling with kids. The only drawback is the location in the new section of Salé, so you'll need a car.

**Hôtel Bouregreg** ( ☎ 037720445; bouregreg@magreb net.net.ma; cnr Rue Nador & Ave Hassan II; s/d Dh334/401; P ⓧ ) The Bouregreg is not the most centrally located hotel, but it is an excellent choice for the price. Spacious, modern rooms have spic-and-span new bathrooms and incredible views of the medina.

**Riad Oudaya** ( ☎ 037 702392; www.riadoudaya.com; 46 Rue Sidi Fateh; r/ste Dh1350/1650) Two charming rooms and two luxurious suites make up this tiny guesthouse – one of two operated by the friendly French owner. Fireplaces and balconies overlooking the medina are some of the features that enrich this *riad* experience.

## Eating

In the southwest corner of the medina, the indoor **fruit and vegetable market** (Ave Hassan II) will fill your picnic basket with fresh produce, as well as dried fruits, nuts and prepared salads.

**Café Maure** (Kasbah des Oudaias; ⏰ 9am-5.30pm) In a calm, shady courtyard on the far side of the Andalucían Gardens, Café Maure is a delightful spot for a refresher. The flowering trees and lounging cats create a languid atmosphere to sip a coffee, tea and admire the views over the estuary. Welcoming for women.

**City VIPS** ( ☎ 037 202840; 47 Ave Allal ben Abdallah; mains Dh20-40; ⏰ 11am-11pm) Everyone from VIPs to LIPs (less-important-people) eats at this popular fast-food joint. The wideranging menu has an Italian emphasis. Good for vegetarians too.

**Café Weimar** ( ☎ 037 732650; 7 Rue Sana'a; pizza Dh55) The café-restaurant in the Goethe Institut is among the hottest spots for hip, young Moroccans and expats. The menu is mostly Mediterranean.

**Le Petit Beure – Dar Tajine** ( ☎ 037 731322; 8 Rue Damas; mains Dh65-85; ⏰ closed Sun) This peaceful and pleasant eatery offers tasty food and traditional atmosphere without the fuss (and financial burden) of the more elaborate places in the medina. Servers discretely double as musicians, playing *oued* (lute) music to accompany your meal.

**La Mamma** ( ☎ 037 707329; 6 Rue Tanta; mains Dh80-100) Rue Tanta might be Rabat's 'Little Italy', thanks to the Benenatis family's culinary exploits. Besides the ice cream parlour and the pizza delivery service, they operate this romantic restaurant.

**Restaurant de la Plage** ( ☎ 037 202928; mains from Dh110) and **Borj Eddar** ( ☎ 037 701501; mains from Dh110; ⏰ closed winter) both overlook the wide, sandy beach and the vast ocean beyond (somehow proof that the seafood is fresh and delicious). Follow Blvd Tariq al-Marsa past the kasbah.

MOROCCO

## Entertainment

Nightclubs in Rabat – some of which are attached to the upscale hotels – normally charge at least Dh60 for entry (which includes the first drink). Most clubs are open from around 11pm until 3am or later. Don't forget to dress the part or you won't get past the front door.

Popular clubs include **Amnesia** (Rue de Monastir; admission Mon-Fri Dh60, Sat & Sun Dh100, women free), which was expected to re-open in 2004, and **5th Avenue** ( ☎ 037 775254; 4 Rue Bin Alaouidan, Agdal; cover Dh100; ☺ weekends until 5am).

## Shopping

The traditional craft of carpet weaving centres in Rabat, which specialises in the formal, Islamic style. Rue des Consuls becomes a hive of activity on Tuesday and Thursday mornings, when women descend from the villages to auction their carpets to local salesmen. Salé is known for its ceramics; it's worth a trip across the river to the Complexe des Potiers (right) if you are in the market for dishes, bowls, a vase or platter.

A stroll up Rue des Consuls and further along Blvd Tariq al-Marsa toward the kasbah will reveal the wide range of handicrafts that are still practised and sold in the capital. For comparison, check out the **Ensemble Artisanal** ( ☎ 037 730507; Blvd Tariq al-Marsa; ☺ 9am-noon & 2.30pm-6.30pm).

## Getting There & Away

### BUS

Local bus No 30 makes the 5km trip to the intercity bus station southwest of the centre. **CTM** ( ☎ 037 795124) has buses to Agadir (Dh166, 12 hours), Casablanca (Dh30, 1½ hours), Essaouira (Dh130, eight hours), Fès (Dh50, 3½ hours), Marrakesh (Dh90, five hours), Tangier (Dh76, 4½ hours) and Tetouan (Dh76, five hours). Other bus lines offer cheaper fares to most of these destinations.

### TRAIN

**Rabat Ville train station** ( ☎ 037 736060) is in the centre of town, on Ave Mohammed V at Place des Alaouites. Twice hourly trains run to Casa-Port in Casablanca (Dh28). Other 2nd-class *rapide* fares include: Fès (Dh72, 3½ hours, eight daily) via Meknès (Dh56, 2½ hours), Oujda (Dh134, 10 hours, three daily) via Taza (Dh108, six hours), Tangier (Dh90, 4½ hours, three daily) and Marrakesh (Dh101, 4½ hours, eight daily).

### GRANDS TAXIS

Grands taxis leave for Casablanca (Dh27) from just outside the intercity bus station. Other grands taxis leave for Fès (Dh55), Meknès (Dh40) and Salé (Dh3) from Ave Hassan II (between the city's main local bus station and the Hôtel Bou Regreg).

## Getting Around

The blue petits taxis can be found around the station or outside the medina walls on Ave Hassan II. Useful bus routes include the following:

**No 16** Local bus station (Blvd Hassan II) to Salé
**No 3** Local bus station to Agdal
**No 17 & 30** Bab al-Had to intercity bus station

# AROUND RABAT
## Salé

Although just across the estuary, the white-washed city of Salé has a character distinct from Rabat. Little within the city walls seems to have changed over the centuries. The medina's main point of access is Bab Bou Haja, on the southwestern wall, which opens onto Place Bab Khebaz. From here it's a short walk to the *souqs* on the northwest side of the square. The Grand Mosque and the beautiful 14th-century **medersa** (admission Dh10; ☺ 9am-noon & 2.30pm-6pm) are 500m further northwest along Rue Ras ash-Shajara. Grands taxis and bus No 16 leave from Bab Mrisa to Rabat; you can catch small boats across the river below Bab Bou Haja.

In the village of Oulja, 3km southeast of Salé, the **Complexe de Potiers** (potters' complex; ☺ sunrise-sunset) is a top spot for the souvenir hunter. A huge selection of ceramics is produced and sold here, including *tajine* dishes of every size and colour and complete sets of fine domestic china.

## Beaches

Surfers and sun worshippers will appreciate the clean sandy strip and the serious waves at **Plage des Nations**, 17km north of Rabat off the road to Kenitra (accessible by bus No 28). Other beautiful beaches are even closer to Rabat, such as the wild sandy stretches around **Plage Temara**, 6km south of Rabat. Take Bus No 17 from Bab al-Had.

# CASABLANCA

Casablanca, popularly known as Casa, is a massive, modern city that was developed by the French in the early days of the protectorate. Amid the striking, colonial architecture – and there are some Art Deco and modernist jewels – it is Casablanca's residents that leave the greatest impression.

Women wearing the veil are less common than those wearing suits and high heels. Men and women mix easily here; on the beaches and in the clubs, the bright young things strut their stuff much like the beautiful youth of any European city. But elements of traditional Morocco remain: the marvel of modern religious architecture – the enormous Hassan II Mosque – is a clear reminder.

## Orientation

The relatively small medina sits in the north of the city just south of the port. The heart of the city is south of the medina at the Place des Nations Unies. West of the centre lies the beachfront Blvd de la Corniche, home to several top-end hotels and nightclubs.

## Information

### EMERGENCY SERVICES

**Service d'Aide Médicale Urgente** (SAMU; ☎ 022 252525) Private ambulance service.

**SOS Médecins** ( ☎ 022 444444; house call Dh300; ☻ 24hr) Private doctors who make house calls.

### INTERNET ACCESS

**Gig@net** ( ☎ 022 484810; 140 Blvd Mohammed Zerktouni; per hour Dh10; ☻ 24hr) A flash new cyberclub with two floors of super-fast computers.

**EuroNet** ( ☎ 022 265921; 51 Rue Tata; per hour Dh10; ☻ 8am-11pm)

### MONEY

There are banks with ATMS and foreign exchange offices on nearly every street corner in Casablanca.

**Banque Marocaine du Commerce Extérieur** (BMCE) (Hyatt Regency Hotel; ☻ 9am-9pm) Good for after-hours and weekend services.

### POST

**Main Post Office** (cnr Blvd de Paris & Ave Hassan II)

### TOURIST INFORMATION

**Office National Marocain du Tourisme** (ONMT; ☎ 022 271177; 55 Rue Omar Slaoui; ☻ 8.30am-noon & 2.30pm-6.30pm Mon-Fri)

**Syndicat d'Initiative** ( ☎ 022 221524; 98 Blvd Mohammed V; ☻ 8.30am-noon & 3pm-6.30pm Mon-Fri, till 5pm Sat, 9am-noon Sun)

## Sights & Activities

Rising above the Atlantic northwest of the medina, the **Hassan II Mosque** is the world's third-largest mosque, built to commemorate the former king's 60th birthday. To see the interior of the mosque you must take a **guided tour** ( ☎ 022 440448; adult/student/child Dh100/50/25; ☻ 9am, 10am, 11am & 2pm Sat-Thu).

About 1km southeast of town is the **Quartier Habous**, or district of holy men. Its French architects tried to marry the best features of traditional Moroccan architecture with modern techniques and facilities. The result is an idealised but attractive French version of a Moroccan medina, sometimes called the 'nouvelle medina'. To the south is the old **Mahakma du Pasha** (courts & reception hall; admission free; ☻ 8am-noon & 2pm-6pm Mon-Sat), which has more than 60 elaborately decorated rooms. To get to the nouvelle medina, take bus No 4 or 40 from Blvd de Paris, across from the post office.

In this trendy suburb of Ain Diab, the beachside **Blvd de la Corniche** is lined with beach clubs, four-star hotels, upmarket restaurants, bars, coffee shops, nightclubs and a new multiplex cinema. Take bus No 9 from Place Oued al-Makhazine, just west of Place des Nations Unies.

## Sleeping

### BUDGET

**Youth Hostel** ( ☎ 022 220551; fax 022 227677; 6 Place Ahmed el-Bidaoui; dm with breakfast Dh45, d/tr Dh120/180, sheets Dh5; ☻ 8am-10am & noon-11pm; **P** ) Facing a small square just inside the medina, the youth hostel has good facilities, but readers have complained about poor treatment.

**Hôtel Oued-Dahab** ( ☎ 022 223866; 1 Rue Mohamed Belloul; s/d Dh120/180) This place is pretty basic,

### CASABLANCA IN ONE DAY

First thing in the morning, take a tour of the **Hassan II Mosque** (p671), followed by lunch at nearby **Café Maure** (p674). Spend the afternoon shopping in the **Quartier Habous** (p671), then head to the port for a seafood dinner, followed by a night out on the town along **Blvd de la Corniche**.

MOROCCO

# CENTRAL CASABLANCA

| | 0 | 600 m |
| | 0 | 0.4 miles |

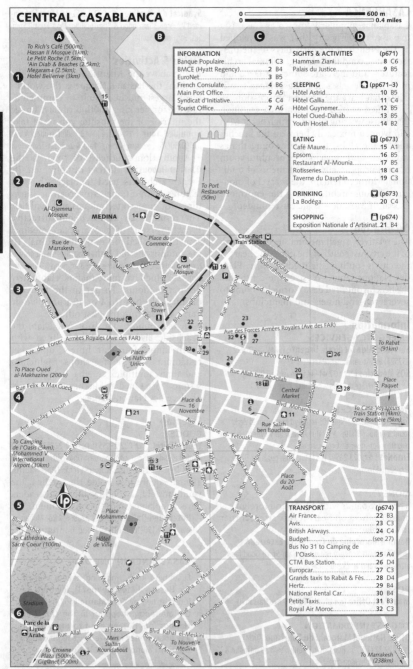

To Rich's Café (500m);
Hassan II Mosque (1km);
Le Petit Roche (1.5km);
'Ain Diab & Beaches (2.5km);
Megarama (2.5km);
Hotel Bellerive (3km)

**INFORMATION**
Banque Populaire...............................1 C3
BMCE (Hyatt Regency)........................2 B4
EuroNet.............................................3 B5
French Consulate................................4 B6
Main Post Office.................................5 A5
Syndicat d'Initiative...........................6 C4
Tourist Office.....................................7 A6

**SIGHTS & ACTIVITIES** (p671)
Hammam Ziani....................................8 C6
Palais du Justice..................................9 B5

**SLEEPING** (pp671–3)
Hôtel Astrid........................................10 B5
Hôtel Gallia........................................11 C4
Hôtel Guynemer..................................12 B5
Hotel Oued-Dahab..............................13 B5
Youth Hostel.......................................14 B2

**EATING** (p673)
Café Maure..........................................15 A1
Epsom.................................................16 B5
Restaurant Al-Mounia...........................17 B5
Rotisseries...........................................18 C4
Taverne du Dauphin.............................19 C3

**DRINKING** (p673)
La Bodéga...........................................20 C4

**SHOPPING** (p674)
Exposition Nationale d'Artisinat..........21 B4

Medina

Al-Djemma
Mosque

MEDINA

Place du
Commerce

Casa-Port
Train Station

Rue de
Marrakesh

Great
Mosque

To Port
Restaurants
(50m)

Clock
Tower

Mosque

Armées Royales (Ave des FAR)

Ave des Forces Armées Royales (Ave des FAR)

To Place Oued
al-Makhazine (200m)

Place
des Nations
Unies

Rue Léon L'Africain

To Rabat
(91km)

Rue Felix & Max Guedj

Place du
16
Novembre

Central
Market

To Casa-Voyageurs
Train Station (4km);
Gare Routière (5km)

Place
Paquet

To Camping
de l'Oasis (5km);
Mohammed V
International
Airport (30km)

Ave Houmane el- Fetouaki

Rue Salah
ben Bouchaib

Place
du 20
Août

Place
Mohammed
V

Hôtel
de Ville

To Cathédrale du
Sacré Coeur (100m)

Blvd Rachidi

**TRANSPORT** (p674)
Air France............................................22 B3
Avis.....................................................23 C3
British Airways.....................................24 C4
Budget.............................................(see 27)
Bus No 31 to Camping de
l'Oasis...............................................25 A4
CTM Bus Station..................................26 D4
Europcar..............................................27 C3
Grands taxis to Rabat & Fès.................28 D4
Hertz...................................................29 B4
National Rental Car..............................30 B4
Petits Taxis..........................................31 B3
Royal Air Maroc...................................32 C3

Parc de la
Ligue
Arabe

Stadium

Mers
Sultan
Roundabout

To Crowne
Plaza (500m);
Giganet (500m)

To Nouvelle
Medina

To Marrakesh
(238km)

but it's clean, friendly and very safe. In the pedestrian zone of the city centre, it is among the more reliable options at the low end of this price range. Rooms with share bathroom are cheaper.

**Hôtel Gallia** ( ☎ 022 481694; 19 Rue Ibn Batouta; s/d/tr Dh150/220/300) This new hotel near the central market is a welcome addition to Casa's sometimes dingy sleeping scene. Fresh, clean rooms and friendly, efficient management make it one of the top budget options.

**Hôtel Astrid** ( ☎ 022 277803; hotelastrid@hotmail .com; 12 Rue 6 Novembre; s/d/tr Dh256/309/405) This surprising gem of a hotel has a grand marble lobby and simple, clean rooms. Each has a colourfully painted door, lending it a touch of character, as well as a TV and telephone.

**Camping de l'Oasis** ( ☎ 022 234257; Ave Mermoz; camp sites per person Dh10, plus per tent/car/camper Dh10/10/15) Popular with campers in vans, Casa's main camping ground is 5km out on the P8 road to El-Jadida, southwest of the centre. Take Bus No 31 from Place des Nations Unies.

### MID-RANGE & TOP END
**Hôtel Guynemer** ( ☎ 022 275764; www.geocities.com/ guynemerhotel; s/d with breakfast Dh450/578, for LP readers Dh372/538; P ⌨ ) This friendly, family-run hotel has 29 stylish rooms that have recently been revamped. More importantly, service at the Guynemer goes above and beyond, from wake-up calls to airport pick-up (Dh200) and city tours.

**Hotel Bellerive** ( ☎ 022797504; reservations@belleriv .com; Blvd de La Corniche, 'Ain Diab; s/d Dh412/500; P ☒ ) This smallish family-run place offers the best value along the Corniche. Most of the rooms – as well as the lovely terrace – have panoramic views of the ocean.

**Crowne Plaza** ( ☎ 022 488000; crowneplaza.casa blanca@ichotelsgroup.com; Hassan II Roundabout; r from Dh650; P ☒ ⌨ ☒ ) Pet-friendly and kid-friendly (they eat for free!), the Crowne Plaza is near the Parc de la Ligue Arabe, where both can romp without restraint. Book on line for the best rates.

## Eating
A good place to find cheap eats, particularly rotisseries (roast chicken places), is opposite the central market on Rue Chaouia. Most restaurants stay open until 2am, and for around Dh15 to Dh25 you can get a generous sandwich with meat, chips and salad.

**Epsom** ( ☎ 022 220746; cnr Rue Tata & Mouftakar; sandwiches Dh25, pizza Dh30-35; ☒ ) Enjoy pizza, pasta and kebabs in the comfy, modern interior or on the more happening sidewalk café.

**Café Maure** ( ☎ 022 260960; Blvd des Almohades; mains Dh60-80; ☒ 11am-7pm) This gem of a restaurant is inside the walls of the *sqala*, the 18th-century fortified bastion. The menu is heavy on seafood and salads, but the speciality is refreshing and exotic fruit juice concoctions.

**Taverne du Dauphin** ( ☎ 022 221200; 115 Blvd Houphouet Boigny; menu Dh110, mains Dh70-90; ☒ closed Sunday) Founded in 1958 by a seafaring French woman, this charming place has been offering fresh *fruits de mer* ever since.

**Restaurant Al-Mounia** ( ☎ 022 222669; 95 Rue Prince Moulay Abdallah; mains Dh110-130) Whether you come for excellent local cuisine or dazzling traditional surroundings, Al-Mounia will not disappoint. The menu features an impressive selection of salads (great for vegetarians) and more exotic fare like chicken *pastilla* and pigeon with raisins.

The fish does not get any fresher than at the two excellent restaurants that are right in the Casablanca port: the aptly named **Restaurant du Port de Peche** ( ☎ 022 318561; entrées Dh50-80, mains Dh60-80); and the more upscale **Ostréa** ( ☎ 022 441390; dozen oysters Dh74, mains Dh90-120; ☒ 11am-11pm).

## Drinking
The city centre is filled with drinking establishments, many in the style of grand French cafés. Most are still the preserve of men, and women may feel uncomfortable.

**Rick's Cafe** ( ☎ 022 274207; 248 Blvd Sour Jdid) Since many travellers visit Casablanca for nostalgic reasons associated with the film, this concept is long overdue. New in 2004, the piano bar claims to have reconstructed the film's Hollywood set. It's sure to be a hit as time goes by.

**La Petite Roche** ( ☎ 022 395748; Blvd de la Corniche, Phare El-Hank) Upstairs from the restaurant, this popular bar is strewn with pillows and lit by candles, creating quite a laid-back but exotic atmosphere. The highlight is the fantastic view across the bay to the Mosquée Hassan II.

## Entertainment
Clubbing in Casablanca centres around the upscale suburb of 'Ain Diab, where Casablanca's beautiful people dress up and get

down. These places are expensive (expect to pay at least Dh100 to get in) and usually guarded by a stern bouncer who practices tough crowd control (and face patrol). If you want to hang with the beautiful people, make sure you dress the part.

**La Bodéga** ( ☎ 022 541842; 129 Rue Allah ben Abdellah; ✹ 12.30pm-3pm & 7pm-midnight) This fun and friendly tapas bar is one of *the* places to see – and be seen with – hip young Moroccans at play. Music ranges from salsa to Arabic to disco, and the downstairs dance floor is packed after 10pm.

**Megarama** ( ☎ 090 102020; www.megarama.info; Blvd de la Corniche; afternoon/evening shows Dh35/40; ✹ 2.15pm, 5pm, 7.45pm, 8.30pm & 10.30pm) This huge new cinema complex in 'Ain Diab has four comfortable theatres that are usually packed.

## Shopping

The most pleasant place to shop is the Quartier Habbous (nouvelle medina), south of the centre. Alternatively, check out the **Exposition Nationale d'Artisanat** ( ☎ 022 267064; 3 Ave Hassan II; ✹ 8.30am-12.30pm & 2.30-8pm), three floors of shops selling high-quality crafts for fixed (but high) prices.

## Getting There & Away
### AIR

From Casablanca's **Mohammed V International Airport** ( ☎ 022 539040), 30km southeast on Marrakesh road, regular flights go to most countries in Western Europe, as well as to West Africa, Algeria, Tunisia, Egypt, the Middle East and North America. Internally, the vast majority of Royal Air Maroc's (RAM) flights go via Casablanca, so you can get to any destination directly from Casablanca.

### BUS

The flash **CTM bus station** ( ☎ 022 541010; 23 Rue Léon L'Africain) has services to Agadir (Dh150, nine hours, seven daily), Essaouira (Dh110, seven hours, two daily), Fès (Dh90, five hours, 10 daily), Marrakesh (Dh70, four hours, seven daily), Meknès (Dh75, four hours, 10 daily), Rabat (Dh30, one hour, 10 daily), Tangier (Dh130, six hours, four daily) and Tetouan (Dh130, seven hours, twice daily).

Ouled Ziane is the bus station for almost all non-CTM services – unfortunately, it's some distance from the city centre. Take a taxi (Dh10), or catch bus No 10 from Blvd Mohammed V.

### TRAIN

Most train departures are from **Casa-Voyageurs train station** ( ☎ 022 243818), 4km east of the city centre. The station is a Dh10 taxi ride, or catch bus No 30 from Blvd Mohammed V. Use Casa-Voyageurs for trains to Mohammed V airport, as well as long-distance destinations, including: Marrakesh (Dh76, three hours, nine daily), Fès (Dh97, 4½ hours, nine daily) via Meknès (Dh81, 3½ hours) and Tangier (Dh117, 5¾ hours, three daily). The quickest and easiest way to get to Rabat (Dh30, one hour) is by the express shuttle trains that run from the **Casa-Port train station** ( ☎ 022 223011).

### CAR

Grands taxis to Rabat (Dh30) and Fès (Dh50 to Dh60) leave from Blvd Hassan Seghir, near the CTM bus station. Many small car-rental agencies are concentrated around Ave des FAR and Blvd Mohammed V and at the airport.

**Tour des Habous** ( ☎ 022 339157; 44 Ave des FAR; Mohammed V International Airport)

**Europcar** ( ☎ 022 313737; Tour des Habous, 44 Ave des FAR) Airport ( ☎ 022 539161; Mohammed V International Airport)

**Hertz** ( ☎ 022 484710; 25 Rue Araibi Jilali) Airport ( ☎ 022 339181; Mohammed V International Airport)

**National** ( ☎ 022 277141; 12 Rue Araibi Jilali) Airport ( ☎ 022 539716; Mohammed V International Airport)

## Getting Around

You can get from Mohammed V International Airport to Casablanca by trains (Dh30, 2nd class, 30 minutes), which leave every hour from 7am to 11pm from Casa Voyageurs. A **shuttle bus** ( ☎ 022 448376) runs from the CTM bus terminal 12 times a day (Dh40, one hour) from 7am to midnight.

There's no shortage of petits taxis in Casablanca. Expect to pay Dh5 for a ride within the city centre with the meter on. Useful bus routes include:

**No 9** From the terminal to 'Ain Diab and the beaches
**No 10** From Place de la Concorde to Ouled Ziane bus station via Blvd Mohammed V
**No 15** From the terminal to the Hassan II Mosque
**No 30** From Blvd Ziraoui to Casa Voyageurs train station via Ave des FAR and Blvd Mohammed V

# ESSAOUIRA

With its picture-postcard ramparts and turrets and its mazelike medina, Essaouira is the most popular of the Atlantic coastal towns. Inside the town walls, it's all light and charm, a labyrinth of narrow lanes, whitewashed houses, tranquil squares and artisan workshops. The snug, fortified harbour is a hive of activity, with nets laid out on the quayside, fishing boats unloading their catch, traditional wooden boats being built and seafood sizzling on grills.

The impressive sea bastion built along the cliffs is known as the **Skala de la Ville**. Down by the harbour, the **Skala du Port** (adult/child Dh10/3; 🕑 8.30am-noon & 2.30pm-6pm) offers more cannons and fantastic views over the fishing port and Île de Mogador. The beach stretches some 10km down the coast to the sand dunes of Cap Sim. The strong coastal wind has made Essaouira Morocco's best-known windsurfing centre, increasingly promoting itself as 'Windy City, Afrika'.

The **Gnawa and World Music Festival** (3rd weekend June) is a four-day musical extravaganza with concerts on Place Moulay Hassan.

## Sleeping

**Camping des Oliviers** ( ☎ 044 475500; fax 044 474574; camp sites Dh41, bungalows from Dh250, 2-person Berber tent Dh100, hot showers Dh5; 🅿 🈂 ) This big, well-maintained four-star site, about 25km out of town on the Marrakesh road, has a small pool and restaurant, and the option of neat little bungalows or Berber tents.

**Hôtel Souiri** ( ☎ /fax 044 475339; 37 Rue al-Attarine; s/d from Dh180/250) A range of spotless rooms, from tiny singles with pine furniture to rooms decked out with wrought-iron sofas and cheerful fabrics. Cheaper rooms with shared bathroom are available.

**Riad Émeraude** ( ☎ /fax 044 473494; www.essaouirahotel.com; 228 Rue Chbanate; s/d Dh310/390) Delightful small *riad* offering excellent value for money. All 12 rooms are light and breezy with spotless white linens and attractive blue-and-yellow decorative touches.

**La Casa del Mar** ( ☎ 044 475091; www.lacasa-delmar.com; 35 Rue D'Oujda s 500, d Dh600-700) Pale greys, terracottas, sea greens and whiter-than-white walls, give La Casa del Mar a stylish, seaside ambience. Downstairs the living area is all open plan, encouraging a friendly social atmosphere.

**Hôtel Villa Bagdad** ( ☎ /fax 044 472023; www.villa-bagdad.com; 12-14 Rue de Bagdad; B&B d Dh550-650, ste Dh1000-1200) Previously a Caid's palace, Villa Bagdad is full of authentic details like the ridiculously sumptuous grand salons with their original ornate plasterwork. The villa also exhibits a stunning collection of artefacts, making this the best museum in Essaouira.

## Eating

The best cheap eats are en route to the port at several outdoor **fish grills** offering a fabulous selection of the day's catch. Just Dh25 will get you an excellent al-fresco lunch.

**Riad Al-Baraka** ( ☎ 044 473561; 113 Rue Mohammed el-Qory; mains Dh35, meals with wine Dh90; 🕑 noon-3pm & 6.30pm-late Tue-Sun) A funky, new-age *riad* with a wonderful courtyard shaded by a huge fig tree. The décor is unconsciously cool and the food is a combination of Middle Eastern and Moroccan flavours with lots of salads.

**Restaurant Ferdaous** ( ☎ 044 473655; 27 Rue Abdesslam Lebadi; mains Dh50, set menu Dh75) The best local restaurant does inventive takes on *tajines* and other local dishes – all depending on what's available in the market.

**Restaurant El-Minzah** ( ☎ 044 475308; 3 Ave Oqba ben Nafii; mains Dh70-90, set menus from Dh95) Well-rated international cuisine. Choose between the elegant dining room or the terrace and watch the changing colours of the ramparts.

**Côté Plage** ( ☎ 044 479000; Blvd Mohammed V; mains Dh150, tapas Dh35) Sit under a white umbrella on the wooden deck and imagine you are in the south of France as you gaze out over the beach. A fabulous lunch spot.

## Shopping

The ramparts of the Skala de la Ville shelter dozens of souvenir shops and **woodcarving workshops** overflowing with exquisite marquetry work made from local fragrant thuya wood (now an endangered species). **Galeries Damgaard** ( ☎ 044 784446; Rue Oqba ben Nafi), run by Frederic Damgaard, a Danish gallerist, promotes the work of local artists, encouraging them to transform their traditonal thuya techniques into more saleable, modern pieces.

## Getting There & Away

The **bus station** ( ☎ 044 784764) is about 400m northeast of the medina across an open parking lot. CTM has buses to Marrakesh (Dh45,

2½ hours), Casablanca (express Dh105, six hours) and Agadir (Dh40, three hours).

**Supratours** ( ☎ 044 475317) runs buses from its office, outside Bab Marrakech, to Marrakesh train station at 6.10am and 4pm (Dh55, 2½ hours) to connect with trains to Casablanca. Book in advance.

# IMPERIAL CITIES

In both culture and climate, the interior of Morocco is worlds away from the coastal region. More traditional, more exotic and more – well – hot, the interior contains some of the country's most exciting and romantic destinations. The biggest drawcard is the ochre-coloured city of Marrakesh. Founded almost 1000 years ago, it is one of the great cities of the Maghreb and is home to its most perfect Islamic monument, the Koutoubia Mosque. The other imperial cities of Fès and Meknès – with their maze-like medinas, grand palaces and Qur'anic schools – typify the majesty and the mystery of contemporary and historical Morocco.

## MARRAKESH

Nomad camp and capital of the south, Marrakesh is the lodestone of central Morocco, once drawing vast camel caravans from the south, for whom the oasis was the finest city they had ever seen. Marrakesh now draws countless travellers under its mesmerising spell, luring them with medieval myths and mystery.

The heat, the dust and the mudbrick ramparts make Marrakesh a uniquely African Moroccan city. Even local legend is full of rude and vigorous turmoil and thunder: stories tell of the city's ochre-red walls being bathed in blood as the soaring minaret of the Koutoubia was planted in the city's heart.

### Orientation

It takes about 30 minutes to walk from the centre of the ville nouvelle to Djemaa el-Fna, the main square in the heart of the old city. The main area of the ville nouvelle is Guéliz, where the bulk of offices, restaurants, cafés and shops, plus a few hotels, are clustered near the main thoroughfare, Ave Mohammed V.

---

**MARRAKESH IN TWO DAYS**

Spend a morning wandering the *souqs*, haggling for souvenirs and exploring the **Ali ben Youssef Medersa** (p677) and the exquisite **Museum of Marrakesh** (p677). After lunch, head to the cool of the **Jardin Majorelle** (p677). In the evening, grab a bite and take in the sights on **Djemaa el-Fna** (p677).

Spend the second day wandering south of the medina, marvelling at the artistry of the **Saadian Tombs** (p677), Dar Si Said and **Palais de la Bahia** (p677). (The Museum of Moroccan Arts is in Dar Si Said). Reward yourself with dinner at a similarly luxurious palace like **Stylia** (p680).

---

## Information
### EMERGENCY
**Ambulance** ( ☎ 044 443724)
**Police** ( ☎ 19; Hôtel de Police; Rue Ouadi el-Makhazine)

### INTERNET ACCESS
**Askmy Café** ( ☎ 044 430602; 6 Blvd Mohammed Zerktouni; per hour Dh10; ☺ 24hr)
**Cyber Club** (Ave Mohammed V; per hour Dh10; ☺ 9.30am-1pm & 3-10.30pm)

### MEDICAL SERVICES
**Polyclinique du Sud** ( ☎ 044 447999; 2 Rue de Yougoslavie, Guéliz; emergency service ☺ 24hr) A private clinic used by nearly all resident expats.
**Night Pharmacy** ( ☎ 044 389564; Rue Khalid ben el-Oualid)

### MONEY
Most banks will change cash or travellers cheques and there's no shortage of ATMs.
**Crédit du Maroc** ( ☺ 8.45am-1pm & 3pm-6.45pm Mon-Sat) After-hours exchange – in the ville nouvelle (215 Ave Mohammed V) and the medina (Rue de Bab Agnaou).

### POST
**Main Post Office** (Place du 16 Novembre; ☺ 8.30am-2pm Mon-Sat)

### TOURIST INFORMATION
**Office National Marocain du Tourisme** (ONMT; ☎ 044 436131; fax 044 436057; Place Abdel Moumen ben Ali, Guéliz; ☺ 8.30am-noon & 2.30-6.30pm Mon-Fri, 9am-noon & 3pm-6pm Sat)
**Syndicat d'Initiative** ( ☎ 044 430886; 170 Ave Mohammed V; ☺ 8.30am-12.30pm & 2.30pm-6.30pm Mon-Fri, 9am-noon Sat)

## Sights & Activities

### MEDINA

The focal point of Marrakesh is **Djemaa el-Fna**, a huge square in the medina, and the backdrop for one of the world's greatest spectacles. According to the author Paul Bowles, without it, Marrakesh would be just another Moroccan city. At dusk, the curtain goes up on rows of open-air food stalls smoking the immediate area with mouthwatering aromas. Jugglers, storytellers, snake charmers, musicians, occasional acrobats and benign lunatics consume the remaining space, each surrounded by jostling spectators.

Southwest of Place Djemaa el-Fna, the 12th-century **Koutoubia Mosque** is the oldest and best preserved of the Almohad mosques. At 70m, its minaret is visible for miles.

The great labyrinth of *souqs* extends from the north side of the Djemaa el-Fna and ends at the Ali ben Youssef Mosque, making the main area of interest comparatively compact and suitable for strolling. The **Ali ben Youssef Mosque** (closed to non-Muslims) and **medersa** ( ☎ 044 390911; Place ben Youssef; Dh20; ☺ 9am-6pm) mark the intellectual and religious heart of the medina.

Nearby, the **Museum of Marrakesh** (☎ 044 390911; Place ben Youssef; adult/child Dh30/10; ☺ 9.30am-6pm) is housed in a beautifully restored 19th-century *riad*, Dar Mnebbi. Changing exhibitions cover the full range of arts and crafts.

### KASBAH (ROYAL QUARTER)

The most famous of the city's palaces, the **Palais el-Badi** (Place des Ferblantiers, Mellah; admission Dh10; ☺ 8.30-11.45am & 2.30-5.45pm) is inside the Kasbah in the south of the medina. At the time of its construction (1578–1602) it was reputed to be one of the most beautiful palaces in the world. Unfortunately, the luxury of the palace did not escape the plundering hand of Moulay Ismail, who spent 12 years stripping it bare.

Long hidden from intrusive eyes, the area of the **Saadian Tombs** (Rue de la Kasbah; admission Dh10; ☺ 8.30am-11.45am & 2.30pm-5.45pm), alongside the Kasbah Mosque, was the original, privileged cemetery for descendents of the Prophet Mohammed. However, the ornate tombs that can be seen today are the resting place of the Saadian princes, most notably Ahmed al-Mansour.

### OTHER PALACES

The exquisite **Palais de la Bahia** ( ☎ 044 389221; Riad Zitoun el-Jedid; admission Dh10; ☺ 8.30am-11.15am & 2.30pm-5.45pm Sat-Thu, 8.30am-11.30am & 3pm-5.45pm Fri) was built towards the end of the 19th century as the residence of the Grand Vizier of Sultan Moulay al-Hassan I.

Further north, the Dar Si Said now houses the **Museum of Moroccan Arts** ( ☎ 044 389564; Riad Zitoun el-Jedid; Dh10; ☺ 9am-11.45am & 2.30pm-5.45pm Mon, Wed, Thu, Sat & Sun, 9am-11.30am & 3pm-5.45pm Fri).

### GARDENS

Owned by the French couturier Yves Saint-Laurent, the sub-tropical **Jardin Majorelle & Museum of Islamic Art** (gardens/museum Dh20/15; ☺ 8am-noon & 3pm-7pm summer, 8am-noon & 2pm-5pm rest of year) provides a wonderful haven. In among the cacti, bamboo and cascades of bougainvillaea is a deep-blue villa, which houses the museum. It contains one of those Moroccan collections you'd love to scoop up and take home to decorate your house with. Exhibits, including carpets, wedding curtains, belts, jewellery and manuscripts are labelled in Arabic and French. There's also a small exhibition of Majorelle's work.

About a 2km walk from the Koutoubia Mosque, is the **Jardin Ménara** (Ave de la Ménara; admission free, pavilion Dh15; ☺ 5am-6.30pm) laid out in the 12th-century by the Almohads. The centrepiece of the olive grove is a large, still pool backed by a pavilion built in 1869.

## Sleeping

### MEDINA

**Hôtel Ali** ( ☎ 044 444979; hotelali@hotmail.com; Rue Moulay Ismail; dm & roof-terrace sleeping Dh40, s/d/tr Dh140/200/260; ☒ ) A stalwart of the budget scene and much favoured by trekking groups. Regulars swear by its cheap rates and friendly service, but it can seem a bit like a bus station. The all-you-can-eat buffet attracts hungry travellers who binge on couscous, salads, fruit and desserts, including lots of options for vegetarians.

**Hôtel Gallia** ( ☎ 044 445913; hotelgalliamarrakech@menara.co.ma; 30 Rue de la Recette; s/d with shared bathroom Dh170/210, d with shower/bath 230/340; ☒ ) One of the medina's most appealing budget hotels carefully run by its French proprietors. There are two lovely courtyards and the entire place is scrubbed from top to toe daily.

MOROCCO

MOROCCO

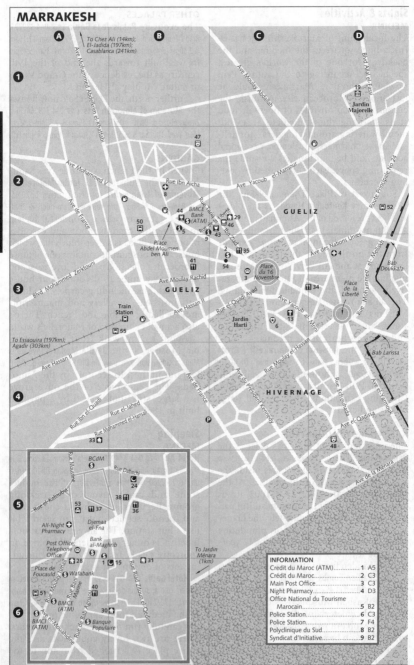

# MARRAKESH

To Chez Ali (14km);
El-Jadida (197km);
Casablanca (241km)

**GUELIZ**

BMCE
Bank
(ATM)

Place
Abdel Moumen
ben Ali

**GUELIZ**

Train
Station

To Essaouira (197km);
Agadir (303km)

Place
du 16
Novembre

Place
de la
Liberté

Bab
Doukkala

Bab Larissa

Jardin
Harti

**HIVERNAGE**

Jardin
Majorelle

BCdM

Rue Dabachi

All-Night
Pharmacy

Djemaa
el-Fna

Post Office;
Telephone
Office

Bank
al-Maghrib

Place de
Foucauld

Wafabank

BMCE
(ATM)

BMCI
(ATM)

Banque
Populaire

To Jardin
Ménara
(1km)

| INFORMATION | | |
|---|---|---|
| Crédit du Maroc (ATM)........................ | 1 | A5 |
| Crédit du Maroc.................................. | 2 | C3 |
| Main Post Office................................. | 3 | C3 |
| Night Pharmacy.................................. | 4 | D3 |
| Office National du Tourisme | | |
| Marocain...................................... | 5 | B2 |
| Police Station.................................... | 6 | C3 |
| Police Station.................................... | 7 | F4 |
| Polyclinique du Sud........................... | 8 | B2 |
| Syndicat d'Initiative........................... | 9 | B2 |

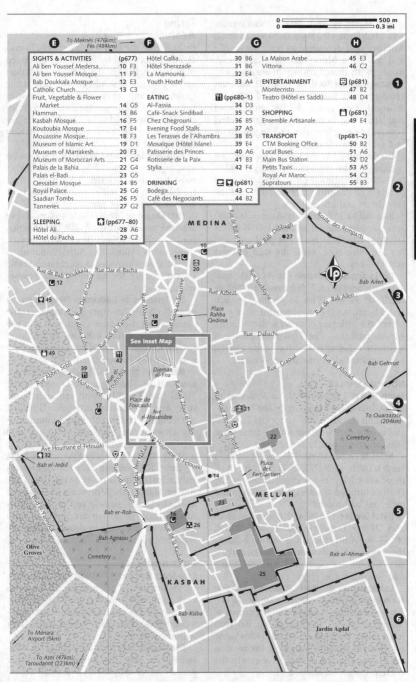

0 — 500 m
0 — 0.3 mi

**SIGHTS & ACTIVITIES** (p677)
Ali ben Youssef Medersa............**10** F3
Ali ben Youssef Mosque..............**11** F3
Bab Doukkala Mosque.................**12** E3
Catholic Church.............................**13** C3
Fruit, Vegetable & Flower
   Market........................................**14** G5
Hamman......................................**15** B6
Kasbah Mosque...........................**16** F5
Koutoubia Mosque......................**17** E4
Mouassine Mosque.....................**18** F3
Museum of Islamic Art...............**19** D1
Museum of Marrakesh.................**20** F3
Museum of Moroccan Arts..........**21** G4
Palais de la Bahia.........................**22** G4
Palais el-Badi..............................**23** G5
Qessabin Mosque........................**24** B5
Royal Palace................................**25** G6
Saadian Tombs............................**26** F5
Tanneries.....................................**27** G2

**SLEEPING**       (pp677–80)
Hôtel Ali.....................................**28** A6
Hôtel du Pacha...........................**29** C2

Hôtel Gallia.................................**30** B6
Hôtel Sherazade..........................**31** B6
La Mamounia...............................**32** E4
Youth Hostel...............................**33** A4

**EATING**           (pp680–1)
Al-Fassia.....................................**34** D3
Café-Snack Sindibad....................**35** C3
Chez Chegrouni...........................**36** B5
Evening Food Stalls.....................**37** A5
Les Terasses de l'Alhambra..........**38** B5
Mosaïque (Hôtel Islane)..............**39** E4
Patisserie des Princes..................**40** A6
Rotisserie de la Paix....................**41** B3
Stylia..........................................**42** F4

**DRINKING**        (p681)
Bodega.......................................**43** C2
Café des Negociants....................**44** B2

La Maison Arabe..........................**45** E3
Vittoria.......................................**46** C2

**ENTERTAINMENT**     (p681)
Montecristo................................**47** B2
Teatro (Hôtel es Saddi)...............**48** D4

**SHOPPING**        (p681)
Ensemble Artisanale....................**49** E4

**TRANSPORT**       (pp681–2)
CTM Booking Office....................**50** B2
Local Buses.................................**51** A6
Main Bus Station.........................**52** D2
Petits Taxis.................................**53** A5
Royal Air Maroc..........................**54** C3
Supratours...................................**55** B3

**MOROCCO**

**Hôtel Sherazade** ( ☎ /fax 044 429305; www.sherazade .com; 3 Derb Djama; s Dh200-450, Dh250-500, apt Dh450) Another *riad* decorated in traditional style and run by a Moroccan–German couple. Rooms with shared bathroom are cheaper.

**Jnane Mogador Hôtel** ( ☎ 044 426323; www.jnane mogador.com; 116 Riad Zitoun Kedim; s/d Dh260/300) A wonderfully restored 19th-century *riad* with attractive rooms and an elegant central courtyard complete with tinkling fountain and grand marble staircase.

**Dar Soukaina** ( ☎ 044 376055; www.komedia.net /soukaina; 19 Derb el-Ferrane, Riad Laârouss; s/d/tr Dh760/ 860/1010) A traditional *riad* lovingly restored to retain all its quirky features, not least the tiny doors and low ceilings.

**Riad Malika** ( ☎ /fax 044 385451; www.riadmalika .com; 29 Derb Arset Aouzal; d B&B Dh800-1000; 🔀 🍴 🍷 ) A fabulous Art Deco *riad*. The pool area and bar are ultra cool, while the staff discreet and low-key.

**Les Jardins de la Medina** ( ☎ 044 381851; www .lesjardinsdelamedina.com; 21 Derb Chtouka; d Dh1950, ste Dh2250; 🅿 🔀 🍷 ) With 36 rooms, this is a small hotel but the management have preserved the intimacy of a *riad* whilst offering superb facilities. The Thai restaurant is a welcome relief after one-too-many *tajines*. Low season reductions are good value.

### NOUVELLE VILLE
**Youth Hostel** ( ☎ 044 447713; Rue Mohammed el-Hansali; dm Dh40, hot showers Dh5; 🕙 8am-9am & 1pm-10pm) This youth hostel is spotlessly clean and boasts a kitchen, but for the same price you can stay closer to the action.

**Hôtel du Pacha** ( ☎ 044 431327; fax 044 431326; 33 Rue de la Liberté; s/d Dh275/350; 🔀 ) Built in 1934, there's a nicely faded colonial air to the Pacha's louvred shutters, high ceilings and generous bathrooms.

**Hôtel Diwane** ( ☎ 044 432216; www.diwanehotel .com; 24 Rue Yougoslavie; s/d/ste Dh500/600/910; 🅿 🔀 🍷 ) A big, flash, flag-waving hotel in the center of Guéliz with all modern amenities. Rooms are decorated with the same flag-waving verve.

**La Mamounia** ( ☎ 044 444409; www.mamounia.com; Ave Houmane el-Fetouaki; d Dh2080-4000; 🅿 🔀 🍷 ) The *grande dame* and jewel in the crown of Marrakesh hotels, the Mamounia, has seen it all from Winston Churchill (who came for the climate and to indulge his passion for painting) and Eric von Stroheim to the current king, Mohammed VI.

## Eating
### MEDINA
By the time the sun sets, much of Djemaa el-Fna is occupied by food stalls, one piled high with kebabs and salads, and the next serving steaming snails. As you peruse the tables, friendly chefs will woo you with promises of fresh produce and free mint tea. Don't be afraid to talk back: the banter is part of the fun. You can eat your fill here for Dh50 or less.

**Pâtisserie des Princes** ( ☎ 044 443033; 32 Rue de Bab Agnaou; 🕙 5am-11.30pm; 🔀 🍴 ) One of the city's most famous patisseries. The small café at the back is a welcome respite for women, or anyone in search of a quiet coffee.

**Chez Chegrouni** ( ☎ 063 434132; 4-6 Djemaa el-Fna; salads Dh5, mains around Dh40; 🕙 7am-11pm) Known for its excellent *tajines* (the best in the city, some locals claim), this little restaurant is almost always crowded. Squeeze into a table on the terrace for an unbeatable people-watching spot.

**Les Terrasses de L'Alhambra** (Djemaa el-Fna; set menus Dh100; 🕙 7am-11pm) The view of the square from the balcony is superb, but patrons sitting inside will also enjoy tasteful, traditional décor. Salads and pizzas are good options for vegetarians.

**Mosaïque** ( ☎ 044 440081; 279 Ave Mohammed V; mains Dh75-85) The elegant restaurant in the Hôtel Islane is filled with artisanal furniture and interesting artwork. Upstairs, the rooftop restaurant offers commanding views of the Koutoubia Mosque and cheaper international cuisine.

**Stylia** ( ☎ 044 440505; 34 Rue Ksour; set menu Dh400; 🕙 dinner; 🔀 ) Speaking gastronomically, this palace restaurant is possibly the top of the line in Marrakesh. Moroccan classics such as flaky chicken *pastilla* and melt-in-your-mouth lamb *tanzhiyya* are prepared with the utmost attention to detail. Follow the signs from Rue Fatima Zohra.

### VILLE NOUVELLE
**Café-Snack Sindibad** (3 Ave Mohammed V; mains Dh25-35; 🕙 6am-11pm) This popular snack shop may look down-at-heel, but the food is as tasty as it is cheap. Try the *tanzhiyya* – a Marrakesh speciality stew – with either lemons or prunes.

**Rotisserie de la Paix** ( ☎ 044 433118; 68 Rue de Yougoslavie; mains Dh80-120) The peaceful summer garden never fails to draw a small crowd on a pleasant day in Marrakesh. The staid menu focuses on grills and seafood.

**Al-Fassia** ( ☎ 044 434060; 232 Ave Mohammed V; mains around Dh100, lunch set menu Dh160) A reminder that the ville nouvelle is still in Morocco, Al-Fassia serves some of the best local cuisine in town.

## Drinking

The number-one spot for a cheap and delicious drink is right on Djemaa el-Fna, where a freshly squeezed orange juice is only Dh2.50.

### CAFÉS

**Café Les Négociants** ( ☎ 044 435762; 110 Ave Mohammed V; ☻ 6am-11pm) The wide Parisian-style terrace is a wonderful place for men to sit and watch the world go by. Women may not feel so welcome.

**Vittoria** ( ☎ 044 431529; 21 Bis Rue de la Liberté; ☻ 8am-10pm) Run by women for women. While away an afternoon over a coffee or tea on comfy couches in the salon or in the sunny courtyard.

### BARS

The bars in Marrakesh are mostly dire, male-oriented places. A few upscale places are patronised by women, most of whom are either tourists or prostitutes.

**Bodega** ( ☎ 044 433141; 23 Rue de la Liberté) This new, wildly popular spot is unique in Marrakesh for its raucous crowd and unassuming atmosphere.

**La Maison Arabe** ( ☎ 044 387010; 1 Derb Assehbe, Bab Doukkala) The one proper bar in the medina.

## Entertainment

### FOLKLORIC SHOWS

Tickets are available through travel agents or hotels.

**Chez Ali** ( ☎ 044 307730; dinner & show Dh400; ☻ 8pm) Out on the Safi road, this folkloric show offers a sampler of traditional singing and dancing.

**Al Menara Reflets & Merveilles** ( ☎ 044 439580; admission Dh250-400; ☻ 9pm Wed-Mon) Each night the Jardin Ménara becomes the stage for a fantastical sound and light show, complete with 50 singers, dancers and acrobats.

### NIGHTCLUBS

Most of the hottest clubs are attached to upscale hotels in the ville nouvelle. Admissions

range from Dh100 to Dh150 (including the first drink). Dress smartly and remember most places don't get going till after midnight.

**Montecristo** ( ☎ 044 439031; 20 Rue Ibn Aicha) This Latin club/salsa bar should be the first stop. If you can't beat the heat on the dance floor, head up to the gorgeous roof terrace.

**Teatro** ( ☎ 044 448811; Hôtel es Saadi, Rue Quadissia; admission Dh150) An old converted theatre, this high-end club pulses to a techno beat. The dance floor is on the former stage – very appropriate for the ladies who now strut their stuff there.

## Shopping

Marrakesh is a shopper's paradise, a city full of skilled artisans producing quality products in wood, leather, wool, metal, bone, brass and silver – the trouble is sifting the gold from the dross. To get a feeling for the quality of merchandise it is always good to start at the government run **Ensemble Artisanal** (Ave Mohammed V), in the ville nouvelle. With a firm idea of prices in mind you may then feel up to tackling the *souqs*, but be prepared to haggle hard.

## Getting There & Away

### AIR

Six kilometres southwest of town is **Ménara airport** ( ☎ 044 447865 flight information). **RAM** ( ☎ 044 425500; www.royalairmaroc.com; 197 Blvd Mohammed V, Guéliz; ☻ 8.30am-noon & 2.30-7pm) has several flights daily to and from Casablanca (Dh935, 40 minutes). There are also international flights to Geneva, London, Madrid and Paris.

### BUS

The main **bus station** ( ☎ 044 433933; Bab Doukkala), where the majority of buses arrive and depart, is just outside the city walls, a 20-minute walk or roughly Dh5 to Dh10 taxi ride from Djemaa el-Fna.

Window No 10 is the **CTM** ( ☎ 044 434402) booking desk. CTM operates daily buses to Fès (Dh145, 8½ hours, one daily), Agadir (Dh75, four hours, nine daily), Casablanca (Dh70, fours hours, three daily) and Essaouira (Dh55, three hours).

You can also buy tickets for any of the above services at the **CTM Booking Office** ( ☎ 044 448328; Blvd Mohammed Zerktouni, Guéliz). This is the arrival and departure point for international buses, including Paris (Dh800

MOROCCO

MOROCCO

to Dh1100, 48 hours) and Madrid (Dh800 to Dh1100, 36 hours).

The office of **Supratours** ( ☎ 044 435525) is west of the train station. The service goes to Rabat (Dh80, six hours, half-hourly) via Casablanca (Dh50, five hours), Tangier (Dh150, 11 hours, once daily) and Essaouira (Dh35, three hours, nine daily).

### TRAIN

The **train station** (information only ☎ 090 203040; Ave Hassan II) lies on the western side of Guéliz. Take a taxi or city bus (Nos 3, 8, 10 and 14, Dh3) into the centre.

There are numerous trains to Rabat (Dh101, four hours) via Casablanca (Dh76, three hours, nine daily); and Fès (Dh171, eight hours, eight daily) via Meknès (Dh154, seven hours). Overnight trains to Tangier (Dh150 to Dh188) leave once daily. Book couchettes two days in advance; they require a supplement of Dh90.

## Getting Around

A petits taxi to Marrakesh from the airport (6km) should be no more than Dh60, but good luck convincing the driver. Alternatively, bus No 11 runs irregularly to Djemaa el-Fna.

The creamy-beige petits taxis around town cost between Dh5 and Dh10 per journey. They're all supposed to use their meters, but you may need to insist, especially coming from the train station or airport.

## FÈS

The oldest of the imperial cities, Fès is arguably the symbolic heart of Morocco. Founded shortly after the Arabs swept across North Africa and Spain, it became the country's religious and cultural centre.

The medina of Fès el-Bali (Old Fès) is one of the largest living medieval cities in the world. Its narrow winding alleys and covered bazaars are crammed with every conceivable sort of workshop, restaurant and market, as well as mosques, *medersas*, dye pits and tanneries – a veritable assault on the senses. It can be totally bewildering, and the constant attention of unofficial guides, touts and shopkeepers does not help.

Fès is a veiled, self-contained city that doesn't easily bare its soul. With time, visitors can glimpse behind the anonymous walls and appreciate the rich culture and spirituality that is Fès.

## Orientation

Fès is neatly divided into three distinct parts: Fès el-Bali (the core of the medina) in the east; Fès el-Jdid (containing the *mellah* and Royal Palace) in the centre; and the ville nouvelle, the administrative area constructed by the French, to the southwest. The main entrance to Fès el-Bali is Bab Bou Jeloud in the northwest corner of the medina.

## Information
### INTERNET ACCESS

**Cyber Club** (Map p684; ☎ 055 626286; Rue Abdelkarim el-Ekattabi; per hour Dh10; ⊙ 9am-midnight)
**London Cyber** (Map p683; Ave de la Liberté; per hour Dh10; ⊙ 10am-10pm)

### MEDICAL SERVICES

**Clinique Ryad** ( ☎ 055 960000; 2 Rue Benzakour, Place Hussein de Jordainie) South of the ville nouvelle.
**Night Pharmacy** (Map p684; ☎ 055 623493; Blvd Moulay Youssef; ⊙ 9pm-6am) Staffed by a doctor and pharmacist.

### MONEY

The majority of banks (and ATMs) are in the ville nouvelle along Ave Hassan II and Blvd Mohammed V.

### POST

**Main Post Office** (Map p684; cnr Ave Hassan II & Blvd Mohammed V)

### TOURIST INFORMATION

**Syndicat d'Initiative** (Map p684; ☎ 055 623460; fax 055 654370; Place Mohammed V; ⊙ 8.30am-noon & 2.30pm-6.30pm Mon-Thu, 8.30am-11.30am & 3pm-6.30pm Fri, 8.30am-noon Sat)
**Office Nationale Marocain du Tourisme** (ONMT; Map p684; ☎ 055 623460; fax 055 654370; Place de la Résistance; ⊙ 8.30am-noon & 2.30pm-6.30pm Mon-Thu, 8.30am-11.30am & 3pm-6.30pm Fri)

## Dangers & Annoyances

Fès has long been notorious for its *faux guides*. The situation has improved with the introduction of a Brigade Touristique (tourist police); still, high unemployment forces many to persist. A few hustlers hang about Fès train station and hotels, but the

# FÈS

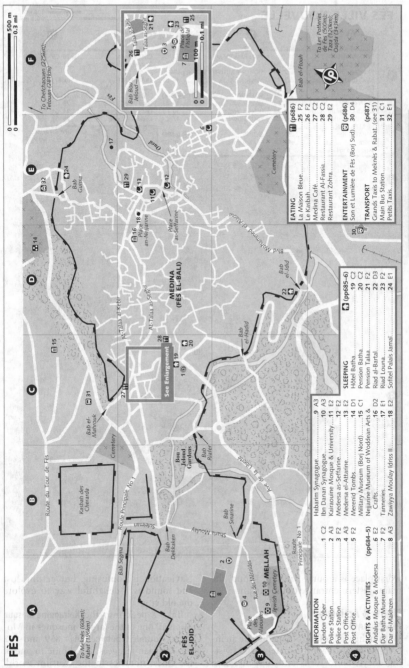

**INFORMATION**

| | |
|---|---|
| London Cyber | **1** C2 |
| Police Station | **2** A3 |
| Police Station | **3** F2 |
| Post Office | **4** A3 |
| Post Office | **5** F2 |

**SIGHTS & ACTIVITIES** (pp684–5)

| | |
|---|---|
| Andalus Mosque & Medersa | **6** E2 |
| Dar Batha Museum | **7** F2 |
| Dar el-Makhzen | **8** A3 |
| Habarim Synagogue | **9** A3 |
| Ibn Danan Synagogue | **10** A3 |
| Kairaouine Mosque & University | **11** E2 |
| Medersa as-Seffarine | **12** E2 |
| Medersa el-Attarine | **13** E2 |
| Merenid Tombs | **14** D1 |
| Military Museum (Borj Nord) | **15** C1 |
| Nejjarine Museum of Woddean Arts & Crafts | **16** D2 |
| Tanneries | **17** E1 |
| Zawiyya Moulay Idriss II | **18** E2 |

**SLEEPING** (pp685–6)

| | |
|---|---|
| Hôtel Batha | **19** C2 |
| Pension Batha | **20** C2 |
| Pension Talaa | **21** F2 |
| Riad al-Bartal | **22** D3 |
| Riad Louna | **23** F2 |
| Sofitel Palais Jamaï | **24** E1 |

**EATING** (p686)

| | |
|---|---|
| La Maison Bleue | **25** F2 |
| Le Kasbah | **26** F2 |
| Medina Café | **27** C2 |
| Restaurant Al-Fassia | **28** C2 |
| Restaurant Zohra | **29** E2 |

**ENTERTAINMENT** (p686)

| | |
|---|---|
| Son et Lumière de Fès (Borj Sud) | **30** D4 |

**TRANSPORT** (p687)

| | |
|---|---|
| Grands Taxis to Meknès & Rabat | (see 31) |
| Main Bus Station | **31** C1 |
| Petits Taxis | **32** E1 |

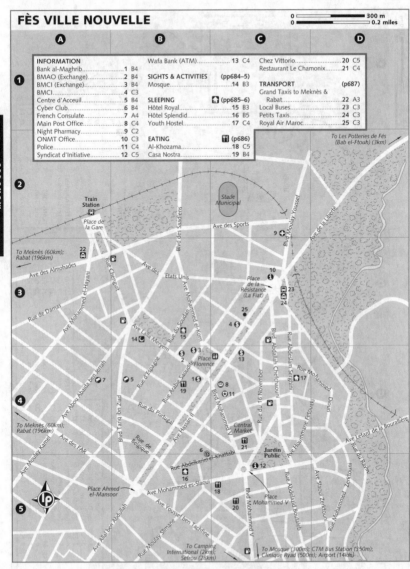

## FÈS VILLE NOUVELLE

0 ——— 300 m
0 ——— 0.2 miles

**INFORMATION**
Bank al-Maghrib.................1 B4
BMAO (Exchange)................2 B4
BMCI (Exchange)................3 B4
BMCI..............................4 C3
Centre d'Acceuil...............5 B4
Cyber Club.......................6 B4
French Consulate...............7 A4
Main Post Office...............8 C4
Night Pharmacy.................9 C2
ONMT Office.....................10 C3
Police............................11 C4
Syndicat d'Initiative..........12 C5

Wafa Bank (ATM)...............13 C4

**SIGHTS & ACTIVITIES** (pp684–5)
Mosque.............................14 B3

**SLEEPING** (pp685–6)
Hôtel Royal.......................15 B3
Hôtel Splendid...................16 B5
Youth Hostel.....................17 C4

**EATING** (p686)
Al-Khozama......................18 C5
Casa Nostra......................19 B4

Chez Vittorio.....................20 C5
Restaurant Le Chamonix.......21 C4

**TRANSPORT** (p687)
Grand Taxis to Meknès &
  Rabat............................22 A3
Local Buses.......................23 C3
Petits Taxis......................24 C3
Royal Air Maroc.................25 C3

---

worst place is around Bab Bou Jeloud, the main western entrance to the medina.

## Sights & Activities

### FÈS EL-BALI

Within the walls of the old medina lie an incredible maze of approximately 9400 twisting alleys, blind turns and hidden *souqs*.

Navigation is confusing, but getting lost and found is a delightful way to explore the old city.

Take a peek into the **Kairaouine Mosque** (Map p683) one of the largest mosques in Morocco, founded between AD 859 and 862 for Tunisian refugees. It is home to one of the finest libraries in the Muslim world.

Non-Muslims are forbidden to enter, but you can explore the **Medersa el-Attarine** (Map p683; admission Dh10; ☻ 8.30am-1pm & 2.30-5pm), the associated Qur'anic school.

The unmistakeable odour of animal excrement and body parts wafts through the streets northeast of Place as-Seffarine. Fork left after about 50m and follow your nose. This is the leather district, the home of the infamous Fès **tanneries**.

Opened in 1998, the **Nejjarine Museum of Wooden Arts & Crafts** ( ☎ 055 740580; Place an-Nejjarine; admission Dh20; ☻ 10am-5pm) is in a beautifully panelled and restored *funduq*, or *caravanserai*. Another excellent collection of traditional arts and crafts is housed in the **Dar Batha Museum** (Museum of Moroccan Arts & Crafts; ☎ 055 634116; Place de l'Istiqlal; admission Dh10; ☻ 8.30am-noon & 2.30pm-6pm Wed-Mon).

### FÈS EL-JDID

In the 14th century, Fès el-Jdid became a refuge for Jews, thus creating a *mellah*, or Jewish quarter. The *mellah's* southwest corner contains the **Jewish Cemetery & Habarim Synagogue** (admission free, donations welcome; ☻ 7am-7pm), where the sea of blindingly white tombs stretches down the hill. The gatekeeper can direct you to the nearby **Ibn Danan Synagogue** (Map p683; admission free, donations welcome), which was restored with the aid of Unesco in 1999.

### BORJ NORD & MERENID TOMBS

For a spectacular view of Fès, walk up to the Borj Nord fortress, where all of Fès is sprawled at your feet. The 16th-century Borj Nord houses a **military museum** ( ☎ 055 645241; admission Dh10; ☻ 8.30am-noon & 2.30-6.30pm Wed-Mon). The **Merenid Tombs** (Map p683), mostly ruins, are dramatic against the city backdrop; sunrise and sunset are spectacular but don't come alone.

## Tours

Both tourist offices can make arrangements for an official guide (Dh250 per day), which will enable you to see and experience much more in the medina. The guides *do* know places to shop, but they will also point out incredible architecture and clandestine corners. Be sure to communicate clearly with your guide so he/she can tailor the tour to your needs.

## Sleeping

### MEDINA

Many cheap hotels are clustered around Bab Bou Jeloud.

**Pension Talaa** (Map p683; ☎ 055 633359; pacohicham@hotmail.com; 14 Talaa Seghira; r with shared bathroom per person Dh75) This tiny place is the best deal in the medina. Unfortunately, it has only four, boxy rooms; but they are spotless, as are the shared toilets (Western) and showers (hot). The English-speaking manager is friendly and efficient.

**Pension Batha** (Map p683; ☎ 055 741150; fax 055 748827; 8 Sidi Lkhayat; s/d with breakfast Dh100/250) Not to be confused with its neighbour of nearly the same name, this smaller pension offers more intimate but less luxurious accommodation. The friendly place is family-owned and run, but the rooms and facilities are not particularly attractive.

**Hôtel Batha** ( ☎ 055 741077; fax 055 741078; Place Batha; s/d with breakfast Dh328/454; P ᔍ ) Though it's a touch run down, this classic hotel still offers spacious, comfortable rooms, attentive service and an unbeatable location. All rooms have private bathrooms.

**Riad Louna** ( ☎ /fax 055 741985; www.riadlouna .com; 24 Derb Serraj; r/ste with breakfast Dh450/950) The traditional house – built in 1389 – has three elegant suites and three smaller rooms set around a lovely, blooming courtyard. The suites are exquisite, done up with fireplaces, *zelij* tile and private Moroccan salons. The rooms are simpler but no less charming.

**Riad al-Bartal** ( ☎ /fax 055 637053; www.riadalbartal.com; 21 Rue Sournas; r/ste with breakfast Dh750/1250; P ᔍ ) This place has a similar deal to the Riad Louna – six suites and one bedroom, an ornate Moroccan salon and a glorious panoramic roof terrace – all refurbished with exquisite, traditional craftsmanship.

**Sofitel Palais Jamaï** ( ☎ 055 634331; www.sofitel .com; s/d with breakfast from Dh2512/2724; P ᔍ ᔍ ᔍ ᔍ ) Once the pleasure dome of a late 19th-century grand vizier to the sultan, Fès' swankiest hotel is set in an Andalucían garden overlooking the medina. Doubles in the new wing have the views, while those in the old palace have more character and a bigger price tag.

### VILLE NOUVELLE

**Youth Hostel** (Map p684; ☎ 055 624085; www.fesyouth-hostel.com; 18 Rue Abdeslam Serghini; dm HI members/nonmembers Dh45/50, tw HI members/nonmembers

Dh55/60; 8am-10am, noon-3pm & 6pm-10pm) One of the best youth hostels in all of Morocco is centrally located in the Fès ville nouvelle. It is very well maintained and efficiently run. No hot water.

**Camping International** (Map p684; ☎ 055 731399; fax 055 731554; camp sites per person Dh40, plus per tent/car/caravan Dh30/30/40; 🚗 ) The newer and more luxurious of Fès' two camping grounds is about 4km south of the centre of town, close to the new football stadium on the Sefrou road.

**Hôtel Royal** (Map p684; ☎ 055 624656; 36 Rue du Soudan; s/d Dh110/140) This reliable choice is convenient to the train station. Despite its age, it is well maintained and deservedly popular.

**Hôtel Splendid** (Map p684; ☎ 055 622148; splendid@iam.net.ma; 9 Rue Abdelkarim el-Khattabi; s/d Dh280/340; P 🍴 🚗 ) This is quite a swish, modern three-star hotel. The rooms are large and comfortable and equipped with telephone, TV and private bath.

## Eating
### MEDINA
The cheap-and-cheerful restaurants and snack stands just inside Bab Bou Jeloud are among the most popular places to eat in the medina, especially as they provide prime seats to watch the passing cavalcade in and out of the medina.

**Médina Café** (Map p683; ☎ 055 633430; 6 Derb Mernissi Bab Bou Jeloud; menus Dh95-105; 8am-10pm) The tiny size is part of the charm at this new restaurant. It is outside the main medina gate, so it has an air of serenity that other nearby places lack.

**Le Kasbah** (Map p683; Rue Serrajine; mains Dh40, menu Dh70) The classiest place inside the Bab Bou Jeloud (which isn't saying too much) is this friendly restaurant on three floors. Head for the roof to get the most fantastic views of the surrounding medina.

**Restaurant Zohra** ( ☎ 055 637699; 3 Derb Ain Nass Blida; menus Dh70-90) Buried in the medina's backstreets to the north of the Kairaouine, this little place is known for its family atmosphere and home cooking. The setting is simple, but warm and welcoming. Phone ahead in the evening to make sure it's open.

**Restaurant al-Fassia** ( ☎ 055 637314; 21 Rue Salaj; mains from Dh70, set menus Dh250-500; 🍴 ) This huge, fancy restaurant is best known for its

elaborate décor and evening floor shows (Dh50, 8pm) featuring folk music to the obligatory belly dancing.

**La Maison Bleue** ( ☎ 055 636052; 2 Place de l'Istiqlal; set menu incl drinks guests/nonguests Dh500/550; dinner) This exquisite *riad* makes an incredibly romantic setting to sample a sultan's feast. Four delectable courses might include an array of traditional salads, *pastilla* and *tajine*; the selection of desserts ranges from simple, fresh oranges with cinnamon to sweet *pastilla au lait*. Reservations are required.

### VILLE NOUVELLE
**Al-Khozama** (Map p684; ☎ 063 374033; 23 Ave Mohammed es-Slaoui; sandwiches Dh15-20, set menu Dh60; 7am-11pm) The draw of this restaurant near Place Mohammed V is the indoor terrace – a comfortable, quiet place for women. There are no surprises on the menu, but the food's tasty and comes in decent portions.

**Restaurant Le Chamonix** (Map p684; ☎ 055 626638; 5 Rue Moukhtar Soussi; set menu Dh52; 10am-10pm) Service is super friendly and the menu ranges from pizza to couscous. One of the few cheap places in this area with a large, welcoming seating area.

**Casa Nostra** (Map p684; ☎ 055 932841; 16 Rue Arabie Saoudite; mains around Dh80, pizza or pasta Dh30-65) This Spanish–Italian restaurant is much frequented by Fès' young, hip crowd. It is a fun upbeat place to come, especially in the evenings.

**Chez Vittorio** (Map p684; ☎ 055 624730; 21 Rue Brahim Roudani; mains from Dh80, salads from Dh30, pizza or pasta from Dh50) The candle-lighting and lovely chequered cloths make the setting for good-value Italian fare and a glass of wine.

## Entertainment
**Son et Lumière de Fès** (Sound & Lights of Fes; Map p683; ☎ 055 763652; fax 055 763654; Borj Sud; admission Dh100; 9.30pm May-Aug; 7.15pm Mar-Apr & Sep-Nov) This laser show recounts 12 centuries of history in 45 minutes.

## Shopping
Fès is and always has been the artisanal capital of Morocco. The choice of crafts is wide, quality is high, and prices are competitive, though you'll need to bargain hard. As usual, it's best to seek out the little shops off the main tourist routes (principally Talaa

MOROCCO

Kebira and Talaa Seghira in Fès al-Bali). Craftsmen's workshops rather than boutiques offer much cheaper prices.

**Les Potteries de Fès** (Bab el-Ftouh) is a fascinating trip if you're after some of Fès' famous blue-and-white pottery, or if you just want to see the production processes. At the time of writing, there was serious talk about moving the potteries further away from the city to limit the environmental damage.

## Getting There & Away
### AIR
**Fès airport** (☎ 055 674712) is 15km south of the city, at Saïss. **Royal Air Maroc** (RAM; Map p684; ☎ 055 625516; 54 Ave Hassan II) operates daily flights to Casablanca (one way Dh864, 45 minutes) and flights to Paris (Dh5073, three hours) a few times a week.

### BUS
The **CTM bus station** (☎ 055 732992) is near Place Atlas, but some buses depart from the main bus station. Seven buses a day go to Casablanca (Dh85, five hours) via Rabat (Dh55, 3½ hours); six go to Meknès (Dh15, one hour); and two go to Marrakesh (Dh130, nine hours). Heading north and east, there are three buses for Tangier (Dh80, six hours); two for Tetouan (Dh70, five hours); and one for Al-Hoceima (Dh82, six hours). International services to Spain and France also depart from the CTM bus station.

Non-CTM buses depart from the **main bus station** (Map p683; ☎ 055 636032) outside Bab el-Mahrouk and travel the same routes for slightly cheaper.

### TRAIN
The **train station** (Map p684; ☎ 055 930333) is in the ville nouvelle, a 10-minute walk northwest of Place Florence. Trains depart every two hours to Casablanca (Dh97, 4¼ hours), via Rabat (Dh72, 3½ hours) and Meknès (Dh17, one hour). Five direct *rapide* trains go to Marrakesh (Dh71, eight hours) and one goes to Tangier (Dh96, five hours).

### TAXI
Grands taxis for Meknès (Dh16) and Rabat (Dh55) leave from in front of the main bus station (outside Bab el-Mahrouk) and from near the train station.

## Getting Around
There is a regular bus service (No 16) between the airport and the train station (Dh3, 25 minutes), with departures every half hour or so. Bus No 47 travels between the train station and Bab Bou Jeloud.

Red petits taxis are metered: you'll pay about Dh10 from the train station to Bab Bou Jeloud. Only grands taxis go out to the airport (Dh80).

## MEKNÈS
From the winding narrow streets of the medina to the grand buildings of the imperial city, Meknès reflects its heritage as the one-time centre of the Moroccan sultanate. Tour programmes may rank Meknès third behind Marrakesh and Fès because it is quieter and smaller, but it is also more laid-back and less hassle. And Morocco's history and its mystery are no less vibrant in this – the third imperial city.

## Information
**Cyber de Paris** (Zankat Accra; per hour Dh6; ☺ 9am-2am)
**Tourist Office** (☎ 055 524426; fax 055 516046; Place de l'Istiqlal; ☺ 8.30am-noon & 2.30pm-6.30pm Mon-Thu, 8am-11.30am & 3pm-6.30pm Fri)
**Main Post Office** (Place de l'Istiqlal) The parcel office is around the corner on Rue Tetouan.
**Quick Net** (28 Ave Emir Abdelkader; per hour Dh8; ☺ 9am-11pm)

## Sights
The heart of Meknès medina lies to the north of the main square, Place el-Hedim, with the *mellah* to the west. To the south, Moulay Ismail's imperial city opens up through one of the most impressive monumental gateways in all of Morocco, **Bab el-Mansour**. Following the road around to the right, you'll come across the **Mausoleum of Moulay Ismail** (admission free, donations welcome; ☺ 8.30am-noon & 2-6pm Sat-Thu), named for the sultan who made Meknès his capital in the 17th century.

Overlooking Place el-Hedim on the north is the 1882 palace that houses the **Dar Jamaï museum** (☎ 055 530863; Place el-Hedim; admission Dh10; ☺ 9am-noon & 3pm-6.30pm Wed-Mon). Deeper in the medina, opposite the Grand Mosque, the **Medersa Bou Inania** (Rue Najjarine; admission Dh10; ☺ 9am-noon & 3pm-6pm) is typical of the exquisite interior design that distinguishes Merenid monuments.

MOROCCO

## Sleeping

With the exception of a few upscale *riads*, the best accommodation options are in the ville nouvelle.

**Youth Hostel** ( ☎ /fax 055 524698; dm with breakfast Dh45, d with breakfast per person Dh60, hot showers Dh5; ☼ 8am-10pm Sep-Jun, 8am-midnight Jul & Aug) The youth hostel is in a quiet residential area just over 1km northwest of the train station. Readers have not been thrilled with the service here, but the setting is pleasant and quiet.

**Camping International d'Agdal** ( ☎ 055 551828; camp sites per adult/child Dh17/12, plus per tent/car/caravan/camper Dh10/17/17/20, hot showers Dh7, electricity Dh15) The camping ground is 2km southwest of the imperial city.

**Hôtel Toubkal** ( ☎ 055 522218; 49 Ave Mohammed V; s/d/tr Dh70/120/200, hot showers Dh10) A recent change of ownership has upgraded this friendly, busy hotel, giving all the rooms a fresh coat of paint and clean linens.

**Hôtel Majestic** ( ☎ 055 522035; fax 055 527427; 19 Ave Mohammed V; s/d Dh189/225) The best budget option is this 1930s hotel close to the train station. Cheaper rooms with shared bathroom are also available.

**Hôtel Akouas** ( ☎ 055 515967; www.hotelakouas.com; 27 Rue el-Amir Abdelkader; s/d Dh308/375; P ⊠ ⬛ 🕿 ) This friendly, family-run three-star has more local colour than its rivals. Rooms, while not huge, are modern, comfortable and very fairly priced.

**Ryad Bahia** ( ☎ 055 554541; www.ryadbahia.ma; Tiberbarine; r/ste with breakfast Dh500/800) This little guesthouse is operated by a husband-and-wife team. They are very enthusiastic about Moroccan history and traditional craftsmanship, and it shows in the careful restoration of their *riad*. There is also a small restaurant in the central courtyard.

**Palais Didi** ( ☎ 055 558590; www.palaisdidi.com; 7 Dar el-Kbira; r/ste with breakfast Dh1200/1500; 🕿 ) Five sumptuous suites and five romantic rooms are set around a sleek marble tiled courtyard. Each one is different, but they are all decked out with antique furniture in the luxurious rooms and deep tubs in the zellij-tiled bathrooms. The owner expects to also open a restaurant on site – worth a splurge for dinner.

## Eating

Meknès is famous for its traditional sweetmeats and you won't find a better choice than in the covered market on Place el-Hadim. There's also good-quality fruit and veggies here, as well as meat, and fish in the adjacent hall.

**La Grotte** (11 Rue de la Votte) This hideaway near the station is an attractive, quiet spot to wait for your train. The cool, shaded 1st-floor sitting area has tile tables and a rustic atmosphere. It attracts young people – women and men alike – for coffee or simple meals.

**Restaurant Oumnia** ( ☎ 055 533938; 8 Ain Fouki Rouamzine; set menus Dh65; ☼ 7am-10pm) This informal restaurant is inside a family home, just off the main drag of the Meknès medina. The Moroccan salon is warm and welcoming, with Mama Oumnia ready to dish up a delicious, homemade *tajine* of the day. This is the next best thing to being invited home for dinner.

**Pizzeria Le Four** ( ☎ 055 520857; 1 Rue Atlas; pizzas Dh38-49, mains Dh65-85) The dark timber and whitewashed walls lend a suitably Italian atmosphere to this popular pizzeria.

**Restaurant Riad** ( ☎ 055 530542; 79 Ksar Chaacha; set menus Dh110 & Dh160) All three *riads* in the Meknès medina have lovely restaurants, but this was the first and remains the largest. Service is friendly and the setting, around a lush green courtyard, is wonderfully romantic.

For a quick bite head to **Sandwich Rossignol** ( ☎ 064 321652; Rue Dar Smen; sandwiches Dh10-20, mains Dh30; ☼ noon-midnight) and **Mo Di Niro** ( ☎ 055 517676; 14 Rue Antserapé; pizzas Dh30-70, burgers Dh15-20; ☼ noon-3pm & 5pm-10.30pm Tue-Sun; ✗ ).

## Shopping

The *souqs* of Meknès are a treasure-trove for the souvenir hunter. While not as huge as the *souqs* of Fès or Marrakesh, they are also less touristy – making it a good place to hunt for a bargain without too much hassle. Check out the **Centre Artisanale** ( ☎ 055 530929; Ave Zine el-Abidine Riad; ☼ 9am-1pm & 3-7pm Mon-Sat) before you head into the *souqs* to find a deal.

## Getting There & Away

### BUS

Take bus No 7 to the smart new **CTM station** ( ☎ 055 522585; Ave des FAR), about 300m east of the junction with Ave Mohammed V. The main bus station lies just outside Bab el-Khemis, west of the medina. Bus routes include Casablanca (Dh65, four hours, six daily), Rabat (Dh35, 2½ hours, seven daily), Fès (Dh15, one hour, six daily), Tangier (Dh75, five hours, three daily) and Marrakesh (Dh140, eight hours, one daily).

### TAXI

The principal grands taxi rank is in a dirt lot next to the bus station, to the west of the medina. There are regular departures to Fès (Dh16), Rabat (Dh40) and Chefchaouen (Dh100). Grands taxis for Moulay Idriss (Dh7) leave opposite the Institut Français.

### TRAIN

From **El-Amir Abdelkader** ( ☎ 055 522763) train station, a total of nine trains go to Fès (2nd-class *rapide* Dh17, one hour) and eight go to Casablanca (Dh81, 3½ hours) via Rabat (Dh56, 2¼ hours). There are five services to Marrakesh (Dh154, seven hours) and one to Tangier (Dh80, four hours).

## AROUND MEKNÈS

In the midst of a fertile plain about 33km north of Meknès, **Volubilis** (Ouailili; admission Dh20, guided tour Dh120; ☼ 8am-sunset) is the largest and best-preserved Roman ruins in Morocco. One of the country's most important pilgrimage sites, **Moulay Idriss**, is only about 4.5km from Volubilis. The simplest and quickest way to get here from Meknès is to hire a grands taxi for the return trip. A half-day outing will cost around Dh300.

# MOROCCO DIRECTORY

## ACCOMMODATION

Camping facilities are available around or near most Moroccan cities, while youth hostels (*auberges de jeunesses*) operate in Casablanca, Chefchaouen, Fès, Meknès, Rabat and Tangier. Hostels are usually safer and more comfortable than the unclassified medina hotels that rival them for price.

Hotels vary dramatically, ranging from dingy dives to gorgeous guesthouses and fancy five-stars (the latter mostly in larger cities). Cities that see many tourists also offer gorgeous guesthouses in the style of a traditional courtyard house, or *riad*.

Price categorisations in this chapter include Budget (up to Dh400), Mid-Range (Dh400 to Dh800) and Top End (Dh800

and up). They are generally listed in order of price. Prices given are for high season and include tax; always check the price you are quoted is TTC (all taxes included).

## ACTIVITIES
### Hammams

Visiting a *hammam* (traditional bathhouse) is a ritual at the centre of Moroccan society (especially for women) and a practical solution for those who don't have hot water at home (or in their hotel). For travellers, it is an authentic local experience akin to visiting a spa – thoroughly cleansing and totally relaxing. Every town has at least one public *hammam*. A visit usually costs Dh10, with a massage costing an extra Dh15 or so. See the boxed text (p656).

### Surfing & Windsurfing

With thousands of kilometres of Atlantic coastline, Morocco has some great surfing spots. Highlights are the beaches in Essaouira (p675) for windsurfing and around Rabat (p667) for surfing.

### Walking

Morocco's many mountain ranges offer a wide array of trekking opportunities. Most travellers head straight for the highest peaks of the High Atlas – treks can be organised from Marrakesh. Chefchaouen is the place to start treks through the Rif Mountains. Spring and autumn are the best seasons for trekking.

## BOOKS

For detailed travel information, see Lonely Planet's *Morocco*. If you're a first-time visitor to Africa, consider checking out Lonely Planet's *Read This First: Africa* for lots of helpful advice.

## BUSINESS HOURS

Tourist information offices are generally open from 8.30am to 12.30pm and then 2.30pm to 6.30pm Monday to Thursday (often closed longer at noon on Friday). Restaurants are generally open from noon to 3pm and 7pm to 11pm daily, while cafés open from 7am to 11pm. Shops open from about 9am to 12.30pm and 2.30pm to 8pm Monday to Saturday (often closed longer at noon on Friday).

## TOP FIVE READS

Morocco inspires great passions, fascination and repulsion, resulting in a rich literary tradition, whose most outstanding member is the late Paul Bowles.

■ **The Spider's House** (Paul Bowles) Fès in the twilight of the French occupation is the arena for this political *tour de force* from Bowles. The daily goings-on of Fès life, with its web-like complexities, provide a fascinating backdrop.

■ **A Year in Marrakesh** (Peter Mayne) A droll account of Peter Mayne's experiences in Marrakesh. His observation of the minutiae is excellent and his detached Englishness makes for some hilarious scenes amidst the local mayhem.

■ **Tangier: City of the Dream** (Iain Finlayson) Intriguing insights into the Beat generation writers such as Paul and Jane Bowles and William Burroughs, as well as Truman Capote and other authors who spent time in Tangier. A highly readable account of the life of this 'seedy, salacious, decadent, degenerate' city.

■ **Hideous Kinky** (Esther Freud) Fresh, clear, funny and sharp. A young hippie takes her children to Marrakesh to find herself and an alternative life. Famously made into a film starring Kate Winslet, Esther Freud's lightness-of-touch is even more engaging.

■ **Lords of the Atlas: The Rise and Fall of the House of Glaoua 1893-1956** (Gavin Maxwell) Recounts the story of Thami al-Glaoui, the pasha of Marrakesh, who even after WWII ordered that the heads of his enemies be mounted on the city gates. An excellent and lively biography.

## DANGERS & ANNOYANCES

Morocco's era as a hippy paradise is long past. Plenty of fine *kif* (dope) is grown in the Rif Mountains, but drug busts are common and Morocco is not a good place to investigate prison conditions.

### Hustlers, Touts & Faux Guides

A few years ago the *brigade touristique* (tourist police) was set up in the principal tourist centres to clamp down on Morocco's notorious *faux guides* (false guides) and hustlers. Anyone convicted of operating as an unofficial guide faces jailtime and/or a huge fine.

This has reduced – but not eliminated – the problem of the faux guides. You'll still find plenty of these touts hanging around the entrances to medinas and outside train stations, especially at the Tangier port and near Bab Bou Jeloud in Fès. Most would-be guides will go away if you ignore them, but some can be persistent and even unpleasant – stay calm and polite, and head for a café or taxi. If you end up with one of these people remember their main interest is the commission gained from certain hotels or on articles sold to you in the *souqs*.

Official guides can be engaged through tourist offices and hotels at the fixed price of Dh120 per half-day (plus tip). It's worth taking a guide in the larger medinas, especially Fès; they have local knowledge and they'll save you from being hassled by others. If you don't want a shopping expedition included in your tour, make this clear beforehand.

## EMBASSIES & CONSULATES
### Moroccan Embassies & Consulates

**Australia** ( ☎ 02-9922 4999; ste 2, 11 West St, North Sydney, NSW 2060)

**Canada** ( ☎ 613-236 7391, www.ambassade-maroc .ottawa.on.ca; 38 Range Rd, Ottawa, Ont KIN 8J4)

**France** ( ☎ 01 45 20 69 35; affgeneral@amb-maroc.fr; 5 Rue Le Tasse, 75016 Paris)

**Germany** ( ☎ 030-206 1240; www.marokko.com/bot schaft; Niederwallstr 39, 1011 Berlin) Consulate-general in Düsseldorf ( ☎ 211-650 4510) *Consulate-general in Frankfurt* ( ☎ 069-955 0123)

**Netherlands** ( ☎ 070-346 9617; www.marokkaanse -ambassade.nl; Oranjestraat 9, 2514 JB, The Hague)

**Spain** ( ☎ 91 563 1090; www.maec.gov.ma/madrid; Calle Serrano 179, 28002 Madrid)

**UK** ( ☎ 020-7581 5001; mail@sifamaldn.org; 49 Queen's Gate Gardens, London SW7 5NE)

**USA** ( ☎ 202-462 7979; embassy@embassyofmorocco.us; 1601 21st St NW, Washington, DC 20009) *Consulate-general* ( ☎ 212-758 2625; 10 E 40th St, New York, NY, 10016)

### Embassies & Consulates in Morocco

Unless otherwise noted, most embassies are open from 9am until noon Monday to Friday.

**Australia** The Australian embassy in Paris has full consular responsibility for Morocco. Consular services to Australian citizens in Morocco are provided by the Canadian embassy.

**Canada** ( ☎ 037 687400; fax 037 687430; 13 Rue Jaafar as-Sadiq, Agdal, Rabat; ⏰ 8am-noon & 1.30pm-5.30pm Mon-Thu, 8am-1.30pm Fri)

**France** ( ☎ 037 689700; www.ambafrance-ma.org; 3 Rue Sahnoun, Agdal, Rabat) Consulate-general ( ☎ 037 268181; Rue Alla Ben Abdallah, Rabat; visa applications ⏰ 8.30am-11.30am, pick-ups ⏰ 1.30pm-3pm Mon-Fri). Consulates also in Agadir, Casablanca, Tangier, Marrakesh and Fès.

**Germany** ( ☎ 037 709662; www.amballemagne-rabat .ma; 7 Rue Madnine, Rabat; ⏰ 9am-noon Mon-Fri) Consulate-general ( ☎ 037 653605; fax 037 653649; 12 Ave Mehdi ben Barka (formerly ben Snassen), Rabat)

**Netherlands** ( ☎ 037 733512; nlgovrab@mtds.com; 40 Rue de Tunis, Rabat) Consulate in Casablanca ( ☎ 022 221820; 26 Rue Nationale)

**New Zealand** The closest embassy is in Madrid, Spain. The UK embassy provides consular support in Morocco.

**Spain** ( ☎ 037 268080; fax 037 707387; 3-5 Rue Madnine, Rabat) Consulate in Agadir ( ☎ 048 845710; fax 048 845643; 49 Rue ibn Batouta) Consulate in Casablanca ( ☎ 022 220752; fax 022 205049; 31 Rue d'Alger) Consulate in Tangier ( ☎ 039 937000; fax 039 932770; 85 Ave Président Habib Bourghiba) Consulate in Tetouan ( ☎ 039 703984; fax 039 704485; Place Moulay el-Mehdi)

**UK** ( ☎ 037 729696; www.britain.org.ma; 17 Blvd de la Tour Hassan, Rabat; ⏰ 8am-4.30pm Mon-Thu & 8am-1pm Fri, visa applications 8am-noon Mon-Fri). Staff will help citizens of the Republic of Ireland and some Commonwealth countries without representation in Morocco. Consulate-general in Casablanca ( ☎ 022 364355; british .consulate@casanet.net.ma) Consulate in Tangier ( ☎ 039 941557; uktanger@mtds.com)

**USA** ( ☎ 037 762265; http://rabat.usembassy.gov; 2 Ave de Marrakesh, Rabat; ⏰ 8.30am-12.30pm & 2.30pm-6.30pm Mon-Fri) Consulate in Casablanca ( ☎ 022 264550; fax 022 204127; 8 Blvd Moulay Youssef; ⏰ 8am-6pm Mon-Fri)

## FESTIVALS & EVENTS

Regilious festivals are of more significance to Moroccans but local *moussems* (saints days) are held all over the country throughout the year and some draw big crowds.

Now more than 40 years old, the annual **Festival of Folklore** ( ☎ 044 446114; www.maghrebarts ma/festivals; Jun) is a unique celebration of Berber culture. The all-singing, folk-dancing extravaganza features the country's best performers.

Each summer the Fès **Festival of World Sacred Music** ( ☎ 055 740535; www.fesfestival.org) brings together music groups from all corners of the globe.

Major festivals include:
**National Folklore Festival** (Marrakesh) May/June
**Gnawa & World Music Festival** (Essaouira)June
**Festival of World Sacred Music** (Fès) June/July
**International Cultural Festival** (Asilah) July/August
**Moussem of Moulay Idriss II** (Fès) September

## GAY & LESBIAN TRAVELLERS

Homosexual acts are officially illegal in Morocco – in theory you can go to jail and/or be fined. However, male homosexuality remains relatively common, although not openly admitted. Platonic affection is freely shown, more so among men than women. Despite this, male homosexuals are advised to be discreet – aggression towards gay male travellers is not unheard of. Lesbians shouldn't encounter any problems, though it's commonly believed by Moroccans that there are no lesbians in their country.

## HOLIDAYS

All banks, post offices and most shops are shut on the main public holidays, including these:
**New Year's Day** 1 January
**Independence Manifesto** 11 January
**Labour Day** 1 May
**Feast of the Throne** 30 July
**Allegiance of Wadi-Eddahab** 14 August
**Anniversary of the King's and People's Revolution** 20 August
**Anniversary of the Green March** 6 November
**Independence Day** 18 November

In addition to secular holidays there are many national and local Islamic holidays and festivals, all tied to the lunar calendar.
**Aïd al-Adha** Marks the end of the Islamic year. Most things shut down for four or five days.
**Aïd al-Fitr** Held at the end of the month-long Ramadan fast, which is fairly strictly observed by most Muslims. The festivities generally last four or five days, during which just about everything grinds to a halt.
**Mawlid an-Nabi (Mouloud)** Celebrates the birthday of the Prophet Mohammed.

## INTERNET RESOURCES

**Al-Bab** (www.al-bab.com/maroc) Fittingly called The Moroccan Gateway this site has an excellent collection of links, particularly good for current affairs and news.
**Maghreb Arts** (www.maghrebarts.com) French-language site with excellent up-to-date coverage of theatre, film, music, festivals and media events in Morocco.

MOROCCO

MOROCCO

**Maroc Tunes** (www.maroctunes.com) Fascinating French-language site – a veritable archive of Moroccan music with lots of reviews and MP3 downloads.

**Mifta Shamali – North Africa Travel Guide** (www.i-cias.com/m.s) Useful virtual guide to the region with some amusing text coverage. Links to Lexicorient, a virtual Maghreb and Arab encyclopaedia.

**Tourism in Morocco** (www.tourism-in-morocco.com) Morocco's official tourist information site; user-friendly, with guided tours, links and news.

## MAPS

Few decent maps of Morocco are available in the country itself, so you are advised to get one before leaving home. Michelin's No 959 map of Morocco is arguably the best.

## MONEY
### ATMs

ATMs (*guichets automatiques*) are now a common sight and many accept Visa, MasterCard, Electron, Cirrus, Maestro and InterBank systems. Major credit cards are widely accepted in the main tourist centres, although their use often attracts a surcharge of around 5% from Moroccan businesses.

### Currency

The Moroccan currency is the dirham (Dh), which is divided into 100 centimes. You will find notes in denominations up to Dh200 and coins of Dh1, Dh2, Dh5 and Dh10, as well as 10, 20 and 50 centimes, though these are becoming rarer. The importation or exportation of local currency is prohibited; there's not much of a black market and little reason to use it. The Spanish enclaves of Ceuta and Melilla now use the euro.

### Tipping & Bargaining

Tipping and bargaining are integral parts of Moroccan life. Practically any service can warrant a tip, and a few dirham for a service willingly rendered can make your life a lot easier. Tipping between 5% and 10% of a restaurant bill is appropriate.

When souvenir hunting, decide beforehand how much you are prepared to spend on an item, but be aware that carpet vendors often start with hugely inflated prices.

An endless supply of small coins is absolutely vital for the payment of taxis, tips, guides and beggars. It is a good idea to load up at a bank when you arrive so you are well prepared.

### Travellers Cheques

American Express (AmEx), Visa and Thomas Cook travellers cheques are also widely accepted for exchange by banks. Australian, Canadian and New Zealand dollars are not quoted in banks and are not usually accepted.

## POST

Post offices are distinguished by the 'PTT' sign or the 'La Poste' logo. You can sometimes buy stamps at tabacs, the small tobacco and newspaper kiosks you see scattered about the main city centres.

The postal system is fairly reliable, but not terribly fast. It takes about a week for letters to get to their European destinations, and two weeks or so to get to Australia and North America. Sending post from Rabat or Casablanca is quicker.

The parcel office, indicated by the sign 'colis postaux', is generally in a separate part of the post office building. Take your parcel unwrapped for customs inspection. Some parcel offices sell boxes.

## TELEPHONE

A few cities and towns still have public phone offices, often next to the post office, but more common are the privately run *téléboutiques*, which can be found in every town and village on almost every corner.

### Mobile Phones

Morocco has two GSM mobile phone networks, Méditel and Maroc Telecom, which now cover 85% of the population (compared to land lines which only 6% of the population has access to). Moroccan mobile numbers start with the codes ☎ 061 to ☎ 068.

### Phone Codes

All domestic phone calls in Morocco require a nine-digit number, which includes the three-digit area code (or GSM code). When calling overseas from Morocco, dial ☎ 00, the country code and then the city code and number. Morocco's country code is ☎ 212.

## TIME

Moroccan time is GMT/UTC all year, so in summer Morocco is two hours behind European time and one hour behind UK time.

## TOILETS

Outside the major cities, public toilets are rare and you will usually need to bring your own paper (papier hygiénique), a tip for the attendant (Dh2 to Dh3), stout-soled shoes and very often a nose clip. Toilets are mostly of the 'squat' variety (referred to as 'Turkish toilets') with a tap, hose or container of water for sluicing.

## TOURIST INFORMATION
### Local Tourist Offices

The national tourism body, **ONMT** (Office National Marocain du Tourisme; www.visitmorocco.com), has offices in the main cities. Regional offices, called Syndicat d'Initiative are to be found in smaller towns. The majority of tourist offices, national and regional, offer only the standard ONMT brochures and the simplest of tourist maps.

### Tourist Offices Abroad

**Australia** ( ☎ 02-922 4999; fax 9923 1053; c/o Moroccan Consulate; 11 West St, North Sydney, NSW 2060)
**Canada** ( ☎ 514-842 8111; onmt@qc.aira.com; Place Montréal Trust, 1800 Rue MacGill, Suite 2450, Montreal, Quebec H3A 3J6)
**France** ( ☎ 01 42 60 63 50; tourisme.marocain@ wanadoo.fr; 161 Rue Saint Honoré, Place du Théâtre Français, 75001 Paris)
**Germany** ( ☎ 0211-370551; marokkofva@aol.com; 59 Graf Adolf Strasse 4000, Düsseldorf )
**Japan** ( ☎ 03-3403 0070; fax 3403 0072; ste 303 2-1-9 Sendagaya, Shibuya-ku, Tokyo 151)
**Spain** ( ☎ 91-542 7431; informacion@turismomarruecos .com; Calle Ventura Rodriguez 24, 28008 Madrid)
**UK** ( ☎ 020-7437 0073; fax 7734 8172; 205 Regent St, London W1R 7DE)
**USA** New York ( ☎ 212-557 2520; mntonyonmt@aol .com; Suite 1201, 20 East 46th St, New York, NY 10017) Florida ( ☎ 407-827 5337; fax 827 0146, inanmrini@aol .com; PO Box 22663, Lake Buena Vista, Orlando, Florida 32830)

## VISAS

Most visitors to Morocco do not require visas and are allowed to remain in the country for 90 days on entry. Exceptions to this include nationals of Israel, South Africa and Zimbabwe. Moroccan embassies have been known to insist that you get a visa from your country of origin. Should the standard 90-day stay be insufficient, it is possible to apply for an extension at the nearest police headquarters (Préfecture de Police). The Spanish enclaves Ceuta and Melilla have the same visa requirements as mainland Spain.

## WOMEN TRAVELLERS

A certain level of sexual harassment is the norm in Morocco. It comes in the form of non-stop greetings, leering and other unwanted attention, but it is rarely dangerous. It is best to avoid overreacting and to ignore this attention. In the case where a would-be suitor is particularly persistent, threatening to go to the police or the brigade touristique is amazingly effective. Women will save themselves a great deal of grief by avoiding eye contact, dressing modestly and refraining from walking around alone at night.

# TRANSPORT IN MOROCCO

## GETTING THERE & AWAY
### Air

Morocco's main international entry point is the **Mohammed V International Airport** ( ☎ 022 539040), 30km southeast of Casablanca. Other international airports include:

**Fès Airport** ☎ 055 674712; 15km south of Fès at Saïss
**Ibn Batouta Airport** ☎ 039 393720; 18km south of Tangier
**Ménara Airport** ☎ 044 447865; Marrakesh
**Rabat-Salé Airport** ☎ 037 808090; 10km east of Salé

For comprehensive information on all Morocco's airports, their facilities and customs log on to website of **Office National des Aéroports** (www.onda.org.ma, no English).

Airlines flying to and from Morocco:
**Air France** (code AF; www.airfrance.com; ☎ 022 294040)
**Alitalia** (code AZ; www.alitalia.it; ☎ 022 314181)
**British Airways** (code BA; www.britishairways.com; ☎ 022 229464)
**Iberia** (code IB; www.iberia.com; ☎ 022 279600)
**KLM-Royal Dutch Airlines** (code KL; www.klm.com; ☎ 022 203222)
**Lufthansa Airlines** (code LH; www.lufthansa.com; ☎ 022 312371)
**Regional Air Lines** (code RGL; www.regionalmaroc.com; ☎ 022 536940)
**Royal Air Maroc** (code RAM; www.royalairmaroc.com; ☎ 022 321122)

## Land

The Moroccan bus company, **CTM** (in Casablanca ☎ 022 45 80 80; www.ctm.co.ma) operates buses from Casablanca and most other main cities to France, Belgium, Spain, Germany and Italy. Buses to Spain leave Casablanca daily except Sunday. Algeciras, Málaga, Granada, Madrid, Valencia, Barcelona and Bilbao are among the destinations. Book at least a week in advance.

Another Moroccan bus service with particularly good links to Spanish networks is **Tramesa** ( ☎ 022 245274; www.tramesa.ma). UK-based companies with service to Morocco include **Eurolines** (www.eurolines.co.uk) and **Busabout** ( ☎ 020 7950 1661; www.busabout.com).

## Sea

Regular ferries run to Europe from several ports along the Moroccan Mediterranean coast. The most trafficked is Tangier, from where there are boats to Algeciras, Spain (€22 to €25, 60 to 70 minutes, hourly); Tarifa, Spain (€2, 35 minutes, five daily); and Sete, France (€53, 36 hours, two weekly). Hourly ferries also run from Ceuta to Algeciras (€18, 35 minutes, hourly). Daily ferries go from Al-Hoceima (summer only), Melilla and Nador to Almería and Malaga in Spain. Bringing a bicycle is an additional €8 to €15, while a car is €50 to €80.

Children travel for half the price. Bringing a bicycle is an additional €8 to €15, while a car is €50 to €80. Tickets are available at the port of departure or from any travel agent in town.

Ferry companies:

**Comarit** (www.comarit.com) Casablanca ( ☎ 022 293320); Blvd d'Anfa); Tangier ( ☎ 039 947402; Tangier Port)
**Ferry Rapidos del Sur** (FRS; www.frs.ma) Spain ( ☎ 956 681830); Morocco ( ☎ 039 942612)
**Transmediterranea** Madrid ( ☎ 902 454645; www .trasmediterranea.es; Calle Alcalá 61)

## GETTING AROUND
### Air

**Royal Air Maroc** (RAM; ☎ 09000 0800; www.royalair maroc.com) dominates the Moroccan air industry – it has only paltry competition from one other domestic airline **Regional Air Lines** (in Casablanca ☎ 022 538080). Both airlines use Casablanca as a hub and many internal flights are routed through Mohammed V airport.

Although many people complain of the rather tired condition of Royal Air Maroc's carriers, their safety record is generally good with only two recorded fatal events since 1970. Recent terrorism fears have also led to increased security in all major airports.

Student and under-26 youth discounts of 25% are available on all RAM domestic flights – but this is only if the ticket is bought in advance from one of their offices. Group reductions are available and children aged from two to 12 travel at half price.

## Bicycle

Mountain biking is becoming an increasingly popular way of travelling in Morocco. At this stage there are no special road rules pertaining to cyclists and they're really not given much consideration by drivers. Distances are great and those on bikes will need to carry all supplies with them (including any spare parts you may need, food and plenty of drinking water). You can transport bikes on both buses and trains. Most camping grounds charge around Dh5 for bicycles.

## Bus

A dense network of buses operates throughout Morocco, with many private companies competing for business alongside the main national carrier, **Compagnie de Transports Marocains** (CTM; in Casablanca ☎ 022 753677; www.ctm .co.ma).

The ONCF train company runs buses through Supratours to widen its train network. Morocco's other bus companies are all privately owned and only operate regionally. It's best to book ahead for CTM and Supratours buses.

Bus travel is relatively cheap considering the distances that have to be covered. Typical fares from Casablanca to Agadir, Marrakesh, Fès and Tangier are Dh150, Dh70, Dh90 and Dh130. More often than not you'll be charged for baggage handling by someone, especially if it's going on top of the bus – Dh5 is common.

## Car & Motorcycle
### BRING YOUR OWN VEHICLE

Taking your own vehicle to Morocco is comparatively straightforward. In addition to your vehicle registration document and an International Driving Permit (although many foreign licences, including US and EU, are acceptable), a Green Card is required from the car's insurer. Not all insurers cover Morocco.

### FUEL & SPARE PARTS

Petrol in the Spanish enclaves of Ceuta and Melilla is tax-free, so drivers heading to Morocco and mainland Spain via the enclaves should arrive with a near-empty tank. Moroccan mechanics are generally extremely good at what they do and all decent-sized towns will have at least one garage (most with an extensive range of spare parts for Renaults and other French cars).

### HIRE

Renting a car in Morocco isn't cheap, starting from Dh3500 per week or Dh500 per day for a basic car with unlimited mileage. Most companies demand a returnable cash deposit (Dh3000 to Dh5000) unless you pay by credit card. The best cities in which to hire cars are Casablanca, Agadir, Marrakesh and Tangier, where the competition is greatest and prices least. However, it is usually cheaper to arrange car rental in advance through a travel agent or international agency.

There are also numerous local agencies and many have booths beside each other at airports – this is an excellent place to haggle. In many cases you can hire the car in one place and leave it elsewhere, sometimes for a fee.

By law, insurance must be sold along with all rental agreements.

### PARKING

In many Moroccan towns, parking zones are watched by *gardiens de voitures* in characteristic blue coats. The going rate is Dh3 for a few hours and Dh10 overnight. In an increasing number of big city centres, parking tickets are issued from blue kerb-side machines (Dh2 per hour for a maximum stay of 2½ hours). Parking is free on Sundays.

### ROAD RULES

In Morocco you drive on the right, as in Continental Europe. On a roundabout, give way to traffic entering from the right. Speed limits in built-up areas range from 40km/h. Outside towns there is a national speed limit of 100km/h, rising to 120km/h on the motorways. It is compulsory for drivers and passengers to wear seat belts in cars, but no-one does.

## Local Transport

### GRANDS TAXIS

The elderly Mercedes vehicles you'll see belting along Moroccan roads and gathered in great flocks near bus stations are shared taxis (*grands taxis* in French). They link towns to their nearest neighbours. Grands taxis take six extremely cramped passengers and leave when full. It can often be to your advantage to pay for two seats to get the taxi going earlier (and give yourself more space). This is particularly useful for lone women as you should get the front seat to yourself.

### PETITS TAXIS

Cities and bigger towns have local *petits taxis*, which are a different colour in every city. Petits taxis are not permitted to go beyond the city limits. They are licensed to carry up to three passengers and are usually metered.

## Train

Morocco's train network is run by the **Office National des Chemins de Fer** (ONCF; www.oncf.org.ma). There are basically two lines that carry passengers: the line from Tangier in the north down to Marrakesh, and the line from Oujda in the northeast, also to Marrakesh, joining with the Tangier line at Sidi Kacem.

The Belgian-made trains are comfortable, fast and preferable to buses. There are different 1st- and 2nd-class fares on all these trains, though there's not much difference in comfort. Second-class is more than adequate on any journey. Couchettes are available on the overnight trains between Marrakesh and Tangier. The compartments fold up into six bunks and they're well worth the extra Dh90.

### COSTS

Couchettes are available on the overnight ordinaire trains between Marrakesh and Tangier. The compartments fold up into six

MOROCCO

bunks (couchettes) and they're well worth the extra Dh90. Sample 2nd-class fares include Casablanca to Marrakesh (Dh75.50, three hours), Rabat to Fès (Dh72, 3½ hours) and Tangier to Marrakesh (Dh190, 9½ hours).

Children aged under four travel free. Those aged between four and 12 years get a reduction of 10% to 50%, depending on the service.

**TRAIN PASSES**
Two types of rail discount cards are available in Morocco. For those aged over 26, the Carte Fidelité (Dh149) gives 50% reductions on eight return or 16 one way journeys in a 12-month period. The Carte Jeune (Dh99) gives the same discounts to those under 26 years. To apply you need one passport-size photo and a photocopy of your passport.

# Regional Directory

The Regional Directory provides information that is valid for Mediterranean Europe as a whole. Here you'll find a general overview of the region that complements both the Getting Started chapter at the beginning of the book and the country Directories, which list details specific to individual countries. So if, for example, you're planning to visit more than one country, refer first to this Regional Directory for the big picture and then to individual country chapters for specific details. For this reason some subjects appear in both the Regional Directory and

the country Directories. Conversely, if you're after information on, say, activities along the Turkish coast, turn straight to the Directory in the Turkey chapter.

## ACCOMMODATION

Throughout this guide, accommodation options have been divided into budget, mid-range and top-end categories. The price range dividing these categories is different for each country, reflecting the different costs of living; all prices quoted include private bathroom facilities unless otherwise stated (the exception to this is the France chapter). For example, for the price of a night in a mid-range *pension* in Rome you might well be able to stay in a top-end hotel in Albania. All prices are quoted in the currency in which they're advertised on the ground – so expect to come across local currencies, euros and US dollars. For an overview of local accommodation options see the Directories in the individual country chapters.

As with the rest of Europe, the cheapest places to stay in Mediterranean Europe are camping grounds, followed by hostels and accommodation in student dormitories. Guesthouses, *pensions* and private rooms often offer good value. Self-catering flats and cottages are worth considering for a group stay, especially if you plan to be based somewhere for a while.

Mediterranean Europe is a hugely popular holiday destination and although the amount of accommodation available is considerable, in the peak holiday periods it can be hard to find. The answer is, wherever possible, to book ahead. Cheap hotels in big destinations (eg Paris, Rome and Madrid), especially the well-run ones in desirable or central neighbourhoods, fill up quickly. It's a good idea to make reservations as many weeks ahead as possible – at least for the first night or two.

In the low season, it's often worth bargaining a little as many places reduce their rates without necessarily advertising the fact.

If you arrive in a country by air and without a reservation, look for an airport accommodation-booking desk, although it rarely covers budget hotels. Tourist offices often have extensive accommodation lists, and the more helpful ones will go out of their way to find you something suitable. In most countries the fee for this service is very low and if accommodation is scarce it can save you a lot of running around. This is also an easy way to get around any language problems. Agencies offering private rooms can be good value. Staying with a local family doesn't always mean that you'll lack privacy, but you may have less freedom to come and go at any hour than you would in a hotel.

Sometimes people will approach you on the street offering a private room or a hostel bed. There's no hard-and-fast rule as to whether this is good or bad – just make sure it's not way out in a dingy suburb somewhere and that you negotiate a clear price. As always, be careful when someone offers to carry your luggage: they might carry it off altogether.

## Camping

Camping is very popular in Mediterranean Europe and, especially in August, camping grounds across the region are packed to the gills. As a general rule of thumb, there's usually a charge per tent or site, per person and per vehicle. National tourist offices should have booklets or brochures listing camping grounds for their country.

Although on paper camping is the cheapest form of accommodation, it's worth noting that, in practice, if you're without your own wheels camping doesn't always save you a whole lot of cash. In large cities, most camping grounds will be some distance from the centre, and if you're on foot, the money you save by camping can quickly be eaten up by the bus or train fares spent on commuting to and from the city centre. You may also need a tent, sleeping bag and cooking equipment. Many camping grounds also hire bungalows or cottages accommodating from two to eight people.

Camping anywhere other than on designated grounds is difficult because the population density of Europe makes it hard to find a suitable spot to pitch a tent away from prying eyes. It is also illegal without permission from the local authorities (the police or local council office) or from the owner of the land (don't be shy about asking – you may be pleasantly surprised by the response).

In some countries (eg France), free camping is illegal on all but private land, and in Greece it's illegal altogether. This doesn't prevent hikers from occasionally pitching their tent for the night, and they'll usually get away with it if they have only a small tent, are discreet, stay only one or two nights, take the tent down during the day and do not light a campfire or leave rubbish. At worst, they'll be woken up by the police and asked to move on.

If you're intending to camp your way around the region you should think about getting your hands on the **Camping Card International** (CCI; www.campingcardinternational.org). It's an 'ID' that can be used instead of a passport when checking into a camping ground and it includes third-party insurance. As a result, many camping grounds offer a small discount (usually 5% to 10%) if you sign in with one of these. CCIs are issued by automobile associations, camping federations and, sometimes, on the spot at camping grounds. In the UK, the **AA** (☎ 0870 5500 600; www.theaa .com) and **RAC** (☎ 0800 550 005; www.rac.co.uk) issue them to their members for UK£6.50.

## Farmhouses

A stay on a working farm is becoming an increasingly popular accommodation choice, particularly in Italy. Ideal for travellers with children – think large open spaces for running about in and cute animals to feed – many are situated in beautiful scenery. This means that without your own transport, your options are limited. However, the advantages are considerable: room rates are usually much less than in hotels of comparable comfort, there are often activities such as horse-riding or hiking, and the food is usually hearty and tasty. If you're after privacy, though, be aware that meals are generally served at communal tables.

Tourist offices should have lists of farmhouses (*agriturismi* in Italian) for specific areas. You should always book ahead as in the high season (May to October) many places are often full while out of season (October to April) many only open on request.

## Guesthouses

The distinction between a guesthouse and a hotel is becoming fairly blurred. The best guesthouses have rooms that are easily as good as any hotel room, while the simpler places usually offer basic rooms with shared bathrooms. In some countries they go under the name of *pensions* (p700), *chambre d'hôte, domatia* and so on. Although the majority of guesthouses are often simple family affairs, there are more expensive ones where you'll find private bathrooms and other luxuries.

## Homestays

In most Mediterranean places offering B&B you're unlikely to get a massive fry-up for breakfast – indeed in some places breakfast is even charged as an extra – but you can find some great bargains. If you're lucky you could find yourself in a magnificent frescoed room in a city-centre townhouse, with your own key and a highly discreet host. In other places, it may be asked of you to be tucked up quietly in your room by a certain hour. Some smarter rooms may have private bathrooms or you might have to share with other guests or the host family.

Contact tourist offices or check on the Internet for lists of local B&Bs, or see www .ibbp.com and www.bedandbreakfastineu rope.com.

## Hostels

Hostels offer the cheapest (secure) roof over your head in Mediterranean Europe, and you don't have to be young to use them. Most hostels are part of the National Youth Hostel Association (YHA), which is affiliated with what was formerly called the IYHF (International Youth Hostel Federation) and has been renamed Hostelling International (HI). In practice it makes no difference – IYHF and HI are the same thing and the domestic YHA almost always belongs to this parent group.

Technically, you're supposed to be a card-holding YHA or HI member to use affiliated hostels, but you can often stay by paying an extra charge. As a nonmember you have to buy what's called a 'welcome stamp' (one per night for up to six nights). Accumulate six welcome stamps and you automatically qualify for full membership valid for a year from the purchase of the first welcome stamp.

To join Hostelling International, ask at any hostel or contact your local or national hostelling office. There's a useful website at www.hihostels.com with links to most HI sites. The offices for English-speaking countries appear below, otherwise, check the individual country chapters for addresses.

**Australia** Australian Youth Hostels Association ( ☎ 02 9261 1111; www.yha.com.au; 422 Kent St, Sydney, NSW 2000)

**Canada** Hostelling International Canada ( ☎ 613 237 78 84; www.hihostels.ca; 205 Catherine St, Suite 400, Ottawa, Ont K2P 1C3)

**England & Wales** Youth Hostels Association ( ☎ 0870 770 8808; www.yha.org.uk; Trevelyan House, Dimple Rd, Matlock, Derbyshire DE4 3YH)

**Ireland** An Óige (Irish Youth Hostel Association; ☎ 01 830 45 55; www.irelandyha.org; 61 Mountjoy St, Dublin 7)

**New Zealand** Youth Hostels Association of New Zealand ( ☎ 03 379 9970; www.stayyha.com; PO Box 436, Level 3, 193 Cashel St, Christchurch)

**Northern Ireland** Hostelling International Northern Ireland ( ☎ 02890 31 54 35; www.hini.org.uk; 22-32 Donegall Rd, Belfast BT12 5JN)

**Scotland** Scottish Youth Hostels Association ( ☎ 01786 89 14 00; www.syha.org.uk; 7 Glebe Crescent, Stirling FK8 2JA)

**South Africa** Hostelling International South Africa ( ☎ 021 424 25 11; www.hisa.org.za; PO Box 4402, St George's House, 73 St George's Mall, Cape Town 8001)

**USA** Hostelling International ( ☎ 202 783 61 61; www .hiusa.org; 733 15th St NW, Suite 840, Washington DC 20005)

At a hostel, you get a bed for the night, plus use of communal facilities, which often include a kitchen where you can prepare your own meals. You are usually required to have a sleeping sheet – simply using your sleeping bag is not permitted. If you don't have your own hostel approved sleeping sheet, you can usually hire or buy one. Hostels vary in character, but the growing number of travellers and increased competition, has led many to raise standards and cut back on regulations. Increasingly, hostels are open all day, curfews are disappearing and the 'warden' with a sergeant-major mentality is an endangered species. In some places you'll even find hostels with single and double rooms.

There are many hostel guides with listings available, including the **HI Europe** (UK£8.50). Many hostels accept reservations by phone or fax, but usually not during peak periods, and they'll often book the next hostel you're heading to for a small fee. You can also book hostels through national hostel offices. Popular hostels can be heavily booked in summer and a limit may be placed on how many nights you can stay.

## Hotels

Hotels in the region range from dodgy flea-pits, with rooms to rent by the hour, to some of the world's grandest five-star palaces with room rates to match. Each country operates its own hotel classification system based on criteria laid down by the government of the individual country. Although there's no region-wide uniformity of the star system, the hotels recommended in this book generally range from one star to three stars. You'll often find inexpensive hotels clustered around bus and train station areas – always good places to start hunting, although rarely the most attractive of areas.

Check your hotel room and the bathroom before you agree to take it, and make sure you know what it's going to cost. Discounts are often available for groups or for longer stays. Ask about breakfast: sometimes it's included but at other times it may be obligatory and you'll have to pay extra for it. And remember that breakfast in many hotels will consist of little more than an espresso and croissant and cost double what you'd pay for exactly the same in the café across the road.

If you think a hotel room is too expensive, ask if there's anything cheaper. (Hotel owners sometimes try to steer you into more expensive rooms – for your own comfort, of course!) In southern Europe in particular, hotel owners may be open to a little bargaining if times are slack. In France and Italy it is now common practice for business hotels (usually the ones rated higher than two stars) to slash their rates by up to 40% on Friday and Saturday nights, when business is slow. Details of weekend discounts are usually advertised on hotel websites.

Well-known hotels in the major destinations fill quickly in high season so always make sure you phone ahead to check room availability. Some hotels insist on a faxed confirmation of your reservation together with a credit card number as a deposit. If you don't have a credit card you'll often be asked to send a money order to cover the first night's stay. Booking over the Internet will usually spare you these hassles. Conversely, many cheaper hotels (and hostels) do not accept reservations unless made on the same day that you arrive.

## Pensions

*Pensions* are effectively modest hotels. Widespread throughout the region, a *pension* was once more personal and smaller than a hotel, often occupying one or two floors in a building housing other similar establishments. Today, however, many former *pensions* classify themselves as hotels.

In a *pension* you can expect to find a fairly basic room, often with a basin and bidet, in a large townhouse. A common problem, especially in older buildings, is to find you have to cart your luggage up the stairs. This is because there is either no lift, or, if there is one, it's so small that the chances of both you and your luggage being in it simultaneously are non-existent.

## Private Rooms

Renting a private room in a local home is often a cheap and pleasant option. It makes more sense for longer stays, as rates for a single night are often subject to surcharges of 50% or more. As with all accommodation, it also works out cheaper if you have someone to share with, as most rooms will be set up as doubles or triples and as a solo traveller you're unlikely to qualify for any discounts. The quality and price of rooms ranges considerably. More expensive rooms offer private bathrooms and some of the larger rooms include cooking facilities. When you book a room, either privately or through an agency (who will charge a fee for their services), make sure you check if the price is per room or per person and whether or not breakfast is included.

It's always worth phoning ahead as, in many cases, the owners will pick you up at the station or port.

## University Accommodation

Some university towns rent out student accommodation during holiday periods. This is popular in France (p147). Accommodation will sometimes be in single rooms (more commonly in doubles or triples) and may have cooking facilities. Inquire at the college or university, at student information services or at local tourist offices.

## ACTIVITIES

Mediterranean Europe is a magnificent outdoor playground. For folk who love their fun in the water, the possibilities are endless.

For those who prefer to stay on *terra firma*, the mountains provide a wonderful arena for any number of outdoor activities.

What follows is a very general overview of some of the many activities on offer. For more detailed local information see the individual country chapters.

## Boating

The idea of boating in the Med invokes images of film stars stepping off gleaming motorboats in an impossibly glamorous Riviera setting. However, to enjoy the wealth of boating opportunities you don't need to be either rich or famous. For a start, the Mediterranean itself is not the only place where you can take to the water. The region's many lakes, rivers and canals offer a variety of boating options unmatched anywhere in the world. These range from yachting in the Aegean to rowing on peaceful Alpine lakes.

## Cycling

Cycling is a popular sport in southern Europe. The great cycle races, such as the Tour de France and Giro d'Italia, are followed by millions of fans, while thousands of enthusiasts regularly take to the roads at the weekend. For the visitor, cycling, along with hiking, is the best way to get close to the scenery and the people, while keeping yourself fit in the process. It's also an environmentally friendly way to get around many cities and towns.

Cycling is a great way to explore many of the Mediterranean islands – the coastal areas of Sardinia (around Alghero), for example, are a popular cycling area. On the mainland, the beautiful hills of Tuscany and Umbria in Italy, and those in the south of France, provide wonderful settings for some leisurely pedalling.

If you are arriving from outside Europe, you can often bring your own bicycle along on the plane. Alternatively, this book lists many places where you can hire one. See p723 for more information on bicycle touring, and the Transport sections in the individual country chapters for rental agencies and tips on places to visit.

If you're planning on cycling in the summer you should never underestimate the effects of the heat. Always cover your head (preferably with a helmet or a cap or sun-hat) and make sure you drink plenty of fluids. Sunburn can be highly unpleasant and heatstroke very serious. See p733 for tips on dealing with heat-induced problems.

## Diving

The limpid azure waters of the Med are ideal for diving. Throughout the region there are hundreds of diving centres offering everything from beginners courses to cave diving to exploring sunken wrecks. Croatia is increasingly becoming something of a diving hotspot; see p532.

## Hiking

Keen hikers can spend a lifetime exploring Europe's many exciting trails. Ranging from severe high-altitude routes to gentle paths suitable for a family stroll, the possibilities are infinite. The spectacular Italian Dolomites are crisscrossed with well-marked trails, and food and accommodation are available along the way in season. Hiking areas that are less well known but nothing short of stunning can be found in Corsica, Sardinia, Crete, Croatia and Turkey.

It's also worth noting that while most high-level Alpine paths are only open in the summer, there are possibilities for hiking in the winter snow. Contact tourist offices for information on routes and local guides.

## Skiing

Skiing is an expensive business. You'll need to budget for ski lifts, accommodation and the inevitable aprés-ski entertainment. Trying to keep costs down by bringing your own kit doesn't always pay dividends either. Equipment hire doesn't always cost the earth and is often a better option than carting your own skis around. As a rule, a skiing holiday in Europe will work out twice as expensive as a summer holiday of the same length. Cross-country skiing costs less than downhill since you don't rely as much on ski lifts.

The skiing season generally lasts from early December to late March, though at higher altitudes in the French and Italian alps it may extend an extra month either way. Snow conditions can vary greatly from one year to the next and from region to region, but January and February tend to be the best, busiest and most expensive months.

Some of the cheapest skiing in Europe can be found in the Sierra Nevada mountain range in the south of Spain and in Greece where the growing ski industry offers skiing at prices that would make the glossier Alpine resorts smirk into their ski lifts.

### Spectator Sports

Mediterranean Europe is a sporty place and if you can get to a big sporting event you're guaranteed an experience. In winter, sport for the most part means football (soccer) and weekend games regularly sell out stadiums that in themselves are often striking examples of modern architecture. Passions run high and a spectacle is assured.

Spring is the time when the great cycle races (the Tour de France and Giro d'Italia) take place. The races are absolutely free – simply find out where and when the race is passing and plonk yourself by the side of the road.

In Spain bullfighting is still popular, especially in the south, and in Turkey the spectacle of greased up chubsters slapping each other through a bout of wrestling is guaranteed to amuse.

Other popular sports in Med Europe include basketball, motor-racing and in the summer, tennis.

### Windsurfing

After swimming and fishing, windsurfing could well be the most popular of the many water sports on offer in Europe. It's easy to rent sailboards in many tourist centres, and courses are usually available for beginners. Two top spots are Tarifa in Spain and Lefkada in Greece, an ideal place for beginners.

## BUSINESS HOURS

Although there are no hard and fast rules respected by all the countries in this guide (or even all the businesses in any one country), the Mediterranean countries do share some similar habits. For example, it's not unusual, especially outside the larger cities, for businesses (including shops) to close for a long lunch. Typically a shop might open early (say 8.30am) until 12.30pm or 1pm when it would lock its doors until 3.30pm or 4pm. It would then open for another three hours or so.

Banks generally open early and either close for the day at around 1.30pm or reopen for a brief two-hour window in the early afternoon, perhaps from 2.30pm to 4.30pm.

Businesses generally operate from Monday to Friday and possibly Saturday morning; Sunday opening is not unheard of, especially in tourist areas, but is extremely rare. It's also worth noting that many museums close on Mondays, especially if they're open over the weekend.

## CHILDREN

Children are adored in Mediterranean countries. There are few taboos about travelling with children in these parts as wherever you go the little ones will be welcomed with open arms and radiant smiles. If you speak the local language, however, you might have to get used to listening to an inordinate amount of advice as to how to dress your children or how to feed them properly.

Travelling with young children requires planning and effort. Don't try to overdo things; even for adults, packing too much into the time available can cause problems. Make sure the activities include the kids as well – balance that day at the Louvre with a day at Disneyland Paris. Include children in the trip planning; if they've helped to work out where you will be going, they will be much more interested when they get there. Lonely Planet's *Travel with Children* by Cathy Lanigan (with a foreword by Maureen Wheeler) is an excellent source of information.

Most car-rental firms in Europe have children's safety seats for hire at a nominal cost, but it's essential that you book them in advance. The same goes for highchairs and cots (cribs); they're available in most restaurants and hotels, but numbers are limited. The choice of baby food, formulas, soy and cow's milk, disposable nappies (diapers) etc is as great in most Mediterranean supermarkets as it is at home, but the opening hours might be different. Run out of nappies on Saturday afternoon and you may be in for a messy weekend.

## CLIMATE

The classical Mediterranean climate consists of long hot summers and mild winters. Summer sunshine is virtually guaranteed between June and September with temperatures topping 40°C in some parts, while the rain tends to wait until autumn and spring. Which is not to say that it doesn't rain much – in fact, Rome regularly receives more annual rainfall than London. The difference is simply that in the Mediterranean the weather generally follows a predictable pattern: in the summer the sun shines and it's hot; in autumn it gets colder and rains, often in short, very sharp bursts; in winter

temperatures drop considerably (it might not be as cold as in northern climes but it still gets distinctly chilly, especially in the mountains); and in spring it starts to get warm again in the build-up to the glorious summer.

Summer storms are distinct possibilities in many places but they tend to be short violent affairs that blow over fairly quickly.

For more detailed analyses of country climates refer to the country chapters.

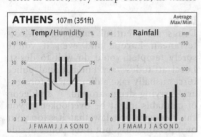

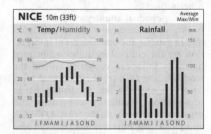

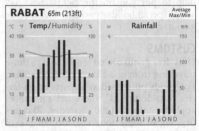

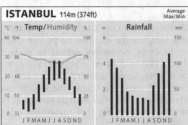

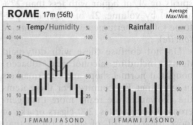

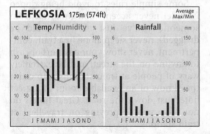

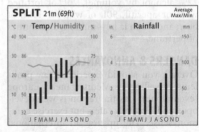

## COURSES

A popular excuse for passing time in the region is to learn the local language. Language courses are widely available to foreigners through universities or private schools, and are justifiably popular since the best way to learn a language is in the country where it's spoken. But you can also take courses in art, literature, architecture, drama, music, cooking, alternative energy, photography and organic farming, among other subjects.

The individual country chapters in this book give pointers on where to start looking. In general, the best sources of information are the cultural institutes maintained by many European countries around the world; failing that, try their national tourist offices or embassies. Student-exchange organisations, student-travel agencies, and organisations such as the YMCA/YWCA and Hostelling International (HI) can also help to put you on the right track. Ask about special holiday packages that include a course.

## CUSTOMS

Duty-free goods are no longer sold to those travelling from one EU country to another. For goods purchased at airports or on ferries outside the EU, the usual allowances apply for tobacco (200 cigarettes, 50 cigars or 250g of loose tobacco), alcohol (1L of spirits or 2L of liquor with less than 22% alcohol by volume; 2L of wine) and perfume (50g of perfume and 0.25L of *eau de toilette*).

Do not confuse these with duty-paid items (including alcohol and tobacco) bought at normal shops and supermarkets in any other EU country. For these items the allowances are really more than generous: 800 cigarettes, 200 cigars or 1kg of loose tobacco; 10L of spirits (more than 22% alcohol by volume), 20L of fortified wine or aperitif, 90L of wine or 110L of beer; and – ooh la la! – unlimited quantities of perfume.

## DANGERS & ANNOYANCES

Overall, you should experience few problems travelling in Mediterranean Europe (even alone) – as the region is well developed and relatively safe – but exercise common sense. The upsurge in international terrorism has not by-passed the Mediterranean region and bomb attacks in Istanbul and Madrid have made world headlines. However, the fact is that you run a far greater risk of being struck by sunburn than by a bomb.

Whatever you do, don't leave friends and relatives back home worrying about how to get in touch with you in case of an emergency. Work out a list of places where they can contact you.

### Drugs

Drugs are plentiful throughout Mediterranean Europe and even if you're sorely tempted you'd do well to desist. Local attitudes vary but national police forces usually take a dim view of foreigners carrying drugs around. A smidgeon of cannabis might be overlooked if you can persuade the law that it's for your own personal use, but if the police decide you have enough to be dealing (and it's often difficult to know how much this is) your trip could take a serious turn for the worse. In some countries the police can hold you for as long as it takes to analyse your case. Hard drugs are rarely overlooked anywhere.

A well-known drugs scam involves a new chum getting you good and stoned, selling you a lump of hash and then threatening to call in the cops unless you pay-up.

### Scams

Mediterranean con-artists are a predatory and imaginative lot. Just as people catch on to cons, new ones appear to replace them. The best defence is generally common sense and a healthy dose of scepticism – if someone seems just a little too friendly or if an offer sounds too good to be true, chances are that something's not quite right.

Some simple rules to avoid being duped include: never accept food or drink from someone you've just met (it could be drugged); never sleep alone in a train compartment; never show your passport or cash to anyone on the street; and be extremely wary of people at train stations who claim they know of an available room in a great hotel just down the road. Great hotels do not have people preying on travellers at train stations.

## Theft

This is the biggest problem facing people travelling in Mediterranean Europe. The most important things to guard are your passport, papers, tickets and money – in that order. It's always best to carry these next to your skin or in a sturdy leather pouch on your belt. Train station lockers or luggage storage counters are useful places to store your bags (but never valuables) while you get your bearings in a new town. Be very suspicious of people who offer to help you operate your locker. Carry your own padlock for hostel lockers.

You can lessen the risks further by being careful of snatch thieves. Cameras or shoulder bags are an open invitation for these operators, who sometimes work from motorcycles or scooters. They will expertly slash the strap before you have a chance to react. A small daypack is better, but watch your rear. Also be very careful at cafés and bars; loop the strap around your leg while seated.

Pickpockets are most active in dense crowds, especially in busy train stations and on public transport during peak hours. A common ploy is for one person to distract you while another whips through your pockets. Beware of gangs of dishevelled-looking kids waving newspapers and demanding attention. In the blink of an eye, a wallet or camera can go missing. Remember also that some of the best pickpockets are often extremely well-dressed.

Be careful even in hotels; don't leave any valuables lying around in your room.

Parked cars containing luggage or other bags are prime targets for petty criminals in most cities, and in particular cars with foreign number plates and/or rental-agency stickers. While driving in cities, beware of snatch thieves when you pull up at the lights – keep doors locked and windows rolled up high. A favourite ploy of scooter snatchers is for a first rider to brush past your car, knocking the side-mirror out of position, then, as you reach out to re-adjust it, an accomplice on a second scooter races past snatching your watch from your wrist as he passes.

In case of theft or loss, always report the incident to the police and ask for a statement. Without one, your travel-insurance company will probably not pay up.

## DISABLED TRAVELLERS

A survey of the facilities available to disabled travellers throughout the region would make for depressing reading. With the notable exception of Croatia, which is improving wheelchair access for the large number of wounded war veterans, the region does not cater well to disabled travellers. On the whole, wheelchair access is limited to the more expensive hotels and major airports. Public transport is usually woefully ill-equipped and museums and tourist sites usually offer little or no wheelchair access.

If you have a physical disability, contact your national support organisation (the 'travel officer' if there is one) and ask about the countries you plan to visit. They often have complete libraries devoted to travel, and they can put you in touch with travel agents who specialise in tours for the disabled.

The British-based **Royal Association for Disability & Rehabilitation** (Radar; ☎ 020 7250 32 22; www.radar.org.uk) publishes a useful guide entitled **A Guide to Long Distance Travel for Disabled People** (UK£5), which gives a good overview of facilities available to disabled travellers in Europe overall.

For on-line information investigate www.bbc.co.uk/holiday/disabled_traveller as it's a highly useful website.

## DISCOUNT CARDS
### International Student & Youth Cards

A handy card to have while travelling is the International Student Identity Card (ISIC), a plastic ID-style card with your photograph, which provides discounts on many forms of transport (including airlines and local public transport), cheap or free admission to museums and sights, and inexpensive meals in some student caféterias and restaurants.

If you're aged under 26 but not a student, you can apply for an International Youth Travel Card (IYTC, formerly GO25) issued by the Federation of International Youth Travel Organisations (FIYTO) or the Euro<26 card. Both go under different names in various countries and give much the same discounts and benefits as an ISIC. All these cards are issued by hostelling organisations, student unions and youth-oriented travel agencies.

See Camping (p698) for information on the Camping Card International.

## Senior Cards

Senior citizens are entitled to many discounts on things like public transport and museum admission fees, provided proof of age can be shown. In some cases a special pass may be required. The minimum qualifying age is generally 60 or 65 for men and slightly younger for women.

In your home country, a lower age may already entitle you to all sorts of interesting travel packages and discounts (eg on car hire) through organisations and travel agents that cater for senior travellers. Start hunting at your local senior citizens advice bureau.

Museums and other sights, public swimming pools and spas, and transport companies frequently offer discounts to retired people, old-age pensioners and those over 60 (slightly younger for women). Make sure you bring proof of age – that suave *signore* in Italy or that polite Parisian *mademoiselle* is not going to believe you're a day over 39.

European nationals aged 60 and over can get a Senior Card. For more information see Train Passes in the Transport chapter (p730).

## DVD & VIDEO SYSTEMS

European DVD discs and players are formatted for the PAL (Secam in France) TV system as opposed to the NTSC system used in the USA and Japan. As a general rule a DVD player bought in a PAL country will play NTSC and PAL formatted discs. On the other hand, most NTSC players can't play PAL discs.

DVDs are also encoded with a regional code (for America and Canada this is 1, for Europe and South Africa 2, and for Australia and New Zealand 3). If you buy a disc in Europe check that its code corresponds with that of your DVD player at home as a player coded 1 or 3 will not play a disc coded 2. A way around this is to look for universally compatible players and discs carrying a 0 code.

If you want to record or buy video tapes to play back home, you won't get a picture if the image registration systems are different. Europe generally uses PAL (Secam in France), which is incompatible with the North American and Japanese NTSC system. Australia also uses PAL.

## ELECTRICITY
### Voltages & Cycles

Most of Mediterranean Europe runs on 220V, 50Hz AC. The exceptions are Malta, which has 240V (such as the UK), and also Spain, which usually has 220V but sometimes still uses the old 110V or 125V, depending on the network (some houses have both). Some old buildings and hotels in Italy, including Rome, might also have 125V. All EU countries are supposed to run off 230V by now, but like many things in the EU, this is taking a bit longer than anticipated.

Check the voltage and cycle (usually 50Hz) used in your home country. Most appliances set up for 220V will handle 240V without modifications (and vice versa); the same goes for 110V and 125V combinations. It's always preferable to adjust your appliance to the exact voltage if you can (some modern battery chargers and radios will do this automatically). Just don't mix 110/125V with 220/240V without a transformer (which will be built into an adjustable appliance).

Several countries outside Europe (such as the USA and Canada) use 60Hz AC, which will affect the speed of electric motors even after the voltage has been adjusted to European values, so CD and tape players (where motor speed is all-important) will be useless. But things like electric razors, hair dryers, irons and radios will be fine.

### Plugs & Sockets

Cyprus and Malta use a design like the one in the UK and Ireland: three flat pins (two for current and one for earth). The rest of Mediterranean Europe uses the 'europlug' with two round pins. Many europlugs and some sockets don't have provision for earth, since most local home appliances are double-insulated. When provided, earth usually consists of two contact points along the edge, although Italy and Greece use a third round pin. In Greece the standard two-pin plug still fits the sockets, but this is not always so in Italy.

If your plugs are of a different design, you'll need an adaptor. Get one before you leave, since the adaptors available in Europe usually go the other way. If you find yourself without one, however, a specialist electrical-supply shop should be able to help.

## EMBASSIES & CONSULATES

See the Directories in the individual country chapters for details of specific embassies and consulates.

As a traveller, it's important to realise what your own embassy – the embassy of the country of which you are a citizen – can and cannot do.

Generally speaking, it won't be much help in emergencies if the trouble you're in is remotely your own fault. Remember that you are bound by the laws of the country you're in. Your embassy will not be sympathetic if you end up in jail after committing a crime locally, even if such actions are legal in your own country.

In genuine emergencies you might get some assistance, but only if other channels have been exhausted. For example, if you need to get home urgently, a free ticket home is exceedingly unlikely as the embassy would expect you to have insurance. If you have had all your money and documents stolen, it might assist with getting a new passport, but a loan for onward travel is almost always out of the question. In genuine emergencies, however, your consulate can help in several ways. Most importantly it can (a) issue an emergency passport (b) help get a message to friends or family and (c) offer advice on money transfers. In exceptional circumstances it might provide a loan for a ticket home.

## GAY & LESBIAN TRAVELLERS

Discretion is the keyword. Although homosexuality is acknowledged and in the large part tacitly accepted, attitudes remain largely conservative, especially outside of the major cities. Open displays of affection between same-sex couples are generally frowned upon and can, in some areas, lead to unpleasant misunderstandings.

Popular gay destinations include the Greek islands of Mykonos and Lesvos; see the boxed text on the poet Sappho (p327). Homosexuality is officially illegal in Morocco and North Cyprus.

This book lists contact addresses and gay and lesbian venues in the individual country Directories. But for European-wide listings, the **Spartacus International Gay Guide** (Bruno Gmünder; US$40) is a good male-only international directory of gay entertainment venues in Europe and elsewhere. It's best when used in conjunction with listings in local gay papers, usually distributed for free at gay bars and clubs. For lesbians, **Women's Travel in Your Pocket** (Ferrari Publications; US$16) is a good international guide.

## HOLIDAYS
### Public Holidays

Most holidays in the southern European countries are based on the Christian calendar. Although not all of the following are celebrated in all of the countries in this guide (see country Directories for specific information) the major holidays are as follows.

**New Year's Day** 1 January
**Epiphany** 6 January
**Easter** Sunday/Monday March/April
**Labour Day** 1 May
**Feast of the Assumption** 15 August
**All Saints' Day** 1 November
**Feast of the Immaculate Conception** 8 December
**Christmas Day** 25 December
**St Stephen's Day** 26 December

In the countries with a Muslim majority (Morocco, Turkey and Albania) the month-long holiday of Ramadan is celebrated.

### School Holidays

The month of August is the prime holiday period for Mediterranean dwellers. The major school holidays generally run from about June to September and many businesses simply shut up shop for much of August. The roads heading towards the southern coastal resorts are not a good place to be in late July, early August.

## INSURANCE

A travel-insurance policy to cover theft, loss and medical problems is a good idea. The policies handled by STA Travel and other student-travel organisations are usually good value. Some policies offer lower and higher medical expense options; the higher ones are chiefly for travellers from countries such as the USA that have extremely high medical costs. There is a wide variety of policies available, so check the small print.

Some policies specifically exclude 'dangerous activities', which can include scuba diving, motorcycling and even trekking. Some even exclude entire countries, such as Serbia & Montenegro. A locally acquired motorcycle licence is not valid under some policies.

You may prefer a policy that pays doctors or hospitals directly rather than you having to pay on the spot and claim later. If you have to claim later make sure you keep all documentation. Some policies ask you to call back (reverse charges) to a centre in your home country where an immediate assessment of your problem is made.

Check that the policy covers ambulance service or an emergency flight home.

For more information on health insurance see the Health chapter (p732) and for car insurance refer to the Transport chapter (p727).

EU nationals can obtain free emergency treatment in EU countries on the presentation of an E111 form, validated in their home country. Note, however, that this form does not provide health cover in Croatia, Malta, Morocco or Slovenia.

## INTERNET ACCESS

The easiest way to access the Internet on the road is to head to the nearest Internet café, of which there are thousands across the region. Most travellers make constant use of these cafés and use free web-based emails such as **Yahoo!** (www.yahoo.com) or **Hotmail** (www.hotmail.com). However, if you're travelling with your own notebook or hand-held computer, remember that your modem may not work once you leave your home country. The safest option is to buy a reputable 'global' modem before you leave home, or buy a local PC-card modem if you're spending an extended time in any one country.

Major Internet service providers (ISPs) such as **AOL** (www.aol.com), **AT&T** (www.att.com) and **CompuServe** (www.compuserve.com) have dial-in nodes throughout Europe; it's best to download a list of the dial-in numbers before you leave home. If you access your Internet email account at home through a smaller ISP or your office or school network, your best option is either to open an account with a global ISP, like those mentioned above, or to rely on Internet cafés and other public access points to collect your emails. See Photography & Video (p711) for information on digital cameras.

If you do intend to rely on Internet cafés, you'll need to carry three pieces of information so you can access your Internet email account: your incoming (POP or IMAP) mail server name, account name and password. Your ISP or network supervisor will give you these. Armed with this information, you should be able to access your Internet email account from any Internet- connected machine in the world, provided it runs some kind of email software (remember that Netscape and Internet Explorer both have mail modules). Most ISPs also enable you to receive your emails through its website, which only requires you to remember your account name and password. It pays to become familiar with the process for doing this before you leave home.

You'll find Internet cafés throughout Mediterranean Europe – check the individual country chapters in this book, and see www.netcaféguide.com for an up-to-date list. You may also find public Internet access in post offices, libraries, hostels, hotels, universities and so on.

## LEGAL MATTERS

The most likely reason for a brush with the law is to report a theft. If you do have something stolen and you want to claim it on insurance you must make a statement to the police as insurance companies are unlikely to stump up the cash without official proof of a crime.

Throughout the region the laid-back atmosphere should not be equated with a laissez-faire free for all. If you are driving, for example, make sure (a) you are sober and (b) you have the correct documents to hand as random road checks are not uncommon.

## MAPS

Good maps are easy to come by once you're in Mediterranean Europe, but you might want to buy a few beforehand to plan and track your route. The maps in this book will help you get an idea of where you might want to go and will be a useful first reference when you arrive in a city. Proper road maps are essential if you're driving or cycling around.

High quality regional maps are produced by Michelin, Freytag & Berndt, Kümmerly + Frey and Hallwag. Widely available in many large bookshops, they can also be bought over the Internet. As a rule, maps published by European automobile associations (for example TCI in Italy, ELPA in Greece etc) are excellent and sometimes free if membership of your local association gives you reciprocal rights. Tourist offices are often another good source for (usually free and fairly basic) maps.

## MONEY

This section looks at the best way of managing your money while on the road.

If you have to have money sent out to you telegraphic transfers are fairly cheap but, despite their name, often quite slow. Be sure to specify the name of the bank and the name and address of the branch where you'd like to pick the money up.

It's quicker and easier to have money wired via an American Express office (which costs around US$60 for US$1000). Western Union's Money Transfer system (available at post offices in some countries) and Thomas Cook's MoneyGram service are also popular.

### THE EURO

On 1 January 2002, the euro became the official currency of the 12 participating euro-zone countries of which France, Greece, Italy, Portugal and Spain feature in this guide.

The euro has the same value in all participating countries. There are seven euro notes (5, 10, 20, 50, 100, 200 and 500) and eight euro coins (1 and 2 euros, then 1, 2, 5, 10, 20 and 50 cents). One side is standard for all euro coins and the other side bears a national emblem of participating countries.

Rates of exchange of the euro and foreign currencies against local currencies are given in the appropriate country chapters.

| country | unit | | euro |
| --- | --- | --- | --- |
| Australia | A$1 | = | €0.59 |
| Canada | C$1 | = | €0.60 |
| Japan | Ÿ100 | = | €0.76 |
| New Zealand | NZ$1 | = | €0.51 |
| South Africa | R1 | = | €0.12 |
| UK | UK£1 | = | €1.49 |
| USA | US$1 | = | €0.83 |

To check the latest currency exchange rates go on-line at www.oanda.com.

## ATMs

ATMs (Automated Teller Machines) are widely available throughout Mediterranean Europe. Be very wary of overly friendly locals at stations or ports who tell you that there are no ATMs at the place you're heading for so you'd best stock up with cash at this convenient ATM – they're almost certainly up to no good.

Cash cards, which you use at home to withdraw money from your bank account or savings account, can be used throughout Europe at ATMs linked to international networks, such as Cirrus and Maestro. This is without doubt the simplest way to handle your money while travelling.

Credit cards can also be used in ATMs displaying the appropriate signs to obtain cash. However, if an ATM in Europe swallows a card that was issued outside of Europe, it can be a major headache. Also, some credit cards aren't hooked up to ATM networks unless you specifically ask your bank to do this.

### Black Market

You're unlikely to receive many whispered approaches offering stupendous exchange rates, as the black market is pretty insignificant in most Mediterranean countries. Where black markets do exist, the rates are only marginally better than bank rates and by dealing with unofficial moneychangers you greatly increase your chances of being duped. You're unlikely to put one over on these guys – they're professionals operating on home turf, and you're not. The best advice is to avoid the black market.

### Cash

Nothing beats cash for convenience, or risk. If you lose it, it's gone forever and very few travel insurers will come to your rescue. Those that will, limit the amount to somewhere around US$300. For tips on carrying your money safely, see Theft p705. As a general rule of thumb, carry no more than 10% to 15% of your total trip money in cash. The remainder could be in travellers cheques which can be replaced in case of loss or theft. Cash cards are better still (see the ATMs section, above).

It's still a good idea, though, to bring some local currency in cash, if only to tide you over until you get to an exchange facility or find an ATM. The equivalent of, say,

US$50 or US$100 should usually be enough. Some extra cash in an easily exchanged currency (eg US dollars) is also a good idea.

## Credit Cards

If you're not familiar with the options, ask your bank to explain the workings and relative merits of credit, credit/debit, debit, charge and cash cards.

A major advantage of credit cards is that they allow you to pay for expensive items (for example, airline tickets or car hire) without you having to carry great wads of cash. They also allow you to withdraw cash at selected banks or from the many ATMs that are linked up internationally (see the ATMs section earlier).

Credit and credit/debit cards such as Visa and MasterCard are widely accepted. MasterCard is linked to Europe's extensive Eurocard system, and Visa (sometimes called Carte Bleue) is particularly strong in France and Spain. However, these cards often have a credit limit that is too low to cover major expenses and can be difficult to replace if lost abroad. Also, when you get a cash advance against your Visa or Master Card credit card account, your issuer charges a transaction fee and/or finance charge. With some issuers, fees can reach as high as US$10 plus interest per transaction so it's best to check with your card issuer before leaving home and compare rates.

Charge cards like American Express and Diners Club have offices in the major cities of most countries that will replace a lost card within 24 hours. However, charge cards are not widely accepted off the beaten track.

Another option is Visa TravelMoney, a prepaid travel card that gives you 24-hour access to your funds in local currency via Visa ATMs. The card is PIN-protected and its value is stored on the system, not on the card. So if you lose the card, your money's safe. Visa TravelMoney can be purchased in any amount from Citicorp and Thomas Cook/Interpayment.

If you want to rely heavily on bits of plastic, go for two different cards – an American Express or Diners Club, for instance, along with a Visa or MasterCard. Better still is a combination of credit or cash card and travellers cheques so you have something to fall back on if an ATM swallows your card or the banks in the area are closed.

A word of warning – fraudulent shopkeepers have been known to quickly make several charge slip imprints with your credit card when you're not looking, and then simply copy your signature from the one that you authorise. Try not to let your card out of sight, and always check your statements upon your return.

## Moneychangers

Within the five countries in the euro-zone, the euro is the single currency (see the boxed text 'The Euro', p709). Travelling between, say, Italy and France no longer involves having to convert Italian lire into French francs.

US dollars, pounds sterling and Swiss francs are easily exchanged in Europe. You lose out through commissions and customer exchange rates every time you change money, so if you only visit Spain, for example, you are better off buying euros straight away from your bank at home.

The importation and exportation of certain currencies (for example, Moroccan dirham and Cypriot pounds) is restricted or banned entirely, so get rid of any local currency before you leave those countries. Try not to have too many leftover Maltese lire as it is impossible to change them back into hard currency. More and more banks and *bureaux de change* will now exchange Croatian Kuna and Slovenian Tolar but usually just in the neighbouring countries.

Most airports, central train stations, some up-market hotels and many border posts have banking facilities outside of working hours, sometimes open on a 24-hour basis. Post offices in Europe often perform banking tasks, tend to have longer opening hours, and outnumber banks in remote places. However, while they'll always exchange cash, they might not be prepared to change travellers cheques unless they're denominated in the local currency.

The best exchange rates are generally offered by banks. *Bureaux de change* usually, but not always, offer worse rates or charge higher commissions. Hotels are almost always the worst places to change money. American Express and Thomas Cook offices usually do not charge commissions for changing their own cheques, but they may offer a less favourable exchange rate than banks.

## Tipping

In many European countries it's common (and is the law in France) for a service charge to be added to restaurant bills, in which case tipping is not strictly necessary. However, as a visitor you'll often be expected to leave something even if it's simply a case of rounding up the bill. See the individual country chapters for details.

Some bargaining goes on in markets, but the best you should hope for is a 20% reduction in the initial asking price (apart from in Morocco, where you can bargain harder).

## Travellers Cheques

The main advantage of carrying travellers cheques rather than cash is the protection they offer from theft, though they are losing popularity as more travellers – including those on tight budgets – deposit their money in their bank at home and withdraw it as they go along from ATMs.

American Express, Visa and Thomas Cook travellers cheques are widely accepted and have efficient replacement policies. If you're going to remote places, it's worth sticking to American Express since small local banks may not always accept other brands.

When you change cheques, don't just look at the exchange rate. Ask about fees and commissions as well. There may be a service fee per cheque, a flat transaction fee or a percentage of the total amount irrespective of the number of cheques. Some banks charge exorbitant fees to cash cheques and not cash; others do the reverse.

Guaranteed personal cheques are another way of carrying money or obtaining cash. Eurocheques, which are available if you have a European bank account, are guaranteed up to a certain limit. When you cash them (eg at post offices), you will be asked to show your Eurocheque card bearing your signature and registration number, and perhaps a passport or ID card. Your Eurocheque card should be kept separately from the cheques. Many hotels and merchants refuse to accept Eurocheques because of the fairly large commissions applied.

## PHOTOGRAPHY & VIDEO

Mediterranean Europe is extremely photogenic, but the weather and where you'll be travelling will dictate what film to use. In overcast, grey conditions where the light is gloomy, photographers should use high-speed film (200 or 400 ISO), but for most of the sunny Mediterranean, slower film is the answer.

Film and camera equipment are available everywhere in the region, but obviously shops in the larger towns and cities will have a wider selection. Avoid buying film at big tourist sites such as the Leaning Tower of Pisa or at the entrance to the Acropolis. It may have been stored badly or have reached its sell-by date and will definitely be more expensive.

---

**GET YOUR MONEY BACK**

Shoppers can save themselves a euro or two by taking advantage of the tax-free shopping available throughout the region.

Value-added tax (VAT) is a kind of sales tax that applies to most goods and services throughout many European countries; it's about 20% in Italy, 19.6% in France, 18% in Greece and 16% in Spain. In most countries, visitors can claim back the VAT on purchases that are being taken out of the country. Those actually *residing* in one EU country are not entitled to a refund on VAT paid on goods bought in another EU country. Thus an American citizen living in Madrid is not entitled to a VAT rebate on items bought in Paris, while an EU passport holder residing in New York is entitled to this rebate.

The procedure for making the claim is fairly straightforward, though it may vary somewhat from country to country, and there are minimum-purchase amounts imposed. First of all make sure the shop offers duty-free sales (often identified with a sign reading 'Tax-Free for Tourists'). When making your purchase, ask the shop attendant for a VAT-refund voucher (sometimes called a Tax-Free Shopping Cheque) filled in with the correct amount and the date. This can either be refunded directly at international airports on departure or stamped at ferry ports or border crossings and mailed back for refund.

REGIONAL DIRECTORY

Properly used, a video camera can give a fascinating record of your holiday. Make sure you keep the batteries charged and have the necessary charger, plugs and transformer for the country you are visiting. In most countries, it is possible to obtain video cartridges easily in large towns and cities, but make sure you buy the correct format. It is usually worth buying at least a few cartridges duty-free at the start of your trip.

Lonely Planet's *Travel Photography* by Richard I'Anson will help you capture the pictures you've always wanted.

Those of you using a digital camera should check that you have enough memory to store your snaps – two 128 MB cards will probably be enough. If you do run out of memory space your best bet is to burn your photos onto a CD. Increasing numbers of processing labs now offer this service.

To download your pics at an Internet café you'll need a USB cable and a card reader. Some places provide a USB on request but be warned that many of the bigger chain cafés don't let you plug your gear into their computers, meaning that it's back to plan A – the CD.

## POST

From major European centres, airmail typically takes about five days to North America and a week to Australasian destinations. Postage costs vary from country to country, as does post office efficiency – the Italian post office, for example, is notoriously unreliable, whereas that of the Vatican is highly efficient.

You can collect mail from poste-restante sections at major post offices. Ask people writing to you to print your name clearly and underline your surname. When collecting mail, your passport may be required for identification and you may have to pay a small fee. If an expected letter is not awaiting you, ask to check under your first name; letters commonly get misfiled. Post offices usually hold mail for about a month, but sometimes less. Unless the sender specifies otherwise, mail will always be sent to the city's main post office.

You can also have mail (but not parcels) sent to you at American Express offices so long as you have an American Express card

or are carrying American Express travellers cheques. When you buy the cheques, ask for a booklet listing all the American Express offices worldwide.

## SOLO TRAVELLERS

Lone travellers should face no special problems in Mediterranean Europe. It's a relatively secure place with plenty of accommodation and an efficient transport network. Security issues for solo travellers are mainly a matter of common sense. Watch your possessions, don't go wandering down dark back alleys at night and be wary of overly friendly people you've just met. For more on possible dangers see the Dangers & Annoyances section (p704) while specific advice for women is included in the Women Travellers section (p715).

If you're thinking about hitting the road on your own, bear in mind that single rooms in hotels are often more expensive than doubles or triples. Seasoned soloists advise staying in hostels as much as possible, not only to save money but also as a means of meeting people.

One of the major advantages to travelling solo is the independence it affords you. You don't have to agree with companions on programmes or times – you just go wherever you want for as long as you want. For many this very real sense of freedom makes up for any feelings of loneliness.

## TELEPHONE & FAX

Telephoning within, or out of, Mediterranean Europe is not difficult. Public pay phones are widespread and, once you've got a phonecard, simple to use. They are also considerably cheaper than calling from a hotel.

To call abroad simply dial the international access code (IAC) for the country you're calling from (most commonly ☎ 00), the country code (CC) for the country you're calling, the local area code (usually, but not always dropping the leading zero if there is one) and then the number. So, for example if you're in Greece (IAC ☎ 00) and you're trying to call Australia (CC ☎ 61), Sydney (area code ☎ 02), number ☎ 1234 5678 – you'd dial ☎ 00 61 2 1234 5678.

Area codes for individual cities are provided in the country chapters. For country codes, see the Phone Codes section (right).

To have someone else pay for your call, you can, from many countries, dial directly to your home country operator and then reverse the charges; you can also charge the call to a phone company credit card. To do this simply dial the relevant Home Direct or Country Direct number to be connected to your own operator. Home Direct numbers, which can often be dialled from public phones without even inserting a phonecard, vary from country to country.

Toll-free numbers throughout Mediterranean Europe generally have an 0800 prefix. You'll find toll-free emergency numbers (eg ambulance, fire brigade, police) in the boxed texts 'Emergency Services' in individual country chapters.

### Fax

You can generally send faxes and telexes from major post offices and large hotels, though they will charge you more. Increasingly outmoded as a means of communication, faxes are still required as confirmation of a reservation by some hotels.

### Mobile Phones

Most European mobile phones operate on the GSM system, which is good news for owners of Australian mobile phones but less so for American travellers. American cell phones are not generally compatible with the European system and if they are they tend to be very expensive to use as service providers charge huge roaming fees.

Throughout the region there are any number of companies through which you can get a temporary or prepaid account if you already own a GSM dual or tri-band phone. Typically, you'd pay around €50 for a SIM card, which would include about €25 worth of prepaid calls. You can then top up the account as you go along.

Travellers planning on visiting various countries should buy a new SIM card in each country to avoid being stung for international calls. However, not all handsets allow use of another SIM card – you'd have to check with your mobile service provider.

Mobile phones are widely available to buy or rent. For more specific information see the individual country chapters.

### Phone Codes

The following is a list of codes which you'll need to call into these countries:

| | |
|---|---|
| Albania | ☎ 355 |
| Croatia | ☎ 385 |
| Cyprus | ☎ 357 |
| North Cyprus (Turkish) | ☎ 90+392 |
| France | ☎ 33 |
| Gibraltar | ☎ 350 |
| Greece | ☎ 30 |
| Italy | ☎ 39 |
| Malta | ☎ 356 |
| Morocco | ☎ 212 |
| Portugal | ☎ 351 |
| Serbia & Montenegro | ☎ 381 |
| Slovenia | ☎ 386 |
| Spain | ☎ 34 |
| Turkey | ☎ 90 |

### Phonecards

You can ring abroad from almost any phone box in the region. Public phones accepting stored value phonecards (available from post offices, telephone centres, newsstands and retail outlets) are virtually the norm now. In some countries (France for example), coin-operated phones are almost impossible to find.

There's a wide range of local and international phonecards. Most international cards come with a toll-free number and a PIN code, which gives access to your prepaid credit. However, for local calls you're usually better off with a local phonecard. It's also worth noting that (a) many cards have an expiry date and (b) those sold at airports and train stations are rarely good value for money.

For local calls you're usually better off with a local phonecard. Without a phonecard, you can ring from a booth inside a post office or telephone centre and settle your bill at the counter. Reverse-charge (collect) calls are often, but not always, possible.

### TIME

Most of the countries covered in this book are on Central European Time (GMT/UTC plus one hour), the same time used from Spain to Italy. Morocco is on GMT/UTC (year-round) while Greece, Turkey and Cyprus are on East European Time (GMT/UTC plus two hours).

Clocks are advanced one hour for daylight-saving time in most countries on the last Sunday in March, and set back on the last Sunday in September. At that time Central European Time is GMT/UTC plus two hours and East European Time is GMT/UTC plus two hours.

## TOILETS

Public toilets are not a feature of the Mediterranean landscape. Even in the major cities you'll often have to walk far and wide to find a toilet and then there's no guarantee that it'll be (a) open, (b) free, or (c) clean enough to use. The best bet is usually to dive into the nearest café, wolf down the cheapest thing on the menu, and use the on-site facilities. Although most loos in the region are of the sit-down Western variety, don't be surprised to find yourself faced with the hole-in-the-ground option. And don't ever assume that public loos will have paper – they almost certainly won't.

## TOURIST INFORMATION

Tourist information is widely available throughout the region. Most towns, big or small, have a tourist office of some description, which at the very least will be able to provide a rudimentary map and give information on accommodation. In the absence of a tourist office, travel agencies and hotel receptionists are two useful sources of information.

In many tourist offices English is spoken and some even offer a hotel reservation service, which might or might not be free.

For more specific details refer to the country chapters.

Many Mediterranean countries also have tourist offices abroad. Again, see country chapters for details.

## TOURS

Tailormade tours abound; see your travel agent or look in the small ads in newspaper travel pages. Specialists include **Ramblers Holidays** (☎ 01707 33 11 33; www.ramblersholidays .co.uk) in Britain for hiking trips and **CBT Tours** (☎ 800 736 24 53; www.cbttours.com) in the USA for bicycle trips.

Young revellers can party on Europewide bus tours. Contiki and Top Deck offer camping or hotel-based bus tours for the 18 to 35 age group. The duration of Contiki's tours are five to 46 days. **Contiki** (☎ 020 8290 67 77; www.contiki.com) and **Top Deck** (☎ 020 7370 45 55; www.topdecktravel.co.uk) have London offices, as well as offices or representatives in Europe, North America, Australasia and South Africa. Check the websites.

For people aged over 50, **Saga Holidays** (www.sagaholidays.com) offers holidays ranging from cheap coach tours to luxury cruises and sells cheap travel insurance. There's a **UK office** (☎ 0800 3005 00; Saga Bldg, Middelburg Square, Folkestone, Kent CT20 1AZ) and a **US office** (☎ 617 262 22 62; 222 Berkeley St, Boston, MA 02116).

National tourist offices in most countries offer organised trips to points of interest. These may range from one-hour city tours to several-day circular excursions. They often work out more expensive than going it alone, but are sometimes worth it if you are pressed for time. A short city tour will give you a quick overview of the place and can be a good way to begin your visit.

## VISAS

Most nationalities will have no major visa problems in the region. With a valid passport you'll be able to visit most of the countries around the Mediterranean for up to three months (sometimes even six), provided you have some sort of onward or return ticket and/or 'sufficient means of support' (money).

Of the countries covered in this book, France, Greece, Italy, Portugal and Spain have all signed the Schengen Convention, an agreement whereby all EU member countries (minus the UK and Ireland and plus Iceland and Norway) agreed to abolish customs checks at common borders. Legal residents of one Schengen country do not need a visa for another. Citizens of the UK and Ireland, are exempt from visa requirements for Schengen countries. Nationals of Australia, Canada, Israel, Japan, New Zealand, Switzerland and the USA do not need visas for tourist visits of up to 90 days to any Schengen country.

All travellers who are non-EU citizens visiting France, Greece, Italy, Portugal and Spain and intending to stay for longer than three days – or to visit another Schengen country from there – are supposed to obtain an official entry stamp in their passport, either at the point of entry or from the local police, within 72 hours. But in general registering at a hotel will be sufficient.

Remember also that stays in the Schengen area are limited, usually to three months (90 days) and that the clock starts ticking from the moment you enter the Schengen area. So, if, for example, you spend two months in Spain and then move onto Italy, you can only stay in Italy for one month.

For those who do require visas (and this includes South African nationals), it's important to remember that these will have a 'use-by' date, and you'll be refused entry after that period has elapsed. Your visa may not be checked when entering these countries overland, but major problems can arise if it is requested during your stay or on departure and you can't produce it.

A Schengen visa issued by one Schengen country is generally valid for travel in other Schengen countries but individual countries may impose restrictions on certain nationalities. It's obligatory to apply for a Schengen visa in your country of residence and you can only apply for two such visas in any 12-month period.

Of the non-Schengen countries covered in this guide, only Turkey requires a visa. Nationals of Australia, Canada, Ireland, South Africa, the UK and the USA need visas to enter Turkey. They can be bought at any point of entry into the country. See the Turkey chapter Directory (p644) for more details.

Visa requirements change, and you should always check with the individual embassies or a reputable travel agent before travelling.

---

**KEEP A COPY**

All important documents (passport data page and visa page, credit cards, travel insurance policy, air/bus/train tickets, driving licence etc) should be photocopied before you leave home. Leave one copy with someone at home and keep another with you.

While you're on the road add the serial numbers of your travellers cheques (cross them off as you cash them) to the photocopies of your important documents and keep all this emergency material separate from your passport, cheques and cash. Add some emergency money (eg US$50 to US$100 in cash) to this separate stash as well. If you do lose your passport, notify the police immediately to get a statement, and contact your nearest consulate.

---

It's generally easier to get your visas as you go along, rather than arranging them all beforehand. Carry spare passport photos (you may need from one to four every time you apply for a visa).

For more information about work visas and permits see Work, p716.

## WEIGHTS & MEASURES

The metric system is in use throughout Mediterranean Europe, which shows decimals with commas and thousands with full stops (for numbers with four or more digits the French use full stops or spaces).

## WOMEN TRAVELLERS

Machismo is alive and well in Mediterranean Europe. As a result, women travellers continue to face more challenging situations when travelling in the region than men do. Hopes of travelling inconspicuously, spending time alone and absorbing the surroundings are often thwarted by men who assume a lone woman desires company, or who seemingly find it impossible to avert their penetrating gaze. Bear in mind that most of this behaviour, which can come across as threatening, is more often than not harmless. Don't let it deter you!

Another problem is wandering hands, particularly on crowded public transport. If you feel someone start to touch you, make a fuss. You'll have the sympathy of the locals as gropers are regarded with as much disgust in the Mediterranean as they are anywhere else.

In Muslim countries, where conservative conceptions of the largely house-bound role of women still tend to prevail, women travelling alone or with other women will certainly be of interest or curiosity to both men and women. Unmarried men rarely have contact with women outside their family unit, which is why men in, for example, Morocco and Turkey, will afford travelling women so much attention. In such areas, women travelling with a male companion will often experience the exact opposite, and may need to pinch themselves as a reminder that yes, they actually exist.

The *Handbook for Women Travellers* by M and G Moss is a good read for women who travel solo.

# WORK

European countries aren't, as a rule, keen on handing out jobs to foreigners. Officially, an EU citizen is allowed to work in any other EU country, but the paperwork isn't always straightforward for long-term employment and after three months they will probably need to apply for a residency permit. Other country/nationality combinations require special work permits that can be almost impossible to arrange, especially for temporary work. That doesn't prevent enterprising travellers from topping up their funds occasionally by working in the hotel or restaurant trades at beach or ski resorts or teaching a little English, and they don't always have to do this illegally either.

In France you can get a visa for work as an au pair if you are going to follow a recognised course of study (eg a French-language course) and complete all the paperwork before leaving your country. Your national student-exchange organisation may be able to arrange temporary work permits to several countries through special programmes. For more details on working as a foreigner, see Work in the Directories of the individual country chapters.

If one of your parents or a grandparent was born in an EU country, you may have certain rights you never knew about. Get in touch with that country's embassy and ask about dual citizenship and work permits – if you go for citizenship, also ask about any obligations, such as military service and residency. Be aware that your home country may not recognise dual citizenship.

If you do find a temporary job, the pay may be less than that offered to local people. The one big exception is teaching English, but these jobs are hard to come by, at least officially. Other typical tourist jobs (picking grapes in France, washing dishes in Alpine resorts) often come with board and lodging but the pay is little more than pocket money.

If you play an instrument or have other artistic talents, you could try busking. As every Peruvian pipe player knows, busking is fairly common in major cities of Mediterranean Europe, especially in France, Spain and Italy. Beware though: many countries require municipal permits that can be hard to obtain. Talk to other buskers first.

Selling goods on the street, apart from at flea markets, is generally frowned upon and can be tantamount to vagrancy; most countries require permits. It's also a hard way to make money if you're not selling something special. In Spain selling goods on the street is fairly common, although officially illegal.

There are several references and websites that publicise specific positions in Mediterranean Europe. **Transitions Abroad** (www .transitionsabroad.com) publishes *Work Abroad: The Complete Guide to Finding a Job Overseas* and the *Alternative Travel Directory: The Complete Guide to Work, Study and Travel Overseas* as well as a colour magazine, *Transitions Abroad*. Its website lists paid positions and volunteer and service programmes. **Action Without Borders** (www .idealist.org) and **GoAbroad.com** (www.goabroad .com) list hundreds of jobs and volunteer opportunities.

*Work Your Way Around the World* by Susan Griffith gives good, practical advice on a wide range of issues. Its publisher, **Vacation Work** (www.vacationwork.co.uk), has many other useful titles, including *Summer Jobs Abroad*, edited by David Woodworth. *Working Holidays*, published by the Central Bureau for Educational Visits & Exchanges in London, is another good source.

If you can afford it, a volunteer work placement is a great way to gain a deeper insight into local culture. If you're staying with a family, or working alongside local colleagues, you'll probably learn much more about life here than you would if you were travelling through the country.

In some instances volunteers are paid a living allowance, sometimes they work for their keep, and other programmes require the volunteer to pay.

There are several Internet sites that can help you search for volunteer work opportunities in Mediterranean Europe. As well as the websites mentioned earlier, **Working Abroad** (www.workingabroad.com) has a good website for researching possibilities and applying for positions.

The **International Willing Workers On Organic Farms Association** (WWOOF; www.wwoof.org) has some organisations in Mediterranean Europe. If you choose to join a WWOOF organisation, you can arrange to live and work on a host's organic farm.

# Transport in Mediterranean Europe

## CONTENTS

### THINGS CHANGE...

The information in this chapter is particularly vulnerable to change. Check directly with the airline or a travel agent to make sure you understand how a fare (and any ticket you may buy) works, and be aware of the security requirements for international travel. Shop carefully. The details given in this chapter should be regarded as pointers and are not a substitute for your own careful, up-to-date research.

Strong competition among airlines means that you should be able to pick up a reasonably priced flight – even if you're coming from as far away as the United States or Australia. If you live in Europe of course you can easily travel overland by car, bus or train.

For websites with information on travel planning and ticket prices, see p12. More detailed information on transport within individual countries is listed in the Transport sections in the dstination chapters.

Throughout the chapter, and unless otherwise specified, the telephone numbers listed are local numbers and do not include international dialling codes.

# GETTING THERE & AWAY

## ENTRY REQUIREMENTS

There are no special entry requirements for nationals of Australia, Canada, Ireland, New Zealand, the UK and the USA. For most places (with the exception of Turkey) a valid passport is all you need for a stay of up to three months. South African nationals, however, require visas for a number of the countries in this book. For further details refer to the individual country chapters.

## AIR

Finding a flight into Mediterranean Europe is not difficult. Most of the world's major airlines fly into the region and with the increase in no-frills airlines operating in the area the number of international flights has grown considerably. In summer the vast number of charter flights – mainly to specific resorts – further adds to the air traffic congestion.

The biggest international airports in the region include the two Paris airports, Orly and Roissy Charles de Gaulle; Leonardo da Vinci (better known as Fiumicino) in Rome; Madrid's Barajas Airport; and Atatürk International Airport in Istanbul. Many of the no-frills airlines fly between the smaller provincial airports dotted throughout the region. Expect to pay high-season prices between June and September; two months either side of this period are the shoulder seasons. Low season is November to March.

### Airports & Airlines

Following is a list of Mediterranean Europe's major international airports.

**Athens** (Eleftherios Venizelos International Airport; code ATH; ☎ 0210 353 0000; www.aia.gr)

**Barcelona** (code BCN; ☎ 93 298 38 38; www.aena.es)

**Casablanca** (Mohammed V Airport; code CMN; ☎ 022 539040; www.onda.org.ma, in French)

**Cyprus** (Lanarca International Airport; code LCA; ☎ 02481 6130)

**Istanbul** (Atatürk International Airport; code IST; ☎ 0212 663 2550; www.ataturkairport.com, in Turkish)

**Lisbon Portela Airport** (code LIS; ☎ 021 841 35 00; www.ana-aeroportos.pt)

**Madrid** (Barajas Airport; code MAD; ☎ 91 393 60 00; www.aena.es)

**Malta** (code MLA; ☎ 21 24 96 00; www.maltaiport.com)

**Milan** (Malpensa; code MXP; ☎ 027 485 22 00; www.sea-aeroportimilano.it)

**Paris** Orly (code ORY; ☎ 01 49 75 15 15; www.adp.fr) Roissy Charles de Gaulle (code CDG; ☎ 01 48 62 22 80; www.adp.fr)

**Rome** (Leonardo da Vinci; code FCO; ☎ 06 659 51; www.adr.it) Also known as Fiumicino.

Following is a list of major airlines that fly to/from Mediterranean Europe:

**Air Canada** (code AC; ☎ 1-888 422 75 33; www.aircanada.ca) Hub: Toronto Pearson International Airport.

**Air France** (code AF; ☎ 08 20 82 08 20; www.airfrance.com) Hub: Roissy Charles de Gaulle Airport, Paris.

**Air Malta** (www.airmalta.com; code KM; ☎ 21 66 22 11) Hub: Malta Airport)

**Air New Zealand** (code NZ; ☎ 0800 73 70 00; www.airnewzealand.co.nz) Hub: Auckland International Airport.

**American Airlines** (code AA; ☎ 1-800 433 73 00; www.aa.com) Hub: Chicago O'Hare Airport.

**British Airways** (code BA; ☎ 08708 509850; www.britishairways.com) Hub: Heathrow Airport, London.

**Cyprus Airways** (www.cyprusairways.com; code CY; ☎ 2236 5700) Hub: Lanarca International Airport.

**Delta Air Lines** (code DL; ☎ 1 800 221 12 12; www.delta.com) Hub: John F Kennedy Airport, New York.

**EasyJet** (code U2; ☎ 08706 000000; www.easyjet.com) Hub: Stansted Airport, London.

**Emirates** (code EK; ☎ 4 2244435; www.emirates.com) Hub: Dubai International Airport.

**Iberia** (code IBE; ☎ 902 40 15 01; www.iberia.com) Hub: Madrid Barajas Airport.

**KLM** (code KL; ☎ 08705 074074; www.klm.com) Hub: Schiphol, Amsterdam.

**Lufthansa** (code LH; ☎ 018 0583 8426; www.lufthansa.com) Hub: Frankfurt Airport.

**Olympic Airways** (www.olympic-airways.gr; code OA; ☎ 2109 267 251) Hub: Eleftherios Venizelos International Airport, Athens.

**Qantas** (code QF; ☎ 02 9691 3636; www.qantas.com.au) Hub: Kingsford Smith International Airport, Sydney.

**Royal Air Maroc** (www.royalairmaroc.com; code AT; ☎ 446444) Hub: Mohammed V Airport, Casablanca.

**Ryanair** (code FR; ☎ 0871 246 00 00; www.ryanair.com) Hub: Stansted Airport, London.

**Singapore Airlines** (code SQ; ☎ 622 388 88; www.singaporeair.com) Hub: Changi Airport.

**South African Airways** (code SA; ☎ 0861 35 97 22; www.saa.co.za) Hub: Cape Town International Airport.

**Virgin Express** (code TV; ☎ 070 35 36 37; www.virgin-express.com) Hub: Brussels National Airport.

## Tickets

Increasingly, the Internet is becoming the place to find cheap tickets. Many airlines offer excellent on-line deals (in fact, many no-frills carriers do the bulk of their business on line), while the profusion of travel agencies with websites means that you can easily shop around for the best fares. There are also hundreds of on-line agencies. Names to look out for include www.travelocity.co.uk, www.cheaptickets.com, www.travelcuts.com and www.expedia.com.

Cheap flights are often advertised by obscure agencies. Most of these firms are honest, but there are some rogue outfits around. Paying by credit card generally offers protection, as most card issuers provide refunds if you can prove you didn't get what you paid for. Similar protection can be obtained by buying a ticket from a bonded agency, such as those covered by the Air Travel Organisers' Licensing (ATOL) scheme in the UK. Agencies that accept cash only should hand over tickets straight away and not tell you to 'come back tomorrow'. After you've made a booking or paid your deposit, call the airline and confirm that the booking has been made.

If you purchase a ticket and later want to make changes to your route or get a refund, you need to contact the original travel agency. Airlines issue refunds only to the purchaser of a ticket – usually the travel agency that bought the ticket on your behalf.

Full-time students and people aged under 26 (under 30 in some countries) have access to discounted fares. You have to show a document proving your date of birth, such as a valid International Student Identity Card (ISIC) or an International Youth Travel Card (IYTC) when buying your ticket and boarding the plane. See the www.istc.org for more information.

## Africa

Nairobi and Johannesburg are probably the best places in East and South Africa to buy tickets to Europe. If you're going to Morocco, you're better off getting a cheap return ticket to Paris, London, Madrid or Amsterdam and getting a cheap flight from there. Some West African countries, such as Burkina Faso, Gambia and Morocco, offer cheap charter flights to France.

Following is a list of reliable agencies.
**Flight Centre** (www.flightcentre.co.za) Discount flight agency present in South Africa and Kenya.
**Rennies Travel** (www.renniestravel.com) Widespread in southern Africa.
**STA Travel** (www.statravel.co.za) Offices across southern Africa.

## Asia

Hong Kong, Singapore and Bangkok are the discount air fare capitals of Asia. STA Travel is common and easily found in the area with branches in **Bangkok** ( ☎ 02 236 0262; www.statravel.co.th), **Singapore** ( ☎ 6737 7188; www.statravel.com.sg), **Hong Kong** ( ☎ 2736 1618; www.statravel.com.hk), and **Japan** ( ☎ 03 5391 2922; www.statravel.co.jp, in Japanese).

In Japan, another option in Japan is **No 1 Travel** ( ☎ 03 3205 6073; www.no1-travel.com). In Hong Kong try **Four Seas Tours** ( ☎ 2200 7760; www.fourseastravel.com/english).

In India, **STIC Travels** (www.stictravel.com) has offices in dozens of Indian cities, including **Delhi** ( ☎ 11 2335 7468) and **Mumbai** ( ☎ 22 2218 1431). Another Indian agency is **Transway International** (www.transwayinternational.com).

## Australia

Cheap flights from Australia to Europe generally travel via southeast Asian capital cities, involving stopovers at Kuala Lumpur, Singapore or Bangkok. If a long stopover between connections is necessary, transit accommodation is sometimes included in the price of the ticket.

Quite a few travel offices specialise in discount air tickets. Saturday's travel sections in the *Sydney Morning Herald* and Melbourne's *Age* have many ads offering cheap fares to Europe. With Australia's large and well-organised ethnic populations, it pays to check special deals in the ethnic press. For on-line bookings, try www.travel.com.au.

Return flights from Sydney to Paris start from about A$1700/1830 low season/high

season. All have frequent promotional fares so it pays to check daily newspapers. Flights from Perth are a couple of hundred dollars cheaper than from east-coast cities.

Following is a list of the major ticket agencies in Oz.
**Flight Centre** ( ☎ 13 16 00; www.flightcentre.com.au) Offices throughout Australia.
**STA** ( ☎ 1300 733 035; www.statravel.com.au) Call to find your nearest branch.

## Canada

Canadian discount air ticket sellers are also known as consolidators and their air fares tend to be about 10% higher than those sold in the USA. The *Globe & Mail, Toronto Star, Montreal Gazette* and *Vancouver Sun* carry travel agencies' ads and are a good place to look for cheap fares. **Airhitch** ( ☎ 212 864 2000; www.airhitch.org) has stand-by fares to/from Toronto, Montreal and Vancouver.

**Travel Cuts** ( ☎ 800 667 2887; www.travelcuts.com) is Canada's national student travel agency. For online bookings try www.expedia.ca and www.travelocity.ca.

## Continental Europe

Though London is the travel discount capital of Europe, there are several other cities in the region where you'll find a wide range of good deals. **STA Travel** (www.statravel.com) has offices throughout Europe as does **Nouvelles Frontières** (www.nouvelles-frontieres.com).

### BELGIUM
**Acotra Student Travel Agency** ( ☎ 02 512 8607; www.acotra.com)
**WATS Reizen** ( ☎ 03 233 7020)

### FRANCE
**Anyway** ( ☎ 08 92 89 38 92; www.anyway.fr)
**Lastminute** ( ☎ 08 92 70 50 00; www.lastminute.fr)
**Nouvelles Frontières** ( ☎ 08 25 00 07 47; www.nouvelles-frontieres.fr)
**OTU Voyages** (www.otu.fr) Specialises in student and youth travellers.
**Voyageurs du Monde** ( ☎ 01 40 15 11 15; www.vdm.com)

### GERMANY
**Expedia** (www.expedia.de)
**Just Travel** ( ☎ 089 747 3330; www.justtravel.de)
**Lastminute** ( ☎ 018 0528 4366; www.lastminute.de)
**STA Travel** ( ☎ 018 0545 6422; www.statravel.de) For travellers under the age of 26.

TRANSPORT IN
MEDITERRANEAN EUROPE

## ITALY
**CTS Viaggi** ( ☎ 064 62 04 31; www.cts.it) Specialises in student and youth travel.

## SPAIN
**Barcelo Viajes** ( ☎ 902 11 62 26; www.barceloviajes.com)
**Nouvelles Frontières** ( ☎ 902 17 09 79; www.nouvelles-frontieres.com)

## SWITZERLAND
**SSR Voyages** ( ☎ 01 297 11 11; www.ssr.ch) Student, youth and budget fares.

## THE NETHERLANDS
**Airfair** ( ☎ 0206 20 51 21; www.airfair.nl)
**NBBS Reizen** ( ☎ 0206 24 09 89) Amsterdam's official student travel agency.
**Malibu Travel** ( ☎ 0206 26 32 30)

## New Zealand
The website www.travel.co.nz is recommended for on-line bookings. Also check the New Zealand *Herald* for ads. The cheapest fares to Europe are routed through Asia. Count on paying around NZ$1950/1850 high/low season for a return ticket from Auckland to Paris.

Ever-dependable operators to check out are in the following list:
**Flight Centre** ( ☎ 0800 243 544; www.flightcentre.co.nz)
**STA Travel** ( ☎ 0508 782 872; www.statravel.co.nz)

## The UK & Ireland
Discount air travel is big business in London. Advertisements for many travel agencies appear in the travel pages of the weekend broadsheet newspapers, in *Time Out*, the *Evening Standard* and in the free magazine *TNT* – often available outside the main train and underground stations.

No-frills airlines **Ryanair** (www.ryanair.com) and **EasyJet** (www.easyjet.com) have cheap flights to Mediterranean countries. Fares from the UK to Madrid, Nice or Rome are highly competitive so you should be able to get a one-way flight for around UK£55.

Charter flights can work out as a cheaper alternative to scheduled flights, especially if you do not qualify for the under-26 and student discounts. See your travel agency for possibilities.

Following is a list of recommended travel agencies.
**Bridge the World** ( ☎ 08704 447474; www.b-t-w.co.uk)
**Flight Centre** ( ☎ 08708 908099; www.flightcentre.co.uk)

**Flightbookers** ( ☎ 08700 107000; www.ebookers.com)
**North-South Travel** ( ☎ 01245 608291; www.north southtravel.co.uk) North-South Travel donate part of their profits to projects in the developing world.
**Quest Travel** ( ☎ 08704 423542; www.questtravel.com)
**STA Travel** ( ☎ 08701 600599; www.statravel.co.uk) For travellers under the age of 26.
**Trailfinders** ( ☎ 02079 381234; www.trailfinders.co.uk)
**Travel Bag** ( ☎ 08708 901456; www.travelbag.co.uk)

## The USA
Discount travel agents in the USA are known as consolidators (although you won't see a sign on the door saying 'Consolidator'). San Francisco is heralded as the ticket consolidator capital of America, although some good deals can be found in Los Angeles, New York and most other big cities.

**STA Travel** ( ☎ 800 781 4040; www.statravel.com) is in all major American cities. The *New York Times*, *LA Times*, *Chicago Tribune* and *San Francisco Chronicle* all have weekly travel sections in which you'll find any number of travel agencies' ads. It's good for travellers under the age of 26.

Flight options across the North Atlantic, the world's busiest long-haul air corridor, are plentiful. You should be able to fly from New York to Paris and back in low season for about US$450; the high season US$815. Equivalent fares from the west coast will cost you roughly US$100 to US$300 higher.

On a stand-by basis, one-way fares can work out to be a cheap deal. New York-based **Airhitch** ( ☎ 212 864 2000; www.airhitch.org) can get you to/from Europe for US$165/199/233 each way from the east coast/Midwest/west coast, plus taxes and a processing fee of US$29.

The following agencies are recommended for on-line bookings. Note that priceline is an on-line auction service.
**www.cheaptickets.com**
**www.expedia.com**
**www.itn.net**
**www.lowestfare.com**
**www.orbitz.com**
**www.sta.com**
**www.priceline.com**

## LAND
### Bicycle
See Bicycle in Getting Around, p725.

## Border Crossings

The main overland routes into Mediterranean Europe enter the region from the north and east. Countries bordering the region to the north include Switzerland, Austria and Hungary; and to the east, Romania, Bulgaria and Macedonia. France is bordered on the east by Switzerland, Germany, Luxembourg and Belgium. To the east of Turkey lies Iran and to the south Syria and Iraq. Morocco is bordered by Algeria.

For details of overland transport into individual countries, refer to the Transport sections in the individual country chapters.

## Car & Motorcycle

See the Car & Motorcycle section in Getting Around, p725.

## Africa

Discounting the complicated Middle East route, going to/from Africa involves a Mediterranean ferry crossing (p722). Due to unrest in Africa, the most feasible overland routes through the continent have all but closed down.

## Asia

The overland trail to/from Asia passes through Iran, Afghanistan and Pakistan. At the time of writing the extremely difficult situation in Afghanistan and Pakistan made this route inadvisable. However, if you're determined to try it, check with your own foreign office for the latest situation on the ground.

It is possible to get to Mediterranean Europe by rail from central and eastern Asia, although count on travel taking around eight days.

## Continental Europe

**Eurolines** (www.eurolines.com) is a consortium of European coach companies that operate across Europe and have offices in all major European cities. Their multilingual website gives extensive details of prices, passes and travel agencies where you can book tickets. See p725 for bus passes that take in most of Mediterranean Europe.

Another option is **Busabout** ( ☎ 02079 501661; www.busabout.com), which covers at least 60 European cities and towns from its London base. This company offers passes of varying duration allowing you to use their 'hop-on, hop-off' bus network in Western and Central Europe. For details see p724.

## The UK

The Channel Tunnel allows for a land link between Britain and France. Eurostar is the passenger train service that travels between London and Paris; cars travel on the Eurotunnel vehicle service.

The Eurostar service takes three hours to get from London's Waterloo station to the Gare du Nord in Paris. Passport and customs checks take place on board or very cursorily on arrival. There's quite a wide range of tickets; the cheapest are nonrefundable and have restrictions on departure times and length of stay. There are often special deals on offer, so either phone **Eurostar** (UK ☎ 08705 186186, France ☎ 08 92 35 35 39; www.eurostar.com) or check out the website. Tickets are available direct from Eurostar, some travel agencies, Waterloo station, many of the UK's mainline train stations, and from **Rail Europe** ( ☎ 0990 300003; www.rail europe.com), which also sells other European rail tickets. Expect to pay anything from UK£50 to UK£300 for a one-way full fare. You can take a bicycle on Eurostar as part of your luggage only if it is in a bike bag.

The **Eurotunnel vehicle service** (UK ☎ 08705 353535; France ☎ 03 21 00 61 00; www.eurotunnel.com) travels between terminals in Folkestone and Calais. You can just drive into the terminal, buy your ticket and get on the next train but you'll almost always make a saving by buying your ticket in advance. Fares vary with the time of year and day, ranging from UK£150 in February and March to UK£250 in July and August. Bicycles can be taken on only two trains per day and they must be booked 24 hours in advance (use the phone numbers listed earlier). Trains run 24 hours a day, every day of the year, with up to four departures an hour. It takes about an hour from loading to unloading.

There are also train-boat-train combos in association with **Hoverspeed** (UK ☎ 08702 408070; France ☎ 00 800 1211 1211; www.hoverspeed .co.uk) and others from London's Charing Cross station to Paris' Gare du Nord that take between seven and eight hours. Check the website for details.

## SEA

Dividing the UK from Continental Europe, the English Channel is an extremely busy shipping lane. There are several ferry routes that cross the Channel and numerous ferry companies that use them. The resulting service is comprehensive but complicated. The same ferry company can have many different prices for the same route depending on the time of day or year, the validity of the ticket or, if you're driving, the length of your vehicle. Vehicle tickets include the driver and often up to five passengers free. It is worth planning (and booking) ahead where possible as there may be special reductions on off-peak crossings and advance-purchase tickets. On Channel routes, apart from one-day or short-term excursion returns, there is little price advantage in buying a return ticket as opposed to two singles.

The shortest cross-Channel routes between England and France (Dover to Calais or Folkestone to Boulogne) are also the busiest, though there is now competition from the Channel Tunnel. **P&O Stena Line** (www.posl .com) handles the short-hop Dover–Calais routes. **P&O Portsmouth** (www.poportsmouth .com) and **Brittany Ferries** (www.brittany-ferries.com) also sail direct between England and northern Spain, taking 24 to 35 hours. The French line **Seafrance** (www.seafrance.com) operates across the Channel. You can book ferry tickets on line (often at a discount).

Rail-pass holders are entitled to discounts or free travel on some lines and most ferry companies give discounts to disabled drivers.

In the Mediterranean itself there are many ferries between Africa and Europe. Major routes include Spain to Morocco, Italy to Tunisia, France to Morocco and France to Tunisia. There are also ferries between Greece and Israel. Ferries are often filled to capacity in summer, so book well in advance if you're taking a vehicle across. Ferry companies operating on these routes include **Ferrimaroc** (www.ferrimaroc.com) and **SNCM** (www.sncm.fr).

Go online at www.aferry.to for information on European ferry timetables, routes, ports and prices.

To cross the Atlantic by sea you have two alternatives. You can either pay for an expensive passage on a cruise ship or hop on a freighter as a paying passenger. Freighters are far more numerous than cruise ships and there are many more routes from which to choose.

Passenger freighters typically carry five to 12 passengers (more than 12 would require a doctor to be on board) and take about seven to 10 days to cross the Atlantic. Expect to pay about US$1350; vehicles can often be included for an additional fee. You can always get an idea of what's available from www.freighter-travel.com.

# GETTING AROUND

Travel within the European Union (EU) countries of the Mediterranean region, whether by air, rail or car is relatively hassle-free thanks to the Schengen Agreement, a European treaty that abolished border controls between signed-up states (Iceland, Norway and all EU member countries except for the UK and Ireland). You shouldn't have too many problems getting around the non-EU countries either, thanks to a comprehensive transport network and good relations between neighbouring countries. The main exception to this is travelling between the Republic of Cyprus (p554) and North Cyprus (p563) where there is a strict border control policy.

Ensure that you have a valid passport and check any visa requirements before travelling (p714).

## AIR

Travelling within Mediterranean Europe is straightforward and need not always be expensive. Throughout the year there are regular scheduled regional services and in summer the number of charter flights increases dramatically.

Athens is a good place to purchase budget tickets in Mediterranean Europe. From here, you can also get good deals to elsewhere in the region. Depending on the season, there are cheap charter flights from Paris and Madrid to Morocco. For more information, see the Transport sections in the individual country chapters.

Getting between airports and city centres is generally not a problem in Mediterranean Europe. The public transport network system usually works well, albeit slowly on occasion; otherwise you'll often find a ready supply of waiting taxis.

## Airlines in Mediterranean Europe

Air travel lacks the flexibility of ground transport and tends to be expensive for short European hops. However, with the abundance of no-frills airlines (such as Ryanair and EasyJet) in the region, it's always worth checking ticket prices and comparing them with the alternatives, especially if you're looking to go from one end of the region to the other. In some cases you might find that you can fly cheaply from A to B and save yourself days cramped in a sticky coach seat. For further details on Ryanair and EasyJet see the Airports & Airlines section of Getting There & Away, p717.

## Air Passes

If you're planning on flying a lot in Europe and you know where you want to go and when, check out the various air passes that many airlines offer. These are often only available to non-Europeans who must purchase them in conjunction with a long-haul international return ticket. Typically, they involve the purchase of flight coupons (usually around US$100 to US$150 each) for travel between a number of European destinations. Airlines involved in such schemes include Aer Lingus, Air Canada, Air New Zealand, American Airlines, British Airways, British Midland, Iberia, Lufthansa, Singapore Airlines, Thai Airways International and United Airlines.

For further information on airlines serving Mediterranean Europe see p717.

Following are two examples of passes:

**Europe by Air Pass** (www.europebyair.com) Valid for one-way travel between up to 100 cities in 30 European countries, coupons cost US$99 per flight. Coupons are only available for purchase in the USA but are valid for one year and are very flexible – you can decide where and when to use them as you go along.

**Star Alliance European Air Pass** (www.star-alliance .com) When you buy a round-trip international ticket with a Star Alliance operator (Air Canada, Air New Zealand, British Midland, Lufthansa, Singapore Airlines, Thai Airways International, United Airlines) you can buy a minimum of three and a maximum of 10 coupons (US$90 to US$115 each) for one-way flights between 41 European countries. You must book the date of the first coupon flight.

# BICYCLE

Cycling is big in Spain, France and Italy, less so in the eastern Mediterranean countries. There are no special road rules for cyclists, although you'd do well to equip yourself with a helmet and lights.

A basic bike kit might include spare brake and gear cables, spanners, Allen keys, spare spokes of the correct length and strong adhesive tape. Take a good lock and make absolutely sure you always use it when you leave your bike unattended.

If you want to bring your own bicycle to Mediterranean Europe, you should be able to carry it on the plane relatively easily. You can either take it apart and pack everything in a bike bag or box, or simply wheel it to the check-in desk, where it should be treated as a piece of luggage. Check all this with the airline well in advance, preferably before you pay for your ticket.

Within Mediterranean Europe, bicycles are usually transported as luggage on slower trains, subject to a small supplementary fee. Fast trains can rarely accommodate bikes: they might need to be sent as registered luggage and may end up on a different train from the one you take. This is often the case in France and Spain.

The European **Bike Express** (UK ☎ 01642 251 440; www.bike-express.co.uk) is a coach service where cyclists can travel with their bicycles. It runs in the summer from northeast England to France, Italy and Spain, with pickup and drop-off points en route. Return fares range from UK£164 to UK£184.

Further advice is available in the UK from the **Cyclists' Touring Club** ( ☎ 08708 730060; www.ctc.org.uk). They can help you plan your own bike tour or organise guided tours for you. Membership costs UK£31 for adults, UK£11 for those under 25 and UK£19 for those over 65.

For more information on cycling see p701 and the individual country chapters.

## Hire & Purchase

It is not as easy to hire bikes in some parts of Mediterranean Europe as it is elsewhere on the Continent, but where available they are hired out on an hourly, half-day, daily or weekly basis. Local tourist offices will carry information on rental outlets. Occasionally you can drop the bicycle off at a different location so you don't have to double back on yourself. See the individual country chapters for more details.

There are plenty of places to buy bikes in Mediterranean Europe (shops sell new and second-hand bicycles or you can always check local papers for private vendors) but you'll need a specialist shop for a bike capable of withstanding touring. The British Cyclists' Touring Club (see previously) can provide its members with a leaflet about purchasing bikes. European prices are quite high (you can expect to pay between €100 and €200 for a new bike), but non-Europeans can often claim back VAT on the purchase.

## BOAT

There are many ferries across the Mediterranean between southern Europe and North Africa, including routes between France and Spain and Morocco. There are also ferries between Italy and Greece (for example, Brindisi to Corfu, Igoumenitsa and Patra), and between Greece and Israel. Ferries are often filled to capacity in summer, so book well in advance if you're taking a vehicle across.

The Greek islands are connected to the mainland and each other by a spider's web of routes; Lonely Planet's *Greek Islands* guidebook gives details. Ferries also link other islands in the Mediterranean with mainland ports: Corsica with Nice; Sicily and Sardinia with Genoa, Livorno, Naples and Reggio di Calabria in Italy and with Marseille in France; Malta with Sicily, Salerno, Reggio di Calabria and Genoa. See the relevant country chapters in this book for more details.

Following is a list of the main ferry companies (and their principal routes) operating in the region:

**Adriatica di Navigazione** (Italy ☎ 041 781 611; www.adriatica.it) Between Ancona or Bari in Italy and Durrës in Albania.

**Blue Star Ferries** (Italy ☎ 0831 514 484; www.bluestar ferry.com) Between Brindisi in Italy and Patra, Corfu and Igoumenitsa in Greece.

**Corsica Ferries** (Corsica ☎ 04 9550 7882; www.corsica férries.com) Between Ajaccio in Corsica and Toulon or Nice in France.

**Grimaldi Ferries** (Italy ☎ 06 4208 3567; Spain ☎ 93 318 5350; www.grimaldi-ferries.com) Between Barcelona or Valencia in Spain and Civitavecchia or Salerno in Italy.

**Hellenic Mediterranean** (Italy ☎ 0831 528 531; www.ferries.gr) Between Brindisi in Italy and Patra, Corfu and Igoumenitsa in Greece.

**Jadrolinija** (Croatia ☎ 51 211 444; www.jadrolinija.hr) Between Ancona or Bari in Italy and Split or Dubrovnik in Croatia.

**SNAV** (Italy ☎ 021 207 6116; www.snav.it) Between Ancona in Italy and Split in Croatia.

**SNCM** (France ☎ 0836 672 100; www.sncm.fr) Between Marseille in France and Tunis in Tunisia.

**Tirrenia Navigazione** (Italy ☎ 081 3172 999; www .gruppotirrenia.it) Between Genoa or Naples in Italy and Sardinia or Sicily.

**Trasmediterrànea** (Spain ☎ 902 45 46 45; www .trasmediterranea.es) Between Barcelona, Valencia, Palma de Mallorca, Maò and Ibiza City.

**Turkish Maritime Lines** (Turkey ☎ 464 8864; www .tdi.com.tr/eng/index_ing.shtml) Between Çesme in Turkey and Brindisi or Ancona in Italy.

## BUS

Mediterranean Europe is well connected by road. Long-haul coaches are the cheapest way to travel around the region although they are neither particularly quick nor comfortable. Generally speaking you'll do better travelling by train, especially if you've got a rail pass.

Europe's biggest network of international buses is **Eurolines** (www.eurolines.com), a consortium of European coach operators serving destinations throughout the region. They have representatives in all major European cities, including **Paris** ( ☎ 08 92 89 90 91), **Rome** ( ☎ 064 40 40 09) and **Barcelona** ( ☎ 93 490 40 00). Eurolines return tickets are valid for six months, and those under 26 and seniors over 60 pay less.

In conjunction with Eurolines, the Moroccan national bus line, **CTM** (Compagnie des Transports Marocains; www.ctm.co.ma) operates buses from Spain, France and northern Italy to most of the large Moroccan towns.

London-based **Busabout** ( ☎ 02079 501661; www.busabout.com) operates buses that complete set circuits round Europe, stopping at all the major cities. You can start at any city, get unlimited travel per sector, and can 'hop-on, hop-off' at any scheduled stop, then resume with a later bus. Buses are often oversubscribed, so book each sector to avoid being stranded. Departures are every two days from April to October, or May to September for Spain and Portugal. The circuits cover the western countries of Mediterranean Europe, and you can pay to 'add-on' Greece, Morocco and Croatia.

See the individual country chapters for more information about long-distance buses.

## Bus Passes

Bus passes make sense if you want to cover a lot of ground as cheaply as possible. However, to get your money's worth you're going to be spending an awful lot of time squeezed into a coach seat.

Eurolines offers passes, which are cheaper but not as extensive or as flexible as rail passes. They cover 46 European cities with France, Spain and Italy well served in the Mediterranean region. Most of the trips must be international; a few internal journeys are possible between major cities. The cost of a 15-day pass is adult/26 years and under €220/185 low season, €285/240 high season; a 30-day pass adult/26 years and under €310/250 low season, €345/215 high season.

Busabout's **Unlimited Pass** (two-week pass adult/ 26 yrs & under €359/329) allows unlimited travel within the given time period. Passes are also available for four, six, eight weeks, and one month. The **Flexipass** (8 days in 1 month flexipass adult/26 yrs & under €419/379, 20 days in 4 months flexipass adult/26 yrs & under €879/789) allows you to select travel days within the given time period.

## Costs

Bus travel is generally the cheapest form of getting around in Mediterranean Europe. As a rough guide a one-way ticket from Rome to Istanbul costs €116, from Bologna to Casablanca €145, and from Barcelona to Granada €55.

## Reservations

Booking a seat in advance is not obligatory but if you know you want to travel on a given date it makes sense to do so. This is particularly true in summer when buses plying the major international routes are often packed to the gills. Turn up on the day and you risk not getting a seat. Wherever possible, book in advance.

## CAR & MOTORCYCLE

Travelling with your own wheels brings its own pleasures and pains. For many the increased flexibility more than makes up for the congestion, exuberant driving habits and appalling parking problems that drivers have to face in the big cities. However, head away from the major centres and you'll enjoy some stunning roads and magnificent scenery.

Two wheels are often easier to navigate than four. Most of Mediterranean Europe is made for motorcycle touring, with good-quality winding roads and an active motorcycling scene. But bear in mind that the weather is not always reliable so make sure your wet weather gear is up to scratch.

Many of the region's motorways are toll roads. You can generally pay with either cash or credit card and in some cases you can avoid the queues altogether by purchasing a prepaid card. See the individual chapters for details.

On ferries, motorcyclists can sometimes be squeezed in without a reservation although booking ahead is advisable in peak travelling periods. Take note of local customs about parking motorcycles on pavements. Though this is illegal in many countries, the police usually turn a blind eye so long as the vehicle doesn't obstruct pedestrians.

If you're thinking of touring Europe on a motorcycle try contacting the **British Motorcyclists Federation** ( ☎ 0116 254 8818; www .bmf.co.uk) for help and advice. An excellent source of information can also be found at www.horizonsunlimited.com for those who are interested in more adventurous biking activities.

For general motoring information go online at www.ideamerge.com/europa.

### Automobile Associations

Information is available from automobile associations in individual countries. Following is a list of national associations.
**Automobile & Touring Club of Greece** (Greece ☎ 748 8800)
**Automobile Club de France** (France ☎ 01 43 12 43 12)
**Automobile Club d'Italia** (Italy ☎ 06 911 15)
**Automòvel Club de Portugal** (Portugal ☎ 01 56 39 81)
**Cyprus Automobile Association** (Cyprus ☎ 2231 3233)
**Hrvatski Autoklub** (Croatia ☎ 41 45 44 33)
**Real Automòvil Club de España** (Spain ☎ 902 40 45 45)
**Türkiye Turing ve Otomobil Kurumu** (Turkey ☎ 0212 282 8140)

### Bring Your Own Vehicle

To bring a private vehicle into the Mediterranean countries you'll need to have proof of ownership of the vehicle (Vehicle Registration Document for British-registered cars) plus a valid driving licence (see following) and insurance (opposite).

You'll also need to make sure you have certain equipment aboard. Vehicles crossing an international border should display a sticker showing its country of registration. A warning triangle, to be used in the event of breakdown, is compulsory almost everywhere. Recommended accessories are a first-aid kit (compulsory in Greece and several other Mediterranean European countries), a spare bulb kit (compulsory in Croatia and Spain) and a fire extinguisher (compulsory in Greece and Turkey). In the UK, contact the **RAC** ( ☎ 0800 550 005; www.rac .co.uk) or **AA** ( ☎ 08705 500600; www.theaa.com) for more information.

## Driving Licence

An EU driving licence is valid for driving throughout Europe. However, old-style green UK licences are no good for Spain or Italy. If you have one of these or any other type of licence you'll need an International Driving Permit (IDP). Valid for 12 months, they can be obtained for a small fee from your national automobile association – take along a passport photo and your driving licence. An IDP is basically a multilingual translation of the vehicle class and personal details noted on your own licence. When driving you should always carry your home licence together with the IDP, as it's not valid on its own.

An IDP is recommended for Turkey even if you have a European licence. Always check what type of driving licence is required in your chosen destination before you head off.

## Fuel & Spare Parts

European fuel prices vary considerably (reckon on €0.85 for unleaded and €0.72 for diesel in Spain, €1.09 and €0.90 in Italy) and often bear little relation to the general cost of living. You can make significant savings by filling up in the cheapest countries (for example, Spain and Greece). Motoring organisations such as the RAC can supply more details.

Unleaded petrol is now widely available throughout Europe (except in Morocco) and is usually cheaper than super (premium grade, the only 'leaded' choice in some countries). Diesel is cheaper still.

You should have no great problems getting spare parts, although you'll need to exercise common sense. If you're stuck in the middle of nowhere on a Sunday afternoon, chances are that you'll be in for a bit of a wait.

## Hire

The international firms will give you reliable service and a good standard of vehicle. Usually you'll have the option of returning the car to a different outlet at the end of the rental period. Book ahead for the lowest rates. If you walk into an office and ask for a car on the spot, you'll pay over the odds, even allowing for special weekend deals. Conversely, if you book before you leave home you'll get the best deals. Fly-drive combinations and other programmes are also worth looking into.

The major international rental agencies with offices throughout the region are **Avis** (www.avis.com), **Budget** (www.budget.com), **Europcar** (www.europcar.com) and **Hertz** (www.hertz .com). Check the websites for the latest rates and to find the office most convenient for you.

Renting through a broker can often cut the costs. In the UK, **Holiday Autos** ( ☎ 08704 004477; www.holidayautos.com) has lower rates and offices or representatives in over 20 countries. **Autos Abroad** ( ☎ 02072 876000; www .autosabroad.com) also offers very competitive prices. Across the water in the USA, try **Kemwel Holiday Autos** ( ☎ 877 820 0668; www .kemwel.com).

If you want to rent a car and haven't booked, note that national or local firms can often undercut the big international companies.

No matter where, or what you rent, it is imperative to understand exactly what is included in your rental agreement (collision waiver, unlimited mileage etc). Make sure you are covered with an adequate insurance policy which, if you're going to cross any borders, is valid from one country to the next.

The minimum rental age is usually 21 or even 23 and you'll almost certainly need a credit card. Note that prices at airport rental offices are usually higher than at branches in city centres.

Motorcycle and moped rental is common in some countries, such as Italy, Spain, Greece and the south of France. See the individual country chapters for further details.

If you're planning on staying in the region for a long period, leasing can work out cheaper than renting. The **Renault Eurodrive** (www.renault-eurodrive.com) scheme provides new cars for non-EU residents for a period of between 17 and 170 days. Under this arrangement, a Renault Clio 1.4 for 17 days, for example, costs US$839 (if picked up and dropped off in France), including insurance and roadside assistance. Check out the options before leaving home. In the US, Kemwel Holiday Autos arranges European leasing deals.

## Insurance

Third-party motor insurance is compulsory in Europe. Most UK motor insurance policies automatically provide this for EU countries. Get your insurer to issue an International Insurance Certificate, known as a Green Card (which may cost extra), an internationally recognised proof of insurance, and check that it lists all the countries you intend to visit. (If driving in Turkey make sure that it covers both the European and Asian parts.) You'll need the Green Card in the event of an accident outside the country where the vehicle is insured.

Also ask your insurer for a European Accident Statement form, which can simplify things if you have an accident. The European Accident Statement, also known in France as the *Constat Amiable,* is available from your insurance company and is carboned so that each party at an accident can record identical information for insurance purposes. The **Association of British Insurers** ( ☎ 02076 003333; www.abi.org.uk) can give more information. Never sign statements you can't read or understand – insist on a translation and only sign it if it's acceptable.

For non-EU countries make sure you check the requirements with your insurer. For further advice and information contact the Association of British Insurers or check its website.

Taking out a European motoring assistance policy is a good investment, such as the AA Five Star Service or the RAC European Motoring Assistance. With the RAC, you can expect to pay about UK£60 for 14 days cover (there's a 10% discount for association members). Non-Europeans might find it cheaper to arrange international coverage with their national motoring organisation before leaving home. Ask your motoring organisation for details about free services offered by affiliated organisations around Mediterranean Europe.

## Purchase

Buying a car in Mediterranean Europe is often not worth the hassle. For one thing, it's technically illegal for someone who is not an EU resident to buy a car in an EU country. You can, however, get round this is by asking a friend who is a resident to buy one for you.

If you want a left-hand drive vehicle (as is the norm in most of Continental Europe) and can afford to buy a new vehicle, prices are usually reasonable in Greece and France. Paperwork can be tricky wherever you buy, and many countries have compulsory roadworthiness checks on older vehicles.

## Road Conditions

Conditions and types of roads vary across Europe, but it is possible to make some generalisations. The fastest routes are four- or six-lane dual carriageways or motorways (ie two or three lanes either side) – called *autoroutes, autostrade* etc. Some of these roads incur tolls, which are often quite hefty (for example, in France, Paris to Lyon costs about €30, Calais to Marseille €57; in Italy Milan to Venice €11.25, Rome to Naples €8.50; and in Spain, Seville to Cádiz costs about €8.25), but there's usually an alternative route you can take. Motorways and other primary routes are generally in good condition.

Road surfaces on minor routes are not so reliable in some countries (Morocco, Malta and Greece) although normally they will be more than adequate. These roads are narrower and progress is generally much slower.

## Road Rules

Motoring organisations can supply members with country-by-country information on the motoring regulations, or they may produce motoring guidebooks for general sale. The RAC can provide you with comprehensive destination-specific notes.

With the exception of Malta and Cyprus, driving in Mediterranean Europe is on the right-hand side of the road. Vehicles brought over from the UK or Ireland, where driving is on the left, should have their headlights adjusted to avoid blinding oncoming traffic at night (a simple solution on older headlight lenses is to cover up a triangular section of the lens with tape). Priority is usually given to traffic approaching from the right in countries that drive on the right-hand side.

Take care with speed limits, as they vary from country to country. You may be surprised at the apparent disregard for traffic regulations in some places (particularly in Italy and Greece), but as a visitor it is always best to be cautious. Random police checks are common in some countries and many driving infringements are subject to on-the-spot fines. If you're clobbered with a fine, always ask for a receipt.

Drink-driving laws are particularly strict. The blood-alcohol concentration (BAC) limit when driving is generally between 0.05% and 0.08%. See the Transport sections in the individual country chapters for more details on traffic rules.

The wearing of crash helmets for rider and passenger is compulsory everywhere in Mediterranean Europe. It's recommended that motorcyclists use their headlights during the day.

---

**CHAOS RULES**

The one rule to which many Mediterranean drivers seem to adhere is the law of chaos. Vehicles are randomly propelled forward, sometimes in a linear motion, sometimes sideways, but always noisily and generally at some speed. Rules do, however, exist, and are followed. The only problem is that they don't usually correspond to those of the Highway Code and are known only to locals.

The rules you should follow are simple: worry about what's in front of you and not what's coming up your rear end, don't take blasts of the horn personally, make sure you stop at red lights, and don't ever dither. Hesitation merely confuses locals, who respect nothing unless its done with confidence.

---

## HITCHING

Hitching is never entirely safe in any country, and we don't recommend it. Travellers who decide to hitch should understand that they are taking a small but potentially serious risk. People who do choose to hitch will be safer if they travel in pairs and let someone know where they plan to go.

A man and woman travelling together is probably the best combination for hitching. Two or more men must expect some delays; two women together will make good time and should be relatively safe. A woman hitching on her own is taking a big risk, particularly in some parts of southern Europe, Turkey and North Africa.

Don't try to hitch from city centres: take public transport to suburban exit routes. Hitching is usually illegal on motorways – stand on the slip roads, or approach drivers at petrol stations and truck stops. Look presentable and cheerful and make a cardboard sign indicating your intended destination in the local language. Never hitch where drivers can't stop in good time or without causing an obstruction. At dusk, give up and think about finding somewhere to stay. If your itinerary includes a ferry crossing (from mainland France to Corsica, for instance), it's worth trying to score a ride before the ferry rather than after, since vehicle tickets sometimes include all passengers free of charge.

It is sometimes possible to arrange a lift in advance: scan student notice boards in colleges, or contact car-sharing agencies. Such agencies are particularly popular in France – look out for Allostop Provoya and Auto-Partage.

Travellers considering hitching as a way of getting around Mediterranean Europe may find these websites useful: for general facts, destination-based information and rideshare options visit www.bugeurope.com; while www.hitchhikers.org connects hitchhikers and drivers worldwide.

## LOCAL TRANSPORT

The local transport network in Mediterranean Europe is fairly comprehensive, covering most parts of the region. Clearly in some of the more isolated places, especially in rural or mountainous areas, services may be irregular and slow but you'll often find a bus that passes sooner or later.

In many places you have to buy your ticket before you get on the bus/boat/train etc. Once on board you then have to validate it if the driver hasn't already checked it. It's often tempting not to do this – many locals don't appear to – but by not validating your ticket you run the risk of a fine if you're caught.

If you're planning on using public transport a lot, it's worth investigating the daily, weekly and monthly passes available.

### Boat

The diffusion of islands in the Mediterranean means that in many countries local ferry services are an integral part of the local transport network. Perhaps the most obvious example is Venice where *vaporetti* (canal ferries) ply the city waterways as buses do the roads in most other places. In some places ferry tickets cover other means of public transport, in others they don't.

### Bus

Domestic buses provide a viable alternative to the rail network in most countries. Compared to trains they are slightly cheaper and, with the exception of Spain, Portugal and Greece, somewhat slower. Buses tend to be best for shorter hops such as getting around cities and reaching remote villages. They are often the only option in mountainous regions where railway tracks don't exist. Advance reservations are rarely necessary. On many city buses you usually buy your ticket in advance from a kiosk or machine and validate it upon boarding.

See the country chapters and individual city sections for more details on local bus/transport.

### Metro

All the major capital cities (Athens, Paris, Madrid and Rome) have a metro system. It's often quicker to travel underground, as you avoid the traffic congestion on the roads but it can be horrifically hot and crowded, especially in summer rush hours.

### Taxi

Taxis in Europe are metered and rates are uniformly high. There might also be supplements (depending on the country) for things such as luggage, time of day, the location from which you boarded and for extra passengers. Good bus, rail and underground (metro) railway networks make the taking of taxis all but unnecessary, but if you need one in a hurry they can usually be found idling near train stations or outside big hotels. Lower fares make taxis more viable in some countries, such as Spain, Greece and Portugal.

### TOURS

There are any number of companies offering tours of the Mediterranean region. Check newspaper travel pages or consult your travel agent. See p723 for information about bicycle tours and p714 for further information about services offered by the following list of tour operators.

**CBT Travel** (USA ☎ 800 736 2453; www.cbttours.com)
**Contiki** (UK ☎ 02082 906777; www.contiki.com)
**Ramblers Holidays** (UK ☎ 01707 331133; www.ramblersholidays.co.uk)
**Saga Holidays** (www.sagaholidays.com) For people aged over 50.
**Top Deck** (UK ☎ 02073 704555; www.topdecktravel.co.uk)

### TRAIN

Trains are a popular way of getting around: they are comfortable, frequent and generally punctual. The *Thomas Cook European Timetable* is the trainophile's bible, giving a complete listing of train schedules, supplements and reservations information. It is updated monthly and available from **Thomas Cook** (www.thomascook.com) outlets in the UK, and in the USA from **Forsyth Travel Library** (☎ 800 367 7984; www.forsyth.com). In Australia, look for it in the bigger bookstores, which can order copies if they don't have any in stock.

If you're planning to do a lot of train travel in one or a handful of countries – Spain and Portugal, say – it might be worthwhile getting the national timetables published by the state railways. The **European Planning & Rail Guide** (US toll-free ☎ 877 441 2387; www.budgeteuropetravel.com) is an informative annual magazine, primarily geared towards North American travellers. To get a copy, call the toll-free number or check the website.

The speed of your journey depends on the type of train you take. Fast trains include the TGV in France, Spain's AVE and, in Italy, the Eurostar. Supplements can apply on fast trains, and it is often obligatory to make seat reservations at peak times and on certain lines.

Overnight trains will usually offer a choice of couchette or sleeper. Couchette bunks are comfortable enough, if lacking in privacy. There are four per compartment in 1st class or six in 2nd class. Sleepers are the most comfortable option, offering beds for one or two passengers in 1st class, and two or three passengers in 2nd class. Charges vary depending upon the journey, but they are a lot more expensive than couchettes.

Most long-distance trains have a dining (buffet) car or an attendant who wheels a snack trolley through the carriages. If possible, buy your food before travelling as onboard prices tend to be high.

You should be quite safe travelling on most trains in Mediterranean Europe but it pays to be security conscious nonetheless. Keep an eye on your luggage at all times (especially when stopping at stations) and lock the compartment doors at night.

Note that European trains sometimes split en route in order to service two destinations, so even if you're on the right train, make sure you're also in the correct carriage.

### Classes

On most trains there are 1st- and 2nd-class carriages. As a rough guide, a 1st-class ticket generally costs just under double the price of a 2nd-class ticket. In most 1st-class carriages you can expect fewer seats than in 2nd class and more luggage space.

### Costs

In some countries, such as Spain, Portugal and (to some extent) Italy, fares are reasonably low; in others, European rail passes make travel more affordable. How much you pay for a journey depends on numerous factors: the type of train you take (high-speed trains are obviously more expensive), whether you travel 1st or 2nd class, the period (August or January, in some cases it's also cheaper to travel overnight rather than during the day), and whether or not you have a seat or a couchette/sleeper.

As a general guide, a train ticket from Madrid to Barcelona costs €60; from Paris to Marseille €84; and from Rome to Brindisi €44.

### Reservations

Although it's generally not essential to reserve a place on most European trains, it's often a good idea, especially in peak periods and on popular routes. Bookings can be made when you buy your ticket for a small, usually nonrefundable, fee. On certain trains it is, however, obligatory. These include all high-speed trains, long-distance trains in Spain and Portugal and long-distance trains between July and September. You'll also need to reserve sleeping accommodation on overnight trains.

Supplements and reservation costs are not covered by most rail passes.

### Train Passes

There are many European rail passes, covering any number of travelling combinations, but passes are only worth buying if you plan to do a reasonable amount of cross-country travelling within a short space of time. When weighing up options, consider the cost of other cheap ticket deals, including advance purchase deals, one-off promotions or special circular-route tickets. Normal international tickets are valid for two months, and you can make as many stops as you like en route; make your intentions known when purchasing, and inform the train conductor how far you're going before they punch your ticket.

The cost of rail passes varies between different outlets, so shop around before committing yourself. Once purchased, take care of your pass, as it cannot be replaced or refunded if lost or stolen. European passes can be used to get reductions on certain ferries. Pass-holders must always carry their passport for identification purposes.

**Rail Europe** (www.raileurope.com) is an excellent source of information on all sorts of rail passes. You can also purchase online. Rail passes can be bought online or at travel agents.

#### EURAIL

These passes can only be bought by residents of non-European countries, and are supposed to be purchased before arriving in Europe. However, Eurail passes can be purchased within Europe, so long as your passport proves you've been there for less than six months, but the outlets where you can do this are limited, and the passes will be more expensive than buying them outside Europe. If you've lived in Europe for more than six months, you are eligible for an Inter-Rail pass, which is a better buy.

Eurail passes are valid for unlimited travel on national railways and some private lines in the Mediterranean countries of France (including Monaco), Greece, Italy, Portugal and Spain. Eurail is also valid on some ferries between Italy and Greece.

Eurail passes offer reasonable value to those aged under 26. A **Youthpass** (15-/21-day pass US$414/534, 1-/2-/3-month pass US$664/938/1160) gives unlimited 2nd-class travel within a choice of five validity periods. The **Youth Flexipass** (10-/15-day pass US$488/642), also for 2nd class, is valid for freely chosen days within a two-month period. Overnight journeys commencing after 7pm count as the following day's travel. The traveller must fill out (in ink) the relevant box in the calendar before starting a day's travel.

For those aged over 26, the equivalent passes provide 1st-class travel including the standard **Eurail pass** (15-/21-day pass US$588/762, 1-/2-/3-month pass US$950/1340/1655) and **Flexipass** (10-/15-day travel within 2 months US$694/914). Two to five people travelling together can get a 'saver' version of either pass, saving about 15%. Eurail passes for children are also available.

Further information is available at www.eurail.com.

Unless you're planning on covering huge distances by train, `travelling virtually every day, it will make more sense to go with the Eurail Selectpass.

### EURAIL SELECTPASS
Previously the Europass, the **Eurail Selectpass** (per 4 countries 5-day pass adult/youth US$398/279, 10-day pass US$584/409) is also for non-Europeans. You can choose to travel between three, four or five countries (from a choice of 17) for five, six, eight or 10 days within a two-month period. Youth (aged under 26) and adult (solo, or two sharing) versions are available, and purchasing requirements and sales outlets are as for Eurail passes.

### EURO DOMINO
There is a Euro Domino pass for each of the countries covered in the Inter-Rail pass and they're worth considering if you're hom-

ing in on a particular region. They're sold in Europe to European residents. Adults (travelling 1st or 2nd class) and youths under 26 can opt for three to eight days' valid travel within one month. Examples of adult/youth prices for eight days in 2nd class are UK£203/152 in Italy, UK£195/163 in Spain and UK£70/52 in Turkey.

### INTER-RAIL
Inter-Rail passes are available to European residents of at least six months' standing (passport identification is required). Terms and conditions vary slightly from country to country, but in the country of origin there is a discount of around 50% on normal fares. The Inter-Rail pass is split into zones, covering most of the Mediterranean countries: Zone D includes Croatia; E includes France; F includes Spain, Portugal and Morocco; G includes Italy, Greece, Turkey, Slovenia and Italy–Greece ferries.

The standard Inter-Rail pass is for people under 26, although travellers over 26 can get the Inter-Rail 26+ version. The price for any one zone (valid for 16 days) is €210/299 for a standard/26+ pass. Passes for two zones (valid for 22 days) cost standard/26+ €289/409 and the all-zone global pass (valid for one month) will set you back standard/26+ €399/559.

### NATIONAL RAIL PASSES
If you intend to travel extensively within one country, check which national rail passes are available. These can sometimes save you a lot of money; details can be found in the Transport sections in the individual country chapters. You need to plan ahead if you intend to take this option, as some passes can only be purchased prior to arrival in the country concerned. Some national flexipasses, near-equivalents to the Euro Domino passes mentioned previously, are only available to non-Europeans.

### SENIOR RAILCARD
Seniors (those over 60) can get a Rail Europe Senior Card, which is valid for a year for trips that cross at least one border and that entitles you to 30% off standard fares. In the UK the card costs UK£5 but you must already have a **Senior Railcard** ( ☎ 0845 7484 950; www.senior-railcard.co.uk; UK£18).

# Health

## CONTENTS

---

> **WARNING**
>
> Codeine, which is commonly found in headache preparations, is banned in Greece; check labels carefully or risk prosecution. There are strict rules applying to the importation of medicines into Greece, so obtain a certificate from your doctor that outlines any medication you may have to carry into the country with you.

---

## BEFORE YOU GO

Prevention is the key to staying healthy while abroad. Some predeparture planning will save trouble later. See your dentist before a long trip, carry a spare pair of contact lenses and glasses, and take your optical prescription with you. Bring medications in their original, clearly labelled, containers. A signed and dated letter from your physician describing your medical conditions and medications, including generic names, is also a good idea. If carrying syringes or needles, be sure to have a physician's letter documenting their medical necessity.

### INSURANCE

If you're an EU citizen, an E111 form (which is gradually being replaced by the European Health Insurance Card), available from health centres or, in the UK, post offices, covers you for most medical care. E111 will not cover you for nonemergencies or emergency repatriation. Citizens from other countries should find out if there is a reciprocal arrangement for free medical care between their country and the country visited. If you do need health insurance, strongly consider a policy that covers you for the worst possible scenario, such as

an accident requiring an emergency flight home. Find out in advance if your insurance plan will make payments directly to providers or reimburse you later for overseas health expenditures. The former option is generally preferable, as it doesn't require you to pay out of pocket in a foreign country.

### RECOMMENDED VACCINATIONS

No jabs are necessary for Mediterranean Europe. However, the WHO recommends that all travellers, regardless of their destination, should be covered for diphtheria, tetanus, measles, mumps, rubella and polio. Since most vaccines don't produce immunity until at least two weeks after they're given, visit a physician at least six weeks before departure.

### INTERNET RESOURCES

The WHO's publication *International Travel and Health* is revised annually and available on line at www.who.int/ith/. Other useful websites include www.mdtravelhealth.com (travel health recommendations for every country; updated daily), www.fitfortravel. scot.nhs.uk (general travel advice for the layperson), www.ageconcern.org.uk (advice on travel for the elderly) and www.mariestopes.org.uk (information on women's health and contraception).

### FURTHER READING

'Health Advice for Travellers' (which is currently called the 'T6' leaflet) is an annually updated leaflet by the Department of Health in the UK available free from post offices. It contains some general information, legally required and recommended vaccines for different countries, reciprocal health agreements and an E111 application form. Lonely Planet's *Travel with Children* includes advice on travel health for younger children.

# IN TRANSIT

## DEEP VEIN THROMBOSIS (DVT)

Blood clots may form in the legs during plane flights, chiefly because of prolonged immobility. The chief symptom of DVT is swelling or pain of the foot, ankle, or calf, usually but not always on just one side. When a blood clot travels to the lungs, it may cause chest pain and breathing difficulties. Travellers with any of these symptoms should immediately seek medical attention.

To prevent the development of DVT on long flights you should walk about the cabin, contract the leg muscles while sitting, drink plenty of fluids and avoid alcohol and tobacco.

# IN MEDITERRANEAN EUROPE

## AVAILABILITY OF HEALTH CARE

Good health care is readily available and for minor illnesses pharmacists can give valuable advice and sell over-the-counter medication. They can also advise when more specialised help is required and point you in the right direction. The standard of dental care is usually good, however it is sensible to have a dental check-up before a long trip.

## TRAVELLER'S DIARRHOEA

If you develop diarrhoea, be sure to drink plenty of fluids, preferably an oral rehydration solution such as Dioralyte. If diarrhoea is bloody, persists for more than 72 hours or is accompanied by a fever, shaking, chills or severe abdominal pain, you should seek medical attention.

## ENVIRONMENTAL HAZARDS
### Altitude Sickness

Experiencing a lack of oxygen at high altitudes (over 2500m) affects most people to some extent. Symptoms of Acute Mountain Sickness (AMS) usually develop during the first 24 hours at altitude but may be delayed up to three weeks. Mild symptoms include headache, lethargy, dizziness, difficulty sleeping and loss of appetite. AMS may become more severe without warning and can be fatal. Severe symptoms include breathlessness, a dry, irritative cough (which may progress to the production of pink, frothy sputum), severe headache, lack of coordination and balance, confusion, irrational behaviour, vomiting, drowsiness and unconsciousness. There is no hard-and-fast rule as to what is too high: AMS has been fatal at 3000m, although 3500m to 4500m is the usual range.

Treat mild symptoms by resting at the same altitude until recovery, usually a day or two. Paracetamol or aspirin can be taken for headaches. If symptoms persist or become worse, however, *immediate descent is necessary*; even 500m can help. Drug treatments should never be used to avoid descent or to enable further ascent.

Diamox (acetazolamide) reduces the headache of AMS and helps the body acclimatise to the lack of oxygen. It is only available on prescription and those who are allergic to the sulphonamide antibiotics may also be allergic to Diamox.

In the UK, fact sheets are available from British Mountaineering Council, 177–79 Burton Road, Manchester, M20 2BB.

### Heat Exhaustion & Heat Stroke

Heat exhaustion occurs following excessive fluid loss with inadequate replacement of fluids and salt. Symptoms include headache, dizziness and tiredness. Dehydration is already happening by the time you feel thirsty – aim to drink sufficient water to produce pale, diluted urine. Replace lost fluids by drinking water and/or fruit juice, and cool the body with cold water and fans. Treat salt loss with salty fluids such as soup or add a little more table salt to foods than usual.

Heat stroke is much more serious, resulting in irrational and hyperactive behaviour and eventually loss of consciousness and death. Rapid cooling by spraying the body with water and fanning is ideal. Emergency fluid and electrolyte replacement by intravenous drip is recommended.

HEALTH

**HEALTH**

## Insect Bites & Stings

Mosquitoes are found in most parts of Mediterranean Europe. They may not carry malaria but can cause irritation and infected bites. Use a DEET-based insect repellent.

Sand flies are found around the Mediterranean beaches. They usually cause only a nasty itchy bite but can carry a rare skin disorder called cutaneous leishmaniasis.

## Water

Tap water is generally safe to drink in Mediterranean Europe but in Eastern European countries, such as Croatia, it's best to stick to bottled water or purified water. Do not drink water from rivers or lakes as it may contain bacteria or viruses that can cause diarrhoea or vomiting.

## TRAVELLING WITH CHILDREN

All travellers with children should know how to treat minor ailments and when to seek medical treatment. Make sure the children are up to date with routine vaccinations, and discuss possible travel vaccines well before departure as some vaccines are not suitable for children aged under one year.

## WOMEN'S HEALTH

Travelling during pregnancy is usually possible but always seek a medical check-up before planning your trip. The most risky times for travel are during the first 12 weeks of pregnancy and after 30 weeks.

## SEXUAL HEALTH

Condoms are widely available in Mediterranean Europe, however emergency contraception may not be, so take the necessary precautions. The **International Planned Parent Federation** (www.ippf.org) can advise about the availability of contraception in different countries.

When buying condoms, look for a European CE mark, which means they have been rigorously tested. Remember to also keep them in a cool, dry place so that they don't crack and perish.

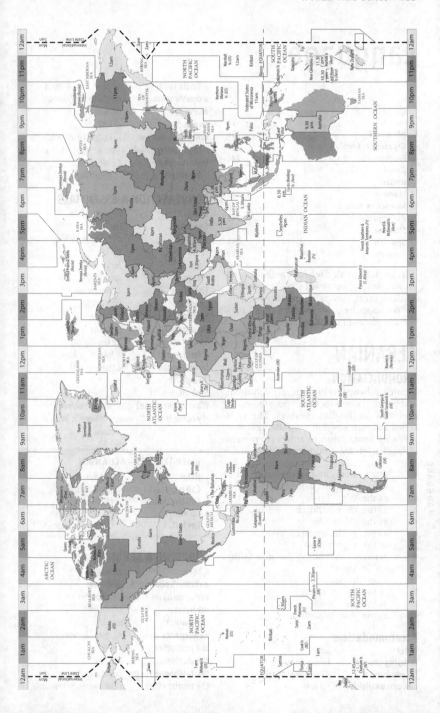

# Language

## CONTENTS

This language guide has basic vocabulary and pronunciation tips to help you get around Mediterranean Europe. For more coverage of the languages here, see Lonely Planet's *Europe* and *Eastern Europe* phrasebooks.

# ALBANIAN

## PRONUNCIATION

Written Albanian is phonetically consistent and pronunciation shouldn't pose too many problems for English speakers. The rr is trilled and each vowel in a diphthong is pronounced. Some Albanian letters are present in English but are pronounced differently.

| | |
|---|---|
| ë | often silent; at the beginning of a word it's as the 'a' in 'ago' |
| c | as the 'ts' in 'bits' |
| ç | as the 'ch' in 'church' |
| dh | as the 'th' in 'this' |
| gj | as the 'gy' in 'hogyard' |
| j | as the 'y' in 'yellow' |
| q | between 'ch' and 'ky', similar to the 'cu' in 'cure' |
| th | as in 'thistle' |
| x | as the 'dz' in 'adze' |
| xh | as the 'j' in 'jewel' |
| zh | as the 's' in 'pleasure' |

## Accommodation

| | |
|---|---|
| hotel | hotel |
| camping ground | kamp pushimi |
| Do you have any rooms available? | A keni ndonjë dhomë të lirë? |
| a single room | një dhomë më një krevat |
| a double room | një dhomë më dy krevat |
| one night | një natë |
| two nights | dy natë |
| How much is it per night/per person? | Sa kushton për një natë/ për një njeri? |
| Does it include breakfast? | A e përfshin edhe mëngjesin? |

## CONVERSATION & ESSENTIALS

| | |
|---|---|
| Hello. | Tungjatjeta/Allo. |
| Goodbye. | Lamtumirë. |
| | Mirupafshim. (informal) |
| Yes. | Po. |
| No. | Jo. |
| Please. | Ju lutem. |
| Thank you. | Ju falem nderit. |
| That's fine. | Eshtë e mirë. |
| You're welcome. | S'ka përse. |
| Excuse me. | Me falni. |
| Sorry. (excuse me, forgive me) | Më vjen keq. or Më falni, ju lutem. |
| Do you speak English? | A flisni anglisht? |
| How much is it? | Sa kushton? |
| What's your name? | Si quheni ju lutem? |
| My name is ... | Unë quhem ... or Mua më quajnë ... |

---

### EMERGENCIES – ALBANIAN

| | |
|---|---|
| Help! | Ndihmë! |
| Call a doctor! | Thirrni doktorin! |
| Call the police! | Thirrni policinë! |
| Go away! | Zhduku!/Largohuni! |
| I'm lost. | Kam humbur rrugë. |

---

## SHOPPING & SERVICES

| | |
|---|---|
| a bank | një bankë |
| a chemist/pharmacy | një farmaci |
| the ... embassy | ... ambasadën |
| my hotel | hotelin tim |
| the market | pazarin |
| newsagency | agjensia e lajmeve |
| the post office | postën |
| the stationers | kartoleri |
| the telephone centre | centralin telefonik |
| the tourist office | zyrën e informimeve turistike |

SIGNS – ALBANIAN

| | |
|---|---|
| **Hyrje** | Entrance |
| **Dalje** | Exit |
| **Informim** | Information |
| **Hapur** | Open |
| **Mbyllur** | Closed |
| **Policia** | Police |
| **Stacioni i Policisë** | Police Station |
| **E Ndaluar** | Prohibited |
| **Nevojtorja** | Toilets |
| Burra | Men |
| Gra | Women |

| | |
|---|---|
| **What time does it open/close?** | *Në ç'ore hapet/mbyllet* |

## TIME, DAYS & NUMBERS

| | |
|---|---|
| **What time is it?** | *Sa është ora?* |
| **today** | *sot* |
| **tomorrow** | *nesër* |
| **yesterday** | *dje* |
| **in the morning** | *në mëngjes* |
| **in the afternoon** | *pas dreke* |
| **Monday** | *e hënë* |
| **Tuesday** | *e martë* |
| **Wednesday** | *e mërkurë* |
| **Thursday** | *e ënjte* |
| **Friday** | *e premte* |
| **Saturday** | *e shtunë* |
| **Sunday** | *e diel* |
| **1** | *një* |
| **2** | *dy* |
| **3** | *tre* |
| **4** | *katër* |
| **5** | *pesë* |
| **6** | *gjashtë* |
| **7** | *shtatë* |
| **8** | *tetë* |
| **9** | *nëntë* |
| **10** | *dhjetë* |
| **100** | *njëqind* |
| **1000** | *njëmijë* |

## TRANSPORT

| | |
|---|---|
| **What time does the ... leave/arrive?** | *Në ç'orë niset/arrin ...?* |
| boat | *barka/lundra* |
| bus | *autobusi* |
| tram | *tramvaji* |
| train | *treni* |

| | |
|---|---|
| **I'd like ...** | *Dëshiroj ...* |
| a one-way ticket | *një biletë vajtje* |
| a return ticket | *një biletë kthimi* |
| **1st class** | *klas i parë* |
| **2nd class** | *klas i dytë* |
| **timetable** | *orar* |
| **bus stop** | *stacion autobusi* |

### Directions

| | |
|---|---|
| **Where is ...?** | *Ku është ...?* |
| **Go straight ahead.** | *Shko drejt.* |
| **Turn left.** | *Kthehu majtas.* |
| **Turn right.** | *Kthehu djathtas.* |
| **near** | *afër* |
| **far** | *larg* |

# CROATIAN & SERBIAN

## PRONUNCIATION

The writing systems of Croatian and Serbian are phonetically consistent: every letter is pronounced and its sound will not vary from word to word. With regard to the position of stress, only one rule can be given: the last syllable of a word is never stressed. In most cases the accent falls on the first vowel in the word.

Serbian uses the Cyrillic alphabet, so it's worth familiarising yourself with it. Croatian uses a Roman alphabet and many letters are pronounced as in English.

The principal difference between Serbian and Croatian is in the pronunciation of the vowel 'e' in certain words. A long 'e' in Serbian becomes 'ije' in Croatian (eg *reka*, *rijeka* (river), and a short 'e' in Serbian becomes 'je' in Croatian, eg *pesma*, *pjesma* (song). Sometimes, however, the vowel 'e' is the same in both languages, as in *selo* (village). There are also a number of variations in vocabulary between the two languages. We haven't marked these differences in pronunciation in the following words and phrases, but you'll still be understood, even with a Croatian lilt to your language. Where significant differences occur, we've included both, with Croatian marked (C) and Serbian marked (S).

## ACCOMMODATION

**hotel**

| | |
|---|---|
| *hotel* | хотел |

**guesthouse**

| | |
|---|---|
| *privatno prenočište* | приватно преноћиште |

## SERBIAN & CROATIAN ALPHABETS

| Cyrillic | Roman | English Pronunciation |
|----------|-------|----------------------|
| А а | A a | as in 'rather' |
| Б б | B b | as in 'be' |
| В в | V v | as in 'vodka' |
| Г г | G g | as in 'go' |
| Д д | D d | as in 'do' |
| Ђ ђ | Đ đ | as the `du' in British 'duty' |
| Е е | E e | as in 'there' |
| Ж ж | Ž ž | as the 's' in 'pleasure' |
| З з | Z z | as in 'zero' |
| И и | I i | as in 'machine' |
| Ј ј | J j | as the 'y' in 'young' |
| К к | K k | as in 'keg' |
| Л л | L l | as in 'let' |
| Љ љ | Lj lj | as the 'lli' in 'million' |
| М м | M m | as in 'map' |
| Н н | N n | as in 'no' |
| Њ њ | Nj nj | as the 'ny' in 'canyon' |
| О о | O o | as the 'aw' in 'shawl' |
| П п | P p | as in 'pop' |
| Р р | R r | as in 'rock' |
| С с | S s | as in 'safe' |
| Т т | T t | as in 'to' |
| Ћ ћ | Ć ć | as the 'tu' in 'future' |
| У у | U u | as in 'plume' |
| Ф ф | F f | as in 'fat' |
| Х х | H h | as in 'hot' |
| Ц ц | C c | as the 'ts' in 'cats' |
| Ч ч | Č č | as the 'ch' in 'chop' |
| Џ џ | Dž dž | as the 'j' in 'judge' |
| Ш ш | Š š | as the 'sh' in 'shoe' |

**youth hostel**
*omladinsko prenoćište*    омладинско преноћиште
**camping ground**
*kamping*    кампинг

**Do you have any rooms available?**
*Imate li slobodne sobe?*
Имате ли слободне собе?
**How much is it per night/per person?**
*Koliko košta za jednu noć/po osobi?*
Колико кошта за једну ноћ/по особи?
**Does it include breakfast?**
*Dali je u cijenu uključen i doručak?*
Дали је у цену укључен и доручак?

**I'd like ...**
*Želim ...*    Желим ...
**a single room**
*sobu sa jednim krevetom*
собу са једним креветом

**a double room**
*sobu sa duplim krevetom*
собу са дуплим креветом

## CONVERSATION & ESSENTIALS
**Hello.**
*Zdravo.*    Здраво.
**Goodbye.**
*Doviđenja.*    Довиђења.
**Yes.**
*Da.*    Да.
**No.**
*Ne.*    Не.
**Please.**
*Molim.*    Молим.
**Thank you.**
*Hvala.*    Хвала.
**That's fine/You're welcome.**
*U redu je/*    У реду је/
*Nema na čemu.*    Нема на чему.
**Excuse me.**
*Oprostite.*    Опростите.
**Sorry. (excuse me, forgive me)**
*Pardon.*    Пардон.
**Do you speak English?**
*Govorite li engleski?*    Говорите ли енглески?
**How much is it ...?**
*Koliko košta ...?*    Колико кошта  ...?
**What's your name?**
*Kako se zovete?*    Како се зовете?
**My name is ...**
*Zovem se ...*    Зовем се ...

## EMERGENCIES – CROATIAN & SERBIAN

**Help!**
*Upomoć!*    Упомоћ!
**Call a doctor!**
*Pozovite (lekara (S)/*    Позовите лекара!
*liječnika! (C)*
**Call the police!**
*Pozovite miliciju (S)/*    Позовите милицију!
*policiju (C)!*
**Go away!**
*Idite!*    Идите!
**I'm lost.**
*Izgubljen/Izgubljena*    Изгубио сам се/
*sam. (m/f)*    Изгубила сам се. (m/f)

## SHOPPING & SERVICES
**I'm looking for ...**
*Tražim ...*    Тражим ...
**a bank**
*banku*    банку

**the ... embassy**

*... ambasadu*     ... амбасаду

**my hotel**

*moj hotel*     мој хотел

**the market**

*pijacu*     пијацу

**the post office**

*poštu*     пошту

**the telephone centre**

*telefonsku centralu*     телефонску централу

**the tourist office**

*turistički biro*     туристички биро

## TIME, DAYS & NUMBERS

**What time is it?**

*Koliko je sati?*     Колико је сати?

**today**

*danas*     данас

**tomorrow**

*sutra*     сутра

**yesterday**

*jučer*     јуче

**in the morning**

*ujutro*     ујутро

**in the afternoon**

*popodne*     поподне

**Monday**

*ponedjeljak*     понедељак

**Tuesday**

*utorak*     уторак

**Wednesday**

*srijeda*     среда

**Thursday**

*četvrtak*     четвртак

**Friday**

*petak*     петак

**Saturday**

*subota*     субота

**Sunday**

*nedjelja*     недеља

| 1 | *jedan* | један |
| 2 | *dva* | два |
| 3 | *tri* | три |
| 4 | *četiri* | четири |
| 5 | *pet* | пет |
| 6 | *šest* | шест |
| 7 | *sedam* | седам |
| 8 | *osam* | осам |
| 9 | *devet* | девет |
| 10 | *deset* | десет |
| 100 | *sto* | сто |
| 1000 | *hiljadu/tisuću* (S/C) | хиљаду |

## TRANSPORT

**What time does the ... leave/arrive?**

*Kada ... polazi/dolazi?*

Када ... полази/долази?

**boat**

*brod*     брод

**bus (city)**

*autobus (gradski)*     аутобус (градски)

**bus (intercity)**

*autobus (međugradski)*     аутобус (међуградски)

**train**

*voz* (S)/*vlak* (C)     воз

**tram**

*tramvaj*     трамвај

---

### SIGNS – CROATIAN & SERBIAN

| | |
|---|---|
| **Ulaz/Izlaz** | Entrance/Exit |
| **Улаз/Излаз** | |
| **Informacije** | Information |
| **Информације** | |
| **Otvoreno/Zatvoreno** | Open/Closed |
| **Отворено/Затворено** | |
| **Slobodne Sobe** | Rooms Available |
| **Слободне Собе** | |
| **Nema Slobodne Sobe** | Full/No Vacancies |
| **Нема Слободне Собе** | |
| **Milicija** (S)/**Policija** (C) | Police |
| **Милиција** | |
| **Stanica Milicije** (S)/ | Police Station |
| **Policije** (C) | |
| **Станица Милиције** | |
| **Zabranjeno** | Prohibited |
| **Забрањено** | |
| **Toaleti** (S)/**Zahodi** (C) | Toilets |
| **Тоалети** | |

---

**one-way ticket**

*kartu u jednom pravcu*     карту у једном правцу

**return ticket**

*povratnu kartu*     повратну карту

**1st class**

*prvu klasu*     прву класу

**2nd class**

*drugu klasu*     другу класу

## Directions

**Where is the bus/tram stop?**

*Gdje je autobuska/tramvajska stanica* (S)/*postaja* (C)?

Где је аутобуска/трамвајска станица?

**Can you show me (on the map)?**

*Možete li mi pokazati (na karti)?*

Можете ли ми показати (на карти)?

**Go straight ahead.**
*Idite pravo naprijed.*
Идите право напред.

**Turn left.**
*Skrenite lijevo.*   Скрените лево.

**Turn right.**
*Skrenite desno.*   Скрените десно.

**near**
*blizu*   близу

**far**
*daleko*   далеко

# FRENCH

## PRONUNCIATION

Most letters in French are pronounced more or less the same as their English counterparts. Here are a few that may cause confusion:

**j**   as the 's' in 'leisure', eg *jour* (day)
**c**   before **e** and **i**, as the 's' in 'sit'; before **a**, **o** and **u** it's pronounced as English 'k'. When undescored with a 'cedilla' (**ç**) it's always pronounced as the 's' in 'sit'.
**r**   pronounced from the back of the throat while constricting the muscles to restrict the flow of air
**n, m**   where a syllable ends in a single **n** or **m**, these letters are not pronounced, but the vowel is given a nasal pronunciation

## ACCOMMODATION

**a hotel**   *un hôtel*
**a guest house**   *une pension (de famille)*
**a youth hostel**   *une auberge de jeunesse*

**Do you have any**   *Est-ce que vous avez des*
**rooms available?**   *chambres libres?*
**for one person**   *pour une personne*
**for two people**   *pour deux personnes*
**How much is it per**   *Quel est le prix par*
**night/per person?**   *nuit/par personne?*
**Is breakfast**   *Est-ce que le petit déjeuner*
**included?**   *est compris?*

## CONVERSATION & ESSENTIALS

**Hello.**   *Bonjour.*
**Goodbye.**   *Au revoir.*
**Yes.**   *Oui.*
**No.**   *Non.*
**Please.**   *S'il vous plaît.*

**Thank you.**   *Merci.*
**That's fine, you're**   *Je vous en prie.*
**welcome.**
**Excuse me.**   *Excusez-moi.*
(to get someone's attention)
**Sorry.** (apology)   *Pardon.*
**Do you speak**   *Parlez-vous anglais?*
**English?**
**How much is it?**   *C'est combien?*
**What's your name?**   *Comment vous appelez-vous?*
**My name is ...**   *Je m'appelle ...*

---

**EMERGENCIES – FRENCH**

**Help!**   *Au secours!*
**Call a doctor!**   *Appelez un médecin!*
**Call the police!**   *Appelez la police!*
**Leave me alone!**   *Fichez-moi la paix!*
**I'm lost.**   *Je me suis égaré/e.*

---

## SHOPPING & SERVICES

**I'm looking for ...**   *Je cherche ...*
**a bank**   *une banque*
**a chemist/pharmacy**   *une pharmacie*
**the ... embassy**   *l'ambassade de ...*
**the market**   *le marché*
**a newsagency**   *un agence de presse*
**the post office**   *le bureau de poste*
**a public telephone**   *une cabine téléphonique*
**a stationers**   *une papeterie*
**the tourist office**   *l'office de tourisme/*
   *le syndicat d'initiative*

**What time does it**   *Quelle est l'heure de*
**open/close?**   *ouverture/fermeture?*

## TIME, DAYS & NUMBERS

**What time is it?**   *Quelle heure est-il?*
**today**   *aujourd'hui*
**tomorrow**   *demain*
**yesterday**   *hier*
**in the morning**   *du matin*
**in the afternoon**   *de l'après-midi*

**Monday**   *lundi*
**Tuesday**   *mardi*
**Wednesday**   *mercredi*
**Thursday**   *jeudi*
**Friday**   *vendredi*
**Saturday**   *samedi*
**Sunday**   *dimanche*

**1**   *un*
**2**   *deux*

## SIGNS – FRENCH

| | |
|---|---|
| **Entrée** | Entrance |
| **Sortie** | Exit |
| **Renseignements** | Information |
| **Ouvert** | Open |
| **Fermée** | Closed |
| **Chambres Libres** | Rooms Available |
| **Complet** | Full/No Vacancies |
| **(Commissariat de) Police** | Police Station |
| **Interdit** | Prohibited |
| **Toilettes, WC** | Toilets |
| **Hommes** | Men |
| **Femmes** | Women |

| | |
|---|---|
| **3** | *trois* |
| **4** | *quatre* |
| **5** | *cinq* |
| **6** | *six* |
| **7** | *sept* |
| **8** | *huit* |
| **9** | *neuf* |
| **10** | *dix* |
| **10** | *dix* |
| **11** | *onze* |
| **12** | *douze* |
| **1000** | *mille* |

## TRANSPORT

| | |
|---|---|
| **When does (the next) ... leave/arrive?** | *À quelle heure part/arrive (le prochain) ...?* |
| **boat** | *bateau* |
| **bus (city)** | *bus* |
| **bus (intercity)** | *car* |
| **tram** | *tramway* |
| **train** | *train* |

| | |
|---|---|
| **the bus stop** | *l'arrêt d'autobus* |
| **the ferry terminal** | *la gare maritime* |
| **the left luggage office** | *la consigne* |
| **a timetable** | *un horaire* |
| **the train station** | *la gare* |
| **the tram stop** | *l'arrêt de tramway* |

| | |
|---|---|
| **I'd like a ... ticket.** | *Je voudrais un billet ...* |
| **one-way** | *aller simple* |
| **return** | *aller retour* |
| **1st-class** | *de première classe* |
| **2nd-class** | *de deuxième classe* |

| | |
|---|---|
| **I'd like to hire a car/ bicycle.** | *Je voudrais louer une voiture/ un vélo.* |

## Directions

| | |
|---|---|
| **Where is ...?** | *Où est ...?* |
| **Go straight ahead.** | *Continuez tout droit.* |
| **Turn left.** | *Tournez à gauche.* |
| **Turn right.** | *Tournez à droite.* |
| **near** | *proche* |
| **far** | *loin* |

# GREEK

## PRONUNCIATION

Pronunciation of Greek letters is shown in the Greek alphabet table on p742. The pronunciation guides use the closest-sounding English letter to represent the Greek.

### Letter Combinations

Some pairs of vowels are pronounced separately if the first has an acute accent (eg **ά**), or the second has a dieresis (eg **ï**). All Greek words of two or more syllables have an acute accent which indicates where the stress falls.

| | | |
|---|---|---|
| **ει, οι** | **i** | as in 'marine' |
| **αι** | **e** | as in 'bet' |
| **ου** | **u** | as in 'plume' |
| **μπ** | **b** | as in 'be' |
| | **mb** | as in 'amber' (or as the 'mp' in 'ample') |
| **ντ** | **d** | as in 'do' |
| | **nd** | as in 'bend' (or as the 'nt' in 'sent') |
| **γκ** | **g** | as in 'go' |
| **γγ** | **ng** | as the 'ng' in 'angle' |
| **γξ** | **ks** | as in 'yaks' |
| **τζ** | **dz** | as the 'ds' in 'suds' |

The suffix of some Greek words depends on the gender of the speaker, eg *asthmatikos* (m) and *asthmatikya* (f), or *epileptikos* (m) and *epileptikya* (f).

## ACCOMMODATION

| | |
|---|---|
| **a hotel** | *ena xenothohio* |
| **a youth hostel** | *enas xenonas neoitos* |
| **a camp site** | *ena kamping* |

| | |
|---|---|
| **I'd like a ... room.** | *thelo ena dhomatio ...* |
| **single** | *ya ena atomo* |
| **double** | *ya dhio atoma* |

| | |
|---|---|
| **How much is it ...?** | *poso kostizi ...?* |
| **per person** | *ya ena atomo* |
| **per night** | *ya ena vradhi* |

**LANGUAGE**

## THE GREEK ALPHABET

| Greek | English | Pronunciation |
|---|---|---|
| A α | a | as in 'father' |
| B β | v | as in 'vine' |
| Γ γ | gh, y | like a rough 'g', or as the 'y' in 'yes' |
| Δ δ | dh | as the 'th' in 'then' |
| E ε | e | as in 'egg' |
| Z ζ | z | as in 'zoo' |
| H η | i | as in 'marine' |
| Θ θ | th | as in 'throw' |
| I ι | i | as in 'marine' |
| K κ | k | as in 'kite' |
| Λ λ | l | as in 'leg' |
| M μ | m | as in 'man' |
| N ν | n | as in 'net' |
| Ξ ξ | x | as the 'ks' in 'looks' |
| O o | o | as in 'hot' |
| Π π | p | as in 'pup' |
| P ρ | r | a slightly trilled 'r' |
| Σ σ | s | as in 'sand' ('ς' at the end of a word) |
| T τ | t | as in 'to' |
| Y υ | i | as in 'marine' |
| Φ φ | f | as in 'fit' |
| X χ | kh, h | as the 'ch' in Scottish *loch*, or as a rough 'h' |
| Ψ ψ | ps | as the 'ps' in 'lapse' |
| Ω ω | o | as in 'lot' |

| | |
|---|---|
| **for one night** | *ya mia nichta* |
| **for two nights** | *ya dhio nichtes* |
| **Is breakfast included?** | *simberilamvanete to proiono?* |

## CONVERSATION & ESSENTIALS

| | |
|---|---|
| **Hello.** | *yasu* (informal) |
| | *yasas* (polite/plural) |
| **Goodbye.** | *andio* |
| **Yes.** | *ne* |
| **No.** | *okhi* |
| **Please.** | *sas parakalo* |
| **Thank you.** | *sas efharisto* |
| **That's fine/You're welcome.** | *ine endaksi/parakalo* |
| **Excuse me. (forgive me)** | *signomi* |
| **Do you speak English?** | *milate anglika?* |
| **How much is it?** | *poso kani?* |
| **What's your name?** | *pos sas lene/pos legeste?* |
| **My name is ...** | *me lene ...* |

## SHOPPING & SERVICES

| | |
|---|---|
| **Where is a /the ...?** | *pu ine ...?* |
| **bank** | *mia trapeza* |
| **... embassy** | *i ... presvia* |

| | |
|---|---|
| **hotel** | *to ksenodhokhio* |
| **market** | *i aghora* |
| **newsagency** | *to efimeridhon* |
| **pharmacy** | *to farmakio* |
| **post office** | *to takhidhromio* |
| **telephone centre** | *to tilefoniko kentro* |
| **tourist office** | *to ghrafio turistikon pliroforion* |
| **What time does it open/close?** | *ti ora aniyi/klini?* |

## EMERGENCIES – GREEK

| | |
|---|---|
| **Help!** | *voithia!* |
| **Call a doctor!** | *fonakste ena yatro!* |
| **Call the police!** | *tilefoniste tin astinomia!* |
| **Go away!** | *fighe/dhromo!* |
| **I'm lost.** | *eho hathi* |

## TIME, DAYS & NUMBERS

| | |
|---|---|
| **What time is it?** | *ti ora ine?* |
| **today** | *simera* |
| **tomorrow** | *avrio* |
| **yesterday** | *hthes* |
| **in the morning** | *to proi* |
| **in the afternoon** | *to apoyevma* |

| | |
|---|---|
| **Monday** | *dheftera* |
| **Tuesday** | *triti* |
| **Wednesday** | *tetarti* |
| **Thursday** | *pempti* |
| **Friday** | *paraskevi* |
| **Saturday** | *savato* |
| **Sunday** | *kiryaki* |

| | |
|---|---|
| **1** | *ena* |
| **2** | *dhio* |
| **3** | *tria* |
| **4** | *tesera* |
| **5** | *pende* |
| **6** | *eksi* |
| **7** | *epta* |
| **8** | *okhto* |
| **9** | *enea* |
| **10** | *dheka* |
| **100** | *ekato* |
| **1000** | *khilya* |

## TRANSPORT

| | |
|---|---|
| **What time does the ... leave/arrive?** | *ti ora fevyi/ftani ...?* |
| **boat** | *to plio* |
| **bus (city)** | *to leoforio (ya tin poli)* |

| SIGNS – GREEK | |
|---|---|
| Είσοδος | Entrance |
| Έξοδος | Exit |
| Πληροφορίες | Information |
| Ανοικτο | Open |
| Κλειστο | Closed |
| Αστυνομικο Τμημα | Police Station |
| Απαγορευεται | Prohibited |
| Τουαλετες | Toilets |
| Ανδρων | Men |
| Γυναικων | Women |

| | |
|---|---|
| **bus (intercity)** | *to leoforio (ya ta proastia)* |
| **tram** | *to tram* |
| **train** | *to treno* |

| | |
|---|---|
| **I'd like a ... ticket.** | *tha ithela isitirio ...* |
| **one-way** | *horis epistrofi* |
| **return** | *me epistrofi* |
| **1st-class** | *proti thesi* |
| **2nd-class** | *dhefteri thesi* |

| | |
|---|---|
| **left luggage** | *horos aposkevon* |
| **timetable** | *dhromologhio* |
| **bus stop** | *i stasi tu leoforiu* |

## Directions

| | |
|---|---|
| **Go straight ahead.** | *pighenete efthia* |
| **Turn left.** | *stripste aristera* |
| **Turn right.** | *stripste dheksya* |
| **near** | *konda* |
| **far** | *makria* |

# ITALIAN

## PRONUNCIATION
### Vowels

**a**    as in 'art', eg *caro* (dear); sometimes short, eg *amico/a* (friend)

**e**    short, as in 'let', eg *mettere* (to put); long, as in 'there', eg *mela* (apple)

**i**    short, as in 'it', eg *inizio* (start); long, as in 'marine', eg *vino* (wine)

**o**    short, as in 'dot', eg *donna* (woman); long, as in 'port', eg *ora* (hour)

**u**    as the 'oo' in 'book', eg *puro* (pure)

### Consonants

**c**    as the 'k' in 'kit' before **a**, **o** and **u**; as the 'ch' in 'choose' before **e** and **i**

**ch**    as the 'k' in 'kit'

**g**    as the 'g' in 'get' before **a**, **o**, **u** and **h**; as the 'j' in 'jet' before **e** and **i**

**gli**    as the 'lli' in 'million'

**gn**    as the 'ny' in 'canyon'

**h**    always silent

**r**    a rolled 'rr' sound

**sc**    as the 'sh' in 'sheep' before **e** and **i**; as 'sk' before **a**, **o**, **u** and **h**

**z**    as the 'ts' in 'lights', except at the beginning of a word, when it's as the 'ds' in 'suds'

Note that when **ci**, **gi** and **sci** are followed by **a**, **o** or **u**, the 'i' is not pronounced unless the accent falls on the 'i'. Thus the name 'Giovanni' is pronounced joh-*vahn*-nee.

A double consonant is pronounced as a longer, more forceful sound than a single consonant.

### Word Stress

Stress is indicated in our pronunciation guide by italics. Word stress generally falls on the second-last syllable, as in spa-*ghet*-ti, but when a word has an accent, the stress falls on that syllable, as in cit-*tà* (city).

## ACCOMMODATION

| | |
|---|---|
| **hotel** | *albergo* |
| **guesthouse** | *pensione* |
| **youth hostel** | *ostello per la gioventù* |
| **camping ground** | *campeggio* |

| | |
|---|---|
| **Do you have any rooms available?** | *Ha delle camere libere/C'è una camera libera?* |
| **How much is it per night/person?** | *Quanto costa per notte/ persona?* |
| **Is breakfast included?** | *È compresa la colazione?* |

| | |
|---|---|
| **a single room** | *una camera singola* |
| **a twin room** | *una camera doppia* |
| **a double room** | *una camera matrimoniale* |
| **for one night** | *per una notte* |
| **for two nights** | *per due notti* |

## CONVERSATION & ESSENTIALS

| | |
|---|---|
| **Hello.** | *Buongiorno.* (polite) |
| | *Ciao.* (informal) |
| **Goodbye.** | *Arrivederci.* (polite) |
| | *Ciao.* (informal) |
| **Yes.** | *Sì.* |
| **No.** | *No.* |
| **Please.** | *Per favore/Per piacere.* |
| **Thank you.** | *Grazie.* |
| **That's fine/You're welcome.** | *Prego.* |

LANGUAGE

| | |
|---|---|
| Excuse me. | *Mi scusi.* |
| Sorry. (excuse me/ forgive me) | *Mi scusi/Mi perdoni.* |
| Do you speak English? | *Parla inglese?* |
| How much is it? | *Quanto costa?* |
| What's your name? | *Come si chiama?* |
| My name is ... | *Mi chiamo ...* |

---

**EMERGENCIES – ITALIAN**

| | |
|---|---|
| Help! | *Aiuto!* |
| Call a doctor! | *Chiama un dottore/ un medico!* |
| Call the police! | *Chiama la polizia!* |
| Go away! | *Vai via!* |
| I'm lost. | *Mi sono perso.* (m) |
| | *Mi sono persa.* (f) |

---

## SHOPPING & SERVICES

| | |
|---|---|
| a bank | *una banca* |
| a chemist/pharmacy | *una farmacia* |
| the ... embassy | *l'ambasciata di ...* |
| my hotel | *il mio albergo* |
| the market | *il mercato* |
| a newsagency | *un'edicola* |
| post office | *la posta* |
| a stationers | *un cartolaio* |
| the telephone centre | *il centro telefonico* |
| the tourist office | *l'ufficio di turismo* |
| What time does it open/close? | *A che ora (si) apre/chiude?* |

## TIME, DAYS & NUMBERS

| | |
|---|---|
| What time is it? | *Che ora è?/Che ore sono?* |
| today | *oggi* |
| tomorrow | *domani* |
| yesterday | *ieri* |
| morning | *mattina* |
| afternoon | *pomeriggio* |
| | |
| Monday | *lunedì* |
| Tuesday | *martedì* |
| Wednesday | *mercoledì* |
| Thursday | *giovedì* |
| Friday | *venerdì* |
| Saturday | *sabato* |
| Sunday | *domenica* |
| | |
| 1 | *uno* |
| 2 | *due* |
| 3 | *tre* |
| 4 | *quattro* |
| 5 | *cinque* |

---

**SIGNS – ITALIAN**

| | |
|---|---|
| **Ingresso/Entrata** | Entrance |
| **Uscita** | Exit |
| **Informazione** | Information |
| **Aperto** | Open |
| **Chiuso** | Closed |
| **Camere Libere** | Rooms Available |
| **Completo** | Full/No Vacancies |
| **Polizia/Carabinieri** | Police |
| **Questura** | Police Station |
| **Proibito/Vietato** | Prohibited |
| **Gabinetti/Bagni** | Toilets |
| **Uomini** | Men |
| **Donne** | Women |

---

| | |
|---|---|
| 6 | *sei* |
| 7 | *sette* |
| 8 | *otto* |
| 9 | *nove* |
| 10 | *dieci* |
| 100 | *cento* |
| 1000 | *mille* |

## TRANSPORT

| | |
|---|---|
| When does the ... leave/arrive? | *A che ora parte/arriva ...?* |
| boat | *la barca* |
| bus | *l'autobus* |
| ferry | *il traghetto* |
| tram | *il tram* |
| train | *il treno* |
| | |
| bus stop | *fermata d'autobus* |
| train station | *stazione* |
| ferry terminal | *stazione marittima* |
| 1st class | *prima classe* |
| 2nd class | *seconda classe* |
| left luggage | *deposito bagagli* |
| timetable | *orario* |
| | |
| I'd like a one-way/ return ticket. | *Vorrei un biglietto di solo andata/di andata e ritorno.* |
| I'd like to hire a car/bicycle. | *Vorrei noleggiare una macchina/bicicletta.* |

### Directions

| | |
|---|---|
| Where is ...? | *Dov'è ...?* |
| Go straight ahead. | *Si va sempre diritto.* |
| Turn left. | *Giri a sinistra.* |
| Turn right. | *Giri a destra.* |
| near | *vicino* |
| far | *lontano* |

# MALTESE

You'll have no problems getting around Malta using English, but if you know a few words in Maltese it'll always be welcome.

## PRONUNCIATION

| ċ | as the 'ch' in child |
| g | as in good |
| ġ | 'soft' as the 'j' in job |
| għ | silent; lengthens the preceding or following vowel |
| h | silent, as in 'hour' |
| ħ | as the 'h' in 'hand' |
| j | as the 'y' in 'yellow' |
| ij | as the 'igh' in 'high' |
| ej | as the 'ay' in 'day' |
| q | a glottal stop; like the missing 't' in the Cockney pronunciation of 'bottle' |
| x | as the 'sh' in shop |
| z | as the 'ts' in 'bits' |
| ż | soft as in 'buzz' |

## ACCOMMODATION

| Do you have a room available? | Għandek kamra jekk jogħġobok? |
| Do you have a room for ...? | Għandek kamra għal ...? |
| one person | wieħed |
| two people | tnejn |
| one night | lejl iljieli |
| two nights | żewġt iljieli |

**Is breakfast included?** Il-breakfast inkluż?

## CONVERSATION & ESSENTIALS

| Hello. | Merħba. |
| Good morning/ Good day. | Bonġu. |
| Goodbye. | Saħħa. |
| Yes. | Iva. |
| No. | Le. |
| Please. | Jekk jogħġobok. |
| Thank you. | Grazzi. |
| Excuse me. | Skużani. |
| Do you speak English? | Titkellem bl-ingliż? |
| How much is it? | Kemm? |
| What's your name? | X'ismek? |
| My name is ... | Jisimni ... |

## SHOPPING & SERVICES

| the bank | il-bank |
| chemist/pharmacy | l-ispiżerija |

**EMERGENCIES – MALTESE**

| Help! | Ajjut! |
| Call a doctor. | Qibgħad ghat-tabib. |
| Police! | Pulizija! |
| I'm lost. | Ninsab mitluf. |
| hospital | sptar |
| ambulance | ambulans |

| the ... embassy | l'ambaxxata ... |
| the hotel | hotel/il-lakanda |
| the market | is-suq |
| the post office | il-posta |
| a public telephone | telefon pubbliku |
| shop | ħanut |
| stamp | timbru |

**What time does it open/close?** Fix'ħin jiftaħ/jagħlaq?

## TIME, DAYS & NUMBERS

| What's the time? | X'ħin hu? |
| today | illum |
| tomorrow | għada |
| yesterday | il-bieraħ |
| morning | fil-għodu |
| afternoon | nofs in-nhar |

| Monday | it-tnejn |
| Tuesday | it-tlieta |
| Wednesday | l-erbgħa |
| Thursday | il-ħamis |
| Friday | il-gimgħa |
| Saturday | is-sibt |
| Sunday | il-ħadd |

| 0 | xejn |
| 1 | wieħed |
| 2 | tnejn |
| 3 | tlieta |
| 4 | erbgħa |
| 5 | ħamsa |
| 6 | sitta |
| 7 | sebgħa |
| 8 | tmienja |
| 9 | disgħa |
| 10 | għaxra |
| 11 | ħdax |
| 100 | mija |
| 1000 | elf |

## TRANSPORT

**When does the boat leave/arrive?** Meta jitlaq/jasal il-vapur?

LANGUAGE

| SIGNS – MALTESE | |
| --- | --- |
| Dhul | Entrance |
| Hrug | Exit |
| Informazjoni | Information |
| Miftuh | Open |
| Maghluq | Closed |
| Tidholx | No Entry |
| Pulizija | Police |
| Toilets | Toilets |
| Rgiel | Men |
| Nisa | Women |

| | |
| --- | --- |
| **When does the bus leave/arrive?** | *Meta titlaq/jasal il-karozza?* |

| | |
| --- | --- |
| **I'd like a ... ticket.** | *Nixtieq biljett ...* |
| **one-way** | *'one-way'* |
| **return** | *'return'* |
| **1st-class** | *'1st-class'* |
| **2nd-class** | *'2nd-class'* |

| | |
| --- | --- |
| **left luggage** | *hallejt il-bagalji* |
| **bus/trolleybus stop** | *xarabank/coach* |

| | |
| --- | --- |
| **I'd like to hire a car/ bicycle.** | *Nixtieq nikri karozza/rota.* |

## Directions

| | |
| --- | --- |
| **Where is ...?** | *Fejn hu ...?* |
| **Go straight ahead.** | *Mur dritt.* |
| **Turn left.** | *Dur fuq il-lemin.* |
| **Turn right.** | *Dur fuq il-ix-xellug.* |
| **near** | *il-vicin* |
| **far** | *il-boghod* |

# MOROCCAN ARABIC

## PRONUNCIATION

Arabic is a difficult language to learn, but even knowing a few words can win you a friendly smile from the locals.

## Vowels

| | |
| --- | --- |
| **a** | as in 'had' |
| **aa** | as in 'far' |
| **e** | as in 'bet' |
| **i** | as in 'hit' |
| **ee** | as the 'e' in 'here', only softer |
| **o** | as in 'hot'; sometimes as in 'for' |
| **u** | as the 'oo' in 'book' |
| **oo** | as the 'oo' in 'food' |

## Vowel Combinations

| | |
| --- | --- |
| **aw** | as the 'ow' in 'how' |
| **ai** | as the 'i' in 'high' |
| **ei, ay** | as the 'a' in 'cake' |

## CONSONANTS

Many consonants are the same as in English, but there are some tricky ones:

| | |
| --- | --- |
| **j** | as in 'John' |
| **H** | a strongly whispered 'h', almost like a sigh of relief |
| **q** | a strong guttural 'k' sound |
| **kh** | a slightly gurgling sound, like the 'ch' in Scottish *loch* |
| **r** | a rolled 'r' sound |
| **s** | as in 'sit', never as in 'wisdom' |
| **sh** | as in 'she' |
| **z** | as the 's' in pleasure |
| **gh** | similar to the French 'r', but more guttural |

## GLOTTAL STOP (')

The glottal stop is the sound you hear between the vowels in the expression 'oh oh!'. In Arabic it can occur anywhere in a word – at the beginning, middle or end. When the glottal stop occurs before a vowel (eg 'ayn), the vowel is 'growled' from the back of the throat. If it is before a consonant or at the end of a word, it sounds like a glottal stop.

## ACCOMMODATION

| | |
| --- | --- |
| **hotel** | *ootel* |
| **youth hostel** | *dar shabbab* |
| **camping ground** | *mukhaym* |

| | |
| --- | --- |
| **Is there a room available?** | *wash kayn shee beet khaweeya?* |
| **How much is this room per night?** | *bshaHal al-bayt liyal?* |
| **Is breakfast included?** | *wash lftur mhsoob m'a lbeet?* |

## CONVERSATION & ESSENTIALS

| | |
| --- | --- |
| **Hello.** | *ssalamu 'lekum* |
| **Goodbye.** | *m'a ssalama* |
| **Yes.** | *eeyeh* |
| **No.** | *la* |
| **Please.** | *'afak* |
| **Thank you (very much).** | *shukran (jazilan)* |
| **You're welcome.** | *la shukran 'la wezhb* |
| **Excuse me.** | *smeh leeya* |
| **Do you speak English?** | *wash kat'ref negleezeeya?* |

| What's your name? | asmeetek? |
|---|---|
| My name is ... | smeetee ... |
| I understand. | fhemt |
| I don't understand. | mafhemtsh |
| How much (is it)? | bish-hal? |

### EMERGENCIES – MOROCCAN ARABIC

| Help! | 'teqnee! |
|---|---|
| Call a doctor! | 'ayyet 'la shee tbeeb! |
| Call the police! | 'ayyet 'la lboolees! |
| Go away! | seer fhalek! |

## SHOPPING & SERVICES

| the bank | al-banka |
|---|---|
| the ... embassy | as-seefara dyal ... |
| the market | as-sooq |
| the police station | al-koomeesareeya |
| the post office | al-boosta |
| a toilet | beet lma |

## TIME, DATES & NUMBERS

| What time is it? | shal fessa'a? |
|---|---|
| today | al-yoom |
| tomorrow | ghaddan |
| yesterday | al-bareh |
| in the morning | fis-sabaH |
| in the evening | fil-masa' |

| Monday | (nhar) letneen |
|---|---|
| Tuesday | (nhar) ttlat |
| Wednesday | (nhar) larb" |
| Thursday | (nhar) lekhmees |
| Friday | (nhar) zhzhem'a' |
| Saturday | (nhar) ssebt |
| Sunday | (nhar) lhedd |

Arabic numerals are simple enough to learn and, unlike the written language, run from left to right. In Morocco, European numerals are also often used.

| 1 | wahed |
|---|---|
| 2 | zhoozh |
| 3 | tlata |
| 4 | reb'a |
| 5 | khamsa |
| 6 | setta |
| 7 | seba'a |
| 8 | tmenya |
| 9 | tes'ood' |
| 10 | 'ashra |
| 20 | 'ashreen |
| 100 | mya |
| 1000 | alf |

## TRANSPORT

| What time does the ... leave/arrive? | wufooqash katwsul/keiwsul ...? |
|---|---|
| boat | flooka |
| bus (city) | ttubees |
| bus (intercity) | lkar |
| train | tran |

| bus stop | blasa dyal tobeesat |
|---|---|
| train station | lagaar |
| 1st class | ddarazha lloola |
| 2nd class | ddarazha ttaneeya |

| Where can I hire a car/bicycle? | feen yimken li nkri tumubil/bshklit? |
|---|---|

### Directions

| Where is (the) ...? | feen ...? |
|---|---|
| I'm looking for ... | kanqellab 'la ... |
| Go straight ahead. | seer neeshan |
| Turn right. | dor 'al leemen |
| Turn left. | dor 'al leeser |

# PORTUGUESE

Portuguese uses masculine and feminine word endings, usually '-o' and '-a' respectively – to say 'thank you', a man will therefore use *obrigado*, a woman, *obrigada*.

## PRONUNCIATION
### Vowels

| a | short, as the 'u' in 'cut'; long, as the 'ur' in 'hurt' |
|---|---|
| e | short, as in 'bet'; long, as in 'there' |
| é | short, as in 'bet' |
| ê | long, as the 'a' in 'gate' |
| i | short, as in 'it'; long, as the 'ee' in 'see' |
| o | short, as in 'pot'; long as in 'note' or as the 'oo' in 'good' |
| ô | long, as in 'note' |
| u | as the 'oo' in 'good' |

### Nasal Vowels

Nasalisation is represented by an 'n' or an 'm' after the vowel, or by a tilde over it, eg ã. The nasal 'i' exists in English as the 'ing' in 'sing'. You can practise by trying to pronounce vowels while holding your nose, as if you have a cold.

### Diphthongs

| au | as the 'ow' in 'now' |
|---|---|
| ai | as the 'ie' in 'pie' |

**ei**   as the 'ay' in 'day'
**eu**   as 'e' followed by 'w'
**oi**   similar to the 'oy' in 'boy'

## Nasal Diphthongs

Try the same technique as for nasal vowels. To say *não*, pronounce 'now' through your nose.

**ão**   nasal 'ow' (owng)
**ãe**   nasal 'ay' (eing)
**õe**   nasal 'oy' (oing)
**ui**   similar to the 'uing' in 'ensuing'

## Consonants

**c**   as in 'cat' before **a**, **o** or **u**; as the 's' in 'sin' before **e** or **i**
**ç**   as the 'c' in 'celery'
**g**   as in 'go' before **a**, **o** or **u**; as the 's' in 'treasure' before **e** or **i**
**gu**   as in 'guest' before **e** or **i**
**h**   never pronounced when word-initial
**nh**   as the 'ni' in 'onion'
**lh**   as the 'lli' in 'million'
**j**   as the 's' in 'treasure'
**m**   not pronounced when word-final – it simply nasalises the previous vowel, eg *um* (oong), *bom* (bõ)
**qu**   as 'k' before **e** or **i**; elsewhere as in 'queen'
**r**   when word-initial, or when doubled (**rr**) within a word it's a harsh, guttural sound similar to the 'ch' in Scottish *loch*; in the middle or at the end of a word it's a rolled 'r' sound. In some areas of Portugal it's always strongly rolled.
**s**   as in 'so' when word-initial and when doubled (**ss**) within a word; as the 'z' in 'zeal' when between vowels; as 'sh' when it precedes a consonant, or at the end of a word
**x**   as the 'sh' in 'ship', as the 'z' in 'zeal', or as the 'x' in 'taxi'
**z**   as the 's' in 'treasure' before a consonant or at the end of a word

## Word Stress

Word stress is important in Portuguese, as it can affect meaning. It generally occurs on the second-to-last syllable of a word, though there are exceptions. In words with a written accent, the stress always falls on that syllable.

## ACCOMMODATION

| | |
|---|---|
| hotel | *hotel* |
| guesthouse | *pensão* |
| youth hostel | *pousada da juventude* |
| camping ground | *parque de campismo* |

| | |
|---|---|
| Do you have any rooms available? | *Tem quartos livres?* |
| How much is it per night/per person? | *Quanto é por noite/por pessoa?* |
| Is breakfast included? | *O pequeno almoço está incluído?* |
| a single room | *um quarto individual* |
| a twin room | *um quarto duplo* |
| a double room | *um quarto de casal* |
| for one night | *para uma noite* |
| for two nights | *para duas noites* |

## CONVERSATION & ESSENTIALS

| | |
|---|---|
| Hello. | *Bom dia.* |
| Goodbye. | *Adeus.* |
| Yes. | *Sim.* |
| No. | *Não.* |
| Please. | *Se faz favor.* |
| Thank you. | *Obrigado/a.* (m/f) |
| You're welcome. | *De nada.* |
| Excuse me. | *Com licença.* |
| Sorry. (forgive me) | *Desculpe.* |
| Do you speak English? | *Fala Inglês?* |
| How much is it? | *Quanto custa?* |
| What's your name? | *Como se chama?* |
| My name is ... | *Chamo-me ...* |

---

**EMERGENCIES – PORTUGUESE**

| | |
|---|---|
| Help! | *Socorro!* |
| Call a doctor! | *Chame um médico!* |
| Call the police! | *Chame a polícia!* |
| Go away! | *Deixe-me em paz!* (pol)/ *Vai-te embora!* (inf) |
| I'm lost. | *Estou perdido/a.* (m/f) |

---

## SHOPPING & SERVICES

| | |
|---|---|
| a bank | *um banco* |
| a chemist/pharmacy | *uma farmácia* |
| the ... embassy | *a embaixada de ...* |
| the market | *o mercado* |
| the newsagents | *a papelaria* |
| the post office | *os correios* |
| the stationers | *a tabacaria* |
| the tourist office | *o (posto de) turismo* |
| What time does it open/close? | *A que horas abre/fecha?* |

## SIGNS – PORTUGUESE

| | |
|---|---|
| **Entrada** | Entrance |
| **Saída** | Exit |
| **Informações** | Information |
| **Aberto** | Open |
| **Fechado** | Closed |
| **Quartos Livres** | Rooms Available |
| **Posto Da Polícia** | Police Station |
| **Proíbido** | Prohibited |
| **Lavabos/WC** | Toilets |
| **Homens (h)** | Men |
| **Senhoras (s)** | Women |

## TIME, DAYS & NUMBERS

| | |
|---|---|
| What time is it? | *Que horas são?* |
| today | *hoje* |
| tomorrow | *amanhã* |
| yesterday | *ontem* |
| morning | *manhã* |
| afternoon | *tarde* |
| | |
| Monday | *segunda-feira* |
| Tuesday | *terça-feira* |
| Wednesday | *quarta-feira* |
| Thursday | *quinta-feira* |
| Friday | *sexta-feira* |
| Saturday | *sábado* |
| Sunday | *domingo* |
| | |
| 1 | *um/uma* (m/f) |
| 2 | *dois/duas* (m/f) |
| 3 | *três* |
| 4 | *quatro* |
| 5 | *cinco* |
| 6 | *seis* |
| 7 | *sete* |
| 8 | *oito* |
| 9 | *nove* |
| 10 | *dez* |
| 11 | *onze* |
| 100 | *cem* |
| 1000 | *mil* |

## TRANSPORT

| | |
|---|---|
| What time does the ... leave/arrive? | *A que horas parte/chega ...?* |
| boat | *o barco* |
| bus (city/intercity) | *o autocarro/a camioneta* |
| tram | *o eléctrico* |
| train | *o combóio* |
| | |
| bus stop | *paragem de autocarro* |
| train station | *estação ferroviária* |
| timetable | *horário* |

| | |
|---|---|
| **I'd like a ... ticket.** | *Queria um bilhete ...* |
| one-way | *simples/de ida* |
| return | *de ida e volta* |
| 1st-class | *de primeira classe* |
| 2nd-class | *de segunda classe* |
| | |
| **I'd like to hire ...** | *Queria alugar ...* |
| a car | *um carro* |
| a bicycle | *uma bicicleta* |

## Directions

| | |
|---|---|
| Where is ...? | *Onde é ...?* |
| Go straight ahead. | *Siga sempre a direito/ Siga sempre em frente.* |
| Turn left. | *Vire à esquerda.* |
| Turn right. | *Vire à direita.* |
| near | *perto* |
| far | *longe* |

# SLOVENE

## PRONUNCIATION

Slovene pronunciation isn't difficult. The alphabet consists of 25 letters, most of which are very similar to English. It doesn't have the letters 'q', 'w', 'x' and 'y', but the following letters are added: **ê, é, ó, ò, č, š** and **ž**. Each letter represents only one sound, with very few exceptions, and the sounds are pure and not diphthongal. The letters **l** and **v** are both pronounced like the English 'w' when they occur at the end of syllables and before vowels.

Though words like *trn* (thorn) look unpronounceable, most Slovenes add a short vowel like an 'a' or the German 'ö' (depending on dialect) in front of the 'r' to give a Scot's pronunciation of 'tern' or 'tarn'.

| | |
|---|---|
| **c** | as the 'ts' in 'its' |
| **č** | as the 'ch' in 'church' |
| **ê** | as the 'a' in 'apple' |
| **e** | as the 'a' in 'ago' (when unstressed) |
| **é** | as the 'ay' in 'day' |
| **j** | as the 'y' in 'yellow' |
| **ó** | as the 'o' in 'more' |
| **ò** | as the 'o' in 'soft' |
| **r** | a rolled 'r' sound |
| **š** | as the 'sh' in 'ship' |
| **u** | as the 'oo' in 'good' |
| **ž** | as the 's' in 'treasure' |

## ACCOMMODATION

| | |
|---|---|
| hotel | *hotel* |
| guesthouse | *gostišče* |

**youth hostel**       *počitniški dom*
**camping ground**     *kamping*

**Do you have a ...?**   *Ali imate prosto ...?*
  **bed**           *posteljo*
  **cheap room**    *poceni sobo*
  **single room**   *enoposteljno sobo*
  **double room**   *dvoposteljno sobo*

**for one night**      *za eno noč*
**for two nights**     *za dve noči*
**How much is it per** *Koliko stane za eno*
**night?**             *noč?*
**How much is it per** *Koliko stane za eno*
**person?**            *osebo?*
**Is breakfast included?**   *Ali je zajtrk vključen?*

## CONVERSATION & ESSENTIALS
**Hello.**             *Pozdravljeni. (polite)*
                       *Zdravo/Živivo. (informal)*
**Good day.**          *Dober dan!*
**Goodbye.**           *Nasvidenje!*
**Yes.**               *Da. or Ja. (informal)*
**No.**                *Ne.*
**Please.**            *Prosim.*
**Thank you (very**    *Hvala (lepa).*
**much).**
**You're welcome.**    *Prosim/Ni za kaj!*
**Excuse me.**         *Oprostite.*
**What's your name?**  *Kako vam je ime?*
**My name is ...**     *Jaz sem ...*
**Where are you from?** *Od kod ste?*
**I'm from ...**       *Sem iz ...*

### EMERGENCIES – SLOVENE
**Help!**              *Na pomoč!*
**Call a doctor!**     *Pokličite zdravnika!*
**Call the police!**   *Pokličite policijo!*
**Go away!**           *Pojdite stran!*
**I'm lost.**          *Izgubil/Izgubila sem se. (m/f)*

## SHOPPING & SERVICES
**Where is the/a ...?**  *Kje je ...?*
  **bank**         *banka*
  **consulate**    *konzulat*
  **embassy**      *ambasada*
  **exchange**     *menjalnica*
  **post office**  *pošta*
  **telephone centre** *telefonska centrala*
  **tourist office**   *turistični informacijski urad*

## TIME, DAYS & NUMBERS
**today**              *danes*
**tonight**            *nocoj*

### SIGNS – SLOVENE
**Vhod**            Entrance
**Izhod**           Exit
**Informacije**     Information
**Odprto**          Open
**Zaprto**          Closed
**Prepovedano**     Prohibited
**Stranišče**       Toilets

**tomorrow**            *jutri*
**in the morning**      *zjutraj*
**in the evening**      *zvečer*

**Monday**              *ponedeljek*
**Tuesday**             *torek*
**Wednesday**           *sreda*
**Thursday**            *četrtek*
**Friday**              *petek*
**Saturday**            *sobota*
**Sunday**              *nedelja*

**1**                   *ena*
**2**                   *dve*
**3**                   *tri*
**4**                   *štiri*
**5**                   *pet*
**6**                   *šest*
**7**                   *sedem*
**8**                   *osem*
**9**                   *devet*
**10**                  *deset*
**100**                 *sto*
**1000**                *tisoč*

## TRANSPORT
**What time does ...**   *Kdaj odpelje/pripelje ...?*
**leave/arrive?**
  **boat/ferry**   *ladja/trajekt*
  **bus**          *avtobus*
  **train**        *vlak*

**one-way (ticket)**    *enosmerna (vozovnica)*
**return (ticket)**     *povratna (vozovnica)*
**bus stop**            *avtobusno postajališče*
**train station**       *železniska postaja*

## Directions
**Where is ...?**       *Kje je ...?*
**Go straight ahead.**  *Pojdite naravnost naprej.*
**Turn left.**          *Obrnite levo.*
**Turn right.**         *Obrnite desno.*
**near**                *blizu*
**far**                 *daleč*

# SPANISH

## PRONUNCIATION
### Vowels

An acute accent (as in *días*) generally indicates a stressed syllable and doesn't change the sound of the vowel.

| | |
|---|---|
| **e** | as in 'met' |
| **i** | as in 'marine' |
| **o** | as in 'or' (without the 'r' sound) |
| **u** | as in 'rule'; the 'u' is not pronounced after **q** and in the letter combinations **gue** and **gui**, unless it's marked with a diaeresis (eg *argüir*), in which case it's pronounced as English 'w' |
| **y** | (see Consonants below) |

### Consonants

| | |
|---|---|
| **b** | a cross between English 'b' and 'v' |
| **c** | a hard 'c' as in 'cat' when followed by **a**, **o**, **u** or a consonant; as the 'th' in 'thin' before **e** and **i** |
| **ch** | as in 'church' |
| **d** | as in 'do' when word-initial; elsewhere as the 'th' in 'then' |
| **g** | as in 'get' when word-initial and before **a**, **o** and **u**; elsewhere much softer. Before **e** or **i** it's a harsh, breathy sound, similar to the 'h' in 'hit' |
| **h** | silent |
| **j** | a harsh, guttural sound similar to the 'ch' in Scottish *loch* |
| **ll** | as the 'lli' in 'million'; some pronounce it more like the 'y' in 'yellow' |
| **ñ** | a nasal sound, as the 'ni' in 'onion' |
| **q** | as the 'k' in 'kick'; **q** is always followed by a silent **u** and is combined only with the vowels **e** (as in *que*) and **i** (as in *qui*) |
| **r** | a rolled 'r' sound; longer and stronger when initial or doubled |
| **s** | as in 'see' |
| **v** | the same sound as **b** |
| **x** | as the 'ks' sound in 'taxi' when between vowels; as the 's' in 'see' when it precedes a consonant |
| **y** | at the end of a word or when standing alone (meaning 'and') it's pronounced like the Spanish **i**. As a consonant, it's somewhere between the 'y' in 'yonder' and the 'g' in 'beige', depending on the region. |
| **z** | as the 'th' in 'thin' |

## ACCOMMODATION

| | |
|---|---|
| hotel | *hotel* |
| guesthouse | *pensión/casa de huéspedes* |
| youth hostel | *albergue juvenil* |
| camping ground | *camping* |

| | |
|---|---|
| Do you have any rooms available?? | *¿Tiene habitaciones libres* |
| How much is it per night/per person? | *¿Cuánto cuesta por noche/por persona?* |
| Is breakfast included? | *¿Incluye el desayuno?* |

| | |
|---|---|
| a single room | *una habitación individual* |
| a double room | *una habitación doble* |
| a room with a double bed | *una habitación con cama de matrimonio* |
| for one night | *para una noche* |
| for two nights | *para dos noches* |

## CONVERSATION & ESSENTIALS

| | |
|---|---|
| Hello. | *¡Hola!* |
| Goodbye. | *¡Adiós!* |
| Yes. | *Sí.* |
| No. | *No.* |
| Please. | *Por favor.* |
| Thank you. | *Gracias.* |
| You're welcome. | *De nada.* |
| I'm sorry. | *Lo siento/Discúlpeme.* |
| Excuse me. | *Perdón/Perdóneme.* |
| Do you speak English? | *¿Habla inglés?* |
| How much is it? | *¿Cuánto cuesta?/¿Cuánto vale?* |
| What's your name? | *¿Cómo se llama?* |
| My name is ... | *Me llamo ...* |

---

### EMERGENCIES – SPANISH

| | |
|---|---|
| Help! | *¡Socorro!/¡Auxilio!* |
| Call a doctor! | *¡Llame a un doctor!* |
| Call the police! | *¡Llame a la policía!* |
| Go away! | *¡Váyase!* |
| I'm lost. | *Estoy perdido/a.* (m/f) |

---

## SHOPPING & SERVICES

| | |
|---|---|
| a bank | *un banco* |
| chemist/pharmacy | *la farmacia* |
| the ... embassy | *la embajada ...* |
| the market | *el mercado* |
| newsagents | *el quiosco* |
| stationers | *la papelería* |
| the post office | *los correos* |
| the tourist office | *la oficina de turismo* |
| What time does it open/close? | *¿A qué hora abren/cierran?* |

LANGUAGE

LANGUAGE

### SIGNS – SPANISH

| | |
|---|---|
| Entrada | Entrance |
| Salida | Exit |
| Información | Information |
| Abierto | Open |
| Cerrado | Closed |
| Habtaciones Libres | Rooms Available |
| Completo | Full/No Vacancies |
| Comisaría | Police Station |
| Prohibido | Prohibited |
| Servicios/Aseos | Toilets |
|   Hombres | Men |
|   Mujeres | Women |

## TIME, DAYS & NUMBERS

| | |
|---|---|
| **What time is it?** | *¿Qué hora es?* |
| today | *hoy* |
| tomorrow | *mañana* |
| yesterday | *ayer* |
| morning | *mañana* |
| afternoon | *tarde* |
| | |
| Monday | *lunes* |
| Tuesday | *martes* |
| Wednesday | *miércoles* |
| Thursday | *jueves* |
| Friday | *viernes* |
| Saturday | *sábado* |
| Sunday | *domingo* |
| | |
| 1 | *uno, una* |
| 2 | *dos* |
| 3 | *tres* |
| 4 | *cuatro* |
| 5 | *cinco* |
| 6 | *seis* |
| 7 | *siete* |
| 8 | *ocho* |
| 9 | *nueve* |
| 10 | *diez* |
| 11 | *once* |
| 100 | *cien/ciento* |
| 1000 | *mil* |

## TRANSPORT

| | |
|---|---|
| **What time does the next ... leave/arrive?** | *¿A qué hora sale/llega el próximo ...?* |
| boat | *barco* |
| bus (city/intercity) | *autobús, bus/autocar* |
| train | *tranvía* |
| | |
| **I'd like a ... ticket.** | *Quisiera un billete ...* |
| one-way | *sencillo/de sólo ida* |
| return | *de ida y vuelta* |

| | |
|---|---|
| 1st-class | *de primera clase* |
| 2nd-class | *de segunda clase* |
| | |
| left luggage | *consigna* |
| timetable | *horario* |
| bus stop | *parada de autobus* |
| train station | *estación de ferrocarril* |
| | |
| **I'd like to hire ...** | *Quisiera alquilar ...* |
| a car | *un coche* |
| a bicycle | *una bicicleta* |

### Directions

| | |
|---|---|
| **Where is ...?** | *¿Dónde está ...?* |
| **Go straight ahead.** | *Siga/Vaya todo derecho.* |
| **Turn left.** | *Gire a la izquierda.* |
| **Turn right.** | *Gire a la derecha/recto.* |
| **near/far** | *cerca/lejos* |

# TURKISH

## PRONUNCIATION

The new Turkish alphabet is phonetic and thus reasonably easy to pronounce once you've learned a few basic rules. Each Turkish letter is pronounced, there are no diphthongs, and the only silent letter is ×.

## VOWELS

Turkish vowels are pronounced as follows:

| | |
|---|---|
| **A a** | as the 'a' in 'art' or 'bar' |
| **E e** | as in 'fell' |
| **İ i** | as 'ee' |
| **I ı** | as the 'a' in 'ago' |
| **O o** | as in 'hot' |
| **U u** | as the 'oo' in 'moo' |
| **Ö ö** | as the 'ur' in 'fur' |
| **Ü ü** | as the 'ew' in 'few' |

Note that both **ö** and **ü** are pronounced with pursed lips.

## CONSONANTS

Most consonants are pronounced as in English, with a few exceptions:

| | |
|---|---|
| **Ç ç** | as the 'ch' in 'church' |
| **C c** | as English 'j' |
| **Ğ ğ** | not pronounced; draws out the preceding vowel a bit |
| **G g** | as in 'gun' |
| **H h** | as the 'h' in 'half' |
| **J j** | as the 's' in 'treasure' |

S s    as in 'stress'
Ş ş    as the 'sh' in 'shoe'
V v    as the 'w' in 'weather'

## ACCOMMODATION

| | |
|---|---|
| hotel | otel(i) |
| guesthouse | pansiyon |
| student hostel | öğrenci yurdu |
| camping ground | kampink |
| Do you have any rooms available? | Boş oda var mı? |
| a single room | tek kişilik oda |
| a double room | iki kişilik oda |
| one night | bir gece |
| two nights | iki gece |
| How much is it per night/per person? | Bir gecelik/Kişibaşına kaç para? |
| Is breakfast included? | Kahvaltı dahil mi? |

## CONVERSATION & ESSENTIALS

| | |
|---|---|
| Hello. | Merhaba. |
| Goodbye. | Allahaısmarladık/ Güle güle. |
| Yes. | Evet. |
| No. | Hayır. |
| Please. | Lütfen. |
| Thank you. | Teşekkür ederim. |
| That's fine/ You're welcome. | Bir şey değil. |
| Excuse me. | Affedersiniz. |
| Sorry/Pardon. | Pardon. |
| Do you speak English? | İngilizce biliyor musunuz? |
| How much is it? | Ne kadar? |
| What's your name? | Adınız ne? |
| My name is ... | Adım ... |

### EMERGENCIES – TURKISH

| | |
|---|---|
| Help!/Emergency! | İmdat! |
| Call a doctor! | Doktor çağırın! |
| Call the police! | Polis çağırın! |
| Go away! | Gidin/Git!/Defol! |
| I'm lost. | Kayboldum. |

## SHOPPING & SERVICES

| | |
|---|---|
| a bank | bir banka |
| a chemist/pharmacy | bir eczane |
| the ... embassy | ... büyükelçiliği |
| my hotel | otelimi |
| the market | çarşı |

| | |
|---|---|
| the newsagency | haber agensı |
| the post office | postane |
| the stationers | kırtasiyeci |
| the telephone centre | telefon merkezi |
| the tourist office | turizm danışma bürosu |
| What time does it open/close? | Ne zamam açılır/kapanır? |

## TIME, DAYS & NUMBERS

| | |
|---|---|
| What time is it? | Saat kaç? |
| today | bugün |
| tomorrow | yarın |
| yesterday | dün |
| morning | sabah |
| afternoon | öğleden sonra |
| Monday | Pazartesi |
| Tuesday | Salı |
| Wednesday | Çarşamba |
| Thursday | Perşembe |
| Friday | Cuma |
| Saturday | Cumartesi |
| Sunday | Pazar |
| January | Ocak |
| February | Şubat |
| March | Mart |
| April | Nisan |
| May | Mayıs |
| June | Haziran |
| July | Temmuz |
| August | Ağustos |
| September | Eylül |
| October | Ekim |
| November | Kasım |
| December | Aralık |
| 1 | bir |
| 2 | iki |
| 3 | üç |
| 4 | dört |
| 5 | beş |
| 6 | altı |
| 7 | yedi |
| 8 | sekiz |
| 9 | dokuz |
| 10 | on |
| 11 | on bir |
| 12 | on iki |
| 13 | on üç |
| 100 | yüz |
| 1000 | bin |
| one million | bir milyon |

LANGUAGE

## TRANSPORT

| | |
|---|---|
| **What time does the next ... leave/arrive?** | *Gelecek ... ne zaman kalkar/gelir?* |
| ferry/boat | *feribot/vapur* |
| bus (city) | *şehir otobüsü* |
| bus (intercity) | *otobüs* |
| train | *tren* |
| | |
| **I'd like ...** | *... istiyorum.* |
| a one-way ticket | *gidiş bileti* |
| a return ticket | *gidiş-dönüş bileti* |
| 1st-class | *birinci mevkii* |
| 2nd-class | *ikinci mevkii* |
| | |
| **left luggage** | *emanetçi* |
| **timetable** | *tarife* |
| **bus stop** | *otobüs durağı* |
| **tram stop** | *tramvay durağı* |
| **train station** | *gar/istasyon* |
| **ferry/ship dock** | *iskele* |
| **I'd like to hire a car/bicycle.** | *Araba/bisiklet kirala mak istiyorum.* |

| SIGNS – TURKISH | |
|---|---|
| **Giriş** | Entrance |
| **Çikiş** | Exit |
| **Danişma** | Information |
| **Açik** | Open |
| **Kapali** | Closed |
| **Boş Oda Var** | Rooms Available |
| **Dolu** | Full/No Vacancies |
| **Polis/Emniyet** | Police |
| **Polis Karakolu/ Emniyet Müdürlüğü** | Police Station |
| **Yasak(tir)** | Prohibited |
| **Tuvalet** | Toilets |

### Directions

| | |
|---|---|
| **Where is a/the ...?** | *... nerede?* |
| **Go straight ahead.** | *Doğru gidin.* |
| **Turn left.** | *Sola dönün.* |
| **Turn right.** | *Sağa dönün.* |
| **near** | *yakın* |
| **far** | *uzak* |

Also available from Lonely Planet:
*Europe* and *Eastern Europe Phrasebooks*

# Behind the Scenes

## THIS BOOK

Many people have helped to create this 7th edition of *Mediterranean Europe. Mediterranean Europe* is part of Lonely Planet's Europe series, which includes *Western Europe, Eastern Europe, Central Europe, Scandinavian Europe* and *Europe on a shoestring*. Lonely Planet also publishes phrasebooks to these regions.

## THANKS from the Authors

### Duncan Garwood

I'd like to thank Heather Dickson in London who gave me the job and helped me with her sound advice and unruffled common sense. Thanks also to all the authors who I worked with on this title: Andrew Stone, Fiona Adams, Josephine Quintero, Amy Marr, Terry Carter, Jeanne Oliver, Vesna Maric, Tom Parkinson, Joe Bindloss and Carolyn Bain. On a personal note, grazie a Rosella, Gerardo e Viviana and as always to Lidia and little Ben.

### Fiona Adams

I would like to thank all the staff in the tourist offices throughout southern Spain for their help and patience, in particular Caty Serra and Rita Hunziker in Ibiza. In Marbella I owe a special thanks to Salvador and his charming family. Many thanks as well to Felicity in the *hostal* in Valencia. In Tarifa, Joe and Lucy – thanks for all your help and may the *poniente* always be with you. Also in Tarifa, a warm thank you to Frans de Man. Special thanks as well to Sarah Andrews, my co-author on the Spain chapter in *Western Europe*, and to all the LP staff who worked on this edition of *Mediterranean Europe*. To Loli Cabarcos and Juan Balan, *besos y abrazos* once again for all your help and friendship. And Mum, thank you so much for looking after Gaucho while I was away (again). Most of all I would like to thank my husband Jamie, the biggest star of them all. I couldn't have done it without you.

### Carolyn Bain

Many thanks to LPUK's Michala Green for sending me off to Malta, thereby allowing me to continue my LP-subsidised search for the perfect Mediterranean island! Various locals, expats and tourists in Malta gave freely of their time, answered my questions and kindly shared with me their local knowledge – I'm grateful to all of them, especially

Tony at the tourist office in Valletta, Jean Paul at the YMCA, Charlie at Coronation Guesthouse and Joseph on Gozo. Thanks also to Charmaine Saliba for the chance to see Portomaso from a local's perspective, and for an excellent night out. And last but not least, warmest thanks to the fabulous Kelvin Adams for his company on much of this trip.

### Joe Bindloss

My thanks as always to Linda Nylind for putting up with me going away. In the Republic of Cyprus, my thanks to the Cyprus Tourism Organisation, Liz and Dimitri in Lefkosia and Efthymia at Cyprus Antiquities. In the north, my thanks to the staff at Sun Car Hire in Lefkosia and the helpful people of Karpasia. Credit to the people on both sides of the line who are striving for peaceful reunification and a fair settlement for refugees.

### Vesna Maric

A million thanks go to Rafael (¡gracias amor!) because of whom I enjoyed every single moment of the journey and who was such a help. Great big thank yous to Gabriel for his grammar fascism, patience and kindness; also to Tom for being a friend and answering all my boring questions and to Imogen Franks for taking me on. Big thanks to Balina for showing us her country and taking care, and to Blerina and Andi for being so kind. More thanks to Beni Andoni in Tirana and Koli and his scary driving. Special thanks to Ines, Gianfranco and Annalisa for all their care in Bari. My eternal thanks to my mama.

### Amy Marr

*Mille grazie* to everyone who offered essential information, kindness on the road, patient conversation and good company over a meal or vino. So many people extended invaluable support, advice, regional insights and answers to my litany of questions, from Rome to Sicily and back again. Special thanks to Franco, Ferdinando, Marianne, Virginia, Giulia, Lucca, Vincenzo, Mimmo & Gabriella, Luigi, Nick, Armando, Viola, Roberta, Armando & Rosalba, Joel & Kathy, Cristian, Salvatore, Millie, Enzo & Emanuela. At Lonely Planet, thank you to Sam Trafford, Mark Griffiths, Heather Dickson, Duncan Garwood, and Loretta Chilcoat. *Grazie* to my home team posse and my *vado pazzo* cohorts in New Mexico. Lastly, *auguri e amore* to my parents for their unrelenting love, support, and tolerance of my giddiness for Italy.

## Jeanne Oliver

Innumerable people in Croatia went out of their way to make my stay enjoyable and my work smoother. Among them were Andrea Petrov of the National Tourist Board, Mark van Bloeman and the Begovićs in Dubrovnik, Tomislav Vukusić in Opatija and Radenko Sloković in Pazin. At home, I'd like to thank David and Ginna Zoellner for looking after Raymond, and John and Cédric Enée for their love and support during the course of this project.

## Tom Parkinson

Big shouts to the many, many people I met en route in Turkey: Connie, Simon, Gemma & Karin, Diana, Alp, Çelebi, Linda & Patricia, Mehmet, Pip, Dayman et al, Beth, Nancy, Jan & Sarah, Derviş et al, Hasan & Dilek, the Irish teachers, Bri, Segg & the boat people, Florent & pal, Jodie & boyf, Aiça, Selda & John, Jacky, Mustafa & Elif, Darcy & the girls, Yaşnır and anyone else I've temporarily forgotten. Special thanks go out to Tarun and Dan Richards for some great travellers' tips, Anthea & Catherine for a top weekend in Kuşadası (Elvis lives!), and Pat Yale for the benefit of her expertise. Finally, a big *gel buraya tatlnım* to Nina K, for the Kensington Close and other surprises.

## Josephine Quintero

I'd like to thank Robin Chapman for sharing my enthusiasm for Portuguese wines and custard tarts, Terry and Colin Geary for their invaluable input, Heather Dickson for encouraging me while on the road, and all the helpful staff of the local tourist associations. Thanks also to Kevin Hawthorn in Silves for his spare bed and insight into the nightlife nuances of the Algarve.

## Andrew Stone

For all the visits over the years and all the hospitality, my main thanks go to the Foucaults and Pere de Fabregues and in particular to Evelyn, Xavier, Michael and Sharmion. Thanks also to Ruth and Paulo at the Hub Lot, to Michel Caraisco and Jean-Jaques Benetti, for the whistlestop wine tour. Thanks also to all the helpful tourism offices, in particular Fabienne Fertilati in Nice and Nathalie Steinberg in Marseille.

## Mara Vorhees

I can testify that all those axioms about Moroccan hospitality are true, and I can't possibly mention everyone who showered it on me. Special thanks go to Mike & Terri Rhodes and Ilham, all in Marrakesh; Mustapha in Casablanca; Naoufel Uariachi and Garland Green in Rabat; Bouchra Jamai and her family in Meknès; Khalil Tassi in Tangier; and proud new parents Abdeslam & Naima Mouden in Chefchaouen. Heartfelt thanks go to all of my guides, especially Amina Zakkari in Fès. Far from faux, you defied my preconceptions and truly enhanced my travelling experience.

Paula Hardy was my absolute gem of a co-author on *Morocco* who made invaluable contributions to that title. I am always grateful to all my friends and family who keep in touch while I am on the road, especially my favourite correspondent and history consultant Jerry Easter.

## CREDITS

*Mediterranean Europe* 7 was developed in Lonely Planet's UK office by Heather Dickson and commissioned with the help of Imogen Franks. Thanks also go to Stefanie di Trocchio. The book was coordinated by Meg Worby (editorial) and Jolyon Philcox (cartography). Sally Steward, Laura Gibb, Sally O'Brien and Nina Rousseau assisted with editing and proofing. Tony Fankhauser, Kim McDonald, Amanda Sierp, Tadhgh Knaggs, Csanad Csutoros and Adrian Persoglia assisted with cartography. Mark Griffiths oversaw cartographic development for this title. Natasha Velleley and Wayne Murphy produced the backcover map. Laura Jane laid the book out in record time with help from Steven Cann. Yvonne Bischofberger designed the colour content and Maria Vallianos designed the cover. Tamsin Wilson, Sally Darmody, and Jacqui Saunders assisted Adriana Mammarella and Kate McDonald with layout checking. Quentin Frayne prepared the Language chapter; and Katie Lynch, Laura and Meg prepared the index. The health chapter was adapted from material written by Dr Caroline Evans, a GP specialising in travel medicine. Overseeing production were Ray Thomson (project manager) Darren O'Connell (managing editor) and Mark Griffiths (managing cartographer). The series was designed by James Hardy, with mapping development by Paul Piaia.

## THANKS from Lonely Planet

Many thanks to the following travellers who used the last edition and wrote to us with helpful hints, useful advice and interesting anecdotes.

**A** Rene Allen, Unal Altinyay, Lainie & Craig Anderson, Phil & Hilary Andre, Eva Appelman, Hilmir Ásgeirsson **B** Gord Barentsen, Lisa

Barnes, Luisa Bezzola, Ami Bhatt, Jane & Steve Bland, Paul Brians, David Bugden **C** Armando Cabrera, Simone Candido, Julie Capsalis, Juan Casabonne, Iclal Cetin, Hanno Christ, Darren Clarke, Charles & Anne Clayton, Ursula Cornu **D** Bruce Davis, Phill Dellow, Walter Derks, Katrijn De Ronde, John Douglas, Laurent-jan Dullaart **E** Ben Earl, Jason Earle, Reinhard Enne **F** Sia Frederick **G** Matthew Garfein, Jane Golding, Luca Grassi, Brian Gue, Efe Gulagaci, Rene Gulden **H** Claudia Hackh, Paul Hagman, Dr Franz Hebestreit, Hagay Hochman, Michelle Hodge, John Holevoet, Tomas Homann, Erik Hoogcarspel, Mary-Ellen Howard, Aline Huppi **K** Minte Kamphuis, Joakim Karlsson, Ayla Karmali, Colin Kenworthy, Petra van der Klaauw, Bronwen Koolik **L** Milan Lazarevic, Ellen Livermore, Anna Lochmann, Espen Loken **M** Kjell J Madsen, Louise Mair, Vince Malarbi, Christine Martens, Dave Mason, Stefano Materassi, Howard Mathers, Mike Mcgee, Ralph McLean, Tale Meyer, Rachel Miller, Terry Murphy **N** Karen Nalbandyan, Klara Novakova **O** Christine Louise Oddy, Susan Orr, Julie & Sener Otrugman **P** John & Dina Pawlowicz, Richard Perry, Alison Phillips, Mirjana Plazonic, Aleksandar Popovic, Steve Pyle **R** Volker Reichhardt, Patrick Reinquin, Maike Rudolph, Esa Ruotsalainen, Wouter Rutten **S** Annelie Scheider, Simon & Georgie, Owen Smith, Deanie Sultana **T** Eric Telfer, Stefano Tona, Brian Travers **U** Cagri Uyarer **V** Chris Vickery **W** Leslie Waldorf, Jan Wergeland, Caroline White **Z** K Zoglin

## ACKNOWLEDGMENTS

Many thanks to the following for the use of their content:

Map data contained in colour highlights map & globe on back cover – Mountain High Maps® © 1993 Digital Wisdom, Inc

**BEHIND THE SCENES**

# Index

**000** Map pages
**000** Location of colour photographs

# THE LONELY PLANET STORY

The story begins with a classic travel adventure: Tony and Maureen Wheeler's 1972 journey across Europe and Asia to Australia. There was no useful information about the overland trail then, so Tony and Maureen published the first Lonely Planet guidebook to meet a growing need.

From a kitchen table, Lonely Planet has grown to become the largest independent travel publisher in the world, with offices in Melbourne (Australia), Oakland (USA) and London (UK).

Today Lonely Planet guidebooks cover the globe. There is an ever-growing list of books and information in a variety of media. Some things haven't changed. The main aim is still to make it possible for adventurous travellers to get out there – to explore and better understand the world.

At Lonely Planet we believe travellers can make a positive contribution to the countries they visit – if they respect their host communities and spend their money wisely.

## SEND US YOUR FEEDBACK

We love to hear from travellers – your comments keep us on our toes and help make our books better. Our well-travelled team reads every word on what you loved or loathed about this book. Although we cannot reply individually to postal submissions, we always guarantee that your feedback goes straight to the appropriate authors, in time for the next edition. Each person who sends us information is thanked in the next edition – and the most useful submissions are rewarded with a free book. See the Behind the Scenes section.

To send us your updates – and find out about Lonely Planet events, newsletters and travel news – visit our award-winning website: **www.lonelyplanet.com/feedback.**

Note: We may edit, reproduce and incorporate your comments in Lonely Planet products such as guidebooks, websites and digital products, so let us know if you don't want your comments reproduced or your name acknowledged. For a copy of our privacy policy, go to www.lonelyplanet.com/privacy.

## Published by Lonely Planet Publications Pty Ltd

ABN 36 005 607 983

© Lonely Planet 2005

© photographers as indicated 2005

Cover design by Pepi Bluck. Artwork by Maria Vallianos. Front cover: Blue and white striped beach huts on Barril beach, Portugal; photographer: Abbie Enock/Travel Ink Photo Library. Back cover: Delivering foccacia in Venice, Italy; photographer: Alan Benson/Lonely Planet images. Many of the images in this guide are available for licensing from Lonely Planet Images: www.lonelyplanetimages.com.

All rights reserved. No part of this publication may be copied, stored in a retrieval system, or transmitted in any form by any means, electronic, mechanical, recording or otherwise, except brief extracts for the purpose of review, and no part of this publication may be sold or hired, without the written permission of the publisher.

Printed through Colorcraft Ltd, Hong Kong. Printed in China.

Lonely Planet and the Lonely Planet logo are trademarks of Lonely Planet and are registered in the US Patent and Trademark Office and in other countries.

Lonely Planet does not allow its name or logo to be appropriated by commercial establishments, such as retailers, restaurants or hotels. Please let us know of any misuses: www.lonelyplanet.com/ip.

## LONELY PLANET OFFICES

**Australia**
Head Office
Locked Bag 1, Footscray, Victoria 3011
☎ 03 8379 8000, fax 03 8379 8111
talk2us@lonelyplanet.com.au

**USA**
150 Linden St, Oakland, CA 94607
☎ 510 893 8555, toll free 800 275 8555
fax 510 893 8572, info@lonelyplanet.com

**UK**
72–82 Rosebery Ave,
Clerkenwell, London EC1R 4RW
☎ 020 7841 9000, fax 020 7841 9001
go@lonelyplanet.co.uk

Although the authors and Lonely Planet have taken all reasonable care in preparing this book, we make no warranty about the accuracy or completeness of its content and, to the maximum extent permitted, disclaim all liability arising from its use.